THE FAMILY EXPERIENCE

COVER ART

Charles H. Alston. *Family.* (1955). Oil on canvas. 48 1/4 × 35 3/4 inches.
    Collection of Whitney Museum of American Art. Purchase,
    with funds from the Artist and Students Assistance Fund
    55-47
    (Photography Credit Bill Jacobson Studio, N.Y., N.Y.

THE FAMILY EXPERIENCE

A Reader in Cultural Diversity

Edited, and with Introductions by

Mark Hutter
Glassboro State College

Macmillan Publishing Company
NEW YORK
Collier Macmillan Canada, Inc.
TORONTO

Editor: Bruce Nichols

Production Supervisor: Publication Services

Production Manager: Aliza Greenblatt

Text Designer: Publication Services

Cover Designer: Fern Logan

Cover Illustration: Charles H. Alston / Whitney Museum of American Art

This book was set in Times Roman by Publication Services, Inc.,
and printed and bound by Book Press.
The cover was printed by Phoenix Color Corp.

Macmillan Publishing Company
866 Third Avenue, New York, New York 10022

Collier Macmillan Canada, Inc.
1200 Eglinton Avenue, East, Suite 200
Don Mills, Ontario M3C 3N1

Library of Congress Cataloging-in-Publication Data

The Family experience : a reader in cultural diversity / edited, and
    with introductions by Mark Hutter.
        p.   cm.
    ISBN 0-02-359235-4
    1. Family—United States—Cross-cultural studies.   2. Sex—United
States—Cross-cultural studies.   3. Intergenerational relations—
United States—Cross-cultural studies.   4. Problem families—United
States—Cross-cultural studies.   I. Hutter, Mark, 1941– .
HQ536.F3655   1991
306.85—dc20   90-39396
                                                          CIP

Printing: 2 3 4 5 6 7   Year: 1 2 3 4 5 6 7

To the Memory
of My Father

Preface

There is at present a great debate in higher education regarding the nature and quality of the college curriculum and what, if any, place "outsiders"—women, people of color, and ethnic groups—should have in it. In many ways the current debate is a continuation of the major redirection of historical study that began about 25 years ago. The "new social history" stressed day-to-day experiences of ordinary people. It sensitized us to the importance of studying women, the poor, working people, and racial and ethnic minorities in order to get a better understanding of our past. No longer would history be restricted to the study of great men and of epochal events that emphasized the powerful and neglected the rest of us.

In the past decade, colleges and universities have become concerned with the integration of issues regarding gender, race, class, and ethnicity. Often the resolution of this concern tries to achieve a balance between the traditional core curriculum, which emphasized white, male-dominated Western culture, and the more recent diversified curriculum that reflects global concerns, the study of non-Western cultures, and the inclusion of women, minorities, and persons of color.

Sociology formally recognizes the importance of internationalizing the curriculum and integrating issues of gender, race, class, and ethnicity. What sociology has actually attained, however, is the "ghettoization" of that curriculum. In terms of internationalization, sociology has developed separate and distinct courses under the general rubric "Comparative Sociology"; more specifically, courses with such titles as "Sociology of the Middle East," or "Sociology of India." Regarding gender, race, class, and ethnicity, we often find separate and distinct courses with such titles as Gender Roles, Sociology of Women, Ethnic Studies, and Black Studies. The introductory sociology courses, including the sociology of the family, continue to devote their attention to what often proves to be white middle class concerns. When cross-cultural materials are introduced into institutional courses such as the family, they are often perceived as upper level courses.

The undergraduate sociology of the family course has begun to incorporate a greater awareness of gender. Matters of ethnicity, race and class, however, are often separated out of the curriculum and are either not discussed or they are relegated to peripheral study topics. The result is that a major characteristic of the American family—its class and cultural diversity—is omitted from discussion.

The aim of this anthology is to provide the student with materials integrating gender, class, race, and ethnicity into the introductory sociology of the family curriculum. These readings will reveal both historical trends and unique variations that widen our understanding of the diversity of the family. Taken together, they will inform and increase understanding of the continuities and changes of the American family.

The selected readings reflect my concern for materials that get at the "guts" of the family experience. They are biased toward an ethnographic, qualitative orientation. A conscious attempt has been made to avoid using articles that are overly quantitative and "number crunching." The goal is to provide the reader with scholarly materials that are interesting and free of unnecessary jargon.

The organizational structure follows the traditional format of sociology of family courses. Each part of the book contains an introductory essay that outlines pertinent major issues and concerns. For each article a brief overview is provided to orient the reader and highlight its sociological significance. The goal is an anthology that can be used either with or without an accompanying textbook in sociology of the family courses.

ACKNOWLEDGMENTS

Glassboro State College and its students, faculty, and administration have fostered the viewpoint expressed in this anthology. In recent years, I have had the wonderful opportunity to work in a number of different academic settings that have enhanced my understanding of matters educational. These include a residential summer institute sponsored by the Institute for Research on Women, at Douglas College of Rutgers University; a National Endowment of the Humanities summer seminar in urban history under the direction of Kenneth T. Jackson at Columbia University; an Andrew Mellon Fellowship to participate in a seminar under the directorship of David Reimers on race and nationality at New York University; and a Faculty Fellowship to participate in the New Jersey State College Faculty Fellowship Program at Princeton University under the directorship of Theodore K. Rabb. In addition, the Society for the Study of Symbolic Interaction, the Balch Institute for Ethnic Studies, the Ethnic Studies Association of the Delaware Valley, and the Garden State Immigration History Consortium have been vital to me. Through these activities I have been able to extend my understanding of curriculum matters and I am most grateful.

The Sociology Editor at Macmillan, Bruce Nichols, his predecessor, Chris Cardone, and the entire Macmillan production staff provided the support needed to assure the completion of this project. Much thanks is expressed to the reviewers, who include Ronald Rindfuss, University of North Carolina; Jill Quadagno, Florida State University; John Mahoney, University of Richmond; Christine Hope, College of Charlestown; David Olday, Moorehead State University; and Steven Schada, Oakton College. The authors and publishers of these articles are thankfully acknowledged for granting permission to reprint their work.

My wife, Lorraine, and my children, Daniel and Elizabeth, continue to provide an emotional and intellectual haven and I am most appreciative. My parents and my parents-in-law have taught me to value and understand the immigrant family experience, and by so doing, have enriched my life.

Mark Hutter

Contents

PART IV / FAMILIES IN CRISIS AND CHANGE   639

Chapter Eleven / Family Violence and Stress   644

Chapter Twelve / Divorce, Single Parenthood, and Remarriage

THE FAMILY EXPERIENCE

GENERAL INTRODUCTION

The average man—or woman—of fifty years or more ago had the greatest respect for the institution called the family, and wished to learn nothing about it. According to the Victorian ideology, all husbands and wives lived together in perfect amity; all children loved the parents to whom they were indebted for the gift of life; and if these things were not true, they should be, and even if one knew that these things were not true, he ought not to mention it. Everything that concerned the life of men and women and their children was shrouded, like a dark deed, from the light.

Today all that is changed. Gone is the concealment of the way in which life begins, gone the irrational sanctity of the home. The pathos which once protected the family from discussion clings to it no more. Now we do not want to be ignorant about the family; we want to learn as much about it as we can and to understand it as completely as possible. We are engaged in the process of reconstructing our family institutions through criticism and discussion (Waller 1938, p. 13).

Willard Waller was one of the most prominent American family sociologists of the mid-twentieth century. These words, written more than fifty years ago in his seminal work, *The Family: A Dynamic Interpretation*, are reflective of his gadfly status in American sociology. His contemporaries did not agree with his critical— some would say scathing—look at the middle-class American family. Most had a much more sanguine view of the American family system that reflected their own middle-class biases. They saw harmony and concord, not tension and discord. Their perspective was shared by the popular media which typified the American family as exclusively Caucasian, affluent, and residing in suburban and rural areas in peaceful harmony.

Indeed, American sociology was so uncritical of the family that it failed to foresee the revolution that swept across America beginning in the early 1960s and continues to the present. Social protest movements called for equality and civil rights for all those "forgotten" in affluent America. These movements, led by "outsiders"—people of color, ethnic groups, feminists, and gays—ushered in a wave of new thought in the study of the family that stressed the diversity of the American experience. These outsiders led American sociology to at last follow the

1

call made by Willard Waller to engage "in the process of reconstructing our family institutions through criticism and discussion."

New conceptual frameworks allowed us to "see" family phenomena formerly hidden from view. We began to understand patterns and dynamics of family violence that we once did not even know existed. Further, new family structures— including dual career families, single-parent families, and families reconstituted by divorce and remarriage—increases in the rates of desertion and divorce, teenage pregnancy, abortion, singlehood, voluntary childlessness, and the feminization of poverty underwent sociological scrutiny and analysis.

The nature of marriage, family, and kinship systems in American society has undergone a new examination. Conventional assumptions about the necessity of maintaining kinship relations and the role of the nuclear family in today's world are being questioned: What are the proper gender roles for women and men? Is parenthood an inevitable and desirable consequence of maturation? A new, more permissive sexual morality led to the re-examination of previously held beliefs and attitudes regarding premarital and extramarital sexual relations, out-of-wedlock pregnancies, and abortions.

Family structures have fluctuated considerably in the last 25 years. More couples than ever before have voluntarily chosen to have fewer children. Many have voluntarily chosen childlessness. Still others have reconsidered that decision and opted to have children in later years. Divorce rates that were accelerating in the 1970s have leveled off and stabilized but remain at a higher rate than ever before in U.S. history.

New family patterns have emerged. That cohabitation has, for many, become an American way of life that comments not only on premarital or nonmarital relationships but has implications for marital relationships as well. For those who eventually marry, the full implications of cohabitation as a facilitator for, or a hindrance to, marital adjustment and happiness is still unknown. Singlehood is accepted by many. Media discussion of the "marriage squeeze" raises questions on whether singlehood is a voluntary permanent option, or a state caused principally by the relatively low number of eligible men for "career" women. Regardless, singlehood involves a different series of life commitments than marriage and family.

Women have been particularly affected by and have affected family life. The number of single-parent families headed by women has been steadily growing. Much of this increase was caused by the rising divorce rate, but another major factor was the rising illegitimacy rate, especially among poor teenage females. These trends have led to the feminization of poverty. Women's labor force participation has been constantly rising in the last fifty years. Further, a significant number of working wives have children, especially young children. Because mothers are generally the primary caretakers, women have had to juggle their career aspirations and family responsibilities. This has led to the demand for increased day care facilities and to talk of a "mommy track" career ladder depending on the ages of children and the husband's occupational and familial career patterns.

The legitimacy of abortion has become the crystallizing issue in reaction to changes in family behavior. Passions ignite over the issue. A polarization has developed between "pro-choice" and "pro-life" advocates that has as its fundamental basis the nature of family values and individual options. Homosexuality is yet another area that has become a debating ground for issues regarding changes in the family. The debate on the acceptability of homosexuality as a legitimate alternative family life-style has been exacerbated by the deadly disease AIDS. Fear of AIDS has been used to incite the expression of homophobia and the rejection of gay rights.

The controversy surrounding sexuality, marriage, and the family has entered the world of politics and public policy more than ever before. Laws regarding abortion and homosexuality are continually argued, challenged, and changed. Laws regarding illegitimacy, and regulations regarding welfare for single-parent households are being written, argued, rewritten, and reargued. Politics continues to intrude on the government's responsibility to provide public support for child-care facilities. Arguments and counterarguments continue on this issue between traditionalists, who seek to preserve "natural" family values, and proponents of individual options in a family system more amicable to family diversity. The divorce revolution brought about by no-fault legislation has had the unintended consequence of dramatically improving the economic situation of divorcing husbands/fathers while at the same time leading to the povertization of wives/mothers and children. Economic discrimination of women justified by a traditional belief in women's "natural" role in the family and the inappropriateness of their participating in the workplace still exists. Although increased attention has recently been given to parallel concerns regarding men's roles, this has not generated nearly the same attention and controversy as women's commitments and options.

As a result of all these changes, debates, and controversies, there has been great discussion about the future of the family. A widespread view declares that the family is a dying institution and expresses much concern about the implications for the "American way of life." A counter view holds that the "family" itself is not dying, but rather that one form of the family is declining and being replaced by new types of families that are supportive of individuals of both sexes and of all ages. These new family forms will usher in emancipatory and egalitarian transformations in sexual relations that include, but are not limited to, marital and family relations.

To understand the contemporary status of the American family, and to be able to predict its future, is vital. Unfortunately, American sociology has only recently recognized the importance of studying the historical and cultural diversity of family systems. In the last ten years, American sociology has increasingly realized that comparative and multicultural analysis can frequently help in understanding things that are so near to us they are difficult to see. Ignoring such diversity, in fact, distorts analysis of the American family; diversity in American families is the very essence of the American family.

The aim here is to develop understanding of the causes, conditions, consequences, and implications of American family diversity for individual, family, and society. This book looks at the diversity of the family experience through time. A multicultural approach is the best way to answer questions about family processes and structures and their relationship to other societal institutions. The family is a prime reflector of the major societal changes experienced in the twentieth century. The study of the family experience allows us to see the impact of broader patterns of societal change on individuals and their everyday lives. The rapid economic, political, and social changes characteristic of present times make such a comparative perspective crucial.

REFERENCE

Waller, Willard. 1938. *The Family: A Dynamic Interpretation*. New York: Dryden.

PART I

MULTICULTURAL PERSPECTIVES

As we enter the last decade of the twentieth century, we can look back at more than two centuries of continual economic, religious, political, and social upheavals throughout the world. Massive modifications and breakdowns of social structures and cultural values have been associated with social and individual crises in which everyday experiences could no longer be taken for granted. Conventional assumptions regarding gender role relationships, marriage, and the family have been under scrutiny and challenge. The sociological perspective is vital to understand these social forces that have affected people's lives.

Throughout history, the family has been the social institution that has stood at the very center of society. For most people, the family is the most important group to which they belong throughout their lives. The family provides intimate and enduring relationships and acts as a mediator between its members and the larger society. It transmits the traditional ways of a culture to each new generation. It is the primary socializing agent and a continuing force in shaping people's lives. Through the family women and men satisfy most of their interpersonal, emotional, and sexual needs. Children are raised in families, providing a tangible link among past, present, and future generations. The family provides the setting in which individuals are socialized and motivated for integration into occupational, religious, political, and social positions that ensure the continuation of societal institutions and structures.

These prefatory remarks suggest why the family is vital to the society and to the individual. It should, therefore, be apparent that changes in the family will have serious ramifications for a given society and its people. Sociology as a discipline developed in the early nineteenth century as a response to the major changes that occurred first in Western Europe and the United States and then rapidly spread through the rest of the world as a consequence of Western colonization. The sociological perspective on marriage and the family was to view it in terms of the social forces that affect people's lives.

Prior to the nineteenth century, Western thought generally held to a biblical belief in the origins of the family stemming from God's creation of the world, including Adam and Eve. Although there was a recognition of relatively minor familial changes over time, the biblical family form and its underlying patriarchal ideological precepts were seen as continuing intact into the nineteenth century. Western thought clung to uniformity throughout the world in terms of family structures, processes, and underlying familial beliefs and values. These governed the behavior of men, women, and children in families.

This belief in the worldwide uniformity of the family underwent severe challenge and was finally discarded as a result of a number of important factors. Western societies were industrializing and urbanizing at a rapid rate, destroying the old societal class systems as a new social class structure developed. Individual rights, duties, and obligations were redefined, and the relationships of the individual to the family and the family to the larger community were reworked. Western colonial expansionism and imperialism fostered a new economic system that had global implications for all cultures. Contacts were being made with people whose systems of family life were markedly different from each other. The recognition of worldwide family diversity led to the overthrow of the belief that there was a single family form. What was needed was an alternative theoretical perspective to reevaluate the origins of the family. This alternative perspective took the form of evolutionary theory.

The theory of evolutionary change developed by Charles Darwin in his *Origin of Species* in 1859 was the culmination of an intellectual revolution begun much earlier that promoted the idea of progressive development. As the theory of evolution became the dominant form in explaining biological principles, social scientists of the nineteenth century developed belief that there was a link between biological and cultural evolution. These social scientists were called Social Darwinists. Their basic tenet was that since biological evolution proceeded through a series of stages (from the simple to the complex), the same process would hold for cultures.

Henry Sumner Maine, Lewis Henry Morgan, J. J. Bachofen, and Herbert Spencer were among those who applied evolutionary theories to the study of the human family. Social Darwinists seemingly dealt with such nonimmediate concerns as the origins and historical development of the family, yet their theories had social and political implications. Social Darwinism provided "scientific" legitimation for Western colonization and exploitation of "primitive" peoples through the erroneous belief that Western culture represented "civilization" and and non-Western cultures, particularly among nonliterate, low-technology societies, represented a primeval state of savagery or barbarity. And through its advocacy of evolutionary progress, Social Darwinism provided laissez-faire guidelines that supported neglect of the poorer classes of American and Western European societies. It also had implications for the roles of men and women in nineteenth-century family systems. By arguing for a patriarchal evolutionary theory of male supremacy and dominance over females, Social Darwinists gave implicit support to the Victorian notions of male supremacy and female dependency.

An important rebuttal to Social Darwinism that in part also developed out of evolutionary theory was made by Friedrich Engels ([1884]1972) in *The Origins of the Family, Private Property, and the State*. Concerns for gender role egalitarianism, as opposed to patriarchy and male sexual dominance, achieved their fullest evolutionary theory expression in this work. Engels' evolutionary theory saw economic factors as the primary determinants of social change and linked particular technological forms with particular family forms. Echoing Lewis Henry Morgan, Engels depicted the stage of savagery as one with no economic inequalities and no private ownership of property. The family form was group marriage based on matriarchy. During the stage of barbarism, men gained economic control over the means of production. In civilization, the last stage, women became subjugated to the male-dominated economic system and monogamy. This stage, in Engels' view, rather than representing the apex of marital and familial forms, represented the victory of private property over common ownership and group marriage. Engels speculated that the coming of socialist revolution would usher in a new evolutionary stage marked by gender equality and by common ownership of property.

Engels' main achievement was in defining the family as an economic unit. This has become a major focus in much of the subsequent historical research on the family and is of great theoretical importance in the sociology of the family. But, insofar as Engels' Marxist view constituted a branch of evolutionary thought, it was subject to many of the same objections (see below) raised against other evolutionary theories.

By the end of the nineteenth century, the popularity of Social Darwinism was rapidly declining. Contributing to the decline were the methodological weaknesses of the approach (data obtained by nontrained, impressionistic, and biased travelers and missionaries) and growing rejection of both its explicit value assumptions on the superiority of Western family forms and its belief in unilinear evolutionary development of the family. More importantly, the shift in the focus of the sociology of the family was at least in part precipitated by the sweeping changes in American and European societies during the nineteenth century. There was a dramatic increase of awareness to such conditions as poverty, child labor, desertions, prostitution, illegitimacy, and abuse of women and children. Social scientists were appalled by the excesses of industrial urban society and the calamitous changes in the family system.

The Industrial Revolution dramatically changed the nature of economic and social life. The factory system developed, and with its development there was a transformation from home industries in rural areas to factories. Rural people were lured by the greater economic opportunities that the city promised. The domestic economy of the preindustrial family disappeared. The rural- and village-based family system no longer served as a productive unit. The domestic economy had enabled the family to combine economic activities with the supervision and training of its children; the development of the factory system led to a major change in the the division of labor in family roles.

Patriarchal authority was weakened with urbanization. Previously, in rural and village settings, fathers reigned supreme; they were knowledgeable in economic skills and were able to train their children. The great diversity of city life rendered this socialization function relatively useless. The rapid change of industrial technology and the innumerable forms of work necessitated a more formal institutional setting—the school—to help raise the children. Laws came into existence to regulate the amount of time children were allowed to work and their work conditions. Laws also required that children attend school. These legal changes reflected the change in the family situation of the urban setting; families were no longer available or able to watch constantly over their children.

The separation of work from the home had important implications for family members. Increasingly, men became the sole provider for the family and the women and children developed a life centered around the family, the home, and the school. Their contacts with the outside world diminished, and they were removed from community involvements. The family's withdrawal from the community was characterized by its hostile attitude toward the surrounding city. The city was thought of as a sprawling and planless development bereft of meaningful community and neighborhood relationships. The tremendous movement of a large population into the industrial centers provided little opportunity for the family to form deep or lasting ties with neighbors. Instead, the family viewed neighbors with suspicion and wariness. Exaggerated beliefs developed on the prevalence of urban poverty, crime, and disorganization.

Social scientists began to see the decline in the importance of kinship and community involvements and the changes in the makeup of the nuclear family as more important areas of investigation than the study of the evolutionary transformations of the family. Their research and theories focused on the causal connections relating family change to the larger industrial and urban developments occurring in the last two centuries. Much attention has also been given to theoretical analyses of the effects these changes have had on the individual, on women, men, and children, on the family, on kinship structures, and on the larger community and the society.

For almost 200 years sociologists have wrestled with these concerns. The readings in the first part of this book focus on the relationship between societal change and the family. Chapter One opens with Cynthia Fuchs Epstein's rebuke of the neo-evolutionary theory of Stephen Goldberg (1974) expressed in his polemical book, *The Inevitability of Patriarchy.* Her piece captures contemporary concerns with theories regarding the origins and implications of patriarchy. As discussed previously, the evolutionary theory of the Social Darwinists ostensibly dealt with such nonimmediate concerns as the origins and historical development of the family. But embedded in their theorizing were implications for the roles of women and men in contemporary nineteenth-century family systems. Indeed, their twentieth-century evolutionary counterparts continue to put forth these same evolutionary arguments. The initiative for this rebirth of interest in the evolutionary reconstruction of family forms has been the development of arguments and counterarguments stemming from the women's movement concern with and attacks on the notions of the inevitability and origins of patriarchy and male dominance.

Cynthia Fuchs Epstein takes issue with the position that argues for the primacy of patriarchy. She examines and finds wanting the tenets of sociobiology—the theory that believes much of human social behavior has a genetic basis. Epstein also examines research on sex hormones and anthropological ethnographic research to prove how erroneous are the beliefs that the sexual division of labor is innate and that patriarchy is inevitable.

Article 2, "The Family and Modern Society," by Brigitte Berger and Peter L. Berger, puts forth the provocative thesis that the nuclear family is not simply a product of the modernization processes and urbanization but actually antedates these processes by centuries. This leads Berger and Berger to hypothesize that the nuclear family may in fact be a precondition rather than a consequence of modernization. They further contend that the family has been undergoing continual change that should be seen not as a breakdown, but as a vital factor in the transformation of modernity.

Robert V. Wells in Article 3, "Demographic Change and Family Life in American History: Some Reflections," examines demographic change and family life within the context of American history. Wells observes that the central life events of birth, death, marriage, and migration not only are experienced by most people within the context of the family but also are controlled and altered by family living as well. In his historical examination of the relationship between demography and family life, Wells contends that there is no such thing as *the* American family. He urges us to have great flexibility in our expectations about and interpretations of family life. He concludes on an optimistic note by observing that family life has been characterized by great vitality and the ability to adapt to changes in demographic and economic patterns that have characterized American history.

Steven Mintz and Susan Kellogg (Article 4) provides a social historical examination of the American family since 1960. They argue that, in the last 30 years, American families have undergone as wide sweeping a historical transformation as the one at the beginning of the nineteenth century. They spell out the changes in behavior and value for both the middle class and the poor. They focus on the New Morality, African American families in poverty, the feminization of poverty, children, and the revolution in family law. They broaden their analysis by examining the political and economic ramifications of these changes in family values and behavior.

The concluding article (5) in Chapter One extends the discussion on the politics of the family. Susan Cohen and Mary Fainsod Katzenstein approach this subject by analyzing the diversity within feminism and within right-wing conservatism, which advocates traditional familial roles. Although the battle is presumably fought over the needs of children, the authors view the nature of gender roles and values as the underlying issue. Further, they treat the different views regarding female autonomy, individualism, and community involvement as the heart of the debate.

The readings in Chapter Two, "The Family in the Community," focus on the relationship of the nuclear family to both the extended family and the larger community. Family historians have emphasized that changes in Western society resulted in the gradual separation of the public institution of work and the community from the private sphere of the family. Middle-class family life since the nineteenth century has been distinguished by this removal from the community setting. And the American suburb has continued to foster this privatizing process. Kenneth T. Jackson (Article 6) in the opening selection of this chapter provides an historical overview of the interrelatedness of the private family ideology and the suburbanization of the United States.

Many sociologists see the privatization of the middle-class family as antithetical to women's independence. More specifically, the spatial segregation of residence from home and the development of the single-family house led to the increased dependence of women on income-earning husbands. In addition, and most significantly, the house became the setting that required the full involvement of women. As Ruth Schwartz Cowan (1983) and Susan Strasser (1982) have demonstrated, women's domestic labor paradoxically increased with the development of mechanized techniques e.g., vacuum cleaners and sewing, washing, and dishwashing machines that were designed supposedly for efficiency's sake but in fact have set new housekeeping standards. In addition, the automobile fostered the end of home delivery services for all kinds of goods and services, thus requiring that families own an automobile to perform these services. These new tasks included driving spouses to commuter transportation stations, picking up and delivering children to school and after-school activities, and taking sick family members to doctors, who no longer made house calls.

One technological advance that ran counter to the prevailing "more work for mother" pattern was the residential telephone. Claude S. Fischer in Article 7 examines how the telephone was used by women to foster gender-linked social relationships and involvements. He looks at the development of the residential telephone in its first 50 years (1980–1940) to emphasize that the relationship between gender and technology may be more complex than initially thought.

In contrast to the relative separation of the nuclear family from extended kinship ties and community involvements is the family life of working class and ethnic groups. As shown in Chapter Three, the family structures of many immigrant and ethnic family groups in the United States are characterized by a developed social network comprising extended kin and neighbors. This social support structure is often an important mediating factor in a given family's involvement with the larger community. The concluding article (Article 8) in Chapter Two, by Ruth Horowitz, examines contemporary patterns of family life that occur among people living in a Chicano community in Chicago. She provides a vivid portrayal of how the important symbols of Mexican family life—solidarity, male domination, virginity, motherhood, and respect—are articulated in the context of an American industrial and urban community. The reading provides a dramatic illustration of the difficulties that a juxtaposition of different cultures imposes on family dynamics that include people of different ages and sexes.

Chapter Three, "Immigrant Families," continues the examination of the immigrant and ethnic family experience in the United States. The rise of American suburbia in the late nineteenth century can also be seen as a response to mass immigration and the massive industrial growth of American cities. Underlying these responses was the desire for class segregation. In particular, the middle classes were frightened of the immigration of people from southern and eastern Europe into the United States during the period from 1880 to 1924. In Article 9, written by the editor of this anthology, Mark Hutter, there is an examination of the urban ways of life of some of these immigrant family groups.

Immigrants from these areas concentrated in the industrial cities of the Northeast and the Midwest, where job opportunities were plentiful and chances of success were greatest. The ultimate success of an immigrant group depended in large part on its ability to re-establish a normal pattern of family life in America. However, popular as well as sociological opinion saw the emerging immigrant ghettos as settings of social disorganization, with alienation, anomie, social isolation, juvenile delinquency, crime, mental illness, suicide, child abuse, separation, and divorce as inherent characteristics of urban life. The social reform movement that developed during this time period saw family disorganization as pervasive and as a consequence arising from governmental nonsupervision of industrial and unban institutions. In Article 9, the nature of the social organizational patterns that were developing among these immigrant groups is examined.

The next two articles also center on the immigration experiece and its impact on families. However, they both have a contemporary time frame and are concerned with recent events. Article 10, by Robert J. Young, discusses the complexity of factors that ultimately affect immigrants in their assimilation into American society. Young studied the Asian-American immigrant experience in the Philadelphia, Pennsylvania, metropolitan area (the Delaware Valley); he examines the interplay of family and economic involvements in the context of community life.

The story of Rosa Marcos Guerro's life in Peru and her migration to New York City (Article 11) conveys the experience shared by hundreds of thousands of Latin American women. Skillfully blending Rosa Guerro's autobiographical materials with their own sociological descriptions and analyses, Thomas Kessner and Betty Boyd Caroli shed much light on the new realities of immigration, on the lives and cultures of an important new segment of our population, and on the continued diversity of the American family.

Chapter Four, "Social Policy and Poverty Families," which concludes Part I, continues our examination of the diversity of the family experience by presenting three articles on families living under poverty conditions. Articles in the preceding chapters analyzed the relationship of the modernization processes, industrialization and urbanization, with processes of family change. Articles in Chapter Four investigate poor families in contemporary industrial and urban societies. Article 12, by William Julius Wilson (with Kathryn Neckerman), is an investigation and discussion of social policy implications for poor black families.

There is great social class diversity of African American families. The majority of black families have both parents present, and the vast majority of adult black males work and provide family support. Yet there are significant differences between black families and white families in the United States. For example, a larger proportion of black families than families of other races have children within the household. A large and continually growing number of single-parent households are maintained by women. Further, blacks marry later and are more likely to remarry after divorce. These prevailing variations in black family dynamics have been interpreted, in part, as adaptations to the special circumstances in which blacks find themselves and, in part, as the result of certain values attributable to these circumstantial variations. The growing diversity within the black community has been explained by two somewhat contradictory theories put forth by Wilson and Charles V. Willie.

Charles V. Willie is an important social scientist who has extensively studied the black family. Willie (1988), in the third edition of his influential book, *A New Look at Black Families*, puts forth the opinion that economic factors in themselves can provide only partial explanation for black poverty. He argues that racism still permeates American society, affects all social institutions, and controls entry to all desirable positions in education, employment, housing, and social status. Wilson, on the other hand, makes the argument that racial distinction is not as important a factor in determining the economic opportunities of blacks as is their social class. Wilson does not claim that racism has completely vanished, but he does contend that economic and class differences have become more important than race for determining access to positions of power and privilege and for entering middle-class and upper-class social groups. Wison critically examines public policy approaches to the ghetto underclass and calls for comprehensive public policy attention to the connection between the poverty status of female-headed families and black male prospects for stable employment.

Article 13, by Harrell R. Rodgers, Jr., extends the analysis of social policy and its implications for the family by looking at European approaches. Western European social welfare policies have fundamental differences from American policies. They emphasize preventive health care, housing, and child and family allowance programs to inhibit the development of social problems associated with poverty. Similar innovative programs detailed in Rodgers' article can provide insightful guides to American social policy formulations in preventing and dealing with poverty families.

In recent years, persistent patterns of gender inequality have resulted in the "feminization of poverty," or the growing impoverishment of women and their children. Sex discrimination in the workplace, a stratified job market that places women in lower-paying positions, and the high divorce rate associated with unanticipated negative consequences in divorce laws are all associated with the increased number of women and their children living at or under poverty levels. The economic consequences of divorce concern Lenore Weitzman (Article 14) This article is the concluding chapter of her very important book, *The Divorce Revolution*. The book's subtitle, "The Unexpected Social and Economic Consequences for Women and Children in America," indicates the major theme of Weitzman's 10-year research project, in which she studied the impact of no-fault divorce laws. No-fault divorce is a new legal viewpoint on divorce that was designed to reduce accusation, acrimony, and artificial marital misconduct during divorce proceedings. Here, Weitzman outlines the larger cultural themes of individualism, personal fulfillment, and self-sufficiency that are reflected in no-fault divorce laws. She concludes by discussing the necessary steps and provides policy recommendations to alleviate the unanticipated problems and the devastating economic effects of no-fault legislation.

REFERENCES

Cowan, Ruth Schwartz. 1983. *More Work For Mother: The Ironies of Household Technology from the Open Hearth to the Microwave*. New York: Basic Books.

Engels, Friedrich. 1972. *The Origins of the Family, Private Property, and the State*. New York: Pathfinder Press.

Goldberg, Stephen. 1974. *The Inevitability of Patriarchy*. New York: William Morrow and Company.

Strasser, Susan. 1982. *Never Done: A History of American Housework*. New York: Pantheon.

Willie, Charles Vert. 1988. *A New Look at Black Families*, 3rd ed. Dix Hills, NY: General Hall.

<table>
| CHAPTER ONE |
</table>

The Changing Family: Origins, History, and Politics

1

Inevitabilities of Prejudice*

Cynthia Fuchs Epstein

Is there any reason to believe that patriarchy is more inevitable than anti-Semitism, child abuse, or any other mode of oppression that has been around for as long as anyone can remember? On the basis of his own experience, Aristotle believed that slavery was inevitable; and although it is still around in some countries, few reasonable people now believe it must be inevitable. Unfortunately, people with credentials for reasonableness, such as a new school of sociobiologists and their popularizers—among them Steven Goldberg—feel comfortable believing that the subordination of women is inevitable, programmed into human nature.

Many forms of oppression seem inevitable because they are so difficult to dislodge. History shows us that. It is easier to maintain oppression than to overthrow it. This is because when a group has a power advantage (which may emerge by chance, or historical accident), even if it is small, it may escalate rapidly if those in power can monopolize not only material resources but the avenues of communication as well. The Nazis did so effectively. Karl Marx cautioned that the owners of production were also the owners of the production of ideas. This means that the values and knowledge of a society usually reflect the views of those who rule, often by convincing those in subordinate statuses that they deserve what they get. The Nazis argued that they belonged to the "master race" and tried to build a science to prove it. They were less subtle than other rulers, but their case is instructive: beware the thesis of any powerful group that claims its power is derived solely from "divine right" or from its genes.

If anything is inevitable, it is change. Change in history is characteristic of human experience and reflects the human capacity to order and reorder it, to

*Epstein, Cynthia Fuchs. 1986. "Inevitabilities of Prejudice." *Society* 23 (September/October): 7–15. Published by permission of Transaction Publishers. Copyright © 1986 by Transaction Publishers.

understand the processes of its ordering, and to sweep away old superstitions. As Robert K. Merton pointed out in the *American Journal of Sociology* in 1984: "What everyone should know from the history of thought is that what everyone knows turns out not to be so at all."

Some twelve years have passed since Steven Goldberg published his book, *The Inevitability of Patriarchy*, more than a decade which has produced thousands of studies of gender differences and similarities, an extensive reanalysis of the relationship and applicability of primate behavior to human behavior, and debate and analysis of sociobiological interpretation. Goldberg has offered us once again, a view of women's subordination as inevitable simply because it has always existed. The thesis, unchanged from his formulation of a decade ago, is uninformed about the rich body of scholarship that has been published—much of it disproving his assumptions about significant differences in men's and women's emotions, cognitive capacities, and situation in the structure of the social hierarchy. In these intervening years, there have also been changes in the statuses and roles of women in the United States and in other parts of the world—these also invalidate Goldberg's perspective on the constancy and universality of his observations about the subordination of women.

Women in the United States, as elsewhere, have been elected and appointed to positions of power. They have joined the ranks of the prestigious and the powerful in the domains of law and medicine, and are entering specialties and practices to which they were denied admission and discouraged from pursuing only a decade ago. Women are now judges at every level of the judiciary in the in the United States, as well as prosecutors in the courts engaging in adversarial and assertive behavior, exhibiting what may be termed as "dominant behavior." There is considerable evidence that woman perform well; sometimes even better than do men, in examinations that determine admission to all fields in professional and graduate schools, where women constitute from a third to half of all students. Each year sees an increase in the number of women admitted to schools of engineering and science in spite of men's supposed greater social orientation toward careers in these fields.

Women have also become university professors and researchers and have thus been empowered to challenge many biased views about human nature and to fill gaps left by male scholars who have characteristically had little interest or inclination to do research in this field. Therefore, a revised view of what is "natural" or "inevitable" is part of the contemporary intellectual agenda.

Women are also making inroads in blue-collar technical work, heretofore denied them because of restrictions in apprenticeship programs made yet more difficult because of personal harassment. Women have experienced the same exclusionary mechanisms exercised against all minority groups who have had the audacity to compete with white males for the privileged positions guarded by "covenants" instituted by unions and ethnic clusters. According to a 1985 Rand Corporation research study by Linda Waite and Sue Berryman, *Women in Non-Traditional Occupations: Choice and Turnover*, women behave similarly to men in that they exhibit similar work force commitment and turnover rates once involved in nontraditional jobs such as those of the blue-collar crafts or in the army.

These researchers emphasize that policies equalizing work conditions for men and women also equalize commitment to the job.

Increasing convergence of gender role behavior is also seen in studies of crime. Girls' crime rates show increasing similarity to that of boys. Girls and boys both commit violent crimes and exhibit increasingly similar criminal histories.

Certainly much of the challenge and change is due to the women's movement and the insistence of women on their rights to equality. Sizable numbers of women in every sphere of society have taken an aggressive role in contesting the domination of men in personal, political, and intellectual life. Given the short period of time in which women have been active on their own behalf and in which they have succeeded in engaging the support of sympathetic men, their strides have been great both with regard to social rank and intellectual accomplishment.

This movement has evolved within the historical context still affected by centuries of oppression that have created and perpetuated the sense that women's inequality is natural. Yet no society, no social group, and especially no ruling group, has ever left gender hierarchy (nor any other form of hierarchy) to nature. It has not been women's incompetence or inability to read a legal brief, to perform brain surgery, to predict a bull market, or to make an intonation to the gods that has kept them from interesting and highly paid jobs. The root of discrimination against women, preventing their access to a variety of fields, has been a rule system replete with severe punishments for those who deviate from "traditional" roles. Access is now achieved through political and social action, and not at all through genetic engineering.

Sociobiologists, on the other hand, argue that the division of labor by sex is a biological rather than a social response. If this were so, sex-role assignments would not have to be coercive. Social groups do not actually depend on instinct or physiology to enforce social arrangements because they cannot reliably do so. Societies assign groups to be responsible for such social needs as food, shelter, and child care: nowhere do they depend on nature to meet these requirements. The types of work that men and women perform in each society are stipulated by society, allowing few individuals to make choices outside the prescribed range. The assignments are justified on the basis of ideologies claiming that they are just and reflect popular, cultural opinions that the arrangement is good (or that, if not, little can be done about it).

Such ideologies and popular views suppose that a fit exists between the job and worker—a fit that makes sense. This argument relies on the maintenance of gender differences. Division according to sex is reinforced by requirements that men and women dress differently (whether it is to don the veil or a skirt if female; and trousers or a *doti* if male), learn different skills (women's literacy rates are considerably lower than those of males in the Third World; in the Western world males and females still are "encouraged" to choose "sex-appropriate" subjects) and engage in different forms of activity. Violators are punished for infractions. Sometimes a raised eyebrow will keep a woman in line; in the extreme she may even face being stoned to death or burned alive (as in the recent outbreak of deaths over dowries in India).

The literal binding of women's feet or the constraint of their minds by law and social custom is part of the process by which the gender division of human beings perpetuates a two-class system. The hierarchy is kept in place subtly by the insistence that people behave in the way society's opinion molders say they should. Thus, "ideal" roles mask real behavior. If we look at what men and women actually do—or *can* do without the distorting mirror of "ideal" gender roles—there is a fundamental similarity in personalities, behavior, and competence, given equal opportunity and social conditions. This is what the vast array of scholarship in psychology, sociology, and physiology has revealed in the last decade.

The research has been so extensive that it is impossible to summarize it here, although I shall review it in my forthcoming book, *Deceptive Distinctions*. By now, reviewers have reanalyzed thousands of articles on gender differences in every attribution and behavior imaginable. Despite what everyone believes, the similarities far outweigh the differences, even in considering aggression. As for the differences that census takers count—frequencies of women and men in different jobs and leisure activities—these clearly seem to be a result of social rules and habits.

No one disagrees that habit, custom, laws, and force are used to position groups of all kinds into social institutions. Goldberg and others have claimed that social rules and customs are mere overlays of a more basic biological set of conditions. I focus on that set of assumptions in this article.

One school of thought labeled the "pop sociological" perspective by Philip Kitcher, a philosopher of science at the University of Minnesota who argues that many forms of human social organization and behavior, including altruism, the traditional family, the double standard of sexual behavior, rape, racism, and male dominance, may be interpreted according to the reproductive strategies of men and women in the evolutionary process.

This school is attributed in large part to the Harvard entomologist Edward O. Wilson. He defines sociobiology, in *Sociobiology: The New Synthesis on Human Nature*, as "the study of the biological basis of social behavior," holding that "sociology and the other social sciences, as well as the humanities," are the last branches of biology to be drawn into a "modern synthesis." Sociobiologists claim insights into the relationship between evolutionary process and human behavior from observations of animal behavior. This perspective stands in a long tradition of attempts to discern the elements of human nature in the behavior of nonhuman animals to account for social organization. Much of this sociobiologically oriented thinking uses Darwin's theory of evolution as its organizing paradigm, which also provides the framework for all of the biological sciences. Evolutionary theory hypothesizes about the development of the human species and African apes from some primate ancestor and offers the paradigm that, within a given species, individuals who possess traits most adaptive in the species' environment are likely to stay alive until they can reproduce and pass on their genes to a new generation. The natural environment "selects" individuals with these adaptive traits. Wilson's work, and that of his disciples, is, as the psychologists Carol Tavris and Carole Wade have put it, in *The Longest War: Sex Differences in Perspective:* "Darwin with a twist." Darwin speculated that within a given species, the most well adapted individuals are likely to stay alive and reproduce, passing on their genes to the next generation. For Wilson and his followers, the attention shifts from species to individual and from physiological characteristics to psychological ones. Thus, sociobiologists believe that nature has bred into humans the desire to pass on their genes, and that much, and possibly most, of behavior is motivated by this innate impulse to see the genetic code survive. Men and women follow reproductive "strategies" which maximize the continuity of their "line."

According to this perspective, the genetic code has affected the brains, the hormones, and ultimately the behavior of men and women whose relationship to each other and place in the social order reflect the "selection" of evolutionary focus. Male dominance is seen as an evolutionary response to the maximizing strategy of men to procreate with as many females as possible to ensure continuity of the male line, and women's passivity as a strategy that maximizes the survival of offspring of the female line.

The argument that men and women are motivated differently in their reproductive strategies accounts for their different placement in the division of labor and in the social hierarchy. A recurrent suggestion in this work is that like some primate groups, human ancestors grouped together in small bands, defended by "dominant" males prepared to act with violence. Dominant males are likely to be fathers or close relatives of the weaker individuals they defend. On the basis of this review of the behavior of baboons, rhesus monkeys, macaques, vervets, as well as some other animals, human male dominance is regarded as ordained by nature.

Some sociobiologists distrust the idea that the theory of evolution offers any direct insight into human nature; but the sociobiologists who have received the most attention are those whose analysis extends to inequality between human males and females by explaining that there are genetic constraints on gender roles. See, for example, Edward O. Wilson, Rechard Alexander, Robert Trivers, Richard Dawkins, David Barash, Pierre Van den Berghe, and Napolean Chagnon.

The contention of sociobiologists challenges the contentions of sociologists who explain much of human behavior as the result of culture and social learning. Not that sociologists and other social scientists dismiss the importance of biology. Biological factors create differences between men and women and "cause" certain kinds of behavior. Reproduction is a biological process; body structure is determined by the genes and creates opportunities for some people to perform better or worse in activities such as playing basketball or crawling through a small space.

The broader claims of sociobiologists assert many more links between social behavior and genetic makeup. Much of their speculation is based on studies of the social life of animals which, in their natural habitat, manifest patterns of behavior seemingly analogous to that of humans: "Sociobiology has two faces" according to Philip Kitcher who has reanalyzed the studies offered as evidence for their theories by those of the Wilson school in his book *Vaulting Ambition*. According to Kitcher, "One looks toward the social behavior of non-human animals. The eyes are carefully focused, the lips pursed judiciously. Utterances are made only with caution. The other face is almost hidden. . . . With great excitement, pronouncements about human nature blare forth." He and other critics from the physical sciences, critics of the sociobiology that "blares forth" about human nature, are wary of the anthropomorphism and speculative conclusions offered. As Kitcher puts it, the implications of their assumptions "are grave" for their view "fosters the idea that class structures are socially inevitable, that aggressive impulses toward strangers are part of our evolutionary heritage, that there are ineradicable differences between the sexes that doom women's hopes for genuine equality." Kitcher maintains that one face of sociobiology has produced "interesting results about the social lives of insects, birds and mammals," but believes that the building of "grand conclusions about ourselves is premature and dangerous."

Today's resurgence of biologically deterministic explanations of gender behavior, such as the reissue of Steven Goldberg's book, competes with social explanations of a wide array of social phenomena. Biological explanations have been used to support inequality between the sexes as they have been used to support inequality between the races and other dominant and subordinate groups. The psychologist Naomi Weisstein stated in *Ms.* in 1982: "Biology has always been used as a curse against women. From Darwin to Desmond Morris, From Freud to Robin Fox, from animal behaviorists who consider themselves open minded but 'realistic,' to the sober professors of ethology, the message has rarely changed: men are biologically suited to their life of power, pleasure, privilege, and women must accept subordination, sacrifice, and submission."

There are no clear-cut camps. Various positions have been taken, but the weight of most evidence and critical analysis does make a convincing argument for resisting simplistic biological explanation and models of "man" which indicate an evolutionary and genetic basis of hierarchy affixed to sex status. This is not only because the political perspective of many sociobiologists—justifying male dominance and social hierarchy—is objectionable to the egalitarian minded, but because the argument is said to rest on a dubious structure of inappropriate, highly selective,and poor data, oversimplification in logic and inappropriate inferences by use of analogy. Many scientists have made the case in great detail. They include Marian Lowe and Ruth Hubbard; Ruth Hubbard, Mary Henefin, and Barbara Fried; Nancy Tanner and Adrienne Zihlman; Janet Sayers; Donna Haraway; Anne Fausto-Sterling; Stephen J. Gould; Ruth Bleier; and Richard Lewontin, Steven Rose and Leon Kamin. I refer to only some of the issues here.

Size, shape, and lateralization of the brain have been used to explain intellectual differences between women and men, blacks and whites, and Asians and Europeans. Nineteenth century anatomists and anthropologists attempted to link brain size to intelligence. They claimed that smaller female brains accounted for differences in intellect compared to men, and that blacks had smaller brains than whites and therefore were less intelligent. The obsession with brain size continued into the twentieth century. The inaccuracy of these views and the faulty evidence on which they are based have been exposed in detailed reevaluation by the paleontologist and historian of science Stephen J. Gould in his book *Mismeasure of Man*.

Today, the work of Norman Geschwind on differences between left and right hemispheric dominance in women and men has received a great deal of attention and is regarded by many social as well as natural scientists as having established a cause of perceived differences in men's and women's orientations and capacities. He believes that the male brain is more lateralized (each half works independently) while women's are less lateralized (the two halves interact more than do those of men). Thus, it is argued, that men can do different types of things simultaneously whereas women can only do one thing at a time without getting confused. Investigators have also claimed that a connection exists between brain lateralization and sex differences in verbal and spatial abilities, mathematical ability, cognitive style, and reproductive function. Critics of this view, including many brain researchers, dispute these views as being unsupported by evidence and completely speculative. Marian Lowe and Anne Fausto-Sterling have both analyzed the history and dispute about brain lateralization research.

Carol Tavris reports that the argument that hemispheric differences account for different abilities between women and men is rapidly becoming dated among brain researchers. The objections of the scientists I have noted have been reinforced by a number of reviews of research literature that indicate a lack of information to support the relationship of brain lateralization to behavioral differences between the sexes.

Sex Hormones

Neuroendocrinological differentiation between the sexes is also interpreted as a cause of the division in the social order, and particularly in patriarchy. Attempts to create a society in which males are not in dominant positions must fail, is the view expressed by sociologist Steven Goldberg in *The Inevitability of Patriarchy*. Goldberg claims that this is so because of "the inexorable pull of sexual and familial biological forces which eventually overcome the initial thrust of nationalistic, religious, ideological or psychological forces that had made possible the temporary implementation of Utopian ideas." Domination by men is thus ensured in groups, and in pairs with women and children. Biologists such as David Barash, who in *The Whisperings Within* reasons that male domination is inexorable and that "the exclusion of women from major policy roles is an international, species-wide phenomenon," argue that genes may produce differences in behavior or ability by programming the activities of the sex hormones, which create noticeable distinctions between the sexes during fetal development and at puberty. The "male" hormone, testosterone, is said to affect the fetal brain at a particular phase of development, predisposing boys to show greater physical activity and to exhibit more aggressive behavior than do girls, which accounts for males' higher social ranking (a process also true for nonhuman primates). The biologist Anne Fausto-Sterling explains in *Myths of Gender* that it is clear that hormones play a part in developing sex characteristics, but not at all clear that they play a role in creating social behavior, or even nurture sexual behavior. She points out that high testosterone levels may not cause aggression, nor low levels reduce aggression. For example, studies of male sex offenders who have been chemically castrated "conclude that the procedure is not particularly effective."

Marian Lowe, in Lowe and Hubbard's *Women's Nature: Rationalizations of Inequality*, warns that in humans no correlations have been found between levels of testosterone and social rank or aggression. Further, although hormones are produced by gene-initiated processes they are subject to change in the social environment, such as exercise, stress, and so on. For example, Fausto-Sterling points out that "elevated testosterone levels may, in fact, result from aggressive behavior."

Since experimenters tend to use the findings of animal studies to make claims that male hormones produce dominance, it should be noted that scientists have also found evidence for the effect of environment on hormones. In experiments with monkeys, Patricia K. Barchas and Robert Rose, and Thomas Gordon and Irwin Bernstein have shown that social position can alter hormonal ratios. Monkeys whose hierarchical positions shift because of removal of the dominant member of the group manifest a change in their testosterone levels.

The question relevant to gender in society is the meaning of differences. For Goldberg, there is an unbroken line between "androgen binding sites in the brain, rough and tumble play in infants, and the male domination of state, industry and the nuclear family." E. O. Wilson is more cautious: "we can go against it if we wish, but only at the cost of some efficiency." If the hormone testosterone is supposed to make men aggressive and thus fit for public office, "female" hormones and the cycles attached to them are seen as detrimental to women's participation in public life. Edgar Berman, medical adviser to the late Senator (and Vice President) Hubert Humphrey, warned against women's participation in public affairs because of their "raging hormones." (Berman later published a book, *The Compleat Chauvinist*, in which he provided "biological evidence" for his views that menopausal women might create havoc if they held public office. Chapter titles from his book are: "The Brain That's Tame Lies Mainly in the Dame," "Testosterone, Hormone of Champions," and "Meno: The Pause that Depresses.") More recently, United Nations Ambassador Jeane Kirkpatrick reported that White House critics resisted her advancement into a higher political post because of the "temperament" she exhibited as a woman. No similar attributions of hormonal barriers to decision-making posts have been offered for men, although they have been excused from infidelity that is explained in popular culture by "male menopause," or by the sociobiologists who see it as an evolutionary response of men.

Many sociobiologists of the Wilson school have been committed to a model of inequity as a product of the natural order, arguing that male domination (patriarchy) is the most adaptive form of society, one that has conferred an advantage on individuals who operate according to its precepts. This thesis—put forth by E. O. Wilson, Lionel Tiger, Robin Fox, and Steven Goldberg—maintains that the near universality of male dominance arose because of the long dependence of the human infant as a result of hunting and gathering, the early modes of obtaining food. Male-based cooperation was expressed through dominance relations. Men guarded the bands and thus ensured survival. There was pressure on men to perfect hunting skills and on women to stay home and mind the children. Each sex would have developed cognitive abilities attached to these activities. A socially imposed hierarchical division of labor between the sexes gradually became genetically fixed.

Anthropological accounts are important for the study of human societies because they provide important crosscultural and intra-cultural analysis from small-scale nonliterate societies to large complex societies. Physical anthropologists also engage in cross-species analysis that demonstrates how much variation is possible in all primate societies. Those who have compared only modern societies to ascertain the sources of human traits and social arrangements are limited by the fact that they are sufficiently related to one another by philosophy, economy, and even political system. So, some forms of social organization would appear to be universal if analysis were confined to modern societies, but even these comparisons indicate the wide variety of social forms and of variation between individuals, between and among groups, races, and sexes. Certain questions about social organization—such as "Is the family universal?"; "Is the sexual division of labor universal?"; "Is hierarchy characteristic of all human societies?"—can only be answered with the help of anthropologists who consider a wider range of societies than do other social scientists, and who also interpret the material evidence of prior human and animal societies and extant primate societies.

Nonliterate cultures have been explored to provide clues about what we can expect of our own societies. Margaret Mead first made popular the notion that societies could vary considerably in the ways their members exhibited sex-role behavior, thus suggesting the extent to which sex roles were socially created rather than biologically dictated. Although Mead's field work supporting these views has been questioned, I do not believe the criticism has sufficient merit to undermine her conclusions and general principles. Mead opened the discussion, but it was still some time before anthropologists, who, like other social scientists have been affected by methodological problems and biases, engaged in widespread rethinking of past models and methods.

Man the Hunter; Woman the Gatherer

In recent years, anthropologists have reevaluated the perspective of "man the hunter," which long served as a model of the origins of human society. Posed as complementary, or in some cases contradictory, the model of "woman the gatherer," which emerged in the 1970's, revealed new insights into what early human society might have been like, what its sources might have been for present social organization and the evolutionary development of the human species. A further refinement of models, viewing both men and women as hunters and gatherers, provides another perspective on the division of labor. The man-the-hunter mode had been a source of speculation about the development of human intelligence and of male dominance. Using this model, primatologists and anthropologists such as Sherwood Washburn and Irven De Vore in *The Social Life of Early Man* and Desmond Morris in *The Naked Ape* had reasoned that hunting, a male activity, was a creative turning point in human evolution—that it required intelligence to plan and to stalk game, and to make hunting and other tools. It also required social bonding of men, the use of language to cooperate in the hunt, and then the distribution of meat and the development of tools for hunting and cutting the meat. According to Washburn and Lancaster in Lee and De Vore's *Man the Hunter*, "In a very real sense our intellect, interests, emotions and basic social life—all are evolutionary products of the success of the hunting adaptation." (Yet Donna Haraway points out that Washburn later opposed sociobiology "for ruining social science by biologizing" in an essay in Michael Gregory, Anita Silvers, and

Diane Sutch's *Sociobiology and Human Nature)*. Women, the breeders of children, fed and protected by the men, were relatively passive standbys in this process. As Stephen J. Gould put it in the *New York Review of Books* in 1984, the myth of "man the hunter" and "woman as nothing in particular" was created. Genetic and social selection for these attributes created the soceity and human nature as we know it today. The model featured hunting, aggression, and a division of labor based on sex. In the sociobiological explanation, this division of labor became genetically fixed. The analysis of this model has an importance beyond its usefulness in explaining the course of human history. The notion of male bonding as a product of evolution has been used continually to justify the behavior of men in discriminating against women in professional and business activity, in clubs and sports. Bonding has been considered a process that prepares men (better than women) to engage in corporate life and public affairs. The question is, what merit is there to the model and the explanations derived from it?

Among others, Frances Dahlberg in *Woman the Gatherer* suggests the account can only be considered a "just-so story" in the light of new scholarship. Beginning in the 1960s, research on primates, on hunter-gatherer societies, and archaeological and fossil records made this story obsolete. For example, the paleoanthropological myth of man the hunter was deflated when the "killer ape" of Robert Ardrey's *The Hunting Hypothesis*, the presumed australopithecine forebear of humans, turned out to be predominantly vegetarian. Ardrey had hypothesized that unique among primates, men alone "killed for a living," and he explained human social behavior such as male privilege and private property as an extension of this behavior. Richard Lee and Irven De Vore, editors of *Man the Hunter*, did not depend on a view of man as a killer. They showed that gathering was an important part of the foraging way of life for nonliterate groups, and probably so for "early man." New evidence indicated that both women and men gathered food for the group. In this analysis, however, women were hardly seen as social movers. Their contributions to society were conceptualized only in their roles as child bearers and mates. A greater challenge to the man-the-hunter model came from Sally Linton in Sue Ellen Jacobs's *Women in Cross-Cultural Perspctive*. Linton attacked the validity of theories of evolution that excluded or diminished women's contributions to human culture and society. She noted that women contribute the bulk of the diet in contemporary hunting and gathering societies, that small-game hunting practiced by both sexes preceded large-game hunting practiced by men, and that females as well as males probably devised tools for their hunting and gathering and some sort of carrying sling or net to carry babies. According to this view, the collaboration and cooperation of women was probably as important to the development of culture as that of men. Nonhuman primate behavior was used to provide clues to the most likely path of hominid evolution in support of the man-the-hunter thesis by indicating that a humanlike dominance system was to be found among our ape "relatives." Like the maligned australopithecine, other primate groups were slandered (or extolled) according to selective human bias.

Erik Eckholm, a science writer for the *New York Times*, wrote in a review of primate studies in 1984, "Soon after the advent of modern primate studies in the early '1960s, many scientists believed that they had discovered the key to primate social systems when they described hierarchies of aggressive males competing for the right ot mate with seemingly passive females, whose roles appeared limited to the bearing of young." Primatologist Sarah Blaffer Hardy was quoted by Eckholm as saying, "It was as if scientists had projected onto primates a mirror image of the social structure of an American corporation or university." New data on nonhuman primates has changed perspectives on male dominance, hierarchy, and aggression in primate societies. The historian of science Donna Haraway, in Kann's *The Future of American Democracy*, points out that Sherwood Washburn, in collaboration with his former student Irven De Vore, grounded "the first development of the baboon comparative model for interpreting hominid evolution from the viewpoint of man-the-hunter." Their early grant proposal to the National Science Foundation in 1961 cited the relevance of baboon social behavior studies to human psychology and psychiatry.

Today, studies of primates invite other interpretations. Male baboons, for example, had been observed to be very aggressive and to form alliances with other males. These observations were used to "prove" that men were naturally aggressive and bonded with other men in social clubs. But the choice of baboons has been questioned as an appropriate model for human behavior. W. C. McGrew, in Dahlberg's *Woman the Gatherer*, and others have pointed out that it is more useful to consider chimpanzees as a model of human behavior because they are probably the nonhuman primate closest to human beings. Their brains are generally similar to that of humans except for size; they have cognitive capacities for symbolic communication and self-recognition and therefore possess a rudimentary concept of self. They make tools (as opposed to simply using tools) for feeding, grooming, and investigation; build nests for sleeping; and they share food. Although these findings about chimpanzees had been reported in the past, scientists in the 1970s discounted the insights claimed by primatologists using other species and urged the use of the chimpanzee model for insights into human social organization. This model offered, for example, different perspectives on male and female behavior. New data show that male chimpanzees keep closer emotional attachments to their siblings than do females, but not with their offspring. Females frequently initiate mating and do so with a number of partners.

Even the utility of studying the chimpanzee is proposed with the warning that the chimpanzee, like all other nonhuman primates alive today, is not now and never has been a forebear of early or modern *Homo sapiens*. Among the primatologists doing work in the field there is general agreement summed up by one of them, Jane Lancaster, in Eckholm's 1984 review, "It is virtually impossible to generalize about what [all] male primates do, or how female primates act." For each species, sex roles have been shaped differently.

The new anthropological literature has also provided revised views of the differential status of women. In the search for universals, women's work in food production has become an important issue in discussions about the status of women. Eleanor Leacock, in *Current Anthropology* in 1978, proposed that equality was probably the original mode in society and that it persisted well into early horticulture, when hunting and gathering were replaced with domesticated plants and animals. Following a Marxist interpretation, Leacock maintains that inequality arose with the advent of private property and the alienation of the worker from the ownership and control of the means of production.

The analyses of hunting and gathering groups have limitations. For one thing, hunters and gatherers do not predate us in history: they live, as we do, now. For another, the bands are small, including fewer than 100 members. Nevertheless, whatever their limitations in describing the origins of human society, hunting and gathering groups demonstrate a variety of ways in which both women's and men's roles have been broader and less rigid than those created by stereotypes. For example, the Agta and Mbuti are clearly egalitarian and thus prove that equalitarian hunting and gathering societies exist in which women are not subordinate to men. Anthropologists who study them claim that there is a separate but equal status of women at this level of development.

The body of recent anthropological studies does not support the idea that women are valued less than men because of the universal restrictions of maternity or because of their lesser economic contributions. It also disputes the necessity of hierarchy in all social organization. In the realms of ritual activity and symbolic values, the evidence shows flexibility and diversity that produce interdependent cooperation between the sexes. Humans, unlike animals, have a particular kind of intellect and language that permits learning and communication which alter the environment and change the rules for survival.

By any system of accounting, how social groups perceive themselves through their use of a collective imagination far exceeds what raw physiology might indicate. In "nature" our bodies give us the capacities to be more than we can observe, even in the societies that exist today. Human imagination also limits what we can be and how we see ouselves. Social evolution, a process measured in millennia, can be hastened or at least altered by humans. Cultural and technological change can influence the impact of a group's biological heritage. Even those most devoted to identifying our biological roots recognize how our physiology may be manipulated and the consequences of its structure altered through technology and the control of fertility.

Ideology often runs counter to experience, and today as in the past we still find women and men persuaded by cultural stereotypes to believe that women have a different orientation to the world despite their demonstrated competence in spheres in which they were once believed to be inept, or that women eschewed their quest and desire for attainment. Correlatively, although most men do not climb the ladder of success and most lead quite ordinary lives not in the least characterized by dominance and status, social scientists still follow the lead of propaganda merchants who see a Horatio Alger in every man. At present, Kai Erikson of Yale University and I are conducting research on working-class communications workers which already shows clearly that men, like women, often put family life, community connection, and leisure time pursuits such as hunting and fishing far above opportunities for promotion. Our study is one of many indicating the same findings.

Today, even a strain of feminist social science literature following the work of Carol Gilligan, in *In a Different Voice: Psychological Theory and Women's Development*, claims that women are different from men in their orientation to the world. An example of this outlook—the notion of women's presumed greater "caring"—is a throwback to the Victorian era. There also have been serious objections to the methodology and interpretation of Gilligan's work, with the suspicion that her conclusions have been generalized far beyond the limited and highly specialized samples (such as pregnant women contemplating an abortion) on which the research is based. In fact, most studies of emotional and cognitive sex differences have relied on experimental situations set up on college campuses using only college students or young children as the database. Far fewer studies have been based on the performance and attitudes of men and women in the real world, but those that have indicate the strong influence of social manipulation. The recent report of the National Academy of Sciences on sex segregation in the workplace is further evidence of that.

People persist in wanting to view the world in terms of sex differences. They insist that individuals conform to ideal roles and turn away from their real roles, common interests, and goals, and from their mutual fate. These people disregard the obvious truth that most things that most people do most of the time can be performed equally well by either sex. The persistence of the view, as well as the persistence of physical and symbolic sex segregation, is created and maintained for a purpose, which is to maintain the privileges of men who predictably resist claims to the contrary. I suspect that the debates will continue and may do so as long as one group derives advantage from suppressing another. But evidence is mounting that supports equality between the sexes and which no truly reasonable people can continue to deny.

READINGS SUGGESTED BY THE AUTHOR:

Bleier, Ruth. *Science and Gender: A Critique of Biology and Its Theories on Women.* Elmsford. NY: Pergamon Press, 1984.

Epstein, Cynthia Fuchs. *Women in Law:* New York: Basic Books, 1981.

Epstein, Cynthia Fuchs. "Ideal Roles and Real Roles, or the Fallacy of the Misplaced Dichotomy." *Research in Social Stratification and Mobility* 4 (1985): 29–51.

Fausto-Sterling, Anne. *Myths of Gender: Biological Theories about Women and Men.* New York: Basic Books, 1985.

Lewontin, R. C.: Rose, Steven and Kamin, Leon. *Not in Our Genes.* New York: Pantheon Books, 1984.

2

The Family and Modern Society*

Brigitte Berger and Peter L. Berger

Various viewpoints concerning the family . . . have contradictory implications for the way in which this institution is to be understood today. There is the view that the family and its values are in a steep decline. This decline is variously interpreted in terms of its causes—broad social trends or specific ideological movements or changes in religion and morality—but most of those holding this view agree that the alleged decline of the family is harmful both to the individual and to society. This viewpoint can be summed up in the proposition that the family is in decline because of decadence. There is also the diametrically opposite point of view to the effect that changes in the overall society have revealed the outmoded character of the family. Supposedly, the family as it is now constituted will not be able to deal with this situation and will either disappear or have to be radically refashioned. And this is supposed to be a good thing, because of the allegedly harmful, pathogenic effects of the family in its peculiar, "nuclear" form. Here, too, there is the idea that the family is in decline, but the opposite implication is drawn from this assumed fact. The decline of the supposedly harmful institution is cheerfully applauded. In between these two opposite interpretations is the more moderate view (probably held by the majority of family analysts) that social changes have had a massive impact on the family, which has shown itself to be a remarkably robust and adaptable institution but which is nevertheless in a state of crisis. Data on divorce, the rise in single-headed households, and the like are used to undergrid this idea of crisis. All three interpretations of the current state of the family can be used to demand government intervention, albeit for differing reasons and in differing ways.

It is not difficult to see the common *empirical* base of these three viewpoints, despite the great and (between the two polar views) contradictory interpretations: The family is in bad shape—and that is a terrible thing; the family is in bad shape—and that is just great; the family is in reasonably good shape—but it has very serious problems, and these will get worse unless something is done about them. What is interesting is that spokesmen for these various viewpoints have accused those holding other views of "mythologizing" the family, in the present or the past or both. Thus those holding the "decline and decadence" view have been accused as having fallen prey to the myth of "the classical family of Western nostalgia."[1] Those believing in the "bad is great" thesis have been accused of seeking mythological solutions that have no chance of success. And the moderates in the debate have been faulted for not understanding that they themselves are part of the problem, because they do not take with becoming seriousness the

*Berger, Brigitte and Peter L. Berger. 1983. "The Family and Modern Society." Pp. 85–104 in *The War Over the Family: Capturing the Middle Ground*. Garden City, NY: Anchor Press/Doubleday. Copyright © 1983 by Brigitte and Peter L. Berger. Reprinted by permission of Doubleday, a division of Bantam Doubleday Dell Publishing Group, Inc.

concerns of the other two parties. In consequence of these all-around accusations of "mythologizing," the watchword for much recent work on the family has been (logically enough) "*de*mythologizing." Every aspect of the academic as well as the popular understanding of the family—its nature, history, present function, and future course—should be subjected to revisionist scrutiny. but there is a cheering aspect of this "demythologizing" thrust: It has indeed produced some very valuable research, which indeed helps us to acquire a "revised" understanding of many facets of the family in modern society. Perhaps ironically, this "revisionism" puts in question precisely some of the common empirical assumptions mentioned above.

The most important "revisions" have been due to new historical research. The 1960s and 1970s have produced a considerable body of new research into the origins and early development of the family in the modern world.[2] This has yielded interesting insights of various sorts, but the insight most revelant to our present topic is this: The notion that the nuclear family is an exclusive product of modernity can itself be shown to have been a myth. This is all the more important in that, as we have indicated above, the alleged problems of the nuclear family (most of them ascribed precisely to its "nuclearity") constitute the common empirical base for all the major participants in the current debate over the family. It is perhaps noteworthy that the most recent revisions of this view have been a case of historians debunking sociologists. In any case, what has happened is that the demythologizers have themselves been demythologized.

Recent research into the history of the family, both in Western Europe and in northern America, shows that the nuclear family, far from being a product of modernization processes (such as urbanization and industrialization), *antedates* these processes by *centuries*. This means that the extended family, for which there has been so much nostalgia, has not existed in those parts of the world at least since the high middle ages. Thus, for example, the brilliant study of Montaillou, a fourteenth-century village in what is now southern France, by Emmanuel Ladurie, makes this point very clearly: The families described in this study show striking similarities with the nuclear type discovered by sociologists as specific to modernity.[3] Even more interestingly, there is some evidence that this nuclear family was common in *Western* Europe, while *Eastern* Europe did indeed have the sort of extended family that Westerners have been so nostalgic about.[4] One could perhaps develop a theory of nostalgia out of this paradox. For our purposes, though, it suggests a striking hypothesis. It could well be that the nuclear family is a *precondition*, rather than a *consequence*, of modernization. This hypothesis, needless to say, would stand on its head many of the assumptions that sociologists have operated with since the 1920s.

The central idea of the nuclear family, of course, is that a household consists of only a married couple and their children. Thus most of the historical data just referred to concern the membership of households.[5] It is this facet of family life that has been found to be dominant all the way back to Montaillou. The presence of servants in the more-well-to-do households has tended to obfuscate the nuclearity of the family structure. With servants, of course, a pre-modern household would have many more members than the typical middle-class family today—but the addition of the servants to the nuclear unit of spouses and children can hardly be called an extended family. What is more, this pre-modern nuclear pattern did not break down under the impact of modernization. On the contrary, it appears as a *continuing* structure (one is tempted here to employ the Marxist term "infrastructure") of Western societies before, during, and since the great transformations of modernity.

It cannot be said that the earlier views of the relation of the family to modernization have been irrevocably falsified. However, the new research suggests that the family in the West was not, as had been thought before, simply a passive recipient of modernizing changes but, rather, an active participant in the modernization process. It is also much more plausible to say now that the peculiar family type of Western societies has been one of the factors *fostering* modernization.[6] Looked at cross-culturally, it then appears that the premodern family an be *either* a block to modernization, as sociologists had so often assumed and as they may have been right in assuming with regard to non-Western patterns, *or* a conduit for modernization, as the new research suggests. In the latter case, one important contribution of the family to the modernization process may have been the protection of individuals against the dislocations and transformations taking place in the larger society.[7] The Western nuclear family was small and mobile enough to allow individuals to participate in modernization, and at the same time tightly knit enough to make this participation humanly tolerable. But even the non-Western, extended family patterns have a considerable capacity to survive in urban-industrial settings and indeed to provide individuals protection and succor in the face of modernizing changes. This is suggested both by studies of immigrants to America (especially from Eastern Europe) and by studies of the family in various Third World societies today.[8] In these cases what often takes place is what could be described as a very "creative schizophrenia": The individual in the modern urban-industrial situation can be "modern" at work and "traditional" at home, alternating between these two worlds of his life in a manner that is not only quite comfortable but actually productive. To be sure, this kind of alternation between worlds also produces tensions. But it is possible that analysts, especially social scientists, have overemphasized the negative aspects of these tensions, overlooking their creative potential.[9] It is still an open question, though, *how long* such "creative schizophrenia" can be maintained, and we are open to the possibility that those who have argued for the convergence of family types all over the world as a result of modernization may be proved correct in the long run.[10] One of the most important cases in this regard is modern Japan, where for a long time a "creative schizophrenia" between modern and traditional spheres of life was successfully maintained—and where analysts disagree on the continuing viability of this synthesis.[11] But a pursuit of these broad questions would exceed our present purpose.

In any case, in Western societies, it now appears, the impact of urbanization and industrialization on the family has been greatly overestimated.[12] Thus new research suggests that there has not been a decline of family ties (including ties to kin beyond the nuclear family unit), *not* a mounting isolation of the family in the urban situations, *not* a general loss of functions of the family (but rather, a transfer of functions). On the contrary, when one looks at the strength of family ties and the importance of those ties to the individual, one is struck by the remarkable continuity over the recent centuries of Western history. As one analyst recently summarized these findings: "In a period of rapid and radical change in most aspects of economic and social life, it is odd that in many ways the European family should have changed so little."[13] To be sure, this statement loses some weight if one distinguishes between classes within Western societies, but it remains correct in suggesting a major modification in the earlier view, which understood modernization as having hit the family like a convulsive cataclysm.

We should not go overboard on this. Major changes *did* take place. There have been the separation of work from the home, the transformation of housework by technological innovations, the disappearance of servants, the revolution brought about by effective methods of birth control—to name just a few. It is important therefore to find an explanatory model that will include both change and continuity in the modern Western family.

We believe that modernization theory broadly understood is capable of doing this. However, we must distance our own position from those who understand modernization primarily in terms of structural and functional changes, with ideation in all its forms reduced to a dependent variable. Curiously, this reductionist bias is common to both sociologists who consider themselves structural-functionalists and to Marxists.[14] We can agree with *some* of the theoretical presuppositions of both schools. Thus we can agree with William Goode that "explanations for social behavior must be found in the social structure."[15] We can also agree with the Marxists that the "mode of production" of any society must be given primary attention in any explanation of social change. But our own version of modernization theory puts much greater stress on ideas, values, and structures of *consciousness* as factors in social change. This does not make us "idealists." Rather, we see social change as the result of the interaction (or, if one prefers, of a *dialectic*) of institutions and consciousness.[16] To which of the two sides of the interactive, or dialectical, process is attributed causal primacy will depend not on some theoretical *a priori* but on the empirical evidence concerning the situation under study. Thus it can be plausibly argued, in a Marxist vein, that the onset of industrial production dramatically transformed all aspects of social life, *including* consciousness. But this particular "mode of production" did not suddenly appear in history as a total innovation. It was the result of a long historical process— which included far-reaching changes in human consciousness. If industrialization caused great changes in consciousness, the advent of industrialization was in turn rooted in specific changes in consciousness (which, if Max Weber was right, may go back as far as the origins of the Judeo-Christian religious world view). And the future course of industrialization may in turn be affected by changes of consciousness. As to modernity, it is a constellation of structures both in the institutional order and in human consciousness, and the interrelation of these structures must be analyzed anew in each empirical situation.

This is highly relevant to our understanding of the relation of the family to modern society. We must distinguish between modern institutions and modern consciousness. It is quite correct that modern institutions produce modern consciousness. Thus, as the family is subjected to such modern processes as urbanization and industrialization, family values, norms, and concepts undergo changes. This does not mean, as we have indicated before, that all premodern forms of ideation simply disappear; with whatever modifications, or even with very few modifications, these traditional structures of consciousness may survive long into the modern period. But what is more, we can find (both historically and today) that modern structures of consciousness antedate their "realization" in modern institutions. Logically, of course, this had to be so in the beginning. Thus modern science and (at least by implication) modern technology had first to appear in the minds of innovative individuals before they began to be realized in the transformation of the external social world. But even today there can be a "cultural lag" in the opposite way from the usual sociological understanding of this phrase — that is, modern institutions may "lag behind" the appearance of certain elements of modern consciousness. A good example of this is the effect on consciousness of even a very minor injection of modern mass media communication into a traditional situation, in consequence of which modern ideas begin to circulate in this situation *prior* to any concrete institutional change.[17] In just this way, the new historical research on the family suggests that the Western nuclear family, long before the advent of modernization, fostered mind-sets and values that were instrumental in bringing about institutional modernization, perhaps even in a very decisive way.

More specifically, the new research suggests that at least *one* of the sources of modern "rationalization" (to use Max Weber's term) may have been the peculiar Western nuclear family. If so, the reason for this is probably to be sought in the patterns of socialization in such a family: in the closer relationship between parents and children, in greater parental influence, and in greater individuation (always as compared with non-nuclear, or extended, family types). The most dramatic way of putting this would be to say that modernity did not produce the nuclear family but, on the contrary, the nuclear family produced modernity. Let us hasten to add that we do not believe in such simple, monocasual explanations of social change. But the dramatic reversal of the usual formulation of the relationship has a certain heuristic use, as a corrective to the conventional view.

In any case, we are persuaded by those historians of the family who argue that a society might become modernized before becoming industrialized and that this was probably the case in Western Europe in the sixteenth century if not earlier.[18] This would mean that modern structures of consciousness were fostered by the European family and that these structures were necessary, or at least very important, preambles to the industrial revolution that followed a considerable time later. The most important point to be made is that one ought to move away from the conventional, one-sided view of the relation of the family to modernity in all its aspects. With this important reservation, we can now look at the institutional changes that have affected the family in the West. A summary will be useful at this point in our argument.

The economic changes have been, if not paramount, of very great importance. The rise of wage labor, at the very beginning of modern capitalism and prior to the coming of the industrial revolution, changed the relation of the household to economic production. Already in the late middle ages one can discern differences in family patterns between peasants and the classes out of which, later, the bourgeoisie was to emerge: the quasi-urbanized artisans and merchants. Family life among the latter appears to have been more open, individuated, and less ritualized than among the peasants. In the same way, there were differences between peasant families continuing to work their own land (whether owned or tenanted) and peasant families whose members hired themselves out for wage labor. When industrialization did come, of course, the nature of work was changed fundamentally. Most important, productive work was progressively taken out of the household. The family changed from being a unit of production to being a unit of consumption, with far-reaching consequences for its values and bonds. Also, with the industrial revolution, for some classes, there came about an increase in real *per capita* income, vesting earning power in the individual as detached from the family, further encouraging economic independence, mobility, and individuation. Again for some classes, this also meant a rising standard of living, from which the family derived immediate benefits. Greater material well-being, in these classes, allowed for new interests to develop within the family, including the "luxury" of new attitudes to spouses and children. Changes in socialization patterns were probably the most important aspect of this.

The "invention of childhood," as described by Philippe Ariès and other historians, was one of these "luxuries."[19] Beginning with the urban classes and the bourgeoisie that sprang from them, there appeared a new tenderness toward children, an interest in their development, and a prolongation of the period considered proper to childhood. Beginning in these classes, children came to be removed from the family for purposes of education. The school, as a separate educational institution standing over against the household, came into being. Later, of course, increasingly as a matter of state policy, this bourgeois pattern came to be extended to the entire population. These changes can be interpreted as a "loss of functions" for the family, if compared with its earlier character as an economic and educational institution. But, as Talcott Parsons correctly pointed out, the same changes can also be interpreted as a "freeing" of the family for other, partially new functions. These latter, however, belonged mainly to the private sphere; to some extent, at least, the family as an institution became "privatized."

The political changes were just as important, or nearly as important, as the economic changes, in their impact on the family. If capitalism and industrialism were the potent new realities in the economic area, the rise of the modern state was the immensely powerful new political reality. The feudal system, from top to bottom, was essentially an organization of households, and was aptly legitimated in familistic images. With the modernization of government, the household lost political functions. Patriarchal power within the household was progressively restricted. but, more fundamentally, *the individual* abstracted from all family relationships, increasingly became the basic political unit, first as subject, then as citizen. Increasingly this affected women as well as men, culminating in the demand for universal suffrage independent of sex or family status. Parental control over the lives of children diminished not only with the development of independent educational institutions (increasingly administered and coercively recruited for by the state) but with the proliferation of economic opportunities not dependent on parental arrangements and with the progressive extension of political rights to individuals of all social classes. Of course, even today parents continue to be the "gatekeepers" of certain opportunities for their children—by "purchasing" the right kind of education, by other forms of financial support, and by contacts and influence. But, compared to earlier times, this parental control over the future of children is greatly attenuated. With the reduction of control, probably inevitably, came a reduction of authority. Where previously parental authority (especially, of course, the authority of the father) was taken for granted, it now rests on the relatively feeble pillars of personal affection, and must be ongoingly "renegotiated." In consequence, there appear new forms of intergenerational conflict, sometimes very intense in quality.

Finally, the declining influence of religion, as a result of the peculiarly modern phenomenon of secularization, also impacted upon the family. In the medieval world view the family was ultimately legitimated in terms of this connection with the sacramental apparatus of the church. The weakening of its legitimation could not but reduce the authority of the family. To a considerable extent the church as an institution was also "privatized." Other institutions now competed with it in providing moral guidance and authority for individual life. The most important institution doing this was, again, the modern state, increasingly arrogating to itself the final authority in the determination of the obligatory moral standards for society. One might say that, in a certain analogy to the economic change, the family became a consumer, rather than a producer, of moral values. To be sure, to put it this way tends to exaggerate the *degree* of change; the family continues to be a very important source for the moral constitution of individuals; but, compared with earlier periods, there has been a good deal of change in this area as well.

We must now look in somewhat greater detail at the most important feature of modern social change in terms of the history of the family—to wit, the victory of the so-called bourgeois family. As just argued, the great social transformations that are part and parcel of the modernization process are deeply rooted in the history of Western civilization—not only in its peculiar social, political, and economic structures but, above all, in its beliefs and values. And as more recent historical research emphasizes, these great changes appear to be rooted in the practices and values of many small groups, predominantly in rule and provincial communities. As these changes occurred, formerly backward areas were turned into bustling commercial and manufacturing centers—in England (notably in the Midlands), Scotland, France (notably around Lyon and La Rochelle), and in parts of the Netherlands, Germany, and Austria. It appears in this perspective that the cataclysmic changes that transformed Europe were the end products (one is almost tempted to say, the marginal products) of a specific way of life, in which the family played a paramount part. What was this specific way of life, and which strata of the population were its "carriers"? The answer, by now, is fairly clear. The "carrier" class of the great revolution was that middle stratum that later on came to be called the bourgeoisie, and the specific way of life underlying the revolution was what we now know as bourgeois culture (though, as we have seen, this has historical antecedents that could only awkwardly be given this designation).

The bourgeoisie already existed in embryonic form in the medieval social order, grew slowly over centuries, spread in ever larger measure to other social strata (both above and below itself), and reached the working class by the end of the nineteenth century. An essential element in this process was a particular type of the family. This type can be viewed as a significant deviation from the "common human pattern"—to use the apt term coined by Jan Romein to designate broad cross-cultural patterns of human life. The distinctive features of this deviation became more pronounced over time, as they visibly benefited those who adhered to it.[20]

One of the basic features of this deviant family type was the separation of the public and the private spheres—or, if one prefers, the *invention* of private life rooted in the family. This innovation already appears in merchant and artisan strata of the late middle ages, especially in urban or urbanizing areas (as Max Weber already saw). As this deviance developed, a great rupture appeared in what had been the common pattern. Until this ruptured the household had been an economic, as well as a conjugal unit. The master of a craft, for instance, presided over a "family" consisting not only of his wife and children (and whatever other blood relatives shared the household) but also of a fluctuating number of servants, journeymen, and apprentices, all living together. Thus his functions as husband, parent, and head of the enterprise tended to be fused. In this example, an urban household did *not* deviate significantly from its rural cognate; households of this type are common in peasant societies all over the world. This type of family functions very well in situations (again, very common cross-culturally) where there is no, or only a very rudimentary, public authority providing the security of social order. This (as we today conceive it) public function was provided by the family, disciplining its own members and "negotiating" the rules of order with other, similar families. It is important that the members of one family consist of blood relatives and others not so related; that is, membership in a family is determined not only by descent or marriage but by the sharing in a common economic enterprise. All these individuals were bonded together in an "almost perpetual community of life."[21]

In a household of this older type, life was "ungraded," in the sense that individuals of all ages participated in the same activities. childhood, in other words, was not yet relegated to a distinctive and increasingly segregated category of life. Work was loosely organized, without the regulation of schedules so characteristic of modern life. In all likelihood, most people worked considerably less than they do today. (We will not pursue here, as tangential to our main topic, the interesting implication that, if this historical research is valid, the notion that modernity has brought about a quantum leap in the availability of leisure time would be false.) And, very important, privacy in the modern sense was virtually unknown. Life was communal in most respects, and only very rarely did or could individuals withdraw into solitude from this common web of living. Our modern sense of shame about such activities as elimination (to be engaged in increasingly in the privacy of the "privy") and sex, and, last but not least, our attitude toward death are very much related to the rupture of an earlier, communal way of life.[22]

The family and the economy changed in tandem. As early as the fourteenth century, in the very early stages of European capitalism, there emerged trading associations no longer based on domestic cooperation only. These trading associations were marked by two important features: the formation of capital based on the pooling of funds by several families, and the separation of economic activities from family life dictated by this. Concomitantly, a distinctive private sphere began to come into being, separated from economic activity and (necessarily) giving new prominence to the interaction between the members of each family. Also concomitantly, contractual relationships gained in importance, since the larger economic units could no longer be held together by an informal "patriarchal" authority. The ancient role of the father began to be undermined. The limits of allegiance implicit in the very notion of contract liberalized social life. This has been a commonplace of sociological theory for a long time (central, for instance, to the views of modernity of Émile Durkheim and Ferdinand Tönnies, as well as of Henry Maine). But, less commonplace, the same liberalization affected life within the family as well. Sons became contractual partners of their fathers, increasingly with equal rights. They were no longer bound to live in the parental household or, if they did live there, to work in the parental enterprise. Individuals thus began to gain economic independence from their families. To a lesser extent, this is also true of daughters, who tended to be "silent partners" but who came to acquire the legal right of withdrawing their inherited capital from the parental enterprise. This new kind of extra- or supra-familial enterprise was increasingly protected by the law. Thus the legal recognition of companies with limited liability separated personal or family funds from business capital, further solidifying the separation of private and public spheres.

As these processes matured, the old unity of the household was dissolved, with enormous consequences for the family. The individual became increasingly independent of the family. Privacy and individualism developed together. And, in consequence, the interaction within the family also had to change dramatically. With the loosening up of what Philippe Ariès has called the "density of social life" in an earlier period, and with the emergence of a distinctive and family-centered private sphere, individuals within the family were "liberated" to experiment with novel and even revolutionary roles. This "liberation" affected the relations between spouses, and between the latter and their children.

As the family became "liberated," it became "domesticated" —a historical correlation all the more important to emphasize, as the two terms are widely perceived today as antithetical. Philippe Ariès has been very influential in our understanding of the process of "domestication," basing himself on French sources from the fifteenth to the end of the seventeenth centuries. While Ariès' views have been criticized by other historians, there are some aspects of his perspective that are difficult to challenge. The emergence of the concept of childhood in its modern sense, with the removal of children into a separate category of life and the introduction of "age grading" into the family, is probably the most important aspect. The rise of education consequent to this "invention of childhood" is another very important aspect, allying family and school in a grand "conspiracy" to remove the child from adult society. Then there is the development of a new sensibility in the family, strongly linked to children and their education but then spreading far from the nursery and the schoolroom in its new notions of love, morality, and propriety. And Ariès was almost certainly correct in seeing all these changes as occurring first and foremost within the rising bourgeoisie, thus giving empirical validity to the common phrase of the "bourgeois family."

However, much of what Ariès described belongs in a larger picture of societal change, over and beyond the French history on which he concentrated. Also, his critical view of modernity reduced him to a mocking tone when describing the new bourgeois domesticity; a very different attitude to the latter is possible, even while granting the validity of most of Ariès' data. In any case, the larger picture into which these data should be fitted is the transformation of Western society by the economic and political forces of modernization. Although the domestic family emerged in the West during the sixteenth and seventeenth centuries among the merchant and artisan strata of the towns and somewhat later in the landed nobility, its most vigorous expression was in the eighteenth century in the class of small producers working their own property—the class from which the bourgeoisie of the industrial revolution sprang.[23] This *petite bourgeoisie* managed most effectively to merge the new family values with the new ideas of private property and individualism that legitimated its social aspirations. In saying this, we are not at all implying a quasi-Marxist understanding of the family values being nothing but ideological constructions in the service of class interests; rather, we understand the relationship, in Max Weber's sense, as one of "affinity" between ethos and class interests, with each influencing the other. During this period, the new family ethos was often linked to religion: Puritanism, Presbyterianism, and later Methodism in England and the American colonies, Calvinism and Jansemism in France, Pietism in Germany. And we agree with Weber in his understanding of the role of Protestantism in the genesis of modern capitalism—though Weber could not have known the equally important role of the family, as uncovered by recent research.

At least since the late-eighteenth century, the history of the West is, in a very basic sense, the history of the bourgeois class and its culture. The great historical transformations of the subsequent two centuries, which, in the aggregate, have produced what we now know as modernity, have been overwhelmingly the products of this class. Since for about half of this period, since the triumph of the bourgeoisie in the nineteenth century (in the major countries of the West, that is), this class and its culture have been identified with the *status quo* against which every rebel worth his salt would define himself, it is all the more important to understand the revolutionary character of this class in its deviation from age-old human patterns. (It may be remarked here, incidentally, that Marx understood this much better than many of his present disciples.) It is very important *not* to confuse this new, culture-producing bourgeoisie with the bourgeoisie of seventeenth- and eighteenth-century France, who made their entry into the court of power as of the reign of Louis XIV. This older bourgeoisie did not create its own culture and ethos but was imitative, in virtually all aspects of life, of the ruling aristocracy. This was derisively described, in his famous *Memoirs,* by Louis, Duc de Saint-Simon, who can be said to exemplify the aristocrat looking down on the social climbers of his age. This older, as it were culturally derivative bourgeoisie, was very different from the "new" bourgeoisie, which was originally predominantly Protestant. It was these people and their descendants who developed "an ethos, a culture peculiar to the industrial bourgeoisie."[24] This culture created the modern world. One of its major characteristics was a fine balance between revolutionizing activity in the larger society (the public sphere) and a zone of domesticity (the private sphere) into which the individual could ongoingly withdraw—for rest and recreation, as it were. The bourgeois family, we would contend, has been the pivotal institution making this balance possible. In this lies its most fundamental relationship to modernity, at least in the shape this has developed in the West. And for this reason the future of modernity is very much linked to the future of the family.

We will return to this point in later chapters. For now, to continue the historical sketch, we would emphasize once more the character of the early bourgeoisie as a community of dissenters. Dissent always requires forceful legitimations, without which the dissenting individual simply lacks the self-assurance and courage to defy the existing structures. This is why the religious qualities of the rising bourgeoisie were so important. Especially Protestantism, in its more unbending varieties, provided these people with an almost unshakable confidence in the righteousness of their values, culture, and political causes. It goes without saying that this often had an aspect of rigidity and fanaticism, inevitably so. It so appears to the retrospective today; it also looked that way to many observers at the time (such as good, moderate Catholics). Revolutionaries are not given to moderation. They pursue their aims with a minimum of self-questioning. This same single-mindedness was expressed in the pursuance of the bourgeois virtues—such as hard work, simple living, and moral propriety—within the bosom of the new bourgeois family.[25] If this produced "repression" in the children growing up in this milieu, it also gave them an inner resilience we can only look back to with wonder. To understand history, here as elsewhere, is to appreciate trade-offs.

If the historical perspective outlined in this chapter is valid, as we are inclined to think, then it no longer holds that the bourgeois family was the *product* of the industrial revolution: instead, it must now be understood as one of the important *preconditions* of this technological cataclysm. To say this, however, is not at all to deny that, once the industrial revolution was under way, there were far-reaching effects back upon the family. As industrialization proceeded through the nineteenth century in the major Western countries, the bourgeois vision of life was given the facility to penetrate ever-wider sectors of society. In the area that concerns us here, the bourgeois family and its norms became the standard for *all* classes. This was the beginning of the "evangelistic," or missionary, phase of the bourgeois family ethos. . . . And increasingly this ethos was coercively spread, not only by the voluntary efforts of well-meaning bourgeois individuals and institutions, but by the power of the state.

Within the bourgeoisie itself, the rise in standards of living made possible by industrial technology progressively transformed the household. This had a very important consequence for the way of life of bourgeois women. Sheila Rothman has described this very well for American society in the last decades of the nineteenth century: "Almost every technological invention in the period 1870–1900 significantly altered the daily routine of middle-class women. During these years, city after city, responding to the demands of engineers and real estate promotors, constructed and extended water and sewage lines. . . . By 1890, even moderate-priced homes in many cities were equipped with hot and cold water, water closets, and bathrooms."[26] This technological transformation of the household leaped forward of course with the advent of electricity, the effects of which are still continuing today with gadget after gadget. All of this led to an extraordinary reduction in women's menial tasks, to be sure first in higher-income households but in the twentieth century penetration massively into the working class. With this, the bourgeois "liberation" of women took on a new character, one of far-reaching and enduring physical comfort. By now, needless to say, this physical comfort is taken for granted by everyone above the poverty line—and claimed as a basic human right by those below it. On the basis of this physical comfort, every sort of life-style innovation and experiment.

But what was diffused to all social classes was not only the external accoutrements of bourgeois life but, more important, its peculiar vision of family life. This vision can be spelled out without much difficulty.[27] Family life is supposed to be attractive. Thus the home becomes a major focus of concern and attention. The home is supposed to be "nicely" furnished, comfortable, an expression of the "good taste" of its inhabitants. Living space is separated by function, and there is special space (typically, the living room) in which the family does things together. For the working father (and, later, the working mother), the home becomes the locale of withdrawal from the tensions and worries of the job, a place of refuge and renewal where the "real life" of the individual can unfold.

Naturally enough, as the home became more attractive and the key locale for the "self-realization" of the individual, sociability came to be centralized there. In other words, sociability moved out of the streets, out of public places; it, too, became "domesticated." This has been criticized as a distortion of social life, as a diminishment of the public sphere, just as the increase of physical comfort and its accoutrements has been attacked—the former as "privatization," the latter as "consumerism." Such criticism is plausible on the basis of specific values—such as a classical vision of the primacy of the public, or an ascetic ideal of personal, life. We are not interested at the moment in challenging these values (though we are skeptical of them); the point here is, rather, to emphasize that both affluence and domesticity have been very important ingredients in what, for generations, was experienced as the "liberating" quality of bourgeois life.

The new bourgeois ethos, while being diffused, retained its central features as these were formed in an earlier period. The concern for children remained in the foreground. Linked to this, there was the concern for education, both as a general social value and as applying specifically to one's own children. The intimate life of the family remains as the focus of personal values and identity, both for men and women. The idea of romantic love continues as the major motive for marriage. The relation between spouses is to be one of intense mutual affection and respect. Within the household, at least, the woman is seen as equal if not dominant. In view of the recent feminist interpretation of this process, the last point ought to be stressed. To be sure, the domestic sphere came to be seen as women's "proper place." This is now frequently interpreted as an economic, and in consequence sociopolitical, disenfranchisement of women. With the modern organization of work, it is argued, men working outside the household were paid, while women performed unpaid work within the household. Ivan Illich has coined the phrase "shadow work" for this type of unpaid labor: "The woman, formerly the mistress of a household that provided sustenance for the family, now became the guardian of a place where children stayed before they began to work, where the husband rested, and where his income was spent."[28] This interpretation rests on the unstated assumption that only paid work is to be considered as supplying status. Almost certainly, this is a projection onto the situation of very new perceptions by intellectuals, which did not prevail at all in an earlier period and still do not prevail in wide areas of society. On the contrary, for many women, especially below the upper middle class, this alleged "disenfranchisement" is precisely what they consider to be "liberation" from the discontents of work in the marketplace.

Be this as it may, in the bourgeois vision of the family the woman is paramount in the home.[29] It is her domain. The husband/father continued for a while as a figure of power and authority in the household, but this status was very successively undermined by the emancipated bourgeois wife/mother, increasingly in conjunction with outside experts such as clergy, doctors, and teachers, more recently psychotherapists and counselors of various types. Today, where this family vision continues to hold, the family regime is largely a regime of women, and the old paternal ideal is the subject of caricature, rather than realistic perception (as, say, American soap operas of the 1950s vividly expressed). It is ironic that just this father figure of diminished and comic status should become the object of feminist wrath. The woman of the bourgeois family has, above all, a "civilizational" mission, both within and beyond the household. Within the household, the woman is the "homemaker"—companion and helper to her husband, supervisor and "facilitator" of her children's development and education, arbiter of taste, culture, and all the "finer things of life." But this civilizing mission also extends beyond the home, into social and cultural activities of an "edifying" nature, and (especially in America) into reformist politics. The role of bourgeois women in the building of cultural institutions (museums, libraries, symphony orchestras, and so on) and in political reform (take, for example, such organizations as the League of Women Voters) has been staggering in its society-wide impact. Far from being imprisoned within the family, we would argue, bourgeois women have been prime builders of bourgeois civilization.

Perhaps it should not surprise us that some women became disenchanted with this role, quite apart from the feminist movement as such. Civilization-building is a weary-making task, with its own psychic costs. In the (somewhat misleading) language of the critics, it can become tiresome to be "on a pedestal." Also, the very values of the bourgeois family ethos, from the beginning, had within them the seeds of their own destruction. Individualism, brought forth within the family, would turn against it. Education would free itself of its family linkage and burgeon into powerful institutions with an anti-family animus, or at least with vested interests antagonistic to those of the family. The experts who started out as allies of the bourgeois family would develop interests and viewpoints of their own that put them at odds with the family. Again not surprisingly, these disintegrative developments became intense in the upper middle class (the original social location of the bourgeois family ethos) just after the patterns of that class were effectively diffused to the lower classes. If one prefers a different language, "decadence" always sets in first in the higher strata of society, those strata whose "virtues" originally shaped the society. (The same phenomenon could be observed in the aristocracy of *ancien régime,* as it weakly tried to defend itself against the vigorously rising bourgeoisie.) Thus today, ironically, a more "intact" bourgeois family ethos can be found in the working classes of most Western societies than in that upper middle class which is still identified with the "bourgeoisie" by its radical critics!

The diffusion of the bourgeois family "downwards" is itself a fascinating topic of historical research.[30] There have been few well-documented arguments as yet as to the precise nature of this process. But it can be confidently stated that by the middle of the twentieth century the main features of the bourgeois family ethos, as outlined above, had spread to virtually all classes in Western societies. Especially the women of the lower classes saw in this ethos the great promise of their own fulfillment and "liberation" from the drudgery of low-prestige and low-paid jobs. In these classes, too, women more than men have been the great "civilizers." This can be seen, for instance, in the black family in America, which has been misleadingly characterized as a thoroughly disorganized and pathogenic social milieu.[31] One of the final ironies of our contemporary situation is this: that the "helping professions," offsprings of the bourgeois family ethos, are now trying to police the lower classes in the name of values quite antagonistic to that ethos—those same lower classes whose vision of the good life is mostly closer to the old bourgeois patterns than the vision of the professionals! It is as if, in the truly "decadent" fashion, the bourgeois ethos had turned upon itself.

NOTES

1. William J. Goode, *After Divorce* (New York: Free Press, 1956).

2. *Daedalus,* Journal of the American Academy of Arts and Sciences, Spring 1977 issue, *The Family,* contains a number of essays that reflect the use and the implications of the new historical data on early history of the family in Europe and America.
    Peter Laslett, *The World We Have Lost,* 2nd ed. (New York: Scribner, 1971), first pub. 1965.
    ———, *Family Life and Illicit Love in Earlier Generations* (New York: Cambridge University Press, 1977).
    ———, ed., *Household and Family in Past Time* (New York: Cambridge University Press, 1972).
    William J. Goode, *World Revolution and Family Patterns* (New York: Free Press, 1963).
    Jean-Louis Flandrin, *Families in Former Times: Kinship, Household and Sexuality* (New York: Cambridge University Press, 1979).
    Lawrence Stone, *The Family, Sex and Marriage in England 1500–1800,* abridged ed. (New York: Harper, 1979).
    D. V. Glass and D. E. C. Eversley (eds.), *Population in History* (London: Edward Arnold, 1965).

3. Emmanuel Ladurie, *Montaillou* (New York: Vintage, 1979).

4. See Laslett's extensive footnote on the Great Russian pattern, p. 14 of his *Family Life and Illicit Love in Earlier Generations, supra,* and there in particular the entire chapter on "Characteristics of the Western Family."

5. See Laslett, *Family Life and Illicit Love in Earlier Generations, supra,* but also the contradictory materials and arguments presented by Lutz K. Berkner, "Recent Research on the the History of the Family in Western Europe," *Journal of Marriage and the Family,* Vol. 35, Aug. 1973, pp. 395–445, as well as by Andrejs Plakan, "Seigneurial Authority and Peasant Family Life: The Baltic Area in the Eighteenth Century," *Journal of Interdisciplinary History,* Vol. 4, Spring 1975, pp. 629–54.

   Robert Wheaton, "Family and Kinship in Western Europe: The problem of the Joint Household," *Journal of Interdisciplinary History,* Vol. 4, Spring 1975, pp. 601–28.

6. William J. Goode, *World Revolution and Family Patterns, supra.*

7. See the convincing argument made by Tamara K. Hareven, "Family Time and Historical Time," *Daedalus,* Spring 1977 issue: *The Family.*

8. Nathan Glazer and Daniel P. Moyniban, *Beyond the Melting Pot* (Cambridge, Mass.: M.I.T. Press, 1963).

   L. Grebler et al., *The Mexican-American People* (New York: Free Press, 1970).

   Herbert G. Gutman, *The Black Family in Slavery and Freedom* (New York: Pantheon, 1976).

   Charles H. Mindel and Robert W. Habenstein, (eds.), *Ethnic Families in America* (New York: Elsevier, 1976).

9. We (with Hansfried Kellner) have discussed this problem, and the phenomenon of carry-over from one social world to another, in our book *The Homeless Mind, supra.* We still stand by the main features of this analysis, but we are now inclined to think that we, too, may have over-emphasized the negative aspect of "homelessness" as against the creative possibility of being "at home" in more than one world.

10. William J. Goode, *World Revolution and Family Patterns, supra,* and Alex Inkeles, *Modernization and Family Patterns: A Test of Convergence Theory,* unpublished MS.

11. Cf., e.g., R. P. Dore, *City Life in Japan* (Berkeley: University of California Press, 1965), and Hiroshi Wagatsuma, "Some Aspects of the Japanese Family," *Daedalus,* Spring 1977, pp. 171–210, as well as Tsuneo Yamane, "The Nuclear Family Within the Three-Generational Household in Modern Japan," in Lois Lenero-Otero, ed., *Beyond the Nuclear Family Model: Cross-Cultural Perspectives* (Beverly Hills, Calif.: Sage Publications, 1977).

12. This argument is well documented by Mary Jo Bane in *Here to Stay, supra,* as well as in the Preface to the *Daedalus* issue on *The Family, supra.*

13. E. Anthony Wrigley, "Reflections on the History of the Family," *Daedalus,* Spring 1977.

14. The best-known representatives of the structural-functional perspective on the family are Talcott Parsons and Robert F. Bales, who spelled out this approach in their *Family Socialization and Interaction Process, supra.* This perspective has greatly influenced contemporary sociology and has become very much a building block in the majority of recent studies on the family.

   The Marxist approach to the family was first spelled out by Friedrich Engels, *The Origins of the Family, Private Property, and the State* (1884) (New York: International Publishers, 1972). A contemporary up-date of this approach can be found in Eli Zaretsky, *Capitalism, the Family and Personal Life, supra,* and a quasi-Marxian approach in Christopher Lasch, *Haven in a Heartless World* (New York: Basic Bks., 1977).

15. William J. Goode et al., *Social Systems and Family Patterns* (New York: Irvington Publishers, 1971).

16. For a general statement of this approach, cf. Peter Berger and Thomas Luckmann, *The Social Construction of Reality* (Garden City, N.Y.: Doubleday, 1966).

Our aforementioned book *The Homeless Mind* is an attempt to apply this approach to the special problem of modern consciousness.

17. For a dynamic case study of this, in a village in Tunisia, cf. Jean Duvignaud, *Change at Shebika* (New York: Pantheon, 1970).

18. Wrigley, op. cit., makes a similarly intriguing argument making the useful distinction between modernization and industrialization, whereby the first has to precede the second.

19. Cf. Ariès, *Centuries of Childhood, supra.*

20. In very different contexts and for very different purposes, similar expositions of available historical data have been made by such diverse scholars as Max Weber, "Household, Enterprise and Oikos," in *Economy and Society* (New York: Bedminster Press, 1968), and in particular his "Zur Geschichte der Handelsgesellschaften im Mittelalter," in Max Weber, *Gesammelte Aufsätze zur Sozial- und Wirtschaftsgeschichte* (Tübingen: Morh & Siebecke, 1924), pp. 353 ff.; Max Horkheimer, "Allgemeiner Teil" to "Theoretische Entwürfe über Autorität und Familie," in *Autorität und Familie: Studien aus den Institute für Soziolforschung* (Paris: Librairie Félix Alcan, 1936); Arnold Gehlen, *Man in the Age of Technology* (New York: Columbia University Press, 1980); Edward Shorter, *The Making of the Modern Family, supra;* E. P. Thompson, *The Making of the English Working Class* (London: Gollancz, 1963); Laslett's various writings cited earlier; Jean-Louis Flandrin, *Familles: parenté, maison, sexualité dans l'ancienne société* (Paris: 1976); Donzelot, *the Policing of Families, supra.*

21. Ariès, op. cit., p. 414.

22. Norbert Elias, *The Civilizing Process* (New York: Urizen Bks., 1977).

23. Ian Bradley, *The Call to Seriousness: The Evangelical Impact on the Victorians* (London: Macmillan, 1976).

24. Bergier, *The Industrial Bourgeoisie, supra.*

25. Bradley, op. cit.

26. Sheila Rothman, *Woman's Proper Place, supra.*

27. Edward Shorter, op. cit., makes a plausible argument along these lines in his *The Making of the Modern Family,* in the chapter "The Rise of the Nuclear Family."

28. Ivan Illich, *Shadow Work* (London: Boyars, 1981).

29. Both Donzelot, in *The Policing of Families, supra,* and Douglas, in *The Feminization of American Culture, supra,* have made this argument the central theme of their books.

30. John M. Cuddihy, in his *The Ordeal of Civility* (New York: Basic Bks., 1975), has made an interesting argument, in a somewhat different context, along these lines.

31. Robert B. Hill, among others, has made a strong counterargument to the pathological view of the black family in his *Strengths of Black Families* (New York: Emerson Hall, 1973).

3

Demographic Change and Family Life in American History: Some Reflections*

Robert V. Wells

DEMOGRAPHY AND FAMILIES

Demographic history has many connections with other aspects of American history. Politics, society, and the economy have all been affected by . . . extraordinary demographic changes. . . . However, no aspect of American life has been more profoundly influenced by the demographic structures and changes . . . than the family. By the middle of the nineteenth century, Americans were already debating what was happening and what ought to happen to their families. that debate continues today, often with passion and nostalgia for family patterns that exist more in myth than in history. . . .

One of the most obvious links between demography and the family is that the central life events of birth, death, marriage, and migration occur within the context of family life. Marriage, for example, frequently marks the passage of a young man or woman out of one family into another. The newly formed family becomes a new reproductive unit for society, since throughout American history most children have been born within families. Death is not always as directly linked to family life as marriage or childbirth, but this most fundamental of all changes frequently occurs within the context of the family. Likewise, migration may be common among isolated individuals, but frequently migrants have been part of a family moving either together or sequentially, with one family member leading the way to a new community, to be followed at a future time by the others.

The central life events experienced by most people in a society not only occur within families but also are controlled by families and alter family living as well. In the past, already existing families often controlled the creation of new families by marriage, partly to help mark the transition of the young to adulthood, and partly to limit the number of potential reproductive units laying claim to scarce resources. Similarly, the sexual activity of children often was expected to be regulated, if not completely postponed, by parents until children had reached a certain age. Death was not managed by families as effectively as some other aspects of demographic behavior, although in the twentieth century parents generally are expected to provide immunities available to children through medical attention. Nevertheless, death can alter families by removing members from the household, sometimes in a fashion that can be quite abrupt and unexpected. In addition, family members often provide support and comfort both for the dying

*Wells, Robert V. 1985. "Demographic Change and Family Life in American History: Some Reflections." Pp. 145–167 in *Uncle Sam's Family: Issues and Perspectives on American Demographic History*. Albany: State University of New York Press. Reprinted by permission of the State University of New York Press.

and for each other to make the resulting transition as easy as possible. Finally, migration obviously alters families by both increasing and decreasing the numbers of people who live together, and by changing the environment in which family life takes place. In turn, the needs of families to send sons or daughters out into the world to seek their fortunes, or perhaps even to send a father off in search of a new community where the family might better prosper helps to shape the size and direction of streams of migration.

The expectations that the young acquire about having children, facing death, marrying, and moving, and the interpretations that they assign to their actual experiences with these phenomena frequently are connected to values that are taught by and implemented through families. Given the undeniably pleasant effects of sexual relationships, families have been remarkably effective in limiting, if not completely curtailing, sexual activity outside of marriage. One of the most remarkable aspects of life in seventeenth- and early eighteenth-century New England was the extent to which young men and women allowed their families to dictate the age at which they might marry by means of control over property, even where a community existed in the midst of large amounts of land on which new families could have set up housekeeping. In the past, parents have paid attention to preparing children to accept not only their own mortality, but also the fact that eventually their parents would depart from the face of the earth. The capacity to handle this major transition in an acceptable psychological fashion is perhaps one of the most important lessons that every child should learn. The values taught by one generation to another have sometimes reflected either myth or the past more than current demographic realities. Maris Vinovskis, for example, has suggested that nineteenth-century Americans often assumed that they faced a much harsher future than was warranted, according to his analysis of the mortality statistics of the time. Thus, families help to celebrate, mourn, and give recognition to major transitions in the life of every person brought about by their own demographic experiences and those of individuals closely associated to them.

A second major link between demographic history and the history of the family comes through the sources that demographers rely on for the study of past patterns of population. Family reconstitution, a technique that has been fundamental in allowing historians and demographers to describe and examine demographic behavior in the past, is a very close cousin of genealogy. both of these techniques depend on the ability of a student to piece together from lists of births, marriages, and deaths an array of details about individual families. The genealogist may be interested in tracing his or her lineage back into the past, whereas the demographer or historian may have no special interest in a particular family name. Nonetheless, family reconstitution requires skills that are remarkably close to those of individuals interested in the study of particular families. In addition, demographic history becomes especially interesting when the demographic patterns of particular families can be linked to other aspects of family life through tax lists, church rolls, voting lists, and other documents recording the relationships of individuals in a particular community. A number of seventeenth- and eighteenth-century New England communities have been studied in this fashion, including Andover, Massachusetts, in the colonial period, and Concord, Massachusetts, during the

Revolution. Mary Ryans's similar work on Utica, New York, in the nineteenth century will be examined shortly.

Censuses, in which information is recorded by household or family head, also provide important links between demographic and family history. The same records that provide data about population totals and age and sex composition on a large scale also may enable the researcher to explore such fascinating topics as the geographic and social mobility of individual families, the extent of fertility control within a population, and the size and structure of families at any particular point in time.

Finally, it should be noted that many of the important issues in family history require at least a basic knowledge of demographic patterns if they are to be understood. Scholars interested in the extent of nature of patriarchal control over families in the past must take into account such basic demographic phenomena as the number of children for which a father might have to provide, as well as how marriage patterns might reflect the control of one generation over another. Women's roles within families and society at large have been profoundly influenced by the number of children a woman might expect to have, at what ages she might expect to have them, and how early she might cease to bear children. Similarly, the migration of young women from rural New England into the textile towns in eastern Massachusetts during the mid-nineteenth century is of interest not only because of its effect on the demographic structure of those towns but also because of what it tells about the willingness of families to let their daughters leave home earlier than in previous generations, and may, in fact, have influenced the attitudes those women brought to the relationships they formed later on in their lives.

Family historians often have been interested in the changing economic roles of families in society in the nineteenth and early twentieth centuries. Although many of the new roles were clearly related to economic structures and modes of production that were unfamiliar in the eighteenth century, basic demographic changes were also important in creating new relationships. Rural families moved into urban environments to take up new and often unfamiliar jobs. As the number of children in the family declined, women may have found themselves freer to pursue work outside the home. Improved life expectancy at the end of the nineteenth century was accompanied by better health. This made it possible for the individual members of the nation's work force to be on the job more regularly and to be better able to provide a full day's work simply because they felt better. This, in turn, meant that many families were no longer as exposed to the threat of uncertain wages simply because they could count on family members being able to work. Families were increasingly protected from the catastrophic results of epidemic illness and death. Business cycles become more important in determining a family's fortune; more and more American families prospered and suffered together.

Given the close links between demographic history and the history of the family, it would be possible to write a complete book exploring the many and varied connections. Since that is neither possible nor desirable in the context of this essay, only two broad points will be explored. First, it is interesting to examine how thinking about the nature of families has evolved over the last two decades, providing more sophisticated and useful means of analyzing both family and demographic processes. After this has been done, some of the effects that the major demographic transitions of the last two centuries have brought to family life will be examined.

THINKING ABOUT FAMILIES

Since 1960, historians, demographers, and sociologists have altered the ways in which they think about families. Two decades ago, most families in the past were commonly thought to have been extended. That is, three or more generations, and perhaps brothers, sisters, and cousins as well, all were assumed to live closely together. The explanation for the much smaller families, consisting typically of a husband and wife and their own children, that were found in the mid-twentieth century in the United States, was that such nuclear families had emerged in response to industrial society. We now know that this is not true. Nuclear families have been common for the last three or four centuries.

In thinking about the family, it is clear that the word "family" has several possible meanings, each of which may be appropriate to particular forms of family or demographic history, but all need to be more precisely defined. There are at least four commonly used definitions. One is that of a reproductive unit consisting of a husband and wife and their children. A second definition of a family is frequently used in conjunction with census data and involves the concept of a household—that is, a group of people who reside together in the same dwelling. A somewhat broader definition of a household that is appropriate for certain times and places in American history involves all those individuals who lived in close proximity to each other, engaging in some common economic pursuit under the directon of one particular individual. The most clearcut example of this kind of family is the plantation in the South when slavery was still common. Although slaves and their white masters rarely, if ever, actually resided in the same house, the whites frequently referred to the whole group as a family. Whether black slaves considered the residents of the plantation to be all one family is another matter. A third definition of the family involves the notion of kinship, that is, all those individuals to whom we consider ourselves somehow or other related. In English, we refer to them as fathers and mothers, children, brothers and sisters, grandparents, uncles and aunts, or cousins of some sort. Records in other languages from other cultures sometimes use words that may be translated directly into English with little distortion of meaning, but it is important to be sensitive to possible subtle, but significant, differences among cultures in the variety of words they use to describe kinship when studying the family patterns among Indians, Afro-Americans, and non-English speaking Europeans. For example, an older, and presumably wiser, male of an earlier generation might be referred to by a word that could appropriately be translated into English as "father," "uncle," or "wise elder." However, each of those meanings in English is quite different. In addition, there is a more limited group of kin to which the term family is also applied, namely those individuals to whom we would turn for assistance in time of trouble. In general, the circle of kin with whom we have expectations of mutual obligations and responsibilities is somewhat smaller than the array of individuals we recognize ourselves to be related to through blood or marriage. How wide this circle is depends on time, culture, and the intimate history of individual families.

The simplest way of looking at families is by descriptions or pictures of structures or patterns at a particular moment in time. Thus, demographers and family historians have studied the number of children ever born to a particular husband and wife by the end of their marriage. Likewise, censuses provide snapshots of what households looked like in terms of size and structures in a given year. Each of these views of the family has its own merits, yet both are limited because they provide no sense of how families have grown, changed, and declined over a long period of time. The children born to an eighteenth-century American couple may have arrived in that family over the span of twenty to twenty-five years, a much longer period of time than is spent in childbearing in the second half of the twentieth century. Death, marriage, and migration might have worked at a much slower pace to shrink the same family. Thus, it has become clear that static views of the family are not always adequate either for demographic or family historians. Family life was and is a process of change and adaptation to both the arrival and departure of new individuals, and the growth and development of the individuals who remain within the family for a prolonged period of time.

The value of taking a dynamic rather than a static view of family life has been brought home through several important studies. One of the most interesting, by Lutz Berkner, examined eighteenth-century European families. By grouping households according to the age of the head of the household, Berkner discovered that, although the size of families remained remarkably constant, their structures changed rather dramatically with the age of the head. Therefore, he argued, families passed through distinct stages depending on how long the family had been in existence and its ability to command economic resources within a community. Berkner raised the question of which, if any, of the various stages of the family was closest to the ideal. Although he agreed that nuclear families were quite common in eighteenth-century Europe, he pointed out that they may not, in fact, have been the preferred way to live. Possibly, families in which there were three generations or perhaps a boarder present were, for one reason or another, more preferred by the people of that time than the nuclear pattern, but demographic conditions made it difficult for most families to exist in the ideal state. Berkner also concluded that most individuals who lived more than a few years would have experienced a variety of family types over the course of their lives and so could not be analyzed as having been born, brought up, and matured within a particular household structure.

The explorations of household structures by this author, using censuses compiled in late-seventeenth-century New York and in Louisiana in the 1760s have reenforced the conclusion that it is necessary to pay attention to the development of households over time rather than to look at them as static units. For example, small households often reflected a variety of circumstances. A family recorded in a census as containing three people may be composed of a young husband and wife who have just had their first child, or, such a family could be a husband and wife who have had a number of children, all but one of whom had died from endemic or epidemic diseases. Finally, a three-person household may simply be an older couple with only one of their children still living with them. In Louisiana, in the 1760s, several communities studied by Andrew Walsh and myself had families that were surprisingly small. Close study showed that these communities were relatively new, and hence were composed of families in which most householders were relatively young. Older communities with older households had larger families. Although the average size of the household in the new communities remained remarkably constant over the span of three or four years, relatively few of the individual households remained unchanged. In one instance, it was possible to trace fifty-two families between 1766 and 1769. Of these fifty-two households, only four remained unaltered in both size and membership. The other forty-eight changed in size and/or composition in the space of three years.

Students of seventeenth-century Chesapeake families, such as Lois Carr and Lorena Walsh, or Darrett and Anita Rutman, have reenforced the importance of examining the development of households as well as their structures at any point in time. In early Virginia and Maryland, households frequently were complex combinations of parts of previous families coexisting with new members of the current household. A simple structural analysis of a seventeenth-century Chesapeake household might provide evidence of a husband and wife and four children living in a household. But with a dynamic perspective, we might learn that this was the second or third marriage for both husband and wife. In addition, the four children, instead of all being born to that particular marriage, might include a child of the father's, a child of the mother's, each from a previous marriage, one child who was the product of this union, and a fourth child who might be an indentured servant or the child of one of the brothers or sisters of the husband or wife who had been taken in either to learn an occupation or because of dislocation in that child's own immediate family.

The need to introduce a dynamic perspective to the study of the family has led historians to choose among several forms of life-cycle analysis. Figure 1 summarizes some of the most fruitful approaches. After using this diagram to consider how thinking about family history has become more complex and sophisticated over the last several decades, there are some brief comments on how readers might use the model presented here as a starting point for their own personal study of family history.

One dynamic perspective is to study the life cycle of the individual. Complete or partial life cycles of individuals of four successive generations have been represented in the figure by the lines labeled "Grandparent," "Parent," "First Child," "Child of First Child," and "Last Child." They are intended to be studied in conjunction with the rectangle in the middle of the figure, labeled "Family Cycle," but can, for the moment, be considered by themselves. Historians looking at family life from this perspective have examined how individuals move through a series of stages and changes from being a very small child, to an adolescent, to a young adult, to a mature adult, and ultimately to an older adult. This can be done with greater or less sophistication, examining, among other things, various changes an individual experiences in family and social roles as he or she moves from one age level to another. With data from several decades or centuries, it is possible to

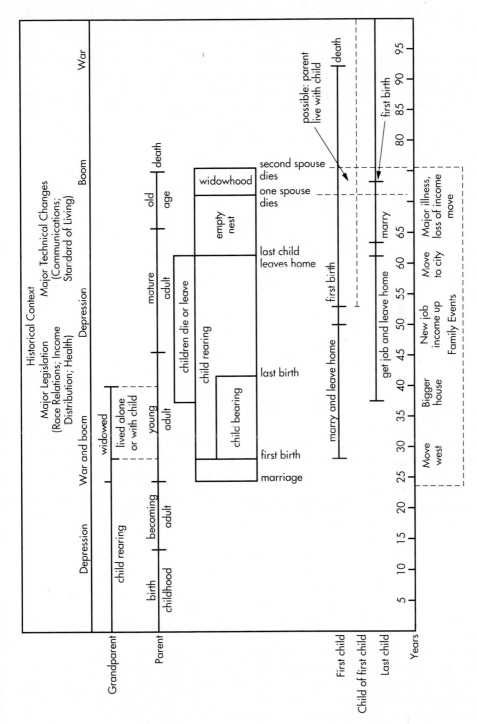

Figure 1. Dynamic approaches to studying families.

study how various stages of development have expanded and contacted or perhaps even multiplied over time. One important result of these kinds of studies has been an increasing awareness that, at least in the past, the life cycle of the individual depended greatly on the sex, race, and cultural heritage of the individual. In the twentieth century, individual life cycles have become increasingly similar.

A second life-cycle approach studies not individuals but families. This technique is based on the concept that families go through stages that profoundly affect the experiences and behavior of each of the individual family members. One simple form of the life cycle of the family, represented by the rectangle in the middle of Figure 1, begins with the creation of the family via marriage, followed by a brief stage in which husband and wife live together without children. The arrival of the first child marks the start of a much longer stage involving childbearing and childrearing, two closely related aspects of family life that may or may not be separated for analytic purposes. When all the children have married, moved, or died, parents are faced with what is known as the "empty nest" stage of family life in which two older adults will live together. With the death of one spouse, the family continues with the widowhood of either the husband or wife until the surviving spouse finally dies, bringing to an end the complete cycle of a family.

Anyone who adopts some kind of life-cycle analysis in their study of demographic or family history will have to make several adjustments according to the period he or she is studying. To begin with, it is necessary to be aware of both stages of transitions. Regarding stages, it must be decided, for example, how many significant divisions there are in the life cycle of a family. For example, is it useful to differentiate between childbearing and childrearing? Students of twentieth-century American families frequently have divided the childrearing stage of family life into two periods according to whether or not there are children under six in the family. Six is, of course, the age at which all children begin to attend public school. Such a division would obviously make little sense in the absence of mandatory schooling for young children. The number of stages that need to be examined and their duration may change dramatically over a long period of time. As is evident from Tables 1 and 2, the duration of the childrearing stage of family life in the eighteenth century was frequently forty years or more. In contemporary America, the childrearing stage of family life is at least ten years shorter. Conversely, in eighteenth-century America, death was so common a phenomenon that many couples missed the empty nest stage of family life because at least one spouse had died before all the children left home. In the second half of the twentieth century, husbands and wives frequently can expect ten to fifteen years of life together after their last child has departed. Consider how different the rectangle in Figure 1, representing eighteenth-century expectations, would look from one depicting a twentieth-century family.

Transition points are as important to study as the stages those transitions define. In recent years, John Modell and others have discovered major changes over the centuries in the age at which individuals experienced transitions, the number of transitions they may go through, the sequence of those transitions, the amount of time between one transition and another, and how common all transitions are to a particular generation. Consider, for example, what it means for a young person to leave home. In modern America, individuals frequently

TABLE 1. Median Age of Wives at Stages of the Life Cycle of the Family

Stage of the Life Cycle of the Family	Wives Born		
	Before 1786 (Quakers)	1880–1889	1920–1929
A. First marriage	20.5*	21.6	20.8
B. Birth of last child	37.9	32.9	30.5
C. Marriage of last child	60.2	56.2	52.0
D. Death of first spouse to die	50.9	57.0	64.4

*The overall patterns of marriage, birth of last child, and duration of marriage seem to have been much the same, from one group to another. To the extent that one group was different from the other two, it is the wives born between 1920 and 1929 who seem to be somewhat unusual and not the Quakers.

SOURCE: Robert V. Wells, "Demographic Change and the Life Cycle of American Families," Appendix. Reprinted from *The Journal of Interdisciplinary History*, II (1971): 281–282, with permission of *The Journal of Interdisciplinary History* and The M.I.T. Press, Cambridge, Massachusetts. Copyright 1971, by the Massachusetts Institute of Technology and the editors of *The Journal of Interdisciplinary History*.

leave home to attend school. After they have graduated from college, they may then get their first job and marry several years later. This sequence is common for both sons and daughters. A century ago, however, a daughter might occasionally leave home for several years to take a job. Going to college for a girl was highly unusual. More likely, she left her parents only upon marriage. A son, on the other hand, might leave home to take a job, marrying relatively quickly thereafter. In fact, historians have discovered a remarkable tendency in the twentieth century for all young people to experience all the transitions that mark the passage between being a child in one's parents' household to establishing a household of one's own. The young who go through the entire sequence do so more quickly than was common in the late nineteenth century.

Because most life-cycle approaches seek to define the average experience, it is important to ask how common was the average pattern. Historians can most easily describe what the average life cycle of a family or of an individual might look like. However, in periods in which there were wide variations in age at marriage, the number of children born to a family, and the expectation of life of any one individual, the expected pattern might differ quite significantly from an individual's actual experience. Peter Uhlenberg, for example, has discovered that in the nineteenth century, only about one of every five females born actually passed through the entire life cycle of an average family. Although a few women lived long lives without marrying, and fewer still were divorced, death commonly intruded to make it impossible for the others to experience the full array of transitions and stages. In a family with six children, the life cycle of the first born child was quite different from that of the sixth child, both in terms of the number of people that child had to relate to in the life of the family and the conditions

TABLE 2. Median Length of Selected Stages of the Live Cycle of the Family (in years)

Stage of the Life Cycle of the Family	Wives Born		
	Before 1786 (Quakers)	1880–1889	1920–1929
1. Childbearing	17.4	11.3	9.7
2. Childrearing	39.7	34.6	31.2
3. Duration of marriage	30.4	35.4	43.6
4. Old age together	– 9.3	0.8	12.4
5. Widowhood			
Female	13.7	18.7	—
Male	12.5	14.2	—
6. Marriage of last child to death of last spouse, when last is			
Female	4.4	19.5	—
Male	3.2	15.0	—

The above table was derived as follows:
Table 2.
   Line 1 = Line B − Line A
   Line 2 = Line C − Line A
   From Table 1
   Line 3 = Line D − Line A
   Line 4 = Line D − Line C
   Line 5 = The figures for the husbands and wives born before 1786 were calculated directly from my data. For the others, see Glick and Parke, "New Approaches," 195.
   Line 6 = Line 4 and Line 5

SOURCE: Robert V. Wells, "Demographic Change and the Life cycle of American Families," Appendix. Reprinted from *The Journal of Interdisciplinary History,* II (1971): 281–282, with permission of *The Journal of Interdisciplinary History* and The M.I.T. Press, Cambridge, Massachusetts. Copyright 1971, by the Massachusetts Institute of Technology and the editors of *The Journal of Interdisciplinary History.*

under which he or she might be raised. Not surprisingly, first borns generally had a greater expectation of having parents around through most of their lives than would a sixth child who was born when the parents had already reached their early forties. The lines labeled "First Child" and "Last Child" in Figure 1 can be looked at in conjunction with the "Family Cycle" in the middle in order to make this difference clear.

In order to take into account these complexities, historians of the family have begun to study what is termed the life course rather than the life cycle. This approach recognizes that individual lives do not intersect in equal ways with family life cycles. Even though two individuals may have been alive during the mid-nineteenth century, and were members of the same family, their lives may have been quite different simply because one of them was a first born and one of them was born last in a large family.

Recognition that different historical circumstances can further influence the way the life cycle of individuals and the life cycle of families intersect to produce different life courses adds an equally important perspective to this mode of analysis. Thus, every generation presumably has its own unique experiences. For example, husbands and wives who married in the early 1930s faced quite different economic prospects than those couples who married in the midst of World War II. In turn, couples who married in the early 1950s had prospects for a stable, prosperous family life that were much more promising than those facing the cohorts of the early 1930s or 1940s. This author's study of Quaker families in the late eighteenth century has indicated that their childbearing patterns changed rather abruptly about the onset of the American Revolution, suggesting that the generation immediately preceding the Revolution saw no reason to curtail childbearing, but those who married and began to create their own family in the midst of the revolutionary situation found reason to try and control the size of the family. The top of Figure 1, labeled "Historical Context," presents some of the possible national events that might affect the life cycles of individuals and families. At the bottom, the rectangle titled "Family Events" includes some of the possible elements of a family's private history that might also affect members of a family in different ways.

Although there have been relatively few studies exploring the interactions of individual life cycles with family life cycles taking into account the specific historical content, it is obvious that the analysis produced by such a perspective is much more sophisticated and much more complex than that involving a simple description of the static structures of the size of a family or household at any one point in time. That is not to say that simple static descriptions do not have their merit, for under certain circumstances they describe the way in which a society is put together. Nonetheless, over the last several decades scholars have become increasingly sophisticated in their understanding of both the factors that shape an individual's development within his or her family, and how family life can change because of historical circumstances and because of the conditions an individual experiences within the family in the course of his or her lifetime.

Figure 1 depicts the dynamic perspective on individuals and families in a very general form. Its immediate purpose was to make some of the preceding discussion clearer. However, readers should be able to use this model to gain a fuller understanding of the lives of some real people. For example, try creating the equivalent diagram for your own family. If genealogies are available, the life cycles of different historical families can be drawn. On a more abstract level, readers could diagram families and individuals in which the transitions and stages vary in number and duration, and place them in real historical contexts. Other possibilities should suggest themselves, including differences arising from sex or cultural heritage.

Not all aspects of family history that are closely related to demographic history make use of the life-cycle perspective. Two of the most interesting recent works in family history have a basic demographic core, but have somewhat different theoretical orientations. One is Carl Degler's recent book, *At Odds,* in which the author argues a basic conflict has existed over the last two centuries between women's needs and efforts to develop themselves as individuals and the demands that women subordinate themselves to the interest of their family. As part of his examination of the tensions that emerged between women and their families, Degler found it desirable to explore in some detail the extent to which fertility was controlled between the late eighteenth century and the present, and the means by which that control was achieved. It is of some significance that women had a great deal of influence over the introduction of contraception, and were not entirely dependent on men and male-controlled modes of birth control.

In her impressive study of the origins of middle-class family structures and values of Oneida County in New York between 1790 and 1865, Mary Ryan has paid as much attention to basic demographic behavior as Degler. Although Ryan's main concern is the articulation and dissemination of a new set of values that helped to define middle-class society, and to perpetuate that society into the late nineteenth and early twentieth centuries, she has remained sensitive to the basic demographic changes that accompanied the changes in attitudes and perceptions. Thus, she provides detailed explorations not only of migration patterns into emerging industrial communities but also of such basic demographic structures as age and sex composition, and household patterns. The evolution of Oneida society is a superb example of how demographic structures interacted with family patterns and cultural values to alter the way in which Americans went about their lives. Ryan argues effectively that the emergence of new values by 1865, although shaped by the demographic changes that occurred over the previous three-quarters of a century, were by no means the only values that could have worked within the contours of the basic demographic structures. Thus, she demonstrates clearly that the connection between value and demographic behavior is close but is not deterministic. The men and women who lived in Oneida County in the early nineteenth century had to adapt to new demographic structures and did so successfully, but they did so on their terms rather than as pawns in some kind of gigantic demographic chess game.

DEMOGRAPHIC CHANGE AND FAMILY LIFE *Know This*

What have been the effects of major demographic changes between the eighteenth century and the present on family life? It is not possible here to deal with all of the possible and probable results, and with the impact of demographic changes on the broader contours of American life in terms of the economy, politics, and society. However, some comment on a few of the major alterations in family life is possible.

When looking at the meaning of the fertility decline for American men and women between the eighteenth and the twentieth centuries, several points stand out. One of the most notable has been the decrease in the average size of households. In the late eighteenth century, an average household contained about six people. Today, households average around three individuals. Much of the difference is the result of the extraordinary decline in childbearing that occurred during the nineteenth and early twentieth centuries, although it will be noted shortly that there are other factors to be considered. In addition, the fact that an average couple had fewer children over the course of their life cycle has had several effects in terms of family life. Perhaps the most notable is that couples can anticipate the empty nest stage of the family cycle to be a much longer and more important part of their lives. With fewer children, childbearing ends at an earlier age, and the last child marries and leaves home when the mother and father are younger than was the case in the past.

What has been the impact on individual lives of this extraordinary reduction in childbearing? Obviously, having fewer children has put considerable less burden on American women in the twentieth century than was the case 200 years ago. Having two children as opposed to six has implications not only for a woman's health but also for the amount of time she will have to devote to the care and raising of others, at considerably sacrifice to her own personal development. As a result, women in the twentieth century are much freer to pursue whatever line of personal development they desire, whether that be a career in the business world or simply providing better maternal care.

From the point of view of the child, the reduction in fertility has had several significant effects. Obviously, a child in a two-person family ought to receive greater attention from his or her parents than one who grows up in the midst of eight or ten competitors for adult attention. The benefits of this depend on the character of the parents, but in general children will develop more rapidly and will acquire greater verbal and numerical skills as a result of greater contact with educated parents than they will if much of their contact is with children of only slightly differing age. A second less obvious but no less important benefit to a child is that women who have fewer children generally have children who are healthier. Thus, children in the twentieth century probably have benefitted in a physical as well as a psychological sense from being born into smaller families.

In addition, a combination of larger houses, made possible by extraordinary economic growth during the nineteenth and twentieth centuries, plus fewer children has meant that each member of an American Family today generally has greater chances for privacy than was the case in the past. A rough rule of thumb to describe the change is that in the eighteenth century that were approximately two people for every room in a typical American house. By the second half of the twentieth century, this ratio has changed so that there are approximately two rooms per person. It would have been a rare child in the eighteenth century who could have expected his or her own separate bedroom to which to retire for whatever purposes he or she felt necessary. This is a quite common phenomenon today.

Improved life expectancy also has had a considerable impact on family life, both directly and through the better health that accompanies most reductions in the death rate. One obvious point is that families are less frequently disrupted by death. Whereas in seventeenth-century America, families commonly experienced abrupt dislocations because of epidemic and endemic diseases, in the twentieth century, a couple who marry can expect a long life together. Possibly, the rapid increase in divorce that began about 1890 is at least partially linked to this improvement in life expectancy simply because a husband or wife caught in an unpleasant marital situation could no longer hope for salvation through the death of the other spouse. The most dramatic increases in life expectancy have occurred during exactly the same period in which divorce has become more common in American society. This relationship is particularly interesting because, in general, improved life expectancy made families more stable or at least predictable; departures from the family are, in the twentieth century, more likely to be by choice, whether by divorce or migration, rather than by the chance appearance of smallpox, cholera, dysentery, influenza or diphtheria.

One trend of special interest to twentieth-century Americans has been the emergence of a much older society which has increased the possibility of grand-parents being a regular part of the family. The increasingly older American popu-lation is primarily the result of declining fertility, which is the principle cause of changes in the age structure of any population, but it is also true that grandparents now live longer than was the case two hundred years ago. One might assume that the emergence of a sizable proportion of the population over the age of sixty (the change has been from approximately four percent in the eighteenth century to about twelve percent today) would mean that more households would include three generations, or possibly even four for relatively short periods of time. In fact, this does not seem to have occurred as often as might be expected. One explanation for this is simply that as life expectancy has improved older Amer-icans have maintained much better health than was the case two hundred years ago, and so they are able to maintain their independence much longer than would have been normal in 1800 or 1850. In the early nineteenth century, the association between advanced age and physical disability would have been almost automatic; that no longer is true. As a result, older Americans are able to maintain their independence in separate households well up into their seventies and eighties. In fact, the dramatic increase in single-person households from seven percent in 1940 to twenty-three percent in 1980 is at least partially explainable by widows and widowers maintaining their households after their children have left home and their spouse has died, and not by young Americans leaving home early.

One other alternative that has emerged because of improved life expectancy deserves attention, although there is little evidence to indicate that this will be a major trend in American society. In the past, when life expectancy was short, any society that survived had to develop patterns of behavior that would guar-antee relatively high levels of reproduction. When half of one generation might die before reaching marriageable ages, most of the survivors had to marry and have children. Any society that allowed significant deviations from this pattern would disappear if the birth rate fell below the death rate for any prolonged pe-riod. Since the death rate in the United States today is slightly under 9 per 1,000 people, compared to between 25 and 30 per 1,000 two hundred years ago, Amer-icans can now experiment in alternate patterns of family living that once threat-ened the survival of society. The last two decades have seen considerable in-crease in communal families, in young men and women living together without marrying or having children, and in homosexual alliances. It seems doubtful that any of these patterns will significantly challenge, let alone replace, the age-old norm of heterosexual marriages leading to reproduction. Nonetheless, improved life expectancy makes it possible for individuals to experiment with alternate liv-ing styles without severely threatening the actual existence of their society. The major obstacle they will have to overcome is presented by those individuals who are worried, not about the physical survival of society, but about the need to pro-tect the values that have been required to produce satisfactory levels of reproduc-tion in the past. At issue is the extent to which the fundamental values of any society are inseparable from attitudes about marriage and childbearing. Are heterosexual, reproductive unions essential to the continuity of an American way of life?

The patterns of migration that have been so important in American demographic history also have had important effects on family life. The process of moving, whether across the Atlantic Ocean, from east to west across the United States, or into an urban environment, has frequently produced either permanent or temporary dislocations of families and households. Lasting changes in families occur when young men or women leave home as a result of marriage, especially since young women often also leave the communities in which they were raised to travel to the towns where their new husbands reside. Before slavery was abolished, black families were vulnerable to separation when whim or economic necessity led a white master to sell some of his people. A more temporary dislocation of families can result from serial migration, in which the head of the household leaves his or her family behind to establish housekeeping in a new community, and then over the span of several months or years will bring along the remaining family members. Under certain circumstances, serial migration can last over a number of years when an individual nuclear family becomes established in a particular community and then aids related families to move to that community. Migrants from abroad have used this pattern, as have families in New England in the late nineteenth century who assisted each other as they moved from one textile town to another.

In new communities, family sizes and structures have undergone rather interesting changes as the result of migration patterns. In towns that have just been established, or which have experienced rapid growth, household structures frequently differ from the normal American pattern by being both smaller and larger. The smaller families are often the temporary product of serial migration or relatively young householders, whereas unusually large households may be the result of newly arrived individuals boarding with families already resident in the town. Gradually, these initial distortions in family life disappear and life in the mature community settles into a fairly standard pattern of family existence. Often life in a more stable community has meant improved economic standing for those families that remain. This should not be too surprising because one of the significant motivations in migration, whether from across the Atlantic or from one town to another in the United States, has been the hope for economic prosperity.

In general, in both the nineteenth and twentieth centuries, families seldom have traveled any long distances in any one move, but because they move several times in the course of the family cycle, rather long distances have been covered in the life of one family. Thus, a household formed in Ohio in the early part of the nineteenth century could end up in Oregon, but only after stops in Illinois, Missouri, and Iowa along the way. Similarly, black migrants from the Georgia Sea Islands frequently moved onto the mainland, and then into Georgia's urban areas, before they began the trek north to New York City and a life style quite different from that which characterized rural Georgia. As was common throughout much of American history, the individual black males who pioneered this trek from the Sea Islands to the northern cities frequently brought along other members of their family after they were established in the northern urban environment.

Migration has also served to emphasize differences among various groups of families. This has happened in several ways. The occupational structure of an individual town has been one of the most important forces in selecting who might migrate to a particular community. For example, Lowell, Massachusetts, in the early nineteenth century, was characterized by highly unusual demographic and residential patterns because the cotton mills there recruited young single women who lived in housing provided by the mills themselves. Cohoes, a milltown a few miles north of Albany, New York, had an unusually high proportion of families headed by women because women who had lost a husband were able to maintain their families there since they were able to find work in the textile mills for both themselves and their older children. In other communities, they might not have been able to survive independently or keep their families together. In contrast, Homestead, Pennsylvania, a town slightly north of Pittsburgh, dominated by a steel mill, was characterized at the start of the twentieth century by families that were nuclear. In the case of Homestead, work in the steel mills was largely restricted to adult males, and so women and children frequently were not employed outside the home. At the same time, most steel mill workers had families with them.

Because the various groups of immigrants who arrived in the United States, each with their own set of attitudes and customs about family life, did not distribute themselves evenly across the country, family patterns in any one particular American community have differed considerably from those in another community depending on which immigrant group settled there. In Homestead, Pennsylvania, for example, Polish-born workers and their families generally spent their money in different patterns, amused themselves differently, and even ate differently than did American or English workers in the steel mills. In Buffalo, New York, Italian and Polish families responded quite differently to the same community. Virginia Yans-McLaughlin has shown that cultural preferences had as much to do with women working as the economic opportunities available in Buffalo. The very nature of the force producing migration from Europe might well affect family life. Irish immigrants of the 1840s and Jewish migrants from Russia in the 1890s frequently moved in family units, with no intention of returning to their original society because of either unhappy religious or economic prospects in the old world. In contrast, Italian and Chinese immigrants tended to be younger, single males who either brought families over much later or moved to the United States temporarily, with every intention of returning to the old country after they had made a satisfactory amount of money. As a result, stable patterns of family life were established much more quickly among Irish and Jewish immigrants than among the Chinese or Italians.

Although such communities were not numerous, nineteenth-century towns that incorporated utopian ideals often developed distinctive arrangements for and attitudes about family life. Shaker communities in western Massachusetts and eastern New York organized society around a life that basically denied the family. Men and women who were attracted to Shaker settlements were required to be celibate, and any kind of sexual or family relationship was generally discouraged. Shakers commonly lived in sexually segregated dormitories. In contrast, Oneida, also a utopian community in upstate New York, fostered the creation of much larger families, in which sexual relations were not only permitted but were encouraged. Men and women were no longer expected to be monogamous. Free love was an important value in this society, though it required rigorous forms of sexual relations in which self-control was considered essential as the means to achieving limited levels of reproduction. The Mormons, who migrated from New York to Utah, with stops in Missouri and Illinois, in order to preserve their religious integrity and escape persecution by their neighbors, also created distinct family patterns. The best known was the practice of polygamy, which allowed a Mormon man to have more than one wife. Not surprisingly, Mormon families were relatively large, not only because there was more than one wife able to bear children but also because Mormons espoused high fertility values. Although relatively few Americans actually practiced such unusual family patterns, these nineteenth-century experiments with new family forms attracted considerable attention because many Americans were aware of the major demographic changes going on around them and were involved in a widespread debate about whether they should be encouraged, discouraged, or ignored.

Migration has influenced how and when different branches of a family interact through a variety of mechanisms. As part of a highly mobile American society, family members had to accept separation as they moved considerable distances from each other. This has affected ties and relationships based on kinship. In the seventeenth century, kin were expected to provide considerable aid to one another, and this was possible so long as families lived relatively short distances apart. It is interesting, therefore, to ask what has happened in terms of kinship when one brother may live in New York City, his sister lives in San Francisco, and a third sibling resides in Dallas? On the surface, it would appear that kinship ties should have been significantly reduced as the result of such distances among families. On the other hand, technological changes in our ability to communicate rapidly via the telephone and in our ability to travel long distances in relatively short periods of time may mean that kinship ties have not been reduced as much as we might suspect. It is possible to telephone a relative across the country faster than you can walk next door to visit a neighbor. Similarly, it seldom takes more than seven or eight hours to cross the country by air today, a time that compares to a journey of twenty to thirty miles in the seventeenth or eighteenth centuries. The day-to-day and hour-to-hour contacts that were common in close-knit communities in the past may no longer exist; however, kinship ties have probably not been as dramatically altered by migration as one might expect. Probably interactions with one's kin now occur more often in the context of special events such as holidays, births, marriages, or deaths rather than in ongoing contact as part of daily activity. No doubt, choice plays a greater role in family contact under such circumstances. In addition, lines between family and community, once blurred when individuals lived in small towns or villages among cousins, uncles, and aunts, have perhaps been more sharply defined, so that we can identify what is public and what is private in our lives. However, these changes have not necessarily eliminated kinship ties but have only altered them.

Perhaps of greater consequence to the day-to-day existence of life of an American family has been the movement to suburban communities with the associated separation of economic and domestic activity. In the suburbs, frequently the adult males, and increasingly adult females, leave home to go to work elsewhere in the large urban area. As a result, the home has become a place of recreation, rest, and retreat, rather than economic activity. The home is where economic goods are consumed rather than produced. In addition, whereas families on small farms frequently worked within eyesight of each other, if not necessarily at the same tasks, now family members are separated from each other for significant parts of the day. Each individual family member, whether husband, wife, or child, once he or she begins attending school, develops numerous contacts with individuals with whom the other members of the family seldom, if ever, interact. Thus, families in twentieth-century America are increasingly composed of individuals who both share a life, but who also have lives that are almost entirely separate from each other. This latter condition would have been extremely unusual two hundred years ago.

CONCLUSION

The effects of demographic changes on American family life already have been numerous and significant. Because the changes are not yet complete, and because Americans have not yet decided what new family patterns they consider to be desirable, considerable experimentation with, and debate over, new and old family patterns will continue over the next several decades. Nonetheless, in examining the relationship between demography and family life one overriding conclusion emerges. There is no such thing as *the* American family; there are only families in America that vary considerably according to the historical period in which they existed, the place in which they are located, and the class and cultural background of the individuals composing those families. We would do well not to be too rigid in our expectations about and interpretations of family life. Families have been, and will continue to be, a vital and important part of American society, but that vitality has come more from their capacity to adapt to remarkable changes in demographic and economic patterns than from any power to maintain rigid adherence to traditional patterns in the face of extraordinary changes. Lower levels of childbearing and improved life expectancy may make experimentation with new forms of family life more possible than it was in the past, but that does not mean that any new patterns will prove ultimately to be more desirable than older family relationships. It should be interesting to both observe and experience family life in America over the next several decades.

REFERENCES

Berkner, Lutz K. 1972. "The Stem Family and the Developmental Cycle of the Peasant Household: An Eighteenth-Century Austrian Example." *American Historical Review* 77: 398–418.

Byington, Margaret. 1974. *Homestead: The Households of a Mill Town.* Reprinted from 1910 edition. Pittsburgh, PA: University of Pittsburgh.

Carr, Lois G. and Lorena S. Walsh. 1977. "The Planter's Wife: The Experience of White Women in Seventeenth-Century Maryland." *William and Mary Quarterly* 34: 542–571.

Degler, Carl. 1980. *At Odds: Women and the Family in America from the Revolution to the Present*. New York: Oxford University Press.

Demos, John. 1970. *A Little Commonwealth: Family Life in Plymouth Colony*. New York: Oxford University Press.

Demos, John and Sarane S. Boocock (eds.). 1978. *Turning Points: Historical and Sociological Essays on the Family*. Chicago: University of Chicago Press.

Easterlin, Richard A. 1980. *Birth and Fortune: The Impact of Numbers on Personal Welfare*. New York: Basic Books.

Elder, Glen, Jr. 1974. *Children of the Great Depression: Social Change in Life Experience*. Chicago: University of Chicago Press.

———. 1981. "Scarcity and Prosperity in Postwar Childbearing: Explorations from a Life Course Perspective." *Journal of Family History* 6: 410–433.

Fischer, David H. 1977. *Growing Old in America*. New York: Oxford University Press.

Glick, Paul C. 1957. *American Families*. New York: John Wiley and Sons.

Glick, Paul C. and Robert Parke, Jr. 1965. "New Approaches in Studying the Life Cycle of the Family." *Demography* 2: 187–202.

Gordon, Michael (ed.). 1983. *The American Family in Social-Historical Perspective*. 3rd ed. New York: St. Martin's Press.

Greven, Philip J., Jr. 1970. *Four Generations: Population, Land, and Family in Colonial Andover, Massachusetts*. Ithaca, N.Y.: Cornell University Press.

Gross, Robert A. 1976. *The Minutemen and Their World*. New York: Hill and Wang.

Hareven, Tamara K. (ed.). 1977. *Family and Kin in Urban Communities, 1700–1930*. New York: New Viewpoints.

———. 1978. *Transitions: The Family and the Life Course in Historical Perspective*. New York: Academic Press.

Hareven, Tamara K. and Maris A. Vinovskis (eds.). 1978. *Family and Population in Nineteenth-Century America*. Princeton, N.J.: Princeton University Press.

Laslett, Barbara. 1975. "Household Structures on an American Frontier: Los Angeles, California, in 1850." *American Journal of Sociology* 81: 109–128.

Laslett, Peter (ed.). 1972. *Household and Family in Past Time*. Cambridge: Cambridge University Press.

Modell, John, Frank F. Furstenberg, Jr., and Theodore Hershberg. 1976. "Social Change and Transitions to Adulthood in Historical Perspective." *Journal of Family History* 1: 7–32.

Rabb, T. K. and Robert I. Rotberg (eds.). 1976. *The Family in History: Interdisciplinary Essays*. New York: Octagon Press.

Rutman, Darrett B. and Anita Rutman. 1979. " 'Now-Wives and Sons-in Law': Parental Death in a Seventeenth-Century Virginia County." Pp. 153–182 in *The Chesapeake in the Seventeenth Century*, edited by Thad W. Tate and David L. Ammerman. Chapel Hill, NC: University of North Carolina Press.

Ryan, Mary P. 1981. *Cradle of the Middle Class: The Family in Oneida County, New York, 1790–1865*. New York: Cambridge University Press.

Stannard, David E. 1977. *The Puritan Way of Death: A Study of Religion, Culture, and Social Charge*. New York: Oxford University Press.

Thornton, Arland and Deborah Freedman 1983. "The Changing American Family." *Population Bulletin* 38.

Uhlenberg, Peter R. 1969. "A Study of Cohort Life Cycles: Cohorts of Native Born Massachusetts Women, 1830–1920." *Population Studies* 23: 407–420.

Vinovskis, Maris A. 1976. "Angels' Heads and Weeping Willows: Death in Early America." *American Antiquarian Society Proceedings* 86: 273–302.

Walsh, Andrew S. and Robert V. Wells. 1978. "Population Dynamics in the Eighteenth-Century Mississippi River Valley: Acadians in Louisiana." *Journal of Social History* 11: 521–545.

Wells, Robert V. 1971. "Demographic Change and the Life Cycle of American Families." *Journal of Interdisciplinary History* 2: 273–282.

———. 1980. "Illegitimacy and Bridal Pregnancy in Colonial America." Pp. 349–361 in *Bastardy and its Comparative History,* edited by Peter Laslett, Karla Oosterveen, and Richard M. Smith. Cambridge, MA: Havard University Press.

Yans-McLaughlin, Virginia. 1971. "Patterns of Work and Family Organization: Buffalo's Italians," *Journal of Interdisciplinary History* 2: 299–314.

4

Coming Apart:
Radical Departures since 1960*

Steven Mintz and Susan Kellogg

A generation ago Ozzie, Harriet, David, and Ricky Nelson epitomized the American family. Over 70 percent of all American households in 1960 were like the Nelsons: made up of dad the breadwinner, mom the homemaker, and their children. Today, less than three decades later, "traditional" families consisting of a breadwinner father, a housewife mother, and one or more dependent children account for less than 15 percent of the nation's households. As American families have changed, the image of the family portrayed on television has changed accordingly. Today's television families vary enormously, running the gamut from traditional families like "The Waltons" to two-career families like the Huxtables on

*Mintz, Steven and Susan Kellogg. 1988. "Coming Apart: Radical Departures since 1960." Pp. 203–237 in *Domestic Revolutions: A Social History of American Family Life*. New York: Free Press. Reprinted with permission of the Free Press, a Division of Macmillan, Inc. Copyright © 1988 by The Free Press.

"The Cosby Show" or the Keatons on "Family Ties"; "blended" families like the Bradys on "The Brady Bunch," with children from previous marriages; two single mothers and their children on "Kate and Allie"; a homosexual who serves as a surrogate father on "Love, Sidney"; an unmarried couple who cohabit in the same house on "Who's the Boss?"; and a circle of friends, who think of themselves as a family, congregating at a Boston bar on "Cheers."[1]

Since 1960 U.S. families have undergone a historical transformation as dramatic and far reaching as the one that took place at the beginning of the nineteenth century. Even a casual familiarity with census statistics suggest the profundity of the changes that have taken place in family life. Birthrates plummeted. The average number of children per family fell from 3.8 at the peak of the baby boom to less than 2 today. At the same time, the divorce rate soared. Today the number of divorces each year is twice as high as it was in 1966 and three times higher than in 1950. The rapid upsurge in the divorce rate contributed to a dramatic increase in the number of single-parent households, or what used to be known as "broken homes." The number of households consisting of a single woman and her children has doubled since 1960. A sharp increase in female-headed homes was accompanied by a steep increase in the number of couples cohabiting outside marriage; their numbers have quadrupled since 1960.[2]

Almost every aspect of family life seems to have changed before our eyes. Sexual codes were revised radically. Today only about one American woman in five waits until marriage to become sexually active, compared to nearly half in 1960 who postponed intercourse. Meanwhile, the proportion of births occurring among unmarried women quadrupled. At the same time, millions of wives entered the labor force. The old stereotype of the breadwinner-father and housewife-mother broke down as the number of working wives climbed. in 1950, 25 percent of married woman living with their husbands, worked outside the home; in the late 1980s the figure is nearly 60 percent. The influx of married women entering the labor force was particularly rapid among mothers of young children. Now more than half of all mothers of school-age children hold jobs. As a result, fewer young children can claim their mother's exclusive attention. What Americans have witnessed since 1960 are fundamental challenges to the forms, ideals, and role expectations that have defined the family for the last century and a half.[3]

Profound and far-reaching changes have occurred in the American family—in behavior and in values. Contemporary Americans are much more likely than their predecessors to postpone or forego marriage, to live alone outside familial units, to engage in intercourse prior to marriage, to permit marriages to end in divorce, to permit mothers of young children to work outside the home, and to allow children to live in families with only one parent and no adult male present. Earlier family norms—of a working father, a housewife, and children—have undergone major alterations. The term "family" had gradually been redefined to include any group of people living together, including such variations as single mothers and children, unmarried couples, and gay couples.[4]

All these changes have generated a profound sense of uncertainty and ambivalence. Many Americans fear that the rapid decline in the birthrates, the dramatic upsurge in divorce rates, and the proliferation of loose, noncontractual sexual relationships are symptoms of increasing selfishness and self-centeredness incompatible with strong family attachments. They also fear that an increased proportion of working mothers has caused more children to be neglected, resulting in climbing rates of teenage pregnancy, delinquency, suicide, drug and alcohol abuse, and failure in school.[5]

Today fear for the family's future is widespread. In 1978 author Clare Boothe Luce succinctly summarized fears about the fragility of the family that continue to haunt Americans today:

> Today 50% of all marriages end in divorce, separation, or desertion. . . . The marriage rate and birth rate are falling. The numbers of one-parent and one-child families are rising. More and more young people are living together without benefit of marriage. . . . Premarital and extra-marital sex no longer raises parental or conjugal eyebrows. . . . The rate of reported incest, child molestation, rape, and child and wife abuse, is steadily mounting. . . . Run-away children, teenage prostitution, youthful drug addiction and alcoholism have become great, ugly, new phenomena.[6]

What are the forces that lie behind these changes in family life? And what are the implications of these transformations?

NEW MORALITY

The key to understanding the recent upheavals in family life lies in a profound shift in cultural values. Three decades ago most Americans shared certain strong attitudes about the family. Public opinion polls showed that they endorsed marriage as a prerequisite of well-being, social adjustment, and maturity and agreed on the proper roles of husband and wife. Men and women who failed to marry or who resented their family roles were denigrated as maladjusted or neurotic. The message conveyed by the broader culture was that happiness was a by-product of living by the accepted values of hard work and family obligation.[7]

Values and norms have shifted. The watchwords of contemporary society are "growth," "self-realization," and "fulfillment." Expectations of personal happiness have risen and collided with a more traditional concern (and sacrifice) for the family. At the same time, in addition to its traditional functions of caring for children, providing economic security, and meeting its members' emotional needs, the family has become the focus for new expectations of sexual fulfillment, intimacy, and companionship.[8]

Today a broad spectrum of family norms that prevailed during the 1950s and early 1960s is no longer widely accepted. Divorce is not stigmatized as it used to be; a large majority of the public now rejects the idea that an unhappily married couple should stay together for their children's sake. Similarly, the older view that anyone who rejected marriage is "sick," "neurotic," or "immoral" has declined sharply, as has the view that people who do not have children are "selfish." Opinion surveys show that most Americans no longer believe that a woman should not work if she has a husband who can support her, that a bride should always be a virgin when she marries, or that premarital sex is always wrong.[9]

Economic affluence played a major role in the emergence of a new outlook. Couples who married in the 1940s and 1950s had spent their early childhood years in the depression and formed relatively modest material aspirations. Born in the late 1920s or 1930s, when birthrates were depressed, they faced little competition for jobs at maturity and were financially secure enough to marry and have children at a relatively young age. Their children, however, who came of age during the 1960s and 1970s, spent their childhoods during an era of unprecedented affluence. Between 1950 and 1970, median family income tripled. Increased affluence increased opportunities for education, travel, and leisure, all of which helped to heighten expectations of self-fulfillment. Unlike their parents, they had considerable expectations for their own material and emotional well-being. [10]

In keeping with the mood of an era of rising affluence, philosophies stressing individual self-realization flourished. Beginning in the 1950s, "humanistic" psychologies, stressing growth and self-actualization, triumphed over earlier theories that had emphasized adjustment as the solution to individual problems. The underlying assumption of the new "third force" psychologies—a name chosen to distinguish them from the more pessimistic psychoanalytic and behaviorist psychologies—of Abraham Maslow, Carl Rogers, and Erich Fromm is that a person's spontaneous impulses are intrinsically good and that maturity is not a process of "settling down" and suppressing instinctual needs but of achieving one's potential. [11]

Even in the early 1960s, marriage and family ties were regarded by the "human potential movement" as potential threats to individual fulfillment as a man or a woman. The highest forms of human needs, contended proponents of the new psychologies, were autonomy, independence, growth, and creativity, all of which could be thwarted by "existing relationships and interactions." Unlike the earlier psychology of adjustment, associated with Alfred Adler and Dale Carnegie, which had counseled compromise, suppression of instinctual impulses, avoidance of confrontations, and the desirability of acceding to the wishes of others, the new humanistic psychologies advised individuals to "get in touch" with their feelings and freely voice their opinions, even if this generated feelings of guilt. [12]

The impulse toward self-fulfillment and liberation was further advanced by the prophets of the 1960s counterculture and New Left, Norman O. Brown and Herbert Marcuse. Both Brown and Marcuse transformed Sigmund Freud's psychoanalytic insights into a critique of the constraints of liberal society. They were primarily concerned not with political or economic repression but rather with what they perceived as the psychological repression of the individual's instinctual needs. Brown located the source of repression in the ego mechanisms that controlled each person's instincts. Marcuse, in a broader social critique, believed that repression was at least partially imposed by society. [13]

For both Brown and Marcuse, the goal of social change was the liberation of eros, the agglomeration of an individual's pleasure-seeking life instincts, or, as Marcuse put it, the "free gratification of man's instinctual needs." Brown went so far as to challenge openly the basic tenets of "civilized sexual morality," with its stress on genital, heterosexual, monogamous sex, and extolled a new ideal of bisexualism and "polymorphous perversity" (total sexual gratification). For a younger, affluent, middle-class generation in revolt against liberal values, the ideas of Brown and Marcuse provided a rationale for youthful rebellion. [14]

An even more thoroughgoing challenge to traditional family values was mounted by the women's liberation movement, which attacked the family's exploitation of women. Feminists denounced the societal expectation that women defer to the needs of spouses and children as part of their social roles as wives and mothers. Militant feminist activists like Ti-Grace Atkinson called marriage "slavery," "legalized rape," and "unpaid labor" and denounced heterosexual love as "tied up with a sense of dependency." The larger mainstream of the women's movement articulated a powerful critique of the idea that child care and housework was the apex of a woman's accomplishments or her sole means of fulfillment. Feminists uncovered unsettling evidence of harsher conditions behind conventional familial togetherness, such as child abuse and wife beating, wasted lives and exploited labor. Instead of giving the highest priority to their families, women were urged to raise their consciousness of their own needs and abilities. From this vantage point, marriage increasingly came to be described as a trap, circumscribing a woman's social and intellectual horizons and lowering her sense of self-esteem. Homemaking, which as recently as the early 1960s had been celebrated on such television shows as "Queen for a Day," came under attack as an unrecognized and unpaid form of work in contrast to more "serious" occupations outside the home. And, as for marital bliss forevermore, feminists warned that divorce—so common and so economically difficult for women—was an occurrence for which every married woman had to be prepared. In general the feminists awakened American women to what they viewed as the worst form of social and political oppression—sexism. The introduction of this new awareness would go far beyond the feminists themselves.[15]

The challenge to older family values was not confined to radical members of the counterculture, the New Left, or the women's liberation movement. Broad segments of society were influenced by, and participated in, this fundamental shift in values.

Although only a small minority of American women ever openly declared themselves to be feminists, there can be no doubt that the arguments of the women's movement dramatically altered women's attitudes toward family roles, child care, marital relationships, femininity, and housework. This is true even among many women who claim to reject feminism. Polls have shown a sharp decline in the proportion of women favoring large families and a far greater unwillingness to subordinate personal needs and interests to the demands of husbands and children. A growing majority of women now believe that both husband and wife should have jobs, both do housework, and both take care of children. This represents a stunning shift of opinion in a decade and a half. A new perception of woman in the family has taken hold. In extreme imagery she is a superwoman, doing a full-time job while managing her home and family well. The more realistic image is of the wife and mother who works and struggles to manage job and family with the help of spouse, day care, and employer. Thus, as women increasingly seek employment outside the home, the family itself shifts to adjust to the changing conditions of its members while striving to provide the stability and continuity it has traditionally afforded.[16]

During the 1960s a sexual revolution that predated the counterculture swept the nation's literature, movies, theater, advertising, and fashion. In 1962,

Grossinger's resort in New York State's Catskill mountains introduced its first singles-only weekend, thereby publicly acknowledging couples outside marriage. That same year, Illinois became the first state to decriminalize all forms of private sexual conduct between consenting adults. Two years later, in 1964, the first singles bar opened on New York's Upper East Side; the musical *Hair* introduced nudity to the Broadway stage; California designer Rudi Gernreich created the topless bathing suit; and bars featuring topless waitresses and dancers sprouted. By the end of the decade, a growing number of the nation's colleges had abolished regulations specifying how late students could stay outside their dormitories and when and under what circumstances male and female students could visit with each other.[17]

One of the most important aspects of this latter-day revolution in morals was the growth of a "singles culture"—evident in a proliferation of singles bars, apartment houses, and clubs. The sources of the singles culture were varied and complex, owing as much to demographic shifts as to the ready availability of birth control, cures for venereal diseases, and liberalized abortion laws. The trend toward postponement of marriage, combined with increased rates of college attendance and divorce, meant that growing numbers of adults spent protracted periods of their sexually mature lives outside marriage. The result was that it became far easier than in the past to maintain an active social and sex life outside marriage. It also became more acceptable, as its patterns became grist for the popular media and imagination.[18]

Sexually oriented magazines started to display pubic hair and filmmakers began to show simulated sexual acts. *I Am Curious (Yellow)* depicted coitus on the screen. *Deep Throat* released in the 1970s, showed cunnilingus and fellatio. Other manifestations of a relaxation of traditional mores included a growing public tolerance of homosexuality, a blurring of male and female sex roles, increasing public acceptance of abortion, the growing visibility of pornography, a marked trend away from female virginity until marriage, and a sharp increase in the proportion of women engaging in extramarital sex. Within one decade the cherished privacy of sexuality had been overturned and an era of public sexuality had been ushered in.[19]

Increasingly, values championed by the women's movement and the counterculture were adopted in a milder form by large segments of the American population. A significant majority of Americans adopted permissive attitudes on such matters as premarital sex, cohabitation outside of marriage, and abortion. Fewer women aspired to motherhood and homemaking as a full-time career and instead joined the labor force as much for independence and self-fulfillment as from economic motives. The preferred number of children declined sharply, and to limit births, the number of abortions and sterilizations increased sharply. A revolution had occurred in values and behavior.[20]

BLACK FAMILIES IN POVERTY

At the same time as the attitudes and behavior of middle-class white Americans were transformed as a result of increasing affluence, the impact of feminism, and a revolution in sexual mores, the circumstances of the black family also shifted, but in very different ways. The situation of poor black families significantly worsened during the 1960s and 1970s. Illegitimate births increased dramatically, and the proportion of young blacks living in poverty climbed steeply. Today, half of all black children grow up in poverty, more than half are born outside wedlock, and nearly half live in female-headed households.[21]

The plight of the black family came to public attention early in the fall of 1965, when the federal government released a confidential report written by Daniel Patrick Moynihan, then an obscure assistant secretary of labor, called *The Negro Family: The Case for National Action*. In his report Moynihan argued that the major obstacle to the advancement of the black community lay in a vicious and self-perpetuating cycle of despair in the urban ghettos. "The fundamental problem," Moynihan maintained, was the breakdown of the black family. "The evidence—not final, but powerfully persuasive—is that the Negro family in the urban ghettos is crumbling." The black middle class had managed to create stable families, "but for the vast numbers of the unskilled, poorly educated city working class, the fabric of conventional social relationships has all but disintegrated."[22]

To support his thesis, Moynihan cited startling statistics. Nearly 25 percent of all black women were divorced, separated, or living apart from their husbands, compared to 7.9 percent of white women. Illegitimacy among blacks had risen from 16.8 percent in 1940 to 23.6 percent in 1963, while the white rate had only climbed from 2 to 3 percent. The proportion of black families headed by women had climbed from 8 percent in 1950 to 21 percent in 1960, while the white rate had remained steady at 9 percent. The breakdown of the black family, Moynihan contended, had led to a sharp increase in welfare dependency, delinquency, unemployment, drug addiction, and failure in school.[23]

The Moynihan Report attributed the instability of the black family to the effects of slavery, Reconstruction, poor education, rapid urbanization, and thirty-five years of severe unemployment, which had undermined the role of the black man in the family. Unable to support their families, many black fathers simply disappeared, leaving the women to cope and rule. In Moynihan's view, children raised in female-headed families, deprived of a male role model and authority figure, tended to remain trapped in a cycle of poverty and disadvantage:

> From the wild Irish slums of the 19th-century Eastern seaboard, to the riot-torn suburbs of Los Angeles, there is one unmistakable lesson in American history; a community that allows a large number of men to grow up in broken homes, dominated by women, never acquiring any stable relationship to male authority, never acquiring any set of rational expectations about the future—that community asks for and gets chaos.[24]

The report concluded with a call for national action to strengthen the black family through programs of jobs, family allowances, and birth control. It did not support the belief that enforcement of civil rights laws would be sufficient to bring about equality. Only new and special efforts by the federal government could alleviate conditions within urban ghettos and strengthen the black family.[25]

Release of the Moynihan Report in August 1965 unleashed a storm of public criticism. Critics feared that the report would reinforce white prejudice by suggesting that sexual promiscuity and illegitimacy were socially acceptable within the black community and that the instability of the black family was the basic cause of racial inequality. Others accused the report of diverting attention from the underlying problems of racism and poverty and of blaming the victims for their own distress.[26]

How accurate was Moynihan's assessment of the black family? On the one hand, he was prescient in identifying single-parenthood, illegitimacy, and poverty among children as major social issues. Indeed, these problems have so worsened since Moynihan wrote his report that they now affect the entire society and can no longer be addressed solely in terms of race. At the same time, however, in important respects Moynihan's analysis was flawed. The problems of illegitimacy and absent fathers were exaggerated, the strengths of the black family were ignored, and the differences between the black family and the white family were overestimated.[27]

Contrary to the impression conveyed by the report of the prevalence of "matriarchy," "deviance," and "family disorganization" among blacks, the overwhelming majority of black families during the 1960s, 1970s, and 1980s were composed of two spouses. In 1960, 75 percent of black children lived with two parents; a decade later, 67 percent did. Today six out of every ten black families have two parents, and two-parent families remain the norm in the black community. The report's discussion of illegitimacy also seriously distorted the facts. Far from increasing, as Moynihan implied, the black illegitimacy rate—the proportion of unmarried women bearing children—had actually been declining consistently since 1961 and has, in fact, continued to decline up until today. In 1960, ninety-eight out of every thousand single black women gave birth to a baby. In 1980 only seventy-seven did. The proportion of black births that were illegitimate increased, but this was the result of a sharp drop in the birthrate of married black women. The report further exaggerated the difference between black and white illegitimacy rates by ignoring the fact that white women were much more likely than black women to use contraceptives, to have premarital pregnancies terminated by abortion, or to put babies born out of wedlock up for adoption.[28]

Moynihan tended to downplay the role of unemployment and the welfare system in producing family instability. Low wages and the unstable, dead-end occupations available to black men contributed to a sense of frustration and powerlessness that prevented many lower-class men from becoming stable husbands and fathers. And the welfare system added to the breakup of families since in half the states welfare benefits could only begin after a father deserted his family.[29]

Much of the disparity between white and black family patterns—in 1965 and today—is simply a result of poverty. The statistical gap between the races largely disappears when one compares blacks and whites of the same economic level. Blacks with incomes above the poverty line differ little from white families in their proportion of female-headed households. Furthermore, a significant part of the disparity in family patterns is explained by the skewed sex ratio of the black population: The number of black men of marriageable age is significantly smaller than the number of black women of marriageable age. The 1970 census indicated that there were only 86 black males for every 100 black females aged twenty to twenty-four and just 84 black males for every 100 females aged twenty-five to thirty-four.[30]

Although many poor families do not conform in structure to middle-class norms, it is important not to underestimate the strength and durability of the lower-class black kinship system. By focusing on the instability, weakness, and pathology of lower-class black families, the Moynihan Report failed to recognize that lower-class black family patterns were a rational response to conditions of severe deprivation. Moynihan underestimated the competence of black mothers in rearing and supporting their children and the support black families received from an extended kinship network. Although Moynihan regarded lower-class black families as "disorganized" and "father-deprived" because they failed to conform to middle-class ideals of the nuclear family, later researchers found an extensive network of kin and friends supporting and reinforcing the lower-class black family. In urban ghettos, destitution and the inability of individual households to fulfill basic needs led lower-class blacks to form "domestic networks," which tended to replace the nuclear family as the fundamental unit of social organization. Friends and relatives helped mothers, took the place of fathers, provided child care, and shared resources.[31]

When President Lyndon B. Johnson announced the War on Poverty in 1964, his diagnosis of the problem of poverty was profoundly influenced by the Moynihan Report. Drawing on Moynihan's argument that poverty and unemployment had undermined the black family and that family disorganization perpetuated social and economic inequality, President Johnson pledged that a primary goal of federal antipoverty programs would be "to strengthen the family and create conditions under which most parents will stay together." Unless the family was strengthened, the president declared, all other legislation "will never be enough to cut completely the circles of despair and deprivation." A unique political commitment to the family had been made by the federal government.[32]

When Lyndon Johnson left the presidency in 1969, he left behind a legacy of a transformed federal government. At the end of the Eisenhower presidency in 1961, there were only 45 domestic social programs. By 1969 the number had climbed to 435. Federal social spending, excluding Social Security, had risen from $9.9 billion in 1960 to $25.6 billion in 1968. Johnson's "Great Society" represented the broadest attack Americans had ever waged on the special problems facing poor and disadvantaged families. It declared decisively that the family-related problems of the poor—problems of housing, income, employment, and health—were ultimately a federal responsibility.[33]

During the 1960s the federal government showed an increasing commitment to improving the welfare of the nation's poor families. To improve their economic status, government greatly expanded public assistance programs. In 1959 there was essentially only a single welfare program providing public assistance to the poor—Aid to Families with Dependent Children (AFDC). Payments were small, amounting to only about a quarter of the median income, and relatively few poor families participated in the program. During the 1960s and early 1970s, AFDC rolls grew rapidly as a result of a sharp increase in the number of female-headed families and changes in eligibility requirements, including a 1961 law that allowed states to grant assistance to families containing an unemployed father and a 1968 Supreme Court ruling that it was unconstitutional for states to deny AFDC benefits to households containing a live-in adult male.[34]

To assure adequate health care coverage to persons receiving federally supported public assistance, in 1965 Congress established Medicaid and in 1968 enacted the Child Health Improvement and Protection Act providing for prenatal and postnatal care. To combat hunger and malnutrition among the poor while disposing of surplus agricultural commodities, the federal government created the Food Stamp program in 1961 and subsequently added school breakfast and lunch programs. To address the problems of crowded and dilapidated housing, Congress in 1961 began to subsidize builders of low-income housing and in 1965 made rent supplements available to poor families. To reduce infant and maternal mortality, the numbers of unwanted children, and physical and mental handicaps among the poor, Congress in 1967 extended Medicaid coverage to include family planning services and required that they be provided to AFDC mothers. To train poorer Americans for new and better jobs, Congress adopted the Manpower Development and Training Act in 1962 and the Economic Opportunity Act in 1964 to provide vocational training, basic education, and summer employment for disadvantaged youth. To encourage adult AFDC recipients to enroll in job-training programs and seek work, Congress in 1967 required states to provide day care or child development facilities for the children of such women. To promote education in 1964 Congress established Head Start, a program of compensatory preschool education for poor children.[35]

Johnson promised to reduce poverty, alleviate hunger and malnutrition, expand community medical care, provide adequate housing, and enhance the employability of the poor. When he left office in 1969, he could legitimately argue that he had kept his promise. Contrary to the widespread view that "in the war on poverty, poverty won," substantial progress had been made. During the 1960s the incidence of poverty was reduced, infant mortality was cut, and blighted housing was demolished. In 1960, 40 million persons, 20 percent of the population, were classified by the government as poor. By 1969, their number had been reduced to 24 million, 12 percent of the population. Infant mortality among the poor, which had barely declined between 1950 and 1965, fell by one-third in the decade after 1965 as a result of the expansion of federal medical and nutritional programs. Implementation of Medicaid and Medicare helped to improve the health of the poor. Before 1965, 20 percent of the poor had never been examined by a physician; by 1970 the figure had been cut to 8 percent. The proportion of families living in substandard housing—usually defined as housing lacking indoor plumbing—also declined steeply, from 20 percent in 1960 to 11 percent a decade later.[36]

Few questions of public policy have evoked greater controversy than the impact of government welfare programs on the families of the poor. Political conservatives have generally argued that public assistance, food subsidies, health programs, and child care programs weakened poorer families. President Ronald Reagan voiced a common conservative viewpoint when he declared, "There is no question that many well-intentioned Great Society-type programs contributed to family breakups, welfare dependency, and a large increase in births out of wedlock."[37]

Belief in a causal connection between increased government welfare expenditures and family breakdown rests on a close chronological correlation between rising welfare spending and dramatic increases in female-headed households and illegitimacy among the poor. Back in 1959, just 10 percent of low-income black Americans lived in a single-parent household. By 1980 the figure had climbed to 44 percent. It was during the late 1960s, a time of rapid economic growth and increasing antipoverty expenditures, that the prevalence of two-parent black families declined most steeply, from 72 percent in 1967 to 69 percent in 1968 to just 63 percent in 1973. Today 59 percent of black families have two parents present. At the same time, the number of illegitimate births among the poor grew substantially. Had the number of single-parent families remained at the 1970 level, the number of poor families in 1980 would have been 32 percent lower than it was. [38]

What was the impact of massive federal intervention on the families of the poor? Did the expansion of state services contribute to rising rates of illegitimacy and single-parent families? The answers to these questions are still uncertain. On the one hand, there is little empirical evidence that welfare policies encourage family breakup. Statistical studies have found no correlation between the level of AFDC benefits and the proportion of black children in single-parent households. What other studies have shown is that increases in wages produce a sharp drop in female-headed households, reinforcing the view that low wages and unstable employment are major contributors to family instability. [39]

It seems clear that some of the apparent deterioration in black family patterns is illusory. The dramatic increase in black single-parent families living on welfare is not so much a result of a dramatic increase in the number of unmarried women having illegitimate babies as that fewer unmarried mothers live with their parents or other relatives than was the case in the past. Nearly two-fifths of the increase in female-headed households between 1950 and 1972 is explained by the movement of existing single-parent families out of households of parents or other relatives. Public assistance allowed female heads of poor families greater opportunity to set up independent homes. If female-headed families made up a growing proportion of the poor, this partly reflected a sharp reduction in poverty among other groups. One of the consequences of government policy was to alter dramatically the profile of the poor. Increases in Social Security payments dramatically reduced the incidence of poverty among the elderly. The Supplemental Social Security program introduced in 1973 sharply reduced poverty among the disabled. As a result of reductions in poverty among the elderly and disabled and increases in the number of single-parent, female-headed households, poverty has been increasingly feminized. [40]

THE FEMINIZATION OF POVERTY

Today families headed by women are four and a half times as likely to be poor as families headed by males. Teenagers who have children out of wedlock are seven times as likely to be in poverty. Although female-headed families constitute only 15 percent of the U.S. population, they account for over 50 percent of the poor population. Teenagers and women in their early twenties who bear illegitimate children constitute a large segment of the population that remains poor and dependent on welfare for long periods of time.[41]

And yet the picture is not quite so bleak as it might seem at first glimpse. Although a majority of poor families are female-headed, it is no longer true that most female-headed families are poor. Over the past two decades, the poverty rate of female-headed families has declined steeply, as women have succeeded in obtaining better-paying jobs in the labor force. Back in 1960, 50 percent of all female-headed families lived in poverty. By 1970 the figure had fallen to 38 percent and down to 19 percent in 1980. Meanwhile, few female-headed families remain in poverty for very long. Most mothers who receive public assistance are self-supporting individuals who have recently experienced a sudden divorce or separation. Most of these women leave the welfare rolls within two years. And finally, many poor women eventually marry, leaving poverty. Nearly three-quarters of young black women who bear a child out of wedlock marry by the age of twenty-four, usually ending their poverty.[42]

Still, there can be little doubt that the nation's welfare policies actually provide incentives to the poor to avoid marriage. Under present law, if an AFDC mother marries, the stepfather assumes financial responsibility for supporting her children, which may deter the couple from marrying. In twenty-nine states, unemployed fathers are ineligible for assistance, which may encourage an unemployed father to desert his family so that his wife and children can obtain AFDC benefits. The discouragement of marriage in American welfare law contrasts sharply with European policies. In such countries as France, Hungary, Sweden, and East and West Germany, which have adopted explicit "family policies," the national government subsidizes families in a variety of ways, including the provision of family allowances to supplement parents' income and direct cash payments to parents when they have children.[43]

CHILDREN IN A NEW AGE

Along with a mounting federal commitment to shore up the nation's poor families came another domestic revolution, a radical new self-consciousness about child rearing. Over the past quarter century, Americans have grown progressively more concerned about the plight of the nation's young people. Alarmed by sharp increases in delinquency, alcohol and drug abuse, pregnancy, and suicides among children and adolescents, parents became uneasy about the proper way to raise children. They also worried about the effects of day care, the impact of divorce, and the consequences of growing up in a permissive society in which premarital sex, abortion, and drugs are prevalent.

The past two decades have witnessed significant changes in the experience of childhood and adolescence. Since 1960 the proportion of children growing up in "traditional families" in which the father is the breadwinner and the mother is a full-time homemaker has fallen dramatically while the number growing up in single-parent, female-headed households or in two-worker, two-parent households has risen steeply. Before 1960 divorce was an occurrence experienced by relatively few children. Of children born during the 1970s, in contrast, 40 percent will experience a divorce before their sixteenth birthdays, and nearly 50 percent will spend at least part of their childhood in a single-parent home. [44]

At the same time as marriages grew less stable, unprecedented changes took place within families. The proportion of married women with preschoolers who were in the labor force jumped from 12 percent in 1950 to 45 percent in 1980. Families grew smaller and, as a result, children have fewer siblings. Families also became more mobile, and hence children have less and less contact with relatives outside the immediate family. According to one estimate, just 5 percent of American children see a grandparent regularly. Young children spend more of their time in front of the television set or in the care of individuals other than their parents—in day-care centers, preschool programs, or the homes of other families—and more and more teenagers take parttime work. [45]

Each of these changes has evoked anxiety for the well-being of children. Many adults worry that a high divorce rate undermines the psychological and financial security of children. Others fear that children who live with a single female parent will have no father figure with whom to identify or to emulate and no firm source of guidance. Many are concerned that two-career parents with demanding jobs substitute money for affection, freedom for supervision, and abdicate their parental roles to surrogates. Still others fret that teenage jobs undermine school attendance and involvement and leave young people with too much money to spend on clothing, records, a car, or drugs. Today's children and adolescents, many believe, are caught between two difficult trends—decreasing parental commitment to child nurture and an increasingly perilous social environment saturated with sex, addictive drugs, and alcohol—that make it more difficult to achieve a well-adjusted adulthood. [46]

According to many Americans, children have paid a high price for the social transformations of the 1960s and 1970s—spiraling divorce rates, the rapid influx of mothers into the work force, a more relaxed attitude toward sex, and the widespread use of television as a form of child care. They are afraid that these patterns have eroded an earlier ideal of childhood as a special, protected state—a carefree period of innocence—and that today's permissive culture encourages a "new precocity" that thrusts children into the adult world before they are mature enough to deal with it. They worry about the deleterious effects of divorce, day care, and overexposure—through television, movies, music, and advertisement—to drugs, violence, sex, and pornography. They are concerned that parents have absorbed a far too egalitarian view of their relationship with their children and have become incapable of exercising authority and discipline. [47]

Giving credence to these fears are a variety of social indicators that appear to show an erosion in the parent-child bond and a precipitous decline in children's well-being. Public opinion polls indicate that two-thirds of all parents believe that they are less willing to make sacrifices for their children than their parents were. Other social statistics—ranging from college entrance examination results to teenage suicide rates—suggest that the decline in parental commitment to children has been accompanied by a sharp increase in problems among young people. Since 1960 the high-school dropout rate has increased until roughly one student in four drops out before graduation; juvenile delinquency rates have jumped 130 percent; the suicide rate for young people fifteen to nineteen years old has more than tripled; illegitimate births among white adolescent females have more than doubled; and the death rate from accidents and homicides has grown sixteenfold. Half a million adolescent females suffer from such eating disorders as anorexia nervosa or bulimia. American teenagers have the highest pregnancy rate of any industrialized nation, a high abortion rate and a high incidence of such venereal diseases as syphilis, gonorrhea, and genital herpes.[48]

Of course, it is easy to exaggerate the depravity of today's youth. Such problems as drug abuse, illegitimacy, and suicide affect only a small fraction of young people, and millions of others are raised in strong, caring homes by supportive and loving parents. Despite this, however, there is a widespread perception that American society is experiencing great difficulty in preparing children for adulthood.[49]

To a growing number of Americans, parenthood has become an increasingly frightening prospect. Fathers who once drag raced in hot rods and guzzled beer illegally are frightened by the idea of their children using drugs. Mothers who once made out with their boyfriends in parked cars are alarmed by statistics showing that teenage girls run a 40 percent change of becoming pregnant and run three times the risk of contracting venereal disease that they did. One result is that parents have become progressively more self-conscious, anxious, and guilt-ridden about child rearing; fearful that even a single mistake in parenting might inflict scars that could last a lifetime. To address parents' mounting anxiety, a veritable torrent of child-rearing manuals has appeared.[50]

Although most discussions of child rearing in the 1960s and 1970s dwell on Dr. Benjamin Spock, his era of influence was even then coming to an end. Until 1960, American child-rearing literature was dominated by a handful of manuals, notably Spock's *Baby and Child Care* and the publications of Dr. Arnold Gesell and the Yale Child Development Clinic, which traced the stages of children's physical, cognitive, and emotional development. The arena rapidly grew more crowded and confused during the 1960s with the publication of a spate of new child-rearing books. By 1981 more than 600 books were in print on the subject of child development. These new manuals tended to convey a sense of urgency absent in earlier child care books, rejecting the easy going approach championed by Dr. Spock. One child care expert, Dr. Lee Salk, addressed the subject in words typical of the new child-rearing literature: "Taking parenthood for granted can have disastrous results."[51]

As the number of child-rearing books multiplied during the 1960s, a fundamental schism became increasingly apparent. At one pole were those echoing concerns voiced by Vice President Spiro T. Agnew that overpermissiveness—that is, too much coddling of children and overresponsiveness to their demands—resulted in adolescents who were anarchic, disrespectful and undisciplined. An extreme example of this viewpoint could be found in James Dobson's *Dare to Discipline*, which called on parents to exercise firm control of their children through the use of corporal punishment. At the other pole were writers like Mark Gerzon, author of *A Childhood for Every Child*, who took the position that the characteristic American child-rearing techniques stifled creativity, generated dependence, instilled sexist biases, and produced repressed and conformist personalities. Authors like Gerzon called on parents to reject control through power and authority and to foster an environment based on warmth and understanding. Most child-rearing books, however, fell between the two, calling on parents to balance firmness and love and to adapt their methods to the unique temperament, needs, and feelings of each child.[52]

Although the authors of the burgeoning new child-rearing literature disagreed vehemently on such specific issues as the desirability of day care or whether mothers of young children should work outside the home, they did agree that successful child raising presents a much more difficult challenge today than it did in the past, noting that even parents with a deep commitment to their offspring confront difficulties that their parents did not have to face.[53]

Among the most potent new forces that intrude between parents and children is television. The single most important caretaker of children in the United States today is not a child's mother or a babysitter or even a day-care center but the television set in each child's home. Young children spend more time watching television than they do in any other activity other than sleep. The typical child between the ages of two and five spends about thirty hours a week viewing television, nearly a third of the child's waking time. Older children spend almost as much time in front of the TV. Indeed, children aged six to eleven average twenty-five hours a week watching TV, almost as much time as they spend in school. Since 1960 the tendency has been for children to become heavier and heavier television viewers.[54]

The debate about television's impact on children has raged furiously since the early 1950s. Critics are worried about parents' use of the television set as a baby-sitter and pacifier and as a substitute for an active parental role in socialization. They argue that excessive television viewing is detrimental because it encourages passivity and inhibits communication among family members. They express concern that children who watch large amounts of television tend to develop poor language skills, an inability to concentrate, and a disinclination to read. Moreover, they feel that television viewing tends to replace hours previously devoted to playtime either alone or with others. And, most worrisome, they believe that violence on TV provokes children to emulate aggressive behavior and acquire distorted views of adult relationships and communication.[55]

Research into the impact of television on children has substantiated some of these concerns and invalidated others. Television does appear to be a cause of cognitive and behavioral disturbances. Heavy television viewing is associated with reduced reading skills, less verbal fluency, and lower academic effort. Exposure to violence on television tends to make children more willing to hurt people and more aggressive in their play and in their methods of resolving conflicts. Time spent in front of the TV set does displace time previously spent on other activities and, as a result, many games and activities—marbles, jacks and trading cards, for example—are rapidly disappearing from American childhood.[56]

However, television also introduces children to new experiences easily and painlessly and stimulates interest in issues to which they might not otherwise be exposed. For many disadvantaged children, it provides a form of intellectual enhancement that deprived homes lacking books and newspapers could not afford.

And, for many children, television programs provide a semblance of extended kinship attachments and outlets for their fantasies and unexpressed emotions.[57]

While some television shows, such as *Sesame Street* and *Mr. Rogers' Neighborhood*, do appear to improve children's vocabularies, teach them basic concepts, and help them verbalize their feelings, overwhelming evidence suggests that most television programs convey racial and sexual stereotypes, desensitize children to violence, and discourage the kinds of sustained concentration necessary for reading comprehension. On balance, it seems clear that television cannot adequately take the place of parental or adult involvement and supervision of children and that the tendency for it to do so is a justifiable reason for increased public concern.[58]

The single most profound change that has taken place in children's lives since 1960 is the rapid movement of millions of mothers into the labor force. In the space of just twelve years, the number of mothers of children five or under who work outside the home tripled. Today nearly half of all children under the age of six have a mother who works. Many factors have contributed to this trend, including a rising cost of living and a declining rate of growth in real family income; increased control of fertility through contraception and abortion, which has meant that careers are less likely to be disrupted by unplanned pregnancies; and women's rising level of educational achievement, which has led many women to seek work not only as a way of getting a paycheck but as a way of obtaining personal independence and intellectual stimulation.[59]

The massive movement of mothers into the work force presented a major social problem: How should young children be cared for when their mothers work outside the home? This question gave rise to more controversy than almost any other family-related issue during the late 1960s and early 1970s.[60]

The event that first precipitated this debate was the publication in 1964 of a Department of Labor study that found almost one million latchkey children in the United States, unsupervised by adults for significant portions of the day. As the number of working mothers climbed in the late 1960s, many family experts advocated day care as a necessary response to the large number of mothers who had gone to work. At first the national debate focused on the child care problems of single mothers—widowed, divorced, and unmarried—and on whether they should be encouraged to enter the labor force.[61]

Liberals, led by Senator Walter Mondale, argued on behalf of a national system of comprehensive child development and day-care centers. Building on the model of the Head Start program, Mondale proposed in 1971 that the federal government establish a national system of services that included day-care programs, nutritional aid for pregnant mothers, medical and dental care, and after-school programs for teenagers. President Richard Nixon vetoed the bill in a stinging message that called the proposal fiscally irresponsible, administratively unworkable, and a threat to "diminish both parental authority and parental involvement with children." The president warned against committing "the vast authority of the national government to the side of communal approaches to child rearing over against the family-centered approach."[62]

Following the presidential veto, congressional support for a federally funded system of day care evaporated. Nevertheless the actual number of children enrolled in nursery schools or group day-care centers grew dramatically. At the time of the president's veto, less than one-third of all mothers with children one year old or younger held jobs. Today half of such women work, three-quarters of them full-time. As a result a majority of all children now spend some of their preschool years in the care of someone other than their mother.[63]

The trend is toward formal group day-care programs. Back in 1970 just 21 percent of all three- and four-year-olds were cared for in day-care centers or nursery schools. But between 1970 and 1983 the proportion virtually doubled, climbing to 38 percent. Today over two-thirds of all three- to four-year-olds are in a day-care, nursery school, or prekindergarten program.[64]

The single largest provider of day care now is the federal government, which offers child care, health, and educational services to some 400,000 low-income children through the Head Start program and which subsidizes private day-care facilities through child care tax credits, state block grants, and tax breaks for employers who subsidize day-care services. Nonetheless, the great majority of preschool child care arrangements in the United States are private, ranging from informal baby-sitting arrangements to private day-care centers run by national chains. Today two-thirds of all children are cared for in private facilities, and day care is an eleven-billion-dollar industry. The largest private corporation, Kinder-Care, has more than a thousand centers licensed to care for as many as a hundred thousand children.[65]

The drive for expanded day-care programs has its principal roots in the growing number of working mothers, the proliferation of single-parent homes, and the belief that access to day care is necessary to guarantee women's equal right to pursue a career. But the trend has also been fueled by new theories of child development, which emphasize the psychologically beneficial effects of a stimulating peer environment, by mounting evidence that children can assimilate information earlier than previously thought, and by research that has shown that disadvantaged children who participated in Head Start were more likely to graduate from high school, enroll in college, and obtain self-supporting jobs and were less likely to be arrested or register for welfare than were other children from low-income families.[66]

As formal child care programs proliferated, parents, educators, and social scientists began to examine the impact of day care on children's social and psychological growth, their intellectual development, and their emotional bond with their mother. The effects of day care remain the subject of intense controversy. Expert opinion varies widely, from those who fear that such programs provide an inadequate and unsatisfactory substitute for the full-time care and devotion of a mother to those who stress the resilience and adaptability of children. On one side, Jerome Kagan, a Harvard developmental psychologist, concludes that recent research reveals "that group care for young children does not seem to have much effect, either facilitating or debilitating, on the cognitive, social or affective development of most children." On the other side of the debate, Michael Rutter, a child psychologist at London's Institute for Psychiatry, states that "although day care for very young children is not likely to result in serious emotional disturbance, it would be misleading to conclude that it is without risks or effects."[67]

At present, knowledge about the impact of day care in children's intellectual, social, and emotional development remains limited. Research has suggested that quality day care has "neither salutary nor adverse effects on the intellectual development of most children"; that early entry into full-time day care may interfere with "the formation of a close attachment to the parents"; and that children in group day care are somewhat more aggressive, more independent, more involved with other children, more physically active, and less cooperative with adults than mother-raised children.[68]

The most pressing problem for parents at the moment is an inadequate supply of quality day care. The quality of day-care centers varies widely. The nature of care ranges from family day care, in which a woman takes children into her home for a fee, and cooperatives staffed or administered by parents, to on-site company nurseries, instituted by approximately one hundred corporations, and child care chains. High-quality centers, which can charge as much as $500 a month to care for a child, usually enroll only a small group of children and provide a great deal of individual attention. Low-quality centers, in contrast, tend to have a high ratio of children to caretakers, a high level of staff turnover, a low level of parental involvement, and a high noise level.[69]

Another serious problem is the lack of access to day care on the part of poorer children. Access to day care varies enormously according to family income. Seventy-five percent of all children from families with incomes of more than $25,000 a year participate in day-care or preschool programs by the age of six, compared to just a third of children from families with incomes of less than $15,000. Today, as a result of limited public funding, just a fifth of all eligible children are enrolled in Head Start. Children from poorer families are also less likely to participate in programs with an educational component.[70]

The United States lags far behind major European nations in assuming public responsibility for children's welfare. Today most European countries offer a variety of programs designed to assist working mothers, including paid maternity and paternity leaves for mothers and fathers who hold jobs, financial allowances for families with children, and subsidized public nurseries and kindergartens. Finland and Hungary go even further, paying mothers who stay at home with their children. The United States, with its long tradition of private-sector approaches to public problems and ingrained hostility toward state intervention in the family, has yet to come to terms with the problems presented by the massive influx of mothers into the workplace. The burden of coping with child care remains with the individual family.[71]

Of all the dramatic changes that have taken place in children's lives in recent years, the one that has aroused the deepest public concern is the spiraling divorce rate. Since 1960 the number of children involved in divorce has tripled, and in every year since 1972, more than a million children have had their homes disrupted by divorce. Of the children born in the 1970s, 40 percent will experience the dissolution of their parents' marriage before they themselves are sixteen. As one expert noted, "Children are becoming less and less of a deterrent to divorce."[72]

As divorce became a more pervasive part of the American scene, researchers began to ask penetrating questions about the psychological and emotional implications of divorce for children. Back in the 1920s, authorities on the family, using the case-study method, had concluded that children experienced the divorce of their parents as a devastating blow that stunted their psychological and emotional growth and caused maladjustments that persisted for years. Beginning in the late 1950s and continuing into the early 1970s, a new generation of researchers argued that children were better off when their parents divorced than when they had an unstable marriage; that divorce disrupted children's lives no more painfully than the death of a parent, which used to break up families just as frequently; and that the adverse effects of divorce were generally of short duration. [73]

Recent research has thrown both of these points of view into question. On the one hand, it appears that conflict-laden, tension-filled marriages have more adverse effects on children than divorce. Children from discordant homes permeated by tension and instability are more likely to suffer psychosomatic illnesses, suicide attempts, delinquency, and other social maladjustments than are children whose parents divorce. As of now, there is no clear-cut empirical evidence to suggest that children from "broken" homes suffer more health or mental problems, personality disorders, or lower school grades than children from "intact" homes. [74]

On the other hand, it is clear that divorce is severely disruptive, at least initially, for a majority of children, and a significant minority of children continue to suffer from the psychological and economic repercussions of divorce for many years after the breakup of their parents' marriage. It is also apparent that children respond very differently to a divorce and to a parent's death. When a father dies children are often moody and despairing. During a divorce, many children, and especially sons, exhibit anger, hostility, and conflicting loyalties. [75]

Children's reactions to divorce vary enormously, depending on their age and gender and, most important of all, their perception of their parents' marriage. Children who viewed their parents' marriage as unhappy tend to adjust more easily to divorce than those who regarded their home life as basically happy. [76]

For many children initial acceptance of their parents' separation is followed by a deep sense of shock. Although some children react calmly on learning that their parents are divorcing, a majority of children of all ages are vulnerable to feelings of pain, anger, depression, and insecurity. Family breakups often result in regressive behavior and developmental setbacks that last at least a year. [77]

Studies that followed children five years after a divorce found that a majority of children show resilience and increased maturity and independence. But, for a significant minority, the emotional turmoil produced by divorce proves to be long standing, evident in persistent feelings of hostility, depression, sexual anxiety, and concern about being unloved. Among a minority of children, the apparent consequences of divorce include alcohol and drug abuse, outward-directed despair and aggression, and sexual promiscuity. [78]

Clearly, divorce is an extremely stressful experience for children, whose economic and emotional costs continue to run high long after the parents' separation. Economic disruption is the most obvious consequence of a divorce. In the immediate aftermath of a divorce, the income of the divorced woman and her children falls sharply, by 73 percent in the year following divorce, while the father's income rises by 42 percent. Adding to the financial pressures facing children of divorce is the fact that a majority of divorced men evade court orders to support their children. Recent surveys indicate that only 40 percent of support orders are fully complied with during the first year after a divorce and that by the tenth year after separation, the figure falls to 13 percent. [79]

Other sources of stress result from the mother's new financial responsibilities as her family's breadwinner, additional demands on her time as she tries to balance economic and child-rearing responsibilities, and, frequently, adjustment to unfamiliar and less comfortable living arrangements. Burdened by her new responsibilities as head of her household, a mother often devotes less time to child rearing, forcing her to rely more heavily on neighbors, relatives, and older children.[80]

The emotional and psychological upheavals caused by divorce are often aggravated by a series of readjustments children must deal with, such as loss of contact with the noncustodial parent. Many children of divorce have to deal with feelings of abandonment by their natural fathers. More than nine of every ten children are placed in their mother's custody, and recent studies have found that two months following a divorce fewer than half the fathers see their children as often as once a week and, after three years, half the fathers do not visit their children at all.[81]

Further complicating children's adjustment to their parents' divorce is the impact of remarriage. Roughly half of all mothers are remarried within approximately two years of their divorce, thus many children of divorce live only briefly in single-parent homes. Today there are over 4 million households—one of every seven with children—in which one parent has remarried and at least one child is from a previous union. These reconstituted families often confront jealousies and conflicts of loyalty not found in families untouched by divorce, leading a number of investigators to conclude that "homes involving steprelationships proved more likely to have stress, ambivalence, and low cohesiveness" than did two-parent homes. At the same time, other researchers have found that most children of divorce favored remarriage.[82]

Today's children are growing up in an unstable and threatening environment in which earlier sources of support have eroded. They live in a permissive culture that exposes them from an early age to drugs, sex, alcohol, and violence. The increasing divorce rate, the entry of many mothers into the full-time work force, high rates of mobility, and the declining importance of the extended family all contribute to a decline in support and guidance. As a society the United States has largely failed to come to grips with the major issues facing children, such as the need for quality care while parents work and the need for a stable emotional environment in which to grow up.[83]

REVOLUTION IN FAMILY LAW

As the nation's families have changed, America's courts have become increasingly embroiled in disputes that pit wives against husbands and children against parents. Today nearly half of all civil court cases in the United States involve questions of family law. The courts are struggling with such questions as whether, in cases of divorce, the mother should be presumed to be the parent best suited to rear young children or whether grandparents should be granted visitation rights to a grandchild whose parents have divorced. The courts have also had to decide whether a husband can give the couple's children his surname over his wife's objections, whether husbands and wives should be permitted to sue each other, and whether children have a right to "divorce" their parents or to choose where they will live, independent of their parents' wishes.[84]

A revolution has taken place in the field of family law, and equally sweeping changes have occurred in divorce law. State legislatures, responding to the sharp upsurge in divorce rates during the 1960s and 1970s, radically liberalized their divorce statutes, making it possible to end a marriage without establishing specific grounds, and, in many states, allowing one spouse to terminate a marriage without the consent of the other. As the number of divorces mounted, every state adopted reforms designed to reduce the acrimony and shame that accompanied the divorce process.[85]

Until 1970, when California adopted the nation's first "no-fault" divorce law, a basic legal assumption was that marital relationships could only be ended for serious cause. Under fault statutes, divorce could only be granted on such grounds as desertion, nonsupport, cruel and abusive treatment, adultery, alcoholism, or a long prison term, and the division of property in a divorce was to reflect the share of guilt attributed to each partner. A man who wanted a divorce was expected to pay lifetime alimony to his wife, the purpose of which was to reward the woman's devotion to her family and to punish the husband who would abandon his wife.[86]

Within a span of just five years, all but five states adopted the principle of no-fault divorce. Today every state except South Dakota has enacted some kind of no-fault statute. Under no-fault divorce laws, a couple can institute divorce proceedings without first proving that either was at fault for the breakup. Rather than sue the other marriage partner, a husband or wife can obtain a divorce simply by mutual consent or on such grounds as incompatibility, living apart for a specified period, or "irretrievable breakdown" of the marriage. In complete no-fault states, a single partner can obtain a divorce unilaterally, without regard for the wishes of the other partner.[87]

The goal of no-fault divorce was to provide couples with a way to avoid long, acrimonious legal battles over who was to blame for a failed marriage and how marital property was to be divided. In an effort to reduce the bitterness associated with divorce, many states changed the terminology used in divorce proceedings, substituting the term "dissolution" for the word "divorce" and eliminating any terms denoting fault or guilt.[88]

Recently courts have also sought to overturn the so-called "tender years" doctrine that a young child is better off with the mother unless the mother is proved to be unfit. The current trend is for the courts not to presume in favor of mothers in custody disputes over young children. Most judges now only make custody awards after considering psychological reports and the wishes of the children. To spare children the trauma of custody conflict, many judges award divorced parents joint custody, in which both parents have equal legal rights and responsibilities in decisions affecting the child's welfare.[89]

Likewise, courts have moved away from the concept of alimony and replaced it with a new concept called "spousal support" or "maintenance." In the past, courts regarded marriage as a lifelong commitment and, in cases in which the husband was found guilty of marital misconduct, held that the wife was entitled to lifelong support. Now maintenance can be awarded to either the husband or the wife, and it can be granted for a limited time to permit a spouse to go to school, acquire skills, and become self-supporting.[90]

As the legal system has moved away from the principle of lifelong alimony, growing attention has been placed on the distribution of a couple's assets at the time of divorce. One state, Mississippi, still awards property on the basis of the name of the title to the property. Four "community property" states divide property acquired during the marriage equally, while the remaining states allow judges to award property "equitably." In dividing up property, a majority of states now require the courts to place monetary value on the wife's contribution as homemaker and mother and require judges to consider such sources of family wealth as insurance policies, pensions, deferred income, and licenses to practice a profession.[91]

Today many women's groups, which initially favored no-fault divorce, are calling for sharp modifications of such laws. They maintain that under present law "divorce is a financial catastrophe for most women." Legal rules that treat men and women equally, critics argue, tend to deprive women of the financial support they need. Under no-fault laws, many older women, who would have been entitled to lifelong alimony or substantial child support payments under the old fault statutes, find it extremely difficult to support their families. Today, the courts award only 15 percent of divorced women alimony, and in most cases the amounts are small (averaging approximately $250 a month) and granted temporarily until a wife reenters the work force. Also, courts, following the principle of equality, generally require ex-husbands to pay only half of what is needed to raise the children, on the assumption that the wife will provide the remainder. To make matters worse, many men are remiss on court-ordered alimony or child support payments.[92]

Another problem results from the expectation that women will reenter the labor force. Courts generally assume that a woman will be able to support herself following a divorce. In reality, however, the earning capacity of many divorced women is quite limited, especially if they have been longtime housewives and mothers. According to one study, only about one-third of wives worked regularly before the divorce, many part-time or sporadically for relatively low incomes. Many of these women find it difficult or impossible to obtain jobs that will allow them to maintain a standard of living approaching the one they had while married.[93]

Cases in which husbands and wives are pitted against each other have increasingly found their way onto the nation's court dockets. Among the issues facing the courts are these: Can a husband be criminally prosecuted for raping his wife? Can a husband give his children his surname over his wife's objections? Can an expectant mother obtain an abortion despite her husband's opposition? Until recently the law considered the father to be "head and master" of his family. His surname became his children's surname, his residence was the family's legal residence, he was immune from lawsuits instituted by his wife, and he was entitled to sexual relations with his spouse. Today the nation's courts have called all of these legal presumptions into question. The Massachusetts Supreme Court has ruled that husbands and wives can sue each other, the supreme courts of Massachusetts and New Jersey have said that husbands can be prosecuted for raping their wives, and the California Supreme Court has ruled that a husband cannot give his children his surname without his wife's agreement.[94]

Another dramatic change in the field of family law is the courts' tendency to grant legal rights to minor children. In the past, parents enjoyed wide discretionary authority over the details of their children's upbringing. More recently the nation's courts have held that minors do have independent rights that can override parental authority. The issues being brought before the courts include these:

> Should an unmarried fifteen-year-old Utah girl be able to obtain an abortion without her parents' knowledge?
>
> Should a twelve-year-old Ukrainian boy and a fifteen-year-old Cuban girl have a right to choose where they will live, even if this means living apart from their natural parents?
>
> Should a fifteen-year-old Washington State girl, unhappy with her parents' restrictions on her smoking, dating, and choice of friends, be allowed to have herself placed in a foster home against her parents' wishes?
>
> Should children be encouraged to turn in their parents for drug use, as in a recent California case?[95]

In deciding such cases, the courts have sought to balance two conflicting traditions: the historic right of parents to control their childrens' upbringing and the right of all individuals, including children, to privacy, due process, and equal rights. In some cases the courts have sided with the parents; in other cases they have supported children; in still others the rulings have been mixed. The U.S. Supreme Court has struck down state laws that give parents an absolute veto over whether a minor girl can obtain an abortion but upheld a Utah statute that required doctors to notify parents before performing an abortion. The Court ruled in the Utah case that a compelling state interest in maintaining the integrity of the family was more important than the girl's right to privacy. Two states—Iowa and Utah—have enacted laws greatly expanding minors' rights. These states permit children to seek temporary placement in another home if serious conflict exists between the children and their parents, even if the parents are not guilty of abuse or neglect.[96]

Recent decisions in family law have been characterized by two seemingly contradictory trends. On the one hand, courts have modified or struck down many traditional infringements on the right to privacy. They have prohibited laws regulating consenting sexual relations between spouses and restricting the right of parents to obtain contraceptive information or pass it on to their children. Since 1970, twenty states have decriminalized all forms of private sexual conduct between consenting adults, and in four other states, judicial decisions have invalidated statutes making such conduct a crime.[97]

On the other hand, courts have permitted government intrusion into areas traditionally regarded as bastions of family autonomy. Shocked by reports of abuse against children, wives, and the elderly, state legislatures have strengthened penalties for domestic violence and sexual abuse. Courts have reversed traditional precedents and ruled that husbands can be prosecuted for raping their wives. A

1984 federal law gave states new authority to seize property, wages, dividends, and tax refunds from parents who fail to make court ordered child support payments. Other court decisions have relaxed traditional prohibitions against spouses testifying against each other.[98]

What links these two apparently contradictory trends is a growing sensitivity on the part of the courts toward the individual and individual rights even when family privacy is at stake. Many recent court decisions are consistent with a greater regard for the autonomy of the individual. Thus, in recent cases, the courts have held that a husband cannot legally prevent his wife from having an abortion, since it is the wife who must bear the burden of pregnancy, and have also ruled that a wife's legal domicile is not necessarily her husband's home. Court decisions on marital rape reflect a growing recognition that a wife is not her husband's property.[99]

One ironic effect of these legal decisions has been a gradual erosion of the traditional conception of the family as a legal unit. In the collision between two sets of conflicting values—individualism and the family—the courts have tended to stress individual rights. For example, the Supreme Court recently struck down a Wisconsin law that forbids remarriage by divorced spouses until they have made arrangements for the financial care of their children on the grounds that it would encourage the birth of children out of wedlock, discriminate against the poor, and violate rights to personal freedom. Earlier in time the law was used to reinforce relationships between spouses and parents and children, but the current trend is to emphasize the separateness and autonomy of family members. The Supreme Court has repeatedly overturned state laws that require minor children to receive parental consent before obtaining contraceptive information or an abortion, and the lower courts have been unwilling to grant parents immunity from testifying against their own children. Similarly, state legislatures have weakened or abolished earlier laws that made children legally responsible for the support of indigent parents, while statutes that hold parents accountable for crimes committed by their minor children have been ruled unconstitutional.[100]

The nation's courts did not choose to become involved in family questions. The current legal ferment is a legacy of dramatic changes that have occurred in the nature of family life as divorce rates have soared, family patterns have grown less uniform, and the bonds connecting parents and children have loosened. These changes have resulted in novel disputes that have found their way into lawyers' offices. What is clear is that in a wide range of areas—including child custody, children's rights, spousal support, and property division—the nation's courts will continue to wrestle with a host of problems spawned by America's changing families.[101]

THE PRO-FAMILY MOVEMENT

Recent changes in family life have produced bewilderment, apprehension, and alarm, and many Americans believe that the consequences of these changes have been disastrous. A Gallup poll conducted in 1977 found that almost half of all Americans surveyed believed that family life has deteriorated in recent years.

This sense of unease has generated a political crusade among Americans who fear that climbing rates of divorce, working mothers, and single parents represent a breakdown of family values. These people, who have adopted the label "pro-family," have built a powerful political coalition out of a series of disparate elements including religious conservatives, such as the Moral Majority, the Religious Roundtable, and Christian Voice; traditional political conservatives; and single-issue groups concerned about a variety of family-related issues such as legalized abortion, ratification of the Equal Rights amendment to the Constitution, feminism, access of teenagers to contraception, sex education in schools, homosexuality, pornography, school busing for racial integration, and eroticism on television.[102]

Although the pro-family movement has drawn support from men and women of every social and economic background, it has appealed largely to women of lower economic and educational status who hold strong religious beliefs, whose self-esteem and self-image are bound up with being mothers and housewives, and who want to ensure that women who devote their lives to the family are not accorded lower status than women who work outside the home.[103]

Despite many disagreements in strategy and belief, the pro-family movement is united in its assessment of blame for the purported deterioration of family life. The issues that ignite the most passionate outrage on the part of the pro-family movement include feminism, which is viewed as primarily responsible for encouraging women to work outside the home; "secular humanism," believed to be responsible for eliminating all traces of religious values in public life; and the youth movement of the 1960s, which is held responsible for propagating a gospel of erotic experimentalism and self-gratification, sanctioning any form of behavior no matter how unconventional. The pro-family movement is also united in agreement on how the beleaguered American family can be helped. Among other things, the movement has sought the restoration of prayer in schools, screening of textbooks, limits on teenagers' access to contraceptives, and reversal of the Supreme Court's decisions on abortion.[104]

The pro-family movement has waged political battles on several fronts. One part of its strategy has been an effort to overturn the landmark 1973 *Roe* v. *Wade* ruling, in which the Supreme Court declared that the decision to have an abortion was a private matter of concern to a woman and her physician, and that only in the later stages of pregnancy could the government limit the right to abortion. Opposition to abortion has taken many forms, from calls for a constitutional amendment that would declare that from the moment of conception a fetus is a full human being entitled to constitutional protections, to efforts to restrict the use of government funds for abortions, to lobbying for local statutes limiting access to abortion by requiring waiting periods before abortions could be performed and parental consent for abortions for minors. The major legislative success of the "right to life" movement was adoption by Congress of the so-called Hyde amendment, which permitted states to refuse to fund abortions for indigent women. Despite this legislative effort, some fifteen states and the District of Columbia continue to fund abortions for poorer women.[105]

Another goal of the pro-family movement is to limit teenagers' access to contraceptive information. One proposal, put forward by the Reagan administration, was the "squeal rule," which would require family planning agencies that receive federal funds to notify the parents of minor children of requests for contraceptives. Another battle has been fought over the Equal Rights Amendment. Those who oppose the amendment have argued that it poses a threat to the family because it would eliminate all discrimination on the basis of sex, including the prohibition of marriages between persons of the same sex, and guarantee access to abortion and family planning services.[106]

The major legislative aim of the pro-family movement has been enactment of the Family Protection Act, which combines the disparate concerns of the movement into a single piece of legislation. This act would prohibit the use of legal aid funds in cases dealing with abortion, divorce, and gay rights and would restore prayer to the public schools.[107]

Arguments between the pro-family movement and its critics reached a peak in 1978, when President Jimmy Carter convened a White House Conference on Families to develop coherent policies to assist American families. The conference quickly became a battleground over such issues as legalized abortion, the Equal Rights Amendment, and gay rights and revealed the deep schism of values that had developed around family issues. The pro-family movement charged that feminists and ethnic minorities had won a disproportionate share of slots at the conference and accused the delegates of a bias against "traditional Judeo-Christian values concerning the family." At the conclusion of the conference, the White House issued a report recommending ways that government could strengthen American family life. Among the proposals were calls for the ratification of the Equal Rights Amendment, the right to abortion, and sex education in the schools, but, because of the opposition spearheaded by the pro-family movement, implementation of these measures proved impossible.[108]

A DEEP SENSE OF AMBIVALENCE

As the 1978 White House Conference on Families dramatically illustrated, American society today is deeply divided by conflicting conceptions of what constitutes a family and how government can best strengthen families to deal with contemporary problems. Yet, despite the furor generated by these disputes, an important point should not be missed. Public opinion polls indicate that while only a minority of Americans supports the legislative proposals of the pro-family movement, a large majority agrees with their belief that the family is an institution in deep trouble.[109]

Recent transformations in American family life have left Americans with a deep ambivalence about their familial roles. A substantial majority of Americans today say that they are less willing to make sacrifices for their children than their parents were and believe that unhappy parents should not remain married simply for the sake of the children. Yet, at the same time, an almost equal majority believes that "parents now have a reduced commitment to their children and their children to them" and want "a return to more traditional standards of family life." Unable to assimilate fully the domestic revolution of the past two decades, Americans are struggling to find a fair way to juggle individual, familial, and social demands.[110]

The American family today, like the family at the end of the eighteenth century and again at the end of the nineteenth, is in the midst of a profound historical transformation. Older assumptions—such as the idea that marriage is a lifetime commitment and that a proper family contains a breadwinner father and a housewife mother—have eroded. The older definition of the paternal role that equated a "real man" with a "good provider" who single-handedly supported his family has increasingly given way to a new ideal—honored as much in the breach as in the observance—that he should take an active role in family life, child care, and housework. Similarly, the older ideal of womanhood that defined a "real woman" as a good mother, wife, and hostess has been diluted by a sharp decline in the number of children in each family and women's growing participation in the world of wage work. Meanwhile, new notions of "children's rights" have challenged traditional assumptions that parents should, rightly or wrongly, dictate important decisions in their children's lives.[111]

Ours is an age of transition. Our families have grown less stable and uniform; traditional family role definitions and expectations have been thrown into question. And, like earlier ages of transition, ours is also an age of conflict. This includes conflicts between groups that hold competing ideals of a proper family but also deep internal conflicts that rage within individuals. Today a large majority of Americans feel torn between a continuing commitment to and nostalgia for older ideals of family life, stressing lifelong marriage and full-time mothering of children, and a newer, more flexible but less dependable conception of the family that allows for greater freedom and self-absorption.[112]

There is little point in looking nostalgically to the past for a solution to current problems. The 1950s pattern of family life—characterized by high rates of marriage, high fertility, and stable rates of divorce—which many continue to regard as an ideal, was the product of a convergence of an unusual series of historical, demographic, and economic circumstances unlikely to return again. Every barometer indicates that families in the future will be small, fragile, and characterized by late marriage and low birthrates. Today about half of all married women with minor children participate in the labor force. Today most working wives are part-time workers; in the future, many more will be likely to be full-time workers, as families become increasingly dependent on a wife's income.[113]

The challenge facing Americans in the years to come is not to hope wistfully for a return to the "normality" of the 1950s—which was actually inconsistent with long-term trends—but a much more difficult and much more concrete predicament. This challenge is to institute new social arrangements that will help moderate the effects of women's entry into the work force, of divorce, and of women's increasing need for autonomy. Possible solutions lie before us. These range from flexible working arrangements to enable employees to be effective parents to adequate supplies of affordable quality substitute care when parents work, maternity and paternity leaves to assist parents who are starting families, revision of welfare policies that encourage the flight of husbands, custody and visitation agreements that will facilitate continuing contact between divorced parents and their children, legal guarantees that children of divorce will receive an adequate and secure income, and monetary incentives for parents who stay home with their children. Americans agree on the desirability of strong families; the ultimate question is whether the nation has the political will to create conditions that will foster stronger families.[114]

NOTES

1.   The statistics on changes in family composition can be found in Daniel Yankelovich, *New Rules: Search for Self-Fulfillment in a World Turned Upside Down* (New York, 1981), xiv–xv.

2.   Stephen L. Klineberg made a similar argument in a public lecture "American Families in Transition: Challenges and Opportunities in a Revolutionary Time" delivered at Rice University, February 15, 1983. Also see Andrew Hacker, *The End of the American Era* (New York, 1971), 174; James J. Lynch, *The Broken Heart: The Medical Consequences of Loneliness* (New York, 1977), 8–10; *Time* (December 2, 1985), 41; *New York Times*, June 27, 1979, I, 1; *NYT*, May 26, 1981, I, 1.

It must be emphasized that despite the dramatic changes that have taken place, the institution of the family is not an endangered species. Today, commitment to marriage remains strong and 90 percent of young Americans marry. Despite rising divorce rates, the majority of marriages do not end in divorce, most divorced individuals remarry, and only a small percentage marry more than twice. Even when divorces occur, they do not necessarily produce grave social problems. Forty percent of all divorces occur within four years of marriage and usually involve no children. At the same time, the desire to have children remains as high as ever. Today only 1 percent of American women say that the ideal number of children in a family is none. And despite concern about the fragility of family ties, the increase in the divorce rate has been largely offset by a decline in death rates. As a result, marriages today are only slightly more likely to be disrupted by divorce, desertion, or death than they were earlier in the century. Indeed, even with the rising divorce rate, fewer children today are raised in institutions or by relatives or by mothers barely able to support them than formerly. In spite of the rising divorce rate, the prevalence of single-parent households has not increased markedly among the middle class because women today are much more likely to remarry after a divorce.

Even in the controversial areas of child care and sexuality, behavior has changed less than newspaper headlines suggest. Today most preschoolers are cared for by full-time mothers or mothers who work part-time. Most mothers of young children accommodate their work schedules to the needs of their children. Continuity is also apparent in sexual behavior. Despite the increasing incidence of premarital sex and widespread public discussion of swinging, wife swapping, and illegitimacy, the overwhelming majority of women who have premarital sex have just one or two partners, usually a fiance or a steady date. Nor has the proportion of unmarried white women having babies increased dramatically. In 1950, 99.5 percent of white teenage women did not have illegitimate births; thirty years later, 98.1 percent of this group did not. See Mary Jo Bane, *Here to Stay: American Families in the Twentieth Century* (New York, 1976), 12–13, 30; Sar A. Levitan and Richard S. Belous, *What's Happening to the American Family?* (Baltimore,

1981), 21, 63; Mary Jo Bane et al., "Child Care Settings in the United States" in *Child Care and Mediating Structures*, eds. Brigitte Berger and Sidney Callahan (Washington, D.C., 1979), 19; Carol Tavris and Carole Offir, *The Longest War: Sex Differences in Perspective* (New York, 1977), 64–69.

3. Tavris and Offir, *The Longest War*, 64–69; Peter Uhlenberg and David Eggebeen, "Declining Well-Being of American Adolescents," *The Public Interest* (Winter 1986), 32–33; Lynch, *Broken Heart*, 8–10; *Time* (December 2, 1985), 41; *NYT*, June 27, 1979, I, 1; *NYT*, May 26, 1981, I, 1; *NYT*, March 16, 1986, I, 18.

4. The impact of these changes is most readily apparent in the lives of a key "pace-setting" segment of the population: educated career women. These women are four times less likely to marry than women of lower economic and educational status and 50 percent more likely to divorce. See Andrew Hacker, "Goodbye to Marriage," *New York Review of Books* (May 3, 1979), 23–27; Peter Clecak, *America's Quest for the Ideal Self: Dissent and Fulfillment in the 60s and 70s* (New York, 1983), 93–94.

5. Yankelovich, *New Rules*, 104, 184.

    It is easy to exaggerate the significance of rising rates of divorce, working mothers, and single-parent households and to conclude that these changes are bad for the family. But it is also possible to view these developments in a more favorable light. Declining birthrates mean that Americans are less likely to bear children by accident or because it is socially expected than earlier Americans, while rising divorce rates mean that people today are less willing to tolerate unhappy and empty marriages. See Klineberg, "American Families in Transition."

6. Ben J. Wattenberg, *The Good News is the Bad News is Wrong* (New York, 1985), 290–91.

7. Joseph Veroff, Elizabeth Douan, and Richard A. Kulka, *The Inner American: A Self Portrait from 1957 to 1976* (New York, 1981), 191, 192, 194, 196; Yankelovich, *New Rules*, 5, 68, 97, 99.

8. Yankelovich, *New Rules*, 5. The rapid rise in the divorce rate is clearly a legacy of changing social values. When individuals are asked why they have decided to get a divorce, a new set of reasons predominates. A survey conducted by the Family Service Association found that the major source of conflict in marriages involved "communications." Conflict over sex was another reason commonly cited in explanations of divorce. More traditional areas of conflict, such as disputes over children or family finances, lagged far behind. See *NYT*, January 3, 1974, I, 16.

    It should be noted, however, that the best predictors of a marital breakup remain what they have always been: a teenage marriage, a wife pregnant before marriage, and a low level of family income. Psychological stress continues to be a leading cause of divorce, since many marriages fail following an acutely stressful experience, such as an unexpected death in the family, revelation of an infidelity, or loss of a job. See Arthur J. Norton and Paul C. Glick, "Marital Instability in America: Past, Present, and Future," in *Divorce and Separation: Context, Causes, and Consequences*, eds. George Lebinger and Oliver C. Moles, (New York, 1979), 6–19; Bane, *Here to Stay*, 22, 32–33, 36.

    Traditional causes of marital stress were aggravated by social and legal changes during the 1970s. Economic instability produced conditions conducive to high divorce rates. Instability in a husband's employment or earnings is a major source of strain in the marriages of poorer couples, producing friction because of the husband's inability to fulfill his family's expectations. Divorce is more likely as well when a wife's earnings are higher than her husband's, in part because independent earnings add to a woman's sense of self-esteem and in part because this contributes to the husband's sense of insecurity. As more wives entered the labor force after 1970, this factor became a growing source of marital strain. Increased rates of social mobility across ethnic, religious, and geographical lines also contributed to the rising rates of marital instability. Census statistics disclose that more and more people are marrying partners who come from outside their ethnic or religious group or their area of birth. After marriage an increasing number of couples pull up stakes and move to new parts of the country, particularly to the Sunbelt, disrupting ties with family and friends. Divorce statistics show that the twelve metropolitan areas with the highest divorce rates are all located in Southern and Western states. Victor R. Fuchs, *How We Live* (Cambridge, Mass., 1983), 147–50; *NYT*, November 13, 1981, I, 12.

Changes in law also contributed to the rising number of divorces. Legal changes that made it easier to obtain a divorce included enactment of no-fault divorce laws in every state except South Dakota, "do-it-yourself" divorce kits that allow couples to dissolve a marriage without the help of a lawyer, a tendency toward lower alimony awards, and a trend toward making property settlements less contingent on who was at fault in breaking up the marriage. *NYT*, January 5, 1974, I, 16; *NYT*, March 19, 1975, I, 33; *NYT*, February 7, 1983, I, 1; Joan Anderson letter, *NYT*, December 5, 1981, I, 24; Lenore J. Weitzman and Ruth B. Dixon, "The Transformation of Legal Marriage Through No-Fault Divorce: The Case of the United States," in *Marriage and Cohabitation in Contemporary Societies: Areas of Legal, Social, and Ethical Change*, eds. John M. Eekelaar and Sanford N. Katz (Toronto, 1979), 143–53; Lynne Carol Halem, *Divorce Reform: Changing Legal and Social Perspectives* (New York, 1980), 233–83.

Finally, the current upsurge in divorces may be a product of the early marriages contracted during World War II and the early postwar period, when an unprecedented number of very young couples were joined together in wedlock. The high number of divorces during and after the World War II may have contributed to the high divorce rate during the 1970s, because the children of divorce face a substantially higher risk than others of having their own marriages fail. Norton and Glick, "Marital Instability in America," 6–19; *NYT*, November 27, 1977, I, 1; *NYT*, April 13, 1982, C1.

9. Veroff, Douan, and Kulka, *The Inner American*, 191, 192, 194, 196; Yankelovich, *New Rules*, 5.

10. Richard A. Easterlin, "The American Baby Boom in Historical Perspective" Occasional Paper no. 79 (Washington, D.C., National Bureau of Economic Research, 1962); "Relative Economic Status and the American Fertility Swing," in *Social Structure, Family Life Styles, and Economic Behavior*, ed. Eleanor B. Sheldon (Philadelphia, 1972); Easterlin, "The Conflict Between Aspirations and Resources," *Population and Development Review*, 2 (September/December 1972), 417–26; Arthur A. Campbell, "Baby Boom to Birth Dearth and Beyond," *Annals*, 435 (January 1978), 52–53.

11. Russell Jacoby, *Social Amnesia: A Critique of Conformist Psychology from Adler to Laing* (Boston, 1975); Ehrenreich, *Hearts of Men*, 89–98, 122, 147, 164–65; Yankelovich, *New Rules*, 235.

12. Refer to note 11. For an example of the new viewpoint on marriage and divorce, see a popular textbook *Essentials of Life and Health* (New York, 1972): "Far from

being a wasting illness, divorce is a healthful adaptation, enabling monogamy to survive in a time when patriarchal powers, privileges and marital systems have become unworkable; far from being a radical change in the institution of marriage, divorce is a relatively minor modification of it. . . . "; quoted in Lynch, *The Broken Heart*, 10.

13. Allen J. Matusow, *The Unraveling of America: A History of Liberalism in the 1960s* (New York, 1984), 277–80, 321–23.

14. Refer to note 13, If a single term gave expression to the growing influence of young people during the 1960s, it was the phrase the "generation gap." It referred to the appearance among the young of a separate culture, a distinct language, and a distinctive outlook, apart from the world of adults. A shift in generational experience may have contributed to the perceived gulf between old and young. Young people of the 1960s, unlike their parents, had escaped the years of hardship, austerity, and sacrifice of the depression and World War II. Also contributing to a generation gap was the rising level of education attained by younger Americans. Many studies conducted during the 1960s concluded that those who had attended college were generally more liberal in their social, religious, and moral attitudes than those who had not.

It would be a mistake, however—a mistake made by many social commentators—to exaggerate the dimensions of the generation gap during the 1960s. Little persuasive evidence was uncovered during the sixties showing extensive alienation between adolescents and their parents. Survey research found a deep cleavage within the younger generation itself, dividing young college students from those who had entered blue collar jobs directly from high school, who were reportedly appalled "by the collapse of patriotism and respect for the law." Altogether, little evidence was found to indicate that younger Americans had abandoned traditional moral frameworks. Even in the most controversial and highly publicized areas of change—sex and drug-taking—truly dramatic shifts would have to wait for the 1970s. Studies of sexual behavior in the late 1960s detected only a modest liberalization in sexual practices compared to findings of twenty years before, while surveys of drug use found that only about 10 percent of young Americans had experimented with marijuana.

A number of influential studies of college students also argued that younger people's rejection of the strict norms that prevailed in the 1950s did not constitute a generation gap. According to these studies, students were simply giving expression to suppressed elements in their parents' lives. See Yankelovich, *New Rules*, 174; Kenneth Keniston, *Young Radicals* (New York, 1968); *NYT*, February 4, 1971, I, 1; *NYT*, January 17, 1972, I, 33; *NYT*, August 18, 1977, C13; *NYT*, December 1, 1968, VI, 129; *NYT*, November 2, 1969, VI, 32ff.; *NYT*, January 18, 1970, VI, 10.

15. William Manchester, *The Glory and the Dream: A Narritive History of America (1932–1972). (Boston, 1974).* 1221, 1355, 1464–68. The literature on the women's movement is vast. A useful introduction is William H. Chafe, *Women and Equality: Changing Patterns in American Culture* (New York, 1977). On the ideology of feminism, see Barbara Sinclair Deckard, *The Women's Movement: Political, Socioeconomic, and Psychological Issues* (New York, 1975); Sara Evans, *Personal Politics: The Roots of Women's Liberation in the Civil Rights Movement and the New Left* (New York, 1979); Jo Freeman, *The Politics of Women's Liberation: A Case of an Emerging Social Movement and Its Relation to the Public Policy Process*

(New York, 1975); Judith Hole and Ellen Levine, *Rebirth of Feminism* (New York, 1971); *Radical Feminism*, eds. Anne Koedt, Ellen Levine, and Anita Rapone (New York, 1973); Gayle Graham Yates, *What Women Want: The Ideas of the Movement* (Cambridge, Mass., 1971).

16. On the impact of feminism, see Judith M. Bardwick, *In Transition: How Feminism, Sexual Liberation, and the Search for Self-Fulfillment Have Altered America* (New York, 1979); Chafe, *Women and Equality*, ch. 5; Cynthia Fuchs Epstein, "Ten Years Later: Perspectives on the Women's Movement," *Dissent*, 22 (Spring 1975), 169–76; Janet Giele, *Women and the Future: Changing Sex Roles in Modern America* (New York, 1978); Elinor Lenz and Barbara Myerhoff, *The Feminization of America: How Women's Values Are Changing Our Public and Private Lives* (Los Angeles, 1985); Jane de Hart Mathews, "The New Feminism and the Dynamics of Social Change," in *Women's America: Refocusing the Past*, eds. Linda Kerber and Jane de Hart Mathews (New York, 1981), 397–421.

17. Manchester, *Glory and the Dream*, 1035–36. On the sexual revolution, see "Sex and the Contemporary American Scene," *Annals of the America Academy of Political and Social Science*, 376 (March 1968).

18. *NYT*, February 10, 1971, I, 48. On the growth of a "singles culture," see *NYT*, January 3, 1974, I, 16; *NYT*, April 21, 1977, C1. Homosexual rights ordinances were adopted in Ann Arbor, Michigan; Berkeley, California; Columbus, Ohio; Detroit, Michigan; Minneapolis, Minnesota; San Francisco, California; Seattle, Washington; and Washington, D.C., between 1972 and 1974. In 1973, the American Psychiatric Association removed homosexuality from its list of mental disorders.

19. Manchester, *Glory and the Dream*, 1035–36; "Sex and the Contemporary American Scene," *Annals of the America Academy of Political and Social Science*, 376 (March, 1968); *NYT*, February 10, 1971, I, 48; *NYT*, January 3, 1974, I, 16; *NYT*, April 21, 1977, C1.

20. Yankelovich, *New Rules*, xiv, 88, 97, 99, 100, 103, 104.

21. Daniel Patrick Moynihan, *Family and Nation: The Godkin Lectures, Harvard University* (San Diego, 1986); *NYT*, September 27, 1977, reprinted in *The Family*, ed. Gene Brown (New York, 1979), 353. For a helpful discussion of factors that have prompted concern for the family, see Nathan Glazer, "The Rediscovery of the Family," *Commentary* (March 1978), 49–56.

22. Lee Rainwater and William L. Yancey, *The Moynihan Report and the Politics of Controversy* (Cambridge, Mass., 1967), includes the full text of *The Negro Family: The Case for National Action* as well as responses to the report by government policymakers, journalists, civil rights leaders, and academic social scientists. For other responses to the report, see *NYT*, July 19, 1965 and April 28, 1967, reprinted in Brown, ed., *The Family*, 356–57.

23. Rainwater and Yancey, *Moynihan Report and the Politics of Controversy*, 51–60, 75–91.

24. Ibid., 75–80. For the comparison with Irish immigrants, see Moynihan, *Family and Nation*, 27–28.

25. Rainwater and Yancey, *Moynihan Report and the Politics of Controversy*, 93–94.

26. Ibid., 133–215; Andrew Billingsley, *Black Families in White America* (New York, 1968); R. Farley and A.I. Hermalin, "Family Stability: A Comparison of Trends Between Blacks and Whites," *American Sociological Review*, 36 (1971); J. Heiss,

"On the Transmission of Marital Instability in Black Families," *American Sociological Review*, 37 (1972), 82–92; Robert B. Hill, *Strengths of Black Families* (New York, 1971); Joyce Ladner, *Tomorrow's Tomorrow* (Garden City, N.Y., 1972); R. Staples, "Toward a Sociology of the Black Family: A Theoretical and Methodological Assessment," *Journal of Marriage and the Family* 33 (1971), 119–38.

27.   *NYT*, April 7, 1985, I, 1.

28.   Thomas Meehan, "Moynihan of the Moynihan Report," *NYT*, July 31, 1966, VI, 5; *NYT*, July 29, 1971, I, 16; Rainwater and Yancey, *Moynihan Report and the Politics of Controversy*, 347–49.

The debate over the sources of difference in white and black illegitimacy rates remains shrouded in controversy. The Kinsey Institute studies of human sexuality, conducted in the 1940s and 1950s, suggested that black women tended to become sexually active at a somewhat earlier age than white women. At the age of fifteen, Kinsey reported, 50 percent of all non-college-educated black women had had premarital intercourse, compared to ten to fifteen percent of white women of similar educational backgrounds. Kinsey also reported that young black women had a greater frequency of intercourse, which he suggested could account for one-third to one-half of the difference in illegitimacy rates.

Other studies attributed the difference in illegitimacy rates to the fact that a higher proportion of black women spent their child-rearing years in an unmarried state, reflecting higher rates of nonmarriage, divorce, desertion, and widowhood. Other researchers suggested that higher black illegitimacy rates reflected the greater use of contraceptives and greater resort to abortion by unmarried white women, underreporting of white illegitimate births, and the greater prevalence of "shotgun" marriages among whites.

What studies have found is that white women were more likely to legitimate children conceived before marriage. In 1971, 34 percent of white children were born within eight months of marriage compared to 26 percent of black children. Research found that the proportion of women who legitimate children by shotgun marriages correlates closely with education. When the education factor is controlled for, the same proportion of black and white women who have a premarital pregnancy marry before the child's birth. Other studies indicate that black women were more likely to have unplanned or unwanted births because they were less likely to use contraceptives or abortions. Kinsey found that three times as many non-college educated unmarried white women had abortions as similarly situated black women. Black women were also less likely to put children up for adoption. In 1971, two-thirds of illegitimate white children were put up for adoption or placed into foster care, as opposed to 7 percent of illegitimate black children. See Sar A. Levitan, William B. Johnston, and Robert Taggart, *Minorities in the United States: Problems, Progress, and Prospects* (Washington, D.C., 1975), 38; Rainwater and Yancey, *Moynihan Report and the Politics of Controversy*, 223–35, 348–49.

29.   Rainwater and Yancey, *Moynihan Report and the Politics of Controversy*, 219, 235, 354–68, 436–37, 454.

30.   Thomas Meehan, "Moynihan of the Moynihan Report," *NYT*, July 31, 1966, 6, 5; *NYT*, July 29, 1971, I, 16; Rainwater and Yancey, *Moynihan Report and the Politics of Controversy*, 318–20.

31.   Carol B. Stack, *All Our Kin: Strategies for Survived in a Black Community* (New York, 1974); *The Extended Family in Black Societies*, eds. Demitri B. Shimkin, Edith M. Shimkin, and Dennis A. Frate (Chicago, 1978), especially essays by Bert

N. Adams, Regina E. Holloman and Fannie E. Lewis, Lenus Jack, Jr., Kiyotaka Aoyagi, and Vera M. Green; Hill, *Strengths of Black Families*, 5–8.

32. Rainwater and Yancey, *Moynihan Report and the Politics of Controversy*, 1–3.

33. *NYT*, December 9, 1968, I, 1.

34. Charles Murray, "No, Welfare Isn't Really the Problem," *Public Interest*, no. 84 (Summer 1986), 5–6; Sar A. Levitan, *Programs in Aid of the Poor*, 5th ed. (Baltimore, Md., 1985), 34.

35. Levitan, *Programs in Aid of the Poor*, 1–154; Levitan, *The Great Society's Poor Law: A New Approach to Poverty* (Baltimore, Md., 1969); Levitan and Robert Taggart, *The Promise of Greatness* (Cambridge, Mass., 1976); *On Fighting Poverty: Perspectives from Experience*, ed. James L. Sundquist (New York, 1969); *The Great Society: Lessons for the Future*, eds., Eli Ginzburg and Robert M. Solow (New York, 1974).

36. Levitan, *Programs in Aid of the Poor*, 5–6; John E. Schwartz, *America's Hidden Success: A Reassessment of Twenty Years of Public Policy* (New York, 1983), 32–50; *Fighting Poverty: What Works and What Doesn't*, eds. Sheldon H. Danzinger and Daniel H. Weinberg (Cambridge, Mass., 1986).

37. Sar A. Levitan and Clifford M. Johnson, *Beyond the Safety Net: Reviving the Promise of Opportunity in America* (Cambridge, Mass., 1984), 60–61.

38. Ibid., Charles Murray, *Losing Ground: American Social Policy, 1950–1980* (New York, 1984), 129–33.

39. Government studies have found that a 10 percent increase in AFDC benefits was associated with a 2 percent increase in the number of female-headed families, while a 10 percent increase in male wages was accompanied by an 8 percent decline in female-headed families. Levitan and Johnson, *Beyond the Safety Net*, 64; Robert Lerman, "The Family, Poverty, and Welfare Programs: An Introductory essay on Problems of Analysis and Policy," in U.S. Congress, Joint Economic Committee, *Studies in Public Welfare* (Washington, D.C.: U.S. Government Printing Office, 1974), 18–19; Marjorie Honig, "The Impact of Welfare Payment Levels on Family Stability," in *Studies in Public Welfare*, 37–53. See essays on poverty and family structure by Mary Jo Bane, William Julius Wilson, and Kathryn M. Neckerman in *Fighting Poverty*, eds. Danziger and Weinberg. For a contrasting view, see Murray, *Losing Ground*, 124–33.

40. *Progress Against Poverty: A Review of the 1964–1974 Decade*, eds. Robert D. Plotnick and Felicity Skidmore (New York, 1975), 13, 62–63, 104–5; Levitan and Taggart, *The Promise of Greatness*, 49, 51; *NYT*, July 18, 1971, IV, 12.

41. Levitan, *Programs in Aid of the Poor*, 13–14, 34–38, 94–95.

42. Welfare mothers divide into at least two identifiable groups, Most single women on welfare are older women seeking temporary assistance while recovering from the loss of a spouse through divorce, desertion, or death. These women account for 85 to 90 percent of all single women who ever go on welfare. Another group of single women on welfare are younger, less-educated mothers, particularly those who bore an illegitimate child during their teens or early twenties, who are more likely to remain dependent on public assistance for long periods. Roughly 10 to 15 percent of the people who ever go on welfare remain on public assistance for eight years or more; they constitute more than half of the people on welfare at any one time. See Mickey Kaus, "Welfare and Work: A Symposium," *New Republic*

(October 6, 1986), 22; *NYT*, September 25, 1986, I, 26. Ben J. Wattenberg, *The Good News is the Bad News is Wrong* (New York, 1985), 191, 240, 243.

43. Sar A. Levitan, *Programs in Aid of the Poor for the 1970s* (Baltimore, Md., 1969), 29; *Family Policy: Government and Families in Fourteen Countries*, eds. Sheila B. Kamerman and Alfred J. Kahn (New York, 1978), 428–503.

44. *Families That Work: Children in a Changing World*, eds. Sheila B. Kamerman and Cheryl D. Hayes (Washington, D.C., 1982), 12–36; Joan Beck, "Growing Up in America is Tough," *Houston Chronicle* (April 2, 1986), A10; Glazer, "Rediscovery of the Family," 50.

     Growing anxiety over children and adolescents was, of course, related to the postwar baby boom. Census statistics showed an explosion in the number of young Americans during the 1960s. The number of young people aged fourteen to twenty-four jumped 47 percent in a decade, reaching forty million in 1970. At the end of the 1960s, young people accounted for 20 percent of the American population, a third more than in 1960. Because teenagers and young adults constituted a growing proportion of the population, as a result of depressed birthrates during the 1930s followed by the postwar baby boom, young people exerted a disproportionate influence on public opinion.

     The 1960s witnessed major gains in income, education, and employment by teenagers. Teenagers were far more likely to finish high school or attend college than were their parents. The proportion of young Americans receiving college degrees tripled in the three decades after 1940—climbing from 6 to 16 percent—while the proportion receiving high school diplomas doubled—from 38 percent to 75 percent. *NYT*, February 4, 1971, I, 1; *NYT*, January 17, 1972, I, 33; *NYT*, August 18, 1977, C13.

45. Today, as many as two-thirds of all American high school junior and seniors hold part-time paying jobs. See Ellen Greenberger and Laurence Steinberg, *When Teenagers Work: The Psychological and Social Costs of Adolescent Employment* (New York, 1986), 3–46.

46. Joan Beck, "Growing Up in America is Tough," *Houston Chronicle* (April 2, 1986), A10.

47. Marie Winn, *Children Without Childhood* (New York, 1983); David Elkind, *The Hurried Child: Growing Up Too Soon* (Reading, Mass., 1981); Vance Packard, *Our Endangered Children: Growing Up in a Changing World* (Boston, 1983). Similar fears were already being voiced in the 1950s. See Eda LeShan, *The Conspiracy Against Childhood* (New York, 1967).

48. Peter Uhlenberg and David Eggebeen, "The Declining Well-Being of American Adolescents," *Public Interest*, no. 85 (Winter 1986), 25–38.

49. While it is true that the suicide rate for white male adolescents increased 260 percent between 1950 and 1976, the illegitimacy rate of illegitimate births among white adolescent females increased 143 percent over the same period, and the rate of death by homicide among white adolescent males increased 177 percent between 1959 and 1976, actual rates remained at low levels. The white male adolescent homicide rate rose from 3 per 100,000 in 1959 to 8 per 100,000 in 1976; the white male adolescent suicide rate climbed from 4 per 100,000 in 1959 to 13 per 100,000 in 1976; and illegitimacy among white teenage women rose from 5.1 per 1,000 to 12.4 per 1,000. It is also easy to exaggerate drug usage. Seventeen percent of all high school seniors have tried cocaine once in their life; 54 percent have

tried marijuana at least once. See Ira S. Steinberg, *The New Lost Generation: The Population Boom and Public Policy* (New York, 1982), 7–19; Adam Paul Weisman, "I Was a Drug-Hype Junkie," *New Republic* (October 6, 1986), 14–17.

50. *NYT*, October 26, 1969, I, 57; *NYT*, April 2, 1967, VI, 112ff.

51. *NYT*, September 11, 1973, I, 50; *NYT*, December 25, 1969, I, 37.

52. *NYT*, April 14, 1974, VII, 3; *NYT*, November 8, 1968, I, 54; *NYT*, January 7, 1973, I, 22, 23; *NYT*, February 16, 1969, VII, Pt. 2, 4; *NYT*, June 27, 1976, VI, 26ff.; *NYT*, December 3, 1973, I, 54; *NYT*, March 16, 1981, II, 8; *NYT*, September 11, 1973, I, 50.

53. *NYT*, December 3, 1973, I, 54; *NYT*, March 16, 1981, II, 8; *NYT*, September 11, 1973, I, 50.

54. Fuchs, *How We Live*, 51, 55–56, 69–71; Bane, *Here to Stay*, 15; John P. Murray, *Television and Youth: 25 Years of Research and Controversy* (Stanford, Wash., 1980), 67.

55. Marie Winn, *The Plug-In Drug* (New York, 1977); Murray, *Television and Youth*, 18–57.

56. Murray, *Television and Youth*, 18–57; *NYT*, January 6, 1959, March 2, 1969, September 18, 1969, September 28, 1969, September 4, 1971, January 11, 1972, April 20, 1980, reprinted in *Childhood, Youth and Society*, ed. Gene Brown (New York, 1980), 70–94.

57. Refer to note 56.

58. Refer to note 56.

59. Fuchs, *How We Live*, 126–33, 150, 166, 169, 173–74, 190, 204; *NYT*, November 30, 1977, I, 1. One set of factors that propelled married women into the labor force was a rising cost of living and a declining rate of growth in real family income. Income, adjusted for inflation, rose 38 percent during the 1950s and 33 percent in the 1960s, but dropped 9.2 percent between 1973 and 1982. At the same time that real income fell, other costs, especially for housing, climbed steeply. Back in 1971, it took an income of just $6,770 to afford a median-price house, which then cost just $24,800. Actual median income that year was $10,300, 51.9 percent more than was required. A decade later, the median price of a house had climbed to over $70,000 and a family that earned the median family income was unable to afford such a house. Other economic factors that led many married women to seek a paycheck included rising real wages for women workers, which increased the attractiveness of work outside the home and the growth of service industries, such as retail trade, education, and health. Such service jobs have traditionally offered more opportunities to women than other occupations because they do not rely on physical strength, their work hours are usually flexible, and the workplace is often located in residential areas.

60. Sheila Kamerman and Alfred Kahn, "The Day-Care Debate: A Wider View," *Public Interest*, no. 54 (1979), 76–93.

61. *NYT*, November 30, 1970, I, 1; *NYT*, April 1, 1973, IV, 9; *NYT*, January 9, 1976, I, 18.

62. Edward B. Fiske, "Early Schooling is Now the Rage," *NYT*, April 13, 1986, XII, 24–30; *NYT*, December 10, 1971, and April 30, 1972, in *The Family*, ed. Gene Brown, 337–43.

63. Fiske, "Early Schooling," 25; Kamerman and Kahn, "The Day-Care Debate," 76–93.

64. Fiske, "Early Schooling," 25.

65. Ibid., 25–26. A 1985 Conference Board study estimated that 120 companies and 400 hospitals and public agencies sponsored day-care centers at or near their facilities. Another 2,500 firms provide financial support for child care. *NYT*, June 21, 1985, 25: 2.

66. Fiske, "Early Schooling," 25–26.

67. Packard, *Our Endangered Children*, 137–38; Jerome Kagan, "The Effects of Infant Day Care on Psychological Development," *The Growth of the Child* (New York, 1978), 78.

68. Packard, *Our Endangered Children*, 139–41, 146, 166–72; Jay Belsky and Laurence D. Steinberg, "The Effects of Day Care: A Critical View," *Child Development*, 49 (1978), 929–49; Belsky and Steinberg, "What Does Research Teach Us About Day Care?" *Children Today* (July-August, 1979); Sally Provence, Audrey Naylor and June Patterson, *The Challenge of Day Care* (New Haven, 1977).

69. Packard, *Our Endangered Children*, 144–58.

70. Fiske, "Early Schooling," 30.

71. *Family Policy*, eds. Kamerman and Kahn, 428–503; *NYT*, June 9, 1979, 17: 2; Packard, *Our Endangered Children*, 162–66; *Houston Chronicle*, March 2, 1987, A7.

    Ten states—California, Connecticut, Hawaii, Illinois, Kansas, Massachusetts, Minnesota, New Hampshire, Ohio, and Washington—currently require employers to grant special leaves to pregnant women and to reinstate them in their jobs or comparable positions when they return. In all other states, maternity policies are governed by the 1978 federal Pregnancy Discrimination Act, which made it illegal to discriminate on the basis of pregnancy or childbirth in hiring, reinstatement, termination, and disability benefits.

    Five states—California, Hawaii, New Jersey, New York, and Rhode Island—provide temporary disability insurance, which provides half the wage the female worker earned during a six to ten week maternity leave.

72. Packard, *Our Endangered Children*, 185; Uhlenberg and Eggebeen, "The Declining Well-Being of American Adolescents," 37.

73. Levitan and Belous, *What's Happening to the American Family*, 69–72; Halem, *Divorce Reform*, 191–93.

74. Packard, *Our Endangered Children*, 189–201; Halem, *Divorce Reform*, 174–81; Levitan and Belous, *What's Happening to the American Family?*, 69–72; Judith S. Wallerstein and Joan B. Kelley, *Surviving the Breakup: How Children and Parents Cope With Divorce* (New York, 1980); Cynthia Longfellow, "Divorce in Context: Its Impact on Children" in *Divorce and Separation*, 287–306.

75. Refer to note 74.

76. Refer to note 74.

77. Refer to note 74.

78. Refer to note 74.

79. Fuchs, *How We Live*, 73–75, 149–50, 214; Levitan and Belous, *What's Happening to the American Family?*, 72–75; *NYT*, April 2, 1974, I, 34; Lenore Weitzman,

The Divorce Revolution: The Unexpected Social and Economic Consequences for Women and Children (New York, 1985).

80. Refer to note 79.

81. *NYT*, May 22, 1983, VI, 48–57; *NYT*, November 23, 1980, I, 28.

82. Packard, *Our Endangered Children*, 294; Halem, *Divorced Reform*, 187–91; Levitan and Belous, *What's Happening to the American Family?*, 70, 74.

83. Winn, *Children Without Childhood*; Elkind, *The Hurried Child*; Packard, *Our Endangered Children*.

84. *NYT*, May 3, 1981, IV, 9.

85. Weitzman and Dixon, "The Transformation of Legal Marriage Through No-Fault Divorce," 143–53; Halem, *Divorce Reform*, 233–83; Andrew Hacker, "Post-Marital Economics," *Fortune* (December 23, 1985), 167, 170.

    Hacker divides divorces into three classifications. One group, comprising about 40 percent of all divorces, involves marriages dissolved within four years of a wedding. Usually, these marriages involve no children. A second group, comprising another 40 percent of divorces, occurs when a woman is in her mid-to-late-thirties. Most of these divorces involve children. The remaining 20 percent of divorces involve long-term marriages with wives typically in their 40s and 50s.

86. Refer to note 85.

87. Refer to note 85; *NYT*, February 7, 1983, A14; *NYT*, January 3, 1974, I, 16.

88. Refer to note 85; *NYT*, March 19, 1975, I, 33.

89. *NYT*, February 7, 1983, A14; *NYT*, April 18, 1982, C1.

90. Mary Ann Glendon, *The New Family and the New Property* (Toronto, 1981), 47, 52, 54–55; *NYT*, February 7, 1983, A14.

91. Glendon, *New Family and the New Property*, 57; *NYT*, March 31, 1978, F11; *NYT*, November 3, 1972, I, 24; *NYT*, March 17, 1974, IV, 7; *NYT*, March 5, 1979, I, 1. The four community property states are California, Idaho, Louisiana, and New Mexico.

92. Weitzman, *Divorce Revolution*; Hacker, "Post-Marital Economics," 167–76.

93. Refer to note 92.

94. *NYT*, May 3, 1981, IV, 9.

95. *NYT*, October 11, 1980, I, 21; *NYT*, May 3, 1981, IV, 9; *NYT*, October 6, 1980, II, 8.

96. Refer to note 95; *NYT*, January 15, 1975, I, 71. A new source of contention lies in the conflict between the rights of a pregnant mother and the rights of the fetus she is carrying. Several courts have ruled that the state has the power to require a woman to give birth by cesarean section or to have a blood transfusion in order to save a fetus. One count, in Maryland, required a pregnant woman who was taking narcotics to enter a drug rehabilitation program and undergo weekly urine tests to prevent the birth of an addicted infant. The difficult question that the courts are being forced to resolve is the extent to which government can intervene to protect a fetus against maternal negligence in order to ensure the birth of a healthy baby. Among the questions stirring controversy is whether protection of a fetus would justify laws barring the sale of alcohol to pregnant women or statutes requiring genetic testing, like amniocentesis, of pregnant women who are at risk of giving

birth to a child suffering from a condition such as Tay-Sachs disease, sickle-cell anemia, or Down's syndrome. See *Wall Street Journal*, April 12, 1985, II, 1.

97. G. Sidney Buchanan, *Morality, Sex, and the Constitution* (Lanham, Md., 1985); Glendon, *New Family and the New Property*, 43.

98. *NYT*, May 3, 1981, IV, 9.

99. Glendon, *New Family and the New Property*, 43.

100. Ibid., 11, 38, 49, 71–73.

   One area in which the nation's courts have recently shown increasing sensitivity to "informal" familial relationships involves the custody rights of stepparents. Today, one American child in five lives in a stepfamily, and six states have adopted statutes providing visitation rights for stepparents. In states without such statutes, divorce agreements have provided for visit is between children and stepparents, awards of custody to stepparents, and, in a few instances, financial support for stepchildren. See *NYT*, March 2, 1987, I, 1.

101. Glendon, *New Family and the New Property*, 61; *NYT*, February 7, 1983, I: 4.

102. *NYT*, June 3, 1980, II, 12.

103. Kristin Luker, *Abortion and the Politics of Motherhood* (Berkeley, 1984), 126–215; Glazer, "Rediscovery of the Family," 50.

104. *NYT*, January 15, 1983, I, 18.

105. Ibid.

106. *NYT*, January 7, 1980, IV, 8; *NYT*, March 26, 1980, III, 18; *NYT*, June 6, 1980, II, 4; *NYT*, June 9, 1980, III, 16; *NYT*, June 22, 1980, I, 24; *NYT*, July 14, 1980, I, 12.

107. Refer to note 106.

108. Gilbert Y. Steiner, *The Futility of Family Policy* (Washington, D.C., 1981).

109. Andrew Hacker, "Goodbye to Marriage," *New York Review of Books* (May 3, 1979), 23–27.

110. Yankelovich, *New Rules*, 103, 104.

111. Ibid., 101, 103.

112. Ibid., 104, 131.

113. George Masnick and Mary Jo Bane, *The Nation's Families, 1960–1990* (Boston, 1980); *NYT*, May 23, 1980, I, 18.

114. For proposals to strengthen the family, see Packard, *Our Endangered Children*, 343–63; Kenneth Keniston and the Carnegie Council on Children, *All Our Children: The American Family Under Pressure* (New York, 1977), 216–21.

5

The War over the Family
Is Not over the Family*

Susan Cohen and Mary Fainsod Katzenstein

The War over the Family (Berger and Berger 1983), *In Defense of the Family* (Kramer 1983), and *Rethinking the Family* (Thorne and Yalom 1982) are but a few of the books produced over the last decade in the political encounters between feminists and traditionalists. Curiously, the battle is not fundamentally about the family, but rather a conflict over the roles and relationships of men and women. Moreover, the differences of opinion over the needs and interests of children constitute a skirmish more than a war. This essay advances an argument: Feminists and traditionalists disagree deeply about issues fundamental to the nature of society and the role of men and women within it. Finding a middle ground is neither easy nor perhaps even possible. But to say that the controversy is over who is pro- or antifamily obscures rather than illuminates the issue. The debate is fundamentally about the places in society of men and women. The discourse about what is good for children is simply not so polarized; to see it as such would be to misspecify the nature of the feminist–traditional division.

We recognize, of course, that there is a close connection between children's interests and the interests of adults. Suppositions about the roles and relationships of men and women have implications for the upbringing of children. How we raise our children depends on our conceptions of the adults we want them to become. At the same time, people who otherwise have widely varying world views may hold similar ideas about the kind of care children should receive and the persons from whom they should receive it.

In this essay, we will analyze the arguments about the family that have preoccupied the American public over the last decade or so. Our intention is threefold:

1. To convey an understanding of the multiplicity of views among both traditionalists and feminists that, while they do not deny the differences between the two ideological camps, do complicate the easy stereotypes to which popular debate so readily resorts;
2. To explore the idea that the rift between feminists and traditionalists revolves largely around issues of adult roles rather than children's needs;
3. To explicate the tensions that exist among both feminists and traditionalists in their attempts to reconcile the sometimes conflicting values embodied within their writings on the family.

*Cohen, Susan and Mary Fainsod Katzenstein. 1988. "The War over the Family Is Not over the Family." Pp. 25–46 in *Feminism, Children, and the New Families*, edited by Sanford M. Dornbusch and Myra H. Strober. New York: The Guilford Press. Reprinted by permission of the Guilford Press.

Feminism and the traditionalist Right are terms that require definition if our discussion is to proceed. When we speak of feminism and the Right, we will be distinguishing between two theoretical perspectives that are themselves extraordinarily heterogeneous. By feminist views, we refer to arguments that start from the premise that society now and in the past has been arranged hierarchically by gender and that such arrangements must be challenged. Within this feminist perspective, however, we discuss a range of views: revisionist theories, such as those of Jean Elshtain (1982) that exhort feminists to return to "female-created and -sustained values" of mothering and nurturance, as well as the more radical views of such theorists as Adrienne Rich (1976), that insist on a basic restructuring of family life.

By rightist, traditional, or conservative views (we use the terms interchangeably), we refer to writings of wide-ranging perspectives on the economic, social, and moral responsibility of the state to its citizens. What these writings share is a belief either in the different natures of men and women, or in the desirability of a continued division of labor by gender whatever might be the similarity or difference in men and women's nature (Christensen 1977). Thus the writings of the New Right speak of the religious and biologically mandated differences in the life callings of men and women. Neoconservatives, by contrast, emphasize the desirability of gender-neutral, nonintrusive laws that afford equal educational and job opportunities for men and women even as they "prefer" that women elect different life priorities from those men choose (see Berger and Berger 1983). Absolutely central to both views is the assumption that the government has now done all it can do, that virtually all antidiscrimination laws that might provide guarantees of equal opportunity are now in place.[1]

THE REAL WAR OVER THE FAMILY: GENDER ROLES AND THE VIEW FROM THE RIGHT

Diverse as different components of the Right are, they are united around an idealization of the traditional nuclear family. Contained in this idealization is a particular view of men's and women's roles that is absolutely crucial to an understanding of the ideological divide between feminism and the Right.

The Right's view of gender roles is remarkably invariant across neoconservative and New Right positions. A man's responsibility to his family is best met by his success in the market, his ability as a wage earner to support his wife and children; a woman's worth is measured by her dedication to her role as wife and mother. This case is made with evangelical conviction by Phyllis Schlafly in *The Power of the Positive Woman* (1978) and *The Power of the Christian Woman* (1981). Motherhood is a woman's calling. If a woman wants love, emotional, social, or financial security, or the satisfaction of achievement, no career in the world can compete with motherhood. That is not to say that women can never find fulfillment outside the home. The rare woman (Mother Theresa is one example that Schlafly offers) may find fulfillment in life's other options, and some may successfully pursue both marriage and career. But this pursuit of dual responsibilities is possible only if two conditions are met: (1) if a woman relies on her own resourcefulness rather than expecting others, the government in particular, to come to her assistance; and (2) if she does not allow her primary role as wife and mother to be superseded by other interests or responsibilities. Here Schlafly offers the example of "Mrs." Thatcher, who managed both to become Prime Minister of Great Britain and to cook breakfast every morning for her husband (in contrast to Mrs. Betty Ford "who stayed in bed while her husband cooked his own breakfast during the many years he was Congressman" (1978, p. 44).

Brigitte Berger and Peter Berger, who have written in defense of the bourgeois family from a neoconservative perspective, are less proselytizing but no less convinced:

> Individual women will have to decide on their priorities. Our own hope is that many will come to understand that life is more than a career and that this "more" is above all to be found in the family. But however individual women decide, they should not expect public policy to underwrite and subsidize their life plans. (1983, p. 205)

The emphasis on the primacy of motherhood and the secondary concession to women's other sources of identity and fulfillment (as long as women don't expect any special help) are common to New Right and neoconservative perspectives alike.

Greater differences do exist within the Right over the question of why this arrangement of gender roles is socially desirable. Schlafly and the evangelical Right accept a traditional sexual division of labor as natural—biologically destined and God-given. Schlafly (1978, pp. 17, 33, 49–50) and Falwell (1980, p. 150) both speak of an "innate maternal instinct," of a "natural maternal need," and of God-given roles. The Bergers are less sure. Whether or not there is a maternal instinct in the human species, it should still be evident, the Bergers argue, that the division of labor embodied in the bourgeois family is preferable to any other arrangement (Berger and Berger 1983, p. 152). The bourgeois family produced individuals whose traits made possible both capitalism and a democratic order (1983, p. 157).[2] The more secular, supply-side exponents of the New Right, as evidenced in the writing of George Gilder (1981, pp. 69–71), make a similar argument, proposing that the heterosexual nuclear family is essential to an efficient and productive society. Married men form stable work patterns and contribute more productively to the economic well-being of the nation than do bachelors who have no family responsibilities and dissipate their energies in nonproductive sexual and economic concerns.

Gender Roles and Public Policy

According to the Right, the traditional bourgeois family as it is now constituted offers women and men nearly all the options they should want. In contrast to the feminist position, the Right seeks a roll-back of state initiatives, maintaining that there is little the state should do beyond what it has already done to lend support to women or men who might seek to alter the traditional gender arrangements both within and outside the family. The list of public policy measures that most feminists would see as essential to the enlargement of life options for men and women (legalized abortion . . . , expanded day-care services, programs to assist victims of domestic violence, insurance provisions for maternity/paternity leaves, protection of homosexual rights) are either actively opposed or simply ignored by virtually all sections of the Right. The New Right's position on these issues is well known: opposition to federal legislation on domestic violence, opposition to the legalization of abortion, and support for the Family Protection Act (barring governmental recognition of homosexual rights, and the use of educational materials that question traditional family roles). The New Right does not oppose an activist state. As feminist scholar Zillah Eisenstein (1982) explains, the New Right share the neoconservative opposition to the expansion of the welfare state but departs from the neoconservative position in its enthusiastic support of a state that seeks to assert its influence over the social and sexual mores of its citizens. The New Right encourages the state to engage in moral leadership but certainly in ways that would pressure or reestablish the breadwinner system. . . .

This is one important distinction between the New Right exponents such as Schlafly or Gilder, and neoconservatives, such as the Bergers, Nathan Glazer, and Irving Kristol. While the former exhort the state to actively exercise moral authority, the latter generally eschew such expectations. The Bergers, for example, go to some lengths to distinguish themselves from moral majority activists. They aver that they are not part of the chorus arguing for the dismantling of the welfare state, and they indict those who would use the state to "influence or control behavior within the family" (1983, p. 207). They thus do not share the New Right's enthusiasm for patrolling antifamily educational materials; they also do not display anything like the almost ecclesiastical tone of George Gilder's case for returning to the era of the male breadwinner. Nevertheless, the Bergers' search for the middle ground lands them closer to the New Right than to feminism. Although they support a (restricted) version of legalized abortion, they insist that abortion has nothing to do with family policy. They therefore refuse to make a case for abortion in their discussion of policies needed to "strengthen" the family; nor do they give even a mention to the desirability of legislation for programs to extend child care or reduce domestic violence. Homosexual rights, they argue, are in no way related to family policy. They write: "It is not a function of the state, at least in a democracy to regulate the arrangements by which 'consenting adults' arrange their private lives—AS LONG AS THEY ARE UNENCUMBERED BY CHILDREN" (1983, p. 206). Hence the neoconservative position, at least as espoused by the Bergers, appears to reject expanded day care, additional funding of services for victims of battering, abortion, or homosexual rights, as long as any of those claims are related to the needs of family members. The position is strongly suggestive of John Stuart Mill's 19th-century argument (progressive for its time) that women should have rights similar to men—except when they choose to marry and have children. In the course of his long essay otherwise decrying the subjection of women, Mill wrote:

Like a man when he chooses a profession, so, when a woman marries it may in general be understood that she makes choice of the management of a household and the upbringing of a family, as the first call upon her exertions . . . and that she renounces not all other objects and occupations, but all which are not consistent with the requirements of this. (Mill 1859/1970, p. 179)

The policies that the Bergers say would help to strengthen the bourgeois family—redressing the heavier tax burden on married couples; providing child allowances; furnishing special allowances for the care of the sick, handicapped, and aged family members; offering vouchers that would empower families to make educational choices for their children—are also policies that the New Right would find easy to support because they in no way threaten the gender-based traditional division of labor. In their common belief that public policy has no place in facilitating the abilities of men and women to depart from their traditional roles within and outside the family, both neoconservative and New Right perspectives stand in direct opposition to the position of most feminists. It is to feminist views on the family—and the roles of men and women—that we now turn.

THE REAL DEBATE OVER THE FAMILY: FEMINISM AND THE AUTONOMY OF WOMEN WITHIN THE FAMILY

According to the Right, feminists are against the family. This antifamily charge is basically a slogan that muddles rather than clarifies the true political issue. The real debate is over women's autonomy within and outside the family.

While the Right idealizes the traditional nuclear family in which the man works for wages and the woman stays home to raise the children, feminists reject the claim that this particular version of family life is the only acceptable form. As Barrie Thorne says in her introduction to *Rethinking the Family*, "Feminists have challenged beliefs that any specific family arrangement is natural, biological, or 'functional' in a timeless way" (1982, p. 2). Thus if one is asking who is for the family and who against it, one must also ask, "Which family?"

A profound disagreement between the Right and feminists does exist—one that focuses on the relationship of women to the family. It is this, rather than the debate over the needs and interests of children, that has fueled the feminist-Right conflagrations. Feminism has been the source of serious criticisms of the traditional family. Yet, in exploring feminist critiques of the traditional family, it is at once apparent that feminist thought is anything but monolithic. At some level, all feminists have insisted that the traditional nuclear family has deprived women of autonomy and in so doing has been an oppressive force that must be altered. But the broad and widely divergent set of views within that position needs to be acknowledged.

A number of the early feminist writings of the late 1960s and early 1970s condemned the nuclear family as the institution centrally responsible for the denial of women's freedom. The writings of Shulamith Firestone (1970) and Kate Millet (1969) argue that the biological family is basic to women's oppression; thus for women to be free within a reconstituted nonbiological family, they must reject their biologically given childbearing role. A revolution in the technology of childbirth (test-tube babies) for Firestone and a separatist, lesbian politics for Millet were the necessary prerequisites of women's liberation from the traditional family.

Yet other feminists writing in the same period took a quite different view. Autonomy for women *could* occur within the biological/heterosexual family provided certain changes in the traditional family could be realized. According to the politics of the National Organization for Women (NOW) in the early 1970s, the demand for autonomy meant, among other things, the right to define and express a woman's own sexuality, economic independence, and a sense of identity not wholly dependent on relationships to other people (Freeman 1975, p. 20). These views translated into demands for equal pay, equality of education and job opportunities, reproductive choice, and personal sexual choice. The thrust of NOW's politics was quite different, however, from the radicalism of Firestone and Millet. For the latter, autonomy was impossible without women divorcing themselves from the biological and heterosexual family. For many NOW members, gay sexuality was an option women might choose, but it was not the *sine qua non* of female autonomy. For some groups within NOW, the issue was how to realize greater autonomy for women within rather than apart from the heterosexual and biological family. For others it was how to constitute a family, but one not defined by traditional heterosexual/biological norms.

The writings of other feminists made it clear that a critique of heterosexuality was not identical with the rejection of motherhood. Adrienne Rich, like Millet, protested the tyranny of traditional gender roles and the fact that heterosexuality occupied the exalted status of an "institution," instead of being one of many legitimate sexual choices. Yet Rich found much to celebrate in the mother-knot, unlike Firestone, whose negative view of motherhood suffuses the pages of her writings. There is a resonant image in *Of Women Born* (Rich 1976) of what the abolition of motherhood as an institution might mean: Rich and her three young sons, alone in a summer house in Vermont, living temporarily joyous and anarchic lives. "We were conspirators, outlaws from the institution of motherhood; I felt enormously in charge of my life" (p. 193). The picture is one of attentive love, but love freed of compulsion and the incessant guilt that comes of not being the perfect mother mythologized by the institution of motherhood. Clearly Rich believes that restructuring motherhood to be free of all vestiges of patriarchal control is both necessary and possible.

Nancy Chodorow explores the issue of autonomy at considerable depth in the *Reproduction of Mothering* (1978). She argues that the subordination of women derives from a pattern of upbringing in which women are the primary caregivers— a pattern that prohibits young girls from experiencing a necessary independence, just as it forces young boys into an excessive independence that deprives them of the capacity for nurturance. What is needed to break this cycle is a new mode of childrearing in which both parents play a substantial role. The fruits of such an arrangement would be more autonomy for mothers, as well as for their female children. Both male and female children would become more whole and ultimately more capable of satisfying relationships than their parents were.

More recent feminist writings (mistakenly characterized by some as feminist capitulation to the Right [Barber 1983]) echo the earlier sentiments of Chodorow and others that autonomy for women is ultimately possible within the biological and heterosexual family. Betty Friedan's *The Second Stage* (1981) makes an argument that is hardly new to feminism, although it has been seen by the media as a redirection of contemporary feminist thinking. In the early years of women's movement, she says (castigating herself along with others), feminists believed that work alone could make for a meaningful life. But this was a mistaken, unbalanced view since all people need love as well as work. Based on this insight, *The Second Stage* is above all a reaffirmation of the family. While Friedan tries to encourage the growth of new kinds of family ties, it is clear that she still sees the heterosexual biological family as the norm, the major change from old patterns being the sharing of child care and household tasks.

Friedan's argument is not explicitly an argument for autonomy, but it is highly individualistic in character, and it clearly rests on the assumption that the vision of family life presented is compatible with autonomy for both men and women. Demands such as flex-time (flexible working hours), reproductive rights, and quality day-care can be seen as mechanisms by which women's range of choices is expanded.

Like Friedan, Jean Elshtain believes that family life is extremely important and that women can be autonomous within the blood-tied family, or at least autonomous enough that one can say that they are not oppressed. At the same time, much of what Elshtain writes appears to echo the Right's view of the family: Her rejection of androgyny, her suggestion that women are particularly suited to mothering, her inattention to abortion and homosexuality, and her insistence on the separation of private and public spheres (see also Rossi 1977). And although she writes of the importance of parenting (close child–parent bonding) in gender-neutral terms, she caps her discussion by calling on not all men and women but rather the feminist thinker, to "ask at what price she would gain the world for herself or other women, utterly rejecting the victories that come at the cost of the bodies and spirits of human infants" (1981, p. 331).

How close is the affinity between Elshtain and the Right? Parallels with the Bergers, for example, are striking: Even as all three allow for variations on the traditional theme, their highest praise is reserved for families where women are responsible for the care of their children. And yet, there are serious differences. Elshtain's work is self-consciously feminist. It is interesting to contrast her concern with the political resonance of language, and the language she herself uses (e.g., her references to the "isolation and debasement of women under terms of male-dominated ideology and social structures" [1982, p. 333]) to the Bergers' sarcastic discussion of "Femspeak" (i.e., nonsexist language).

Elshtain can be seen as traditional in her stress on the private sphere (Stacey 1986). Yet she wants to revitalize the private, not only for its own sake but also for its potential to change public values and structural arrangements. In this Elshtain is linked to 19th-century feminists, as well as to contemporary feminist thinkers like Carol Gilligan. The Bergers praise the traditional (bourgeois) family for producing the sort of people who do well in a liberal capitalist order; Elshtain sees the family as a place from which to challenge that order.

Finally, it is important to recognize that Elshtain is not without objections to the traditional family. She speaks of a need to "articulate a *particular ideal* of family life that does not repeat the earlier terms of female oppression and exploitation" (1982, p. 323). She repeatedly expresses a concern that women be viewed as autonomous subjects, and that the voices that relate women's experience of their lives not be silenced. Unlike the Right, she does not simply evoke the past; instead she asks people to forge links with it through traditions that do not oppress women. The point here is that even that part of feminist thinking that is closest to the Right's view of the family and women's role within it rejects those conceptualizations of the family that give little attention to the value of women's autonomy.

The policy demands that stem from feminist conceptions of women's autonomy include quality day care, reproductive rights and rights of sexual preference, shelters for battered women, programs for displaced homemakers, incentives for industry to make available parental leaves and flex-time, and the Equal Rights Amendment (ERA). Various feminist writings reveal, of course, different emphases. Elshtain hardly talks about policy at all. Friedan says most women "do not want impersonal 'government day care'" (1981, p. 260); she urges the widespread adoption of flex-time and job sharing and speculates on new forms of domestic architecture that would be conducive to communal cooking, housework, and child care. Adrienne Rich warns against looking to public day care or communal living arrangements for an easy solution to the problem of women's oppression; what is needed, she says, is a transfiguration of society for which there is no exact blueprint. Firestone writes of the need for a technological revolution in reproductive biology. However diverse the policy issues addressed, the basic idea underlying feminist discourse is to give women greater autonomy than that provided by the family in which husband is breadwinner and wife homemaker.

THE DEBATE OVER CHILDREN'S INTERESTS

Feminist views do, then, stand in clear opposition to the perceptions of the Right about the relationship of women to the family and to society. These views of women in family roles are separated by a deep ideological chasm from those of the right. The argument of this section, however, is that there is no such vast divide between the views of feminism and the Right over the interests and needs of children.

The views of the Right are well known. Children's interests are met best in a heterosexual, two-parent family where the mother stays home to raise her children. This is the optimal situation, at least. If it were also the absolute requisite of decent childbearing, then the views of the Right and of feminism would be entirely uncongenial. But in fact the views of the Right and, as we shall see later, those of feminism are neither monolithic nor unbending.

Most conservative exponents are prepared to recognize the exigency of some variations on the theme of full-time mother's care. Phyllis Schlafly makes it as clear as anyone on the Right that a child is best brought up by the biological mother. Having recently become a grandmother, Schlafly says, she has been able to observe first hand that babies' needs "are the same now as they always have been."[3] Babies are constantly demanding and need the love, care, and attention of someone who will be a steadfast part of their lives. But as Schlafly recognizes, the presence of a biological mother as the chief caretaker is not always possible. She acknowledges the mothering capacities of the nonbiological mother who has adopted a child; and she observes that there are occasions when the mother may need to work outside the home, where families "must accommodate themselves to such situations." In that case, the person caring for the child may be, at best, "a grandmother, an aunt, a relative or some other person." What is harmful to a child, she says, is government-funded day care, because staff is constantly changing, as well as situations where "women, the feminists, argue for day care simply out of a desire to justify their own life styles."

Schlafly's arguments about the needs and interests of children insist on children being raised by a devoted and constant caretaker. Her emphatic view that a child suffers in the hands of government-funded day care or feminists out to justify their own life-styles may have at least as much to do with her antipathy towards government intrusion and feminist ideologies as it does with the needs and interests of children. If these needs and interests were her sole or even primary concern, she would presumably be more interested in whether the "bonding between mother and child" can occur alongside government day care settings or within feminist households. The argument here is as much about society and the place of men and women as it is about the needs and interests of children.

The Bergers' preference for the mother assuming the primary task of infant and child care is only somewhat less explicit. They write, however, that "the anthropological evidence suggests that the precise form [of the family] does not matter for the infant as long as the minimal imperatives are not violated—most important as long as the structure is stable and allows for the expression of love toward the infant" (1983, p. 152).

The Bergers then go on to note that the evidence leaves open the possibility that a female need not play the role of mother figure (they do not address the analogous possibility that the male need not play the role of father figure). But their speculation ends there. Because arrangements where males predominate as childrearers have not been known historically, they conclude that it is unlikely that alternate family forms would be equally viable. The Bergers' preference for the biological mother as childrearer[4] does at least leave open the possibility of a less than always-present mother, and even of some other gender-structured arrangement as long as it could be demonstrated to be stable and loving.

An enormous body of feminist writing on the family focuses on the importance of mothering, but from the primary perspective of its impact on women. Adrienne Rich's *Of Woman Born* (1976) is one such work whose principal concerns is the experience of mothering for women. But her description of children's needs, like Schlafly's comment about the unrelenting demands of her new grandchild, evokes the passion of small children for unconditional love ("from dawn to dark, and often in the middle of the night" [1976, p. 4]). Rich's book is largely about the way in which mothering in a patriarchal society imprisons women, and about the need to release mothering from patriarchal burdens, although not from children. This is closely connected to her argument about children's needs: Mothering, she argues, when it is imbedded in patriarchal society, cannot meet children's needs—daughters learn to resent the powerlessness of their mothers, sons grow to be sent either literally or figuratively into the fields of battle.

Throughout Rich's analysis of mothering, there is little discussion, however, of the needs of children apart from the adults they will become. What needs infants or children may have, independent of their gender socialization is hardly addressed.[5]

Chodorow's book on mothering is similarly structured to address the question of how sex roles get reproduced through the mothering process; children "mothered" within patriarchal society grow up less than whole. Girls emerge as dependent women; boys grow into adults who experience difficulty in their ability to relate to others. Children thus need the parenting of both male and female—parenting that provides "consistency of care and the ability to relate to a small number of people stably over time" (1978, p. 217).

More recent feminist writing critical of "first stage" feminism—allegedly preoccupied with the emancipation of women—makes an explicit case for the primacy of children's needs. And yet even this writing has little to say about what actually constitutes the needs and interests of children. This brand of feminism is represented by Jean Elshtain, who comes closer than most feminists to associating the traditional family structure with the capacity of the adult world to meet the needs of infant and child. Elshtain asserts (and there would be many feminists and conservatives who would agree) that children need "strong early attachment to specific adult others" (p. 320). She continues,

> Not every neglected and abused child becomes a Charles Manson but every Charles Manson was an abused and neglected child. "The jailhouse was my father," Charles Manson cried. (1981, p. 329)

In sketching a feminist theory that calls for a newly strengthened but nonoppressive family, Elshtain says, "Responsibilities for children are paramount . . . social feminist of the sort I propose places children in the center of its concern" (1982, p. 448). Elshtain's argument does not require women to take on the primary task of childrearing, nor does she explicitly, as do the Bergers, hail the success of the traditional bourgeois family. Rather abstractly, however, she insists on the preservation of the "[private] sphere that makes [such] a morality of responsibility possible" (1982, p. 336). Traditional feminine virtues of nurturance and compassion must be maintained, both for the sake of children and for the construction of a moral society. This restructuring of the private sphere (whatever it may look like—and Elshtain is less than clear on this) will have enormous ramifications. The rediscovery of "maternal" values will serve women because, by strengthening the private, the public life that has excluded and debased women (and the poor) will be challenged. Children will benefit from the love and compassion now surrounding them, and society will be altered in desirable ways by the infusion of feminine values.[6]

The isomorphism of children's, family's, women's, and societal needs in feminist writings—writings as different as those of Chodorow, Rich, and Elshtain—is extraordinary. Perhaps this coincidence of interests can be explained by the possibility that views concerning the interests of children are derivations of an ideal-ization about the lives of the adults that these children are to become. Children's needs are not identified independent of the adult qualities (autonomy, sensitivity, compassion—all strikingly adult in sound) that these authors hope children will acquire. In most feminist writings, there is little concerned attempt to explore the needs of children apart from the models of adulthood it is hoped that children will later fulfill.

The failure of feminist theory to properly address ideas of children's needs and interests is recognized in an essay by Chodorow and Contratto. They exhort feminists to rethink ideas about mothering and the family based on a more fully elaborated exploration of child development. They call for theories that are:

> interactive and that accord the infant and child agency and intentionality, rather than characterize it as a passive reactor to drives or environmental pressures. We need to build theories that recognize collaboration and compromise as well as conflict, theories in which needs to not equal wants; in which separation is not equivalent to deprivation and in which autonomy is different from abandonment. We must begin to look at times other than infancy in the developmental life span and relationships over time to people other than the mother to get a more accurate picture of what growing up is about. (1982, p. 71)

In an article titled "Re-visioning Women and Social Change: Where Are the Children?" (1986), Barrie Thorne undertakes the beginning of such an analysis. She observes that feminists have seen children largely as threats to an ordered society, as victims of a disordered society, or as learners of adult culture. She argues instead for a conceptualization that attributes agency to children.

Most feminists and conservatives would agree on a "bottom line" of childrearing—that infants and young children need constant, committed devotion from a stable cast of adults. Nor does there appear to be an irremediable polarization over how such basic children's needs are to be met. The right prefers the full-time presence of the biological mother but is not implacably opposed to at least a limited array of alternative arrangements. Some feminists are deeply opposed to the institution of full-time motherhood under conditions of patriarchy (e.g., Rich and Chodorow). Others, such as Elshtain, celebrate the possibility of the reconsecration of mothering in a domestic setting that may or may not involve shared parenting (Elshtain is unclear). Some feminist theories appear to prefer dual, heterosexual parenting; others reject or do not require such arrangements.

Kristin Luker's (1983) fascinating study of pro-life and pro-choice activists lends support to the claim that the usual pro- and antifamily slogans applied to the Right and to feminism are not useful labels. Almost counterintuitively, pro-choice activists, Luker observes, are often *preoccupied* with planning for the care and education of their children. They insist that parenting must be purposeful, designed to give the child maximum parental guidance and every possible advantage. Pro-life activists, by contrast, tend to be laissez-faire individualists in their attitude towards child upbringing. Advocates of large families, pro-life activists assert that the individual qualities of the particular child, rather than parental planning, or material advantage, will determine the child's destiny.[7]

But the beliefs of such activists aside, what is most remarkable about the *writings* of both the Right and of feminism on the family is the scarcity of attention paid to the identification of children's needs. Common to both is the tendency to derive conceptions about children's needs from assumptions about desirable gender arrangements to which those children are expected later to conform. There appears to be a dual agenda for both feminists and conservative writings on the family. In the construction of this agenda, children's needs seem all too readily subsumed by the eagerness to win acceptance for a particular preferred arrangement of men's and women's place in adult society.

What feminists are about

AUTONOMY, COMMUNITY, AND SOCIETY

In their writings about the kind of society in which children attain adulthood, both conservatives and feminists struggle to reconcile the often conflicting goals of autonomy and community. The fostering of individualism and the creation of community are themes that preoccupy both feminism and the Right, and the tensions between these dual goals are a constant source of problems for both theoretical perspectives.

The Bergers' *The War over the Family* (1983) treats these themes at some length. Their defense of the bourgeois family rests on what they believe to be the particular strength of that institution: its capacity to provide community and a sense of belonging while at the same time creating in its members the spirit of individualism. "Human beings," they write, "cannot live without community any more than they can live without institutions" (1983, p. 146). The family, better than other institutions, can create sharing, trust, and identity. At the same time, they argue, the great contribution of the bourgeois family has been the promotion of individualism. The bourgeois family fosters self-assertion, the belief in the individual's ability to control the world through rational calculations. They write: "Put simply, the bourgeois family socialized individuals with personalities and values conducive to entrepreneurial capitalism on the one hand and democracy on the other" (1983, p. 157).

It would be surprising if a single institution that bred moral harmony and community on the one hand and individualism on the other were not to experience the tension that derives from reconciling these potentially conflicting values. And indeed, as the Bergers acknowledge, the family as the locale where both harmony and individualism are to be nurtured does find itself under seige. Although they accede explicitly to the importance of this problem, they do no more than acknowledge it:

> Also the very values of the bourgeois family ethos from the beginning, had within them the seeds of their own destruction. Individualism brought forth within the family, would turn against it. (1983, p. 103)

They acknowledge that individualism bred in the bourgeois family has led to educational institutions that can challenge the family and to a middle class that is far more skeptical than lower-income populations about reigning values. The efflorescence of individualism, by this argument, may be at the very root of feminist discontent with the family. They acknowledge this idea in a single flippant observation:

> Perhaps it should not surprise us that some women become disenchanted with this role [within the household] quite apart from the feminist movement as such. Civilization building is a weary-making task, with its own psychic costs. In the (somewhat misleading) language of the critics; it can become tiresome to be "on a pedestal." (1983, p. 103)

Beyond this passing acknowledgement, there is little discussion by the Bergers of how the inculcation of individualism in the family may affect male and female members differently. Self-assertion and rational calculation are mentioned as qualities that families breed in their members, presumably without regard to gender. There is absolutely no discussion of battering or incest, experiences that curtail the "autonomy" of male and female family members in quite different ways.

The potential tension between individualism spawned within the bourgeois family and the sense of community that the family is also expected to transmit is reconciled only when the range of individualist aspirations is limited. Individualism that promotes, as the Bergers describe it, "the ideal of the 'swinging single,' with no ties on his or her project of endless self-realization; the idealization of abortion, once and for all eliminating the vestigial risk of pregnancy, the insistence that a 'gay life style' is as socially legitimate as heterosexual marriage" (1983, p. 135) is individualism that cannot be reconciled with the harmony of the bourgeois family. The possibility of reconciling community and autonomy within the bourgeois family is, then, entirely dependent on the creation of individualist values that conform to standards that do not fundamentally undermine the traditional nuclear, heterosexual family.

A central motif in feminist discussion is, likewise, the idea of autonomy. Most of the changes sought by feminists can be understood as means toward, or aspects of, this end. But the idea of autonomy has some problematic implications in spite of its pivotal role in feminist theory.

Autonomy can take different shapes. One involves "the right of all individuals to develop their highest potential" (Gordon 1982, p. 50). A classic presentation of this notion of autonomy can be found in John Stuart Mill's 1859 essay, *On Liberty*. Going further back in time, to the philosophical origins of liberalism, one finds a somewhat different version of autonomy: In Hobbes and Locke the emphasis is on acquisitions and competition. This egoistic and often aggressive type of autonomy is a *modus operandi* that many feminists explicitly reject, and that they perceive as a serious threat to another feminist goal—egalitarian communities.

Liberal feminists are prone to overlook the issue of community and instead tend to portray feminism in almost wholly individualistic terms. Betty Friedan writes,

> feminism is threatening to despots of fascism, communism, or religious fundamentalism, Third World or American brand, because it is an expression of individualism,

human autonomy, personal freedom, which once freely experienced, can never be erased or completely controlled. (1981, p. 329)

The primary concern of *The Second Stage* is the needs of the individual. While it is true that Friedan gives much attention to our needs for connectedness, her focus remains on the individual. Moreover, she sees the need for connection being met primarily within the nuclear family. Friedan seems to attach little importance to the notion of political community, or to communities of women.

Many feminists write about individualism in a more guarded way than does Friedan. Linda Gordon, in her essay in *Rethinking the Family*, expresses an "ambivalence between individualism and its critique" (1982, p. 50). The task of feminism, she says, is

to develop a feminist program and philosophy that defends individual rights and also builds constructive bonds between individuals to defend all the gains of bourgeois individualism and liberal feminism, while transcending the capitalist-competitive aspects of individualism with a vision of loving, egalitarian communities. (1982, pp. 51–52)

Many feminist writers would find themselves in accord with this formulation of feminist goals. However, the uncomfortable question arises as to whether the transcendence that Gordon envisions can ever actually be achieved.

Jean Elshtain has written on this issue in a sobering if not pessimistic way. She makes a case for the primacy of community over individualism, arguing that much of feminism rejects the possibility of community within the bonds of traditional ethnic family life that provided a basic identity to women like her grandmother. She goes on to argue that, in this world at least, it is impossible to establish both individual autonomy and strong communal ties: "Feminism of the sort I propose recognizes that there is no final resolution to the twin goals of individual and social good" (1982, p. 448).

Many radical, Marxist, and social feminists would dispute Elshtain's claim, or grant that while it may be true now, it will not be so after the revolution (of whatever sort). Unfortunately this issue is addressed directly far too infrequently by feminists of the Left. Instead of explicit discussion, there is often an underlying assumption that once the revolution takes place, each person will have the freedom to realize her- or himself fully and at the same time will naturally join others in creating egalitarian communities.

Among less revolutionary feminists there is a tendency to see the tension between individual freedom and social good as an inevitable, if unfortunate, aspect of the human condition. According to this view, political life is an arena in which compromises are always necessary. Decisions must be made as to how much freedom one is willing to give up for the sake of a strong community, and how far one is willing to weaken communal authority for the sake of individual freedom.

Elshtain's argument, though, is not merely that these two important ends are contradictory, but also that they are in a fundamental sense dependent on one another. In a discussion of Dostoyevsky's "Grand Inquisitor," she comments,

In the Inquisitor's world, there is *neither* freedom *nor* community. Dostoyevsky's mass are "pitiful" and "childlike" in the worse sense—hardly a community, hardly exemplars of mutuality. They have security but the price they pay is the loss of *both* community and liberty. (1983a, pp. 251–252)

Freedom requires roots and roots involve communities and no community has ever existed without constraints of some kind. (1983a, p. 253)

It is thus not just that perfect freedom and perfect community are impossible. Freedom paradoxically requires constraints, including the constraints that are inevitably an aspect of family life. While Elshtain clearly doesn't equate community with family—she stresses the importance of political participation and a sense of political purpose beyond the family—she does see strong families as an essential element of communal life: "There is no way to create real communities out of an aggregate of 'freely' choosing adults" (1982, p. 442). Not only is community impossible without families, freedom (paradoxically) is impossible without families; as she states above, "Freedom requires roots." Roots are composed of family, ethnic, and religious ties, ties that are largely involuntary.

One way in which families nourish freedom, says Elshtain, is by fulfilling our needs for intimacy, security, and a sense of purpose that, if unmet by the family, will be met elsewhere, in ways that may prove disastrous.

Cults moved into the vacuum created by the "thinning-out" of community and family ties, even as they further eroded those ties to preclude any outside locus for human relations. In an argument that eerily replicates radical claims that attachment to the family vitiates commitment to "the Cause," Jim Jones rejected a request by two members of his doomed cult for a Thanksgiving visit to the family of one of them in these words: "It's time for you to cut your family ties. . . . Blood ties are dangerous because they prevent people from being totally dedicated to the Cause." (1982, pp. 444–445)

Yet many feminists would reject Elshtain's contention that freedom and community require the blood-tie of the family. Her argument about the threat from cults might well be met with the response that some families are cult-like in the way they treat individual members. Linda Gordon states:

Feminism has undermined the family as it once existed faster than it has been able to substitute more egalitarian communities. This is not a criticism of the women's movement. Perhaps families held together by domination, fear, violence, squelched talents, and resignation should not survive. (1982, p. 50)

Elshtain recognizes that families have often restricted freedom for women and says this must be changed (1981, pp. 144, 323). However, she disagrees with many feminists on the extent to which "domination, fear, violence, squelched talents, and resignation" have marked family life.

Elshtain makes another argument as to why families are essential to freedom, and it rests on a particular conception of freedom. Her understanding of freedom is not the classical liberal one centering around an absence of restraint, nor is it freedom to fulfill one's potential, although it includes elements of both these ideas. Elshtain's conception of freedom includes the idea of moral responsibility. For her, to be free is above all to be free to act morally. Here the family is crucial; as a place where moral responsibility is taught to children, and is part of the experience of family members in their relations with one another.

> My vision holds that if we are to learn to care for others, we must first learn to care for those we find ourselves joined to by *accident* of birth. Such commitments are essential to a social order grounded in the image of a social compact or covenant rather than in contract and self-interest. (1983b, p. 108)

She says,

> The social compact is a different notion from that of contract. It is inseparable from ideals of civic virtue and retains a hold on working-class, religious, and rural culture. A compact is no contingent agreement but a solemn commitment to create something "new" out of disparate elements—a family, a community, a polity—whose individual members do not remain "as before" once they become part of this social mode of existence. Within the social compact, community members, ideally, share values that are sustained by moral suasion, not enforced by coercion. (1982, p. 446)

This is a vision that involves both freedom and morality. "Morality" is a term rarely used by feminists of the Left, except in a negative way. Moral systems are frequently portrayed as part of the array of tools men have used to deprive women of their autonomy. There is little discussion of possibilities for creating a new morality to replace the codes that in the past have been so oppressive to women. Rather, there seems to be an underlying assumption that if people—especially women—are finally allowed the autonomy that is their right, moral behavior will somehow flow from that. Women allowed autonomy will bring into the public sphere values of caring and nurturance. What sanctions will be needed, which moral precepts will define the rules governing who is "cared for," how, by whom, and why, are less fully examined.[8] Thus we return to the view that individual autonomy and social good are not in tension, that genuine autonomy for all entails the social good.

Clearly, this debate over the relation between autonomy and community is of utmost importance for feminist theory. Further exploration of this issue—both for what it can tell us about how to view the family and for its overall implications for feminism—is essential.

It is of no less importance for the Right. Both perspectives are troubled by the problems of creating an institutional setting (the "family" or some alternative structure) in which children can be raised and that can foster the qualities of individualism within the supportive parameters of community.

CONCLUSION

In the struggle between feminists and the Right the family has been a battleground, but it is not, in fact, the real source of conflict. Feminism is not antifamily; the

Right is not simply pro-family. To recognize that there has been a misnaming of the issue is, we hope, to introduce a note of calm into the conflict, a conflict that has frequently been tinged with hysteria. There *are* serious, deep differences between feminism and the Right. These cannot be minimized. However, there are differences not primarily over what children need or whether the family ought to be abolished, but over the place of men and women in society. Looking past the turmoil, one finds this common ground: an acceptance of the family as an arrangement that is, at least potentially, productive for the human spirit as well as the body, and a recognition that all children need stable affectionate care.

Where feminists and conservatives part ways, often bitterly, is over the traditional sexual division of labor. In a fundamental sense this question of gender roles is a question about autonomy.

"Autonomy" is a term often heard in liberal democracies, and in this country both feminism and the Right claim to value it highly. But it is a protean word. One finds widely varying notions about what it means, who has a right to it, in what ways, and what it has to do with public policy. Conservatives, many of whom are in reality laissez-faire liberals, tend to think in terms of "being left alone." Feminists, on the other hand, are far more likely to hold government responsible for giving people *tools* for autonomy; public policy is to increase life-options.

The central question today, of course, is autonomy for women. Recognizing that neither feminism nor the Right represents monolithic entities, we generalize in the following way: The New Right sees a natural sexual order outside the realm of autonomy; in it, biology determines how we live. What it mandates for women is not only the physical act of giving birth but a female essence, a female place in society, flowing almost entirely from that physical act (or the capacity for it) and from the rearing that follows childbirth. The neoconservative Right avoids the implication that biology is destiny. Women and men are said to choose their destiny, to affect through individual effort and talent the course of their own life careers. Yet both implicitly and explicitly, neoconservatives express their expectations that men and women will choose differently.

Feminists, with the exception of those such as Firestone, gracefully, often joyfully, accept the gift of biology, but respond to it so as to preserve women's autonomy as much as possible. The capacity to bear children is seen as a gift to be used when motherhood is genuinely desired; it should not mean an unwanted child. Most feminists are reluctant to draw neobiological conclusions from biological facts. That is to say, having the capacity for childbirth says little about who one is or how one is to find meaning in life or what sort of freedom one has or should have. Although feminists such as Elshtain are exceptions, most feminists assiduously avoid the advocacy of a social or moral division of labor lest it appear to evoke the traditional strictures of biological destiny.

With the exception of radical thinkers like Millet and Firestone, most feminists believe that a large measure of autonomy is possible for women, whether they are mothers or not, within the confines of the nuclear (not necessarily heterosexual or dual-parenting) family. The traditional family has to be rethought and refashioned. Feminist visions of the family are far more varied than the vision of the family that is idealized by the Right (in which the woman meets her destiny by channeling all energy into motherhood). Feminism calls on people to give up such cherished but mistaken notions as: all women have a vocation in motherhood; a child needs constant care from her or his biological mother; lesbians are morally inferior mothers; men aren't suited to be the nurturers of small children. A sharing of child care and household tasks, and day care arrangements in which there is stable, affectionate attention, are two ways in which family life can be reshaped so as to make it possible to be both a woman and a person who is economically, politically, psychologically, and spiritually autonomous.

While insisting on autonomy as perhaps the most essential of feminist goals, most feminists recognize other important goals, including that of community. The family, in fact, represents one attempt to achieve both of these. But there is widespread criticism both external to and within feminism that denies the easy possibility of reconciling autonomy and community within a restructured family institution. Autonomy and community are in constant tension, this criticism claims, even as they might nourish each other in certain ways.

The Right also endorses the twin goals of individuality and community, though their definitions and arguments are quite different from those of feminists. Individualism, for the Right, is encouraged by the family even as it must be, in another sense, sacrificed to the family. The Right maintains that the family is uniquely qualified to instill norms of independence and freedom in its young. Yet the exercise of this individualism is to happen outside, not within, the family. Within the family, community supersedes individuality. The choices men and women make inside the family are to be curtailed by the parameters of biology and tradition. Outside the family, however, individualism may flourish—but an individualism (feminist critics charge) that embraces only men. The Right, then, seeks to reconcile the goals of community and autonomy by assigning community to the family and individuality to society; such an equation, its critics maintain, aggravates rather than reconciles the tension between individualist and community values.

Much more work needs to be done by feminists as well as conservatives about what individualism and community mean, about the complicated ways they relate to each other, and about how people try to realize them in daily life. In the meantime, we must recognize the debate over the family for what it is: true discordance about the roles and values of men and women—rather than a contest over the needs and interests of children.

ACKNOWLEDGMENTS

The authors thank Gretchen Ritter for her bibliographic help and ever insistent questioning, as well as Diana Meyers and Helene Silverberg for their comments on an earlier draft. Mary Katzenstein is grateful to the Jonathan Meigs Fund and to the Ford Foundation funding of the Stanford project which provided research support.

NOTES

1. For a particularly helpful discussion of the New Right and neoconservatism, see Zilah Eisenstein (1982, Spring), "The Sexual Politics of the New Right: Understanding the

'Crisis of Liberalism' for the 1980s," *Signs*, 7(3). Her focus on the antifeminism of the Right adds an absolutely crucial dimension to existing analyses. Her description of neoconservatism as bent on conservatizing as opposed to dismantling the welfare state (as the New Right intends) does however, raise the question of how neoconservatism can be distinguished from Carter liberalism, which also wanted to restrict the "excesses" of the welfare state.

2. Robert Coles' review of the Bergers' book questions whether the causal order might be the other way around: *New York Times Book Review*, May 15, 1983, p. 7.

3. The quotations in this paragraph are from a telephone interview Mary Katzenstein had with Mrs. Schlafly, Nov. 8, 1983.

4. The Bergers do not state this explicitly but the idea comes through clearly when they state that women, not men, should give priority to the family.

5. She discusses the liberating experience of living during a Vermont vacation without rules and without her husband, who was then in Europe, an experience liberating both for herself and her sons. But Rich does not generalize from this to children's needs in ordinary times.

6. This is similar but not identical to the 19th-century argument that women's entrance into the *public sphere* would enhance domestic and public life.

7. The laissez-faire view of the pro-life activists was described by the author to Mary Katzenstein in a separate conversation and does not appear in the book.

8. See Jessie Bernard's discussion of the difference that women's participation in the public sphere could make (1981, pp. 546–557).

REFERENCES

Barber, B. R. 1983. "Beyond the Feminist Mystique." *The New Republic*. July 11: 26–32.

Berger, B., and P. L. Berger. 1983. *The War over the Family: Capturing the Middle Ground*. New York: Anchor Press/Doubleday.

Bernard, J. 1981. *The Female World*. New York: The Free Press.

Chodorow, N. 1978. *The Reproduction of Mothering: Psychoanalysis and the Sociology of Gender*. Berkeley: University of California Press.

Chodorow, N., and S. Contratto. 1982. "The Fantasy of the Perfect Mother." In *Rethinking the Family: Some Feminist Questions*, edited by B. Thorne and M. Yalom. New York: Longman.

Christensen, H. T. 1977. "Relationship between Differentiation and Equality in the Sex Role Structure." In *Beyond the Nuclear Family Model*, edited by L. Lenevo-Otevo. Beverly Hills: Sage.

Coles, R. 1983. "Honoring Fathers and Mothers." *New York Times Book Review*. May 15: 1.

Eisenstein, Z. 1982. "The Sexual Politics of the New Right: Understanding the Crisis of Liberalism for the 1980s." *Signs*, 7: 567–588.

Elshtain, J. B. 1981. *Public Man, Private Woman: Women in Social and Political Thought*. Princeton: Princeton University Press.

Elshtain, J. B. 1982. "Feminism, Family, and Community." *Dissent*, 29: 442–449.

Elshtain, J. B. 1983a. "Feminism, Community, Freedom." *Dissent*, 30: 247–255.

Elshtain, J. B. 1983b. "Feminism, Family, and Community." *Dissent*, 30: 103–109.

Falwell, J. 1980. *Listen America*. New York: Doubleday.

Firestone, S. (1970). *The Dialectic of Sex: The Case for Feminist Revolution*. New York: Bantam Books.

Freeman, J. 1975. *Politics of Women's Liberation*. New York: Longman.

Friedan, B. 1981. *The Second Stage*. New York: Summit Books.

Gilder, G. 1981. *Wealth and Poverty*. New York: Basic Books.

Gordon, L. 1982. "Why Nineteenth-Century Feminists Did Not Support 'Birth Control' and Twentieth-Century Feminists Do: Feminism, Reproduction, and the Family." In *Rethinking the Family: Some Feminist Questions*, edited by B. Thorne and M. Yalom. New York: Longman.

Katzenstein, M. 1983. Telephone interview with Mrs. Schlafly from the Schlaflys' home in Illinois. November 8.

Kramer, R. 1983. *In Defense of the Family: Raising Children in America Today*. New York: Basic Books.

Luker, K. 1983. *Abortion and the Politics of Motherhood*. Berkeley: University of California Press.

Mill, J. S. 1869/1970. "On Liberty." In *Essays on Sex Equality*, edited by A. S. Rossi. Chicago: University of Chicago Press.

Mill, J. S. 1869/1970. "The Subjection of Women." In *Essays on Sex Equality*, edited by A. S. Rossi. Chicago: University of Chicago Press.

Millet, K. 1970. *Sexual Politics*. New York: Avon Books. (*Sexual Politics* was revised a year after its original publication.)

Rich, A. 1976. *Of Women Born: Motherhood as Experience and Institution*. New York: W. W. Norton.

Rossi, A. 1977. "A Biosocial Perspective on Parenting." *Daedalus*, 106: 1–27.

Schlafly, P. 1978. *The Power of the Positive Woman*. New York: Jove Publications.

Schlafly, P. 1981. *The Power of the Christian Woman*. Cincinnati: Stanford Publications.

Stacey, J. 1986. Are Feminists Afraid to Leave Home? The Challenge of Conservative Pro-Family Feminism. In *What is Feminism?*, edited by J. Mitchell and A. Oakley. New York: Pantheon.

Thorne, B. 1987. "Re-Visioning Women and Social Change: Where Are the Children?" *Gender and Society*, 19: 85–109.

Thorne, B., and M. Yalom. (eds). 1982. *Rethinking the Family: Some Feminist Questions*. New York: Longman.

<table>
<tr><td>CHAPTER
TWO</td><td></td></tr>
</table>

| CHAPTER TWO | The Family in the Community |

The Family in the Community

CHAPTER TWO

6

Home, Sweet Home:
The House and the Yard*

Kenneth T. Jackson

In 1840 suburbs had not yet developed into a recognizable entity, distinct from either the city or the farm. Peripheral towns were merely lesser versions of small cities. Outlying residents looked upon urban centers as agents of progress and culture. It was in the cities that the latest innovations developed: Philadelphia with a marvelous public waterworks in 1799, Boston with free public education in 1818, New York with public transportation in 1829. The eastern cities imported the elegant style of the Georgian London town house, they provided gas lamps and public health systems, and in every way they offered urban services superior to those of any suburb.[1]

William Dean Howells (1837–1920), America's foremost man of letters after the Civil War, experienced firsthand the relative advantages of city, small town, and suburb. An outlander from Martins Ferry and Hamilton, Ohio, Howells located in Boston as a young adult and rose with spectacular speed to become editor of the *Atlantic Monthly*. Moving successively to suburban Cambridge, to the Back Bay near the center of Boston, back to Cambridge, to suburban Belmont, back to an apartment hotel in Cambridge, to the old Beacon Hill neighborhood, and finally and permanently in the 1890s to New York City, Howells knew better than most the problems caused by the lack of urban services in the suburbs. Writing in 1871 of residence just a few miles from Boston, he noted, "We had not before this thought it was a grave disadvantage that our street was unlighted. Our street was not drained nor graded; no municipal cart ever came to carry away our ashes;

there was not a waterbutt within half a mile to save us from fire, nor more than a thousandth part of a policeman to protect us from theft."[2]

Peripheral towns patterned themselves after urban models and sought to project an image of dynamic growth; with the right combination of luck, grit, and leadership, any one of them could grow into a really big city. The example of Brooklyn, vigorously competing with mighty New York, was an inspiration. Although known by the sobriquet "City of Churches," the upstart community was not simply an "overgrown village" or a "bedroom" for Gotham. Brooklyn early developed the institutions that enabled it to become a leading metropolis in its own right—colleges, art museums, opera companies, music academies, libraries, and fire, police, and sanitation systems.

Even the nomenclature of outlying communities suggested connections with a metropolis or aspirations to urban greatness. Thus the nineteenth century produced in a single region a South Chicago, North Chicago, South Chicago Heights, and Chicago Heights. Meanwhile, a few miles distant from Detroit, founders of a new community took the name of Birmingham, after a smoky English industrial metropolis, even though in the next century it would become not a center of manufacture but a leafy residential retreat for wealthy executives. This predeliction for urbanism led some boosters to incorporate their dreams into town names—as in Oklahoma City, Carson City, and Kansas City—in the hope that the wish might father the fact.

By 1890, however, only half a century later, the suburban image was quite distinct from that of large cities. No longer mini-metropolises, peripheral communities, like Brookline outside of Boston, followed a different path. Moreover, the expectations about residential space shared by most Americans today had become firmly implanted in middle-class culture. This shift had many dimensions and sprang from many causes, but the suburban ideal of a detached dwelling in a semirural setting was related to an emerging distinction between *Gemeinschaft*, the primary, face-to-face relationships of home and family, and *Gesellschaft*, the impersonal and sometimes hostile outside society. In 1840 only New York and Philadelphia had as many as 125,000 residents, and the factory system was in its infancy. The typical urban worker toiled in an establishment employing fewer than a dozen persons. By 1890, when the Bureau of the Census announced that the Western frontier no longer existed, the United States had become the world's leading industrial nation. In that year the country was already one-third urban and the population of the Northeast was well over one-half urban (defined by the census as communities of 2,500 or more persons). New York was closing on London as the world's largest city, while Chicago and Philadelphia each contained about one million inhabitants. Minneapolis, Denver, Seattle, San Francisco, and Atlanta, which hardly existed in 1840, had become major regional metropolises. Perhaps more important was the rise of heavily layered government bureaucracies and of factories employing hundreds and sometimes thousands of workers. As more people crowded together in public spaces, families sought to protect home life by building private spaces. Conviviality and group interaction, despite the massive growth of fraternal societies in the late nineteenth century, gave way to new ways of thinking about the family, the house, and the yard, and ultimately, to new ways of building cities.

FAMILY AND HOME

In both Christian and Jewish culture, the family has always occupied an exalted station. It represents the chosen instrument of God for the reproduction of the species, the nurturing of the young, and the propagation of moral principles. But as the French social historian Philippe Ariès has noted, the family as a tightly knit group of parents and children is a development only of the last two hundred years. Prior to the eighteenth century, the community was more important in determining an individual's fate than was his family. In pre-Napoleonic Europe, about 75 percent of the populace lived in sqaulid hovels, which were shared with unrelated individuals and with farm animals. Another 15 percent lived and worked in the castles and manor houses of the rich and powerful, where any notion of the nuclear family (father, mother, and children in isolation) was impossible. In cities the population was arrayed around production rather than biological units. Each household was a business—a bakery, hotel, livery stable, countinghouse—and apprentices, journeymen, servants, and retainers lived there along with assorted spouses and children. Much of life was inescapably public; privacy hardly existed at all. In every case, the image of the home as the ideal domestic arrangement was missing. Even the word *home* referred to the town or region rather than to a particular dwelling.[3]

In the eighteenth century, however, the zone of private life began to expand, and the family came to be a personal bastion against society, a place of refuge, free from outside control. Ariès notes how the arrangement of the house and the development of individual rooms reflected this desire to keep the world at bay and made it possible, in theory at least, for people to eat, sleep, and relax in different spaces. The new social and psychological concept of privacy meant that both families and individuals increased their demand for personal rooms. In the United States, especially in the suburbs, intricate floor plans soon allowed for distinct zones for different activities, with formal social spaces and private sleeping areas.[4]

Although this attitudinal and behavioral shift characterized much of European and Oriental culture, the emerging values of domesticity, privacy, and isolation reached fullest development in the United States, especially in the middle third of the nineteenth century. In part, this was a function of American wealth. In Japan the family, and especially the household, has been the central socioeconomic unit since the fifteenth century, a notion that fits with the Buddhist ideal of suppressing individual desires if they are not in conformity with the best interests of the house. Social and economic conditions in Japan, however, imposed such severe restrictions on residential space that dwellings there were (and continue to be) dwarfishily small in comparison with the West. Houses there are regarded as little more than shells required to keep out the rain, for the focus is the business of living going on within the structure.[5]

Aside from America's greater wealth, an important cultural dimension to the shift should be noted. In countless sermons and articles, ministers glorified the family even more than their predecessors had done, and they cited its importance as a safeguard against the moral slide of society as a whole into sinfulness and greed. They made extravagant claims about the virtues of domestic life, insisting that the individual could find a degree of fulfillment, serenity, and satisfaction in the house that was possible nowhere else.[6] As the Reverend William G. Eliot, Jr., told a female audience in 1853: "The foundation of our free institutions is in our love, as a people, for our homes. The strength of our country is found, not in the declaration that all men are free and equal, but in the quiet influence of the fireside, the bonds which unite together in the family circle. The corner-stone of our republic is the hearth-stone."[7]

Such injunctions took place as industrial and commercial capitalism changed the rhythm of daily life. Between 1820 and 1850, work and men left the home. The growth of manufacturing meant that married couples became more isolated from each other during the working day, with the husband employed away from home, and the wife responsible for everything connected with the residence. The family became isolated and feminized, and this "woman's sphere" came to be regarded as superior to the nondomestic institutions of the world. Young ladies especially were encouraged to nurse extravagant hopes for their personal environment and for the tendering of husband and children. For example, Horace Bushnell's *Christian Nurture*, first published in 1847, described how the home and family life could foster "virtuous habits" and thereby help assure the blessed eternal peace of "home comforts" in heaven.[8]

Whether women regarded the family as a training ground for the real world or as an utter retreat from the compromises and unpleasantries of competitive life, they were told that the home ought to be perfect and could be made so. Through the religious training and moral behavior of its inhabitants and the careful design of the physical structure, a simple abode could actually be a heaven on earth. "Home, Sweet Home," a song written by John Howard Payne in 1823, became the most widely sung lyrics of the day, as Americans identified with the restless wanderer yearning for his childhood home.

Although most celebrations of the private dwelling were written by men, if any one person presided over the new "cult of domesticity," it was Sarah Josepha Hale, editor of *Godey's Lady's Book*, a Philadelphia-based periodical intended for middle-class readership. Her verse in praise of the home found its way into many publications and was typical of a broad effort to institutionalize the female as homemaker and queen of the house. Hale's vision, and that of almost everyone else, assumed that man's was the coarser sex; women were softer, more moral and pure. The only respectable occupation for adult females (unless they were governesses) was that of wife and mother. Dependence was not only part of woman's supposed nature, but also of English and American law. Married women had scant legal identity apart from their husbands, whose control over their wives' bodies, property, and children was all but absolute.

Like verse and prose, pictures and prints with domestic themes were published in millions of copies and in considerable variety. At midcentury, the new technology of reproducing pictures encouraged the craft businessmen Currier and Ives to establish a firm producing lithographs for magazines and books. Among the most popular of the early Currier and Ives series was one of four prints on the "seasons of life," which clearly associated happiness and success with home settings and the family.

Although most writers were too sentimental and mawkish to talk about such matters as mortgage financing and structural engineering, at the core of their thought were new notions about the actual and symbolic value of the house as a physical entity. Yale theologian Timothy Dwight was especially blunt:

> The habitation has not a little influence on the mode of living, and the mode of living sensibly affects the taste, manners and even the morals, of the inhabitants. If a poor man builds a poor house, without any design or hope of possessing better, he will . . . conform his aims and expectations to the style of his house. His dress, his food, his manners, his taste, his sentiments, his education of his children, and their character as well as his own, will all be seriously affected by this ugly circumstance. [9]

The single-family dwelling became the paragon of middle-class housing, the most visible symbol of having arrived at a fixed place in society, the goal to which every decent family aspired. It was an investment that many people hoped would provide a ticket to higher status and wealth. "A man is not a whole and complete man," Walt Whitman wrote, "unless he owns a house and the ground it stands on." Or, as *The American Builder* commented in 1869: "It is strange how contentedly men can go on year after year, living like Arabs a tent life, paying exhorbitant rents, with no care or concern for a permanent house." The purchase of one's home became more than a proxy for success; it also conferred moral rectitude. As Russell Conwell would later note in his famed lecture, "Acres of Diamonds," which he repeated thousands of times to audiences across the country:

> My friend, you take and drive me—if you furnish the auto—out into the suburbs of Philadelphia, and introduce me to the people who own their homes around this great city, those beautiful homes with gardens and flowers, those magnificent homes so lovely in their art, and I will introduce you to the very best people in character as well as in enterprise in our city, and you know I will. A man is not really a true man until he owns his own home, and they that own their homes are economical and careful, by owning the home. [10]

On the simplest and most basic level, the notion of life in a private house represented stability, a kind of anchor in the heavy seas of urban life. The American population, however, was very transitory. The United States was not only a nation of immigrants, but a nation of migrants. Alexis de Tocqueville observed in 1835, "An American will build a house and sell it before the roof is on," and recently urban historians have demonstrated that in fact residence at the same address for ten years was highly unusual in the nineteenth century. The best long-term data on mobility concerns Muncie, Indiana, site of the classic *Middletown* studies. During the five years between 1893 and 1898, some 35 percent of Muncie families moved; between 1920 and 1924, the proportion rose to 57 percent; during a five-year period in the 1970s, it dropped to 27 percent. Compared to other advanced societies the figures seem to be substantial. [11]

Despite such mobility, permanent residence was considered desirable, and, then as now, homeownership was regarded as a counterweight to the rootlessness of an urbanizing population. The individual house was often no more than one in a series of houses, yet it assumed to itself the values once accorded only the ancestral house, establishing itself as the temporary representation of the ideal permanent home. Although a family might buy the structure planning to inhabit it for only a few years, the Cape Cod, Colonial Revival, and other traditional historical stylings politely ignored their transience and provided an architectural symbolism that spoke of stability and permanence.

Business and political leaders were particularly anxious for citizens to own homes, based on the hope, as Friedrich Engels had feared, that mortgages would have the effect of "chaining the workers by this property to the factory in which they work." A big employer like the Pennsylvania Railroad reportedly was unafraid of strikes because its employees "live in Philadelphia and own their homes, and therefore, cannot afford to strike." Or, as the first president of the Provident Institution for Savings in Boston remarked, "Give him hope, give him the chance of providing for his family, of laying up a store for his old age, of commanding some cheap comfort or luxury, upon which he sets his heart and he will voluntarily and cheerfully submit to privations and hardship."[12]

Marxists and feminists saw this threat because they did not share the vision of tranquil, sexually stratified domesticity in isolated households. In Europe Charles Fourier agreed with Engels that the family was based on the domestic enslavement of women, while in the United States, Charlotte Perkins Gilman, Melusina Fay Peirce, Victoria Woodhull, and a group of *material feminists* proposed a complete transformation of homes and cities to end sexual exploitation. Their formula for a "grand domestic revolution" included kitchenless houses and multi-family dwellings. The idea was that some women would cook all the food or do all the laundry, and that regular salaries would attend such duties. On both sides of the Atlantic Ocean, communitarian socialists conducted hundreds of experiments with alternative lifestyles, and many of the most active spokesmen specifically denounced the ideal of the female as the full-time homemaker and the man as absent bread-winner. As a Fourierist journal remarked in 1844, the semirural cottage "is wasteful ineconomy, is untrue to the human heart, and is not the design of God, and therefoi it must disappear." As Fourier wished, in many areas of the world and among working class and minority populations in the United States, larger groupings would often be more important than the nuclear unit for reproduction, child-raising, and the economic functioning of the individual.[13]

The isolated household became the American middle-class ideal, however, and it even came to represent the individual himself. As Clare Cooper has noted, just as the body is the most obvious manifestation and encloser of a person, so also is the home itself a representation of the individual. Although it is only a box and often the unindividualized result of mass production and design, it is a very particular box and is almost a tangible expression of self. Men and women find in their homes the greatest opportunity to express their personal taste. Gaston Bachelard has gone further and suggested that much as the house and nonhouse are the basic divisions of geographical space, so the self and the nonself represent the basic divisions of psychic space. Not surprisingly, Anglo-Saxon law and tradition regard a man's home as his castle and permit him to slay anyone who breaks and enters his private abode. The violation of the house is almost as serious as the violation of the self.[14]

NOTES

1. A careful study of the pre-Civil War suburban economy is Henry Claxton Binford, "The Suburban Enterprise: Jacksonian Towns and Boston Commuters, 1815–1860" (Ph.D. dissertation, Harvard University, 1973).

2. William Dean Howells, *Suburban Sketches* (New York, 1871), 11–12.

3. Philippe Aries, *Centuries of Childhood* (New York, 1965), 8–12; Aries, "The Family and the City," in Alice S. Rossi, ed., *The Family* (New York, 1978), 227–35; and Elizabeth Janeway, *Man's World, Woman's Place* (New York, 1971), 9–26.

4. One thrust of the recent work of French sociologists and cultural historians has been to deny that the family is the meeting ground for social and biological necessity. Instead, they have viewed it as an instrument of oppression and disaster. Jacques Donzelot, *The Policing of Families*, trans. Robert Harley (New York, 1979), 3–87. The notion of privacy and overcrowding, as Colin Duly has noted, is relative and in different cultures cannot simply be measured by counting the number of individuals sharing a house. Duly, *The Houses of Mankind* (London, 1979), 5–27.

5. Heinrich Engel, *The Japanese House: A Tradition for Contemporary Architecture* (Rutland, Vermont, 1964), 221–29; and Lewis Mumford, *The City in History; Its Origins, Its Transformations, and Its Prospects* (New York, 1961), passim.

6. For especially perceptive inquiries into these changes, see Kirk Jeffrey, "The Family as Utopian Retreat From the City: The Nineteenth Century Contribution," *Soundings*, LV (Spring 1972), 21–42; Philippe Aries, "The Family and the City," *Daedalus*, CVI (Spring 1977), 227–35; and David P. Handlin, *The American Home: Architecture and Society, 1815–1915* (Boston 1979), passim.

7. William G. Eliot, Jr., *Lectures to Young Women* (Boston, 1880, first published in 1853), 55–56. Quoted in Jeffrey, "Family as Utopian Retreat," 21.

8. Gwendolyn Wright, *Building the Dream: A Social History of Housing in America* (New York, 1981), chapters 5 and 6.

9. Quoted in Wright, *Building the Dream*, chapter 5. On the other side of the issue, see Betty Friedan, *The Feminine Mystique* (New York, 1963), 307, which called the home "a comfortable concentration camp."

10. *The American Builder*, September 1869, p. 180. Although faith in rising property values is traditional in the United States, housing prices have not kept pace with inflation over the past century. Matthew Edel, Elliott D. Sclar, and Daniel Luria, *Shaky Palaces: Homeownership and Social Mobility in Boston, 1870–1970* (New York: Columbia University Press, 1984).

11. Stephan A. Thernstrom and Peter R. Knights, "Men in Motion: Some Data and Speculation About Urban Population Mobility in Nineteenth Century America," *Journal of Interdisciplinary History*, I (Autumn 1970), 7–35. Theodore Caplow, et al., *Middletown Families: 50 Years of Change and Continuity* (Minneapolis, 1982), 104.

12. Quoted from Edel, *Shaky Palaces*, chapter 8.

13. Dolores Hayden, *The Grand Domestic Revolution: A History of Feminist Designs for American Homes, Neighborhoods, and Cities* (Cambridge, Mass., 1981), 34–38. Friedrich Engels, *The Origin of the Family, Private Property, and the State* (Moscow: Progress Publishers, 1977), 73–75. Jonathan Beecher and Richard Bienvenu, eds., *The Utopian Vision of Charles Fourier* (Boston, 1971).

14.   Clare Cooper, "The House as Symbol of the Self," in Lan, Jen, et al., eds., *Designing for Human Behavior: Architecture and Behavioral Sciences* (Stroudsburg, Pa., 1974), 130–46.

7

Gender and the Residential Telephone: 1890–1940*

Claude S. Fischer

The telephone is one of the most prominent technologies to enter the American home in the twentieth century, an era of rapid change both in technology and in women's roles. The residential telephone has been associated, in popular stereotype and in (sometimes misogynist) humor, with women. This paper explores gender differences in telephone use during the half-century before World War II, the social meaning of those differences, and its implications for understanding the nexus of gender and technology.

Two prefatory comments are needed. One: This topic *does* have a humorous dimension. It also carries for some, as it did for leaders of the early telephone industry, an implied derogation of women: that chatting on the telephone is "one more female foolishness." Social scientists know better. Conversation, even so-called "gossip," is an important social process, serving, among other ends, to renew networks and communities (see, for example, Paine 1967; di Leanardo 1984; pp. 194ff.; Spacks 1986). Those who might treat the subject as trivial or focus on its apparent sexism would be echoing, ironically, the dismissive attitude of male critics who ignored the seriousness with which women themselves took conversation.

Two: As a historical study, this paper must rely on evidence that is necessarily fragmentary and often impressionistic—reports in industry archives, advertising copy, comments of journalists, testimonials, and the like. We are fortunate, however, in also having a few governmental studies and other surveys to draw upon. While we might wish for more data that meet modern standards, we must use what we can. In addition to the archives and studies, I draw upon Lana Rakow's (1987) interviews about telephone use with women in a small, midwestern town and upon a handful of oral histories conducted by John Chan in San Rafael, California.[1]

*Fischer, Claude S. 1988. "Gender and the Residential Telephone: 1890–1940." *Sociological Forum* 3(2): 211–233. Reprinted by permission of the Eastern Sociological Society. © 1988. All rights reserved.

The argument, in brief, is that women "appropriated" a practical, supposedly masculine technology for distinctively feminine ends. This "gendering" of the telephone may have simultaneously reinforced gender differences and also amplified women's abilities to attain both their normatively prescribed and personally preferred ends.

THE STUDY OF DOMESTIC TECHNOLOGIES

In recent years, historians of women have energized the study of technology and society. In household tools and the gender division of labor, social historians are seriously examining, both empirically and theoretically, the neglected topic of consumer technologies in everyday life (see Cowan 1987; Fischer 1985). Most of this scholarship has contested the notion that mechanization of housework "liberated" women—notions promulgated by advertisers, Progressive-era commentators, home economists, and many women themselves. "Verily," wrote a Women's Club leader in 1905, "the march of mechanical invention has been the emancipation of women. The freeing of their hands has led to the freeing of their minds" (quoted by Wilson 1979, p. 95; see also Andrews and Andrews 1974; Marchand 1985). Instead, argue recent scholars, "industrialization of the home", although easing the arduousness of housework, nevertheless continued and even solidified women's disproportionate responsibility for domestic labor. For example, advances in cleaning technology raised the standards for cleanliness that housewives must attain (Cowan 1983; Strasser 1982; Vanek 1978; Bose, Bereano, and Malloy 1984; Walker 1964; Thrall 1982; McGraw 1982; Bereano, Bose, and Arnold 1985).

As a debunking literature, some of this work understandably tends to be contentious. Rothschild (1983, p. 79) asserts: "Technology has aided a capitalist-patriarchal political order to reinforce the gender division of labor and lock women more firmly into their traditional roles in the home." And she provides speculative scenarios for how that might have happened.[2] Even Ruth Cowan, who firmly rejects such functionalist explanations (1983, pp. 147–150), stresses the burdens that household mechanization placed on women in contrast to the burdens they lifted from men.

Having gained much from the openings these studies provided, we should perhaps now move on to ask more complex and probing questions: How did people actually *use* domestic technologies? For what purposes? With what results? And specifically with regard to gender, how did men and women differ in their reactions to and uses of new tools, with what consequences for technological change and gender roles (Cowan 1979)?

THE TELEPHONE

The case I examine here is the *telephone* in North America, briefly glancing at two other technologies later. The concern is with the residential telephone, setting aside the role of telephone use in economic organizations. The telephone, for all its pervasiveness in the contemporary home, has been subject to virtually no serious study as a household tool; even students of the domestic sphere have made, at best, only passing remarks about it. And yet there appears to be something—as suggested by the popular stereotypes—that links the domestic telephone more to women than to men.

We focus on 1890 to 1940, when the telephone became common, outside the South, in middle-class urban homes and on very many farms, as well. The percentage of all homes in the United States with telephones grew from about 2 percent in 1890 to 35 in 1920 and 41 in 1930, shrinking to 31 in 1933 and then rebounding to 37 percent in 1940 (U.S. Bureau of Census 1975, p. 783). Household budget studies indicate that home economists expected to find telephones in urban middle-class homes beginning about the 1910s (see Horowitz 1985). At the same time, many farm households outside the South and especially in the Midwest and West had also obtained telephones. By 1920, farm households were *more* likely, at 39 percent, to have telephones than were urban households; in the Plains region, the farm subscription rate was about 70 percent.[3] It was not until the 1960s and 1970s that telephones became virtually universal in North America, but in the pre- war era people developed what the industry termed the "telephone habit" and gender differentiation emerged.

AN "AFFINITY" FOR THE TELEPHONE

Although apparently no one has conducted a public opinion poll on the matter, North Americans seem to associate women with extensive use of the telephone. Anecdotal observations suggest so, and more systematic contemporary data do, as well.

Research, largely by American Telephone and Telegraph (AT&T), indicates that today women are more likely to have telephones at home than are men (Wolfe 1979); that the number of women or teenage girls in a household especially predict its frequency of calling (Mayer 1977, p. 231; Brandon 1981, Ch. 1); and that women initiate most of households' long-distance calls (Arlen 1980, pp. 46–47). An Ontario survey of people forty and older showed that women were two to three times more likely to telephone their friends than were men, although less than one-and-a half times more likely than men to see their friends face-to-face (Synge, Rosenthal, and Marshall 1982). And Lana Rakow (1987, p. 142) found that in rural Wisconsin, "both women and men generally perceive the telephone to be part of women's domain." The comments of a younger woman with whom Rakow spoke give the flavor of the perceived gender difference:

> I never remember my dad talking on the phone. To this day, if I call up and say, "What are you up to," he'll say, "Nothin', you wanna talk to Mom?" He's real hard to talk to on the phone.... That was one of the things my [ex-] husband said later... "One of the things I hated the most was that you were on the phone from nine until I went to bed at night: you were on the phone with your mother." I *never* knew it bothered him, *never*. I said "John, you never said anything." He said "I hated that. It was just like you were ignoring me." I'm sure if he had said something I would have cut down at least.... [*Question:* Did he use the telephone?] Very seldom, other than to make plans, but never just to visit. I would even say, "Call your mom up." He'd say, "Well, you call her." My son is the same way. (Rakow 1987, pp. 267–270)

Comparable historical research is harder to come by, but a few items point to a similar affinity two or three generations ago. As part of a larger project, we used 1900 and 1910 U.S. Census manuscripts to randomly sample a few hundred households in three northern California towns: Antioch, Palo Alto, and San Rafael. We then identified those that had residential telephones. In 1900, only 12 of 351 households had phones. None of the 39 households with unmarried male heads had residential telephones; 3 percent of the 203 households with male heads with wives but not daughters eighteen or older at home did; but 9 percent of the 35 households with husbands, wives, and at least one adult daughter had telephones. In 1910, the estimates were 12 percent of the 33 households headed by single males, 28 percent of the 229 with husband and wife but no adult daughters, and 44 percent of the 27 households with husband, wife, and daughter had telephones. (Households headed by females were few and unusual. These were excluded.) In other words, the probability of a residential telephone increased noticeably with the number of adult women in the home.

Logit analysis of the 1900 data showed that the number of adult women, but not of adult men, in the household correlates with telephone subscription. Adding controls for socioeconomic variables makes the effect of women drop just below statistical significance, but the patterns are maintained. Including or excluding households headed by females makes no difference. Regression analyses of the 1910 data showed the same pattern: significant or near-significant independent effects of adult women on residential telephone subscription with nil (or even negative) independent effects of the number of adult men on probability of subscription. For 1920, 1930, and 1936, we drew samples for the towns from city directories and voter lists. Again, the presence of a spouse added to the odds of having a telephone. Unfortunately, we did not record the genders of additional adults in the household. Nevertheless, the number of adults strongly predicted telephone subscription. Given the patterns or 1900 or 1910, it is likely that women in the household contributed most to the effect.

National data collected during World War I provides different, yet confirmatory, results. In 1918 and 1919, the Bureau of Labor Statistics surveyed the spending patterns of over twelve thousand families headed by wage earners and low-level salaried workers. (Bureau of Labor Statistics 1924). We randomly drew 20 percent of the cases from the original list, yielding a working sample of 2,588. We defined telephone subscription as a reported expenditure on telephones in the prior twelve months of at least five dollars. The range of household types was limited to husband-and-wife families with at least one child who were above severe poverty and not recent immigrants. Those households with at least one adult son at home were *less* likely to have a telephone than were those without an adult son (15.4 percent versus 20.4; p < .05). But households with an adult daughter were *more* likely to have a telephone than those families without such a daughter at home (26.5 percent versus 19.8; p < .05). We also performed OLS regression analyses, controlling for income, region, housing, and demographic factors. In these equations, the curious result was that additional household members of *any* kind *depressed* the probability of telephone subscription—but males did so far more than females. An adult son at home depressed the probability by −.17, a daughter by a nonsignificant $-.05$; a male lodger changed it by $-.09$, a female lodger by a nonsignificant $+.01$. In any event, a shift in the gender *proportion* of the family toward women increased the odds of a telephone.

A massive survey conducted by the General Federation of Women's Clubs in the early 1920s revealed that more homes had telephones and automobiles than had toilets. Club president Mary Sherman attributed that to women: "Before toilets are installed or washbasins put into homes, automobiles are purchased and telephones are connected . . . because the housewife for generations has sought to escape from the monotony rather than the drudgery of her lot" (Sherman 1925, p. 98). And two small surveys of farm families reported that wives made the great bulk of the households' calls, even those for farm business (Borman 1936; Robertson and Amstutz 1949, p. 18).

This "affinity" of women for the telephone apparently bothered the nineteenth-century men who developed the industry. Emerging from the telegraph trade, telephone companies for many years considered their major market to be businessmen—calling one another or clients, calling home from the office, or calling the office from home or a resort. Women—that is, the wives of the businessmen—were also a market, but a more limited one.

Telephone advertisements counseled women to use the instrument at home to manage the household, in particular to order supplies, call service people, and issue and respond to invitations (see Steele 1905). A 1904 advertisement by the Delaware and Atlantic Company depicts a homemaker in an elegant Victorian dress speaking into a wallmounted telephone. The text reads: "The modern way is to save one's time and temper by telephoning. The telephone makes housekeeping simple and emergencies no longer terrifying."[4] Themes of emergency and crime also appeared in advertisements before World War II. Bell companies recommended that a man order an extension telephone for his wife's bedside should she hear a prowler while he was away on business. But the dominant theme in marketing the telephone to women into the 1920s (Fischer 1988) was the suggestion that women, in their roles as "chief executive officers" of the household, use the instrument to order goods and services. This was consistent with the emerging image of the housewife-administrator in both advertising and home economics (Marchand 1985; Cowan 1983). At the same time, the industry stimulated this use of the telephone from the other end: It encouraged merchants to organize, invite, and advertise telephone ordering (see, for example, Printers' Ink 1910; Shaw 1934).

The stereotypical woman's telephone call of today—a *conversation* with friends or family—was a problem for the industry at the turn of the century (Fischer 1988). And it was a general source of hostile humor. For example, a contributor to *Lippincott's Monthly* wrote in 1909: "Has not the telephone become the favorite pastime of the woman with nothing to do? It has. Does it not accelerate gossip? Aid the flirt and the wayward, constantly? It does. . . . A telephone in a residence should be for the convenience of the user, for imperative needs, for exceptional social emergencies. . . . But for the exchange of twaddle between foolish women . . . it has become an unmitigated domestic curse" (Antrim 1909, pp. 125–126; Bennett 1912).

From the 1910s into the Depression, however, women appeared increasingly often in the advertising copy and the literature of telephone advertising. And they appeared increasingly in more roles than only that of household manager. Advertisements began showing the woman as a lonely wife called by her hard-working husband or as a grandmother at the ancestral home enjoying a call from her upwardly-mobile children in the city. In the 1920s and 1930s, advertising copy depicted her as a socially active young woman managing her farflung network or as an anxious teenager courting by wire.[5] A sales manual for Bell Canada in the late 1920s advised the following "pitch" to its canvassers: "With her name in the directory, a housewife is in ready contact with friends. They can easily reach her to invite her to teas and other social activities of her circle." (Bell Canada 1928).

By World War II, industry men viewed women as at least coequal users of the telephone, although sales personnel still seemed to assume that men would usually decide whether the household would subscribe to the service. Today, the industry considers women to be the main users of residential telephones (as noted earlier).

WHAT DID WOMEN *DO* WITH THE TELEPHONE?

Why did women so quickly outpace men as customers for the residential tele-phone? To answer that, we initially asked what it was that women used the telephone for. They did use it for the purpose that the early salesmen of the technology advertised: managing the household. But how extensive, in fact, was that use? Despite passing remarks that shopping by telephone was commonplace (Cowan 1976; Asmann 1980, pp. 279–280), evidence suggests that fewer than half of urban women with telephones ordered goods over the lines. In material circulated to merchants in 1933, the Bell Company claimed that over 50 percent of housewives in Washington "would rather shop by telephone than in person" (Printers' Ink 1933). A 1930s Bell survey of 4,500 households in one city found that 40 percent of subscribers were "willing" to buy over the telphone, while in another survey, a bare majority of 800 subscribers answered yes to the question, "Do you like to shop by telephone." The same source reported that telephone orders represented just 5 percent of business in large department stores (Shaw 1934). Discounting these claims somewhat for the obvious self-interest of the telephone company leads to the conclusion that telephone shopping was probably a minority practice, as late as the 1930s.

Few women interviewed by Rakow (1987) or Chan mentioned using the tele-phone for ordering, although many did mention emergencies. A contemporary— although limited—survey in London, Ontario (Canada), found that only 30 percent of the respondents liked ordering goods by telephone (Singer 1981). Telephone shopping did not become nearly as common, at least in urban America, as the industry expected or tried to stimulate. Even today, in the era of toll-free numbers and credit cards, some researchers claim that the desire to handle the merchan-dise and for social activity will always circumscribe "tele-shopping" (see Salomon 1986).

If women were developing an "affinity" for the telephone but not using it that much in their roles as homemakers, what were they using it for? Social purposes—that is, to *converse* with family and friends.

Some original data illustrating the point come from an unusual time-budget study of homemakers conducted in 1930. As part of a widespread, if unsystematic, survey of how women spent their time, federal government home economists asked "Seven Sisters" alumnae to complete time-budgets for a week.[6] I randomly sampled the forms sixty-two respondents had completed for a total of 250 days and tabulated listings of telephone calls. There were only eighty-three such entries, which, considering the probability that virtually all of these high-status housewives had telephones, implies that for most telephone use was unremarkable. (Only one woman mentioned using a neighbor's telephone.) Of all the reported outgoing calls, 30 to 50 percent apparently involved orders for goods and services, and 30 to 50 percent of the outgoing calls involved personal or social matters. Of all noted calls, in- or out- going, 25 to 40 percent were commercial and 30 to 50 percent were social.

Since the women often listed telephone calls with little or no explanation of the purpose, I could only estimate ranges. The low estimates assume that calls fell into a category only if they were explicitly labeled (for example, "called friend"), while the high estimates rest on bolder assumptions (for example, an unexplained outgoing call after 6 P.M. was likely to be social rather than commercial). Almost all the plausible biases in the data would reduce reporting of social calls: the study was explicitly done to assess homemaking, to see just how "hard" women were working (Kneeland 1929); the instructions to respondents clearly imply that the primary interest was in tabulating homemaking activities; the sample is of affluent and busy women (many had part-time paid or unpaid jobs), just the sort presumably most likely to find shopping by telephone attractive; the evident status concerns in some of the responses (one women noted that her evening's reading was in Greek, another that it was on psychology) probably lead many to minimize what might appear frivolous, and in the period, telephone "visiting" probably still had the lingering stigma, fostered by the telephone industry, of triviality (Fischer 1988). On the other hand, perhaps the onerousness of the time-budget task led to an overselection of women with time on their hands. (But shopping by telephone was probably *not* underreported simply because shopping was commonplace; entries describing in-person marketing are very frequent, averaging perhaps one every other day.) In sum, it is reasonable to assume that, even among these upper middle-class and presumably skilled home managers, social use of the telephone was the most common use.

The most explicit reports about women's uses of the telephone concern *farm* women. Repeatedly, observers claimed that telephoning sustained the social relations—and even the sanity—of women on dispersed homesteads.[7] Industry men who sold equipment or service to farmers also claimed this; for example, the North Electric Company, of Cleveland, in 1905: "The evil and oppression of solitude on woman is eliminated" (Telephony 1905, p. 303); and an officer of an Ohio telephone company, the same year:

When we started . . . the farmers thought that they could get along without telephones. . . . Now you couldn't take them out. The women wouldn't let you even if the men would. Socially, they have been a godsend. The women of the country keep in touch with each other, and with their social duties, which are largely in the nature of church work (Kemp 1905, p. 433).

The U.S. Census Bureau made a similar claim in 1910:

There is a sense of community life impossible without this ready means of communication. This is an immense boon in the life of women on the farm, who for days at a time during planting and harvesting seasons may be left alone in the house during working hours. . . . The sense of loneliness and insecurity felt by farmers' wives under former conditions disappears, and an approach is made to the solidarity of a small country town (U.S. Bureau of the Census 1910, p. 78).

Official investigations of rural life, especially of farm women, emphasized its isolation and boredom and—as in the 1909 Country Life Commission (U.S. Senate 1909, pp. 45ff.)—recommended or applauded improved communications, including the telephone. A 1915 inquiry, "Social and Labor Needs of Farm Women" (U.S. Department of Agriculture 1915), highlighted the "loneliness, isolation, and lack of social and educational opportunity" described by its respondents (p. 11) and relayed requests by farm women for improved communications. Most asked for better roads, but some women also mentioned telephones, such as this one from Arkansas: "The worst trouble we have is isolation. Absence of social life. We would rather have free telephones and moving pictures than free seed" (p. 14). Five years later, Florence Ward (1920, pp. 6–7) reported on a survey of ten thousand "representative" northern and western farm families: "Marked progress has been made during the past few years. . . . The telephone [in 72 percent of the homes] and the automobile [62 percent] in large measure free the farm family from isolation."

The many claims and the related anecdotes[8] suggesting that the telephone ended farm women's isolation do not, of course, prove that this was so—only that many people believed it was so. But these accounts do strengthen the assertion that farm women were using the telephone largely for social purposes—despite, one should note, the usual rural problems of poor sound quality, shared party lines, and poverty. In a typical rural community, subscribers shared lines of four or more parties. This worked against social conversations, both because the lines were in demand and because of frequent eavesdropping. On the other hand, companies usually charged a flat rate for unlimited local calls; this would encourage telephone visiting. The evidence suggests that, on the whole, rural callers—mostly women, we have seen—exerted themselves, financially and otherwise, to make these calls. (Rakow's [1987] oral histories provide more ambiguous evidence, as noted later.)

If farm women persevered to use the telephone socially, what about urban women? There are not comparable testimonies about nor investigations of the communications needs of urban women. Fragments of evidence suggest that the town residents also emphasized the use of the telephone for sociability—although perhaps to a lesser degree. These include the advertising pitches of the later years, which featured, for example, drawings of urbane women in affluent settings and texts suggesting calls to friends. They include evidence of a popular perception that women chatted on the telephone.[9] They include the alumnae survey described earlier.

Also, well-off urban women used the telephone to pursue organizational activities. In her study of Chicago "society women," Rosher (1968) found that by 1895 one-fourth of those who were officers in reform groups had telephones, compared to less than one percent of Chicagoans generally; 66 percent of women activists had telephones by 1905, versus 3 percent of Chicagoans. Rosher argues that the club women were quick to adopt the telephone and suggests that it may have been a major factor in the increasing civic activity of Chicago women (1968, p. 110).

Records of women's clubs in affluent Palo Alto, California, provide other illustrations of telephone organizing. For example, the *Bulletins* of the Palo Alto Womens' Business and Professional Club, 1929 to 1933, include entries such as: "Phone the club house for reservations not later than . . ."; "If you can help Grace Martley's trip arrangements, call 21745"; "Last Saturday we had a food sale . . . Mrs. Baldwin did the telephoning"; and "If this is your first notice that you are already named on the committee, it is because you don't answer the telephone."[10]

Courting was another social use of the telephone (see Rothman 1984, pp. 233ff.). An etiquette column in 1930 warns "Patty" that if she wants her boyfriend to "respect and admire her, she does not call him up during business or working hours . . . (and at home) she should not hold him up to the ridicule of his family by holding an absurdly long telephone conversation" (Richardson 1930). (Catherine Bertho 1981, p. 243] claims that in France during "la Belle Epoque," the telephone was viewed as an instrument of seduction and adultery, because it allowed the voice of an "other" man secretly to enter the home.) In Palo Alto, the telephone company found in 1934 that they had to add a switchboard to the Stanford Union, because "with eighty women residing this year in the Union, the telephone congestion has been so great during the 'dating' hours around lunch and dinner that service has been slow."[11] (Of course, in this case, half the speakers were men. But the point here is to determine what women were doing with the telephone.)

These items of evidence ranging from anecdotes to surveys of thousands of women suggest that farm and middle-class women commonly used the telephone for social, personal, civic, and recreational ends. About working-class women we know least. They were least likely to have telephones at home, even less so than comparable farm women. And they were of least interest as customers to the marketers of telephone service. Nevertheless, it seems reasonable to assume that those who had telephones in their homes used it at least as often for social conversations as for shopping, since they would have been less able to afford the tariff for the delivery of goods. Surveys today indicate that, in the general population, telephones are used far more often for social purposes than for household management. For example, over ten thousand respondents to a survey of Pacific Telephone customers (Field Research Corporation 1985, p. 42) estimated that 74 percent of their calls were "personal or social," versus 12 percent for household matters such as repairs or orders and 14 percent for business.

In Singer's (1981) London, Ontario, survey, 77 percent of respondents reported that their calls of the day had been for personal or social reasons versus 20 percent for commercial or business purposes. A small study of thirty-one women in the Bronx in 1970 who were heavy users of the telephone pointed to their isolation in the home and their consequent need to call both service providers and friends and kin as the explanation for their high use (Maddox 1976, p. 263).

To this evidence of female sociability on the telephone, we must add John Chan's and Lana Rakow's (1987) oral histories, which include several elderly women who had been raised on farms. Most interviewees claimed that the telephone was *not* used very much then, from about 1915 to 1940; that when it was used, it was largely for "serious" purposes; that people did not visit on the telephone as often or for as long as they do "nowadays"; and that party lines, poor sound, the lack of someone with a telephone to call, and simple etiquette kept subscribers from having lengthy chats. While visiting by telephone was probably *less frequent* and *briefer* the farther back in time one goes, so that the contrast with current practice is notable, the interviewees nevertheless reported that social calls *did* occur regularly, *were* considered important, and were *more often women's calls than men's* (see, for example, Rakow 1987, p. 230). [12]

The best estimate as to what women actually *did* with the telephone is that, while they used it for emergencies on rare occasions and while many used it regularly for shopping and other household management tasks, they used it most—and in a gender-specific way—as an instrument of sociability. The volume of such use was probably less before World War II than it is now, but it probably took precedence over "practical" uses then, too. Some might criticize the *quality* of telephone sociability, contending that it lacks the intimacy of face-to-face conversation (Strasser 1982, p. 305), but its popularity among women is undoubtable. About men's use of the telephone at home we know comparatively little. The evidence suggests that they used it less often, valued it less, and were perhaps more shy of it than women.

WOMEN AND A TECHNOLOGY OF SOCIABILITY

In sum, North American women seemed to have a special affinity for the household telephone and that affinity seemed to involve sociability. Why?

A simple but insufficient answer is that men had equal appetites for telephone conservation but satisfied it at work. Relatively few men, however, had access to telephones at work. Farmers in the field did not, blue-collar workers rarely did, and probably only a small minority of white-collar workers could chat on the telephone while at work. [13] The great majority of men, too, would have needed the home telephone (or at least, a pay telephone) for their personal calls. Furthermore, bits of data suggest that men and women in comparable situations still differ in telephone use, for example, farm men and women and working men and women (Rakow 1987; Synge, Rosenthal, and Marshall 1982).

I will suggest three mutually compatible answers for the gender differentiation of telephone use. One locates the source in women's structural positions, another in normative gender rules, and the third in personality differences.

One: Women, especially but not only housewives, typically are more isolated from daily adult contact than men are. Current research shows that women, at least in the child-rearing years, tend more often to lose touch with friends. Such isolation was probably greater in the first half of this century when children were more numerous, fewer women were in the paid labor force, more lived on farms, and travel was more difficult. Thus, telephone visiting was probably the means many women used to attain some of the social interaction their husbands obtained in the workplace and marketplace (see Rakow 1987, pp. 63, 166).

But if one can "reach out," one can also be reached. Women may have become subject to more demands from kin and friends than when they were more cut off. Some informants complained to Lana Rakow (1987) that the telephone increased their burdens. General observation and claims of women, such as the pleas of farm wives for telephones and good roads, indicate that, on net, increased social contact was nevertheless preferred. Thus, women may have turned to the home telephone more than did men to find that social contact.

This explanation is probably incomplete. The evidence, allusive as it is, points to gender differences in telephone sociability even among men and women with comparable opportunities for adult contact.[14]

Two: Among the gender-typed responsibilites of women is that of social manager. Both men and women commonly expect the latter to issue and respond to social invitations; to organize the preparations for group dinners, outings, church affairs, and so forth; and more generally, to manage the family's social networks— keeping in touch with relatives (including the husbands' kin), exchanging courtesies and token gifts with neighbors, and the like. On a wider scale, women perform similar "socioemotional" tasks in their volunteer work. As Rakow (1987, p. 297) puts it, "telephone talk is work women do to hold together the fabric of the community." Part of women's affinity for the telephone, then, results from the duties they have: their sociability is in service to the household, the extended family, the friendship circle, and the community. (See also di Leanardo 1984, pp. 194ff.; Ross 1983; Kessler and McLeod 1984; and Leffler, Krannich, and Gillespie 1984, for examples of women's greater responsibility for and sensitivity to social networks.)

This explanation, too, is incomplete. It implies that telephone conversation is more housework, only another burden. It does not capture the degree of voluntary conversation and the pleasure in conversation suggested by the accounts we have of women and telephony. So a third factor may also be in play.

Three: Women are more comfortable on the telephone than men; and this in turn, because North American women are generally more sociable than North American men. There is considerable evidence in the social-psychological and social networks literatures that, holding constant the opportunities or social contacts, women are more sociable than men, whatever the explanation for that one prefers—constitutional, structural, social, or cultural (see, for example, Fischer and Oliker 1983; Hoyt and Babchuck 1983; Kessler and McLeod 1984; Bott

1971; Komarovsky 1967; Pogrebin 1987, Chs. 13,14). Given the difference, the telephone fits the modal female style more than it does the modal male style.

A few items in telephone history are consistent with this third contention. A 1930s survey of 27 "typical" Iowa farm families found that women made 60 percent of the calls, including many regarding the farm business (Borman 1936). Results from a 1940s rural Indiana survey of 166 subscribers explains that pattern in the following way: "Women used the phone most frequently. Many men said they did not like to use the phone, so they had women call for them" (Robertson and Amstutz 1949, p. 18; see also Rakow 1987, pp. 69–70). A Bell survey suggests the sensitivity of women to the social nuances of telephone conversations. When, in the 1920s, Bell asked a sample of "better-class" subscribers why they did not use long-distance more often, the researchers found that "the feeling seemed general with the *housewives* in these groups that a social conversation cannot be limited to the three-minute initial period without the embarrassment of being somewhat abrupt or discourteous" (Wilson 1928, p. 51; emphasis added).

These data are, admittedly, crude. But, added to what sociologists know about gender differences in social relations, they lend weight to this explanation: Women developed a greater affinity for the residential telephone than men did, because it was more useful to them in overcoming isolation, in performing their network tasks, and in pursuing an activity that they typically both enjoyed more and were better at than men—sociable interaction.

IMPLICATIONS

The case of the residential telephone presents a more complex picture of gender and technology than appears in most of the literature. One can argue that the telephone, like the stove or washing machine, facilitated women's designated tasks in the home and thereby increased, or at least helped maintain, an oppressive division of labor. More broadly, telephone use may have accentuated or solidified male-female differences in interpersonal relations.

It would be difficult, however, without engaging in some dubious reasoning, to assert that the telephone was another vehicle for the "capitalist-patriarchal order." The reasoning underlying the greater oppression argument tends to be circular, taking this form: There are oppressive tasks women must perform; *any* change that makes the tasks less oppressive necessarily makes women more able, willing, and likely to perform them and more often; ergo, *any* change—other than removal or "de-gendering" of the task—perpetuates or aggravates the oppression. This deduction can be persuasive in the absence of empirical data. But it is not of much use in understanding actual social change. It is more useful to ask how, within the existing cultural matrix, a technology came to be used and to what ends.

In the current instance, given the extant gender division of labor, it would seem that the telephone made women's work easier. There is little evidence to claim that women performed more (or fewer, for that matter) material tasks in the home because of the telephone. It is reasonable to claim, as did a few women to Lana Rakow, that the telephone made women more vulnerable to requests for their socioemotional labor—to advise, comfort, organize, and so on. Women's tasks in this realm may have grown. But calls go both ways and it is likely that each burdensome call a woman received was matched by at least one help-seeking call a woman made. It is also reasonable to claim that the telephone facilitated work that women were expected to perform anyway. We can say little more without considerably more comparative *evidence*—for example, that in comparable places without telephones, women's duties were more or less onerous.

What is most reasonable to conclude from the evidence, however, is that women also used the telephone, and used it often, to pursue what they *wanted*: sociable conversation. The testimonials and other data suggest that use of the telephone was more often experienced as a pleasure (and more so by women than by men). If so, this is an instance of women "appropriating" a technology to serve their *own* distinctive ends.

There is, of course, the possibility of "false consciousness" on the part of women testifying about the telephone—that it really burdened them more than it eased their burdens, harassed them more than it pleased them, all despite their perceptions. Individual and collective misperceptions are certainly possible. (For example, women may have experienced the purchase of a vacuum cleaner as easing the demands of housecleaning, but not have noticed the upward creep of their standards of cleanliness which may have created more work.) However, such a claim carries a heavy evidentiary burden, since the actors' understandings of their own experience ought to have *prima facie* validity. Simply deducing consequences from a theory of technology is not satisfactory, for plausible deductions can be made in either direction, for more or for less "liberation."

This conclusion implies that we must make careful distinctions among, and even within, technologies. To pursue the point, consider briefly the connection of women's historical experiences to two other technologies that share with the telephone the ability to facilitate sociability.

The few social historians of the *bicycle* seem to agree that many young women used it to shuck Victorian constraints. When mechanics developed a practical "safety bicycle" in the 1890s, middle-class Americans went on a virtual cycling craze. Since riding the contraption in contemporary ladieswear, bustles and all, was difficult, many women adopted risque bloomer outfits and other shape-revealing clothes. (This practice joined with a feminist movement against corsets and for freer garments, as well as an increasing abandonment of Victorian inhibitions elsewhere.) Bicycle outings also allowed young women to lose their chaperons and be alone with their beaus. "More and more women came to regard the bicycle as a freedom machine" (Smith 1972, p. 76). In France, the president of a feminist congress in 1896 toasted the "equalitarian and leveling bicycle" that was about to liberate women (Weber 1896, p. 203). Of course, this was a "liberation" restricted to younger women. (On bicycles, see, for example, Aronson 1968, and Smith 1972; on cultural responses, see, for example, Kern 1983, and Green 1983.)

The social history of the *automobile* is more complex. Cowan (1983) and others (for example, Hawkins and Getz 1986) have argued that common use of the automobile increased housework burdens on women by stimulating new shopping and chauffeuring trips, by undercutting delivery services, neighborhood stores, and other conveniences that had existed for the housebound wife, and indirectly by expediting suburbanization and its consequent requirement for numerous and long trips.

Granting this point (for the moment—we have little solid evidence), there was also another side to the automobile. Many women reportedly viewed the automobile as a device of personal liberation, especially for rural women. Home economist Christine Fredrick wrote in 1912:

> Learning to handle the car has wrought my emancipation, my freedom. I am no longer a country-bound farmer's wife.... The auto is the link which bonds the metropolis to my pastoral existence; which brings me in frequent touch with the entertainment and life of my neighboring small towns—with the joys of bargains, library, and soda-water (quoted by Scharff 1986).

Less literate farm wives said much the same when asked about spending scarce funds for automobiles (see the earlier discussion on studies of farm women; also Interrante 1979; Berger 1979, pp. 65–66; Wik 1972, pp. 25ff.). The theme of ending women's isolation recurs. As in the case of the telephone, we know less about urban women, and urban women were less likely than comparable farm women to drive cars. But there is some evidence that city women, too, enjoyed the personal liberation of the automobile, at least over the alternative, the trolley-car (Scharff 1986). One expression of the liberation was the boom in family touring that followed mass automobility (Belascoe 1979; see also Rothman, 1984, pp. 294ff.).

Perhaps this romance with the automobile turned into a snare. As the automobile became *available* to women, it also became necessary to them (for reasons mentioned above); trips were less often pleasant indulgences and more often unavoidable burdens. Still, in many ways and for many years, the automobile, too, seemed to amplify the ability of women to satisfy their own desires.

What the telephone, bicycle, and this facet of the automobile share in common, it seems, is that they are, in part, *technologies of sociability*; they facilitate personal interaction. Women seemed to have similarly grasped other, comparable, turn-of-the-century social changes, and more eagerly than men. They flocked to department stores (Leach 1984) and to movies (Peiss 1986), both leaving behind the "domestic sphere" and finding sociability. Women's "affinity" then, for such changes is understandable: women, at least in North America, are the sociable gender.

Women seemed to have taken the telephone and used it for their own ends, as well as their families'. Men's jokes about this affinity are perhaps, at base, simply a defensive acknowledgement of this difference between men and women in personal relations.

NOTES

1. Chan conducted these interviews as part of a larger project on the telephone in community history headed by the author.

2. Rothschild (1983, p. 85) asks, *"How has* technology continued to play a role in re-inforcing the gender division of labor and the control of women's household labor?" [emphasis added] and provides many credible but unproven answers— for example, that "technology helps the corporate economy to appropriate the housewife's time. New products and processes demand that the housewife educate herself about them, shop for them and comparison shop, and experiment with them." These speculations, however, beg the prior issues of documenting the causal link. (Another logical prob-lem in this and similar lines of argument, is anthropomorphisizing technology—e.g., "new products . . . demand" [cf. Winner 1977].)

3. These averages mask great variations by region, place, and class. In 1930, for example, estimated telephone subscription rates ranged from 12 percent in Mississippi and South Carolina to over 65 percent in Iowa, Kansas, and Nebraska (Untitled Report, Chief Statistician's Division, AT&T, July 27, 1932, courtesy AT&T Historical Archives; on differential state diffusion, see Fischer and Carroll 1988). Community differences were also great, varying from 22 to 65 percent subscription rates among the one hundred largest AT&T exchanges in 1927 (Wilson 1928, p. 7). Because they are based on specific locales, estimates by economic strata are quite diverse. In 1927, in one Michigan exchange, 24 percent of the bottom quartile (measured by rents paid) had telephones, 48 percent of those in the middle half, and 65 percent of the top quintile had telephones (Wilson 1928, p. 7). In a "typical" southern New England exchange in 1930, half the homes in the bottom two-thirds of the income distribution had telephones, while 93 percent of those in the top third did (Harrell 1931). While these (and similar) estimates are necessarily rough, they suggest that most urban households in the United States above the median income and outside the South had gotten telephones by the Depression. During the Depression, many households, especially those on farms, gave up telephones (see Fischer 1987a, 1987b).

4. Copy in "Advertising and Publicity" folder, AT&T Historical Archives, New York.

5. This summary is based on reviewing much telephone advertising of the period, found in various sources (see Fischer 1988), including archival collections: AT&T Historical Archives, New York City (thanks to Robert Lewis and Mildred Ettlinger); archives of the Pioneer Telephone Museum, San Francisco (Don Thrall, Ken Rolin, Norm Hawker); Museum of Independent Telephony (Peggy Chronister); Bell Canada Historical, Montreal (Stephanie Sykes, Nina Bederian-Gardner); Illinois Bell Infor-mation Center (Rita Lapka); and the N. W. Ayer Collection, Smithsonian Institution, Washington— supplemented by excerpts from a few northern California newspapers gathered by John Chan, Steve Derne, and Barbara Loomis.

6. The time-budget forms and related materials are in Box 653, Record Group 176, Bureau of Human Nutrition and Home Economics, "Use of Time on Farms Study, 1925–1930," Washington National Records Center, Suitland, MD. Despite the title, the raw data that have survived are *not* from farms, but largely from a select sample of urban and suburban housewives. Barbara Loomis alerted me to these records. Kneeland (1929) and U.S.D.A. (1944) summarize some of the data. This sample is obviously unrepresentative of American women generally and the data are vulnerable to numerous errors, particularly for this paper, underreporting of calls. Nevertheless, it provides a rare glimpse of the daily routines of upper middle-class women over a half-century ago, in ways more systematic and comprehensive than even the diaries relied upon by many historians.

7. This has been repeated so often in telephone literature that it has of course been exaggerated. For example, Brooks (1976, p. 94), in his history of telephony, writes,

"By the end of the 1880s, telephones were beginning to save the sanity of remote farm wives by lessening their sense of isolation." But at the end of the 1880s, very few farm homes, effectively no remote ones, *had* telephones.

8. For example, in 1917, the Whitehead Telephone Company pressed the Indiana Public Service Commission to allow an extra charge for lengthy calls so as to discourage gossip on their rural, eight-party lines. But Whitehead's customers packed the hearing and testified that they had no objection to gossip. The Commission found against the company. A similar case occurred in Oregon (MacMeal 1934, p. 224).

9. For instance, a 1926 item from the London, Ontario, *Free Press*: "An anti-telephone gossip union is about to see the light of day in London whose specific purpose is to obtain legislation to charge all telephone gossips after five minutes of the wire, $1.00 a minute. . . . . Roughly 10,000 members have already signed on the dotted line in the Forest City, 90 percent of whom are men." Most of the complaints targeted women (1926: February 11, from "London Community File," Bell Canada Historical).

10. "Palo Alto Womens' Business and Professional Club" folder, Palo Alto Historical Association; collected by Steve Derne.

11. *Palo Alto Times*, 1934:November 15.

12. Chan's respondents similarly downplayed the amount of telephone use, but a common recollection—at least among the men—was the use of the telephone by mothers and sisters for social purposes. Some men reported that they had made rendezvous by telephone, but not that they visited by telephone.

13. Take 1920 as a sample year: Farmers comprised about 30 percent of the male labor force in the United States. Blue-collar workers formed another 48 percent. *At most*, perhaps three-fifths of the remainder, the white-collar workers, could have used a telephone at work freely—which then equals a high guess of 13 percent of all employed men having such access. Put another way, each business telephone had to be "shared" by an average of about eight male workers (or six non-farm, male workers; ten workers of both sexes). And this includes all sorts of "official business only" instruments. At the same time, each residential telephone had to be "shared" by only 2.9 households. In 1930, the business telephone ratio was one per 5.5 male workers and the residential rate was one per 2.4 households. (Data are calculated from U.S. Bureau of the Census 1975, pp. 139–140, 783.)

14. Farm women apparently used the telephone more than did farm men, despite roughly comparable physical isolation. Elderly women today use the telephone more than elderly men do, although both groups are retired (Synge, Rosenthal, and Marshall 1982) and elderly women have more friends than elderly men do (Fischer and Oliker 1983). Various testimonials imply that, after working hours, women with jobs outside the home chat on the telephone more than do working men (e.g., Rakow 1987).

REFERENCES

Andrews, William D. and Deborah Andrews. 1974. "Technology and the Housewife in Nineteenth-Century America." *Women's Studies* 2:309–328.

Antrim, M. T. 1909. "Outrages of the Telephone." *Lippincott's Monthly Magazine* 84 (July): 125–126.

Arlen, Michael J. 1980. *Thirty Seconds*. New York: Farrar, Straus & Giroux.

Aronson, S. H. 1968. "The Sociology of the Bicycle." Pp. 293–303 in *Sociology and Everyday Life*, edited by M. Truzzi. Englewood Cliffs, NJ: Prentice-Hall.

Asmann, Edwin A. 1980. "The Telegraph and the Telephone: Their Development and Role in the Economic History of the United States: The First Century, 1844–1944." Manuscript, Lake Forest College.

Belascoe, W.J. 1979. *Americans on the Road: From Autocamp to Motel, 1910–1945.* Cambridge, MA: MIT Press.

Bell Canada. 1928. "Selling Service on the Job." Document #12223:5. Montreal: Bell Canada Historical.

Bennett, Arnold. 1912. "Your United States." *Harper's Monthly* 125(July):191–202.

Bereano, Philip, Christine Bose, and Erik Arnold. 1985. "Kitchen Technology and the Liberation of Women from Housework." Pp. 162–181 in *Smothered by Invention*, edited by W. Faulkner and E. Arnold. London: Pluto Press.

Berger, Michael L. 1979. *The Devil Wagon in God's Country: The Automobile and Social Change in Rural America, 1883–1929.* Hamden, CT: Archon Books.

Bertho, Catherine. 1981. *Telegraphes et Telephones*. Paris: Livres de Poche.

Borman, R. R. 1936. "Survey Reveals Telephone as a Money Saver on Farm." *Telephony* 111 (11 July): 9–13.

Bose, C., P. L. Bereano, and M. Malloy. 1984. "Household Technology and the Social Construction of Housework." *Technology and Culture* 25 (January): 53–82.

Bott, Elizabeth. 1971. *Family and Social Network*, 2d ed. New York: Free Press.

Brandon, B., ed. 1981. *The Effect of the Demographics of Individual Households on Their Telephone Usage*. Cambridge, MA: Ballinger.

Brooks, John. 1976. *Telephone: The First Hundred Years*. New York: Harper and Row.

Bureau of Labor Statistics. 1924. "The Cost of Living in the United States." Bulletin No. 357, U.S. Department of Labor. Washington, DC: U.S. Government Printing Office. (Data file # ICPSR 8299 provided by the Inter-University Consortium for Political and Social Research, Ann Arbor, MI.)

Cowan, Ruth Schwartz. 1976. "The 'Industrial Revolution' in the Home: Household Technology and Social Change in the 20th century." *Technology and Culture* 17 (January): 1–23.

1979. "From Virginia Dare to Virginia Slims: Women and Technology in American Life." Pp. 30–44 in Dynamos and Virgins Revisited, edited by M. M. Trescott. Metuchen, NJ: Scarecrow Press.

1983. *More Work for Mother*. New York: Basic Books.

1987. "The Consumption Junction: A proposal for Research Strategies in the Sociology of Technology." Pp. 261–280 in *The Social Construction of Technology*, edited by W. E. Bijker, T. P. Hughes, and T. Pinch (eds.), Cambridge, MA: M.I.T. Press.

di Leanardo, Micaela. 1984. *The Varieties of Ethnic Experience*. Ithaca, NY: Cornell University Press.

Field Research Corporation. 1985. *Residence Customer Usage and Demographic Characteristics Study: Summary*. Courtesy R. Somer, Pacific Bell.

Fischer, Claude S. 1985. "Studying Technology and Social Life." Pp. 284–301 in *High Technology, Space, and Society*, edited by M. Castells, Beverly Hills, CA: Sage.

1987a "The Revolution in Rural Telephony." *Journal of Social History* 21 (Fall): 5–26.

1987b "Technology's Retreat: The Decline of Rural Telephony, 1920 to 1940." *Social Science History* 11 (Fall): 295–327.

1988 "Touch Someone: The Telephone Industry Discovers Sociability." *Technology and Culture* 29 (January): 32–61.

Fischer, Claude S. and Glenn Carroll. 1988. "The Diffusion of the Telephone and the Automobile in the United States, 1902 to 1937." *American Journal of Sociology* 93 (March): 1153–1178.

Fischer, Claude S. and Stacey Oliker. 1983. "A Research Note on Friendship, Gender, and the Life Cycle." *Social Forces* 62 (September): 124–133.

Green, Harvey, 1983. *The Light of the Home: An Intimate View of the Lives of Victorian Women in America*. New York: Pantheon.

Harrell, J. E. 1931. "Residential Exchange Sales in the New England Southern Area." Bell System General Commercial Conference on Sales Matters, June. Mf 368B, Illinois Bell Historical, Chicago.

Hawkins, Richard and J. Greg Getz. 1986. "Women and Technology: The User's Context of the Automobile." Paper presented at the American Sociological Association annual meetings in New York.

Horowitz, Daniel. 1985. *The Morality of Spending: Attitudes toward the Consumer Society in America, 1875-1940*. Baltimore, MD: John Hopkins University Press.

Hoyt, D. R. and N. Babchuck. 1983. "Adult Kinship Networks." *Social Forces* 62 (September): 84–101.

Interrante, J. 1979. "You Can't Go to Town in a Bathtub: Automobile Movement and the Reorganization of Rural American Space, 1900–1930." *Radical History Review* 21 (Fall): 151–168.

Kemp, R. F. 1905. "Telephones in Country Homes." *Telephony* 9 (5 May): 432–433.

Kern, S. 1983. *The Culture of Time and Space, 1880–1918*. Cambridge, MA: Harvard University Press.

Kessler, R. C. and J. D. McLeod. 1984. "Sex Differences in Vulnerability to Undesirable Life Events." *American Sociological Review* 49 (October): 620–631.

Kneeland, Hildegarde. 1929. "Is the Modern Housewife a Lady of Leisure?" *Survey* 62 (June):301–302, 331, 336.

Komarovsky, Mirra. 1967. *Blue-collar Marriage*. New York: Random House.

Leach, William R. 1984. "Transformation in a Culture of Consumption: Women and Department Stores, 1890-1925." *Journal of American History* 71 (September): 319–342.

Leffler, Ann, Richard S. Krannich, and Dair L. Gillespie. 1984. "When I'm Not with the Friend I Hate, I Hate the Friend I'm with: Contact, Support and Hostility Networks in Community Life." Paper presented at the American Sociological Association annual meetings in San Antonio, TX.

MacMeal, H. B. 1934. *The Story of Independent Telephony*. Chicago: Independent Pioneer Telephone Association.

Maddox, Brenda. 1977. "Women and the Switchboard." Pp. 262–280 in *The Social Impact of the Telephone*, edited by I. de S. Pool. Cambridge, MA: MIT Press.

Marchand, Roland. 1985. *Advertising the American Dream: Making Way for Modernity, 1920–1940*. Berkeley: University of California Press.

Mayer, M. 1977. "The Telephone and the Uses of Time." Pp. 225–245, in *The Social Impact of the Telephone*, edited by I. de S. Pool. Cambridge, MA: MIT Press.

McGraw, Judith. 1982. "Women and the History of American Technology." *Signs* 7(4):798–828.

Paine, Robert., 1967. "What is Gossip About?" *Man* 2 (June): 278–285.

Peiss, Kathy. 1986. *Cheap Amusements: Working Women and Leisure in Turn-of-the-Century New York*. Philadelphia, PA: Temple University Press.

Pogrebin, Letty Cottin. 1987. *Among Friends*. New York: McGraw Hill.

Printers' Ink. 1910. "Bell Encourages Shopping by Telephone." 70 (19 January).

1933. "Telephone Company Works with Retailers on Campaign." 163 (4 May): 41.

Rakow, Lana F. 1987. "Gender, Communication, and Technology: A Case Study of Women and the Telephone. Ph.D. dissertation, Institute of Communications Research, University of Illinois at Urbana-Champaign.

Richardson, Anna Steese. 1930. "Telephone Manners: Why Not?" *Successful Farming* (March): 46–47.

Robertson, L. and K. Amstutz. 1949. "Telephone Problems in Rural Indiana." Bulletin 548 (September), Purdue University Agricultural Experiment Station, Lafayette, Indiana.

Rosher, A. 1968. "Residential Telephone Usage among the Chicago Civic-minded." Master's thesis, Department of History, University of Chicago.

Ross, Ellen. 1983. "Survival Networks: Women's Neighborhood Sharing in London before World War I." *History Workshop* 15 (Spring): 4–27.

Rothman, Ellen. 1984. *Hands and Hearts: A History of Courtship in America*. New York: Basic Books.

Rothschild, Joan. 1983. "Technology, Housework, and Women's Liberation: A Theoretical Analysis." Pp. 79–93 in *Machina Ex Dea: Feminist Perspectives on Technology*, edited by Joan Rothschild. New York: Pergamon.

Salomon, Ilan. 1986. "Telecommunications and Travel Relationships: A Review." *Transportation Research* 20A.

Scharff, Virginia A. 1986. "Reinventing the Wheel: American Women and the Automobile, 1910–1930." Paper presented at the Organization of American Historians annual meetings in New York.

Shaw, J. M. 1934. "Buying by Telephone at Department Stores." *Bell Telephone Quarterly* 13 (July): 267–288.

Sherman, Mary. 1925. "What Women Want in Their Homes." *Woman's Home Companion*. 52 (November): 28, 97–98.

Singer, B. D. 1981. *Social Functions of the Telephone*. Palo Alto, CA: R & E Research Associates.

Smith, R. 1972. *A Social History of the Bicycle*. New York: McGraw-Hill.

Spacks, Patricia Meyer. 1986. *Gossip*. Chicago: University of Chicago Press.

Steele, G. O. 1905. "Advertising the Telephone." *Printers' Ink* 51 (12 April): 14–17.

Strasser, Susan. 1982. *Never Done: A History of American Housework*. New York: Pantheon.

Synge, J., C. J. Rosenthal, and V. W. Marshall. 1982. "Phoning and Writing as a Means of Keeping in Touch in the Family of Later Life." Paper presented at the Canadian Association on Gerontology annual meetings in Toronto.

Telephony. 1905. "Facts Regarding the Rural Telephone." 9 (5 April): 303.

Thrall, Charles A. 1982. "The Conservative Use of Modern Household Technology." *Technology and Culture* 23 (April): 175–194.

U.S. Bureau of the Census. 1910. *Special Reports: Telephones 1907*. Washington, DC: Government Printing Office.

1975. *Historical Statistics of the United States, 1790–1970*. Washington, DC: U.S. Government Printing Office.

U.S. Department of Agriculture. 1915. *Social and Labor Needs of Farm Women*. Report no. 103. Washington, DC: Government Printing Office.

1944. "The Time Costs of Homemaking—A Study of 1500 Rural and Urban Households." Mimeograph, Agricultural Research Administration, Bureau of Human Nutrition and Home Economics.

U.S. Senate. 1909. *Report of the Country Life Commission*. 60th Congress, 2d Session, Senate Document 705. Washington, DC: U.S. Government Printing Office.

Vanek, J., 1978. "Household Technology and Social Status." *Technology and Culture* 19 (July): 361–375.

Walker, K. E. 1964. "Homemaking Still Takes Time." *Journal of Home Economics* 61 (October): 621–624.

Ward, Florence E. 1920. "The Farm Women's Problems." U.S. Department of Agriculture Circular 148. Washington, DC: Government Printing Office.

Weber, Eugen. 1986. *France: Fin de Siècle*. Cambridge, MA: Harvard University Press.

Wik, R. M. 1972. *Henry Ford and Grass-Roots America*. Ann Arbor: University of Michigan Press.

Wilson, L. B. 1928. "Sales Activities." General Commercial Conference, Bell System. In microfilm 368B, Illinois Bell Historical.

Wilson, Margaret Gibbons. 1979. *The American Woman in Transition*. Westport, CT: Greenwood.

Winner, Langdon. 1977. *Autonomous Technology: Technics-Out-Of-Control as a Theme in Political Thought*. Cambridge, MA: MIT Press.

Wolfe, L. M. 1979. "Characteristics of Persons with and without Home Telephones." *Journal of Marketing Research*, August: 421–425.

8

The Expanded Family
and Family Honor*

Ruth Horowitz

Three months prior to Ana's cotillion, or *quincecañera* (fifteenth birthday celebration),[1] everything appeared to be ready. Sponsors to pay for almost all aspects of the religious ceremony and the party afterward had been found. Relatives, *compadres* (godparents), and friends had been enlisted to help: an uncle was paying for the food, an aunt was paying for the liquor, a grandmother was buying her dress, baptismal godparents were buying the cake, and two of their daughters were going to "stand up" (serve as an attendant) for the church procession. Other relatives and friends were enlisted as godparents to pay for the flowers, a *cojín* (pillow) to kneel on in the church, a *diadema* (diadem or tiara), the bands, the photographs, and several other incidentals. As Ana had chosen to have the dinner and dance in the gym of the local community center, she did not have to rent a hall. An order for two hundred invitations had been placed at the engravers with the names of all the attendants printed on an inserted sheet.

In addition to finding enough relatives and friends of the family to pay for the affair, Ana had found the requisite fourteen young couples, *damas* (women) and *chambelaones* (men), to stand up in matching dresses and tuxedos. This is frequently a difficult task, as each of the young women has to buy her own dress (generally $45 to $100), which Ana, like most celebrants, picked out of a catalog of bridesmaid dresses. The cost of the rented tuxedo is often $40. A cotillion is an expense for everyone. Ana had already stood up for two of the young women, who were returning the favor, and she was scheduled to participate in four more. Finding fourteen couples who could afford and would agree to stand up for the affair was difficult. In addition, she wanted to exclude from the males any potential troublemakers. As it was, two of the young women were standing up with their brothers, who were in different gangs, and another's escort was in a rival gang, but none were known as troublemakers at parties.

Problems began several weeks before the affair. An aunt's family dropped out, claiming they could not afford to pay for the band because they had to attend the funeral of a relative in Mexico. Excuses such as this are common, but the day was rescued when Ana's mother agreed to try to pay for the band herself.

One week prior to the cotillion Ana discovered that her mother had hired only a Mexican *ranchera* (Mexican country music) band and not a rock group. Ana did not want a cotillion without a rock group, and a local band was finally

*Horowitz, Ruth. 1983. "The Expanded Family and Family Honor." Pp. 52–76 in *Honor and the American Dream: Culture and Identity in a Chicano Community*. New Brunswick, NJ: Rutgers University Press. Copyright © 1983 by Rutgers, The State University of New Jersey. Reprinted with permission of Rutgers University Press.

located forty-eight hours before the party. Then one of the couples decided that they could not afford to pay for the clothes and dropped out. Another couple broke up and an escort had to be found on short notice. While anxious about having only thirteen couples, Ana claimed it was better than seven or eight, as some had. Her problems were not over. An aunt informed her mother that she had seen Ana kissing her boyfriend, and her mother threatened to cancel the event because she did not want to endure the questions about Ana's virginity that public knowledge of her activities might engender. If the affair had been cancelled, the strength of the family network might have been questioned.

A cotillion is a public affirmation both of a young woman's virginity and of her kin's ability to work together to pay for such an event. Not all fifteen year olds have cotillions. Many families cannot afford them. Moreover, rumors often claim that a young woman holding a cotillion is trying to prove that she is still a virgin when she no longer is one. On the other hand, failing to have a cotillion is frequently considered a good indication that the young woman is no longer a virgin and may even be pregnant.

The evening before the affair required major organization, as beans and rice had to be prepared for two to three hundred guests and the gym had to be decorated. Retiring at two in the morning, everyone was awake by six. Clothes had to be ironed for her six brothers and sisters and both Ana and her older sister had to buy shoes the day of the affair. Her family congratulated themselves for having chosen to buy fried chicken rather than spending the considerable effort to cook the more traditional *mole* (a spicy baked chicken in sauce), though a few guests later commented on its absence.

Ana marched down the church aisle in her long white dress and veil on the arm of her uncle, following the thirteen couples and the new godparents. As she knelt with her boyfriend before the priest, Ana and the others resembled a wedding party. She did not kiss him but quietly left her flowers at a side altar and prayed there to the Virgin Mary. Her mother was pleased that seventy-five guests attended the church ceremony and that close to two hundred attended the party, many of whom brought presents. Wandering around the room while the photographer took pictures, one could hear compliments about the open bar, the dresses Ana had chosen, and the Mexican band.

Several of the members of the Lions gang arrived after dinner, having learned of the party from their member Ten Pen, whose sister stood up for Ana. On their best behavior and wearing their good clothes, they sat quietly drinking and, when the rock band played slow tunes, got up to dance. No incidents occurred, unlike several weeks before, when a groom fought at his own wedding and was arrested when the fight continued outside the hall. Ana's cotillion was dubbed a success by all. After the party, the photographs were admired over and over.

This event symbolizes much of what is valued in the Chicano family: the close, interdependent family network and the family's success in finances, in containing the sexual activities of the daughter so that she not only remains a virgin but is perceived as such, and in following the proper forms of social interaction. Expectations based on symbols of the expanded family, male domination, virginity, motherhood, and formalism determine the meanings of social relationships within and outside the family. The family relationships should be strong, the males should be dominant, the unmarried women must remain virgins, and the married women should center their lives around motherhood. Courtesy toward and respect for others, particularly elders, is expected of everyone. Some expectations closely resemble those found in Mexican villages,[2] others are affected by United States institutions. In either case, situations of normative ambiguity create dilemmas for concrete action, and the economic status of community residents creates problems for which new cultural resolutions are constantly devised and tested.

While familial social relationships have been somewhat altered, traditional arrangements remain strong. According to Bott (1971, p. 265) "geographical mobility *alone* should be enough to disrupt the sort of close-knit networks one finds in homogeneous working-class areas, and such disruption should be accompanied by greater jointness in the husband-wife relationship."[3] On 32nd Street the move from other areas of the United States or from Mexico has not greatly altered traditional arrangements. The worlds of the men and the women remain largely segregated and traditionally oriented yet interdependent. This is attributable to a number of factors: relatives often came together or followed one another; close networks were expanded to include *compadres* (children's godparents), who were often friends and/or neighbors; and the cultural symbols that give meaning to social relationships were frequently stronger than many of the forces of change. It is situations where the circumstances (ecological, social, or economic) have changed that highlight the strengths and weakness of the collective expectations. What *should* be done may become unclear, be revised, or be reaffirmed. Let us look at these dilemmas and the evolving solutions.

A COHESIVE FAMILY

The kinship network on 32nd Street can best be termed an "expanded family" in the model described by Gans (1962). While many relatives of varying generations tend to live nearby and interact continuously, each household is comprised of a nuclear family unit. A similar structure is found throughout the Chicano population regardless of social class and is the expected standard for families.[4] In Mexico, particularly among the urban poor, the ties of kinship have been augmented to include *compadres* (fictive kin) through treating the godparents of the children as part of the expanded family network.[5] While there is some indication that the importance of fictive kin as an extension of family relationships is lessening in some areas of the United States today,[6] in other communities it remains important.[7] On 32nd Street, the relationship between the godparents of a child's baptism and the child's parents remains particularly important for many families. *Padrinos* (godfathers) and *madrinas* (godmothers) are remembered on mother's and father's day and celebrate birthdays and many holidays with their godchildren. The interaction among generations and the closeness among age groups serve in part to maintain cultural continuity in Mexico and in the United States.

The expanded family is the normative familial form for all classes, whether or not it includes fictive kin in the United States as in Mexico. An important aspect of the expanded family network is one of continuous exchanges that are not governed by laws of supply and demand. Not only is the relationship with friends who have engaged in these exchanges strengthened by being named *compadres*, but the mutual obligations further strengthen the relationship of the entire expanded family unit both as a symbol of their cohesiveness and because they need each other. The content of the exchanges varies slightly by social class among Chicanos (Sena-Rivera 1979). While the extent of economic interdependence and the exchange of personal services vary by social class, the family in all social classes remains the primary source of emotional and social support and is a major source for feelings of self-worth.[8] Sena-Rivera argues that economic interdependence is strongest for the most affluent and the least affluent families, that "interdependence in personal services is universal . . . but . . . follows socio-economic class lines (actual necessity rather than performance as an end in itself)" (p. 127). On 32nd Street the exchange of economic and personal services is frequently necessary for survival. Exchanges of money and individual skills are frequently made among kin and fictive kin. Turning for help to outside agencies such as public welfare or a public employment agency is regarded as a failure of a family's solidarity and worth. Ana's mother, for example, feared a public disgrace for the family when an aunt's family could not assist by paying for the band at the cotillion.

Having a large, close family that can be augmented by *compadres* who can and will readily help in time of need is very highly valued. Being seen as a cohesive family transcends economic success.[9] In such a family on 32nd Street and in other Chicano communities members lend each other money, locate a car mechanic, and help out in innumerable other situations.[10] "We can hardly keep track of all the money that goes around between us anymore. We just assume it's about equal," a young couple declared while discussing the state of their finances and their families' aid.

Much tension and weight are placed on the family relationship, which sometimes cannot support the demands made on it. At times these demands may lead to conflicts. With the lack of economic resources available to a nuclear family unit, its financial situation can easily become overextended, as when Ana's uncle dropped out, leaving her mother with additional expenses that were more than she could afford. This situation strained the family's relationship for several months until Ana's uncle was again able to help them. Economic pressures can disrupt the ongoing flow of resources and social relationships.

Being a cohesive family does not mean that members do not have problems. Amelia's family is close and they help each other frequently by exchanging favors and with mutual social and emotional support. Amelia is one of nine children (aged eight to thirty). Though her mother frequently drinks heavily, which embarrasses her, the children were very close to their mother and were upset at her first absence, when, as a local representative, she went to Washington for a conference. When one of the daughters married and moved into the basement apartment, her sister felt the double bed was too large for one person and had a younger sister sleep with her. A second married sister lives upstairs, another lives ten blocks away, and the sons all live within a few blocks. All the sons and daughters congregate almost daily at their mother's home. Amelia considers her family to be a cohesive one. They constantly help each other, just as Ana's family did in providing aid to make her cotillion successful, and reaffirming their image as a strong family.

Those families who do not have relatives or *compadres* on whom to rely must turn to public welfare in time of financial problems or must ask for support, thereby publicly acknowledging their humiliation. The neighborhood is attuned to such events, and news of them is quickly shared.[11] One of the members of the Lions gang frequently attempted to invite himself to dinner at other homes. The other gang members often refused and laughed at his attempts, ridiculing him for his inability to obtain readily a meal from the usual sources—relatives. While eating at relatives' homes is common, no one *asks* to do so; relatives or *compadres* are expected to offer meals to anyone at their homes at mealtime. A person who can survive without money for a long period by going from relative to relative, is viewed as having a cohesive family. A responsible individual does make some attempt to reciprocate, though no accounting is kept and the help received may not be reciprocated for a long period of time. However, even within the family, overdependence can lead to tension, as there is little money to go around.

Compadres and relatives usually make up an emotional and social support group. Women move freely back and forth between homes—cooking together, talking, taking care of one another's children, shopping, and going out together for entertainment. They have frequent Tupperware, makeup, toy, and clothes demonstrations at relatives' or *compadres'* homes. A young woman described one such party:

> They're lots of fun. We girls get together and play lots of games, talk, laugh a lot, and buy too many things. Our husbands don't always like that when we have to pay up. Everyone dresses up to come and we laugh and gossip a lot.

Holidays, birthdays, and other special occasions are usually celebrated with *compadres*, relatives, and their children. A special dinner is prepared, and people eat in several shifts if no table is large enough to accommodate all the guests. Attending a Thanksgiving dinner, which includes not only turkey and sweet potatoes but rice, beans, and chili sauce, at the Mendoza home with two sets of *compadres* (each of the three families had seven children, then all below seventeen years old), guests ate in three of four shifts. The children played and ran in and out, while the women discussed problems of child rearing in the kitchen and then joined the men to dance to Latin music.

Not everyone is pleased with the close familial ties. For those who wish to do things differently, close ties may be viewed as prying, not helpful. Tina, a twenty-five-year-old mother of two boys explained:

> I hate living around the corner from my mother-in-law. She always wants to know what's happening over here. It's my family and I'll run it as I choose. I like some of my relatives but having them all over here asking for things constantly is too much.

Several months later I bumped into Tina after she had moved from the eastern to the western side of the community. She declared that living so near her mother-in-law had become too unpleasant and she had moved at the first opportunity. Tina gave her sister-in-law all her old dishes and furniture when she moved into the downstairs apartment. Both declared that they were happier in their new apartments in the same building. While a close family is highly valued, privately it displeases those who wish to be different.

The strong network of intergenerational relationships provides a means by which traditions can be readily passed on. Few childrearing manuals are used, and intergenerational aid encourages traditional practices. Young girls spend time helping their mothers and learning the mothering role. Girls frequently take on household responsibilities and care for their younger siblings before becoming mothers themselves.[12] At ten or twelve, girls frequently are party to discussions among their mothers' friends and between their mothers and grandmothers about family life and relationships. The intergenerational interaction and the strong emotional support these relationships provide are a solid basis for the maintenance of traditional sex role relationships within the family, upon which the code of honor is based.

MANHOOD

Manhood is expressed through independence, personal strength, control over situations, and domination. This image of manhood, particularly in relationship to femininity, has been traced by some scholars to the culture of Spain, where the desire for precedence in interpersonal relationships and authority over the family are important symbols of manliness.[13] Others trace it to the culture of the Aztecs, where women were expected to be subordinate and submissive to men, while a third group argues that male domination was a result of colonialism.[14] Though the traditional symbols of manhood have not changed substantially in the transition to 32nd Street and have significant implications for men's relationships as fathers, husbands, sons, and brothers,[15] male domination as worked out within the family does not weaken the critical position of the mother.

The role of the Mexican father/husband has been described as one of domination and control over his wife and daughters. Studies of Mexican towns demonstrate that men are seen as people who cannot be "gotten around."[16] Fathers are seen as rigid, closed, and distant.[17] Sons become independent at an early age.[18] Some of these descriptions are similar to those of relationships for fathers and husbands in the 32nd Street community while others are not. The symbols of manhood articulate many of the salient meanings of social relationships within the family. The father/husband, as the dominant member of the household, must maintain the honor of his wife and daughters. To dishonor them reflects not only on them but also on his ability to maintain his self-respect as an independent and dominant individual. He alone must be responsible for supporting his family and must not publicly appear to become dependent on a working wife. The husband/father as the family head and the son as an independent young man both expect to be served by the women in the household and to come and go as they please. Sara, an eighteen year old, explained:

> My brother, he comes rushing in and sits down at the table expecting a hot dinner no matter what time it is, just like my father. . . . You know he gets it every time and we have to make it.

No one found it extraordinary that one wife, who worked an early shift (7:00 A.M. to 3:00 P.M.), was expected to prepare dinner for her husband, who finished his shift at 11 P.M. and arrived home to eat at 4:00 A.M., after several hours of drinking. If she was asleep he woke her, and she had to cook and still get their seven children ready for school and be at work by 7:00 A.M.. A spotless house was also expected and provided.

Though the men can demand and usually receive services (cooking, cleaning, and so forth) of the women when they want, the men are dependent on the women to provide these services. Men are taught that cooking, washing clothes, and cleaning are women's and *not* men's work. For example, when one male youth pulled out the ironing board to iron his pants, his sisters took it away from him and laughed and teased him for wanting to do "woman's work." They all thought him strange and talked about him behind his back. His father even gave him a lecture. A man who does "woman's work" must be unable to find a woman to do that work, and therefore must be less than a man, or must be unduly controlled by his woman. This male dependence actually gives a woman a significant source of power.

Husbands

While a husband may have extramarital affairs, he should not publicly flaunt them because it would demonstrate lack of respect for his wife.[19] In one family with seven children the mother caught her husband three times with the same fifteen-year-old woman. The oldest son beat his father. "It was OK, my mother doesn't like him either. He tricks [goes out with other women] on her all the time." This man could barely support his family, making the situation worse for him. His wife frequently said she would leave him but she never did. Though this is not typical, similar situations exist.

Moreover, some wives argue that men are "free spirits." A scene at a large community dance illustrated some of the manipulations and interactions that occur between husbands, wives, lovers, and friends. The rock music emanating from the packed gym could be heard several blocks away and eliminated conversation. Margie sat at a table with a girlfriend and a friend of her new husband, Dino, trying not to follow Dino's movements as he wandered around the room. He stopped to slap palms every few feet and pulled a young woman out to the floor to dance a fast dance. Walking by me he complained to a female friend that Margie did not care for him or their new baby properly. He stopped by another young woman and invited her out after the dance. He then sauntered over to his wife and pulled her out to the floor for a slow number. Her expression was sulky as they walked back to the table, where he told her that if they had any money left he was going out with his male friends later. She silently found a few bills. He handed half of them back and wandered away.

Many people were aware of what was going on, but no one said anything. Finally, Dino came back and asked me to take him and his wife to get their baby at his sister's. Margie really did not want to leave yet and was silent in the car. When Dino claimed it was Margie's job to get the baby from his sister, she told him that it was his baby too. Dino got out and said that taking care of the baby was her responsibility; he worked. Looking depressed, Margie said she wished Dino would come home with her.

Dino told me to hurry to take him back to the dance after we dropped off Margie. At the discothèque downtown Dino spent the few dollars he had. Afterward he and his girlfriend went to a married couple's house. When he went home the next day he told his wife that he had passed out at a male friend's. She understood, he said. I heard later from friends that she threw several pots at him. Two years later she left him and went back to school.

While not all husbands have girlfriends, many wives believe that as long as their men come home to them, husbands should be allowed to do what they want. Christina, a friend of Margie's, claimed that Dino left Margie for six months because she tried to keep too many tabs on him.

> You can't control what a man does and you got to accept him the way he is. Men are free spirits and as long as they come home to you, why should you worry? If they bring in some money and you cook, clean, sew, and are ready for them, why should they leave? Margie made a mistake that night at their party. She shouldn't have left when they had that fight, because she should have known that Dino would just stay there with one of his girlfriends. She holds him in too tight.

While wives may not like the fact that their husbands leave them home, many believe men must be free to roam.

As the person who must maintain his dominance and control the household, the husband is responsible for supporting the family without the help of his wife. Given the poorly paid jobs available, the wages of a working wife or daughter frequently become an economic necessity. Over 40 percent of the community women work, though many of them have working husbands or fathers (Schensul 1972).

Within this cultural context, men are caught in what appears to be an unresolvable dilemma. A working wife is a public indication that the husband is unable to support his family and therefore lacks control in the family and dominance over his wife, who could become economically independent. But the alternatives to an employed wife are few and not much better. A hungry and poorly clothed family does not enhance a man's reputation, nor does depending on support from the expanded family for any length of time without reciprocation. Caught in this dilemma, many husbands prefer to let their wives work and explain their actions within the traditional cultural context. By stating that they are still in control, that they *let* their wives work, and then only to pay for incidental expenses while the men remain the main breadwinners, their actions are legitimized. For example, while two men in their thirties were sitting in a bar discussing whether wives should work, one said to the other, "I would never let my wife work while I got this good job, but a lot of guys are getting laid off now and my wife didn't get bad money before we got married." The second responded, "I got her working now 'cause we need a new washer and dryer to help her out. Now she has to go to the laundromat." Both men criticized another man whose wife was working though he had a well-paying job and the couple had a "good home." Only if a man explains that he is still in control is a working wife considered legitimate. The fact that women work is still articulated in terms of male domination, and the women infrequently use their employment to change the husband-wife relationship.

Fathers and Sons

A son, like any man, is expected to be independent and dominant in any social relationship with women. In the family this means he should come and go as he pleases, as his father does. Staying near home is not regarded as proper. One eleven year old who always remained on his front steps was told by his father to "go hang somewhere else." What he does outside with his peers is seen largely as his own business. Some parents do not know that their sons are gang members and may know little of their sons' lives outside the home, to the point of not recognizing their "street names." One gang member told me to tell his parents that I met him in a settlement house because they did not know he was a Lion. Should a son begin to jeopardize his job potential by getting into too much trouble, his parents are faced with a dilemma. To interfere is to question his autonomy and threaten his manhood. Paradoxically, a father who refuses to control his son's behavior fails to fulfill his role as dominant family member. A situation of normative ambiguity exists: if he interferes, he violates his son's independence; if he does not, he demonstrates his lack of control. There is no higher order of rules to resolve this striking moral incongruity. Each situation must be negotiated.

The youths are aware of their parents' dilemma. One son expressed the dilemma in the following manner:

> My old lady [mother] gets really upset with me running around in the street 'til real late 'cause she's got so many things to worry about. I shouldn't do it 'cause of my old lady but can't help it; besides my old man he's out a lot anyways doin' his thing.

Felipe at fifteen was rarely punished, though he was often absent from school. He was a man, according to his father, and should be granted independence outside the home. The father felt that he had no authority over his sons and could not tell them how to organize their lives. Only inside the walls of his home did he feel he had a right to control his sons' activities. If Felipe talked back to his father or mother, or came in noisy and drunk, then his father felt he had a right to act. As a man, he had a right to maintain order in his home; otherwise, he felt he had no say. Another father felt similarly about his son. After trying for a long time to encourage his son to continue his education, the father decided that he could not use punishment to force his sixteen-year-old son to attend school.[20]

> I know my son is real smart, his teachers told me that many times, but he and his friends leave school every day before they finish. He says it's boring. He's a good artist—I told him he could go to art school but he says the teachers are all fags

[homosexuals]. He has to finish school to get anywhere, but I can't force him. He's a man.

Other fathers put their sons in military schools or send them to Mexico, resolving the dilemma. The father remains in control and the son retains some independence by living away from home.

This dilemma is a triggering situation in that either solution carries implications for the parents' (largely the father's) identity in the eyes of their sons and other people in the community. If the father tries to control his son's activities, he will become known as a strict disciplinarian who is denying his son's independence. Community members will see him as someone who takes the American dream seriously but may be making his son into less of a man. If he leaves his son on his own, the son may perceive his father as distant and tough but allowing him to pursue his activities as he sees fit, as an independent man. In that case, community residents may see the father as helping to develop an independent, honorable man but failing to maintain his own manhood by losing control over his son's activities.

Neither resolution is entirely successful and both may add to the distance between the father and his children. Fathers are generally marginally involved in the care of older children except as disciplinarians. This does not mean that there is a lack of mutual respect, only that the relationship is perceived to some degree in terms of discipline and control.[21] "During the week we have fun, but when my father's home on Sunday we can't go nowhere or do anything. He just plays his lousy music," claimed a fifteen-year-old boy. His father works the afternoon shift (he makes more money doing so) and is rarely home and awake when his children are. "When we were young my father always took us places, now he takes us nowhere," explained a twelve-year-old boy. Fathers play with babies and hug their young sons and daughters but remain at some distance from their older children. A fourteen-year-old girl complained:

> My father hardly does anything with us. He gives the little kids anything they want and he lets my oldest brother do anything he wants, but we can't go anyplace and he never takes us anywhere. He doesn't even talk to us and he only talks to my oldest brother at night sometimes.

Faced with a number of dilemmas as fathers, husbands, or sons, men must negotiate situational solutions. As a husband, a man must support his family and not allow his wife to work in order to remain dominant, but he is frequently faced with poor job prospects and an insufficient paycheck. New rationalizations and norms legitimate a wife's work and maintain the man's honor. The father-son relationship is replete with dilemmas of independence and domination, with no culturally acceptable solution to the situation of normative ambiguity. The father must decide in each situation whether to discipline his son or encourage the son's autonomy. His choice affects not only his relationship with his son but how he is viewed publicly. Moreover, most fathers realize the importance of education and the potential for getting into trouble in the streets while they also see the importance of the male peer group and male independence.

VIRGINITY

The Virgin Mother is among the most salient religious symbols in Mexico. She is more important than the adult Christ in many Mexican religious ceremonies. For example, *el día de la Virgen de Guadalupe* (December 12) is an important celebration both in Mexico and on 32nd Street, when even men who rarely attend church go to mass.[22] In Mexico City women walk on their knees the several miles from the downtown to the Virgin in Guadalupe's shrine. The sexual purity of women—the faithfulness of a wife to her husband or the virginity of an unmarried woman—is symbolized by the Virgin Mother. The honor of a man is besmirched if a daughter is not a virgin at marriage or a wife is unfaithful. His honor is inexorably tied to that of his family. In Mexican villages, the role of an honorable woman, both as a mother and as a daughter, is that of a *mujer abnegada*, a self-sacrificing, dutiful woman (Diaz 1966, p. 78). While the symbol of the Virgin Mother is used in evaluating women's relationships on 32nd Street, some expectations have changed from those of the traditional Mexican village.

According to Mexican tradition, maintaining a young woman's public image as a virgin requires that she be accompanied on social occasions by a chaperone (usually an older or younger relative). On 32nd Street, chaperonage of unmarried women has largely been eliminated though wives are often accompanied by their young children when visiting or shopping. The result is that everyone is aware that most women can escape the watchful eyes of their kin. Consequently, maintenance both of a woman's virginity or faithfulness and of community perception of that state are difficult. Most families are concerned with the movements of their daughters but cannot completely restrict their activities, though a few families do attempt to retain tight control.

Brothers and other relatives act as unofficial chaperones for young women. They will often stop young women from drinking, watch their sisters if they are with young men, or tell all their friends to stay away. For example, at a party sixteen-year-old Sara asked me:

> Please tell me if you see my brother because I can't drink with him around, he'll beat me. Me and my sisters are not supposed to drink, he doesn't like that. You know when we go to dances on the north side, we got to sneak 'cause if he ever found out he would follow us around and we'd never get to go anywhere.

The importance that parents give to a daughter's identity as a virgin is revealed in the following example. Alicia, when she was fourteen, hid her pregnancy from her parents until her sixth month. Her parents sent her to an aunt and uncle in Mexico to whom she was supposed to give the child. Realizing how much she wanted to keep the baby, her aunt persuaded Alicia's parents to let her keep the child. When she returned home seven months pregnant, Alicia was not permitted to leave the house. Anytime a visitor arrived, she hid, first under the bed and then, when she became too big, under the sink in the kitchen. Labor pains started when she was hiding in the garage. Later her parents almost took over the upbringing of her son, taking him as a deduction on their income tax even after Alicia went to work and referring to him as their son, though everyone knew who the parents were.

Parents are faced with what seems to many an unresolvable dilemma. If they follow the traditional honor-based code and refuse to allow their daughter to go out unsupervised, then her virginity remains publicly unquestioned and the honor of her family is upheld. The wider society and many of the local institutions, whether organized by members of the wider society or by local residents, provide legitimation for allowing a young woman some degree of freedom. Both the schools and the churches sponsor dances that are sparsely supervised. Local community groups also sponsor dances with American rock bands. Parents are invited to attend yet discouraged from participating or actually attending by the type of music and the dim lighting. This local legitimation of more freedom for young women places parents in a problematic situation. Freedom heightens the risk of the daughter losing her virginity or being perceived as having lost it. But if they closely supervise her activities, they risk alienating her. Again a situation of normative ambiguity exists and the resolution must be situationally negotiated between parents and their daughters.

The parental dilemma is exacerbated by the expectation that men will take what they can from women. Men are defined as dominant and women defined as submissive; consequently, only male relatives can be trusted with women. One father succinctly expressed these views:

> You know what all men are after. . . . It's natural for them to go out and get it anyway they can. I don't trust any of the young punks around here. They take it and run. There are too many unmarried pregnant girls around here. The young girls don't know how to handle themselves.

Parents are confronted directly with the dilemma when young women ask permission to attend a party or dance with friends. Parents often employ the tactic of nondecision. They postpone any decision until the last moment. Then, when their daughter is ready to go out, they deny her permission. Other times the responsibility is shifted back and forth between mother and father and then changed again at the last moment. This lack of resolution can result in dissatisfaction on both sides. Many young women stop asking. "I just go where I please without asking permission. She [her mother] would just stare at me in silence when I asked, so what's the point in asking?" a nineteen year old explained. By going out on their own, young women risk being appraised as nonvirgins.

Some families are able to retain strict control over their daughters. Lana, for example, must ask permission to sit in front of her house and rarely is allowed to go anywhere. She was particularly upset when she was not permitted to go anywhere or do anything on her birthday.

> I don't ever get anything, like one time my father gave me ten dollars five days after my birthday and I threw it back at him and I told him that I don't want his ten dollars. I didn't ask you for money. He said this was a way to pay me back for what I'd done for them. I told them that they didn't owe me anything. All I wanted

for my birthday was some fun like a picnic at the beach. I didn't want any money. I just wanted someone to remember and have some fun. I'm never allowed to go to the movies. I do all the cooking and cleaning. My mother comes in and takes a bath and watches TV.

Another mother timed her daughter's return from school every day; it took eight minutes to walk home and if her daughter was not home within twelve minutes after the last bell, the mother went out looking for her. While this case is extreme, other families only allow their daughters to attend parties or dances under the supervision of a mature older relative. Most of the young women, however, have enough freedom to do what they want during the hours they are permitted outside the house. Many skip school to attend parties or be alone with their boyfriends.

Unable to resolve the dilemma with their parents, many young women marry in order to leave home. Marriage is one of the few culturally legitimate means for young women to leave home and still maintain their honor and that of their families. For example, Mita's parents did not approve of the man she wanted to marry. She resented the fact that they physically restrained her from going out with him. At one point they threatened to send her to Texas to stay with her relatives. They followed through on the threat as far as taking her to the station but did not actually send her. Mita later moved out of her house to live with a married girlfriend and planned a wedding on her own. The week before the wedding her parents took her to Mexico on a false pretext and kept her there for a month. Finally, a few months later they gave up their efforts and let the couple marry. Mita explained:

They want me to marry a doctor or something but I want to get married now. . . . I can't stand my parents telling me do this, do that. At night my mother makes sure we're [Mita and her younger sister] in bed and if we get up for a drink of water, she starts following us around and tells us to get back to bed. We have to sneak anything we do.

Parental permission for their daughter to go out affects the public evaluation not only of the parents but of their daughter. If she is permitted to attend parties, she is at a much greater risk of being appraised as a nonvirgin even if she actually retains her virginity. Parents frequently increase the risk of such erroneous perceptions by failing to take a strong stand if their daughter sneaks out. It is the public perception of her sexual purity that reflects upon the parents. If she is perceived as a nonvirgin, then her family's honor is questioned. Only complete parental control over her behavior minimizes the risk of her being perceived as a nonvirgin or of actually losing her virginity. As such control is difficult to maintain in modern urban society, it is more an ideal than a reality.

MOTHERHOOD

Motherhood is the most culturally acceptable identity available to women. The role of independent career woman is not culturally acceptable. Women must be either wives, sisters, or mothers to men. Motherhood is seen not as a last resort but rather as a highly honored role. The Mexican image of the Virgin Mother, loving and dependable, the person with whom the child satisfies desires for nurturing and acceptance, is the 32nd Street model of motherhood.[23] Motherhood is the basis of the strongest bonds of blood ties.[24] These bonds are much stronger than those of husbands and wives or fathers and children.

The husband-wife bond is based on procreation and expression of love but little on companionship. The expectation that men will dominate in all situations makes it difficult to develop companionable relationships between men and women even in marriage, as sociability usually develops between equals. (Moreover, any time a man and a woman who are not related through blood ties are together, it is expected that they will become sexually involved, because men dominate women and, lacking equality and the possibility of friendship, the only reason they would be together is as sexual partners.)[25] Most socializing occurs in single-sex groups, and the expanded family network fulfills companionship functions. But children's ties with their mothers are natural and lifelong:[26] they never become distant with age, as do ties with their fathers, who discipline and control them. While the dynamics of the father-child interaction is in part determined by the child's willingness to obey him and demonstrate respect for him, mothering places no such conditions on the parent-child relationship.

Loyalty and support for his mother was demonstrated by a young man who had become addicted to heroin and entered a methadone program only after stealing from his mother:

> I used to steal all the time from my brothers and sisters and went through my old man's coat pockets many times . . . even stole his watch once and pawned it, but you know when I took some bread [money] from my old lady, then I knew I had to do something. Taking from your old lady's real bad.

The mother remains the central and most stable feature in a son's life. He depends on her for nurture and emotional support and she on him for support and the ultimate protection of her honor. As a son his honor is dependent on hers; any aspersion cast on her honor reflects on his own.

In an extreme case of maintaining a mother's honor, a son killed his father after repeatedly catching him with teenage women. Some community residents felt the murder was justifiable, that the father's behavior was dishonorable and the resolution culturally acceptable. But the community was not unanimous in defining the situation as one where the family honor was at stake. Some residents felt that murder was not a necessary or legitimate resolution and that the son was a criminal who deserved to be jailed. His mother, though, worked continuously for his release. Sentenced as a juvenile, he was out in less than three years.

Young women vicariously experience the mother role through their continual associations with relatives and *comadres* and their babies. They are frequently enthusiastic about their own mother having additional children. Fifteen-year-old Celia, one of seven children declared:

Man, I want my mother to have a kid so I can take care of it. I love babies. I like to baby-sit for the little kid next door, she's so smart. Now my mother's *comadre* is having a kid so maybe I'll be able to help, but they live all the way by 40th Street, but then maybe I can stay by their house sometimes.

At sixteen, Celia became pregnant and married.

The traditional expectation that a woman's unique role is to be a mother with many children creates a conflict for those young women who have interests outside the home. Some reject motherhood. One nineteen-year-old college student, the eldest of seven, despised the traditional female role of daughter and mother:

I had to change diapers for my three youngest brothers and sisters. They were such a mess and were so much trouble. I hate them for it. I wish my mother didn't have them. What did she need so many kids for anyway? It would have been a lot better without the last two. They were always crying and wanting attention . . . comb their hair, wash them, feed them, change their diapers, and put them to sleep. . . . They're my mother's kids. She should be responsible for them. I'm not their mother . . . if my mother gets married again and has another kid I'll die. One time I told her I wasn't going to have any kids. She really got angry and said God will punish me. It was up to Him, not me. She didn't speak to me for a week. I'm not going to have any kids. They're just trouble.

Celia's oldest sister, a student, added another problem to the list:

It wouldn't be good for my mother to have more kids. They cost money and it would be like the dog; everyone would get excited for a while and then bored and not want to take care of it. [Celia objected here.] I don't want to take care of it. I'd move out.

The view of the two students are not generally accepted and often considered immoral. They violate all expectations of femininity and the family. Though it is becoming more common for young women to desire to limit family size, in part because of the expense of bringing up children, older people and many younger ones see this not only as tampering with "God's will" but also as comparing things that cannot be compared: economics and family. These young women are openly denying the importance of motherhood and appear to equate the family's worth with that of money. For most, social and economic success are not valued above motherhood. Problems arise only for those young women who are beginning to strive for success in the wider society. The exclusion of motherhood is still regarded as deviant.

CHIVALRY AND RESPECT

Chivalry and etiquette are not regarded as critical for most of American society today. Except for some fictional British detectives, such as Dorothy Sayres's Lord Peter Wimsey, symbols of etiquette and chivalry are rare today, but the precise form of social relationships remains important for the residents of 32nd Street.

The formalities of social interaction are essential in an honor-based subculture, where even the slightest word or movement may be seen as placing a person in a demeaning situation.[27] Etiquette "sets limits and protects us from having to expose ourselves in ways which may be detrimental to our public image" (Goodenough 1963, p. 197). Formal rules provide order for everyday social interactions, creating some sense of security and stability in potentially problematic situations. Rules channel impulse, passion, and desire into ways of acting that are recognized as having a particular social meaning in a particular social setting. "Form surrounds and sets bounds to our privacy, limiting its excesses, curbing its explosions, isolating and preserving it" (Paz 1961, p. 32). Formal rules of etiquette create a distance between actors, minimizing the potential for questions about precedence and the need to prove invulnerability in a situation. For example, following rules against staring at others can prevent a person from defining a situation as a challenge to his claim to precedence.[28]

Following an elaborate set of formal rules of etiquette is expected in both Chicano and Mexican families. Foster (1967, p. 96), describing a Mexican village, states, "From early childhood one learns to be 'correct.' Children when confronted with a family friend or a stranger are told *dále la mano* [step up and shake hands]." On 32nd Street swearing is not tolerated in the home by either females or males. Swearing often results in a slap or a belt across the seat, administered by a mother, father, or older sister or brother. Nor is insolence or rudeness tolerated in the home. Doors must be closed nicely. An older person must be greeted and taken leave of with a courtesy that would please Emily Post. The following exchange took place when I brought a male friend to meet the Lions at the park. After I introduced him, each of the Lions greeted my friend with "I'm very glad to meet you" as they shook hands. Courtesies such as taking woman's arm when walking in the street and always walking on the curb side are performed by most men. The first time one of the Lions held my arm as we crossed an icy patch on the sidewalk, I turned to him astounded and asked if he always did such things. He replied that he usually did, as he had been instructed to do so since he was a child. Similar behavior was frequently demonstrated at weddings and cotillions.

Adherence to the rules of etiquette is a sign of respect when dealing with persons older than oneself. Punishment is expected if these rules are not followed. Ronny, a member of the Lions gang, was made to lean over the edge of the bathtub by his mother and was beaten with a belt when he arrived home drunk and telling wild stories. "She only does that when I come home real drunk. I usually sober up before I go home. I deserve it when I come in high." His mother felt she had no control over his drinking, but when he demonstrated a lack of respect by coming inside her home drunk and disorderly, she would and could discipline him.

Not only do formal interactions help youths to maintain order between generations, between the sexes, and between men, but youths who successfully employ the rules of etiquette at home are well received by all adults, while those who demonstrate a lack of manners within the home are denigrated by the community regardless of behavior outside the home. Those who know when to use their manners are those who gain the respect of others, even among gang members. Consequently, the use of common rules of etiquette not only demonstrates respect for others and channels behavior but is also highly valued by others in the community.

It is clear that the important symbols of family life are solidarity, male domination, virginity, motherhood, and respect. In the context of an urban community within a highly industrialized and educated society, some of the expectations derived from these symbols become distorted, are ambiguous, or are in conflict. While some of the problematic situations can be resolved within the traditional culture, for other situations all solutions seem less than perfect. Much of the ambiguity and conflict is found in the expectations concerning sex role behavior and child-parent relationships.

In the urban context youths are granted many freedoms and hold few responsibilities. These expectations are validated and supported by the media, by the schools, and even to some extent by the Catholic church. The situation places continual pressure on parents to allow their children more freedom while encouraging youths to demand those freedoms. Moreover, women are encouraged to work, particularly because of financial need.

The cohesive family with its strong network of relatives and *compadres* provides economic supports to help deal with financial realities, emotional supports to deal with normative ambiguity and conflict, and social supports and mechanisms to maintain the traditional symbols of sex role relationships and nearly traditional behavior patterns. With the support of the expanded family, actors negotiate difficult situations of normative ambiguity and conflict. Sometimes the process is painful, emotionally charged, and the consequence unsatisfactory to both parties; a son is physically punished or a daughter is locked in her room. Members of the expanded family may provide advice and emotional support or may invite the unruly son or daughter of a relative or *compadre* to live with them. Families do their best to keep members out of the social welfare and justice systems.

Youths are caught between the traditional model of social relationships and the Chicago urban reality: the streets, the school, the media, and the job scene. With the freedom they take or are given, the youths are faced with many dilemmas as they venture beyond the confines of the communal and familial order.

NOTES

1. A *quinceañera* is a young woman's fifteenth birthday celebration and is often referred to as a cotillion. It is a special birthday for a young girl in both Mexico and the United States and symbolizes her transition from childhood to adulthood. Traditionally, she then had to be chaperoned and guarded in her behavior. In the small villages of Mexico she is often given some new clothes, while on 32nd Street some of the girls have affairs for several hundred guests, such as the one described in the text.

2. See, for example, Diaz (1966), Foster (1967), Nelson (1971), and Romanucci-Ross (1973).

3. Several empirical studies support Bott's hypothesis. In England, Young and Willmot (1957) studied the problems of wives who moved from the Bethnal Green neighborhood where many of their kin lived and found that only forty years later networks of

friends and kin developed again in Dagenham (Willmott 1963). Studies of the United States such as Handel and Rainwater (1964) and Rainwater and Handel (1964) found that geographic mobility brought an increase in homecenteredness and less sex role segregation between husband and wife in working class families.

Mobility has not affected familial sex roles in this way in the 32nd Street community, nor have lack of propinquity and urbanization affected the strength and importance of family ties. There is evidence that propinquity is not necessary to maintain the cohesion of extended kinship, and urbanization does not entirely destroy it (Coult and Habenstein 1962; Litwak 1960). Both studies found extended kinship among people who lived in different places and in urban areas.

4. For similar findings in other Chicano communities see Alvirez and Bean (1976), Murillo (1971), Sena-Rivera (1979), Sotomayor (1972), and Temple-Trujillo (1974).

5. Mintz and Wolf (1950), in an historical analysis of *compadrazgo*, have documented its changes of function and content since the sixth century. According to Gibson (1966) *compadrazgo* was widely adopted in Mexico during the colonial period, when an epidemic caused significant depopulation and *compadres* became accepted as substitute parents.

Lomnitz (1977), in her study of a Mexico City shantytown, found that the function of the *compadre* relationship from the rural situation and from the "ideal model" had been strengthened and broadened in the shantytown. Rural *compadres* were never cited as necessary for emergency help and close friendship but were "respected" persons. However, through participant-observation, Lomnitz found in the shantytown that not only has the number of *compadre* relationships increased (for example, *compadres* are chosen for saint days, upon graduation from primary school, and so on), but *compadres* are frequently picked from neighbors and friends and are part of the reciprocal obligation network which is necessary for economic survival:

> The *compadrazgo* institution is being used in the shantytown to make preexisting reciprocity relations more solid and permanent. . . . I agree with Safa (1974, pp. 61–64) in that cooperation between equals is a result of necessity born of the social structure. If one lacks a powerful godfather one must make do with *compadres* (Lomnitz 1977, p. 162).

Compadrazgo is a way of legitimizing mutual assistance among neighbors and is judged in its "intensity and trustworthiness of reciprocal exchange" (Lomnitz 1977, p. 173).

6. Keefe, Padilla, and Carlos (1979) and Sena-Rivera (1979) argue that *compadrazgo* is decreasing; however, Carlos (1973) has found that with urbanization and modernization *compadres* still play an important role in Mexico and the relationship remains strong.

7. See Madsen (1964), Moore (1970), and Rubel (1966) for illustrations of its continued importance.

8. See Keefe, Padilla, and Carlos (1979), Murillo (1971), Rubel (1966), and Sena-Rivera (1979) for similar findings in other studies of Chicanos.

9. This "familism" in which individuals subordinate their needs to the collective can be traced back to Aztec culture (Mirandé and Enríquez 1979).

10. Alvirez and Bean (1976) argued that many Chicano families pool their resources, and Carlos (1973) has found that fictive kin help each other by finding jobs, lending money, and giving preferential treatment in business.

11. On some occasions, such as a fire or death, it might be permissible to accept emergency public aid, but it is still better if friends and family help out.

12. A fourteen-year-old girl explained:

    > I stay home until at least one o'clock in the summer every day to wash the kitchen and bathroom floors, otherwise they get dirty and sticky and the little kids crawl around on them all the time. In the winter during school, I do it before I go in the morning. Sometimes I'm late from school. We clean the whole house twice a week and my other sisters do the cooking and the washing.

13. See Pitt-Rivers (1966) for an analysis of male honor in Spain.

14. See Hayner (1966) and Paz (1961), who argue that Aztec women were submissive to men. However, Mirandé and Enríquez (1979) argue that Aztec women had roles beyond wife and mother and that complete male domination occurred through external forces such as those imposed by colonialization (Baca Zinn 1975; Sosa Riddell 1974).

15. Similar patterns have been found in other Chicano communities (Flores 1971; Nieto-Gomez 1974; Vidal 1971).

16. Nelson (1971 p. 51) describes this phenomenon in her study of a Mexican village. In his analysis of psychological studies of the Mexican, Peñalosa (1968) found that they described the father-son relationship as distant and respectful and the father-daughter relationship as distant and conflict-free.

17. Diaz (1966), Fromm and Maccoby (1970), and Nelson (1971) so describe the fathers in the Mexican villages they studied. Rubel (1966) and Goodman and Beman (1971) describe similar findings in Chicano communities.

18. Diaz (1966) found that mothers expected their sons to become independent early in their lives in Tonalá, Mexico.

19. See Pitt-Rivers (1966) for an elaborate analysis of a similar situation in Spain.

20. A parent's problem in dealing with a son's or, for that matter, a daughter's education is exacerbated by problems in dealing with educational institutions and personnel. This is evident in the manner in which parents criticize their children's performances and in their fear of confronting school personnel, because the parents themselves lack education or feel unable to communicate in English. One teacher explained that he saw less than one half of the parents of his students and felt that these parents were immediately on the defensive when they came in. Typically a parent is called only if the teacher thinks there is something wrong with the student. Parents do not know that they can take the initiative, as many middle-class parents do, and demand things for their child, such as remedial aid or placement in a different class.

21. For a similar view of Mexican villages see Diaz (1966), Hayner (1966), and Nelson (1971).

22. The Virgin of Guadalupe symbolizes piety, virginity, and saintly submissiveness. She is the supreme good (Mirandé and Enríquez 1979). Peñalosa (1968) argues that "guadalupanismo," that is, the highly emotional, devout veneration of the Virgin of Guadalupe, is very strong in Mexican culture (see Bushell 1958; Madsen 1960).

23. See Fromm and Maccoby (1970) and Nelson (1971) for analyses of the Virgin Mother.

24. This traditional Mexican situation is similar to that of the Aztecs, who considered the mother the heart of the house, solely responsible for child rearing and cleaning,

dedicated to her husband, and remaining respectable in the eyes of the community (Mirandé and Enríquez 1979, p. 14).

25. Gans (1962) describes a very similar situation among Italians living in the United States.

26. This has been documented in other Chicano communities (Murillo 1971).

27. In the modern media, concern for form and style is often linked to the violence of the cowboy in the movies.

> The gun tells us that he lives in a world of violence; and even that he "believes in violence." But the drama is one of self-restraint, the movement of violence must come in its own time and according to its special laws, or else it is valueless...it is not violence at all which is the "point" of the western movie, but a certain image of a man, a style, which expresses itself most clearly in violence (Warsow 1963, p. 239).

28. One rule of standard etiquette may place a man in a situation in which a claim to precedence is questioned, namely, apologizing profusely for an action already completed. An apology for an act committed is seen as an act of "gripping." If an individual attempts to place another in a demeaning situation, he must follow through on his claim. If a member of the Lions gang shouts "the Nobles suck" and there is by chance a Noble within hearing distance, the Noble will interpret the act as demeaning to his gang's honor and will follow through on the challenge. If the Lion apologizes, asking for forgiveness, he is "gripping," that is, placing himself in a subordinate position to the Noble, because only someone of higher status may grant forgiveness. Consequently, if the original challenger "grips," he loses his claim to precedence in that situation.

REFERENCES

Alvirez, David and F. D. Bean. 1976. "The Mexican American Family." Pp. 271–292 in *Ethnic Families in America,* edited by C. H. Mindel and R. W. Habenstein. New York: Elsevier.

Baca Zinn, Maxine. 1975. "Political Familism: Toward Sex Role Equality in Chicano Families." *Aztlán: Chicano Journal of the Social Sciences and the Arts* 6:13–26.

Bushnell, John H. 1958. "La Virgen de Guadalupe as Surrogate Mother." *American Anthropologist* 60:261–265.

Carlos, Manuel L. 1973. "Fictive Kinship and Modernization in Mexico: A Comparative Analysis." *Anthropological Quarterly* 46:75–91.

Coult, Allen and R. Habenstein. 1962. "The Study of Extended Kinship in Urban Society." *Sociological Quarterly* 3:141–145.

Diaz, May N. 1966. *Tonalá: Conservatism, Authority and Responsibility in a Mexican Town.* Berkeley: University of California Press.

Foster, George. 1967. *Tzintzunztán.* Boston: Little, Brown.

Fromm, Erich and Michael Maccoby. 1970. *Social Character in a Mexican Village.* Englewood Cliffs, NJ: Prentice-Hall.

Gans, Herbert. 1962. *The Urban Villagers.* New York: Free Press.

Gibson, Charles. 1966. *Spain in America*. New York: Harper and Row.

Handel, G. and L. Rainwater. 1964. "Persistence and Change in Working-Class Life-Styles." Pp. 36–41 in *Blue-Collar World*, edited by A. B. Shostak and W. Gomberg. Englewood Cliffs, NJ: Prentice-Hall.

Hayner, Norman. 1966. *New Patterns in Old Mexico*. New Haven: College and University Press.

Keefe, S. E., A. M. Padilla, and M. L. Carlos. 1979. "The Mexican-American Extended Family as an Emotional Support System." *Human Organization* 38:144–152.

Litwak, Eugene. 1960. "Geographic Mobility and Extended Family Cohesion." *American Sociological Review* 25:385–394.

Lomnitz, Larissa Adler. 1977. *Networks and Marginality*. Translated by Cinna Lomnitz. New York: Academic Press.

Madsen, William. 1960. *The Virgin's Children*. Austin: University of Texas Press.

Mintz, S. W. and E. R. Wolf. 1950. "An Analysis of Ritual Co-parenthood." *Southwestern Journal of Anthopology* 6:341–635.

Mirandé, A. and E. Enríquez. 1979. *La Chicana*. Chicago: University of Chicago Press.

Murillo, Nathan. 1971. "The Mexican-American Family." Pp. 97–108, *Chicanos: Social and Psychological Perspectives*, edited by N. N. Wagner and M. J. Haug. Saint Louis: C. V. Mosby.

Nelson, Cynthia. 1971. *The Waiting Village: Social Change in Rural Mexico*. Boston: Little, Brown.

Nieto-Gomez, Anna. 1974. "La Feminista." *Encuentro Feminil* 1:34–37.

Paz, Octavio. 1961. *The Labyrinth of Solitude*. Translated by Lysander Kemp. New York: Grove.

Peñalosa, Fernando. 1968. "Mexican Family Roles." *Journal of Marriage and the Family* 30:680–689.

Pitt-Rivers, Julian. 1966. *Honour and Social Status*. Pp. 19–78 in *Honour and Shame*, edited by J. Peristiany. Chicago: University of Chicago Press.

Rainwater, L. and G. Handel. 1964. "Changing Family Roles in the Working Class." Pp. 70–75 in *Blue-Collar World*, edited by A. W. Shostak and W. Gomberg. Englewood Cliffs, NJ: Prentice-Hall.

Romanucci-Ross, Lola. 1973. *Conflict, Violence and Morality in a Mexican Village*. Palo Alto: National Press Books.

Rubel, Arthur. 1966. *Across the Tracks*. Austin: University of Texas Press.

Seña-Rivera, Jaime. 1979. "The Extended Kinship of the United States: Competing Models and the Case of la Familia Chicana." *Journal of Marriage and the Family* 41:121–129.

Sosa Riddell, Adaljiza. 1974. "Chicanas and el Movimiento." *Aztlán: Chicano Journal of the Social Sciences and the Arts* 5:155–165.

Sotomayor, Marta. 1972. "Mexican American Interaction with Social Systems." *Social Casework* 52:316–322.

Temple-Trujillo, Rita E. 1974. "Conceptions of the Chicano Family." *Smith College Studies in Social Casework* 45:1–20.

Vidal, Mirta. 1971. *Women: New Voice of La Raza*. New York: Pathfinder.

Warsow, Robert. 1963. "The Gentleman with a Gun." In *An Anthology of Encounter Magazine*, edited by M. Lusky. New York: Basic Books.

Willmott, P. 1963. *The Evolution of a Community*. London: Routledge and Kegan Paul.

Young, M. and P. Willmott. 1957. *Family and Kinship in East London*. London: Routledge and Kegan Paul.

Immigrant
Families

9

Immigrant Families in The City*

Mark Hutter

The period of time from 1880 to 1924, when immigration laws placed severe lim-itation on movement into the United States, witnessed a massive exodus of people from southern and eastern Europe. This "new" immigration was from countries like Austria-Hungary, Greece, Italy, Poland, Rumania, Russia, and Serbia (now a part of Yugoslavia). Immigrants from these countries were joined by others from China and Japan, Mexico, French Canada, and the West Indies. It contrasts with the peoples of the "old" immigration, those who arrived between 1820 (when federal statistics of origin were first recorded) and 1880. That was made up al-most entirely of northwest Europeans who came from countries such as England, Ireland, Scotland, France, Germany, Norway and Sweden.

Total immigration in the three decades before the Civil War totaled five million. Between 1860 and 1890 that number doubled, and between 1890 and the beginning of the first world war in 1914, it tripled. The peak years of immigration were in the early twentieth century, with over a million people entering annually in 1905, 1906, 1907, 1910, 1913, and 1914. The main explanation for this massive movement of people to the United States was that the countries of origin of the "new" immigrants were experiencing population explosions and dislocations. By the later part of the nineteenth century, the pressures of overpopulation, combined with the prospects of economic opportunity in the United States and the availability of rapid transportation systems that included railroads and steamships, set the wheels of world migration moving. Maldwyn Allen Jones, whose study *American Immigration* (1960) has been a standard work on the subject, comments on the shared motives of the culturally diversified immigrants for coming to America:

> The motives for immigration . . . have been always a mixture of yearning—for riches, for land, for change, for tranquillity, for freedom, and for something not

*Hutter, Mark. 1986–1987. "Immigrant Families in the City." *The Gallatin Review* 6(Winter): 60–69.

definable in words. . . . The experiences of different immigrants groups . . . reveal a fundamental uniformity. Whenever they came, the fact that they had been uprooted from their old surroundings meant that they faced the necessity of coming to terms with an unfamiliar environment and a new status. The story of American immigration is one of millions of enterprising, courageous folk, most of them humble, nearly all of them unknown by name to history. Coming from a great variety of backgrounds, they nonetheless resembled one another in their willingness to look beyond the horizon and in their readiness to pull up stakes in order to seek a new life. (Jones 1960, pp. 4–5)

There was a great deal of variation in immigrant family migration arrangements. Some immigrant groups coming from Scandinavian societies and from Germany came as nuclear families responding to America's needs to settle and farm the vast lands of middle western America. For these groups settlement often meant the almost complete reconstitution of Old World rural village life and family patterns in rural America (Hareven and Modell 1980). One extreme example of this practice were the Hutterites, a German religious group that lived in Russia and migrated to the United States in the late nineteenth century. They settled in isolated rural agricultural sections in order to maintain their distinctive family patterns. These include early marriage, exceptionally high fertility, and near universal remarriage after widowhood. The Hutterite community was a highly cooperative family economy ruled by a family patriarch that operated through kinship affiliations created by the high fertility and strict laws of intermarriage. This isolated group could and has maintained itself until today because of its ability to find marriage partners within the group.

As agricultural opportunities in rural America declined and as the demand for skilled and especially unskilled urban workers grew, the "new" immigrations from southern and eastern Europe concentrated in the industrial cities of the Northeast and the Midwest. It was in these urban areas where job opportunities were plentiful and where the chances of success were greatest. Young unattached males became the mainstay of the migration population. The ethnic historian Thomas J. Archdeacon (1983) reports that, in the decades between 1840 and 1899, males constituted 58 to 61 percent of the arrivals. By contrast, the importance of single males accounts for the statistic that 70 percent of the newcomers between 1900 and 1909 and that two out of every three between 1910 and 1914 were males. The proportion of males to females did not take place evenly across the immigrant nationalities. Jews displayed the best balance with an almost fifty-fifty split. Southern Italians, on the other hand, had more than three times as many males as females. The sex ratio among Greeks, the most extreme group, indicated that for every one Greek female there were 11 Greek men. Such sex ratio imbalances obviously set limits on the possibility of family life during this time period.

The ultimate success of an immigrant group depended in large part on its ability to reestablish a normal pattern of family life in America. This initially proved quite difficult. Severe problems confronted the immigrant families in America. The huge influx of immigrants to the American cities gave new meaning and visibility to urban poverty. Ghetto housing was awful; inadequate buildings were cheaply and quickly built to meet immediate needs, which proved to be inadequate. People lived in overcrowded, dirty, unsanitary, and poorly ventilated and poorly heated apartment dwellings that were still expensive because of the demand. Boarders and lodgers were numerous and helped provide some of the needed monies to pay the rent. It was not uncommon for beds to be used around the clock, with day-shift workers using them at night and night-shift workers using them during the day.

The horrible living conditions were dramatically exposed in the muckraking works of such novelists as Upton Sinclair, whose famous novel *The Jungle* exposed the grinding poverty in the Slavic communities in Chicago located within the stench of the blood and entrails of cattle being slaughtered in the neighborhood stockyards, and also of the journalistic accounts of newsmen like Lincoln Steffens whose book, *The Shame of the Cities*, refers to the ghetto slums as literally looking like hell. The journalist Jacob Riis, himself an immigrant from Denmark, wrote and photographed the urban poverty of New York's ghetto life in his classic work, *How the Other Half Lives*. His graphic descriptions of the barren and filthy firetraps of New York's tenements startled the nation. The following passage from his book is typical of what life was like in one of these buildings:

> —Cherry Street. Be a little careful please. The hall is dark and you might stumble over the children. . . . Not that it would hurt them; kicks and cuffs are their daily diet. They have little else. Here where the hall turns and dives into utter darkness is a step, and another, another. A flight of stairs. You can feel your way, if you cannot see it. Close? Yes! What would you have? All the fresh air that ever enters these stairs comes from the hall-door that is forever slamming, and from the windows of dark bedrooms that in turn receive from the stairs their sole supply of the elements God meant to be free, but man deals out with such niggardly hand. . . . The sinks are in the hallway, that all the tenants may have access—and all be poisoned alike by their summer stenches. . . . Hear the pumps squeak! It is the lullaby of tenement house babies. In summer, when a thousand thirsty throats pant for a cooling drink in this block, it is worked in vain. But the saloon, whose open door you passed in the hall, is always there. The smell of it has followed you up. Here is a door. Listen! That short hacking cough, that tiny, helpless wail—what do they mean? They mean . . . a sadly familiar story—before the day is at an end. The child is dying with measles. With half a chance it might have lived; but it had none. That dark bedroom killed it. (Riis, 1890/1957, pp. 33–34).

A common theme in the popular literature of that time were stories of wives forgotten in the old country and of families torn asunder by the clash of the old ways of life with the new. The editorial columns of the immigrant press frequently reported on the life struggles of its readers. Many newspapers had "advice" columns with its editors serving as lay clergy, social worker, friend, and relative to those who had nowhere else to turn. The "Bintel Brief" ("Bundle of Letters") of the *Jewish Daily Forward* has become the most famous of these advice columns. Through it, readers wrote of their marital and family problems, the impact of poverty on their lives, religious conflicts in terms of attitudes and behavior, and other life concerns. The following two letters, the first from 1906 and the second from 1910, were reprinted in *A Bintel Brief* (Metzker 1971) and are illustrative of such advice columns:

1906

Worthy Mr. Editor,

I was married six years ago in Russia. My husband had not yet been called up for the military service, and I married him because he was an only son and I knew he would not be taken as a soldier. But that year all originally exempted men were taken in our village. He had no desire to serve Czar Nickolai and since I didn't want that either, I sold everything I could and sent him to London. From there he went to America:

At first he wrote to me that it was hard for him to find work, so he couldn't send me anything to live on. I suffered terribly. I couldn't go to work because I was pregnant. And the harder my struggles became, the sadder were the letters from my husband. I suffered from hunger and cold, but what could I do when he was worse off than I?

Then his letters became fewer. Weeks and months passed without a word.

In the time I went to the rabbi of our town and begged him to have pity on a deserted wife. I asked him to write to a New York rabbi to find out what had happened to my husband. All kinds of thoughts ran through my mind because in a big city like New York anything can happen. I imagined perhaps he was sick, maybe even dead.

A month later an answer came to the rabbi. They had found out where my husband was but didn't want to talk with him until I could come to America.

My relatives from several towns collected enough money for my passage and I came to New York, to the rabbi. They tricked my husband into coming there too. Till the day I die I'll never forget the expression on my husband's face when he unexpectedly saw me and the baby.

I was speechless. The rabbi questioned him for me, sternly, like a judge, and asked him where he worked and how much he earned. My husband answered that he was a carpenter and made twelve dollars a week.

"Do you have a wife, or are you single?" the rabbi asked. My husband trembled as he answered, "I have committed a crime," and he began to wipe his eyes with a handkerchief. And soon a detective appeared in the rabbi's house and arrested my husband, and the next day the story appeared in the Jewish newspapers. Then some good women who had pity on me helped me. They found a job for me, took me to lectures and theaters. I began to read books I had never realized existed.

In time I adjusted to life here. I am not lonely, and life for me and my child is quite good. I want to add here, too, that my husband's wife came to me, fell at my feet and cried, but my own problems are enough for me.

But in time my conscience began to bother me. I began to think of my husband, suffering behind bars in his dark cell. In dreams I see his present wife, who certainly loves him, and her little boy living in dire need without their breadwinner. I now feel differently about the whole thing and I have sympathy for my husband. I am even prepared, when he gets out of jail, to wish him luck with his new life partner, but he will probably be embittered toward me. I have terrible pangs of conscience and I don't know what I can do. I hope you will print my letter, and answer me.

Cordially,
Z.B.

Answer:

In the answer to this letter, the woman is comforted and praised for her decency, her sympathy for her husband and his second wife. Also it is noted that when the husband is released he will surely have no complaints against her, since he is the guilty one in the circumstances, not she.

1910

Worthy Editor

My husband [here the name was given] deserted me and our three small children, leaving us in desperate need. I was left without a bit of bread for the children, with debts in the grocery store and the butcher's and last month's rent unpaid.

I am not complaining so much about his abandoning me as about the grief and suffering of our little children, who beg for food, which I cannot give them. I am young and healthy. I am able and willing to work in order to support my children, but unfortunately I am tied down because my baby is only six months old. I looked for an institution which would take care of my baby, but my friends advise against it.

The local Jewish Welfare Agencies are allowing me and my children to die of hunger, and this is because my "faithful" husband brought me over from Canada just four months ago and therefore I do not yet deserve to eat our bread.

It breaks my heart but I have come to the conclusion that in order to save my innocent children from hunger and cold I have to give them away.

I will sell my beautiful children to people who will give them a home. I will sell them, not for money, but for bread, for a secure home where they will have enough food and warm clothing for the winter.

I, the unhappy young mother, am willing to sign a contract, with my heart's blood, stating that the children belong to the good people who will treat them tenderly. Those who are willing and able to give my children a good home can apply to me.

> Respectfully,
> Mrs. P [The full name and address are given]
> Chicago

Answer:

What kind of society are we living in that forces a mother to such desperate straits that there is no other way out than to sell her three children for a piece of bread? Isn't this enough to kindle a hellish fire of hatred in every human heart for such a system?

The first to be damned is the heartless father, but who knows what's wrong with him? Perhaps he, too, is unhappy. We hope, though, that this letter will reach him and he will return to aid them.

We also ask our friends and readers to take an interest in this unfortunate woman and to help her so that she herself can be a mother to her children. (Metzker 1971, pp. 50–52, 104–105).

In the late nineteenth and early twentieth century as a result of the public outcry generated by the exposures by social-minded individuals like Sinclair, Steffens and Riis, and such tragedies as the Triangle Shirtwaist Factory fire that claimed the lives of one hundred and forty-six people, reforms were directed to change the living and working environments of immigrants. These movements included tenement-house reforms, workmen's compensation, the abolition of child labor, and the protection of women and children in industry.

However, the pervasive poverty in rapidly growing industrial cities led many to the erroneous conclusion that it was the immigrants themselves who were to blame for their poverty. Blame was not placed on the economic circumstances that the immigrants had to confront. This belief led to the development of a wide number of social programs aimed directly in changing the immigrant families themselves. Social reformers created both private and public welfare agencies to help alleviate the problems of the sick, the poor, and the delinquent or criminal. Immigrant families and especially their children became the major targets for discipline and reformation, and programs were designed to intervene in the affairs of immigrant families. The concern was to Americanize them into what they saw as the great American melting pot where the cultural variations of the given immigrant group would be altered to the standard American way of life.

The settlement-house, a private social welfare agency is a typical example of how some of these practices became articulated. The term "settlement" meant giving the immigrant newcomers the wherewithal to survive in a modern industrial city. Located right in the heart of the immigrant communities, it sought to help the immigrant families cope with poverty and improve their living standards. Settlement house workers tried to teach English, American social customs, and, when necessary, the rudiments of household management, health care, and sanitation. They encouraged family member involvement in work and household roles that often conformed to their own middle class standards of family morality. When successful, as in the case of Jane Addams of Chicago's Hull House, they integrated their work without undermining the immigrant's native culture. Unfortunately, much too frequently, workers saw as their primary task the eradication of "non-American" cultural points of view and to family traditions regarding marital roles and parent child relationships.

Education was seen as the key institution to eradicate immigrant cultures and to achieve Americanization. For example, in the years before World War I Henry Ford required all of his foreign workers to attend English school. For a five year period, 1915–1920, the federal Bureau of Education subsidized a Division of Immigrant Education, which encouraged school districts throughout the nation to establish special Americanization programs. The response was favorable and many state governments provided funds for the education of immigrants. During this period and continuing afterwards, numerous public school systems instituted night classes in which foreign students could learn English and gain knowledge of American government to acquire citizenship (Archdeacon 1983).

For the Americanization of immigrant children, the school system became the prime vehicle to help accomplish this task. Education meant more than simply teaching proper English and the three "Rs" of reading, "riting," and "rithmetic," but also meant socializing children to "American" ways of life, habits of cleanliness, good housekeeping, nutrition, and social graces. Children were also graded on their level of acculturation to American values, as measured by behavior in school. State legislation was passed making compulsory attendance laws more stringent to help ensure that children were adequately exposed to the assimilative influences of the schools. Settlement house workers also played a role here by assisting in the supervision of school attendance and observance of child labor laws.

However, it was the immigrants themselves, especially the immigrant family system that was primarily responsible for the success of the "new" immigration in "making it" in America. Let's see how this came about. By 1920 almost sixty percent of the population of cities of more than 100,000 inhabitants were first or second generation ethnic Americans (Sellers 1977). The immigrant settled in ethnic enclaves which people referred to as "Little Italys," "Polanias," "Little Syrias," and "Jewtowns." Each enclave reflected its distinctive ethnic flavor with its own church, stores, newspapers, clothing, and gestural and language conventions. The Chicago newspaper journalist, Mike Royko, reminiscing on his own Slavic community background recalls that you could always tell where you were "by the odors of the food stores and the open kitchen windows, the sound of the foreign or familiar language, and by whether a stranger hit you in the head with a rock" (Seller 1977, p. 112).

The establishment of immigrant "ghettos" in cities reflects a stage in the development of American cities where there was a great need for occupational concentration as a result of the expansion of the industrial economy in the late 19th century (Yancey, Ericksen, and Juliani 1976). Low-paid industrial immigrant workers were forced by economic pressures to live close to their places of work. The particular choice of residence and occupation was strongly influenced by the presence of friends and relatives in a process that has been called "chain migration." Chain migration refers to the connections made between individuals in countries of origin and destination in the process of international migration and to the process in which choices of residence and occupation were influenced by friends and relatives.

Networks of friends and relatives established in America maintained their European kinship and friendship ties and transmitted assistance across the Atlantic. Relatives acted as recruitment, migration, and housing resources, helping each other to shift from the often rural European work background to urban industrial work. A number of social historians (Anderson 1971; Hareven 1975; Yans McLaughlin 1971) have observed that nineteenth as well as twentieth century migrants chose their residential and occupational destinations in large part because of the presence of kin group members in the new area.

Chain migration can be seen as facilitating transition and settlement. It ensured a continuity in kins contacts, and made mutual assistance in cases of personal and family crises an important factor in the adjustment of immigrants to the new urban American environment. Workers often migrated into the new industrial urban centers keeping intact or reforming much of their kinship ties and family traditions. As previously mentioned, a prevalent practice was for unmarried sons and daughters of working age, or young childless married couples to migrate first. After establishing themselves by finding jobs and housing they would tend to send for other family members. Through their contacts at work or in the community they would assist their newly arrived relatives or friends with obtaining jobs and housing.

The fact that so many single individuals came to America alone accounts for the fact that turn of the century urban households of immigrants often included people other than the nuclear family. These people were not kinship related but were strangers. These strangers were boarders and lodgers who for various reasons came to America alone and for a period of time lived with fellow immigrants. This practice of taking in boarders and lodgers proved extremely valuable in allowing new migrants and immigrants to adapt to urban living (Hareven 1983).

The family can be seen as being an important intermediary in recruitment of workers to the new industrial society. Family patterns and values often carried over to the urban setting, and provided the individual with a feeling of continuity between ones rural background and new industrial city. Initially, selected individuals migrated, then families migrated in groups, and often entire rural communities reconstituted themselves in ethnic enclaves. They helped recruit other family members and countrymen into the industrial work force. Migration to industrial communities, then, did not break up traditional kinship ties; rather the family used these ties to facilitate their own transition into industrial life. Tamara Hareven (1983) after examining the historical evidence concludes that it is grossly incorrect to assume that industrialization broke up traditional kinship ties and destroyed the interdependence of the family and the community.

In summary, the 50 year dramatic growth period of 1876–1925 of the industrial urban centers of the northeast and midwest can be attributed to the social and family organization of the newly arriving immigration groups. Rather than view this period in terms of social disorganization we would argue that insufficient attention has been placed on the nature of social interactional patterns that were developing among the immigrant groups in American cities. We owe the spectacular rise of world cities like New York City to the vitality of the immigrants and their social support structures.

REFERENCES

Anderson, Michael. 1971. *Family Structure in Nineteenth Century Lancashire*. Cambridge: Cambridge University Press.

Archdeacon, Thomas. 1983. *Becoming American: An Ethnic History*. New York: The Free Press.

Hareven, Tamara K. 1975. "Family Time and Industrial Time: Family and Work in a Planned Corporation Town, 1900–1924." *Journal of Urban History* 1 (May): 365–389.

Jones, Maldwyn Allen. 1960. *American Immigration/* Chicago, University of Chicago Press.

Metzker, Isaac (ed.) 1971. *A Bintel Brief*. New York: Ballatine Books.

Riis, Jacob A. 1957/1890. *How the Other Half Lives: Studies Among the Tenements of New York*. New York: Hill and Wang.

Seller, Maxine. 1977. *To Seek America: A History of Ethnic Life in the United States*. Englewood, New Jersey: Jerome S. Ozer, Publisher.

Yancey, William. L., Eugene P. Ericksen, and Richard N. Juliani. 1976. "Emergent Ethnicity: A Review and Reformulation." *American Sociological Review* 4 (June): 391–402.

Yans-McLaughlin, Virginia. 1971. "Patterns of Work and Family Organization." Pp. 111–126 in *The Family in History: Interdisciplinary Essays*, edited by Theodore K. Robb and Robert I. Robb. New York: Harper Torchbooks.

10

What Kinds of Immigrants Have Come to the Philadelphia Area, Where Did They Settle, and How Are They Doing?*

Robert J. Young

Dramatic changes in the Immigration Law of 1965, fully implemented in grad-ual stages by 1968, struck at the very roots of an oppressive immigration policy mandated by national legislation between 1921 and 1924. The National Origins Immigration Act, legislated and consolidated in those years, blatantly enshrined the racial and ethnic prejudices of national policymakers. Those ethnic and racial groups designated as less desirable, mainly Southern and Eastern European, were virtually eliminated from the immigrant stream. The Italian, Polish, and other eastern European groups that had been dominant elements in the pre-WWI immi-grant flow were limited after 1921 to numbers so low that these and virtually all other immigrant communities atrophied. Philadelphia, like other major metropoli-tan areas, experienced the end of an era of massive immigration that had created one of this city's greatest strengths and resources—its patchwork of stable eth-nic neighborhoods clustered around churches, synagogues, schools, and shopping districts.

As oppressive as the National Origins Act had been it had little effect on the Asian-American communities. For all practical purposes they had been so consistently discriminated against in immigration legislation that they had long since been effectively eliminated from the immigrant flow. Discriminatory legis-lation on the West Coast, from the 1880s onward into the first decade of the 20th century, compounded by the Chinese Exclusion Act at the national level in 1882 and the 1907 Gentlemen's Agreement in Theodore Roosevelt's administration, not only brought Asian immigration to a halt but resulted in a reverse flow. Therefore, by 1921, Asian-American communities were already isolated, inward looking, or virtually on their way to extinction by death or intermarriage with other minority groups, for example, the Asian-Indian-Mexican pattern in California.[1] Philadel-phia's only recognizable Asian-American community, the Chinese, clustered in its Chinatown, was a rather typical example of a national phenomenon of an ag-ing, disproportionately male Asian-American population, numerically in decline.[2]

*Young, Robert J. 1989. "What Kinds of Immigrants Have Come to the Philadelphia Area, Where Did They Settle and How are They Doing?" A version of this paper was presented at the conference, *"Who Are These Strangers Among Us?"; Recent Immigration to the Delaware Valley*. Sponsored by The Balch Institute for Ethnic Studies and The Nationalities Service Center of Philadelphia, PA.

Only in isolated Japanese-American enclaves on the West Coast, in San Francisco or the territory of Hawaii, was the situation different.

I note these historical details not only because, as an historian, I recognize the value of reflecting on the historical experiences of immigrant communities to understand how we and they interpret their presence, but because I wish to emphasize the Asian-American immigrant experiences in the Delaware Valley in the post-1965 period. I leave it to others to discuss the equally important experiences of other recent arrivals, largely of European origins, who are making their contributions to our society. Certainly a significant Greek immigration which crested in the 1970s, successive and continuing waves of Russian-Jewish immigrants and the more recent phenomenon of renewed Irish migration, are all significant developments in the increasingly complex ethnic mix in the Delaware Valley. However, I have chosen to center my attention on the Asian immigrant populations not only because of my on-going relationship with several Asian communities in both official and unofficial capacities but because they represent a particularly unique experience in the recent history of immigration in the Delaware Valley. Moreover, since, unlike the aforementioned ethnic groups, they did not arrive to find established religious, education, or cultural institutions ready to welcome them, they have gone through the immigrant experience without the initial assistance, mentors, and expertise often available to these others.

A new era of massive immigration was ushered in when the National Origins immigration legislation was replaced by the Immigration Act of 1965. Not even the most farseeing national legislators anticipated the dramatic demographic changes that would result and the inherently positive impact this would have on American society. Responding largely to issues of social justice, in an era that turned its back on racism, the framers of the 1965 legislation created an immigration policy that rejected national origins as a criterion, fostered reunification of families, and allowed special consideration for the highly skilled. Only belatedly did it become apparent that this legislation, which was undoing historic bias that had largely blocked Asian immigration, was simultaneously creating an elitist migration that would, within a decade, establish a significant Asian-American presence in or around every major city in the United States.[3] Asian communities never before represented in U.S. society, as well as those which had been previously present but not widely distributed, grew suddenly and dynamically. Obviously, a new era in the history of Asian-Americans had begun not only at the national level but in the Delaware Valley. It was the beginning of an era both unprecedented and dramatic in its implications!

In virtually all instances those Asian immigrants who arrived after 1965 found themselves on new ground without established social, religious, or cultural institutions that older established European immigrant communities had long since developed. In other instances newly arrived Asian immigrants found remnants of earlier Asian-American communities and their institutions more American than Asian. Often a gap of thirty of forty years between immigration experiences created tensions as new met old. Philadelphia, much like other American cities with small but established Asian-American communities, experienced some of this. Anyone familiar with the politics and concerns of Philadelphia's Chinatown could quickly list numerous instances in which new arrivals and older residents differ sharply over issues of land usage, commercial development, or the direction of cultural institutions. Such differences were to be expected not only because of "turf" issues but because of the size and diversity of the arriving immigrant flow.

The first great surge of Asian immigration, which followed the implementation of the Immigration Act of 1965, had special characteristics that dominated the picture of arriving Asian immigrants nationally and locally for much of the next decade. These special characteristics were a result of several factors not least of all a critical shortage of medical personnel, at the regional and national level, which generated a need for nurses and doctors. Additionally, since the Immigration Act of 1965 included a provision that gave preference to immigrants with critical skills there was little impediment and often numerous incentives for Asian professionals to migrate. These arrivals were clearly an elite in terms of education and professional backgrounds.[4] Largely college-educated, with disproportionate numbers of doctors and engineers among them, they found little difficulty in establishing themselves. Almost overnight, Asian-Indian, Chinese, Korean, and Filipino professional communities emerged where none had really existed before. Initially in Philadelphia, as at the national level, the new arrivals clustered around the academic institutions, hospitals, and research centers, which either provided employment or opportunities for "recredentialing"—a significant problem in the various medical fields. Only briefly clustered around the University of Pennsylvania, Drexel Institute, Einstein Northern Division, and Temple University, they soon departed for the suburbs to enjoy the upper-middle class lifestyle which their education and incomes made possible. By and large this "First Wave" did not cluster in the city or suburbs; they initially created few cultural institutions and quickly got on with the task of enjoying the American dream in every economic sense of the word. Dispersed to the close suburbs in Bucks, Delaware, and Montgomery counties and South Jersey, their regular contact with ethnic communities was often the Saturday trip to the ethnic grocery store and Sunday visits with friends. Widely scattered and economically integrated, they formed no recognizable or distinguishable ethnic concentrations. With both husband and wife typically employed in professional level jobs, the new arrivals had relatively easy access to society in the work-a-day world. Placing absolutely no pressure on community resources or social services, the First Wave passed into the mainstream without serious difficulties and barely noticed. Not only were they an unmitigated blessing in terms of skills and as taxpayers but a virtual reverse foreign aid program. As noted by one distinguished Asian ambassador,[5] the thousands of fully trained doctors and engineers emigrating the the U.S. in the 1960s and 1970s represented a massive pool of skills on which the U.S. economy came to depend as did its medical and public health facilities.

As the Immigration Act of 1965 was fully implemented between 1965 and 1968, the size and composition of all Asian immigrant communities grew nationally as they did in the Delaware Valley. The entire 10,000 per nation special visa quota was utilized by China, India, Korea, and the Philippines by the mid-1970s. Fueled by the national doctors' shortage and an equally significant shortage of engineers, this elitist flow continued to the point that in the Delaware Valley as well as in numerous areas across the country every hospital emergency room and all colleges teaching engineering had become dependent on the immigrant flow. By

1975 it was also apparent that the earlier arrivals, many of whom had intentions to return after their U.S. experience, were making a decision to stay and were deeply involved in the process of raising families. It is at about this time, and at least partially in response to the Bicentennial Celebration, that numerous ethnic groups consciously began to ponder the issue of being a "hyphenated" American and the task of raising their children as Asian-Americans. An enormous number of ethnic cultural and educational efforts emerged at this point in all Asian immigrant communities in the Philadelphia area.[6]

Subtle changes in patterns of immigration were beginning to occur as this First Wave began the process of establishing educational, cultural, and religious institutions. The First Wave, as they became citizens, became significant sponsors of relatives in keeping with immigration statues that encouraged reunification of families. In essence a point had been reached that allowed for immigration patterns familiar in past U.S. history—family members bringing family members. This "Second Wave," still very much an elite in terms of past U.S. immigration patterns, was made up almost entirely of high school and college-educated individuals[7] who either settled into white collar jobs of a clerical nature or business in instances where language skills stood in the way of lateral moves. It is this Second Wave that was responsible for the sudden growth nationally of ethnically identifiable neighborhoods in major cities such as New York's Queens or Los Angeles' "Korea Town." Although nothing equivalent developed in the Philadelphia area, several Asian ethnic clusters began to emerge and widely distributed business activities became observable. In West Philadelphia the cluster of food, clothing, and service-related shops and restaurants on or adjacent to 41st and Walnut, which represent a growing Asian-Indian presence, a hub of Korean activity in Logan on and adjacent to Broad Street, which provided the usual ethnic grocery-restaurant mix but also a network of banking and business facilities and most notable, the rapid expansion of Chinatown, were signs of change. An even more significant presence was manifested in the neighborhoods of Philadelphia, Center City, and in the older suburbs as Asian merchants—especially Korean—made significant investments in "Mom and Pop" type businesses, the ubiquitous fruit stands of Center City and various services, especially dry cleaning establishments. Intent upon a future in business, many of these capital-short, college-educated merchants seized the opportunities at the bottom and moved rapidly to fill gaps in the neighborhoods left by the departure of an earlier generation of shopkeepers, largely immigrants or the children of immigrants. In many instances this resulted in linkages with traditional business communities anxious to retire from the city. The speed with which the transition to Korean ownership occurred in some areas of the city is attributable also to a growing recognition that old and new immigrants shared certain common values, which led each to seek out the other. In Logan, the West Girard Avenue business area, the Columbia Avenue district, and many others, retiring Jewish businessmen sought out Korean merchants through informal contacts. There was also a parallel development that was having equally important implications. Although it has been little referred to by those studying Asian immigration in the 1970s, the arrival of prosperous and even wealthy immigrants who took advantage of the possibilities to do business was a significant development. Special legislation in the Immigration Act of 1965 had allowed foreign investors able to prove assets of at least $40,000 and an immigrant visa. Traditional business communities in India, Hong Kong, and the Philippines reacted immediately! Massive investments were made in real estate and banking. Even as the investment capital requirement was raised from $40,000 to $250,000, this visa category was fully utilized. Even more important, it represented an entree for future growth of dynamic business communities able to function at a regional or even national level. The much commented upon "motel Patels"[8] were only one of the most observable of many such traditional business communities to have emerged during this period as both a national and regional phenomenon.

Collectively the First Wave and Second Wave shifted traditional centers of Asian-American influence ever eastward. In the process, cities such as New York and Chicago became centers of the so-called "New Immigration" while the Delaware Valley shared in this development. As the First Wave subsided when the doctor and engineer shortages ended in the mid-1970s, a significant change occurred as the Second Wave, with its entrepreneurial and white-collar elements, came to dominate the flow. Another observable change at this point was a shift in the age composition of all of the Asian-American communities as earlier elements aged and elderly dependents arrived to join immigrant adult children. In the process, the rate of immigration did not slacken but surged. By the end of the 1970s the four Asian countries responsible for most Asian immigrants (China, India, Korea, and the Philippines) were utilizing the entire 20,000 visas[9] allotted to each state, with some being represented by thousands more on the basis of skills that resulted in special preference visas.

It is during the 1970s that this Second Wave played a significant role in the creation of ethnic neighborhoods in many American cities. Although, for a variety of reasons, this phenomenon is not well represented in Philadelphia, the ethnic clusters referred to earlier were lesser examples of this pattern. The huge stock of affordable housing in the Delaware Valley and accessibility to the automobile are certainly part of the reason why clustering was less practical or necessary. However, an equally important element is the rapid social mobility of virtually all the Asian immigrant communities in the Philadelphia area. The 1970s and, even more so, the 1980s saw rapid movement to better areas within the city and, for many, outside the city. By the late 1970s the Northeast section of Philadelphia was a major magnet for inner-city moves as was the Olney area. Older inner suburbs such as Cheltenham and Upper Darby, as well as areas in Lower Bucks county, received significant numbers of relocating Asian immigrants. All Asian immigrant communities shared in this restructuring.

Political events in Vietnam in 1975 radically changed the mix of Asian immigration to the United States and Philadelphia as the initial surge of hundreds of thousands of refugees from Southeast Asia joined the immigrant stream. Unlike groups that had preceded them, and traumatized by war and flight, they arrived destitute and remained subject to the whims of relocation agencies. The proximity of Philadelphia to Indiantown Gap Resettlement Camp made the Delaware Valley one of the major receiving areas for Vietnamese refugees. Despite an inhospitable climate and limited employment opportunities at the time, Philadelphia became and remained a major resettlement center.[10] Throughout the period 1975–1981 the area received tens of thousands of refugees. And even after 1981 there has been a steady, although lesser flow, which includes a significant but undocumented number of "internal migrants" drawn by the potential for entry level jobs.

The 1975 arrivals, impoverished to the extreme—but eminently middle-class in skills and education—were poured into decaying areas of West, North, and South Philadelphia by various resettlement agencies. Lacking English-language skills and with few job related skills, they competed with other minorities in deteriorating areas of the city that faced economic decline and rising rates of unemployment. Traumatized by multiple problems of adaptation and sudden downward mobility, large numbers of these refugees suffered something close to communal depression.[11] Probably the greatest burden, however, was the absence of mentors to "translate" the society to the newcomers and complete absence of familiar institutions. Throughout the remainder of the 1970s and 1980s, the continual arrival of ever more refugees, often not as well educated or resourceful,[12] compounded the problems of earlier arrivals.

The particularly heavy renewed influx of refugees from Southeast Asia, between 1979 and 1981, also tended to leave the earliest arrivals very much to their own resources. Having been involved in resettlement efforts in those days, I remember vividly the poor living conditions of recent arrivals, the constant pressures of adjustment, destabilization of family life, and the almost frenetic movement and relocation of people within the city, the state, and the country as the new arrivals sought better conditions and family reunification. I also well remember the terrible realities that many faced after the meager resettlement allowance and the first month's advance on rent ran out.[13] But what I remember most was the ill-advised policy of dispersing the refugees throughout the Delaware Valley just as an informal national policy advocated distribution of that population throughout the nation.[14] In each case these policies delayed the stabilization of the refugee population, which regrouped anyway in the next few years. For Philadelphia the regroupment lead to Vietnamese clusters in the vicinity of St. Francis de Sales parish in West Philadelphia, which increasingly functioned as a center for educational and cultural activities. For many Vietnamese, large numbers of whom were Catholic, the presence of a Vietnamese priest at a parish such as this, or the existence of a neighborhood parochial school, served as an initial linkage to the larger society and a base of support.[15]

The continuing influx of Southeast Asian refugees from Vietnam, Cambodia, and Laos into West Philadelphia and South Philadelphia eventually created the largest identifiable Asian clusters, which took place along side the Korean enclave in Logan and Chinatown as the closest Philadelphia examples of Asian ethnic neighborhoods. However, even these enclaves showed few signs of permanence and may yet be but passing phenomena unless there are sudden infusions of new arrivals. As I will note a bit later most of these concentrations of Asian ethnic populations that developed between 1975 and 1985 are showing significant signs of mobility, which may challenge their existence, with the one notable exception of Chinatown.

As this discussion has implied, the story of recent Asian immigration to the United States and the Delaware Valley is complex and subject to numerous variables. Even in providing this brief historical background, it is obvious that it is important to note not only which state the immigrant came from but also when he came, and under what conditions. As we are now almost 25 years removed from the initial change in immigration law that resulted in the dynamic growth of Asian immigrant communities, we must begin to consider "generations" in each community based on chronological age and years of residence in the United States. To discuss where these immigrants settled and how they are doing, I must consider "generations" as one of the most important of many significant elements. In each Asian immigrant community resident in the Philadelphia area, there are obvious, if not yet documented, signs of upward mobility in terms of housing, income, and, in virtually all groups, education. If we are to go beyond generalizations to specifics, it is important to note which immigrant community we are discussing and when they arrived as well as under which conditions they arrived. The experiences of the Vietnamese refugee population are notably different from those of the Asian-Indian. The younger brothers and sisters of Asian professionals who came in the First Wave, and constitute the Second Wave, also have significant differences in their experience. Likewise even if the refugee populations there are notable differences in the experiences depending on whether one arrived in 1975, 1980, or recently.

Although it will take the national census in 1990 to document many of the observations I am about to make about the Asian immigrant communities in the Delaware Valley, I have no doubt about the outcome. I am sure that the 1990 census will show an extraordinarily local success story even more graphic than my experiential observations and very much in accord with national patterns among Asian immigrants. Even though the numbers of Asian immigrants involved in the Philadelphia area are dwarfed by those in Los Angeles, New York, and Chicago, I am sure that the overall results are at least as positive and in some instances better here.

Perhaps the easiest group to deal with is the First Wave. They arrived as an elite to fill well compensated jobs at a time when the United States and the region enjoyed full employment. Largely affluent suburbanites, clustered in the near suburbs, and favoring locations such as Cherry Hill, Cheltenham, Lower Merion, and areas in Delaware, Chester, and Bucks counties, are almost universally homeowners with children who were born or at least raised in the United States. These groups, regardless of national origins, are characterized by their emphasis on quality education for their children and often disproportionate expenditures on the same. Now pretty much the older generation in every sense of the word, they tend to be the office-holders in the numerous cultural, religious, and educational organizations that each national group created. Secure in their professions, affluent, and long resident in the United States, their greatest collective concern seems to be the on-going adjustment to being the parents of children growing up in two cultures. In the last few years many of these have also had to accept the unexpected and often unplanned for arrival of elderly relatives who lack the language or social skills to adjust to living in the United States. Although this problem may sound like merely a variation on the growing problem of elder care in America, it has complex elements especially if the grandchildren at home no longer speak the mother tongue or traditional expectations for care of a parent are impossible. Remember that none of the Asian immigrant communities accept nursing homes as an answer. Often the result is an elderly parent spending long hours in isolation at home. As these communities age, this is an obvious emerging problem.

If there is a "sameness" to the experience of the First Wave, there is a notable diversity to the experience of the Second Wave. One of the most notable variables was the level of English language skills acquired prior to arrival. Arrivals from India and the Philippines, by and large, had these and found it relatively easy to enter white collar occupations. Large numbers of Koreans, who represented the fastest growing Asian immigrant community in the Delaware Valley,[16] did not. Problems with English largely explain why the Korean community, despite an overwhelmingly college-educated population, moved into retail sales. Once again this was both a regional and a national phenomenon. Moreover, arriving at a time when numerous small business properties were available due to retirement or abandonment, this was an opportunity available for a limited capital outlay. The Korean version of the Horatio Alger story, which saw progression from sidewalk fruitstand to inner city "Mom and Pop" grocery store to wholesaler/distributor or suburban storeowner, was played out hundreds of times in the 1970s and 1980s in the Philadelphia area. As the Korean immigrant population increased there was almost no inner city neighborhood without a Korean "Mom and Pop" grocery store. Columbia Avenue, Girard Avenue, North Broad Street, and, eventually, areas in West and South Philadelphia were blanketed by the increasingly obvious examples of Korean entrepreneurship. By the end of the 1970s this became a suburban phenomenon as well—with clusters of Korean-owned shops radiating out from the city along Lancaster Pike and in aging shopping areas in the older suburban communities of Delaware, Montgomery, and Bucks counties. Most of these businesses had in common long hours and labor intensive activities often requiring total family involvement. The typical Korean-owned business is a six-day-a-week job. Korean businessmen's associations, which only formed in the 1970s, soon boasted thousands of members.[17] Most recent estimates are that there are over 5,000 Korean-owned businesses in the Delaware Valley. Over 2,000 of these are in the suburbs, while approximately 3,000 are in Philadelphia.[18] This continued increase in Korean-owned business in the Delaware Valley since 1980 shows no sign of diminishing. The fact that virtually all these businessmen either own businesses or are acquiring them, where virtually none existed as recently as twenty years ago, says volumes about how they are doing economically.

Upward mobility in economic terms has also translated into residential mobility. Residential enclaves such as those adjacent to 4600–4800 North Broad Street are rapidly giving way to new enclaves in better neighborhoods in Olney, the far Northeast, Cheltenham, and Upper Darby. I foresee the possibility that, before long, that area will remain only as a center for business activities and social organizations even though there is a continuing stream of new arrivals. The near future will show a growing trend of Koreans commuting to their stores from city neighborhoods perceived to be safer or from nearby suburbs. Above all, the shift to the suburbs will be influenced by the quality of schools. As one educator in Delaware county told me, "Koreans choose schools, not neighborhoods."[19] The shift to the suburbs is so pronounced that several realtors in Delaware County now engage a Korean salesman for properties in the 69th Street business area and the adjacent residential area because of the recent influx of Korean businessmen either leaving homes in Philadelphia or leaving Philadelphia entirely. The same pressures also explain selective hiring of Asian-Indian salesmen.

The shift to the suburbs, which we noted as a growing movement among Korean immigrants, is also apparent in each of the other Asian immigrant communities. An older, inner suburb such as Upper Darby—an historic stepping-stone out of the city for earlier immigrant groups—appears to be functioning in much the same way for the newest arrivals. It is in areas like this that we are seeing the development of Pan-Asian enclaves adjacent to existing European immigrant communities, which have also expanded since 1965. The basic attraction is affordable housing in safe neighborhoods with viable public school systems. In neighborhoods such as Millborne and Upper Darby the Second Wave flows together with significant elements of the refugee population that arrived in the period shortly after 1975. The most graphic illustration of this trend can be gleaned from, among other things, school records in Upper Darby and adjacent areas. A particularly dramatic example of this trend is offered by enrollment figures at the Upper Darby Middle School, which has historically received the bulk of school-aged immigrant children or the children of immigrants.[20] Between 1982 and 1985 the Asian-American population increased from 5.0 percent to 8.1 percent. In 1986 it increased to 12.4 percent. In 1988 the figure reached 14.9 percent. This school, which has foreign-born students representing thirty-four countries, has thirty-two students born in Vietnam, twenty-two from Korea, eighteen from India, and twelve from Cambodia as its four largest Asian groups. What is interesting, although it is too recent a statistic to be able to evaluate, is the slight drop in Asian-American representation in 1989 to 12.1 percent. An interesting observation, which came through in interviews, may eventually explain this. It was observed that earlier arrivals—especially Koreans—are now able to afford the larger homes and more expensive real estate further out. Broomall has become the destination for many Koreans these last two years, while others, especially Vietnamese, are shifting to more affluent areas of Upper Darby such as Drexel Hill, where they are often attracted by the large homes, which provide room for extended-family living. A possible additional factor may be the rapid increase in formerly low-cost housing prices in Upper Darby since 1986, which has largely resulted in Asian-American demand. These pressures may in the short run delay the suburban move for some and encourage yet further the parallel trend, especially among more recent refugees from Southeast Asia, to acquire homes within Philadelphia adjacent to declining ethnic neighborhoods in Southwest and South Philadelphia or along Roosevelt Boulevard. The rapid development of a Vietnamese enclave in Southwest Philadelphia during the last three or four years and Vietnamese and Cambodian enclaves in South Philadelphia and the lower Northeast, is paralleled by movements of all Asian immigrant groups who have the means into the Oxford Circle area or the far Northeast. Areas in Northeast Philadelphia have become almost the equivalent of a move to older suburbs for middle-income groups in the Second Wave and refugee populations.

Despite obvious signs of rapid residential mobility each of the groups has created institutions that draw on surrounding communities. The Korean community is probably the most dynamic and visible in this regard because its businessmen's, cultural, and religious organizations are present almost everywhere in the

Delaware Valley. More than a dozen Korean Protestant churches in Philadelphia and congregations in Bucks and Delaware counties are the most obvious and visible manifestations of new permanent institutional structures.[21] Korean businessmen organized along lines of specialization are equally important as a source of community mobilization.[22] Less visible are the signs of cooperation with existing institutions, which for inner-city Asian immigrants who are Catholic often take the form of ties to the local parishes. Many of these such as Holy Child in North Philadelphia, Holy Redeemer in Chinatown, St. Francis de Sales in West Philadelphia, or St. Alice's in Delaware county offer services in regional or national languages, at regular intervals, some utilizing clergy from Asian communities. Recently arrived priests from Korea and India, together with established Vietnamese clergy, represent a return to a pattern of the past when immigrant clergy followed immigrant congregations to the new country.[23]

In the midst of this glowing picture of upward mobility on the part of recent Asian immigrant and refugee populations, we must pause to acknowledge that even the most successful populations have problems and difficulties. The tensions that arise in families caught between cultures,[24] the pressure on children to excel, racial incidents, and, in many if not most cases, the six-day-a-week or two-career pattern all take a toll. It is also necessary to consider those who are not part of this pattern of upward mobility. The presence of special programs at University City High, Furness High, and at South Philadelphia High School, to encourage Asian students to stay in school and avoid drugs says something about other realities.[25] Those refugees who arrived without literacy skills in their own language and no English language skills have often languished on the bottom rungs of the ladder of success. Groups such as the Hmong, as well as large numbers of formerly rural Cambodians and Laotians, are faced by serious continuing problems of adaptation, while their younger generation is often deeply influenced by sometimes negative peer pressures from the surrounding American environment. There is also the growing concern in all the Asian communities that the public schools do not treat their cultures adequately or sympathetically, which often results in racist stereotyping bred from ignorance.[26]

In all Asian-American immigrant and refugee communities the maturation of an American-born generation is a major concern as parent-child relations and issues such as marriage often create tension-filled interludes.[27] Although it may seem to be appropriate to say that these and all the other problems noted were also faced by most earlier immigrant populations, this does not make the present experience less difficult for those experiencing the pressures now.

What is the future of Asian migration to and the growing complexity of Asian-American populations in the Delaware Valley? First, and most apparent, is the fact that a critical mass has emerged. Each of the Asian refugee and immigrant populations in the area has sunk roots, established citizenship, and now serves as a base for future immigration into the area. We can assume the Chinese, Indian, Korean, and Filipino populations will continue to grow at rates approaching the national levels, with larger proportions of those representing the attributes of the Second Wave. Each of these Asian ethnic populations will probably show fewer signs of elitism in terms of earning power and education as the principle of family reunification, as enshrined in the Immigration Act of 1965, becomes dominant.

Given the labor shortage in the Delaware Valley and the continuing need for entry level employees in the service and business industries, there will be plenty of opportunities for these—especially as the second generation provides linkages and expanded opportunities. The fact that the Delaware Valley is already attracting significant numbers of internal migrants of Southeast Asian origins testifies to a growing recognition of these local possibilities.[28]

When speaking of Southeast Asian communities we should also note the future possibility of renewed massive immigration from Vietnam under the Orderly Departure Program (O.D.P.). Although the recent closing of refugee camps in Thailand has probably brought to an end significant emigration of Cambodians and Laotians, the O.D.P. flow from Vietnam shows not only no sign of ending but real possibilities for sudden expansion. Although so far the number of arrivals in the Delaware Valley has been largely limited to Amer-Asians and their families, recent improvements in U.S.-Vietnam relations show signs that a rapid expansion of the O.D.P. may be in the offing—and at a time when budget cutbacks have stripped refugee resettlement programs of adequate funding.[29] As American officials began to interview freed political prisoners in Ho Chi Minh City on October 5, 1989 in preparation for the departure of the first 3,000 for the United States, it was revealed that "another 100,000 former prisoners and their families have requested entry into the United States."[30] Since it is estimated that these refugees, for which the U.S. government acknowledges a responsibility, totals over 500,000, it can be assumed that the Vietnamese community in the Delaware Valley will soon experience yet another wave of new arrivals.

As we look to the future then, we can clearly see that the Asian-American presence in the Delaware Valley is well established and growing. I anticipate that the 1990 Census will show growth rates that have more than doubled the size of each of the Asian-American ethnic populations since 1980[31]—a trend that will most certainly continue through the 1990s. Along with these developments it is to be anticipated that these ethnic groups, whether individually or at times collectively, will function as ethnic groups that have preceded them. One should expect political mobilization to meet group goals as an increasingly obvious Americanization process proceeds alongside the development of a critical mass of political leadership talents. The recent rash of publicized concerns[32] of Asian ethnics and Asian-Americans with regard to schools and police, among others, are to be viewed as the beginning of a greater and more complete community involvement, which represents the maturation of an immigrant experience.

NOTES

1.   In most areas of California and the Pacific Northwest the sizable Asian-Indian population virtually disappeared during the first half of the twentieth century due to restrictive immigration legislation, which denied resident males marriage partners of their own community. By the mid-1950s virtually the only legacy of that migration was an aged Asian-Indian community, cantered in the Imperial Valley, intermarried with Mexican women.

2.   In the Philadelphia area, the pattern often saw Chinese male populations remaining unmarried or producing children who were absorbed into the Afro-American community.

3. "Suburbs Absorb More Immigrants, Mostly the Educated and Affluent," *New York Times*, December 14, 1986.

4. The economic implications of the census data for 1980 showed the four largest Asian immigrant populations (Asian-Indian, Chinese, Filipino, and Korean) with family incomes above the national median. "We, the Asian and Pacific Islander Americans." U.S. Department of Commerce, Bureau of Census, 1988, p. 9.

5. Calculated on the basis of an estimated expenditure of $250,000 necessary to train a physician in the United States, the 2,000 plus annual flow of Asian Indian doctors in the early 1970s—to say nothing of the additional thousands of engineers—represented an "Aid Package" worth hundreds of millions. Address by Ambassador Nayar, Republic of India, in a speech to the Kerala Association, Philadelphia, PA, October 1984.

6. The Bicentennial celebrations acted as a catalyst for not only the first formal contacts between Philadelphia's administration and several newly established Asian-American organizations but also the beginning of several organizations locally and nationally began the process of political mobilization of immigrant populations. A notable example was the Association of Indians in America, which lobbied successfully for a new category in the 1980s Census—Asian-Indian.

7. "We, The Asian and Pacific Islander Americans," U.S. Department of Commerce, Bureau of Census, 1988, p. 6.

8. The reference is to a traditional business community, originally from Gujarat State in India and now widely represented in the motel business and in Seven-Eleven store franchises throughout the eastern and western United States. They are also a significant business community in East Africa and the Carribean.

9. These same four Asian nationalities also rank in the top four positions for Delaware Valley immigrants. *American Demographics*, cited in the *Philadelphia Inquirer*. August 4, 1988.

10. Through the 1980s the Philadelphia area, which ranks sixteenth in total number of arriving immigrants, ranks eight in terms of refugee resettlement. *Refugee Reports*, July 28, 1989.

11. The initial refugee flow in 1975 and 1976 was largely Vietnamese elites but included increasing percentages of Cambodians and Laotians by 1977. The elite nature of the Vietnamese flow is corroborated by the 1980 Census which noted that 75.1 percent of the adult population twenty-five years and older had a high school education or better. Unfortunately few had an education in English. See "We, the Asian and Pacific Islander Americans," U.S. Department of Commerce, Bureau of the Census, 1988, p. 11.

12. "Who are the Refugees, and Who's Going to Pay?" *The New York Times*, October 15, 1989.

13. The resettlement allowances that were provided by the federal government via resettlement agencies—usually not more that $500 per person—guaranteed poor housing conditions, since these funds barely covered the cost of a security deposit and the first month's rent, even in declining areas of Philadelphia. Many who settled in the suburbs initially had to move into the city.

14. Although in 1975 refugee resettlement was based on the availability of sponsors, it is equally apparent that political and economic considerations eventually resulted in a de facto policy that discouraged refugee concentrations and, in many cases, disallowed refugee movement to perceived islands of security such as California.

This policy of "steering," ill-advised from the beginning, failed almost from its inception.

15. "Facing the Challenge of Asian Immigrants," *Catholic Standard and Times*, October 26, 1989.

16. Both personal interviews and demographic statistics note the substantial increase in the Korean-American community of the Delaware Valley, which community leaders estimate at 50,000 and growing. Interview with Mr. Yoan Kim cited above. Also see footnote 9.

17. If anything small business ownership may be higher in the Delaware Valley than on the West Coast where 30 percent to 40 percent of Korean immigrants are in business. See "The Koreans Big Entry Into Business," *New York Times*, September 24, 1989.

18. From a speech by Mr. Yoan Kim, President, Korean Businessmen's Association of Greater Philadelphia, Aug 10, 1989.

19. For an interview with Dr. Brotsky, Principal, Beverly Hills Middle School, September 15, 1989.

20. Beverly Hills Middle School interview.

21. There is also an interesting overlap with existing Protestant churches in the Delaware Valley, which results in dual congregations—one ethnic and one traditional—sharing facilities. There are at least five such Korean congregations and two Chinese in Delaware County alone. "Churches within Churches Now on the Local Scene," *Press Focus*, October 25, 1989.

22. The comprehensive organization of Korean business organizations, which includes seven subsets—from jewelers' to grocerymen's associations—makes possible communication throughout the Korean-American community via newsletters and publications.

23. Distribution of Asian Catholics throughout the region, however, presents problems of alienation for many new arrivals, especially those with language problems. Nationally and regionally this issue is being discussed. See "Facing the Challenge of Asian Immigrants," *Catholic Standard and Times*, October 26, 1989.

24. "Becoming a Second Generation," *India Abroad*, October 13, 1989.

25. S.E.A.M.A.A.C. Schools Outreach Program.

26. The recently initiated suit by the Asian-American Coalition, charging racism in the public schools of Philadelphia, whether correct or not, is an obvious sign of tensions.

27. "Dating, A Scary Cultural Gap," *India Abroad*, October 13, 1989.

28. From an interview with Mr. Samlien Nol, Executive Director, S.E.A.M.A.A.C. of Philadelphia, May 10, 1989.

29. "Who are the Refugees and Who's Going to Pay," *New York Times*, October 15, 1989.

30. "A New Wave from Vietnam: Out of the Prison Camps," *New York Times*, October 15, 1989.

31. See Appendixes A and B.

32. "Disorganized interpreter system hurts Asian-American, panel says," *The Philadelphia Inquirer*, November 1, 1989.

APPENDIX: ASIAN/PACIFIC
ISLANDERS/1980 PHILADELPHIA REGION

Population All Races	1980 Asian/Pacific Islanders	Percentage	1970 Asian/Pacific Islanders
United States	226,545,805	3,726,440	1.6	1,538,721
Pennsylvania	11,863,895	70,514	0.6	20,081
New Jersey	7,364,823	109,383	1.5	23,333
Maryland	4,216,975	67,949	1.6	17,944
Delaware	594,338	4,627	0.8	1,495

Breakdown by Nationality				
	United States	Pennsylvania	New Jersey	Maryland	Delaware
Chinese	812,178	13,769	23,492	15,037	1,174
Filipino	781,894	9,640	24,470	15,037	1,174
Japanese	716,331	4,422	10,263	4,656	412
Asian Indian	387,223	17,230	30,684	13,788	1,227
Korean	357,393	12,597	13,173	14,783	501
Vietnamese	245,025	8,127	2,846	4,162	171
Hawaiian	172,346	909	579	630	77
Samoan	39,520	87	112	6	5
Guamaian	30,695	164	199	323	45
Other Asians					
Total	183,835	4,569	3,565	2,721	226
Asian	166,377	4,426	3,489	2,660	226
Pacific Islanders	17,005	133	76	58	—

SOURCE: U.S. Census Bureau, Philadelphia Office, August 15, 1986.

11

Ten Years Is a Long Time: A Woman from Rural Peru*

Thomas Kessner and Betty Boyd Caroli

"My mother is a *Quechua* Indian, I am a *chola* [half-breed] but my sons are American and we live in the Bronx. In 1968 we were still in Lima, Peru—my mother worked as a domestic and I had just graduated from high school. Neither of us could speak a word of English and we had never heard of the Bronx. I tell you everything has changed—Lima, New York, and us. Ten years is a long time."

Five hundred years ago, the Inca civilization spread over thousands of miles of South America. An intricate tangle of communications and government, the Inca society was considerably advanced for its times. But further development was abruptly cut short when Pizarro and the Invading Spaniards brought the cross and the flag of Catholic Spain to South America. They also brought the cannon and centuries of Spanish domination. Its power now a memory, its buildings now ruins, the Inca empire today endures only as an untravelled maze, a dynamic of contradictions.

By one set of standards the Inca civilization never attained more than a modest level of development. It does not appear, for example, to have evolved a written alphabet. Yet attesting at least to its engineering genius was the Machu Picchu, that magnificent fortress city on a high mountain ridge, which stood firm for half a millennium. The Incas appear not to have known about the wheel. Nonetheless, their period system formed a perfect wheel, with lines of power and authority radiating out from the capital city, Cuzco, along amazingly distant spokes. From the Inca king at the center out to an inner ring of chieftains, out again to a series of wider command rings, the Incas demonstrated themselves to be highly advanced in their political organization. Facilitating this political network was an equally extensive road network stretching thousands of miles and including suspension bridges and tunnels. Even at the peak of their influence, the Incas lacked fast animals for communication and transport. Ingeniously, however, even here they developed a reasonably successful substitute system, one relying on a system of human relay runners, called *chasquis* who operated at more than eight miles per hour. Each man marked off a mile and a half in the oxygen-poor air of Peru's high altitudes before he passed his load on to a successor. The system worked so well, it is reported, that fish from the coast arrived at the emperor's table within hours, and messages moved along at almost two hundred miles a day.

The Incas' use of fertilizer, especially the nitrogen-rich guana manure, and their knowledge of terracing to prevent soil erosion remain impressive even to

*Kessner, Thomas and Betty Boyd Caroli. 1982. "Ten Years Is a Long Time: A Woman from Rural Peru." Pp. 105–122 in *Today's Immigrants, Their Stories: A New Look at the Newest Americans*. New York: Oxford University Press. Copyright ©1981 by Thomas Kessner and Betty Boyd Caroli. Reprinted by permission of Oxford University Press. Inc.

twentieth-century agronomists. They were able to construct sixty-foot-high walls of locked stone that withstood earthquakes. But ultimately it was the crucial process of making iron that escaped them, leaving them vulnerable to European conquest. The mixture of the two worlds, one advanced and the other less so, is the locked enigma of Inca history.

Pizarro claimed Peru in 1533 and the outmatched Incas saw the end of their empire. But the people and their rich culture lived on. Rosa Marcos Guerro, living in the Bronx with her *Quechua* mother and her American sons, testifies to that. But Rosa's story stretches back, far before her birth, into the intricacies of Spanish colonial policy in the New World.

Sixteenth-century Spanish law attempted to keep families together and races apart by requiring that Spanish men sailing for the Americas secure special permission to leave their households behind. Husbands could begin their journeys only with the approval of their wives and then the separation might not exceed three years. But the sexual imbalance in the overwhelming male immigration (ten men to one woman) and the distances that stretched stays of years into decades led to frequent cohabitation between Spanish men and Indian women. Before bed went baptism, at least a ritual conversion to Catholicism, and this particular step was carefully noted in the records of time. As a result of frequent intermarriages between the races, half the population of twentieth-century Peru is mixed Spanish and Indian. Peruvians call these mixed-blooded people *cholos* to distinguish them from the Spanish *criollos* and the Indian *indigenas*. Today almost everybody is Catholic.

Rosa Marcos Guerro tells how intermarriage affected her life: "I don't really know much about my father. He was Spanish. I know that, but my mother never talks about him. A miner, I think. First, he lost his eyesight in a work accident and then, when I was only a year old, he died. His family, who didn't like the idea of an Indian daughter-in-law, just forgot about us. My mother had to raise us alone—two sisters, two brothers, and me. Really only four because one brother died from pneumonia when he was only two. I am the youngest.

"My mother had many different jobs. First selling fruits and vegetables and then later she worked as a domestic. Without any education—she cannot even write her name—she had to take the worst jobs. She is not stupid. She can do accounts in her head faster than anybody I ever saw. The *Quechuas* have a system of knots, called *quipu*, a way to communicate numbers and messages without writing anything down, but my mother says she doesn't use that. She is just smart.

"We never had much money. I remember when I was a child, I had no toys and so I played with dirt. Made little castles and people—like my sons play in the sand at Coney Island. But dirt is different from sand. You cannot do the same things with it. My dolls were just pieces of cloth I rolled up. Their arms and legs, even their faces, I had to see in my mind.

"One of my mother's jobs for a while was taking care of the rooms where people came to do their laundry and bathing. In La Oroya, where I was born, people didn't have their own bathrooms. That was how it was then—it's probably different now. A dirty job. My mother wanted something better so she went to work for a rich family. As their domestic. When they moved to Lima, they took us all.

"I must have been about ten when we left La Oroya. I know I had already started school. I remember that because boys and girls went to school together there. In Lima we had separate classes. Very proper. When you have money, you can be proper but in La Oroya where everybody seemed so poor, nobody thought so much about things like that.

"In Lima we lived with our godparents—it's a different system in Peru. Godparents aren't just chosen for babies. They are picked for children on many occasions—first haircutting or ear-piercing. Not so much anymore and not in the capital, but in the country it was like that. The richest, most successful are godparents even if they aren't such good friends. That way the children maybe will take on some of the good luck of the godparents. Besides, if anything happens to the real father and mother, the godparents can take over the children.

"It was lucky we went to live with them in Lima. Some of the people I knew had to live in those 'new towns' just outside the city. Circles of huts where country people live. In the last about thirty years—my mother remembers when it began—lots of people have been moving to Lima from the country. Better jobs, they think. Or modern houses. They say they just want to make money to take back to the country. But most of them end up staying. There are lots of clubs—each one has people from a different town—and these are supposed to help people get used to the city. But it's awful living in these 'new towns.' No sewers or telephones or buses. The lucky ones have radios running on batteries, but they don't have electricity. Maybe it's different now. My sister—she still lives in Lima—she says everything's changed. She even has a telephone, but it cost a lot of money. About a hundred dollars. The other things I have—mixer, blender, toaster—she doesn't dream to have.

"In the center city where my godparents lived, everything was much nicer. They were Spanish, you see, and in Peru the best you can be is Spanish. Then *chola* like me. The bottom is like my mother—Indian.

"My godparents treated us pretty well but some of their relatives used to complain that we were spoiled. 'What's that *chola* doing sitting on the sofa?' they used to say. Oh I hated to be called *chola*. It's a bad name—means a person from the country. How do you say? Hick? I tried so hard not to look *chola*. I remember my cheeks were very red and cracked when I first got to Lima. La Oroya is so high in the mountains that it's cold and dry. Of course we didn't have lotions or creams. I hated my red cheeks—like a big sign, they said, *chola*. There are other ways to tell who is *chola*. The people in the capital can tell by how you speak—your accent and how you dress. Everybody tried very hard to look *criollo*.

"For my mother that change was hard. She stopped wearing the *pujeros* [pajamas] and the *panyalon* [shawl] that Indian women wear on the streets. Even tried to talk like the city people. *Quechua* is her language but she never taught it to us. Said she wanted something better for us. That's why she made us go to school and study Spanish. I took commercial subjects—bookkeeping and accounting—but I never liked them. Somehow my mother thought I would. Maybe that's what she wanted to do herself.

"I went to public school but my sisters went to Catholic school with the nuns. They were always getting in trouble. I was a good girl, so I stayed in public school. When I graduated in 1968, I couldn't find a job. A friend of ours, a Japanese girl my sister knew, started talking about New York. Her family had a restaurant in Lima so they weren't poor. But she had gotten into some kind of trouble—wanted to marry a man that her parents didn't like or something like that. I never knew the whole story. In the travel agency where she worked she found out a lot about New York and how to get here.

"You know what I heard about New York? Two things. First: you got paid by the week instead of the month and that sounded so big. In Lima my mother was making fifty dollars a month. Of course she got food and a place to live but I heard that in New York you could make fifty dollars a week. The other thing I heard was that education was free. You could go to school at night and it didn't cost anything. That sounded so good.

"My friend, Kumi, said for me to get money for the ticket and she would take care of the tourist visas. In the travel agency she had learned how to do it. I asked everybody for money—my sister, my mother, my aunt, my godmother. They all gave a little and it was just enough for the ticket.

"But I wasn't worried. We knew a man in Brooklyn. He used to live across the street from Kumi's family in Lima and he said he would help us. We went right to him and he got us an apartment for ninety dollars a month. Jobs were easy to get, too. I remember he took us out the first day and we found two jobs—two jobs for each of us! from 8 A.M. until 4 P.M. I worked in a plastic factory making bottles. Then at 5, I went to another job in a factory making clothes—stayed there until midnight. For each job I got seventy dollars a week. A week! More than I could make in a month in Lima! And I had two jobs! That was really a lot of money and I still don't know what I did with it. A little bit I sent back to my mother, but not much. Ten dollars a few times. I just can't think where it went. Even today I say, 'Where is my money?' I guess I was making so much that it didn't matter.

"In a few months I met my husband and we went to live in the Bronx. It is funny. When I first came to New York I said I would never live in the Bronx. It was the worst. Queens, Brooklyn, Manhattan. They were all right. Not the Bronx. But my husband's family lived there so that's where we went.

"My husband was Puerto Rican. Maybe somebody who wasn't Spanish would think we were the same but it's not true. We both spoke Spanish but his was a very funny kind, not like in Peru. In every way we were different. He was more than six feet tall and I am only five. He was very skinny with almost no chest at all. We Peruvians have big chests, I think because we lived where there was not much air.

"After we were married he went to Vietnam and was killed there just two months after our sons were born. They're twins. We named them Foster—that was my husband's name—and Emanuele—that's for my side. Because my husband was Puerto Rican, my sons are American citizens and I want something special for them. When I came to the United States I was not thinking about my family. It wasn't for them that I left—but for me. I wanted something better for myself and

I found it. But life will be much better for my sons. Here they can go to college. They can do anything they want. I won't push them, but I know their lives will be very good.

"I have never become an American citizen. Most of the rights are mine anyway because my husband was American, but I cannot pass these on to my mother and sister. Now this is a problem. When my husband died, I had to bring my mother here to help. I had already paid for my sister and my brother to come to New York and I found them jobs when they got here. But my mother was still in Peru, and I needed her here to take care of my sons so I could work, too. I didn't have anybody else to help me. Well, it wasn't so hard to bring my mother then, but now everything is much stricter and I don't know what to do. She wants to go back to Lima to visit. My oldest sister still lives there. But, I am afraid that if she goes, she won't get back in. So we hired a lawyer. I paid him $700. He said, 'Rosa, it would be so easy if you would become an American citizen.' He doesn't understand what it means to change citizenship. I feel Peruvian.

"Maybe you are thinking that I want to go back to Peru one day to live but that is not true. When I left, I knew I would never go back and it did not make me sad at all. I would like to see my sister, yes, but only for that I would go back. I like to see things change, and my life here is really changed. Besides, I can't return because of *soroche*. That's a sickness people get in the mountains when they are not used to being up high. Me—I never get it because I grew up in the mountains—but my sons will get it, I know. And it's terrible. Causes vomiting and headaches. So you see, my sons really are American and we can't go back.

"Not all parts of our lives have changed here in New York. We have a mixture—like in religion. My mother is Catholic, a really strong Catholic. She goes to mass every week but she still believes in things that the Catholic Church doesn't like. Sort of magic and part of this carries over into medicine.

"My mother always says not to eat hot foods when you are sick. If you have an operation or an infection, you shouldn't eat fish. I think it's true because when I was little I was very sick. Somebody gave me fish and I got much worse. Then last year my friend has an operation and when she was just ready to come home from the hospital they gave her tuna fish. Yes, and it almost killed her. Things doctors do not know about, my mother teaches me. When I have indigestion, she tells me to drink tea made from oregano or celery leaves. It works much better than any medicine the doctor gave me.

"In Peru only the rich go to doctors. Most people take care of things at home—we have many cures. I use them here. If my sons are really sick, I take them to the best doctor I can find. Not a clinic, but a private doctor. Last year I paid forty dollars for the best eye doctor to look at Foster. But simple things I take care of at home. For colds, I still use my mother's remedy—I make a syrup out of grated onion with sugar dissolved in it.

"Some of the *Quechua* ideas are primitive and we don't use them anymore. Maybe they don't even use them anymore in Peru—at least not in the capital. A long time ago—well, not so long ago because my mother remembers hearing about it—they took the urine of the llama and used it for special baths, like washing your hair. Said it made your hair shiny and healthy. For babies, too. Gave their children baths in llama urine to make them healthy. Of course the llama has many uses—for meat and wool. They even burned the manure for fuel. Maybe they had to find some purpose for the urine and that's how it started. I don't know.

"Another habit they had in the country, but not anymore I think, is the way they made *chicha*. That's a special beer made from corn. Women used to chew the kernels a while and then spit them out into a big pot. Their saliva and the corn would ferment and that made *chicha*. I never drank it made that way but my mother remembers people saying it was good.

"Of course everybody has heard about the cocoa leaves they chew. In the country, but not in the capital, they get three or four ounces—whatever you want. Some people start chewing in the morning and they keep a big ball in their mouths all day. Say it helps them feel better, especially if they are sick or have a toothache. Instead of going to the dentist, they just let the teeth come out when they are ready. Well, I want something better for my sons and I take them to the best dentist every year for a checkup. Whether they have a toothache or not. I don't have much money, but I have enough for that. It is always more than in Peru.

"After my husband died, I had to work and since I didn't know English very well, I got a job as a domestic. Made good money and worked only for people I liked. I kept my apartment—nobody even suggested I should live in.

"Sometimes people ask me if I wasn't tempted to steal things when I worked in those nice apartments but they don't understand my people. For the *Quechuas,* the worst thing you can do is to take something that doesn't belong to you. I remember once I was in a supermarket here in New York and I said the wrong word for corn-on-the-cob. I got it mixed up, and a woman corrected me. Then she said, 'Don't be ashamed. Everybody makes mistakes.' I said, 'I'm not ashamed. My mother taught me the only time I need to be ashamed is if I take something that doesn't belong to me.' I don't think the woman understood.

"I made good money as a domestic but I worried about insurance and what would happen to my sons if I got sick and couldn't work. So I changed to a job in an office—a bank cafeteria. I clean up and help with the salads. They pay me well and I get insurance too. They even pay me for my English classes at New York University. When I first came here, the high schools gave free English lessons but now it costs money. So it's good my company helps. It's really funny in my class. There's an architect from Belgium and an Italian lady–I think they are very rich because they talk about all the places they travel to. But the teacher treats us just the same. That's the way Americans are.

"Another thing I like about Americans is their attitude toward sex. You know when I came to New York, I was almost twenty years old but I did not know where babies came from. I remember when my sister married, I was about fifteen. She started talking to my godmother about sex and they told me to leave the room.

"I don't want that for my sons. When they ask me something, I tell them. Undress in front of them. At first they paid attention. Now they don't even notice. I still don't undress in front of my mother because I have respect for her, but I want my sons to be more open. I hear people talk about going to bed on their first date. I think that is too much. I like change but for me that is too fast change.

"Change is something you have to go along with. You know many Puerto Ricans decide they don't like New York after a while and they want to go back. Well, that's not easy. I hear about it from my husband's family. If you go back to Puerto Rico, they call you *Americano*. If you stay here they call you Puerto Rican. I always say, stay here. Things changed after you went away. You can't stop it. That's just the way it is. A few years means a long time."

Rosa Guerro's immigration to New York City is not unlike that of hundreds of thousands of other women who have abandoned the islands of the Caribbean and the lands of Central and South America to earn more money. Fifty years ago it might have been Rosa's older brother, Miguel, who made the journey first, but now it is more often the women in the family who come. This pattern, more and more pronounced since 1950, reverses a much older tradition, one in which men were the ones to leave their families to enter America's unskilled work force. For some nationalities the disproportionate male ratio occasionally reached 80 or even 90 percent. Further, these men often came to work, not to live—to save up American dollars and return to their native countries to buy land or start small businesses back home.

This large immigration of men depended on an abundance of unskilled jobs, and when New York's employment scene changed, immigration did, too. Jobs that had earlier been wide open to immigrant men became tightly unionized and in some cases, skilled, An applicant needed a recommendation, an acquaintance, and sometimes, even a diploma. Those fortunate enough to follow countryment already here reaped benefits. Italian construction companies looked out for *paesani,* Jewish manufacturers hired Russian Jews as tailors, and Irish camaraderie softened entry for new men from Dublin.

Latin men who came north in the 1960s and 1970s encountered a scene very different from that which European men found in the early part of the twentieth century. Because routes north—from the Caribbean and South America—became well traveled only after the United States cut off the flow across the Atlantic, there were few Colombians and Peruvians in important places in the 1960s and 1970s to smooth the way for others. The American economy had changed too. While the old industrial boom had welcomed brawn and the willingness to lift a shovel, more sophisticated labor requirements were not common. Opportunities still exist at the bottom—for doormen, porters, day laborers—and some Latin men with little education, such as Rosa's brother, Miguel, put on the uniforms and go to work. But earning with one's hands has, in the meanwhile, become less acceptable and South American men get that message.

Those who take manual or service jobs can save enough for a car, perhaps even a house, especially if several members of the family earn. Or if they are like Rosa's brother, who spends reluctantly if at all, they may do even better. "Miguel's going to buy a house," Rosa says with some pride. "He never spends his money. Just saves. Works and saves. For him that is enough. Much better than he would have had in Peru. I know another man from Peru who just bought part of a delicatessen—he saved his money and had all his children working too."

But today for man other Latin men, the climb seems too slow. Taxes, inflation, and higher expectations claim a larger chunk of family income today than they did fifty years ago. The old promise, "Save and you can get ahead quickly," appears more hollow to Latin men (Miguel and a few others, obvious exceptions) than it did to Europeans and Asians in their mass immigration periods.

But for Latin women, the promise still holds. Immigration today draws them out of their native countries as it drew European males fifty years earlier. Some have argued that the difference lies partly in the fact that unionization has not taken so total a hold on "female" occupations, making entry into such occupations far more informal. Others point to changes in mechanization that have put work that once required great muscle power within women's reach. And the definition of women's work has altered, too, with American-born women moving into jobs higher on the ladder, leaving a gap at the bottom to be filled by new arrivals.

Wives and sisters of European immigrants can refuse the worst jobs. Their families have already served apprenticeships and these women wait for something better. Irish young women turn down cleaning jobs to take work as governesses while second- and third-generation Italian women claim secretarial and teaching jobs. An old plot replays itself with different characters. The last to arrive on stage get the least desirable parts and, after 1965, the wings have been full of Latin women. In dark Manhattan lofts, they paste feathers on designer pillows; in Chinatown clothing factories or toy plants in Queens, they work "off the books," if they are illegal or undocumented. Sometimes their employment occurs with the tacit cooperation of law officers, even when their earnings fall below the minimum wage and social security and income taxes, whose benefits will never be claimed, are collected. One priest, familiar with the employment of women in factories, explained: "Of course it happens all the time. Women work. Pay taxes and social security, but most of them don't know how to file for refunds or how to apply for social security benefits. Many of them know little English. A lot of them don't want to call attention to themselves because they're here illegally or somebody in their family is. They're just happy they have a job."

New and broader job opportunities for women make up only half the changed picture. Social conditions have altered, too. Today, women living alone or in groups draw no special attention to themselves as they would have had they come half-a-century ago. Landlords and neighbors accept female tenants. Protective agencies intrude less on their lives, and families do not insist on placing their single daughters with "good" families as live-in help.

Some women take jobs as domestics, but when they do, it is by choice, and if they live in, they maintain their own network of information about such rights as weekends off, bonuses at Christmas, "Don't do windows," and are thereby able to protect themselves better than any law or army of investigators could do. Their negotiating power lies, very plainly, in their scarcity. They do the work that others shun.

No one knows how many Latin women arrive in New York each year because, like their brothers, they have learned about nonlegal entry. Rosa's case is typical—not illegal, but not entirely honest either. In her tourist visa application she promised to visit relatives, and even gave names and addresses. Then she agreed to go back to Lima after a period in the United States not to exceed six months. But her return ticket, offered as proof of her intentions, was cashed in within a week, its proceeds put down as deposit on a Queens apartment. Other women come as students, take jobs, and melt into the city's neighborhoods.

When Rosa packed her bag to leave Lima, she had few national statistics of how much people earned in Peru but she knew how much her mother made and that her friends, just out of high school, were accepting jobs paying less than three dollars a day. Then she heard of New York's very different scale and her mind was made up. Wages, for Rosa, pointed the way to a better life than her mother had had, and work opportunities in Peru for women appeared limited. Single women in their early twenties were most likely to work while they considered marriage and prepared for their first child. But even among this age group, more than half did not work. America seemed much better to Rosa. At fifty dollars a week, who wouldn't work? The contrast appeared striking. In agricultural Peru, unskilled women with little education earned so little that all except the poorest did not bother. And those who took employment the first years of marriage looked forward to the time when they could stop.

In the United States, working had become more and more acceptable for women, both for middle class and blue collar women. The wives of senators and the widows of former presidents of the country saw that their job histories were included in publicity releases. Not only had work lost the stigma for American women that it still carried in Peru, it had become a badge of competence. The constrast in attitudes presented Latin American women with new alternatives, and many of them decided to break out of their restrictive molds and compete for better paying jobs in the north.

When Rosa's plane landed in New York in 1969, she joined these thousands of other women seeking to change their lives; but immigration officials checking arrivals had little to go on in trying to ascertain her real intentions. At large airports, signs above passport control divide international arrivals into categories and the lines behind them are of unequal length. Peruvians at the immigrant gates numbered only about twelve hundred in 1969, a low year for the decade; but almost two-thirds of them were female. Another gate, for "non-immigrant aliens," is usually much busier. Ten times the number of immigrant Peruvians line up here, Rosa among them. Most in this category claim to be on a pleasure trip, generally to one of two places—either Miami, Florida or New York City. No one checks the progress of their visits, but if someone were to do so, he or she would see how little time is passed at the tourist sites of Manhattan and how much at the factories of Queens and Brooklyn. Permanent "temporary visitors" escape detection because they are so many and inspectors assigned to question them so few. Adding to the difficulty is their diversity; among the "non-immigrant" Peruvians who came to the United States in 1969 were businessmen, students, wealthy tourists, and Rosa.

Officially, the Peruvian population in New York at the time Rosa arrived was still very small. Only 3,400 Peruvians registered that year as aliens, but many thousands of others lost themselves in the Spanish sectors of the city. This "melting in" is easy in a metropolitan area such as New York city, where 25 percent of the city speaks Spanish, even easier in some parts of the Bronx that are solidly Spanish speaking.

Ironically, it was this northernmost New York borough that Rosa, who has made the Bronx her home for most of her American sojourn, perceived as the worst when she first arrived. Walking down its streets one is painfully aware of how many are unschooled here and how little each family lives on. There are pockets of welath in such elite areas as the Riverdale section, where such arriviste as former Deputy Mayor Herman Badillo live. But the South Bronx is ravaged by crime and arson, the pocked streets so much turf to competing gangs and drug pushers. One large slum.

But the Spanish flavor extends throughout the city and Rosa could have settled down in any one of its other boroughs, raising her family without learning a word of English. While to the outsider, they are all Spanish, for those inside, there are immense differences between the many Spanish-speaking residents of the barrios of New York. More than two-thirds are Puerto Rican. Another 6 percent are Cuban, and about 300,000 come from other areas of Central and South America, with just a sprinkling from Mexico and the Iberian peninsula. Distinctions often blur between them, except to those most familiar with accents and vocabulary variations.

Julio Rodriguez, a real estate agent in Corona, Queens, tells why he is never fooled: "When I have them fill out forms, many tell me they are Puerto Rican but they are not. I am Puerto Rican and I know our dialect. These people are really Dominicans or other Hispanics trying to pass as Puerto Rican since Puerto Ricans have full rights as American citizens. But people who don't speak Spanish would believe them. They think anyone who speaks Spanish is Puerto Rican. But we are all so different."

Within Spanish-speaking communities in Brooklyn—in the Williamsburg and Crown Heights sections—and in the Inwood section of Manhattan, enclaves of separate Hispanic nationalities have grown. Parts of the old stronghold of the European immigrants on the Lower East Side of Manhattan have turned increasingly Hispanic, along with Washington Heights on the Upper West Side. These Spanish-speaking enclaves do not stop at the city limits but reach out on Long Island to Freeport and Hempstead, up the Hudson to Mount Vernon.

While the total picture remains fluid, one element appears distinct and clear: Spanish women have helped make New York increasingly female. While 51 percent of the nation is female, New York's figure is 53 percent, with every borough except Richmond reporting this percentage or higher. In Rosa's age group, the female preponderance is most marked.

Immigration only partially explains the imbalance. Women also hold an advantage in longevity, outliving their male contemporaries by seven years or so. Among people over fifty-five, women hold a large edge, especially among blacks. (Puerto Ricans offer the one exception, their elderly women evidently preferring the sunshine of their native island.) Only among children under fifteen does New York report more males than females. In every other age group, women hold the edge.

Whatever the current numbers imply, some observers say Latin women will not stay in New York. As soon as their savings books reach a certain goal, they will leave for warmer, more familiar towns, where they grew up, just as European men did in the early twentieth century.

Rosa's observation and objectives refute this view. "I know there are lots of women in New York," she says. "My mother and I notices how our building is mostly women. I guess I won't find another husband here. Probably makes it harder for me to get a job, too. But I'm not worried. I've done okay. Why do I need a husband if I have a job? You know I always got paid in cash when I cleaned for people. Sometimes they gave me food or a dress or something. At Christmas I got a bonus from everybody. If they didn't give me a bonus, I quit. I saved that for the summer—to rent a house in New Jersey on the shore. I even started checking on charter flights to Lima."

As Rosa's sons grew up, they acquired toys unlike those their mother remembers from her childhood. Trains, fire engines, and cowboy hats—an American arsenal. When they were four, she enrolled them in a daycare center with an American teacher who did her job so well that within months the boys began to ridicule their mother's English. Rosa tried to improve her grasp of English by reading the newspaper when she had time and by making a list of unfamiliar words, but she had little opportunity to speak English. Her mother, who came to live with Rosa, did not want to try a new language, and Rosa could not keep up with her sons.

Rosa's feelings about her lack of progress with her new language led her to change jobs, but the position yielded other benefits besides free English classes. Employees in the bank were generous with tips on where to shop and gifts of surplus from the kitchen. They even insisted that she take a cab when she went on errand around the city for them. Rosa observed the clothes and hairstyles of those around her. She imitated them.

She learned fast. Like other immigrants, Hispanic women enroll in language courses, sign up for classes at the community colleges, and join the banks' Christmas clubs. They learn about discount stores but they prefer carrying cast-off shopping bags from Saks or Bergdorf's. These paper status symbols are reused day after day until the corners open up. The women can distinguish one designer signature wallet from another and the fake from the real. They buy the imitation, but they covet the real. Women's liberation and feminist causes hardly touch them. They have little or no interest in the Equal Rights Amendment and Title VII. For them equality is simply the chance to work and collect a check at the end of the week. As long as they have that, New York seems attractive.

Some do not work, preferring the city's welfare system, but Rosa claims that the women from Central and South America who take this route are few. Her old argument still stands strong—at this wage, who wouldn't work? She collects insurance because of her husband's death in Vietnam but welfare is another matter. She angrily defends her Hispanic sisters from the charge that their decision to immigrate was predicated on the availability of welfare payments. She believes most want to work.

"I didn't mind the work. It was kind of an adventure. Even when we went to the Bronx, I kept my job—one job. I bought lots of things. Everybody had lots. A TV set. Some people had two. A lot of women even had washing machines so they could do their clothes at home. I thought laundromats were wonderful—not like those rooms my mother kept in La Oroya so people could wash their things by hand. But my own washing machine in my own kitchen! That was really America!"

Rosa emerges from the mid-Manhattan office building where she works and, raising one index finger, she summons a taxi. In careful English, she gives her destination and then settles back, a used Bergdorf shopping bag beside her, to enjoy the ride. Her hair is cut in a fashionable flip and her makeup reflects the latest style. Occasionally she looks left or right but mostly she keeps her eyes straight ahead. She never looks back.

12

Poverty and Family Structure: The Widening Gap Between Evidence and Public Policy Issues*

William Julius Wilson (with Kathryn Neckerman)

In the early and mid-1960s social scientists such as Kenneth B. Clark, Lee Rainwater, and Daniel Patrick Moynihan discussed in clear and forceful terms the relationship between black poverty and family structure and sounded the alarm even then that the problems of family dissolution among poor blacks were approaching catastrophic proportions.[1] These writers emphasized that the rising rates of broken marriages, out-of-wedlock births, female-headed families, and welfare dependency among poor urban blacks were the products not only of race-specific experiences, but also of structural conditions in the larger society, including economic relations. And they underlined the need to address these problems with programs that would attack structural inequality in American society and thereby, in the words of Moynihan, "bringing the Negro American to full and equal sharing in the responsibilities and rewards of citizenship."[2]

There is a distinct difference in the way the problems of poverty and family structure were viewed in the major studies of the 1960s and the way they are viewed today, however. Unlike the earlier studies, discussions in the current research of the relationship between black family instability and male joblessness have been overshadowed by discussions that link family instability with the

*Wilson, William Julius (with Kathryn Neckerman). 1986. "Poverty and Family Structure: The Widening Gap Between Evidence and Public Policy Issues." Chapter 10 in *Fighting Poverty: What Works and What Doesn't*, edited by Sheldon H. Danziger and Daniel H. Weinberg. Cambridge, MA: Harvard University Press. Copyright © 1986 by the Board of Regents of the University of Wisconsin System. Reprinted by permission of Harvard University Press.

growth of income transfers and in-kind benefits. Because, as we demonstrate in this essay, the factors associated with the rise of single-parent families—not only among blacks, but among whites as well—are sufficiently complex to preclude overemphasis on any single variable, the recent trend among scholars and policy makers to neglect the role of male joblessness while emphasizing the role of welfare is especially questionable. But first let us examine the problem of poverty and family structure in its historical context.

POVERTY AND FAMILY STRUCTURE
IN HISTORICAL PERSPECTIVE

In the early twentieth century the vast majority of both black and white low-income families were intact. Although national information on family structure was not available before the publication of the 1940 census, studies of early manuscript census forms of individual cities and counties make it clear that even among the very poor, a substantial majority of both black and white families were two-parent families. Moreover, most of the women heading families in the late nineteenth and early twentieth centuries were widows. Evidence from the 1940 census indicates that divorce and separation were relatively uncommon. [3]

It is particularly useful to consider black families in historical perspective because social scientists have commonly assumed that the recent trends in black family structure that are of concern in this essay could be traced to the lingering effects of slavery. E. Franklin Frazier's classic statement of this view in *The Negro Family in the United States* informed all subsequent studies of the black family, including the Moynihan report. [4] But recent research has challenged assumptions about the influence of slavery on the character of the black family. Reconstruction of black family patterns from manuscript census forms has shown that the two-parent, nuclear family was the predominant family form in the late nineteenth and early twentieth centuries. Historian Herbert Gutman examined data on black family structure in the northern urban areas of Buffalo and Brooklyn, New York; in the southern cities of Mobile, Alabama, of Richmond, Virginia, and of Charleston, South Carolina; and in several counties and small towns during this period. He found that between 70 percent and 90 percent of black households were "male-present" and that a majority were nuclear families. [5] Similar findings have been reported for Philadelphia, for rural Virginia, for Boston, and for cities of the Ohio Valley. [6] This research demonstrates that neither slavery, nor economic deprivation, nor the migration to urban areas affected black family structure by the first quarter of the twentieth century.

However, the poverty and degraded conditions in which most blacks lived were not without their consequences for the family. For the most part, the positive association between intact family structure and measures of class, such as property ownership, occupation, or literacy, generally reflected the higher rate of mortality among poor men. [7] Widowhood accounted for about three-quarters of female-headed families among blacks, Germans, Irish, and native white Americans in Philadelphia in 1880. [8] In addition, men sometimes had to live apart from their families as they moved from one place in another in search of work. [9] Given their disproportionate concentration among the poor in America, black families were more strongly affected by these conditions and therefore were more likely than white families to be female headed. For example, in Philadelphia in 1880, 25.3 percent of all black families were female headed, compared to only 13.6 percent of all native white families.

The earliest detailed national census information on family structure is available from the 1940 census. In 1940 female-headed families were more prevalent among blacks than among whites, and among urbanites than among rural residents for both groups. Yet, even in urban areas, 72 percent of black families with children under eighteen were male headed. Moreover, irrespective of race and residence, most women heading families were widows.

The two-parent nuclear family remained the predominant type for both blacks and whites up to World War II. As shown in Table 1, 10 percent of white families and 18 percent of black families were female headed in 1940. The relative stability in gross census figures on female-headed families between 1940 and 1960 obscures the beginnings of current trends in family breakup. More specifically, while widowhood fell significantly during those two decades, marital dissolution was rising.[10] Furthermore, the proportion of out-of-wedlock births was growing.

TABLE 1. Percentage of Female-Headed Families, No Husband Present, by Race and Spanish Orgin, 1940–1983

Year	White	Black	Spanish Origin	Total Families
1940	10.1	17.9	—	—
1950	8.5	17.6[a]	—	9.4
1960	8.1	21.7	—	10.0
1965	9.0	24.9	—	10.5
1970	9.1	28.3	—	10.8
1971	9.4	30.6	—	11.5
1972	9.4	31.8	—	11.6
1973	9.6	34.6	16.7	12.2
1974	9.9	34.0	17.4	12.4
1975	10.5	35.3	18.8	13.0
1976	10.8	35.9	20.9	13.3
1977	10.9	37.1	20.0	13.6
1978	11.5	39.2	20.3	14.4
1979	11.6	40.5	19.8	14.6
1980	11.6	40.2	19.2	14.6
1981	11.9	41.7	21.8	15.1
1982	12.4	40.6	22.7	15.4
1983	12.2	41.9	22.8	15.4

Sources: U.S. Bureau of the Census, *Current Population Reports*, series P-20, nos. 153, 218, 233, 246, 258, 276, 291, 311, 326, 340, 352, 366, 371, 381, and 388, "Household and Family Characteristics" (Washington, D.C.: Government Printing Office, 1965, 1970–1984); and idem, *Current Population Reports*, series P-20, nos. 267 and 290 "Persons of Spanish Origins in the United States" (Washington, D.C.: Government Printing Office, 1974 and 1975).

[a] Black and other.

By the 1960s, the proportion of female-headed families had begun to increase significantly among blacks, rising from 22 percent in 1960 to 28 percent in 1970, and then to 42 percent by 1983. This proportion also rose among white families, from 8 percent in 1960 to 12 percent in 1983. The increase in female-headed families with children under eighteen is even more dramatic. By 1983, almost one out of five families with children under eighteen were headed by women, including 14 percent of white families, 24 percent of Spanish-origin families, and 48 percent of black families.[11] To understand the nature of these shifts, it is necessary to disaggregate these statistics and consider factors such as changes in fertility rates, marital status, age structure, and living arrangements.

CHANGING FAMILY STRUCTURE
AND DEMOGRAPHIC CORRELATES

The unprecedented increases in the proportion of births out of wedlock are a major contributor to the rise of female-headed families in the black community. In 1980, 68 percent of births to black women ages fifteen to twenty-four were outside of marriage, compared to 41 percent in 1955. According to 1981 figures, almost 30 percent of all young single black women have borne a child before the age of twenty.[12] The incidence of out-of-wedlock births has risen to unprecedented levels for young white women as well, although both rates and ratios remain far below those for black women (see Table 2).

These increases in births outside of marriage reflect trends in fertility and marital status, as well as changes in population composition. Age-specific fertility rates for both white and black women have fallen since the peak of the baby boom in the late 1950s. Even fertility rates for teenagers (ages fifteen to nineteen) have fallen overall. What these figures obscure, however, is that the fertility rates of young unmarried women have risen or declined only moderately, while those of married women of these ages have fallen more substantially (see Table 2). In addition, growing proportions of young women are single. For instance, the percentage of never-married women increased dramatically between 1960 and 1980, from 29 percent to 47 percent for whites, and from 30 percent to 69 percent for blacks.[13] Recent data show not only that the incidence of premarital conception has increased, but also that the proportion of those premarital pregnancies legitimated by marriage has decreased.[14] Thus, out-of-wedlock births now comprise a far greater proportion of total births than they did in the past, particularly for black women (see Table 2). The black "illegitimacy ratio" has increased so precipitously in recent years not because the rate of extramarital births has substantially increased, but because the percentage of women married and the rate of marital fertility have both declined significantly.

The decline in the proportion of women who are married and living with their husbands is a function of both a sharp rise in separation and divorce rates and the substantial increase in the percentage of never-married women. The combined impact of these trends has been particularly drastic for black women as the proportion married and living with their husbands fell from 52 percent in 1947 to 34 percent in 1980.[15] As set out in Table 3, black women have much higher

TABLE 2. Fertility Rates and Ratios by Race and Age, 1960–1980

Age-group and Year	Fertility Rate		Marital Fertility Rate		Nonmarital Fertility Rate		Illegitimacy Ratio	
	Black	White	Black	White	Black	White	Black	White
Ages 15–19								
1960	158.2	79.4	659.3	513.0	76.5	6.6	421.5	71.6
1965	136.1	60.7	602.4	443.2	75.8	7.9	492.0	114.3
1970	133.4	57.4	522.4	431.8	90.8	10.9	613.5	171.0
1975	106.4	46.4	348.0	311.8	86.3	12.0	747.2	229.0
1980	94.6	44.7	344.0	337.6	83.0	16.0	851.5	329.8
Ages 20–24								
1960	294.2	194.9	361.8	352.5	166.5	18.2	199.6	21.9
1965	247.3	138.8	293.3	270.9	152.6	22.1	229.9	38.4
1970	196.8	145.9	267.6	244.0	120.9	22.5	295.0	51.8
1975	141.0	108.1	192.4	179.6	102.1	15.5	399.5	60.9
1980	145.0	112.4	232.8	198.2	108.2	22.6	560.2	114.9
Ages 25–29								
1960	214.6	252.8	225.0	220.5	171.8	18.2	141.3	11.4
1965	188.1	189.8	188.6	177.3	164.7	24.3	162.8	18.8
1970	140.1	163.4	159.3	164.9	93.7	21.1	180.6	20.7
1975	108.7	108.2	130.8	132.4	73.2	14.8	226.8	26.2
1980	115.5	109.5	149.7[a]	148.4[a]	79.1	17.3	361.7	50.2

SOURCES: National Center for Health Statistics, *Vital Statistics of the United States*, annual volumes 1960–1975 and 1984 (Washington, D.C.: Government Printing Office).

[a] Marital fertility rates for 1980 are unavailble; 1979 figures are substituted.

separation and divorce rates than white women, although the differences are exaggerated because of a higher rate of remarriage among white women.[16] Whereas white women are far more likely to be divorced than separated, black women are more likely to be separated than divorced. Indeed, a startling 22 percent of all married black women are separated from their husbands.[17]

Just as important a factor in the declining proportion of black women who are married and living with their husbands is the increase in the percentage of never-married women. Indeed, as shown in Table 3, the proportion of never-married black women increased from 65 percent in 1960 to 82 percent in 1980 for those ages fourteen to twenty-four and from 8 percent to 21 percent for those ages twenty-five to forty-four. On the other hand, while the proportion of black women who are separated or divorced increased from 22 percent in 1960 to 31 percent in 1980 for those ages twenty-five to forty-four, and from 17 percent to 25 percent for those ages forty-five to sixty-four, the fraction divorced or separated actually fell for younger women.

For young women, both black and white, the increase in the percentage of never-married women largely accounts for the decline in the proportion married with husband present (see Table 3). For black women ages twenty-five to forty-four, increases in both the percentage of never-married women and in marital dis-

TABLE 3. Marital Status of Women by Race and Age, 1947–1980

Age-group and Marital Status	1947 White	1947 Black	1960 White	1960 Black	1970 White	1970 Black	1980 White	1980 Black
Ages 14–24								
Married[a]	33.5	30.9	33.6	25.7	29.6	21.3	26.8[b]	13.1[b]
Never married	62.9	59.5	63.3	65.0	66.4	72.3	68.6	82.4
Separated/divorced/ husband absent	3.3	8.4	3.0	9.0	3.8	6.2	4.5	4.3
Widowed	0.4	1.3	0.1	0.3	0.1	0.1	0.1	0.2
Ages 25–44								
Married	80.3	67.2	85.1	64.9	85.0	62.0	75.5	44.7
Never married	11.5	10.5	6.8	8.2	6.3	12.2	9.8	21.3
Separated/divorced/ husband absent	5.8	14.4	6.3	22.4	7.6	22.2	13.6	30.8
Widowed	2.4	8.0	1.8	4.5	1.2	3.6	1.1	3.2
Ages 45–64								
Married	70.2	57.6	74.1	52.8	73.5	54.1	74.0	46.0
Never married	8.0	5.3	6.4	5.3	5.9	4.7	4.4	6.8
Separated/divorced/ husband absent	5.0	8.3	5.7	16.6	7.3	20.4	9.8	25.4
Widowed	16.8	28.5	13.7	25.3	13.3	20.4	11.8	21.8

SOURCES: U.S. Bureau of the Census, *Current Population Reports*, series P-20, no. 10, "Characteristics of Single, Married, Widowed, and Divorced Persons in 1947" (Washington, D.C.: Government Printing Office, 1948); idem, *Current Population Reports*, series P-20, nos. 153 and 218, "Marital Status and Family Status" (Washington, D.C.: Government Printing Office, 1960 and 1970); idem, *Current Population Reports*, series P-20, no. 365, "Marital Status and Living Arrangements, March 1980" (Washington, D.C.: Government Printing Office, 1981).

[a] Married, husband present.

[b] Includes only ages 15–24.

solution were important; for white women of the same age-group, marital dissolution is the more important factor. Marriage has not declined among white women ages forty-five to sixty-four; however, among black women in the same age-group, the proportion married with husband present has fallen, due mainly to increases in marital dissolution.

Although trends in fertility and marital status are the most important contributors to the rise of female-headed families, the situation has been exacerbated by recent changes in the age structure, which have temporarily increased the proportion of young women in the population, particularly in the black population. Whereas in 1960, only 36 percent of black women ages fifteen to forty-four were between fifteen and twenty-four years of age, by 1975 that proportion had increased to 46 percent; the comparable increase for white women was from 34 percent in 1960 to 42 percent in 1975.[18] These changes in the age structure increase the proportion of births occurring to young women and, given the higher out-of-wedlock birth ratios among young women, inflate the proportion of all births that occur outside of marriage as well.

Finally, the rise in the proportion of female-headed families reflects an increasing tendency for women to form independent households rather than to live in subfamilies. Until recently, Census Bureau coding procedures caused the number of subfamilies to be significantly underestimated;[19] therefore, an accurate time series is impossible. However, other research suggests that women are becoming more likely to form their own households. For example, Cutright's analysis of components of growth in female-headed families between 1940 and 1970 indicates that 36 percent of the increase in numbers of female family heads between the ages of fifteen and forty-four can be attributed to the higher propensity of such women to form their own households.[20] Bane and Ellwood show that these trends continued during the 1970s.[21] In the period 1969 to 1973, 56 percent of white children and 60 percent of black children born into single-parent families lived in households headed by neither mother nor father (most lived with grandparents). During the years 1974 to 1979, those proportions declined to 24 percent for white children and 37 percent for black children.

Thus, young women comprise a greater proportion of single mothers than ever before. For example, while in 1950, only 26 percent of black female family heads and 12 percent of white female family heads were under the age of thirty-five, in 1983 those proportions had risen to 43 percent for blacks and 29 percent for whites. The number of black children growing up in fatherless families increased by 41 percent between 1970 and 1980, and most of this growth has occurred in families in which the *mother has never been married.*[22] This is not surprising, according to Bane and Ellwood's research: whereas the growth of the number of single white mothers over the last decade is mainly due to the increase in separation and divorce, the growth of the number of single black mothers is "driven by a dramatic decrease in marriage and increase in fertility among never-married women."[23] In 1982 the percentage of black children living with both parents had dipped to 43 percent, only roughly half of the proportion of white children in two-parent homes.

As Bane and Ellwood point out, "Never married mothers are more likely than divorced, separated or widowed mothers to be younger and be living at home when they have their children."[24] Younger mothers tend to have less education, less work experience, and thus fewer financial resources. Therefore they are more likely initially to form subfamilies, drawing support from parents and relatives. However, it appears that most children of single mothers in subfamilies spend only a small part of their lives in such families. On the basis of an analysis of data from the Panel Study of Income Dynamics (PSID) for the period 1968 to 1979, Bane and Ellwood suggest that by the time children born into subfamilies reach age six, two-thirds will have moved into different living arrangements. Among blacks, two-thirds of the moves are into independent female-headed families, whereas among whites two-thirds are into two-parent families. However, whether the focus is on subfamilies or on independent female-headed families, less than 10 percent of white children and almost half of the black children born into non-two-parent families remain in such families "for their entire childhood."[25] And, as discussed in the next section, these families are increasingly plagued by poverty.

THE POVERTY STATUS OF FEMALE-HEADED FAMILIES

As emphasized in the previous chapter, the rise of female-headed families has had dire social and economic consequences because these families are far more vulnerable to poverty than are other types of families. Indeed, sex and marital status of the head are the most important determinants of poverty status for families, especially in urban areas. The poverty rate of female-headed families was 36.3 percent in 1982, while the rate for married-couple families was only 7.6 percent. For black and Spanish-origin female-headed families in 1982, poverty rates were 56.2 percent and 55.4 percent respectively.[26]

Female-headed families comprise a growing proportion of the poverty population. Individuals in female-headed families made up fully a third of the poverty population in 1982. Forty-six percent of all poor families and 71 percent of all poor black families were female headed in 1982. These proportions were higher for metropolitan areas, particularly for central cities, where 60 percent of all poor families and 78 percent of all poor black families were headed by women.[27] The proportion of poor black families headed by women increased steadily from 1959 to 1977, from less than 30 percent to 72 percent, and has remained slightly above 70 percent since then. The total number of poor black female-headed families continued to grow between 1977 and 1982, increasing by 373,000; the proportion of the total number of poor black families did not continue to increase only because of the sharp rise in the number of male-headed families in poverty during this period (from 475,000 to 622,000 in 1982). The proportion of poor white families headed by women also increased from less than 20 percent in 1959 to a high of almost 40 percent in 1977, and then dropping to 35 percent in 1983.

Female-headed families are not only more likely to be in poverty, they are also more likely than male-headed families to be persistently poor. For example, Duncan reports, on the basis of data from the Michigan PSID, that 61 percent of those who were persistently poor over a ten-year period were in female-headed families, a proportion far exceeding the prevalence of female-headed families in the general population.[28]

CAUSES OF THE RISE IN FEMALE-HEADED FAMILIES

As the foregoing discussion suggests, to speak of female-headed families and out-of-wedlock births is to emphasize that they have become inextricably tied up with poverty and dependency, often long term. The sharp rise in these two forms of social dislocation is related to the demographic changes in the population that we discussed in the previous section. For example, the drop in the median age of women heading families would lead one to predict a higher rate of poverty among these families, all other things being equal. We only need to consider that young women who have a child out of wedlock, the major contributor to the drop in median age of single mothers, are further disadvantaged by the disruption of their schooling and employment.

However, while a consideration of demographic changes may be important to understand the complex nature and basis of changes in family structure, it is hardly sufficient. Indeed, changes in demographic factors are generally a function of broader economic, political, and social trends. For example, the proportion of out-of-wedlock births has risen among young black women, as a result of a decline in both marriage and marital fertility, coupled with relative stability of out-of-wedlock birth rates (i.e., the number of births per 1,000 unmarried women). This increase in the proportion of extramarital births could be mainly a function of the increasing difficulty of finding a marriage partner with stable employment, or of changes in social values regarding out-of-wedlock births, or of increased economic independence afforded women by the availability of income transfer payments. Broader social and economic forces may also be influencing married women to have fewer children.... In this section we will delineate the role of broader social and economic forces not only on trends in family formation in the inner city, but on national trends in family formation as well. In the process we hope to establish the argument that despite the complex nature of the problem, the weight of existing evidence suggests that the problems of male joblessness could be the single most important factor underlying the rise in unwed mothers among poor black women. Yet, this factor has received scant attention in recent discussions of the decline of intact families among the poor. Let us first examine the contribution of other factors, including social and cultural trends and the growth of income transfers, which in recent years has become perhaps the single most popular explanation of changes in family formation and family structure.

The Role of Changing Social and Cultural Trends

Extramarital fertility among teenagers is of particular significance to the rise of female-headed families. Out-of-wedlock birth rates for teens are generally not falling as they are for older women. Almost 40 percent of all illegitimate births are to women under age twenty.[29] Moreover, adolescent mothers are the most disadvantaged of all female family heads because they are likely to have their schooling interrupted, experience difficulty finding employment, and very rarely receive child support. They are also the most likely to experience future marital instability and disadvantages in the labor market.

Any attempt to explain the social and cultural factors behind the rise of out-of-wedlock teenage fertility must begin with the fact that most teenage pregnancies are reportedly unwanted. Surveys by Zelnik and Kantner have consistently shown that the majority of premarital pregnancies are neither planned nor wanted. In 1979, for instance, 82 percent of premarital pregnancies in fifteen- to nineteen-year-olds (unmarried at the time the pregnancy was resolved) were unwanted.[30]

However, unpublished tabulations from a recent Chicago study of teenage pregnancy indicate that adolescent black mothers reported far fewer pregnancies to be unwanted than did their white counterparts. Moreover, as Dennis Hogan has stated, the Chicago data suggest that "it is not so much that single motherhood is unwanted as it is that it is not sufficiently 'unwanted.' Women of all ages without a strong desire to prevent a birth tend to have limited contraceptive success.[31] This argument would seem especially appropriate to poor inner-city black neighborhoods. In this connection, Kenneth Clark has argued that

In the ghetto, the meaning of the illegitimate child is not ultimate disgrace. There is not the demand for abortion or for surrender of the child that one finds in more privileged communities. In the middle class, the disgrace of illegitimacy is tied to personal and family aspirations. In lower-class families, on the other hand, the girl loses only some of her already limited options by having an illegitimate child; she is not going to make a "better marriage" or improve her economic and social status either way. On the contrary, a child is a symbol of the fact that she is a woman, and she may gain from having something of her own. Nor is the boy who fathers an illegitimate child going to lose, for where is he going? The path to any higher status seems closed to him in any case.[32]

Systematic evidence of expected parenthood prior to first marriage is provided in two studies by Hogan. Drawing upon data collected in a national longitudinal survey of high school students conducted for a National Center for Educational Statistics study (described from here on as the High School and Beyond data), Hogan found that whereas only 1 percent of the white females and 1.4 percent of the white males who were single and childless in 1980 expected to become parents prior to first marriage, 16.5 percent of black females and 21 percent of black males expected parenthood before first marriage. In a follow-up study that focused exclusively on black female adolescents and excluded respondents "who were pregnant or near marriage at the time of the initial interview [1980]," Hogan found that only 8.7 percent expected to become single mothers in 1980, and of these, 19.5 percent actually became unmarried mothers by 1982.[33] On the other hand, of the 91 percent who reported that they *did not* expect to become unmarried mothers, only 7.4 percent gave birth to a child by 1982. Unpublished data from this same study reveal that 20.1 percent of the black girls becoming single mothers by 1982 *expected* to do so in 1980.[34] Thus, although only a small percentage of these adolescent girls expected to become single mothers, those who expressed that view were almost three times as likely to become single mothers as the overwhelming majority who did not.

A number of social structural factors that may influence the development of certain behavior norms may also be directly related to single parenthood. Hogan's research shows that girls from married-couple families and those from households with both mother and grandparent are much less likely to become unwed mothers than those from independent mother-headed households or nonparental homes. The fact that the rate of premarital parenthood of teens who live with both their single mothers and one (usually the grandmother) or more grandparents is as low as that of teens who live in husband-wife families suggests that "the critical effects of one-parent families are not so much attributable to the mother's example of single parenthood as an acceptable status as to the poverty and greater difficulty of parental supervision in one-adult families."[35] Furthermore, Hogan and Kitagawa's analysis of the influences of family background, personal characteristics, and social milieu on the probability of premarital pregnancy among black teenagers in Chicago indicates that those from nonintact families, lower social class, and poor and highly segregated neighborhoods have significantly higher fertility rates. Hogan and Kitagawa estimated that 57 percent of the teenage girls from high-risk social environments (lower class, poor inner-city neighborhood residence, female-headed family, five or more siblings, a sister who is a teenager mother, and loose parental supervision of dating) will become pregnant by age eighteen compared to only 9 percent of the girls from low-risk social backgrounds.[36]

Social structural factors also appear to affect the timing of marriage. Hogan reports that although black teenagers expect to become parents at roughly the same ages as whites, they expect to become married at later ages. Analysis of the High School and Beyond data reveals that when social class is controlled, black adolescents have expected age-specific rates of parenthood that are only 2 percent lower than those of whites, but expected age-specific rates of marriage that are 36 percent lower.[37] While Hogan notes that many whites are delaying marriage and parenthood because of educational or career aspirations, he attributes blacks' expectations of late marriage to the poor "marriage market" black women face. Indeed, available research has demonstrated a direct connection between the early marriage of young people and an encouraging economic situation, advantageous government transfer programs, and a balanced sex ratio.[38] These conditions are not only more likely to apply for young whites than for young blacks, but as we try to show, they have become increasingly problematic for blacks.

This evidence suggests therefore that attitudes and expectations concerning marriage and parenthood are inextricably linked with social structural factors. Since we do not have systematic longitudinal data on the extent to which such attitudes and aspirations have changed in recent years, we can only assume that some changes have indeed occurred and that they are likely to be responses to broader changes in the society. This is not to ignore the import of normative or cultural explanations, rather it is to underline the well-founded sociological generalization that group variations in behavior, norms, and values often reflect variations in group access to channels of privilege and influence. When this connection is overlooked, explanations of problems such as premarital parenthood or female-headed families may focus on the norms and aspirations of individuals, and thereby fail to address the ultimate sources of the problem, such as changes in the structure of opportunities for the disadvantaged.

It is also important to remember that there are broader social and cultural trends in society that affect in varying degrees the behavior of all racial and class groups. For instance, sexual activity is increasingly prevalent among all teenagers. Growing proportions of adolescents have had sexual experience: according to one survey, the proportion of metropolitan teenage women who reported having premarital intercourse increased from 30 percent in 1971 to 50 percent in 1979. These proportions have risen particularly for white adolescents, thereby narrowing the differentials in the incidence of sexual activity. And they have more than offset the increase in contraceptive use over the past decade, resulting in a net increase in premarital pregnancy.[39] Rising rates of sexual activity among middle-class teens may be associated with various social and cultural trends such as the "sexual revolution," the increased availability of birth control and abortion, and perhaps the growing sophistication of American adolescents, or their adoption of adult social behavior at an increasingly early age. While these trends may also have influenced the sexual behavior of teens from disadvantaged backgrounds, it is difficult to assess their effects independent of the complex array of other factors.

Our meager state of knowledge permits us only to say that they probably have some effect, but we do not have even a rough idea as to the degree.

Although our knowledge of the effect of social and cultural trends on the rise of extramarital fertility is scant, we know a little more about the effect of some of these trends on marital dissolution. Multivariate analyses of marital splits suggest that women's labor-force participation and income significantly increase marital dissolution among white women.[40] Labor-force participation rates of white women have nearly doubled from 1940 to 1980 (from 25.6 percent to 49.4 percent), in part due to a decline in marriage and in part to an increase in labor-force participation among married women, particularly those with children. The labor-force participation of black women has also increased, but not as dramatically (from 39.4 percent in 1940 to 53.3 percent in 1980);[41] black women have always worked in greater proportions than white women, a pattern that still holds today for all age-groups except women ages sixteen to twenty-four, an age category with high fertility rates.

Accompanying the increasing labor-force participation of women has been the rise of the feminist movement, which validates work as a source of both independence from men and personal fulfillment, and which has provided practical support not only through legal and political action but also through its role in promoting organizational resources for women in the labor market. Feminism as a social and cultural movement may have directly influenced the marriage decisions of women; it may also have indirectly affected these decisions through its role in womens' more active participation in the labor market. In the absence of systematic empirical data, the effect of the feminist movement on the marital dissolution of women, particularly white women, can only be assumed.

It can be confidently asserted, however, that women's increasing employment makes marital breakup financially more viable than in the past. Although marital dissolution means a substantial loss of income, and sometimes severe economic hardship—median income of white female-headed families in 1979 was $11,452, compared to $21,824 for white married-couple families[42]—most white women can maintain their families above poverty with a combination of earnings and income from other sources such as alimony, child support, public-income transfers, personal wealth, and assistance from families. In 1982, 70 percent of white female-headed families were living above the poverty line.[43] In addition, many white single mothers remarry. For most black women facing marital dissolution, the situation is significantly different, not only because they tend to have fewer resources and are far less likely to remarry, but also because the major reasons for their increasing rates of marital disintegration have little to do with changing social and cultural trends.

The Role of Welfare

A popular explanation for the rise of female-headed families and out-of-wedlock births has been the growth of liberal welfare policies, in particular, broadened eligibility for income transfer programs, increases in benefit levels, and the creation of new programs, such as Medicaid and food stamps. Charles Murray, for example, argues that relaxed restrictions and increasing benefits of AFDC enticed lower-class women to forego marriage or prolong childlessness in order to qualify for increasingly lucrative benefits.[44] Likewise, Robert Gordon depicts "welfare provisions as a major influence in the decline in two-adult households in American cities."[45]

The effect of welfare on out-of-wedlock births and marital instability became even more of an issue after the costs and caseloads of public assistance programs dramatically increased during the late 1960s and early 1970s. Since that time, a good deal of research has addressed this issue. Because all states have AFDC and food stamp programs, there can be no true test of the effects of welfare on family structure: there is no "control" population that has not been exposed to these welfare programs. However, substantial interstate variations in levels of AFDC benefits and in eligibility rules have provided opportunities for researchers to test the effects of program characteristics. Most studies have examined the level of welfare benefits as one of the determinants of a woman's choice between marriage and single parenthood. Some use aggregate data; others use individual-level data; still others examine the effect of providing cash transfers to intact families under special conditions, such as the Income Maintenance Experiments. But whether the focus is on the relationship between welfare and out-of-wedlock births or that between welfare and marital dissolution, the results have been inconclusive at best.

Many of the studies concerning welfare and out-of-wedlock births have compared illegitimacy rates or ratios across states with varying AFDC benefit levels. Cutright found no association between out-of-wedlock birth rates and benefit levels in 1960 or 1970. Using aggregate data, Winegarden's state-level analysis showed no association between measures of fertility and benefit levels, although he did report a small positive association with benefit availability. Fechter and Greenfield and Moore and Caldwell both used state-level cross-sectional data in a multivariate analysis and found no effects of welfare benefit levels on out-of-wedlock births. Finally, Vining showed that for blacks, the illegitimacy ratio in the South was only slightly lower than in non-southern states, despite levels of AFDC payments that were less than half those of the rest of the country; for whites, the difference was somewhat larger.[46]

This type of research is vulnerable to the criticism that, in Vining's words, "the overall incidence of illegitimacy could have been rising over time in concert with an overall rise in welfare payments, despite the lack of correlation between cross-state variation of illegitimacy and cross-state variation in welfare levels at any point in time."[47] However, despite frequent references in the literature to rising welfare expenditures, benefit levels have fallen in real terms over the past ten years, while illegitimacy ratios have continued to rise. Both Cutright and Ellwood and Bane examined changes over time in state benefit levels and in illegitimate birth rates and found no association.[48]

Other studies using different approaches and data sets have also yielded inconclusive, largely negative, results. Placek and Hendershot analyzed retrospective interviews of three hundred welfare mothers and found that when the women were on welfare, they were significantly *less* likely to refrain from using contraceptives, *less* likely to desire an additional pregnancy, and *less* likely to become pregnant. Similarly, Presser and Salsberg, using a random sample of New York women who had recently had their first child, reported that women on public assistance desired fewer children than women not on assistance, and were less likely to have planned their first birth. Based on a longitudinal study of low-income New York City women, Polgar and Hiday reported that women having an additional birth over a two-year period were no more likely to be receiving welfare at the start of the period than women who did not get pregnant. Moore and Caldwell reported no relationship between characteristics of AFDC programs and out-of-wedlock pregnancy and childbearing from a microlevel analysis of survey data.[49] Ellwood and Bane examined out-of-wedlock birth rates among women likely and unlikely to qualify for AFDC if they became single mothers, and found no significant effect of welfare benefit levels; a comparison of married and unmarried birth rates in low- and high-benefit states also yielded no effects.[50]

Finally, results from the Income Maintenance Experiments have been inconclusive. Reports from the New Jersey experiments indicate no effect. In the Seattle and Denver experiments, effects of income maintenance payments on fertility varied by race/ethnicity: white recipients had significantly lower fertility, Mexican-Americans had higher fertility, and blacks showed no effect.[51] Because of the relatively short duration of the study, it is not clear if maintenance payments affected completed fertility or simply the timing of births.

The results of studies focusing on the relationship between welfare and family stability have also been inconclusive. Researchers using aggregate data ordinarily look for correlations between rates of female family headship and size of AFDC payments, while controlling for other variables. In some studies, the unit of analysis is the state; in others, most notably Honig and Ross and Sawhill, various metropolitan areas where examined.[52] Analytic models used in most of these studies are similar, but disagreement over specification of the variables and other aspects of the analysis has produced mixed results. Honig found positive effects for AFDC payments on female family headship, although by 1970 the effects had diminished; Minarik and Goldfarb reported insignificant negative effects; Ross and Sawhill found significant positive effects for nonwhites, but not for whites; and Cutright and Madras found that AFDC benefits did not affect marital disruption, but did increase the likelihood that separated or divorced mothers would head their own households.[53]

As Ellwood and Bane observed, despite the sophistication of some of these multivariate analyses of aggregate data, the analyses have "largely ignored the problems introduced by largely unmeasurable differences between states."[54] Introducing a unique and resourceful solution to these problems, they present estimates of welfare effects based on comparisons of marital dissolution and living arrangements among mothers likely and unlikely to be AFDC recipients, and among women who are or are not mothers (and thus eligible for AFDC), in high- and low-benefit states. They also examine changes over time in benefit levels and family structure. The findings based on these three different comparisons are remarkably similar. Ellwood and Bane estimate that in 1975, a $100 increase in AFDC benefits would have resulted in a 10 percent increase in the number of divorced or separated mothers, with a more substantial effect for young women; the same increase in AFDC benefits would have contributed to an estimated 25 percent to 30 percent increase in the formation of independent households, again with much more substantial effects for young mothers.[55]

Studies using individual-level data have yielded mixed results, with some finding modest effects, and some reporting no effect at all of welfare on marital dissolution or family headship. Hoffman and Holmes analyzed Michigan PSID data and reported that low-income families living in states with high AFDC benefits were 6 percent more likely than the average to dissolve their marriages, while similar families in states with low-benefit levels were 6 percent less likely to do so. Ross and Sawhill, in a similar analysis of the same data, found no significant welfare effects, even in a regression performed separately for low-income families. In a recent study, Danziger et al. modeled headship choices using data from 1968 and 1975 *Current Population Surveys* and concluded that a reduction in welfare benefits would result in only a slight decrease in the number of female household heads; the authors also reported that the increase in female-headed families between 1968 and 1975 was greater than the model would have predicted given the changes in the relative economic circumstances of female heads and married women occurring during that period.[56] It seems likely that the decreasing supply of "marriageable men" (examined below) is a constraint on women's marriage decisions that is not accounted for in the model.

Studies of intact families receiving income transfers under the Income Maintenance Experiments show that providing benefits to two-parent families did not tend to reduce marital instability: the split rates for these families were higher, not lower, than those of comparable low-income families, although the results were not consistent across maintenance levels. The Income Maintenance Experiments "increased the proportion of families headed by single females. For blacks and whites, the increase was due to the increase in dissolution; for Chicanos, the increase was due to the decrease in the marital formation rates." Groeneveld, Tuma, and Hannan speculate that nonpecuniary factors such as the stigma, transaction costs, and lack of information associated with the welfare system caused the income maintenance program to have a greater effect on women's sense of economic independence.[57]

To sum up, this research indicates that welfare receipt or benefit levels have no effect on the incidence of out-of-wedlock births. Aid to Families with Dependent Children payments seem to have a substantial effect on living arrangements of single mothers, but only a modest impact on separation and divorce. The extent to which welfare deters marriage or remarriage among single mothers is addressed only indirectly, in studies of the incidence of female-headed households, and here the evidence is inconclusive.

However, if the major impact of AFDC is on the living arrangements of single mothers, it could ultimately have a greater influence on family structure. As we emphasized in our discussion of Hogan's research on the premarital parenthood of adolescents, young women from independent mother-headed households are more likely to become unwed mothers than those from married-couple families and those from female-headed subfamilies living in the homes of their grandparents.[58]

Nonetheless, the findings from Ellwood and Bane's impressive research, and the inconsistent results of other studies on the relationship between welfare and family structure, and welfare and out-of-wedlock births, raise serious questions about the current tendency to blame changes in welfare policies for the decline in the proportion of intact families and legitimate births among the poor. As Ellwood and Bane emphatically proclaim, "Welfare simply does not appear to be the underlying cause of the dramatic changes in family structure of the past few decades."[59] The factor that we have identified as the underlying cause is discussed in the next section.

The Role of Joblessness

Although the structure of the economy and the composition of the labor force have undergone significant change over the last forty years, the labor-force participation patterns of white men have changed little. The labor-force participation rate of white men declined from 82 percent in 1940 to 76 percent in 1980, in part because of a drop in the labor-force activity of men over the age of fifty-five (from 83.9 percent to 72.2 percent for those ages fifty-five to sixty-four).[60] Labor-force participation of white men ages twenty-four and under actually increased over the past decade.

For blacks, the patterns are different. The labor-force participation of black men declined substantially, from 84 percent in 1940 to 67 percent in 1980.[61] Labor-force trends for older black men parallel those of white men of the same ages. But a decline in labor-force participation of young black men and, to a lesser extent, prime-age black men has occurred, while the participation of comparable white men has either increased or remained stable.

Economic trends for black men, especial young black men, have been unfavorable since the end of World War II. While the status of young blacks who are employed has improved with the percentage of white-collar workers among all black male workers, rising from 5 percent in 1940 to 27 percent in 1983, the proportion of black men who are employed has dropped from 80 percent in 1930 to 56 percent in 1983. Unemployment rose sharply for black male teenagers during the 1950s and remained high during the prosperous 1960s; similarly, unemployment rates for black men twenty to twenty-four years of age rose sharply during the mid-1970s and have remained high. In 1979, when the overall unemployment rate had declined to 5.8 percent, the rate for black male teenagers was 34.1 percent.[62] In addition, while blacks have historically had higher labor-force participation levels, by the 1970s labor-force participation of black men had fallen below that of white men for all age-groups, with particularly steep declines for those ages twenty-four and younger . . .

The adverse effects of unemployment and other economic problems of family stability are well established in the literature. Studies of family life during the Great Depression document the deterioration of marriage and family life following unemployment. More recent research, based on longitudinal data sets such as the PSID and the National Longitudinal Study or on aggregate data, shows consistently that unemployment is related to marital instability and the incidence of female-headed families. Indicators of economic status such as wage rates, income, or occupational status may also be related to marital instability or female head-edness, although the evidence is not as consistent. For instance, while Cutright's analysis of 1960 census data indicates that divorce and separation rates are higher among lower-income families, Sawhill et al. find that unemployment, fluctuations in income, and lack of assets are associated with higher separation rates, but that the level of the husband's earnings has an effect only among low-income black families. However, Cohen reports that when the husband's age is controlled, the higher the husband's earnings, the less likely both black and white couples are to divorce.[63]

Nonetheless, the weight of the evidence on the relationship between the employment status of men, and family life and married life suggests that the increasing rate of joblessness among black men merits serious consideration as a major underlying factor in the rise of black single mothers and female-headed households. Moreover, when the factor of joblessness is combined with high black-male mortality and incarceration rates,[64] the proportion of black men in stable economic situations is even lower than that conveyed in the current unemployment and labor-force figures.

The full dimensions of this problem are revealed in Figures 1 through 6, which show the effect of male joblessness trends, in combination with the effects of male mortality and incarceration rates, by presenting the rates of employed civilian men to women of the same race and age-group.[65] This ratio may be described as a "male marriageable pool index." The number of women is used as the denominator in order to convey the situation of young women in the "marriage market." Figures 1 to 3, for men sixteen to twenty-four years of age, show similar patterns: a sharp decline in the nonwhite ratios beginning in the 1960s, which is even more startling when compared with the rising ratios for white men. Figures 4 to 6, for men twenty-five to fifty-four years of age, show a more gradual decline for black men relative to white men. Clearly, what our "male marriageable pool index" reveals is a long-term decline in the proportion of black men, and particularly young black men, who are in a position to support a family.

As we noted above, the relationship between joblessness and marital insta-bility is well established in the literature. Moreover, available evidence supports the argument that among blacks, increasing male joblessness is related to the ris-ing proportions of families headed by women.[66] By contrast, for whites, trends in male employment and earnings appear to have little to do with the increase in female-headed families. Although lower-income families have higher rates of marital dissolution, trends in the employment status of white men since 1960 cannot explain the overall rise in white separation and divorce rates.

It seems likely that the chief cause of the rise of separation and divorce rates among whites is the increased economic independence of white women as indicated by their increasing employment and improving occupational status. It is not that this growing independence gives white women a financial incentive to separate from or to divorce their husbands; rather, it makes dissolution of a bad marriage a more viable alternative than in the past. That the employment status of white males is not a major factor in white single motherhood or female-

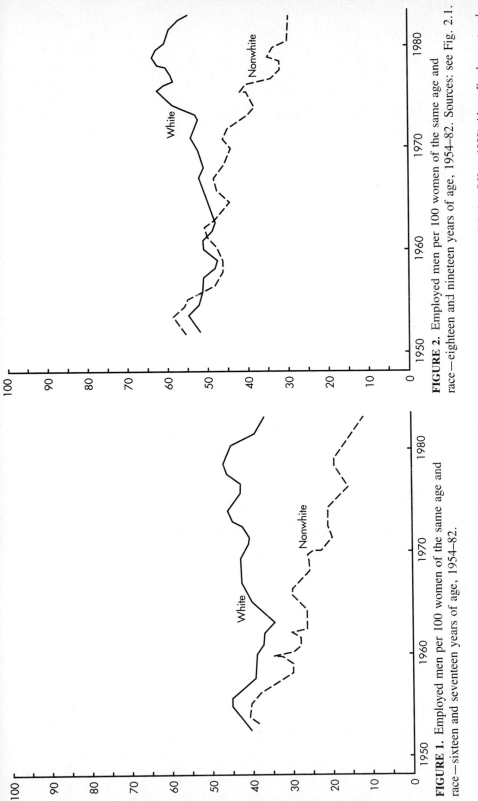

FIGURE 1. Employed men per 100 women of the same age and race—sixteen and seventeen years of age, 1954–82.

FIGURE 2. Employed men per 100 women of the same age and race—eighteen and nineteen years of age, 1954–82. Sources: see Fig. 2.1.

SOURCES: U.S. Bureau of Labor Statistics, *Handbook of Labor Statistics*, Bulletin 2070 (Washington, D.C.: Government Printing Office, 1980); idem, *Employment and Earnings*. The denominators, the number of women by age and race, are taken from U.S. Bureau of the Census, *Current Population Reports*, series P-25, no. 721, "Estimates of the United States by Age, Sex, and Race, 1970 to 1977" (Washington, D.C.: Government Printing Office, 1978); and idem, *Current Population Reports*, series P-25, "Estimates of the Population of the United States by Age, Sex, and Race, 1980 to 1982" (Washington, D.C.: Government Printing Office, 1983).

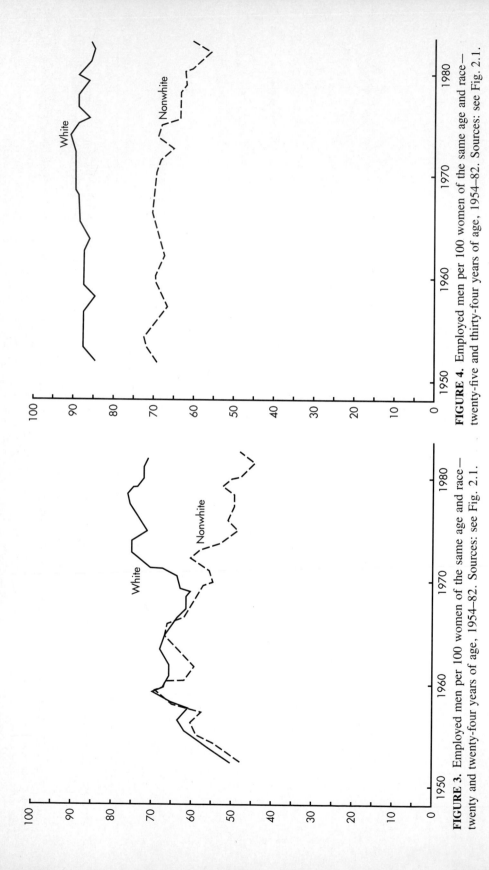

FIGURE 3. Employed men per 100 women of the same age and race—twenty and twenty-four years of age, 1954–82. Sources: see Fig. 2.1.

FIGURE 4. Employed men per 100 women of the same age and race—twenty-five and thirty-four years of age, 1954–82. Sources: see Fig. 2.1.

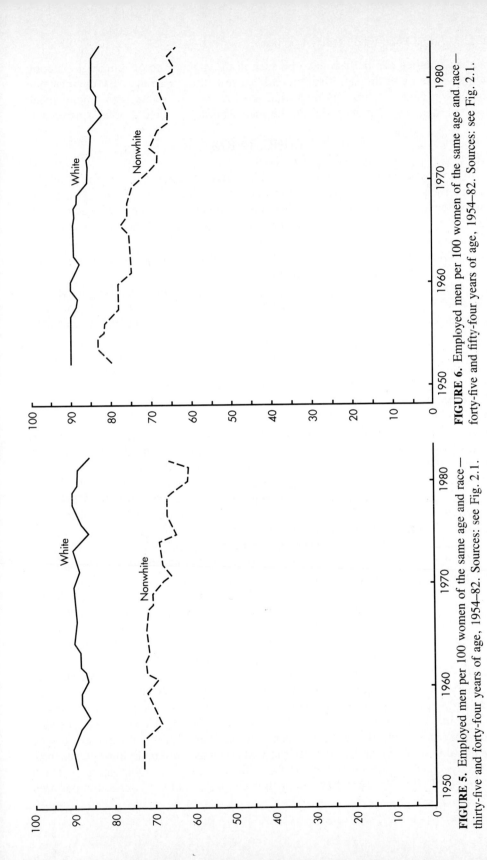

FIGURE 5. Employed men per 100 women of the same age and race—thirty-five and forty-four years of age, 1954–82. Sources: see Fig. 2.1.

FIGURE 6. Employed men per 100 women of the same age and race—forty-five and fifty-four years of age, 1954–82. Sources: see Fig. 2.1.

headed families can perhaps also be seen in the higher rate of remarriage among white women and the significantly earlier age of first marriage. By contrast, the increasing delay of first marriage and the low rate of remarriage among black women seem to be directly tied to the increasing labor-force problems of men.

CONCLUSION

In the 1960s scholars readily attributed black family deterioration to the problems of male joblessness. However, in the last ten to fifteen years, in the face of the overwhelming focus on welfare as the major source of black family breakup, concerns about the importance of male joblessness have receded into the background. We argue in this essay that the available evidence justifies renewed scholarly and public policy attention to the connection between the disintegration of poor families and black male prospects for stable employment.

We find that when statistics on black family structure are disaggregated to reveal changes in fertility rates, marital status, age structure, and residence patterns, it becomes clear, first of all, that the black "illegitimacy ratio" has increased rapidly not so much because of an increase in the incidence of out-of-wedlock births, but mainly because both the rate of marital fertility and the percentage of women married and living with their husbands has declined significantly. And the sharp reduction of the latter is due both to the rise in black divorce and separation and to the latter is due both to the rise in black divorce and separation and to the increase in the percentage of never-married women. Inextricably connected with these trends are changes in the age structure, which have increased the faction of births to young women and thereby inflated the proportion of all births occurring outside of marriage. The net result has been a 41 percent increase in the number of black children growing up in fatherless families during the 1970s, with most of this increase occurring in families in which the mother has never been married. Furthermore, the substantial racial differences in the timing of first marriage and the rate of remarriage underscore the persistence of black female headedness. And what makes all of these trends especially disturbing is that female-headed families are far more likely than married-couple families to be not only poor, but mired in poverty for long periods of time.

Although changing social and cultural trends have often been invoked to explain some of the dynamic changes in the structure of the family, they appear to have more relevance for shifts in family structure among whites. And contrary to popular opinion, there is little evidence to provide a strong case for welfare as the primary cause of family breakups, female-headed households, and out-of-wedlock births. Welfare does seem to have a modest effect on separation and divorce, especially for white women, but recent evidence suggests that its total effect on the size of the population of female householders is small. As shown in Ellwood and Bane's impressive study, if welfare does have a major influence on female-headed families, it is in the living arrangements of single mothers.[67] We explained why this could ultimately and indirectly lead to an increase in female family headship.

By contrast, the evidence for the influence of male joblessness is much more persuasive. Research has demonstrated, for example, a connection between the early marriage of young people and an encouraging economic situation. In this connection, we have tried to show that black women are more likely to delay marriage and less likely to remarry. We further noted that although black teenagers expect to become parents at about the same ages as whites, they expect to marry at later ages. And we argue that both the black delay in marriage and the lower rate of remarriage, each of which is associated with high percentages of out-of-wedlock births and female-headed households, can be directly tied to the labor-market status of black males. As we have documented, black women, especially young black women, are facing a shrinking pool of "marriageable" (i.e., economically stable) men.

White women are not faced with this problem. Indeed, our "male marriageable pool index" indicates that the number of employed white men per one hundred white women in different age categories has either remained roughly the same or has increased since 1954. We found little reason, therefore, to assume a connection between the rise in female-headed white families and changes in white male employment. That the pool of "marriageable" white men has not shrunk over the years is reflected, we believe, in the earlier age of first marriage and higher rate of remarriage among white women. For all these reasons, we hypothesize that increases in separation and divorce among whites are due chiefly to the increased economic independence of white women and related social and cultural factors.

Despite the existence of evidence suggesting that the increasing inability of many black men to support a family is the driving force behind the rise of female-headed families, in the last ten to fifteen years welfare has dominated explanations of the increase in female headship. The commonsense assumption that welfare regulations break up families, affirmed by liberals and conservatives alike, buttressed the welfare explanations of trends in family structure. The Subcommittee on Fiscal Policy of the Joint Economic Committee initiated a program of research on the topic in 1971; according to Cutright and Madras, recognition of the increasing monetary value of noncash benefits, in the context of economic theories of marriage,[68] persuaded the subcommittee that welfare was related to the rise of female-headed families despite inconclusive evidence. And despite frequent references to rising social welfare expenditures, the real value of welfare benefits has declined over the past ten years while the number and proportion of female-headed families continues to climb.

Only recently has it been proposed that the rise in female-headed families among blacks is related to declining employment rates among black men.[69] Evidence such as that displayed in Figures 1 to 6 and in other studies discussed in this essay makes a compelling case for once again placing the problem of black joblessness as a top-priority item in public policy agendas designed to enhance the status of poor black families.

NOTES

1. Kenneth B. Clark, *Dark Ghetto: Dilemmas of Social Power* (New York: Harper and Row, 1965); Lee Rainwater, "Crucible of Identity: The Negro Lower-Class Family,"

Daedalus 95 (Winter 1966): 176–216; and Daniel P. Moynihan, *The Negro Family: The Case for National Action* (Washington, D.C.: Office of Policy Planning and Research, U.S. Department of Labor, 1965).

2. Moynihan, *Negro Family,* p. 48.

3. F. F. Furstenberg, Jr., T. Hershberg, and J. Modell, "The Origins of the Female-Headed Black Family: The Impact of the Urban Experience," *Journal of Interdisciplinary History,* 6 (1975): 211–33; E. H. Pleck, "The Two-Parent Household: Black Family Structure in Late Nineteenth-Century Boston," *Journal of Social History* 6 (Fall 1972): 3–31; Reynolds Farley, *The Growth of the Black Population* (Chicago: Markham, 1970); and R. Farley and A. I. Hermalin, "Family Stability: A Comparison of Trends between Blacks and Whites," *American Sociological Review* 36 (1971): 1–8.

4. E. Franklin Frazier, *The Negro Family in the United States* (Chicago: University of Chicago Press, 1939). Cf. A. H. Walker, "Racial Differences in Patterns of Marriage and Family Maintenance, 1890–1980," in *Feminism, Children, and New Families,* ed. S. M. Dornbush and M. H. Strober (New York: Guilford Press, 1985).

5. Herbert Gutman, *The Black Family in Slavery and Freedom, 1750–1925* (New York: Pantheon Books, 1976).

6. Furstenberg, Hershberg, and Modell, "Origins of Female-Headed Black Family"; C. A. Shifflett, "The Household Composition of Rural Black Families: Louisa, County, Virgina, 1880," *Journal of Interdisciplinary History* 6 (1975): 235–60; Pleck, "Two-Parent Household"; P. J. Lammermeir, "The Urban Black Family in the Nineteenth Century: A Study of Black Family Structure in the Ohio Valley, 1850–1880," *Journal of Marriage and the Family* 35 (August 1973): 440–56.

7. Pleck, "Two-Parent Household"; and Furstenberg, Hershberg, and Modell, "Origins of Female-Headed Black Family."

8. Furstenberg, Hershberg, and Modell, "Origins of Female-Headed Black Family."

9. Pleck, "Two-Parent Household."

10. Farley and Hermalin's "Family Stability" age-standardized figures show that between 1940 and 1960 the proportion of widows in the population dropped from 14 percent to 12 percent for white women, and from 24 percent to 17 percent for black women. During these two decades, however, the number of divorced women per 1,000 married women rose from 27.2 to 36.8 for whites, and from 29.1 to 71.3 for blacks. U.S. Bureau of the Census, *Census of the Population* (Washington, D.C.: Government Printing Office, 1943); and idem, *Current Population Reports,* Series P-20, "Marital Status and Family Status, March 1960" (Washington, D.C.: Government Printing Office, 1960).

11. U.S. Bureau of the Census, *Current Population Reports,* Series P-20, no. 388, "Household and Family Characteristics, March 1983" (Washington, D.C.: Government Printing Office, 1984).

12. National Office of Vital Statistics, *Vital Statistics of the United States,* vol. 1 (Washington, D.C.: U.S. Department of Health, Education, and Welfare, 1957); and National Center for Health Statistics, "Advanced Report of Final Natality Statistics, 1980," in *Monthly Vital Statistics Report* (Washington, D.C.: U.S. Department of Health and Human Services, 1982); and U.S. Bureau of the Census, *Current Population Reports,* Series P-20, "Fertility of American Women, June 1981" (Washington, D.C.: Government Printing Office, 1983).

13. U.S. Bureau of the Census, "Marital Status, March 1960"; and idem, Current Population Reports, Series P-20, "Marital Status and Living Arrangements, March 1980" (Washington, D.C.: Government Printing Office, 1981).

14. M. O'Connell and M. J. Moore, "The Legitimacy Status of First Births to U.S. Women Aged 15–24, 1939–1978," *Family Planning Perspectives* 12 (1980): 16–25; and A. Cherlin, *Marriage, Divorce, Remarriage* (Cambridge, Mass.: Harvard University Press, 1981).

15. U.S. Bureau of the Census, *Current Population Reports,* Series P-20, "Characteristics of Single, Married, Widowed, and Divorced Persons in 1947" (Washington, D.C.: Government Printing Office, 1948); and idem, "Marital Status and Living Arrangements, March 1980."

16. Abundant evidence indicates that whites are more likely to remarry than blacks. For instance, a 1975 Current Population Survey showed that of women ages thirty-five to fifty-four who had been divorced or widowed, 53 percent of whites had remarried and were currently married and living with their husbands, as compared with only 38 percent of blacks (U.S. Bureau of the Census, *Current Population Reports,* Series P-20, "Marriage, Divorce, Widowhood, and Remarriage by Family Characteristics, June 1975" [Washington, D.C.: Government Printing Office, 1977]). In addition, National Center for Health Statistics data show that a higher proportion of white than black marriages are *remarriages,* despite the fact that blacks have higher rates of martial dissolution (National Center for Health Statistics, "Marriage and Divorce," in *Vital Statistics of the United States,* 1978, vol. 3 [Washington, D.C.: U.S. Department of Health and Human Services, 1982]).

17. U.S. Bureau of the Census, "Marital Status and Living Arrangements."

18. U.S. Bureau of the Census, *Current Population Reports,* Series P-25, "Population Estimates" (Washington, D.C.: Government Printing Office, 1965); and idem, *Current Population Reports,* Series P-25, "Population Estimates" (Washington, D.C.: Government Printing Office, 1981).

19. Mary Jo Bane and David T. Ellwood, "The Dynamics of Children's Living Arrangements," working paper, supported by U.S. Department of Health and Human Services grant, contract no. HHS-100-82-0038, 1984.

20. P. Cutright, "Components of Change in the Number of Female Family Heads Aged 15–44: United States, 1940–1970," *Journal of Marriage and the Family* 36 (1974): 714–21.

21. Bane and Ellwood, "Dynamics of Children's Living Arrangements."

22. U.S. Bureau of the Census, *Current Population Reports,* Series P-23, "The Social and Economic Status of the Black Population in the United States: A Historical View, 1790–1978" (Washington, D.C.: Government Printing Office, 1979); and idem, *Current Population Reports,* Series P-20, "Marital Status and Family Status, March 1970" (Washington, D.C.: Government Printing Office, 1971); and idem, "Marital Status and Living Arrangements, March 1980."

23. Bane and Ellwood, "Dynamics of Children's Living Arrangements," p. 3.

24. Ibid., p. 23.

25. Mary Jo Bane and David T. Ellwood, "Single Mothers and Their Living Arrangements," working paper, supported by U.S. Department of Health and Human Services grant, contract no. HHS-100-82-0038, 1984, quote on p. 27.

26. U.S. Bureau of the Census, *Current Population Reports,* Series P-60, no. 144, "Characteristics of the Population below Poverty Level, 1982" (Washington, D.C.: Government Printing Office, 1983).

27. Ibid.

28. G. J. Duncan, *Years of Poverty, Years of Plenty* (Ann Arbor: Institute for Social Research, University of Michigan, 1984).

29. U.S. Department of Health and Human Services, "Advance Report of Final Natality Statistics, 1980," in *Monthly Vital Statistics Report* (Washington, D.C.: Government Printing Office, 1982).

30. M. Zelnik and J. F. Kantner, "Sexual Activity, Contraceptive Use and Pregnancy among Metropolitan-Area Teenagers, 1971–1979," *Family Planning Perspectives* 12 (1980): 230–37.

31. Dennis P. Hogan, personal communication, 1984.

32. Clark, *Dark Ghetto,* p. 72.

33. Dennis P. Hogan, "Demographic Trends in Human Fertility and Parenting across the Life-Span," paper prepared for the Social Science Research Council Conference on Bio-Social Life-Span Approaches to Parental and Offspring Development, Elkridge, Md., May 1983; and idem, "Structural and Normative Factors in Single Parenthood among Black Adolescents," paper presented at the Annual Meeting of the American Sociological Association, San Antonio, Tex., August 1984.

34. Hogan, personal Communication, 1984.

35. Hogan, "Structural and Normative Factors," p. 21.

36. Dennis P. Hogan and Evelyn M. Kitagawa, "The Impact of Social Status, Family Structure, and Neighborhood on the Fertility of Black Adolescents," *American Journal of Sociology* 90 (1985): 825–55.

37. Hogan, "Demographic Trends."

38. R. Easterlin, *Birth and Fortune: The Impact of Numbers on Personal Welfare* (New York: Basic Books, 1980); Dennis P. Hogan, *Transitions and Social Change: The Early Lives of American Men* (New York: Academic Press, 1981); and M. D. Evans, "Modernization, Economic Conditions and Family Formation: Evidence from Recent White and Nonwhite Cohorts," Ph.D. dissertation, University of Chicago, 1983. Cf. Hogan, "Demographic Trends."

39. Zelnik and Kantner, "Sexual Activity."

40. S. Hoffman and J. Holmes, "Husbands, Wives, and Divorce," in *Five Thousand American Families: Patterns of Economic Progress,* ed. J. N. Morgan, vol. 4 (Ann Arbor: Institute for Social Research, University of Michigan Press, 1976); S. Danziger, G. Jakubson, S. Schwartz, and E. Smolensky, "Work and Welfare as Determinants of Female Poverty and Household Headship," *Quarterly Journal of Economics* 97 (August 1982): 519–34; and H. L. Ross and I. Sawhill, *Time of Transition: The Growth of Families Headed by Women* (Washington, D.C.: Urban Institute, 1975).

41. U.S. Bureau of the Census, *Census of the Population,* 1980 (Washington, D.C.: Government Printing Office, 1984).

42. Ibid.

43. U.S. Bureau of the Census, "Characteristics of the Population below Poverty Level, 1982."

44. Charles Murray, *Losing Ground: American Social Policy, 1950–1980* (New York: Basic Books, 1984).

45. Cited in M. Feldstein, ed., *The American Economy in Transition* (Chicago: University of Chicago Press, 1980), p. 341.

46. P. Cutright, "Illegitimacy and Income Supplements," *Studies in Public Welfare,* paper no. 12 prepared for the use of the Subcommittee on Fiscal Policy of the Joint Economic Committee, Congress of the United States (Washington, D.C.: Government Printing Office, 1973); C. R. Winegarden, "The Fertility of AFDC Women: An Economic Analysis," *Journal of Economics and Business* 26 (1974): 159–66; A. Fechter and S. Greenfield, "Welfare and Illegitimacy: An Economic Model and Some Preliminary Results," working paper 963–1037 (Washington, D.C.: Urban Institute, 1973); Kristin Moore ad Steven B. Caldwell, "Out-of-Wedlock Pregnancy and Child-bearing," working paper no. 999–1002, Urban Institute, Washington, D.C., 1976; and D. R. Vining, Jr., "Illegitimacy and Public Policy," *Population and Development Review* 9 (1983): 105–10.

47. Vining, "Illegitimacy and Public Policy," p. 108.

48. Cutright, "Illegitimacy and Income Supplements"; David T. Ellwood and Mary Jo Bane, "The Impact of AFDC on Family Structure and Living Arrangements," prepared for the U.S. Department of Health and Human Services under grant no. 92A-82, 1984.

49. P. J. Placek and G. E. Hendershot, "Public Welfare and Family Planning: An Empirical Study of the 'Brood Sow' Myth," *Social Problems* 21(1974): 660-73; H. B. Presser and L. S. Salsberg, "Public Assistance and Early Family Formation: Is There a Pronatalist Effect?" *Social Problems* 23 (1975): 226–41; S. Polgar and V. Hiday, "The Effect of an Additional Birth on Low-Income Urban Families," *Population Studies* 28 (1974): 463–71; and Moore and Caldwell, "Out-of-Wedlock Pregnancy and Childbearing."

50. G. Cain, "The Effect of Income Maintenance Laws on Fertility in Results from the New Jersey–Pennsylvania Experiment," in *Final Report of the Graduated Work Incentive Experiment in New Jersey and Pennsylvania* (Madison, Wis., and Princeton, N.J.: Institute for Research on Poverty, University of Wisconsin, and Mathematica Policy Research, 1974).

51. M. C. Keeley, "The Effects of Negative Income Tax Programs on Fertility,"*Journal of Human Resources* 9 (1980): 303–22.

52. Cutright and Madras, "AFDC and the Marital and Family Status of Ever-Married Women"; J. J. Minarik and R. S. Goldfarb, "AFDC Income, Recipient Rates, and Family Dissolution: A Comment," *Journal of Human Resources* 11 (Spring 1976): 243–50; M. Honig, "AFDC Income, Recipient Rates, and Family Dissolution, *Journal of Human Resources* 9 (Summer 1974): 303–22; and Ross and Sawhill, *Time of Transition.*

53. Honig, "AFDC Income, Recipient Rates, and Family Dissolution"; Minarik and Goldfarb, "AFDC Income, Recipient Rates, and Family Dissolution: A Comment"; Ross and Sawhill, *Time of Transition;* and Cutright and Madras, "AFDC and the Marital and Family Status of Ever-Married Women."

54. D. T. Ellwood and M. J. Bane, "Impact of AFDC on Family Structure and Living Arrangements," report prepared for the U.S. Department of Health and Human Services under grant no. 92A-82 (John F. Kennedy School of Government, Harvard University, 1984), p. 2.

55. In this connection, Ellwood and Bane state that "women in this group will tend to have married and had children at a very young age. Such marriages tend to be unstable, and thus it is plausible that welfare benefits might have an important impact on this group. Welfare may offer an alternative to an unhappy early marriage. . . . One should keep in mind, however, that even a sizable increase such as this one need not imply a very sizable increase in the number of single mothers. Among younger nonwhite women, divorced or separated mothers represent just 20% of all single mothers. A 50% increase in this group translates to only a 10% increase in the number of single mothers under 24. Thus even though welfare might have a significant impact on ever-married mothers, if welfare does not influence births to nonmarried women, its overall impact on the fraction of all women who are single mothers would be small. . . . By contrast nearly 60% of all young white mothers report themselves as divorced or separated. A 50% increase here implies a much larger change in the number of single mothers. A large impact on divorce and separation then implies a much larger change in the number of women who are single mothers for whites than for nonwhites." Ellwood and Bane, "Impact of AFDC on Family Structure," p. 42.

56. Hoffman and Holmes, "Husbands, Wives, and Divorce"; Ross and Sawhill, *Time of Transition;* and Danziger et al., "Work and Welfare."

57. J. H. Bishop, "Jobs, Cash Transfers, and Marital Instability: A Review and Synthesis of the Evidence," *Journal of Human Resources* 15 (Summer 1980); 301–34; L. P. Groeneveld, M. Hannon, and N. Tuma, *Marital Stability: Final Report of the Seattle–Denver Income Maintenance Experiment,* vol. 1, Design and Result, pt. 5 (Menlo Park, Calif.: SRI International), p. 344; and L. P. Groeneveld, N. B. Tuma, and M. T. Hannon, "The Effects of Negative Income Tax Programs on Marital Dissolution," *Journal of Human Resources* 15 (1980): 654–74.

58. Hogan, "Demographic Trends"; and idem, "Structural and Normative Factors."

59. Ellwood and Bane, "Impact of AFDC on Family Structure," p. 8.

60. U.S. Bureau of the Census, *Census of the Population,* 1980.

61. Ibid.

62. Duncan, *Years of Poverty, Years of Plenty;* U.S. Bureau of the Census, "Social and Economic Status of the Black Population"; and U.S. Bureau of Labor Statistics, *Employment and Earnings* (Washington, D.C.: U.S. Department of Labor, January 1984).

63. W. E. Bakke, *Citizens without Work* (New Haven, Conn.: Yale University Press, 1940); M. Komarovsky, *The Unemployed Man and His Family* (New York: Octagon Books, 1940); G. H. Elder, Jr., *Children of the Great Depression* (Chicago: University of Chicago Press, 1974); Honig, "AFDC Income, Recipient Rates, and Family Dissolution"; Ross and Sawhill, *Time of Transition;* I. Sawhill, G. E. Peabody, C. A. Jones, and S. B. Caldwell, *Income Transfers and Family Structure* (Washington, D.C.: Urban Institute, 1975); and Hoffman and Holmes, "Husbands, Wives, and Divorce"; Bishop, "Jobs, Cash Transfers, and Marital Instability"; P. Cutright, "Income and Family Events: Marital Instability," *Journal of Marriage and the Fam-*

ily 33 (1971): 291–306; and A. Cohen, "Economic, Marital Instability and Race," Ph.D. dissertation, University of Wisconsin, Madison, 1979.

64. R. Farley, "Homicide Trends in the United States," *Demography* 17 (May 1980): 177–88; A. Blumstein, "On the Racial Disproportionality of United States' Prison Populations," *Journal of Criminal Law and Criminology* 73 (Fall 1982): 1259–81.

65. Several objections might be raised to these figures. First, it might be argued that the ratios are biased downward because of an undercount of young black men. This may be true, but it would seem that unenumerated men are not counted precisely because they do not have a stable attachment to labor force and family, and thus would be unlikely to be included in these figures even if they had been enumerated. Second, the employment figures are for the civilian labor force only and do not include men in the armed forces. Including men who are in the armed forces would smooth out the graph for men twenty to twenty-four years of age during the late 1960s, and would narrow the black-white gap a little because of slightly higher enlistment levels among blacks, but would not change the basic trends. The slight upturn in the index after 1954 for men twenty to twenty-four is likely to represent the return of men in the armed forces to the civilian labor force following the Korean War. Finally, although some women may marry men other than employed men of their own age and race category, the figures are intended to convey the "marriage market" constraints facing most women.

66. While rising average incomes are likely to have enhanced family stability for black men who are employed, the more dramatic trends in unemployment and labor-force participation have outweighed increases in earnings to produce a net decline in family stability among blacks.

67. Ellwood and Bane, "Impact of AFDC on Family Structure."

68. Cutright and Madras, "AFDC and the Marital and Family Status of Ever-Married Women"; cf. G. S. Becker, E. M. Landes, and R. T. Michael, "An Economic Analysis of Marital Instability," *Journal of Political Economy* 85 (1977): 1141–87.

69. Center for the Study of Social Policy, "The 'Flip-Side' of Black Families Headed by Women: The Economic Status of Black Men," working paper, 1984; and Walker, "Racial Differences in Patterns of Marriage and Family Maintenance."

13

Some Social Welfare Lessons from Europe*

Harrell R. Rodgers, Jr.

The major industrial countries of Western Europe have not eradicated poverty, but their poverty rates tend to be lower than the U.S. rate (Beckerman 1979; Commission of the European Communities 1981; OECD 1976). This is especially true of the Scandinavian countries, West Germany, Switzerland, and the Netherlands. The rate of poverty in France is similar to the U.S. rate, and Great Britain has a higher incidence of poverty (Townsend 1979).

The major Western countries are also experiencing increases in the numbers of female-headed families, which tend to have low incomes (Finer et al. 1974; Commission of the European Communities 1982). But almost all of these countries have comprehensive social welfare programs that provide more assistance and security for low-income, poor, and single-parent families than similar groups receive in the United States. Some of the countries do a much better job than the United States of assisting lone-parent families with children and aiding women, married and unmarried, who combine work with parenting. The programs of these countries are the focus of this essay.

SOME LIMITS OF COMPARATIVE ANALYSIS

Comparative analysis can provide interesting and even important insights about both positive and negative approaches to social policy, but conclusions must be tempered by caution. Three points should be kept in mind when comparing the successes of various countries in preventing, alleviating, or eradicating poverty. First, social welfare programs are not the only predictors of rates of national poverty. Countries with very healthy economies (especially very low rates of unemployment) have less need for assistance programs. Countries with more complex economic problems may employ imaginative and costly social welfare programs and economic strategies but still have serious problems with poverty. The smaller industrial countries—Switzerland, Austria, Sweden, and Denmark, for example—have healthier economies and less poverty than those with larger populations. These smaller countries may have more success, in part, because they have less complex problems.

Second, just because a particular program works well in one country does not mean that it could be adopted or would work as well in another. The national health

*Rodgers, Harrell R., Jr. 1986. "Some Social Welfare Lessons from Europe." Pp. 95–111 in *Poor Women, Poor Families: The Economic Plight of America's Female-Headed Households*. Armonk, NY: M. E. Sharpe. Reprinted by permission of M. E. Sharpe, Inc., Armonk, New York 10504.

insurance systems in most Western European countries, for example, were adopted before health-care professionals became well organized and politically powerful. Since the end of World War II medical associations in the United States have been well organized and powerful enough to defeat proposals for major reform of the health-care system. Neither the Democratic nor the Republican party would seriously consider proposing the creation of a national health insurance program in the United States today.

Third, there is a critical difference between maintaining families at a low-income level and helping them achieve a normal standard of living. Great Britain is an example of a country that uses social welfare programs to maintain large numbers of families far below median family income levels for long periods of time. This approach keeps the families from suffering absolute deprivation, but it does not solve their problems (such as the need for a decent job). Because the productive value of the recipients is lost, this type of welfare system also creates a serious drag on the economy. Modeling reform on Great Britain's approach would be a serious mistake.

THE WEST EUROPEAN APPROACH

America's approach to social welfare policy is fundamentally different from that of most other Western industrial countries (Furniss and Mitchell 1985). There are three major differences. First, most of the latter emphasize prevention of social problems, including poverty, by mean of such policies as national health systems, extensive housing programs, and child or family allowances. Second, there is a belief that problems are best prevented if the most important programs are universal. Thus, these countries are much less likely to use means tests for program eligibility. Universal programs are not only more effective in preventing social ills, they generally enjoy broader public support and do not carry the social stigma often associated with means-tested welfare programs. Third, many of the countries try to ameliorate social problems by public intervention to keep the economy healthy. The Scandinavian countries, for example, use public resources to keep the unemployment rate as low as possible. Low rates of unemployment play a significant role in ameliorating poverty.

Comparing U.S. social welfare programs for low-income families with those of Western Europe reveals how significantly these differences manifest themselves in public policy. The United States is the only major Western industrial country that:

- does not have a uniform cash-benefit program for poor families;
- restricts cash-welfare benefits almost exclusively to single-parent families headed by women;
- has designed its main cash-welfare program to discourage mothers from working;
- has no statutory maternity benefits;
- has no universal child-rearing benefits; and
- has no universal health-care benefits (Kamerman 1984).

Some of the implications of these differences are fairly obvious. In the United States:

- The emphasis is on dealing with families or individuals after they become poor or seriously ill.
- Assistance is temporary, varies significantly by state, and is limited mostly to families headed by single women who must remain single to receive help.
- Little or nothing is done to move most welfare mothers into the job market, and in fact most are discouraged from seeking work by loss of benefits and lack of supportive services (e.g., child care).
- Poor families can receive critical assistance (e.g., medical care) only if they stay on welfare.
- Most employed women cannot have a child without suffering serious wage loss, or even their job.

The remainder of this essay examines some major European programs and discusses the insights that might be applied in reforming American social welfare programs.

Child and Family Allowances

Every Western industrialized country except the United States provides a package of cash and in-kind programs to supplement the income of families with children (Kamerman and Kahn 1981). Many countries call this set of programs a "family benefit" package. A central component is the child or family allowance, which can be found in sixty-seven countries (Kamerman 1984, p. 263). In most of them, including Canada, Belgium, and the Scandinavian countries, the allowances are universal and tax free to all families, regardless of income or family structure. In some countries (e.g., Great Britain and France) they are limited to families with two or more children, and sometimes they are means-tested (e.g., West Germany). The allowances vary by the number of children in the family, and sometimes by the age of the children. France, for example, provides a larger supplement to families with young children. In all the major Western countries a special supplement is provided to single-parent families. None of the countries excludes families from these benefits because they are intact or because a parent is in the labor force.

The allowances were originally designed to increase the birth rate. Whether the grants ever had a significant impact on childbearing is problematical, but they remain popular because they supplement the cost of raising children. By sharing the cost of childrearing the society helps insure that the basic needs of children are met. The general belief is that children raised in a more financially sound environment will be healthier, better educated, and more productive members of society.

The size of the grants is generally small, but the evidence suggests that they are a significant aid to low-income, especially single-parent, families (Kamerman 1984, p. 263). This is especially true since the allowance is larger when there is a lone parent.

Housing Assistance and Allowances

Governments in Western Europe use a wide range of policies to subsidize the construction, purchase, and rental of quality housing. Their role in housing tends to be substantially greater than that of the U.S. government (Headey 1978; Leichter and Rodgers 1984; McGuire 1981). Many of the West European governments became involved in housing policy in an effort to overcome the destruction brought about by two world wars. Once involved they tended to stay involved. Both conservative and liberal political parties in Western Europe generally support an extensive role for the government in housing. The conservatives believe that government programs subsidize and stimulate the private housing market and the economy, while liberal parties add that decent housing for all should be a societal goal. Quality housing is a national resource because it is a durable good which also provides a healthier environment for families.

The governments of Western Europe use a wide range of housing policies, including public housing, saving bonuses to help families accumulate the down payment for a home, subsidies to builders or nonprofit housing cooperatives, assistance to home mortgage lenders, and housing allowances. Great Britain, for example, stresses public housing and housing allowances. About 20 percent of all housing in Britain is publicly owned. A wide range of income groups live in this public housing, with rents reflecting the size and income of the family. Housing allowances are also used to assist families living in privately owned housing.

In Sweden some 45 percent of all housing was built with public funds, about 20 percent is owned by consumer cooperatives, and about 35 percent is privately owned. Regardless of sector, about 90 percent of all housing in Sweden is financed by the government. This policy lowers the costs of housing, making it generally more affordable. In addition, Sweden has a very generous housing allowance policy. About 50 percent of all families with children are eligible for a housing allowance.

The governments of France, West Germany, and the Netherlands all play a major role in housing. Like Sweden, these countries stimulate the housing market through quasi-public housing—housing subsidized and financed by the government and run by quasi-public authorities. Public and quasi-public housing is not limited to low-income families in these countries; it is commonly occupied by middle-income families. This takes away any stigma on public housing and promotes a healthier housing environment. these countries also use housing allowances to assist families with limited incomes. West Germany and France provide larger grants to single-parent families; the Netherlands and Britain increase the grants to families whose rent is high in relationship to their income.

Single-parent families benefit greatly from the housing programs in all these countries. They are given preference in public or quasi-public housing and receive housing allowances. In some countries they receive a larger allowance to make up for the loss or lack of a second adult earner. In most of these countries the housing allowance, along with the family or child allowance, constitutes a significant income grant to single-parent families. As Kamerman (1984, pp. 264–65) notes:

If one adds the value of the housing allowance to the family allowance allotted a non-wage-earning mother, the total accounts for almost half of her income in France, more than a third in Sweden, and more than a quarter in Germany and the United Kingdom; for the working mother, the transfers together constitute almost 40 percent of her income in France, more than 25 percent in Sweden, and close to that in the United Kingdom and Germany.

One obvious result of the use of family and housing allowances is that single-parent and other low-income families are much less dependent upon cash means-tested welfare programs.

Child Support

In recent years some countries have adopted a new approach to child support when one parent is absent. Austria, France, Denmark, and Sweden now use "advance maintenance payments" (Kamerman and Kahn 1983). Under this program, all absent parents are taxed a certain proportion of their income each month. The proceeds are accumulated and used to provide a minimum monthly grant to all children with an absent parent. If the absent parent is unemployed or cannot be found or identified, the child or children still receive the minimum grant. An absent parent may also make additional contributions directly to the children.

The advance maintenance payments program enjoys growing popularity, for it has several advantages. First, the policy greatly increases the chance that an absent parent will make regular payments for child support. The program does so not by penalizing the absent parent, but by assessing the absent parent at a fair and regular rate. The burden on the absent parent is often reduced by the monthly tax which keeps the parent from falling behind and then being obligated to pay a burdensome amount to catch up. Second, children are not penalized if the absent parent cannot pay or cannot be located. Third, requiring absent parents to meet their child-care obligations reduces the likelihood that the custodial parent and children will need public assistance.

The advance maintenance approach may work better in the four West European countries than it would in the United States. The reason, as noted above, is that many of the European social welfare programs that support and assist low-income families are universal, with no means tests. By contrast, a single-parent family in the United States often becomes ineligible for health or nutritional assistance when income from a job or child support increases, even very modestly.

Maternity Benefits

Most of the major West European industrial countries have programs that protect the jobs and incomes of women for a period of time before and after childbirth. Maternity leaves are generally covered by the country's social insurance program. This approach assures that a woman will receive the assistance regardless of the wealth of her employer. There is no means test for the program, benefits are in cash, and they are usually wage-related. In most cases a woman receives at least

90 percent of her normal wage up to some cutoff point. The leave lasts sixteen weeks in France and thirty-six weeks in Sweden, but most countries set the leave at twenty-four to twenty-six weeks, allowing for extensions for specified periods if the mother or child is ill (Kamerman and Kahn 1981, pp. 71–73). Some countries allow a mother to extend the leave for a few weeks at her discretion, but at a reduced benefit level. Sweden allows the parents to decide, after the birth of the child, which of them will take the leave.

The social insurance programs also usually allow a mother to take a paid leave to care at home for a sick child. The mother usually receives 90 percent of her normal pay for a certain number of days. If the child's illness is extended, the mother is sometimes covered at the rate specified for personal illness under the social insurance program. Sweden allows either parent to take this leave.

Child Care

The issue of child care provides interesting insights into social welfare philosophy. In many of the West European countries, as in the United States, there has been intense debate about the role that public authorities should play in child care. The family policies or family benefit packages that exist in Western Europe were built on the assumption that most mothers would remain at home until their children reached school age. As women have become more career oriented and formed a larger percentage of the work force, child-care policy has had to be reexamined. A few countries, especially in Scandinavia, have in recent years concluded that women should be given the support they need to be mothers and career employees at the same time (Kamerman and Kahn 1981; Rosengren 1973). This decision reflects the existence of both a more liberal social philosophy and a labor shortage in these countries.

By contrast, other European countries have traditionally encouraged mothers to stay at home with their children until they are enrolled in preschool (around age three). In recent years some countries have accepted the change in women's roles and have begun to develop policies designed to accommodate mothers who want to return to the job market before their children enter preschool or who need child care during nonschool hours. Some countries have established publicly supported or subsidized child-care centers, with fees scaled to income. Only France has created enough facilities to match demand to any significant degree. In West Germany and Great Britain there are long waiting lists for the facilities that have been established and there is continued reluctance about facilitating the return to the job market of women with small children. In most of the countries the mothers must pay for family or center care.

In Scandinavia the governments tend to play a much larger role in providing child care, but facilities are still inadequate to meet demand. The publicly supported centers in Sweden, for example, have long waiting lists. Still, the obligation of providing child-care assistance has been accepted and the facilities are being expanded. In Sweden the public centers are neighborhood based and run by certified child-care specialists. A board composed of center employees and parents sets board policy and supervises the operation of the center. Fees reflect the salary of the parent, the number of children in the family, and how long the center cares for the child each day. Fees are kept modest to encourage center use, and they are lower for single-parent families. All of the centers have a developmental, as opposed to custodial, orientation. Each child receives educational, nutritional, and health-care assistance. Some centers are open twenty-four hours a day for parents who work nights. Often the centers share facilities with programs for retired citizens who can, if they wish, help out with the children.

In sum, it is in child-care policy that other Western industrial countries most resemble the United States. Although in France and in Scandinavia there has been acceptance of the need for a larger public role in child care, in none of the countries is the demand for child-care assistance currently being met.

Health Care

Most advanced industrial countries in the West—except the United States—have a universal program of national health insurance or a national health service (Leichter 1979; Roemer 1977; Simanis and Coleman 1980). These programs provide comprehensive health care to all citizens regardless of income, age, family structure, or employment status. While all individuals and families have the same benefits under the programs, low-income citizens and families certainly receive a higher level of health assistance than they would if care were based on ability to pay. Additionally, a family struggling on limited income cannot be made poorer by health-care costs, nor does the family have to be officially designated as poor—and then stay poor—to receive health-care assistance. Thus, the health-care system is one method by which these countries prevent poverty.

All the countries place emphasis on preventive health care, which is considered less costly than an acute health-care approach where people seek medical care only after they become ill. In a preventive system emphasis is placed on health education and on such services as basic medical screening for early detection of conditions that can cause serious illness, maternity care, and prenatal and postnatal care. Most of the countries have networks of neighborhood centers that specialize in maternity and child health care. In France, mothers cannot receive their child or family allowance unless they schedule regular visits to these clinics for themselves and their children.

With the exception of Great Britain, all the major West European industrial countries have national health insurance systems. Under these systems, most citizens become a member of the national health insurance program through their employment. All employers are obligated to enroll their employees in an approved insurance plan that provides comprehensive health-care coverage to the employee and any dependents. Both the employer and the employee pay a monthly fee, which provides most of the funding for the system. Any citizen who is unemployed or aged is enrolled in a health plan financed by the federal and/or local government.

Under national health insurance, participants select a doctor of their choice, who either treats them or, if necessary, refers them to a specialist. The doctors charge on a fee-for-service basis, but the government establishes the reimbursement rate. The patient may pay a small fee for services, especially if medical appliances or drugs are prescribed.

Germany was the first Western country to adopt a health insurance program, the Sickness Insurance Law of 1883 (Flora and Heidenheimer 1981; Sulzbach 1947). Originally the act covered industrial wage earners but not their families. In 1885 and 1886 the law was amended to bring some workers in commercial enterprises and farm work into the program. The program, financed by a tax on workers and their employers, provided medical care, cash sickness benefits, maternity benefits, and a cash grant for funeral expenses. The program was administered by sickness funds, a type of cooperative organization that had long existed in Germany. In 1885 there were almost 19,000 such funds.

During the first two decades of the twentieth century, the program changed in two major ways. Eligibility was extended to more workers and increasingly to their dependents, and benefits became more comprehensive. National standards for the sickness funds encouraged them to consolidate, greatly reducing their numbers. Hundreds of amendments strengthened and expanded the program over the years. Currently almost all West German citizens are covered by the program. Employees make monthly contributions, which are matched by employers. Some of the costs are financed out of general revenues. All citizens earning less than a regularly adjusted minimum income standard are required to participate in the program, and their dependents are automatically covered. Those earning above the standard may participate on a voluntary basis. Pensioners and citizens receiving unemployment compensation are covered by public programs.

Medical benefits under the German program are comprehensive, with modest cost sharing. In addition to comprehensive health care, the program provides sickness allowances, a household allowance so that families can hire assistance during an illness, a lump-sum maternity payment, and a cash grant to cover funeral expenses. Doctors are paid on a fee-for-service basis, with fee schedules determined by the federal government.

The national health insurance systems in other Western industrial countries work very much like the German system. National health insurance is not inexpensive, but it provides comprehensive coverage for all citizens for about the same per capita cost as the American system (Simanis and Coleman 1980, p. 5).

Great Britain established a national insurance plan in 1911. The initial plan covered workers, but not their dependents. The 1911 act was designed to supplement and, in part, take the place of worker organizations known as friendly societies, cooperative organizations that pooled fees to provide workers with cash benefits during illness, medical care by a contracted physician, and an allowance to cover funeral expenses.

The 1911 act covered only workers earning less than an established income standard. The program was financed by worker and employer contributions and general tax revenues. Covered workers received physician care (but not hospitalization) and sickness, disability, and maternity benefits. The friendly societies were pacified by being allowed to administer all but the medical benefits. By the 1940s only about 40 percent of the population was covered under the act (Leichter 1979, p. 167).

To overcome many of the inadequacies of this approach, the National Health Service Act was passed in 1948. Under it the government assumed responsibility for financing hospital and clinic construction and for training and hiring medical personnel. Unlike a national health insurance system, the government became the owner of the country's hospitals and clinics and the employer of most doctors and other medical personnel. Some 85 percent of the cost of the program is financed by the central and local governments. Employers and employees pay modest insurance premiums that finance another 10 percent of costs. Cost-sharing and user fees provide the other 5 percent of financing.

Every British citizen is covered under the act, and the benefits are comprehensive. Citizens receive routine medical care by registering with a physician of their choice. General practitioners receive a fee for each patient registered with them. As a cost-cutting incentive, group practitioners are allowed to have more patients than solo practitioners. Hospital and surgical care is provided by physicians who are salaried employees of publicly owned hospitals. Patients pay a small fee for dental and ophthalmic services and for prescriptions. There are normally no fees associated with routine medical and hospital services.

The British Health Service has been plagued by a very weak national economy, preventing the nation from increasing funding to upgrade medical services. Still, the British National Health Service, like the health-care programs found in the other Western nations, provides comprehensive health care to all citizens, regardless of their income.

Market Strategies

Many Western industrial countries use economic strategies to reduce the need for social welfare assistance. One of the most common strategies is the use of economic policies and public programs to keep unemployment as low as possible. Norway and Sweden, for example, have been successful in keeping unemployment below 3 percent (Office of Economic Research 1981, p. 10). They do so through the manipulation of interest rates, public investments in the private sector, and government job training, relocation, and employment programs (Furniss and Tilton 1979, pp. 134–38). By contrast, American administrations have used economic policies to increase the unemployment rate, as a method of reducing or controlling the rate of inflation.

Keeping unemployment low is often part of a more complex economic strategy. Sweden, for example, has made economic efficiency a key element in its market approach. The Swedes believe that their industry must be modern and highly productive in order to remain competitive in international markets. This means that industry must constantly innovate to promote productivity, and that weak, inefficient businesses must be weeded out. The maintenance of obsolete or inefficient jobs is not allowed because this would reduce efficiency. Workers and unions do not have to struggle to protect obsolete jobs, for workers whose jobs are abolished are assured of other, equally good positions. If the worker needs retraining or relocation he or she receives this help with pay during the transition period. Thus, full employment is part of a larger economic strategy designed to keep the economy healthy, competitive, and prosperous. Sweden recognizes that only this type of economy can produce the surpluses needed to provide a wide range of supportive human services.

SUMMARY AND CONCLUSIONS

The social welfare systems of other major Western industrial societies differ from the American system in several important respects. First, most of these countries provide a broader core of universal, non-means-tested assistance programs to all citizens. The most obvious example is the package of programs provided to all citizens through the health-care system. Second, the countries have programs specifically designed to assist families with children. These programs are either universal or provided to almost all middle- and low-income families. All the countries make this package available to lone-parent families, with many giving such families a larger supplement. Third, none of them denies assistance to intact families or requires a lone parent to stay unemployed, single, or poor to qualify for, or remain qualified for, critical assistance such as housing or health care. Fourth, the cash-benefit programs are uniform for all poor families, regardless of family structure.

Because of the benefits that citizens receive from programs such as national health insurance, family allowances, varied housing programs, and maternity leaves, fewer low-income families need income-tested cash-welfare assistance. The universal and other broadly provided assistance programs thus increase the security, independence, and presumably the dignity of low-income families, allowing them more options for work, training, or education. France has specifically altered and expanded its social welfare package in recent years to give greater assistance to lone-parent families and to allow low-income women a choice of staying home with their children or entering the labor force. Sweden has designed its system to facilitate management of simultaneous work and parenting roles by both parents.

This review suggests that for several reasons the social welfare programs of Western Europe are better designed than the U.S. programs. First, they better meet many of the basic, critical needs of citizens. This is especially true of health-care and housing programs. The universal financing of such programs as health care and maternity leaves allows all citizens to enjoy these benefits regardless of the wealth of their employer. Second, they do not require a parent to be single or remain single or unemployed to receive needed assistance. These negative incentives are built into the American system. Third, they provide a uniform level of benefits to all poor families, including intact or single-parent families that fall on hard times. There are lessons here that could inform alternations in the American approach to social welfare.

Some West European programs are particularly imaginative and provide cues about how American programs could be improved. most obvious is the advance maintenance payments program now in effect in a number of countries. Sweden's universally financed maternity leave, which can be used by either parent, and the broadly available housing allowances found in West Germany, France, and Sweden are other good examples.

Last, the market strategy of some of these countries yields a critical insight. The health of a country's economy is the key predictor of the poverty rate. Public policies designed to keep unemployment low, productivity high, and industries competitive, and to support, retrain, and relocate those out of the job market are critical means by which a nation can limit poverty.

REFERENCES

Beckerman, W. 1979. "The Impact of Income Maintenance Payments on Poverty in Britain, 1975."[*The Economic Journal* (June): 261–79.

Commission of the European Communities. 1981. *Final Report from the Commissioners to the Council on the First Programme of Pilot Scheme and Studies to Combat Poverty,* Brussels.

———. 1982. *One-Parent Families and Poverty in the EEC.* Copenhagen.

Finer, M. et al. 1974. *Report on the Committee on One-Parent Families.* London: Her Majesty's Stationery Office.

Flora, P. and J. J. Heidenheimer (eds.). 1981. *The Development of Welfare States in Europe and America.* New Brunswick, NJ: Transaction.

Furniss, N. and N. Mitchell. 1984. "Social Welfare Provisions in Western Europe: Current Status and Future Possibilities." In *Public Policy and Social Institutions,* edited by H. Rodgers. Greenwich, CT: JAI Press.

Furniss, N. and T. Tilton. 1979. *The Case for the Welfare State: From Social Security to Social Equality.* Bloomington: Indiana University Press.

Headey, B. 1978. *Housing Policy in the Developed Economy: The United Kingdom, Sweden, and the United States.* London: Croom Helm.

Kamerman, S. B. and A. J. Kahn. 1981. *Child Care, Family Benefits, and Working Parents.* New York: Columbia University Press.

———. 1984. "Child Support: Some International Developments." In *Parental Support Obligations,* edited by J. Cassetty. Lexington, MA: Lexington Books.

Leichter, H. M. 1979. *A Comparative Approach to Policy Analysis: Health Care Policy in Four Nations.* New York: Cambridge University Press.

Leichter, H. M. and H. R. Rodgers, Jr. 1984. *American Public Policy in a Comparative Context.* New York: McGraw-Hill.

McGuire, C. C. 1981. *International Housing Policies: A Comparative Analysis.* Lexington, MA: Lexington Books.

Office of Economic Research. 1981. *U.S. Economic Performance in a Global Perspective.* New York: New York Stock Exchange.

OECD. 1976. *Public Expenditures on Income Maintenance Programmes.* Paris.

Roemer, M. 1977. *Comparative National Policies on Health Care.* New York: Marcel Dekker.

Rosengren, B. 1973. *Pre-School in Sweden.* Stockholm: Swedish Institute.

Simanis, J. G. and J. R. Coleman. 1980. "Health Care Expenditures in Nine Industrial Countries." *Social Security Bulletin* 43 (January): 3–8.

Sulzbach, W. 1947. *German Experience with Social Insurance.* New York: National Industrial Conference Board.

Townsend, P. 1979. *Poverty in the United Kingdom.* Los Angeles: University of California Press.

Wagner, L. M. and M. Wagner. 1976. *The Danish National Child Care System.* Boulder, CO: Westview.

Young, D. R. and R. R. Nelson (eds.). 1973. *Public Policy for Day Care of Young Children.* Lexington, MA: Lexington Books.

14
Divorce and the Illusion of Equality*

Lenore Weitzman

ILLUSION AND REALITY

I began this research in a spirit of great optimism. I expected to discover that California's pioneering divorce law was all its formulators hoped it would be—a law that would bring the divorce process out of the shadows of outmoded tradition into the just light of the twentieth century. The legal reforms, in the words of Professor Herma Hill Kay, could be a triumph of "honesty over perjury, a concern for the individual over legal fictions, and a commitment to understand and deal fairly with the realities of family interaction, rather than to pursue an artificial search for fault, and an unproductive assignment of blame."[1]

Equally important was the law's promise of equality for men and women. Here, finally, was a law that would shed the anachronistic assumptions about women's roles and women's capacities that permeated traditional family law, and would free women from the so-called protections they had enjoyed—protections that in reality served to make them second-class citizens, and perpetuate their dependence on their husbands.[2] The no-fault divorce law promised the abolition of all sexist, gender-based rules that failed to treat wives as equals in the marital partnership.

I assumed the reformers were correct in their belief that only good could come from the reform of the fault-based divorce process. The sham testimony and vilification that were required to prove fault insulted the dignity of the law, the courts, and all the participants. How much better to construct a legal procedure that would eliminate vicious scenes and reduce, rather than increase, the antagonism and hostility between divorcing spouses. How much better to lessen the trauma

---

*Weitzman, Lenore. 1985. "Divorce and the Illusion of Equality." Pp. 357–401 in *The Divorce Revolution: The Unexplored Consequences.* New York: The Free Press. Copyright © 1985 by The Free Press. Reprinted with permission of The Free Press, a division of Macmillan, Inc.

of divorce for both parents and children. And how much better to end a marriage in a nonadversarial process that would enable the parties to fashion fair and equitable financial arrangements. If I, as a researcher, had a personal or political goal beyond my stated aim of "analyzing the effect of the new law on the social and legal process of divorce," it was to discover what made this law successful so that potential reformers in other states could learn from the California experience.

In the early days of exploratory research, I began to confront cases of upper-middle-class women who had been married for twenty-five years and were being cut off with only a few years of alimony and hardly any property. There were forced to move so their homes could be sold. With little or no job experience, and minimal court-ordered support, it seemed that they were headed for near-poverty. I assumed they were exceptions—women who had incompetent lawyers or who "got the wrong judge."

But as we conducted more interviews, and as the systematic data from the court dockets became computer printouts with statistical results, a disquieting pattern emerged, a pattern that pointed to substantial hardship for women and children. Somehow the elimination of grounds, fault, and consent, and the institution of gender-neutral standards for financial awards were having unanticipated and unfortunate consequences.

It gradually became clear that an ostensibly equal division of property is not in fact equal when women have the responsibility for child care in nine out of ten divorces involving children. To divide the property equally between husband and wife typically means that one-half of the family assets are awarded to one person, the husband, while the other half are left to an average of three people, the wife and two children.

It also became clear that judges were interpreting the equal division rule as requiring the forced sale of many family homes. Accepting the well-intended goal of allowing the parties to make a "clean break" after divorce, many of them probably believed, in those early days, that the wife was "better off" without a home that tied her down to old neighborhoods and children's schools and children's friends, that locked her into the suburbs and restricted her personal, social, and economic options. But it soon became evident how much more hardship the new solution caused: it was much worse for a woman to have no home at all, and to be evicted from her neighborhood and its social supports. If equal division of property meant the sale of the family home, it also meant disruption, dislocation, and distress in the lives of women and children. And it meant they were forced to shoulder a disproportionate share of the financial hardships of divorce.

Nor was it only younger women with children who were suffering from the forced sale of the family home. Some of the most tragic victims were older homemakers who not only lost their residence of twenty-five or thirty-five years, but also lost their whole social structure in a forced move to the other side of town.

As I became more aware of the disparities in the lives of men and women after divorce I realized that the assets and property that they had acquired during marriage were not, in fact, being divided equally. This was partially a result of major changes in the nature of property that had occurred in our society. Husbands and wives were increasingly investing in careers and human capital— most particularly in the husband's education and career. The new property resulting from this kind of investment was often the family's major asset. Yet this property was not being divided equally upon divorce. (Indeed, in many states it was not being divided at all.) If the law allowed men to retain their career assets—their professional licenses, their health insurance, and their earning capacities—then their wives were not in fact being awarded an equal share of the property, despite the equal division rule.

It did not take long to see that many sex-based assumptions that were ridiculed a decade ago—assumptions about women's economic dependence, their greater investment in children, their need for financial support from their ex-husbands— were ironically not so ridiculous after all. Rather, they reflected, even as they reinforced, the unfortunate reality of married women's lives, and they softened the economic devastations of divorce for women and children.

In the early days of the women's movement, and in the rush to embrace equality in all its forms, some feminists thought alimony was a sexist concept that had no place in a society in which men and women were to be treated as equals. Alimony was an insult, a symbolic reflection of the law's assumption that all women were nonproductive dependents. Similarly, some viewed the maternal preference in custody decisions as an encumbrance: it perpetuated a divorced woman's responsibility for children and restricted her opportunities in the world of work and economic mobility.

But it soon became clear that alimony was a critical mechanism for realizing the goal of fairness in divorce. To a woman who had devoted twenty-five years of her life nurturing a family and who at age fifty had no job, no career, no pension, and no health insurance, alimony was not an insult. It was often her lifeline— her sole means for financial survival. As Betty Friedan explained the reversal in feminist thinking:

> The women's movement had just begun when the so-called divorce reform law was passed. At that time, we were so concerned with principle—that equality of right and opportunity had to mean equality of responsibility, and therefore alimony was out—that we did not realize the trap we were falling into. . . . We fell into a trap when we said, 'No alimony!' because housewives who divorced were in terrible straits. We fell into another trap by accepting no-fault divorce without provision for mandatory economic settlements.[3]

Along with this attitude came the realization that most of these women not only needed alimony, they had *earned* it. Alimony is a woman's due, her entitlement, and part of her compensation for her contributions to her husband's and children's welfare. Alimony is an essential part of the reciprocity in the marriage contract: it is the share of the family income that the wife was promised for her contributions to the marital partnership.

These concepts of entitlement, need, compensation, and sharing also applied to the mothers of preschool children. Women who had the full-time job of caring for the couple's children after divorce had taken over many of their husband's family responsibilities and faced greater burdens and greater expenses as single parents. Even if many young mothers wanted to be self-sufficient, their economic reality compelled support from their former husbands. But it was not need alone that justified their support: they had earned it—and continued to earn it as the children's primary caretaker after divorce.

Perhaps the word should not be alimony—perhaps the term should reflect the concepts of entitlement and compensation, but the need for postdivorce support was apparent. Again, consider Betty Friedan's words:

> Alimony? It's a sexist concept, and doesn't belong in a women's movement for equality. But that economic equality we seek is not a reality yet. Half of all women are unpaid housewives still, and the ones who work still earn barely half what men earn, and are still expected to take the entire responsibility of the kids, as well. Maintenance, reimbursement, severance pay—whatever you want to call it—is a necessity for many divorced women, as is child support.[4]

Another insight that mocked the laudable goals of legal equality for men and women came in the custody arena. It gradually became evident that legal "equality" in custody decisions could backfire in some circumstances and create more hardship than the traditional maternal preference. If the automatic legal assumption that the mother would have custody engendered guilt in some women who wanted to give up or share custody, far greater numbers so feared losing their children that they were willing to give up the money or the property they were due if they were threatened with a custody fight.

Thus, "sex-neutral" custody laws meant women might be forced to bargain for custody to their own financial loss. Fathers with superior legal resources, knowledge, money, and negotiating skills now also had the legal leverage to threaten to deprive mothers of their children unless they agreed to relinquish their claims to alimony or property or child support. Faced with such a threat, most women would choose children over money or property or child support. As they said in our interviews, "It's only money." But the ironic results of these negotiations were even greater economic hardships for the women and their children than would have been the case under the traditional maternal preference laws.

Similarly disillusioning were the consequences of the well-intended experiment with joint custody and its vision of fathers and mothers sharing the care of their children after divorce. Although joint custody laws hold the promise of men assuming equal responsibility for postdivorce parenting, in practice these laws have given men equal authority, but not equal responsibility. Since most children in what the courts label "joint custody" continue to live with their mother, and since fathers are not required to share the day-to-day tasks of child rearing (or to even assume regular visitation), laws that force custodial mothers to consult with and gain the father's approval on all major decisions about their children serve primarily to give fathers more power and control over their former wives. The father's right to veto the mother's decisions gives him the power to veto her lifestyle as well. Joint legal custody laws also give fathers a new justification for reducing their child support: men can more easily persuade a court that they are sharing the child rearing expenses because they are "sharing" custody.

In sum, this research reveals that the law does not provide an effective mechanism 1) to recognize and accommodate the differences in the structural position of most men and women in our society today; 2) to honor and reward women's work in the home and their contributions to their husbands and children; 3) to offset the impairment of women's earning capacities during marriage, and 4) to recognize that women who are caring for children after divorce need extra support because they do not have equal skills and resources to support themselves and their children. The result is that women are unequally disadvantaged by divorce. Divorce laws that treat women "equally" and assume that all women are equally equipped to survive the breakup of their families without support from their ex-husbands or society, only serve to enlarge the gap between men and women and create even greater inequalities.

Why were these realities not immediately apparent? Why did it take so long for those concerned with social justice to realize that the new laws placed an unequal and unconscionable burden on women?

One reason was simply lack of information. No one knew just how devastating divorce had become for women and children. Few people were aware of the fact that only 17 percent of the divorcing women were awarded alimony, or that more than half of the women were not able to collect the child support they had been awarded. Few knew that the standard of living of divorced women and their children dropped 73 percent in the first year after divorce, while that of divorced men increased 42 percent. Nor was it generally understood that divorcing couples had so little property that an equal division of marital property would mean the forced sale of the family home.

While individual women complained of the hardships they faced, they did not know that they were not alone. Nor did they realize that their plight was not a result of the failure of their lawyers, or the skill of their husbands' lawyers, or the bias of the judge, but rather part of *a systematic pattern* by which women were routinely denied the support and property they and their children needed.

My research is the first to examine systematically the effects of the new divorce laws. These data, which took years to collect and analyze, provide the first comprehensive portrait of the results of the new provisions for property, alimony, custody, and child support awards—and of their combined effects. Moreover, it was not until 1978 that the U.S. Census Bureau began to collect national data on alimony and child support and only in the early 1980s that these data were analyzed and published. Thus, the consequences of the divorce law reforms are just coming to light.

A second reason for the slow acknowledgment of the law's effects is that these consequences were largely unanticipated. In retrospect, this seems somewhat surprising. How could the original reformers have been so oblivious to the potential for inequality in the new law?

While a definitive answer to this question is impossible, one explanation lies in the concerns of the coalition of reformers who launched the divorce law revolution in California. They were totally *preoccupied* with the negative aspects of the traditional adversarial system. They wanted to eliminate the perjury and hypocrisy in the traditional divorce process, the hostility and acrimony generated in the course of establishing grounds and fault, and the law's incentives for spouses to exaggerate charges of fault in order to maximize their property or alimony awards. And, most important, they wanted to eliminate the detrimental effects of the adversarial process on spouses and their children.[5]

The reformers assumed that the abolition of fault, grounds, and consent would eliminate the abuses of the old law and bring civility and honor to the divorce court.*

To the extent that they considered the question of equality, they believed that the new law would foster the "emerging equality" of women. Recall their conviction that women were protected by the community property system in California. They truly believed that the elimination of fault as the basis for financial awards would better serve justice and equity. If property were divided equally, it seemed no one would be deprived of a fair share. If alimony awards were based on need and ability to pay, standards reflecting economic reality, the interests of both parties would be protected. If men and women were treated equally, neither spouse would be given an unfair advantage in divorce.

In light of the aims and goals of those who formulated California's no-fault divorce law, it is not surprising that no one focused on the potential economic impact of the legal changes on women and children. Ironically, one might say the reformers were too busy looking backward at the multiple abuses engendered by the old law, and too busy looking forward to the specter of increased acrimony, hostility, and trauma with an ever-rising divorce rate.

Another explanation for the reformers' failure to anticipate the results of their reforms was their own *misinformation* about the reality under the old law. Recall the testimony of divorced men before the Assembly Judiciary Committee who contended that it was men who were routinely "taken to the cleaners" by wives who demanded and got exorbitant alimony and property awards.[7] We now understand how this myth was conceived and why it was perpetuated: the very men who were testifying and reforming the law were the ones who were most likely to be paying alimony and to know others who were. These men assumed their own experience was universal. They did not know that less than one-fifth of divorced women were awarded alimony under the old law, because their wives and their friends were among this small minority of women who did receive some alimony.

Nor did they know how little property the average divorcing couple owned so they did not realize that the common practice for dividing property under the old law merely allowed a woman to keep the family home and have a small cushion against postdivorce financial strains. Their assumptions about what was likely to happen in divorce settlements were again based largely on their personal

---

*In fact, if one examines the impact of the legal reforms from the perspective of the legal profession, it becomes evident that the profession is a major beneficiary of the no-fault reforms: lawyers and judges are no longer required to systematically compromise their professional ideals by assisting parties in collusion and perjury.[6]

observations of the small percentage of couples who had substantial property; to award more than half of the property to the women in those cases seemed to them an unjust deprivation for the men. Thus the goal of equality—of giving each spouse a one-half share—seemed eminently reasonable.

In light of these erroneous beliefs, it is not surprising that the profession did not foresee how drastic the effects of an equal division rule could be. Nor did they see what a loss their female clients would incur when no-fault took away their legal leverage to bargain as aggrieved parties.

When the California law was being reformulated in the 1960s, there were no organized feminist groups to participate in the debates, which were largely confined to the legal community.[8] The relatively few female attorneys who took part in those discussions believed that the removal of fault-based awards would guarantee fair treatment for all wives, including the "guilty" ones who were severely punished for deviating from traditional morality under the old law. If alimony was based on need, they reasoned, those wives who needed it would receive it. If property was divided equally, they reasoned, women would be guaranteed their half share. Thus the reforms were seen as an assurance that wives would be treated fairly and equally—in accord with more liberal concepts of fairness—rather than be judged (and sometimes punished) by traditional notions of morality.

Although California's no-fault law was passed by an almost all-male legislature, four women (out of 20) were members of the Governor's Commission which proposed the new law.[9] At least one of these women, Professor Herma Hill Kay, was keenly aware of women's concerns and had played a major role in the recent liberalization of the state's abortion law.[10] But all members of the Commission were so deeply convinced of the fairness of the new law that they did not forsee how *de jure* equality might not result in equity in a society lacking *de facto* equality.

It is also possible that the reformers were simply too quick to assume that the "approaching equality" in the larger society would be swift in coming. As they wrote:

> When our divorce law was originally drawn, woman's role in society was almost totally that of mother and homemaker. She could not even vote. Today, increasing numbers of married women are employed, even in the professions. In addition, they have long been accorded full civil rights. Their approaching equality with the male should be reflected in the laws governing marriage dissolution and in the decisions of the courts with respect to matters incident to dissolution.[11]

The concept of equality had a compelling appeal. The new divorce laws held the promise of fulfilling a dream: they projected a vision of a world in which men and women could be truly equal. This shining vision dazzled the reformers' perceptions of the real world in which we live.

A major reason for their miscalculation doubtless lies in the American belief that we can legislate equality. Americans have always believed in equality before the law, and in the late 1960s and early 1970s many reformers assumed that they could create equality by legislation alone—without changing the social realities that promote inequality. The new divorce laws give us a heartbreaking refutation of this belief, for in this case, the legislation of equality actually resulted in a worsened position for women and, by extension, a worsened position for children.

It is now obvious that equality cannot be achieved by legislative fiat in a society in which men and women are differently situated. As long as women are more likely than men to subordinate their careers in marriage, and as long as the structure of economic opportunity favors men, and as long as women contribute to their husband's earning capacities, and as long as women are likely to assume the major responsibilities of child rearing, and as long as we want to encourage the care and rearing of children, we cannot treat men and women as "equals" in divorce settlement. We must find ways to safeguard and protect women, not only to achieve fairness and equity, but also to encourage and reward those who invest in and care for our children and, ultimately, to foster true equality for succeeding generations.

We do not have to abandon the nonadversarial aims of the no-fault reforms to accomplish these goals. Nor do we have to return to the charade of the fault-based traditional system. The reformers correctly diagnosed many of the problems in the traditional system and correctly prescribed remedies to eliminate them. What they failed to do in the process was to address the disjunctures that these changes would create in the *other* parts of the system of divorce—most notably in the terms of the economic settlement. Even though many divorced women were not very well off after divorce under the old law, the levers of fault and consent gave them some power to bargain for a better financial settlement. The reformers did not realize that without these levers women would need alternative provisions in the law to enable them to negotiate adequate financial settlements.

Nor did the reformers anticipate the profound impact of the women's movement on the consciousness of all the participants in the divorce process. Since the California legal reforms came before the forceful organizational efforts of the women's movement in the 1970s, the reformers did not realize that the concept of "equality," and the sex-neutral language of the new law, would be used by some lawyers and judges as a mandate for "equal treatment" with a vengeance, a vengeance that can only be explained as a backlash reaction to women's demands for equality in the larger society. Thus the reformers did not forsee that the equality they had in mind for a childless divorcee of twenty-five would be used to terminate alimony for a fifty-five-year-old housewife who had never held a paying job.

The challenge that now lies before us is that of refashioning the current legal system so that we can retain the positive aspects of the no-fault reforms while we alter its present economic results. To that end, we would do well to stand back and assess the larger issues and implications of these legal changes on the status of marriage in our society. As the twentieth century draws toward its end, we might ask how our laws view that venerable institution, how the present views compare with past perceptions, how these views are reflected in the current divorce laws, and how today's divorce laws are likely to influence our future outlook toward marriage.

THE TRANSFORMATION
OF MARRIAGE

The divorce law revolution transformed more than the traditional legal assumptions about divorce. It transformed the legal norms for marriage by articulating, codifying, and legitimating a new understanding of the marital partnership and marital commitment in our society. The new laws reflected, among other things, altered social realities, evolving social norms, and everyday legal practice. Ideally, that is as it should be: if law is to be effective, it must accord with social and practical reality. However, because the present laws do not *adequately* or accurately reflect social reality, they are exacerbating some of the grossest inequities in our society.

Traditional family law established a clear moral framework for both marriage and divorce: marriage was a partnership, a lifelong commitment to join together "forsaking all others," for better or for worse. Husbands and wives were assigned specific roles and responsibilities, and these obligations were reinforced by law: men remained legally obligated to support wives and children, while women remained responsible first and foremost for the care and custody of the children. The moral obligations of marriage were, in theory, reinforced by alimony and property awards so that spouses who lived up to their marriage contract were rewarded, and those who did not were punished.

Of course we now know that the reality of divorce settlements often diverged from this theoretical ideal. Alimony was the exception rather than the rule, and fathers often honored their responsibility for child support in the breach. But the old structure did give the spouse who wanted to remain married considerable bargaining power, and to that extent it reinforced marriage as against the alternative of divorce. The required grounds and the need to prove fault created effective barriers to divorce by making it difficult. In addition, because the old structure linked fault to the terms of the economic settlement, divorce was expensive for men of means. If she was "innocent," the wife of a man with money and property could expect to be awarded a lifetime alimony, the family home, and other property to meet her needs. In addition, her husband would remain responsible for her financial support. (So, too, could the guilty wife expect to be punished and be denied alimony and property.)

The new reforms altered each of the major provisions of the traditional law — and, in the process, redefined the norms of legal marriage. No-fault laws abolished the need for grounds and the need to prove fault in order to obtain a divorce. They abandoned the gender-based assumptions of the traditional law in favor of standards for treating men and women "equally" in alimony and property awards. They negated the traditional role that fault played in financial awards and instead decreed that awards should be based on the divorcing parties' current financial needs and resources. And finally, the new rules shifted the legal criteria for divorce — and thus for viable marriage — from fidelity to the traditional marriage contract to individual standards of personal satisfaction. They thereby redefined marriage as a time-limited, contingent arrangement rather than a lifelong commitment.

From State Protection of Marriage
to Facilitation of Divorce

The divorce law reforms reflect an underlying shift in the role of the state from a position of protecting marriage (by restricting marital dissolution) to one of facilitating divorce.

The new divorce laws adopt a laissez-faire attitude toward both marriage and divorce. They leave both the terms of the marriage contract—and the option to terminate it—squarely in the hands of individual parties. The pure no-fault states also eliminate the traditional moral dimension from the divorce: guilt and innocence, fidelity and faithlessness, no longer affect the granting of the decree or its financial consequences.

The individual's right to freely choose to end his or her marriage is further bolstered in some states by no-consent rules which give either party the right to obtain a divorce without the other's agreement. Since pure no-fault no-consent rules allow one spouse to make a unilateral decision to terminate the marriage, they transfer the economic leverage from the spouse who wants to remain married to the spouse who wants to get divorced. This is an important difference. Under the traditional divorce law the party who wanted a divorce might well have to make economic concessions or "buy" a spouse's agreement. But under the no-consent rule it is the one who hopes to preserve the marriage who must do the bargaining. Apart from the economic implications, which are considerable, the outstanding effect of these laws is to empower the party who seeks the divorce, and this increases the likelihood that divorce will in fact occur.

From a Lifetime Contract to an Optional,
Time-limited Commitment

The new divorce laws no longer assume that marriage is a lifelong partnership. Rather, it is now seen as a union that remains tenable only so long as it proves satisfying to both partners. In addition, the traditional obligations of marriage, like the institution itself, are increasingly being redefined by the new divorce laws as optional, time-limited, contingent, open to individual definition, and, most important, terminable upon divorce.

In contrast to the traditional marriage contract whereby a husband undertook lifelong responsibility for his wife's support, the new divorce laws suggest that this and other family responsibilities can—and may—be terminated upon divorce, or soon after divorce. Thus we see time limits for alimony, which is now awarded for a limited number of years under the no-fault divorce laws. Throughout the United States alimony has been redefined as short-term, transitional support and the new standards of self-sufficiency define women as "dependents" for shorter and shorter periods of time. (Current awards in California run an average of two years.)

Similar in its effect is the emphasis on a speedy resolution of the spouses' property claims. There are many more forced sales of family homes than in the past, to hasten the day when each spouse can "take his (or her) money and leave." Arrangements that delay the sale of the home so that minor children do not have to move are viewed with disfavor by the courts because they "tie up the father's money." The judges we interviewed asserted that each spouse is entitled to his or her share of the property and should not have to wait for it. This view is also reflected in the tendency to "cash out" other shared long-term investments such as pensions and retirement benefits. Such practices are designed to provide a "clean break" by dividing the family's property completely and finally at the time of the divorce.

The severing of family obligations is also reflected in the lax enforcement of alimony and child support awards. While this is certainly not condoned in the law itself, it is the practical result of the attitudes and behavior we observed among judges and attorneys, and their obvious reluctance "to bother" with enforcement of court-ordered support. (Although the 1984 child support enforcement law suggests a possible improvement in this area, it is important to recall that the wage assignments mandated by the federal law were already required in California at the time of this research, but the judges chose to ignore them.)

Even parenting is becoming increasingly optional. Indeed, the *de facto* effect of the current laws is to deprive children of the care, companionship, and support of their fathers. This is implicit in the courts' treatment of postdivorce visitation and parenting. Since national data show that 52 percent of the children of divorce (who are not currently living with their father) had not seen him at all in the past year, it is evident that the majority of divorced fathers are abandoning much of their parental role after divorce and are being allowed to do so without legal sanction.[12]

In fact, one of the strongest supports for the assertion that fathers are legally allowed to abandon their children is the lack of a legal course of action to compel a father to see his children. The implicit message is that joint parenting—and even parenting itself—is an "optional" responsibility for fathers.

This conclusion is also evident in the law's tolerance for fathers who abandon their children financially. It is reflected in the meager amounts of child support the courts award to begin with, thereby allowing fathers to rid themselves of much of their financial responsibility for their children, and by the courts' failure to enforce child support awards once they are made, thereby giving tacit approval to fathers who abandon altogether their financial responsibilities for their children.

Professor Samuel Preston contends that the current "disappearing act of fathers" is part of a larger trend: the conjugal family is gradually divesting itself of care for children in much the same way that it did earlier for the elderly.[13] To date, indications of parental abandonment have focused on fathers. Thus far, most analysts have seen mothers as firmly committed to their children. But as the norms of the new divorce law permeate popular awareness, this picture may also change.

The import of the new custody laws, especially those that remove the maternal presumption and institute a joint custody preference, is to undermine women's incentives to invest in their children. As women increasingly recognize that they will be treated "equally" in child custody decisions, that caretaking and nurturance of children find no protection in the law and are punished by the job market, and that joint custody awards may push them into difficult, restrictive, and unrewarding postdivorce custodial arrangements, they may increasingly take to heart the new laws' implied warning that they not become so invested in their children.

It is evident that the concepts of optional and time-limited marital commitments embodied in the new divorce laws have a differential effect on men and women. While they free men from the responsibilities they retained under the old system, they "free" women primarily from the security that system provided. Since the traditional system channeled men and women in different directions, most women are now ill-equipped to take advantage of the new norms. Their investments in home, family, and children have typically meant lost opportunities in the paid labor force and have made them more dependent on the long-term protection and security that the traditional law promised them. Thus it is not surprising that this research reveals that women are "suffering" more under the new laws, for these laws have removed the financial safeguards of the old law—with a decline in alimony awards and a decrease in women's share of the community property—at the same time that they have increased the financial burdens imposed on women after divorce.

For men, by contrast, the new legal assumption of time-limited commitments is likely to mean a new freedom from family financial obligations. In fact, as noted earlier, the new laws actually give men an incentive to divorce by offering them a release from the financial burdens of marriage. The wealthier a man is, and the longer he has been married, the more he has to gain financially from divorce.

From Protection for Housewives and Mothers to Gender-neutral Rules

The ways in which alimony, property, child custody, and child support rules are administered under the new divorce laws reflect profoundly altered assumptions about the roles of husbands and wives in marriage. These new assumptions reflect changing social reality as well as a new ideological commitment to allow both men and women more options and more latitude to define their marital roles.

If the new legal assumptions were accompanied by provisions that in fact enabled both spouses to choose the extent to which they would assume breadwinning and homemaking roles, and if they then gave each spouse "credit" for the roles they in fact assumed during marriage, then the law would accurately reflect the complexity and variety of marital roles in these years of "transition." But the present legal system seems to leave no room for such flexibility. Nor does it leave any room for individual choice.

Rather, it suggests that a woman who chooses to be a housewife or mother risks a great penalty because if she is later divorced she will pay heavily for that choice. Even if she and her husband agree to form an equal partnership in which they give priority to his career while she assumes the larger share of the housework and child care, and even if they agree that he will share his earnings and career assets with her, their agreement apparently will have no legal standing. The woman will still be expected to be self-sufficient after divorce, and the man's promise—the promise of continued support and a share of his earnings that is implied in most marriages with a traditional division of labor—will be ignored in most courts.

The penalty is equally severe for the woman who works during marriage, or who works part time, but who nevertheless gives priority to her family over her work. Her claims to share her husband's income through spousal support fall on deaf ears in courts that base awards solely on her "capacity for gainful employment."

Under the new legal assumptions the average divorced woman in California will be awarded no alimony, a minimal amount of child support (which she is often unable to collect), exactly half of the joint tangible assets (an average of less than $10,000 worth of property) and an explicit directive to become immediately self-supporting. Chances are that even if she was married under the old law, and lived her life by the letter of the traditional marriage contract, and even if she is forty-five or fifty-five at the time of divorce, the court will apply the new standards of self-sufficiency to her as well.

Especially disadvantaged by these new assumptions are mothers of young children and older homemakers. Today, instead of recognizing their years spent in homemaking and child care, and instead of compensating them for years of lost career opportunities and impaired earning capacities, the divorce courts accord them "equality" and presume them to be as capable as any man to support themselves after divorce.

Thus one clear implication of the present allocation of family resources at divorce is that women had better not forgo any of their own education, training, and career development to devote themselves fully or even partially to their families. The law assures that they will not be rewarded for their devotion, either in court or in the job market, and they will suffer greatly if their marriage dissolves. This is a powerful message at a time when half of all U.S. marriages are expected to end in divorce and when under the no-fault and no-consent laws in many states, a woman may have no choice about the divorce and no legal leverage to effect her financial settlement.

The concept of marital roles embodied in the new divorce laws carries an equally sobering message about motherhood. Divorcing mothers of preschool children have experienced a greater decline in alimony awards than any other group of women since the no-fault was instituted. We have seen that the vast majority of these mothers, 87 percent, are awarded no alimony: they are expected to find jobs immediately, to support themselves completely and, for the most part, to support their children as well.

In addition, since the age of majority for children has dropped from twenty-one to eighteen, the divorced mother of teenage children confronts the fact that her former husband is not legally required to support their children once they reach age eighteen even if they are still in their senior year of high school, much less through college. However both high school and college students in these post-child support years typically remain financially dependent on their parents. It is their mothers who are much more likely to respond to their needs and to support them, even though they are typically financially less able to do so.

Finally, the woman who has raised her children to maturity and who, as a result of the priority she has given to motherhood, finds herself with no marketable skills when she is divorced at forty-five or fifty-five, typically faces the harshest deprivations after divorce. The courts rarely reward her for the job she has done.

Rather, the new assumptions imply that her motherhood years were wasted and worthless for she too is measured against the all-important new criterion of earning capacity.

The treatment that housewives and mothers receive under the new laws convey a clear message to the young woman who is planning her future. They tell her that divorce may send her into poverty if she invests in her family ahead of—or even alongside of—her career.

Thus the new divorce laws are institutionalizing a set of norms which may be as inappropriate in one direction as the old norms were in another direction. The old law assumed that all married women were first and foremost housewives and mothers. The new law assumes that all married women are employable and equally capable of self-sufficiency after divorce. Both views are overly simplistic, impede women's options, and exert a rigidifying influence on future possibilities.

For most women in our society, marriage and careers are no longer either/or choices. Most women do not expect to choose between work and marriage, or between a career and motherhood. The vast majority of American women want all three. But, as Vassar economist Shirley Johnson observes, when "women who have both worked full time and carried the lioness's share of the household management and child rearing responsiblities, find out that their dual role is not recognized or rewarded in divorce settlements, the effect of the new divorce laws is to encourage women to . . . shift their energies into the labor market."[14] Johnson goes on to explain why, in economic terms, it no longer pays for a woman to "invest in marriage-specific skills" since such investments have a relatively lower payoff in our society, because of the risk of marital dissolution. Rather, the economic lesson in the new divorce laws is that women should give first priority to maintaining "marketable skills over the increasingly uncertain life-time of their marriage."[15]

From Partnership to Individualism

The new divorce laws alter the traditional legal view of marriage as a partnership by rewarding individual achievement rather than investment in the family partnership. Instead of the traditional vision of a common financial future within marriage, the no-fault and no-consent standards for divorce, and the new rules for alimony, property, custody, and child support, all convey a new vision of independence for husbands and wives in marriage. In addition, the new laws confer economic advantages on spouses who invest in themselves at the expense of the marital partnership.

This focus on the individual underlies many of the changes discussed above. It reflects not only a shift in the legal relationships between the family and its adult members, but also a shift in the court's attitudes and practices in meting out rewards at divorce.

The traditional law embodied the partnership concept of marriage by rewarding sharing and mutual investments in the marital community. Implicit in the new laws, in contrast, are incentives for investing in oneself, maintaining one's separate identity, and being self-sufficient. The new stress is on individual responsibility for one's future, rather than the partnership assumption of joint or reciprocal responsibilities.

Once again, it is easy to see how these new assumptions reflect larger cultural themes: the rise of individualism, the emphasis on personal fulfillment, the belief in personal responsibility, and the importance we attach to individual "rights."[16] These trends have at once been applauded for the freedom they offer and criticized as selfish, narcissistic, and amoral.[17] Whether this change represents a decline or an advance depends on our personal values: are we more concerned with the security and stability that the old order provided, or with the misery it caused for those who were forced to remain in unhappy marriages?

Our evaluation will also depend on how we see the past. The belief that the rise of individualism has fostered a decline in the family rests on the assumption that the family was stable and harmonious in the past. But, as Dr. Arlene Skolnick notes, despite massive research in recent years, historians have not yet identified an era in which families were stable and harmonious and all family members behaved unselfishly and devoted their efforts to the collective good.[18] That "classical family of western nostalgia," to use Professor William J. Goode's term for the stereotype,[19] has been one of the major casualties of recent research in family history.[20]

But historical research does suggest a change in the psychological quality of family life. Within the family itself, relationships have become more emotionally intense. On the other hand, the ties between the family and the larger community have become more tenuous.

Historian Lawrence Stone's term "affective individualism" captures the trend.[21] Stone is referring to a growing awareness of the self as unique and a growing recognition of the individual's right to pursue his or her own goals. The rise of affective individualism has brought emotional closeness between nuclear family members, as well as a greater appreciation for the individuality of each person in the family. Historically, this trend strengthened the husband-wife unit at the expense of the larger family and the kinship network in which it was embedded.[22] More recently, as rising divorce rates demonstrate, the strength of the husband-wife unit has declined and values of "pure" individualism are emerging. The new divorce laws reflect this evolution in that they encourage notions of personal primacy for both husband and wife.

Today's individualistic norms imply that neither spouse should invest too much in marriage or place marriage above self-interest. This view supports marriage as a means of serving individual needs, reversing the traditional dictum that individuals should submerge their personal desires wherever they conflict with the "good of the family." It also challenges traditional norms of reciprocity and mutual dependence. If men are no longer soley responsible for support, and if women are no longer responsible for homemaking and child care, then neither sex can count as much on the other for support or services. By the same token, it is arguable that to the extent both spouses come to rely on themselves, both gain less from the union. Indeed, a pattern of less stable relationships when spouses are less interdependent has already been observed among both cohabitating and married couples in a recent study of American couples.[23]

Not only do the new rules for spousal responsibility undermine the marital partnership, the new property rules do so as well. In spite of the partnership principles on which they are based—that is, the idea that property accumulated during marriage is to be shared equally at divorce—the current bases for dividing property belie such principles.

If the major breadwinner is allowed to retain most of the new property or career assets he (or she) has acquired during marriage (assets such as a professional education, good will, health benefits, and enhanced earning capacity), *the law's implicit message is that one's own career is the only safe investment.* This encourages both spouses to invest in themselves before investing in each other, or their marriage, or their children.

This is one area in which the new legal assumptions are not congruent with the attitudes and assumptions of the divorced men and women we interviewed. Our interviewees rejected the limited definition of alimony as based on "need" and minimal self-sufficiency, and instead saw alimony as a means of sharing their partnership assets—the income and earning capacity they had both invested in, and the standard of living they expected to share. These "sharing principles" for alimony were seen as an essential element in their implicit partnership "contract."

The legal incentive to place career before family has parallels in law professor Mary Ann Glendon's suggestion that the sources of "standing and security" in society have shifted from family to work.[24] That is, as employment relationships have moved away from concepts of termination-at-will, and have become more secure and predictable, family relationships—particularly the husband-wife relationship—have moved in the other direction and have become tenuous and insecure because they are terminable-at-will with no-fault divorce.

Thus the legal entitlements to one's job and the security of employment are being strengthened in our society at the same time that legal security in the family is being weakened.[25] In fact, Glendon has said that the only employment situation to which termination-at-will "applies more than ever is the unpaid labor force, namely to homemakers."[26] Since homemakers facing divorce are also less likely than men to have gained security in the labor force, they may be falling into a void between the family system and the work system, deprived of the protection or security of either one.

One implication of these changes is that marriage is likely to become increasingly less central to the lives of individual men and women. The privileged status of marriage in traditional family law, and the protections and restrictions placed on its inception and dissolution, reinforced its importance and encouraged husbands and wives to invest in it and to make it the center of their lives. The new laws, in contrast, discourage shared investments in marriage and thereby encourage both husbands and wives to dissociate from investments in the partnership. As more men and women follow the apparent mandate of the new laws, it seems reasonable to predict that marriage itself will lose further ground.

Indeed, sociologist William J. Goode persuasively argues that the trend is already well in progress. He observes that marriage is simply less important today than it was in the past for both men and women, and he foresees the further "decline of individual investments in family relationships over the coming decade" because investments in one's individual life and career pay off better in modern society.[27] As more women seek to follow men in the path of acquiring status, self-esteem, and a sense of individual accomplishment from their jobs, the importance of marriage will rest increasingly on its ability to provide individuals with psychic and emotional sustenance. This, Goode observes, is a difficult and fragile bond.[28] In these trends he sees profound implications for the future of intimate relationships and the bearing and rearing of children in Western nations.

The Clouded Status of Children

A final feature of the new divorce laws is the ambiguity they convey about parental responsibility for children. Under traditional law, the sustained well-being of the children of divorce was assumed to be the state's primary concern in any legal proceedings involving children. Indeed, it was from this concern that most of the traditional divorce law protections for women stemmed: women were recognized as the primary custodians of children, and in that capacity were to be accorded preferences and support to ensure the fulfillment of their responsibilities. Similarly, women who had devoted the productive years of their lives to child rearing were to be rewarded for that appropriate and honorable effort.

Under the new laws, the state's concern for the welfare of children is far less evident. Rather, it appears that in the law's practical application, at least, the children have been all but forgotten in the courts' preoccupation with parental "equality."

The same rules that facilitate divorce, facilitate the disruption of children's lives. The gender-neutral rules that encourage or force mothers to work also deprive children of the care and attention they might otherwise have. (Effectively, the fate of divorcing mothers is still the fate of the children of divorce because sex-neutral custody standards notwithstanding, mothers still remain the primary caretakers of children after divorce.) Equally important, the *de facto* effects of the current laws deprive children of both the care and the support of their fathers.

In sum, the current laws, in effect, provide that divorced fathers *may* participate more in the lives of their children if they choose to do so, but they need not so choose. The laws also decree that mothers *must* work outside the home whether they wish it or not, and thus *must* divide their energies between jobs and children. One might well ask what legal protections remain to insure parenting for children after divorce.

Before we move on to policy recommendations, it is useful to note the important role that the law can play in shaping individual options and social reality. Even as the law over time evolves to reflect social reality, it also serves as a powerful force for creating social reality.

Although the divorce law reformers knew that equality between the sexes was not yet a reality when they codified assumptions about equality in the law, they had seen trends in that direction and believed the new law would accelerate those trends. Throughout this book we have seen, however, how the law actually helped to impede any trend toward economic equality that may have been developing. The law worsened women's condition, improved men's condition, and widened the income gap between the sexes. Thus the law has moved us toward a new reality, to be sure, but it is not, in the economic sphere at least, the hoped-for reality.

So long as the laws remain in force in their present form and their present application, postdivorce equality between the sexes will remain an impossibility. For without equality in economic resources, all other "equality" is illusory.

THE NEXT STEPS

Most of the hardships occasioned by the present system are not inevitable consequences of divorce. What is required to alleviate them is a commitment to fairness, an awareness of the greater burdens that the system imposes on women and children, and a willingness to require fathers to should their responsibility for their children.

Although the changes in divorce law were originally welcomed as enlightened reforms that, among other things, would support the emerging equality of men and women, this research shows that they have effected little real equality between the sexes and have brought a host of unanticipated, unintended, and unfortunate consequences for women and children.

As we embark on a discussion of new remedies, it is natural to be leery of their unanticipated consequences and to be fearful of the dislocations they may create. To minimize these risks insofar as possible, I have confined the suggestions that follow to specific cases of injustice under the present laws, and have not undertaken proposals for broad-scale societal reforms.

What are the most serious cases of injustice in the present system? Where should we direct our efforts? There are four groups that deserve our special attention.

First, there are the children of divorce. The policy recommendations for them are relatively straightforward, although they require not just legislation but also more effective administration and enforcement of the law. The children of divorce need more financial support and more effective means of securing the support they are awarded.

Child support awards should be based on the income-sharing approach because this formula is most likely to equalize the standards of living in the custodial and noncustodial household after divorce. Since it is evident that children share the economic status of their custodial parent, the goal of equalizing the standards of living in the two households should be made an explicit aim of child support awards. There should also be explicit recognition of the child's entitlement to share the standard of living of the higher-earning parent. (The Wisconsin legislation that recognizes the child's entitlement to a fixed share of the father's income provides one potential model for such legislation.)

In addition, all support awards should include automatic adjustments for cost-of-living increases. Children would also benefit from the use of more effective techniques to enforce these awards, including wage assignments from the inception of the award, income tax intercepts, national location services, property liens and bonds, and, where necessary, the threat and use of jail.

The college-age children of divorce also need "child" support if they are financially dependent on their parents past age 18. In most states legislation is needed to extend their legal minority and to require their parents to support them if they are full-time students (and financially dependent) until they complete their undergraduate education. The current rules in New York and Washington, discussed below, provide two potential models for such legislation.

Although a child's interest in family property is not recognized in the United States today, many states have special rules for the family home when there are minor children. When these rules are optional, as they are in California, their use depends on judicial discretion, and they are often ignored. What is needed in California (and similar states) is a legislative directive that requires judges to maintain the family home for minor children after divorce.

The children of divorce would also benefit from a primary caretaker presumption for sole custody awards, and laws that allow joint custody only upon the agreement of both parents. Such clear standards for custody awards would make it more difficult to use children as "pawns" in divorce negotiations, and would reduce both the threat and use of custody litigation in order to gain financial advantages in property or support awards. Since custody litigation and the prolonged hostility it typically generates are likely to have an adverse psychological and financial impact on the welfare of children, custody laws that designate clear priorities and minimize litigation are clearly preferable.

The second type of clear injustice involves the long-married older housewife with little or no experience in the paid labor force, who has devoted herself to her husband, home, and children in the expectation that she would share whatever income and assets the couple acquires. This woman needs rules that require (rather than allow) judges to redistribute the husband's postdivorce income with the goal of equalizing the standards of living in the two households.

This recommendation rests on the same principle that underlies community property rules; it is the assumption that marriage is an equal partnership in which all the assets should be shared. This principle, as we have seen, is strongly supported by the divorced men and women we interviewed. They view the sharing of income through alimony—or whatever name we choose for income transfers after divorce—as the means for providing the wife with her share of the fruits of their joint endeavors. These sharing principles are fundamental elements in the "marital contract" that most married couples agreed to and lived by during marriage.

Older women should not be measured by the new standards of equality and self-sufficiency after divorce. It is both impractical and unfair to expect women who married and lived most of their lives under a different set of social and legal rules to be forced to find employment and to support themselves. They have earned an interest in their husband's income for the rest of their lives and require a legislative presumption of permanent (i.e., continuing, open-ended) support.

Long-married older wives must also be assured of equal share of all of their husband's career assets. While courts in most states now recognize their entitlement to share pensions and retirement benefits, few states guarantee older women the right to health and hospital insurance. Since we have seen the hardships this creates, legislation should require that divorced wives be allowed to remain insured as group members (and pay group premium rates).

Women who divorce after longer marriages are also entitled to maintain their homes. If the family home and the husband's pensions are the only major assets of the marriage, the older wife should be allowed to maintain her home without forfeiting her share of the pension. Similarly, if the home is the *only* major asset of the marriage, the long-married wife who has a limited earning capacity and few other resources should not be evicted from her home so that the property can be divided equally. Rather, she should be allowed to continue living in the family home.

In summary, we need "grandmother clauses" for the long-married older women who married and lived their lives under the traditional rules. *It is unfair to change the rules on them in the middle of the game. Rather, they have earned the right to an equal share of the fruits of the marital partnership.* They are entitled to one-half of the property and income it has produced and are entitled to maintain the same standard of living as their former husbands.

The third case that merits a new approach is that of the mother who retains major responsibility for the care of minor children after divorce. Whether the custody award is labeled "sole custody" or "joint legal custody" or even "joint physical custody," if this woman assumes most of the day-to-day caretaking, she requires a greater share of the family's resources. These include the continued use of the family home (which should be viewed as part of the child support award rather than as an unequal division of property) and a significant portion of her ex-husband's income so that the two households maintain, insofar as practical, equal standards of living after divorce.

Since employment will play a critical role in the postdivorce lives of younger divorced mothers, and thus in their ability to contribute to their children's and their own support, they should be awarded full support in the early years after divorce to enable them to maximize their long-range employment prospects. This means generous support awards and balloon payments immediately after divorce to finance their education, training, and career counseling. Insofar as possible, every effort should be made to provide them and their children with full support in the transitional years so that forced employment does not interfere with their training and child care.

The fourth type of injustice is perhaps the most difficult because it raises most poignantly the conflict between the old rules and the new—and the special problems of the transitional generation. This is the case of the woman who is about forty years old at the time of her divorce. Although it is often asserted that the most tragic victims of the new divorce laws are the older women, from a policy perspective their situation is much easier, because the steps to rectify the injustice they suffer are clear. But this is not so for women who divorce in their middle years. Many divorcing women of forty have been employed during marriage and have also raised children who are now approaching majority or have reached it. The chances are good that although these women may have worked part or full time during marriage, they have given priority to their families and their husbands' careers, rather than their own interests. Since these women are rarely able to command a salary anywhere near their husbands', and since they have passed the point where they can recapture lost career opportunities, it is manifestly unfair to hold them to the new standards of self-sufficiency at the point of divorce, as the courts do now. In addition, the courts are insensitive to the triple load that many of these women have carried during marriage, managing home, work, and family. They deserve some special recognition and compensation for their contributions, not harsher treatment.

On the other hand, a woman who divorces at forty is young enough to have at least twenty productive years ahead of her, and it seems inappropriate to expect her former husband to maintain her standard of living for all those years and the retirement to follow. And yet, since her chances of remarrying are low, her economic future rests on just this choice—her future earning capacity or his.

In these cases justice requires a complex adjustment of equities that defies easy prescription in the closing pages of this book. But at least the principles for the solution are evident, and they are the same as those enunciated above: this woman should *be awarded* an equal share of the marital partnership by fully sharing her husband's career assets, including his enhanced earning capacity, through both property and support awards; *be helped* to resume or begin paid employment with additional training, counseling, and education where necessary; and, where appropriate, *be compensated* for the detriment to her own career.

We now move on to consider the major features of the current law and more specific policy recommendations.

No-Fault, No-Consent and the Climate of Divorce

This research has shown that the no-fault reforms have generally had a positive effect on the divorce process: there is clearly less hostility and acrimony and, on the whole, all of our respondents—California men and women, and lawyers and judges—express positive feelings about the no-fault law. They strongly approve of the principles of divorce without fault, grounds, or consent, and they overwhelmingly consider this aspect of the present legal system to be appropriate and fair. Few want to return to the traditional system.

These findings do not necessarily suggest that a pure no-fault system is the most desirable form of divorce law. We have seen that feelings of guilt and responsibility continue to influence men's and women's perceptions of what is fair, and that the abolition of grounds and fault has increased the power of the party who wants to terminate the marriage and typically removed the bargaining power of the economically weaker party. Since this research underscores the connection between seemingly distinct rules dealing with grounds, fault, property, and support, it would be unwise for states that do not have a pure no-fault system to read the California results of a pure no-fault system across the board. If this research has generalizable findings it is that *reforms should not be undertaken without a careful consideration of the economic consequences* of the abolition of grounds and fault and certainly not without careful consideration of the provisions necessary to provide adequate economic protection for dependent wives and children.

Thus while a pure no-fault system is not suggested for states that currently have a hybrid system, it is clear that it would be unwise and inappropriate to suggest that California return to a more traditional system. The current no-fault rules enjoy widespread support and legitimacy, and the dissatisfaction with the present regime can be dealt with through other remedies.

What concerns many laymen and professionals alike is that the abolition of fault and consent has given new leverage to the party seeking divorce, and this, coupled with the lack of financial safeguards for women and children, allows a great many men to walk away with impunity from financial responsibilities for their families. The solution, at least for California today, is not to reintroduce fault and its penalties, but rather to strengthen the economic provisions of the new laws to assure adequate protection for wives and children.

One lesson of this research is that the means to assure this economic protection cannot rely exclusively on "the law on the books." They must also include ways to mobilize the law in action—the law as it is interpreted, administered, and enforced. Here, then, are some of these means.

Property: The Equal Division Rule

There is widespread approval of the California rule that requires an equal division of all property acquired during marriage. All categories of our respondents—judges, lawyers, men and women—support the equal division rule in principle, and consider it fair and just. The vast majority believe that each spouse is *entitled* to one-half of the property acquired during marriage, and almost no one prefers the old system of awarding more property to the "innocent" party while penalizing the guilty party with a lower property award.

These attitudes provide strong support for retaining California's equal division rule. Further support for the present system comes from the finding that California wives are typically awarded a larger share of the marital property than wives in states with equitable distribution rules (who typically receive about a third, rather than a half, of the marital property).

The only major source of dissatisfaction with the equal division rule has been with its effects on the family home. But the forced sale of the family home is, as we have seen, not required by the law. Rather the law is flexible enough to permit a delay in the division of assets. What is therefore needed is not a change in the law but a change in the way judges are applying the law.

Thus the first policy recommendation of this research is for the California legislature to retain the equal division rule but to require judges to delay the sale of the family home in specific circumstances (which are discussed below).

A parallel recommendation applies to states with equitable distribution laws. It recommends the adoption of a presumption that an equal division is most equitable. That presumption would establish the important principle of each spouse's entitlement to one-half of the marital property, and yet still be flexible enough to permit special treatment for the matrimonial home as recommended below.

The Family Home. The major complaint about the equal division rules concerns judges who have interpreted it as requiring a forced sale of the family home. This has created great hardships for families with minor children and for long-married couples whose only assets are the family home and the husband's pension.

Two issues need to be considered in fashioning policy for the family home. The first concerns the use of the home, the second concerns its ownership.

The easier issue involves the use of the family home. Since there are compelling reasons for maintaining the family home for minor children, and since a delayed sale of the family home is already permissible under California law, the problem here is one of inducing judges to utilize this option. Since this research has shown that most judges refuse to delay the sale of the home in most cases, a legislative directive is needed *to require* judges to delay the sale of the family home in the interests of maintaining a stable home for minor children and their custodian.

One alternative is to require judges to postpone the sale and division of the family home until the youngest child reaches eighteen. Another alternative is to require a postponement for an initial period (for example, the rule in Cincinnati, Ohio, allows the custodial parent to live in the home rent free and interest free for five years after the divorce) and to allow the court to extend the period after reviewing the family circumstances after that period of time.

The more complicated issue concerns the ownership of and equity in the family home. On the one hand, there are sound reasons for awarding the home outright to the custodial parent, as was normally done under the old law. The parent with custody can justly assert a greater need for the family's resources which an award of the home would provide. In addition, an outright award of the family home could be seen as a form of compensation for the responsibilities of child rearing. Moreover, since women are more likely than men to be custodial parents, and are less likely to be able to buy another home, such an award would help to offset the discrepancy between the parents' standards of living after divorce. In addition, if family income is limited, an award of the home might be considered compensation for forgone spousal or child support. A final justification for awarding the home to a mother with custody is to protect her against the dismal long-range prospects that divorced women face in finding comparable housing if the family home is sold ten or fifteen years later, after the children reach majority.

On the other hand, there are also sound reasons for allowing the noncustodial parent to retain his or her ownership share of the home. If the home is the only major family asset, and most of the couple's savings are invested in it, it seems inequitable to deprive the noncustodial parent of his or her interest in the investment. This consideration alone would not dissuade me from the more compelling needs of the children and custodial parent. However, an award of the entire equity in the home to one party has another practical difficulty; it creates a strong incentive to seek custody in order to acquire the home. Since wise public policy should discourage the use of children as pawns for financial gains, and should seek to minimize litigation over children, lawmakers should make every effort to avoid creating financial incentives that encourage custodial claims and disputes. Consequently, an outright award of the family home to the custodial parent at the time of the divorce is not recommended at this time.

Obviously, the rules for the family home must be considered in conjunction with rules for determining child custody. If, as suggested below, a primary caretaker presumption is adopted for custodial decisions, then there would be less risk of an uninterested parent seeking custody in order to get the house because his or her chances of success would be minimal. However, the risk of such suits is substantial under the "best interest" standard currently used in most states.

How then should the equity in the home be apportioned? There are two solutions with considerable appeal. The first solution has already been approved by the California appellate courts: the custodial parent retains possession of the home, but the equity in the home is valued and divided at the time of divorce. The custodial parent gives the other a note for his or her share of the equity to be paid when the house is sold. Although most California courts currently require the custodial parent to pay interest on the note, courts in other states use interest-free notes which they consider part of child support.

This solution has several advantages. The custodial parent is solely responsible for maintaining the home and realizes the appreciation in the value of the home. This eliminates the potential for conflict between divorced parties who are forced to remain joint owners of a house but cannot agree on expenditures for maintenance, improvements, or repairs. It also eliminates the prospect of disagreements about whether another man or woman may reside in the house. A final advantage of this solution is that the noncustodial parent's equity in the house serves as a form of collateral to ensure child support payments.[29]

The second solution is to maintain the home in joint ownership but to allow the custodial parent and children to live there "rent free" or "interest free" as part of the child support award. Joint ownership has more appeal in a fluctuating or declining real estate market where a division of equity at the time of the divorce may saddle the custodial parent with too large a note. Although the prospects of a declining real estate market appear unlikely in California at this time, a rule that requires the parties to share the risk may be considered preferable in some counties—as well as in other states.

Since the major disadvantage of joint ownership is the prospect of disagreements about maintenance and repairs, cohabitants, and the terms of the sale, an agreement about these issues could be drawn up in advance. (Such an agreement should allow the resident parent the right to manage and control the property but should provide for financial sharing of nonroutine repairs.)

In Cincinnati, Ohio, for example, courts maintain the family home in joint ownership and allow the custodial parent and children to live there for five interest-free and rent-free years after divorce. The custodial parent makes all of the decisions about the home during her or his tenancy and is responsible for its maintenance.

Similar provisions are necessary to assure an older housewife continued use and possession of the family home. Since judges may delay the sale of any asset under the current law, an explicit presumption for them to do so after a long marriage (where the home, or the home and the pension, are the only assets) should be sufficient to attain this goal within the framework of the present law. It is easy to argue, however, that an outright award of the family home would be preferable. In light of the precarious economic circumstances of most of the women divorced after long marriages, I prefer the following type of rule: if an older woman has little or no earning capacity, and has limited resources with which to buy another home at the time of the divorce, and if an equal division of family assets would require the sale of the family home, or if it would require an older housewife to "trade" her interest in her husband's pension in order to retain the family home, then the law should be amended to allow an explicit exception to the equal division rule to enable an older woman to retain the family home after divorce. Such a rule could be flexible enough to accommodate a move to a smaller but comparable residence in the same neighborhood if that would enable her to maintain her standard of living, but it would preclude the unconscionable forced sale of the family home and the eviction of the older wife that we have seen under the present legal rules.

Career Assets and the New Property

One of the most important policy recommendations suggested by the findings of this research concerns the recognition of career assets and other forms of new property as marital assets. Career assets are the tangible and intangible assets that are acquired in the course of a marriage as part of either spouse's career or career potential—pensions and retirement benefits, a professional education, license to practice a profession or trade, enhanced earning capacity, the goodwill value of a business or profession, medical and hospital insurance, and other benefits and entitlements.

Three findings of this research underscore the ways in which these assets affect the *de facto* equality of property division. First, we have seen that most couples acquire various career assets in the course of their marriage in the same way that they acquire other assets that the courts currently recognize as marital property, and that these forms of new property are typically more valuable than any of their tangible community assets at the time of divorce. Second, since these assets are commonly excluded from the division of property at divorce, the courts are not dividing the property equally or equitably. And third, since these assets are typically treated as the husband's separate property, he is thereby allowed to retain a considerably greater share of the marital assets after divorce.

These findings lead to the recommendation that all states expand the definition of marital property to include career assets such as those enumerated above, and divide these assets as part of the marital property upon divorce.

The past decade has brought a rapid increase in states that recognize pensions and retirement benefits as valuable assets to be divided at divorce. This suggests that the principles for recognizing career assets have already been established in most states. Although a small but growing minority of states also allow some form of compensation for the spouse who supports the family while the other acquires a professional education, other states still reject such claims. In addition, many valuable career assets, such as medical and dental insurance, are simply ignored in most states.

The hardships that result from the omission of these and other yet unrecognized career assets [have been] poignantly documented. . . . When these assets are omitted from the pool of marital property to be divided upon divorce, the husband is typically allowed to keep these assets as if they were his alone. It is . . . like *promising to divide the family jewels equally but allowing the husband to keep all of the diamonds.* The omission of the career assets from the pool of marital property makes *a mockery of the equal division rule.*

Alimony

One of the ironic findings of this research is that the current alimony laws seek to protect the very same women whom we have cited as the clearest victims of injustice under the new law. In this arena the problem seems to be in the interpretation of the law and, in particular, the way in which judges balance a husband's needs against those of his former wife.

In theory, the current law guarantees support for three groups of women: mothers with custody of young children, older homemakers incapable of self-sufficiency, and women who need transitional support are theoretically exempted from the new standards. Despite the guarantee, however, the new norms of self-sufficiency are in fact being applied to all of these women.

For example, under the new law alimony awards to mothers of preschool children have dropped more than for any other group of women under the new rules. Judges and lawyers report that they "encourage" mothers of preschoolers to enter the labor force as soon as possible.

Similarly, older women who have been housewives and mothers throughout marriages of long duration are being held to the new law's standards of self-sufficiency. Although a higher percentage of these women are awarded spousal support, still one out of three gets nothing at all. In addition, even those who are awarded alimony often receive comparatively low awards and are admonished to try to get a job and become self-sufficient despite their obvious inability to do so. Judges approach these cases mindful of the husband's need for "his income" and his limited capacity to support two families. Thus, despite the law's theoretical assurance of protection for long-term homemakers, in reality they are often denied that protection in court.

The findings of this research reveal a wholesale shift from permanent alimony awards, based on the premise of the wife's continued dependency, to time-limited transitional awards, based on the new assumption of self-sufficiency. The median duration of these awards is twenty-five months, just about two years. Thus the average award carries an expectation of a short transition to self-sufficiency.

The major impact of the no-fault's alimony reforms has fallen on middle-class and upper-middle-class women because they were the women who could (and did) count on alimony under the old law. Thus, in contrast to the old law's assumption that these women would remain dependent after divorce and were therefore in need of permanent alimony, no-fault has brought an expectation that they should become both independent and self-sufficient. These women are increasingly being denied alimony altogether, especially if they have earned even minimal incomes in the past, or they are being awarded small amounts for short periods solely to "ease the transition." However, an award of $350 a month in 1984 dollars for a period of two years is not likely to be seen as a great boon to the newly divorced middle-class woman. Rather is conveys a message: find a job right away, any job, and start supporting yourself.

These observations lead to additional policy recommendations.

The inequities visited upon older women should be eliminated by support rules that aim at equalizing the standards of living of the two parties after divorce. Since this research has demonstrated that we cannot rely on judges' interpretations of the relative "needs" of the two spouses, clear legislative directives are in order. They should specify that women who married and lived under a different set of social and legal rules have earned the right to share their husbands' income for the rest of their lives and to maintain a standard of living that is equal to theirs.

Clearly it is a perversion of the concept of equality to deny older homemakers alimony and expect them to be as equally capable of supporting themselves after divorce. It is also a violation of the deeper meaning of equality in marriage—that marriage is an equal partnership in which the contributions of the two spouses are of equal worth. If the husband's earning capacity is their major asset, and if it is treated as his alone at divorce, the essence of the equal partnership is violated.

One lesson from this research is that a woman who is divorced after fifteen or twenty or thirty years of marriage *can not* recapture the years she has lost in the labor force. But an equally important lesson is this: she should not be expected to because she was promised by both her husband and the larger society that her husband would share his income with her. That was their marriage contract, both implied and expressed, and it is simply not fair to change the rules on her in the last quarter of the game, after she has fulfilled her share of the bargain.

Thus support rules for women divorced after a marriage of long duration should specify that she will not be required to seek employment and support herself. In light of the great inequities created by the punitive treatment of these women, judicial discretion to evaluate their "needs" or to consider their earning capacities should be limited. Rather, what is required are rules that create a presumption that their needs are equal to those of their former husbands and that their marital pension, in the form of permanent alimony, is guaranteed for the rest of their lives.

Thus support awards following long marriages should be guided by four presumptions: a presumption that future earning capacity and the income it produces are assets of the marital partnership, a presumption that these assets should be shared by the two spouses after divorce, a presumption that support awards should equalize the standards of living of the two parties after divorce, and a presumption that such support shall be permanent.

In the practical application of these presumptions the courts will have to define what is a "long marriage" and an "older woman" and that definition will and should depend on the circumstances of the parties.*

A different set of support rules is required for younger women who have been housewives and mothers and have subordinated their own careers for their husbands and families. Here too, sharing principles and an effort to equalize the standards of living in the two households are essential in the early years after divorce, and for an extended period if there are minor children. But there is an

---

*Some courts have adopted a twenty-year rule of thumb because of the precedent set by military and police pensions, while others have recognized the ten-year precedent set by the security system.

additional goal for these women—the goal of helping them to maximize their earning capacities. Even if these women have been employed during marriage, it is likely that marriage has had a detrimental effect on their careers. What they need now are spousal support awards that allow them to take advantage of the benefits of counseling, education, and retraining, and enable them to fully invest in their careers. Since we have seen the payoffs of high support in the early postdivorce years for long-term earning capacity, their support awards should begin with several years of balloon payments to subsidize training or retraining so that they can maximize their long-term employment potential.

In both cases, the postdivorce support award should provide for cost-of-living increases so that their real values do not erode with each passing year. In addition, penalties and interest should be assessed on late payments.

Child Support

Current child support awards are too low, poorly enforced, and place a disproportionate financial burden on mothers.

Several steps could be taken to improve this situation. First, courts should establish realistic guidelines for child support awards based on the income sharing approach and the assumption that children are entitled to maintain the standard of living of the higher-income parent insofar as possible. Thus each parent should contribute to child support according to his or her ability to pay—with due consideration given to the caretaking contribution of the custodial parent. (The innovative guidelines established in Delaware, Minnesota, and Wisconsin provide potential models.)[30]

A second set of child support issues concerns the support of children over age eighteen. Under the present California law they are treated as adults (even if they are still high school students), and their parents are not legally obligated to contribute to their support. The *de facto* result of this rule is that mothers' more limited resources are further strained. The policy recommendation in this sphere is to require parents to support children until they complete their college education. Parental contributions for such support could be apportioned according to the parents' relative incomes, just as it is for minor children.

One model for new legislation is the New York rule that presumes support lasts until the child reaches age 21 unless the child becomes emancipated. A second model is the rule in the State of Washington which permits divorce courts to order parents to support their college age children past majority (until they complete their undergraduate education if they are full-time students).

A third necessity for child support awards is that they include provisions for automatic cost of living adjustments (COLA), as do many private and government stipends (such as social security awards). Since the purchasing power of child support awards is eroded in an inflationary economy, awards must be linked to the consumer price index or to some other basic economic indicator that will allow for automatic adjustments that maintain a steady standard of living. In addition, penalties and interest should be assessed on late payments.

Fourth, to improve child support we must distinguish and emphasize the question of enforcement. Since fathers who earn between $30,000 and $50,000 a year are just as likely to default on their child support as those who earn $20,000, it is evident that the father's ability to pay is not what determines compliance. Rather, it is the system of enforcement—and that system clearly needs to be strengthened.

One way to improve the system of enforcing child support is to shift the burden of monitoring and securing compliance from the recipient to the state. An ideal system would follow the Swedish model in which the state itself pays the full amount of the child support to the recipient and takes the full responsibility for collecting it from the donor.[31]

Short of this, however, there are other known, effective means of increasing compliance which should be adopted on a national scale: automatic wage assignments that begin with the inception of the order; channeling support payments through administrative arms of the court that monitor compliance and rapidly initiate enforcement action as soon as a single payment is overdue; intercepting state and federal income tax refunds to secure past-due support from delinquent fathers; expanding location and tracking procedures through Social Security and the Internal Revenue Service; and securing payment through the posting of bonds and obtaining liens on property. While many of these enforcement procedures are incorporated into the federal legislation of 1984, they have yet to be adopted by and fully utilized by most states.

Fifth, since we have seen repeated examples of judges choosing not to enforce the laws on the books—refusing to issue wage assignments, "forgiving" arrearages for past-due support, excusing flagrant offenders with no more than repeated "warnings" and refusing to require a bond or other form of security from fathers with a history of noncompliance—it is evident that the system of enforcement itself requires monitoring. One solution that has been suggested follows the Michigan model of establishing an administrative division within the court to receive and monitor payments and to initiate enforcement action.[32] Since we know that a substantial increase in compliance can be achieved by the adoption of a system that includes both the threat and practice of incarceration for noncompliance, it is essential that these remedies not be left solely to the discretion of judges. Rather, sentencing guidelines and judicial monitoring are necessary to ensure that judges do not undermine the system of enforcement.

Finally, more imaginative means of securing voluntary compliance ought to be considered. For example, several counties have obtained a dramatic increase in voluntary compliance after they begin publishing the names of noncomplying fathers in local newspapers.[33]

Custody

Although the laws governing custody have changed considerably, actual custodial arrangements have not. Despite the sex-neutral laws, mothers remain the primary caretakers of children after divorce. However, joint custody legislation, especially in states such as California where it is strongly favored, has significantly affected the relative bargaining positions of men and women. Women are more likely to forgo their claims to support and property if threatened with loss of custody or with custodial arrangements that they see as untenable or harmful to their children, and the new laws give men greater power to make such demands. In addition, as joint legal custodians, men not only have more control over their children; they also have more control over the postdivorce lives of their ex-wives.

One problem with the current custody laws is that they treat all men and all women as if they were equally capable of caring for their children after divorce. This ignores the social reality that in most families one parent, typically the mother, has been the primary caretaking parent. Children are likely to suffer a greater loss if they are separated from the primary caretakers and primary caretakers are likely to suffer more if they lose their children.[34] Laws that ignore these social facts place a cruel and unnecessary pressure on primary caretakers to trade away financial benefits for fear of losing their children.

Two alternatives are recommended in setting standards for custody awards: a primary caretaker presumption for sole custody awards, and a joint custody option only upon the agreement of both parties.

Consider first a rule that would create a presumption that custody will be awarded to the primary caretaker. This would serve to maintain the child's bond to the parent more directly involved in child care during the marriage, and thus would ensure optimal continuity and stability for the child. Moreover, because it is a sex-neutral rule it accommodates cases in which the father has been the primary parent. In fact, it makes it evident that parenting during marriage, by both mothers and fathers, is to be valued and rewarded. Thus another advantage of this rule is that it encourages and rewards child caretaking during marriage. Finally, this rule provides a more clear-cut criterion than the present "best interest of the child" standard and thereby discourages the use of a custody threat as a bargaining chip.

The second policy recommendation calls for laws that permit joint custody only when both parents agree. We have seen that coercive joint custody laws, such as the preference for joint custody in the California law, give men equal rights without equal responsibility. Although they hold the promise of enabling men to share the responsibility of caring for children after divorce, in practice most children continue to live with their mothers. By the same token, fathers have a new justification for reducing child support and for increasing control over their former wives' decisions and lifestyle.

In addition to changing the rules for custody, it is clear that stronger social and economic supports are needed for custodial parents, whether male or female, in the larger society. The possible range and nature of such supports are suggested by the following statement from a Norwegian social scientist who was herself recently divorced:

> Everyone [in Norway] knows that divorced [custodial] parents need more money and more social support because of the additional pressures involved in raising children as a single parent. As soon as I got divorced my income went up: both the local and national government increased my mother's allowance, my tax rate dropped drastically as I was now taxed at the lower rate of a single head of household, and my former husband contributed to child support. It also helped to have . . . day care and a husband who was willing to take some of the responsibility for parenting during the week.[35]

The advantages of a legal (and social) system that takes seriously its responsibility to provide protection and support for parents and their children after divorce is evident. For example, in another Scandinavian country, Sweden, the state assures custodial parents of steady child support payments (custodial mothers receive the amount of child support awarded to them from the state, which then collects the money from the noncustodial parent).[36] In addition, in Sweden and Norway all mothers are given a special mother's allowance to ensure that every child is raised in a household with an adequate standard of living. The state also provides universal health and hospital coverage and a wide range of other social benefits (such as subsidized housing) that further ensure that all children have the basic necessities of life. Finally, both local and national tax laws give the custodial mother special benefits so that she retains a larger portion of the income she earns.[37] As a result of these extensive benefits and the protected legal treatment they receive, divorced women and their children in Sweden live, on the average, at 90 percent of their predivorce standard of living.[38] They are spared the economic hardships that befall so many American women and children.

The Role of Judges and Lawyers

Since all these policy recommendations focus on legislative reforms, one might ask whether judicial education and continuing education of the bar might not provide equally useful routes to bring about change. One hopeful indication of the prospects for change comes from my own experience in judicial education seminars. When I first began presenting the data from this research, the findings were greeted with some skepticism. Each judge insisted that he (the overwhelming majority of judges who hear family law cases are male) was not awarding low amounts of alimony and/or child support. Further, most judges insisted that they were not awarding a larger proportion of the family income or property to the husband.

I soon learned to begin my talks by presenting a few hypothetical cases and asking the judges to set awards for Ann Thompson, the fifty-three year old housewife, and Pat Byrd, the young mother of preschool children. After collecting and tabulating their responses in front of the audience (i.e., their awards of child and spousal support, and their disposition of the family home when that home was the sole asset of a family with preschool children), we proceeded to "trace out" the implications of the awards they had just made. The results of their awards were compared to the costs of raising children, to state welfare and poverty levels, and to the husbands' disposable income after divorce. Women's job prospects and average wages were examined, and the probable postdivorce income of husband and wife were compared.

When it became clear that awards that seemed fair in the abstract—awards that would "allow" a man to keep "enough" of his income and yet effect an "equal" division of family income and assets—actually served in these concrete cases to severely disadvantage women and children, the judges were more receptive to the notion that they should reconsider the consequences of their decisions and begin to think about what awards-setting standards might lead to more equitable results.

While this suggests the potential benefits of judicial education, it is clearly not a panacea. The pervasive pattern of judicial attitudes and practices . . . —the judges' open disregard of the law requiring them to order wage attachments for fathers who are not paying child support; their willingness to forgive the arrearage on past-due child support because it "unfairly burdens" the father; their readiness to attribute earning capacity to an older housewife; and their assumption that it is fair to divide family income so that the wife and children share one-third, while the husband keeps the other two-thirds for himself—make one hesitate to rely on any prescription that seeks to change judges instead of changing the law itself.

It is also impossible to ignore the implicit sex bias in the way many judges define what is reasonable or unreasonable. For example, judges rarely grant a wife's request for a forced sale of the family business so that she can obtain her share of the equity, because they see an overriding interest in preserving the "husband's" business intact. However, when a husband requests an immediate sale of the family home so he can cash out his share of the equity while the wife seeks to delay the sale to ensure housing for the children, the judges tend to see the overriding interest as, again, the *husband's* need for *his* share of the equity. In the first case they tell the wife that it is reasonable to make *her* wait for her share of the equity, but in the second case they say it is unreasonable to make a husband wait for his share.

Consider also what judges consider a reasonable arrangement for the management and control of a family business or closely held "family" corporation. Here the judges typically acknowledge that to compel divorced spouses to jointly manage an ongoing business would be disruptive and impractical; rather, *one* person has to be empowered to make the final decisions. They therefore award the business management and control (as well as outright ownership, in some cases) to one spouse, invariably the husband. They simply overlook the *wife's right* to share equally in the control of a business or company that she partially owns.

However, when the same issues are raised about joint child custody, judges see no problem about compelling divorced spouses to cooperate in an ongoing relationship to make decisions. Nor do they see the impracticability of divided authority, or the disruption that this may cause for children. Rather, they focus on the *father's right* to share parental authority.

Finally, consider judicial attitudes towards the goodwill value of a business or a profession. Many judges frankly admit that they are reluctant to recognize the goodwill in a profession because it would be too difficult for the husband to raise the capital to "buy back his wife's share." However, when an older housewife who has spent twenty or thirty years in the family home points out that it is virtually impossible for her to raise the capital to buy out her husband's share of the home, judges say her practical difficulties are irrelevant.

These attitudes underscore the need for the type of explicit judicial directives that have been suggested above.

Several other recommendations on the judiciary were originally suggested by attorneys in our sample and have been reiterated at virtually every meeting I have had with attorneys and bar association groups. The first is for a specialized judiciary with an interest and expertise in the family law area. It is openly acknowledged that many California judges are political appointees with primary experience in criminal courts: they have no interest or experience in family law; and they resent hearing divorce cases and being assigned to the domestic relations calendar.* Such judges may "endure" the assignment but make no effort to keep up with recent case law developments or to master the body of knowledge necessary to make competent judgments. Thus attorneys complain of having to educate judges in the course of presenting their cases, and of facing judges who do not want to bother to read briefs or hear case law precendents.

It is therefore recommended that judges assigned to family law cases have prior experience, knowledge and interest in family law. In addition, courts could hire special commissioners with such expertise. Since these recommendations may be at odds with the current system of judicial appointments and the structure of the courts in many counties, an alternative is to require *mandatory judicial education before* judges are assigned to hear divorce cases. In addition, once a judge is assigned to the domestic relations calendar, continuing education courses, on an annual basis, should be mandatory.

Along with the need for a specialized bench and for compulsory judicial education, there is clearly a need for more judges to be assigned to hear family law cases. These cases now comprise one-half of all the cases in most counties, yet they are typically rushed through the judicial process because they are assigned only one-tenth (or less) of judicial time. Since the judges who are assigned to domestic relations can rarely handle the entire caseload of pending divorces, it is common practice in many counties to assign divorce cases that require more than a half day or day of court time to the "master calendar" where they are given the next available superior court judge. It is, as one attorney put it, "like playing Russian roulette with my client's future because we can be assigned to a judge who doesn't have a clue about family law, hasn't heard a case in 3 years, and has never dealt with a complicated pension case in his life."

This appalling situation would also be alleviated by the establishment of a specialized family law bench with knowledgeable, experienced, and interested judges who participate in annual judicial education programs. In addition, sufficient judicial personnel should be assigned to the family court so that all of the divorce cases can be heard by those judges.

A final suggestion for the judiciary involves awards of attorneys fees and legal costs. Attorneys frequently cited the difficulties they face in obtaining awards for appraisers' and experts' fees when they represent the lower-earning or unemployed spouse. Although the law allows judges to award attorneys' fees and legal costs, judges typically award only a fraction of the costs requested or refuse to award any fees at all. This puts a greater burden on the attorney who represents the lower-earning spouse, or the spouse who has less access to family resources, who is usually the wife. An attorney's vigorous representation of the interests of the lower-income spouse is undermined if the attorney does not have the money to pay

---

*The central Los Angeles court is unique in having a system of specialized commissioners with expertise in family law and the attorneys in that community rate the competence of the judiciary as high.

for depositions, investigative accountants, and independent appraisals. (These are serious handicaps when added to the initial handicaps of a spouse who typically has less knowledge of the family's finances.) Thus it is urged that judges be encouraged to award attorneys' fees and legal costs to the attorney representing the lower-earning spouse so that person is not disadvantaged in the legal process.

The prospects for change through individual attorneys are also problematic. Even those attorneys who spontaneously commented on the ways the present system of divorce disadvantages women, felt there was little they could do—as individual attorneys—to change it. In their own practices, they felt they must be "realistic" in advising their clients, and this meant giving clients reliable information about how the system operates in practice. For example, one male attorney said:

> I have to think of my reputation. I don't want to be known as a woman's lawyer. I have to be fair to my male clients and let them know what the court expects of them. No man will listen to me if I tell him to give his wife half of his income or to turn the house over to her—and he could sue me for malpractice.

Another explained his advice to female clients in this way:

> I'm not doing my client any good if I lead her to believe she can maintain her life style. I have to prepare her for the worst. . . . Then if we're lucky enough to get any alimony, she'll think I'm terrific—which I am.

The lawyer's concern with maintaining his or her reputation, avoiding malpractice claims, and establishing realistic expectations to assure satisfied clients, all discourage taking risks and trying to "buck the system." In addition, since most negotiations are done with other attorneys who also "know the system," an attorney stands little chance of persuading them to deny the best interests of their own clients. Rather, an attorney who persists in trying to obtain more alimony or property for disadvantaged female clients simply risks damaging his or her own reputation as a competent lawyer.

The structure of the legal profession links attorneys to individual clients and rewards them for representing the client's interests. One particularly poignant example of this reality involved an attorney who, at the time of our interview, was struggling with the question of a wealthy doctor's support for his college-age children. While the doctor could well afford to support his children through college and graduate school, and was ready to sign an agreement to do so, the attorney had a professional responsibility to tell the doctor that the law did not require him to support his children past age eighteen. In this case the attorney felt the doctor might later regret the agreement he was about to sign, and might then allege malpractice because his attorney had not clearly informed him of the extent to which his choice was voluntary and exceeded the norms. On the other hand, the last time this attorney had handled a similar case, he wrote a letter to the client outlining his legal options (to protect himself from a future malpractice claim) and asked the client to countersign the letter. The letter had such a negative impact that the client decided not to agree to pay for these college expenses after all.

These examples suggest, once again, that the route to divorce law reform must have a strong legislative focus.

CONCLUSION

My research reveals that the economic consequences of the present system of divorce are unfair to women and children. Divorce today spells financial disaster for too many women and for the minor children in their custody. The data reveal a dramatic contrast in financial status of divorced men and divorced women at every income level and every level of marital duration. Women of all ages and at all socioeconomic levels experience a precipitous decline in standard of living within one year after divorce, while their former husbands' standard of living improves. Older women and women divorced from men in the higher-income brackets experience the most radical downward mobility.

These economic changes have drastic psychosocial effects on the children of divorce. The sharp decline in mothers' standard of living forces residential moves with resulting changes in schools, teachers, neighbors, and friends. Mothers pressured to earn money have little time and energy to devote to their children just when the children need them most. Moreover, when the discrepancy in standard of living between children and father is great, children feel angry and rejected and are likely to share their mother's feelings of resentment.

These findings make it clear that, for all its aims at fairness, the current no-fault system of divorce is inflicting a high economic toll upon women and children. The time has come for us to recognize that divorced women and children need greater economic protection, and to implement the legal changes necessary to achieve that goal.

We do not have to tolerate the hardships that the present legal system inflicts in order to achieve the long-range goal of equality: true equality cannot evolve while these abuses persist. Nor do we have to return to the traditional fault-based system to obtain economic settlements that better protect dependent wives and children. The no-fault law took a major step forward by reducing the acrimony and hostility in the legal process of divorce, but because it did not provide economic protection for women and children, it failed to achieve its loftier goals of fairness, justice, and economically based equality.

The lesson of this experience is not that the goals of divorce law reforms were unworthy, but rather that the means used to achieve them were not in all ways appropriate. The law requires a continuous process of correction and refinement. We should not lose sight of the fact that it is the means that need correcting—not the ends.

We now have the knowledge and experience to fashion remedies that can promote those goals and, at the same time, protect women and children from the economic devastations of divorce. As our awareness of the inequities of the present system has increased, so too has our knowledge of the changes that are necessary to correct these inequities. The paths before us are clear. It is now time for us to follow through on the road to fairness, equity, and equality in the legal process of divorce.

NOTES

1. Herma Hill Kay, "A Family Court: The California Proposal," in *Divorce and After*, Paul Bohannan, ed. (New York: Doubleday, 1970), p. 248.

2. See generally, Leo Kanowitz, *Women and the Law* (Albuquerque, New Mexico: University of New Mexico Press, 1969); Barbara A. Babcock, Ann E. Freedman, Eleanor Holmes Norton, Susan D. Ross, *Sex Discrimination and the Law: Causes and Remedies* (Boston: Little Brown & Co., 1975); Herma Hill Kay, *Sex-Based Discrimination in Family Law* (St. Paul, Minn.: West Publishing Co., 1974); and Lenore J. Weitzman, *The Marriage Contract: Spouses, Lovers, and the Law* (New York: The Free Press, 1983).

3. Betty Friedan, *It Changed My Life* (New York: Random House, 1976), p. 325 (hereafter cited as Friedan, *It Changed My Life*).

4. Friedan, *It Changed My Life*, p. 326.

5. See Herma Hill Kay, "The California Background," unpublished paper written for the California Divorce Law Research Project, Center for the Study of Law and Society, University of California, Berkeley, September 1977 (on file at the author's office in the Boalt Hall School of Law, University of California, Berkeley) (hereafter cited as Kay "California Background").

6. Ibid.

7. See Kay "California Background," p. 21.

8. This point is made by attorney Riane Eisler, who notes that the California law was changed *before* the feminist movement began to have an impact:

   > It has been said, sometimes even by the men drafting these laws, that no-fault is a product of women's liberation, or of what some people call the "male backlash." But the first no-fault divorce laws in this country were passed in California early in 1969, by almost all-male legislature, before most people had even heard of the women's liberation movement.

   Dissolution: No-Fault Divorce, Marriage and the Future of Women (New York: McGraw-Hill, 1977) p. 11. I am indebted to Mary Sylvester who checked twelve sources on the legal history of the California legal reform and was unable to find any mention of feminist participation or women's issues, with the exception of the Eisler observation quoted above and Professor Kay's statement that no organized women's groups participated. Kay, "The California Background," pp. 78, 79.

9. Kay, "The California Background," p. 45.

10. Ibid., pp. 79–80.

11. Assembly Committe Report on Assembly Bill No. 530 and Senate Bill No. 252 (The Family Law Act) submitted by Committee on the Judiciary, James A. Hayes, Chairman, August 8, 1969, printed in *Assembly Daily Journal* (Sacramento, California, Aug. 9, 1969).

12. See Frank F. Furstenburg, Christine W. Nord, James L. Peterson, and Nicholas Zill, "The Life Course of Children of Divorce: Marital Disruption and Parental Contact," *American Sociological Review* Vol. 48, October 1983, pp. 656–668.

13. Samuel H. Preston, "Children and the Elderly: Divergent Paths for America's Dependents," *Demography* Vol. 21, no. 4, November 1984, pp. 435–457.

14. Shirley Johnson, "The Economic Position of Divorced Women," *Fairshare*, 1985.

15. Ibid.

16. Barbara Ehrenreich offers a fascinating explanation for the recent "flight from commitment": it was men, she argues, who first rebelled against their traditional sex roles and abandoned the breadwinner ethic for the individualism of the "me" generation. See Barbara Ehrenreich, *The Hearts of Men* (Garden City, New York: Anchor Press/Doubleday, 1983).

17. See, for example, Christopher Lasch, *The Culture of Narcissism* (New York: Norton, 1979).

18. Arlene S. Skolnick, *The Intimate Environment: Exploring Marriage and The Family*," third edition (Boston: Little Brown, 1983), p. 22 (hereafter cited as Skolnick, *Intimate Environment*).

19. William J. Goode, *World Revolution in Family Patterns* (New York: The Free Press, 1986), pp. 6–7.

20. Skolnick, *Intimate Environment*, p. 22.

21. Lawrence Stone, *The Family, Sex and Marriage in England, 1500–1800* (New York: Harper and Row, 1977).

22. Ibid. For a summary of Stone's thesis, see Lawrence Stone, "The Historical Origins of the Modern Family," The O. Meredith Wilson Lecture in History published by the Dept. of History, University of Utah, Salt Lake City, Utah, 1982, pp. 11–12.

23. Pepper Schwartz, master lecture presented at the National Council on Family Relations, October 18, 1984, drawing on data from Philip Blumstein and Pepper W. Schwartz, *American Couples: Money, Work, Sex* (New York: William Morrow & Co., 1983).

24. Mary Ann Glendon, *The New Family and The New Property* (Toronto: Butterworths, 1981).

25. Ibid.

26. Ibid.

27. William J. Goode, "Individual Investments in the Family Collectivity," *The Tocqueville Review* Vol. 6, no. 1, Summer 1984.

28. Ibid.

29. The 1984 child support enforcement legislation explicitly approves of the use of property as security to ensure child support payments.

30. Interview with Susan Paikin, Delaware Family Court, August 1984.

31. See Anders Agell, "Paying of Maintenance in Sweden," 1981. Paper presented at the International Conference on Matrimonial and Child Support, May 27–30, 1981, The Institute of Law Research and Reform (Edmonton, Alberta, Canada: University of Alberta, 1982) (hereafter cited as Agell, "Maintenance").

32. See David Chambers, *Making Fathers Pay* (Chicago: University of Chicago Press, 1979).

33. Report of John Schambre, Program Specialist, Office of Child Support Enforcement, Region IX, San Francisco, at Hawaii Child Support Enforcement Judicial Education Seminar, January 18, 1985.

34. This position is asserted in Joseph Goldstein, Anna Freud, and Albert J. Solnit, *Beyond the Best Interests of the Child* (New York: The Free Press, 1973) and Nancy D. Polikoff, "Gender and Child Custody Determinations: Exploding the Myths," in *Families, Politics and Public Policy: A Feminist Dialogue on Women and the State*, Irene Diamond, ed. (New York: Longman, 1983), pp. 183–202.

35. Personal interview on file at author's office.

36. Agell, "Maintenance."

37. Ibid.

38. Sheila B. Kamerman and Alfred J. Kahn, "Child Support: Some International Developments," in *The Parental Child-Support Obligation*, Judith Cassetty, ed. (Lexington, Mass.: D. C. Heath and Co., 1983), pp. 227–239.

PART II

GENDER RELATIONS: INEQUALITY, SEXUALITY, AND INTIMACY

Gender relations both within and outside of marriage and the family have been influenced by the ideology of patriarchal authority, which has been deeply entrenched in political, social, and economic institutions. Patriarchy has affected premarital, marital, and familial relationships and has been articulated in attitudes and behavior regarding sexuality, intimacy, power, and privilege.

However, the ideological revolutions regarding marriage and the family combined with the processes of industrialization and urbanization have produced a major reconceptualization of gender role relations within the last two hundred years. Social scientists (Ariès 1962; Shorter 1975; Stone 1977) have observed that prior to that period, the Western European and American nuclear family was not intimate and did not encourage domesticity or privacy. The inseparable and indistinguishable facets of social life were family and community. The notion of family privacy was practically unknown. Indeed, the very concept of the nuclear family did not emerge until the seventeenth century. The low valuation of the family in preindustrial Western society occurred because of the individual's almost total involvement with the community. The general situation was one in which most activities were public and one where people were rarely alone. The lack of privacy attributed to this overwhelming community sociability hindered the development of the family as we know it.

The family in this preindustrial period and extending into much later periods was patriarchal and authoritarian, and demanded deference. Husbands had virtually absolute power and control over wives and children. The relationship between husband and wife was not as intimate or private as it is today. In addition, the status and treatment of women varied with their involvement in economically productive work. When a woman contributed economically, she had more power and control over her own life. When she did not, her life was that of a domestically confined slave, servile and subservient to her master—her husband. The absolute power of the husband held true not only in economic terms but also in moral matters. Both women and children were relegated to subordinate legal positions that were based on the economic and political control of the husbands and fathers.

The rise of the national state, ideological changes (see Berger and Berger, Article 2) that included emerging ideas about liberty and the importance of the individual, combined with the Industrial Revolution all contributed to changes in the way marriage and the family was conceptualized. Traditional patriarchal relations were gradually replaced by romantic love, companionate marriage, and an affectionate and permissive mode of child rearing. Edward Shorter (1975) labels the changes in the period after 1750 as the "Sentimental Revolution." The Sentimental Revolution ushered in a new emotional component to gender relations in three areas: courtship, the mother-child relationship, and the relationship of the family with the community.

The emergent emphasis on affection, friendship, and the romantic love ideology began to characterize courtship. As a result, marriage became more and more a matter of free choice rather than an arrangement determined by the parents on the basis of economic and social considerations. Attitudes toward children underwent a similar change, with new sentiments of affection and love emerging and neglect and indifference decreasing. An increase in the growth of maternal care and the development of a more loving attitude toward children by their mothers resulted. These shifting sentiments brought about a change in the relationship of the family to the community. Affection and caring tied the husband-wife relationship tighter and began to replace lineage, property, and economic considerations as the foundation of the marriage. Simultaneously, the couple's involvement with the community lessened.

In summary, the historical evidence illustrates two processes at work: the first is the couple's almost complete withdrawal from the community; the second is the corresponding strength of the ties of the couple with each other and with their children and close relatives. Taken together, these processes are often seen to have disturbed the grip of patriarchy on marriage and the family. The readings in this part of the book will investigate whether this has in fact occurred in the areas of dating and courtship (Chapter Five), sexuality and intimacy (Chapter Six), power and intimacy (Chapter Seven), and in the interrelationship of family and workplace (Chapter Eight).

Most social historians believe that the modern American family emerged with the American Revolution and formed its major components by 1830. The four predominant characteristics of the American family are marriage based on affection and mutual respect, low fertility, child-centeredness, and what historian Carl Degler (1980) has called the "doctrine of the two spheres." This doctrine held that the primary role of the wife was child care and the maintenance of the household (the private sphere) while the husband's was work outside the home (the public sphere). Anchoring this doctrine was the belief that while the wife may be the moral superior in the relationship, legal and social power rests with the husband. The direct consequence is the subordination of women's roles to their husbands'. To deal with subordination, women carved out a source of power based on the emerging importance of mutual affection, love, and sexuality as integral components of modern marriage. As we shall see, a number of our readings will examine this development within an analysis of dating and courtship processes and in the expressions of sexuality.

An analysis of American courtship processes reflects historical changes that have shifted decision making from parental control to the couple themselves. This shift reflects the emerging nineteenth-century attitude that marriage should be based on personal happiness and the affection of the partners for each other. As marriage began to be equated with love and individualism, the growing acceptance of affection as the primary ground for marriage became an essential factor in the change in women's roles and a potential source of power and autonomy within the family. A woman could appeal to her husband's affection for her, and she, in turn, could manipulate that affection to increase her power or influence within marriage and the household.

Similarly, the expression of sexuality both within and outside of the courtship process took on a power component. The Victorian notion of the "passionlessness" woman can be seen as serving to improve women's status. Nancy Cott (1977) contends that the downplaying of sexuality could be used as a means of limiting male domination. The de-emphasis of feminine sexuality was replaced by an emphasis on women's moral and spiritual superiority over males and was used to enhance their status and widen their opportunities.

The doctrine of the two spheres that developed in the nineteenth century defined the essence of maleness as occupational involvement and the pursuit of worldly and material success. Women, on the other hand, were defined in terms of home—wife and mother—involvement and moral virtue. As a consequence, the idealization of masculine and feminine behavior affected courtship to the extent that romantic love took on greater importance as the criterion for marriage than ever before. Yet, ultimately, the doctrine of the two spheres continued to foster obstacles to friendship between the sexes, often resulting in a reliance on same sex friendships. Further, it severely handicapped the development of emotional bonds within courtship.

In the opening article (15) of Chapter Five, Dating and Courtship, Beth L. Bailey examines the economy of dating in the first three decades of the twentieth century. Her analysis reflects, in part, the work of Willard Waller, who in an influential 1937 article discussed the "rating and dating complex" that seemed to exist in colleges. Waller described a mutually exploitative dating system in which male students sought sexual gratification while women sought to enhance their prestige by going out with the more desirable men and being taken to restaurants, theaters, amusements, etc. As a result, dating became a bargaining relationship with exploitative and antagonistic overtones. Waller further speculated that the gender role antagonisms generated by the dating system were continued in courtship, love, and marriage and led to undesirable emotional tensions throughout the couples' lives. He conceptualized the "principle of least interest" to describe how unequal emotional involvement could lead to the person with "least interest" exploiting the other throughout their relationship.

Michael Moffatt (Article 16) updates the current college dating scene by reporting on the expression of sexuality among undergraduates at Rutgers University in New Jersey. The sexual experiences range from casual sex to "caring" sexual relationships. As noted by Moffatt, there is no necessary correlation between sexual experience and involvement in happy or satisfying sexual relationships. Moffatt believes that collegiate sex is but a variation on modern American suburban sex.

Egon Mayer's discussion (Article 17) of intermarriage between Jews and Christians revolves around the issues of individualism and love versus tradition and family continuity. An underlying issue is the maintenance of ethnic identity in intermarriages and the continuation of that identity in future generations.

The readings in Chapter Six, Sexuality and Power, focus on the theme of sexuality and intimacy. Ira Reiss (Article 18) has been a leading scholar in the sociological study of sexuality. Here, Reiss calls for a comprehensive sociological theory of human sexuality. In articulating such a theory, Reiss believes that sexuality must be seen as intrinsically linked with marital jealousy, gender role power, and ideological beliefs about normality.

The next reading employs a social-historical perspective in examining aspects of sexuality and intimacy in twentieth-century America. John D'Emilio and Estelle B. Freedman in their selection, "The Sexualized Society" (Article 19), perceive a major reshaping of sexuality in the 1960s and 1970s. They contend that the emphasis on individuality and the pursuit of happiness is extended into the realm of sexuality. Sexuality now ceases to be defined primarily in terms of reproduction and, further, is no longer limited to expressiveness within marriage. Affection, intimacy, and sexuality have become more and more a matter of individual choice; not only is it no longer solely defined in terms of the family but it also is no longer solely defined in terms of heterosexuality.

Francesca M. Cancian explores the "feminization of love," in Article 20. The feminized perspective defines love in terms of emotional expressiveness, verbal self-disclosure, and affection. Women are identified with this perspective. In contrast, the definition largely ignores love manifested by instrumental help or the sharing of physical activities that has been identified with masculine behavior. She argues that, by conceptualizing love in this manner, polarized gender role relationships that contribute to social and economic inequality occur. She calls for an androgynous perspective that rejects the underlying ideology of separate spheres and validates masculine as well as feminine styles of love.

The concluding article (21) in this chapter is Adele Bahn and Angela Jaquez's "One Style of Dominican Bridal Shower." The authors provide an ethnographic account of what, at first glance, seems as a festive celebration with no serious intent. However, the underlying meaning of bridal showers for these Dominican women living in New York City revolves around the anticipatory socialization of the prospective wife into four roles. The shower is seen to reflect old and new norms that prescribe and reinforce the traditional roles for the bride, including the role of a woman among women, the sexual role, the homemaker role, and the subservient role of the wife vis-a-vis the husband.

Chapter Seven, Power and Intimacy, opens with a social-historical examination of etiquette books (Article 22). The authors, Pearl Bartelt, Mark Hutter, and David W. Bartelt, argue that etiquette books have played an instrumental role in developing a gender-specific behavioral guideline for women. Etiquette books are examined to see how they have articulated rules regarding gender role behavior in public places, at work, and in the home. These books are seen to have perpetuated the power and status of men and maintain women in subordinate positions.

Mary Feld Belenky and her associates (Article 23) examine the "politics of talk," the forms of discourse that family members permit or minimize, encourage or prohibit in family life. A series of questions regarding the rules of conversational discourse and expressing feelings and intimacies among parents and children are articulated and considered in order to shed light on the kinds of domestic environments that "nurture and constrain the development of a sense of mind and voice in women." The authors' work includes an analysis of families from different social class backgrounds.

The concluding selection (Article 24) is an ethnographic account of marital sexuality written by Lillian B. Rubin. In an earlier book, *Worlds of Pain*, Rubin (1976) recounted the experiences of fifty white working class families. Neither the husbands nor the wives had more than a high school education. The men all had blue-collar jobs and most of the women held part-time jobs. Major family decisions, whether to buy a house or a car, where and when to take vacations, and how to spend money, were seen by men as their prerogative. Economic concerns are a major factor in the general level of dissatisfaction that both felt, but women in particular felt particularly trapped in their houses and with their never-ending housework. Rubin wanted to know the extent to which these problems and conflicts had affected their sexual adjustment. She found strong dissatisfactions felt by both men and women that were seen to reflect the fundamental differences in the ways that these men and women conceptualize sexuality and emotional expressivity.

In "The Sexual Dilemma," a chapter from her more recent book, *Intimate Strangers*, Rubin extends her analysis to a more diversified sample of American marriages. Her analysis is based on 15 years of research, many as a psychotherapist, and on interviews with 150 couples between the ages of 25 and 55 who have lived together for at least 5 and as many as 35 years. Rubin is concerned with the marital, familial, and sexual revolutions of recent years and how these have affected the gender role relationships between wives and husbands. Here again, Rubin sees that differential attitudes toward sexuality and emotional attachment are often a fundamental source of problems within marriages. To further demonstrate her point, Rubin compares the sexual behaviors of lesbians and homosexual men, concluding that for both homosexuals and heterosexuals "the character of the split between sex and emotion is the same."

Chapter Eight, Family and Workplace Organization, contains three articles (25, 27, 28) focusing on gender relationships in terms of the different allocations and divisions of labor that exist between outside work and the home. In various ways the readings selected here all illustrate the continued pervasiveness of patriarchal ideology. We find that the notion of the two spheres of men's place in the work force and women's place in the home affects the nature and character of marital and familial relationships and involvements.

Jesse Bernard, in her often cited work on the "good provider" (Article 25), traces the historical development of male familial roles in the United States. Essentially, the good-provider role defined a man as one whose wife did not have to, or should not, enter the labor force. The good-provider role is seen to have implications for both men and women. For men, the consequence of the good-provider role helped develop the predominant concept of male identity in terms of work and career activities. Consequently, the development of this specialized male role removed women from labor-force participation and income-producing activities and made possible their total involvement with child-rearing and domestic household activities. The results of changes in the good-provider role in the last 20 years for both men and women are examined by Bernard.

Barbara Levy Simon in her Book, *Never Married Women*, studied the lives of 50 women from 66- to 101-years old and from diverse ethnic, religious, and social class backgrounds who have in common an uncommon marital status. Simon (Article 26) is concerned with destroying the popular images of the "old maid" by introducing us to the actualities of single women's daily lives. A rapidly increasing number of women in the last 10 years have been delaying marriage until their mid-to late thirties, and a significant number will never marry. In this light, the insights gained from Simon's study of these women who have rejected the societal norm of marriage and child bearing have particular relevancy. Further, the cultural diversity and the age of her sample further documents the diversity of life cycle experiences among women in twentieth-century America.

Arlie Russell Hochschild (Article 27) examines the contemporary dual-career family. This paper was later elaborated in her widely praised book, *The Second Shift*, published in 1989. Hochschild is concerned with how cultural definitions of "appropriate" domestic roles and labor-force roles affect marital dynamics. She observes that contemporary economic trends have altered women's lives much more so than they have altered men's lives.

Women have found themselves in new circumstances: they are working full time in the paid labor force, yet, at the same time, they are seen as primarily involved in domestic work. As a result, women are experiencing a "culture lag" in the larger world, and a "gender lag" in the home. There is a lag regarding both attitudes and behavior towards women's paid work and domestic work. Women are confronted with a "second shift" of domestic labor because husbands are generally not increasing their work involvement with the home. Further, men have not emotionally supported women's role change to the same extent that women have. Hochschild analyzes this phenomenon through her concept of the "economy of gratitude." The concept is used to analyze whether husbands and wives have the same reality definitions about whether a given act requires an expression of appreciation and gratitude or not. The implications of differential reality definitions are then discussed by Hochschild.

REFERENCES

Ariès, Philippe. 1962. *Centuries of Childhood: A Social History of Family Life.* Translated by Robert Baldick. New York: Knopf.

Cott, Nancy. 1979. "Passionlessness: An Interpretation of Victorian Sexual Ideology, 1790–1850." Pp. 162–181 in *A Heritage of Her Own,* edited by Nancy F. Cott and Elizabeth H. Pleck. New York: Simon and Schuster.

Degler, Carl N. 1980. *At Odds: Women and the Family in America from the Revolution to the Present.* New York: Oxford University Press.

Hochschild, Arlie (with Anne Machung). 1989. *The Second Shift: Working Parents and the Revolution at Home.* New York: Viking.

Rubin, Lillian B. 1976. *Worlds of Pain.* New York: Basic Books.

Shorter, Edward. 1975. *The Making of the Modern Family.* New York: Basic Books.

Stone, Lawrence. 1977. *The Family, Sex and Marriage in England 1500–1800.* Abridged edition. New York: Harper/Colophon Books.

Waller, Willard. 1937. "The rating and Dating Complex." *American Sociological Review* 2:727–734.

Dating and Courtship

15

The Economy of Dating*

Beth L. Bailey

The "date" made its transition from lower-class slang to upper-crust rebellion and into middle-class convention with relative ease. To most observers, the gradual change from calling to dating looked like a natural accommodation to the new realities of twentieth-century life. Dating filled a need in an urban society in which not all respectable young women had parlors in their homes and childhood friends infrequently grew up to become husband and wife. Dating quickly became, and remains, the dominant mode of American courtship.

In the early twentieth century, the gloomiest critics feared only that this new system would make it harder for youth to negotiate the true business of courtship: marriage. Poor but ambitious and worthy young men could not attract suitable partners without spending vast sums on entertainment, and every theater ticket and late supper meant less money set aside toward that minimum figure needed to marry and start a family.

The critics were right, but in some ways their criticisms were irrelevant. Dating was not about marriage and families. It wasn't even about love—which is not to say that American youth didn't continue to fall in love, marry, and raise families. But before World War II, long-term commitments lay in the future for youth, clearly demarcated from from the dating system. In the public realm, in the shared culture that defined the conventions of dating and gave meaning and coherence to individual experience, dating was not about marriage. Dating was about competition.

Through at least the first two-thirds of the twentieth century, Americans thought of courtship as a system governed by laws of scarcity and abundance,

*Bailey, Beth L. 1988. "The Economy of Dating." Pp. 25–30 in *From Front Porch to Back Seat: Courtship in Twentieth-Century America*. Baltimore and London: The Johns Hopkins University Press.

and acted in accordance with that perception. Furthermore, America's system of courtship, as much as any other sphere of national life, mirrored the vicissitudes of economic and social opportunity and demands. In the 1920s, dating provided a new frontier for public competition through consumption, and in the 1930s it accepted competitive energies denied outlet elsewhere. In the postwar years, however, youth looked to courtship for a respite from the demands of a competitive society.

These different attitudes toward the role of competition in courtship before and after World War II are expressed in two distinct forms of dating. Before the war, American youth prized a promiscuous popularity, demonstrating competitive success through the number and variety of dates they commanded. After the war, youth turned to "going steady," saying that the system provided a measure of security and escape from the pressures of the postwar world. The courtship experience and ideals of those who grew up before the war were profoundly different from those of teenagers in the postwar years, and the differences created much intergenerational conflict. Yet, for all their disagreement, both groups understood dating in the same terms: competition, scarcity, abundance. This understanding of dating, as much as the system itself, was an accommodation to modern life.

Shortly after World War II ended, Margaret Mead gave a series of lectures on American courtship rituals. Although the system she described was already disappearing, she captured the essence of what dating meant in the interwar years. Dating, Mead stressed, was not about sex or adulthood or marriage. Instead, it was a "competitive game," a way for girls and boys to "demonstrate their popularity." This was not a startling revelation to the American public. Americans knew that dating was centered on competition and popularity. These were the terms in which dating was discussed, the vocabulary in which one described a date.[1]

In 1937, in the classic study of American dating, sociologist Willard Waller gave this competitive system a name: "the campus rating complex." His study of Penn State detailed a "dating and rating" system based on very clear standards of popularity. To be popular, men needed outward, material signs: an automobile, the right clothing, fraternity membership, money. Women's popularity depended on building and maintaining a reputation for popularity. They had to *be seen* with popular men in the "right" places, indignantly turn down requests for dates made at the "last minute" (which could be weeks in advance), and cultivate the impression that they were greatly in demand.[2]

Waller gave academic legitimacy to a practice and a label commonly employed since the early 1920s.[3] The competitive system of rating and dating flourished on college campuses well before Waller's study. It was a product of many long-term trends that had produced an awareness of youth as a discrete and definable experience and had fostered the development of a national youth culture. In the 1920s, youth most extravagantly celebrated their culture (for themselves and for the nation, through the attentions of national newspapers and magazines) on college campuses. While their numbers were relatively small, the doings of college youth carried much symbolic weight with adults and their nonstudent peers, who viewed youth culture sometimes with suspicion, sometimes with envy, almost always with fascination.

As Paula Fass argues in her study of American college youth in the 1920s, "Competition within conformity and conformity in the service of competition were the structuring facts of campus life in the twenties." Competition and conformity, the individual and the group, held each other in a delicate balance. Conformity to peer group standards set the limits of competition—and unleashed the forces of competition within the limits of peer culture. Sports, school spirit, organizational rivalry, social life, and consumption allowed full play of competitive urges. But because youth and its institutions were a separate culture in which one could participate for only a few years, competition was without significant long-term risk. This protected competition was seen as a training ground for the struggles young people would soon face in the world outside college. Moreover, and paradoxically, this competition expressed itself through conformity; conformity was the ultimate sphere of competition. It was a self-contained, self-regulating, self-limiting system.[4]

Fass explores these issues primarily in terms of organizational and institutional competition, but youth's evolving system of courtship also perfectly expressed them. The rating-and-dating system *was* individual competition expressed through conformity. The competition was individual, but in the 1920s success in courtship came to be defined by the peer group. Success was popularity. Popularity was—and could only be—defined and allocated by others.

By the 1930s, the competitive system of courtship was well entrenched. However, though the rating-and-dating system stayed much the same, it was fed from different sources in the Depression years of the 1930s. No longer was competitive youth culture seen as the training ground for success-bound youth. Instead, success in social competition compensated for fears that other avenues of competition were closed off. But that a system based on abundance, consumption, and relative protection from the realities of adult life could persist and grow stronger in the face of a national depression shows how completely it had replaced the older systems of courtship.

No matter how people conducted their private lives, from the mid-1920s to World War II the rating-dating system dominated public discourse on courtship.[5] Waller's model is validated by countless examples from the popular media. College campuses, the peer cultures in which the rating-dating complex originated, offer textbook cases. In *Mademoiselle's* 1938 college issue, a Smith senior advised incoming freshmen that they must cultivate an "image of popularity" if they wanted dates. "During your first term," she wrote, get "home talent" to ply you with letters, telegrams, invitations. College men will think, "She *must* be attractive if she can rate all that attention."[6] And at Northwestern University in the 1920s, the competitive pressure was so intense that coeds made a pact not to date on certain nights of the week. That way they could preserve some time to study, secure in the knowledge that they were not losing ground in the race for popularity by staying home.[7]

Although Waller did not see it, the technique of image building was not always limited to women. For men, too, nothing succeeded like success. A *Guide Book for Young Men about Town* advised: "It's money in the bank to have lots of girls on the knowing list and the date calendar. . . . It means more popularity for you." As proof, the author looked back to his own college days, recalling how a classmate won the title of "Most Popular Man" at a small coed college by systematically going through the college register and dating every girl in the school who wasn't engaged.[8]

At some schools, the system was particularly blatant. In early 1936, a group of women at the University of Michigan decided to rate the BMOCs (Big Men on Campus) according to their "dating value." Men had to have dated several women even to be considered for the list. Those qualifying were rated either "A—smooth; B—OK; C—pass in a crowd; D—semigoon; or E—spook." As the Damda Phi Data sorority, these women made copies of the rating list and left them around campus. The *Michigan Daily* reported that the lists were being used "quite extensively" by women to check the ratings of potential blind dates.[9] This codification helped women to conform to peer judgments of dating value (and also to gain some kind of power over the most powerful men).

The concept of dating value had nothing to do with the interpersonal experience of a date—whether or not the boy (or girl, for that matter) was fun or charming or brilliant was irrelevant. Instead, the rating looked to others: "pass in a crowd" does not refer to any relationship between the couple, but to public perceptions of success in the popularity competition. Dating a "spook" could set you back, but the C-rater would hold your place, keep you in circulation.

Subtle manifestations of the rating-dating complex reveal the stress on competition even more clearly. In 1935, the Massachusetts *Collegian* (the Massachusetts State College newspaper) ran an editorial against using the library for "datemaking." The editors concluded: "The library is the place for the improvement of the mind and not the social standing of the student."[10] Social standing, not social life: on one word turns the meaning of the dating system. That "standing" probably wasn't even a conscious choice shows how completely people took for granted that dating was primarily concerned with status, competition, and popularity. Dates were markers in this system of exchange. Success—the only goal structurally possible—was to acquire enough popularity to continue to compete.

Popularity was clearly the key—and popularity defined in a very specific way. It was not earned directly through talent, looks, personality, or importance in organizations, but by the way these attributes translated into dates. These dates had to be highly visible, and with many different people, or they didn't count. In the mid-1930s, for instance, an etiquette book for college women compared a Northwestern University organization of campus "widows" (who showed they were faithful to faraway lovers by wearing yellow ribbons around their necks and meeting to read letters and share mementos while others dated) to women who were "pinned" to one man. The author made just one caveat: the widows "stay home all the time, and the pin wearers *at least* have steady dates" (emphasis added).[11] One man was only marginally better than none.

The rating-dating system, and the definition of popularity on which it was based, was not restricted to college campuses. Originally, popular magazines and advice books had described it as a college phenomenon, but during the 1930s, the college campus ceased to be the determining factor. In 1940, a *Woman's Home Companion* article explained the modern dating system (with no mention of college campuses) to its readers: "If you have dates aplenty you are asked everywhere. Dates are the hallmark of personality and popularity. No matter how pretty you may be, how smart your clothes—or your tongue—if you have no dates your rating is low. . . . The modern girl cultivates not one single suitor, but dates, lots of them. . . . Her aim is not a too obvious romance but general popularity."[12]

The tone of the article is unqualified approval. As the popularity-ideal passed from college youth into the culture at large, it lost its aura of difference, its suspectness. For one thing, college youth raised on rating-dating were, by the late 1930s, the ones writing the advice columns for young people. In national magazines, they standardized and perpetuated the competitive dating system.

High school students of the late 1930s and 1940s, then, were raised on rating and dating. Not only did they imitate the conventions of older youth, they were advised by some young columnists, who spoke with distinctly nonparental voices, that these conventions were natural and right. *Senior Scholastic,* a magazine used in high schools all over the United States, began running an advice column in 1936. "Boy Dates Girl," written under the pseudonym Gay Head, quickly became the magazine's most popular feature. [13]

Gay Head's advice always took the competitive system as a given. She assumed that girls would accept any *staightforward* offer of a date if not already "dated" for the evening, and that boys, in trying for the most popular girl imaginably possible, would occasionally overreach themselves. She once warned girls never to brush off any boy, no matter how unappealing, in a rude way, since "he may come in handy for an off-night."[14] An advice column for "sub-debs" in the *Ladies' Home Journal* struck the same note. The columnist advised that shunning blind dates as "public proof" of a slow social life was bad policy. Even if "imperfect," she wrote, blind dates would "help keep you in circulation. They're good press agents. They even add to your collection."[15]

Teenagers had little argument with this advice. Early debates on "going steady" in *Senior Scholastic* (which show that some students, at least, wanted a "single suitor") overwhelmingly rejected the steady-date plan. Negative responses were blunt: "If a girl goes steady she loses her gift of gab; she doesn't need to compete with others of her species" (Chicago); "Going steady is like buying the first car you see—only a car has trade-in value later on" ("Two Boys," Milwaukee); "One is a bore—I want more!" ("A Girl," Lynwood, California). A girl from Greensboro, North Carolina summed it all up:

> Going steady with one date
> Is okay; if that's all you rate. [16]

Rating, dating, popularity, competition: catchwords hammered home, reinforced from all sides until they seemed a natural vocabulary. You had to rate in order to date, to date in order to rate. By successfully maintaining this cycle, you became popular. To stay popular, you competed. There was no end: popularity was a deceptive goal. It was only a transient state, not a trophy that could be won and possessed. You competed to become popular, and being popular allowed you to continue to compete. *Competition* was the key term in the formula—remove it and there was no rating, dating, or popularity.

NOTES

1.　Margaret Mead, *Male and Female* (New York: William Morrow, 1949; reprint ed., New York: Morrow Quill Paperbacks, 1967), p. 285. Mead first gave the substance of this book as the Jacob Gimbel Lectures in Sex Psychology in 1946. The *Ladies' Home Journal* also ran much of Mead's discussion in 1949, including her description of dating as a "competitive game." (Margaret Mead, "Male and Female." *LHJ*, September 1949, p. 145.)

2.　Willard Waller, "The Rating and Dating Complex," *American Sociological Review* 2 (1937): 727–34. Woman's popularity was described as associational—she received status as the object of man's choice. Undoubtedly, the right clothes, the right connections, and all the intangibles that come from the right background purchased male attention in the first place, but popular and scholarly accounts consistently slighted this angle.

3.　Paula Fass, *The Damned and the Beautiful* (New York: Oxford University Press, 1977), p. 201.

4.　IBID., p. 226.

5.　Michael Gordon, "Was Waller Ever Right?" *Journal of Marriage and the Family (JMF)* 43 (February 1981): 67–75. Gordon questions the validity of Waller's model based on the atypicality of his sample. I do not insist that rating-dating actually governed individual acts and choices of either Penn State students or the population at large (although it may have), but it did provide a vocabulary for and a way of understanding the dating system for participants and observers alike. The language of rating-dating appears widespread in both college and noncollege sources, though with a significant time lag between colleges and the general population.

6.　May Ellen Green, "Advice to Freshmen," *Mademoiselle,* August 1939, p. 88.

7.　Fass, *Damned and Beautiful*, p. 200. Fass found the Northwestern arrangement reported in the *UCLA Daily* (13 November 1925). I found an apocryphal version of the story in "If Your Daughter Goes to College," *Better Homes and Gardens (BH&G)*, May 1940.

8.　Norton Hughes Jonathon, *Guidebook for the Young Man about Town* (Philadelphia: John C. Winston Co., 1949), pp. 129–31.

9.　Betty Strickroot, "Damda Phi Data Sorority Rates BMOC's by Their Dating Value," *Michigan Daily,* 25 March 1936.

10.　Editorial, "Where Do You Make Your Date?" Massachusetts *Collegian,* 10 October 1935, p. 2.

11.　Elizabeth Eldridge, *Co-ediquette* (New York: E. P. Dutton & Co., 1936), p. 224. The author based her book on personal research and experience at several U.S. colleges and universities. This volume went through four printings in June-August 1936.

12.　Anna Streese Richardson, "Dates in Christmas Socks," *Woman's Home Companion (WHC)*, January 1940, p. 7.

13.　Usage does change. The name Gay Head comes from the cliffs of Martha's Vineyard, where, as *Senior Scholastic (SS)* revealed in its teachers' supplement, Gay had been christened by a male editor with a bottle of raspberry soda (20 February 1937). In 1937 *Senior Scholastic* was used by 6,200 teachers in high school classrooms, and the teachers reported that "Boy Dates Girl" was extremely popular with students (Teachers' Supplement, 29 May 1937, p. A-3).

14. Gay Head, "Boy Dates Girl: The First Reel," *SS*, 19 September 1936, p. 18.
15. "Blind as a Bat," *LHJ,* December 1944, p. 8.
16. Gay Head, "Boy Dates Girl Jam Session," *SS* 22–27 February 1943, p. 29; "Should High School Students Go Steady?" *SS*, 20 October 1941, p. 38; "Jam Session," *SS*, 28 February–4 March 1944, p. 32. *Senior Scholastic* began its jam session polls in 1941; the first was on dutch dating.

16

Sex in College*

Michael Moffatt

> *[College] seems to be such a decadent place . . . It seems that everyone here is always talking about sex or the person they've been having sex with.*
> —Sophomore female, anonymous paper, 1986

College was the place, or so the dean had proposed back in orientation, where the students should try to broaden themselves by seeking out new and different experiences. This was the meaning of a liberal education. And college authorities as well as undergraduates often took pride in the diversity of Rutgers, in the wide range of choices available to those students who wanted the broadening experiences of college. On the evidence of the students' anonymous sexual self-reports,[1] Rutgers as a sexual institution—presumably without its policymakers exactly thinking of it this way—did indeed give its undergraduates an opportunity to realize these institutional values. Not all the students did so, however. Not every student enrolled in the whole sexual extracurriculum, and there were even some nonmatriculators. What were the crude Kinseyian facts of undergraduate sexual behavior in the college as they were reported in these papers? How might a numbers-oriented sexologist, reading these papers, have summarized these Rutgers students sexually?

WHO WAS DOING WHAT TO WHOM, AND HOW OFTEN . . . ?

The simplest statistical generalization from the sexual self-reports is that there was no typical Rutgers woman or typical Rutgers man in terms of sexual behavior. Sexual meanings might have been largely uniform and consensual among the students . . . . Sexual actions, on the other hand, were distinctly idiosyncratic . . . .

*Moffatt, Michael. 1989. "Sex in College." Pp. 247–270 in *Coming of Age in New Jersey: College and American Culture*. New Brunswick, NJ: Rutgers University Press. Copyright © 1989 by Rutgers, The State University. Reprinted with permission of Rutgers University Press.

Behaviorally, the students reported as many different levels and patterns of sexual activity as there were undergraduate writers of these papers. Some women and men described years of sexual experience before arriving at Rutgers; others said they were still virgins in their last year in college. Some started early and then went through long dry spells, even up to the present; others started late and made up for lost time; and still others started late and progressed slowly. The majority of these self-reporters said they had restricted themselves, by and large, to sex with commitment and to conventional heterosexual practices. A minority, on the other hand, suggested that they had sampled from virtually every sexual elective in the modern erotic curriculum.

Some enthusiasts in casual sex sounded as if they were out every night, or at least every weekend night; others said they took their tastes of casual sex only every now and then. Some boyfriend-girlfriend pairs reported having intercourse on a daily basis; others said that it was difficult to make love more than three or four times a month because of different academic schedules, roommates, off-campus jobs, and so on. A few heterosexual couples hardly ever had intercourse for fear of unwanted pregnancy. No student writer of these papers said she or he was ready, even hypothetically, to deal with pregnancy or childbirth.

About one in five of both the women and men who wrote these papers said that they were still virgins. Of those who were not, most of the women and about half the men indicated when they had lost their virginity, and the various years in which persons of both sexes said they had first had "real" sex fell on a near-perfect bell-shaped curve. The left tail of the curve was on eighth grade, in the junior high school years. The right tail was on the senior year in college. And the apex, the period at which about half the sexually experienced students had already "lost it," was at the life juncture "going away to college": the senior year of high school and the freshman year of college. If these figures were at all representative, then, we can guess from them that almost half the freshmen (women and men) at Rutgers were still virgins, and that the collegiate virginity rate then declined for both sexes until it was somewhat less than one in five for Rutgers seniors (the one-in-five virgins in the overall sample included some lowerclassmen).[2]

The women's papers were more comprehensive and more honest-sounding than the men's about frequencies and types of sexual engagement. Two-fifths of fifty-five sexually experienced women who gave the precise details of their sexual ontogenies said that—independent of their reported practice of casual sex—they had had only one long-term boyfriend or lover since loss of virginity. Slightly less than two-fifths mentioned two such boyfriends; slightly less than one-fifth mentioned three or more long-term partners. Only 8 percent (or three) of these women described sex lives that had occurred with casual partners only.[3] One of these women later decided that she was a lesbian.

As for casual sex, one-third of the fifty-five women who evidently told all said that they had never tried it; they stated or implied that they had been involved only in long-term, "caring" sexual relationships. Two-thirds of these fifty-five women, on the other hand, did mention what they referred to variously as "mistakes," "pickups," "experiments," "flings," or "affairs." Thirty percent mentioned one of them; 22 percent mentioned two to four; 38 percent indicated an indefinite number ("a few friends, a few friends of friends," "more than I should have," "a series of pickups," "quite a few," "many"). And 8 percent once again described, undefensively or with some relish, ten to thirty casual sexual liaisons to date.[4] Most of these women were juniors and seniors, and they suggested that they had practiced perhaps three-quarters of this casual sex during their years in college.

However, according to these student self-reports, to be sexually experienced was not necessarily to be in a happy or satisfying sexual relationship or set of relationships at present. Sixty-five percent of the sexually experienced women indicated that they were involved in ongoing relationships or other erotic networks at the moment of writing. Only 40 percent of the sexually experienced men suggested the same—once again, mostly juniors and seniors.

The majority of undergraduate writers who described their current sexual practices discussed the themes and variations of conventional one-on-one, privately conducted heterosexual intercourse. Reported frequencies ranged widely, from " 6 or 7 times a week" to "any time we have a chance." "Conventional" sex (my category, implicit in the students' accounts) meant, under the new orthodoxy: mutual oral sex as foreplay followed by heterosexual intercourse, preferably to mutual orgasm (alternatively, orgasm during foreplay could substitute for orgasm during intercourse, especially for females). Most undergraduates reported that they liked to experiment with different positions during intercourse: "missionary," "woman-on-top," "doggy style," "Oceanic";[5] and so on. Some otherwise conventional students said that they considered heterosexual anal sex just one more variant of nonkinky sex; others said that it was "disgusting" or "unthinkable."

Conventional couples also said they enjoyed different settings for sex—in a bubble bath, in a rented hot-tub, at a motel for a thrill. More than a dozen wrote with delight of the occasional lovemaking out-of-doors or almost-in-public, with the added spice of possibly being caught in the act. One could draw from these descriptions a Woody Allenesque map of the sexual campus. In wooded glades or under bridges or on the university golf course. Under the official gates of the university. On campus buses following lightly traveled routes. In lonely classrooms reserved for study, late at night. In dorm basement corridors and stairwells and bathrooms and laundry rooms, also late at night. Fellatio by a girlfriend while sitting in a study carrel in a campus library. Two different students even bragged about stealing into the private dining room of the president of the university after hours and fornicating on his carpet. (This room, though often locked, might have been accessible to student workers in Dining Services.)

Advanced sexual practices were those techniques that most students classified as "kinky," even if they engaged in them themselves. ("With Sue I experienced the whole spectrum of kink."—Senior male) Some combined sex and food ("Hagendaus and cunnilingus"—cf. (Canaan 1986). A few alluded to costumes and role-playing: Milkman, Hitchhiker, Sorority Girl Losing It to Fraternity Jock, High School English Teacher, Hooker, and so on. A half dozen mentioned "light" B and D; a few referred in passing to S and M. (Seven or eight students mentioned using drugs, or "illegal substances," to enhance sexual pleasure; two specified crack.) Seven women and eight men said in their sexual chronologies that they had experimented with different kinds of group sex once or more, two-thirds of the time in college. Most of these incidents, fraternity gang bangs aside, were two-on-ones of either variety. And three homosexual students mentioned enjoying the occasional homosexual or bisexual "group grope."

Any readers whose sensibilities are offended by these advanced sexual practices can possibly comfort themselves by concentrating on what the great majority of the students' sexual self-reports were in fact reporting: either no "real" sex at all (those one-in-five virgins) or (most sex for most undergraduates most of the time) sex that was one-on-one, heterosexual, in private, conventional in technique and caring in emotional style. In other words, for the most part, modern American suburban sex in its adolescent variant.

SEX AND OTHER COLLEGIATE VALUES

According to the new orthodoxy, sexuality, perhaps the central private fact of modern personal identity as it is thought of in American culture, was an *autonomous* zone of physical, psychological, and emotional sensibility. It did not necessarily refer outside of itself; there was no reason why sexual development should be directly relevant to anything else in one's personal ontogeny. And, in these sexual self-reports, very few students writers spontaneously referred to more formal collegiate values—to the relation of sex to studying, or to academic success, or to the life of the mind. Sexual development and intellectual development in college, these papers implied, ought to be parallel but independent processes. They both ought to occur during the same years, but there was no need for any systematic connections between the two of them.

As a physical versus an intellectual behavior, as an "animalistic" versus a "higher human" activity, sexuality *was* mildly opposed to life of the mind in student ideation. Thus, a favorite undergraduate locker-room expression for vigorous fornication, used symmetrically by females and males, was "I fucked his/her brains out" (short form; "I fucked his/her brains"). But there was no indication in these papers that these contemporary young Americans thought that sexual and intellectual activities conflicted with one another in any way. There was no suggestion that chastity or abstinence might enhance the higher processes of collegiate cerebration. Sexuality and mental hard work, on the contrary, were seen as values, which, like "college life" and "academics," should be balanced during one's college years. All work and no play . . . Women and men implied that happy, fulfilling sex lives made them happier and more successful students. Men . . . sometimes said that any sex at all, loving or casual, relaxed them so that they did better in the classroom. No one said that an active sex life interfered with academic success or achievement.[6]

By the implication of these papers, then, these undergraduates, like students in earlier American college generations, ascribed to the old college value mens sana in corpore sano. But they had a rather different idea than did the vigorous student athletes of yore about the particular activities that would ensure the health and happiness of their bodies.[7]

COLLEGE AS A SEXUAL NONCOMMUNITY

After high school . . . I met Judy. Now Judy was one of my younger sister's friends: she was beautiful: she was infamous: she was a sex machine . . . and I was ripe and ready for the challenge. We did it everywhere; on the road behind Kilmer Campus, outside one of the churches in town, but most often on my fathers motorboat. . . . But now, Judy is in college, and when I last spoke with her, she was happily seeing one guy. (Oh, how college can change a person). She was, so far the best sex partner I have had, and I was deeply saddened by her switch to a monogamous relationship. — Senior male

I enjoy being at a large university where one is not subjected to constant scrutiny by the entire student body. — Senior female

Though intellect and sexuality were autonomous, separate, complementary cultural domains in the implicit conceptions of most of these undergraduates, "college" nevertheless did occur all the time in their sexual self-reports as the institutional context or setting for the student writers' sexualities. Rutgers in particular had two opposite meanings as a sexual environment in these papers. In one of its meanings, interestingly, the conventional values of American "community" were inverted. When the subject was the human side of college, Rutgers was often excoriated by undergraduates for being a large, anonymous institution in which hardly anyone really knew anyone else "as a person." When the subject was sexuality, on the other hand. Rutgers as these undergraduates described it in the sexual self-reports was often admired and appreciated for precisely these same institutional properties.

For sexually, many students pointed out, hardly anyone knew what you were up to at so vast an institution. No adults supervised your behavior. There were eight thousand potential players in the game of undergraduate sex in Rutgers College alone, and many more thousands on the other undergraduate campuses of Rutgers-New Brunswick; you would never know all these undergraduates and they would never all know you. Moreover, after four years you yourself would move on to other sexual environments. You did not need to be labeled indefinitely as having any one sexual reputation at Rutgers. If you were embarrassed in the eyes of old friends by a change in your sexual style, then you could always find a new set of friends.

Thus, impersonal Rutgers provided the undergraduates with an open, flexible sexual environment through which individual women and men could maneuver with some freedom. Neotraditional women could try being "sluts" and then retreat to the comfort of romantic commitment to one male, or they could decide that they are guilt-free experimentalists and evolve in other ways. Romantic men could change their stripes and become liberals; conceivably, liberal men could decide they are not really liberals and fall back into romance. Heterosexuals, if so inclined, could quietly check themselves out against bisexuality and homosexuality. Even Neanderthals could experience conversion — to pure romantics, to liberals, conceivably even to radicals.

THE SEXUAL ORGANIZATION OF
THE UNDERGRADUATE COLLEGE

Actual Rutgers, on the other hand, was not an entirely anonymous social environment. It did have its undergraduate collectivities, its networks of personal acquaintanceship and knowledge. Since Rutgers abandoned its older in loco parentis reponsibilities for the sexual moralities of its undergraduates in the 1960s, college authorities were no longer personally significant in influencing or controlling student sexuality on a daily basis. But as in the sixteenth- and seventeenth-century French villages analyzed by social historian Natalie Zeemon Davis, youthful peer groups were significant (cf. Davis 1971). Student collectivities could encourage some types and rates of sexual activity and discourage others. What sorts of regular influences did the different forms of undergraduate society have on student sexuality as it was described in these papers?

Going Away to College

Boy oh boy was [Rutgers] an eye opening experience after a lifetime of Catholic school education!!!—Senior Female

Before I came to college, my views on sexual relationships were very old-fashioned, prudent ones. Although I had urges, I refused to let myself act on them. I felt that sexual intercourse was for married couples only and that girls who slept with their boyfriends were cheap. . . . However, [in my freshman year] I looked around and realized that *most* of the girls my age were sexually active. I began to look at sex differently; I realized that feeling horny was normal, and that it wasn't something bad.—Sophomore woman

The erotic values of Rutgers students were constructed almost entirely from sources in American mass culture, and many incoming freshmen were already familiar with these values when they first arrived at Rutgers. But some were not; some came from politer or more sexually restricted backgrounds. And in the reports of these undergraduate writers, going away to college was sometimes remembered as a moment of sexual shock. Even those youths who were familiar with contemporary sexuality in theory occasionally remembered their first contact with the actualities of collegiate sex with a sense of surprise, whether unhappily or happily:

I remember the shock an disgust I felt [freshman] year when I mentioned one of my friends to someone and he said, "Oh is she the one who's fucking Fred?" . . . I think if someone said it this year I wouldn't think twice.—Sophomore female

My third night of school, as a freshman, I met a girl and within 15 minutes I was in bed with [her] treating her like a piece of meat. I was [in a dorm corridor] at about 3 A.M. and a drunk blond stumbled out of the elevator. I smiled but did nothing. She came over said hi and stole my hat. She started running around the lounge saying come and get me, so I did. I caught up to her and grapped her belt loop to stop her. She said "wooooo" so you wanna get in my pants. I was shocked and blushing. She ran down the hallway and into her room, I followed. In no time we were fucking like lunatics, well she was anyway. I said I have to come and asked if I could blow it in her. She pushed me off, grabbed my cock and started sucking until I erupted my love juice into her hot steamy mouth. It was then I knew college was for me. — Senior male

One woman recalled allowing an upperclassman to pick her up on her second night at college as a freshman and take her back to his room on another campus, where she let him to teach her how to give a "blowjob." Then, she wrote with surprise, he maintained his one-way oral-sex relationship with her for several more weeks: "Strangely he didn't dump me" right away.[8] Another woman told of going to the fraternity in which she was to be a "little sister" the third night of her freshman year, when she was still a virgin. A male friend introduced her to a friend of his; she got very drunk; and the next morning she decided, from pains in places where she had never hurt before, that this new acquaintance had raped her.

These student memories were in the great minority among all the writers of these self-reports, however. They came from perhaps a dozen of the 144 sample papers. In many more reports, going away to college was not recalled as a particularly sexually marked event. Most Rutgers undergraduates came from hometowns within fifty miles of college. Some students confined their sexual relations to a hometown girlfriend or boyfriend for their first months or even years in college. As one sophomore male wrote, "I haven't cheated on my [hometown] girlfriend (yet)."

Others stayed with a hometown partner for a certain period *while* cautiously sampling from the movable feast of Rutgers sex. Some women who came to Rutgers as virgins let the new collegiate sexual ambience work on them slowly and changed their sexual styles only when they felt ready to do so. ("By the end of my freshman year, I decided I had had enough of my virginity." — Sophomore female) And many undergraduates simply saw college as the next stage in their steady sexual development:

> For me, highschool served as a trial and error period where I learned what was the right thing to do and what was wrong. The first weekend of college, I met my boyfriend and we began getting serious. The college atmosphere allows one to get to know another fairly easily because there is no adult supervision or restrictions. One is basically on his/her own and can do whatever he/she chose to do. The relationship between my boyfriend and I grew strong and stable. Sexually, we took it slow . . . . Eventually (six months later) we had sex for the first time together (the first time for me but not him). — Sophomore female

Dorm Fantasies, Dorm Realities. The coed dorm floor, the basic personal collectivity for most students in their freshman and sophomore years at Rutgers, was described sexually in these papers much as I saw it in my two years of participant observation in the dorms . . . . "This place is gossip-city," one woman resident observed of Hasbrouck Fourth in 1984. Most women did not want their sexual practices widely discussed among the various floor friends and acquaintances with whom they had to live for a year; most of them said they tried to find their erotic partners elsewhere. Younger men did not necessarily make the same effort; they had less to lose by local sex, or so they felt. But the women were still the no-sayers in sex, especially between floor friends.

Which is not to say that such no-saying always came easily between female and male coresidents or that coresidence always produced reliably nonerotic, brotherly-sisterly sensibilities between opposite-sex neighbors. Consider the following woman's account of an apparent sexual adventure with the boy next door on her coed dorm floor. Following a common pattern, she and her female roommate had been friends with the two males in the next room—but that was all they had been in public definition, "just friends." And the woman narrator had a boyfriend of her own who presumably lived elsewhere. But friendship was not in fact quite the only thing that had gone on between her and the boy next door. Other emotions simmered:

> I went to bed early that night because I had early class the next morning. I wasn't tired so I just lay there thinking. I kept thinking about the time he kissed me when I was in his room. I was talking to his roommate and mine when suddenly he came behind me, pulled me into his arms and kissed me hard. I was taken aback and just left the room without a word. I've been avoiding him since but I kept thinking of him instead of my boyfriend.
>
> Hours had gone by and I wasn't getting any tired just horny.

She had a problem, however. A known sexual relationship with a local male would be very complicated. Discretion was necessary. Any liaison had to be carefully hidden from everyone else on the floor, including the closest associates (and, presumably, friends) of the two principals, her roommate and his roommate. Not only that; she had to figure out a way to seduce the male in question. It was very late now. Everyone else on the floor had gone to bed. She figured out her gambit and made her opening move:

> I had concocted a great but "innocent" way to feel his touch on my body. I quietly—very quietly—so as not to wake my roommate, got out of bed. I took off my heavy pajamas and my underwear and excitedly slipped on my thin red velour bathrobe that accented by nakedness underneath especially my shapely bottom . . . . I snook out of my room and walked over to the hall phone. I had the operator call me back. After the phone had rung three times. I answered it.
>
> I went to his door and knocked quietly but firmly. . . . Well what seemed like hours, he finally came to the door—in just his underwear.
>
> Although I had seem him dressed or undressed as it may be, I looked at him through new eyes. His shoulders were wide, muscular and tan, and his stomach was pretty tight . . . and the bulge in his shorts was "very nice." I had never felt that way the other times I saw him undressed. . . .
>
> Once his roommate could not hear I said, "I need a favor. Will you come with me, please?" He nodded and went back into his room and came out with his robe and slippers on. He still looked sexy.

Note how the participants in this account were following the correct sartorial etiquette of the dorm. The young woman wore a proper bathrobe over her nakedness; the young man, even when faced with a well-known female standing all alone on his doorstep late at night, went back into his room and politely dressed to a point of minimum decency. She apparently had glimpsed him in his underwear before ("undressed" in this context probably did not mean entirely nude); such glimpses were not uncommon between friends in the familiarity of the dorm. But the glimpse had probably been accidental, not the result of a deliberate display on the male's part. And now her look was being transformed by her new intentions; now, atypically between dorm coresidents, the glimpse was becoming sexual, for her at any rate.

The narrator had a moment of doubt, but she concentrated and heroically carried on. She had chosen one of the commoner, more trustworthy female ploys: The Massage. But where? She had this worked out as well:

> I started feeling silly for doing this but when I closed my eyes for a second I remembered my plan. So I took his hand and led him down the hall and up three flights of stairs to the laundry room. I said, "I'm sorry to bother you but I can't sleep. I need a massage and you are the only one I could think of that could give me a good one . . . and besides you owe me!" He didn't look happy but he didn't protest. He asked me what to do and shyly I suggested that I lie down across the washing machines so it would be easier to massage my whole back.

From this point on, as the male got the idea and rapidly became much more enthusiastic about their nocturnal exercise together, the text narrated a standard seduction, well within the limits of sexual explicitness found in many of the other female and male undergraduate sexual self-reports. This particular account was unusually well plotted, however. Its moments of possible awkwardness and embarrassment were well imagined, realities such as birth control were kept firmly in mind, and the female narrator always remained in control of the action, calling virtually every shot. Consistently, in the tones of a guiltless female experimentalist, she as protagonist was the agent. Her male partner was only the tool of her sexual pleasure:

> Well I layed down and he started massaging my shoulders. I could feel his eyes on my bottom. He started rubbing lower. . . . It felt good and I started opening my legs a little. He then murmured "now what?" I knew he had weakened but I was enjoying the teasing too much so I said "now my legs." He started with my feet and then went onto my calfs. I was really starting to get wet and even started moving slowly back and forth. . . . I pulled my robe up to just where he could glimpse my cheeks and my red lips . . . he started rubbing my thighs higher and even "accidentally" touched my lips. I couldn't take anymore and wipped around onto my back. Doing so one of my breasts and my mound became exposed. I quickly covered them up but barely and I said, "now my arms and . . . my chest." He wouldn't look me in the eye but said, "I should get up there 'coz I can't do your right arm right." I said, "Whatever you say" and closed my eyes.

He got on me and boy was he hard!...My breasts were dying to be licked, sucked and squeezed any my pussy was aching to be penetrated—hard, real hard! He started tracing my breast through my robe and then he put his hand through my robe and started playing with my lips.

I started calling his name, slightly groaning, and arched my back so that my lips were rubbing the rod in his underwear. He jumped off me and took off his underwear and started to climb back up but I said "No!" and sat up exposing both breasts. I jumped off the washers and stood close to him facing him. I started kissing his neck, rubbing his check and just above his hard cock....

...He picked me up and started to put me on the washer. I said, "No, I can't that way I haven't been taking my pill."...He kept trying to shove his cock into my pussy but I kept him at bay until he knelt down and started licking and sucking my pussy.

Oh that got me really going. I wanted to feel something hard in there so I said, "Your finger—oh please! put your fingers in me!" He obliged and oh he knew where to rub. While he was slowly going in and out with two fingers his pinky kept touching my other whole and wetting it, though I know it wasn't intentional. That really made me want to be fucked so I pulled away from his fingers and slowly pulled him up so that he was standing with his cock pointing straight for my pussy. I smiled and turned around. I walked over to the washer and pulled him close.

I leaned over the washer and quietly said, "Fuck me." He didn't understand so I pulled his cock and started rubbing it between my checks. Then I said, "Come on I know you'd love to fuck me there and I want to feel you there. I want you to ram me." I separated my cheeks and I said, "Fuck me." He smiled shyly and made his way into my whole. I said, "Fuck me hard!" He grabbed my waist and started pumping hard. I said, "Harder!" I felt my insides starting to vibrate and tingle and then I felt his cock surge and come in me. I yelled and..."

And now, in the last sentence, we discover that the conventional sexual restraints of the coed dorm floor had in fact ruled even this account. Not only had its female narrator told this adventure in an anonymous paper, possibly as a fantasy; not only had she safeguarded herself as protagonist within the narrative by keeping the encounter a secret from everyone else on her floor. But the tale was, it turned out, only a dream. And her sole remaining anxiety in the text was the fear that she would disturb her roommate when she woke up:

...I woke up disappointed and hoping I hadn't woke my roommate.—Senior female

To say that most undergraduates tended to avoid actual sexual relations with floor coresidents is not to say that college residence halls—or, more precisely, the private rooms in college residence halls—were chaste, asexual places. There were not too many other places to "do it" with your off-floor erotic partner if you were a freshman or sophomore dorm resident. In this sense, the fundamental sexual constraint imposed by the overcrowded undergraduate dorms was, Where and when can one find a little sexual privacy?:

I mean I absolutely hated it when my boyfriend and I would be in the middle of sex and my roommate walked in and nearly ripped the door off its hinges because we chained the door shut. — Senior female

[My] dorm was so overcrowded that sexual activities seldom got a chance. But when everyone went home for the weekend the place would go quiet except for the squeaking of bed frames. It was always so obvious because everyone would have tossled hair when they went for Sunday brunch and the doors always have strange messages on them like "Your aunt from Florida called" or Smiley faces . . . or flowers . . . — Junior female

Different roommates had different arrangements. Most roommates had private codes among themselves, apparently innocent message-board scribblings that really meant, Would you please go away for awhile? I've got someone in here. Some roommates worked around one another's daily schedules and grabbed their opportunities when they could. Sometimes an amiable roommate agreed to spend an occasional night in another room, camping out on the floor of a neighbor or using a spare bed left vacant by other nocturnal peregrinations. A few students reported that their roommates sometimes stayed in the rooms in which they were sleeping with a sex partner. Sometimes this was literally all the narrator was doing: sleeping with a sex partner simply for closeness and convenience, without intercourse.[10] Other times, writers said, they waited until it sounded as if their roommates were asleep, and then went at it as quietly as possible.

Virtually all coed dorm floors at Rutgers, by all indications, were aggressively heterosexual in their erotic ambiences. Both heterosexual and homosexual subjects widely agreed that gay, lesbian, and bisexual dorm residents either had to remain entirely in-the-closet on the average coed dorm floor, or risk having to live with real social ostracism all year long.[11] Most heterosexual men said they would find it very hard to handle the revelation from a new roommate-friend that he was gay, even if he made it very clear that his erotic interests were directed elsewhere. Many heterosexual women, on the other hand, thought they could deal with the same revelation from a lesbian roommate more calmly. Almost all heterosexual women and men said they would worry, however, about what other people on the floor would think about *them* if they discovered their roommates were homosexuals. One or two gay students did report in other contexts, however, that they had first decided they were homosexuals when gay roommates, other years, initially turned them on — very quietly, without the knowledge of anyone else on their floors.

Fraternities and Sororities

Some people believe that fraternal social events are just orgies where guys + girls get real drunk and fuck each others brains out. This is so far from the truth that it makes me laugh. . . . I've met a great deal of very nice girls through my association with the house and feel these girls would no more like to be termed sluts as I would a playboy. Please don't misunderstand, we do have our share of "wild adventures." . . . I think a lot of these so called sexual adventures are because of our reputations as sex animals. I'm not familiar with the proper psychological term but to describe it—*we become in peoples' minds what they expect us to be.* This is where the fun part begins.

There are alot of undersexed liberal women who want to meet men, have a good time etc. . . . but not get involved in long-term relationships. Alot of guys from the house get involved in these types of affairs—Including myself. But you know, even us fraternity boys have feeling and I know I've been hurt afew times by such relationships—this kind of shoots down the idea that were sex animals. . . . —Senior male

Seven identified fraternity members wrote about sex and the fraternities in their sexual self-reports, and many other students described them in passing. Three of the fraternity members have been quoted . . . —one on thirteen-on-one gang fornication, the second on his "list," and the third on the new distinction between good women and sluts. A fourth narrated the pleasures of pickup sex; a fifth wrote a possible fantasy or put-on about "abusing" a "young voluptuous, erotic, CHERRY, blond starlet" whom he had picked up at a party in his fraternity one night and taken up to his room (he also described her as a "frat rat," a "slut," a "cunt," and a "horbag"); and a sixth celebrated "doing a nigger" while his friends in the next room played "Back to Black" on their stereos (and one "stuck his head under my door and watched").

The earnest apologist quoted above was the only writer who attempted to deny or to give nuance to the salient sexual connotation of the fraternity in contemporary undergraduate erotic culture. And in trying to do so, even he reaffirmed it. In virtually all these reports, by brothers and by nonmembers alike, the fraternities, and the wild parties on Thursday and Friday nights that characterized them, were uniformly described—simply and without qualification in most cases—as the biggest and most available sexual "meat markets" on the campus.

Which is not to say that every young woman or man who went to such parties was looking for sleazy sex or for guilt-free experimental sex, depending on the subject's moral stance. Nor is it to say that everyone who was looking for these erotic delights necessarily succeeded in finding them. As the fraternity apologist quoted above added, "Believe me, more guys go home with 'blue balls' so to speak than picking up girls." But it was clear that if you were a male or female undergraduate and pickup sex was what you wanted, then the many parties in the many nearby fraternities were the most likely places to go to look for it.[12]

The same sort of generalization could be made about the sexual moralities of those male students who belonged to the fraternities, on the evidence of these papers. There were neotraditionalist men outside the fraternity system; and there may have been male liberals and perhaps a few pure romantics—but certainly very few known gays—within it. It was not absolutely necessary to be a brother in order to be a sexual Neanderthal at Rutgers. But if you wanted to be a Neanderthal with good peer-group support, if you wanted to be surrounded by other men who also thought that sleazy sex with sluts was the way to prove your manhood, then the fraternities, or some of them at any rate, were the places for you. In them, by all evidence in these papers, you could escape the complicated and relatively more egalitarian contemporary gender relations of the coed dorm floors. You could escape the tensions of dealing with female next-door neighbors as friends. Once again, as in the good old days, only other men needed to be your friends. Women were once more at a safe distance. Some fraternity members may indeed have had real woman friends, but if they did so, they had them very much on their own time. As far as fraternity values went, at least as they came through almost without exception in these papers, women once again came in two types; good women (present or future girlfriends and/or wives) and sluts.

Sororities were newer and less developed at Rutgers than fraternities, with only one or two residential houses in the mid-1980s. One senior woman's paper described the erotic policies of a sorority in detail. Her sorority sounded well-matched to the fraternities, and her paper provided a handy woman's guide to the subtleties of being a good woman under the neotraditional version of the new sexual orthodoxy:

At the time that I was a [sorority] pledge . . . morality played a large role in my chapters' pledge program. This was do to the fact that my chapter was attempting to change its image after a sister had been a willing participant in a "gang bang" incident with a fraternity. Consequently, we as pledges were under the watchful ey our elder and seemingly musch wiser sisters. . . .

This did not mean tat the members of the sisterhood became celibate. Far from it, we now had to be discreet about our comings and goings. An unofficial list of rules and regulations became the key to successful sorority sex.

1. No prolonged making out on the dance floor, porch or other public area. Take it upstairs.
2. No public display of affection with anyone other than one's boyfriend while wearing one's pin, letters, or crest.
3. When staying at a fraternity be discrete. Do not make a scene for the entire party as you go upstairs. Do not roam the halls half naked or in a state of undress covered up only by a brother's. Mostimportantly, do not stay for breakfast with the brothers. If you can smell the bacon you've obviously overstayed your welcome.
4. Never participate in group sex. It will make you as well as everyone else in the house extremely famous.
5. Attempt to avoid riding on campus transportation the morning after your fraternal slumber party. No one wants to have dogs follow them or fellow greeks yell "Hey Bimbo!" at them. . . .
6. Most importantly, use some reliable method of birth control. One's collegiate years are no time to be creating legacies.

OFF-CAMPUS LIFE:
PREFIGURATIONS OF ADULT SEXUALITY

In their first years in college, most undergraduates traded the sexual supervision of parents and other adults for the gossipy peer-group controls of the coed dorm floor. After their sophomore years, however, they almost invariably decided that they had had enough of the dorms. Some of the males then moved into the fraternities with their sexually curious, and differently coercive, male cohorts. Other males and females, most of the upperclassmen, moved into off-campus housing. And here for the first time they began to escape the strong influence of their age-mates upon their sexual behavior. For the first time since they had left home to go away to college, they were sexually on their own to act as they wished, with something like the autonomy of adults in the real world.

Undergraduates did live with some of their peers in off-campus residences. Because of the high rents in housing-poor New Brunswick, students often had to share houses, apartments, and even rooms with varying numbers of roommates. But now their roommates were much more likely to be their chosen friends, youths who were sexually similar to themselves. One's off-campus roommates were not as likely to gossip with others about one's own sexuality; and there were not so many others around all the time with whom to gossip. Women who enjoyed themselves with sexual experimentalism or with sexual liberalism and women who reported fairly easy, frank woman-to-woman sex talk were usually older undergraduates who lived in off-campus housing or possibly in the apartments the university made available to older students. And lesbian, gay, and bisexual students, in these papers and in other research, universally said that off-campus housing was the only reasonable residential setting for their particular sexualities.

Most off-campus housing, three-quarters of it or more, was a single-sex arrangement. Students said this was because of the wishes of New Brunswick landlords. They also said it was due to the greater intimacy of off-campus living arrangements. It was not the same to share a small apartment with a single bathroom with opposite-sex roommates as it was to share a large dorm floor with separate bathrooms. But some women and men did live together in off-campus housing as friends, or as acquaintances, who were simply sharing space. And some lived together as "boyfriend and girlfriend," enjoying their new erotic freedom, living *almost* like married couples:

> This summer I lived with my boyfriend [in an off-campus apartment]. Before living together, sex was fairly regular, but often there were times when we both wanted to, but often couldn't for various reasons—his parents were home, my roommate was there, too much homework, exams, pressure, tensions, interruptions etc. But this summer changed everything.
>
> . . . anytime either of us felt the urge, we merely had to wander into our room and have sex. . . . Now I know what old-fashioned people mean when they say; "They're just itching to hop into bed" . . . —Senior female

Almost all Rutgers undergraduates eventually did intend to marry, according to other interviews. But in these papers, only a few of the writers alluded to marriage, and then only in indefinite, romantic terms for the most part:

> I never thought that a relationship with sex could be as comfortable as the one I'm in now . . . and will be in forever. —Junior female

The undergraduates' lack of planning was an accurate projection of their immediate sexual futures. Like most middle-class Americans in the 1980s, most of them would defer marriage into their mid-twenties or later, until they had finished further schooling or until they were settled into the work world. [13]

Some of them sounded as if they would be happy to stay pair-bonded to their present lovers until they were finally ready to start thinking seriously about marriage. Others sounded as if they felt they were just getting started sexually, or, in the case of the unintentional virgins, as if they were still waiting to get started. They were just beginning to enjoy themselves; the last thing they wanted to do was to become tied down prematurely. Most of these writers seemed to assume that, when married, they would be sexually faithful to one partner. But however much they were looking forward to marriage for other reasons, they were not especially looking forward to marriage for the sex. It got boring pretty fast, many of them imagined:

> Where else [but in college] can you have sex with 14 different girls in six months, when you are married?—Junior male

Only one student in these 144 sample papers, a woman, wrote a specific fantasy about sex in later years. Here it is, in conclusion, one young woman's version of the sorts of carryings-on she apparently thought would be necessary in order to ward off the inevitable monotony of sex in the adult world—the erotic future under the new sexual orthodoxy, adolescent point of view:

> He lay there naked upon my bed. Arms and legs tied to the bed posts. My whip cracked loudly—powerfully. He started as I crossed the room. The blazing fire threw an interesting glow out to my leather pants and halter.
>
> . . . I stroked his chest lightly for several moments and then in a swift motion broke through his skin with my sharpened nails, leaving long red trails . . . My tongue, drawn to the deep rich red of the blood, lowered to his flesh. Slowly, enjoying every drop, I licked and teased—my hands clutching his chest. A chill of excitement, like electricity, shot through me.
>
> . . . I leaned forward so that my breasts smothered his face. He licked wildly at my cleavage. . . . My halter fell open. He rubbed his face on my naked breasts. I lifted my shoulders and arched my back so that my nipples dangled just above his mouth. His tongue darted out and his neck strained forward as he tried desperately to reach them. A smile crossed my lips then; I threw my head back in laughter. Beg for it, motherfucker, beg for it!
>
> . . . My hand slid to his pubic hair and began to play as I licked his balls. That familiar musky scent filled my nostrils and I began to get excited. My tongue followed the length of his dick—up and down, up and down . . . Then, in one motion, my mouth engulfed him. I then withdrew and repeated once more before I got up.
>
> . . . I looked up ans reached to the night table where the switch blade sat waiting . . . Quickly, I slashed the ropes that held his left hand and then his right. . . . After a short while he lifted his body and I saw the flash of the switch blade as it fell upon the ropes that tied his feet. He threw the blade across the room and fell upon me. . . . Our bodies pressed and rubbed against each other. My nails dug into the flesh on his back as his hands kneaded my buttocks. My back arches towards him. I grasped the back of his head with my hands and my lips found his. He entered me as we kissed. He held me tightly against him, his chest pressing against mine. We fucked wildly. His hips pumped madly between my own legs. We then climaxed together.

There we lay, our arms and legs intertwined, my face buried in his chest. He lifted my chin and told me how much he loved me. After twelve years of marriage, we could still have a great sex life. — Senior female

NOTES

1. [Papers] are quoted without correction of spelling, punctuation, or grammar.

2. These figures were based on what the students chose to say in their papers in 1986. . . . in 1987 I circulated a more conventional, more directive sex questionnaire through an undergraduate class taking the same course, and the curve of reported ages for first times showed a slightly different distribution. Both for women and for men it peaked earlier, in the eleventh- and twelfth-grade years of high school, with males reporting earlier sexual comings-of-age than females. Of the reporting nonvirgins, 70 percent of the men and 62 percent of the women said they had lost their virginity before arriving at college. . . . among students with about the same college-age distributions as those in the 1986 class, the reported virginity rate at the time the papers were written was the same for women on the 1987 questionnaire as in the 1986 papers (one in five) but lower for men (one in eight). Ninety-six women and fifty-five men returned these questionnaires in 1987, less than half the students enrolled in the course.

   In his 1980 data from Douglass, Weis had a reported women's virginity rate of 35 percent, higher than in my sample. But he does not indicate the ages or college classes of his respondents (Weis 1985). If they were mostly freshmen and sophomores, his figures would be comparable to those suggested here.

   Working with a 1981 collegiate data set from almost eight hundred female and male subjects in northern California, most of them freshmen and sophomores, Hildebrand and Abramowitz (1984) found that 40 percent of the females reported they were virgins and 30 percent of the males made the same admission.

3. Data on this sexual variable were similar on the 1987 questionnaire, though the spread was a little wider. Forty percent of the women who were sexually active reported one boyfriend only since loss of virginity; 15 percent reported two; 14 percent reported three; 18 percent reported four; 10 percent reported five or more; and 3 percent indicated that they had had all their sexual relationships with casual partners only.

4. Female figures for 1987: 27 percent of the sexually active women reported never having tried casual sex; 43 percent reported trying it with one to three different partners; 15 percent reported four to six partners; 12 percent reported seven to twelve partners; and 4 percent reported more than twelve (twelve, twenty-five, and twenty-nine). Male figures from 1987: of nonvirgins, 16 percent said they had never tried casual sex; 24 percent had tried it with one to three partners; 20 percent with four to six partners; 16 percent with seven to twelve partners; and 22 percent reported sexual encounters with over a dozen different partners (with highs up into the fifties).

5. *Oceanic:* a native sexual position reported by anthropologists from the south Pacific, one requiring good thigh muscles. The male squats or kneels between the legs of the half-supine female, and both of them move freely during intercourse. One young woman told me proudly in her report in 1986 that she and her boyfriend had discovered this position on their own, six months before learning about it in my class.

6. The emotions of an unhappy sexual relationship *could* throw you off your academic stride, of course, but the culprit in this case was not sex itself, but bad sex.

7. This comparison is not an idle one. Late-nineteenth-century ideologues of collegiate "manliness" were very worried about the impure and enervating activities to which adolescent males might apply their "animal spirits" if they did not exhaust themselves through vigorous athletics: loose women, homosexuality, or, worst of all, masturbation!

8. The generalization [is] offered . . . that oral sex rarely arouses guilt among these student writers. This woman was an exception. She evidently thought that the male who taught her to perform fellatio on him should then have thrown her over for being a slut.

9. It seems very unlikely that this text actually had been a dream, at least the way the narrator told it here; it was entirely too carefully and conventionally plotted. Rather, it seems to belong to a common set of American colloquial stories and jokes with a particularly elementary twist at the end—an unbelievable event told in the first-person singular, ending with "and then I woke up!"

10. With some regularity, particularly before their "first time," women reported that they slept with boyfriends without intercourse for weeks or even months—partly to get used to the whole idea, partly to see if the boyfriend "really cared."

11. An exception, at least one year, was Erewhon Third. . . . Another exception was Nelson Hall, a special-interest dorm set up for students at Rutgers who, for various reasons, wanted to live in a different ambience than that found on the average coed dorm floor. In this dorm, at least in 1984—1985, lesbian and gay students tended to report more tolerance for their sexualities than on the average dorm floor. This tolerance was well known on other dorm floors, however, so much so that Nelson had a minor reputation among the students for being the "fag dorm" (and nonhomosexual students who lived in Nelson sometimes felt they had to protest that they were not "guilty" by association).

    As for the atmosphere on the average coed dorm floor, one of Pete's old sophomoric friends burst into his room on Hasbrouck Fourth one day in early September 1984 and greeted him excitedly: "Hey dickhead, I've been lookin' all over for you!" Before Pete could introduce him to me, he burst out with the story he had come to tell. He now lived in Gates Hall. He and a few friends had been in an adjacent high-rise dorm the night before, he said, and one of the residents had had a pair of binoculars, so they started using them voyeuristically, to peep into the windows of the private student rooms in Gates.

    > And we see this guy in one room, with about five other guys, curtains wide open, and they're all dickin' each other up the ass! I couldn't *believe* it. Then I counted the floors, and this guy lives on *my floor!* So I call up on the hall phone and ask for him, I say to tell him his mother's calling. But he won't come to the phone.
    > But I couldn't *believe* it. What's this place turning into? *My* dorm's turning into another Nelson!

    Whereupon Pete replied, in a very even tone, "X, have I introduced you to *Professor* Moffatt?"

    Then, later in the semester, when I was doing research with some students who belonged to the Lesbian/Gay Alliance at Rutgers, I head their version of the same story and met the protagonist:

    > I'd just met this guy, and we went back to my room. And we started to make out. We were just taking off our clothes. I *had* left my curtains open. Well, apparently some people were watching from [the adjacent dorm] and they saw us. And I guess they called some people on the phone. I'd already decided I wasn't going to answer the phone if it rang. So when I didn't respond to the door, they hammered on it and

someone yelled, "Hey, put your pants on!" I couldn't *believe* it. Then someone went downstairs and hollered up at me in a effeminate voice. After that, I had some nasty stuff put on my door, and once a guy walking past my room said, "I can't stand *fags!*"

I couldn't believe they'd do that, look into my room. . . . If I'd seen the guys who did it, I'd have given their names to the deans and tried to have them thrown out of housing.

By the end of the semester, *he* had moved out of Gates, however, into an off-campus apartment.

12. In theory, these parties were open only to other members of the fraternity-sorority system and to invited guests. In practice, however, virtually any roving male who tried a few houses on a Thursday and Friday night could crash such a party. Or he could find a friend or acquaintance who would invite him in as a guest. High school students from neighboring towns commonly got in. Women, collegiate or otherwise, were generally given a quiet pulchritude test at the door of a fraternity, and any of them who met that house's particular standards or needs were readily admitted as instant invited guests.

13. For about twenty years following World War II, the ages for marriage and initial parenthood declined into the late teens and early twenties among middle-class Americans, atypically youthful years in recent American and British demographic history. These ages had returned to historical Anglo-American levels by the 1970s and 1980s, however: marriage and parenthood in the mid to late twenties and early thirties (see Gillis 1974; Kett 1977; Stone 1977). In past centuries, delayed marriage in middle-class western culture also often meant delayed sexuality, but obviously no longer. It has been the case once again, however, that delayed marriage means youths wait a number of years past their early twenties for full economic adulthood; most of them defer marriage until they acquire the additional schooling to become established in the professional occupations they dream of, and many of them plan a few more free years after that to enjoy modern affluent young adulthood. (To be strictly correct, then, the title of this book ought to be *Coming Partly Of Age in New Jersey*.)

REFERENCES

Canaan, Joyce. 1986. "Why a 'Slut' is a 'Slut'; Cautionary Tales of Middle-Class Teenage Girls' Morality." Pp. 184–208 in *Symbolizing America* edited by Herve Varenne. Lincoln: University of Nebraska Press.

Davis, Natalie Z. 1971. "The Reasons of Misrule: Youth Groups and Charivaris in Sixteenth-Century France." Pp. 97–123 in *Society and Culture in Early Modern France*. Stanford: Stanford University Press.

Gillis, John R. 1974. *Youth and History: Tradition and Change in European Age Relations 1700–Present*. New York: Academic Press.

Hildebrand, M. and S. Abramowitz. 1984. "Sexuality on Campus: Changes in Attitudes and Behaviors in the 1970s." *Journal of College Student Personnel* 25:534–46.

Kett, Joseph F. 1977. *Rites of Passage: Adolescence in America 1790 to the Present*. New York: Basic Books.

Stone, Lawrence. 1977. *The Family, Sex and Marriage in England, 1500–1800*. New York: Harper and Row.

Weis, David L. "The Experience of Pain during Women's First Sexual Intercourse: Cultural Mythology about Female Sexual Initiation." *Archives of Sexual Behavior* 14: 421–437.

17

Two Can Make a Revolution*

Egon Mayer

Paul's grandmother, Ba Thi Tu, had been cooking for the Bar Mitzvah for days alongside her daughter, Josephine Tu Steinman. The menu included veal with black mushroom sauce, Vietnamese meatballs, beef chow fun, chicken and cashew nuts, rice noodles, and other Oriental delicacies. A dish calling for pork had to be eliminated, along with shellfish dishes, because they were not kosher.

This was no ordinary Bar Mitzvah fare: no chopped herring, stuffed derma, or matzoh ball soup here. This was the home-catered Bar Mitzvah feast of Paul Steinman—the son of Ron Steinman, an executive at NBC-TV News— and Josephine Steinman, formerly Ngoc Suong Tu, a Vietnamese Buddhist who converted to Judaism after she came to the United States with her husband.

That *The New York Times* chose to report on the "Bar Mitzvah with a Viet-namese Flavor" (June 29, 1983) is ample indication, of course, that such cere-monies are far from common. Indeed, such families are far from common. Jews and Vietnamese are generally not found together in large enough numbers to pro-duce more than one or two intermarriages. But the story highlights what have become increasingly common facts of family life for Jews, as well as other mi-norities, since the early part of the twentieth century. America is blending, and out of its cultural caldron are emerging life-styles and new customs that defy age-old distinctions. When it comes to mate selection and the family forms that follow from it, love triumphs over tradition; inclinations triumph over timeless customs; and even religious rituals are transfigured to meet private needs and desires.

In that simple human interest story in *The Times*, which focused on the menu rather than on the ironies of the occasion, one can see reflected centuries of tension, and the fermenting of cultural forces and contending human drives coming to fruition.

Paul's Hebrew teacher was *kvelling* (rejoicing) at what appeared to her to be the fulfillment of the American dream. "A blending of two ancient cultures have met here today," Ms. Saletsky said. One is almost moved to the clichéd exultation "Love Conquers All." But as we shall see, such simple generalizations are defied by the complex realities of intermarriages.

Here, and in most other cases, too, love is no blind conqueror. It does not vanquish all other bonds or loyalties. Ron Steinman's Jewishness was important enough for him to have Ngoc Suong convert; important enough to have his children raised as Jews and educated in a Hebrew school; and important enough to have his firstborn son go through the traditional Jewish rite of passage. In subsequent personal conversation with Ron and Josephine, it became apparent that those same

*Mayer, Egon. 1987. "Two Can Make a Revolution." Pp. 23–58 in *Love and Tradition: Marriage Between Jews and Christians*. New York: Schocken.

Jewish sentiments were not a salient consideration in Ron's mind when he chose to marry the then Ngoc Suong. Moreover, Josephine observed that one of her deeply felt reasons for wanting to become Jewish was her Vietnamese heritage that obliges a married woman to join her fate entirely to her husband and his family. Thus, for her, conversion to Judaism was a traditional wifely obligation. At the same time, for Ron, marriage to a Vietnamese woman was very much a break from his Brooklyn Jewish family tradition. For both, albeit for different reasons and in different ways, love and marriage entailed not following the customary path of their respective families, at least as far as mate selection was concerned.

The modern vocabulary of motives for marriage emphasizes love, compatibility, and mutual fulfillment. It leaves but little room for such considerations as duty, respect for tradition, and responsibility to one's ancestors and parents. Individualism, personalism, and privatism form the cornerstones of contemporary family relationships—at least that is the conventional wisdom. In the light of that wisdom, the very concept—intermarriage—is an anachronism. What should it matter, as the question is often asked, what a person's religious, ethnic, racial, etc., background is? Only one man and one woman are united in a marriage. Ron and Ngoc Suong no doubt underwent such questioning before their marriage; at least in their own minds, if not with one another and their respective parents.

Yet their very life as a modern Reform Jewish family is a testimonial to the persistence of tradition, albeit in modern garb. The fact that she became Jewish, an American, and changed her name to Josephine is an indication of just how important it was for both of them to bridge the cultural and religious differences that many think should not matter any more to modern men and women living in the age of hi-tech.

The brief story of Paul's Bar Mitzvah points to a multitude of insights about what it means to be a Jew in modern America; about what it means to be a member of a religious or ethnic minority in a liberal, pluralistic society; about what it means to be a family today; and, indeed, about the very nature of identity in modern society.

The story symbolizes the simultaneous drive of individuals to pursue their own individual happiness under circumstances that are made unpredictable by the impersonal forces of history (e.g., war). At the same time, the story also symbolizes the deeply rooted tenacity of traditions and the capacity of free individuals to blend and connect the most time-honored traditions in the most unconventional ways. In a sense, the story of Paul's Bar Mitzvah epitomizes the irony of Jewish survival.

The image of love emerging out of the ashes of war has always been one of profound irony. That an American-Jewish bureau chief for NBC, covering the war in Vietnam, should return to the United States with a Buddhist wife who becomes a Jew, and that they should, in turn, raise Jewish children, is truly newsworthy. At least one of the sources of the irony is war itself. That love should emerge from it is somewhat understandable, but that it should leave intact two people's attachments to their heritage, despite their experience of the war and despite their love across vastly different heritages, is remarkable. To be sure, the Steinmans' experience is virtually unique, and hardly generalizable. Yet it recalls for me my own first encounter with Jewish intermarriage as a child, in the person of one of our closest family friends—Allen Feher, or Sándor bácsi, as I called him—in my childhood in Budapest.

Sándor had been one of my father's closest friends, ever since they were teenagers in Komárom (a small town in southwestern Czechoslovakia). They had attended yeshiva together, both being from Orthodox Jewish families. Sándor had married a few years before World War II and lived a traditional Orthodox Jewish life as a small merchant. When the Nazis entered Hungary in 1944 he happened to be away from home on business. His wife and two children were deported and never returned from the concentration camp. Sándor had gone into hiding in Budapest in the apartment of a Christian friend. There he was befriended by Irene, the daughter of a high-ranking officer in the Hungarian military, naturally, a Christian.

At the end of the war, Sándor and Irene married and had a child. Sándor abandoned his Orthodoxy and even joined the Communist Party—at least for appearance's sake. It helped him advance in the nationalized shop in which he worked. Yet, he continued to cling to a lifelong desire to go to Israel. In Communist Hungary in the late 1940s and early 1950s, that was—for all intents and purposes—a Messianic hope. But Irene, using her family contacts in the government, was able to obtain an exit visa for the three of them. In 1953 (at the close of the Stalinist era), Sándor—an intermarried Jew with a Catholic wife and daughter—immigrated to Israel, the land of his Jewish dreams. Irene never converted. She felt that she had returned to the land of Jesus and continued to live her life as an Israeli Catholic, as did her daughter.

A different war, a different continent and, surely, different personalities, yet one cannot help but feel that the same forces were working their curious chemistry in the lives of the Steinman and the Feher families. Ron and Sándor drew from the same well of tradition. And, for some as yet mysterious reason, Ngoc Suong and Irene both found it to be their desire to link their lives and fates to the ways in which their men would come to grips with their heritages. Ngoc Suong joined Ron Steinman's religion; Irene joined Allen Feher's nation.

Surely neither couple sought to make a social revolution of any kind and would probably be surprised to see themselves spoken of as "revolutionaries." Yet their relationships, along with the multitude of other similar relationships, continue to exert transformative pressures on the ancient culture of the Jewish people, as well as on the laws of a modern nation-state, Israel.

Allen and Irene's daughter, for example, has remained a Christian, but as a young, dynamic woman, she has also served in the Israeli army. Naturally, she met and socialized with Israeli young men, virtually all of whom were Jews. For her, it was hardly a break with any social convention to fall in love with a Jewish man. But marriage for the two of them in Israel was out of the question, since matrimonial law in Israel is determined by Jewish religious regulations that prohibit such marriages. Ironically, they had to "elope" to Cyprus to marry in a Greek civil ceremony so as to be able to live as a legitimately married couple in Israel. Their case, along with untold others, remains a source of festering tension in Israeli political life.

Bar Mitzvahs like that of the Steinmans' also stretch the meaning of the ancient Jewish ritual. According to the *halacha* (the body of Jewish law made up by the commendments in the *Five Books of Moses* and their rabbinic interpretations in the Talmud and subsequent exigetical texts), Bar Mitzvah refers to the ancient legal status of adulthood at which point an adolescent is obligated to abide by the laws. The term applied only to young men who were regarded as having reached their Bar Mitzvah at the age of thirteen. There had been no comparable status for Jewish women, nor a celebration thereof, until the Conservative movement institutionalized the Bat Mitzvah in the 1920s.

Interestingly enough, the Bar Mitzvah was one of the many observances the Reform movement abandoned in the nineteenth century. The Reform movement, born out of the spirit of the enlightenment and German nationalism at the end of the eighteenth century, sought to do away with all those Jewish religious customs that could not be rendered plausible in the light of modern reason and contemporary life-style. The notion that a pubescent young man at the tender age of thirteen should somehow be regarded as a legal adult responsible for his actions was one of those implausible customs in the eyes of the Reform movement.

Consequently, some of the oldest and most respectable Reform temples in America would not permit Bar Mitzvahs to be performed as late as the 1950s, nor were Bat Mitzvahs permitted.

But ancient traditions die hard, and sometimes not at all. The need on the part of Jewish families to signify to themselves and their communities that their children are part of the Jewish fold through some kind of joyous public ceremony could not be eradicated by rational philosophy. The Bar Mitzvah has gradually made its return into the Reform movement since the 1950s. In fact, with the increasing incidence of marriages between Jews and non-Jews, particularly in the Reform community, the Bar Mitzvah has emerged as the signal Jewish ceremony by which an intermarried family publicly proclaims that their child is being raised as a Jew.

In a twist of modern Jewish family history, the Steinmans, as Reform Jews, were celebrating the Bar Mitzvah, which had lost its apparent meaningfulness for Reform Jews earlier. It now serves a highly potent social and psychological function precisely as a result of intermarriage. To be sure, not all children of intermarriages go through a Bar or a Bat Mitzvah ceremony. Indeed, most do not. My own studies have shown that in those intermarried families in which the non-Jewish spouse does not convert to Judaism, only about 15 percent of the children will go through that symbolic Jewish life cycle ceremony. In what we call conversionary families, in which the formerly non-Jewish spouse converts to Judaism, as in the case of the Steinmans, nearly 75 percent of the children go through the ceremony; it apparently does not take many to stimulate cultural reforms.

The Steinmans' Bar Mitzvah menu also hints at an unfolding cultural revolution. Although most of America's Jews have relinquished the ethnic distinctiveness of their daily diet over the past few generations (hardly anyone really lives on chopped herring, *gefilte* fish, or *chulent* any more), such Jewish ceremonial occasions as weddings and Bar Mitzvahs are still marked by highly traditional food. For most modern American Jews, that is probably one of the salient features of these occasions: the opportunity to recollect the flavors and images of the past through their palates. But because most typical Jewish homes no longer prepare traditional Jewish foods as part of their normal diet, professional Jewish catering has emerged as an industry in its own right. Ostensibly, the function of the industry is to provide food and style consistent with the middle-class consumer values of American Jews. However, its more subtle, latent function is to serve up a feast of traditions through culinary inventiveness: to blend the taste of the immigrant with the style of the successful American.

In "olden days," it was not the caterer, but rather the women of the family who prepared the food for days and weeks before a Bar Mitzvah or a wedding. One of the objects of the ceremony was to exhibit before the larger invited community the mastery of the family of shared food values. "Look at my *kugel*," or *strudel,* or *gefilte* fish, the proud mother of a Bar Mitzvah boy would exclaim to her friends. And recipes, memories of mothers, and culinary techniques would be exchanged. But who asks a caterer for a recipe or memories of his mother?

Not surprisingly, it was Paul Steinman's Vietnamese grandmother and mother who spent their days cooking in preparation for the Bar Mitzvah. After all, where do you get a kosher caterer who cooks Vietnamese style? And the arousal of sensory memories through food is evidently no less important to the Vietnamese than it is to Jews—even if it is at a Bar Mitzvah. But the irony is this: Given the obvious importance attached to the memories of the palate by both Jews and Vietnamese, and probably all other ethnic Americans as well, what kind of memories are being built into young Paul's palate, and what kind of a Bar Mitzvah feast will he lay out for his own son?

The old adage that an army marches on its stomach may be true, but, at least from the brief account of Paul Steinman's Bar Mitzvah feast, it may also be surmised that cultural revolutions can be instigated in the kitchen.

The ironies of Paul's Bar Mitzvah and the late Sándor bácsi's marriage to Irene and immigration to Israel all point to the historical tension between love and tradition; between the drive of the individual for self-expression and fulfillment and his affinity for the norms and values of his heritage. This tension, of course, is not unique to intermarriages. It is endemic to all modern marriages. It is therefore appropriate and necessary to turn our attention briefly to the role of love and tradition in the making of modern family life.

Modern marriages, generally, and intermarriages, most particularly, are based on the feeling that two people share by being in love. In a brilliantly argued essay, Franceso Alberoni, the Italian sociologist, has suggested that the experience of falling in love is very much akin to the birth of a social movement; it is the moment that signals the birth of a new collective "we."

> In an existing social structure, the movement divides whoever was united and unites whoever was divided to form a new collective subject, a "we" which, in the case of falling in love, is formed by the lover-beloved couple.[1]

"No experience of falling in love exists without the transgression of a difference," writes Alberoni, and therefore, "falling in love challenges institutions on the level of their fundamental values."[2] The potential of two individuals to make a revolution is realized through love.

But love, like any other revolutionary force, can only transform people or social institutions if it is harnessed in some kind of ongoing collective enterprise such as marriage. Perhaps for this reason, love had not been allowed to play a significant role in mate selection in most societies until the last 200 years.

In a collection of essays with the title *Romanticism: Definition, Explanation and Evaluation* (1965), the historian John B. Halsted informs us that "the term Romanticism came into currency at the very beginning of the nineteenth century" and referred primarily to the works of poets and writers, later artists and composers, who gave primacy in their works to moods, feelings, passions, and enthusiasms.[3] They saw themselves as rebelling against the structures of Classicism and Rationalism. Historians of the modern family, such as Edward Shorter and Ellen K. Rothman, have shown that at more or less the same time that Romanticism was emerging as a thematic force in the world of the arts, romance—the primacy of empathy and spontaneity as well as sexuality between men and women—was emerging as an ideology on the basis of which couples would seek to form marriages and families.[4] It is in its latter, more layman's sense that we will use the terms *romance* and *romantic*.

Whereas love unites, tradition divides. The feelings of love burst through walls and spill over boundaries of conventionality. The feelings toward a tradition are quite different. No matter how passionately one may be committed to it, the sentiments inspired by tradition can be expressed only in forms and rituals that were established by others long ago. Tradition inspires conformity, just as surely as love inspires inventiveness. Tradition makes careful distinctions in time, in space and, most importantly, between categories of people. Love is oblivious to all that.

In point of fact, modern marriages are not merely based on love. More importantly, they are based on a belief; an ideology of romance that regards the deep psychological and sexual attachments that are experienced as love as socially legitimate and desirable; an adequate basis for the making of a complex relationship called marriage. A related tenet of this ideology of romance is that the social identity or group background of the beloved has no place in the emotional calculus of the loving relationship, nor should it have a role to play in the organization and quality of the marriage that ensues from loving.

But as we shall see in this, as well as in subsequent chapters, the heritages, traditions, cultural memories, and group identities of individuals who fall in love and marry do continue to play a significant role in the individuals' self-concepts and also in the life-styles of their families.

Thus, love is only the spark that may start a revolution. But real social transformation occurs precisely when the energy of love is harnessed and integrated in the flux of established situations: the family, religion, the state, and the community. That the love of two should have such far-reaching consequences, that is a real revolution.

For all these reasons, love and tradition have never lived comfortably with one another. Tracing the history of love in the West since the time of the ancient Greeks, Morton Hunt—a historian—shows vividly, and with some sense of both its drama and its humor, that the "joining of romantic passion, sensuous enjoyment, friendship and marriage" took nearly 2,000 years to evolve to its modern form.[5]

The general lovelessness of ancient marriages is captured in a somewhat cruel Greek adage of the sixth century before the Christian era: "Marriage brings a man only two happy days: the day he takes his bride to his bed, and the day he lays her in her grave."[6] But as late as our own twentieth century, the fictional Goldie, wife of Sholom Aleichem's *Tevyeh, The Milkman* (popularized in America as *Fiddler on the Roof*), is perplexed when her husband asks her, "Do you love me?" She replies:

> For twenty-five years I've washed your clothes, cooked your meals, cleaned your house, given you children, and milked the cow. After twenty-five years, why talk about love right now?[7]

Goldie's words are virtually a mirror image of the ancient Greek view of matrimony attributed by Morton Hunt to the famous orator Demosthenes: "Mistresses we keep for pleasure, concubines for daily attendance upon our needs, and wives to bear us legitimate children and to be our housekeepers."[8]

Undoubtedly, many more wives and husbands probably loved one another, before, as well as during the course of their married life, than one finds recorded in the annals of history. But it is also true, and far more widely established historically, that love has been but rarely considered an acceptable reason, much less an expected forerunner, of matrimony. If love was to be found at all, it was most often to be found briefly before, and frequently outside of, marriage, generally in forbidden relationships.

Marriage, however, was a moral duty and a social responsibility particularly incumbent upon men. It was through marriage that a family name, the family heritage, and property would be passed, unto posterity. Singlehood was as much frowned upon in the ancient Jewish tradition as it was in the ancient Greek and Roman traditions. Indeed, even in colonial America, bachelors were highly suspect and, in most colonies, were burdened with special taxes and generally kept under the watchful eyes of their neighbors. In Connecticut, William Kephart reports, "every kind of obstacle was put in the way of a bachelor keeping his own house. . . . Unless a bachelor had authority to live alone he was fined one pound (£) a week."[9]

But although marriage was a duty almost universally honored by most adults since ancient times, who actually married whom was not left to the individual. Such decisions were too important to be left in private hands, subject to personal whim or fancy. Given its strong social, moral, and religious objectives, marriages were arranged throughout most of history, in both the East and West, by parents, older siblings, and other guardians of family tradition. They made certain that the marriage partners who were chosen for their young ones were consistent with the needs and values of the family and the larger community. Naturally, under such a controlled mate selection system, marriages between Jews and Christians were virtually out of the question on both sides; only social deviants would intermarry.

To be sure, even under such a system, a son or daughter might be granted veto power by a permissive parent over a particular choice. But it is highly unlikely that more than a rare few ever had the freedom to choose a mate based entirely on their private emotional preference and without due regard to the broad conventional preferences of their families and communities. Those who violated the imperatives of custom or clan, the Romeos and Juliets of history, most often paid the price. In short, for much of our history, the dictates of tradition clearly dominated the inclinations of the heart when it came to marriage. It is more than likely that the ancestors of Ron Steinman—as well as those of his wife, Ngoc Suong Tu—were married off in their early teen years to mates chosen by their parents.

It took several far-reaching revolutions, and about two centuries, to dismantle traditional constraints upon mate selection and to replace them with romantic idealism. By the end of the eighteenth century, writes Edward Shorter, "young people began paying much more attention to inner feelings than to outward considerations, such as property and parental wishes, in choosing marriage partners." [10]

The onset of the Industrial Revolution in the latter half of the seventeenth century began to unsettle the closely bunched lives of people in villages and farms, forcing increasing numbers to leave their highly traditional rural enclaves for larger towns and cities.

The feudal West was beginning to stir, shaking the age-old foundations of family organization. Of course, for most Jews, those early stirrings were barely noticed. They would continue to live in restricted isolation from their Christian neighbors for yet another two centuries. But a few famous "court Jews" were beginning to enter intimate political and economic arrangements with dukes and princes in Germany, which, in due time, would lead to even greater intimacies between their children and grandchildren, as one can see among the illustrious Rothschilds. Selma Stern's colorful account of the adventurous lives of the seventeenth-century court Jews amply hints at the advance of the industrial age that was beginning to pave the way for a growing intimacy between Jews and non-Jews. [11] But whether the intimacy would lead to love and marriage would depend on the relative power of tradition and love in the prevailing social norms.

With the benefit of hindsight, we now know that romanticism followed closely on the heels of the American and French revolutions, the two epoch-making revolutions at the end of the eighteenth century that ushered in the modern era. As Edward Shorter put it, in the years after 1750, "the libido unfroze in the blast of the wish to be free." Gradually the idea gained currency that marriage should be much more than a joining of hands, of fortunes, and of families—that it should be a joining of hearts.

At least as it applies to the making of marriages, the romanticism that followed in the wake of two great political revolutions probably advanced much further in the United States than elsewhere in the West. In a delicately drawn history of courtship in America, Ellen Rothman shows that parents increasingly allowed and expected their children to freely choose their own marriage partners. [12] In turn, young men and women recognized that in order to find a mate, they must first find love. Perhaps Thomas Jefferson himself might be credited (or blamed) for the ascendancy of love. After all, it was he who changed the famous slogan of liberty attributed to John Locke ("Life, Liberty, and Property") to "Life, Liberty, and the Pursuit of Happiness."

In a profound analysis of that Jeffersonian turn of phrase, Jan Lewis, a historian, has shown that the freedom to pursue personal happiness soon became a moral as well as a psychological imperative, with wide-ranging effects on both family life and religion.[13] Put succinctly, "in the decades after the Revolution, the head fell victim to the heart." Marriage was now to grow out of passionate desire and was to lead to mutual emotional fulfillment and inner peace, and not simply to outer stability and respectability.

In their *Manifesto of the Communist Party,* Karl Marx and Friedrich Engels argued that the purely economic forces of capitalism that they saw all around them in the Europe of 1848 were sweeping away age-old customs that had governed religion, family life, and social relations in general. However, a closer look at the surge of Romanticism in that era—be it in the form of sublime poetry read in the drawing rooms of the bourgeoisie or in the form of the unbridled sexuality of the lower classes—suggests that it was not the power of capital alone (or even primarily) that was transforming social norms. Rather, it was the revolutionary new idea that each individual had the right to pursue his or her own personal happiness: that society could be so ordered that people might find true happiness in their choice of mates, and that they might try to exploit their own talents to their best possible advantage.

Today, the unconditional value of conjugal love as both the basis for and the proper object of marriage is so thoroughly taken for granted that it is difficult to imagine that it was ever otherwise, or that any alternate view of that tender emotion might be equally valid. But if such social historians as the Frenchman, Philippe Aries; or the Canadian, Edward Shorter; or the American, Morton M. Hunt, are correct, the popular infatuation with romantic love and its close connection in the popular mind with marriage is a relatively recent phenomenon. For most of history, men and women were joined in matrimony out of more practical considerations, such as the demands of social conventionality or the needs for security.

Looking back upon traditional patterns of courtship, Shorter writes,

> All situations in which boys and girls met for the first time were monitored by some larger group.... Young women simply did not encounter young men without other people around.[14]

The opportunity for the spontaneous involvement of members of the opposite sex with one another was rigorously controlled so as to prevent undesirable amorous entanglements. The "other people around" were most often parents, older siblings, or even peers who could safeguard the individual against "stepping out" of the bounds of social propriety—emotionally or otherwise. Arranged marriages, which often took place among well-to-do families in Europe, be they Jews or Christians, were the surest way to prevent romance from intruding into the all-important process of family formation. Continuing his backward glance, Shorter continues,

> The most important change in the nineteenth- and twentieth-century courtship has been the surge of sentiment.... People started to place affection and personal compatibility at the top of the list of criteria in choosing marriage partners. These new standards became articulated as romantic love. And secondly, even those who

continued to use the traditional criteria of prudence and wealth in selecting partners began to behave romantically within these limits.[15]

Like stardust in the trail of a comet, the romantic revolution followed in the wake of twin social revolutions of the eighteenth and nineteenth centuries: the industrial and the democratic.

In the United States, love and the pursuit of happiness had yet another major role in transforming the society. It was to be the flame under the melting pot.

> What, then, is the American, this new man? He is neither a European, nor the descendant of a European; hence that strange mixture of blood, which you will find in no other country. I could point out to you a family whose grandfather was an Englishman, whose wife was Dutch, whose son married a French woman, and whose present four sons have now four wives of different nations.[16]

This often-quoted passage, from the pen of French-American Jean De Crevocouer in his *Letters from an American Farmer* (1782), presaged by some 120 years the theme if not the title of the Jewish-American Israel Zangwill's play, *The Melting Pot* (1908).[17] As some critics of the period observed, Zangwill captured in a phrase the spirit of the nation.

The Melting Pot was a drama about a romance, a thinly veiled imitation of Shakespeare's *Romeo and Juliet,* only with a happy ending—at least for the couple. David Quixano, a Russian-born Jewish immigrant, falls in love with Vera Revendal, a Russian-born Christian; both work on the Lower East Side of New York—that quintessential immigrant ghetto of the turn of the century. For some reason, Zangwell chose the most un-Russian last names for his principal characters. Perhaps he thought that they would blend better if they were not burdened with more distinctive names. Be that as it may, the young lovers were determined to marry, despite the turbulance of their emotions and opposition of their relatives. They put off their marriage only when it was learned that Vera's father, a colonel in the Tsar's army, was personally responsible for the killing of David's family in the Kishinev *pogrom* of 1903.

However, by the end of the play love prevails over all the sorrow, bitterness, and prejudice. To paraphrase Zangwill, the shadows of Kishinev melt away in the American crucible. The young lovers walk hand in hand into the sunset against the skyline of lower Manhattan, to the background strains of "My Country 'Tis of Thee."

The play opened at the Columbia Theater in Washington, D.C. with President Theodore Roosevelt in attendance. In fact, the play was dedicated to Roosevelt. When the final curtain fell, Arthur Mann, the historian, writes, the President shouted from his box, "That's a great play, Mr. Zangwill! That's a great play!" *The Melting Pot* went on to become a huge popular success, continues Mann.

> After showing in the nation's capital, it ran for six months in Chicago, and then for 136 performances in New York City. Thereafter, for close to a decade, it played in dozens of cities across America. In 1914 it was produced in London, again before full houses and admiring audiences.[18]

The play became a text in high schools and colleges; it was produced by amateur theatrical groups frequently, and its publisher, Macmillan, reprinted it at least once a year until 1917.

One does not need a great deal of historical insight to understand why that play should have become so popular and, particularly, so highly praised by the official champions of American culture. Between 1870 and 1924 (when the Johnson Act finally stemmed the tide of mass immigration), the population of America more than doubled from about 45 million to about 110 million.[19] The growth was fueled by the entry of about 25 million immigrants, overwhelmingly from southern, eastern, and middle Europe: Jews, Slavs, Poles, Italians, Serbs, Croats, etc. In some of the larger American cities, nearly 40 percent of the population was comprised of the foreign-born and recently arrived immigrants: "The tired, the poor, the wretched refuse of the earth," as Emma Lazarus described them on the base of the Statue of Liberty.

Lincoln Steffens voiced the central question of the period in a title of an article, "What Are We Going to Do with Our Immigrants?"[20] Perforce, the answer had to be assimilation. The pervasive and troubling division between blacks and whites, which continues as the single most salient social division in America, inevitably drew all immigrants into the general society and made their gradual assimilation a popular social goal. Ralph Waldo Emerson gave poetic voice to this sentiment.

> As in the old burning of the Temple at Corinth, by the melting and intermixture of silver and gold and other metals a new compound more precious than any, called Corinthian brass, was formed, so in this continent—asylum of all nations— the energy of the Irish, Germans, Swedes, Poles, Cossacks, and all the European tribes—of the Africans, and the Polynesians—will construct a new race, a new religion, a new state, a new literature, which will be as vigorous as the new Europe which came out of the smelting pot of the Dark Ages.[21]

Although social scientists make useful distinctions between such concepts as assimilation, amalgamation, and pluralism, it is clear from all the studies of the great immigration of that period that the process of Americanization was to involve both the relinquishing of many old-world traditions and the acquisition of many new ones.

How rapidly the process would occur in the lives of particular individuals, and in the collective history of one ethnic group or another, was to vary according to biographical and social circumstances. The peddler who found himself in the hinterlands of Pennsylvania was surely Americanized more rapidly than his cousin who manned a pushcart on New York's Lower East Side. But what would ultimately make America a true amalgam—an embodiment of the ideal printed on her coinage, *E Pluribus Unum*—was to be a universal human emotion: love.

Zangwill's play owed its popularity to the fact that it held out a promise that both the masses of immigrants yearning to become full-fledged Americans and the guardians of American culture, trying to cope with the massive influx of foreign multitudes, dearly wished to believe. The fire that was to heat the melting pot was none other than love—not the love of nation or folk, nor the love of abstract ideas, but the entirely private kind of love between a man and a woman.

It was expected that contact between different ethnic groups would lead to acculturation: borrowing a custom here and there, sharing recipes, and the like. The practical necessity of working and living in America would lead to assimilation in such matters as language, education, and political and economic aspirations. But what would forge the blended American, as Roosevelt, Emerson, or Steffens envisioned him, would be none other than marriage—the union of diverse groups through the power of romantic love.

In Jewish communities, the social revolutions of the nineteenth century socially emancipated the individual Jew, thus enabling him to become an equal citizen. As the German historian Heinrich Graetz put it,

> The hour of freedom for the European Jews dawned in the revolutions of February and March, 1848, in Paris, Vienna, Berlin, in Italy, and other countries. An intoxicating desire for liberty came over the nations of Europe, more overpowering and marvelous than the movement of 1830. With imperious demands the people confronted their princes and rulers. Among the demands was the emancipation of the Jews. In all popular assemblies and proclamations, the despised Jews of yesterday were admitted into the bond of "Liberty, Equality, and Fraternity" (the slogan of the French Revolution of 1789).[22]

As a result of those revolutions, Jews streamed from confined settlements in backward towns and villages into the capitals of Europe; from narrowly restricted occupations into the full range of modern pursuits that were being opened up by the Industrial Revolution; and into a new kind of relationship with Christians— one that, at least in principle if not in fact, was based on a doctrine of social equality.

Intermarriages between free-thinking Jews and Christians followed on the heels of emancipation in an inexorable sequence. Historians surmise that the salons in the homes of Jewish bankers in Berlin and Vienna offered the first common meeting places for liberated Jews and Christians, and it was from these sociable acquaintanceships that the first intermarriages resulted. First the privilege of only the well-to-do Jews, intermarriage between Jews and Christians gradually became an available option for the broad masses of urban middle-class Jews.

Although statistics on the rate of Jewish intermarriage at the beginning of the modern era are spotty and imprecise, there are some available that clearly buttress the general impressions. In a study of marriage records right after the American Revolution, the historian Malcolm H. Stern found that in 699 marriages of Jews, 201, or about 29 percent, were intermarriage between a Jew and a Christian.[23] Similar patterns are reported by others elsewhere in the Western World.

Citing the work of such early students of Jewish social life as Drachsler, Engelman, Fishberg, and Ruppin, Milton L. Barron reports, for instance, that the percentage of intermarriages as a proportion of all marriages in which Jews were involved increased in Switzerland from 5 percent in 1888 to about 12 percent by 1920; in Hungary, the rate increased from about 5 percent in 1895 to about 24 percent by 1935; and in Germany, the rate increased from about 15 percent in

1901 to about 44 percent by 1933, on the eve of the Nazi rise to power and the passage of the draconian Nuremberg Laws that forbade marriage between Jews and Christians. [24]

Citing the work of the French demographer E. Schnurmann, Moshe Davis similarly reports that in Strasbourg, the rate of intermarriage between Jews and Christians increased from an undetermined "very low rate" to over one-third of all marriages of Jews between 1880 and 1909. The French city of Strasbourg had a substantial Jewish population at the time, so the increase in intermarriage could not be attributed to a dearth of eligible Jewish marriage partners. [25]

Jews were apparently eager to enter the mainstream of modern society through the portals of romance and matrimony with their Christian neighbors, and they were also being more readily accepted in their host societies. The separation of church and state following the revolutions in America and France, and the availability of civil marriage—there as well as in much of the rest of the Western World—further hastened the incidence of intermarriages that would not have been legal in earlier generations.

Although the statistics are spotty, as we have seen, and not as precise as most social scientists would prefer, their message is unmistakable. Jews were choosing Christian mates (most often a Jewish man choosing a Christian woman), as well as being chosen by them, in ever-increasing number. They were breaking sharply with one of the oldest and most deeply held norms of Jewish life: the norm of endogamy—the *halachic* requirement (based on biblical injuctions) that Jews only marry other Jews.

The one sleeping-giant exception to this trend at the turn of the twentieth century was the Jew of Eastern Europe, about half of the world's approximately 8 to 9 million Jews at the time. They lived in the infamous Pale of Jewish Settlement, a territory about the size of Texas on the periphery of Russia and Poland. [26] In these small, isolated, economically backward and politically enfeebled villages, they were barely touched by the great revolutions of the previous two centuries. Whereas the lives of Western Jews had undergone significant transformations since the end of the seventeenth century, particularly rapidly from the mid-eighteenth century, the lives of Eastern European Jews in the 1880s did not differ much from what they might have been in the Middle Ages. Indeed, some might say that they were probably better off in the Middle Ages than they were in the last decades of the nineteenth century.

As described by many writers, in varying hues of pain, humor, and bitterness, as well as some nostalgia, Eastern European Jewry lived a cloistered, virtually medieval existence until the first decades of the twentieth century.

Their language, Yiddish; their religious life, a highly ritualized and fundamentalist form of Orthodox Judaism laced with the mysticism of the Hasidic Jews; their economy, pre-industrial and progressively rendered impoverished by anti-Semitic decrees; their host culture, Polish and Russian peasantry wantonly anti-Semitic and given to periodic orgies of organized violence against Jews; their self-image, a moral kingdom of priests and philosophers who were destined to attain a loftier existence someday. All these features of their life served to erect an almost impregnable barrier between Jews and Christians who lived as neighbors in the villages (or *shtetlach,* as they were called in Yiddish). Social intimacy at the level of friendship was almost non-existent between them. Therefore, the possibility of intermarriage was virtually unthinkable.

And yet, if the story of *Tevyeh, the Milkman* is any indication of social realities, despite those great barriers some Jews and Catholics or Russian Orthodox peasants did fall in love; did go against the prevailing social norms and did marry, although often they did so by eloping to the West. Clearly the inclination of the individual to pursue his or her own personal happiness, even in the face of powerful opposing social norms, could not be entirely suppressed.

Nevertheless, the central point remains — marriages between Jews and Christians were far less common in the ghettoized areas of Eastern Europe than they were for Western Jewry. Arthur Ruppin, one of the early sociologists of world Jewry, has amply documented that, for instance, the proportion of intermarriages in one hundred Jewish marriages was less than 1 percent in Galicia as late as 1929. By contrast, the rate in places like Germany was 23 percent, and it was 13 to 27 percent in Budapest and Vienna. Elsewhere in Eastern Europe — in Latvia, Lithuania, White Russia, and the Ukraine — mixed marriages rarely occurred. [27] Moreover, it stands to reason that they were not any more frequent at the end of the nineteenth century than they were in the first decades of the twentieth.

However, it must be recalled that between the 1880s and the 1920s, about half of the approximately 5 million Jews who lived in Eastern Europe immigrated to the United States. Beginning with the pogroms of 1881, masses of *shtetl* Jews were quite literally chased into the modern world by the whips and swords of Russian Cossacks. Rather than try to bear it stoically, dying martyrs' deaths as their ancestors might have done, millions of Jews from the Pale chose the path of migration to the West, specifically to the United States.

Between 1881 and 1923, approximately 2.8 million Jews entered through Ellis Island, the "golden door" to America. They quickly overwhelmed the 250,000 Jews, mostly of German descent, who had comprised American Jewry up to that time. As is well known from Irving Howe's popular *World of Our Fathers,* the first generation of Eastern European immigrants settled in such densely Jewish ghettos as the Lower East Side in New York, Maxwell Street in Chicago, and similar enclaves in Philadelphia, Baltimore, and Washington, D.C. [28]

Their settlement patterns, their economic circumstances, their dependence on *mameloschen* (mother tongue, i.e., Yiddish), and the rising tide of anti-Semitism in America soon resulted in the re-establishment of the kind of ghettoized mode of social life that they had all just recently left behind in the Old World. The convergence of all these social factors resulted in a dramatic decline in the overall rate of mixed marriages for American Jews.

In contrast to the approximately 30 percent rate of Jewish mixed marriages discovered by Malcolm Stern among American Jews in the Federal period (when there were no more than 100 thousand Jews in the country, representing about one-quarter of 1 percent of the total population), the proportion of intermarriages among Jews in the first decades of this century (when they were about 3.5 percent of the total U.S. population) was less than 2 percent. [29]

At the very historical moment when Israel Zangwill was rhapsodizing about the power of love, and intermarriage in particular, and as the great emotional fire flamed under the "melting pot," more of his own people were huddling together—as were immigrant Italians, Poles, Irish, Greeks, and Chinese—than they might have been a half century earlier. The tough realities of immigrant life, and traditions of the Old-World culture that most immigrants brought with them, placed a powerful check on the romanticism of the nineteenth century; but not for long.

In a popular compilation of letters to the editor of the *Jewish Daily Forward,* the preeminent Yiddish newspaper in America since 1890, we find that from the earliest times their readers were writing to the illustrious editor of the paper about problems having to do with marriage, particularly between Jews and non-Jews. Isaac Metzker, who published the popular compilation in 1971 under the title *A Bintle Brief* (a bundle of letters), gives us a vivid flavor of some of their concerns.

1908

Worthy Editor:

I have been in America almost three years. I came from Russia where I studied in yeshiva. . . . At the age of twenty I had to go to America. Before I left I gave my father my word that I would walk the righteous path and be good and pious. But America makes one forget everything.

Here I became a (machine) operator, and at night I went to school. In a few months I entered a preparatory school, where for two subjects I had a gentile girl as teacher. . . . Soon I realized that her lessons with me were not ordinary . . . she wanted to teach me without pay. . . . I began to feel at home in her house . . . also her parents welcomed me warmly. . . . Then she spoke frankly of her love for me and her hope that I would love her.

I was confused and I couldn't answer her immediately. . . . I do agree with her that we are first human beings, and she is a human being in the fullest sense of the word. She is pretty, educated, intelligent, and has a good character. But I am in despair when I think of my parents. I go around confused and yet I am drawn to her. I must see her every day, but when I am there I think of my parents and I am torn by doubt.

Respectfully,
Skeptic from Philadelphia[30]

Reading this poignant letter nearly 80 years after it was written, and with the hindsight of history, one wonders what the nameless correspondent was skeptical about. Was it about his faith, about the wisdom of his parents, or the wisdom of his attachment to them? Was it about his love for the girl or her love for him, or was it perhaps about love itself?

Another correspondent, writing to the editor just about a year later, had other problems, but seemed to be unperturbed by any skepticism.

1909

Dear Editor:

I come from a small town in Russia. I was brought up by decent parents and got a good education. I am now twenty years old and am a custom-peddler in a Southern city. Since my customers here are Colored people, I became acquainted with a young Negro girl, twenty-two years of age, who buys merchandise from me. . . . She is a teacher, a graduate of a Negro college, and I think she is an honorable person.

I fell in love with the girl but I couldn't go around with her openly because I am White and she is Colored. However, whenever I deliver her order, I visit with her for awhile.

In time she went away to another city to teach, and I corresponded with her. When she came home for Christmas, I told her I loved her and intended to marry her and take her North to live. But she refused me and gave me no reason. Perhaps it was because I am a White man.

I spoke about my love for her to my friends, who are supposedly decent people, and they wanted to spit in my face. To them it appeared that I was about to commit a crime.

Therefore I would like to hear your answer as to whether I should be condemned for falling in love with a Negro woman and wanting to marry her. And if you can, explain to me also her reason for refusing me.

Respectfully,
Z.B.[31]

One wonders how many young Jewish peddlers, machine operators, and night school students who had recently come to America were having their first taste of the bittersweet pulls and pinches of romance with Italians, Irish, WASPs, and blacks. One wonders, and wishes for more data. But even in the absence of such data, it is safe to say that there were many more such matches, resulting in marriages (and even occasional conversions to Judaism), than there had been in Eastern Europe.

Writing in 1920, Julius Drachsler reported that the rate of intermarriage for Jews in New York City was 2.27 percent between 1908 and 1912. However, the trend was clearly upward as one looked past the immigrant generations and outside the ghettoized areas of Jewish Settlements.[32]

The trend became most clearly defined for American Jews only as recently as 1971. It was in that year that the Council of Jewish Federations and Welfare released its landmark study of the U.S. Jewish population known as the National Jewish Population Study, or NJPS. Table 1 succinctly presents the key finding of

TABLE 1. Percentage of Jewish Persons Marrying Someone Who Was Not Born Jewish, out of All Jews Who Married at Given Time Periods

Time period	Jews marrying non-Jews
1900–1920	2.0
1921–1930	3.2
1931–1940	3.0
1941–1950	6.7
1951–1955	6.4
1956–1960	5.9
1961–1965	17.4
1966–1971	31.7

that study with regard to the intermarriage trend. Although there is some scholarly debate about the precise, most current intermarriage rate, there is no debate about the direction of the trend.

It took about sixty years, or roughly three generations, for the descendants of the Eastern European immigrants (who constitute approximately 75 to 80 percent of the total American Jewish population) to catch up in their rate of mixed marriage with those of their brethren in America and Western Europe who had been modernized in the eighteenth and nineteenth centuries.

The magnitude of the most recent rates, and the speed with which they had increased, rang out like a thunderclap in the Jewish community. In a seminal work, *Assimilation in American Life* (1964), Milton Gordon had argued that "if marital assimilation . . . takes place fully, the minority group loses its ethnic identity in the larger host or core society."[33] The findings of NJPS rang a powerful alarm in the minds of those concerned with Jewish group survival.

The convergence of Gordon's sociological insights and the statistical patterns discovered by the NJPS led many learned observers to a foreboding conclusion. American Jewry might become an "extinct species" as a result of marital assimilation. At the very least, so it was feared, the size and significance of an already small minority in the American mosaic might be further reduced to ultimate insignificance as a result of intermarriage. In a carefully calculated analysis, Harvard demographer Elihu Bergman cautioned in 1977 that the net effect of the increased rate of intermarriage projected out over a century would be to reduce the size of the American-Jewish population from the approximately 5.7 million in 1976 to as few as about 10 thousand by the time of the American tricentennial, in the year 2076.[34]

Nor have the concerns been based upon Jewish facts alone. In the wake of Vatican Council II, the *Decree on Ecumenism* (1966) proposed that the Catholic Church mitigate its historically rigorous opposition to mixed marriages. By 1970, the Church no longer required in such marriages that the non-Catholic partner promise to raise the children as Catholics—much less to convert to Catholicism. The result of the liberalizing trend in the Church was to see a steady increase in Catholic intermarriages and a corresponding decline in conversions to Catholicism. Indeed, as Andrew Greeley has shown in his *Crisis in the Church* (1979), "by far the largest numbers of those who have disidentified from the Roman Catholic Church have done so in connection with a mixed marriage."[35]

If religious tradition was steadily losing its grip on cupid's arrows, the once restraining influence of ethnic traditions was faring even worse. In an influential article in the *American Sociological Review,*[36] Richard Alba showed that marriage across ethnic lines among Catholics had increased significantly with the coming of age of successive generations of the descendents of immigrants. Ethnic in-group marriage among the immigrant generations of English, Irish, German, Polish, French, and Italian Catholics quickly yielded to ethnic mixing among the second and third generations, according to Alba's deft analysis.

Among Jews, too, the breaching of the previous generations' ethnic divisions was nearly total by the end of the 1950s. As recently as the 1910s, Konrad Bercovici reports, intermarriage between a Sephardic Jew and a Russian Jew was as rare, if not rarer (and more frowned upon), as marriage between a Jew and a non-Jew.[37] Indeed, Bavarian Jews even hesitated to marry German Jews who came from nearer the Polish border, derisively referring to them with the ethnic slur "Pollacks." In turn, the Russian Jews looked down upon the Polish Jews as well as upon the Galicians and would not permit their children to marry them, reports Milton Barron. But by mid-century the inter-ethnic aversions had largely disappeared in the Jewish community, in much the same way as they had among Catholics.

In retrospect, it would seem that the wholesale crossing of ethnic boundaries *within* religious groups paved the way for the crossing of religious boundaries. The walls of tradition were being battered down by sentiment and emotional attachments, one cultural building block at a time. If those trends would continue unabated for even a few successive generations, Israel Zangwill's play about the melting pot would prove to be prophetic. The romantic ideology of the eighteenth and the nineteenth centuries would indeed sweep away the last vestiges of traditional constraint on the individual's choice of a mate. Such a fundamental change in the making of family life would prove a more profound point as well. It would prove that happiness—and, indeed, identity itself—is quite possible in the modern world without any significant rootedness in a shared tradition.

However, alongside the increasing rates of intermarriage for Jews and others, mid-century modernity was marked by other cultural trends as well. Perhaps none is more notable than the Americans' search for their diverse heritages. The period saw a spate of publications, both in the social sciences and popular literature, extolling the virtues of ethnicity and tradition. Opposing Zangwill, Michael Novak heralded *The Rise of the Unmeltable Ethnic* (1972) and the age of "White ethnicity."[38] Earlier, Herbert Gans and Michael Parenti had also seen the signs amidst the suburban and urban transitions of the 1950s and 1960s.[39] Ethnic group ties continued to play a powerful role in shaping the residential as well as friendship preferences of people long after ethnicity had been declared irrelevant in American life by the conventional wisdom.

In popular literature, the enthusiasm for nearly lost heritages reached its crescendo with the publication and subsequent serialization on TV of Alex Haley's *Roots*. It is particularly ironic that Haley dedicated his book to America's bicentennial, since it was published in 1976. The "nation of many nations," in which the culture was to blend and render indistinguishable the diversity of cultures that it comprised, was being greeted, on its bicentennial, with a massive outpouring of interest in ethnic distinctiveness and family heritage. The interest in "roots" spawned a virtual cottage industry in genealogy as a family pastime for several years. It was being fed by such books as Bill R. Linder's *How to Trace Your Family History* (1978) and, for Jews, Arthur Kurzweil's popular *Tracing Your Jewish Roots*.[40] As recently as 1984, no less a personage than the President of the United States, Ronald Reagan, created a significant "media event" by visiting the village in Ireland from whence his ancestors emigrated to the United States in the 1840s.

The "Bar Mitzvah with the Vietnamese flavor" with which this chapter began, now points to an even deeper irony. It purports to blend two cultures, Jewish and

Vietnamese, very much in keeping with the American ideal of the melting pot. But it simultaneously speaks to the persistence of an unalloyed attachment to the traditions of those cultures. It particularly speaks to the persistence of Jewish identity and ritual in the lives of people—some born Jewish, some newly so— who, at least on the basis of their choice of marriage partners, would seem to have agreed that love is more important than tradition.

The Steinman Bar Mitzvah underscores the emergence of two apparently contradictory trends among modern American Jews, in particular, and perhaps among all modern ethnic Americans, in general. One is the trend described by Shorter, by Lewis, by Rothman, and by other students of the romanticization of the modern family: the triumph of the heart over the head, of love over tradition in matters of mate selection. The other is the trend of resurgent ethnicity described by Novak, by Parenti, by Glazer and Moynihan, and by others since the 1960s. These two contradictory trends have been made even more puzzling since the mid-1970s with the resurgence of religious emotionalism and fundamentalism among those very segments of society—the young, professional, educated, and middle class—who had been thought to be immune to spiritual matters because of their modern consciousness and life-style.

As do all profound contradictions, these contradictory trends raise several compelling questions that strike at the very core of the meaning of intermarriage. Why do people choose to celebrate particular symbols or rituals of a larger tradition whose main tenets they have rejected? For example, why did Josephine Steinman want her son's Bar Mitzvah to have a "Vietnamese flavor" when she had converted to Judaism and presumably now sees herself as part of the Jewish people? Why did Ron Steinman want his wife to become Jewish, as do tens of thousands of other young Jews who marry Christians, when his sense of equality was such that he was able to fall in love with a woman who was a Buddhist? Why do the hundreds of thousands of Jews and Christians, who marry one another in defiance of their age-old ethnic and religious traditions, persist in memorializing many of those very same traditions in their holiday celebrations, in the way they rear their children, in what they read and what they eat, and in their very concept of themselves as human beings? Particularly among American Jews who have experienced such a great and rapid increase in intermarriages, why has the trend toward intermarriage *not* been accompanied by a comparable trend of disidentification from the Jewish people?

Perhaps Josephine Steinman herself was answering some of those deep questions in her own mind when she commented on the unique Bar Mitzvah menu to *The Times'* reporter, "It was a desire to put on a party in one's own image. That became particularly important with the kind of family we have. After all, there aren't many Vietnamese-Jewish families."

Of course, Mrs. Steinman is right. There aren't many Vietnamese-Jewish families, but, until the 1950s, it is not likely that one would have found culturally blended Jewish families of even less exotic mixture, such as Italian-Jewish or Irish-Jewish, which are far more common. It is not that such marriages did not occur. Of course, they did. Jews have been marrying non-Jews since biblical times. But the social stigma attached to such marriages usually compelled intermarried couples to become more or less socially invisible—at least in the eyes of the Jewish community and often in the eyes of the Christian community as well.

What stands out as remarkable about the Steinman's Bar Mitzvah is that this family has no desire or need to "pass" as either exclusively Jewish or Vietnamese, or exclusively anything else. They can create a party in their own image, indeed an entire social identity in their own image. Moreover, they can find a Reform Jewish congregation (of which they are members) that seems not only to accept but also to actually delight in this family's ability to express their Jewishness in their own unique idiom.

Rose Epstein, an old friend of the family, is quoted as commenting on the celebration, "It's a new world, isn't it? I can't get over how nice it is when people accept." Her comment is almost liturgical. It recalls the well-known Hebrew song "Hine Ma Tov U'Manaim, Shevet Achim Gam Yachad" (Behold, how good and pleasant it is when brethren dwell in unity).[41] One almost has to pinch one's self to realize that the unity of brethren rhapsodized by the Hebrew poet certainly did not envision the celebration of Bar Mitzvahs with Vietnamese cousins or chicken with cashew nuts.

Some might say the the desire, as Josephine put it, to "put on a party in one's own image" proclaims nothing more profound than the contemporary consumerist values of modern upper-middle-class Americans—young, professional urbanites—whose numbers are legion in New York City and other major metropolitan areas. Perhaps they merely reflect the narcissism of the postwar baby-boomers coming of age and expressing their passionate individualism in a traditional idiom. Perhaps tradition here is nothing more than yet another vehicle for their highly personal "ego trip." Perhaps.

But, in fact, Ron and Josephine Steinman went through a long period of searching within themselves, as well as through various Jewish institutions on two continents, before they could arrive at a form of religious identification and affiliation that was harmonious with their view of life. Josephine was searching for the compassion and respect for life she had learned as a child. Ron wanted to belong to a community that reflected tolerance and social responsibility. Their personal outlooks, although drawn from vastly different cultures, were surprisingly similar. What the two wanted was to be able to link their inner felt similarity to a single tradition; in this instance, the Jewish tradition—to link the personal feelings shared by two to a tradition shared by many. The particular resolutions they have made in dealing with their dual family heritage have come at the cost of great effort and, at times, the suffering of callousness and intolerance from those closest to them.

Their search, and particular resolution, reflects an apparent need on the part of many intermarried couples to not dismiss their heritages, but, rather, to integrate them into some kind of harmonious whole. Who has such needs and why is an issue that will be explored in subsequent chapters. Suffice it to say, here, that the Steinmans are not alone, even if their particular cultural blend is a bit more unusual than that of others.

Amidst the general alarm among American Jews over the increasing rate of intermarriage throughout the 1970s, relatively little attention was paid to the fact that unprecedented numbers of non-Jews were becoming Jewish by choice. The National Jewish Population Study had found that about one-third of the contemporary intermarriages involved the conversion of the non-Jewish partner. My own study of intermarried couples, conducted on behalf of the American Jewish Committee (1976–1977), confirmed those figures and also found that in about 20 percent of the intermarriages in which no conversion to Judaism had taken place, the non-Jewish spouse had more or less "assimilated" into the Jewish community through the Jewishness of the family.

Other demographic studies of Jewish communities, such as those of Floyd Fowler in Boston (1975), of Albert Mayer in Kansas City (1977), of Bruce Phillips in Denver (1982), and of Steve Cohen and Paul Ritterband in New York (1983), all show that the rate of conversion into Judaism has increased along with the increase in intermarriage.[42] In fact, the percentage of conversions from among the intermarriers has tended to run ahead of the rate of intermarriage itself. Taken together, these studies show that the rate of conversion into Judaism during the past thirty years has increased by about 300 percent.

In 1954, Rabbi David Eichhorn published a report estimating that the Reform and Conservative movements were producing between 1,500 to 1,750 "new Jews" each year through conversions.[43] In 1984, Rabbi Sanford Seltzer of the Reform Union of American Hebrew Congregations estimated, in a personal conversation, that his movement was producing between 7,000 to 8,000 "new Jews" each year. Although increases among the Conservative and Orthodox have not been as great, knowledgeable observers in those movements also point to significant increases in their conversion activities—all this, by the way, without any direct efforts by any of the movements thus far to seek out converts actively.

As . . . in the great majority of such conversionary families, a high value is placed on the maintenance of Jewish traditions, as in the Steinman family. But there appears also to be an inclination to express those values in a life-style and cultural idiom that reflects the non-Jewish heritage of the family as well, at least in some respects. In those intermarried families in which no conversion has taken place, considerably less value is placed on the maintenance of Jewish traditions, as one might expect. Yet even in those families, there is a tendency in a great many cases to include certain Jewish traditions in the life-style of the home, along with such non-Jewish traditions as the celebration of Christmas with Christian relatives, and possibly other Christian holidays and life-cycle events.

One Jewish-Catholic couple—the husband had actually studied for the priesthood before he became an agnostic social worker—used the occasion of their honeymoon to travel to some of the small villages of southern Italy to try to trace the husband's ancestors. Yet this couple's son had a Bar Mitzvah thirteen years later. At the time of our meeting in 1980, their home offered a comfortable display of Italian-Catholic memorabilia; reproductions of Gothic portraits of saints alongside Diane's menorah, a reproduction of Chagall's famous fiddler on the roof picture, and Danny's Hebrew books from which he was studying for his Bar Mitzvah. And Frank—who is a master of Italian cuisine—also did much of the cooking for his son's Bar Mitzvah. Apparently the Leone family also wanted a party in their own image, a Bar Mitzvah with an Italian flavor.

Perhaps one has to be a bit narcissistic to make such casual use of divergent cultural symbols to satisfy one's own sense of the good fit between traditional and personal life-style. But such an invidious psychological label as narcissism is hardly adequate to account for the lingering attachments of contemporary intermarrieds to greater or lesser fragments of their ancestral traditions. Nor are the other explanations of intermarriage as helpful as they once might have been. The proverbial power of love, which popularly accounts for the incidence of intermarriage itself, should have rendered all previous tribal loyalties for naught. Or as Zangwill put it, the melting pot should have so alloyed the couple's traditions that the new amalgam would not betray traces of its origins.

Finally, any understanding of how intermarrieds merge their ancestral traditions with their contemporary life-style must encompass the ways in which modern families, Jewish families especially, incorporate tradition into their lives. After all, the life-styles of all ethnic groups have been greatly influenced by one another, as well as by the general patterns of American culture. Just as "you don't have to be Jewish to love Levy's real Jewish rye bread,"[44] so, too, you don't have to be intermarried to have a Jamaican calypso band at a Jewish wedding or to have kosher Chinese food at a Bar Mitzvah.

At the heart of the matter lies the cardinal principle of modern consciousness: that, in American society as in most other modern societies, the individual enjoys simultaneous membership in a great variety of groups and cliques—from work to community to leisure—and yet is freer from the constraints of any of those memberships than at any previous time in history. But that very freedom impels many to seek linkages with the timeless traditions of their ancestors.

NOTES

1. Francesco Alberoni, *Falling in Love* (New York: Random House, 1983), p. 6.

2. Ibid., p. 17.

3. John B. Halsted, *Romanticism: Definition, Explanation, and Evaluation* (Lexington, MA: D.C. Heath and Company, 1965).

4. Edward Shorter, *The Making of the Modern Family* (New York: Basic Books, Inc., 1975); Ellen K. Rothman, *Hands and Hearts: A History of Courtship in America* (New York: Basic Books, Inc., 1984).

5. Morton M. Hunt, *The Natural History of Love* (New York: Alfred A. Knopf, Inc./Minerva Press, 1959, 1967).

6. Ibid., p. 26.

7. Joseph Stein, *Fiddler on the Roof*. Broadway musical.

8. Hunt, *The Natural History of Love*, p. 25.

9. William M. Kephart, *The Family, Society, and the Individual*, 3d Ed. (New York: Houghton Mifflin Company, 1972), p. 137.

10. Shorter, *The Making of the Modern Family*, p. 148.

11. Selma Stern, *Court Jew* (Philadelphia, PA: Jewish Publication Society, 1951).

12. Rothman, *Hands and Hearts*, pp. 28–29.

13. Jan Lewis, *The Pursuit of Happiness: Family and Values in Jefferson's Virginia* (New York: Cambridge University Press, 1983).

14. Shorter, *The Making of the Modern Family,* pp. 121–122.

15. Ibid., p. 148.

16. J. Hector St. John Crevecoeur, *Letters of an American Farmer* (New York: Dolphin Books, n.d.), pp. 49–50.

17. Israel Zangwill, *The Melting Pot* (New York: Macmillan Company, 1908).

18. Arthur Mann, *The One and the Many* (Chicago: Chicago University Press, 1979), p. 100.

19. Ibid., p. 75–76.

20. Ibid., p. 111.

21. Ibid., p. 117.

22. Heinrich Graetz, *History of the Jews* (Philadelphia, PA: The Jewish Publication Society, 1956), v. 5, p. 697.

23. Malcolm H. Stern, "Jewish Marriage and Intermarriage in the Federal Period, 1776–1840," *American Jewish Archives* (November 1967), pp. 142–143.

24. Milton L. Barron, "The Incidence of Jewish Intermarriage in Europe and America," *American Sociological Review* 11:1 (February 1946), pp. 6–13.

25. Moshe Davis, "Mixed Marriage in Western Jewry," *Jewish Journal of Sociology* 10:2 (December 1968) pp. 177–210.

26. Ande Manners, *Poor Cousins* (Greenwich, CT: Fawcett Publications, 1972), p. 25.

27. Arthur Ruppin, *The Jews in the Modern World* (New York: Arno Press, 1973), pp. 318–321.

28. Chaim I. Waxman, *America's Jews in Transition* (Philadelphia, PA: Temple University Press, 1983), pp. 29–31.

29. National Jewish Population Study, "Intermarriage" (New York: Council of Jewish Federations, 1971). Mimeograph.

30. Isaac Metzker, *A Bintle Brief* (New York: Ballantine Books, 1971), pp. 76–77.

31. Ibid., pp. 91–92.

32. Julius Drachsler, *Democracy and Assimilation* (New York: Macmillan Company, 1920), p. 126.

33. Milton M. Gordon, *Assimilation in American Life* (New York: Oxford University Press, 1964), p.80.

34. Elihu Bergman, "The American Jewish Population Erosion," *Midstream* 23:8 (October 1977).

35. Andrew M. Greeley, *Crisis in the Church* (Chicago: Thomas More Press, 1979), p. 150.

36. Richard D. Alba, "Social Assimilation among American Catholic National Origin Groups." *American Sociological Review* 41:6 (1976), pp. 1030–1046.

37. Konrad Bercovici, *Crimes of Charity* (1917).

38. Michael Novak, *The Rise of the Unmeltable Ethnics* (New York: Macmillan Publishing Company, 1971).

39. Herbert J. Gans, *The Levittowners* (New York: Vintage Books, 1969); Michael Parenti, "Ethnic Politics and the Persistence of Ethnic Identification," *American Political Science Review* 61 (September 1967), pp. 717–726.

40. Bill R. Lindner, *How to Trace Your Family History* (New York: Dodd Mead Company, 1978); Arthur Kurzweil, *From Generation to Generation: How to Trace Your Jewish Geneology* (New York: Morrow, 1980).

41. United Jewish Appeal, *Book of Songs and Blessings* (New York: United Jewish Appeal, 1980), p. 25.

42. Floyd J. Fowler, *1975 Community Survey: A Study of the Jewish Population of Greater Boston* (Boston: Combined Jewish Philanthropies, 1977); Albert Mayer, *The Jewish Population Study of the Greater Kansas City Area* (Kansas City: Jewish Federation, 1977); Bruce A. Phillips, *Denver Jewish Population Study* (Denver: Allied Jewish Federation, 1982).

43. David M. Eichhorn, *Conversion to Judaism* (New York; Ktav Publishing House, Inc., 1965), p. 213.

44. Slogan from a popular bill board advertisement in the New York area for Levy's Real Jewish Rye Bread.

Sexuality and Intimacy

18

A Sociological Journey into Sexuality*

Ira L. Reiss

This article presents a brief overview of a book-length societal-level explanation of sexuality that I have recently completed (Reiss 1986). As a sociologist I have been dissatisfied with the Freudian explanation of universal stages of psychosexual development. Such an approach was too psychological and too much simply a reflection of Vienese culture in the early 20th century to permit us to explain many of the differences in sexuality that exist among various societies. Another popular approach is the Marxian view, stressing the importance of the economic system in the exploitation of one group by another. I have perceived the Marxian view of sexuality as, among other things, being unable to explain the many differences in sexuality that exist in cultures with similar economic systems. The orthodox Marxian approach also has difficulty in explaining the exploitation of one gender by the other that exists in societies without private property, such as hunting and gathering societies, or for that matter, the present-day People's Republic of China (Stacey 1983). Nevertheless, the relationship of sexuality to positions of social power is one that I have developed in other ways in my own work, and so I do retain some elements of Marxism. The more recent sociobiological explanation has little relevance for explaining cross-cultural variations and changes over a few generations. Sociobiology deals with biological determinants that operate over many thousands of years and thus cannot explain a change in sexual customs that occurs in one generation, nor can it explain variations in sexual customs that occur within the same genetic sex in different societies.

*Reiss, Ira L. 1986. "A Sociological Journey into Sexuality." *Journal of Marriage and the Family* (May): 233–242. Copyrighted 1986 by the National Council on Family Relations, 1910 West County Road B, Suite 147, St. Paul, Minnesota 55113. Reprinted by permission.

But if one rejects most of these dominant explanatory schemas, what does one substitute? During the last 25 years or so there have only been a few attempts in sociology at theory building concerning sexuality, and even those have not attempted an overall, cross-cultural explanation of all types of sexuality (Reiss 1960, 1967, 1979, 1980; Gagnon and Simon 1973; Christensen 1962; Ehrmann 1959; Delamater and MacCorquodale 1979). These efforts have consisted of partial or minitheories applying only to specific types of sexuality or to just our own society. No comprehensive sociological theory of human sexuality has been formulated.

I began to work upon this task some five years ago. It was indeed a massive undertaking, for it presumed extensive knowledge of cultures around the world as well as of existing explanatory sociological propositions. The challenge was not only to become familiar with this literature but somehow to integrate it conceptually with new propositions into a macro-level, societal explanation of sexuality.

I stress a macro-level approach in my theory. Research and theory at micro level of analysis focuses on interaction and socialization processes. Such an approach could examine sexuality in terms of such things as individual adjustments in sexual scripts. Analysis at this level has been quite modest in terms of theory development (Singer 1985; Simon and Gagnon 1984). I have integrated some aspects of a micro-level analysis into my explanation, but basically it is built upon a macro foundation that comparatively examines and seeks to explain different sexual behaviors and attitudes in various groups and societies. I chose this macro-level approach because it was related to some of my previous theorizing, it was of primary interest to me, and it is the most distinctively sociological tradition. I also felt it had been the most neglected by other theorists.

I spent the better part of four years reading, discussing, and formulating my ideas for this venture. Given the stage of development of sociological explanations of sexuality, my theory is of necessity based considerably on its logical structure; empirical evidence is not available to test all of its parts. Nevertheless, I did examine what evidence was available to test my ideas. The Standard Cross Cultural Sample of 186 nonindustrial societies around the world (Murdock and White 1969) was useful in this regard. In addition, my own reading of other nonindustrial societies as well as of Western industrial societies allowed me to examine the fit of my thinking with these additional data. In this paper I will present an overview and point out the major features of the theory I discuss in my book (Reiss 1986). Finally, I should note that I developed this sociological theory of sexuality not only for sociologists, but for anyone with a serious intellectual interest in understanding sexuality.

A SOCIETAL CONCEPTION OF SEXUALITY

First we must clarify what we mean by concepts like sex, gender, and sexuality so that we may communicate clearly. The word *sex* has multiple meanings in our society. The term sometimes refers to genetic sex, sometimes to gender, and sometimes to sexual activity: for example, "Her sex is female"; "Her sex role is that of a woman"; "She had sex with him." These different potential meanings must be clarified if we are to have a shared, societal-level definition of sexuality.

We cannot change the way the word *sex* is used in public discourse but we can clarify our scientific usage. I suggest that in our scientific discourse we use the word *sex* to mean only genetic sex, that is XX, (female) or XY (male). For the sake of clarity, I would use the phrase *gender role*, and not *sex role*, to refer to the rights and duties assigned to those called males and females in a society.

Such clarification is sufficient for our use of the terms *genetic sex* and *gender role*, but we still need a definition of the word *sexuality* that is precise and measurable, because sexuality is the focus of my sociological theory. *I would define human sexuality as consisting of those cultural scripts aimed at erotic arousal that produce genital responses.* I believe this definition would hold for any type of society. It can be tested by seeing if this is indeed what people mean by sexuality in various societies. It can further be examined to discern whether the genital responses that occur in all societies can be largely related to the sexual scripts aimed at erotic arousal rather than to biological or individualistic factors.

According to my sociological definition, sexuality is learned and it is learned in a societal context. Sexuality is thus not "natural," nor is it individualistic; rather, it is a social outcome that we learn to achieve in much the same way as we do our friendship and love relationships. In this sense I am qualifying the assertion frequently made by Masters and Johnson that if you "remove the road blocks, sex will work" (Master and Johnson 1970). That statement seems to imply that there is a natural sexual outcome that will flow forth. I believe sexuality is programmed just as other social behavior, and it will not "work" unless that social programming has occurred. It is not just a matter of removing road blocks from an innate pathway; rather, it is primarily a matter of having been socially taught how to create a pathway that will lead to sexual interaction with others.

Presuming we agree upon this definition of sexuality, the next question concerns the place of sexuality in the social structure of human societies. I would start by asserting that in all cultures, sexuality is viewed as important. This is so in cultures that attempt to restrict it as well as those that encourage it. In short, no culture is indifferent to sexuality. Why is this so? My answer rejects the common reply that sexuality is seen as important because of its reproductive consequences. Allow me to explain.

In most nonindustrial societies the connection of sexuality to pregnancy is not as direct as we perceive it to be in industrial societies today. Pregnancy is often seen as not simply resulting from acts of intercourse but rather as an outcome of one particular type of sexuality, such as repetitive coitus with one's marriage partner. Further, pregnancy only occurs in many cultures if the husband, in addition to copulating, gives the "spirit child" to his wife (Berndt and Berndt 1951). In addition, the production and care of children is often seen as a group activity of many related kin and not just the concern of one couple (Levy 1973). In this sense reproduction is not an individual biological act but a group undertaking. In the above ways, then, what we in the West scientifically view as the biological connection of sexuality to reproduction is seriously modified in the shared thinking of people in other cultural settings.

Even in our type of society, where we stress the biological connections and reproductive outcomes of sexuality, the importance we place on sexuality is not only due to that perspective. Consider the fact that, although 10-year-olds cannot become pregnant, we are more restrictive of 10-year-olds having coitus than of 20-year-olds. That surely points to our assigning importance to some aspect of sexuality other than reproduction. Think also of the importance placed upon sexuality by homosexuals—pregnancy is not even an issue there. In addition, would a husband with a sterile wife view sexuality as less important than would a husband with a fertile wife? All of this is not to deny that the reproductive capacity of sexuality is usually one factor in the importance placed upon sexuality, but rather, it is to assert that in many societies reproduction is perceived differently and is often not the most crucial factor.

Two other major factors, in my view, are more central and universal features of sexuality than is reproduction. I submit that they are the key reasons for the importance all societies place upon sexuality. If all reproductive outcomes of sexuality were to vanish, these two factors would still maintain its universal importance. The first characteristic of sexuality that contributes to its evaluation as important is the obvious one of physical pleasure. Clearly, human beings value physical pleasure, and sexuality has a good probability of yielding pleasure in some degree. The second characteristic is perhaps not quite so obvious; it is self-disclosure, or the revelation to others of intimate aspects of the self. I do not necessarily imply affectionate ties when I speak of self-disclosure. Consider that one does not typically have orgasms in public, and thus the simple act of experiencing orgasm in front of another human being is an uncommon disclosure of oneself. That kind of self-disclosure may lead to disclosure on levels other than the sexual, such as the intellectual, emotional, or affectionate. Cultures differ as to which outcomes they choose to encourage and under what conditions. But the basic self-disclosure of showing passion is a most common (though, of course, not guaranteed) outcome of sexual relationships.

Why should physical pleasure and self-disclosure make sexuality important in all societies? The answer is, I believe, that those are the key characteristics of important social relationships. To illustrate, think of friendship and kinship relationships. They are everywhere valued and they too, at their core, entail physical pleasure and self-disclosure. There is physical pleasure in the embraces (nonsexual) that occur in friendship and kinship relationships, and there is self-disclosure in what such friends and kin are willing to reveal to each other. What kind of close relationship would it be if there were no physical contact and no self-disclosure? Such pleasure and disclosure elements are the nucleus of almost all valued human relationships. Therefore, since sexuality possesses, in pleasure and disclosure, the building blocks of human relationships, it is universally recognized that sexuality has within itself the components that are valued in human relationships. Not all forms of sexuality are equally valued, but the relationship potential of sexual encounters is widely recognized. It is for that reason, I contend, that sexuality is everywhere viewed as important. Given this key place of sexuality in human interaction, we will explore how it is woven into the social fabric of different societies.

UNIVERSAL LINKAGES

In both its logical and empirical aspects, my investigation supported the view that in all societies sexuality is linked in some fashion to three elements of the social structure: (a) marital jealousy, (b) gender role power, and (c) beliefs about normality. These three areas are subdivisions, respectively, of the broader kinship, power, and ideological components found in all social systems. I will try to detail the linkages for each of these three components of social systems.

The first linkage of sexuality is to marital jealousy. Here it is proposed that jealousy, on a macro level, is most accurately seen as a boundary-maintenance mechanism that aims at protecting those relationships socially viewed as important. Since we have already asserted that sexuality is universally considered important, it follows that at least some types of sexual relationships will be protected by jealousy boundaries. Furthermore, since marriage is also everywhere valued, when one combines sexuality with marriage it surely will produce a relationship viewed as worthy of protection by jealousy boundaries. In case you may question whether sexuality outside of marriage is deemed important enough to deserve the protection of jealousy customs, think about jealousy in homosexual and hetero-sexual cohabiting relationships. Recent evidence in the United States indicates that jealousy is strongly present in such relationships (Blumstein and Schwartz 1983). On a social-psychological or micro level, jealousy is a negative emotional response to a felt threat from an outsider to a valued relationship. The society we live in informs us as to which relationships are supposed to have the boundary mechanism of jealousy. Some forms of sexual relationships are always among those relationships that societies choose to protect.

I investigated those cultures such as the Lepcha and the Greenland Eski-mos that others have asserted are lacking in marital sexual jealousy (Gorer 1967; O'Kelly 1980; Sanders 1956). My examination led me to the conclusion that despite the claims of some, all these cultures do indeed have marital sexual jeal-ousy. To be sure, there are variations in the jealousy boundaries, for in many nonindustrial societies extramarital sexuality with people other than one's mate is permitted. For example, in many societies the levirate custom permits such extramarital relationships with an older brother's wife. But even there the relation must be carried out with low social visibility and great tact. In such cases there still clearly are boundaries protecting the priority of the marital relationship, even though some extramarital sexual partners are on occasion permitted.

Jealousy is obviously present in such societies, and although it is structured somewhat differently than in the Western world, it surely is tied to marital sex-uality. My investigation led me to conclude that although the intensity varies, sexual jealousy protecting the priority of marriage would appear to be, in some form, universally present. There is a common feeling that sexual relationships outside the marriage may be intrusive and may violate the priority of the marital dyad. The self-disclosure and pleasure aspects of sexuality in a stable relation-ship endow it with the aura of a private confidence that should not be casually disrupted. Thus, even when extramarital relationships are legitimated, they occur as controlled satellites of the more important marital dyad.

In line with some of my theoretical propositions on power, I concluded that those who were more powerful in economic and political terms would be more likely to react to jealousy with greater violence and aggression. I tested this out by comparing male and female jealousy patterns under various conditions of gender inequality. The results indicated considerable support for my beliefs. Males were much more likely to express agression in response to jealousy, in accord with the extent to which they were more powerful than females. Females in a great many cultures most often responded to jealousy-provoking situations with depression rather than aggression against others.

The second societal linkage area for sexuality is to gender roles, particularly in relation to the relative power of each gender. It follows from the assertion that sexuality is viewed as important that those in power will seek to get as much of this valued element as their culture would permit. The underlying proposition is that those in power control whatever the society views as important, and thus, since sexuality is viewed as important, those in power will have greater access to that area of social life. Further, since in most societies males have greater power than females, it follows that males will have greater sexual rights than females.

In testing out the relationship of sexual rights to male power in the Standard Sample, I found that patrilineal societies (tracing descent only through the paternal grandfather's line) displayed more male as opposed to female sexual rights than did matrilineal societies (tracing descent only through the maternal grandmother's line). I also found that when, in addition to tracing descent through the male line, males lived together, there was a greater likelihood of a low evaluation of the female gender. Social systems that promote common male residence seem to lower the status of females. This lower status may well be a result of increased male power in such societies. Relevant to this power linkage are my findings, previously cited, concerning the relationship of the relative power of each gender to the likelihood of an aggressive response to marital jealousy. That finding is congruent with the role of power as a key determinant of sexual customs.

The third societal linkage of sexuality is to ideology. I use *ideology* here to refer to the strongly held, shared beliefs about fundamental human nature that exist in a society. Such beliefs are relevant to sexuality, for they imply how equal or nonequal females are to males and how similar their sexual rights should be. Sexual ideologies are subtypes of the general ideology in a society, and they revolve about two dimensions: (a) overall gender equality and (b) the relative sexual permissiveness allowed to each gender.

Regarding sexual ideologies, the evidence from recent studies indicates that females in America have endorsed overall gender equality in political, economic, religious, and family institutions more fully than they have accepted equality in terms of sexual rights. This pattern is most obvious in the degree to which females as opposed to males still hesitate to endorse casual or body-centered sexuality (Lottes 1985). In contrast to this are the findings that males have accepted sexual equality for both genders but show some reluctance to endorse overall gender equality. The trend between males and females is toward a convergence of these beliefs, but clearly we are still in transition.

Other cultures reflect these same differences, which are related to the fact that males are in most societies more powerful in the political, economic, and other institutions and thus believe that this is a "natural" state of affairs. They resist giving up their power and accepting full gender equality, even though they favor promoting greater acceptance of sexual behavior on the part of females. All these perspectives appear to be logically based on Western beliefs about sexuality and gender concerning what is "natural" for males and and females to do. We believe it is natural for females to be less interested in casual sexuality, and sociobiologists are quick to think up underlying evolutionary advantages to account for this condition. Their theories overlook those cultures where the human female doesn't appear to have such beliefs. Although there are general trends in our society toward new types of gender roles and new sexual orientations, some hesitancies about male and female role changes seem to reflect our conformity to older ideological beliefs. Ideology seems to be important in delaying as well as promoting change, both in the direction of those in power and in opposing directions. These findings are one reason why I have modified the orthodox Marxian position that ideologies basically support those groups that are in power.

I assume that in general it is our ideological beliefs that promote our popular perspectives on sexual normality. We can see this clearly in our views in the Western world about homosexuality. There homosexual behavior is viewed as competitive with heterosexuality, and accordingly it is condemned, restricted, and viewed as "abnormal." I speak here of homosexual *behavior* because there is so little cross-cultural evidence on homosexual *preference*. In some parts of the world, as in the New Guinea Highlands, homosexual behavior is viewed as a pathway to heterosexuality and is widely supported (Herdt 1981). Herdt reports that, in the Sambia, preadolescent boys are taught to fellate older unmarried males and ingest their sperm in order to be able to produce their own sperm in adulthood and thereby be able to impregnate their wives. After marriage, Herdt estimates, over 95% of these males give up their homosexual behavior because they perceive such behavior as predominantly a pathway to the heterosexuality that they now have achieved in marriage.

In such a society the sexual ideology would judge homosexual behavior as not competitive with heterosexuality but as supportive of it. The explanatory proposition that applies to the Sambia case as well as to societies in the West would be that sexuality is socially approved in accord with the degree to which it is seen as supportive of accepted gender and kinship roles. People in Sambia and in the United States do not agree on how homosexual behavior and heterosexuality relate, but both societies seem to afford priority to whatever sexual relationships they see as supportive of the gender and kinship roles in that society.

Another interpretation concerning homosexuality emerged from my examination of the Standard Sample. I found that homosexual behavior was highest in those societies wherein the mother was heavily involved with infants and the father was not so involved. A Freudian would look at such a situation and claim that is was the psychodynamics of a dominant mother and an absent father that led to homosexuality. My interpretation of these same data is different. I see the close mother and distant father involvement with infants as an indirect measure of male power. Such gender roles reflect a male-dominant society in which men are occupied in the political and economic institutions and thus are only peripherally involved in child care. That type of institutional involvement creates a narrow, segregated male gender role while at the same time giving little opportunity for the very young male child to interact with male models. Further, such narrow male roles will likely lead to more males finding such a restricted role uninteresting or difficult to achieve. It may be in part from such pressures that increased nonconformist homosexual behavior occurs in societies like our own.

Note, however, that in societies like the Sambia, homosexual behavior would not be so likely to function as an alternative to heterosexuality for those who are unhappy with the narrow male gender role. In the Sambia type of society, homosexual behavior would be an expected part of the sexual upbringing model and not a deviant choice. I believe that homosexual behavior may be encouraged by the close male groupings and living arrangements that go along with such male-dominant societies. We have evidence that among rhesus monkeys, bringing up infants with only their own genetic sex increases the likelihood of homosexual behavior (Goldfoot, Wallen, Neff, McBriar, and Goy 1984). My point here is that a cross-cultural and sociological approach affords interpretations that are at odds with our culture's traditional views of homosexuality and its relationship to heterosexuality. The cross-cultural approach forces us to consider other explanations of even those sexual customs we may have felt we fully understood. It surely calls into question the validity of many of our traditional theories of homosexuality that clearly do not apply across cultures.

Our common views concerning what is "normal" sexually can easily influence our scientific views. This may be particularly applicable to those who provide therapy. The case of premature ejaculation is illustrative. A generation ago very few people were going to therapists for treatment of premature ejaculation. The concept of premature ejaculation is based upon an equalitarian view of heterosexual coital relationships. It is predominantly when the female's orgasm is of concern that a male will view himself as a premature ejaculator. He is "premature" in terms of the cultural ideal that his partner should have a coital orgasm if he does. In cultures with a more prominent double standard, such concerns are not so strongly felt and thus do not drive people to enter therapy. In some societies, as East Bay in Melanesia, males are expected to reach orgasm in 15 to 30 seconds or else it is felt that they have a problem of "delayed ejaculation" (Davenport 1965). Such "problems" appear to be less a matter of a disrupted personality system than a matter of conformity to sexual norms. Finally, note that in our society a female who reaches orgasm in seconds after vaginal penetration is not considered to be prematurely orgasmic; rather, she is often praised as "responsive." This may well be so because in male-dominated societies there is little cultural concern that she will leave her partner unsatisfied, and her speedy orgasm may satisfy his desire to view himself as a "good" lover.

Think about the way that premature ejaculation is commonly treated and it will become even more obvious how our cultural values and not any scientific criterion of "abnormality" define this behavior. The squeeze technique is the most common method used to "correct" the problem of premature ejaculation. This highly effective method involves the female partner squeezing the penis when the man is close to ejaculation, thereby stopping the ejaculation and teaching the man that he can control it. To those raised in our culture, where heterosexual coitus is the epitome of sexuality, this seems a natural solution to the problem. But think about the alternative approaches that could be suggested to a client by a therapist.

The therapist could inform the client that the male can aid the female in reaching climax orally or manually, either before or after his orgasm. That would be a way of "equalizing" the orgasmic outcomes. But our society teaches that coitus should be the central sexual act, and most often both partners want orgasm in coitus. To be sure, young people today are somewhat less focused on coitus only, but the emphasis is still there. Freudian analysts and others may well define as abnormal any focus on oral, anal, or manual sexuality in preference to or equal with coitus. It is easy to speculate why Western societies have placed such great importance upon this aspect of sexual behavior. Because it is the way to produce future soldiers, servants, workers, and citizens, many societies that seek power emphasize coitus.

Perhaps of equal interest is the fact that in the name of equality we promote a sexual act, coitus, that clearly produces orgasm more easily in the male than in the female. Many women report much more difficulty in achieving orgasm coitally than they have in oral or manual sexual acts (Masters and Johnson 1966, 1970). Thus, ironically, the therapy for producing orgasmic equality involves promoting a sexual act not equally suited to female orgasm. The fact that females also prefer orgasm in coitus does not dispute this statement but merely points to how females have been indoctrinated into a male type of sexuality.

The significance of our examination of premature ejaculation is that it demonstrates how we can politicize therapy. To be sure, many younger therapists would not call premature ejaculation a disorder, an abnormality, or a dysfunction, but many others such as Freudian analysts would. The fact of the matter is that we lack in therapy a clear scientific standard for declaring some actions abnormal. Because of that the ideological beliefs about abnormality that are commonly held in the society may easily be adopted by the therapist and used as if they were based on scientific evidence. This possibility is most likely to occur in an area as emotionally charged as is sexuality. The strength of our views concerning the wrongness of certain sexual acts may make it easy for us to feel that there must be some scientific basis for calling such an act abnormal.

As a step in the direction of not allowing our private ideological beliefs to seduce us into believing that they constitute a scientific basis for classifying certain sexual acts as abnormal, I would suggest that we hesitate to label as abnormal any sexual act that can be found as an accepted act in another culture. By the same token, those sexual acts that we find to be unacceptable in all cultures may provide a starting point for a theory of psychological abnormality. The sadistic sexual murderer would be performing such a universally condemned sexual act. I know of no culture that would accept such an action. Even with this conception of normality, we must be careful not to assume that no new forms of sexual acts can be normal. But using such a cross-cultural basis prevents us from simply adopting our own society's view of sexual normality and endowing it with scientific validity.

This approach is not without its problems, but it does at least demand evidence and reasoning before a particular act can be labeled abnormal.

There may well be other scientific bases for defining a sexual act as abnormal, but until it is clearly established as such by scientific evidence and reasoning, we had better not use such labels freely if we are to avoid the politicization of therapy. If we wish, we can as private citizens still strongly condemn and put people in jail for many sexual acts our culture does not approve of. But that is different from saying that we can scientifically show that those people are "sick." Such people may simply be nonconformists, for whatever reason.

For scientists or therapists to use the label "paraphilia" or "dysfunctional" for all sexual acts that are socially disapproved of or unusual is to undermine the scientific basis of their approach. I would suggest it is better to call such clients nonconformists and then search for scientific theories that can measure the "illness" component, if any, of their noncomformity. I do not go as far as Thomas Szasz did in calling mental illness a myth, for I do not reject the possibility of finding a scientific basis for defining abnormality such as the one I suggest, that is, the inability to perform in an acceptable fashion in any type of known society. But I do agree with Szasz that a great many of the acts we today label as abnormal are simply acts of nonconformity that happen to upset other people (Szasz 1974). A therapist who labels his or her client as a paraphiliac or as dysfunctional is promoting a desire for a "cure." Few clients would want to maintain a paraphilia or a dysfunction. Calling the client a nonconformist opens up more clearly the possibility of not changing. The therapist could try to give insight into the range of choices that are open and also help the client understand the societal basis of the conformity desire. Such an approach might not satisfy people's desire to condemn what they disapprove of, but would it not be a more objective form of therapy?

Much of the same politicization of sexuality occurs in our reactions to erotica. There, too, the terms, "abnormal" and "sick" are commonly used for those acts that are unpopular in some group. This radical feminist distinction between erotica and pornography is more a private moral judgment of what one likes than a scientific distinction. *Pornography* has become a "bad" word, just like *fornication* and *adultery*. Social scientists have stopped using words like fornication and adultery because of their moral implications and have instead spoken of premarital intercourse and extramarital intercourse in order to minimize the intrusion of private moral biases. Many of the scientific researchers on erotica have done the same and are not using the term *pornography* because it implies only "bad" erotica to some people, such as the radical feminists. Instead, many researchers have elected to use the word *erotica* for all materials designed to arouse one sexually. Individual persons can express any private judgment about which forms of erotica they personally prefer or condemn because they judge it to be subordinating to women, or not gender equal in the relationship portrayed, or just plain obnoxious. But such subjective distinctions do not serve as a scientific basis for classifying erotica.

There is much misinformation on erotica because of the strong emotions associated with it. The amount of violence in X-rated films has been exaggerated by some. For example, a recent analysis of 650 X-rated videotapes found that only 10% could be classified as showing "deviational sadistic, violent and victimized sex" (Rimmer 1984). In another recent study, it was reported that films rated PG and R have many more murders and rapes than do X-rated films (Radecki 1984). My cross-cultural analysis indicates that attitudes favorable to gender equality go with an acceptance of a wide range of erotica. My analysis further indicates that even the rate of nonsexual violence is not a good predictor of rape rates in the United States and in other cultures. We need careful and not cavalier judgments in this area if we are to be scientifically informed. We need to be aware of the possible substitution of private ideological judgments of "abnormality" for scientific judgments of the nature of erotica. This analysis of erotica is developed much further in my recent book (Reiss 1986, chap. 7).

My point throughout this discussion of erotica, homosexuality, and premature ejaculation has been that sexuality is linked with the strong emotional ideologies of a society. We need to distinguish our private judgments from our scientific judgments. The scientific explanations can act as a clarification of our private judgments, if people make the effort to become aware of them.

THE OVERALL SOCIOLOGICAL THEORY

My explanation of sexuality began with the assertion that our ability to participate in sexual relationships is basically a social product that is learned much as we learn how to develop friendship and love relationships. This is not to deny that biological or psychological factors are relevant. They are surely relevant if you ask questions focusing upon psychological and biological systems. But I am writing as a sociologist and I pose my questions in terms of how we can explain similarities and differences among human societies. On such questions I believe sociological theory can provide the answers better than can any other discipline. My own approach has particularly emphasized comparative sociology, which in my judgment is very similar to cultural anthropology.

Sexuality is everywhere viewed as important because of its social bonding power. This ability is based predominantly on the physical pleasure and self-disclosure components that at least to some degree most often accompany sexual acts. It is such bonding that is encouraged by societies in relationships such as marriage that the society wishes to support. In this sense, sexual bonding promotes the formation of kinship ties and helps form the gender role concepts of a society.

All societies have customs that place boundary mechanisms around important relationships such as sexual relations in marriage. This is accomplished by means of jealousy norms that are taught to group members. The more powerful members seek to maximize their control of that which is important in their group. Hence, the more powerful one gender is over the other, the more likely it is that those persons also possess greater sexual rights and privileges.

Our sexual ideologies support as "natural" those sexual customs that embody the society's ideological views concerning our fundamental human nature and condemn as "unnatural" those sexual customs that do not conform to these beliefs. A scientific theory is expected to develop verifiable indices of abnormality and not simply to accept the popular views concerning abnormal behavior or attitudes. One fundamental basis of our personal ideological judgment seems to be whether it is felt that the sexual practice in question will support or harm our kinship and gender systems. Note that this social opinion may be factually incorrect. For example, many Westerners would say that homosexuality must be competitive with heterosexuality—a person pursues either one or the other. Not only is this a stereotype of our own sexual behavior, but the Sambia and other similar cultures illustrate how a society may judge homosexual behavior to be essential to the creation of heterosexual behavior. One way to judge the worth of a scientific theory of sexuality is the degree to which it extends our vision beyond the cultural blinders we are each given by our society.

I have noted above that the three specific parts of a social system that are always linked to sexuality are marital jealousy, gender role power, and concepts of normality. More generally, these three linkage areas are located in the social structures of kinship, power, and ideology. Changes in sexual customs would occur to the extent that these areas were affected. Clearly, our economic, political, religious, and family institutions are involved in any such changes. Perhaps the economic system is more flexible than the others mentioned, because it is designed more for pragmatic subsistence outcomes than for moral guidance. But all institutions have a possible role in social change, and their causal influence should not be prejudged. The casual directions may well work two ways, with sexual customs on occasion initiating change in basic institutional areas. To illustrate, the greater sexual activity by young people in the 1965–75 decade was, I believe, one major cause of the change in the political acceptability of contraception and abortion services for young people.

In my book I have devised 25 specific propositions that afford a predictive basis for understanding social change and the precise ways in which sexuality may be linked to kinship, power, and ideological structures in particular types of societies (Reiss 1986). These propositions predict the conditions under which certain variations in the linkages of sexuality to the three key areas of the social structure would occur. I have referred to a goodly number of them informally in this paper. Figure 1 further illustrates the basic theoretical ideas I have been addressing.

Note that the casual direction as indicated in this diagram goes two ways and involves causal relationships among the variables on each of the concentric circles as well as between the various factors on different concentric circles. One starts with sexual behavior at the center of the diagram and notes that it leads to the outcomes of "sexual importance" and "sexual bonding." These in turn are causally related to the linkages to kinship, power, and ideology and to the creation of sexual scripts, noted in the next concentric circle. Finally, at the outer circle are the social institutions that are both shaped by these other factors and that in turn shape them. This diagram is simply a graphic version of the general way these various factors relate to each other. It is no substitute for the specific propositions I have formulated that explain societal variations in detail. Rather, this diagram illustrates the logical foundation for my sociological theory of human sexuality.

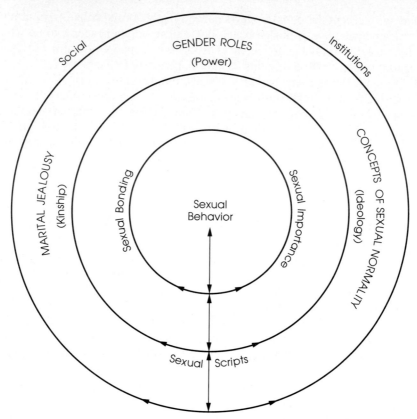

FIGURE 1. A Sociological Overview of Human Sexuality

Source: Reiss, 1986: 214, Reprinted by permission of Prentice-Hall, Inc., Englewood Cliffs, New Jersey.

The empirical foundation for the basic logic and the specific propositions that explain similarity and variation in sexual customs are surely not complete. I have discussed some of the evidence in this paper, and much more is contained in my book. Many concepts require better measurement and further clarification. This is particularly true for the crucial concept of power in relation to sexuality. Evidence on several of the variables in my propositions is yet to be gathered. At this point, parts of the theory rest on its logical and reasoning foundations. This article puts forth the overall logical conception of my explanation of sexuality as it currently stands.

Perhaps of greatest importance, this theory allows us to answer questions that prior approaches could not adequately handle. Those fundamental questions, concerning the explanation of why various groups differ or are alike in their sexual customs, are important to us both as individuals and as social scientists. In this new sociological explanation, I am not obliged to nor limited by the belief systems of older theories, even though I do not totally reject everything they assert. This is a fresh start and one that is rooted predominantly in the assumptions of sociology.

As we utilize this explanation, we will have more to share with scientists in biology and psychology who have for a longer period of time been working on explanations of human sexuality that are relevant to the type of questions they pose concerning personality and biological systems. Of course, interrelationships are possible among disciplines. But sociology is a young science, and for now I believe it will yield the greatest scientific understanding if we nurture it separately and thereby develop its ability to explain the place of the social system in our sexual lives.

REFERENCES

Berndt, Ronald and Catherine Berndt, 1951. *Sexual Behavior in Western Arnhem Land.* New York: Viking Fund.

Blumstein, Philip and Pepper Schwartz. 1983. *American Couples.* New York: Morrow.

Christensen, Harold T. 1962. "Value Behavior Discrepancies Regarding Premarital Coitus in Three Western Cultures." *American Sociological Review* 27: 66–74.

Davenport, William. 1965. "Sexual Patterns and Their Regulation in a Society of the South West Pacific." Chap. 8 in *Sex and Behavior,* New York: John Wiley.

Delamater, John and Patricia MacCorquodale. 1979. *Premarital Sexuality: Attitudes, Relationships, Behavior.* Madison: University of Wisconsin Press.

Ehrmann, Winston W. 1959. *Premarital Dating Behavior.* New York: Hold, Rinehart and Winston.

Gagnon, John H. and William Simon. 1973. *Sexual Conduct.* Chicago: Aldine.

Goldfoot, David A., K. Wallen, D. A. Neff, M.C. McBriar, and R. W. Goy. 1984. "Social Influences upon the Display of Sexually Dimorphic Behavior in Rhesus Monkeys: Isosexual Rearing." *Archives of Sexual Behavior* 13: 395–412.

Gorer, Geoffrey. 1967. *Himalayan Village: An Account of the Lepchas of Sikkim,* (2nd edition). New York: Basic Books.

Herdt, Gilbert, 1981. *Guardians of the Flutes: Idioms of Masculinity.* New York: McGraw-Hill.

Levy, Robert I. 1973. *Tahitians: Mind and Experience in the Society Islands.* Chicago: University of Chicago Press.

Lottes, Ilsa. 1985. "The Use of Cluster Analysis to Determine Belief Patterns." *Journal of Sex Research* 21: 405–421.

Masters, William H. and Virginia F. Johnson. 1966. *Human Sexual Response.* Boston: Little, Brown.

Masters, William H. and Virginia F. Johnson, 1970. *Human Sexual Inadequacy.* Boston: Little, Brown.

Murdock, George P. and Douglas R. White. 1969. "Standard Cross Cultural Sample." *Ethnology* 8: 329–369.

O'Kelly, Charlotte G. 1980. *Women and Men in Society.* New York: D. Van Nostrand.

Radecki, Thomas. 1984. Quoted in "Pornography: Love or Death?" *Film Comment* 20 (November/December): 43–45.

Reiss, Ira L. 1960. *Premarital Sexual Standards in America.* New York: Free Press.

Reiss, Ira L. 1967. *The Social Context of Premarital Sexual Permissiveness.* New York: Holt, Rinehart and Winston.

Reiss, Ira L. 1986. *Journey into Sexuality: An Exploratory Voyage.* New York: Prentice-Hall.

Reiss, Ira L., Ronald E. Anderson, and G. C. Sponaugle. 1980. "A Multivariate Model of the Determinants of Extramarital Sexual Permissiveness. *Journal of Marriage and the Family* 42: 395–411.

Reiss, Ira L. and Brent C. Miller. 1979. "Heterosexual Permissiveness: A Theoretical Analysis." Chap. 4 in *Contemporary Theories about the Family,* vol. 1, edited by Wesley Burr, Revoen Hill, F. Ivan Nye, and Ira L. Reiss. New York: Free Press.

Rimmer, Robert H. 1984: *The X-Rated Videotape Guide.* New York: Arlington House.

Sanders, Irwin T. (ed.). 1956. *Societies Around the World.* New York: Dryden.

Simon, William and John H. Gagnon. 1984. "Sexual Scripts: Permanence and Change." *Society* 22 (November/December): 53–60.

Singer, Barry. 1985. "A Comparison of Evolutionary and Environmental Theories of Erotic Response (Part 1): Structural Features." *Journal of Sex Research* 21: 229–257.

Stacey, Judith. 1983. *Patriarchy and Socialist Revolution in China.* Berkeley: University of California Press.

Szasz, Thomas. 1974. *The Myth of Mental Illness,* revised edition. New York: Harper and Row.

19

The Sexualized Society*

John D'Emilio and Estelle B. Freedman

Toward the end of the 1960s John Williamson, a successful engineer in southern California, purchased a fifteen-acre retreat in the Santa Monica mountains. Graced with a view of the ocean, the secluded site sported a two-story mansion, several smaller houses, and a building that contained an Olympic-sized pool. Williamson intended to make the property the setting in which to implement an experiment in sexual freedom. For years, a group of people "had met regularly at his house to discuss and explore ways of achieving greater fulfillment in marriage." They were all "middle-class people," many of them prosperous professionals like himself, "who held responsible jobs in the community [and] were integrated in the social system."[1] Over time, the discussions led to action, including the swapping of marital partners for sexual excitement and group sex. Williamson's newly acquired property, Sandstone, would give the venture institutional expression.

In the succeeding years, Sandstone became something of an underground tourist attraction, bringing through its doors upper-middle-class adventurers in search of new kinds of personal fulfillment and erotic delights. Those who made the trek could take off their clothes or leave them on. They could sip wine, smoke marijuana, and converse by the fireplace upstairs, or wander downstairs where they would find, in the words of one visitor, "a parlor for pleasure-seekers, providing sights and sounds that . . . [they] had never imagined they would ever encounter under one roof during a single evening." They would see

> shadows and faces and interlocking limbs, rounded breasts and reaching fingers, moving buttocks, glistening backs, shoulders, nipples, navels, long blond hair spread across pillows, thick dark arms holding soft white hips, a woman's head hovering over an erect penis. Sighs, cries of ecstasy could be heard, the slap and suction of copulating flesh, laughter, murmuring, music from the stereo, crackling black burning wood.

Perhaps the only thing more surprising than Sandstone itself was the fact that a prominent journalist would write about it. Gay Talese's *Thy Neighbor's Wife,* from which this description is taken, became a widely reviewed, much discussed best-seller.[2]

Although Sandstone was unusual, the attraction of successful professionals to it and the marketing of it by Talese suggest that the liberal consensus about sex had dissolved. Feminists and gay liberationists were not the only ones challenging its assumptions. By the late 1960s the belief in sex as the source of personal meaning had permeated American society. The expectation that marriage would fulfill the quest could no longer be sustained. Aided by the values of a consumer culture and encouraged by the growing visibility of sex in the public realm, many Americans came to accept sexual pleasure as a legitimate, necessary component of their lives, unbound by older ideals of marital fidelity and permanence. Society was indeed becoming sexualized. From the mid-1960s to the 1980s, as the liberal consensus disintegrated, the nation experienced perhaps the greatest transformation in sexuality it had ever witnessed. The marketing of sex, important shifts in attitudes, and major changes in the life cycle of Americans all encouraged alterations in patterns of sexual behavior.

THE BUSINESS OF SEX

One unmistakable sign of the reorganization of sexuality came through the large-scale invasion by entrepreneurs into the field of sex. The tension in sexual liberalism, between the celebration of the erotic as the peak experience in marriage and the effort to contain its expression elsewhere, made sex ripe for commercial exploitation. Since the mid-nineteenth century, the erotic had attracted entrepreneurs. But, as we have seen, it mostly remained a marginal, illicit industry. As the Supreme Court in the 1950s and 1960s shook the legal edifice that kept sexual imagery within certain limits, the capitalist impulse seized upon sexual desire as an unmet need that the marketplace could fill. Wherever Americans looked, it seemed, the erotic beckoned in the guise of a commodity.

Pornography provides one convenient measure of the dynamic that was underway. Long confined to a shadowy underground, and formerly taking the shape of a home industry, it became in the 1970s highly visible. Thousands of movie houses featuring triple-"X"-rated films dotted the country, ranging from drive-ins on the outskirts of towns, and theaters in the central city, to fancy establishments in modern shopping malls. North Carolina and South Carolina boasted the largest concentration of adult theaters, belying the notion that pornography was the product of big-city decadence. Some of the films, such as *Deep Throat* and *The Devil in Miss Jones*, achieved respectability of sorts, becoming cult favorites that attracted large audiences. In most cities, adult bookstores sold hard-core sex magazines and paperbacks without the literary pretensions or journalistic substance to which *Playboy* and its competitors aspired. A substantial portion of newsstand sales came from publications that the police would have seized a decade earlier. Technological advances offered new opportunities and new audiences for the distribution of pornography. The introduction of video-cassette recorders in the late 1970s opened the door to a booming business in sex films for home consumption. As one maker of pornographic videos remarked, "there are some people who would like to frequent sex theatres, but for various reasons they don't. They're either ashamed to be seen going in, they don't want to take their wives with them, or whatever. This way, they're able to see the X material in the privacy of their own home, and it doesn't seem so distasteful to them." Men brought their wives or girlfriends to help them select the evening's viewing fare. Soon, the rental of pornographic movies was providing the essential margin of profit for many video stores. The spread of cable television, meanwhile, allowed producers to avoid the constraints of the federally regulated networks. A subsidiary of Time, Inc., for instance, used cable television to distribute a weekly program, *Midnight Blue*, that featured couples having sex.[3]

By the 1980s, economic analysts were referring to the "sex industry." A multi-billion-dollar endeavor, it featured high-salaried executives, a large work force, brisk competition, board meetings, and sales conventions. Al Goldstein, the publisher of *Screw* who "diversified" in the 1970s, remarked on the contrast between the sleazy image of the industry and its more prosaic—and profitable— reality. "People come into my office," he said, "and they think there are supposed to be 12 women under my desk. If there is anybody under there, it's 12 tax accountants. Or 12 attorneys. I'm a capitalist. I'm good at what I do." Industry boosters promoted the field as they would any other. Dennis Sobin, who edited *The Adult Business Report,* the chief trade magazine of the industry, commented that "the sex business has the same potential for sales and profits as the food industry. It is a growth industry that cannot go backwards."[4]

One reason, perhaps, for the confidence of this new breed of entrepreneur was that they could arguably see themselves as simply the least hypocritical of an entire spectrum of marketers of sexuality. Not only had pornography moved into the light of day, but sexual imagery had become incorporated into the mainstream of American life. Advertisers broke new ground in their use of the erotic to excite consumers. In newspaper ads, clothing manufacturers and department stores featured pre-pubescent girls in flirtatious poses. Record companies enticed buyers with sexually suggestive album covers. Calvin Klein commissioned billboards with models naked from the waist up, their buttocks snugly fitted into his designer jeans. "The tighter they are, the better they sell," he commented.[5] By the 1980s, male bodies, too, were being used to promote sales. On television, commercials for any number of products projected the message that consumption promised the fulfillment of erotic fantasies and appetites.

The visual entertainment media also made sex a staple of their shows. An evening of television might begin with game shows in which attractive female models draped themselves over prizes representing a consumer's dreams, progress to situation comedies where the plot revolved around the titillating possibilities of sexual encounters, and end with steamy adult dramas. Instead of *I Love Lucy,* viewers laughed at the innuendo of *Three's Company,* in which a man and two women cohabited, or they might wonder when Sam and Diane, the main characters in *Cheers,* would make it into bed. Rather than the simple cops-and-robbers plots of *The Untouchables,* the award-winning *Hill Street Blues* closed many episodes in the bedroom of its chief protagonists. Popular nighttime soap operas combined the themes of money, power, and sex into high Nielsen ratings. Potboiler novels became mini-series, with titles such as *Sin,* or *Hollywood Wives,* in which the characters trotted around the globe in search of sexual adventure. Multi-million-dollar budgets and the absence of frontal nudity were about the only differences between these network specials and their prodigal pornographic cousins.

The permeation of sex throughout the culture made itself felt in other ways. In the morning newspapers, "Dear Abby" and Ann Landers found themselves addressing more and more explicit sexual scenarios. A series of articles in one midwestern daily advised single men and women that "there is nothing wrong with sharing physical pleasure with somebody else. Sure, old moralistic rules flash by, but for a growing number of us they can satisfactorily be put aside. For once, it's exhilarating to be the 'bad' kid. . . . By having a variety of partners we learn there are interesting variations on the theme."[6] In the early 1980s, Dr. Ruth Westheimer, a radio personality with a grandmotherly wholesomeness, became something of a national hero, as well as a highly paid lecturer, through her enthusiastic prescriptions for sexual happiness. Magazines made space for pages of personal ads where a "DWM" (divorced white male) might seek "SF" (single female) for walks, talks, and an afternoon affair. Cars sported bumper stickers ("firemen have long hoses," "elevator operators like to go down," "teachers do it with class") that jocularly associated occupational identity with sexual prowess.

So much openness about sexuality had an impact on the prescriptive literature to which Americans were so partial. By the 1970s, marital advice books were fast losing their audience to popular sex manuals. Many of them—*Everything You Always Wanted to Know about Sex, The Sensuous Man, The Sensuous Woman*— became runaway best-sellers. Dispensing with the genteel language and scientific descriptions characteristic of midcentury books for the married, they endorsed sexual experimentation in language that twenty years earlier had been the province of pornography. "Put your girl in a soft, upholstered chair," the author of *The Sensuous Man* advised,

> and kneel in front of her so your head comes about to the level of her breasts. . . . Now slide her off the chair and right onto that beautiful erect shaft. The feeling is dizzying. She is wet and very, very hot; you are face to face and in about as deep as you can be. . . . [It's] an exciting way to come, When you do explode, you'll find yourself in each other's arms—exhausted, wet, beautiful—a total state of A.F.O.—all fucked out.[7]

Alex Comfort's *The Joy of Sex* played on the theme of a popular cookbook by offering menus of its own for the sexual gourmet. Liberally illustrated with erotic drawings, it depicted naked men and women in an endless variety of sexual positions. Comfort's success propelled publishers to commission companion volumes for gay men and lesbians. Even books aimed at supposedly traditional Americans dispensed with reticence. Marabel Morgan's *The Total Woman* may have held that woman's place was in the home, but it also instructed housewives to greet their husbands at the end of the day dressed in a transparent nightgown.[8]

CHANGING LIFE CYCLES
AND NEW SEXUAL PATTERNS

As entrepreneurs were weaving sexuality into the fabric of public life, Americans were simultaneously experiencing dramatic demographic changes. Between the 1960s and the 1980s, the life cycle of many Americans became considerably more complex and unpredictable. The timing of marriage and childbearing, control over fertility, the instability of the traditional nuclear family, and innovations in living arrangements all encouraged a reorganization of sexual standards.

The unusual demographic patterns of the baby-boom era reversed themselves with startling rapidity in the 1970s. Between 1960 and 1980, the marriage rate declined by a quarter. By 1985, the median age of marriage for men had risen to 25.5 years, while for women it jumped to 23.2. Along with later marriage came an overall decline in fertility. Beginning in the mid-1970s, the fertility of American women hovered at the replacement level, far below the peaks reached in the late 1950s. The accessibility of legal abortions, the accelerating trend toward sterilization, and the availability of reliable contraceptives put absolute control of fertility within reach for the married. Especially within the middle class, childlessness emerged as a serious option to consider. As one couple noted, "we are the only people we know who have a child, or at least the only people we know well. . . . Some [of our friends] are married, a few might as well be, others aren't totally opposed to the idea—and they have all either ruled out families entirely or postponed them until the very distant future." By the end of the 1970s more than a quarter of married women in their late twenties remained childless.[9]

Not only were Americans marrying later and having fewer children, but families were much less likely to remain intact. Aided by the liberalization of state laws, the divorce rate began a steep climb in the mid-1960s. Between 1960 and 1980, the number of divorced men and women rose by almost two hundred percent; the divorce rate itself jumped ninety percent. For blacks, the impact of divorce was even more widely felt. In 1980, over a quarter of black men and women between the ages of twenty-five and fifty-four were divorced, in comparison to less than ten percent of whites. Many of the divorced remarried eventually, yet second marriages had even less chance of surviving. Although the rush to divorce had slowed somewhat by 1980, marriages of the late seventies had only a one-in-two chance of surviving.

All of these shifts affected the size and structure of American households, which tended to grow smaller and become more diversified in composition. During the 1970s, over half of the new households created were nonfamily ones. The traditional two-parent family with children accounted for only three-fifths of all living arrangements by 1980. Even that figure tended to overstate its predominance, since many of those families would experience dissolution, and most Americans could expect to spend a portion of their childhood and adult years in "nontraditional" situations.

One widely touted demographic innovation of the 1970s was the rise of cohabitation among men and women. Hardly noted by 1960 census-takers, it became a highly visible phenomenon in the 1970s, tripling in frequency. Although cohabiting couples constituted only three percent of American households, the chances of an individual participating in such an arrangement were much higher. One study found that almost one in five American men had lived for at least six months with a woman other than their spouse. The phenomenon was more common among blacks than whites, and a majority of the men had been previously married. Surveying the changing nature of American life-styles, the sociologists Philip Blumstein and Pepper Schwartz confidently predicted that cohabitation "will probably become more visible and more common."[10]

In the midst of this reorganization of household and family structure, one element of change elicited special comment—the rise of the working mother. White married women had been steadily entering the labor force since World War II, and for black wives work outside the home had always been a common experience. But the rapid movement of mothers into paid employment surprised most observers. By the early 1980s a majority of mothers, including those with children of preschool age, were working for wages. Some of this change owed its origin to feminism, which validated the choices of mothers who sought employment. Some of it was due to financial necessity. As inflation escalated in the 1970s, and the changing structure of economic and social life raised the consumption needs of many families, the pressure for mothers to work mounted. Among married couples in 1980, wives with family incomes between twenty-five thousand and fifty thousand dollars were most likely to be employed. The absence of female employment consigned many families to subsistence living. Moreover, as the divorce rate mounted and more women found themselves heading households, many mothers had no choice but to work.

Whatever the motives, the high proportion of women in the work force promised upheavals in the realm of personal life and heterosexual relations. Working women were both cause and effect of many demographic changes—the rising age of marriage, later childbearing, the decline in fertility, the spread of single-person households, and cohabitation. Unhappy marriages, in which spouses felt compelled out of duty or desperation to remain together, might more readily dissolve. As Paul Glick, a Census Bureau demographer who had studied marriage and divorce for a generation, commented, "women who enter the marketplace gain greater confidence, expand their social circles independent of their husbands' friends, taste independence and are less easy to satisfy, and more likely to divorce." Or, as one Indiana wife put it, "women don't have to put up with [men's] crap—they can support themselves."[11] Working women brought greater confidence and more power to their relationships with men. Although conflict might ensue as couples readjusted their expectations, surveys indicated nevertheless that younger males in particular preferred the more egalitarian results that came with the modification of traditional sex roles.

These demographic shifts hit the black community with special force. Although black-white differentials in family structure actually narrowed in the 1970s, nontraditional living arrangements still appeared with much greater frequency among blacks. Overall incidence rates of divorce, female-headed households, and out-of-wedlock births remained higher. By 1980 almost half of black households were female-headed, a majority of black infants were born to unmarried women, and only a minority of black children were being raised in two-parent households. Approximately half of black adults were not married and living with their spouse. In assessing these statistics, one sociologist was moved to comment that "all is not well between black men and women." In contrast to the mid-1960s, when the Moynihan report provoked so much controversy within the civil rights movement, black leaders in the eighties felt freer to air their own concerns. By the early 1980s, many were rating the issue of family life equally with jobs and education as a critical concern of the community. Eleanor Holmes Norton, who served in the Carter administration, called it "the most serious long-term crisis in the black community."[12]

When combined with the invasion of sexuality into so much of the public realm, these new demographic patterns among Americans presaged a major shift in sexual behavior and attitudes. The later age of marriage increased the likelihood that women as well as men would enter the institution sexually experienced. The rise in divorce meant that more and more Americans would be searching for new sexual partners as mature adults. Children and adolescents would know that their parents were having sex outside of marriage; the openness with which heterosexual cohabitation, lesbianism, and male homosexuality were discussed provided visible alternatives to marriage. Postponed childbearing and low fertility made obvious the distinction between sex for procreation and for pleasure. Women who worked and had more sexual experience were better placed to negotiate the terms of a sexual relationship with a partner. The new explicitness of so much popular literature about the erotic almost guaranteed that many Americans would have their sexual repertoires greatly enhanced. Perhaps most significantly, the growing complexity of the American life cycle substantially weakened the hegemony of marriage as the privileged site for sexual expression. As one longitudinal study of families in Detroit concluded, "the decision to marry or remain single is now considered a real and legitimate choice between acceptable alternatives, marking a distinct shift in attitude from that held by Americans in the past."[13]

Survey data from a variety of sources confirm a striking shift in sexual values toward approval of nonmarital sexuality. As late as the 1950s, for instance, polls suggested that fewer than a quarter of Americans endorsed premarital sex for men and women. By the 1970s, these figures had been reversed. Especially among the young, substantial majorities registered their approval. Although males, blacks, the college-educated and higher-income families were more likely to accept premarital sexuality, the differences between groups were disappearing. Only older Americans and religiously devout whites tended to maintain a stance of moral disapproval. The generation gap was especially pronounced over some of the more radical departures from past orthodoxy. One study found that three-quarters of Americans over sixty-five opposed the practice of cohabitation, while the figures were reversed for the under-thirty population. Similarly, when confronted with the contemporary openness of the gay community, younger Americans proved more than three times as likely as their seniors to display tolerance for homosexuality. In their study of American couples, Blumstein and Schwartz found that among married couples, cohabiting heterosexuals, gay men, and lesbians, majorities of everyone except wives expressed approval for sexual relationships devoid of love.[14]

One important ideological source for the revamping of sexual beliefs was feminism. Particularly among younger heterosexuals, traditional notions of male and female differences weakened in the 1970s. Most looked forward to marriages in which roles blurred. Many younger males abandoned the allegiance to a double standard of behavior for their female peers. For both men and women, expectations about sexuality and intimacy changed. As Sophie Freud Loewenstein, a Boston social worker, explained it,

> Women who have taken it for granted that their sexual satisfaction was unimportant are now reading about women having multiple orgasms. Many men realize that they've been ripped off by being programmed to deny their expressive aspects. It becomes a possibility to throw out some of the old sex roles and change drastically. That change can be very frightening, but the atmosphere makes it more permissible.[15]

As its critique of sex-role conditioning spread throughout the culture, feminism altered the attitudes of Americans about the proper behavior of men and women.

Demographic change, shifts in attitudes, and the eroticism that so much of the public realm displayed contributed to a major alteration in the sexual life of many Americans. Unmarried youth as well as conjugal pairs, urban male homosexuals as well as heterosexual couples, experienced important modifications in their patterns of sexual behavior. Among other things, sexual experience was beginning at a younger age, acts once considered deviant were more widely incorporated into heterosexual relations, and the gap between the sex lives of men and women was narrowing.

The behavior of the young and the unmarried dramatically illustrates the extent of change. From the mid-1960s onward the incidence of premarital intercourse among white females zoomed upward, narrowing substantially the disparity in experience between them and their male peers. Survey after survey of white college students in every part of the country confirmed this shift. By 1980 large majorities of female students were engaging in coitus, often in relationships that held no expectation of marriage. Among black women, too, there was evidence of change, though primarily in the age at which coitus began. Between 1971 and 1976, fifteen- and sixteen-year-olds were half again as likely to have engaged in intercourse. In the early 1970s, a much broader survey that included men and women of varying educational levels also documented the rise in premarital coitus among women. By then young women were as likely to have sex as were the men in Kinsey's study a generation earlier. Morton Hunt, the author, also confirmed a greater variety in practices. Where Kinsey had found few heterosexuals who had tried fellatio or cunnilingus, by the 1970s it was a commonplace experience among those in their twenties. The frequency of intercourse for young men and women was also substantially higher, while masturbation, especially among women, was starting earlier and had become more widespread.[16]

Evidence of other sorts substantiates these survey findings. On college campuses, health services routinely distributed contraceptive information and devices to students. For those who began having intercourse earlier, or who did not attend college, Planned Parenthood clinics offered an alternative source of assistance. In Muncie, Indiana, for example, a third of teenage girls used the services of Planned Parenthood in 1979. The rise in births to unmarried teenagers, as well as the large number who sought abortions, also suggests that a growing proportion of the young were sexually active.[17]

These changes in patterns of behavior took place in a social context different from that which had shaped the behavior of youth between the 1920s and the 1960s. For one, formal dating evinced a sharp decline. Teenage youth socialized casually in groups without pairing off; friendships between males and females were more common. As one high school boy described it, in drawing a contrast between himself and his father:

> Once he told me that he wasn't brought up to think about women the way guys like me do, and it was vice versa back then. 'We were scared of each other; we didn't really have *friends* of the opposite sex' is the way he said it to me. Now that's changed! I can talk with girls I'm not dating—I mean, be real friendly with them. There's one girl at school who's the person I feel easiest with there. We're pals, but I've never wanted to make out with her!

This ease of interaction had implications for the progress of sexual experience. When the young did pair off, it tended to signal an already serious relationship. They were less likely to move gradually through the stages of kissing, necking, and petting before deciding to have intercourse. In fact, one observer of the young concluded that petting, so important in the sexual initiation of midcentury adolescents, "seems destined to take its place as a historical curiosity."[18]

The demographic patterns of the late 1960s and 1970s, as well as the less measurable effects of feminist ideology, also contributed to the shape of change. As women became sexually active earlier in life, as the age of marriage rose, and their participation in the labor force promised greater autonomy, more of them could approach sexual experience with different expectations. One twenty-eight-year-old blue-collar female, cohabiting with a male partner, firmly expressed her right to an erotic life. "I may have had an unusual upbringing, but it never occurred to me that a man wouldn't let me be sexy," she said. "I have the same needs and moods as a man, and I am not going to let some chauvinist pig stifle them." Another single woman, also in her twenties, justified nonmonogamy on the basis of her strong sexual desires. "I have a roving eye and sometimes I give in to it. . . . I consider myself a very sexual person and I need an adventure from time to time. And I think [my cohabiting partner] does too. But that's all it is—fun and a little bit of an ego thrill."[19] Their comments suggest that at least some women had moved a long distance from the 1950s, when sexual intercourse had to be justified as a sign of an abiding romantic attachment.

Not surprisingly, the erotic dimension of marriage also changed profoundly during these years. Although some elements of the past persisted, especially concerning gender differences in initiating sex, the conjugal relationship was moving rapidly in the direction of greater variety, higher levels of satisfaction, and more frequent intercourse. For instance, a study comparing the sexual practices of married couples in the early 1970s with those in the Kinsey reports found twice as many couples departing from the missionary position. Except among black couples, oral sex—both cunnilingus and fellatio—had been incorporated into the sexual repertoire of husbands and wives to such an extent that the author of the study, Morton Hunt, called the change an "increase . . . of major and historic proportions." Among whites, the move toward variety in technique and position extended across the social spectrum, narrowing considerably the class differences that Kinsey had noted. The frequency of intercourse had also risen, in a reverse of the trend displayed by Kinsey's respondents. As Hunt explained,

> Although in [Kinsey's] time the frequency of marital coitus was declining due to the wife's rising status and her growing right to have a voice in sexual matters, the regularity of her orgasm in marital intercourse was rising. . . . This increase in orgiastic reliability and overall sexual satisfaction eventually offset the forces that caused the initial drop in coital activity.

Only ten percent of the wives in Hunt's survey described their sexual relations of the preceding year as unpleasant or of no interest to them. Of the ninety percent claiming satisfaction, three-quarters were content with the frequency while one-quarter wished for more.[20]

The visibility of sex in the culture certainly contributed to these trends. Not only did it encourage an interest in the erotic, but it also made information much more readily available to adults. Particularly among working-class wives, who as late as the 1940s and 1950s were often dependent on their husbands to lead the way, the barriers to active sexual agency were dropping. A waitress in her mid-thirties described the initiative she took:

> What changed our sex life was that a bunch of us girls on the same block started reading books and passing them around—everything from how-to-do-it sex books to real porno paperbacks. Some of the men said that the stuff was garbage, but I can tell you that my husband was always ready to try out anything. . . . Some of it was great, some was awful . . . and some was just funny, like the honey business.

Another woman, married to a blue-collar worker, had him buy sex manuals to spice up their love life. "We found all different ways of caressing and different positions, and it was very nice because we realized that these things weren't dirty," she explained. "Like I could say to my husband 'Around the world in eighty days!' and he'd laugh and we'd really go at it." Moreover, much of the literature written in the 1970s, such as *The Hite Report* and Nancy Friday's *My Secret Garden*, presented sex from women's vantage point. The emphasis in these works shifted from simultaneous orgasm through intercourse to forms of pleasuring suitable for women, or what one commentator called "separate but equal orgasms." Thus, even the supposedly immutable "sex act" underwent redefinition in ways that weakened a male monopoly over the nature of sex.[21]

As couples experimented with different techniques of lovemaking, the erotic became a vehicle for exploring new realms of intimacy and power. Some men enjoyed the sensation that came from knowing they were satisfying their partners. "The whole process [of oral sex] makes me feel good about myself," said one husband. "I take serious pride in being a good lover and satisfying my partner, giving her pleasure." A businesswoman remarked that "I like oral sex very much because it is extremely intimate and I'm moved by it as an act of intimacy." For some women, oral sex evoked feelings of power. "I do feel powerful when he does it. I feel quite powerful," said one. "Sort of the Amazon mentality—all powerful woman." Another experienced similar emotions when performing fellatio. "I'm exerting power. I'm rewarding him," she commented. "The giving of pleasure is a powerful position, and the giving of oral sex is a real, real gift of pleasure."[22]

The cultural validation of erotic pleasure also contributed to a historic shift in expectations. Among earlier generations, men and women had found themselves at odds about the frequency of sex in marriage. At the turn of the century, at least among the white middle class, many women submitted to their husband's desires; by midcentury, many men felt themselves sexually deprived. But a survey of couples conducted in the late 1970s found virtual agreement among men and women about sexual satisfaction and frequency. Eighty-nine percent of married men and women who had sex three or more times a week expressed contentment with their sex life; among those who had sex once a week or less, the figure dropped to fifty-three percent for each gender. The responses of unmarried cohabiting couples provided roughly similar findings. Not only were most men and women indicating similar preferences, but they expected relatively high frequencies of sex. According to Blumstein and Schwartz, among all the couples they studied—heterosexual, gay male, and lesbian—"a good sex life is central to a good overall relationship," and infrequent sex provoked discontent with all aspects of the relationship. Even the readers of a mainstream women's magazine such as *Redbook* had incorporated high expectations about sex into their lives. After polling 100,000 women, the editors found that "women are becoming increasingly active sexually and are less likely to accept an unsatisfactory sex life as part of the price to be paid for marriage."[23]

One reason, undoubtedly, for the shifts in heterosexual relationships was the availability of birth control. The dramatic move in the 1960s toward effective contraception continued into the 1970s. By mid-decade three out of four married couples relied on the pill, the IUD, or sterilization.[24] Then, too, the legalization of first-trimester abortions provided a measure of last resort for wives whose contraceptive efforts failed. Though it is difficult to know how great an increase in the incidence of abortion took place in the seventies, the fact that it was medically safe and legal at least removed the dangers that formerly attached to it. The near universality of birth control practices had virtually eliminated the constraints that fears about pregnancy had imposed on the sex life of married women. It also highlighted the degree to which the erotic had been divorced from procreation.

The separation of sex from reproduction also emerged from another quarter. Not only could couples safely have sex without the expectation of conception, but technological innovations were making it possible to have babies without sex. Science was upsetting age-old certainties about the natural connection between sex and procreation. "Remember when there was only one way to make a baby?" an advertisement for a 1979 CBS special report asked. "That was yesterday. Today, nature's role is being challenged by science. Conception without sex. Egg fertilization outside the womb. 'Surrogate' mothers who can bear other couples' children. Frozen embryos stored in 'supermarkets' for future implantation."[25] Among other things, scientific change was allowing lesbian couples to have children, without choosing marriage, through the cooperation of male sperm donors. Public policy added another dimension to technological change, as welfare agencies allowed single women and single men to adopt children, thus emphasizing the distinction between biological and social parenting. Though the new technology would raise some vexing problems of its own, as the controversy over Baby M revealed, people were nonetheless making choices that seemed to confirm that making love and making babies were not the same.

The new visibility that gay life achieved in the 1970s also emphasized the weakened link between procreation and the erotic. Although it is difficult to measure change in this area with any degree of precision, certainly the social life of gay men and lesbians had altered considerably. The many organizations that existed throughout the country allowed greater ease in making friends and acquaintances, and in embarking upon relationships. Less police harassment made it safer for bars to open and stay in operation. Regional music festivals brought thousands of lesbians together for several days of companionship; annual rituals such as the gay pride marches each June became celebrations of community cohesiveness even as they made a political statement. Church attendance, political club membership, and professional caucuses all contributed to a broadening of an identity in which the erotic played a prominent role. But the historic invisibility of gay male and lesbian life makes it impossible to compare the erotic dimension of gay experience from one generation to another. Even in the 1970s there were few studies that moved beyond the impressionism of journalistic observations.

A study that did, the work of Philip Blumstein and Pepper Schwartz, is interesting in part because of the comparison it allows between men and women, and between heterosexuals and homosexuals. The researchers found that a good sexual adjustment was as important to a successful relationship among gay male and lesbian respondents as among heterosexuals, and that the higher the frequency of sex the greater the sense of satisfaction. But lesbians seemed content to have sex less often, and after two years in a relationship, the lesbian couples tended to see a significant decline in the frequency of sex. Young lesbians were more likely to engage in oral sex than were older women, and among all the couples, gay men placed the greatest stock in variety in sexual technique. Lesbians proved very similar to heterosexual men and women in the extent of nonmonogamy—twenty-eight percent of lesbians, twenty-five percent of husbands, and twenty-one percent of wives—whereas for gay men, nonmonogamy was a way of life. Furthermore, among couples that did not practice monogamy male homosexuals tended to have sex with a far larger number of partners. One percent of the lesbians, seven percent of the husbands, but more than two-fifths of the gay men, had sex with more than twenty partners while living with a mate.[26]

Even in an era that witnessed an expansion of erotic opportunities, the experience of some urban gay men appeared to stand outside the norm. When Kinsey undertook his study in the 1940s he found that although male homosexuals on average had sex less frequently than heterosexual men, some of them had far more partners in the course of a lifetime. In the 1970s, as the urban gay subculture became larger and more accessible, the chances for sexual encounters multiplied. Heterosexuals may have had their singles bars where they could meet a partner for an evening of sex, but in large cities, gay bathhouses, bars with back rooms, and stores showing pornographic films allowed gay male patrons to have sex with a series of men in rapid succession. For many, sexual promiscuity became part of the fabric of gay life, an essential element holding the community together. Yet the fact that such sex businesses could operate in the 1970s relatively free of police harassment and that the media could spotlight them in discussions of gay life says as much about heterosexual norms as about those of gay men. In the larger metropolitan areas, male homosexuals were no longer serving as symbols of sexual deviance; their eroticism no longer divided the good from the bad. Heterosexuals sustained a vigorous singles nightlife, and advertised in magazines for partners; suburban couples engaged in mate-swapping; sex clubs were featuring male strippers, with women in the role of voyeur. By the end of the decade, some "straight" men and women were even patronizing a heterosexual equivalent of the gay bathhouse, as the success of places like Plato's Retreat in New York demonstrated. The experience of the urban gay subculture stood as one point along a widened spectrum of sexual possibilities that modern America now offered.

Although it would be foolhardy to deny the depth and breadth of the changes that had occurred by the end of the 1970s, one must also acknowledge the continuities with the past. Blumstein and Schwartz, for instance, found that "there *are* new men and new women, among both heterosexual and homosexual couples, who are dealing with sexual responsibilities in new ways and trying to modify the traditions that their maleness and femaleness bring to their relationships." But they were fewer in number than the pair of sociologists expected to find, and the persistence of tradition was particularly hard for some heterosexual women whose partners proved "less 'liberated' than she—or he—thought he was."[27] Marriages were happier and more intimate than a generation earlier, but partly because so many unhappy ones ended in divorce. In a culture that was coming to identify frequent, pleasurable, varied, and ecstatically satisfying sex as a preeminent sign of personal happiness, the high rate of marital dissolution could easily mean that large numbers of Americans were failing to reach these standards. The differences in the patterns of behavior of gay men and lesbians also pointed to the continuing salience of gender in shaping sexual meanings. Moreover, while lesbians and male homosexuals had carved out some space for themselves in society, the frequency of physical assaults upon visibly gay men and women suggested that their form of nonprocreative sex still provoked outrage. Feminism, too, may have opened new realms of sexual expressiveness for women, but the extent of rape and other forms of male sexual violence still made sex an arena of danger for them. The much-vaunted "sexual revolution," though real in many ways, was hardly complete.

Two issues, in particular, were emerging by the end of the 1970s to suggest the contradictory emotions that still enshrouded sex. Since the advent of penicillin in the 1940s, the threat of venereal disease had, to a significant degree, faded as an inhibitor of nonmonogamous sexual expression. But, in the midst of Americans' recently acquired sexual "freedom," the media spotlighted a new venereal scourge. Herpes, which *Time* magazine labeled "today's scarlet letter" and the "new leprosy," was reaching epidemic proportions among young urban heterosexuals. Though the condition posed far less physical danger than syphilis, it provoked guilt and panic as well as a pulling back from erotic encounters for some. A medical professional reported that "we hear it over and over: I won't have sex again." Among victims, the disease elicited feelings of self-pollution— "you never think you're clean enough," said one. The *Soho Weekly News,* a New York paper popular among young professionals in the city, was moved to proclaim "current sexual practice" as "the real epidemic." For many, the spread of herpes came to symbolize the inherent flaws in an ethic of sexual permissiveness. Pleasure brought retribution; disease became a marker of weak moral character.[28]

Another "epidemic," that of teenage pregnancy, also highlighted ambivalence about the erotic. Although most Americans tended to look benignly upon sex between unmarried adults, the spread of sexual experience among teenagers troubled them. To a large extent, adolescents were pursuing the erotic without the approval or the guidance of their elders. Despite the visibility of sex in the culture, the acquisition of knowledge by the young remained sporadic and haphazard, largely "a private, individually motivated and covert affair," in the opinion of one sex researcher. Some parents felt it was simply wrong, despite their own experience. As one middle-class mother in Muncie had phrased it, "just because it was right for me doesn't make it okay for my kids." A survey of high school youth in the early 1980s found that almost half had learned nothing about sex from their parents. Nor were schools rushing to fill the gap. By the late 1970s only half a dozen states mandated sex education; in most places, curriculum remained up to the local school districts, which generally displayed the same caution or disregard that occurred in the home. In one New York City suburb, a high school principal refused to let the editor of the school paper print an article about birth control methods. A California school district provided sex instruction in conjunction with drivers education, indicating how marginal it was to the academic curriculum. "In order to avoid controversy," according to the authors of *Sex and the American Teenager,* "schools embrace boredom."[29]

The result of this abdication of responsibility by schools and parents was that the young were often left to drift into sexual activity without guidance and with little knowledge. Teenagers whose parents were unwilling to talk with them about sex, or who did not receive sex education in school, were more prone to engage in intercourse. Yet they were also likely to be ignorant of how conception occurred or how to prevent it. Even when schools did provide instruction, they often acted too late. One North Carolina fifteen-year-old learned about condoms in a junior high school class, after he had been having intercourse for two years. "And then I realized, man, I've been taking a lot of chances. Thirteen, fourteen, fifteen . . . Lord's been good to me," he said. Others were not so lucky, as the incidence of teenage pregnancy revealed. In 1976, among the premaritally sexually active, twenty-seven percent of white girls and forty-five percent of blacks had become pregnant by the age of eighteen. Ironically, in view of the laissez-faire stance that adults seemed to take, the young were looking for advice. As Robert Coles and Geoffrey Stokes concluded on the basis of their work with high school students,

it seems clear from our interviews that some kids who are planning to enter sexual relationships *want* to be told to wait. But those who can't talk to their parents hear either nothing or a ritualized naysaying that has no bearing on their *imme-diate* situation—and those who can may find their parents unwilling to take the responsibility for saying anything more than "Be careful."[30]

Meanwhile, for those who had made their choice to have sex, accurate information about reproduction, conception, and birth control might at least save them from the tragedy of unwanted pregnancies.

That so many teenage girls were becoming pregnant in an age when reli-able contraception was available says much about the contradictions within the sexually permissive culture of the 1960s and 1970s. From everywhere sex beck-oned, inciting desire, yet rarely did one find reasoned presentations of the most elementary consequences and responsibilities that sexual activity entailed. Youth had more autonomy from adult supervision than ever before, allowing them to explore the erotic at a time of profound physiological changes, but adults seemed to respond by implicitly drawing a boundary at sexual activity during adolescence. Perhaps one could not stop the young from experimenting, but neither would so-ciety endorse their behavior. The result was a social problem of tragic dimensions, one that placed in bold relief the ambivalence of American society toward sex. And, the fact that young girls were left to pay a higher price for sexual activity served as a poignant commentary on the persistence of gender in the structuring of sexuality in the postliberal era.

The reshaping of sexuality in the 1960s and 1970s was of major proportions. The marketing of sex, new demographic patterns, and the movements of women and homosexuals for equality all fostered a substantial revision in attitudes and behavior. In some ways, the process of sexualization represented pushing the logic of sexual liberalism to its extreme: once sex had been identified as a critical aspect of happiness, how could one justify containing it in marriage? Even before the 1960s, the behavior of youth and the commercial manipulation of the erotic had suggested the vulnerability of the liberal consensus. By the end of the 1970s, it was obvious that the consensus had dissolved. As Americans married later, postponed childbearing, and divorced more often, and as feminists and gay liberationists questioned heterosexual orthodoxy, nonmarital sexuality became commonplace and open. And, all of this took place in a social environment in which erotic imagery was ubiquitous.

The collapse of sexual liberalism did not, however, lead to a new, stable consensus. By the end of the 1970s, conservative proponents of an older sexual order had appeared. Their efforts to stem the tide of change and, indeed, to re-store sexuality to a reproductive marital context would demonstrate the continuing power of sex to generate controversy.

NOTES

1. Gay Talese, *Thy Neighbor's Wife* (Garden City, N.Y., 1980; paperback, 1981), p. 188.

2. *Ibid.*, p. 398.

3. New York *Times,* April 5, 1979, p. B15.

4. New York *Times,* February 10, 1981, p. B6, and February 9, 1981, p. B6.

5. New York *Times,* February 9, 1981, p. B6.

6. Theodore Caplow et al., *Middletown Families* (Minneapolis, 1982), pp. 173–74.

7. Quoted in Morton Hunt, *Sexual Behavior in the 1970s* (New York, 1974), p. 9.

8. Alex Comfort, ed., *The Joy of Sex: A Gourmet Guide to Love Making* (New York, 1972); Marabel Morgan, *The Total Woman* (Old Tappan, N.J., 1975).

9. *New York Times Sunday Magazine,* May 25, 1975, p. 10. Unless otherwise noted, the demographic information in this and the following paragraphs is from Andrew Hacker, ed., *U/S: A Statistical Portrait of the American People* (New York, 1983).

10. Richard R. Clayton and Harwin L. Voss, "Shacking Up: Cohabitation in the 1970s," *Journal of Marriage and the Family* 39 (1977), pp. 273–83; Philip Blumstein and Pepper Schwartz, *American Couples: Money, Work, Sex* (New York, 1983; paperback, 1985), p. 36.

11. New York *Times,* November 27, 1977, p. 74; Caplow et al., *Middletown Families,* p. 131.

12. Robert Staples, *Black Masculinity* (San Francisco, 1982), p. 115; New York *Times,* August 13, 1984, p. B4.

13. New York *Times,* December 23, 1982, p. C5.

14. See Hunt, *Sexual Behavior in the 1970s,* p. 21; B. K. Singh, "Trends in Attitudes toward Premarital Sexual Relations," *Journal of Marriage and the Family* 42 (1980), pp. 387–93; New York *Times,* November 27, 1977, p. 75; Norval D. Glenn and Charles N. Weaver, "Attitudes Toward Premarital, Extramarital, and Homosexual Relations in the U.S. in the 1970s," *Journal of Sex Research* 15 (1978), pp. 108–18; Blumstein and Schwartz, *American Couples,* pp. 255, 272.

15. New York *Times,* November 28, 1977, p. 36.

16. Ira E. Robinson and Davor Jedlicka, "Change in Sexual Attitudes and Behavior of College Students from 1965 to 1980: A Research Note," *Journal of Marriage and the Family* 44 (1982), pp. 237–40; Robert R. Bell and Kathleen Coughey, "Premarital Sexual Experience Among College Females, 1958, 1968, and 1978," *Family Relations* 29 (1980), pp. 353–57; Melvin Zelnick, Young J. Kim, and John F. Kanter, "Probabilities of Intercourse and Conception Among Teenage Women, 1971 and 1976," *Family Planning Perspectives* 11 (1979), pp. 177–83; Hunt, *Sexual Behavior in the 1970s,* pp. 150, 166, 77, 87.

17. Caplow et al., *Middletown Families,* pp. 169–70, 185.

18. Robert Coles and Geoffrey Stokes, *Sex and the American Teenager* (New York, 1985), p. 7; Hunt, *Sexual Behavior in the 1970s,* p. 142.

19. Blumstein and Schwartz, *American Couples,* pp. 208, 282.

20. Hunt, *Sexual Behavior in the 1970s,* pp. 202, 198, 187, 192.

21. *Ibid.,* pp. 183–84; Barbara Ehrenreich, Elizabeth Hess, and Gloria Jacobs, *Re-Making Love: The Feminization of Sex* (Garden City, N.Y., 1986), p. 100.

22. Blumstein and Schwartz, *American Couples,* pp. 232, 236.

23. *Ibid.,* pp. 201–3; Ehrenreich et al., *Re-Making Love,* p. 164.

24. New York *Times,* July 22, 1977, p. 1.

25. New York *Times,* October 31, 1979, p. C19.

26. Blumstein and Schwartz, *American Couples*, pp. 202–3, 236, 273. For another study see Karla Jay and Allen Young, *The Gay Report: Lesbians and Gay Men Speak Out About Sexual Experiences and Life Styles* (New York, 1979).

27. Blumstein and Schwartz, *American Couples*, p. 305.

28. Allan M. Brandt, *No Magic Bullet: A Social History of Venereal Disease in the United States Since 1880* (New York, 1985), pp. 170–74, 179–82.

29. Hunt, *Sexual Behavior in the 1970s*, p. 130; Caplow et al., *Middletown Families*, p. 171; Coles and Stokes, *Sex and the American Teenager*, p. 38.

30. Coles and Stokes, *Sex and the American Teenager*, pp. 37, 99.

20.
The Feminization of Love*

Francesca M. Cancian

A feminized and incomplete perspective on love predominates in the United States. We identify love with emotional expression and talking about feelings, aspects of love that women prefer and in which women tend to be more skilled than men. At the same time we often ignore the instrumental and physical aspects of love that men prefer, such as providing help, sharing activities, and sex. This feminized perspective leads us to believe that women are much more capable of love than men and that the way to make relationships more loving is for men to become more like women.[1] This paper proposes an alternative, androgynous perspective on love, one based on the premise that love is both instrumental and expressive.[2] From this perspective, the way to make relationships more loving is for women and men to reject polarized gender roles and integrate "masculine" and "feminine" styles of love.

THE TWO PERSPECTIVES

"Love is active, doing something for your good even if it bothers me" says a fundamentalist Christian. "Love is sharing, the real sharing of feelings" says a divorced secretary who is in love again. In ancient Greece, the ideal love was the adoration of a man for a beautiful young boy who was his lover. In the thirteenth century, the exemplar of love was the chaste devotion of a knight for another man's wife. In Puritan New England, love between husband and wife was the ideal, and in Victorian times, the asexual devotion of a mother for her

*Cancian, Francesca M. 1986. "The Feminization of Love." *Signs: Journal of Women in Culture and Society* 11(4): 692–709. © 1986 by the University of Chicago. All rights reserved.

child seemed the essence of love.[3] My purpose is to focus on one kind of love: long-term heterosexual love in the contemporary United States.

What is a useful definition of enduring love between a woman and a man? One guideline for a definition comes from the prototypes of enduring love—the relations between committed lovers, husband and wife, parent and child. These relationships combine care and assistance with physical and emotional closeness. Studies of attachment between infants and their mothers emphasize the importance of being protected and fed as well as touched and held. In marriage, according to most family sociologists, both practical help and affection are part of enduring love, or "the affection we feel for those with whom our lives are deeply inter-twined."[4] Our own informal observations often point in the same direction: if we consider the relationships that are the prototypes of enduring love, it seems that what we really mean by love is some combination of instrumental and expressive qualities.

Historical studies provide a second guideline for defining enduring love, specifically between a woman and a man.[5] In precapitalist America, such love was a complex whole that included work and feelings. Then it was split into feminine and masculine fragments by the separation of home and workplace. This historical analysis implies that affection, material help, and routine cooperation all are parts of enduring love.

Consistent with these guidelines, my working definition of enduring love between adults is a relationship wherein a small number of people are affectionate and emotionally committed to each other, define their collective well-being as a major goal, and feel obliged to provide care and practical assistance for each other. People who love each other also usually share physical contact; they communicate with each other frequently and cooperate in some routine tasks of daily life. My discussion is of enduring heterosexual love only; I will for the sake of simplicity refer to it as "love."

In contrast to this broad definition of love, the narrower, feminized definition dominates both contemporary scholarship and public opinion. Most scholars who study love, intimacy, or close friendship focus on qualities that are stereotypically feminine, such as talking about feelings.[6] For example, Abraham Maslow defines love as "a feeling of tenderness and affection with great enjoyment, happiness, satisfaction, elation and even ecstasy." Among healthy individuals, he says, "there is a growing intimacy and honesty and self-expression."[7] Zick Rubin's "Love Scale," designed to measure the degree of passionate love as opposed to liking, includes questions about confiding in each other, longing to be together, and sexual attraction as well as caring for each other. Studies of friendship usually distinguish close friends from acquaintances on the basis of how much personal information is disclosed, and many recent studies of married couples and lovers emphasize communication and self-disclosure. A recent book on marital love by Lillian Rubin focuses on intimacy, which she defines as "reciprocal expression of feeling and thought, not out of fear or dependent need, but out of a wish to know another's inner life and to be able to share one's own."[8] She argues that intimacy is distinct from nurturance or caretaking and that men are usually unable to be intimate.

Among the general public, love is also defined primarily as expressing feelings and verbal disclosure, not as instrumental help. This is especially true among the more affluent; poorer people are more likely than they to see practical help and financial assistance as a sign of love.[9] In a study conducted in 1980, 130 adults from a wide range of social classes and ethnic backgrounds were interviewed about the qualities that make a good love relationship. The most frequent response referred to honest and open communication. Being caring and supportive and being tolerant and understanding were the other qualities most often mentioned.[10] Similar results were reported from Ann Swidler's study of an affluent suburb: the dominant conception of love stressed communicating feelings, working on the relationship, and self-development.[11] Finally, a contemporary dictionary defines love as "strong affection for another arising out of kinship or personal ties" and as attraction based on sexual desire, affection, and tenderness.[12]

These contemporary definitions of love clearly focus on qualities that are seen as feminine in our culture. A study of gender roles in 1968 found that warmth, expressiveness, and talkativeness were seen as appropriate for women and not for men. In 1978 the core features of gender stereotypes were unchanged although fewer qualities were seen as appropriate for only one sex. Expressing tender feelings, being gentle, and being aware of the feelings of others were still ideal qualities for women and not for men. The desirable qualities for men and not for women included being independent, unemotional, and interested in sex.[13] The only component perceived as masculine in popular definitions of love is interest in sex.

The two approaches to defining love—one broad, encompassing instrumental and affective qualities, one narrow, including only the affective qualities—inform the two different perspectives on love. According to the androgynous perspective, both gender roles contain elements of love. The feminine role does not include all of the major ways of loving; some aspects of love come from the masculine role, such as sex and providing material help, and some, such as cooperating in daily tasks, are associated with neither gender role. In contrast, the feminized perspective on love implies that all of the elements of love are included in the feminine role. The capacity to love is divided by gender. Women can love and men cannot.

SOME FEMINIST INTERPRETATIONS

Feminist scholars are divided on the question of love and gender. Supporters of the feminized perspective seem most influential at present. Nancy Chodorow's psychoanalytic theory has been especially influential in promoting a feminized perspective on love among social scientists studying close relationships. Chodorow's argument—in greatly simplified form—is that as infants, both boys and girls have strong identification and intimate attachments with their mothers. Since boys grow up to be men, they must repress this early identification, and in the process they repress their capacity for intimacy. Girls retain their early identification since they will grow up to be women, and throughout their lives females see themselves as connected to others. As a result of this process, Chodorow argues, "girls come to define and experience themselves as continuous with others; . . . boys come to define themselves as more separate and distinct."[14] This theory implies that love is feminine—women are more open to love than men—and that this gender difference will remain as long as women are the primary caretakers of infants.

Scholars have used Chodorow's theory to develop the idea that love and attachment are fundamental parts of women's personalities but not of men's. Carol Gilligan's influential book on female personality development asserts that women define their identity "by a standard of responsibility and care." The predominant female image is "a network of connection, a web of relationships that is sustained by a process of communication." In contrast, males favor a "hierarchical ordering, with its imagery of winning and losing and the potential for violence which it contains." "Although the world of the self that men describe at times includes 'people' and 'deep attachments,' no particular person or relationship is mentioned. . . . Thus the male 'I' is defined in separation."[15]

A feminized conception of love can be supported by other theories as well. In past decades, for example, such a conception developed from Talcott Parsons's theory of the benefits to the nuclear family of women's specializing in expressive action and men's specializing in instrumental action. Among contemporary social scientists, the strongest support for the feminized perspective comes from such psychological theories as Chodorow's.[16]

On the other hand, feminist historians have developed an incisive critique of the feminized perspective on love. Mary Ryan and other social historians have analyzed how the separation of home and workplace in the nineteenth century polarized gender roles and feminized love.[17] Their argument, in simplified form, begins with the observation that in the colonial era the family household was the arena for economic production, affection, and social welfare. The integration of activities in the family produced a certain integration of expressive and instrumental traits in the personalities of men and women. Both women and men were expected to be hard working, modest, and loving toward their spouses and children, and the concept of love included instrumental cooperation as well as expression of feelings. In Ryan's words, "When early Americans spoke of love they were not withdrawing into a female byway of human experience. Domestic affection, like sex and economics, was not segregated into male and female spheres." There was a "reciprocal ideal of conjugal love" that "grew out of the day-to-day cooperation, sharing, and closeness of the diversified home economy."[18]

Economic production gradually moved out of the home and became separated from personal relationships as capitalism expanded. Husbands increasingly worked for wages in factories and shops while wives stayed at home to care for the family. This division of labor gave women more experience with close relationships and intensified women's economic dependence on men. As the daily activities of men and women grew further apart, a new worldview emerged that exaggerated the differences between the personal, loving, feminine sphere of the home and the impersonal, powerful, masculine sphere of the workplace. Work became identified with what men do for money while love became identified with women's activities at home. As a result, the conception of love shifted toward emphasizing tenderness, powerlessness, and the expression of emotion. [19]

This partial and feminized conception of love persisted into the twentieth century as the division of labor remained stable: the workplace remained impersonal and separated from the home, and married women continued to be excluded from paid employment. According to this historical explanation, one might expect a change in the conception of love since the 1940s, as growing numbers of wives took jobs. However, women's persistent responsibility for child care and housework, and their lower wages, might explain a continued feminized conception of love. [20]

Like the historical critiques, some psychological studies of gender also imply that our current conception of love is distorted and needs to be integrated with qualities associated with the masculine role. For example, Jean Baker Miller argues that women's ways of loving—their need to be attached to a man and to serve others—result from women's powerlessness, and that a better way of loving would integrate power with women's style of love. [21] The importance of combining activities and personality traits that have been split apart by gender is also a frequent theme in the human potential movement. [22] These historical and psychological works emphasize the flexibility of gender roles and the inadequacy of a concept of love that includes only the feminine half of human qualities. In contrast, theories like Chodorow's emphasize the rigidity of gender differences after childhood and define love in terms of feminine qualities. The two theoretical approaches are not as inconsistent as my simplified sketches may suggest, and many scholars combine them, [23] however, the two approaches have different implications for empirical research.

EVIDENCE ON WOMEN'S "SUPERIORITY" IN LOVE

A large number of studies show that women are more interested and more skilled in love than men. However, most of these studies use biased measures based on feminine styles of loving, such as verbal self-disclosure, emotional expression, and willingness to report that one has close relationships. When less biased measures are used, the differences between women and men are often small.

Women have a greater number of close relationships than men. At all stages of the life cycle, women see their relatives more often. Men and women report closer relations with their mothers than with their fathers and are generally closer to female kin. Thus an average Yale man in the 1970s talked about himself more with his mother than with his father and was more satisfied with his relationship with his mother. His most frequent grievance against his father was that his father gave too little of himself and was cold and uninvolved; his grievance against his mother was that she gave too much of herself and was alternately overprotective and punitive. [24]

Throughout their lives, women are more likely to have a confidant—a person to whom one discloses personal experiences and feelings. Girls prefer to be with one friend or a small group, while boys usually play competitive games in large groups. Men usually get together with friends to play sports or do some other activity, while women get together explicitly to talk and to be together. [25]

Men seemed isolated given their weak ties with their families and friends. Among blue-collar couples interview in 1950, 64 percent of the husbands had no confidants other than their spouses, compared to 24 percent of the wives.[26] The predominantly upper-middle-class men interviewed by Daniel Levinson in the 1970s were no less isolated. Levinson concludes that "close friendship with a man or a woman is rarely experienced by American men."[27] Apparently, most men have no loving relationships besides those with wife or lover; and given the estrangement that often occurs in marriages, many men may have no loving relationship at all.

Several psychologists have suggested that there is a natural reversal of these roles in middle age, as men become more concerned with relationships and women turn toward independence and achievement; but there seems to be no evidence showing that men's relationships become more numerous or more intimate after middle age, and some evidence to the contrary.[28]

Women are also more skilled than men in talking about relationships. Whether working class or middle class, women value talking about feelings and relationships and disclose more than men about personal experiences. Men who deviate and talk a lot about their personal experiences are commonly defined as feminine and maladjusted.[29] Working-class wives prefer to talk about themselves, their close relationships with family and friends, and their homes, while their husbands prefer to talk about cars, sports, work, and politics. The same gender-specific preferences are expressed by college students.[30]

Men do talk more about one area of personal experience: their victories and achievements; but talking about success is associated with power, not intimacy. Women say more about their fears and disappointments, and it is disclosure of such weaknesses that usually is interpreted as a sign of intimacy.[31] Women are also more accepting of the expression of intense feelings, including love, sadness, and fear, and they are more skilled in interpreting other people's emotions.[32]

Finally, in their leisure time women are drawn to topics of love and human entanglements while men are drawn to competition among men. Women's preferences in television viewing run to daytime soap operas, or if they are more educated, the high-brow soap operas on educational channels, while most men like to watch competitive and often aggressive sports. Reading tastes show the same pattern. Women read novels and magazine articles about love, while men's magazines feature stories about men's adventures and encounters with death.[33]

However, this evidence on women's greater involvement and skill in love is not as strong as it appears. Part of the reason that men seem so much less loving than women is that their behavior is measured with a feminine ruler. Much of this research considers only the kinds of loving behavior that are associated with the feminine role and rarely compares women and men in terms of qualities associated with the masculine role. When less biased measures are used, the behavior of men and women is often quite similar. For example, in a careful study of kinship relations among young adults in a southern city, Bert Adams found that women were much more likely than men to say that their parents and relatives were very important to their lives (58 percent of women and 37 percent of men). In measures of actual contact with relatives, though, there were much smaller differences: 88

percent of women and 81 percent of men whose parents lived in the same city saw their parents weekly. Adams concluded that "differences between males and females in relations with parents are discernible primarily in the subjective sphere; contact frequencies are quite similar."[34]

The differences between the sexes can be small even when biased measures are used. For example, Marjorie Lowenthal and Clayton Haven reported the finding, later widely quoted, that elderly women were more likely than elderly men to have a friend with whom they could talk about their personal troubles—clearly a measure of a traditionally feminine behavior. The figures revealed that 81 percent of the married women and 74 percent of the married men had confidants—not a sizable difference.[35] On the other hand, whatever the measure, virtually all such studies find that women are more involved in close relationships than men, even if the difference is small.

In sum, women are only moderately superior to men in love: they have more close relationships and care more about them, and they seem to be more skilled at love, especially those aspects of love that involve expressing feelings and being vulnerable. This does not mean that men are separate and unconcerned with close relationships, however. When national surveys ask people what is most important in their lives, women tend to put family bonds first while men put family bonds first or second, along with work.[36] For both sexes, love is clearly very important.

EVIDENCE ON THE MASCULINE STYLE OF LOVE

Men tend to have a distinctive style of love that focuses on practical help, shared physical activities, spending time together, and sex.[37] The major elements of the masculine style of love emerged in Margaret Reedy's study of 102 married couples in the late 1970s. She showed individuals statements describing aspects of love and asked them to rate how well the statements described their marriages. On the whole, husband and wife had similar views of their marriage, but several sex differences emerged. Practical help and spending time together were more important to men. The men were more likely to give high ratings to such statements as: "When she needs help I help her," and "She would rather spend her time with me than with anyone else." Men also described themselves more often as sexually attracted and endorsed such statements as: "I get physically excited and aroused just thinking about her." In addition, emotional security was less important to men than to women, and men were less likely to describe the relationship as secure, safe, and comforting.[38] Another study in the late 1970s showed a similar pattern among young, highly educated couples. The husbands gave greater emphasis to feeling responsible for the partner's well-being and putting the spouse's needs first, as well as to spending time together. The wives gave greater importance to emotional involvement and verbal self-disclosure but also were more concerned than the men about maintaining their separate activities and their independence.[39]

The difference between men and women in their views of the significance of practical help was demonstrated in a study in which seven couples recorded their interactions for several days. They noted how pleasant their relations were and counted how often the spouse did a helpful chore, such as cooking a good meal or repairing a faucet, and how often the spouse expressed acceptance or affection. The social scientists doing the study used a feminized definition of love. They labeled practical help as "instrumental behavior" and expressions of acceptance or affection as "affectionate behavior," thereby denying the affectionate aspect of practical help. The wives seemed to be using the same scheme; they thought their marital relations were pleasant that day if their husbands had directed a lot of affectionate behavior to them, regardless of their husbands' positive instrumental behavior. The husbands' enjoyment of their marital relations, on the other hand, depended on their wives' instrumental actions, not on their expressions of affection. The men actually saw instrumental actions as affection.[40] One husband who was told by the researchers to increase his affectionate behavior toward his wife decided to wash her car and was surprised when neither his wife nor the researchers accepted that as an "affectionate" act.

The masculine view of instrumental help as loving behavior is clearly expressed by a husband discussing his wife's complaints about his lack of communication: "What does she want? Proof? She's got it, hasn't she? Would I be knocking myself out to get things for her—like to keep up this house—if I didn't love her? Why does a man do things like that if not because he loves his wife and kids? I swear, I can't figure what she wants." His wife, who has a feminine orientation to love, says something very different: "It is not enough that he supports us and takes care of us. I appreciate that, but I want him to share things with me. I need for him to tell me his feelings."[41] Many working-class women agree with men that a man's job is something he does out of love for his family,[42] but middle-class women and social scientists rarely recognize men's practical help as a form of love. (Indeed, among upper-middle-class men whose jobs offer a great deal of intrinsic gratification, their belief that they are "doing it for the family" may seem somewhat self-serving.)

Other differences between men's and women's styles of love involve sex. Men seem to separate sex and love while women connect them,[43] but, paradoxically, sexual intercourse seems to be the most meaningful way of giving and receiving love for many men. A twenty-nine-year-old carpenter who had been married for three years said that, after sex, "I feel so close to her and the kids. We feel like a real family then. I don't talk to her very often, I guess, but somehow I feel we have really communicated after we have made love."[44]

Because sexual intimacy is the only recognized "masculine" way of expressing love, the recent trend toward viewing sex as a way for men and women to express mutual intimacy is an important challenge to the feminization of love. However, the connection between sexuality and love is undermined both by the "sexual revolution" definition of sex as a form of casual recreation and by the view of male sexuality as a weapon—as in rape—with which men dominate and punish women.[45]

Another paradoxical feature of men's style of love is that men have a more romantic attitude toward their partners than do women. In Reedy's study, men were more likely to select statements like "we are perfect for each other."[46] In a survey of college students, 65 percent of the men but only 24 percent of the women said that, even if a relationship had all of the other qualities they desired, they would not marry unless they were in love.[47] The common view of this phenomenon focuses on women. The view is that women marry for money and status and so see marriage as instrumentally, rather than emotionally, desirable. This of course is at odds with women's greater concern with self-disclosure and emotional intimacy and lesser concern with instrumental help. A better way to explain men's greater romanticism might be to focus on men. One such possible explanation is that men do not feel responsible for "working on" the emotional aspects of a relationship, and therefore see love as magically and perfectly present or absent. This is consistent with men's relative lack of concern with affective interaction and greater concern with instrumental help.

In sum, there is a masculine style of love. Except for romanticism, men's style fits the popularly conceived masculine role of being the powerful provider.[48] From the androgynous perspective, the practical help and physical activities included in this role are as much a part of love as the expression of feelings. The feminized perspective cannot account for this masculine style of love; nor can it explain why women and men are so close in the degrees to which they are loving.

NEGATIVE CONSEQUENCES OF
THE FEMINIZATION OF LOVE

The division of gender roles in our society that contributes to the two separate styles of love is reinforced by the feminized perspective and leads to political and moral problems that would be mitigated with a more androgynous approach to love. The feminized perspective works against some of the key values and goals of feminists and humanists by contributing to the devaluation and exploitation of women.

It is especially striking how the differences between men's and women's styles of love reinforce men's power over women. Men's style involves giving women important resources, such as money and protection that men control and women believe they need, and ignoring the resources that women control and men need. Thus men's dependency on women remains covert and repressed, while women's dependency on men is overt and exaggerated; and it is overt dependency that creates power, according to social exchange theory.[49] The feminized perspective on love reinforces this power differential by leading to the belief that women need love more than do men, which is implied in the association of love with the feminine role. The effect of this belief is to intensify the asymmetrical dependency of women on men.[50] In fact, however, evidence on the high death rates of unmarried men suggests that men need love at least as much as do women.[51]

Sexual relations also can reinforce male dominance insofar as the man takes the initiative and intercourse is defined either as his "taking" pleasure or as his being skilled at "giving" pleasure, either way giving him control. The man's power advantage is further strengthened if the couple assumes that the man's sexual needs can be filled by any attractive woman while the woman's sexual needs can be filled only by the man she loves.[52]

On the other hand, women's preferred ways of loving seem incompatible with control. They involve admitting dependency and sharing or losing control, and being emotionally intense. Further, the intimate talk about personal troubles that appeals to women requires of a couple a mutual vulnerability, a willingness to see oneself as weak and in need of support. It is true that a woman, like a man, can gain some power by providing her partner with services, such as understanding, sex, or cooking; but this power is largely unrecognized because the man's dependency on such services is not overt. The couple may even see these services as her duty or as her response to his requests (or demands).

The identification of love with expressing feelings also contributes to the lack of recognition of women's power by obscuring the instrumental active component of women's love just as it obscures the loving aspect of men's work. In a culture that glorifies instrumental achievement, this identification devalues both women and love.[53] In reality, a major way by which women are loving is in the clearly instrumental activities associated with caring for others, such as preparing meals, washing clothes, and providing care during illness; but because of our focus on the expressive side of love, this caring work of women is either ignored or redefined as expressing feelings. Thus, from the feminized perspective on love, child care is a subtle communication of attitudes, not work. A wife washing her husband's shirt is seen as expressing love, even though a husband washing his wife's car is seen as doing a job.

Gilligan, in her critique of theories of human development, shows the way in which devaluing love is linked to devaluing women. Basic to most psychological theories of development is the idea that a healthy person develops from a dependent child to an autonomous, independent adult. As Gilligan comments, "Development itself comes to be identified with separation, and attachments appear to be developmental impediments."[54] Thus women, who emphasize attachment, are judged to be developmentally retarded or insufficiently individuated.

The pervasiveness of this image was documented in a well-known study of mental health professionals who were asked to describe mental health, femininity, and masculinity. They associated both mental health and masculinity with independence, rationality, and dominance. Qualities concerning attachment, such as being tactful, gentle, or aware of the feelings of others, they associated with femininity but not with mental health.[55]

Another negative consequence of a feminized perspective on love is that it legitimates impersonal, exploitive relations in the workplace and the community. The ideology of separate spheres that developed in the nineteenth century contrasted the harsh, immoral marketplace with the warm and loving home and implied that this contrast is acceptable.[56] Defining love as expressive, feminine, and divorced from productive activity maintains this ideology. If personal relationships and love are reserved for women and the home, then it is acceptable for a manager to underpay workers or for a community to ignore a needy family. Such behavior is not unloving; it is businesslike or shows a respect for privacy. The ideology of separate spheres also implies that men are properly judged by their instrumental and economic achievements and that poor or unsuccessful men are failures who may deserve a hard life. Levinson presents a conception of masculine development itself as centering on achieving an occupational dream.[57]

Finally, the feminization of love intensifies the conflicts over intimacy between women and men in close relationships. One of the most common conflicts is that the woman wants more closeness and verbal contact while the man withdraws and wants less pressure.[58] Her need for more closeness is partly the result of the feminization of love, which encourages her to be more emotionally dependent on him. Because love is feminine, he in turn may feel controlled during intimate contact. Intimacy is her "turf," an area where she sets the rules and expectations. Talking about the relationship as she wants, may well feel to him like taking a test that she made up and that he will fail. He is likely to react by withdrawing, causing her to intensify her efforts to get closer. The feminization of love thus can lead to a vicious cycle of conflict where neither partner feels in control or gets what she or he wants.

CONCLUSION

The values of improving the status of women and humanizing the public sphere are shared by many of the scholars who support a feminized conception of love; and they, too, explain the conflicts in close relationships in terms of polarized gender roles. Nancy Chodorow, Lillian Rubin, and Carol Gilligan have addressed these issues in detail and with great insight. However, by arguing that women's identity is based on attachment while men's identity is based on separation, they reinforce the distinction between feminine expressiveness and masculine instrumentality, revive the ideology of separate spheres, and legitimate the popular idea that only women know the right way to love. They also suggest that there is no way to overcome the rigidity of gender roles other than by pursuing the goal of men and women becoming equally involved in infant care. In contrast, an androgynous perspective on love challenges the identification of women and love with being expressive, powerless, and nonproductive and the identification of men with being instrumental, powerful, and productive. It rejects the ideology of separate spheres and validates masculine as well as feminine styles of love. This viewpoint suggests that progress could be made by means of a variety of social changes, including men doing child care, relations at work becoming more personal and nurturant, and cultural conceptions of love and gender becoming more androgynous. Changes that equalize power within close relationships by equalizing the economic and emotional dependency between men and women may be especially important in moving toward androgynous love.

The validity of an androgynous definition of love cannot be "proven"; the view that informs the androgynous perspective is that both the feminine style of love (characterized by emotional closeness and verbal self-disclosure) and the masculine style of love (characterized by instrumental help and sex) represent necessary parts of a good love relationship. Who is more loving: a couple who confide most of their experiences to each other but rarely cooperate or give each other practical help, or a couple who help each other through many crises and cooperate in running a household but rarely discuss their personal experiences? Both relationships are limited. Most people would probably choose a combination: a relationship that integrates feminine and masculine styles of loving, an androgynous love.

NOTES

1. The term "feminization" of love is derived from Ann Douglas, *The Feminization of Culture* (New York: Alfred A. Knopf, 1977).

2. The term "androgyny" is problematic. It assumes rather than questions sex-role stereotypes (aggression is masculine, e.g.); it can lead to a utopian view that underestimates the social causes of sexism; and it suggests the complete absence of differences between men and women, which is biologically impossible. Nonetheless, I use the term because it best conveys my meaning: a combination of masculine and feminine styles of love. The negative and positive aspects of the concept "androgyny" are analyzed in a special issue of *Women's Studies* (vol. 2, no. 2[1974]), edited by Cynthia Secor. Also see Sandra Bem, "Gender Schema Theory and Its Implications for Child Development: Raising Gender-aschematic Children in a Gender-schematic Society," *Signs: Journal of Women in Culture and Society* 8, no. 4 (1983): 598–616.

3. The quotations are from a study by Ann Swidler, "Ideologies of Love in Middle Class America" (paper presented at the annual meeting of the Pacific Sociological Association, San Diego, 1982). For useful reviews of the history of love, see Morton Hunt, *The Natural History of Love* (New York: Alfred A. Knopf, 1959); and Bernard Murstein, *Love, Sex and Marriage through the Ages* (New York: Springer, 1974).

4. See John Bowlby, *Attachment and Loss* (New York: Basic Books, 1969), on mother-infant attachment. The quotation is from Elaine Walster and G. William Walster, *A New Look at Love* (Reading, Mass.: Addison-Wesley Publishing Co., 1978), 9. Conceptions of love and adjustment used by family sociologists are reviewed in Robert Lewis and Graham Spanier, "Theorizing about the Quality and Stability of Marriage," in *Contemporary Theories about the Family*, ed. W. Burr, R. Hill, F. Nye, and I. Reiss (New York: Free Press, 1979), 268–94.

5. Mary Ryan, *Womanhood in America*, 2d ed. (New York: New Viewpoints, 1979), and *The Cradle of the Middle Class: The Family in Oneida County, N.Y., 1790–1865* (New York: Cambridge University Press, 1981); Barbara Ehrenreich and Deirdre English, *For Her Own Good: 150 Years of Experts' Advice to Women* (New York: Anchor Books, 1978); Barbara Welter, "The Cult of True Womanhood: 1820–1860," *American Quarterly* 18, no. 2(1966): 151–74; Carl N. Degler, *At Odds* (New York: Oxford University Press, 1980).

6. Alternative definitions of love are reviewed in Walster and Walster; Clyde Hendrick and Susan Hendrick, *Liking, Loving and Relating* (Belmont, Calif.: Wadsworth Publishing Co., 1983); Ira Reiss, *Family Systems in America*, 3d ed. (New York: Holt, Rinehart & Winston, 1980), 113–41; Margaret Reedy, "Age and Sex Differences in Personal Needs and the Nature of Love" (Ph.D. diss., University of Southern California, 1977).

7. Abraham Maslow, *Motivation and Personality*, 2d ed. (New York: Harper & Row, 1970), 182–83.

8. Zick Rubin's scale is described in his article "Measurement of Romantic Love," *Journal of Personality and Social Psychology* 16, no. 2 (1970): 265–73; Lillian Rubin's book on marriage is *Intimate Strangers* (New York: Harper & Row, 1983), quote on 90.

9. The emphasis on mutual aid and instrumental love among poor people is described in Lillian Rubin, *Worlds of Pain* (New York: Basic Books, 1976); Rayna Rapp, "Family

and Class in Contemporary America," in *Rethinking the Family*, ed. Barrie Thorne (New York: Longman, Inc., 1982), 168–87; S. M. Miller and F. Riessman, "The Working-Class Subculture," in *Blue-Collar World*, ed. A. Shostak and W. Greenberg (Englewood Cliffs, N.J.: Prentice-Hall, Inc., 1964), 24–36.

10. Francesca Cancian, Clynta Jackson, and Ann Wysocki, "A Survey of Close Relationships" (University of California, Irvine, School of Social Sciences, 1982, typescript).

11. Swidler.

12. *Webster's New Collegiate Dictionary* (Springfield, Mass.: G. C. Merriam Co., 1977).

13. Paul Rosencrantz, Helen Bee, Susan Vogel, Inge Broverman, and Donald Broverman, "Sex Role Stereotypes and Self-Concepts in College Students," *Journal of Consulting and Clinical Psychology* 32, no. 3 (1968): 287–95; Paul Rosencrantz, "Rosencrantz Discusses Changes in Stereotypes about Men and Women," *Second Century Radcliffe News* (Cambridge, Mass., June 1982), 5–6.

14. Nancy Chodorow, *The Reproduction of Mothering* (Berkeley: University of California Press, 1978), 169. Dorothy Dinnerstein presents a similar theory in *The Mermaid and the Minotaur: Sexual Arrangements and Human Malaise* (New York: Harper & Row, 1976). Freudian and biological dispositional theories about women's nurturance are surveyed in Jean Stockard and Miriam Johnson, *Sex Roles* (Englewood Cliffs, N.J.: Prentice-Hall, Inc., 1980).

15. Carol Gilligan, *In a Different Voice* (Cambridge, Mass: Harvard University Press, 1982), 32, 159–61; see also L. Rubin, *Intimate Strangers*.

16. Talcott Parsons and Robert F. Bales, *Family, Socialization and Interaction*, Glencoe, Ill., Free Press, 1955). For a critical review of family sociology from a feminist perspective, see Arlene Skolnick, *The Intimate Environment* (Boston: Little, Brown & Co., 1978). Radical feminist theories also support the feminized conception of love, but they have been less influential in social science, see, e.g., Mary Daly, *Gyn/Ecology; The Metaethics of Radical Feminism* (Boston: Beacon Press, 1979).

17. I have drawn most heavily on Ryan, *Womanhood*, (n. 5 above), Ryan, *Cradle* (n. 5 above), Ehrenresch and English (n. 5 above), Welter (n. 5 above).

18. Ryan, *Womanhood*, 24–25.

19. Similar changes occurred when culture and religion were feminized, according to Douglas (n. 1 above). Conceptions of God's love shifted toward an image of a sweet and tender parent, a "submissive, meek and forgiving" Christ (149).

20. On the persistence of women's wage inequality and responsibility for housework, see Stockard and Johnson (n. 14 above).

21. Jean Baker Miller, *Toward a New Psychology of Women* (Boston: Beacon Press, 1976). There are, of course, many exceptions to Miller's generalization, e.g., women who need to be independent or who need an attachment with a woman.

22. In psychology, the work of Carl Jung, David Bakan, and Bem are especially relevant. See Carl Jung, "Anima and Animus," in *Two Essays on Analytical Psychology: Collected Works of C. G. Jung* (New York: Bollinger Foundation, 1953), 7:186–209; David Bakan, *The Duality of Human Existence* (Chicago: Rand McNally & Co., 1966). They are discussed in Bem's paper, "Beyond Androgyny," in *Family in Transition*, 2d ed., ed. A. Skolnick and J. Skolnick (Boston: Little, Brown & Co., 1977), 204–21. Carl Rogers exemplifies the human potential theme of self-development through the search for wholeness. See Carl Rogers, *On Becoming a Person* (Boston: Houghton Mifflin Co., 1961).

23. Chodorow (n. 14 above) refers to the effects of the division of labor and to power differences between men and women, and the special effects of women's being the primary parents are widely acknowledged among historians.

24. The data on Yale men are from Mirra Komarovsky, *Dilemma of Masculinity* (New York: W.W. Norton & Co., 1976). Angus Campbell reports that children are closer to their mothers than to their fathers, and daughters feel closer to their parents than do sons, on the basis of large national surveys, in *The Sense of Well-Being in America* (New York: McGraw-Hill Book Co., 1981), 96. However, the tendency of people to criticize their mothers more than their fathers seems to contradict these findings; e.g., see Donald Payne and Paul Mussen, "Parent-Child Relations and Father Identification among Adolescent Boys," *Journal of Abnormal and Social Psychology* 52 (1956): 358–62. Being "closer" to one's mother may refer mostly to spending more time together and knowing more about each other rather than to feeling more comfortable together.

25. Studies of differences in friendship by gender are reviewed in Wenda Dickens and Daniel Perlman, "Friendship over the Life Cycle," in *Personal Relationships*, vol. 2, ed. Steve Duck and Robin Gilmour (London: Academic Press, 1981), 91–122, and Beth Hess, "Friendship and Gender Roles over the Life Course," in *Single Life*, ed. Peter Stein (New York: St. Martin's Press, 1981), 104–15. While almost all studies show that women have more close friends, Lionel Tiger argues that there is a unique bond between male friends in *Men in Groups* (London: Thomas Nelson, 1969).

26. Komarovsky, *Blue-Collar Marriage* (New York: Random House, 1962), 13.

27. Daniel Levinson, *The Seasons of a Man's Life* (New York: Alfred A. Knopf, 1978), 335.

28. The argument about the middle-aged switch was presented in the popular book *Passages*, by Gail Sheehy (New York: E. P. Dutton, 1976), and in more scholarly works, such as Levinson's. These studies are reviewed in Alice Rossi, "Life-Span Theories and Women's Lives," *Signs* 6, no. 1 (1980): 4–32. However, a survey by Claude Fischer and S. Oliker reports an increasing tendency for women to have more close friends than men beginning in middle age, in "Friendship, Gender and the Life Cycle," Working Paper no. 318 (Berkeley: University of California, Berkeley, Institute of Urban and Regional Development, 1980).

29. Studies on gender differences in self-disclosure are reviewed in Letitia Peplau and Steven Gordon, "Women and Men in Love: Sex Differences in Close Relationships," in *Women, Gender and Social Psychology*, ed. V. O'Leary, R. Unger, and B. Wallston (Hillsdale, N.J.: Lawrence Erlbaum Associates, 1985), 257–91. Also see Zick Rubin, Charles Hill, Letitia Peplau, and Christine Dunkel-Schetter, 'Self-Disclosure in Dating Couples," *Journal of Marriage and the Family* 42, no. 2 (1980): 305–18.

30. Working-class patterns are described in Komarovsky, *Blue Collar Marriage*. Middle-class patterns are reported by Lynne Davidson and Lucille Duberman, "Friendship: Communication and Interactional Patterns in Same-Sex Dyads," *Sex Roles* 8, no. 8 (1982): 809–22. Similar findings are reported in Robert Lewis, "Emotional Intimacy among Men," *Journal of Social Issues* 34, no. 1 (1978): 108–21.

31. Rubin et al., "Self-Disclosure."

32. These studies, cited below, are based on the self-reports of men and women college students and may reflect norms more than behavior. The findings are that women feel and express affective and bodily emotional reactions more often than do men, except

for hostile feelings. See also Jon Allen and Dorothy Haccoun, "Sex Differences in Emotionality," *Human Relations* 29, no. 8 (1976): 711–22; and Jack Balswick and Christine Avertt, "Gender, Interpersonal Orientation and Perceived Parental Expressiveness," *Journal of Marriage and the Family* 39, no. 1 (1977): 121–128. Gender differences in interaction styles are analyzed in Nancy Henley, *Body Politics: Power, Sex and Non-verbal Communication* (Englewood Cliffs, N.J.: Prentice-Hall, Inc., 1977). Also see Paula Fishman, "Interaction: The Work Women Do," *Social Problems* 25, no. 4 (1978): 397–406.

33. Gender differences in leisure are described in L. Rubin, *Worlds of Pain* (n. 9 above), 10. Also see Margaret Davis, "Sex Role Ideology as Portrayed in Men's and Women's Magazines" (Stanford University, typescript).

34. Bert Adams, *Kinship in an Urban Setting* (Chicago: Markham Publishing Co., 1968), 169.

35. Marjorie Lowenthal and Clayton Haven, "Interaction and Adaptation: Intimacy as a Critical Variable," *American Sociological Review* 33, no. 4 (1968): 20–30.

36. Joseph Pleck argues that family ties are the primary concern for many men, in *The Myth of Masculinity* (Cambridge, Mass.: MIT Press, 1981).

37. Gender-specific characteristics also are seen in same-sex relationships. See M. Caldwell and Letitia Peplau, "Sex Differences in Same Sex Friendship," *Sex Roles* 8, no. 7 (1982): 721–32; see also Davidson and Duberman (n. 30 above), 809–22. Part of the reason for the differences in friendship may be men's fear of homosexuality and of losing status with other men. An explanatory study found that men were most likely to express feelings of closeness if they were engaged in some activity such as sports that validated their masculinity (Scott Swain, "Male Intimacy in Same-Sex Friendships: The Impact of Gender-validating Activities" [paper presented at annual meeting of the American Sociological Association, August 1984]). For discussions of men's homophobia and fear of losing power, see Robert Brannon, "The Male Sex Role," in *The Forty-nine Percent Majority*, ed. Deborah David and Robert Brannon (Reading, Mass.: Addison-Wesley Publishing Co., 1976), 1–48. I am focusing on heterosexual relations, but similar gender-specific differences may characterize homosexual relations. Some studies find that, compared with homosexual men, lesbians place a higher value on tenderness and verbal self-disclosure and engage in sex less frequently. See e.g., Alan Bell and Martin Weinberg, *Homosexualities* (New York: Simon & Schuster, 1978).

38. Unlike most studies, Reedy (n. 6 above) did not find that women emphasized communication more than men. Her subjects were upper-middle-class couples who seemed to be very much in love.

39. Sara Allison Parelman, "Dimensions of Emotional Intimacy in Marriage" (Ph.D. diss., University of California, Los Angeles, 1980).

40. Both spouses thought their interaction was unpleasant if the other engaged in negative or displeasureable instrumental or affectional actions. Thomas Wills, Robert Weiss, and Gerald Patterson, "A Behavioral Analysis of the Determinants of Marital Satisfaction," *Journal of Consulting and Clinical Psychology* 42, no. 6 (1974): 802–11.

41. L. Rubin, *Worlds of Pain* (n. 9 above), 147.

42. See L. Rubin, *Worlds of Pain*; also see Richard Sennett and Jonathon Cobb, *Hidden Injuries of Class* (New York: Vintage, 1973).

43. For evidence on this point, see Morton Hunt, *Sexual Behavior in the 1970s* (Chicago: Playboy Press, 1974), 231; and Alexander Clark and Paul Wallin, "Women's Sexual Responsiveness and the Duration and Quality of Their Marriage," *American Journal of Sociology* 21, no. 2 (1965): 187–96.

44. Interview by Cynthia Garlich, "Interviews of Married Couples" (University of California, Irvine, School of Social Sciences, 1982).

45. For example, see Catharine MacKinnon, "Feminism, Marxism, Method, and the State: An Agenda for Theory," *Signs* 7, no. 3 (1982): 515–44. For a thoughtful discussion of this issue from a historical perspective, see Linda Gordon and Ellen Dubois, "Seeking Ecstacy on the Battlefield: Danger and Pleasure in Nineteenth Century Feminist Thought," *Feminist Review* 13, no. 1 (1983): 42–54.

46. Reedy (n. 6 above).

47. William Kephart, "Some Correlates of Romantic Love," *Journal of Marriage and the Family* 29, no. 3 (1967): 470–74. See Peplau and Gordon (n. 29 above) for an analysis of research on gender and romanticism.

48. Daniel Yankelovich, *The New Morality* (New York: McGraw-Hill Book Co., 1974), 98.

49. The link between love and power is explored in Francesca Cancian, "Gender Politics; Love and Power in the Private and Public Spheres," in *Gender and the Life Course*, ed. Alice S. Rossi (New York: Aldine Publishing Co., 1984), 253–64.

50. See Jane Flax, "The Family in Contemporary Feminist Thought," in *The Family in Political Thought*, ed. Jean B. Elshtain (Princeton, N.J.: Princeton University Press, 1981), 223–53.

51. Walter Gove, "Sex, Marital Status and Mortality," *American Journal of Sociology* 79, no. 1 (1973): 45–67.

52. This follows from the social exchange theory of power, which argues that person A will have a power advantage over B if A has more alternative sources for the gratifications she or he gets from B than B has for those from A. See Peter Blau, *Exchange and Power in Social Life* (New York: John Wiley & Sons, 1964), 117–18.

53. For a discussion of the devaluation of women's activities, see Michelle Rosaldo, "Woman, Culture and Society: A Theoretical Overview," in *Woman, Culture and Society*, ed. Michelle Rosaldo and Louise Lamphere (Stanford, Calif.: Stanford University Press, 1973), 17–42.

54. Gilligan (n. 15 above), 12–13.

55. Inge Broverman, Frank Clarkson, Paul Rosenkrantz, and Susan Vogel, "Sex-Role Stereotypes and Clinical Judgments of Mental Health," *Journal of Consulting Psychology* 34, no. 1 (1970): 1–7.

56. Welter (n. 5 above).

57. Levinson (n. 27 above).

58. L. Rubin, *Intimate Strangers* (n. 8 above); Harold Rausch, William Barry, Richard Hertel, and Mary Ann Swain, *Communication, Conflict and Marriage* (San Francisco: Jossey-Bass, Inc., 1974). This conflict is analyzed in Francesca Cancian, "Marital Conflict over Intimacy," in *The Psychosocial Interior of the Family*, 3d ed., ed. Gerald Handel (New York: Aldine Publishing Co., 1985), 277–92.

21

One Style of Dominican Bridal Shower*

Adele Bahn and Angela Jaquez

Unlike American bridal showers, which are used as a means of helping the couple furnish their home, or to give personal gifts to the bride, the Hispanic shower, particularly the Dominican shower, is often the means of socialization for the bride in her future status as wife. Gifts are also presented at the Dominican shower, but gifts are not the primary purpose of the shower. While seemingly frivolous and festive, the customs and activities at showers reveal serious content when analyzed for their underlying meaning—content that reflects the norms and values of society and societal expectations about the young woman about to make the transition from fiancée and bride to wife.

One important factor in Dominican culture is the Roman Catholic church, but just as important are the historical ties with Spain (and thence with Arab culture); these underlie Dominican culture and translate into two basic values that are paramount in the coming nuptials: virginity for the woman and *machismo* (a culturally specific type of virility or manliness) for the man. These values are interrelated and in fact are the reason for the socialization at the shower.

*Bahn, Adele and Angela Jaquez. 1988. "One Style of Dominican Bridal Shower." Pp. 131–146 in *The Apple Sliced: Sociological Studies of New York City*, edited by Victoria Boggs, Gerald Handel and Sylvia Fava. Prospect Heights, IL: Waveland Press. Copyright © 1984. Reissued 1988 by Waveland Press, Inc., Prospect Heights, Illinois.

METHODOLOGICAL NOTE: The research reported here was done through observation of bridal showers and interviews with guests, former guests, and women who had given showers.

Seven showers were attended in New York City; the brides were in the age range 19–22. Information was obtained on thirty-two additional showers through open-ended interviews in Spanish with fifty women who described showers they had given or attended in New York City or in the Dominican Republic. The interviews took place, in groups of up to eight women at a time, over coffee or tea in the junior author's apartment. The women were primarily of Dominican background, but some were of Puerto Rican, Cuban, San Salvadoran, or Colombian origin. Invitations to the showers and introductions to the women interviewed were obtained through a "snowball sample."

Our research process illustrates some special approaches needed to study ethnic phenomena in the city to which access is limited by language, sex, and age. The senior author had studied earlier the changes and continuities in the status of American brides, through a content analysis of United States bridal magazines from 1967 to 1977, the decade of the women's movement; British, French, and Italian bridal magazines were also examined. The analysis covered family patterns, marriage customs, sex roles, sexual behavior, birth control and family planning, consumption patterns, images of the wedding, prescriptions for wifehood, concepts of beauty, and symbols and images of the wedding. This provided a framework for the study of Dominican bridal showers in New York City. The senior author participated in some of the interviews when sufficient conversation was in English.

The junior author, a graduate student in sociology, is Dominican in background, bilingual, and in her 20s, characteristics that enabled her to attend the showers and conduct the interviews. She was able to establish rapport and believes that the events and conversations were not significantly affected by her presence. Rarely was she treated as an "outsider," although on one occasion the participants deliberately did not share with the researcher their pornographic pictures and written jokes. In most instances events at the showers were tape-recorded and photographed. The interviews were also recorded, transcribed, and later translated into English.

The young woman is expected to be a virgin when she marries. Although some norms are changing, this remains an important one. She is expected to be innocent, virginal, and inexperienced. Although more freedom is allowed her here in this country, and although it varies from one Hispanic culture to another, virginity remains the ideal. Therefore, the shower functions as an introduction and socialization for the bride to a number of her future roles, particularly the sexual role.

> One is therefore led to think that most of these rites whose sexual nature is not to be denied and which [are] said to make the individual a man or woman or fit to be one—fall into the same category as certain rites of cutting the umbilical cord, of childhood, and of adolescence. These are rites of separation from the sexual world, and they are followed by rites of incorporation into the world of sexuality, and in all societies and all social groups, into a group confined to persons of one sex or the other. This statement holds true especially for girls, since the social activity of a woman is much simpler than that of a man.[1]

SOCIAL FUNCTIONS OF THE SHOWER

The primary functions of the shower had to do with socialization, socialization to at least four roles that are components of the wifely status in traditional Dominican family life. These (1) the role of a woman among women, (2) the sexual role, (3) the homemaker role, and (4) the subservient role of the female in the marital relationship. The socialization is both implicit and explicit.

A Woman among Women

The shower itself is attended only by women (although often men are invited to come in at the end of the shower, at which time it becomes a party with music, drinking, and dancing). However, what has happened before the men arrive is kept secret from them, and all sexual decorations and related materials will have been removed.

The women are dressed in their best. Decorations, food, entertainment, and the order of festivities have been planned by women, usually close friends or relatives of the bride. There are limitations on who is invited. No one who is either too young or too old—or too staid—is invited. Often the mother and older aunts of the bride are not invited because it is felt that such guests would put a damper on the activities; the shower would have to be "too respectable." A number of middle-aged women even denied that this type of shower takes place at all! It seems out of consonance with the continuing norms for women of respectability and sexual innocence and indifference. Only women from about sixteen to thirty-five or forty are present at the showers, with the ages of most guests, as might be expected, clustering around the age of the bride.

Some of the women who plan the shower have a consciousness of tradition and duty to the bride: to inform her of what she needs to know and what is likely to happen to her.

Not all the guests are friends of the bride. Sometimes a woman who is particularly adept at being mistress of ceremonies at the shower, or who is known to have had experience at running showers, is invited even though she may not be a particular friend of the bride or even well known to the organizer of the shower, except by reputation. These women take pride in their ability to invent and create activities and decor and to set the order and sequence of the shower.

There may be a handwritten "book," a collection of dirty jokes, sayings, and tricks that is borrowed and lent for showers. New material that is particularly successful is added to the book and it even travels from New York to the Dominican Republic in the luggage of guests invited to showers there. The essence of the book is that it is shared lore passed from women to women. Some of the respondents referred to the "dirty papers" that are part of the collection (for example, the "Memorandum" set forth a little later in this essay). However, some of the women who are particularly adept at organizing showers took pride in *not* using such materials. They felt they were experienced and creative enough not to need it.

Learning the Sexual Role

The Dominican-Spanish term for "bridal shower" is *"despedida de soltera,"* which is literally translated, "Good-bye to singlehood." It is a ceremony that rarely takes place earlier than two weeks prior to the marriage ceremony and is planned by the closest friends of the bride-to-be or her relatives but not by her parents.

Formal invitations are rarely used since the planners prefer to invite the bride-to-be's friends by word of mouth. This gives them the opportunity to make suggestions about bringing something that is sexually explicit, which will embarrass the bride.

The planners make arrangements to decorate the living room of the apartment where the shower will take place either on a Friday or Saturday evening. An umbrella is affixed to a decorated chair, which is usually placed in the corner of the room. Often pornographic pictures taken from magazines are taped on the walls around the chair. The scenes they depict are both conventional and unconventional, and a number of postures are shown. The balloons that may decorate the room turn out, on closer inspection, to be condoms, blown up and tied to hang satirically from the ceiling and walls.

For the New York shower, special items may have been bought in Times Square sex shops: a plastic banana that, when opened, reveals a pink plastic penis in a constant and impossible state of erection; or a "baby pacifier" that turns out to be a tiny penis.

The refreshments may consist—besides the cakes and sandwiches prepared by friends and relatives of the guest of honor—of sausage and hot dogs arranged to look like the male sex organs and served to the guest of honor. Sometimes a root vegetable, *yautia*, which resembles a long potato, is arranged and decorated with corn silk and two small potatoes to resemble male genitalia. The vegetables are hairy and exaggerated and may also be smeared with condensed milk and ketchup or tomato paste to symbolize the semen and blood that are expected to flow on the bride's wedding night.

The guests arrive at least thirty minutes before the bride-to-be is brought in. While waiting for her, the guests engage in a lively discussion about their first night's experience. When they suspect that she is at the door, they get together in the center of the room and turn off the lights. When she enters, she is surprised. Sometimes one of the guests throws a glass of water on her, which is supposed to give her good luck. From the doorway she is led to the decorated chair, where she remains for the rest of the ceremony. As the shower continues, the bride-to-be is prepared and informed about her future roles as a wife. This includes the giving of gifts that underline her role as a housewife. She is expected to be a virgin and sexually unknowledgeable, and these expectations color the rest of the ceremony. It is also expected that she will blush and show embarrassment, horror, and astonishment at the "dirty jokes," "red tales," and "fresh tricks" that follow.

A "corsage" made of stockings in the shape of male genitalia is pinned to the bride's bosom. A dildo, sausage, or plastic hot dog may also be used. She may be forced to eat the sausage or to keep the plastic effigy in her mouth. She may be undressed to her underwear and told to put on a "baby doll" nightgown.[2] A vibrator may be used on her breast and intimate parts but no penetration occurs. The bride is shown pictures of a variety of sexual scenes and told that this is what she may expect—that this could happen to her, that she must be ready and supply "anything he wants." Typically, one of the participants is dressed like a man and imitates the groom's actions on the wedding night. If no one dresses as a man, a dildo is tied around the waist of one of the guests and this "male impersonator" "attacks" the bride. The dildo is rubbed on her face and all over her body. Aside from these overt "sexual" acts, there are guests who give her "tips" about how to please a man sexually, such as how to perform fellatio successfully.

One respondent tells of a woman dressed as a man with a dildo attached, who jumped out of the closet and enacted a rape scene. The respondent, at whose bridal shower this had occurred, claimed that it had been a valuable experience in that it had "prepared" her for her wedding night, which had been "rough." But because of these scenes, some of the guests protest that they "don't *ever* want a shower."

At any time during the shower, any of the participants can draw the bride-to-be's attention and tell her a "red joke" or read a litany to her. Litanies are anonymously written poems that use pseudonyms for the saints and contain a great deal of vulgarity. A popular litany that is used at showers both here and in the Dominican Republic is called "A Virgin's Bedside Prayer." The main character of this litany, who is supposed to be the bride-to-be, asks the saints for a man who will be sexually satisfied by her.

Double-entendres are popular at the showers. The following example was obtained from a respondent and had been translated from the Spanish.

MEMORANDUM

For the ultimate goal of maintaining the high standard of social hygiene in our city, the Honorable City Mayor along with the City Council have decreed the following:

TO ALL LOVERS AND COUPLES

As of the 16th September 1980, the Mayor and City Council in a unanimous decision have declared that all lovers and couples caught in a theater, movie, park, beach,

street or avenue, empty building or even in an alleyway, committing such acts
as mentioned below, will be punished to the fullest extent of the law and fined
accordingly:

1. With the hand on the thigh ....$ 5.00
2. With the hand on the thing $10.00
3. With the thing in the hand $15.00
4. With the thing in the mouth $20.00
5. With the mouth on the thing $25.00
6. With the thing in the thing $30.00
7. With the thing inside the thing $35.00
8. With the thing on the thing $40.00
9. With the thing in the front of the thing $45.00
10. With the thing behind the thing $50.00

For those who are curious about what "the thing" means:

a. It is not a bat, but it lives most of the time hanging down.
b. It is not an accordion; however, it shrinks and stretches.
c. It is not a soldier, but it attacks in the front and in the back.
d. It does not think, but it has a head.
e. It is not attractive; however, occasionally it's called "beautiful."
f. It is not analgesic, but it can be used as a tranquilizer.
g. It is not a palm tree, but it has nuts.
h. It does not belong to any club or organization; however, it's known as a member.
i. It does not produce music, but is called an organ.
j. It is not a gentleman, but it will stand up for ladies.

Any comments made by the bride-to-be during the shower are recorded or
written down by one of the participants. At the end of the shower they are either
read aloud or played back for the couple in a private room. The comments that
she makes during the ceremony are interpreted sexually. For example, she may
be forced to place her finger in a glass of ice cubes for a long time, and she may
cry out, "Please take it out!" By this comment, it is understood that she will be
saying the same thing to the groom on her wedding night.

Typically, home-made snacks and refreshments are served while the ceremony
goes on. As the climax of the shower, the bride is told to open the gifts that she
has received. The gifts consist of kitchen utensils, linen, porcelain figurines, and
personal items such as nightgowns. When she opens them, she is expected to
thank each donor individually and to exhibit the gifts so that the others can see
what she has received. Afterward, her best friend helps her to change into her
street clothes.

The role of the bride-to-be at the shower is very clear, underscoring the
appropriateness of her reaction to the sexual aspects of the proceedings. She is
expected to scream and show horror and surprise. The response of the girl is
scripted and socially prescribed. She is expected to cry and scream to be let
go, and to beg for her mother to rescue her. She is expected to be modest and
maidenly. Should the bride not show the proper surprise and horror, the order of

festivities changes. The tricks stop and the shower becomes more conventional.[3] Such a bride is believed by many to be perhaps "experienced" and not a virgin.

If a girl is pregnant or is known to have had sexual experience, the shower takes on a more conventional form. There are gifts and some joking, but it is mild. Interestingly, some of the respondents admit that the original purpose of the shower, to socialize and educate for sex and for the anticipated first night, may not be as necessary as before.[4] Still, they feel that it should be done "for the fun of it"—for the sociability.

Homemaker Role

The women at the older edge of the age range who are attending the shower may have a different socializing purpose. Although Dominican girls are taught from an early age to cook and perform domestic tasks at home, it was the duty of the older women at the showers, especially in the Dominican Republic, to give advice on the care of house and husband, particularly the presentation of food and the treatment of the husband in terms of comfort. They may propose the ironing of sheets, for example. Their gifts are more likely to have some relationship with cleaning and housekeeping.

At the showers observed, there was very little discussion of the housekeeper role, but participants at showers in the Dominican Republic mention that it is still a component there. In the Dominican Republic the future bride is advised to talk with her future mother-in-law in order to find out what the future husband likes or dislikes, especially with regard to food. Along similar lines, she is advised to clean the house well, particularly the bedroom and bathroom since these are the two rooms that men use the most. She is advised to serve his meals properly and make sure that he has everything he needs at the table, including toothpicks, napkin, and cold water. She is also told that she should keep herself well groomed in order to hold his interest in her as a woman. She should be tolerant, kind, understanding, show him compassion, and be sweet all the time. This type of premarital conversation with the future mother-in-law does not seem to take place in this country.

The Subservient Status of Women

The marriage is said to be in the bride's hands. She is said to be solely responsible for its success and for the happiness and comfort of her husband. Traditionally, she was dependent upon him for financial and emotional support. It will be her fault if the marriage breaks up. The woman internalizes these norms and is expected to conform. If the man leaves, it is believed that she was responsible. If he strays, that is to be expected: it is "natural" for a man to have others. And as for nagging, or even mentioning the man's misbehavior, that is worse than anything he may do. The proper role is for a wife to act even more loving and understanding.

The internalization of these values is associated with the concept of machismo,[5] the superiority of the male over the female in every area. A frequent theme is the wife's inadequacy as a sexual partner. If the husband is unfaithful and needs an excuse, or is impotent, or feels some dissatisfaction, it is her fault. Her vagina is too big rather than that he is an inept lover. The size of the women's vagina is believed to be critical to the sexual satisfaction of both. She may be told to use ointments that will shrink her vagina temporarily before having sex. The size of the vagina is a subject of conversation among the girls and women and a good deal of anxiety is reflected in the conversation and jokes. There is little acknowledgment that the clitoris is the primary area of female pleasure and that more expert manipulation or adjustment might make sexual satisfaction a reality for both. Blaming the size of the vagina allows the man to say that it is the woman's fault for being "so big"—and she, internalizing his perspective, agrees.

Some respondents speak of the old days in the Dominican Republic when, in the event proof of virginity was lacking, the wife could be sent back to her parents. One respondent, whose husband trained as a physician in the Dominican Republic, notes that even recently operations have been performed, primarily on upper-middle-class women who might have had sexual experience, to restore their hymen or to at least make penetration seem difficult. Another respondent, who was a virgin at the time of her marriage ten years ago but did not bleed, notes that her husband (who is not a Dominican) still mentions it and that it is the last word in any argument they have.

The concept of *machismo* is broader than explicit sexual relations. It also covers the wife's contact with men and women in general. Under the rules of *machismo*:

1. No males are allowed to visit a woman when her husband is not at home.
2. She is not allowed to "'hang out" with a group of friends.
3. She is to restrict her friendship to females.
4. She should not be too friendly with others of either sex.

Many jokes told at the shower are forms of reactions to *machismo*. Most jokes are antimale and tend to fall into two categories. The first has to do with sexual inadequacy on the part of the husband. The second has to do with his cuckoldry. In both cases, the women may be expressing the laughter of the oppressed. The jokes are a way to say that which is unsayable, that there is an unequal distribution of power. The jokes constitute an ideological attack on a system, and make manifest another ideology: that the weaker one may also have a weapon; that "he" is not so powerful after all and "she" may have a weapon at her disposal. The antimale joke that follows has been translated from the Spanish:

APARTMENT FOR RENT

A prosperous businessman propositioned a prostitute, and she agreed to spend the night with him for the sum of five hundred dollars. When he departed the following morning, he told her that he didn't carry money with him, but he would tell his secretary to send a check with the indication that the check was for renting an "apartment." On the way to his office, he felt that the "program" did not warrant the fee and was not worth the amount agreed upon, and for that reason he ordered his secretary to send a check for two hundred dollars with the following note:

Dear Mrs.:
I am sending you a check for the renting of your apartment. I am not sending the amount agreed upon because when I rented your apartment, I was under the impression

1. That it had never been used;
2. That it had heat; and
3. That it was small.

But last night, I noticed that it had been used, that it did not have heat, and that it was excessively big.

The prostitute had hardly received the note before she sent back the check with the following note:

Dear Sir:
I am sending back your check of two hundred dollars, since I do not understand how you can have imagined that such a pretty apartment would not have been previously occupied. In reference to the heat, I want to tell you that you didn't know how to turn it on, and as for the size, I am not at fault that you did not have sufficient household goods to fill it.

ETHNIC ADAPTATION IN THE BRIDAL SHOWER

In New York City, the Dominican bridal shower appears in two forms, the "pure" Dominican shower and the American-Dominican shower. A "pure" shower is characterized by Dominican hospitality and warmth shown to people in general. The Dominican tendency to share, to talk, to open themselves up makes everyone feel at home. Fewer commercially purchased items are used. For decorations, pictures taken from pornographic magazines are usually used. The dildoes are all homemade rather than bought in sex-item stores. The snacks and refreshments are personally served and the souvenirs are individually pinned on the guests. This is not always true at American-Dominican showers.

The language spoken at the "pure" Dominican showers is Spanish, whereas at the American-Dominican one, bilingualism is quite prevalent. Here the guests are found forming little social groups who chatter among themselves. They also help themselves to the snacks and refreshments. The difference, it appears, is that the "pure" shower is more strongly characterized by collectivism, while the American adaptation reflects more individualism.

The Americanized bride-to-be seems to show less shock and astonishment at the goings-on than does the "pure" Dominican bride, whose reaction is very strong, spontaneous, and full of tears. The sexually explicit material that is shown her often brings about refusals to look at or to participate in the acts. However, the American-Dominican bride-to-be responds less dramatically and seems to enjoy it all. This "take-it-on-the-chin" attitude of the Americanized bride seems to be the result of having been exposed to much more sexual information, either in school, at work, on television, or at the movies.

Another important distinction between American-Dominican showers and their "pure" counterparts is the integration of different ethnic features in the ceremony. There is a considerable influence of Puerto-Rican and Cuban culture in some showers held in New York City, whether they are "pure" or American-Dominican. This is illustrated by the types of litanies and dirty poems read at the showers. Most of the vulgar words used to describe sexual organs and acts are slang from Puerto Rico or Cuba. For example, the word *"pinga"* is Cuban slang for "penis" and *"chocha"* is a Puerto Rican slang word for "vagina." The Dominican immigrants have learned the words through social interaction with other Hispanic groups domiciled in the city. In fact, many Dominican males were nicknamed *"Chicho"* at home, but are not called that here, since for Puerto Ricans it is the slang word for "sexual intercourse." As has already been noted, vulgarity is not commonly used by Dominican women, but is quite acceptable and indeed pertinent at the showers in both countries.

The showers are rapidly being affected by the technology of modern society. The tape recorder is taking the place of written notes; the film projector is beginning to replace the sex education "classes" held at most ceremonies; and cameras are being used to record these events. This is happening not only here, but also in the Dominican Republic, probably introduced there by Dominican immigrants who travel constantly between the two places.[6]

CONCLUSION

Exploration of the showers suggests that they might be a good indicator of the degree of assimilation to American values of marital egalitarianism, even allowing for class differences within the Dominican family structure, particularly in New York but also perhaps in the Dominican Republic.[7] It used to be that *"New Yorkinas"*—girls who grew up in or came to New York—were seen to be on the track of a loose life: corrupted somehow, nonvirginal, or at least on the way to being that way. But the true "corruption" may be nonacceptance of the traditional subservient role, a major change that immigration has brought. There is a continuous exchange between the Dominican Republic and Dominicans in New York. People go back and forth. When they first came here, the old norms remained strong at first. But changes in the family structure having to do with economic and social life here in New York have changed some of the norms and have at least made others the focus of conflict.

Both men and women work here in New York. In fact, the employment opportunities for women in factories and the garment district may be better than for men. More women go to school than men. Many young women serve as the brokers for their families, dealing with city officials and social agencies and thus gaining experience and autonomy. The broker role, traditional for men in the Dominican Republic, serves here to give women power in their families; but it may also cause conflicts. For example, a woman's fiancée may retain the traditional values of Dominican family life, even though he may be earning no more than she and may be less educated. The shower, whether reflecting old or new norms, prescribes and reinforces some of the traditional roles for the bride. But she, while enjoying the attention her friends are paying her, may be making an adjustment that will not necessarily be helpful to her in her new status as a married woman in a family structure that is in flux. Changes in the social context in which the marriage will be embedded, as well as the urban environment in which she lives, require education, independence, and aggressiveness on the part of both men and women.

A CASE STUDY: MARIA'S SHOWER

José and Maria, who met at a party in Upper Manhattan, have now been going out for eight months. Their relationship had to be approved by Maria's parents, who ultimately agreed that José could visit her regularly at her home. Since they decided to have a steady relationship, it was expected that a formal engagement would follow. José bought Maria an engagement ring and presented it to her in front of her parents. Their next step was to set up a wedding date. Maria decided to get married in spring. Maria's friends and relatives were anxious to learn the exact date of the wedding. Her best friend and her future sister-in-law wanted to give her a shower. They felt that it would be good for her to participate in one, since it would be a time for her to have fun with all her friends before she got married. Two weeks prior to the wedding, the word was spread, at her job, at the church, at the local bodega, and throughout the neighborhood that she was going to have a shower. Nobody was supposed to reveal to Maria that such an event was being planned for her. It could not take place at her home because the preparations might make her suspicious. It would no longer be a surprise, as it is supposed to be. Her best friend offered her apartment in Washington Heights (Manhattan), which she and two other friends cleaned and decorated, particularly the living room. On a Saturday evening in March, one week before the wedding, the shower was held. When the planners invited other friends, they suggested that they bring dirty jokes, "fresh" gifts, and anything else that would amuse and embarrass the bride-to-be. They divided up the work, and two women made kipper and pastelitos; these were the snacks that would be served at the shower along with Pepsi-Cola and orange soda.[8]

One hour before the shower everything was ready. During this time, the guests, all females, arrived and awaited the bride-to-be's entrance at seven o'clock. Thirty-four well-dressed women of all ages, most of them in their twenties, were present at the ceremony. However, one young girl fifteen years of age was in attendance. The living room contained a decorated chair with an umbrella placed above it, a wishing well, and a table with an elaborately decorated pink cake on it. Under the chair was a tape recorder. On the wall were pornographic pictures of nude white men and women with abnormally large genitalia and of couples engaged in various stages of sexual intercourse. In the center of these pictures, a large home-made penis had been placed. It was made by one of the participants out of a nylon stocking and paper. (The woman who made it is Cuban; she stated that she loved to go to bridal showers.) Next to the cake was a doll dressed in pink with a hot dog on its head.

All of the participants were from Latin America. They began discussing their own experiences on their wedding nights. A Dominican said that she almost died of a heart attack when she saw her husband naked for the first time: "He had a big member." Another participant replied, "It's quality not quantity that counts."

Some of the women admitted that they were afraid on their wedding night, and others said that they were anxious to find out what it really was like to have sex for the first time. All of the participants engaged in this type of conversation.

At the moment of the bride-to-be's arrival, one of the women said, "She's coming. Silent! Quiet!" There was a lot of tension in the air, as people tried to decide where to place themselves so as to completely surprise the bride. The light was turned off. One of the women was standing in the middle of the room with a glass of water in her hands. When the bride appeared in the doorway, the water was thrown in her face and everyone shouted, "Surprise!" The bride covered her face and began to cry. She said, "José and I have an appointment with the priest right now, but I guess that we will have to go another day."

Everyone was speaking Spanish, telling jokes, and generally having fun. The only words spoken in English were "Okay" and "Nice." A young woman took the penis from the wall and pinned it on the bride as a corsage. The bride-to-be begged, "No, please. It's ugly!" The woman replied, "You have to wear it because from now on, you're always going to have one chasing you and following you around." Another woman asked the bride to put it into her mouth. She refused to do so. Another woman took it and forced it into Maria's mouth. "There's nothing to be afraid of! Just be a good girl. This is harmless in comparison to what you're marrying." Another person asked, "Do you like it the way it is—hard like a rock?" Whenever the bride touched it, other women would say, "Oh, look how she caresses it. I knew you were going to like it."

One woman took a glass filled with ice and forced the bride's finger into it. She had to keep her finger in it until it hurt so that she could beg and scream for them to stop, saying things like, "Please stop doing this to me. I hate you. Are you crazy or something? I didn't know you were going to do this to me." Meanwhile, everything she was saying was being recorded. This was later played back for the groom at the shower's end. The women then said to him, "Listen to all the things she's going to say to you on your wedding night."

A woman picked up a penis that she had made from the protective rubber of her sewing machine and dropped it in Maria's lap, saying, "This thing loves to be between legs. You have to get accustomed to it." Another woman said, "Do you know which number is going to be your favorite? You mark my words, it will be sixty-nine." Another participant showed Maria a red baby-doll nightgown and told her, "Come on and put it on! Take off your panty-hose." Maria seemed surprised and said, "I am okay in my dress." A woman told her, "No, you have to wear the gown, now." Two women helped her to undress and to put on the nightgown while others applauded and commented, "She is going to look good. Not bad! You're going to drive him crazy. Sexy. That's the way he wants you." A woman picked up the home-made dildo and quickly rubbed it on the bride-to-be's vulva. Another young woman who was standing up said to her, "I am going to show you the woodpecker style, but you have to be drunk to do it." She stuck her tongue in and out and said, "Pick, pick, with the tip of your tongue. Touch his ass simultaneously right in the hole." Everyone laughed, and the bride-to-be, although laughing with them, was amazed. A woman in her late thirties approached Maria, who said to the women, "Look, auntie, what these women are doing to me." Her aunt smiled at her and another woman stood up and said, "Listen to Maria's prayer. She used to say this prayer every night before she met José." A litany was read aloud and everyone laughed at each sentence. The name of the litany was "A Virgin's Bedside Prayer." After the litany had been read, the reader asked the bride-to-be, "Is this true? No, don't answer because we know it's true." Maria told them that they were "a bunch of fresh women." She was beginning to feel more comfortable. Meanwhile a copy of *Playgirl* magazine was being passed around and the women made jokes about the naked men, the size of their penises, etc. Suddenly, someone cried out, "José is coming!" Immediately, a young woman impersonating a man walked in. Everyone began to laugh. She had a home-made penis hanging from the zipper of her pants. She came up to the bride and wiped the penis across her face. Then she took Maria's hand and made her squeeze the penis. "This is yours, my love." Laughing, the bride pushed her away. Then the young girl with the "penis" began chasing all the women in the room. Everyone was having fun.

A native of Colombia had brought a film projector along to show some X-rated films. Everyone sat on the floor and the first film was shown. It was about two women engaged in a homosexual relationship. Most of the women protested and one of them said, "We don't want to see homosexuals. We want to see the real thing." Finally, the woman changed the film. Another woman said to Maria, "Pay attention, Maria!" The film showed two women engaged in various sexual acts with a man who was in a bathtub. Someone said to Maria, "You have to be ready to do it anywhere at anytime, Maria." The film showed the man ejaculating, and someone said to the bride, "Look at all that milk. You have to get accustomed to it. And look at how vulnerable a man can be when he comes!" The film ended and the kipper and pastelitos were served to the guests by two of the women in attendance.

At the time that this was happening, a thirty-five-year-old Dominican woman was giving Maria advice and telling her to wear something blue, something old, and something new on her wedding day for good luck. (It is part of the Dominican folklore to do this.) Two young women suggested that she should start opening her gifts. The first gift that she opened was a table set. Then she opened a box containing kitchen utensils and other boxes containing bathroom towels, an automatic broom, a nightgown, etc. On the whole, the gifts were household gifts, mainly items for use in the kitchen or bathroom. (There seemed to be a great deal of curiosity about who brought which gift.) The bride thanked everyone for their gifts and at 10 P.M. she was helped into her street clothes and prepared for the arrival of José. Then someone said to her, "Maria, guess who's here?" José shook hands with all the women and some of the male relatives, who came in when it was clear that the shower had ended. No one discussed what had gone on during the shower and at 11 P.M. everyone went home, including the bridal couple.

NOTES

1. Arnold van Gennep, *The Rites of Passage* (Chicago: Univ. of Chicago Press, 1960), p. 67.

2. Of the seven showers observed, there was nudity or near-nudity of the bride-to-be in six cases. There was some discrepancy in the reports of the respondents about its

occurrence at showers. Some respondents said that it was not typical and, in fact, violated strong norms of personal modesty.

3. The word "conventional" represents what the respondents say is more like an "*American* shower" (emphasis ours).

4. The respondents noted that some girls had attended sex education classes in school in New York City. Some said they had gotten information from friends and had attended other showers. Many made a point of saying that their mothers had told them nothing.

5. For a general discussion, see Manuel de Js. Guerrero, *El Machismo en Republica Dominica* (Santo Domingo, R.D.: Amigo del Hogar, 1975).

6. See Glenn Hendricks, *The Dominican Diaspora* (New York: Teachers College Press, 1974).

7. Comparative family structure, including Latin America, is described in Betty Yorburg, *Sexual Identity: Sex Roles and Social Change* (New York: John Wiley & Sons, 1974). See also Vivian Mota, "Politics and Feminism in the Dominican Republic: 1931–45 and 1966–74," in June Nash and Helen Icken Safa (eds.), *Sex and Class in Latin America* (Brooklyn: J. F. Bergin, 1980).

8. At the showers, alcoholic beverages are typically served only to the bride-to-be.

ACKNOWLEDGMENTS

The authors would like to thank Carmen Salcedo and Altagracia Mejia for the initial invitations and Vernon Boggs for his encouragement of the study.

| CHAPTER SEVEN | # Power and Intimacy |

22

Politics and Politesse: Gender Deference and Formal Etiquette*

Pearl W. Bartelt, Mark Hutter, and David W. Bartelt

In the persistently hierarchical relationship between men and women, the mechanisms of control range from the wage-scale to the legal system, and from expressly sexist regulations to verbal forms of disapproval and censure. In this catalog of controls, the etiquette handbook plays a significant role. At once both an arbiter to social propriety and a guide to attaining a mystical ideal of perfect domestic order, these handbooks have played, and continue to play, a significant part in developing a gender-specific behavioral ideal for women. In this paper, we report the results of an analysis of these handbooks, and argue that these works both describe "proper" behavior for women and delimit those situations within which women should appear, and in what roles. They describe, in short, the deferential behavior necessary for women to move in an acceptable fashion in a male-dominated social structure.

The prescription of deferential behavior for women by women could be analyzed as another example of simple adaptation to structural inequality, with etiquette books providing the guidelines for "getting by," as it were. While a part of this may well be accurate, we have chosen to focus on a different aspect of the handbook. We feel that these handbooks provide an excellent example of what Mills (1940) termed "situated actions and vocabularies of motive." That is, these handbooks provide a case in which normative structures become part of a vocabulary of motives which rationalize and defend deferential behavior as it oc-

*Bartelt, Pearl W., Mark Hutter, and David W. Bartelt. 1986. "Politics and Politesse: Gender Deference and Formal Etiquette." *Studies in Symbolic Interaction* 7, Part A: 199–228. Copyright © 1986 by JAI Press, Inc., Greenwich, Connecticut. Reprinted by permission.

curs. Thus, etiquette handbooks, while playing an important structural role in the persistence of male-female hierarchies, also have an interactional meaning within the day-to-day behavior of women who defer to a male-ordered world.

As can be expected, we have addressed this analysis from the specific theoretical perspective of symbolic interactionism. We have also borrowed from the fields of literary criticism and hermeneutics in our attempt to analyze a deeper structure of etiquette texts. We feel that the symbolic interactional perspective, while traditionally astructural and ahistorical in nature (Meltzer, Petras, and Reynolds 1975), has shown a marked facility for interpreting the internal dynamics of a social relationship. There have been, in fact, attempts to broaden the perspective with analyses of face-to-face inequality (Goffman 1956), social definitions reflective of superordinate positions (Blumer 1958), and external status identifiers (Braroe 1970; Stone 1970, pp. 256–59). Work focusing on gender inequality is also present in Goffman's (1977) analysis of sexual "arrangements."

We assume in this paper that there is a persistent structural inequality involved in the social relationships between males and females. We examine here a major component of that inequality—the development of formal rules of conduct (etiquette) which provide a ready-made, and standardized, vocabulary of motives for major social situations which persistently involve women as major actors. These rules of etiquette, we assert, have inherent in them a subordinating status. These rules, further, are persistent through time—they make the subordination of women a historical feature of multiple situations, transcending any specific situation and any specific rule. Perhaps most significantly, they make the subordinate status of women an integral part of the social definition of propriety.

THE HISTORICAL CONTEXT

The Industrial Revolution shattered the domestic economy where work and family activities were integrated in the household. The rise of industrial and monopolistic capitalism separated men and women into two isolated worlds: the world of work and the world of the household. This had the effect of separating the life of the husbands from the intimacies of everyday domestic activities and estranging them from their wives and children. Economic factors coincided with a misguided Victorian partriarchialism that saw economic employment as a threat to womanly virtue and to her physical and emotional well-being (Hutter 1981).

Nineteenth-century Victorian society was organized in such a way that it heightened the dichotomy between private and public, domestic and social, female and male. Through the restrictions of the conjugal family, women tended to be relegated to the domestic sphere. Yet, when the society placed values on men's and women's work, the tendency was to place greater value and higher priority on the public work associated with men rather than the domestic work associated with women.

Engels in his *The Origin of the Family, Public Property and the State* ([1884] 1972) was quick to point out the alienating character of women's domestic work. The gradual loss of women's economic independence led to an increased division of labor between men and women and to the subservience of women to men.

Engels spells out the implications of the development of the "privatization of the family" for women:

> her being confined to domestic work now assured supremacy in the house for man; the woman's housework lost its significance compared with the man's work in obtaining a livelihood; the latter was everything, the former an insignificant contribution . . . (Engels, [1884] 1972 p. 152)

The privatization of the family with its withdrawal from economic and community activities led to the development of inequality within the family. This inequality was based on the sexual differentiation of labor. In the private sphere, this differentiation was encouraged by the admonitions placed on women to cease work and take almost exclusive care of small children and to sacrifice their career aspirations to those of their husbands. In the public sphere, in addition to women's forced withdrawal from the marketplace and the work force, urban public places and facilities were designed, for the most part, to inhibit or discourage women's participation in them. Normative strictures supported the social and legal constraints to perpetuate the assignment of women to the domestic, private sphere. They justified the almost exclusive involvement of men in the higher valued and higher status activities of the public sphere. The role of etiquette books in the articulation of these normative strictures is the focus of this paper.

THEORETICAL ELEMENTS: SYMBOLIC INTERACTIONISM MEETS SEXUAL POLITICS

Most interactionist treatments of normative aspects of behavior refer back to Goffman's basic essays "On Face Work: An Analysis of Ritual Elements in Social Interaction" (1955) and "The Nature of Deference and Demeanor" (1956), in which he is concerned with rules of conduct. Rules of conduct are seen as guiding behavior in two ways: as obligations they provide moral constraints on an individual's behavior; and as expectations they provide information on the behavior of others also guided by those constraints. Thus, rules of conduct are mutual and reciprocal and provide operational guidelines for participants' behaviors in social interaction.

Goffman delineates two types of rules of conduct—that between "substance" and "ceremony." Substantive rules which guide conduct are expressed in law, morality, and ethics while ceremonial rules which guide conduct are expressed in etiquette. Goffman focuses his attention on the rules of etiquette, applying what Lindesmith, Strauss, and Denzin (1977, pp. 398–403) refer to as an "interactional loss" analysis of human interaction. That is, the participants of the interaction are concerned with assuring the regularity and order of the interaction and the maintenance of "face" or self-esteem of the participants.

Norms, or the concept of normative structures, have always been troublesome elements in theories accounting for structured social relationships—particularly ones based on conflict or inequality. Put briefly, norms are not always consistent, not always followed, and not always applied, and are seldom clear-cut and unambiguous. The concept implies, then, a structure of power and enforcement for the development, application, interpretation, and change of norms. Further theoretical problems arise when one adopts an interactionist approach, which makes the individual's adherence to social norms problematic rather than automatic. Mills, in an early article, presents one resolution of this issue, adopted as well by Lindesmith et al. (Mills 1940; Lindesmith et al. 1977, p. 275). Mills begins with the proposition that behavior does not occur in a vacuum, but in a social situation whose parameters are mutually defined by the actors in a situation. Once a situation is understood, the behavior that takes place is symbolically interpreted by the participants according to a vocabulary of motives — a set of explanations of behavior which a person attaches to himself or herself and to others in the situation. Norms are, in the context of this vocabulary, explanations of behavior conforming to some actor or actors' expectations.

Placed within a hierarchical relationship, published codes of conduct, such as etiquette, are best understood as formalized, public statements which explain the deferential behavior of subordinates, both to themselves and others. Etiquette texts provide these vocabularies for social situations which persistently involve women as major actors, and act as a set of authoritative behavioral guideposts on the social landscape. As such, they constitute an accessible indicator of persistence and change in the nature of the relationships of inequality between men and women, as well as viable illustrations of the propriety of subordination.

Goffman (1977) offers an analysis of sexual arrangements which supplements the argument we have developed thus far. He notes, "The sociologically interesting thing about a disadvantaged category is not the painfulness of the disadvantage but the bearing of the social structure on its generation and stability. The issue then, is not that women get less but under what arrangements this occurs and what symbolic reading is given to the arrangement" (1977, p. 307). Goffman considers women as a disadvantaged group with particular distinctions. First, unlike other disadvantaged adult groups women are not sequestered off into entire families or neighborhoods; they are an integral part of the family. But, through their extensive involvements with the family of orientation and the family of procreation they develop ideological commitments with their menfolk which are supportive of the advantaged position of men in society. "Women are . . . separated from one another by the stake they acquire in the very organization which divides them" (Goffman 1977, p. 308). Secondly, they are held in high regard. Through ritualized conduct they are defined as being fragile and valuable and consequently they have to be sheltered through the harsher things in life. Here Goffman (1977, p. 311) articulates the importance of the "courtesy" system in expressing this condition:

> In terms of what interpersonal rituals convey, the belief (in Western society) is that women are precious, ornamental, and fragile, uninstructed in, and ill-suited for, anything requiring muscular exertion or mechanical or electrical training or physical risk; further, that they are easily subject to contamination and defilement and to blanching when faced with harsh words and cruel facts, being labile as well as delicate. It follows, then, that males will have the obligation of stepping and helping (or protecting) whenever it appears that a female is threatened or taxed in any way,

shielding her from gory, grisly sights, from squeamish-making things like spiders and worms, from noise, and from rain, wind, cold, and other inclemencies. Intercession can be extended even to the point of mediating her contacts with officials, strangers, and service personnel.

Goffman's explicit enumeration of the several ways in which men intervene on women's behalf contains an implicit message as well. The multiple specific instances of male "protection" of women generate, in their very multiplicity, a sense of permanent dependence and subordination.

In a later work, *Gender Advertisements* (1979), Goffman notes the same principle of deference expressed in multiple forms. While predominately a visual text, this work examines the implicit gender deference found in the realm of advertising. The case Goffman makes is fairly straightforward, namely that the advertisement of products reproduces gender inequality in its imagery as a significant aspect of the sales process. Thus, mirroring his earlier analysis, while multiple products are advertised, and multiple forms of body language are catalogued, one must assume that the persistence of male gender dominance in virtually all gender-based advertising represents an idealization of male dominance. (The interested reader is referred to Winter, 1981, for a more systematic treatment of the reading of visual "texts" and the determination of structural relations from them.)

In this paper we wish to examine the rules of etiquette which govern the face-to-face interaction of males and females in everyday life. Etiquette books will be used as our indicator since they provide one systematic source of these rules. Our logic is consistent with that of Sherri Cavan, who states "while all appropriate rules of etiquette are not actualized in all situations at all times, these books can serve at least as a partial codification of the precepts of befitting modes of general conduct" (1970 p. 556). We will be looking at etiquette books written since early in the century to see how the rules of conduct have provided guidelines to regulate that relationship.

In particular, we will focus our attention on the hierarchical characteristics of that relationship and how it is handled in etiquette books. A major component ordering the male-female relationship is the superordinate and subordinate positions; we are interested in how this is articulated in etiquette books.

In etiquette books, the concepts of superordinate and subordinate positions are very interesting because at first glance it often appears that the subordinate is really the superordinate. The potential for confusion occurs if one equates placement on a pedestal as superordinate.

Thus, while etiquette books indicate that men should show deference and respect to women in actuality this is a subterfuge for an underlying reduction in status for women. While they advocate the "benefits" they downplay the inherent inferiority and fail to recognize that they actually limit female options. Games of deference, however, often act to keep someone in their place, namely, in a subordinate position.

Another interesting point is that the books are written for the subordinate. Paradoxically, it becomes the task of the person in this subordinate position to impose the strictures of etiquette upon others. It may be that language implying the superordinate position (respect, deference, etc.) is used to gain cooperation of women. The books themselves may be a contributing factor in the acceptance of this subordinate position.

An additional explanation illustrates why females need the etiquette books and males do not. Daniels (1975, p. 343) states that "Those in the superordinate status will find this structure undergirding their privileged condition natural or even virtually invisible. Those who are below them are more cognizant of the costs of the system and so are less likely to feel that the system is natural." Since it is not natural for them the women need to be taught etiquette.

Henley and Freeman (1975) have observed that everyday interaction patterns reflect the subordination of women to men and are a fundamental source of social control employed by men against women. Further, by constant repetition these patterns become habitual and are taken for granted; the hierarchical power significance which underlies these patterns becomes obscure:

> By being continually reminded of their inferior status in the interaction with others, and continually compelled to acknowledge that status in their own patterns of behavior, women learn to internalize society's definition of them as inferior so thoroughly that they are often unaware of what their status is. Inferiority becomes habitual, and the inferior place assumes the familiarity—and even desirability—of home (1975 p. 391).

Henley and Freeman argue that if women are to fully understand the nature of sexual politics in everyday interactional patterns they must systematically analyze how they are affected by them and how they perpetuate the power and status of men. This same position of the women's involvement in the process is a part of our paper in the examination of etiquette.

Henley, in her later work (1977), discussed nonverbal behavior between males and females that involves power. She examines address, demeanor, posture, personal space, time, touching, eye contact, facial expression, and self-disclosure. Differential gesture behavior between females and males follow the same relationship as gestures between status nonequals with males following the behavior of the superior and females following the behavior of the subordinate (Henley 1977, p. 181). Indeed, even when women follow patterns to assert dominance (as in the case of eye make-up to increase staring) the assumption of the gesture becomes interpreted sexually rather than as a gesture of dominance.

One of the more interesting techniques employed to show the importance of gesture in subordinate, superordinate positioning of females and males is a set of exercises designed for males by Williamette Bridge (Henley 1977, pp. 143–44). Here men are directed to sit, bend, run, and walk in the fashion appropriate for a female. These kinesics that are appropriate for females are just those postures which connote submission rather than power.

A similar orientation to our study is that of Gordon and Shankweiler (1971) who view marriage manuals in terms of sexual ideology. They note that the traditional definition of ideology refers to a body of beliefs and values which have a legitimating function for the status quo. Ideology tends to support and give substance to the position of dominance of one group over another. Translated into the study of sexual ideology, males are seen as the dominating group with females subservient and subordinate to them.

METHODOLOGY

After presenting the method used in this study we will turn our attention to these etiquette books and see in more illustrative detail how etiquette manuals articulated this sexist ideology. As noted earlier, our areas of concern will be behavior in public places and everyday life, domestic relations, and women and work. The preselection of these categories derived from the perspective that assumes there is a division of major worlds within which women participate—the public arena, the home, and the workplace, (See, for example, Siltanen and Stanworth 1984.)

(It should be noted that while recent etiquette books have dealt with more "modern" conditions, such as single parenting and divorce situations, these areas did not allow for the kind of historical analysis we were concerned with. Clearly, these and many other topics in these texts may prove amenable to a similar analysis. Given our concern with continuity, such a consideration lies outside the purview of this analysis.)

Obviously the etiquette books in the sample covered a large range of materials. We found that the three main areas we had selected were covered in all of the books and consistently addressed male–female relations.

The etiquette books that are in this study form a purposive sample. The books that are presented were collected from a variety of public and academic libraries throughout the Philadelphia–southern New Jersey area. The variety included a large urban university, a private liberal arts college, a four-year state college, a large urban public library, and small county affiliated borough libraries. We felt that this diversity would provide the depth of materials needed for a qualitative analysis of the materials.

These works are an indication of these libraries' current holdings and reflect a variety of historical periods. We selected library holdings since the library historically serves as a reference place for etiquette materials. We systematically extracted anecdotal records from all of the works and selected all etiquette admonition procedures that involved males and/or females specifically. We then selected those items that best illustrated the composite and diversity of all the data for a particular topic.

It was decided that only those books published from the turn of the century to the present would be used. They therefore range from a publication date of 1899 to the present and include one author's continuing updating (Vanderbilt 1957, 1972, 1974).

A HISTORY OF AMERICAN ETIQUETTE BOOKS

A brief overview of the history of American etiquette books beginning within the context of nineteenth-century industrial urban society may be of value here. As we noted at the beginning of this paper, the Industrial Revolution had a profound effect on women. For the mid-nineteenth-century family it meant the separation of men and women into two isolated worlds: the world of work and the world of the household.

In terms of involvement in city life, Victorian partriarchal ideology developed the belief that it would be best for the protection of women that they minimize their contact with it. Women were directed to develop a life comprised solely of concerns centered around the family, the home, and the school. Their contacts with the outside world, particularly economic employment, diminished and they were removed from other community involvements as well. The family's withdrawal from the community was tinged by its hostile attitude toward the surrounding city (Hutter 1983). The city was depicted as a sprawling and planless development bereft of meaningful community and neighborhood relationships. The tremendous movement of a large population into the urban industrial centers was seen to provide little opportunity for the family to form or develop deep or lasting ties with neighbors. Instead the family viewed their neighbors with suspicion and wariness. Exaggerated beliefs developed on the prevalence of urban poverty, crime, and disorganization. The perceived chaotic world of the city was countered by the family turning in onto itself—what Karl Marx has described as the privatization of the family.

The effects of urban industrial growth combined with what Barbara J. Berg (1978) has labeled the "women-belle ideal." The tenets of this creed held that women were inferior, that they should be denied access to the institutions of knowledge and given little responsibility. The result was the production of "an anomalous sector of society: the useless lady" (Berg 1978, p. 96). Sheila M. Rothman (1978) makes a similar observation. Rothman (1978, p. 21) argues that the consequence of the technological innovation and urban living for women was to provide them with leisure and to become consumers, not producers, of the new technology. The downtown department store was literally designed for the woman consumer. It was the notable exception that allowed for women's involvement in public urban places (Rothman 1978; Hutter 1983).

Virtuous womanhood was defined in similar ways by ministers, moralists, writers of advice books, and public lecturers as one in which there were distinct and separate tasks and reponsibilities for the sexes. The appropriate sphere for women was nurturance and caretaking. It is interesting to note that both Berg and Rothman see that the role of caretaker and nurturer was eventually extended outside the home to involvement in social welfare groups and agencies. Rothman cites Catherine Beecher, a very influential writer of advice books in the 1860s and 1870s who urged women to obtain "appropriate scientific and practical training for her distinctive profession as housekeeper, nurse of infants and the sick, educator of childhood, trainer of servants and minister of charities" and by so doing they would "develop the intellectual, social and moral powers in the most perfect manner" (1978, p. 22).

Etiquette books played an important role in the socialization process of the Victorian lady. They emphasized the importance of proper modes of acting to socially conscious Americans whether they were part of the upper class or not in the areas of deference, demeanor, and manners.

Arthur M. Schlesinger (1946), in an insightful monograph entitled *Learning How to Behave,* observed that etiquette manuals were published at the rate of five or six a year between 1870 and 1917. Their aim was to instill a more aristocratic style of behavior in the emerging middle classes. They also served to reinforce the "relative duties of superior and subordinate" (Schlesinger 1946, p. 34). A third factor, according to Schlesinger (p. 35), was desire to cultivate and sensitize American people to the social graces which were seen to lag behind their European counterparts.

> The emphasis on sophisticated manners led to exhaustive specifications of what to do in every conceivable situation: how high to lift one's skirt when crossing a street ("A lady should gracefully raise her dress a little above her ankle"); when and how to bow ("The head should be bent; a mere lowering of eye-lids, affected by some people, is rude"); how to shake hands (avoid either the "pump handle shake" or the "cold clammy hand" resembling a fish); how and when to write acceptances and regrets; how to make calls ("The formal call should not exceed fifteen minutes"); what to wear at morning functions, in the afternoon and at the ball or opera; and so on *ad infinitum*. Little wonder that one mentor proudly remarked that "not even a saint could, from his 'inner consciousness' alone, evolve a conception of the thousand and one social observances of modern fashionable life."

Esther B. Arestz (1970), in a popular account of etiquette notes that American etiquette books flourished during the first decade of the twentieth century; 71 etiquette books and twice that number of magazine articles were published. However, a significant change characterized these books. No longer did etiquette books claim to be written for "Society." Arestz attributed this to the low regard Americans had for the upper classes. "Society's reputation for vulgar spending and tasteless antics had gone from bad to shocking with millionaires staging dinner parties where guests in formal attire dined on horseback or drank toasts to a monkey as guest of honor" (Arestz 1970, p. 275). The focus of the new etiquette books was generally to improve the manners of middle class America.

After World War I, a major transition occurred in American social values. New wealth generated from the war was accompanied by the rejection of the rigidities of America's Victorian conventions. In addition, Prohibition, the automobile, and movies and radio, all encouraged the development of a more informal relationship between the sexes. These changes became incorporated into etiquette books without changing their basic orientations.

Etiquette books continued to be popular. Schlesinger (1946) reports that from 1918 to 1929 no less than 68 etiquette books were published and an additional 78 were published in the period from 1930 to 1945. The two most influential, Lillian Eichler's (1922) *Book of Etiquette* and Emily Post's *Etiquette: The Blue Book of Social Usage* written in 1922, sold over a million copies in the ensuing years. Schlesinger (1946) believes that their popularity stems from the continued social mobility of the social classes and "the need many earnest souls felt for a steadying hand in a period of bewildering flux in social conventions (p. 51). The publication of numerous etiquette books has continued since the end of World War II. Amy Vanderbilt's (1957, 1974), *McCall's Magazine's* (1960), and *Vogue's* (1948) and others have been quite popular, as have the continued revised editions of Emily Post's books. Baldrige (1978) has continued Vanderbilt's tradition and Ford (1980) and Martin (1982) have entered the field. Martin, as Miss Manners, has experienced considerable popularity.

While these manuals and others of the same ilk bowed to emerging new attitudes, i.e., women smoking in public, no chaperones, the proper usage of "Ms.," there can still be seen the perpetuation and continuation of traditional social values and particularly of patriarchal ideology. They still maintain the underlying sexist ideology of female subservience. Further, for American women, the rules of etiquette are particularly demeaning. Stemming from the sexist pedestal model of their English counterparts, American etiquette books continue a patriarchal viewpoint from the Victorian era to the present. An unbroken tradition of female subservience most symbolically represented in the restriction of the women to the home in relative isolation and of courtesy based on femininity continues.

The placement of American women on the pedestal has been particularly perfidious. Unlike England where social power frequently accompanied rules of etiquette, no vestige of social power can be claimed or articulated by American etiquette rules.

We have isolated three areas where these rules are most consistent over time; behavior in public places, at work, and in the home. The ubiquity of day-to-day situations contained in these three categories, combined with the significance of everyday interactions in maintaining deference in sexual politics, leads us to argue that etiquette guides contribute significantly to the subordination of women in American society.

BEHAVIOR IN PUBLIC PLACES AND IN EVERYDAY LIFE

David Reisman (see Reisman, Glazer, and Denney 1961) has observed that in societies which are relatively stable, peoples' conformity reflects their membership in particular age groupings, clan and caste groups. Behavior patterns are well established and have endured through a considerable period of time. However, in societies undergoing rapid social change such normative guidelines are inoperative. Etiquette rules are then established to control and regulate the important relationships of life.

In everyday life situations—walking, taking a streetcar, dining in public restaurants, the theater and cultural events, traveling—there arises the necessity to develop rules governing one's behavior and to provide predictability in such relatively anonymous situations. This was particularly true in the United States during the turn-of-the-century period. America was undergoing major social and industrial changes. Cities were expanding at a phenomenal rate. People were moving to urban areas from the rural areas of the South and Midwest. There was an unprecedented wave of immigration from eastern and southern Europe. To control this disparate population in these emerging communities, etiquette manuals were developed as one attempt to teach these norms of conduct and to do so explicitly. This was an attempt to maintain the status quo.

Lyn Lofland (1973) found in a review of etiquette books from 1881 to 1962 that there was a concentration on explicit instructions for public behavior during the earlier period and a gradual decreasing concern with these matters during the later one. This reflects the instability and unpredictability which people felt in the emerging industrial cities in the United States and the growing felt regularities in the cities of the mid-twentieth century. These concerns of the early etiquette books are demonstrated in such topics as:

> Street Etiquette: Recognizing friends on the street—Omitting to recognize acquaintances—Shaking hands with a lady—Young ladies conduct on the street—Accompanying visitors... —Conduct while shopping... —Carriage of a lady in public... —Meeting a lady acquaintance... —Riding and Driving... —Travelers and Traveling

These early guidebooks provide the reader with explicit instructions on how to behave in these public places. The general pattern of admonitions revolve around the areas of controlling the relationship of males and females who are strangers to each other. The following excerpts from Lillian Eichler's etiquette book in 1922 is illustrative:

> If a women drops her bag or gloves and they are retrieved by a passing man, it is necessary only to smile and say "Thank you." No further conversation is permissible (p. 194).
> When a gentleman sees that a woman passenger is having difficulty in raising a window he need feel no hesitancy in offering to assist her. However, the courtesy ends when the window has been raised (p. 224).

Green (1922) reaches a similar position:

> A man bowing and joining a woman on the street must ask permission to do so. She is at perfect liberty to gracefully decline (p. 47).
> A man may offer his services to a woman in crossing a crowded thoroughfare and should raise his hat and bow when she is safely over, but should make no comment unless she does so first. He may also offer his assistance in getting on or off a car, raising his hat and bowing without remark (p. 241).

These restrictions on peoples' behavior in public places continues to the present in more recent etiquette books. Boykin (1940, p. 229) states:

> A girl traveling alone should be especially reserved with members of the opposite sex. If not her attitude may be misunderstood and she may find herself in a situation she will not enjoy.

And, again, Amy Vanderbilt (1967, p. 167) continues to argue for the control of interaction among strangers in public places:

> A man touches his hat but does not look more than briefly at a woman to whom he gives up his seat (in a streetcar). He then stands as far away from her as possible and does not look in her direction.

When we shift our attention to other areas of public life—pedestrian behavior, shaking hands, opening doors, smoking in public, restaurant behavior, women's dress—we see a pattern which continues to be enunciated in contemporary etiquette books. The underlying rationale for this pattern is giving deference to women—opening doors, walking on the outside of sidewalks (to possibly prevent women being littered by splashes from the street or by garbage), asking women for permission to smoke. Underlying these deferential patterns is imputation of women's helplessness and frailty. This is, of course, accompanied by the more subtle but direct premise of women's subservience. This is the price exacted. The following guidelines illustrate this:

SEXUAL TRAFFIC

A man should always give a woman the right of way whenever it is possible, and cross behind her instead of in front of her (Hathaway 1928, p. 35).

Naturally a man always opens a door for a woman. She should draw aside when she is preceding him and permit him to do so. No gentleman is happy walking through a door a woman has opened (Wilson 1940, 18).

A man accompanying a woman "opens the door for her and holds it for her to go through. At a revolving door, he starts it off with a push and waits for her to go through." Also he "allows a woman to precede him, if single file formation is necessary, unless there is some service he can do for her by going first" (Fenwick 1948, p. 29).

Traditionally, a man preceded a woman through a revolving door in order to push the door for her. He was also the first one on the escalator, to be in a position to help the woman on and off. This ritual may still be practiced for form's sake, but if a woman reaches the conveyance first she needn't stand and wait unless she is elderly or is carrying packages and does in fact need help (Ford 1980, p. 60).

Gentlemen, to this very day, walk on the street side of the sidewalk, unless they are European gentlemen, in which case they walk to the lady's left. Miss Manners, who can bear the idea that styles of clothing change, but not that the small courtesies of life do, firmly believes that the only reason men do not tip their hats is the same as the reason they no longer smack one another across the face with their gloves when they are angry: They don't have the sartorial equipment (Martin 1982, p. 84).

GREETING RITUALS

Men always shake hands . . . A woman does not shake hands with a man unless he happens to be an intimate friend. In this case she may offer her hand if she wishes. However, under no circumstances may she ignore the overture should the hand be extended (Gardner and Farren 1937, p. 65).

A man always removes his hat when he meets a woman and keeps it off as long as they stand talking, unless the weather is very bad (Stephenson and Millett 1936, p. 72).

A man kissing a lady on the street—in greeting or farewell (only)—should always remove his hat, no matter what the weather. He should be careful concerning this courtesy even—or perhaps I should say especially with his wife or daughter (Vanderbilt 1974, p. 20).

Men should always stand, and most women prefer to, when being introduced to older people or to high officials. A man always stands when being introduced to another man or a woman, and today at small gatherings more and more women feel comfortable standing when the men stand to be introduced to a newcomer. I think it shows both consideration and a special interest to stand and devote your full attention to someone new. It is not out of place for a woman in a group of women to stand when introduced to someone new (Ford 1980, p. 30).

A gentleman must, in these circumstances, take what he is offered. If it is a hand, shake it. If it is a cheek, kiss it. If it is a pair of lips, kiss it. If it keeps reappearing, it must be rekissed. Remember that we are talking about a formal, public gesture, and the fact that parts of the body and ways they are used may duplicate private expressions of emotions is irrelevant. Just because gentlemen no longer have the exclusive right to initiate private kissing does not mean that they may now share in the ladies' privilege of initiating—or withholding—public kissing (Martin 1982, p. 79).

COSTUME

Women dress in keeping with their companion, not vice-versa (Hathaway 1928, p. 43).

When a man can't or won't dress for an occasion it is bad taste for the woman who he escorts to be dressed to the hilt, and while I feel a certain informality in entertaining tends to relax us all, it shouldn't relax us so much that we become completely graceless (Vanderbilt 1974, p. 268).

SMOKING

Well-bred women do not smoke when it will make them conspicuous, or when it will embarrass or offend anyone who is with them (Hathaway 1928, p. 43).

A man lights a woman's cigarette first unless there is a high wind, in which case he lights his own first, and his female companion's from his cigarette (Vanderbilt 1974, p. 19).

Underlying all these admonitions is the philosophy of female helplessness, weaknesses, and frailties. Bevans in the 1960 edition of *McCall's Etiquette Book* states that "Man's treatment of women is based on a time when women were considered muscularly (hence mentally) the inferior sex. In return for knuckling under to this attitude of male superiority, women demanded and got many special considerations based on their weaknesses and helplessness. Manners of men toward women are still to a great extent based on this ancient blackmail, although the reason for it has long since been disproven" (Bevans 1960, p. 11). A similar conclusion was reached by Elizabeth Post (1975): "Femininity is still more attractive in a woman than masculine capability and in no way denies the fact that her helplessness is a thing of the past" (Post 1975, p. 156).

We believe that this type of thinking still pervades contemporary etiquette books. The authors of these books fail to see that these deferential patterns are in reality forms of social control which perpetuate and continue the power and superior status enjoyed by men. While it is true that "wiser" people know that women are not weak and helpless and continuation of these patterns for whatever motive—femininity, courtesy, or whatever—when it is solely based on sexual differentiation criteria continues to serve as a common means of social control employed against women. The fixing of these patterns into codified vocabularies defining propriety in inherently inequitous terms, in day-to-day situations, links these definitional processes to the overarching structure of sexual politics—the persistent power differential between the sexes.

DOMESTIC RELATIONS

In the Victorian era there developed a systematic rationale for keeping women in the home. For the upper classes, domestic confinement was seen as essential for women in their societies' role of controlling and regulating social gatherings. As newly rich families began to gain eminence, these families through individual achievement in industry and commerce were supplanting the traditional rich whose positions were based on hereditary and family connections. To govern the social mobility of these new personnel an elaborated formalized society developed.

Influenced by the male dominating patriarchal ideology, women were exhorted to act as guardians of the home; men were exhorted to leave the home for the struggles of the business world, the army, the church, or politics. Women's duties were to regulate and control social gatherings and thus keep order in the ever-changing social scene. However, their sequestration in the home and the confinement of their activities to domesticate and "society" matters occurred at the same time men were expanding their influence and involvement in the new industrial world. This, ultimately, proved disastrous for women's independence and autonomy.

Having woman relegated to the home regardless of training had another disastrous effect. Her individuality and uniqueness are discounted and she is molded into a conforming domestic identity. She is never judged by or allowed to expand on her talents but is judged instead by her "housewifery." Bem and Bem share this view in their statement that "a women's unique identity determine(s) only the periphery of her life rather than its central core" (1979, p. 34).

The rules governing sexual behavior for women were also paradoxical. The emphasis was on respectability through control of sexual behavior and desire. Victorian women gained status by denying their own sexuality and in treating the Victorian masculine sex drive as sinful. Beliefs in purity and the elaborated etiquette norms which stressed modesty, prudishness, and cleanliness and the rules governing demeanor and appearance served to provide a sense of order, stability, and status in the everyday world. However, it also served to be psychologically stultifying. Further, the placing of woman on the "virginal pedestal" and limiting her involvements to the home and excluding her from the economic sphere served to reinforce the patriarchal ideology. Through idolatry subservience emerged.

This normative pattern carried over to the less affluent classes without the same rationale. Patriarchal ideology—the placing of women on a pedestal—supported this pattern. Men's affairs were primarily in the outside world, where they had to provide the income to support the family. This financial dependency tied with the ideological dependency was effective in keeping women in their place. Etiquette books were the major supports to this philosophy. An examination of their stances over the years reflect this. What changes have occurred in more recent books is a toning down of the more explicit sexist statements to the more subtle form. The most typical assertion is that man is the provider, woman, the domesticator. The following are illustrative:

Man is the worker and provider, protector and the law giver; woman is the preserver, the teacher or inspirer, and the exemplar (Hale 1899, p. 31).

Man's work is to subdue the earth; women's to take charge of the home, to nourish and bring up children. Woman has her work and her duties but these are neither man's work nor man's duties; and just in proportion as he seeks to impose his own burdens upon her, will he find his own character degraded and debased by so doing (Hale 1899, p. 297).

After listening and looking the most important of a woman's accomplishments is the ability to maintain an intelligent, vivacious conversation with family friends and guests (Hardy 1910, p. 232).

This attitude continues from the 1920s through the 1940s:

There are a few things for girls to remember, too. Avoid the things that show a possessive instinct, such as helping a man with his coat, straightening his necktie, brushing a bit of lint from his coat, or hanging on to his arm in public. Don't call him on the telephone unless it is necessary to change some arrangements you had made with him previously (Stephenson and Millett 1936, p. 119).

The ideal attitude which should underlie all women's manners, express kindness, gentleness, good will, sensitive understanding, self respect and when it is appropriate, deference (Fenwick 1948, p. 33).

Deference is perhaps too strong a word to describe the perfect attitude, but certainly there should be a noticeable deferring on the part of the wife, toward the husband as head of the home (Fenwick 1948, p. 34).

Finally, when we would expect major reformations in the 1960s and 1970s we found none:

Although husbands should try to help with the household chores his wife should, I think, try her best to spare him the too feminine chores—washing the dishes, setting the table, or sweeping the floors (Vanderbilt 1972, p. 648).

Society holds a wife accountable to a large extent for the presence or lack of agreeable attributes in a husband. If his manners are boorish, she is expected to correct them, one way or the other, to help him get ahead. If his clothes are ill-kept and shabby, the fact is usually attributed to his wife's negligence or lack of thrift. If he's blatantly attentive to other women, society asks where his wife has failed—and it may be right (Vanderbilt 1957, p. 47; 1967, p. 511; 1972, p. 647).

There is no place where manners are more important than in marriage. We should all encourage husbands to maintain the traditional gallantry toward us, not so much for our own sakes, but for theirs. It helps a man, I think, to maintain his status at a time when so much—I'm thinking of the independence of women—threatens him (Vanderbilt 1974, p. 27).

In sum, these manuals and others of the same ilk can be seen as perpetuating and continuing traditional social values and particularly patriarchal ideology. They still maintain the underlying sexist ideology of female subservience and continue a patriarchal viewpoint from the Victorian era to the present. As explicit behavioral guideposts, these normative vocabularies directly place a woman into a subservient role within the home. As ideal models to which many women refer, they provide an almost perfectly self-contained system of domestic labor–management relations.

WOMEN AND WORK

Let us now turn our attention to the role of women in the business world. Women particularly have found a place in the tertiary sector (office work and service jobs) and in occupations that are clearly related to traditional female sex-role activities and personality traits. There is an overwhelming concentration of women in canning and clothing factories, teaching, nursing, social work, dietetics, and at occupational levels which require little or no organizational or leadership characteristics (Yorburg 1974, p. 68). Women's employment can thus be categorized in terms of occupations which are extensions of domestic involvements (i.e., teaching, nursing, waitress, etc.) or in occupations which have a dead-end aspect to them (e.g., clerical, retail sales).

In addition to the above described characteristics the business world is structured by men. This is reflected in selective hiring practices which ensure that males are likely to find themselves working with relatively young and attractive females. Goffman (1977, p. 318) points out that "the world that men are in is a social construct, drawing them daily from their conjugal milieu to what appear to be all male settings: but these environments turn out to be strategically stocked with relatively attractive females, there to serve in a specialized way as passing targets for sexually allusive banter and for diffuse considerateness extended in both directions."

The rules of etiquette depict women in terms of the ideals of femininity which preclude them becoming involved in or competing with men on an equal footing in the business world. So these ideals have, then, a political consequence, that of relieving persons who are males from half the competition they would otherwise face (Goffman 1977, pp. 325–26).

Etiquette books are instructive on how they have perpetuated the exclusion of women from equality in the world of work. One area that might be indicative of the changing view of women and work is the advice involving the woman as wife/mother. It is interesting that in the earlier references (Hathaway 1928, pp. 31–32) one sees the wife's role as external to the business world:

> During business hours a considerate wife does not interrupt her husband's work by unnecessary telephone calls and messages, nor does she treat her husband as a superior sort of errand boy who is expected to be on call at all hours of the day and night. And neither does she expect a man to jump up and do a bit of carpentry or furniture moving after he comes home tired from a day's work. If a woman could only realize the severe tension under which the average man has to work, she would be more careful to fit her demands for his help into his more leisurely moments.

In the 1950s, however, the woman is being cautioned not to let her career take precedence over her husband and family.

It's hard to face this, but no woman can find happiness putting career above her husband and family. Once she has taken on women's natural responsibilities, whatever work she undertakes must be done in a way that deprives the family the *least*—for some deprivation they must endure if she works at all . . . the hard truth is that more women with young children fail at making happy homes while working full-time than succeed (Vanderbilt 1957, p. 206; 1967, p. 159; 1972, p.247).

It is important to note that this same citation is maintained in the more recent issues of her work (Vanderbilt, 1967, 1972).

The woman in business is presented as "giving up" certain aspects of femininity. This pattern is maintained throughout the literature.

Women in business should expect from men only the same courtesy that businessmen of a fine type pay to each other . . . Just because she is a woman she should not expect special privileges, nor should she let the feminine—that is, the coquettishly feminine—side of her nature be evident. This actually repels rather than attracts the man of sense and breeding, who realizes how out of place such an attitude is in a business environment (Hathaway 1928, p. 329).

Women in business should expect from men only the same courtesy that businessmen of a fine type pay to each other. . . . If we stop to consider it, this is usually rather a high grade of courtesy with which any woman should be satisfied. . . . Moreover, it might be added that in business a woman should in general behave herself with about the same manner that a high grade gentleman does. Applying make-up conspicuously at one's post . . . preening oneself generally and indulging in coquettish or kittenish ways are not according to the rules of etiquette, say the experts (Stevens 1934, p. 118).

While she should be charming and womanly at all times, the feminine office worker should not expect full drawing-room courtesy from her employer and co-workers. Wise is she who realizes that in the office she is on the same footing as a man. . . . If she has tact, courtesy and poise, and conducts herself as a "lady," she will at all times receive the respect to which she is entitled (Gardner and Farren 1937, p. 108).

A woman in business is supposed to be a woman, not one of the boys. On the other hand, you must avoid being so female that you embarrass your co-workers (Bevans 1960, p. 69).

Notice that this is important because if she does not preserve her femininity she might "repel rather than attract males" (Hathaway 1928), or "embarrass co-workers" (Bevans 1960). The woman is still functioning in her day-to-day interactions for others rather than herself.

The Bevans (1960) etiquette book effectively illustrates that the status of secretary involves a change of deference patterns:

If the employer is a man and his secretary a woman, the secretary doesn't expect him to rise, when she enters, and she properly treats him with the kind of respect she might expect from a man in a drawing room (p. 69).

A man's relationship to his secretary is very different from that of a man and woman socially. He doesn't rise when she enters the room. He may precede her through doors (though most men don't). He doesn't introduce her to visitors unless there is a specific reason they should become acquainted. He calls her "Martha" before she calls him "Henry" and he invites her to use his first name if he wants her to, rather than the other way around. He is the one who starts a conversation, too. If it is a business one, she may properly open it, but chatting about outside things should wait until the boss indicates that he has time for a talk (p. 74).

If a man and his secretary must work together during their stay (on a business trip), the proper thing is for the secretary to go to her employer's room, not the other way around (p. 356).

Even in the more modern works where it is stated that a secretary is not always a female, the choice of using gender-specific language is maintained. Baldrige's (1978) chapter on General Office Manners concentrates on the secretary rather than the executive:

> A good secretary is usually a firm's most important and perhaps least appreciated segment of the business. A good secretary bears a tremendous responsibility in the success of any operation with which he or she is associated. (A secretary may, of course, be male or female; the employer also. For the sake of brevity, we will refer to the secretary as "she" and the employer as "he.") (p. 474).
>
> She helps her employer do the gracious thing in his office relationships—including writing thank-you notes, sending gifts, and calling someone when the occasion warrants it—both inside the office and out of it (p. 474).
>
> Most good secretaries I know have never minded doing work that involves the personal side of their bosses' lives. In fact, most of them enjoy doing it. A woman easily becomes a member of his family in many ways, and takes vicarious enjoyment in the family's activities. However, in some firms a secretary is not supposed to perform any functions of a personal nature. If she feels her employer is loading her with too many personal things, she should speak to him about it in a very nice but frank way, so that he will not feel offended or guilty (p. 475).

This status designation really formalizes the subordinate position.

Look at how the woman in other than the secretarial role is not free from the subservient position. She is told she must guard against letting this superordinate role take over her life:

> A woman who achieves executive status of some kind must guard against being dictatorial at home as well as in the office. . . . [W]hen a woman does arrive she tends to become irritatingly important. . . . [S]he forgets the feminine graces and cajoleries and tries to meet him man-to-man (Vanderbilt 1957, pp. 207–208; 1967, p. 181; 1972, p. 276).

Names and titles are also a part of the business world. The suggestion is made in some of the materials that a woman retain her business name:

> It is better taste for a business woman to be known professionally as "Miss Maiden Name" in public life, and "Mrs. James L. Jones" in private life (Wilson 1940, p. 136).

It has always seemed wise to me for a woman who establishes herself in business or a profession to use her maiden name. I believe this gives protection, too, to her husband, should she engage in any activities that might run counter to his own professional or business interest (Vanderbilt 1974, p. 79).

It is interesting that in the Vanderbilt (1974) reference the justification is for the protection of the male.

Even when the justification is not subservience she is cautioned to be sensitive to her "husband's ego":

A woman who keeps her maiden name professionally (or even if she retains it for everything) should be very sensitive to her husband's ego when they are in social situations where she is known and he is not. People who do not know them well will tend to assume the woman and her husband bear the same name. It is important for the wife to introduce her husband proudly and distinctly. If Mary Branton, for example, is accompanied by her husband to her firm's annual convention, she should always introduce him as John Kushell, saying his name slowly and carefully so the difference is clear. Then people will not introduce John Kushell around as John Branton (Baldrige 1978, p. 725).

The other area that one must pursue is how to address a husband and wife if she has a title such as a physician. Notice how her professional role is subservient to her social role:

A woman physician uses her Christian name with her title on her cards . . . Her title as physician cannot be indicated on a joint card with her husband's name (Wilson 1940, p. 136).

On a married woman doctor: If she uses husband's name professionally and he is not a doctor himself, it would seem a little belittling for her to use a joint card, which read "Mr. James Pike and Dr. Mary Pike." A joint card in his case would read "Mr. and Mrs. James Pike." If both are doctors their joint card should read Dr. and Mrs. James Pike" (Vanderbilt 1957, p. 567; 1967, p. 598; 1972, p. 765).

If he (her husband) is not a doctor (and she is) she must decide whether or not she wishes to retain the title socially, which means that letters must be addressed to "Dr. Mary and Mr. Simon Fling"—an awkward and lengthy address . . . so for the sake of convenience many women doctors do prefer to be addressed as "Mrs." on social correspondence (Post 1975, p. 73).

A different solution is presented by Martin (1982). One can see, however, that the solution did not come about because of the recognition of the women's professional role:

Illicit love has given us, if nothing else, the two-line method of address, which may also be applied to married couples with different titles or names. The doctor and Mr. May be addressed as:

Dr. Dahlia Healer
Mr. Byron Healer

and the doctor and academician, if he uses his title socially, which not all holders of doctorates do, as:

Dr. Dahlia Healer

Dr. Bryon Healer

or as:

The Doctors Healer

or as:

The Doctors Bryon and Dahlia Healer (p. 515).

A woman must, therefore, not let her career be more important than her family, not give up her femininity, and not let her title supersede that of wife. All of this relates back to the earlier discussion of the woman maintaining her femininity and how this acts as a form of social control that maintains her subservient position. It also further demonstrates the ways in which gender-based definitions of propriety supersede, or at least supplement, work rules in the subordination of women in the workplace.

INTERACTION: SYMBOLS AND STRUCTURE

In the idealized world of the etiquette text, we have come to recognize a world of women's automatic deference to male prerogatives. Thus far, we have treated these works as normative points of reference on certain interactional states—public, domestic, and workplace. In this regard, they occupy the same societal position as a host of other such guidebooks, covering self-improvement, success, sexuality, and the stock market, to name the most obvious parallels. We prefer, however, to extend our analysis beyond this point, starting with the observation that the role of women remained consistent in the etiquette texts during almost the entire twentieth century. While the manners and mores of the society were changing, and while the specifics of many earlier social situations no longer obtain, the deference of female to male embodied in these texts has remained constant.

On the one hand, this could be simply handled as a case of cultural persistence, and further evidence for the school of thought which maintains the virtual inevitability of female subjugation (e.g., Stephens 1963; Ortner 1974). This persistence is so striking, however, that we feel that a closer look at the structure of these texts is warranted. Borrowing from the fields of literary criticism and hermeneutics, we shall attempt to analyze a deeper structure to the etiquette text (Said 1983; Ricouer 1981). For the time being we adopt the common assumption of these fields, that the organization and form of presentation of a text is at least as important as its explicit content.

Earlier in the paper, for instance, we noted that in the areas of sexual traffic, greeting rituals, costume, smoking, domestic relations, and the workplace that women were explicitly expected to defer to males. We have also noted earlier that at least one form of textual structure is remarkable, namely that public and business arenas are male-determined. Women are external to them, and surrender a part of their sexuality if they participate fully in them, especially in the world of work. In a complementary fashion, the domestic world is presented as an adjunct to the world of work, and appropriate behaviors justified in terms of that work.

At one level, this analysis simply reestablishes the points brought out a century ago by Engels, cited earlier. But the family as adjunct to the production system, and the male dominance of these worlds is still too easily viewed as the explicit aspect of the etiquette messages. We would argue that there are three additional points deserving of attention. First, aside from a persistence of deference, there is a persistence of style of the text. That is, the entire discussion of the proper form of behavior is cast in a similar nominative structure, or naming convention. The subject of etiquette is not the behavior of individuals, but the behavior of the generalized others, if you will, of "men" and "women." This stylistic device serves to objectify the nature of gender as a base for normative prescription. It places the roots for appropriate behavior not in the social order, but implicitly in a more fundamental, biological order.

This brings us to a second observation. The effect of objectifying the subjects of etiquette, i.e., men and women in concrete social situations become males and females, is to accept a system of natural law as a basis for deference and demeanor. It makes the relations between men and women a function of chromosonal makeup—a transhistorical inequality rooted in the nature of things, as it were. The force of etiquette becomes reinforced by the "laws of nature" without specific reference to these laws, simply by the process of objectifying the gender classification scheme. In short, the internal force of an etiquette text rests on its ability to present the species *Homo sapiens* as if it were in fact two species. [We should also note that is not restricted only to the etiquette text. Hubbard (1979) has argued that the structure of evolutionary theory in biology makes a similar assumption.]

Finally, the form of the etiquette prescription is also of interest. Consistent with the above arguments, we find that specific behavioral situations are analyzed and prescribed for in terms of some general set of principles, which we may call "propriety." In this sense, the etiquette text resembles nothing so much as dialectic of circumstance and code, specific behavior and normative generalization. In itself, this is not revealing. Combined with the natural law tendencies of that general code, especially regarding gender-based propriety, it becomes more significant. We would argue, however, that the greatest significance in this relationship of behavior to code is its implicit similarity to two widely different normative structures: tort law and religious canon.

More specifically, tort law is essentially a system of jurisprudence which rests on a case system. General principles of law are applied to specific circumstances as they arise. Litigious situations are always interpreted with respect to their similarity with previous situations, and if they are truly unique, with respect to the general principles of law. Similarly, religious laws in Western society have been caught in the dilemma of orthodoxy vs. social change on the one hand, and differential orthodoxies, based on textual interpretation, on the other. Both dilemmas have resulted in the establishment of a sort of religious propriety—a general set of principles or beliefs which become translated into specific doctrines attached to specific situations. In religious law, doctrine is an equivalent to etiquette; in tort law, private property to propriety. The underlying textual organization is shared, as specific behaviors or situations are contextualized, as representations of a universal set of principles.

These equivalences are not argued to be identities. Nonetheless, they are powerful symbolic links which seem woven into the very fabric of the etiquette text. It is as if the etiquette text is written in a style which encourages it being seen as another form of natural law. While we may view the application of etiquette guidelines as being somewhat trivial, it is still significant that the style of presentation brings with it the heavy rhetorical baggage of both the legal and judicial system.

There are several links between this essentially hermeneutic analysis and other approaches to gender dominance and conflict which deserve mention. Of special note are the potential ties of this analysis to recent conceptualizations present in feminist theory. A strong parallel exists between our concept of property and propriety and MacKinnon's (1982, 1983) analysis of the objectification of sexual categories, especially as they are reflected in the legal system. Building and expanding upon works of recent French feminists (Marks and de Courtivron 1980) and the works of de Beauvoir (1953; see also Schwartzer 1984), MacKinnon argues persuasively that the process of gender objectification implicitly serves to ground male dominance in the natural order, as it were: "Sexual objectification . . . is at once epistemological and political" (1983 p., 635–36). Just as MacKinnon is able to relate the legal text to behavioral consequence and to structural antecedents, it should be possible to take the analysis of etiquette texts as a further modality of control based on a similar textual/categorical assumption.

A work which is somewhat less directly theoretical, but which provides a slightly different perspective, is that of Hochschild (1983). In her analysis of the commercialization of human feeling, she points out that roughly half of women's jobs in the work force consist of public contact work—work which essentially deals with emotional impression management. Just as on-the-job training emphasizes a fictional emotional deference (particularly in the airline industry), etiquette texts assume the necessity of managing human relationships virtually as if they were public contact occupations. This similarity might prove useful in explaining selective recruitment into "women's work," based on the presocialization already present for situations requiring gender-based deferential behavior.

Alternatively, Collins has advanced a non-Marxian conflict theory of sexual stratification (1975, pp. 225–58), based on these systems of inequality having some roots in biological gender differences. His argument, while not a form of genetic determinism, assumes that differences in average size become socially magnified into gender stratification. While we do not necessarily agree with either the form or the substance of his theoretical argument, he has provided an alternative approach which needs to be assessed independently of this specific analysis. Indeed, some of the comments he has made regarding the status context of deference and demeanor are largely supportive of the arguments we have raised regarding the reinforcement of privilege through behavioral guidelines (1975, pp. 161–68, 187–209).

We leave the theoretical discussion, then, at a point of divergence. We feel that our analysis of etiquette texts can be fit into either conflict perspective as they represent theories of the larger social structure. Beyond the specifics of etiquette texts lie other specific areas of analysis to which symbolic interactionist techniques, or their derivatives, might be applied. It is hoped that this attempt to isolate structural and historical factors has demonstrated the utility of symbolic interaction for such analyses.

CONCLUSION

"Modern . . . lives are a series of traps," Mills once argued (1959, p. 3), and proceeded to describe a sociology whose purpose was to illuminate and resolve these traps as a way of humanizing society. His was a reminiscent echo of Marx's argument that people "made history, but seldom of their own choosing" ([1869] 1959, p. 320) as he too called for an end to coercive ideologies which masked social relationships for subordinate classes. We have argued that formal etiquette constitutes one of those traps—a vocabulary of motives which conceals politics behind politesse, and sexism behind propriety. Just as Blood noted that Victorian chivalry made "the ladies feel like queens . . . (while) the king still wielded the royal sceptre" (1972, p. 427), we have argued that the woman's pedestal found in etiquette as elsewhere conceals the real power reflected in the norms of "proper" behavior. While the evidence we have provided is anecdotal in nature, the persistence of gender-specific controls over time in our sample (dating from 1899 to the present) reveals a consistency and a pervasiveness of these norms in a variety of social situations.

In behavior in public places and in everyday life women must control their interactions with strangers and be treated in a subservient manner (door openings, cigarette lightings, etc.). In business a woman must guard against losing her femininity or letting her career supersede her family. She also must relinquish her professional title in social settings. Etiquette books are in many ways telling her to remain a female and to remain in the subordinate position in the business world. In the area of interpersonal relations the major emphasis is on the man being the provider and the woman being involved in the domestic aspects of life. Once again women are cut off from the world at large. Goffman (1977, p. 326) summarizes our position:

> Apologists can, then, interpret the high value placed on femininity as a balance and compensation for the substantive work that women find they must do in the domestic sphere and for their subordination in, if not exclusion from, public spheres. And the courtesies performed for and to women during social occasions can be seen as redress for the retiring roles they are obliged to play at these times. What could be thought good about their situation, then seems always to enter as a means of cloaking what could be thought bad about it. And every indulgence society shows to women can be seen as a mixed blessing.

The authors must conclude that etiquette books have acted to perpetuate the power and status of men and maintain women in the subordinate, subservient role. The totality of the subordination of women in this set of rules, the persistence of these rules over time, and their linkage to situations which involve extensive male-female interactions make these etiquette rules virtually an ideology of sexual subservience. It is obviously only one of many ideological elements operating in the sphere of male-female "arrangement" and, as such, is basically reflective of a more universal justification of sexual inequality. The analysis we have offered demonstrates how this particular normative vocabulary of motives operates to justify and perpetuate this type of inequality. While these etiquette books may have a limited readership, this in no way vitiates their importance in the larger context of sexual politics. Indeed, they may be taken as symbolic of prevalent attitudes regarding sexual relationships in twentieth-century American society.

ACKNOWLEDGMENTS

The authors would like to thank Lynn Kahn formerly of the Glassboro State College Women's Studies Office for the collection and review of materials and Michael Gordon for his comments on an earlier draft of the paper.

REFERENCES

Arestz, Esther B. 1970. *The Best Behavior,* New York: Simon & Schuster.

Baldrige, Letitia. 1978. *The Amy Vanderbilt Complete Book of Etiquette: A Guide to Contemporary Living.* New York: Doubleday.

Bem, Sandra L. and Daryl J. Bem. 1979. "Training the Woman to Know her Place: the Power of a Nonconscious Ideology," Pp. 29–38 in *Social Interaction,* edited by Howard Robboy et al. New York: St. Martin's Press.

Berg, Barbara. 1978. *The Remembered Gate: Origins of American Feminism.* New York: Oxford University Press.

Bevans, Margaret. 1960. *McCalls Book of Everyday Etiquette.* New York: Golden Press.

Blood, Robert. 1972. *The Family.* New York: Free Press.

Blumer, Herbert R. 1958. "Race Prejudice as a Sense of Group Position." *Pacific Sociological Review* 1:3–7.

———. 1966. "Sociological Implications of the Thought of G. H. Mead." *American Journal of Sociology* 71(March):535–44.

Boykin, Eleanor. 1940. *This Way Please.* New York: Macmillan.

Braroe, Nels Winther. 1970. "Reciprocal Exploitation in an Indian-White Community," Pp. 240–250 in *Social Psychology Through Symbolic Interaction,* edited by Gregory P. Stone and Harvey A. Farberman. Waltham, MA: Ginn-Blaisdell.

Cavan, Sherri. 1970. "The Etiquette of Youth," Pp. 554–565 in *Social Psychology Through Symbolic Interaction,* edited by Gregory P. Stone and Harvey A. Farberman. Waltham, MA: Ginn-Blaisdell.

Collins, Randall. 1975. *Conflict Sociology*. New York: Academic Press.

Daniels, Arlene Kaplan. 1975. "Feminist Perspectives in Sociological Research" Pp. 340–380 in *Another Voice,* edited by Marcia Millman and Rosabeth Moss Kanter. New York: Anchor Books.

Davidoff, Lenore. 1975. *The Best Circles: Society Etiquette and the Season*. Totowa, NJ: Rowman & Littlefield.

De Beauvoir, Simone. 1953. *The Second Sex*. New York: Knopf.

Eichler, Lillian. 1922. *Book of Etiquette,* Vol. 2. Garden City, NY: Doubleday.

Engels, Friedrich. [1884] 1972. *The Origin of the Family, Private Property, and the State*. New York: Pathfinder Press.

Fenwick, Millicent. 1948. *Vogue's Book of Etiquette*. New York: Simon & Schuster.

Ford, Charlotte. 1980. *Book of Modern Manners*. New York: Simon & Schuster.

Gardner, Horace and Patrician Farren. 1937. *Courtesy Book*. Philadelphia: Lippincott.

Goffman, Erving. 1956. "The Nature of Deference and Demeanor." *American Anthropologist* 58: 473–502.

———1955. "On Facework: an Analysis of Ritual Elements in Social Interaction." *Psychiatry* 18(August):213–223.

———1977. "The Arrangement Between the Sexes." *Theory and Society* 4(Fall):301–331.

———1979. *Gender Advertisements*. Cambridge,MA: Harvard University Press.

Gordon, Michael and Penelope Shankweiler. 1971. "Different Equals Less: Female Sexuality in Recent Marriage Manuals." *Journal of Marriage and the Family* 33(August):459–466.

Green, W. C. 1922. *The Book of Good Manners*. New York: Social Mentor Publications.

Hale, Sara J. 1899. *Manners, Happy Home and Good Society*. Boston: Lee & Shepard.

Hardy, E. J. 1910. *How to Be Happy Though Civil: A Book on Manners*. New York: Scribner.

Hathaway, Helen. 1928. *Manners*. New York: Dutton.

Haupt, Enid. 1963. *The Seventeen Book of Etiquette and Entertaining*. New York: McKay.

Henley, Nancy M. 1977. *Body Politics*. Englewood Cliffs, NJ: Prentice-Hall.

Henley, Nancy and Jo Freeman. 1975. "The Sexual Politics of Interpersonal Behavior." Pp. 391–401 in *Women: A Feminist Perspective,* edited by Jo Freeman. Palo Alto, CA: Mayfield.

Hochschild, Arlie. 1983. *The Managed Heart: Commercialization of Human Feeling*. Berkeley: University of California Press.

Hubbard, Ruth. 1979. "Have Only Men Evolved?" Pp. 7–36 in *Women Look at Biology Looking at Women,* edited by Ruth Hubbard, Mary Sue Henifin, and Barbara Fried. Boston: Schenkman.

Hutter, Mark. 1981. *The Changing Family: Comparative Perspectives*. New York: Wiley.

————1983. "Urban Identification and the Rise of the Downtown Department Store." Presented at the annual meeting of the Society for the Study of Symbolic Interaction.

Lindesmith, Alfred, Anselm Strauss, and Norman Denzin. 1977. *Social Psychology,* 5th edition New York: Funk & Wagnalls.

Lofland, Lyn. 1973. *A World of Strangers.* New York: Basic Books.

MacKinnon, Catharine A. 1982. "Feminism, Marxism, Method and the State: An Agenda for Theory," *Signs* 7(3):515–544.

————. 1983. "Feminism, Marxism, Method and the State: Toward Feminist Jurisprudence." *Signs* 8(4):635–658.

Marks, Elaine and Isabelle de Courtivron (eds.). 1980. *New French Feminisms.* Amherst: University of Massachusetts Press.

Martin, Judith. 1982. *Miss Manners' Guide to Excruciatingly Correct Behavior.* New York: Antheneum.

Marx, Karl. [1869] 1959. *The Eighteenth Brumaire of Louis Bonaparte.* Pp. 314–338 in Lewis S. Feuer's *Marx and Engels: Basic Writings on Politics and Philosophy.* Garden City, NY: Doubleday Anchor.

Meltzer, Bernard N., John W. Petras, and Larry T. Reynolds. 1975. *Symbolic Interactionism: Genesis, Varieties, Criticisms.* London and Boston: Routledge & Kegan Paul.

Mills, C. Wright. 1940. "Situated Actions and Vocabularies of Motive." *American Sociological Review* 5(December):904–913.

————1959. *The Sociological Imagination.* New York: Grove.

Ortner, Sherry. 1974. "Is Female to Male as Nature is to Culture?" Pp. 67–87 in *Woman, Culture and Society,* edited by Michelle Zimbalist Rosaldo and Louise Lamphere. Stanford, CA: Stanford University Press.

Post, Elizabeth. 1975. *The New Emily Post's Etiquette.* New York: Funk & Wagnalls.

Ricouer, Paul. 1981. *Hermeneutics and the Human Sciences.* New York: Cambridge University Press.

Riesman, David, Nathan Glazer, and Reuz Denney. 1961. *The Lonely Crowd.* New Haven, CT: Yale University Press.

Rosaldo, Michelle Zimbalist. 1974. "Woman, Culture and Society: A Theoretical Overview." Pp. 17–42 in *Woman Culture and Society,* edited by Michelle Zimbalist Rosaldo and Louise Lamphere. Stanford, CA: Stanford University Press.

Rothman, Sheila M. 1978. *Woman's Proper Place.* New York: Basic Books.

Said, Edward. 1983. *The World, the Text and the Critic.* Cambridge, MA: Harvard University Press.

Schlesinger, Arthur M. 1946. *Learning How to Behave.* New York: Macmillan.

Schwartzer, Alice. 1984. *After the Second Sex: Conversations with Simone de Beauvoir,* New York: Pantheon.

Siltanen, Janet and Michelle Stanworth (eds.). 1984. *Women and the Public Sphere: A Critique of Sociology and Politics.* New York: St. Martin's Press.

Stephens, William N. 1963. *The Family in Cross Cultural Perspective*. New York: Holt, Rinehart & Winston.

Stephenson, Margaret and Ruth Millett. 1936. *As Others Like You*. Bloomington, IL: McKnight & McKnight.

Stevens, Carilyn. 1934. *Etiquette in Daily Living*. Chicago: Associated Authors Service.

Stone, Gregory P. 1970. "The Circumstance and Situation of Social Status," Pp. 250–59 in *Social Psychology Through Symbolic Interaction,* edited by Gregory P. Stone and Harvey A. Farberman Waltham, MA: Ginn-Blaisdell.

Vanderbilt, Amy. 1952. *New Complete Book of Etiquette*. Garden City, NY: Doubleday.

———. 1957. *Amy Vanderbilt's Complete Book of Etiquette*. Garden City, NY: Doubleday.

———. 1967. *New Complete Book of Etiquette: The Guide to Gracious Living*. Garden City, NY: Doubleday.

———. 1972. *Amy Vanderbilt's Etiquette,* Garden City. NY: Doubleday.

———1974. *Amy Vanderbilt's Everyday Etiquette*. Garden City, NY: Doubleday.

Winter, Irene. 1981. "Royal Rhetoric and the Development of Historical Narrative in Neo-Assyrian Reliefs. *Studies in Visual Communication* 7(2):2–38.

Wilson, Margery. 1940. *The New Etiquette*. New York: Stokes.

Yorburg, Betty. 1974. *Sexual Identity*. New York: Wiley.

23

Family Life and the Politics of Talk*

Mary Field Belenky

I've begun to appreciate what a family means. I think that if I am committed to anything right now, it is to nourishing those bonds with my family, making them strong, getting them to understand me more, making an effort to understanding them more from the point of view of greater honesty.

—Bridget
Senior year of college

The descriptions of family life that the women shared with us suggest that Tolstoy's observation that "happy families are all alike; every unhappy family is unhappy in its own way" is not quite right. The daughters from happy fami-

*Belenky, Mary Field, Blythe McVicker Clinchy, Nancy Rule Goldberger, and Jill Mattuck Tarule. 1986. "Family Life and the Politics of Talk." Pp. 155–189 in *Women's Ways of Knowing: The Development of Self, Voice, and Mind*. New York: Basic Books. Copyright © 1986 by Basic Books, Inc. Reprinted by permission of Basic Books, Inc., Publishers.

lies told stories that seemed very much alike, but daughters from unhappy families also told stories that were very similar to one another. Indeed, the women who held each of the different ways of knowing we described tended to tell a common story of family life. Only a few—usually with the help of supportive friends, neighbors, and excellent schools—were able to move far beyond the epistemological atmospheres depicted in their family histories. [Here] we will recapitulate our scheme and describe the shared family histories held by women who utilized each way of knowing.

Given that we have been describing frameworks for meaning-making that evolve and change rather than personality types that are relatively permanent, it is curious that people who share an epistemological position would have so much family history in common. The following are among the many ideas that may account for the phenomenon:

> The families as described accurately reflect the environments that give rise to each of these ways of knowing. Individuals are typically supported by their families to develop only to a certain point, lingering on at that level throughout much of their adult lives.
>
> The social forces that operate on a family during the daughter's formative years continue to shape her experience. Thus the families, schools, and jobs that involve poor women are likely to be very hierarchically arranged, demanding conformity, passivity, and obedience—all unsupportive of continued intellectual growth. The same institutions that are provided for the privileged are more likely to encourage active, creative thinking and lifelong intellectual development. (See, for example, Kohn 1977, 1980.)
>
> Being a construction, family histories are rewritten from the perspective of each new epistemological era. Daughters at each position tell a similar family story because people who share common ways of knowing construe the world similarly. Thus, a person who believes that truth comes only from authorities may describe a parent in terms that can only be characterized as dictatorial. Later, this same woman, being more able to imagine an inner life, may become aware of her parents' deep interest in the truths that she might offer. (See, for example, Kegan 1982.)
>
> Both the story and the actualities of family life change because parents and children evolve in tandem, supporting and challenging each other to develop ever more complex ways of knowing as they play out their lives together. Children encourage the development of parents as much as parents encourage the development of children. (See, for example, Galinsky 1981; Gutmann 1975; Rossi 1980.)

The distinctive family patterns common to each epistemological position were revealed to us most clearly when we looked for themes that focused on the "politics of talk." By this we mean those forms of discourse that a family permits and encourages and those that they minimize and prohibit. To lay bare these politics we asked ourselves the following kinds of questions as we examined the family histories:

> What are the rules about speaking and listening that can be inferred from a family story? Are children to be seen but not heard in the day-to-day life of the family? Or do both parents and children listen to one another with care?

Do parents assume only the role of teacher? Or do they actively try to learn from and with their children as well?

Do parents teach by asking as well as by telling? Are the questions asked genuine, rhetorical, or reproachful? Do the questions draw out and enlarge feelings, ideas, plans, and the possibilities for compromises? Or do the questions squelch and constrict?

Are feelings and intimacies permitted? Does the intellectual and the impersonal reign? Or are the two intertwined?

Are conversations seen as a means that collaborators have for sharing and building, block by block, on one another's ideas? Are conversations held for nurturing ideas and people? Or are debates staged for honing the individual's logic? For outdoing others?

Do the forms and content of conversations that daughters have with their mothers differ, in regular ways, from those that they hold with their fathers?

By considering these questions we hope to deepen our understanding of the kinds of environments that nurture and constrain the development of a sense of mind and voice in women. By focusing our attention on the family and the mothering role—an institution and relationship devoted to care, connection, and human development, we might help bring a different language into the study of psychology. This study, traditionally grounded in the premise of separation, has evolved a language Gilligan describes as unparalleled in its depersonalization, in which people are "objects" and relationships are "holding environments . . . creating an imagery of love that is indistinguishable from the imagery of war." The study of mothers, Gilligan holds,

> is of particular interest for the psychology of love, holding in it the promise of elucidating a love that combines intensity and wisdom, a love that is neither exclusive nor finite but at once constant and changing. In contrast to the image of women as either self-absorbed or self-effacing, the study of women may bring the psychology a language of love that encompasses both knowledge and feelings, a language that conveys a different way of imagining the self in relation to others. (1984, p. 91)

STORIES OF FAMILY LIFE AS TOLD BY THE SILENT

Not imagining that they can understand and remember the words of others, silent women do not see themselves participating in the give-and-take of talk with others. They have little inkling of their intellectual powers or of the possibilities of an inner voice and dialogue.

These women essentially lived their lives in silence or din, looking for nourishment in the most barren soil. Their family histories suggest only the sparsest opportunity for dialogue. Bonnie's story captures the essence of the tales.

> If you just knew my parents. You couldn't talk to them. They weren't talking parents. They were parents that said, "You shut up to everyone. You don't tell nobody

nothing." I couldn't go to dances. I couldn't do this or that. Nothing involved with other people. They were to themselves. The don't want nothing to do with other people. That was the way I was supposed to be. No friends, no phone calls, no nothing. Just to yourself. That's all that they wanted.

Talk had little value or was actively discouraged in the homes in which they grew up. When conversations did occur they were quite limited in nature. The way Cindy described conversing with her mother and sister since she became pregnant was characteristic of the fleeting mechanical images of "two-way talk" that we found in this first group of stories.

We've grown closer in the last few months. We talk more than we did. My mother helps me a lot, telling me what she went through when she was that way [referring both to being raped and pregnant] and I tell her what I went through. And with my sister, we have got something in common now. My sister tells me how she felt when she was pregnant and I tell her how I feel being pregnant.

Violence Instead of Dialogue

Because the families of silent women see words as having an impact on others only when they are uttered with force and violence, they yell rather than talk when they wish to influence one another. They do little to help each other think through and articulate the problems of the moment, not to mention long-range plans and hopes for the future: "Whenever he would get mad at me about something, he could never come to me and tell me what he was mad about. He would just flare up, all out of proportion. He would not ever try to talk to me or anything." Without conversation, these families use violence—out of necessity—as the primary means for getting what they need and want from each other. Failing that (and in the long run, violence does fail to produce what they want), they withdraw or "exit," the remaining alternative to "voice" or dialogue for coping with conflict (Gilligan 1986).

Because silent women use either/or, dualistic thinking, they often liken the world to a zero-sum game in which all the players compete with one another for scarce resources, believing that if one wins the other will lose, because they think the pool of spoils is predetermined and limited (Boulding 1962; Rapapport 1960). Thus it is not surprising that the silent women we interviewed depicted the marriages of their parents—if they endured—as relationships of great inequality. One parent—usually, but not always, the father—lorded it over the other. As one woman put it, "Men dominate women. In my family there is a lot of that. They rules [sic] over the house. And woman submits and children obey. That's cut and dry. That's where it is at." The images of the powerful are stark, brutal—and wordless.

Silent women frequently described their parents as chaotic and unpredictable. Everyone is this small group of women experienced some form of gross neglect and physical and/or sexual abuse, by one or both of their parents. Some had essentially been abandoned by one or both parents; others experienced the death of parents or siblings at a very early age. Much more often than not, alcoholism fueled the parents' uncontrolled emotions. Many of the women described their parents as volatile, a few as extraordinarily violent. Undoubtedly, Bonnie provided the most horrifying example.

> My father used to do the weirdest things to me. I hate him. He was in the navy, back in the war and stuff like that. I guess he picked up weird things like that. He used to put me in a corner and put a bag over my head and every time he'd walk by he'd kick me—just like a dog. My mom told me once he put a tick on my stomach and let the tick suck my blood. Things like that—really gross, things that a father would never do to their daughter. He'd stick toothpicks up my fingernails until it would bleed. [*Did he sexually abuse you, too?*] Oh, yeah. When I was six. Had to get me to the hospital. I had twenty stitches. I just can't talk about it.

The ever-present fear of such volcanic eruptions and catastrophic events leaves children speechless and numbed, unwilling to develop their capacities for hearing and knowing. Children develop their intellectual capacities for finding order in the world only if they have some basis for trusting that order does, indeed, exist. It is no wonder that these women imagine a world where everyone is preoccupied with survival of their single, isolated selves, where everyone acquiesces to authority or runs for cover. (See Lifton 1976, on psychic numbing.)

Family psychiatrist Salvador Minuchin and colleagues (1967) depict a pattern of family life among the urban poor that is remarkably similar to the pattern we found in these families among the rural poor. They describe disorganized slum families unable to withstand the demoralizing and shattering effects of poverty. The children tend to be action-oriented, with little insight into their own behaviors or motivations. Since they do not expect to be heard, and if heard they expect no response, the volume of their voices is more important than the content. They lack verbal negotiating skills and do not expect conflicts to be resolved through nonviolent means.

Families that are relegated to the bottom of the social class structure are often shaken by the collapse of an outmoded way of life. Values, symbol systems, and patterns of communication are torn asunder. Parents feel they have lost their way and have nothing to teach. One generation no longer tells its stories to the next.

While violent families often suffer from the stresses of poverty, family violence occurs at all levels of the social class structure. Researchers have repeatedly found violent families, whether rich or poor, to be characterized by high levels of social isolation, rigid sex-role stereotyping, poor communication, and extreme inequalities in the distribution of power among family members. These characteristics are consistently noted, whether the studies are of wife battering, child abuse, or abuse of the elderly (Finkelhor 1983).

The Allocation of Life Chances

Occasionally women of lower-class origins who grew up in families characterized by silence, hierarchy, and violence were able to find strengths elsewhere—from other relatives, neighbors, and excellent schools—that helped them transcend the epistemological atmospheres of their families. On the whole, however, when poor families fail their children, the society provides precious little help; while children of privilege are more likely to find rich sources of sustenance to promote their development elsewhere.

The stories of two women—Liz, born into privilege, and Mimi, born into poverty—illustrate the difference that social class can make in the distribution of life chances. Each woman described her father as tyrannical and her mother as unavailable. Each woman suffered sexual assaults from her father, which they believed began in the third or fourth year of life. Each sought help to end the incest in their thirteenth year. Each was disbelieved by her mother. From that point on the similarities stop.

The father from the poor home was jailed. The mother blamed the daughter. When Mimi ran away, the authorities caught her and placed her in a shelter home. "The shelter mother was really mean to me. I was afraid of the dark so she used to take the light bulbs out at night and lock me in my room." From there Mimi was moved through a series of foster homes and residential schools. While she occasionally met people who were kindly, she met no one who believed in her, drew her out, sponsored her, or educated her. At twenty-six she lives with her two babies and no husband. Having no skills she looks to welfare, not her own efforts, for maintenance.

Liz's father, "the biggest tyrant and the most indifferent man who ever lived," committed an identical crime but was not sent to jail. While Liz's mother was "like a loose limb, like an arm that is all shriveled up." there were many others to receive, encourage, counsel, and educate Liz. While the first daughter remained mired in silence, the second was, at the time of the interview, a constructivist who had a well-developed sense of voice and mind.

Among the many who helped Liz transcend her family, some were not even human. "When I was really feeling cast off I had my dog and me. That was my world. Then I started riding horses. That became my world. It was completely detached from my family. I didn't want anything from them. I just wanted my pony. I wanted to ride. I wanted to ride all day. And I'd do it." Her animals and the woods surrounding the family's vacation house offered her solace and escape. Her animals helped her develop capacities that are cultivated only in loving relationships.

> My relationship with my horse is amazing. He would save your life for you, if you needed it. He loves to do things for you. He loves to please. From him I learned reciprocity. I mean the reason that we were so great together was because we understood give-and-take with one another. How can you talk about a horse this way? He taught me a lot about responsibility, about what it would be like having a child.

Like a good teacher, her horse gave her confidence in herself and in her ability to learn. "I have a feeling that I'm good with horses, that I know horses pretty well, that I am sensitive and I am pigheaded—*but I can learn when I decide I want to learn"* (emphasis added).

She also found good teachers in the therapists and counselors she consulted, who were able to provide much of the information and the language that she needed to make sense of her family. She also found good teachers in the schools she attended. Some of her teachers even opened their homes to her, making themselves available as a "surrogate family." "They showed me what parents ought to be like. They taught me a lot about loving relationships that I don't think I would ever have learned otherwise. They have been great for me. They gave me confidence in myself. I have been using them as a model of what I want out of my own life."

The arts seemed particularly important in helping her develop the powers of her own voice and mind. In the schools that she attended she was helped to cultivate her abilities in almost all of the expressive arts, winning "a whole bunch of awards" and accolades as a dancer, actor, and singer. The arts, she said, "took care of me emotionally so well. It was something you could do, that you love, that you work at." Her schools and her home also had extensive libraries, so she could read and reread her favorite books—mostly about artists and the unfolding of their personhood and their gifts. But most of all, some of the schools she attended gave her "a love of learning." "Learning for learning's sake, not learning for an A or B. It helped me feel like there was a world out there that I could have and be interested in." Having cultivated her capacities as a knower, she could make sense of her experience, put it in perspective, and move on. "You can't really move on in your life until you've accepted certain things about your parents and have integrated them and then started moving on. It is the only way you can face the world and walk into it with an open heart and an open mind." The daughter from the poor family, having no inkling that hearts and minds could be opened, walks nowhere.

Breaking the Cycle

Indeed, the women we interviewed who moved far beyond the epistemological atmospheres depicted in their histories had much in common with Liz. Each learned to immerse herself in at least one symbol system from a very early age. This might have been music or art, but most often they found another world through books and literature. Frequently they kept a diary. Whatever the medium, as children these women were producers as well as consumers in the medium that they chose to develop. The schools they attended supported such activities and helped them cultivate the life of the mind. They often had younger siblings who looked up to them and needed their care. Most found important, decent human relationships outside of the home—in their neighborhood, school, or among distant relatives. A few created such relationships for themselves through the sheer power of their imaginations, by endowing their pets and imaginary playmates with those attributes that nourish the human potential.

It has been the accepted wisdom that emotional problems are central causes of psychopathology and that only by alleviating emotional difficulties can intellectual deficits be ameliorated. Our stories and the works of Réuven Feuerstein (1980), Nicholas Hobbs (1982), and Myrna Shure and George Spivack (1978) all suggest the central importance of intellectual development if emotional difficulties are to be prevented or overcome. "Gaining a voice" and developing an awareness of their own minds are the tasks that these women must accomplish if they are to cease being either a perpetrator or a victim of family violence. It is also necessary if these women are to stop passing down these patterns from one generation to the next. Many of the young women who viewed the world from silence began raising families of their own. Unfortunately they were replicating the same patterns of family life that they themselves experienced. Cindy, pregnant at fifteen, tried to imagine herself as a teacher to her child. She was reminded of her sister's child who had a "rear end like leather." "We figured, you know, if you spanked him every time he did something wrong, he would straighten himself up as he gets bigger." Cindy could imagine wielding force but not words when teaching and influencing her child. Another adolescent mother, who was under investigation for child abuse, had similar views: "I try to make them mind the best I can without beating them to death. You know that they still don't understand it. They just blurt out what they want to blurt out." She also assumed that beatings would "straighten them up." She did not realize that it was hard for the children to understand what was wanted of them if they were not told. She could not imagine that what they might "blurt out" could have value.

Mothers who have so little sense of their own minds and voices are unable to imagine such capacities in their children. Not being fully aware of the power of words for communicating meaning, they expect their children to know what is on their minds without the benefit of words. These parents do not tell their children what they mean by "good"—much less why. Nor do they ask the children to explain themselves. (See also Bernstein 1964; Ward 1971.)

We observed these mothers "backhanding" their children whenever the child asked questions, even when the questions seemed to stem from genuine curiosity and desire for knowledge. It was as if the questions themselves were another example of the child's "talking back" and "disrespect." Such a mother finds the curious, thinking child's questions stressful, since she does not yet see herself as an authority who has anything to say or teach.

THE FAMILIES OF THOSE WHO
LISTEN TO THE VOICES OF OTHERS

The women who sought ideas and ideals and listened to others in order to fill their storehouses full of truths told a different story.

One-Way Talk

The parents of these women were certainly not uncommunicative. Typically, they told their children everything. These parents assumed that their daughters should and would listen to them, that they would understand them, and that they would obey. A student from a community college illustrates the point.

Learning under my mother was—powerful. She could figure people out. She wasn't one to be beating you and knocking you all the time. She talked and talked and talked. Every time she opened her mouth she would be telling you something that would really do you some good. It wasn't a lot of frivolous talk. Me and my mother would sit down and she would talk. She taught me the facts of life. I would tell my mother everything and she would tell me what to do and what not to do, what was right and what wasn't right. I would go out on dates and come back and relate the whole story to her. She would go, "This is good and this was bad. Don't do this the next time."

Although the stories show more effective communication patterns that those of the silent women, these parents used only "one-way" conversations as the predominant mode of operating with their children. The parents did most of the talking, while the children did most of the listening. While some of the women described their parents as warm and supportive, others as cold and sometimes abusive, almost all of the women in this second group had at least one parent whom they depicted as being only "one way."

These parents said what was on their minds, but they did not strive to understand what was on their daughters' minds. They did all the active thinking and talking about the ins and outs and the rights and wrongs of the situation. The parents expected their daughters to absorb their ideas, but they seldom encouraged their daughters to think things through for themselves. Because they were children, they were expected to hear but not to be heard.

Inequality

These daughters and their parents accepted the inherent inequality built into the parent-child relationship as a permanent condition. In comparison, the women who cultivated more elaborate modes of meaning-making assumed that the inequality between parent and child was only temporary. Indeed, as we shall see, the creation of a relationship of equality, collegiality, and intimacy between daughters and parents—especially mothers—becomes valued as a central achievement by most of those who come to understand that all knowledge is constructed.

The women who assumed that knowledge came from outside the self brought these same patterns of speaking and listening to their new families as they began to raise children of their own. One adolescent mother had begun lecturing her infant. She said, "I am going to teach Nellie right from wrong. I am going to tell her what I think is best. Then I am going to hope and pray that she will listen.

The marriages created by these women and those of their parents conformed to the sex-role stereotypes the culture upheld. The women almost always depicted them as being very hierarchical, with talking and listening being unevenly divided between the partners. It was typically the husband who did the speaking and the wife who listened. As one woman recounted, "Women were more or less to be seen and not heard. The men were supposed to be the ones with the voice of the family, the go-getter, the breadwinner. I think a man feels he is superior to women—most women." Only rarely were these roles reversed, with the wife being dominant and the husband subordinate. As one woman said of her father, "He recedes into a vast degree of silence." The widespread tendency for men to do the talking and for women and children to do the listening has been repeatedly documented in the studies of social scientists, who have only recently begun to focus attention on the politics of discourse in family life (Bernard 1981; Engle 1980; Fishman 1978; 1983; Gleason and Greif 1983; Greif 1980; West and Zimmerman 1983).

When these women described their mothers as wives, they seldom depicted them as speaking up and speaking out. If their mothers departed from the conventional pattern of quietness and submissiveness, the daughters almost always described them as being shrill and destructive. One adolescent illustrated how upsetting it could be to have a mother who was "gaining a voice": "When others told her off my mother used to take it and just walk off. Now she will just tell them where to put it. She's just different since she and my father got a divorce. I don't understand her at all."

Rebellions—Adolescent and Otherwise

In the stories the received knowers told, there were no images of rebellion against adult authority. These daughters took it and just walked off quietly, exactly as they wanted their mothers to do. Although a few of these women, like most of the silent women, lived socially deviant lives guided primarily by impulse, none described themselves as ever questioning parental authority. None spoke of efforts to overrule their parents and to become self-directed. There were no accounts of adolescent rebellions. Even though many of them told of beatings, incest, abandonment, and foster placements, none protested. Such things just happened. These women did not try to explain why. They did not sit in judgment of their parents. They never mentioned begin angry.*

Only one of these women ever spoke of fighting back. At the age of fifty she recalled her stepfather trying to rape her when she was thirteen. She had bit him and he never tried again. Almost four decades later she recounted only shame and confusion that she had become an aggressor in that long-ago incident: "I've never been that type of person that wants to hurt other people. I'd rather take the hurt myself than to hurt other people." This woman, as is characteristic of others in this group, extended care and protection to others but not to herself. She might be hurt, but she would not inflict hurt—whatever the cost. She was still ashamed that she stood up for herself. She recalled no images of pride for having been brave and victorious. She expressed no sense of outrage at what her stepfather attempted, at a trust violated.

In denying her own selfhood this woman provided a classic example of the conventional feminine voice that Gilligan (1982) was able to hear in women's moral judgments. In actuality, these women do not speak in a different voice. They have no voice at all. Conventional feminine goodness means being voiceless as well as selfless.

---

*In their studies of the authoritarian personality, Adorno, Frenkel-Brunswik, Levinson, and Sanford (1950) found that inmates in San Quentin prison espoused more deference to parental and other authorities than did any other population they studied.

Men As Speakers, Women as Listeners

The continued injunction against articulating needs, feelings, and experiences must constrain the development of hearts and minds, because it is through speaking and listening that we develop our capacities to talk and to think things through. The fact that women are expected to curtail their voice may account for the greater prevalence of clinical depression and learned helplessness among women than among men (Al-Issa 1980; Weissman and Paykel 1974).

The tendency to allocate speaking to men and listening to women impairs the development of men as well. The frequent failure of men to cultivate their capacity for listening has a profound impact on their capacity for parenting, for it is mothers more than fathers who are most likely to still their own voices so they may hear and draw out the voices of their children. Fathers and daughters more often stand at a great distance, literally, because many, many of these fathers are absent, and figuratively, because fathers and daughters seldom try to understand each other or to stand in each other's shoes. One teenager described how it was with many fathers. "My father is all right to talk to—but he's got to realize where everybody else stands, too. Like every now and then he thinks that where he stands is the only place to be, and nobody else is supposed to stand where they want to be."

As dialogue is the primary means for preventing or resolving conflicts, not listening and imagining the other invites coercion or withdrawal. Indeed, if our interviews are an index of current trends, it appears that fathers are having great difficulty fulfilling their parental roles at this point in history. To a degree that surprised and disturbed us, we found women describing their fathers as unable to see others in their own terms, as dictatorial and sometimes violent, and as fleeing from family life and their children.

FAMILY HISTORIES OF THOSE WITH AN INNER VOICE

The subjectivists, finding an inner source for truth, turned from their parents' words and sought self-direction by listening to their own "infallible gut." "I didn't seem to get along with my parents at all. I just did not want to hear their side of the story—or what they had to say about anything." Realizing that there were as many sides to a story as there were storytellers, these women often ignored the stories that their parents told so that they might concentrate on creating their own.

Those who focused on cultivating their own intuitive voice admired their parents only to the extent that the parents listened to them. The parents had to still their own voices and listen with a nonjudgmental, unconditionally accepting ear if these women were to feel heard. What their parents had to say in return was the least of their concerns. Proper talk as envisioned by them was still one-way talk. Any advance over the previous position was that it was the daughter who talked and the parent who listened. Again, mothers more than fathers were likely to be available as listeners.

Questioning Parental Authority

Unlike the more passive listeners, these women tried to wrest control for their own lives out of the hands of their parents or other authorities. "I was very rebellious—not wanting to be told what to do. I thought I was old enough to know right from wrong." If the subjectivists' parents did not support their efforts to become self-directed, the daughters often began an educational campaign to bring the parents around to their way of thinking. A college student, who went through childhood "never disagreeing," remembered a confrontation with her mother that stood out for her as a major turning point. "I sat her down and told her, 'Look, the only way I am going to learn is for me to experience it for me. Let me find out. God knows, you found out. So let me find out. I will even let you say, "I told you so." Please!'"

If their parents did not yield power willingly, the subjectivist daughters grabbed the reins for themselves. Some even imagined taking them by force.

My mother used to hit me. She doesn't hit me anymore. I think it is because I've outgrown her and I'll hit her back. Before I was very trapped. I never went out. I was too scared to go out. Now my horizons have broadened. I have seen that there is more than just being at home, being scared of everything, being the baby of the family with someone always hovering over me—always telling me what to do.

In sharp contrast to the numbness and muteness inherent in the previous positions, the subjectivists see themselves finding and venting their inner feelings—even rage. While the others remain resigned and remarkably uncomplaining in the face of even great injustices, the subjectivists are overtaken by fury if wronged by their parents. For the most part, these stories were told in the present tense and with the heat of the battle still in the air. One of the women who held this perspective imagined that some day—far in the future—she would likely forgive her parents and put her anger aside. Another spoke of the anger that persisted beyond her mother's death and prayed that she might be able to find room in her heart to forgive her father before he, too, passed away.

Sometimes the women remembered experiencing an outpouring of rage over an ongoing injustice they had previously accepted. A college student described her earlier passivity and how she had acquiesced to her father's incestuous demands throughout her childhood. Then things changed about the time she reached early adolescence. Most likely she, too, was recounting a time when she began to find inner sources of knowing.

So when he tried to have sex with me when I was thirteen, *I did know the difference.* After that I remember being really furious with him. I remember just fury running through my veins. I remember wanting to run out and scream to him, "Don't you ever touch my sister like this or I will kill you!" He betrayed one of the most precious things a human being has—a sense of faith in the people who brought you up (emphasis added).

Why are subjectivists able to revolt and rebel against their parents, while the women who see themselves only as receivers of knowledge remain so acquiescent?

The subjectivists' ability to imagine an "infallible gut" provides guidance and standards independent of parents. With an "inner gut" subjectivists can imagine themselves having some sort of a voice and a right to speak out—even against authorities.

The subjectivists are advantaged in still another important way. They imagine the world and themselves in a state of constant flux. They can even imagine themselves initiating some of the changes. The silent and received knowers, however, see everything as static and stationary—including themselves. They understand the world as arbitrary, unamenable to analysis, and unalterable. If their parents are unjust, that is how it is. To protest would only increase their own difficulties.

Many of the subjectivists we interviewed were fortunate enough to have parents who supported their efforts to become independent. These women frequently reported that their parents became less dictatorial as they grew older. While it might have been that these daughters constructed their view of their parents differently as they themselves grew more mature, it was also likely that their parents had actually undergone change. Jane Loevinger (1962, 1976) found a decline in authoritarian family attitudes in parents as they aged and raised more children (even after having considered the parent's age). Many children reported that their parents became more flexible with each succeeding child.

Adult development regularly proceeds in the direction that supports the developmental progress of children. Indeed, the process of promoting the growth and development of children is an important source of growth and development for parents (Bell and Harper 1977; Galinsky 1981; Loevinger 1976). Furthermore, there is some historical evidence of a broad, current trend away from authoritarianism and dualism toward relativism; an increased awareness of inner emotional and intellectual capacities; and a prolonged capacity for change and adaptation occurring during the adult years (Hagen 1962; Perry 1970; Riesman, Denney, and Glazer 1961; Veroff, Douvan, and Kulka 1981). Indeed, two major shifts in the study of psychology suggest an accomodation to such a trend. Adult development as a field of study has become a rapidly growing area of concentration, although in the past is was assumed that development was confined to the childhood and adolescent years. Cognitive psychology has increasingly attracted attention away from the behaviorist perspective where the individual is seen as a passive agent reacting only to external stimulus. Concern with the memorization process is being replaced by studies of how knowledge is constructed all along the life span (Gardner 1985). Educational practice—at least for the privileged—appears to be following the trend.

The subjectivists who struggle to overcome parental authority are often successful. When parents do actively support their daughters' efforts to become self-directed, a renewed sense of connection often occurs between the generations. Some subjectivists described how they started talking with their parents—most often their mothers—as if they were peers. It is just this kind of shift that regularly moves the daughter to begin another revision of the family history. "I always thought of her more as an authority. She was my mother and I was a kid. Now it's more like friends. We are on a friendship level instead of two generations. (Laughs.) Now I listen a lot better to my mother than I used to. I find out later, she was right all along! (Laughs.)" These daughters, feeling more heard, more in control of their own destinies, and more able to maintain an equal footing, could once again afford to listen to their parents.

However, it is a different story if subjectivists' parents remain dictatorial and unable to appreciate their daughters' unique points of view. These daughters are likely to dismiss their parents as narrow-minded and look elsewhere for support and conversation.

> When I was little I thought my father was the smartest person on the planet. I thought he knew everything. That has changed dramatically. Now I get real frustrated with his narrow-minded view of the world; with his demands that I live up to his preconceived notions. I think he views the world through a real small scope.

Another woman echoed,

> I once say my mother as a woman who was very good. A woman who drew a very fine line between what was right and what was wrong. And she lived on the right side of the line. Then I began to see my mother as a very narrow-minded woman. I began to see my mother as a bigot.

Subjectivists love their parents if they perceive them as responsive, open, flexible; they reject their parents if they see them as doctrinaire and rigid.

Unlike any of the women who held the previous perspectives, some of the subjectivists depicted parents as having inner sources of knowing, such as intellect or intuition. A community college student said of her father,

> I have always thought of my father as a man who was very wise. I did then and I do now. He was a lover of humanity. He would watch and think about people—why they do the things that they do. He was a lover of porches and rocking chairs. Even though he was barely literate, he had a quick mind. He could separate out the trivial.

Another woman described her mother: "My mother is very strong-minded. She knows what she is talking about." There are several reasons why subjectivists are more likely to notice such capacities in their parents. It is possible that their parents involve themselves more in utilizing their inner resources for constructing knowledge than do the parents of the women from the previous perspectives. It is also possible that the daughter herself has to adopt the subjectivists' perspective before she can begin to conceptualize and describe the inner life that her parents may have been drawing on all along.

As images of parents' cultivating and utilizing their inner sources of knowing increased, we see a corresponding decrease in images of impulsive, chaotic, and violent behavior on the parents' part—at least in the descriptions the daughters offered. The parents' behavior is either becoming more subordinated to the parents' own symbolic processes or the daughter is becoming more capable of conceptualizing such a possibility, or both. Taking the stories at face value, it seems as if both the subjectivist women and their parents were more able to replace anarchy and despotism with self-government than were the more voiceless women and their parents.

Fathers and Mothers As Knowers

When we examined the subjectivists' stories to see if they attributed different capacities to fathers than to mothers, a pattern did emerge. If, for instance, a subjectivist described her father as being intelligent, she left it at that; but if she depicted her mother as being intelligent, she would, as likely as not, add a qualifier suggesting that the mother's intellectual gifts came to naught. For example,

> My mother is a smart, creative, beautiful woman who is wasting away.

> You'd never know that my mother is so intelligent as she was always hiding it.

> My mother is smart. She never finished grade school but I always sensed a real common sense about her. But she refuses to face the truth about my dad. Whenever there was any sort of problem [that is, incest], she always blamed me.

Supermoms

When daughters strove to stand on their own two feet—as they often did in the subjectivist period—they scrutinized their mothers for signs of independence and self-sufficiency. They frequently described their mothers as powerful, even if they did not specifically attribute intelligence to them. Many of these mothers "pulled themselves up from the bottom" and, with fathers unavailable or inadequate, became the primary or sole supporters of their children. One woman, whose mother supported eight people, suggested the admiration that these women could have for such powerhouses—and how cherished such mothers made them feel. "She really raised herself up. She works for us. She is very, very pushy and ambitious for us."

Admiration for powerful mothers is a theme that recurs again and again in the fiction that depicts the lives of American blacks. Such images appeared in the stories of the black women we interviewed as well. The theme, however, is prominent in many of the interviews of women, black or white, whose mothers raised their children without the help of fathers—if their mothers were not broken by the burden. As the phenomenon of fathers abandoning responsibility for the raising of children becomes more widespread, so does the image of mothers as saviors and superwomen.

That the images of uncompromised power in women are so often associated with being abandoned by men lends some credence to Barbara Ehrenreich's argument in *The Hearts of Men* (1983) that the current wave of feminism is a response of women to the withdrawal of men from family life. Women are becoming so strong and independent because their survival and the survival of their children depend on it.

Images of mothers in intact families reflect a different pattern. Subjectivists whose parents never divorced also depicted their mothers as being powerful. However, the images of the power held by mothers with husbands often involved discomfort and subterfuge: "My mother is a very fierce woman. She is very strong. She yields and yields—just until she gets what she wants. She goes after things. I like that about her. When she sets herself a goal she reaches it by any means possible." Another woman described her mother trying to contain her own power while bolstering that of her husband. "She tries her best to let my father be the man of the house. Sometimes it doesn't work. Sometimes she is the man of the house—so to speak. Sometimes she needs to be—in my opinion." While the women from the previous positions criticized their mothers if they became strong, independent, and outspoken, the subjectivists criticized their mothers if they did not. One woman expressed her disdain by saying, "Her whole life was molded around my dad and making him happy."

Selflessness Questioned

For the first time criticism of conventional feminine goodness entered the stories. At this juncture, mothers who exhibited selflessness, dependence, and avoidance of speaking out were held in contempt. Mothers who rejected this mode of relating to others were increasingly described with images of pleasure and pride. As we will show, the image of the "little woman" disappeared by the time we reached the stories told by constructivists.

Essentially, the subjectivists began to question the traditional role women played in the zero-sum game. They were no longer willing to lose or to curtail their own chances so that the fortunes of others might be enhanced. A woman spoke of the conflict she experienced between the demands of her family and the demands of her career: "There is always an emergency when something I am doing is important to me. I resent giving that time to anybody else. Every time there is something that is important to me, somebody wants part of me. I resent it a lot." For the subjectivists, however, the win/lose model still prevailed. The only advance over the previous positions was that the subjectivists now claimed the right to be one of the winners.

Subjectivists As Parents

Not only did the view of subjectivists' parents evolve and change with epistemological development, but their relationships with their own child went through similar transformations. Only as a mother begins to find in herself sources of knowledge is she likely to look for such resources in her child. The woman we called Inez provided us with an example. It was she who gave us the "infallible gut" metaphor that we have used to suggest the essence of the subjectivist's inner voice. Inez, like many who were delayed in development, grew up in a family where the father was dictatorial and abusive. The mother, concerned about community opinion, continually denied his incestuous behavior and failed to protect her daughters. Inez, like others raised by parents who fail to acknowledge the truths of what is going on and of what the children are thinking and feeling—or even that the children can think and feel—grew up believing that she was "dumb," good only as a "doormat," and "that I am not worth anything. That my opinion ain't worth shit. Until recently I didn't realize that I could think and be smart and still be a woman. I had no faith in myself. I didn't trust my judgment at all." This woman who saw no interior strengths began to find within herself an "infallible gut." This discovery was followed by changes in the way she was able to perceive her children as well. As we shall see, however, such changes take time. This is how she began the first of two interviews: "What stands out for me is that I'm learning how to make a good home. . . . I care a lot about my kids and the people close to me. When I care, I really care. Before I didn't think I could be loved or that anybody would care."

"To make a good home" can mean many things. When we first talked, Inez was trying to become less passive with her children, to become more comfortable with her authority as a parent. She was pleased to learn that she could make her kids obey by using a variety of punishments: confining them to their rooms, denying meals, and washing their mouths out with soap. She said,

> My impression of power was what my father was—abusive, destructive, and unloving. Everything was win or lose. Either you were on top or you're the dummy on the bottom. I had to become the boss of the family. Now I see that I'm the mother and I have some knowledge that my kids don't have. I've lived longer than they. I've got more information than they do. Now, if they look at me cross-eyes, I stick a bar of soap in their mouths. I learned that I can be the authority figure in my kids' lives and still be loved. I can set down the rules because I love them.

After a year of much hard work with therapists, college courses, and several self-help groups, Inez's second interview had a new focus. Although she was still very concerned about exercising her authority as a parent, Inez now showed some concern for helping the children "be smart," "to think things through themselves," and "to make their own decisions." To do that she saw that she had to curtail her lectures to them and let them find their own voices. Inez then said, "I still don't talk with my kids enough. I still dictate." The previous year she mentioned only the use of force in influencing her children. Then she began to see the difference between discourse and dictation. Inez's own voice appeared in their relationship and she began to understand that she could and should tell them what she wanted and why. Inez was also beginning to see the importance of drawing forth the children's own voices. It is likely that the time lag we observed between the development of Inez's ability to conceptualize her own mind and power of voice and being able to imagine such capacities in her children is a regularly occurring phenomenon: that you must first begin to hear your own inner voice in order to understand the importance of drawing out the voices of others, whether the other is your child, spouse, student, client, or friend.

FAMILY LIFE AND INTEGRATING THE
VOICES OF REASON AND FEELING

The women who questioned the infallibility of the gut and who were consciously cultivating and integrating the voices of reason and emotion wove still another pattern in the family story. While not all these women came from happy homes, they were much more likely than the women who held other perspectives to describe family relationships characterized by images of connection, care, mutuality, and reciprocity. Because the themes in the family histories told by the procedural and the constructivist knowers were so similar, we combined their stories, noting the exceptions when they occur.

Mothers and Dialogue

Daughters who integrated the voices of reason and feelings were likely to be interested in the quality of the voices of their mothers. Many noted with admiration that their mothers developed strong, clear voices of their own. As one young woman said, "My mother is only five feet tall, but if you heard her over the phone, why you would think that she is at least five feet and seven inches."

Again we see that it is important to daughters that parents have a voice. Those who receive knowledge from others look to their parents for truth and direction and often feel helped when their voices are loud and clear. At this new juncture daughters wish their parents to have voices of their own so that they might be full participants in an ongoing conversation. A twenty-three-year-old college alumna described such talk. "I was her confidante. She would tell me things about herself. It was sort of a relationship of equals." It was only in this last collection of stories that family conversations routinely involved two-way talk. In these stories both parents and daughters were given a voice, each spoke and listened, each had an equal say.

These daughters were disappointed if their mothers did not have the courage to speak their minds straight out, or if their mothers only provided others "with a forum for discussion, but is never a participant in that discussion herself."

Some noticed their fathers listening with care. When that occurred it was highly valued. However, none of these daughters particularly admired their fathers for speaking out. For fathers to have a voice was a given—not an achievement. For fathers to develop a listening ear and for mothers to "gain a voice" were the feats that those who were integrating the voices of reason and feeling noted and appreciated.

Connectedness Between Mothers and Daughters

Although the basic themes of attachment and autonomy were interwoven, a greater sense of connection and of commonalities pervaded the daughters' portraits of mothers, while the sense of distance and difference continued to predominate in the descriptions of life with father. This pattern was also observed by James Youniss and Jacqueline Smoller (1985) in their extensive study of adolescents' perceptions of mothers and fathers. This pattern was also reflected in the descriptions of family life Lillian Rubin heard in the interviews she conducted with husbands and wives in her study of lower-class family life, *Worlds of Pain* (1976). Chodorow (1978) argued that the basic sense of living connected or separated from others— different conceptions of self and the self-world relationship—is deeply rooted in the experience of the infant's earliest relationships with his or her caregiver. Universally, mothers and/or other women attend to the care of the young, with fathers and other men remaining on the periphery. Chodorow maintains that when caregivers primarily from only one sex nurture infants, the stage is set for two distinctive developmental consequences, depending on the match or mismatch of the caregiver's and the infant's gender. The female infant nurtured by her mother has only to affirm her connectedness and sense of sameness as she begins to develop an understanding of gender and of her own identity as a person in the world. The male baby, on the other hand, has to declare his separateness from his mother, his primary caregiver and first source of identification, in order to build a conception of his gender and identity.

Chodorow's argument is compelling and helps explain the differing sense of connectedness and separateness that can readily be observed in well-developing boys and girls from the earliest ages on. However, as we reexamined these stories of family life, two considerations emerged that threw Chodorow's argument into a different light. With an increasing awareness of how much the sense of connectedness to others deepens with maturity, we believe that important casual factors that occur later in the life cycle must also be considered. For many women being a mother as well as having a woman as a mother provides a profound experience of human connection. That adult experiences as well as childhood experiences contribute to the evolution of a sense of connection is consistent with our observations that connectedness with others is one of the most complicated human achievements, requiring a high level of development. As Jerome Kagan (1984) suggests, there is a general tendency to attribute characteristics to the infant that are opposite to those that are prized in adults in the culture. Thus, he argues, Americans valuing independence and individuality in adults tend to see the baby as being dependent and undifferentiated from others. In contrast, the Japanese, valuing a close interdependence between people, see the infant as too autonomous and needing to be coaxed into a dependent role in order to encourage the mutual bonding necessary for adult life. The more we come to understand and value attachment and connectedness in adults, the more likely we will conceptualize autonomy and independence as part of the infant's nature and act to encourage the development of the capacity for connection with others.

Guiding Metaphors

Whatever the roots of connectedness, communal and family life is threatened whenever members fail to see the interdependence of all. As Gilligan and her colleagues suggest, the individual who conceptualizes the self as basically connected to others sees the bonds that knit human relationships together as bonds of attachment. They spin visions of the ties between persons, which can best be suggested by the metaphors of webs and nets. Webs and nets imply opposing capacities for snaring or entrapment and for rescuing or safety. They also suggest a complexity of relationships and the delicate interrelatedness of all so that tension and movement in one part of the system will grow to be felt in all parts of the whole. In the complexity of a web, no one position dominates over the rest. Each person—no matter how small—has some potential for power; each is always subject to the actions of others. It is hard to imagine other ways of visioning the world that offer as much potential for protection to the immature and the infirm.

In contrast, the self premised in autonomy sees individuals relating through bonds of agreements, such as contracts, laws, and the like. Their metaphors for suggesting the world are more often images of pyramids and mountains. On the metaphorical mountain the few at the top dominate the many on the bottom. Those near the base must move the whole mountain to affect those near the apex; in the image of the net, even the least can affect all others by the slightest pull on the gossamer thread.

Those on a mountain find it easier to maintain the view that some must lead and others must follow, that some will win while the rest will lose. In the hierarchial world that the players with these limited epistemologies construct, the game is rigged. Typically, it is the men who dominate the women and the parents who hold sway over the children. Mothers taking this either/or stance believe that they must choose to lose in order for their children to succeed. Thus mothers try to remain voiceless, powerless, and selfless so that their children will prosper (Miller 1976).

Carole Klein (1984), in *Mothers and Sons*, tells us that the mothers of sons feel more guilt and receive more condemnation from others when they pursue their own interests than do the mothers of daughters. Because women are expected to subordinate themselves to males, it may take longer for mothers and sons to realize that the win/lose model is not the best model for most human relationships than it takes mother and daughters. It is the relationship between mothers and daughters in which the possibility of common interests and a win/win game is most likely to become apparent. Because mothers and daughters can affirm and enjoy their commonalities more readily, they are more likely to see how they might advance their individual interests in tandem, without one having to be sacrificed for the other—an understanding that most of the constructivist women and their mothers have achieved.

Healing the Split Between Intellect and Emotion

When the procedural knowers first began to cultivate the voice of reason, they were more likely to see intrapsychic powers being allocated to their parents according to the conventional pattern. They saw their fathers as imbued with intelligence, while they portrayed their mothers as warm and sensitive. While they saw each of their parents as having developed one aspect of their powers rather fully, they portrayed them as denying other aspects of their selfhood.

Occasionally when this bifurcation was sharply drawn, the volcanic eruptions that were so typical of the earlier stories remained a theme, albeit the theme was now largely muted and the level of violence greatly diminished. While these mothers were depicted as hot-tempered and hysterical, it was the cold, unemotional fathers who erupted with volcanic force. The fathers relied on their wives to mediate and interpret their feelings to others. Such fathers were unemotional only in the sense that they did not articulate feelings. Indeed, it often appeared that it was the mother who was actually the thinker and the father who was the feeler— at least in terms of dealing with the personal and the interpersonal. A smooth relationship between such fathers and their daughters was often dependent on the mediation services provided by sensitive, feeling mothers. Such mothers tried to imagine, understand, and articulate each person's feelings. The conversations of these fathers and daughters could enter into the personal only when the mother became an interpreter and supplied them with the language of emotions.

It may be that the father's unmet need for the absent mother to intercede as an intermediary and translator explains why marital separation is so often followed by the abandonment of children by fathers. When a separation or divorce occurs, a father has to face his children directly, without the services of a mediator. Some fathers may feel so uncomfortable without an intermediary that they withdraw altogether. Teaching children and fathers to talk with each other directly might go a long way toward reducing the amount of intensity of such estrangements.

The descriptions of volcanic activity, alcoholism, violence, and abandonment were markedly diminished in the stories of family life told by procedural and constructivist knowers—in terms of both prevalence and virulence—when compared with the stories told by women who held the earlier perspectives. While fully 75 percent of the silent and the received knowers depicted one or both of their parents as alcoholic, only two (6 percent) of the reflective and constructivist knowers combined gave a parent this label. A third woman had a mother she proudly called a "sober alcoholic." "I really respect her for her progress in stopping drinking and being successful at it. That's one of the great accomplishments of her life. Being able to accept that she had a problem and that she could be doing something about it and being successful in it."

While a few of these women had parents who were separated or divorced, none of the fathers abandoned the father-daughter relationship altogether—an event that occurred with remarkable frequency in the previous collection of stories. When all family members were encouraged to draw on their whole range of capacities to deal with both the personal and the impersonal, they no longer needed to rely on the use of either power or abandonment for the resolution of conflicts. Instead, talking things through—however heatedly—became the preferred alternative. As Patti, the adolescent mother who helped us understand procedural knowing, said, "My mother and I can fight, argue, and scream about different points of things and yet end up saying, 'Well, thank you!' You know, appreciating each other no matter how much we disagree."

Mothers and Developing the Voice of Reason

The tendency to allocate intellectual capacities to fathers and emotional ones to mothers was largely overcome in the stories told by women who were integrating the voices of reason and emotions themselves. These women were much more likely to see mothers and fathers as endowed with both intellectual and emotional capacities. Almost all of them portrayed their mothers as having good minds and many of their fathers as having some capacity to acknowledge and articulate their feelings.

While subjectivists' mothers had the ability to speak from the gut and say what they felt, it was only in this last group of stories that the daughters consistently depicted their mothers as also having the ability to speak from the mind and to say what they thought. As Patti said,

> My mother is a wonderful person to talk to. I can talk to her about anything now. She is the type that can draw stuff out of a person. *She stands up for what she thinks* (emphasis added).

Another elaborated,

> My mother is very independent, very strong—a very verbal kind of person. She has got her opinions and she is not the least bit afraid to express them. When she gets into arguments there is a lot of love—but there is that independence of thought.

Mildred illustrates the pleasure that constructivist women and their mothers often take in each others's intellectual powers.

> My mother is a liberated woman who has a wonderful mind. After getting a Ph.D. in philosophy, she produced nine children and became the perfect housewife. About the age of forty she realized that she spent her whole life making other people happy and there are a lot of other things for women out there. She has gotten a second degree and now she teaches. She is very successful. Her students adore her and her children adore her.

Another college student saw her mother in similar terms.

> My mother is a wonderful person! She is really a miracle. Very creative, very political, very involved with life. She is complicated. I was always her friend. She included me in her life. She always comes to something with understanding.

These women portrayed their intelligent mothers as being very active learners.

> My mother always wants to be on top of the news. She is always questioning, investigating, and looking for something else, making challenges and demands on herself, in her job and with her children.

Like their daughters, these mothers had two inner voices at their command: a voice for expressing emotions and a voice for sharing reasons. Both could be heard. The use of one did not drown out the other.

Fathers and Developing the Voice of Emotions

As these women came to value their mothers for their good minds, many also began to find in their fathers emotional capacities that they never knew existed. As Patti said, "My father is trying to be more understanding, which makes it easier for me to express myself. He realizes now that emotions play a much larger part than logical thinking." While Patti saw her father changing, others saw that it was their own view of their fathers that was undergoing change. As one college student said, "My father is an emotional man who doesn't let you know that he is emotional. He is very intelligent, very logical, and very accepting. I can see now that he really has a depth of emotions that I've never really seen before."

The shift that these women noticed—where fathers became more tolerant of their nurturant and affiliative responses and mothers became more active and agentic—has been documented in many studies of adult men and women approaching mid-life (Cumming and Henry 1961; Gurin, Veroff, and Feld 1960; Gutmann 1964; 1975; Lowenthal, Thurnher, and Chiriboga 1975; Neugarten 1969; Rossi 1980). Again, it appears that when all goes well parents and children develop in tandem, that in the natural course of things the different generations can provide each other with the mutual supports that each requires for continued growth and development.

The Mother-Daughter Relationship and the Development of Connected Knowing

However much the parents of these women moved toward developing and integrating their intellectual and emotional capacities, distinctive differences remained between the ways the women depicted their mothers and fathers and related to them as knowers. While fathers served as models of separate knowing, it was in the relationships with mothers that these daughters found the most developed models of and opportunities for connected knowing. Connected knowing arises out of the experience of relationships; it requires intimacy and equality between self and object, not distance and impersonality; its goal is understanding, not proof.

Most of the procedural knowers reported that they talked with their mothers about personal things and they talked to their fathers—if they talked at all—about relatively impersonal topics. (In no case did this pattern reverse.) For example, a woman in her mid-twenties said,

> My mother is the one that I have more intimate discussions with. I can talk with her about stuff that I don't discuss with my father. . . . My mother deals more with that part of me which is able to deal with people, and sympathize with people, and communicate with people. My father has more to do with my intellectual development and my appreciation of literature.

And Faith said, "My dad has this dislike of what he calls 'idle chitchat,' but that's sort of necessary for a person." Faith's father liked to talk about "world affairs and crossword puzzles."

When fathers do talk to their daughters about matters of personal importance to the daughters, they tell them what they ought to do. One senior told us that her father was "still in the advice-giving mode." The father offered his advice out of loving concern. He wanted his daughter to major in economics in order to get a good job in business and become financially secure. But to the daughter, who was interested in painting and taking care of animals, the father's advice felt cold and controlling. When she failed to pursue her father's goals, she was aware that she had disappointed him. "My father categorizes me, and he always finds me wanting."

The intelligent mothers these women depicted were more like students, trying to understand; and they spoke of their intelligent fathers as being more like conventional teachers, bent on passing out truths. Linda's description of her parents provided an outstanding example. Both of her parents were psychiatrists involved as researchers and practitioners with adolescents and young adults (Linda's age group). Linda's mother looked to Linda as an expert she could consult. "She asks me—We talk a lot about her cases and her work. I kind of help her see the point of view of my generation—or whatever." Linda's mother asked, she did not tell. To her father, Linda was not an expert but a case that proved his points. She believed that her father was not interested in her as a unique person but as a general case for fitting into his "little classifications." She believed that he had little interest in the classifications that she might offer. "He makes me a case study. I'm just a little piece of evidence. . . . He is not interested in what goes on in my head." As Linda saw it, her father did not look to her for help to expand his understanding of her age group. Instead of asking her about her experience, he told her what she was experiencing. "Since I'm in this position, I must feel this way, this way, and this way. He has all of these little classifications which he fits everything into." She also believed that he was only interested in proving his old theories, not in generating new ones. She tested out this hunch: "I said, 'Dad, are you still learning new things?' And he goes, 'Well, not particularly.' " To her mother, Linda was a colleague or a teacher; to her father, Linda was a research subject, a student, or a child.

That such differences between mothers and fathers are so common may be accounted for by the fact that many men are used to being the expert, while many women are used to consulting others; many men are interested in how experience is generalized and universalized, while many women are interested in what can be learned from the particular; and the work of men frequently involves maintaining or increasing the status differential between persons, while the life work of many women focuses on maternal practice, where the main goal is to bring the smallest, least members up into relations of equality. While mothers and daughters slip into chairs around the kitchen table with ease, only occasionally do fathers abdicate their platforms without pressure from below.

To see themselves as equals, daughters often had to cut their fathers down to size. As one college alumna recounted,

> I am awed by my father. He is very smart, very intelligent, and very articulate. He can really pop the bubble. I can pop his bubble now and then! (Both laugh.) I never knew it before, but I can throw it right back to him—and he can be devastating!

By being devastating herself, she could meet him on equal ground. She continued,

> Eventually I began to realize that my father wasn't perfect. That he was a human being—with frailties and problems of his own. If my father said something, that was

that. You never argued with him. I began to realize that he could be wrong about stuff and that he did have deficiencies as a person. I think that helped our relationship in the sense that I could be a little more equal to him and able to communicate with him more. I think that's when we really started being very good friends.

Another woman definitely had seen her father, the professor, as God. She had once called him "Zeus" and said he was " a magnificent sight to look at." She agreed with one of his students that if her father "was running for God," she, too, would have voted for him. This father seemed to have campaigned for such a role. "He tends to have the approach that he is better than anyone else. He really has an overinflated ego. I think that any person will admit that early on in life parents are God—the authority. Later on they don't know a damn thing. And then after a while, you realize that they are reasonable people after all." In saying this, she paraphrased the words that Mark Twain put in the mouth of a young man: "My parents were so dumb when I was seventeen and so much smarter when I was twenty-one; I can't believe how much they learned in just four years."

While fathers of the constructivists occasionally still required dethroning, such images were largely absent from their stories of mothers. Indeed, the women in this group characterized the relationship between mothers and daughters as one of great intimacy, equality, and collegiality. While one might worry that such close, personal ties might hamper the individuation and development of these women, it was rare for women in this group to express such concerns. Indeed, Bertram Cohler and Henry Grunebaum (1981), in their study of daughter, mothers, and grandmothers, were also surprised at the intimate relationships they observed between different generations of women and revised their opinions about the difficulties such closeness might necessarily entail.

Not only did these women tend to cultivate relationships with their mothers that were very close and collegial, such relationships served as models for guiding and assessing many other relationships. As such, most of the constructivists were able to turn at least one of their professors into a colleague/friend of the highest order. Whenever such relationships took place, the sense of pleasure and accomplishment was unmistakable. Bridget shared her delight in the changes that even she and her father were able to bring about. "I tease him about the fact that I am finally getting myself established in life and that now he can start learning things from me. (Laughs.) I am going to love it! (Laughs.) It makes me feel great! He laughs! He agrees!" These women, along with many of their mothers, some of their professors, and a few of their fathers, became perpetual students *and* perpetual teachers. In trading these roles back and forth, they made colleagues of one another.

Maternal Conversation

"Gossip," Spacks says, "proceeds by a rhetoric of inquiry rather than of authority" (1982, pp. 33–34). The same is true of maternal conversation. Mothers interview their daughters. Mothers try to enter into their daughters' heads. Patti, for example, said of her mother, "She's the type of person that can draw stuff out of a person." A college student also described how her mother interviewed her. "She makes me question. I think that is intelligence. She is always asking me, 'Why?' She sees what I am doing." These mothers posed questions and took care to hear their daughters' answers. They valued the answers that their daughters gave. The parents— particularly the mothers—of these women even brought their own questions to the daughters for answers. "My parents are always telling me about dilemmas where they don't know what to do. They never know what to do!" The daughters, having developed the capacity for problem posing, interviewed their mothers as well. As one said, "My mother probably gets tired of me asking her hard questions. I suppose that I challenge her morals sometimes. That might annoy her about me." This daughter might like to know that such interviews, unlike lectures, are often appreciated.

Some of the women at the previous epistemological positions undoubtedly had parents who were also adept at question posing, but they did not describe such behavior. There may be a regular unfolding of the abilities to conceptualize and to articulate the processes involved in dialogue. "Telling" is understood long before the complexities of "asking" are comprehended (Arlin 1975). We feel that in most cases, mothers are no more caring than fathers, but their caring is more likely to take place in the connected mode. They try to help their daughters on the daughters' own terms, while fathers try to help in the fathers' terms. The effort to see others in their own terms is typical of the people Gilligan (1982) and her colleagues (Attanucci 1984; Lyons 1983) describe—mostly women—who are grounded in the responsibility mode of moral reasoning. Those who operate out of response strive to understand others in their own terms, while those oriented to a morality of rights see others in terms of social roles, norms, standards, and principles. Linda provided a good example when describing her mother.

> She trusts me. Any decision that I make. . . . We have a constant understanding of one another, a constant trust of each other's judgment. I could do just about anything, and if I sat down and explained it to her she would see my point of view and trust that I was doing it right—as I would for her. If I felt uncomfortable about something that she was doing, she would explain it to me and I'd feel comfortable. I'd trust her.

Both suspended judgment, listened to one another, and found their trust rewarded. Another women could even trust her mother with the trouble that she was only anticipating. "She is interested in what I am doing. I can talk to her about the trouble that I have gotten into and the trouble I am getting into. She is able to receive what I have to say."

These daughters often felt that their mothers heard and valued them in their own terms, even when they were in disagreement. Many talked about a father who basically wanted his daughter to fit into his categories, that her own terms had no value unless they were congruent with his.

> My father assumed all sorts of things about me. He evaluated me in five minutes, just like any old surgeon. "Hip bones, this and that and the next thing." He

judged me and then he categorized me. Sort of slotted me away nicely into the little mesh grid system he had for his little children. He never knew what was going on in my mind, but he was certain that he did. He never asked. I despise being categorized.

Linda assumed that her father just talked and never asked questions because he could not tolerate her point of view if it were to disagree with his. "He won't listen, 'cause it's like he refuses to trust us. It's like he refuses to believe that anything we would do is right, if it is different from what he would do." Really listening and suspending one's own judgment is necessary in order to understand other people in their own terms. As we have noted, this is a process that requires trust and builds trust.

Just as these daughters are seen in their own terms by their mothers, the daughters strove to see their mothers in their mothers' terms. Their success suggested that these daughters rejected the conventional expectation that mothers should remain selfless in their dedication to others. Indeed, almost all the mothers of these women are deeply committed to work outside the family, suggesting that the mothers also rejected the notion of selflessness and made a considerable investment in their own self-development as well as the development of others. The fact that these daughters showed only pride in the mothers' achievements, while other daughters often felt slighted by the mothers' outside commitments, suggests that these mothers were relatively successful in taking their own needs into consideration without sacrificing those of their families.

Just as it takes a long while to develop the capacity to pose questions for yourself, it takes a good deal of time before you can imagine and appreciate the questions that others pose for you; and it takes even longer to understand the importance of posing questions to others.

Patti was one of the few adolescent mothers we interviewed who acknowledged the importance of drawing out and listening as well as speaking to her child. About helping her child in trouble, Patti said that she would inquire and argue but that she would not dictate.

I hope that we will sit down and argue about everything until we can finally understand each other. I will try to understand why she did it, but I don't ever want to dictate to her. It is very important that you look at things in all aspects. To understand your daughter, you have to have a broad view over everything, an overlook of every possible aspect. Sometimes it is hard to understand what your kid is going through. That is where it is really difficult being a parent.

Patti saw talk—not rewards and punishments—as the most important teaching tool that she had at her disposal. She strove to understand what her child was thinking and why she did what she did. She realized that understanding another person—especially a small child—is an awesome and important responsibility. She asked the child questions so that the child could explain herself. Her questions encouraged the child to consider the consequences of her actions and to evaluate her choices of behavior. She wished that her child would be guided by her own understanding and choices, not by parental dictates. Patti was not simply child-centered, however. While she strove to understand her child and to meet her needs, she continued to request the child also to consider the needs and honor the perspective of others.

Women pose questions more than men, they listen to others, and they refrain from speaking out—these have long been considered signs of the powerlessness, subjugation, and inadequacy of women. When women's talk is assessed against standards established by men's behavior, it is seen as tentative, vacillating, and diminutive (Lakoff 1975).

The pattern of discourse that women have developed, however, may best be considered as an appropriate response to women's work. The care of children, or maternal practice, gives rise to maternal thought and particular modes of relating to the world (Ruddick 1980). Any speaker appreciates listeners who will still their own voices and pose good questions. To the small child, just beginning to frame ideas with words, such help is indispensable. Even Socrates abstained from sharing his thoughts with the educated men of Athens for fear that his ideas might prevent the men from working out ideas of their own. In "talking cures," therapists listen and refrain from speaking as they, too, understand the value of drawing out the human voice.

Many mothers interview their children, rather than lecture, possibly because they are genuinely fascinated by the child's thoughts and feelings and enjoy drawing the child out. Also, mothers may intuit that drawing out the child's ideas helps him or her articulate and develop emotions and thoughts. Ultimately, it is the receiving of the child and hearing what he or she has to say that develops the child's mind and personhood. There is now considerable evidence that this is the case. Parents who enter into a dialogue with their children, who draw out and respect their opinions, are more likely to have children whose intellectual and ethical development proceeds rapidly and surely (Baumrind 1971; Bayley and Schaefer 1964; Haan, Smith, and Block 1968; Hauser, Powers, Noam, Jacobson, Weiss, and Follansbee, 1984; Hess and Shipman 1965; Hoffman 1975; Holstein 1968; Kohlberg 1984; Lickona 1983; Parikh 1975; Shure and Spivack 1978).

Question posing, as we have seen, is central to maternal practice in its most evolved form. Question posing is at the heart of connected knowing. We argue that women's mode of talk, rather than being denigrated, should become a model for all who are interested in promoting human development. It is through attentive love, the ability to ask "What are you going through?" and the ability to hear the answer that the reality of the child is both created and respected.

REFERENCES

Adorno, T. W., E. Frenkel-Brunswick, D. J. Levinson, and R. N. Sanford. 1950. *The Authoritarian Personality.* New York: Harper & Row.

Al-Issa, I. 1980. *The Psychopathology of Women.* Englewood Cliffs, NJ: Prentice-Hall.

Arlin, P. 1975. "Cognitive Development in Adulthood." *Developmental Psychology* 11:602–606.

Attanucci, J. S. 1984. "Mothers in Their Own Terms: A Developmental Perspective on Self and Role." Unpublished doctoral dissertation. Harvard University.

Baumrind, D. 1971. "Current Patterns and Parental Authority." *Development Psychology Monographs* 4(1, part 2).

Bayley, N. and E. S. Schaefer, 1964. "Correlations of Maternal and Child Behaviors with the Development of Mental: Data from the Berkeley Growth Studies." *Monograph of the Society for Research in Child Development* 29(6, Serial no. 97).

Bell, R. Q. and L. V. Harper, 1977. *Child Effects on Adults*. Hillsdale NJ: Lawrence Erlbaum.

Bernard, J. 1981. *The Female World*. New York: The Free Press.

Bernstein, B. 1964. "Elaborated and Restricted Codes: Their Social Origins and Consequences." Pp. 55–69 in *The Ethnography of Communication*, edited by J. Gumperz and D. Hymes. *American Anthropologist* special publication 66 (6, pt. 2.).

Boulding, K. 1962. *Conflict and Defense: A General Theory*. New York: Harper & Row.

Chodorow, N. 1978. *The Reproduction of Mothering*. Berkeley: University of California Press.

Cohler, B. and H. Grunnebaum, 1981. *Mothers, Grandmothers, and Daughters*. New York: Wiley & Sons.

Cuming, E. and W. H. Henry. 1961. *Growing Old: The Process of Disengagement*. New York: Basic Books.

Ehrenreich, B. 1983. *The Hearts of Men: American Dreams and the Flight from Commitment*.

Engle, M. 1980. "Language and Play: A Comparative Analysis of Parental Initiatives." In *Language: Social Psychological Perspectives*, edited by H. Giles, W. P. Robinson, and P. M. Smith. Oxford: Pergamon Press.

Feverstein, R. 1980. *Instrumental Enrichment: An Intervention Program for Cognitive Modifiability*. Baltimore: University of Maryland Press.

Finkelhor, D. 1983. "Common Features of Family Abuse." Pp. 17–28. in *The Dark Side of Families: Current Family Violence Research*, edited by D. Finkelhor, R. J. Gelles, G. T. Hotaling, and M. A. Strauss. New York: Sage.

Fishman, P. 1978. "What Do Couples Talk About When They're Alone?" Pp. 11–22 in *Women's Language and Style*, edited by D. Butturff and E. L. Epstein. Akron, OH: L & S Books.

———. 1983. "Interaction: The Work Women Do." Pp. 89–102 in *Language, Gender, and Society*, edited by B. Thorne, C. Kramarae, and N. Henley. Rowley, MA: Newbury House.

Galinsky, E. 1981. *Between Generations: Stages of Parenthood*. New York: Berkley.

Gardner, H. 1985. *The Mind's New Science: A History of the Cognitive Revolution*. New York: Basic Books.

Gilligan, C. 1982. *In a Different Voice: Psychological Theory and Women's Development*. Cambridge, MA: Harvard University Press.

————. 1984. "The Conquistador and the Dark Continent: Reflections on the Psychology of Love." *Daedalus* 113: 75–95.

————. 1986. "Exit-Voice Dilemmas in Adolescent Development." In *Development, Democracy, and the Art of Trespassing: Essays in Honor of Albert O. Hirschman*, edited by A. Foxley, M. McPherson, and G. O'Donnell. Notre Dame, IN: University of Notre Dame Press.

Gleason, J. B. and E. B. Greif. 1983. "Men's Speech to Young Children." Pp. 140–150 in *Language, Gender and Society*, edited by B. Thorne, C. Kramarae, and N. Henley. Rowley, MA: Newbury House.

Greif, E. B. 1980. "Sex Differences in Parent-Child Conversations." Pp. 253–258 in *The Voices and Words of Men and Women*, edited by C. Kramarae. New York: Pergamon Press.

Gurin, G., J. Veroff, and S. Feld. 1960. *Americans View Their Mental Health*. New York: Basic Books.

Gutmann, D. 1964. "An Exploration of Ego Configurations in Middle and Later Life." Pp. 114–148 in *Personality in Middle and Later Life*, edited by B. L. Neugarten, New York: Atherton.

————. 1975. "Parenthood: A Key to the Comparative Study of the Life Cycle." Pp. 167–184 in *Life-Span Developmental Psychology: Normative Crisis*, edited by N. Datan and L. Ginsberg. New York: Academic Press.

Haan, N., M. B. Smith, and J. H. Block. 1968. "The Moral Reasoning of Young Adults: Political-Social Behavior, Family Background, and Personality Correlates." *Journal of Personality and Social Psychology* 10:183–201.

Hagen, E. V. 1962. *On the Theory of Social Change: How Economic Growth Begins*. Homewood, IL: Dorsey Press.

Hauser, S., S. I. Powers, G. Noam, A. M. Jacobson, B. Weiss, and D. J. Follansbee. 1984. "Familial Contexts of Adolescent Ego Development." *Child Development* 55:195–213.

Hess, R. D. and V. C. Shipman. 1965. "Early Experience and the Socialization of Cognitive Modes in Children." *Child Development* 36:869–886.

Hobbs, N. 1982. *The Troubled and Troubling Child: Reeducation in Mental Health, Education and Human Service Programs for Children and Youth*. San Francisco: Jossey-Bass.

Hoffman, M. L. 1975. "Moral Internalization, Parental Power, and the Nature of Parent-Child Interaction." *Developmental Psychology* 11:228–239.

Holstein, C. 1968. "Parental Determinants of the Development of Moral Judgement." Doctoral dissertation, University of California, Berkeley.

Kagan, J. 1984. *The Nature of the Child*. New York: Basic Books.

Kegan, R. 1982. *The Evolving Self*. Cambridge, MA: Harvard University Press.

Klein, C. 1984. *Mothers and Sons*. Boston, Houghton Mifflin.

Kohlberg, L. 1984. *The Psychology of Moral Development*. New York: Harper & Row.

Kohn, M. L. 1977. *Class and Conformity: A Study in Values*, 2nd edition. Chicago: University of Chicago Press.

————. "Job Complexity and Adult Personality." Pp. 193–212 in *Themes of Work and Love in Adulthood*, edited by N. J. Smelser and E. H. Erikson. Cambridge, MA: Harvard University Press.

Lakoff, R. 1975. *Language and Woman's Place*. New York: Harper & Row.

Lickona, T. 1976. *Moral Development and Behavior: Theory, Research, and Social Issues*. New York: Holt, Rinehart & Winston.

Lifton, R. J. 1976. *The Life of the Self*. New York: Simon & Schuster.

Loevinger, J. 1962. "Measuring Personality Patterns of Women." *Genetic Psychology Monographs* 65:53–136.

————. 1976. *Ego Development*. San Francisco: Jossey-Bass.

Lowenthal, M. F., M. Thurnher, and D. Chiriboga. 1975. *The Four Stages of Life*. San Francisco: Jossey-Bass.

Lyons, N. 1983. "Two Perspectives on Self, Relationship and Morality." *Harvard Educational Review* 53:125–145.

Miller, J. B. 1976. *Towards a New Psychology of Women*. Boston: Beacon Press.

Minuchin, S., B. Montalyo, B. G. Gurney, B. L. Rosman, and F. Schomer. 1967. *Families of the Slums: An Exploration of Their Structure and Treatment*. New York: Basic Books.

Neugarten, B. L. 1969. "Continuities and Discontinuities of Psychological Issues into Adult Life." *Human Development* 12:121–130.

Parikh, B. 1975. "Moral Judgment Development and Its Relation to Family Environment Factors in India and in the United States." Unpublished doctoral dissertation, Boston University.

Perry, W. G. 1970. *Forms of Intellectual and Ethical Development in the College Years*. New York: Holt, Rinehart & Winston.

Rappaport, A. 1960. *Fights, Games and Debates*. Ann Arbor: University of Michigan Press.

Riesman, D., R. Denney, and N. Glazer. [1950] 1961. *The Lonely Crowd*, 2nd edition. New Haven, CT: Yale University Press.

Rossi, A. 1980. "Aging and Parenting in the Middle Years." In *Life-Span Development and Behavior*, vol. 3, edited by P. Baltes and O. G. Brim. New York: Academic Press.

Rubin, L. 1976. *Worlds of Pain: Life in the Working-Class Family*. New York: Basic Books.

Ruddick, S. 1980. "Maternal Thinking." *Feminist Studies* 6:70–96. Reprinted in A. Cafagna, R. Peterson, and C. Staudenbaur (eds.). 1982. *Child Nurturance: Volume 1, Philosophy, Children, and the Family*. New York: Plenum Press.

Shure, M. and G. Spivack. 1978. *Problem Solving Techniques in Childrearing*. San Francisco: Jossey-Bass.

Spacks, P. 1982. "In Praise of Gossip." *Hudson Review* 35:19–38.

Veroff, J., E. Douovan, and R. A. Kulka. 1981. *The Inner American: A Self-Portrait from 1957–1976*. New York: Basic Books.

Ward, M. C. 1971. *Them Children: A Study in Language Learning.* New York: Holt, Rinehart & Winston.

Weissman, M. and E. Paykel. 1974. *The Depressed Woman.* Chicago: University of Chicago Press.

West, C. and D. H. Zimmerman. 1983. "Small Insults: A Study of Interruptions in Cross-Sex Conversations Between Unacquainted Persons." Pp. 103–118 in *Language, Gender and Society*, edited by B. Thorne, C. Kramarae, and N. Henley. Rowley MA: Newbury House.

Youniss, J. and J. Smoller. 1985. *Adolescent Relations with Mothers, Fathers and Friends.* Chicago: University of Chicago Press.

24

The Sexual Dilemma*

Lillian B. Rubin

WIFE: I say that foreplay begins in the morning.

HUSBAND: It seems to me being sexual would make us closer, but she says it works the other way—if she felt closer, there'd be more sex.

It's a common complaint in marriages—wives and husbands all too often divided as these two are. We wonder about it, ask each other questions, try to persuade the other with reason, and, when that fails, we argue. Sooner or later we make up, telling each other that we'll change. And, in the moment the words are said, we mean them. We try, but somehow the promises aren't fulfilled; somehow, without thought or intention, we slip back into the old ways. The cycle starts again; the struggle is resumed.

We're told by the experts that the problem exist because we don't communicate properly. We must talk to each other, they insist—explain what we need and want, what feels good, what bad. So "communication" has become a household word, the buzzword of the age. We think about it, talk about it, read books, take courses, see therapists to learn how to do it. We come away from these endeavors with resolutions that promise we'll change our ways, that we'll work without our partner on being more open and more expressive about what we're thinking and feeling. But too often our good intentions come to naught, especially when it comes to reconciling our sexual differences.

*Rubin, Lillian B. 1983. "The Sexual Dilemma." Pp. 98–119 in *Intimate Strangers: Men and Women Together*. New York: Harper & Row. Copyright © 1983 by the author. Reprinted by permission of Harper & Row, Publishers, Inc.

These are difficult issues, not easily amenable to intervention by talk, no matter how earnest, how compelling our efforts at honesty may be. One couple aged thirty-three and thirty-five, married eight years and the parents of two children, told of these differences. Speaking quickly and agitatedly, the wife said:

> Talk, talk, talk! He tries to convince me; I try to convince him. What's the use? It's not the words that are missing. I don't even know if the problem is that we don't understand each other. We understand, all right. But we don't like what we know; that's the problem.

Her husband's words came more slowly, tinged as they were with resignation and frustration.

> I understand what she wants. She wants us to be loving and close, then we can have sex. But it's not always possible that way. We're both busy; there are the kids. It can't be like a love affair all the time, and if we have to wait for that, well [his words trailing off] . . . what the hell, it'll be a long wait.

The wife, speaking more calmly but with her emotional turmoil still evident just below the surface of her words:

> He complains that I want it to be like a love affair, but that's not it. I want to feel some emotion from him; I want an emotional contact, not just a sexual one.

The husband, vexed and bewildered:

> When she starts talking about how I'm sexual but not emotional, that's it; that's where I get lost. Isn't sex emotional, for Christ's sake?

From both husband and wife, an angry yet plaintive cry. It's not words that divide them, however. They tell each other quite openly what they think, how they feel. It just doesn't seem to help in the ways they would wish. But, if it's not a simple matter of communication, then what is it that makes these issues seem so intransigent, so resistant to resolution even with the best intentions we can muster?

Some analysts of society point to the culture, to the ideologies that have defined the limits of male and female sexuality. Certainly there's truth in that. There's no gainsaying that, through the ages of Western society, women's sexuality has come under attack, that there have been sometimes extreme pressures to control and confine it—even to deny its existence. There's no doubt either that we have dealt with male sexuality with much more ambivalence. On the one hand, it too has been the object of efforts at containment; on the other, we have acknowledged its force and power—indeed, built myth and monument in homage to what we have taken to be its inherently uncontrollable nature.

Such social attitudes about male and female sexuality, and the behavioral ideals that have accompanied them, not only shape our sexual behavior but affect our experience of our own sexuality as well. For culture both clarifies and mystifies. A set of beliefs is at once a way of seeing the world more clearly while, at the same time, foreclosing an alternative vision. When it comes to sex—precisely because it's such a primitive, elemental force—all societies seek some control over it and, therefore, the mystification is greater than the clarification. Thus, for example, Victorian women often convinced themselves that they had no sexual feelings even when the messages their bodies sent would have told them otherwise if they had been able to listen. And, even now, men often engage in compulsive sexual behavior that brings them little, if any, pleasure without allowing themselves to notice the joylessness of it. Both behaviors a response to cultural mandates, both creating dissonance, if not outright conflict, when inner experience is at odds with behavioral expectations.

The blueprint to which our sexuality conforms, then, is drawn by the culture. But that's not yet the whole story. The dictates of any society are reinforced by its institutional arrangements and mediated by the personal experience of the people who must live within them. And it's in that confluence of social arrangement and psychological response that we'll come to understand the basis of the sexual differences that so often divide us from each other.

For a woman, there's no satisfactory sex without an emotional connection; for a man, the two are more easily separable. For her, the connection generally must precede the sexual encounter:

> For me to be excited about making love, I have to feel close to him—like we're sharing something, not just living together.

For him, emotional closeness can be born of the sexual contact.

> It's the one subject we never get anywhere on. It's a lot easier for me to tell her what she wants to hear when I feel close, and that's when I get closest—when we're making love. It's kind of hard to explain it, but [trying to find the words] . . . well, it's when the emotions come roaring up.

The issues that divide them around intimacy in the relationship are nowhere to be seen more clearly than here. When she speaks of connection, she usually means intimacy that's born of some verbal expression, some sharing of thought and feeling:

> I want to know what he's thinking—you know, what's going on inside him—before we jump into bed.

For him, it's enough that they're in the same room.

> To me, it feels like there's a nice bond when we're together—just reading the paper or watching the tube or something like that. Then, when we go to bed, that's not enough for her.

The problem, then, is not *how* we talk to each other but *whether* we do so. And it's connected to what words and the verbal expression of emotion mean to us, how sex and emotion come together for each of us, and the fact that we experience the balance between the two so differently—all of which takes us again to the separation and individuation experiences of childhood.

For both boys and girls, the earliest attachment and the identification that grows from it are much larger, deeper, and more all-embracing than anything we, who have successfully buried that primitive past in our unconscious, can easily grasp. Their root is pure eros—that vital, life-giving force with which all attachment begins. The infant bathes in it. But we are a society of people who have learned to look on eros with apprehension, if not outright fear. For us, it is associated with passion, with sex, with forces that threaten to be out of our control. And we teach our young very early, and in ways too numerous to count, about the need to limit the erotic, about our fears that eros imperils civilization.

In the beginning, it's the same for children of either sex. As the child grows past the early symbiotic union with mother, as the boundaries of self begin to develop, the social norms about sexuality begin to make themselves felt. In conformity with those norms, the erotic and emotional are split one from the other, and the erotic takes on a more specifically sexual meaning.

But here the developmental similarities end. For a boy at this stage, it's the emotional component of the attachment to mother that comes under attack as he seeks to repress his identification with her. The erotic—or sexualized—aspect of the attachment is left undisturbed, at least in heterosexual men. To be sure, the incest taboo assures that future sexual *behavior* will take place with a woman other than mother. But the issue here is not behavior but the emotional structure that underlies it.

For a girl, the developmental requirement is exactly the opposite. For her, it's the erotic component of the attachment to a woman that must be denied and shifted later to a man; the larger emotional involvement and the identification remain intact.

This split between the emotional and the erotic components of attachment in childhood has deep and lasting significance for the ways in which we respond to relationships—sexual and otherwise—in adulthood. For it means that, for men, the erotic aspect of any relationship remains forever the most compelling, while, for women, the emotional component will always be the more salient. It's here that we can come to understand the depth of women's emotional connection to each other—the reasons why nonsexual friendships between women remain so central in their lives, so important to their sense of themselves and to their well-being. And it's here also that we can see why nonsexual relationships hold such little emotional charge for men.

It's not, as folklore has held, that a woman's sexual response is more muted than a man's, or that she doesn't need or desire sexual release the way a man does. But, because it's the erotic aspect of her earliest attachment that has to be repressed in childhood if a girl is later to form a sexual bond with a man, the explicitly sexual retains little *independent* status in her inner life. A man may lust after *women*, but a woman lusts after *a man*. For a woman, sex usually has meaning only in a relational context—perhaps a clue to why so many girls never or rarely masturbate in adolescence or early adulthood.

We might argue that the social proscriptions against masturbation alone could account for its insignificance in girls and young women. But boys, too, hear exhortations against masturbation—indeed, even today, many still are told tales of the horrors that will befall them. Yet, except to encourage guilt and secrecy, such injunctions haven't made much difference in its incidence among them.

It would be reasonable to assume that this is a response to the mixed message this society sends to men about their sexuality. On the one hand, they're expected to exercise restraint; on the other, there's an implicit understanding that we can't really count on them to do so—that, at base, male sexuality cannot be controlled, that, after all, boys will be boys.

Surely such differences in the ways in which male and female sexuality are viewed could account for some of the differences between the sexes in their patterns and incidence of masturbation. But I believe there's something else that makes the social prohibitions take so well with women. For with them, an emotional connection in a relationship generally is a stimulus, if not a precondition, for the erotic.

If women depend on the emotional attachment to call up the sexual, men rely on the sexual to spark the emotional, as these words from a forty-one-year-old man, married fourteen years, show:

> Having sex with her makes me feel much closer so it makes it easier to bridge the emotional gap, so to speak. It's like the physical sex opens up another door, and things and feelings can get expressed that I couldn't before.

For women, emotional attachments without sex are maintained with little difficulty or discomfort; for men, they're much more problematic. It's not that they don't exist at all, but that they're less common and fraught with many more difficulties and reservations.

This is the split that may help to explain why men tend to be fearful of homosexuality in a way that women are not. I don't mean by this that women welcome homosexual stirrings any more than men do. But, for women, the emotional and the erotic are separated in such a way that they can be intensely connected emotionally without fear that this will lead to a sexual connection. For men, where the emotional connection so often depends on a sexual one, a close emotional relationship with another man usually is experienced as a threat.

We can see most clearly how deep these differences run when we compare the sexual behaviors of lesbians and homosexual men. Here, the relationships are not muddied by traditional gender differences, suspicions, and antagonisms, and the differences between men and women are stark—there for anyone to see.

In a series of intensive interviews with gay women and men, I was struck repeatedly by the men's ability to take pleasure in a kind of anonymous sex that I rarely, if ever, saw in the lesbian world. For gay women, sex generally is in the context of a relationship—transient perhaps but, for however long it lasts, with genuine elements of relatedness. There are no "fucking buddies" whose names are irrelevant or unknown among lesbians—a common phenomenon with homosexual men. The public bathhouses so popular with many gay men are practically nonexistent for the women because the kind of impersonal, fleeting sexual encounters such places specialize in hold no attraction for most of them.

Among gay men, a friendship that doesn't include sex is rare. With gay women, it's different. Like their straight sisters, lesbians can have intensely intimate and satisfying relationships with each other without any sexual involvement. Certainly a nonsexual relationship will sometimes slide over into a sexual relationship. But, when it does, it's the emotional aspect of the entire relationship, not just the sexual, that's at center stage for the women.

Whether a person is straight or gay, the character of the split between sex and emotion is the same. But the way it's experienced generally is quite different depending upon whether the sexual partner is a woman or a man. Among straight men, because the sexual involvement is with a woman, it calls up the memory of the infantile attachment to mother along with the old ambivalence about separation and unity, about emotional connection and separateness. It's likely, therefore, that it will elicit an intense emotional response—a response that's threatening even while it's gratifying. It's what men look for in their sexual relations with a woman, as these words from a thirty-four-year-old husband tell:

> It's the one time when I can really let go. I guess that's why sex is so important to me. It's the ultimate release; it's the one place where I can get free of the chains inside me.

And it's also what they fear. For it threatens their defenses against the return of those long-repressed feeling for that other woman—that first connection in their lives. So they hold on to the separation between the sexual and emotional, and thereby keep the repression safe. Thus, moments after speaking of sex as the "one place" where he could feel free, the same man spoke of his apprehensions:

> Much as I look for it, sex can also be a problem for me sometimes. I can get awfully anxious and tense about it. If I don't watch it, so much begins to happen that I get scared, like I don't know where I'm at. So that puts a damper on things. I'm a little ashamed to say it, but I can do a whole lot better sexually with someone else—you know, someone I don't care about—than I can with her. With someone like that, it doesn't mess up my insides and get all that stuff boiling around.

"What is this 'stuff' that upsets you so?" I wondered aloud. Discomfited, he lowered his head and muttered, "I don't really know." "Could you try to figure it out for me?" I prodded gently.

> Well, it's really hard to put it into words, but let's see. The closest I can get is to say it feels like something I don't want to know about—maybe something I'm not supposed to know about. [A thoughtful pause] Jesus, I said that, but I'm not even sure what it means. Let's see! It's something like this. If I let it all happen—I mean, let all those feelings just happen—I don't know where it'll end. It's like a

person could get caught in them, trapped, so that you could never get out. Hell, I don't know. I've heard people say sex is like going back to the womb. Maybe that's it. Only you came out of the womb, and here it feels like you might never get out again. Does that make any sense to you?

Without doubt the sex act evokes a set of complex and contradictory emotional responses for both women and men—responses that leave them each feeling at once powerful and vulnerable, albeit in different ways. For a man, there's power in claiming a woman's body—a connection with his maleness that makes him feel alive, masterful, strong. A thirty-three-year-old man, married eight years, said wistfully:

When things are quiet between us sexually, as they are now, it's not just the sex I miss, it's the contact.

"Do you mean the contact with Marianne?" I asked.

Yeah, but it's what it stands for; it's not just her. I mean, it's the contact with her, sure, but it's how it makes me feel. I guess the best word for that is "alive"; it makes me feel alive and [searching for the word] I guess you could say, potent.

At the same time, there's anxiety about the intense, out-of-control feelings that are moving inside him—feelings that leave him vulnerable again to the will and whim of a woman.

I'm not always comfortable with my own sexuality because I can feel very vulnerable when I'm making love. It's a bit crazy, I suppose, because in sex is when I'm experiencing the essence of my manhood and also when I can feel the most frightened about it—like I'm not my own man, or I could lose myself, or something like that.

It deserves a slight detour to comment on the phrase "the essence of my manhood," used by this man to describe his sexual potency and feelings. It makes intuitive sense to us; we know just what he means. Yet it set me to wondering: What is the essence of womanhood?

Some women, I suppose, might say it lies in nurturance, some might speak about mothering, most probably would be puzzled because there would be no single, simple answer that would satisfy. But one thing is sure: For most women, the "essence of womanhood" would not lie in their genitals or in their experience of their sexual powers. That it's such a common experience among men is, perhaps, an effect of their early difficulties in establishing a male identity. Nothing, after all, more clearly separates a boy from his mother than this tangible evidence of his maleness.

This aside now done, let's return to the complex of feelings a man experiences around a sexual connection with a woman. There's comfort in being in a woman's arms—the comfort of surrender to the feelings of safety and security that once were felt so deeply, the warming sense of being nurtured and nourished there once again. And there are enchantment and ecstasy to be found there as well—the thrill of experiencing the "essence of manhood," the delight of recapturing the unity with another that had to be forsworn so long ago. But it's also those same feelings that can be felt as a threat. For they constitute an assault on the boundaries between self and other he erected so long ago. And they threaten his manliness, as this culture defines it, when he experiences once again his own dependent needs and wishes.

Thus delight and fear play catch with each other—both evident in the words men use to describe the feelings and fantasies that sex elicits. They speak sometimes of "falling into a dark cavern," and at other times of "being taken into a warm, safe place." They say they're afraid of "being drawn into an abyss," and also that it feels like "wandering in a soft, warm valley." They talk about feeling as if they're drowning, and say also that it's like "swimming in warmth and sunshine." They worry about "being trapped," and exult about feeling "free enough to fly."

Sometimes the same man will describe his feelings with such contradictory words:

> It depends. Sometimes I can get scared. I don't even know exactly why, but I feel very vulnerable, like I'm too wide open. Then it feels dangerous. Other times, no sweat, it's just all pure pleasure.

Sometimes it's different men who speak such widely disparate thoughts. No matter. All together they tell us much about the intensity of the experience, of the pleasure and the pain that are part of the sexual connection.

For a woman, there's a similar mix of feelings of power, vulnerability, and pleasure. There's power in her ability to turn this man who usually is so controlled, so in charge, into what one woman called "a great big explosion" and another characterized as "a soft jellyfish." A thirty-four-year-old woman, married eleven years, put it this way:

> There's that moment in sex when I know I'm in control, that he really couldn't stop anymore because his drive is so great, that I feel wonderful. I feel like the most powerful person in that instant. It's hard to explain in words what that feels like—I mean, the knowledge I have at that second of my own sexual power.

And, alongside this sense of her own power, there's vulnerability also. Thus, sighing in bemusement at the intricacies of her own feelings, she continued:

> But it's funny because there's also that instant when he's about to enter me when I get this tiny flash of fear. It comes and goes in a second, but it's almost always there. It's a kind of inner tensing up. There's a second when instead of opening up my body, I want to close it tight. I guess it's like being invaded, and I want to protect myself against it for that instant. Then he's in and it's gone, and I can get lost in the sexual excitement.

The fear that each of them experiences is an archaic one—the remnants of the separation-unity conflict of childhood that's brought to the surface again at the moment of sexual union. The response is patterned and predictable. He fears engulfment; she fears invasion. Their emotional history combines with cultural mandates about femininity and masculinity to prepare them each for their own side; their physiology does the rest.

For men, the repression of their first identification and the muting of *emotional* attachment that goes with it fit neatly with cultural proscriptions about manliness that require them to abjure the emotional side of life in favor of the rational. Sex, therefore, becomes the one arena where it is legitimate for men to contact their deeper feeling states and to express them. Indeed, all too often, the sex act carries most of the burden of emotional expression for men—a reality of their lives that may explain the urgency with which men so often approach sex. For, if sex is the main conduit through which inhibited emotions are animated, expressed, and experienced, then that imperative and compulsive quality that seems such a puzzle becomes understandable.

But the act of entry itself stirs old conflictual desires that must be contained. This is the moment a man hungers for, while it's also the instant of his greatest vulnerability. As a woman takes him into her body, there are both ecstasy and fear—the ecstasy of union with a woman once again; the fear of being engulfed by her, of somehow losing a part of himself that he's struggled to maintain through the years.

For a woman, the repression of her first *erotic* attachment is also a good fit with the cultural proscriptions against the free expression of her sexuality. But, in childhood, there was no need to make any assault on her first identification with mother and the deep emotional attachment that lay beneath it; no need, either, to differentiate herself as fully and firmly as was necessary for a male child. In adulthood, therefore, she remains concerned with the fluidity of her boundaries, on guard against their permeability—a concern that's activated most fully at the moment of penetration.

This is one of those moments in life when the distinction between fantasy and reality is blurred by the fact that the two actually look so much alike. With entry, her boundaries have been violated, her body invaded. It's just this that may explain why a woman so often avoids the sexual encounter—a common complaint in marriages—even when she will also admit to finding it pleasurable and gratifying once she gets involved. For there are both pleasure and pain—the pleasure of experiencing the union, the pain of the intrusion that violates her sometimes precarious sense of her own separateness. Together, these conflicting feelings often create an inertia about sex—not about an emotional connection but about a sexual one—especially when she doesn't feel as if there's enough emotional pay-off in it to make it worth the effort to overcome her resistance to stirring up the conflict again.

This conflict can be seen in its most unvarnished form in the early stages of relations between lesbians. There's a special kind of ecstasy in their sexual relationship just because it's with a woman—because in a woman's arms the boundaries of separateness fall, the dream of a return to the old symbiosis with mother is fulfilled. But the rapture can be short-lived, for the wish for symbiosis belongs to the infant, not the adult. Once achieved, therefore, ecstasy can give way to fear—fear of the loss of self, which is heightened beyond anything known in the sexual bond with a man.

There's anxiety about boundaries in heterosexual sex, of course. But there's also some measure of safety that exists in this union with one's opposite. For, although sex between a man and a woman can be an intensely intimate experience, there's a limit, a boundary between them that can't be crossed simply by virtue of the fact that they're woman and man. It may, indeed, be one of the aspects of sex with a man that a woman finds so seductive—the ability to satisfy sexual need while still retaining the integrity of a separate sense of self. For, in heterosexual sex, the very physical differences help to reassure us of our separateness while, at the same time, permitting a connection with another that's possible in no other act in human life.

Between two women—just as there was with mother—there's likeness, not difference. Lesbians speak often of the pleasure in this identity, telling of their feeling that loving each other is akin to loving self. But this very identity also raises all the old issues of fusion with a woman and sets the stage for the ambivalent oscillation between desire and fear. This is the central conflict in the early stages of a lesbian relationship—the conflict which it must survive if it is to become a lasting one. And it's in their ability to surmount the conflicts these boundary issues produce while, at the same time, maintaining an extraordinary level of intimacy that enduring lesbian relationships may be most instructive for the heterosexual world.

But what about sexual relations between men? Where does male homosexuality fit into this picture? It's different, of course, as these matters of relationship and emotion differ between men and women.

First of all, the boundary problems are not so central for men as for women because, as we have seen a man develops boundaries that are more rigid and inflexible than a woman's. Therefore, the threat of merger that inheres in the identity between two women will not be a serious issue for men. Rather, the central problem between men is more likely to be related to their difficulty in bridging the distance between them, not in how to maintain it. In fact, to the degree that their boundaries can be penetrated,the threat more likely comes in relations with a woman rather than with a man just because this is the connection that has been the denied one.

Second, because the split between the sexual and the emotional is such a dominant characteristic of male sexuality, relations with men relieve the pressure for an emotional connection that's always present in any interaction with a woman—whether sexual or not. It's this split that permits the kind of impersonal sex so common among homosexual men—sex that's erotically stimulating and exciting yet leaves the emotions relatively untouched; "high sensation, low emotion sex" is the way a male colleague characterized it. And it's this split that, at least until now, has made lasting emotional connections between homosexual men so much less common than among lesbians. When men relate to women, they must confront that split, try to heal it, if their relations are to survive. But, without women in their lives to insist upon the primacy of the emotional connection, it will often get attenuated, if not lost.

As I write these pages, some questions begin to form in my mind. "Is all this," I wonder, "just another way of saying that women are less sexual than men? What about the women we see all around us today who seem to be as easy with their sexuality as men are, and as emotionally detached?"

Without doubt there are today—perhaps always have been—some women for whom sex and emotion are clearly split. But, when we look beneath the behavior of even the most sexually active woman, most of the time we'll see that it's not just sex that engages her. It's true that such a woman no longer needs to convince herself that she's in love in order to have a sexual relationship with a man. But the key word here is *relationship*—limited, yes, perhaps existing only in a transitory fantasy, but there for her as a reality. And, more often than not, such relationships, even when they are little more than fleeting ones, have meanings other than sexual for a woman. For the sexual stimulus usually is connected to some emotional attachment, however limited it may be. And what, at first glance, might seem simply to be a sexual engagement is, in reality, a search for something else.

We need only listen to women to hear them corroborate what I'm saying here. When asked what it is they get in their more casual sexual encounters, even those who consider themselves the most sexually liberated will generally admit that they're often not orgasmic in such transient relationships. "When I was single, I'd sleep with someone who appealed to me right away, no problems," said a recently married twenty-seven-year-old breezily. "Did you usually have orgasms in those relationships?" I asked her. Laughing, she replied, "Nope, that was reserved." "Reserved for what?" I wanted to know. Saucily, "For the guy who deserved it." "And what does that mean?" Finally, she became serious. "I guess it means I have to trust a guy before I can come with him—like I have to know there's some way of touching him emotionally and that I can trust him enough to let him into that part of me."

"What's in it for you?" I asked all the women who spoke this way. "Why get involved at all if it's not sexually gratifying?" Without exception, they said they engaged sexually because it was the only way they could get the other things they need from a man. "What things?" I wanted to know. The answer: Something that told of their need for relationship and attachment rather than sex. They spoke of wanting "hugging more than fucking," of how it "feels good to be connected for a little while." They talked almost urgently of the "need to be held," "to feel needed by someone," of how important it is that "there's someone to give something to and take something from."

It's true, men also will speak of the need to be held and hugged. But orgasm generally is not in question and hugging is seldom an end to be desired in and for itself. In fact, it's one of the most common complaints of women that, even in the context of a stable relationship, such tender physical contact becomes too quickly transformed into a prelude to sex. "Why can't he just be happy to hold me; why does it always have to lead to fucking?" a woman complains. "I hold her and we hug and cuddle; I like it and I like her to hold me, too. But there's a natural progression, isn't there?" her husband asks, mystified.

Whether in my research or in my clinical work, I hear the same story told—women who are sexually very active yet who only become orgasmic in the context of a relationship with a man they can trust, as these words illustrate. She's a forty-three-year-old woman in a four-year second marriage after having been single for seven years. Talking about some of the experiences of those years as a divorcee, she said:

> There wasn't any dearth of men in my life most of the time, and I learned a lot about myself and how I relate to them during those years. I found out that going to bed with someone was one thing, but getting satisfied sexually was another.
>
> When I got married the first time, I was practically virginal—hardly any experience with anyone but my husband. So I didn't know much about my own sexuality. I mean, I knew I was a very sexual woman, but I thought having orgasms was practically automatic, you know, just a matter of pushing the right buttons, so to speak. What a surprise when I got divorced and started sleeping around with a lot of guys! [With a rueful grin] All of a sudden it seemed like my body had a mind of its own and I just couldn't make it; I couldn't come, I mean. I'd get all hot and excited and . . . poof, nothing. I couldn't understand it; I mean, I had no idea what was happening.
>
> Then I got involved with a guy I really liked. It was an honest-to-God relationship with a good man who cared about me as a person, and lo and behold, I was orgasmic again. I didn't get it right away, but after a while, even if you're a dimwit, you get the point.

The flow of words stopped, as if she considered the "point" self-evident. Not certain just what she meant, I asked for an explanation. "What was it you finally 'got'?"

> Well, after a couple of those experiences, I began to realize that something in me would withhold having an orgasm when I was with a man I didn't trust. I didn't plan it that way; it just happened. It didn't make any difference how attracted I was to him or how turned on I was, if I didn't trust him in some deep place inside me, then I wouldn't be able to come, and that was that.

Trust is, of course, an issue for men as well. Like the inorgasmic woman, a man, too, can become impotent in a sexual encounter with a woman he fears is untrustworthy. In recent years, we have heard more about such men than ever before—perhaps because there are more of them, perhaps only because these issues are more likely to be part of a public discussion these days. But, whatever their number, it's a much less common phenomenon than it is among women. Moreover, when impotence does hit, it's almost as likely to happen in the context of an emotional relationship as it is with a stranger. A thirty-one-year-old cook, married only a short time, spoke of both these moments when experience has taught him that impotency could become an issue for him:

It's a damned funny business and I can't know exactly when it'll happen. I finally figured out it happens when something scares me—you know, when I figure maybe it's not safe. [Looking perplexed] Sounds a little nuts, doesn't it? What's not safe? I don't know. Sometimes it would be when I was trying to get it on with someone I didn't know—like the first time with a woman. But that's from my past life— [laughing] I mean when I was single. It happens sometimes with LuAnn, too—not a lot, just sometimes. She's great—never makes me feel like I let her down or anything. But it worries me when it happens anyhow. Thing is, I don't really know why, but I think it's the same scared feeling, like something inside me goes, "Uh, oh—better watch out."

"Watch out for what?" I asked. He stood up, paced the room, tried to answer.

That's the thing; it's hard to put it in words. It's just "better watch out." With some person I don't know, I can figure I don't trust her so much so I get scared. After all, when you're at the peak in sex, you're damned vulnerable—right out there with everything hanging out, so to speak. [With a rush] I mean you're there, man! [Stopping then, as if hearing his own words for the first time, then continuing more calmly] Christ, I guess it's the same with LuAnn, isn't it? It's such an intense experience, sex, that you can't help exposing a lot, so sometimes you can't be sure you can trust *any* woman with it.

Obviously, most men as well as women prefer sex in the context of a relationship with a person to whom they have some emotional attachment. But, in contrast to women, for men, most of the time it's just that—a preference that can be put aside when, for whatever reasons, it cannot be honored. The fullness of the emotional experience may be diminished under conditions that are less than ideal for them, but their sexual pleasure and capacity for orgasm generally are not.

Indeed, for some men, sex is easier, less riddled with conflict, when it comes without emotional attachment. For there are still many men who suffer the madonna-whore split inside themselves—men who love the "good" woman but who lust after the "bad" one, men who can experience their sexuality fully only with a woman with whom there is no emotional connection. A thirty-eight-year-old accountant, married two years after having been divorced and single for six, said painfully:

I love Caroline but, damnit, sex just isn't as exciting anymore. I was a regular stud when I was single—always ready, yeah, at your service ma'am, no problems. [Turning to stare out the window which framed a lovely garden] Now it's all changed and I worry like hell about what it's going to do to our marriage. She's patient, but she admits she'd like more sex. But I seem to have lost interest. I go along for a while thinking sex just doesn't matter much to me anymore. Then some woman catches my attention and I feel the flash inside me that says, "Boy would I like to get my hands on *that*." [Bewildered] I don't know! It was the same thing in my first marriage. I'd get it on with women I didn't give a damn about and fly high with it, but with my wife [his words trailing off] . . . I'm scared; I don't want it to happen again. [Retreating suddenly from the obvious emotion in the room, he laughed] What do you think? Do I need a shrink? Am I hiding some deep, dark secret about wanting to fuck my mother? Huh? What about it?

His thirty-one-year-old wife tells her side:

At the beginning, it was wonderful. I'm sexually pretty free. I mean, I'm not some kind of—what'll I say?—some kind of wild woman, but I'm cool. I like sex and there's not much I wouldn't do sexually. And Randy loved it when we were going together—or at least I thought he did. He acted like it anyway. But not long after we got married, it all changed.

"Then you didn't live together before you got married?" I asked.

No, we were in two different cities—about five hundred miles apart. So we had weekends together, when we could manage it, and one week's vacation. But we didn't go together very long before we got married. The five hundred miles seemed to get longer and longer, and in a few months we decided to stop fooling around and just do it. [Sighing as she remembered the past] They were wonderful months, though—especially in bed. It was like an explosion when we came together. And now . . . well, most of the time it's just kind of bloop and blah. I finally convinced him that we ought to try some therapy and we've been seeing someone for the last couple of months. But between you and me, I think he needs to do it alone. It's not like I think I'm perfect or anything, but I really think this is his problem, not mine. I keep having the feeling that now that we're married, he wishes I were a virgin or something. I know it sounds crazy, but that's what I feel.

"Has the couples therapy helped any? Has anything changed at all?" I wondered aloud.

Oh yeah, it's better—at least some of the time it is. But I get discouraged sometimes—and scared, too, I guess. It gets better for a while and I get all revved up and hopeful, then he just poops out again. And that's the way it is right now—up and down, up and down, over and over again.

And so it goes: "up and down, over and over again." We make some changes, and the old issues pop up again in new form. We move ahead, and something comes along to push us back. We think about it, wonder about it, fret about it, argue with each other, often forgetting that each step is a gain—a small one, perhaps, but a movement forward which, while it might not take us as far as we would wish, also doesn't permit an easy return to the old ways. Meanwhile, we continue to reach out to each other in yearning—searching for connection, for unity, for emotional release. And again we confront the central dilemma of our relations with each other. For the unity and connection that's at least momentarily possible in this union of two bodies—that makes sex so deeply satisfying—also touches our deepest and earliest fears.

25

The Good-Provider Role: Its Rise and Fall*

Jessie Bernard

The Lord is my shepherd, I shall not want. He sets a table for me in the very sight of my enemies; my cup runs over (23rd Psalm). And when the Israelites were complaining about hungry they were on their way from Egypt to Canaan. God told Moses to rest assured: There would be meat for dinner and bread for breakfast the next morning. And, indeed, there were quails that very night, enough to cover the camp, and in the morning the ground was covered with dew that proved to be bread (Exodus 16:12–13). In fact, in this role of good provider, God is sometimes almost synonymous with Providence. Many people like Micawber, still wait for him, or Providence, to provide.

Granted, then, that the first great provider for the human species was God the Father, surely the second great provider for the human species was Mother, the gatherer, planter, and general factotum. Boulding (1976), citing Lee and de Vore, tells us that in hunting and gathering societies, males contribute about one fifth of the food of the clan, females the other four fifths (p. 96). She also concludes that by 12,000 B.C. in the early agricultural villages, females provided four fifths of human subsistence (p. 97). Not until large trading towns arose did the female contribution to human subsistence decline to equality with that of the male. And with the beginning of true cities, the provisioning work of women tended to become invisible. Still, in today's world it remains substantial.

Whatever the date of the virtuous woman described in the Old Testament (Proverbs 31:10-27), she was the very model of a good provider. She was, in fact, a highly productive conglomerate. She woke up in the middle of the night to tend to her business; she oversaw a multiple-industry household; *her* candles did not go out at night; there was a ready market for the high-quality linen girdles she made and sold to the merchants in town; and she kept track of the real estate market and bought good land when it became available, cultivating vineyards quite profitably. All this time her husband sat at the gate talking with his cronies.

A recent counterpart to the virtuous woman was the busy and industrious shtetl woman:

> The earnings of a livelihood is sexless, and the large majority of women... participate in some gainful occupation if they do not carry the chief burden of support. The wife of a "perennial student" is very apt to be the sole support of the family. The problem of managing both a business and a home is so common that no one recognizes it as special. . . . To bustle about in search of a livelihood is merely another form of bustling about managing a home; both are aspects of . . . health and livelihood. (Zborowski and Herzog 1952, p. 131)

In a subsistence economy in which husbands and wives ran farms, shops, or businesses together, a man might be a good, steady worker, but the idea that he was *the* provider would hardly ring true. Even the youth in the folk song who listed all the gifts he would bestow on his love if she would marry him—a golden comb, a paper of pins, and all the rest—was not necessarily promising to be a good provider.

I have not searched the literature to determine when the concept of the good provider entered our thinking. The term *provider* entered the English language in 1532, but was not yet male sex typed, as the older term *purveyor* already was in 1442. Webster's second edition defines the good provider as "one who provides, especially, colloq., one who provides food, clothing, etc. for his family; as, he is a good or an adequate provider." More simply, he could be defined as a man whose wife did not have to enter the labor force. The counterpart to the good provider was the housewife. However the term is defined, the role itself delineated relationships within a marriage and family in a way that added to the legal, religious, and other advantages men had over women.

Thus, under the common law, although the husband was legally head of the household and as such had the responsibility of providing for his wife and children, this provision was often made with help from the wife's personal property and earnings, to which he was entitled:

> He owned his wife's and children's services, and had the sole right to collect wages for their work outside the home. He owned his wife's personal property outright, and had the right to manage and control all of his wife's real property during marriage, which included the right to use or lease property, and to keep any rents and profits from it. (Babcock, Freedman, Norton, and Ross 1975, p. 561)

So even when she was the actual provider, the legal recognition was granted the husband. Therefore, whatever the husband's legal responsibilities for support may have been, he was not necessarily a good provider in the way the term came to be understood. The wife may have been performing that role.

In our country in Colonial times women were still viewed as performing a providing role, and they pursued a variety of occupations. Abigail Adams managed the family estate, which provided the wherewithal for John to spend so much time in Philadelphia. In the 18th century "many women were active in business and professional pursuits. They ran inns and taverns; they managed a wide variety of stores and shops; and, at least occasionally, they worked in careers like publishing, journalism and medicine" (Demos 1974, p. 430). Women sometimes even "joined the menfolk for work in the fields" (p. 430). Like the household of the proverbial virtuous woman, the Colonial household was a little factory that produced clothing, furniture, bedding, candles, and other accessories, and again, as in the case of the virtuous woman, the female role was central. It was taken for granted that women provided for the family along with men.

The good provider as a specialized male role seems to have arisen in the transition from subsistence to market—especially money—economies that accelerated with the industrial revolution. The good-provider role for males emerged in this country roughly, say, from the 1830s, when de Tocqueville was observing it, to the late 1970s, when the 1980 census declared that a male was not automatically to be assumed to be head of household. This gives the role a life span of about a century and a half. Although relatively short-lived, while it lasted the role was a seemingly rock-like feature of the national landscape.

As a psychological and sociological phenomenon, the good-provider role had wide ramifications for all of our thinking about families. It marked a new kind of marriage. It did not have good effects on women: The role deprived them of many chips by placing them in a peculiarly vulnerable position. Because she was not reimbursed for her contribution to the family in either products or services, a wife was stripped to a considerable extent of her access to cash-mediated markets. By discouraging labor force participation, it deprived many women, especially affluent ones, of opportunities to achieve strength and competence. It deterred young women from acquiring productive skills. They dedicated themselves instead to winning a good provider who would "take care of" them. The wife of a more successful provider became for all intents and purposes a parasite, with little to do except indulge or pamper herself. The psychology of such dependence could become all but crippling. There were other concomitants of the good-provider role.

EXPRESSIVITY AND THE GOOD-PROVIDER ROLE

The new industrial order that produced the good provider changed not so much the division of labor between the sexes as it did the site of the work they engaged in. Only two of the concomitants of this change in work site are selected for comment here, namely, (a) the identification of gender with work site as well as with work itself and (b) the reduction of time for personal interaction and intimacy within the family.

It is not so much the specific kinds of work men and women do—they have always varied from time to time and place to place—but the simple fact that the sexes do different kinds of work, whatever it is, which is in and of itself important. The division of labor by sex means that the work group becomes also a sex group. The very nature of maleness and femaleness becomes embedded in the sexual division of labor. One's sex and one's work are part of one another. One's work defines one's gender.

Any division of labor implies that people doing different kinds of work will occupy different work sites. When the division is based on sex, men and women will necessarily have different work sites. Even within the home itself, men and women had different work spaces. The woman's spinning wheel occupied a different area from the man's anvil. When the factory took over much of the work formerly done in the house, the separation of work space became especially marked. Not only did the separation of the sexes become spatially extended, but it came to relate work and gender in a special way. The work site as well as the work itself became associated with gender; each sex had its own turf. This sexual "territoriality" has had complicating effects on efforts to change any sexual division of labor. The good provider worked primarily in the outside male world of business and industry. The homemaker worked primarily in the home.

Spatial separation of the sexes not only identifies gender with work site and work but also reduces the amount of time available for spontaneous emotional give-and-take between husbands and wives. When men and women work in an economy based in the home, there are frequent occasions for interaction. (Consider, for example, the suggestive allusions made today to the rise in the birth rate nine months after a blackout.) When men and women are in close proximity, there is always the possibility of reassuring glances, the comfort of simple physical presence. But when the division of labor removes the man from the family dwelling for most of the day, intimate relationships become less feasible. De Tocqueville was one of the first to call our attention to this. In 1840 he noted that

> almost all men in democracies are engaged in public or professional life; and . . . the limited extent of common income obliges a wife to confine herself to the house, in order to watch in person and very closely over the details of domestic economy. All these distinct and compulsory occupations are so many natural barriers, which, by keeping the two sexes asunder, render the solicitations of the one less frequent and less ardent—the resistance of the other more easy. (de Tocqueville 1840, p. 212)

Not directly related to the spatial constraints on emotional expression by men, but nevertheless a concomitant of the new industrial order with the same effect, was the enormous drive for achievement, for success, for "making it" that escalated the provider role into the good-provider role. De Tocqueville (1840) is again our source:

> The tumultuous and constantly harassed life which equality makes men lead [becoming good providers] not only distracts from the passions of love, by denying them time to indulge in it, but it diverts them from it by another more secret but more certain road. All men who live in democratic ages more or less contract ways of thinking of the manufacturing and trading classes. (p. 221)

As a result of this male concentration on jobs and careers, much abnegation and "a constant sacrifice of her pleasures to her duties" (de Tocqueville 1840, p. 212) were demanded by the American woman. The good-provider role, as it came to be shaped by this ambience, was thus restricted in what it was called upon to provide. Emotional expressivity was not included in the role. One of the things a parent might say about a man to persuade a daughter to marry him, or a daughter might say to explain to her parents why she wanted to, was not that he was a gentle, loving, or tender man but that he was a good provider. He might have many other qualities, good or bad, but if a man was a good provider, everything else was either gravy or the price one had to pay for a good provider.

Lack of expressivity did not imply neglect of the family. The good provider was a "family man." He set a good table, provided a decent home, paid the mortgage, bought the shoes, and kept his children warmly clothed. He might, with the help of the children's part-time jobs, have been able to finance their educations through high school and, sometimes, even college. There might even have been a little left over for an occasional celebration in most families. The good provider made a decent contribution to the church. His work might have been demanding, but he expected it to be. If in addition to being a good provider, a man was kind, gentle, generous, and not a heavy drinker or gambler, that was all frosting on the cake. Loving attention and emotional involvement in the family were not part of a woman's implicit bargain with the good provider.

By the time de Tocqueville published his observations in 1840, the general outlines of the good-provider role had taken shape. It called for a hard-working man who spent most of his time at his work. In the traditional conception of the role, a man's chief responsibility is his job, so that "by definition any family behaviors must be subordinate to it terms of significance and [the job] has priority in the event of a clash" (Scanzoni 1975, p. 38). This was the classic form of the good-provider role, which remained a powerful component of our societal structure until well into the present century.

COSTS AND REWARDS OF THE
GOOD-PROVIDER ROLE FOR MEN

There were both costs and rewards for those men attached to the good-provider role. The most serious cost was perhaps the identification of maleness not only with the work site but especially with success in the role. "The American male looks to his breadwinning role to confirm his manliness" (Brenton 1966, p. 194).[1] To be a man one had to be not only a provider but a *good* provider. Success in the good-provider role came in time to define masculinity itself. The good provider had to achieve, to win, to succeed, to dominate. He was a bread*winner*. He had to show "strength, cunning, inventiveness, endurance—a whole range of traits henceforth defined as exclusively 'masculine' " (Demos 1974, p. 436). Men were judged as men by the level of living they provided. They were judged by the myth "that endows a money-making man with sexiness and virility, and is based on man's dominance, strength, and ability to provide for and care for 'his' woman" (Gould 1974, p. 97). The good provider became a player in the male competitive macho game. What one man provided for his family in the way of luxury and display had to be equaled or topped by what another could provide. Families became display cases for the success of the good provider.

The psychic costs could be high:

> By depending so heavily on his breadwinning role to validate his sense of himself as a man, instead of also letting his roles as husband, father, and citizen of the community count as validating sources, the American male treads on psychically dangerous ground. It's always dangerous to put all of one's psychic eggs into one basket. (Brenton 1966, p. 194)

The good-provider role not only put all of a man's gender-identifying eggs into one psychic basket, but it also put all the family-providing eggs into one basket. One individual became responsible for the support of the whole family. Countless stories portrayed the humiliation families underwent to keep wives and especially mothers out of the labor force, a circumstance that would admit to the world the male head's failure in the good-provider role. If a married woman had to enter the labor force at all, that was bad enough. If she made a good salary, however, she was "co-opting the man's passport to masculinity" (Gould 1974, p.98) and he was effectively castrated. A wife's earning capacity diminished a man's position as head of the household (Gould 1974, p. 99).

Failure in the role of good provider, which employment of wives evidenced, could produce deep frustration. As Komarovsky (1940, p. 20) explains, this is "because in his own estimation he is failing to fulfill what is the central duty of his life, the very touchstone of his manhood—the role of family provider."

But just as there was punishment for failure in the good-provider role, so also were there rewards for successful performance. A man "derived strength from his role as provider" (Komarovsky 1940, p. 205). He achieved a good deal of satisfaction from his ability to support his family. It won kudos. Being a good provider led to status in both the family and the community. Within the family it gave him the power of the purse and the right to decide about expenditures, standards of living, and what constituted good providing. "Every purchase of the family—the radio, his wife's new hat, the children's skates, the meals set before him—all were symbols of their dependence upon him" (Komarovsky 1940, pp. 74–75). Such dependence gave him a "profound sense of stability" (p. 74). It was a strong counterpoise vis-á-vis a wife with a stronger personality. "Whether he had considerable authority within the family and was recognized as its head, or whether the wife's stronger personality . . . dominated the family, he nevertheless derived strength from his role as a provider" (Komarovsky 1940, p. 75). As recently as 1975, in a sample of 3,100 husbands and wives in 10 cities, Scanzoni found that despite increasing egalitarian norms, the good provider still had "considerable power in ultimate decision-making" and as "unique provider" had the right "to organize his life and the lives of other family members around his occupation" (p. 38).

A man who was successful in the good-provider role might be freed from other obligations to the family. But the flip side of this dispensation was that he could not make up for poor performances by excellence in other family roles.

Since everything depended on his success as provider, everything was at stake. The good provider played an all-or-nothing game.

DIFFERENT WAYS OF PERFORMING
THE GOOD-PROVIDER ROLE

Although the legal specifications for the role were laid out in the common law, in legislation, in legal precedents, in court decisions, and, most importantly, in custom and convention, in real-life situations the social and social-psychological specifications were set by the husband or, perhaps more accurately, by the community, alias the Joneses, and there were many ways to perform it.

Some men resented the burdens the role forced them to bear. A man could easily vent such resentment toward his family by keeping complete control over all expenditures, dispensing the money for household maintenance, and complaining about bills as though it were his wife's fault that shoes cost so much. He could, in effect, punish his family for his having to perform the role. Since the money he earned belonged to him—was "his"—he could do with it what he pleased. Through extreme parsimony he could dole out his money in a mean, humiliating way, forcing his wife to come begging for pennies. By his reluctance and resentment he could make his family pay emotionally for the provisioning he supplied.

At the other extreme were the highly competitive men who were so involved in outdoing the Joneses that the fur coat became more important than the affectionate hug. They "bought off" their families. They sometimes succeeded so well in their extravagance that they sacrified the family they were presumably providing for to the achievements that made it possible (Keniston 1965).[2]

The Depression of the 1930s revealed in harsh detail what the loss of the role could mean both to the good provider and to his family, not only in the loss of income itself—which could be supplied by welfare agencies or even by other family members, including wives—but also and especially in the loss of face.

The Great Depression did not mark the demise of the good-provider role. But it did teach us what a slender thread the family hung on. It stimulated a whole array of programs designed to strengthen that thread, to ensure that it would never again be similarly threatened. Unemployment insurance was incorporated into the Social Security Act of 1935, for example, and a Full Employment Act was passed in 1946. But there proved to be many other ways in which the good-provider role could be subverted.

ROLE REJECTORS AND ROLE OVERPERFORMERS

Recent research in psychology, anthropology, and sociology has familiarized us with the tremendous power of roles. But we also know that one of the fundamental principles of role behavior is that conformity to role norms is not universal. Not everyone lives up to the specifications of roles, either in the psychological or in the sociological definition of the concept. Two extremes have attracted research attention: (a) the men who could not live up to the norms of the good-provider role or did not want to, at one extreme, and (b) the men who overperformed the role, at the other. For the wide range in between, from blue-collar workers to professionals, there was fairly consistent acceptance of the role, however well or poorly, however grumblingly or willingly, performed.

First the nonconformists. Even in Colonial times, desertion and divorce occurred:

> Woman may have deserted because, say, their husbands beat them; husbands, on the other hand, may have deserted because they were unable or unwilling to provide for their usually large families in the face of the wives' demands to do so. These demands were, of course, backed by community norms making the husband's financial support a sacred duty (Scanzoni 1979, pp. 24–25)

Fiedler (1962) has traced the theme of male escape from domestic responsibilities in the American novel from the time of Rip Van Winkle to the present:

> The figure of Rip Van Winkle presides over the birth of the American imagination; and it is fitting that our first successful home-grown legend should memorialize, however playfully, the flight of the dreamer from the shrew—into the mountains and out of time, away from the drab duties of home . . . anywhere to avoid . . . marriage and responsibility. One of the factors that determine theme and form in our great books is this strategy of evasion, this retreat to nature and childhood which makes our literature (and life) so charmingly and infuriatingly "boyish." (pp. xx–xxi)

Among the men who pulled up stakes and departed for the West or went down to the sea in ships, there must have been a certain proportion who, like their mythic prototype, were simply fleeing the good-provider role.

The work of Demos (1974), a historian, offers considerable support for Fiedler's thesis. He tells us that the burdens thrust on men in the 19th century by the new patterns of work began to show their effects in the family. When "the [spatial] separation of the work lives of husbands and wives made communication so problematic," he asks, "what was the likelihood of meaningful communication?" (Demos 1974, p. 438). The answer is, relatively little. Divorce and separation increased, either formally or by tacit consent—or simply by default, as in the case of a variety of defaulters—tramps, bums, hoboes—among them.

In this connection, "the development of the notorious 'tramp' phenomenon is worth noticing," Demos (1974, p. 438) tells us. The tramp was a man who just gave up, who dropped out of the role entirely. He preferred not to work, but he would do small chores or other small-scale work for a handout if he had to. He was not above begging the housewife for a meal, hoping she would not find work for him to do in repayment. Demos (1974) describes the type:

> Demoralized and destitute wanderers, their numbers mounting into the hundreds of thousands, tramps can be fairly characterized as men who had run away from their wives . . . Their presence was mute testimony to the strains that tugged at the very core of American family life . . . Many observers noted that the tramps had created a virtual society of their own [a kind of counterculture] based on a principle of single-sex companionship. (p.438)

A considerable number of them came to be described as "homeless men" and, as the country became more urbanized, landed ultimately on skid row. A large part of the task of social workers for almost a century was the care of the "evaded" women they left behind.[3] When the tramp became wholly demoralized, a chronic alcoholic, almost unreachable, he fell into a category of his own—he was a bum.

Quite a different kettle of fish was the hobo, the migratory worker who spent several months harvesting wheat and other large crops and the rest of the year in cities. Many were the so-called Wobblies, or Industrial Workers of the World, who repudiated the good-provider role on principle. They had contempt for the men who accepted it and could be called conscientious objectors to the role. "In some IWW circles, wives were regarded as the 'ball and chain.' In the West, IWW literature proclaimed that the migratory worker, usually a young, unmarried male, was 'the first specimen of American manhood . . . the leaven of the revolutionary labor movement'" (Foner 1979, p. 400). Exemplars of the Wobblies were the nomadic workers of the West. They were free men. The migratory worker, "unlike the factory slave of the Atlantic seaboard and the central states, . . . was most emphatically 'not afraid of losing his job.' No wife and family cumbered him. The worker of the East, oppressed by the fear of want for wife and babies, dared not venture much" (Foner 1979, p. 400). The reference to fear of loss of job was well taken; employers preferred married men, disciplined into the good-provider role, who had given hostages to fortune and were therefore more tractable.

Just on the verge between the area of conformity to the good-provider role—at whatever level—and the area of complete nonconformity to it was the non-good provider, the marginal group of workers usually made up of "the under-educated, the under-trained, the under-employed, or part-time employed, as well as the under paid, and of course the unemployed" (Snyder 1979, p. 597). These included men who wanted—sometimes desperately—to perform the good-provider role but who for one reason or another were unable to do so. Liebow (1966) has discussed the ramifications of failure among the black men of Tally's corner: The black man is

> under legal and social constraints to provide for them [their families], to be a husband to his wife and a father to his children. The chances are, however, that he is failing to provide for them, and failure in this primary function contaminates his performance as father in other aspects as well. (p. 86)

In some cases, leaving the family entirely was the best substitute a man could supply. The community was left to take over.[4]

At the other extreme was the overperformer. De Tocqueville, quoted earlier, was already describing him as he manifested in the 1830s. And as late as 1955 Warner and Ablegglen were adding to the considerable literature on industrial leaders and tycoons, referring to their "driving concentration" on their careers and their "intense focusing" of interests, energies, and skills on these careers, "even limiting their sexual activity" (pp. 48–49). They came to be known as workaholics or work-intoxicated men. Their preoccupation with their work even at the expense of their families was, as I have already noted, quite acceptable in our society.

Poorly or well performed, the good-provider role lingered on. World War II initiated a challenge, this time in the form of attracting more and more married women into the labor force, but the challenge was papered over in the 1950s with an "age of togetherness" that all but apotheosized the good provider, his house in the suburbs, his homebody wife, and his third, fourth, even fifth, child. As late as the 1960s most housewives (87%) still saw breadwinning as their husband's primary role (Lopata 1971, p. 91).[5]

INTRINSIC CONFLICT IN THE GOOD-PROVIDER ROLE

Since the good-provider role involved both family and work roles, most people believed that there was no incompatibility between them or at least that there should not be. But in the 1960s and 1970s evidence began to mount that maybe something was amiss.

De Tocqueville had documented the implicit conflict in the American busi-nessman's devotion to his work at the expense of his family in the early years of the 19th century; the Industrial Workers of the World had proclaimed that the good-provider role which tied a man to his family was an impediment to the great revolution at the beginning of the 20th century; Fiedler (1962) had noted that throughout our history, in the male fantasy world, there was freedom from the responsibilities of this role; about 50 years ago Freud ([1930]1958) had analyzed the intrinsic conflict between the demands of women and the family on one side and the demands of men's work on the other:

> Women represented the interests of the family and sexual life, the work of civiliza-tion has become more and more men's business; it confronts them with ever harder tasks, compels them to subliminations of instinct which women are not easily able to achieve. Since man has not an unlimited amount of mental energy at his disposal, he must accomplish his tasks by distributing his libido to the best advantage. What he employs for cultural [occupational] purposes he withdraws to a great extent from women, and his sexual life; his constant association with men and his dependence on his relations with them even estrange him from his duties as husband and father. Woman finds herself thus forced into the background by the claims of culture [work] and she adapts an inimical attitude towards it.(pp. 50–51)

In the last two decades, researchers have been raising questions relevant to Freud's statement of the problem. They have been asking people about the relative satisfactions they derive from these conflicting values—family and work. Among the earliest studies comparing family–work values was a Gallup poll in 1940 in which both men and women chose a happy home over an interesting job or wealth as a major life value. Since then there have been a number of such polls, and considerable body of results has now accumulated. Pleck and Lang(1979) and Hesselbart (1978) have summarized the findings of these surveys. All agree that there is a clear bias in the direction of the family. Pleck and Lang conclude that "men's family role is far more psychologically significant to them than is their work role" (p. 29), and Hesselbart—however critical she is of the stud-ies she summarizes—believes they should not be dismissed lightly and concludes that they certainly "challenge the idea that family is a 'secondary' valued role" (p. 14).[6] Douvan (1978) also found in a 1976 replication of a 1957 survey that family values retained priority over work: "Family roles almost uniformly rate higher in value production then the job role does" (p. 16).[7]

The very fact that researchers have asked such questions is itself interesting. Somehow or other both the researchers and the informants seem to be saying that all this complaining about the male neglect of the family, about the lack of family involvement by men, just is not warranted. Neither de Tocqueville nor Freud was right. Men do value family life more than they value their work. They do derive their major life satisfactions from their families rather than from their work.

It may well be true that men derive the greatest satisfaction from their family roles, but this does not necessarily mean they are willing to pay for the benefit. In any event, great attitudinal changes took place in the 1960s and 1970s.

Douvan, on the basis of surveys in 1957 and 1976, found, for example, a considerable increase in the proportion of both men and women who found marriage and parenthood burdensome and restrictive. Almost three fifths (57%) of both married men and married women in 1976 saw marriage as "all burdens and restrictions," as compared with only 42% and 47%, respectively, in 1957. And almost half (45%) also viewed children as "all burdens and restrictions" in 1976, as compared with only 28% and 33% for married men and married women, respectively, in 1957. The proportion of working men with a positive attitude toward marriage dropped drastically over this period, from 68% to 39%. Working women, who made up a fairly small number of all married women in 1957, hardly changed attitudes at all, dropping only from 43% to 42%. The proportion of working men who found marriage and children burdensome and restrictive more than doubled, from 25% to 56% and from 25% to 58%, respectively. Although some of these changes reflected greater willingness in 1976 than in 1957 to admit negative attitudes toward marriage and parenthood—itself significant—profound changes were clearly in process. More and more men and women were experiencing disaffection with family life.[8]

"ALL BURDENS AND RESTRICTIONS"

Apparently, the benefits of the good-provider role were greater than the costs for most men. Despite the legend of the flight of the American male (Fiedler 1962), despite the defectors and dropouts, despite the tavern habitué's "ball and chain" cliché, men seemed to know that the good-provider role, if they could succeed in it, was good for them. But Douvan's findings suggest that recently their complaints have become serious, bone-deep. The family they have been providing for is not the same family it was in the past.

Smith (1979) calls the great trek of married women into the labor force a subtle revolution—revolutionary not in the sense of one class overthrowing a status quo and substituting its own regime, but revolutionary in its impact on both the family and the work roles of men and women. It diluted the prerogatives of the good-provider role. It increased the demands made on the good provider, especially in the form of more emotional investment in the family, more sharing of household responsibilities. The role became even more burdensome.

However men may now feel about the burdens and restrictions imposed on them by the good-provider role, most have, at least ostensibly, accepted them. The tramp and the bum had "voted with their feet" against the role; the hobo or Wobbly had rejected it on the basis of a revolutionary ideology that saw it as enslaving men to the corporation; tavern humor had glossed the resentment habitués felt against its demands. Now the "burdens-and-restrictions" motif has surfaced both in research reports and, more blatantly, in the male liberation movement. From time to time it has also appeared in the clinicians' notes.

Sometimes the resentment of the good provider takes the form of simply wanting more appreciation for the life-style he provides. All he does for his family seems to be taken for granted. Thus, for example, Goldberg (1976), a psychiatrist, recounts the case of a successful businessman:

> He's feeling a deepening sense of bitterness and frustration about his wife and family. He doesn't feel appreciated. It angers him the way they seem to take the things his earnings purchase for granted. They've come to expect it as their due. It particularly enrages him when his children put him down for his "materialistic middle-class trip." He'd like to tell them to get someone else to support them but he holds himself back. (p. 124)

Brenton (1966) quotes a social worker who describes an upper-middle-class woman: She has "gotten hold of a man who'll drive himself like mad to get money, and [is] denigrating him for being too interested in money, and not interested in music, or the arts, or in spending time with the children. But at the same time she's subtly driving him—and doesn't know it" (p. 226). What seems significant about such cases is not that men feel resentful about the lack of appreciation but that they are willing to justify their resentment. They are no longer willing to grin and bear it.

Sometimes there is even more than expressed resentment; there is an actual repudiation of the role. In the past, only a few men like the hobo or Wobbly were likely to give up. Today, Goldberg (1976) believes, more are ready to renounce the role, not on theoretical revolutionary grounds, however, but on purely selfish ones:

> Male growth will stem from openly avowed, unashamed, self-oriented motivations. . . . Guilt-oriented "should" behavior will be rejected because it is always at the price of a hidden build-up of resentment and frustration and alienation from others and is, therefore, counterproductive. (p. 184)

The disaffection of the good provider is directed to both sides of his role. With respect to work, Lefkowitz (1979) has described men among whom the good-provider role is neither being completely rejected nor repudiated, but diluted. These men began their working lives in the conventional style, hopeful and ambitious. They found a job, married, raised a family, and "achieved a measure of economic security and earned the respect of . . . colleagues and neighbors" (Lefkowitz 1979, p. 31). In brief, they successfully performed the good-provider role. But unlike their historical predecessors, they in time became disillusioned with their jobs—not jobs on assembly lines, not jobs usually characterized as alienating, but fairly prestigious jobs such as aeronautics engineer and government economist. They daydreamed about other interests. "The common theme which surfaced again and again in their histories, was the need to find a new social connection—to reassert control over their lives, to gain some sense of freedom" (Lefkowitz 1979, p. 31). These men felt "entitled to freedom and independence." Middle-class, educated, self-assured, articulate, and for the most part white, they knew they could talk themselves into a job if they had to. Most of them did not want to desert their families. Indeed, most of them "wanted to rejoin the intimate circle they felt they had neglected in their years of work" (p. 31).

Though some of the men Lefkowitz studied sought closer ties with their families, in the case of those studied by Sarason (1977), a psychologist, career changes involved lower income and had a negative impact on families. Sarason's subjects were also men in high-level professions, the very men least likely to find marriage and parenthood burdensome and restrictive. Still, since career change often involved a reduction in pay, some wives were unwilling to accept it, with the result that the marriage deteriorated (p. 178). Sometimes it looked like a no-win game. The husband's earlier career brought him feelings of emptiness and alienation, but it also brought financial rewards for the family. Greater work satisfaction for him in lower paying work meant reduced satisfaction with life-style. These findings lead Sarason to raise a number of points with respect to the good-provider role. "How much," he asks, "does an individual or a family need in order to maintain a satisfactory existence? Is an individual being responsible to himself or his family if he provides them with little more than the bare essentials of living?" (p. 178). These are questions about the good-provider role that few men raised in the past.

Lefkowitz (1979) wonders how his downwardly mobile men lived when they left their jobs. "They put together a basic economic package which consisted of government assistance, contributions from family members who had not worked before and some bartering of goods and services" (p. 31). Especially interesting in this list of income sources are the "contributions from family members who had not worked before" (p. 31). Surely not mothers and sisters. Who, of course, but wives?

WOMEN AND THE PROVIDER ROLE

The present discussion began with the woman's part in the provider role. We saw how as more and more of the provisioning of the family came to be by way of monetary exchange, the woman's part shrank. A woman could still provide services, but could furnish little in the way of food, clothing, and shelter. But now that she is entering the labor force in large numbers, she can once more resume her ancient role, this time, like her male counterpart the provider, by way of a monetary contribution. More and more women are doing just this.

The assault of the good-provider role in the Depression was traumatic. But a modified version began to appear in the 1970s as a single income became inadequate for more and more families. Husbands have remained the major providers, but in an increasing number of cases the wife has begun to share this role. Thus, the proportion of married women aged 15 to 54 (living with their husbands) in the labor force more than doubled between 1950 and 1978, from 25.2% to 55.4%. The proportion for 1990 is estimated to reach 66.7% (Smith 1979, p. 14). Fewer women are now full-time housewives.

For some men the relief from the strain of sole responsibility for the provider role has been welcome. But for others the feeling of degradation resembles the feeling reported 40 years earlier in the Great Depression. It is not that they are no longer providing for the family but that the role-sharing wife now feels justified in making demands on them. The good-provider role with all its prerogatives and perquisites has undergone profound changes. It will never be the same again.[9] Its death knell was sounded when, as noted above, the 1980 census no longer automatically assumed that the male member of the household was its head.

THE CURRENT SCENE

Among the new demands being made on the good-provider role, two deserve special consideration, namely, (1) more intimacy, expressivity, and nurturance—specifications never included in it as it originally took shape—and (b) more sharing of household responsibility and child care.

As the pampered wife in an affluent household came often to be an economic parasite, so also the good provider was often, in a way, a kind of emotional parasite. Implicit in the definition of the role was that he provided goods and material things. Tender loving care was not one of the requirements. Emotional ministrations from the family were his right; providing them was not a corresponding obligation. Therefore, as de Tocqueville had already noted by 1840, women suffered a kind of emotional deprivation labeled by Robert Weiss "relational deficit" (cited in Bernard 1976). Only recently has this male rejection of emotional expression come to be challenged. Today, even blue-collar women are imposing "a host of new role expectations upon their husbands or lovers. . . . A new role set asks the blue-collar male to strive for . . . deep-coursing intimacy" (Shostak 1973, p. 75). It was not only vis-á-vis his family that the good provider was lacking in expressivity. This lack was built into the whole male role script. Today not only women but also men are beginning to protest the repudiation of expressivity prescribed in male roles (David and Brannon 1976; Farrell 1974; Fasteau 1974; Pleck and Sawyer 1974).

Is there any relationship between the "imposing" on men of "deep-coursing intimacy" by women on one side and the increasing proportion of men who find marriage burdensome and restrictive on the other? Are men seeing the new emotional involvements being asked of them as "all burdens and restrictions"? Are they responding to the new involvements under duress? Are they feeling oppressed by them? Fearful of them?

From the standpoint of high-level pure-science research there may be something bizarre, if not even slightly absurd, in the growing corpus of serious research on how much or how little husbands of employed wives contribute to household chores and child care. Yet it is serious enough that all over the industrialized world such research is going on. Time studies in a dozen countries—communist as well as capitalist—trace the slow and bungling process by which marriage accommodates to changing conditions and by which women struggle to mold the changing conditions in their behalf. For everywhere the same picture shows up in research: an image of women sharing the provider role and at the same time retaining responsibility for the household. Until recently such a topic would have been judged unworthy of serious attention. It was a subject that might be worth a good laugh, for instance, as when an all-thumbs man in a cartoon burns the potatoes or finds himself bumbling awkwardly over a diaper, demonstrating his—proud—male ineptness at such female work. But it is no longer funny.

The "politics of housework" (Mainardi 1970) proves to be more profound than originally believed. It has to do not only with tasks but also with gender— and perhaps more with the site of the tasks than with their intrinsic nature. A man can cook magnificently if he does it on a hunting or fishing trip; he can wield a skillful needle if he does it mending a tent or a fishing net; he can even feed and clean a toddler on a camping trip. Few of the skills of the homemaker are beyond his reach so long as they are practiced in a suitably male environment. It is not only women's work in and of itself that is degrading but any work on female turf. It may be true, as Brenton (1966) says, that "the secure man can wash a dish, diaper a baby, and throw the dirty clothes into the washing machine—or do anything else women used to do exclusively—without thinking twice about it" (p. 211), but not all men are that secure. To a great many men such chores are demasculinizing. The apron is shameful in a man in the kitchen; it is all right at the carpenter's bench.

The male world may look upon the man who shares household responsibilities as, in effect, a scab. One informant tells the interviewer about a conversation on the job: "What, are you crazy?" his hard-hat fellow workers ask him when he speaks of helping his wife. "The guys want to kill me. 'You son of a bitch! You are getting us in trouble.' . . . The men get really mad" (Lein 1979, p. 492). Something more than persiflage is involved here. We are fairly familiar with the trauma associated with the invasion by women of the male work turf, the hazing women can be subjected to, and the male resentment of admitting them except into their own segregated areas. The corresponding entrance of men into the traditional turf of women—the kitchen or the nursery—has analogous but not identical concomitants.

Pleck and Lang (1979) tell us that men are now beginning to change in the direction of greater involvement in family life. "Men's family behavior is beginning to change, becoming increasingly congruent with the long-standing psychological significance of the family in their lives" (p. 1). They measure this greater involvement by way of the help they offer with homemaking chores. Scanzoni (1975), on the basis of a survey of over 3,000 husbands and wives, concludes that at least in households in which wives are in the labor force, there is the "possibility of a different pattern in which responsibility for households would unequivocally fall equally on husbands as well as wives" (p. 38). A brave new world indeed. Still, when we look at the reality around us, the pace seems intolerably slow. The responsibilities of the old good-provider role have attenuated far faster than have its prerogatives and privileges.

A considerable amount of thought has been devoted to studying the effects of the large influx of women into the work force. An equally interesting question is what the effect will be if a large number of men actually do increase their participation in the family and the household. Will men find the apron shameful? What if we were to ask fathers to alternate with mothers in being in the home when youngsters come home from school? Would fighting adolescent drug abuse be more successful if fathers and mothers were equally engaged in it? If the school could confer with fathers as often as with mothers? If the father accompanied children when they went shopping for clothes? If fathers spent as much time with children as do mothers?

Even as husbands, let alone as fathers, the new pattern is not without trauma. Hall and Hall (1979), in their study of two-career couples, report that the most serious fights among such couples occur not in the bedroom, but in the kitchen, between couples who profess a commitment to equality but who find actually implementing it difficult. A young professional reports that he is philosophically committed to egalitarianism in marriage and tries hard to practice it, but it does not work. He even feels guilty about this. The stresses involved in reworking roles may have an impact on health. A study of engineers and accountants finds poorer health among those with employed wives than among those with nonemployed wives (Burke and Wier 1976). The processes involved in role change have been compared with those involved in deprogramming a cult member. Are they part of the increasing sense of marriage and parenthood as "all burdens and restrictions"?

The demise of the good-provider role also calls for consideration of other questions: What does the demotion of the good provider to the status of senior provider or even mere coprovider do to him? To marriage? To gender identity? What does expanding the role of housewife to that of junior provider or even coprovider do to her? To marriage? To gender identity? Much will of course depend on the social and psychological ambience in which changes take place.

A PARABLE

I began this essay with a proverbial woman. I close it with a modern parable by William H. Chafe (1978), a historian who also keeps his eye on the current scene. Jack and Jill, both planning professional careers, he as doctor, she as lawyer, marry at age 24. She works to put him through medical school in the expectation that he will then finance her through law school. A child is born during the husband's internship, as planned. But in order for him to support her through professional training as planned, he will have to take time out from his career. After two years, they decide that both will continue their training on a part-time basis, sharing household responsibilities and using day-care services. Both find part-time positions and work out flexible work schedules that leave both of them time for child care and companionship with one another. They live happily ever after.

That's the end? you ask incredulously. Well, not exactly. For, as Chafe (1978) points out, as usual the personal is also political:

Obviously such a scenario presumes a radical transformation of the personal values that today's young people bring to their relationships as well as a readiness on the part of social and economic institutions to encourage, or at least make possible, the development of equality between men and women. (p. 28)

The good-provider role may be on its way out, but its legitimate successor has not yet appeared on the scene.

NOTES

1. Rainwater and Yancey (1967), critiquing current welfare policies, note that they "have robbed men of their manhood, women of their husbands, and children of their fathers. To create a stable monogamous family we need to provide men with the opportunity to be men, and that involves enabling them to perform occupationally" (p. 235).

2. Several years ago I presented a critique of what I called "extreme sex role specialization," including "work-intoxicated fathers." I noted that making success in the provider role the only test for real manliness was putting a lot of eggs into one basket. At both the blue-collar and the managerial levels, it was dysfunctional for families. I referred to the several attempts being made even then to correct the excesses of extreme sex role specialization: rural and urban communes, leaving jobs to take up small-scale enterprises that allowed more contact with families, and a rebellion against overtime in industry (Bernard 1975, pp. 217–239).

3. In one department of a South Carolina cotton mill early in the century, "every worker was a grass widow" (Smuts 1959, p. 54). Many women worked "because their husbands refused to provide for their families. There is no reason to think that husbands abandoned their duties more often than today, but the woman who was burdened by an irresponsible husband in 1890 usually had no recourse save taking on his responsibilities herself. If he deserted, the law-enforcement agencies of the time afforded little chance of finding and compelling him to provide support" (Smuts 1959, p. 54). The situation is not greatly improved today. In divorce child support is allotted in only a small number of cases and enforced in ever fewer. "Roughly half of all families with an absent parent don't have awards at all. . . . Where awards do exist they are usually for small amounts, typically ranging from $7 to $18 per child" (Jones 1976, abstract). A summary of all the studies available concludes that "approximately 20 percent of all divorced and separated mothers receive child support regularly, with an additional 7 percent receiving it 'sometimes': 8 percent of all divorced and separated women receive alimony regularly or sometimes" (Jones 1976, p. 23).

4. Even though the annals of social work agencies are filled with cases of runaway husbands, in 1976 only 12.6% of all women were in the status of divorce and separation, and at least some of them were still being "provided for." Most men were at least trying to fulfill the good-provider role.

5. Although all the women in Lopata's (1971) sample saw breadwinning as important, fewer employed women (54%) than either nonemployed urban (63%) or suburban (64%) women assigned it first place (p. 91).

6. Pleck and Lang (1979) found only one serious study contradicting their own conclusions: "Using data from the 1973 NORC (National Opinion Research Center) General Social Survey. Harry analyzed the bivariate relationship of job and family satisfaction to life happiness in men classified by family life cycle stage. In three of the five groups

of husbands . . . job satisfaction had a stronger association than family satisfaction to life happiness" (pp. 5–6).

7. In 1978, a Yankelovich survey on "The New Work Psychology" suggested that leisure is now becoming a strict competitor for both family and work as a source of life satisfactions: "Family and work have grown less important than leisure: a majority of 60 percent say that although they enjoy their work, it is not their major source of satisfaction" (p. 46). A 1977 survey of Swedish men aged 18 to 35 found that the proportion saying the family was the main source of meaning in their lives declined from 45% in 1955 to 41% in 1977; the proportion indicating work as the main source of satisfaction dropped from 33% to 17%. The earlier tendency for men to identify themselves through their work is less marked these days. In the new value system, the individual says, in effect, "I am more than my role. I am myself" (Yankelovich, 1978). Is the increasing concern with leisure a way to escape the dissatisfaction with both the alienating relations found on the work site and the demands for increased involvement with the family?

8. Men seem to be having problems with both work and family roles. Veroff (1978), for example, reports an increased "sense of dissatisfaction with the social relations in the work setting" and a "dissatisfaction with the affiliative nature of work" (p. 47). This dissatisfaction may be one of the factors that leads men to seek affiliative-need satisfaction in marriage, just as in the 19th century they looked to the home as shelter from the jungle of the outside world.

9. Among the indices of the waning of the good-provider role are the increasing number of married women in the labor force; the growth in the number of female-headed families; the growing trend toward egalitarian norms in marriage; the need for two earners in so many middle-class families; and the recognition of these trends in the abandonment of the identification of head of household as a male.

REFERENCES

Babcock, B., A. E. Freedman, E. H. Norton, and S. C. Ross. 1975. *Sex Discrimination and the Law: Causes and Remedies*. Boston: Little, Brown.

Bernard, J. 1975. *Women, Wives, Mothers*. Chicago: Aldine.

———. 1976. "Homosociality and Female Depression." *Journal of Social Issues* 32:207–224.

Boulding, E. 1976. "Familial Constraints on Women's Work Roles." *SIGNS: Journal of Women in Culture and Society* 1:95–118.

Brenton, M. 1966. *The American Male*. New York: Coward-McCann.

Burke, R. and T. Weir. 1976. "Relationships of Wives Employment Status to Husband, Wife, and Pair Satisfaction and Performance." *Journal of Marriage and the Family* 38:279–287.

Chafe, W. 1978. "The Challenge of Sex Equality: A New Culture or Old Values Revisited?" Paper presented at the Radcliffe Pre-Centennial Conference, Cambridge, MA, April 2–4.

David, D. S. and R. Brannon (eds.). 1976. *The Forty-Nine Percent Majority: The Male Sex Role*, Reading, MA: Addison-Wesley.

Demos, J. 1974. "The American Family in Past Time." *American Scholar* 43:422–446.

Douvan, E. 1978. "Family Roles in a Twenty-Year Perspective." Paper presented at the Radcliffe Pre-Centennial Conference, Cambridge, MA, April 2–4.

Farrell, W. 1974. *The Liberated Man*. New York: Random House.

Fasteau, M. F. 1974. *The Male Machine*. New York: McGraw-Hill.

Fiedler, L. 1962. *Love and Death in the American Novel*. New York: Meredith.

Foner, P. S. 1979. *Women and the American Labor Movement*. New York: Free Press.

Freud, S. [1930] 1958. *Civilization and Its Discontents*. New York: Doubleday-Anchor.

Goldberg, H. 1976. *The Hazards of Being Male*. New York: New American Library.

Gould, R. E. 1974. "Measuring Masculinity by the Size of a Paycheck." In *Men and Masculinity*, edited by J. E. Pleck and J. Sawyer: Englewood Cliffs, NJ: Prentice-Hall. (Also published in *Ms.*, June 1973: 18ff.)

Hall, D. and F. Hall. 1979. *The Two-Career Couple*. Reading, MA: Addison-Wesley.

Hasselbart, S. 1978. *Some Underemphasized Issues About Men, Women, and Work*. Unpublished manuscript.

Jones, C. A. 1976. *A Review of Child Support Payment Performance*. Washington, DC: Urban Institute.

Keniston, K. 1965. *The Uncommitted: Alienated Youth in American Society*. New York: Harcourt, Brace & World.

Komarovsky, M. 1940. *The Unemployed Man and His Family*. New York: Dryden Press.

Lefkowitz, B. 1979. "Life Without Work." *Newsweek* (May 14): 31.

Lein, L. 1979. "Responsibility in the Allocation of Tasks." *Family Coordinator* 28: 489–496.

Liebow, E. 1966. *Tally's Corner*. Boston: Little, Brown.

Lopata, H. 1971. *Occupational Housewife*. New York: Oxford University Press.

Mainardi, P. 1970. "The Politics of Housework." In *Sisterhood Is Powerful*, edited by R. Morgan, New York: Vintage Books.

Pleck, J. H. and L. Lang, 1979. "Men's Family Work: Three Perspectives and Some New Data." *Family Coordinator* 28:481–488.

Pleck, J. H. and J. Sawyer (eds.). 1974. *Men and Masculinity*. Englewood Cliffs, NJ: Prentice-Hall.

Rainwater, L. and W. L. Yancey. 1967. *The Moynihan Report and the Politics of Controversy*. Cambridge, MA: M.I.T. Press.

Sarason, S. B. 1977. *Work, Aging, and Social Change*. New York: Free Press.

Scanzoni, J. H. 1975. *Sex Roles, Life Styles, and Childbearing: Changing Patterns in Marriage and the Family*. New York: Free Press.

———. 1979. "An Historical Perspective on Husband-Wife Bargaining Power and Marital Dissolution." In *Divorce and Separation in America*, edited by G. Levinger and O. Moles. New York: Basic Books.

Shostak, A. 1973. *Working Class Americans at Home*. Unpublished manuscript.

Smith, R. E. (ed.). 1979. *The Subtle Revolution*. Washington, DC: Urban Institute.

Smuts, R. W. 1959. *Women and Work in America*. New York: Columbia University Press.

Snyder, L. 1979. "The Deserting, Non-Supporting Father: Scapegoat of Family Non-Policy." *Family Coordinator* 38:594–598.

Tocqueville, A. de. 1840. *Democracy in America*. New York: J. & H. G. Langley.

Veroff, J. 1978. *Psychological Orientations to the Work Role: 1957–1976*. Unpublished manuscript.

Warner, W. L. and J. O. Ablegglen. 1955. *Big Business Leaders in America*. New York: Harper.

Yankelovich, D. 1978. "The New Psychological Contracts at Work." *Psychology Today* (May): 46–47, 49–50.

Zborowski, M. and E. Herzog. 1952. *Life Is With People*. New York: Schocken Books.

26

Being Marginal:
The Single Woman as Caricature*

Barbara Levy Simon

> How dare I fail to marry? How peculiar. How brazen. How sad. Or so many believe. Were I weak in the knees, I might believe that too. But, fortunately, my knees are steady and hold me up fine when people give me those patronizing looks and commiserating tones.
>
> As an eighty-two-year old, it's easy to ignore the labels attached to those of us who stayed single. It used to be harder. For example, when I was about forty, my boss asked me out of the blue if I was still in love with my father. By then, I knew enough to make jokes about such foolishness. The only alternative to humor that I could think of was committing mayhem or worse. And how could I explain to the judge that I killed my boss because he saw me as a silly spinster? [July 1983]

In Anglo-American culture, the never-married old woman is a stock character, a bundle of negative personal characteristics, and a metaphor for barrenness, ugliness, and death. Her obvious undesirability forms the basis for the children's card game, "Old Maids," in which each player tries to avoid coming to the end of

*Simon, Barbara Levy. 1987. "Being Marginal: The Single Woman as Caricature." Pp. 1–21 and 28 in *Never Married Women*. Philadelphia: Temple University Press. Copyright © 1987 by Temple University. Reprinted by permission of Temple University Press.

Quotations are taken from interviews I conducted with never-married women, aged sixty-six and older, in the Philadelphia and New York City areas between 1982 and 1984. The bracketed information specifies the date of the interview in which the quoted comment was made. The names of all those interviewed are changed or omitted to ensure confidentiality.

the round with the "Old Maid" card in his or her hand. In a phrase, to "get stuck with the Old Maid" is to lose the game.

This view of the never-married woman as an unwanted leftover has inspired more than a parlor game. Such an image enjoys a long history in our language and literature. It stretches from the "spinster" of the fourteenth century, as evidence by the word itself, which is still used in law for a woman who has never married, through an undeniably rich and varied series of characterizations in fiction and poetry. William Wordsworth bemoaned "maidens withering on the stalk"; William Blake called prudence "a rich, ugly old maid, courted by Incapacity." Alexander Pope caught the image in a couplet: "My soul abhors the tasteless dry embrace/Of a stale virgin with a winter face".[1] More contemporary writers extend the theme. William Faulkner writes: "He was as crochety about his julep as an old maid, measuring everything by a recipe in his head."[2] In order to belittle a man, one need only liken him to an old, never-married woman. Nor are women writers exempt from these prejudices. The novels of Barbara Pym, for example, teem with highly idiosyncratic single women in middle and old age who have many of the negative characteristics of the "old maid."

Not just a literary tradition, this stereotype permeated nineteenth-century British popular culture, rendering the never-married woman "redundant." She fares little better in twentieth-century popular imagery.

The classic image is surprisingly pervasive in everyday life. A contemporary travel guide highlights safety and propriety abroad thus: "Many [streets] are as sedate as your proper maiden aunt." In a popular work on corporate sexism, a female employee characterizes never-married women as people immersed in the trivial: "Women bosses have [this fault, which I call] 'old-maid thinking.' It is eternally thinking in terms of details, not in terms of the big thing—more interested in the details of the means than in the general significance of the results."[3] "Old-maid thinking," to the Sunoco Corporation, entails penny pinching. The never-married old woman in Sunoco's 1983 ad exclaims, "I think it's a sin to waste money, but I want a gas I can rely on!"[4] From eighteenth-century poet to contemporary advertiser, a cultural stereotype remains constant—the notion that a woman who never marries misses out on much of life through prim and peevish parsimony.

Yet, there are important shifts across time in cultural receptivity to female singleness to take note of. Historian Lee Chambers-Schiller documents the expansion of respect for white single women of the middle and upper classes and the broadened social role that they carved out for themselves in the United States between 1810 and 1860. The "Cult of Single Blessedness," as it was called, "upheld the single life as both a socially and personally valuable state" and "offered a positive vision of singlehood rooted in Protestant religion and the concepts of woman's particular nature and special sphere."[5] By the time the women interviewed for this book were born, however, a deviant and despised status for never-married women had reemerged.

When I took the single path—the road less traveled—few girls were doing so. Back in the 1930s, when I reached age thirty, I didn't know one single girl my age but me in my hometown who wasn't married by thirty. I remember well since my mother taunted me just about daily with that fact. She would say to me: "Mary, you're the only girl in the county without a husband. I warned you that that would be sure to happen if you act so damn proud all the time. Men don't like that in a woman."

The picture is different now. Single girls are much more numerous than in my day. Their lot is less peculiar, less subject to scrutiny. I wish I could lead the single life all over again, this time starting in 1950 rather than in 1905. The underbrush is cleared away now; people's eyebrows arch less at the sight of a single woman. I don't mean to say that it would be easy now. I mean to say that I walked past marriage when that *wasn't* done. In the 1980s, it *is* done and done by lots of them. [July 1984]

This woman derives the same finding from her impressionistic observations that some social scientists report: A significantly higher proportion of women in the United States is foregoing marriage in the 1980s than at any time in the past hundred years. Twenty-two percent of college-educated women in the United States born in the mid-1950s will never marry, compared with 9 percent of college-educated women born in the mid-1930s.[6]

This projection has even inspired a *People* magazine cover story. Four contemporary celebrities who embody male norms of womanly beauty and sexiness grace the cover of the magazine with the rhetorical question, "Are these old maids?" The text begins,

Spinster. The word conjures up a vivid image in the mind's eye—that of a sharp-tongued, gray-haired lady who is wizened and alone. No children to visit on Thanksgiving. No grandkids to knit booties for. No kindly gent with whom to share those sunset years.[7]

Why are higher percentages of American women remaining single than in the past? Increased female participation in the labor market produces a higher proportion of women who are financially independent, though often that independence is of the economically marginal variety. Increased availability, acceptance, and usage of contraception and abortion make heterosexual intimacy without marriage more likely. These material forces, together with the cultural impact of feminism and of the gay rights movement, open more widely to women the door to single lives of dignity, choice, and meaning.

Nonetheless, many women still seek marriage. For these women, however, an imbalance in the ratio of available unmarried women to unmarried men in their thirties and forties results in a scarcity of marriageable men.[8] This unavailability of eligible men is particularly exaggerated for women who deferred marriage while pursuing their education and careers. They encounter a cultural lag between genders. Educated women who want to marry prefer men with equivalent or superior training and education as mates. However, "the cultural pattern is still for men to choose women who are not their equals."[9]

The projected rising tide of never marrying among contemporary women in the United States heightens the importance of investigating the experience of women who chose single life at much earlier points in this century. The auto-biographical reflections in this book provide long-neglected insights about the symbolic and material worlds of never-married old women. They offer a view from the edge of twentieth-century patriarchy and capitalism, and they reveal much about the processes of domination and marginalization of subject groups in general.

A major contribution that old, single women offer, the firsthand accounts of their daily lives, is a necessary corrective for the distorted images of single women perpetuated by both popular and "high" culture. These self-descriptions (together with interpretations of them) constitute the major focus of this book. Indeed, this study was guided throughout by Clifford Geertz's counsel that the most fitting task of social science is to search for the meanings people ascribe to their own existences, to interpret the "webs of significance" humans have themselves "spun" and in which they are "suspended."[10]

The 50 women whom I interviewed for this study were born between 1884 and 1918, and come from diverse ethnic, religious, and social-class backgrounds. The qualitative records they put forth counter the reductive portrayals of single women that still predominate.

> Nothing is more ridiculous than someone who says, upon learning that I never got married, "Oh, you would like my Aunt —-! She never got married either. You two would have a lot in common."
>
> That sort of comment gives me some idea of what a black person feels like when whites assume that he either knows or would like to know any other black person who happens to be in the vicinity. Common skin color a friendship makes? Common marital status a friendship makes? Wrong in both cases.
>
> Some single women I meet are pearls to be treasured. Others are just plain boring. Some are not to be endured. The fact is that, like married women, single women come in all flavors and styles. [August 1984]

The stories and reflections of the never-married women recorded here replace oversimplification with nuance and substitute first-person observation for presupposition. These women also throw light on the "pushes and pulls" toward both singleness and marriage that Peter Stein has identified.[11]

Another major present that never-married women offer is a view of patriarchal capitalism from its unmarried margins. They discuss in intimate detail the privileged statuses of marriage and of men. Their stories are, in Peter Stein's terms, "a testament to the imperialism of marriage . . . for as singles they are still . . . regarded as a residual category."[12]

For black women who had been raised in poor or working-class families, the twin imperatives of getting out of poverty and of evading white men's sexual demands far outstripped the importance of getting married as familial and cultural commands. Early in their lives, these women understood the intersecting racial and sexual caste systems that required them to sell their labor in dirty work at low pay, in domestic or farm work. They knew firsthand the systematic exclusion of black women from factory jobs, office clerical work, and retail sales positions, which Jacqueline Jones has documented.[13] They also had personal knowledge of the prevalence of rape and sexual harassment of black women by white men. The cultural message given the 12 black women whom I interviewed by their families and communities was to study, work, and pray their way out of economic misery and sexual vulnerability. Most of these 12 women were encouraged to marry, but *not* with the urgency with which they were exhorted to get an education, a steady and respectable job, and to stay close to God. One black woman, raised by parents who were tenant farmers, commented:

> About once a day my parents spelled out what I should become. They talked about me studying to be a school teacher and painted quite a clear picture of the alternatives. If I didn't go to college, I would become a tenant farmer, starving like they were. Or I would become a maid who cleaned up after white people's dirt. Or I would become a "woman of Satan," someone who slept around and drank cheap bourbon on Sunday mornings.
>
> I don't ever remember my folks worrying about my getting a husband. That was *way* down the list of what they cared about. [March 1984]

Elizabeth Higginbotham, in studying the priorities of educated black women in the contemporary United States, has found discernible class differences in their life preferences. Black women from established middle-class families were expected both to marry and to complete college. Those whom she studied from lower middle-class families were expected, above all, to finish college. Only then were they encouraged to secure a husband.[14] Emphasizing demographic considerations in black society, Robert Staples has argued that the severe sex ratio imbalance between black women and men (in favor of women) has drastically limited the opportunities for black women to marry in twentieth-century America. As a consequence, a strong demographic pull toward single status for black women has been created that has not been felt by white women.[15]

The 5 Hispanic women who were interviewed told a very different tale. Regardless of the social-class background from which they came, these women (4 from Puerto Rico and one from Cuba) spoke of extreme pressure from family, church, and community to marry early and bear children. One of the Puerto Rican women noted:

> The aim of my family from the time my sisters and I were tiny was to marry us off well. Since my two sisters did as they were expected, all family eyes began to focus on me, the oldest sister. My life between ages twenty and thirty was a story of hints, insults, warnings, and mother's tears. The year I turned thirty, they stopped putting pressure on me. That year they came to see me as too far gone to redeem. My life got much easier when the family gave up on me. [February 1983]

All the women, regardless of ethnic background, knew the prevailing stereotypes of never-married women well and the sway such images had over the thinking of their neighbors, family members, and colleagues at work. Forty years ago, Everett Hughes captured the essence of stereotyping as a process when he wrote about the "master trait or status" assigned to groups and individuals deemed to be deviant from the dominant culture. In the stereotyping process, one key attribute dominates other attributes in shaping other people's conception and perception of the holder of that attribute. This trait is, in Hughes' analysis, formally expected. Along with the "master trait," a cluster of "auxiliary status traits," or informally expected characteristics, is attributed to the bearer of the master trait. [16] If color is the master trait, laziness, dirtiness, loose morals, and general inferiority are the associated auxiliary traits attached to white people's view of people of color. If old age is the master trait, senility, uselessness, and antiquated thinking are a few of the informal characteristics expected by younger observers.

Old, single women carry with them three master traits—old age, female gender, and never-married status. When an old, single woman in our culture is black, Hispanic, or Asian, she bears at least four master statuses. The same is true for single old women who are physically disabled. Context, of course, determines which trait will stand out and elicit stigma that is felt at a particular moment. Black women may experience their race as their master trait in white-dominated situations, but among their family members and with black neighbors, the same women may find their marital status to be most salient. A woman with cerebral palsy judged her disability to be her primary sign of abnormality, except on those rare occasions when she was in a group of severely disabled people. Small wonder, then, that these never-married women report that a long, unbecoming list of characteristics has been affixed to them, and that a few of the women (though surprisingly few) internalized the judgments.

What fuels this stereotyping process? Why do dominant groups and individuals and their upwardly mobile allies bother to worry about those on the borders of their group? Anthropologist Mary Douglas seeks an answer to such questions in her studies of taboos, pollution, and cross-cultural categories of undesirability. She concludes that:

> So many ideas about power are based on an idea of society as a series of forms contrasted with nonform. There is power in forms and other power in the inarticulate area, margins, confused lines, and beyond the external boundaries.... Where the social system requires people to hold dangerously ambiguous roles, these persons are credited with uncontrolled, unconscious, dangerous disapproved powers. [17]

The very murkiness of marginal people's situation disturbs those in a better-defined position. Douglas suggests words about witches that may well apply to perceptions of never-married old women:

> Witches are social equivalents of beetles and spiders who live in the cracks of the walls and wainscoting. They attract the fears and dislikes which other ambiguities and contradictions attract in thought structures, and the kind of powers attributed to them symbolize their ambiguous, inarticulate status. [18]

Michelle Fine and Adrienne Asch's analysis of disabled women is highly relevant to the situation of never-married old women. They argue that disabled women have fewer socially sanctioned roles than do nondisabled women or disabled men. [19] Such women are perceived as inadequate or unable to perform the economically productive roles traditionally ascribed to men. They are also assumed to be unable, by virtue of their disability, to fill the nurturant and reproductive roles of "able" women. Never-married women are permitted, until old age, the first role, that of economic productivity—at least minimally. Society, however, does not grant them a nurturant role in relation to adults or children outside the family, though, as we shall see, they are heavily relied upon for nurturance within the family. Such a reduction in roles can lead to feelings of worthlessness, to taking on a more traditional version of femininity, or to a high degree of dependence on others and on external institutions for identity and validation. [20]

The stigma of never-married status in a world of married couples or formerly married individuals "spoils the identity," in the words of Erving Goffman, of women who remain single throughout their lives. [21] Once one's identity is spoiled, Goffman speculates, only three strategies are open to reduce the stigmatization. The individual can attempt to correct the deviant trait. (She can find a husband.) Or she can commit much energy to mastering activities considered, in the ordinary course of things, to be beyond her ken as an unmarried woman. (She can devote herself to caring for children, personally or professionally; she can make herself as conventionally attractive as possible, through stylish dressing and make-up; or she can "talk up" an actual or fictional history of popularity with men and romantic adventure.) The third strategic choice of the woman with the spoiled identity is to diverge from the mainstream and adopt an unorthodox, indeed radical interpretation of the nature and value of her identity. [22] (The never-married old woman can proclaim to herself, and the world, the dignity of a chosen single life.) This is Clara Mayo's concept of "positive marginality," and it is, in fact, what many of these 50 very interesting women have done. [23]

All 50 women whom I interviewed were "deviants." In remaining single, they deviated from a powerful cultural norm and an overwhelming demographic pattern, to which 93 to 95 percent of the women in their birth cohorts conformed. Which of Goffman's trinity of strategies did these 50 women use, in the light of such deviancy, to maintain their identities, a project which sociologist Sarah Matthews conceptualizes as a "process of negotiations"? [24] How, in her words, did these 50 "actors mediate those forces" that have labeled and treated them as oddities, that have socially constructed and sustained their marginality? [25]

Some of the women, 8 in number, have fully and uncritically internalized the notion that normal women marry. The women in this group employed the first strategy, trying to become "normal," until they conceived of themselves as too old to marry. All but one of this cluster of 8 then employed the second strategy as a way of adapting to an undesired single role and a judgmental world.

A much more ambivalent orientation toward the deviancy of single status was exhibited by a second subset of 20 women in the group. These women reported that, most of the time, they felt quite clear about their preference for single life. They acknowledged, however, periodic doubts as to whether this clarity and preference was healthy or pathological. Their approach alternated between adopting traditionally "feminine" concerns, postures, and appearances and the more defiant tack of actively ignoring prevailing definitions of acceptability in women. This alternative, of trying to look like "normals," is reminiscent of the approach chosen during the mid-nineteenth century by single women active in reform movements such as antislavery work. These reformers, Chambers-Schiller reports, were especially sensitive to public attitudes concerning the "unnaturalness" of their spinsterhood.[26] They "felt the deviancy of their unmarried state, and often reacted by emphasizing the feminine qualities in their personalities and behavior in ways which limited their contributions to the cause of reform."[27]

Unlike their nineteenth-century predecessors, the never-married women I interviewed risked, by remaining single, "double failure" (a term devised by Suzanne Gordon to express the combination of sexual and emotional demands made on twentieth-century women.)[28] Until the writings of the early sexologists and Sigmund Freud began to permeate American culture in the second and third decades of the twentieth century, Victorian and Edwardian notions of womanhood (that is, *respectable* womanhood—the qualifying term bestowed only upon white, middle-class women) prevailed, which assumed female sexual indifference.[29] As a consequence, nineteenth-century single women in America, if they were white and middle class, failed to marry, but they failed no *sexual* test. (Neither did "less than respectable" women of the nineteenth century—those who were women of color from all classes and white women from poor or working-class backgrounds. Such women, in sharp contrast with white, middle-class women, were considered "animalistic" and lustful. These women did not "fail" to be sexual if they did not marry, for their sexual availability and utility were seen to be traits attached to their color or social class, not functions of their marital status.)

By the time most of the women I interviewed has reached adulthood, in the 1920s or 1930s, married women of all class and racial groups in America were understood to be sexual creatures. Therefore, the term "old maid," when applied to a twentieth-century woman, connoted both sexual and marital lacunae. The 20 women who preferred single life, but vacillated in their belief in its legitimacy and normalcy, were acutely aware of their "double failure." Their defensiveness took several forms. They either conformed (strategy 2) early in life and rebelled at some later point, or they oscillated between periods of conformity and periods of rebellion. Some even attempted strategies 2 and 3 at the same time. They *explicitly* rejected the necessity or preferability of married life for women, yet strove to reassure themselves and others of their likeness to married women. One woman captures this duality:

> Marry? Why would I marry? As a single woman, I had my freedom all of the time. Some relatives hinted every now and then that there was something wrong that I had not ever married. But I wasn't odd. I dressed lacier than a lot of married women I saw on my block. I spent more time with my brothers' kids than a lot of my married neighbors spent with their *own* children. And, I can assure you, I had nothing whatsoever to do with women who didn't like men. Why, on my job, I fired one woman the minute I learned that she was, well, you know, like that tennis star. You know, a "lezzie." I have no truck with those sorts. [February 1984]

The third kind of relation to the deviancy of single status cultivated by some of the women I interviewed was outright and sustained rejection of the marital norm. Twenty-two women took that position in early adulthood and held to it without deviating from strategy 3. Some of these 22 women did so defiantly; others maintained their resistance in a more relaxed and insouciant manner. The latter attitude was expressed well by one of them:

> Heavens, I have had a nice life! Some thinks I would have had a better time if I'd have married. But I don't see it that way. I've just done the things I've wanted to do, money permitting. If I wanted to travel, I found a way. If I got lonely, I made new friends. If I wanted younguns around, I found some. There was never a big deal about happiness. You either make it for yourself or you don't. It doesn't have much to do with marriage. Now, I would have been just as happy if I had married, for, after all, anybody I would have settled down with would have been fun, I can assure you. You see, I would have made sure of that. And if things had gotten nasty in that marriage, I would have ended the nastiness or ended the marriage. [July 1983]

Resistance to conforming to marital norms and to appearing "normal" took many forms among these 22 women who chose strategy 3 as a way of living. For some, the resistance was expressed in their dress. Five of the women reported that they tried to invent a wardrobe that was neither masculine nor traditionally feminine. Others talked about playing sports in a public and competent way to "remind myself and everyone else," as one woman said, "of how active women can be if given the chance to come out of the cage." Many of the 22 reported that they competed at work for promotions and distinction in order to insist on their "place in the sun," as one woman phrased it. This competitiveness, one example of which follows, was a repeated theme among the "resisters":

> Teddy Roosevelt was my idol because he gave everything his all. I have done the same, especially because lots of people expect "spinsters" to sit on the sidelines and meekly resign themselves to life's crumbs. I decided early that if I was going to be a single woman I was going to do it with flair. So I set my sights on being factory foreman. No woman had done that in the eighty-four years of the factory's existence before I did it. Oh, lots of men on the floor had a lot to say about that. They spread lies and accusations that hurt me. Some suggested that I thought I was a man. Some said I was missing some female hormones. Some called me "butch" whenever they talked to me. My skin got thicker and thicker and so did my paycheck. My pride in myself grew all the while. [September 1982]

Others resisted conformity through living with or developing deep friendships with other single women. Several of these women remarked on the risks they took in doing so. They knew that if they had lived with relatives or alone they would have been subjected to pity, but not scandal. Upon sharing a household or most of their observable existence with a special single-woman friend, they made themselves vulnerable to suspicions of homosexuality. One woman commented:

> Elsie and I made no bones to anyone about how important we were to each other. We went everywhere together. We bought a house together and shared forty-one years together. Her mother and father begged her to "consider appearances" and to live with them instead. My boss called me in once to ask me if my pastor approved of my way of living. None of them used the word, but they all worried that we

were homosexuals. Elsie and I made a pact early on that we would never take the easy out and give anyone any answers. To this day, neither of us have betrayed that promise. It is simply no one's business. That holds in this interview, by the way. It's none of your business, either. [May 1984]

It is important, before we conclude this discussion of the resistant 22, to make clear that most of these women had intricate friendship, neighborhood, and kin relations with men as well as women, and with children as well as adults. Thirteen of these 22 women chose work that focused on teaching or delivering services to children and their families. How, then, are these links with nuclear families, men, and children different from those I have categorized as conformist behavior within strategy 2? The distinction is one of perceived motivation. Those women from either the cluster who mixed strategies 2 and 3 or from the group who employed only strategy 3, who appeared to have chosen a job or a relationship out of *commitment* to that work or to that person, have *not*, in my judgment, conformed. Those choices of jobs, activities, or companions that seemed to me to be inspired primarily by fear, the fear that they might be considered odd if they did not act in those directions, I have dubbed "conforming behavior." An example of each, which will help make this admittedly subjective distinction clearer, follows:

From the time I was tiny, I wanted to be a teacher, I loved "playing school" as much as some other kids loved playing hookey. Mostly I wanted to work with little children, the ones between five and eight, who are finding out about the world. You see, I knew early on that I had a certain gift for making little kids laugh and get pleasure from exploring ideas. Happily, that all turned out to be true. My students came back year in and year out to tell me that I had made school a fine place for them. That is enormously gratifying, you know. [December 1983]

Contrast that obvious confidence and commitment with the following:

Why did I choose teaching, you ask? Well, because I didn't dare do what my heart dictated—become a horse trainer. As a child, I had learned to ride and all about caring for horses. My father, you see, had been a horse trainer for a rich family in Glenside. But when I was graduating from high school, I thought a long time about my prospects. I guessed that I would never marry because I seemed to prefer to be alone than to be with boys. I saw, therefore, that I would have to earn my own keep.

Now, very few women became horse trainers. In fact, I had known one married woman who had trained horses. But the thought of being a single woman who did that seemed like asking for trouble. Why, just think of the things people would have said about an "old maid" who did men's work. I knew myself well enough to know that such slights would do me a lot of damage. So I looked around instead for something to do that nobody would give a second thought to. Teaching was it. [October 1983]

Avoidance of stigma motivated this second teacher to join that profession. In a similar way, fear of being called a "man hater" encouraged another woman to find a man friend.

The men and girls at the office thought I was out to lunch one day and started to talk about me. They wondered out loud if I was "strange." They said they had never seen me with a man. Somebody said that I liked women too much.

I was depressed for months. Then I met at a family picnic a man who wasn't what you'd call exciting, but who was pleasant enough. I remember thinking at that picnic that it would help me a lot to show up with this fellow at work a few times. So I engineered a 'lunch relationship." Over two years, we only saw each other at lunch. But let me tell you, that was enough to bring me back into the zone of the acceptable. I'm not proud, you understand, of using that nice man in that way. But it was important to me to change the way they saw me. [January 1984]

This woman's self-consciousness and instrumental pursuit of acceptability sprang from her awareness, still keen at seventy-nine of her membership in a tiny statistical minority.

The vast majority of American women born in this country since the seventeenth century, between 89 and 96 percent, have married.[30] The number of never-married women in the colonial period who lived past forty-five and did not marry was very small—only a small percentage of adult women, according to Chambers-Schiller.[31] During the last quarter of the eighteenth century, the proportion of women who remained single began to increase, and this trend continued through the first three-quarters of the nineteenth century. Of those women born between 1835 and 1838, 7.3 percent remained single; between 1845 and 1849, 8.0 percent; and between 1855 and 1859, 8.9 percent. The trend reached its peak among women born between 1865 and 1875, of whom 11 percent did not marry.[32]

The last two decades of the nineteenth century saw a decline in the proportion of women born in those years who never married. Among the birth cohort of the oldest women in this study, those born between 1884 and 1894, 8.7 percent did not marry. An even more dramatic decline in the never-married rate occurred among American women born in the first two decades of the twentieth century. Between 1915 and 1918, the birth-years of the youngest women studied here, only 4.8 percent remained single. In short, during the forty years between 1875 and 1915 the percentage of women who did not marry shrank to less than half the proportion of those who remained single in 1875.[33]

Singleness among women over thirty-five years old, born between World War I and the U.S. Census of 1980, remained low—5.5 percent or lower. In 1979, only 5.3 percent of women in the United States thirty-five years old or older had never been married.[34] Clearly, women who did not marry in twentieth-century America constitute a statistical minority. One woman, interviewed at age ninety, commented on this minority status:

At thirty, there still were a few of us "left on the vine." By forty, there was no one but Georgia O'Connor and me without a husband from the sixty-four of us here in St. Margaret's parish who took First Communion together. By forty, I was well-accustomed to being a single "goat" outside the "flock" of married sheep. In fact, I could see by age twenty-five that a single path would be an unusual path for a woman in my situation who did not become a nun. So I had to make up my own rules for living, which I found easy to do. [August 1982]

Others in the group of women interviewed reacted to their minority status in different ways. Some railed against it; some ignored it; and some took pride in it, as the woman quoted above did. Some developed critiques of the majority's mores, and a few made the "marriage imperative" a foundation of their self-definition and self-loathing. This broad range of reactions to membership in a never-married minority was relatively easy to discover since most of the women viewed our interviews as opportunities to talk about those parts of their lives most important to them as well as those elements they deemed most misunderstood by others. . . . As women brought up in a society and period that taught them to marry and bear children, they flouted this central cultural rule. They disobeyed patriarchal preference and consequently they have endured the economic hardships and social stigma that women without men face. They have swum upstream, having selected their own stroke and pace. Most have done so with enthusiasm and self-respect that give the lie to all-too-familiar stereotypes.

NOTES

1. William Wordsworth, "Personal Talk," in Alice N. George, ed., *The Complete Poetical Works of Wordsworth* (Boston: Houghton Mifflin, 1932; orig. pub. 1806–7), pp. 346–347; William Blake, "Proverbs of Hell in the Marriage of Heaven and Hell," in Geoffrey Keynes, ed., *The Complete Writings of William Blake* (London: Oxford University Press, 1966; orig. pub. 1790–93), pp. 150–151; Alexander Pope, "January and May: or the Merchant's Tale," in H.W. Boynton, ed., *The Complete Poetical Works of Pope* (Boston: Houghton Mifflin, 1931; orig. pub. 1709), pp. 35–46.

2. William Faulkner, *The Sound and the Fury* (New York: Random House, 1929), p. 167.

3. In Rosabeth M. Kanter, *Men and Women of the Corporation* (New York: Basic Books, 1977), p. 201.

4. Sunoco advertisement, Veterans Stadium scoreboard, Philadelphia, July 12, 1983.

5. Lee Chambers-Schiller, *Liberty, a Better Husband: Single Women in America: The Generations of 1780–1840* (New Haven: Yale University Press, 1984), p. 18.

6. William R. Greer, "The Changing Women's Marriage Market," *New York Times*, February 22, 1986, p. 48. This article reports on a study by Neil Bennett, Patricia Craig, and David Bloom, who made demographic projections, based on parametric modeling techniques, applied to U.S. Census data gathered from 70,000 households in 1982.

7. "The New Look in Old Maids," *People*, March 31, 1986, pp. 28–33.

8. Laurel Richardson, *The New Other Woman: Single Women in Affairs with Married Men* (New York: Free Press, 1985), pp. 2–4.

9. Greer,"Changing Women's Marriage Market," p. 48.

10. Clifford Geertz, *The Interpretation of Cultures* (New York: Basic Books, 1973), p. 5.

11. Peter J. Stein, *Single Life: Unmarried Adults in Social Context* (New York: St. Martin's Press, 1981), pp. 17–18.

12. Ibid., p. 9.

13. Jacqueline Jones, *Labor of Love, Labor of Sorrow: Black Women, Work, and the Family from Slavery to the Present* (New York: Basic Books, 1985), p. 154.

14. Elizabeth Higginbotham, "Is Marriage a Priority? Class Differences in Marital Options of Educated Black Women," in Stein, ed., *Single Life*, pp. 259–267.

15. Robert Staples, *The World of Black Singles* (Westport, Conn.: Greenwood Press, 1981), p. 11.

16. Everett Hughes, "Dilemmas and Contradictions of Status," *American Journal of Sociology* 50 (1945): 353–359.

17. Mary Douglas, *Purity and Danger: An Analysis of Pollution and Taboo* (Boston: Routledge & Kegan Paul, 1966), pp. 98–99.

18. Ibid., p. 102.

19. Michelle Fine and Adrienne Asch, "Disabled Women: Sexism without the Pedestal," *Journal of Sociology and Social Welfare* 8 (1981): 233–240.

20. Ibid., p. 240.

21. Erving Goffman, *Stigma: Notes on the Management of Spoiled Identity* (Englewood Cliffs, N.J.: Prentice-Hall, 1963), pp. 1–5.

22. Ibid., p. 10.

23. Clara Mayo, "Training for Positive Marginality," in *Applied Social Psychology Annual* (Beverly Hills, Calif.: Sage, 1982), pp. 55–73.

24. Sarah H. Matthews, *The Social World of Old Women: Management of Self Identity* (Beverly Hills, Calif.: Sage, 1979), p. 151.

25. Ibid., pp. 19–20.

26. Lee Chambers-Schiller, "The Single Woman Reformer: Conflicts Between Family and Vocation, 1830–1860." *Frontiers* 3 (1978): 41–48.

27. Ibid., p. 41.

28. Suzanne Gordon, *Lonely in America* (New York: Simon & Schuster, 1976), p. 83.

29. Lillian Faderman, *Surpassing the Love of Men* (New York: Morrow, 1981), p. 241.

30. Daniel S. Smith, "Family Limitation, Sexual Control, and Domestic Feminism in Victorian America," in Mary Hartman and Lois Banner, eds., *Clio's Consciousness Raised* (New York: Harper Torchbooks, 1974), pp. 119–136.

31. Lee Chambers-Schiller, *Liberty* p. 3.

32. Smith, "Family Limitations," p. 121.

33. Ibid.

34. U.S. Bureau of the Census, *Marital Status and Living Arrangements: March 1979*, Current Population Reports, Series P-20, No. 349 (Washington, D.C.: U.S. Government Printing Office, 1980), p. 2.

27

The Economy of Gratitude*

Arlie Russell Hochschild

A person is usually grateful to receive a gift. But what is a gift? For a gift to *be* a gift, it must *feel* like one. For it to feel like a gift, it must seem extra— something beyond what we expect normally.[1] The broader culture helps fix in the individual a mental baseline against which any action or object seems extra, and so, like a gift. Changes in the broader culture also shift the many tiny mental baselines which undergird a person's sense of a gift. The sense of genuine giving and receiving is a part of love, and so it is through the conception of a gift that the broader culture makes its way into love.

Take modern marriage. In light of changing cultural ideas about manhood and womanhood, what does a wife expect from her husband? What does she take as a gift, and so feel moved to thank him for? What does he want to be thanked for? What really feels to the husband like a gift from her? Is the gift she wants to give the one he wants to receive? Much depends on how cultural currents influence their "marital baseline"—what each partner consensually, if not consciously, expects of the other. Sometimes couples agree on the definition of a gift. But when strong cultural currents affect men and women differently, a marriage may contain two separate and conflicting baselines.

Take the example of housework in a two-job marriage. A husband does the laundry, makes the beds, washes the dishes. Relative to his father, his brother and several men on the block this husband helps more at home. He also does more than he did ten years ago. All in all he feels he has done more than his wife could reasonably expect, and with good spirit. He has given her, he feels, a gift. She should, he feels, be grateful. However, to his wife the matter seems different. In addition to her eight hours at the office, she does 80% of the housework. Relative to all she does, relative to what she wants to expect of him, what she feels she deserves, her husband's contribution seems welcome, but not extra, not a gift. So his gift is "mis-received." For each partner has perceived this gift through a different cultural prism. By creating different cultural prisms for men and women, larger social forces can impoverish a couple's private *economy of gratitude*.

An *economy of gratitude* is a vital, nearly sacred, nearly bottom-most, largely implicit layer of the marital bond. It is the summary of all *felt gifts*. Some marital economies thrive, others flounder. Crucial to a healthy economy of gratitude is a common interpretation of reality, such that what feels like a gift to one, feels like a gift to the other. A common interpretation of reality, in turn, relies on a shared template of prior expectation, which is laid down by cultural habits of thought. In comparison to this preexisting template of expectation, any newly grasped event or thing spontaneously stands out as more, or less, or different than what, until just now, one had expected.[2] This prior expectation and the newly grasped reality together create feeling. Sometimes we infer the prior expectation (and newly grasped reality) from the feeling, and sometimes we infer the other way around. But when we speak of a shared cultural baseline, it is this we share.

Gratitude is a form of appreciation. We appreciate many acts and objects which we take for granted. But we feel grateful for what seems to us extra. In the *Random House Dictionary of the English Language*, gratitude is synonymous with the term "indebted" or "obliged." But gratitude as used in this paper is different and more: for a person may be burdened with a surfeit of gifts which formally obliges him to return the favor—without wanting to, without gratitude. Gratitude involves a warmth, a thankfulness, a desire to return the favor. According to Joel Davitz, gratitude adds to "Thanks" the feeling of an "intense positive relationship with another person . . .   a communion, a unity, a closeness, friendliness and freedom, mutual respect and interdependence."[3]

The economy of gratitude is Janus-faced. It faces outward to rapid, bewildering changes in the larger society, which filter downward from society, to community, to the two selves that compose a couple. It also faces inward to the individual's experience of gratitude and love. One way to understand the relation of social issues to private troubles, as C. Wright Mills put it, is to explore the place at which they meet—the economy of gratitude.

Let us start at the beginning of a chain of social events—with a mass exodus of women into the cash economy. In 1950, 29% of working-age women worked in the labor force while in 1980, it was 52%. In the 1950s relatively few mothers worked; now more mothers than non-mothers work. Since 1980 women have taken 80% of the new jobs in the economy. Women's movement into the cash economy has drastically changed their lives. Yet, at the same time, the traditional view that childrearing and housework are "women's work" strongly persists. The culture lags behind the economy creating what William Ogburn called a "culture lag."

Because economic trends bear most directly upon women, they change women more.[5] As a result, culturally speaking, men lag behind women in their adaptation to the new economic reality. For women the *economy* is the changing environment, while for men, *women* are the changing environment. Women are adapting more quickly to changes in economic opportunity and need, than men are adapting to changes in women. A culture lag in the wider society, then, echoes as a "gender lag" at home. There is a lag both in behavior and in attitude: while women have gone out to paid work, most men have not increased their care of the home. But, perhaps even more important, men emotionally support this change in women far less than do women.

In uniting men and women, marriage intimately unites a social stratum which has changed less with a with a social stratum that has changed more. Marriage thus becomes an intimate arena in which to negotiate a broader culture lag. Marriage is not a "haven in a heartless world," as Christopher Lasch suggests (1977). Rather, marriage is the major shock absorber of tensions created by wider trends bearing unevenly upon men and women.[6] These shocks are finally absorbed—and felt—as the "mis-receiving" of a gift.

In what follows, I ask how various conditions influence how people attune themselves to gratitude in similar or divergent ways. How do divergences imbalance an economy of gratitude, and so affect love? Examples in this essay are drawn from in-depth interviews with fifty-five two-job families in the San Francisco Bay Area conducted between 1978 and 1983. Both husbands and wives work 35 hours or more and care for at least one child six years or under. Twenty percent of husbands fully shared housework and parenting, while most of the rest "helped out some." I interviewed individuals separately and together.[7]

TRADITIONAL AND EGALITARIAN
ECONOMIES OF GRATITUDE

A gender culture is a matter of beliefs about manhood and womanhood, and of emotive anchors attached to these beliefs. Many discrete beliefs, such as, "a woman's place is in the home," can be understood as positions on central cultural rules about gender honor. The traditional person affirms rules that accord honor to men and women in different ways (asymmetric rules of honor): the egalitarian affirms rules that accord honor in a similar way (symmetric rules of honor). More specifically, the traditional endorses an asymmetrical "conversion rule" according to which a man's status in the public realm can be converted into honor in the private realm, while women's essentially cannot. The traditional believes a woman's honor derives properly from the home, a man's from the public world. A man's public work thus "translates"; a woman's does not. To gauge a woman's honor, then, one asks: Is she married? To a good fellow? How many children? Are her children doing well? Is her home tidy? She may work outside the home, often because she has to, but this adds nothing to her honor as a woman, only something to the family coffers. To gauge a man's honor, on the other hand, one asks how much he earns? What job does he do? At what rank? In which institution? He may do half the parenting of his children, but in the eyes of the traditional, this does not add to his honor as a man; if anything, it subtracts.

To the traditional, a man may also transfer his publicly based honor to his wife. Mr. Jones's promotion at the bank reflects well on Mrs. Jones. Especially if the wife forms part of what Hanna Papanek calls, the "two-person career," a husband's glory reflects on his wife. It is not simply that she is proud of him; in the eyes of others, her own status has risen. But according to the traditional rule, Mrs. Jones cannot, in a parallel way, transfer her own promotion to her husband—because her husband's honor as a man a) cannot depend in any way on his wife's public work, and b) because he must do better than she in *his* realm, her success may therefore *detract* from his honor. Arrangements of gender honor are such that only a man can "do social class" for the family.

In contrast, for the egalitarian, male and female honor is based equally on their participation in the public and private spheres. Women can transfer their honor to men, just as men transfer theirs to women. By these new rules, women like men can "do social class" for their family.

The communities in which most Bay Area two-job couples lived were themselves culturally plural. Most couples had friends who shared their gender rules, but acquaintances who went by different rules. One man captured this sense of cultural pluralism when he commented:

In some social circles, it's high status to have a professional wife. I would say it *is* more high status to have a wife who is a highly regarded professional than one who is home cooking dinner. Yet we have a dentist friend who refuses to let his wife work. After a while, they crossed us off their list, because my wife gave his wife "too many ideas."

Only a minority of Bay Area couples in the late 1970s and early 1980s were what we could call pure traditionals in the sense that their "marital baseline" — their set of cultural assumptions—was squarely set upon traditional gender rules. Living by traditional rules, they established a traditional economy of gratitude. One such couple were Frank and Carmen Delacorte.[8] Frank is a serious, quiet 30-year-old, high school educated, cabinet maker whose national origin is El Savador and who is a Catholic. He feels that it is his job (his only job, and no one else's job) to provide for his family. Frank dislikes the unskilled work he has recently been forced to do in a box factory, but still bases his male pride on the fact that he works, and provides for his family.

Carmen, his wife, is a large voluble, dark haired woman who runs a daycare center in her home for the children of neighboring mothers who work. She does it she explains firmly,"to help Frank":

The only reason I'm working is that every time I go to the grocery store, the bill is twenty dollars more. I'm not working to develop myself or to discover my identity. No way.

Frank feels grateful that Carmen helps him do his job—without complaining. Consider the "not complaining." One evening Frank and Carmen have dinner with another couple, the wife of whom resents *having to* work as a waitress, because "the man should earn the money." To the discomfort of the Delacortes, the wife openly exposes her husband's vulnerability—given their traditional cultural baseline—he could not support his family as a man should.

Frank rides in a carpool with his foreman, an ardently outspoken traditional. As Frank hesitantly explained:

We are talking about needing extra money and I told him about the business that Carmen has (taking children into her home) and I said: "You know, you've got a house. Your wife could have a business like Carmen's. It's not too bad." His attitude was "no! no! no! ... I don't want anybody saying my wife is taking care of other people's children." He feels like he lives the way most people should live—the husband working, the wife at home.

In Frank's social world, the old gender rules hold: the wife of an adequate man should not *need* to work, but to support a family in the urban working class in the early 1980s, men like Frank, in fact do need a wife's salary. Frank's economic circumstances erode the rules on which he bases his identity as a man, and make him, as a man, vulnerable to insult. Frank feels grateful, then, that his wife gives him the real gift of working without complaining about it.

For her part, Carmen feels *her* job is to care for the home and children; she expects Frank to do the outside chores and to help some, when she asks, with the inside ones. Like most working mothers, Carmen averaged fifteen hours longer each week than Frank did—it added up to an extra month a year. But as a traditional, Carmen could not formally define her "double day" as a problem. Like a number of traditional women in my study, Carmen found a way around her dilemma. She claimed incompetence. She did not drive, so Frank had to shop with her. She did not have a mechanical sense, so Frank had to get money from the automatic teller. In this way, Carmen got relief from her burdens but clung to her traditional notion of womanhood. But she did so, as Erving Goffman would note, at the expense of her "moral character." Instead of moving to new gender rules which would honor Carmen for her paid work, and Frank for his contributions at home, Carmen felt Frank's help at home as a continual series of "gifts." And given her incapacities, she felt grateful.

The Delacortes agreed on certain ritually symbolic extras, for which they felt a certain ritual gratitude. Frank occasionally brought flowers to Carmen. From time to time Carmen troubled to bake an apple pie, because it was Frank's favorite dessert. The roses and the pie were their private extras, symbols of other private gifts.

Flowers from a man to a woman, and food from a woman to a man are widely shared symbols of giving: they are *gendered gifts*. Commercial advertising exploits these gender conventions even as it extends and perpetuates them. The floral industry advertises roses as a man's gift of love to a woman. Similarly, Pillsbury advertises its flour with "Nothin' says lovin' like something from the oven—and Pillsbury says it best." Frank felt Carmen baked the pie because she knew that he personally—not 8 million viewers—loved pie. Carmen felt Frank gave her roses because he knew she—not all the women in America—loved roses. Each incorporated public gender conventions into their private economy of gratitude.

In sum, the Delacorte's economy of gratitude was archetypically traditional. Economic times strained their cultural ideas, but Carmen's way of getting Frank to help at home without changing the gender rules—also archetypical—did not break their accord on the rules. Thus what felt like a gift to the giver also felt like one to the receiver. Seldom was a gift "mis-received." Theirs was thus a rich economy of gratitude.

AN EGALITARIAN ECONOMY OF GRATITUDE

Michael Sherman is a thoughtful, upper-middle-class engineer and in the eight years of his marriage he had gradually at his wife's urging,"converted" from traditional to egalitarian gender rules. His wife, Adrienne, is a college professor. By the time their twins were born, their understanding was that both would give priority to the family and would take whatever cuts in income and career they had to.

Adrienne was not helping Michael "do social class" for their family, she was sharing that function. When Michael bathed the twins, he was helping Adrienne: he was doing what a good father and a good man does. Adrienne was not grateful for Michael's help because she expected it. But Adrienne was grateful to Michael because, in their social circle, egalitarian marriages were themselves rare. In that sense, she felt Michael had given her an "extra." Because she had struggled to establish the new rules in her marriage, and because the rules were new in her social circle and in the wider culture itself, Adrienne sensed their social fragility. She felt Michael had given her an appreciable gift in accepting her terms, when he had been brought up in family to whom caring for children was a mere diversion from a man's task of securing the family's social class.

Michael did feel he was getting behind other traditional men whose wives did more than his at home, but he did not complain; he was doing this for himself as well and for her, and for this, Adrienne was grateful.

For his part, Michael was grateful because, despite their egalitarianism, Adrienne had for six years in good spirit moved from city to city, disrupting her professional training in order to follow him.

Just as the need for a woman's wage challenged the old gender rules, so the wage gap between working men and women challenges the new rules. Although Adrienne wanted her husband to treat her work as just as important as his, her salary was half of his. This piece of economic reality undermined her cultural claim to an equal part in the "class-making" of the family. Adrienne was grateful, then, when Michael honored her work despite the wage gap.

Adrienne was, therefore, especially grateful to Michael for the little signs of deference he showed to her contributions to her field. On one occasion, Michael brought the children to a conference at which she was giving a talk. As she rose to give her talk, she saw in the audience, her beaming husband and two squirming children. But in that one moment, she felt Michael had given her a great gift.

The egalitarian woman is oddly similar to the traditional man: for a new economic reality undercuts the cultural identity of each, making each grateful to their partners for passing lightly over the "soft patches" in their gender positions.

The Delacortes and the Shermans each illustrate the tie between a cultural baseline, the definition of a gift and gratitude. For the Delacortes, gratitude emerges along old cultural tracks; for the Shermans, on the new.[9] For each, cultural thinking implies a language by which we "speak gratitude." In this sense, the Delacortes and Shermans speak in different tongues. Just as a meaning in one language is not understood in the other, so gifts in the language of gratitude are not interchangeable. Carmen Delacorte's gift of "non-complaint" is meaningless if set on the cultural baseline of a Michael Sherman. Adrienne would never complain she had to work, having fought so hard for the equal right to want to. Had she complained, Michael would have turned to talk of Adrienne's "hang up" about ambition, Adrienne's "will to fail." Nor could gifts cross the language barrier in the other cultural direction. For a gift *feels like* a gift only if the giving and receiving are defined by the same cultural baseline.

CULTURAL MISALIGNMENTS AND NON-RECEIVED GIFTS

The Delacortes and Shermans describe two cultural poles between which most couples fall into a large, confusing cultural middle ground. Unlike Carmen Delacorte, most Bay Area working women *want* to work, but unlike Adrienne Sherman, most do not fully share the family's "class-making." Unlike Frank Delacorte, most men whole-heartedly support their wives' work, but unlike Michael Sherman, did not fully share the housework and childcare.

More important, most couples differ to some degree in their idea about manhood and womanhood, and so differ in their understandings about the gendering of gifts. The "language barrier" lies *between* husband and wife. The most common form of "mis-giving" occurs when the man offers a traditional gift—hard work at the office—but the woman wants to receive a "modern" one—sharing child-rearing and housework. Similarly, the woman offers a "modern" gift—more money, while the man hopes for a traditional gift—like home cooking. As external conditions create a "gender gap" in the economy of gratitude, they disrupt the ordinary ways in which a man and woman express love.

Many marriages resemble the couple in O'Henry's story, *The Gift of the Magi*. In that story, Della and Jim are very poor but very much in love and at Christmas, each wants to buy the other a fine gift. Della has beautiful long brown hair that hangs below her waist. Jim sells his favorite gold watch in order to buy combs for her beautiful hair. At the same time, Della cuts off her hair and sells it in order to buy a chain for Jim's gold watch. Each makes a sacrifice for the other which makes them unable to receive a gift from the other. The poignance of the story lies not in the mix-up of the gifts which is, after all, farcical. The poignance rises from the reader's fear that each character will fail to *appreciate* the sacrifice of the other. The story ends happily, however, for each finds out and gives thanks. Presently, new economic pressures and old gender rules are creating in marriage a social version of *The Gift of the Magi*, but the endings are not always so happy.

In *The Gift of the Magi*, the couples exchanged gifts on Christmas, a ritual occasion set aside for gift exchange. In the story, each gift was intended and planned. Each gift was also an object, not an activity, and so seemed well removed from the realm of social roles. (Actually, though, Della's hair seems an emblem of beauty, and the feminine role, while Jim's watch seems an emblem of industry, and the male role.) Each wanted to please, and gave to the other what they knew the other would treasure. The "mis-giving" lay only in *external* circumstance—the timing and secrecy of each sacrifice.

In the ordinary domestic life of working couples, on the other hand, little time is set aside for ritual gift giving. The daily round of chores more often feels like flat, neutral, necessary doings than like meaningful gem-like offerings. Yet curiously, in the course of these "flat" doings, flashes of feeling may spontaneously emerge: on one side, "He should love this . . . " or on the other, "God, what a sweetheart." These spontaneous flashes suggest the comparison between the Christmas Eve watch chain on one hand, and a Saturday washing of the dog on the other. The pattern of those flashes along certain social tracks, the feeling of intense personal closeness, and warmth that rises from the realization—"a gift for me"—make up a real working economy of gratitude.

LIGHT AND HEAVY MEANINGS; GRATITUDE TO NURTURANCE

Sometimes a "mis-giving" stays "light" in the sense that a missed exchange does not make one or the other *feel unloved*. At other times, it cuts dangerously deep into signs by which partners know they are loved.

Consider a light "mis-giving" between Peter and Nina Loyola. Married 12 years, the parents of two, Peter is a sensitive, articulate man who ran a book store. His wife, Nina, a tall, lively woman, is a rising star in the personnel division of a large and expanding company. Like the Delacortes, they began their courtship on traditional terms. But as Nina's company grew, and as managerial opportunities for women opened up, Nina was promoted, until she began to earn three times Peter's salary.

Proud of her career and her salary, Nina was glad to contribute that much money to the family coffers. She was glad to enable Peter to do work he loved, such as running a book store rather than work he hated, but would have done for the money, like real estate. As Nina commented: "My salary and benefits make it possible for Peter to take some risks, starting a new store. I'm really glad he can do it." Nina offered Peter her high salary as a gift.

But Peter did not *receive* her high salary as a gift. Peter knew Nina meant it as a gift. He was glad he could do work he loved, and appreciated what her salary allowed them—a new home, car and private education for their eldest daughter. But he could muster only an ambivalent "thanks." For after a certain point, the old gender rule stopped him.

Peter felt *ashamed* that Nina earned much more than he. What was the source of this shame? Peter did not feel competitive with Nina, nor did he sense her competing with him. Peter appreciated her talents and accomplishments. As he put it, "Not all women could do as well as my wife has." He also appreciated her physical appearance. "She's a good looking woman," he volunteered, "I love seeing her in the morning, her hair washed, and shiny, when she's all fresh for the day." He wanted his daughter to be "just like her."

Peter felt proud *for* Nina, and proud *of* Nina, but he could not feel proud *because* of her: he could not *share* her new status. He could not feel "given to" by her. So Nina could not give her new status *to* him. Indeed, her rise in status actively reduced his—not in Nina's eyes, but in the eyes of his relatives and neighbors and old friends—and among them, especially the men. Through Peter, with Peter's consent, these imagined others discredited Nina's gift. For they judged his honor by the old rule of asymmetrical status transfer.

Far from receiving Nina's salary as a gift, then, Peter treated her salary as a miserable secret to manage. They did not tell Peter's parents—his father, Peter explained, "would die." They did not tell Nina's parents because "she even out-earns her father." They did not tell Peter's high school buddies back in his rural home town in Southern California because "I'd never hear the end of it." Her salary was treated as a deviant act, even a bit like a crime. As Nina explained, in a near whisper:

> I was interviewed for an article in Business Week, and I had to call the fellow back and ask him please not to publish my salary. When he interviewed me, I was a little proud of saying what my salary was. Then I thought, "I don't want that in there—because of Peter."

The taboo on talk of Nina's salary finally extended to themselves as well. As Nina explained, "after awhile we stopped talking about my salary. We still don't."

Another matter diminished Nina's gift. Her salary might make her expect more help from Peter at home. As Nina reported:

Occasionally I've wondered if (my salary) bothered him. Because if we're having a disagreement over something, he sometimes indicates he thinks I'm acting high and mighty, like "who do you think you *are*? I say, "You never used to say that." He said, "I do think you've gotten much more assertive [nervous giggle] than you used to be." I do think Peter might equate my assertiveness with my income. I don't know in my own mind if that has anything to do with it. Of if I was just tired of doing all the housework.

If her greater salary meant he would have to do more at home, he would accept it only grudgingly.

In the climate of opinion he sensed himself to be living in, Peter felt like a "one in a hundred" kind of man. For, as he said with great feeling, "most men couldn't take it if their wives outearned them this much!" They both felt Nina was *lucky* to be married to such an unusually understanding man. So the gift, as Peter felt it was not from Nina to Peter, but from Peter to Nina. Nina, too, felt lucky because only with such an unusually understanding man could she be both successful at work and married.

Nina gave Peter the kind of gift it was a "man's place" to give a woman. Peter wanted to give Nina the high salary, and even more, to give her "the *choice* of whether or not to work." But Nina did not need the choice. Given her skills and opportunities, she would always choose to work. Instead, Nina really wanted Peter to share the housework and childcare. As it was, Nina had to ask Peter to help. Having always to ask, Nina felt Peter was doing her a favor: his participation was not a settled matter. Because she had to ask, his help did not *feel* to Nina like a gift.

Given Peter's shame about her salary, however, Nina did not want to push Peter about the housework. So she rarely asked. She herself did the lion's share of it. Nina *made up* for out-earning her husband (and breaking the cultural rule) by working a double day.[10] In this way, the old rules reduced the value of new economic opportunities for women, and introduced an imbalance that might surprise Marx but not Simone de Beauvoir—in the marital economy of gratitude.

In the end, Peter benefited from his wife's salary. But he also benefited from a second order of gifts his wife owed him *because* she had given him the first gift—an "apology" said through housework.

Given how traditional most men are, a liberated man could make a fine marital bargaining chip out of his sympathy with the new rules, or even attempt at sympathy. Peter gave Nina an unusual amount of personal support for her career. What he did not give her was an acceptance of its public reflection on him. Curiously Nina was "doing it all"—being the prime provider and housekeeper too—and felt *grateful* that she could. We have here the emotional underbelly of gender ideology—not, as we might imagine, in its more popular form of anger and resentment, but in its more common form—of apology and gratitude.

Nina and Peter devised a marital dialogue that "lightened" their "mis-giving." They sidestepped the issue and exchanged other gifts. Nina also came to sympathize with Peter's view of the matter, so that they formed a united cultural baseline, according to which Peter's "mis-giving" was not a marital problem, but only Nina's personal problem of "role conflict," her personal weariness from too much to do.

In other marriages, mis-givings run deeper. Seth Stein, for example, was a hard-driving internist who worked eleven hours a day, and on three days, twelve. "I finally arranged to come home at 6:30," he explained, "when I realized I had missed the first two years of my son's growing up." Officially Seth supported his wife's career. As he commented, "I've always known my wife was a career lady." He believed that in general, too, women had as much place in the public world as men. But it was also clear that his outward rhetoric cloaked deeper and different feelings on the matter. There was a lag between his outward attitude toward his wife's career and the emotional anchor to which it was firmly tied.

For Seth acted and felt as though his work mattered far more than his wife's. This was because the reputational talk of fellow doctors, mattered dearly to Seth, and to such doctors—themselves "career-believers"—it did not matter how many times he had to read to his son the "Three Little Pigs." For Jessica, he felt, it must be different.

But Jessica had earned her own way through medical school, and now practiced as an internist. To a certain degree, Seth felt proud of his wife; he did not want her to be a housewife, or even a secretary. But the egalitarian rule stopped there at midpoint. Emotionally he resisted the rest of its social-psychological logic. His wife would be a professional, like himself. But her work would not be as important to the family or to himself, as he wanted his work to be to her and the family. (There would be no symmetrical "Status transfer.") Because his work took priority over hers, its rewards in relaxation and nurturance would take priority over hers, too. In sum, Seth was an egalitarian on the surface and a traditional underneath.[11]

As Seth drove home from a tough, long day at the office, he had the fantasy of a fresh cooked meal, wine, the children in bed, and appreciation, gratitude and nurturance from Jessica—who would be grateful for all his hard work brought her. Much to his wife's dismay, he sought no exit from his extraordinary hours, and insisted on conceiving of them as his gift to her.

Jessica wanted Seth to share the work of the home with her. Failing that, she wanted Seth to feel badly about not sharing. Even if his career could not permit, she wanted Seth *to want* to share. Failing that, she wanted Seth to set aside his concern for his own work, so he could appreciate *her* parenting. In contrast to the traditional Carmen, Jessica most of all wanted Seth to appreciate the fact that she was relinquishing time from her career, so that he could go full steam ahead in his work. As Seth explained:

> Jessica has been very disappointed about my inability to do more in terms of the child rearing and my not doing 50-50. She says I don't do 50-50, that I have left the child rearing to her. Her career has suffered. She cut twice as much time, instead of me cutting time back from my career. She complains that I'm not more like some imaginary other men or men she knows. Such a man does take time with his children because he wants to and knows how important it is. I don't do enough

parenting. So she's disappointed in me for not doing my share. On the other hand, she understands the spot I'm in. So she holds it in, until she gets good and pissed and then she lets me have it.

Their gratitude clash extended to nurturance. I asked Seth what he was not getting from Jessica that he had expected and wanted. He answered ruefully:

> Nurturing. She don't take care of me enough. But the deal was so straight forward from day one that I'm not bitter. But when I do reflect on it, that's the thing I reflect on. I ain't got a wife taking care of me. Every once in a while I will be upset about it and long for someone who might be sitting around waiting to make me comfortable when I get home. Instead, Jessica needs her back massaged just as much as I do.

If Seth played by the cultural rules that made social room for his "career lady" wife, he could not enjoy first claim to nurturance. But Seth badly wanted that first claim, though he was not convinced he had the *right* to want it. This was the first point in the interview that he broke into pigeon English, as if to distance himself from what he was saying, as if to say "someone less educated, someone younger, someone not me is talking."

Jessica proposed a different cultural baseline: If you help me at home, I will feel grateful for *that* and love you." Through their different stances on the gender rules, they created a deep fracture in their understanding about what was not a gift. Both felt they were thanklessly giving gifts that were continually lost on the other. As Seth finally put it, "I work, and I work and I work, and I come home to what? Nothing." As Jessica put it, "I'm making sacrifices he doesn't even see." Their economy of gratitude had gone broke: each felt short-changed. Disappointed and deprived of "gifts," each finally resented the other. In another, yet more adversarial marriage, a similar husband explained miserably:

> I could dig a twenty foot ditch and she would not notice. Barbara complains I am not doing my share. We get into arguments. We are both equally convinced that we are doing our share of chores around the house and Jude (the two year old)—in a sense—is considered a chore. One or the other of us is always thinking we're getting ripped off.

Each spouse failed to give what the other wanted, or to appreciate what the other was trying to give. Perhaps part of the answer lies in some early injury to human character. But mis-givings also seemed to occur to couples who were, in other arenas of their lives, thoughtful and giving. The larger problem lies in gender mixups in our modern *The Gift of the Magi*.

PRAGMATIC AND HISTORICAL
FRAMES ON GRATITUDE

We may trace gratitude to three sources; first, to ideas about gender honor which derive from a *moral* frame of reference. Second, it may be traced to notions about what is, practically speaking, available. When a man compares his wife to other wives "out there" and finds her better or worse, he invokes a *pragmatic* frame of reference. Third, we may compare our fortunes with those of parents and grandparents, and others of the past, and so invoke a *historical* frame of reference.

In describing how gender rules have a ripple effect on marriage, we have already talked of a moral frame of reference. So let us turn now to the pragmatic and historical. When we apply a pragmatic frame of reference, we invoke ideas about how common or rare a desirable attitude or action is within a marketplace of ideas and actions. For example, women married to egalitarian husbands nearly always mentioned how "lucky" they felt they were to have a husband who was "unusually supportive" of their work, or who was "unusually willing" to share household chores, or "unusually involved with the children." Female "luck" was rooted in a comparison to other less lucky women. Compared to other women, they had it good. When men spoke of luck, which they less often did, it was relative to that of other men.

These luck-comparisons fit a certain pattern. When women tried to persuade their husbands to do more in the home, they compared their husbands to other men who did more. Husbands compared themselves to other men who did less. Underlying both comparisons, however, was a question of the gender marketplace: what was the *going rate* for male housework? For pitching in with the child rearing? For support for a wife's work?

Some working mothers also felt grateful for being actively shielded against the disapproval of kin or neighbors. Many working mothers told "shielding stories"—stories of being protected from the dishonor of breaking the traditional gender rules. One working mother was protected by a maid from the disapproval of a neighbor. Another was protected by a co-worker from the disapproval of a boss. Another had earned an advanced degree in nursing much against the advice of her mother, mother-in-law, and sister-in-law, all of whom were ardently traditional "hold-outs" against the mass movement of women into the cash economy. From time to time, her husband shielded her against this hostile microclimate of opinion. As she recounted appreciatively:

> Once when I was at the library working on a lecture, my husband's mother dropped by and asked where I was. Evan told her I was out shopping for Joey's clothes. He covered for me. Otherwise she would have been very critical of me for leaving Evan and Joey on a weekend like that.

To creep off to the library on a Saturday afternoon, leaving one's husband in charge of a three year old, under the cold judging eyes of traditional kin, was a daring act. Given her time and place, she was socially vulnerable. She therefore felt grateful that her husband protected her. For, when the relevant climate of opinion is unfavorable to women's ambitions, some unusual husbandly support becomes an extra chip in the marital bargain. This husband offered more than the "going rate" among males. He was unusual. Pragmatically speaking, his wife was "lucky."

We may also invoke a historical frame of reference. Over all, more women than men among these Bay Area couples mentioned feeling "lucky" or grateful at some aspect of their work and family arrangement. They felt lucky to have a good babysitter, lucky to have an understanding boss, or husband. They felt lucky their child so seldom got sick, lucky they needed so little sleep.

In many ways, men were objectively luckier than women. For roughly the same hours of work, women earned a third of the male wage. In addition to their full time jobs, these working mothers did nearly all the housework and childcare. Were they to divorce, these women were poised—as their husbands were not—for a great class fall. Ironically, though, women talked about luck and men did not. Why?[12]

Perhaps women unconsciously compare themselves favorably to yet more oppressed women of previous eras—their mothers or grandmothers who had fewer opportunities and rights than they. While many men have moved up the class ladder, men, as a gender, have relinquished certain privileges their fathers and grandfathers enjoyed. Relative to men in the past, they may feel "unlucky." To put it another way: (a) if life is divided into a female domestic realm and a male public realm, (b) if the female realm is devalued relative to the male, and (c) if females are now entering the male realm and males are encouraged to enter the female realm, these changes are likely to feel to women like moving "up" and to men like moving "down." History, too, provides a template of prior expectation against which we appraise our luck.

We may receive a gift from a person and feel grateful, or receive a gift from "life in general," and feel lucky. In either case the gift is a profoundly social affair. For to perceive a gift *as* a gift is to apply a background context to the present moment. This background context is partly moral: "how lucky I am compared to what the cultural rules lead me to expect." It is partly pragmatic: "how lucky I am compared to what I might have otherwise." It is partly historical: "how lucky I am compared to people of my kind in the past." We bring to bear these three frames of reference upon the ongoing stream of experience, and from time to time they produce moments of gratitude and luck.

This analysis of the social production of gratitude is not an alternative to an analysis based on power. It is an analysis of just how profound inequalities work emotionally. Power does not work *around* the feeling of gratitude: it works *through* it by establishing a moral, pragmatic and historical frame of reference which lowers a woman's template of prior expectations even as it artificially elevates that of man.

CONCLUSION AND IMPLICATIONS

Changes in the modern family alter how moral, pragmatic, and historical frames of reference are brought to bear on the ongoing flow of domestic life. Contemporary economic trends have drastically altered the reality of women's lives, much less so those of men. These trends have created a "culture lag"— a strain between the economic reality and the cultural code people apply to it. This culture lag bears powerfully on marriage. It makes of marriage a shock absorber of social tensions produced by larger social trends. Drawing on interviews from a larger study of two-job couples, I have contrasted (a) a consensual traditional economy of gratitude, (b) a consensual egualitarian economy of gratitude, (c) a larger number of marriages in which conflicting notions of gender transformed gratitude into an object of struggle.

When couples struggle over the cultural baseline of their economy of gratitude, they partly control the value of the gifts they want to exchange, and partly they do not. If a woman offers a man a home made apple pie, they do not have to consider how the outside culture sees the apple pie. The valuing of the pie is "social" only in the sense that they have adopted an outer symbol of giving as a private one. Once done, the perception of the gift does not hinge upon the opinion of the outer world.

But couples do not have such control over the value of other gifts they may wish to exchange. Nina, in the example above, offered her higher salary to her husband. But his gender ideology prevented him from receiving it—not simply because he had a traditional notion of male honor in his head, but because his social circle was composed of people who have that notion in their heads. If he ignored what his social circle thinks of him, that act of courage enters his marital economy of gratitude. His wife will be grateful—and, in some way, will repay him. The best way to get sexism out of the economy of gratitude, then, might be to get it out of the social circles on which people—mainly men—rely for a good opinion of themselves.

Second, if marriage is the shock absorber of a dissonance between cultural and economic realities, and if this dissonance creates different viewpoints between men and women within marriage, then we need to understand "marital" problems in more broadly social ways. Certainly marriage is a union of two personalities: there's good chemistry and bad. But something fundamentally social also bedevils many modern marriages as well. For marriage is also a joining of two—often different, usually shifting—stances toward gender rules. A stance toward a gender rule affects what feels like a gift, a token of love. Much of marital dialogue is tacitly aligning his idea to her idea of how much a stint of housework, how much disapproval-shielding, or how much "taking it from the boys about your wife's higher salary—counts in the currency of gratitude.

In modern times, the daily realities strain the traditional economy of gratitude—because most women have to work and want to be valued for it. At the same time modern realities also strain the egalitarian economy of gratitude, for many want to be equally valued for work that still earns substantially less. For traditional and egalitarian couples alike, then, the notion of a gift is culturally in flux.

The strain in modern marriage, then, may have less to do with "personal hang-ups" than with the ripple effect of larger social trends upon the understanding of a gift. The happiest of these two-job marriages, shared a common understanding of what a gift would be and their understanding also fit the current realities of their lives: even highly traditional men in happy marriages did not come home, sit at the dining room table and feel he "would be grateful" and "would feel loved" if dinner were waiting on it—for under modern circumstances, often it is not. Each found feasible equivalents for roses and apple pie.

Happy egalitarian couples sought out the social support to fully internalize the new gender rules. Most important, they did not make do with less gratitude: they found a way to exchange more gifts on new terms and in this way solved the problem of *The Gift of the Magi.*

ACKNOWLEDGMENTS

Special thanks to Adam Hochschild, Ann Swidler, Peggy Thoits, Steve Gordon, and David Franks for insightful criticism.

NOTES

1. One of the few social analyses of gratitude comes from George Simmel (Wolff 1950, pp. 379–395) and Marcel Mauss (1967). In a very different tradition, largely based on experimental research, equity theory (though it does not treat gratitude per se) explores the circumstances that lead couples to feel that a social bond is satisfying or fair. (Elaine Walster 1976).

2. See *The Managed Heart: Commercialization of Human Feeling.* (Hochschild 1983, p. 76).

3. See Joel Davitz (1969, p. 60).

4. See William Ogburn, *Social Change* (New York: Viking Press, 1932) pp. 200–13. Ogburn argued that the material culture changed at a faster rate than the nonmaterial culture—e.g., the folk ways, social institutions—including the family. As Ogburn used the term, it obscures the role of power and interest; culture simply "lagged behind" economy, without serving the interests of any particular social group. In this analysis, the lag serves the interests of men who feel they have less than women to gain from the social changes which economic opportunity and need have now opened up.

5. In the nineteenth century, economic trends most directly affected men as industrialization drew them more than women into wage labor. This caused men to change their basic life ways more, and women to "culturally lag." Today, economic changes affect women more, causing women to change faster. Today the changing environment for women is the economy; the changing environment for men is women.

6. Thanks to Eqbal Ahmad for the term "shock absorber."

7. I used three research methods. First, I mailed a short questionnaire on work and family life to every thirteenth name drawn from the personnel roster of the international headquarters of a large manufacturing company in San Francisco. Respondents who fit the research criteria (married, in a two-job family, caring for a child under six) were asked to volunteer for an in-depth follow-up interview. In this way I obtained families from the managerial, clerical, and production ranks. I then used a snowball sample to supplement the original sample, moving "sideways" at each occupational level. I also interviewed daycare workers and babysitters. Finally I did participant observation in selected homes. Data from this larger study will be reported in a forthcoming book, *The Second Shift: Inside The Two Job Marriage* (New York: Viking Press).

8. These and other personal names in this paper are fictitious.

9. The two couples differ in social class, ethnicity, and religion. Other research suggests a greater traditionalism among the working class, among the politically conservative, and among couples in which the wife and husband's mother is a homemaker. Differences in religious culture appear to make little difference: Jews are slightly more egalitarian, Catholics slightly less—but religious differences may also reflect class ones. (See Baruch and Barnett 1983; Pleck 1982; Kimball 1983; Hood 1983.)

10. When men endorsed the new gender rules (of status transfer) they could receive their wive's salary as a gift. Such wives did not have to "make up for" transgressing a rejected rule by a return of "extra" favors. One wife, a word processor, explained the response of her husband (a night watchman) to a recent promotion: "I really don't think it affects anything, because we look at it this way: If I make more than Will, or he makes more than me, we are both reaping the benefits of that. . . . " The gift was offered, and—culturally as well as materially—received.

    Just as many men could not accept their wives salaries if they were higher than their own, so many men could not accept their rises, after a point, in professional status. Men often reacted to a wife's period of occupational training differently from how women reacted to that of their husbands. When men were in training for a career, a working wife treated the training as a promissory note for a future gift. She often therefore took over housework and childcare to let him study. But men did not similarly take their wives occupational training as the promissory note for a future gift. In one extreme example, a husband commented on his wife's writing of a Ph.D. thesis in political science: "I hate it, I can't tell you how I hate it. I feel I'm getting nothing out of it. It isn't a job. It isn't a cooked meal. It's nothing. I just hate it." At the time of the interview there was a glut on the academic market, but no man writing a dissertation in the study was greeted with such a response.

11 Seth was a mixed traditional—or "pseudo egalitarian"—in the sense that his rhetoric was more liberal than his economy of gratitude. This slippage between the surface and depth of an attitude is common adaptation to the pressure to change—which in this case, came from his wife.

12. There is considerable research evidence that women attribute more personal events (e.g., winning a game, doing well on an exam) to "luck" than men do. This finding has often been attributed to women's lower "locus of control." My field observations correspond to the laboratory evidence, and simply add both an explanation for the lower locus of control, and for their social management of it.

REFERENCES

Baruch, Grace and Rosalind Barnett. 1980. "Correlates of Fathers' Participation in Family Work: A Technical Report." Working Paper 106. Wellesley, MA: Wellesley College Center for Research on Women.

Davitz, Joel. 1969. *The Language of Emotion*. New York/London: Academic Press.

Hochschild, Arlie. 1983. *The Managed Heart: The Commercialization of Human Feeling*. Berkeley/Los Angeles: University of California Press.

Hood, Jane. 1983. *Becoming a Two Job Family*. New York: Praeger.

Kimball, Gayle. 1983. *The 50-50 Marriage*. Boston: Beacon Press.

Lasch, Christopher. 1977. *Haven in a Heartless World*. New York: Basic Books.

Mauss, Marcel. 1967. *The Gift: Forms and Functions of Exchange in Archaic Societies*. New York: Norton.

O'Henry, William. 1961. "The Gift of the Magi." Pp. 323–328 in *What is the Short Story?*, edited by Eugene Current-Garcia and Walton R. Patrick. Glenview, IL: Scott, Foresman.

Pleck, Joseph. 1982. "Husbands' and Wives' Family Work: Paid Work and Adjustment." Working Paper 95. Wellesley, MA: Wellesley College Center for Research on Women.

Swidler, Ann. 1986. "Culture in Action: Symbols and Strategies." *American Sociological Review* 15 (April): 273–286.

Walster, Elaine. 1976. "New Directions in Equity Research." In *Advances in Experimental Social Psychology*, vol. 9, edited by L. Berkowitz and E. Walster. New York: Academic Press.

Wolff, Kurt H. 1950. *The Sociology of George Simmel*. New York: The Free Press.

PART III

GENERATIONAL
RELATIONSHIPS

Part II of this reader was largely devoted to examining the marriage and family dynamics of gender relationships. We now shift our attention to articles that study relationships between family members of different ages.

All human societies are differentiated on the basis of age and sex. Throughout history, the social roles of men and women have been separate, as have the roles of children, adults, and the aged. The family is composed of members of various ages who are differentially related. Most sociological accounts of the family have emphasized how age differentiation of family members enhances their solidarity. The interdependence of family members has been seen to foster emotional attachments, structural solidarity, and family cohesion. Yet, inherent in this differential age structure is the potential for conflict and tension.

Differential age structures have always been linked to status discrepancies in power, privilege, and prestige. Just as a power dimension is often articulated in gender relationships, families can be viewed in terms of hierarchical social structures in which older generations or older siblings hold positions of power, authority, and prestige over their younger counterparts. There are various degrees of family stratification by age. But the universal tendency is for the elders to exercise control over younger family members.

The articles contained in the two chapters that make up this part of the book will examine how families define sets of people according to age. These age categories influence family members' relations to one another. Distinguishing family members by age also has implications for the conceptualization of persons placed in particular age groups. The conceptualizations of childhood and adolescence, adulthood, and the aged reflect conceptualizations of the family, and they should be seen in terms of cultural diversity and social-historical context.

Philippe Ariès in his classic study, *Centuries of Childhood: A Social History of Family Life* (1962), put forth the striking theme that Western ideas about childhood and family life have changed and developed from the Middle Ages to modern times. Ariès sought to document how in medieval life the child was integrated into the community. It was not until the development of bourgeois capitalist society that the segregation of children occurred. He argued that, in the earlier period, children were treated as small adults. As soon as they were capable of being without their mothers, children interacted in the adult world, sharing the same world of work and play. By the age of seven or eight, they were treated as if they had the same mental capacities for understanding and feeling as their adult counterparts.

The lack of awareness of the particular nature of childhood and the full participation of children in adult life is associated with the nature of the family and the community. Ariès depicted the medieval community as intense; no one was left alone because the high density of social life made isolation virtually impossible. This sociability practically nullified the reality and the conceptualization of the private home and the private family. The distinct sense of privacy so characteristic of modern-day families was absent.

Ariès saw the transition to the modern conceptualization of the child beginning to emerge during the seventeenth century. Economic changes led to a revival of interest in education. This, in turn, introduced the idea that a period of special preparation was necessary before individuals could assume their place as adults. Children began to be treated differently, they were expected to behave differently, and their nature was viewed as being different. Children were now coddled, and a greater interest and concern for their moral welfare and development became common.

Ariès emphasized that this emerging concept of childhood developed and was given expression in the emergence of the bourgeois family. He argued that, from a relatively insignificant institution during the Middle Ages, there developed a growing belief in the virtue of the intimate and private nuclear family. The rise of the private family and the growth of the sentimental bonds among its members consequently came about at the expense of the public community.

The continued inward development of the family and its creation of a private sphere of life removed from the outside world was intertwined with the increased importance given to children. The outside community came to be viewed with suspicion and indifference. Proceeding into the industrial era, the family began to withdraw its nonproductive members, women and children, from involvement with the surrounding community. The increased division of labor of family members and the consequent isolation of women and children within the home resulted.

Other social historians have reached similar conclusions. Maris A. Vinovskis, in the opening article (28) of Chapter Nine, Patterns of Parenthood, Childhood, and Adolescence, picks up on the work of family historians and utilizes their perspectives to analyze the development of the family and parent-child interactions. Vinovskis focuses primarily on seventeenth-, eighteenth-, and nineteenth-century English and American families whose members reside in a common household. Using the changing nature of the household as his basis, he surveys three aspects of child development: parental love of children, intellectual capabilities of young children, and youth.

Parental responsibilities for early child care, parental control of children, and what they indicate about historical changes in parent-child relations are then analyzed. Vinovskis concludes that there have been historical changes in the perception and treatment of children and adolescents. This has affected the degree of adult attachment to infants and their intellectual training. Further, although parental involvement has grown considerably, the role of the father in caring for young children has notably declined. Finally, parental control over children's behavior in the areas of sexual behavior or choice of career or spouse has lessened.

Viviana Zelizer (1985) in her book *Pricing the Priceless Child* traces the emergence of the modern conceptualization of the child by documenting a shift in the value of American children since the 1870s from economically useful assets to economically "useless" but emotionally "priceless" love objects. In Article 29, she observes that the changing economic character of baby adoption and the more recent use of surrogacy has historically moved from a buyer's market to a bullish baby market. This change is seen to reflect the "profound cultural transformation in children's economic and sentimental values" during this time period. Zelizer further argues that surrogacy is a further extension of the sentimental search for a child to love. By specifying the racial and cultural characteristic of the sought for surrogate mother, parents aim for the "deliberate manufacture of a particular, suitable child."

In addition to historical transformations in the attitudes toward and the conceptualization of children, attitudes and values regarding the saliency of the parental role have also changed. This has been most dramatically evident in the current heated debate regarding abortion. The United States has witnessed a revolution in the abortion situation for the last 20 years or so. Many states have liberalized their abortion laws. As a severe reaction, a "right to life" movement has emerged as the most powerful single-issue force in American politics.

The pro-life movement views the fetus as a human life rather than as an unformed complex of cells. From this position, pro-lifers believe that abortion is essentially murder of an unborn child. In contrast, pro-choicers believe that ultimately women, not legislators, should have the right to decide whether or not and under what circumstances women will bear children.

For a better understanding of the current abortion controversy, we include a selection (Article 30) from Kristin Luker's (1984) important work, *Abortion and the Politics of Motherhood*. Luker argues that female pro-choice and pro-life advocates hold different world views regarding gender, sex, and the meaning of parenthood. Moral positions on abortion are seen to be tied intimately to views on sexual behavior, the care of children, family life, technology, and the importance of the individual. Luker identifies pro-choice women as educated, affluent, and liberal. In contrast, pro-life women support traditional concepts of women as wives and mothers. Luker believes that the abortion debate is so passionately fought "because it is a referendum on the place and meaning of motherhood."

Another major contemporary concern regarding the nature of parenthood, childhood, and adolescence is reflected by the rise in teenage pregnancy and parenthood. In the United States, these teenage mothers are many times as likely as other women with young children to live below the poverty level. Article 31, by Elise Jones and other members of the Alan Guttmacher Institute (a nonprofit research center), reports on a 37-country study that finds the United States leading nearly all other developed nations in its incidence of pregnancy among girls ages 15 through 19. The Guttmacher researchers compare in detail five Western countries with the United States. They found that, although American adolescents were not more sexually active than European adolescents, they were more likely to become pregnant. These researchers believe that the lack of openness in American society about birth control and sex is the major explanatory factor for why America has the highest teenage pregnancy rates. Concomitantly, societies, such as the United States, that have the least open attitudes toward sex are the ones that have the highest teenage abortion rates.

The majority of single teenage parents experience the "feminization of poverty." Teen pregnancy imposes hardships on at least two generations: mothers and children. Article 32 is an ethnographic account of "sneaker mothers." Terry M. Williams and William Kornblum report on teenage mothers living in urban ghettos. Their attitudes toward sexuality is seen as part of a recreational pattern anchored in a poverty environment. Williams and Kornblum further observe that the most serious problems that these people face is how to get sufficient education and/or training to enter the job market and make enough to support themselves and their children.

Chapter Ten, The Family and the Elderly, is concerned with the nature of generational relationships between the elderly and the family. Earlier, we commented that the universal tendency has been for elders to exercise control over younger family members. Indeed, in more traditional societies that are less susceptible to social change, the elderly have been seen as the repositories of strategic knowledge and religious custom, controlling the ownership of property, and having major influence over kinship and extended family rights and obligations. But, with the movement toward modernization, individualism, and the private family there has been a significant decline in the influence, power, and prestige that the elderly have in the family. The elderly have relatively little importance in an industrial society that emphasizes individual welfare, social and economic progress and change, and that is opposed to the ideology of family continuity and tradition.

However, recent research has demonstrated that the significant decline in the mortality rate, especially in the later decades of the twentieth century, has fundamentally changed the character of the relationship among elders, their children, and grandchildren. This decline has given contemporary grandparenthood new meaning and has accounted for the rise of the four-generation family. This demographic change has greatly increased the potential for family interaction across more than two generations.

Ethel Shanas (Article 33) focuses on the "new pioneers" among the elderly and their families—the members of four-generation families. Shanas observes that the implication for the emergence of a four-generation-family system are not fully appreciated. Opportunities exist for the development of innovative and satisfying kinship ties across the generations, but the disruptive potential of the older generations straining the emotional and economic resources of the younger generations is quite real.

Recently, Andrew J. Cherlin and Frank J. Furstenberg (1986) studied a representative nationwide sample of American grandparents. They note that quality-of-life improvements for many older people have brought about changes in the grandparent-grandchild relationship. The authors discuss how grandparents are at a stage where they desire to maintain autonomy while at the same time participate in the family life of their children and grandchildren. They further observe that social class is relatively unimportant in grandparenthood. In Article 34, we reprint a selection from their book *The New American Grandparent*, which has the informative subtitle "A Place in the Family, A Life Apart." In this selection, Cherlin and Furstenberg also discuss the future of grandparenthood.

The last two articles in this chapter focus on elderly with different ethnic backgrounds. Florentius Chan (Article 35) reports on the experiences of elderly Asian and Pacific Islanders, many of whom are foreign-born and are newly arrived immigrants or refugees. The popular image is of the veneration of elders by Asians and Pacific Islanders. However, as Chan observes, problems of cultural adjustment and the shattering of support networks in America results in very disruptive family and social patterns for these people.

Melba Sanchez-Ayendez (Article 36) also examines the support networks of older adults. She analyzes older Puerto Rican women in an urban, low-income community. Her concern is with interplay between values and behavior in family and community. The cultural tradition of these women defines and interprets their relationships and their use of social support networks. The importance of family interdependence and the articulation of gender roles provide the context for her examination of these elderly women.

REFERENCES

Ariès, Philippe. 1962. *Centuries of Childhood: A Social History of Family Life*. Translated by Robert Baldick. New York: Knopf.

Zelizer, Viviana A. 1985. *Pricing the Priceless Child*. New York: Basic Books.

CHAPTER NINE

Patterns of Parenthood, Childhood, and Adolescence

28

Historical Perspectives on the Development of the Family and Parent–Child Interactions*

Maris A. Vinovskis

The perception and treatment of children and parent–child relationships have experienced major changes during the past 300 or 400 years. While most Western families have always been small and nuclear, the sharp boundary between the modern American family and the rest of society is a recent development. Although parents have historically been responsible for their children, they were not always closely attached to them as infants. Nor have young children been perceived and treated the same throughout history. Whether or not children were once seen as miniature adults, it is clear that they were regarded as capable of considerable intellectual training at a very early age. Furthermore, while historians differ amongst themselves on the existence or meaning of adolescence in earlier times, most of them agree that the life course of youth has changed considerably during the past several hundred years.

Parent-child relationships have also changed over time. Parental involvement in early child care has grown considerably since the Middle Ages, but the role of the father in the catechizing and educating of young children has diminished. At the same time, parental control over children has been greatly diminished in areas such as sexual behavior or choice of a career or spouse.

The relationship between parents and children is influenced by many factors and can vary over time. Alterations in the composition and size of the household

*Vinovskis, Maris A. 1987. "Historical Perspectives on the Development of the Family and Parent-Child Interactions." Pp. 295–312 in *Parenting Across the Life Span,* edited by Jane B. Lancaster, Jeanne Altmann, Alice S. Rossi, and Lonnie R. Sherrod. New York: Aldine De Gruyter. Reprinted with permission. © 1987 Social Science Res. Council.

as well as its interactions with the outside can affect the experiences of children growing up within it. Similarly, changes in the roles of parents or servants, for example, may affect the socialization of the young by that household. And any changes in the perceptions of the nature of children or their appropriate role in society is likely to influence their dealings with parents and other adults.

During the past 20 years historians have reexamined the nature of the family as it once was as well as the changes in the perception and treatment of children (Degler 1980b; Vinovskis 1977, 1983a). Most of these efforts, however, have been focused on some particular aspect of the family of the child, with less attention paid to their interaction. This essay will attempt to bring together some of these diverse studies and suggest how parenting and child development may have been different in the past than it is today. Although this analysis will draw upon historical examples from all of Western Europe since the 16th century, its primary focus will be on 17th, 18th, and 19th century England and America. Furthermore, while there are many different possible definitions of family, throughout this essay, family will refer to members of the same kin living under one roof (Stone 1977).

NATURE OF THE FAMILY AND
HOUSEHOLD IN THE PAST

The social context of parenting and child development is very much affected by the nature of the residence in which the child is reared. The traditional assumption (Wirth 1938; Parsons 1943) is that most children in the past grew up in extended households. After marriage, they continued to live with their parents and supported them in their old age. As a result, young children frequently grew up in large households where their grandparents as well as their parents played an important role in their upbringing.

Accordingly, the extended Western preindustrial household was transformed into an isolated nuclear one as the result of the disruptive impact of urbanization and industrialization (often incorrectly combined under the term "modernization") in the 19th and 20th centuries. While this new nuclear household was supposedly better suited to the needs of the modern economy in terms of providing a more mobile and less kin-oriented labor force, the tasks of child rearing and care of the elderly were seen to have suffered in the process.

Recent historical research has cast considerable doubt on the idea that the Western family evolved from extended to nuclear due to the onset of urbanization and industrialization. As Laslett (1972) and his associates have argued, most households in preindustrial Western Europe were already nuclear and therefore could not have been transformed by any recent economic changes. While some variations did exist in household size, these were surprisingly small and mainly due to the presence or absence of servants or boarders and lodgers rather than relatives. Furthermore, instead of the nostalgic view of children growing up in large families, Laslett (1972) contends that most households were actually quite small (mean household size was about 4.75).

Critics (Berkner 1972, 1973) of the use of a mean household size point out that studying the average size of families at any given moment is misleading and incorrect because individual families increase and decrease in size and complexity over time. While only a small proportion are extended at any particular instance, a much larger proportion of them may have been extended at some point. Berkner (1972) in particular notes the prevalence of the stem family in Austria, where one of the male children continues to live with the parents after he marries and then inherits the farm after the father dies.

Although the critics of the use of mean household size are correct in questioning its conceptual and analytical utility, it is not likely that many families in preindustrial England or America had married children routinely living with them (Degler 1980a; Vinovskis 1977, 1983a). While single servants or boarders and lodgers frequently resided in the same household (Demos 1970; Modell and Hareven 1973), it was expected that married couples would establish their own separate, independent households. In some parts of Western Europe, however, such as southern France (Flandrin 1979) or the Baltic provinces (Plakens 1975), multigenerational households were more common. Furthermore, while mean household size was usually quite small in Western Europe (Laslett 1972), it was considerably larger in colonial New England (Greven 1972) because of the higher fertility and lower mortality of that region.

Even if most Western European families had always been small and nuclear, it does not mean that the social context in which children were brought up in a household remained the same. As Ariès (1962) has pointed out, the medieval family was very different from its modern counterpart in that the boundary between the household and the larger society was not as rigidly drawn and the role of parents, servants, or neighbors in the socialization of children was not as differentiated and clear-cut. Stone's (1977) analysis of the late medieval and early 16th century English family confirms and expands upon many of Ariès's findings. While Stone acknowledges that his categorization and periodization of the changes in English families is limited by the sources and the overlapping of these ideal family types to some degree in practice, his framework provides a useful point of departure for this analysis.

The English in the late medieval period maintained only weak boundaries between their families and the rest of society, and family members were oriented more toward kin relationships among the upper classes and toward neighbors among their poorer counterparts (Stone 1977). Marriage among property-owning classes in 16th-century England was a collective decision involving not only the family but also other kin. Individual considerations of happiness and romantic love were subservient to the need to protect the long-term interests of the lineage. Relationships within the nuclear family were not much closer than those with neighbors, relatives, or other friends.

According to Stone (1977), this open lineage family gave way to a restricted patriarchal nuclear family that predominated from 1580 to 1640, during which time loyalties to lineage, kin, and local community declined as allegiances to the state and church and kin within the household increased. As a result, the boundary between the nuclear family and the other members of society increased, while the authority of the father as head of the household within that family was enhanced. Both the state and the church provided new theoretical and practical support for patriarchy within the family, which was coupled with a new interest in children.

Fathers now had added incentive to ensure that their offspring internalized the values of submissiveness to them even if it meant breaking their will at an early age. This drive toward parental dominance was particularly characteristic of the Puritans, who tended to be especially anxious about their children's upbringing. Concern about children continued as they developed, and upper-class parents sought to control their choices of both a career and a spouse.

Finally, Stone (1977) sees the growth of the closed domesticated nuclear family after the mid-17th century among the upper bourgeoise and squirarchy caused by the rise of affective individualism. The family was now increasingly organized around the principle of personal autonomy and bound together by strong affective ties. The separation between the members of the nuclear family and their servants or boarders and lodgers widened, along with the distance between the household and the rest of society. Physical privacy became more important, and the idea of the individual's right to pursue his own happiness became more acceptable.

While the causes of the changes or the exact timing among the different social classes of the move from the open lineage family to the closed domesticated nuclear family are not always clear or agreed upon (Trumbach 1978), the occurrence of that shift is generally accepted. Children growing up in 15th-century England, for example, encountered a very different social environment in their homes, and neighborhoods from those in the 18th and 19th centuries. Thus, the close-knit affective nuclear family that is most prevalent today is really only the latest stage in the longer evolution of households and family life in Western Europe in the past 500 years.

Throughout most of the preindustrial period the household also functioned as the central productive unit of society. Children received training in their own homes regarding their future occupations or were employed in someone else's household (Mitterauer and Sieder 1982). But as the economic functions of the household were transferred in the late 18th and 19th centuries to the shop or the factory, the home environment in which the children were raised changed. Rather than being closely integrated into neighborhood activities and serving as an economic focal point, the household increasingly became a haven or escape from the outside world (Cott 1977; Lasch 1977). Furthermore, as members of the nuclear family increasingly distanced themselves from others, they came to expect and cherish more from each other emotionally (Mitterauer and Sieder 1982). As a result, whereas children growing up in the 15th century were expected and encouraged to interact closely with many other adults besides their own parents, those in the 18th and 19th centuries came to rely more upon each other and their own parents for their emotional needs.

While major changes in the nature of the family occurred in Western Europe, such changes were less dramatic in America due to the fact that when the New World was settled the closed domesticated nuclear family was already prevalent in England (Stone 1977). The families that migrated to the New World, especially the Puritans, brought with them the ideal of a close and loving family (Demos 1970; Morgan [1944] 1966). While the economic functions of the American household were altered in the 19th century, the overall change was less than the shift from an open lineage family to the closed domesticated nuclear family in Western Europe.

Thus, although the relationship between parents and their children, for example, has not remained constant in America during the past 300 years, the extent of that change is probably less than in Western Europe.

CHANGING PERCEPTIONS AND
TREATMENT OF CHILDREN

Having surveyed some of the changes in the nature of the household and the way they might affect the environment in which children were raised, the way those children were perceived and treated will now be considered. Since it is impossible, of course, to survey child development in its entirety, the focus will be confined to only three aspects: (1) parental love of children, (2) intellectual capabilities of young children, and (3) youth.

Parental Love of Children

It is commonly assumed that one of the basic characteristics of human beings is the close and immediate attachment between the newborn child and the parents— especially the mother. Consequently, child abandonment or abuse today is puzzling to many Americans, since these practices seem to contradict what is perceived to be a deeply ingrained feeling toward one's own children.

Maternal indifference to infants, however, may have been common during the Middle Ages (Ariès 1962; Stone 1977). Parents did not pay much attention to newborn infants and did not display much grief it they died. According to Ariès, the lack of affection toward and attention to infants continued until the 16th and 17th centuries, and Shorter (1975) argues that it persisted into the 18th and 19th centuries among the ordinary people of Western Europe. A few studies (Pollock 1983), however, question the extent of maternal indifference and inattention in the past and thereby tend to minimize any of the more recent changes perceived by other historians.

As evidence of parental indifference to infants, scholars point to the casualness with which deaths of young children were accepted and sometimes seemingly encouraged or at least tolerated. Although overt infanticide was frowned upon and increasingly prosecuted in the 16th century, it still may have been quite common in parts of Western Europe (Langer 1975). There also seems to be agreement that the practice of leaving infants at foundling hospitals or with rural wet nurses during the 17th, 18th, and 19th centuries resulted in very high mortality rates (Badinter 1981). The prevalence of wet-nursing is indicated by the fact that in the first two decades of the 19th century approximately half of the infants born in Paris were nursed commercially, even though this often resulted in more than one quarter of those infants dying (Sussman 1977). In addition, the natural children of the wet nurses also suffered and were more apt to die because they did not receive sufficient nourishment (Lehning 1982). Whether the decision to abandon an infant to a charitable institution or to a wet nurse was mainly the result of the mother's economic desperation, the difficulty of raising an out-of-wedlock child, or a lack of attachment for the young infant is not clear. But the fact that many well-to-do, married women casually chose to give their infants to wet nurses, despite the apparent higher risks of mortality, suggests that not everyone using this form of child care was driven to it by dire circumstances (Shorter 1975).

While the practice of overt infanticide and child abandonment may have been relatively widespread in parts of Western Europe (such as France), it does not seem to have been as prevalent in either England or America (Hoffer and Hull 1981; Stone 1977). Indeed, authorities in both those countries prosecuted cases of infanticide in the 16th and 17th centuries more vigorously than most other forms of murder and emphasized the importance of maternal care of the young child. Furthermore, the use of wet nurses (employed by upper-class English women) became unfashionable by the end of the 18th century (Trumbach 1978).

Although there is considerable disagreement on the extent and timing of parental indifference to infants in Western Europe, almost everyone is agreed on its presence as well as its subsequent demise. Though few individuals (Pollock 1983) have begun to challenge this interpretation—at least in its more extreme forms— most observers still concur that by the 17th and 18th centuries (or perhaps even later among French peasants and workers) parents expressed more interest in and affection for their children (Demos 1970; Morgan 1966; Stone 1977, Trumbach 1978). Indeed, the deep affection and attachment to one's own children became one of the major characteristics of the closed domesticated nuclear family. By the 19th century many observers began to even criticize parents for being too child-centered (Wishy 1968).

While the gradual change in the reactions of parents to their newborn un- doubtedly improved the situation of children generally, parents still could, if they chose, abuse their own children as long as such abuse did not result in death. Gradually, however, the state began to intervene to protect the child from harm inflicted at the workplace or at home. Yet it was not until the late 19th century that reformers in England were able to persuade lawmakers to pass legislation to protect children from abusive parents, since the parent–child relationship was re- garded as sacred and beyond state intervention (Behlmer 1982). Ironically, efforts to prevent cruelty against animals preceded those to accomplish the same ends for children by nearly half a century (Turner 1980).

Intellectual Capabilities of Young Children

Child developmentalists sometimes portray the nature and capabilities of the young as invariant across cultures and over time, without taking into consideration how much of the behavior of those children can be explained by parental and societal expectations. Yet historically the perceptions and treatment of the child have been quite varied.

Some of the earliest studies (Earle 1899) of children in colonial America yielded the observation that a distinct phase of childhood did not exist. Children were expected to think and behave as adults from a very early age. As Fleming (1933, p. 60) noted, "Children were regarded simply as miniature adults. . . ." This perception of children received strong reinforcement from Ariès (1962), who argued that medieval society in general did not distinguish between children and adults and that the idea of childhood as a separate and distinct stage did not emerge until the 16th and 17th centuries.

Some recent scholars (Demos 1970, 1974; Zuckerman 1970) of the colonial American family have continued the idea that children were perceived and treated as miniature adults. But others (Axtell 1974; Stannard 1975, 1977; Kaestle and Vinovskis, 1978, 1980) have questioned this interpretation by pointing out that the New England Puritans were aware that children had different abilities and temperaments from adults and that child rearing should be molded to those individual differences (Moran and Vinovskis 1983).

Young children in colonial America, however, were perceived as being more capable intellectually at an early age than their counterparts today. The Puritans believed that children should be taught to read the Bible as soon as possible because it was essential for everyone's salvation. The importance of early reading was reinforced for them by their expectation that children were likely to die at any moment and therefore had to be spiritually prepared for this eventuality (Slater 1977; Stannard 1975, 1977; Vinovskis 1972, 1976, 1981b). Indeed, the notion that children could and should learn to read as soon as they could talk was so commonly accepted by educators (Locke 1964) that they did not feel the need to elaborate upon it in their writings (Kaestle and Vinovskis 1978, 1980).

The idea of early childhood learning received a powerful boost in the first third of the 19th century, when the infant school movement swept the United States (May and Vinovskis 1977; Kaestle and Vinovskis 1978, 1980). The focus on special classes for very young children was imported from England, where infant schools had been created to help disadvantaged poor children. While most infant schools in America were initially intended to help poor children, they were quickly adopted by middle-class parents once it became evident that they were useful in helping children to develop. By the 1830s and 1840s in Massachusetts, for example, nearly 40–50% of 3-year-old children were attending schools and learning to read. Although some infant-school teachers were reluctant to focus on intellectual activities such as reading, pressures from parents forced most of them to provide such instruction.

During the first two centuries of settlement in the New World, the idea that 3- and 4-year-old children were intellectually capable of learning to read had gone virtually unchallenged in theory as well as practice and was reinforced by the infant-school movement of the late 1820s. Yet in the 1830s this viewpoint became strongly and successfully contested. Amariah Brigham, a prominent physician, published a popular book (1833) in which he argued that the early intellectual training of children seriously and permanently physically weakened their growing young minds and often led to insanity in later life. His dire warnings were accepted and repeated by educators as well as writers of child-rearing manuals. As a result, crucial financial support for the infant schools from the middle-class reformers dropped precipitously, and many such institutions were forced to close. Although parents were much slower than physicians and educators in abandoning early childhood education, by the 1850s and 1860s virtually no very young children (3 or 4 year olds) could be found in Massachusetts schools. Interestingly, when the kindergarten movement was popularized in the United States in the 1860s and 1870s by Mary Peabody, a former Massachusetts infant-school teacher, it was restricted to children at least 5 or 6 years old and deliberately avoided intellectual activities such as reading.

This example of the changing attitudes on when a child could and should learn to read illustrates how alterations in the perception of children can greatly affect the type of socialization provided for them in early life. It also demonstrates how sudden and dramatic shifts in the perceptions of the child can alter the basic pattern of child care that had been accepted unquestioningly for several centuries. One might even speculate that as society becomes increasingly willing to incorporate the latest scientific and medical findings in the care of the young, and as social institutions such as the schools become more willing and able to determine how and when parents educate their children, the likelihood of frequent swings in child-rearing practices may increase.

Youth

Although the historical study of youth is now attracting more research (Gillis 1974; Kett 1977), there is still little agreement among scholars on the changes that occur in this phase of the life course. The recognition of adolescence as a particular stage of development in the past, for example, has not been conclusively demonstrated. Some historians (Demos and Demos 1969) see its emergence only in the late 19th or early 20th century, as a result of the introduction of more career choices and the sharper discontinuities in young people's lives due to urban-industrial development. Others (Hiner 1975) have challenged that interpretation by arguing for the presence of adolescence in the early 18th century. Some individuals (Kett 1977) have moved away from the issue of adolescence as a particular stage and focused instead on the changes in the lives of youth as they move from a state of dependence to one of independence, signaled by the establishment of their own household.

Rather than trying to analyze the individual emotional turmoil and tension that is often associated with adolescence today, many historians are studying other aspects of teenage development, such as patterns of school attendance and labor force participation. Here the debate, usually among economic and educational historians, revolves not around the life course experiences of the individual, but on those differences in the experiences among various ethnic groups or classes (Vinovskis 1983). Scholars like Thernstrom (1964) argue that early school leaving in 19th century America was mainly the result of ethnic rather than class differences, as Irish parents were more willing to have their children leave school in order to help the family earn enough money to purchase their own home. Other historians (Katz and Davey 1978; Bowles and Gintis 1976) reject this ethnic interpretation and contend that the real cause of variations in school attendance was class differences. Finally, some analysts (Kaestle and Vinovskis 1980) offer a more pluralistic interpretation that recognizes the importance of both the ethnicity and class of the parents as well as the type of community in which the children are raised.

While historians may be moving toward more agreement on the patterns of school attendance and labor force participation among youth, they are simultaneously beginning to disagree on the importance of that education. Whereas Thernstrom (1964) and most other social historians simply assumed that education was an important factor in the social functioning and mobility of 19th-century teenagers, Graff (1979) questions the benefits and necessity of literacy and education altogether. Thus, historians who have been content to analyze the patterns and causes of teenage school attendance are now being forced to reexamine its actual meaning and impact on the lives of those children.

Although American historians have tried to analyze the patterns of school attendance and labor force participation of teenagers in the past as well as the existence of adolescence as a stage of the life course, surprising little has been done to explore the changes in teenage sexuality, pregnancy, or childbearing (Vinovskis 1982). This is somewhat surprising, since the issue of the so-called "epidemic" of adolescent pregnancy has become so visible and symbolically important to policymakers in Washington today (Vinovskis 1981a).

In early America, adolescent sexuality, pregnancy, and childbearing were not perceived to be particular problems (Vinovskis 1982). Althought the age of menarche in colonial New England biologically was low enough for teenage parenting to occur, few became pregnant because of the stringent 17th-century prohibitions against premarital sexual relations and the fact that few women married in their early teens. Even if teenage girls were sexually active and did become pregnant, their age was less of a factor in how society reacted than their general behavior. In other words, early Americans were more concerned about premarital sexual relations in general than the age of the women involved. Only in the late 19th and early 20th centuries is there differentiation between teenage and adult sexual behavior, with a more negative connotation attached to the former.

Throughout most of the 17th, 18th, and 19th centuries there was little onus attached to teenage marriages as long as the couple was self-supporting. Since opportunities for careers for single or married women outside the home were limited, the handicaps currently associated with early childbearing did not seem as severe. Furthermore, the relatively small number of teenage marriages during these years compared to the situation today also minimized the attention that was paid to teenage childbearing in the past.

Indeed, only in the post-World War II period has the issue of teenage pregnancy and childbearing become such a major public concern. Ironically, the greatest attention to it has come during the late 1970s and early 1980s, even though the rates of teenage pregnancy and childbearing peaked in the United States in the late 1950s (Vinovskis 1981a).

PARENT-CHILD RELATIONS

Thus far this essay has dealt with changes in the nature of the household as well as in the perception and treatment of children over time. Two issues in the relationship between parents and children: (1) parental responsibility for early child care and (2) parental control of children should also be considered.

Parental Responsibility for Early Child Care

In modern American society it is assumed that the parents have the primary responsibility for child care until the children are enrolled in schools where they will receive most of their educational instruction. When the behavior of parents seriously threatens the well-being of the young child, the state can intervene to protect it, but this does not occur frequently. Furthermore, the physical care and early socialization of the child is almost always the responsibility of the mother— even if both parents are employed.

Historically, the primary responsibility for the upbringing of young children belonged almost exclusively to the parents, especially the father. Although in some periods and societies, such as 17th- and 18th-century New England (Moran and Vinovskis 1983), the state or church intervened in order to assure that the children were properly catechized and instructed, it was not until the late 19th and early 20th centuries that the state was willing to remove the young child from the direct supervision of negligent or abusive parents (Behlmer 1982). It should also be noted, however, that although the state valued the family in the past, it was not irrevocably committed to it when that family was incapable of supporting its own members. Thus, in early America destitute families were sometimes disbanded and the children placed in other households in order to reduce the welfare costs to the rest of the community (Rosenkrantz and Vinovskis 1977).

If the responsibility for early child care usually resided with the parents, they did not always provide that care themselves. In the medieval household, for example, servants as well as neighbors complemented the care given the young child by the parents or their older siblings (Ariès 1962; Stone 1977). In addition, as was discussed previously, many women in the past willingly or out of economic necessity relinquished the nurturing of their infants to a wet nurse (Shorter 1975; Sussman 1977).

By the 17th and 18th centuries, particularly in England and America, parents increasingly cared for their own young children and began to limit assistance from nonfamily members (Morgan [1944] 1966; Stone 1977). This trend was caused in large part by the growing affection and self-centeredness among the immediate family members in the closed domesticated nuclear family. Furthermore, parental involvement in the upbringing of their own children was especially evident among the Puritans, who insisted on the importance of the family in providing for the spiritual as well as the physical needs of the young child (Moran and Vinovskis 1982, 1983).

As the family began to play a more active role in the care of its young children, there was often a division of labor between the parents. The mother provided for the physical needs of the child while the father, as head of the household, attended to its spiritual and educational development. Indeed, the Puritans saw the father as the primary catechizer of children and household servants (Moran and Vinovskis 1983).

The importance in these areas of the Puritan father was reversed in the 18th and 19th centuries, as men stopped joining churches and therefore were deemed less suitable for overseeing the religious upbringing of their children (Moran 1979, 1980). New England Puritans came to rely more upon the mothers who, although they were less literate than the husbands, continued to join the churches. By the end of the 18th and early 19th centuries, the mother's role in early childhood care and socialization was clearly established (Kuhn 1947; Moran and Vinovskis 1983). The only major change thereafter was the growing role of the schools in the provision of formal education for the young child, as parents usually willingly relinquished that task to reluctant schoolteachers who had tried to limit the entry of young children into their classrooms (Kaestle and Vinovskis 1980).

Thus, although parents have usually been assigned the primary responsibility for the care and socialization of the young child in Western society, they have not always provided those services themselves. During the past 300 or 400 years, however, parents have increasingly nurtured and socialized, at least to some degree and frequently with the assistance of specialized institutions such as schools or churches, their own children. While the direct involvement of parents in early child care and education has grown, that of other nonrelated members of the household or of the neighbors has diminished; the family today is more private and self-centered than its medieval counterpart. Finally, although the father played a more important role in the catechizing and educating of young children in certain time periods and cultures, the primary provider of care and affection for the young child was usually the mother or her female substitute. The mother's role in the upbringing of the young child increased during the 18th and 19th centuries as fathers became too busy or uninterested in sharing more fully in the raising of their young offspring. While child-rearing manuals continued to acknowledge the importance of the father for the care of the young, they also recognized that the mother had become the major figure in the performance of that task (Demos 1982).

Parental Control of Children

Throughout most of Western development, parents exercised considerable control over children as long as they remained in the home. Children were expected to be obedient to their parents and to contribute to the well-being of the family. During much of this time, parents arranged the marriages of their children and greatly influenced their choice of careers.

In the medieval period, the interests of the lineage and kin were more important than those of the individual (Ariès 1962; Stone 1977). Children were not only expected to acquiesce to the requests of parents, but also to the interests of the larger kinship network. Marriages were arranged in order to further the goals of the family and its kindred.

The emergence of the restricted patriarchal nuclear family weakened the claims of the lineage and kin on the allegiances of the children as the nuclear family grew closer together. The emphasis on the authority of the father as the head of the household, however, reinforced parental control over the children.

It was not until the arrival of the closed domesticated nuclear family that the rights of children as individuals were clearly recognized and acknowledged. Increasingly, children were allowed not only to veto an unsatisfactory marriage partner, but even to choose someone they loved (Stone 1977; Trumbauch 1978). While dating this erosion of parental power in the selection of a child's mate may vary from one society to another, it probably occurred in America between the late 18th and early 19th centuries (Smith 1973).

Parents tried to determine not only whom children should marry, but also when. According to Greven (1970), the second generation in 17th-century Andover, Massachusetts were prevented from early marriages by the unwillingness of their fathers to relinquish legal control over the land they had set aside for their sons. While this argument is plausible, Greven has been unable to establish it statistically (Vinovskis 1971). Indeed, while there is little doubt that parents often tried to influence the timing as well as the partner of their child's marriage, very few of the existing historical studies are able to ascertain the relative importance of the role of the parents—especially since many of the children may have willingly acquiesced in this process anyway. Yet the idea that a child has rights independent of and superior to those of the parents is a relatively recent development in Western society.

In Western Europe children were also often expected to turn over almost all their earnings directly to the parents—sometimes even after they had left home (Shorter 1975). Under these circumstances, the economic value of children to the family was considerably enhanced, since the additional labor or revenue from a grown child could be substantial. Although children frequently contributed some of their outside earnings to their parents in the United States, it does not seem to have been as common as in Western Europe—especially among the native-born population (Dublin 1979). This difference in parental control over the earnings of children probably reflects both the greater individuality and freedom of the child in the 19th-century American family and the fact that these families were not as economically destitute as their European counterparts. Certainly among some immigrant groups in the United States there seems to have been a stronger tradition of children, particularly girls, turning over their pay envelopes to the parents (Hareven 1982).

Over time parental control of children has been significantly diminished. Whereas in the medieval and early modern periods parents had almost unlimited control over the behavior of their children in their own households, such is no longer the case. Although parents may still influence the choice of a child's mate or career, they cannot determine them. In addition, the idea of a child giving most of his/her outside wages to the parents seems anachronistic and inappropriate today. Indeed, the development of children's rights has proceeded so far and rapidly that society is in the midst of a backlash as efforts are being made to reassert parental rights in areas such as the reproductive behavior of minor children.

CONCLUSION

This brief historical survey of the nature of the family and household, the perception and treatment of children, and parent–child relationships suggests that major changes have occurred in these areas during the past 300 to 400 years. While most Western families have always been small and nuclear, the sharp boundary between the modern American family and the rest of society is a recent development.

Although parents have been responsible for their children, they were not always closely attached to them as infants. Nor were young children perceived and treated the same throughout history. Whether or not children were once seen as miniature adults, it is clear that they were regarded as capable of considerable intellectual training at a very early age. Furthermore, while historians differ amongst themselves on the existence or meaning of adolescence in the past, most of them agree that the life course of youth has drastically changed during the past several hundred years.

Finally, parent–child relationships have changed over time as well. Parental involvement in early child care has grown greatly since the Middle Ages, but the role of the father in the catechizing and educating of young children has diminished. At the same time, parental control over the behavior of children has been greatly diminished in areas such as sexual behavior or choice of a career or spouse.

Although there have been major changes in the way society treats children, it would be very difficult to agree on the costs and benefits of those trends from the viewpoint of the child, the parents, or society. While many applaud the increasing individualism and freedom for children within the family, others lament the loss of family responsibility and individual discipline. While an historical analysis of parents and children cannot resolve such issues, it can provide us with a better appreciation of the flexibility and resilience of the family as an institution for raising the young.

SUMMARY

Major changes have occurred during the past 300 to 400 years in the perceptions and treatment of children. Although parents have been responsible for their children, they were not always closely attached to them as infants. Whether or not children were once seen as miniature adults, it appears that they were regarded as capable of considerable intellectual training at a very early age. The existence and definition of adolescence has also changed considerable over time.

Parent-child relationships have changed as well. Parental involvement in early child care has grown considerably since the Middle Ages, but the role of the father in catechizing and educating young children has diminished. At the same time, parental control over the behavior of children has been greatly diminished in areas such as sexual behavior or choice of a career or spouse.

ACKNOWLEDGMENTS

Research was supported by the Program in American Institutions at the University of Michigan.

REFERENCES

Ariès, R. 1962. *Centuries of Childhood: A Social History of Family Life.* Translated by R. Baldick. New York: Vintage Books.

Axtell, J. 1974. *The School Upon a Hill: Education and Society in Colonial New England.* New Haven, CT: Yale University Press.

Badinter, E. 1981. *Mother Love: Myth & Reality.* New York: Macmillan.

Behlmer, G. K. 1982. *Child Abuse and Moral Reform in England, 1870–1908.* Stanford, CA: Stanford University Press.

Berkner, L. K. 1973. "Recent Research on the History of the Family in Western Europe." *Journal of Marriage and the Family.* 35: 395–405.

Berkner, L. K. 1972. "The Stem Family and the Developmental Cycle of the Peasant Household: An Eighteenth-Century Austrian Example." *American Historical Review* 77: 398–418.

Bowles, S. and H. Gintis. 1976. *Schooling in Capitalist America: Educational Reform and the Contradictions of Economic Life*. New York: Basic Books.

Brigham, A. 1833. *Remarks on the Influence of Mental Cultivation and Mental Excitement upon Health*. 2d edition. Boston, MA: Marsh, Capen and Lyon.

Cott, N. F. 1977. *The Bonds of Womanhood: "Woman's Sphere" in New England, 1780-1835*. New Haven, CT: Yale University Press.

Degler, C. 1980a. *At Odds: Women and the Family in America from the Revolution to the Present*. New York: Oxford University Press.

Degler, C. 1980b. "Women and the Family." Pp. 308–326 in *The Past Before Us: Contemporary Historical Writings in the United States*, edited by M. Kammen. Ithaca, NY: Cornell University Press.

Demos, J. 1970. *A Little Commonwealth: Family Life in Plymouth Colony*. New York: Oxford University Press.

Demos, J. 1974. "The American Family in Past Time." *American Scholar* 43: 422–446.

Demos, J. 1982. "The Changing Faces of Fatherhood: A New Exploration in American Family History." Pp. 425–450 in *Father and Child: Developmental and Clinical Perspectives*, edited by S. H. Cath, A. R. Gurwitt, and J. M. Ross. Boston: Little, Brown.

Demos, J. and V. Demos. 1969. "Adolescence in Historical Perspective." *Journal of Marriage and the Family* 31: 632–638.

Dublin, T. 1979. *Women at Work: The Transformation of Work and Community in Lowell, Massachusetts, 1826–1860*. New York: Columbia University Press.

Earle, A. M. 1899. *Child Life in Colonial Days*. New York: Macmillan.

Flandrin, J. L. 1979. *Families in Former Times: Kinship, Household and Sexuality in Early Modern France*. Translated by R. Southern. Cambridge: Cambridge University Press.

Fleming. S. 1933. *Children and Puritanism: The Place of Children in the Life and Thought of the New England Churches, 1620–1847*. New Haven, CT: Yale University Press.

Gillis, J. R. 1974. *Youth and History*. New York: Academic Press.

Graff, H. J. 1979. *The Literacy Myth: Literacy and Social Structure in the Nineteenth-Century City*. New York: Academic Press.

Greven, P. J. 1972. "The Average Size of Families and Households in the Province of Massachusetts in 1764 and in the United States in 1790: An Overview." Pp. 545–560 in *Household and Family in Past Time*, edited by P. Laslett. Cambridge: Cambridge University Press.

Greven, P. J. 1970. *Four Generations: Population, Land, and Family in Colonial Andover, Massachusetts*. Ithaca, NY: Cornell University Press.

Hareven, T. K. 1982. *Family Time & Industrial Time: The Relationship Between the Family and Work in a New England Industrial Community*. Cambridge: Cambridge University Press.

Hiner, N. R. 1975. "Adolescence in Eighteenth-century America." *History of Childhood Quarterly* 3: 253–280.

Hoffer, P. C. and N. E. H. Hull. 1981. *Murdering Mothers: Infanticide in England and New England, 1558–1803*. New York: New York University Press.

Kaestle, C. F. and M. A. Vinovskis. 1978. "From Apron Strings to ABCs: Parents, Children, and Schooling in Nineteenth-Century Massachusetts." Pp. S39–S80 in *Turning Points: Historical and Sociological Essays on the Family,* edited by J. Demos and S. S. Boocock. Chicago: University of Chicago Press.

Kaestle, C. F. and M. A. Vinovskis. 1980. *Education and Social Change in Nineteenth-Century Massachusetts*. Cambridge: Cambridge University Press.

Katz, M. B. and I. E. Davey. 1978. "School Attendance and Early Industrialization in a Canadian City: A Multivariate Analysis. *History of Education Quarterly* 18: 271–294.

Kett, J. F. 1977. *Rites of Passage: Adolescence in America, 1790 to the Present*. New York: Basic Books.

Kuhn, A. L. 1947. *The Mother's Role in Childhood Education*. New Haven, CT: Yale University Press.

Langer, W. 1975. "Infanticide: A Historical Survey." Pp. 55–68 in *The New Psychohistory,* edited by L. deMause. New York: The Psychohistory Press.

Lasch, C. 1977. *Haven in a Heartless World: The Family Beseiged*. New York: Basic Books.

Laslett, P. (ed.). 1972. *Household and Family in Past Time*. Cambridge: Cambridge University Press.

Lehning, J. R. 1982. "Family Life and Wetnursing in a French Village." *Journal of Interdisciplinary History.* 12: 645–656.

Locke, J. 1964. *Some Thoughts Concerning Education*. Abridged and edited by F. W. Garforth. Woodbury, New York: Barron.

May, D. and M. A. Vinovskis. 1976. "A Ray of Millenial Light: Early Education and Social Reform in the Infant School Movement in Massachusetts, 1826–1840." Pp. 62–99 in *Family and Kin in American Urban Communities, 1800–1940,* edited by T. K. Hareve, New York: Watts.

Mitterauer, M. and M. Sieder. 1982. *The European Family: From Patriarchy to Partnership*. Translated by K. Oosterveen and M. Horzinger. Chicago: University of Chicago Press.

Modell, J. and T. K. Hareven. 1973. "Urbanization and the Malleable Household: An Examination of Boarding and Lodging in American Families." *Journal of Marriage and the Family* 35: 467–479.

Moran, G. F. 1980. "Sisters in Christ: Women and the Church in Seventeenth-Century New England." Pp. 47–64 in *Women in American Religion,* edited by J. W. James, Philadelphia: University of Pennsylvania Press.

Moran, G. F. 1979. "Religious Renewal, Puritan Tribalism, and the Family in Seventeenth-Century Milford, Connecticut." *William and Mary Quarterly* 3rd Series, 36: 236–254.

Moran, G. F. and M. A. Vinovskis. 1982. "The Puritan Family and Religion: A critical Reappraisal." *William and Mary Quarterly,* 3rd Series 39: 29–63.

Moran, G. F. and M. A. Vinovskis. April 1983. "The Great Care of Godly Parents: Early Childhood in Puritan New England." Paper presented at Biennial Meeting of the Society for Research in Child Development. Detroit.

Moran, E. S. [1944] 1966. *The Puritan Family: Religion and Domestic Relations in Seventeenth-Century New England.* New York: Harper and Row.

Parsons, T. 1943. "The Kinship System of the Contemporary United States." *American Anthropologist* 45: 22–38.

Plakens, A. 1975. "Seigneurial Authority and Peasant Family Life: The Baltic Area in the Eighteenth Century." *Journal of Interdisciplinary History*, 4: 629–654.

Pollock, L. 1983. *Forgotten Children: Parent-Child Relations from 1500 to 1900.* Cambridge: Cambridge University Press.

Rosenkrantz, B. G. and M. A. Vinovskis, 1977. "Caring for the Insane in Ante-Bellum Massachusetts: Family, Community, and State Participation." Pp. 187–218 in *Kin and Communities: Families in America,* edited by A. J. Lichtman and J. R. Challinor. Washington, DC: Smithsonian Institution Press.

Shorter, E. 1975. *The Making of the Modern Family.* New York: Basic Books.

Slater, P. G. 1977. *Children in the New England Mind: In Death and in Life.* Hamden, CT: Archon Books.

Smith, D. S. 1973. "Parental Power and Marriage Patterns: An Analysis of Historical Trends in Hingham, Massachusetts." *Journal of Marriage and the Family* 35: 406–418.

Stannard, D. E. 1975. "Death and the Puritan Child." Pp. 9–29 in *Death in America,* edited by D. E. Stannard. Philadelphia: University of Pennsylvania Press.

Stannard, D. E. 1977. *The Puritan Way of Death: A Study in Religion, Culture, and Social Change* New Haven, CT: Yale University Press.

Stone, L. 1977. *The Family, Sex and Marriage in England, 1500–1800.* New York: Oxford University Press.

Sussman, G. D. 1977. "Parisian Infants and Norman Wet Nurses in the Early Nineteenth Century: A Statistical Study. *Journal of Interdisciplinary History,* 7: 637–654.

Thernstrom, S. 1964. *Poverty and Progress: Social Mobility in a Nineteenth-Century City.* Cambridge, MA: Harvard University Press.

Trumbach, R. 1978. *The Rise of the Egalitarian Family: Aristocratic Kinship and Domestic Relations in Eighteenth-Century England.* New York: Academic Press.

Turner, J. 1980. *Reckoning with the Beast: Animals, Pain, and Humanity in the Victorian Mind.* Baltimore, MD: Johns Hopkins Press.

Vinovskis, M. A. 1971. "American Historical Demography: A Review Essay." *Historical Methods Newsletter* 4: 141–148.

Vinovskis, M. A. 1972. "Mortality Rates and Trends in Massachusetts Before 1860." *Journal of Economic History* 32: 184–213.

Vinovskis, M. A. 1976. "Angels, Beads and Weeping Willows: Death in Early America." *Proceedings of the American Antiquarian Society* 86: 273–302.

Vinovskis, M. A. 1977. "From Household Size to the Life Course: Some Observations on Recent Trends in Family History." *American Behavioral Scientist* 21: 263–287.

Vinovskis, M. A. 1981a. "An Epidemic of Adolescent Pregnancy: Some Historical Considerations." *Journal of Family History* 6: 205–230.

Vinovskis, M. A. 1981b. *Fertility in Massachusetts from the Revolution to the Civil War.* New York: Academic Press.

Vinovskis, M. A. May 1982. "Adolescent Sexuality, Pregnancy, and Childbearing in Early America: Some Preliminary Speculations." Paper presented at the SSRC Conference on School-Age Pregnancies and Parenthood, Belmont Conference Center, Maryland.

Vinovskis, M. A. 1983a. "American Families in the Past." Pp. 115–137 in *Ordinary People and Everyday Life: Perspectives on the New Social History,* edited by J. B. Gardner and G. R. Adams. Nashville, TN: American Association for State and Local History.

Vinovskis, M. A. 1983b. "Quantification and the Analysis of Antebellum Education" *Journal of Interdisciplinary History* 13: 761–786.

Wirth, L. 1938. "Urbanism as a Way of Life." *American Journal of Sociology* 44: 1–24.

Wishy, B. 1968. *The Child and the Republic.* Philadelphia: University of Pennsylvania Press.

Zuckerman, M. 1970. *Peaceable Kingdoms: New England Towns in the Eighteenth Century.* New York: Alfred A. Knopf.

29

From Baby Farms to Baby M*

Viviana A. Zelizer

The Baby M deal would astonish any nineteenth-century baby trader. Not because of inflation in baby prices and not even because of Baby M's unusual mode of conception. The amazing fact, from a nineteenth-century perspective, is that Baby M has such eager and paying customers. For in the 1870s, there was no such market for babies. The only profitable undertaking was, as the *New York Times* described it in 1873, the "business of getting rid of other people's [unwelcome] babies." For about ten dollars, baby farmers took in these generally illegitimate children. With babies' high rates of mortality, the turnover was quick, and business brisk. Indeed, one report estimated that a "tradeswoman in tiny lives" could make as much as $10,000 a year.

Selling babies, on the other hand, was a rare and largely unprofitable transaction: often no more than a twenty-five-cents deal. In an 1890 case, an agent of the New York Society for the Prevention of Cruelty to Children pretended interest

*Zelizer, Viviana. 1985. "From Baby Farms to Baby M." *Society* 25(3): 23–28. Published by permission of Transaction Publishers. Copyright © 1988 by Transaction Publishers.

in obtaining a two-week-old baby. The baby farmer demanded two dollars but quickly settled for half. "She ... urged [the agent] to take the infant at once and at his own price." It was, unquestionably, a buyer's market.

Yet, by the 1920s and 1930s, "baby-hungry" couples were eagerly paying $1,000 or more to purchase an infant. As a 1939 article in *Collier's* put it: "It's [a] bonanza ... there's gold in selling babies." The trade slogan of one baby seller in Chicago was "It's cheaper and easier to buy a baby ... than to have one of your own." Today, the going rate for a healthy white infant in the black market is up to $50,000. "Special-order" Baby M cost the Sterns $25,000 plus the now surely steep legal fees. And this is just a down payment. It will take at least an additional $150,000 to provide Baby M with the first eighteen years of a proper upper-middle-class upbringing.

Lost in the emotional immediacy of the Baby M dispute are two more general and fundamental issues that underlie the surrogacy controversy. First, what explains our bullish baby market? Why were late-nineteenth-century mothers forced to pay baby farmers to get rid of a baby they did not want or could not afford, while today a Mrs. Whitehead is paid to produce a baby for others? Is it just a matter of the scarcity of babies? Second, what, precisely, defines the legitimacy or illegitimacy of baby markets? Are surrogacy fees necessarily a degrading payment or "dirty money"? Then, are adoption fees, foster care payments, and "gray" baby markets, also "dirty money"?

I argue that the socially and morally problematic nature of the surrogacy baby market is not primarily, as Neuhaus suggests, that sacred items are "placed in a contract and sealed by money," nor even that surrogacy is rigged against poor women. More significantly, surrogacy unequivocally reveals our discriminatory valuation of children. Babies are made on "special-order" because children already available on the adoption market are not "good" enough—too old, too sick, or of the wrong skin color. In this respect, surrogacy is only a technical innovation. In fact, it is just the latest stage of a very special adoption market which began in the 1920s.

CREATION OF A BABY MARKET

The creation of a market for babies in the 1920s was not the result of clever promotion and only partly a consequence of an increasing shortage of infants. The startling appreciation in babies' monetary worth was intimately tied to the profound cultural transformation in children's economic and sentimental value between the 1870s and 1930s; specifically, the emergence of the economically worthless but emotionally priceless child.

In eighteenth-century rural America the birth of a child was welcomed as the arrival of a future laborer and as security for parents later in life. By the mid-nineteenth century, the construction of the economically worthless child was completed among the urban middle class. It took longer among working-class families which, even in the late nineteenth century, depended on the wages of older children and the household assistance of younger ones. Child labor laws and compulsory education gradually destroyed the class lag. By the 1930s, lower-class children joined their middle-class counterparts in a new nonproductive world of childhood, a world in which the sanctity and emotional value of a child made child labor taboo.

The "exchange" value of children changed accordingly. Nineteenth-century foster families took in useful children expecting them to help out with farm chores and household tasks. It was considered a fair bargain. After all, if children worked for their own parents, why not work for surrogate caretakers? Not surprisingly, the premium was for children older than ten, old enough to be useful. In this context, babies were "unmarketable," and hard to place except in foundling asylums or on commercial baby farms.

The redefinition of children's value at the turn of the century challenged established instrumental assumptions. If child labor was no longer legitimate, a working home was an anachronism. If children were priceless, it was obnoxious to profit from their misfortune. Thus, baby farming was singled out as a uniquely mercenary "traffic in children." Child-welfare workers actively sought to replace instrumental parenting of any kind with a new approach to adoption more suitable for the economically "useless' sacred child. Parents were urged by *Children's Home Finder* in 1897 not to take a child "for what you can get out of him, but, rather, for what you can put into him." By the 1920s and 1930s, a new consensus was reached. The only legitimate rewards of adoption were emotional, as the *New York Times* put it in 1926: "an enlargement of happiness to be got in no other way." As one grateful adoptive father told a *Good Housekeeping* reporter in 1927, "Talk about children owing their parents anything! We'll never be able to pay what we owe that baby."

Sentimental adoption created an unprecedented demand for children under three, especially for infants. In 1910, the press already discussed the new appeal of babies, with *Cosmopolitan* warning, "there are not enough babies to go around." The Home-Finding Committee of the Spence Nursery, an agency organized for the placement of infants, was surprised to discover that, "instead of our having to seek these homes, they have sought us, and so great is the demand for babies that we cannot begin to meet it." By 1937, infant adoption was being touted as the latest American fad. *Pictorial Review* noted: "The baby market is booming. . . . The clamor is for babies, more babies. . . . We behold an amazing phenomenon: a country-wide scramble on the part of childless couples to adopt a child." Ironically, while the economically useless nineteenth-century baby had to be protected because it was unwanted, the priceless twentieth-century baby, "needs protection as ever before . . . [because] too many hands are snatching it."

The priceless child was judged by new criteria; its physical appeal and personality charms replaced earlier economic yardsticks. After talking to several directors of orphan asylums, the *New York Times* concluded in 1909 that "every baby who expects to be adopted . . . ought to make it a point to be born with blue eyes. . . . The brown-eyed, black-eyed, or grey-eyed girl or boy may be just as pretty . . . but it is hard to make benevolent auxiliaries of the stork believe so." The greatest demand was for little girls. Soon after launching its popular Child-Rescue Campaign in 1907, promoting foster home care, the *Delineator* commented that requests for boys were half that for girls: "a two-year old, blue-eyed, golden haired little girl with curls, that is the order that everybody leaves. It cannot be filled fast enough."

The gender and age preferences of twentieth-century adoptive parents were clearly linked to the cultural revolution in fostering. While the earlier need for a useful child put a premium on strong, older children, preferably male; the later search for a child to love led to babies and, particularly, pretty little girls. It was not the innate smiling expertise of females, but established cultural assumptions of women's superior emotional talents which made girls so uniquely attractive for sentimental adoption.

PRICING THE PRICELESS CHILD

The sentimentalization of adoption had an unanticipated and paradoxical effect. By creating a demand for babies, it also stimulated a new kind of baby market. While nineteenth-century mothers had paid baby farmers to accept their unwanted baby, twentieth-century adoptive parents were willing to pay to obtain an infant. "Baby traffickers" thus found an additional line of business; making money not only from the surrender of babies, but doubling their profits by then selling them to their new customers. As a result, the value of a priceless child became increasingly monetized and commercialized. Ironically, the new market price for babies was set exclusively by their noneconomic, sentimental appeal.

By 1922, the dramatic findings of "A Baby a Day Given Away," a study conducted by the New York State Charities Aid Association, put commercialized adoption directly in the national public spotlight. The six-months investigation of newspaper advertisements offering and requesting children for adoption, revealed an "indiscriminate exchange of children." An average of a baby a day was being disposed of in New York, "as casually as one would give away a kitten"; many sold at "bargain-counter" prices. It was not a peculiar New York arrangement. In the classified advertisement column of almost any Boston newspaper, noted Ida Parker in *Fit and Proper?* in 1927, "together with items relating to automobiles, animals, amusements . . . may often be found the child offered for adoption."

Three years later, the notorious prosecution of a New York baby farmer shocked the nation, further raising the visibility of commercial child placement. Helen Augusta Geisen-Volk was charged and indicted for child substitution and for starving infants to death. The young wife of a well-to-do manufacturer added fuel to the scandal by publicly confessing that, unknown to her husband, Mrs. Geisen-Volk had sold her an infant for seventy-five dollars. None of the crimes committed by Geisen-Volk were new to the baby-farming business; similar accusations were made as early as the 1870s. More unusual were the severity of the reaction and the degree of public interest in the case.

Commercial child placement emerged as a significant social problem in the 1920s in large part because it violated new professional standards in adoption. Without proper supervision by a licensed child-placing agency, adoption could be dangerous both for children and their adoptive parents. Selling children undermined not only professional adoption; it also betrayed the new standards of sentimental adoption. It was a sacrilege to price a priceless child. Worse than a criminal, Mrs. Geisen-Volk was indicted by the judge as a "fiend incarnate." As a probation officer told *New York Times* reporters, "the woman . . . has no maternal affections . . . [babies] to her . . . are articles of merchandise to be bartered or exchanged. The defendant represents a revolting anomaly in humankind."

Harshly denounced as an "iniquitous traffic in human life," and a "countrywide shame," the black market in babies flourished in the 1930s and 1940s. As demand for adoptable children grew, the booming traffic in infants reached a new stage. It was now a seller's market. Therefore, the mother of an unwanted child no longer needed to pay to dispose of her baby. Instead, entrepreneurial brokers approached her, offering to pay medical and hospital expenses and often a bonus in exchange for her baby. Even in independent placements arranged without profit, it became common practice to pay the hospital and medical expenses of the natural mother.

In 1955 a congressional investigation conducted by Senator Estes Kefauver officially pronounced baby-selling a national social problem. The price tag of a black-market baby climbed, from an estimated $1,000 in the 1930s to $5,000 in the late 1940s. By 1951 some babies sold for as much as $10,000. The rising money value of infants was partly determined by a reduced supply. As the dramatic decline in the national birthrate, which began early in the nineteenth century, continued into the 1930s, fewer babies were available for adoption. Contemporary observers also suggested that the increased demand for babies was partly the result of higher rates of infertility among American couples. Growing concern with the preservation of the family unit further contributed to the baby shortage. After 1911, the mothers' pension movement allowed widows, and in some cases deserted wives or mothers, or keep their children. Reformers also encouraged unmarried mothers to keep their babies. As a result, the supply of adoptable infants shrunk, and the waiting lists of adoption agencies grew longer. Unwilling to wait two or more years for a child, parents turned to the black market.

Scarcity alone does not determine value. A reduced supply raised the price of babies only because there was a growing number of enthusiastic buyers for white, healthy babies. The market capitalized on, but did not create, the infatuation with priceless babies. In sharp contrast, older children found few customers. Deprived of their former labor value, they were excluded from the new emotional market. Therefore, while the agencies' waiting list for babies had the names of hundreds of impatient parents, it was virtually impossible to find homes for children older than six, who had become both economically and sentimentally useless. Handicapped and minority children were also excluded from the adoption market.

PAYING FOR BABIES: A SPECIAL CURRENCY

The sentimentalization of adoption in the twentieth century, thus, led paradoxically to a greater commercialization and monetization of child life. As the market for child labor disappeared, a market price developed for children's new sentimental value. Childless couples were now willing to pay thousands of dollars to obtain a child's love, smiles, and emotional satisfactions. In 1975, a second congressional hearing on black-market practices estimated that more than 5,000 babies were sold each year in the United States, some for as much as $25,000. Sellers retained bargaining leverage. As one black-market lawyer told a prospective customer, "Take it or leave it. I have five other couples." The capitalization of children's value extended into legitimate child placement. Reversing a long-standing policy, many agencies in the 1940s introduced adoption fees.

Today, surrogacy arrangements introduce a new "custom-made" market for children. Fees are paid not just to obtain someone else's baby but to produce a brand new one. For some economists, this further monetization of child life makes sense. Indeed, Landes and Posner advocate the outright legalization of baby-selling as the best solution to the baby shortage. An undiluted price system, they argue, would match adoptive parents with adoptable children more efficiently than agencies. Landes and Posner, in the 1978 *Journal of Legal Studies*, dismiss "moral outrage" or "symbolic" objections against baby sales, as antiquated and impractical.

Yet moral objections to baby payments cannot be easily appeased. For many, the exchange of children should be regulated only by altruism, never for profit. Indeed, money is what makes surrogacy particularly unsavory. Without payment, surrogacy can be an innovative act of altruism; making babies as a gift for child-less couples. But $10,000 turns the giver into a salaried agent, and the baby into commercial chattel. From this perspective, surrogate parenthood can be legitimized simply by making it unprofitable. For instance, last May in Michigan, a sixteen-member national panel of doctors, lawyers, and clergymen, convened by State Senator Connie Binsfield to discuss legislation covering reproductive technologies, recommended that surrogate parenthood not be outlawed, but that the "production of babies for money, or a fee beyond reasonable expenses" be banned. Similarly, in Nebraska, a bill proposed by State Senator Ernest Chambers of Omaha, would accept the legality of surrogate relationships, but would declare that any commercial surrogate contract could not be enforced through the state's judicial system. Surrogate babies, declared Chambers in the *New York Times*, "become commodities like corn or wheat, things which can be purchased in the futures market."

Are surrogacy fees necessarily degrading? Does it only take a payment to transform a baby into a commodity? Ironically, both supporters and opponents of baby-selling answer affirmatively; thus equally accepting the inevitable power of money. They only differ in their evaluation of the process: economists welcome the rationalization of baby exchanges while antimarket ideologists bemoan the monetization of child life. All agree that once money is exchanged, the sale of children is qualitatively indistinct from the sale of cars. After all, in both cases, the payoff is identical: cold cash.

This is a narrow view of money. Money does serve as the key instrument of the modern market, transforming objects or even emotions and the value of life into quantifiable, objective sums. But money also exists outside of the sphere of the market, profoundly shaped by culture and social structure. Despite the physical anonymity of dollar bills, not all dollars are equal. We routinely assign different meanings and uses to particular monies. A paycheck, for instance, is "marked" as a different kind of money than a lottery winning. The money we obtain as compensation for an accident is not quite the same as the royalties from a book. A gift of money from a friend is distinct from our employer's Christmas bonus or a grandparents' Christmas check. Different monies are used differently: for instance, a wife's pin money was traditionally reserved for special purchases such as clothing or vacations and kept apart form the "real" money earned by her husband. Different uses can transform the meaning of money. What if Mrs. Whitehead, for instance, had intended to use her $10,000 as a donation to an infertility clinic? That would certainly mark the money differently than if she planned to use it for a Florida weekend, or simply for groceries. Such distinctions are not imposed by rational economic guidelines, but emerge from our cultural and social context.

Baby payments are a special category of money, shaped by the cultural definition of children as priceless. We also distinguish between legitimate and illegitimate baby purchases. Black-market sales, for example, are unacceptable because they treat children in the same impersonal, economizing manner used for less sacred commercial products. Yet a different kind of market exists which is, in most cases, legal and compatible with sentimental adoption. In this gray market, placements are arranged without profit by parents, friends, relatives, doctors, and lawyers. Within this context, professional fees for legal or medical services are acceptable. Justifying such payments during the 1975 congressional hearings on black-market practices, the executive director of the Child Welfare League of America explained, "Money exchanges hands, but it is only to pay for actual costs. There is no thought of profit." Thus, while the black market is defined as a degrading economic arrangement; a modified, legitimate market exists for the exchange of children.

Adoption fees are another category of "special money." Until the 1940s, agencies only accepted "gratitude donations" from adoptive parents. The Children's Home Society of Virginia, for instance, according to the 1941 *Child Welfare League of America Bulletin*, told parents, "that a gift from them in such an amount as they choose will be gratefully received, but that it must be made as a gift and not as payment for services." The society's directors refused to even discuss any definite sum with foster families. The boundary between adoption and purchase was preserved by defining the money as an elective gift and a symbol of gratitude, not a price.

The shift from donations to fees was, therefore, a sensitive matter. Yet the system was accepted. How was the adoption fee distinguished from a purchase price? In large measure, the differentiation hinged on defining the payment as compensation for professional services, not in exchange for a child. A fee was also legitimized as a symbolic payment, a material expression of gratitude. Adoption fees were usually portrayed as a psychological crutch for parents, rather than a commercial device for agencies; for example, from the *Child Welfare League of America Bulletin*: "For any human being to be in the position of asking another . . . for a child . . . is to admit inadequacy. . . . Payment of the fee may ease some of the discomfort arising from this deeply humiliating experience." Parents' voluntary contributions of additional monies to the agency, beyond the stipulated fee, further reinforced the boundary between the adoption fees and a purchasing price. Their elective gift of money served as a symbolic reminder that adopting a child is not an ordinary business deal.

The uniqueness of payments involving children is also apparent in their "rental." For example, at the beginning of the century, wet nurses employed by the foundling asylums were often accused of regarding their infant boarders simply as a source of income. Yet, while these "pay babies" were indeed a source of much needed income, it was defined as a very special payment. A Russell Sage report in 1914 remarked that "renting" out a baby to these poor New York women was often more a sentimental event than a business deal.

Similarly, when boarding homes for older children were first introduced at the turn of the century, boarding fees were defined as "dirty money," tempting foster parents into taking children for profit. This ambivalence over paid parenting was persistent. For instance, periodic efforts to raise board payments by defining the foster mother as an employee of the agency met with resistance and ultimately failure. In the 1940s, a special committee from the Washington Council of Social Agencies, urged payment of a service fee to foster parents in return for their contributions over and above the physical care and maintenance of the child. But the service fee was opposed because it transformed mothering into a marketable job.

"SPECIAL-ORDER" BABIES

Adequate monetary incentive seems to have an effect on the number of foster homes available and even on the success of fostering. Yet foster parents—most of whom are recruited from lower-middle-class or working-class families—remain uneasy about asking for payment. They often find ways to transcend the instrumental parenting contract. In many cases, for instance, foster parents use their own funds for a foster child's incidental expenses; extra clothing, transportation, allowance, toys, or parties.

The gray market, adoption fees, and board payments illustrate some of the cultural contours of baby payments. Pricing the priceless child is a unique commercial venture; child "rental" and child sales are profoundly constrained by twentieth-century conceptions of children. The money involved is partly payment, but it can also also be a symbolic expression of sentimental concern.

Surrogacy fees are the latest addition to this inventory of special monies. They remain in a definitional limbo. For opponents of surrogacy, surrogacy fees are no different than black-market price tags, unsuitable to measure the value of a child's life. Some see it as a perverse form of pin money for housewives, paying extra expenses by making a baby. But there is a moral arrogance as well as sociological blindness in the absolutist indictment of surrogacy payments. This money can indeed be "dirty" cash, used to entice poor women into renting their wombs for the rich. It can even be used by the surrogate to blackmail childless couples.

Is that how surrogate mothers define their payment? Most do acknowledge that they would not have entered the arrangement without compensation. Some seem to perceive it as an ordinary wage: "We wanted money to pay some bills and take a vacation," explained one housewife. But surrogates clearly mark the special quality of this money, sometimes refusing even to define it as a payment in exchange for a baby. A mother who was paid $10,000 and delivered twins was quoted by the *New York Times* as saying, "Believe me, . . . there are easier ways to make ten thousand dollars that involve a lot less time and a lot less pain."

The fee is defined by many surrogates as the childless couple's expression of gratitude for their special gift of a baby. Indeed, a study of 125 surrogate mothers found that while 89 percent of the women said they would require a fee for their service, in no case was money the only reason for "baby-making." One woman who had had an abortion now wanted, according to *Psychology Today*, "to give the gift of a live baby to a loving couple." Others simply liked being pregnant. Surrogates are well aware of the vulnerable boundary between a noble payment and a mercenary fee. Some mark the special quality of the surrogacy fee by allocating the money to particularly unselfish expenses. Mrs. Whitehead, for instance, intended to use the $10,000 toward a college education for her two other children. As another surrogate mother explained in the *New York Times*: "If the money was just for me I'd feel as if I'd sold her [the baby], and it would be dirty money."

Distinguishing between monies by differential uses occurs with other kinds of special payments. For instance, in cases of compensation for the accidental death of a young child, plaintiffs often ritualize the monetary award by donating it to charity, safety organizations, or scholarships for needy children. Baby payments, much as "death" money, are different than ordinary cash. We need to understand better the meaning of surrogacy fees. How does the father define this money? What about the baby brokers? How do their fees differ from the payment to the mother? How is a "just" surrogacy fee determined? Dr. Richard Levin, the head of Kentucky's Surrogate Parenting Associates (quoted in *The Surrogate Mother* by Noel P. Keane with Dennis L. Breo), explains that he has a "moral problem with paying a surrogate mother too much—as with one woman who . . . wanted $100,000—or not enough." But what makes $10,000 acceptable? Would a small token fee be defined as more appropriate? Or would an extraordinarily large sum—comparable to some wrongful-death settlements in child death cases—be a more dignified quantity?

The moralistic indictment of surrogacy fees obscures the complex reality of such payments. The involvement of money does not necessarily convert all exchanges into ordinary sales. The surrogate payment may be a venal and dehumanizing payoff but it can also symbolize an acceptable retribution. Thus, with proper regulation, money does not necessarily pollute the surrogacy baby market. The class bias in surrogacy arrangements, which is the focus of Neuhaus's argument, is a potentially more damaging feature of the surrogacy market. Poor women, traditionally the wet nurses and baby minders of the rich, would now also become their baby makers. Subsidized surrogacies, much like subsidized adoptions, however, could make the benefits of surrogacy available to poor infertile women. That would only equalize the buyers. It is improbable, although not impossible, that affluent women would serve as surrogates.

In the cases of surrogacy, the inequities between parents are less fundamental than the explicit discrimination between children. Surrogacy is not just a sentimental search for any child to love, but the deliberate manufacture of a particular, suitable child. As one observer has pointed out, the advertisements to hire a surrogate do not follow any affirmative action plan. This "help-wanted" ad specifies: "English background," "Northern European," "white," "Caucasian." The desired product is a white infant, with no physical or mental handicaps. In the 1920s rush to adopt babies, some wealthy Americans had their English-rose, golden-haired baby girls imported from London. Today, they can be made in America. They even carry the genetic insurance provided by the adoptive father's sperm.

Surrogacy further marks the distinction between priceless, desirable children and "unsuitable" children that was established earlier in the century. While babies are made to order, the National Committee for Adoption estimates that a minimum of 36,000 hard-to-place children, some because they are sick, some disturbed, others because they are black, and still others because they are too old, cannot find an adoptive home. Surrogacy contracts often make the concern with quality-control quite explicit. Some contracts include provisions for amniocentesis and obligatory abortion if the results are not agreeable to the genetic father. But what if, despite all precautions, a child is born defective? Would Baby M be disputed with equal passion if she were not a cute, healthy baby—the ultimate priceless child?

Private adoption of unwanted children cannot be mandated by the state. Neither should the search for a child—even through surrogate arrangements—be outlawed by the state, although it must be closely regulated and officially supervised. But we need to collectively recognize the curious and even cruel limits to our sentimentalization of childhood. We must invest emotionally and financially in finding ways to nurture—either in family groups or collective arrangements—those children who need care but are not infants, not white, or not healthy enough. The shortage of such care is as severe as the shortage of cute and healthy white babies.

30
Motherhood and Morality in America*

Kristin Luker

According to interested observers at the time, abortion in American was as frequent in the last century as it is in our own. And the last century, as we have seen, had its own "right-to-life" movement, composed primarily of physicians who pursued the issue in the service of their own professional goals. When abortion reemerged as an issue in the late 1950s, it still remained in large part a restricted debate among interested professionals. But abortion as we now know it has little in common with these earlier rounds of the debate. Instead of the civility and colleagueship that characterized the earlier phases of the debate, the present round of the abortion debate is marked by rancor and intransigence. Instead of the elite

*Luker, Kristin. 1985. "Motherhood and Morality in America." Pp. 192–215 in *Abortion and the Politics of Motherhood*. Berkeley: University of California Press. © 1984 The Regents of the University of California.

male professionals who commanded the issue until recently, ordinary people—and more to the point, ordinary women—have come to predominate in the ranks of those concerned. From a quiet, restricted technical debate among concerned professionals, abortion has become a debate that seems at times capable of tearing the fabric of American life apart. How did this happen? What accounts for the remarkable transformation of the abortion debate?

The history of the debate . . . provides some preliminary answers. Technological advances in obstetrics led to a decline in those abortions undertaken strictly to preserve the life of the woman, using the narrowly biological sense of the word *life*. These technological advances, in turn, permitted (and indeed forced) physicians over time to make more and more nuanced decisions about abortion and eventually brought to the fore the underlying philosophical issue that had been obscured by a century of medical control over abortion: is the embryo a person or only a potential person? [O]nce this question is confronted directly, a unifed world view—a set of assumptions about how the world is and ought to be organized—is called into play. [Clearly] world views are usually the product of values so deeply held and dearly cherished that an assault upon them is a deeply disturbing assault indeed. Thus . . . the abortion debate has been transformed because it has "gone public" and in so doing has called into question individuals' most sacrosanct beliefs.

But this is only part of the story. This [essay] will argue that all the previous rounds of the abortion debate in America were merely echoes of the issue as the nineteenth century defined it: a debate about the medical profession's right to make life-and-death decisions. In contrast, the most recent round of the debate is about something new. By bringing the issue of the moral status of the embryo to the fore, the new round focuses on the relative rights of women and embryos. Consequently, the abortion debate has become a debate about women's contrasting obligations to themselves and others. New technologies and the changing nature of work have opened up possibilities for women outside of the home undreamed of in the nineteenth century; together, these changes give women—for the first time in history—the option of deciding exactly how and when their family roles will fit into the larger context of their lives. In essence, therefore, this round of the abortion debate is so passionate and hard-fought *because it is a referendum on the place and meaning of motherhood.*

Motherhood is at issue because two opposing visions of motherhood are at war. Championed by "feminists' and "housewives," these two different views of motherhood represent in turn two very different kinds of social worlds. The abortion debate has become a debate among women, women with different values in the social world, different experiences of it, and different resources with which to cope with it. How the issue is framed, how people think about it, and, most importantly, where the passions come from are all related to the fact that the battlelines are increasingly drawn (and defended) by women. While on the surface it is the embryo's fate that seems to be at stake, the abortion debate is actually about the meanings of *women's lives.*

To be sure, both the pro-life and the pro-choice movements had earlier phases in which they were dominated by male professionals. Some of these men are still active in the debate, and it is certainly the case that some men continue to join the debate on both sides of the issue. But the data in this study suggest that by 1974 over 80 percent of the activists in both the pro-choice and the pro-life movements in California were women, and a national survey of abortion activists found similar results.[1]

Moreover, in our interviews we routinely asked both male and female activists on both sides of the issue to supply information on several "social background variables," such as where they were born, the extent of their education, their income level, the number of children they had, and their occupations. When male activists on the two sides are compared on these variables, they are virtually indistinguishable from one another. But when female activists are compared, it is dramatically clear that for the women who have come to dominate the ranks of the movement, the abortion debate is a conflict between two different social worlds and the hopes and beliefs those worlds support.

WHO ARE THE ACTIVISTS?

On almost every social background variable we examined, pro-life and pro-choice women differed dramatically. For example, in terms of income, almost half of all pro-life women (44 percent) in this study reported an income of less than $20,000 a year, but only one-fourth of the pro-choice women reported an income that low, and a considerable portion of those were young women just starting their careers. On the upper end of the income scale, one-third of the pro-choice women reported an income of $50,000 a year or more compared with only one pro-life woman in every seven.

These simple figures on income, however, conceal a very complex social reality, and that social reality is in turn tied to feelings about abortion. The higher incomes of pro-choice women, for example, result from a number of intersecting factors. Almost without exception pro-choice women work in the paid labor force, they earn good salaries when they work, and if they are married, they are likely to be married to men who also have good incomes. An astounding 94 percent of all pro-choice women work, and over half of them have incomes in the top 10 percent of all working women in this country. Moreover, one pro-choice woman in ten has an annual *personal* income (as opposed to a family income) of $30,000 or more, thus putting her in the rarified ranks of the top 2 percent of all employed women in America. Pro-life women, by contrast, are far less likely to work: 63 percent of them do not work in the paid labor force, and almost all of those who do are unmarried. Among pro-life married women, for example, only 14 percent report any personal income at all, and for most of them, this is earned not in a formal job but through activities such as selling cosmetics to groups of friends. Not surprisingly, the personal income of pro-life women who work outside the home, whether in a formal job or in one of these less-structured activities, is low. Half of all pro-life women who do work earn less than $5,000 a year, and half earn between $5,000 and $10,000. Only two pro-life women we contacted reported a personal income of more than $20,000. Thus pro-life women are less likely to work in the first place, they earn less money when they do work, and they are more likely to be married to a skilled worker or small businessman who earns only a moderate income.

These differences in income are in turn related to the different educational and occupational choices these women have made along the way. Among pro-choice women, almost four out of ten (37 percent) had undertaken some graduate work beyond the B.A. degree and 18 percent had an M.D., a law degree, a Ph.D., or a similar postgraduate degree. Pro-life women, by comparison, had far less education: 10 percent of them had only a high school education or less; and another 30 percent never finished college (in contrast with only 8 percent of the pro-choice women). Only 6 percent of all pro-life women had a law degree, a Ph.D., or a medical degree.

These educational differences were in turn related to occupational differences among the women in this study. Because of their higher levels of education, pro-choice women tended to be employed in the major professions, as administrators, owners of small businesses, or executives in large businesses. The pro-life women tended to be housewives or, of the few who worked, to be in the traditional female jobs of teaching, social work, and nursing. (The choice of home life over public life held true for even the 6 percent of pro-life women with an advanced degree: of the married women who had such degrees, at the time of our interviews only one of them had not retired from her profession after marriage.)

These economic and social differences were also tied to choices that women on each side had made about marriage and family life. For example, 23 percent of pro-choice women had never married, compared with only 16 percent of pro-life women; 14 percent of pro-choice women had been divorced, compared with 5 percent of pro-life women. The size of the families these women had was also different. The average pro-choice family had between one and two children and was more likely to have one; pro-life families averaged between two and three children and were more likely to have three. (Among the pro-life women, 23 percent had five or more children; 16 percent had seven or more children.) Pro-life women also tended to marry at a slightly younger age and to have had their first child earlier.

Finally, the women on each side differed dramatically in their religious affiliation and in the role that religion played in their lives. Almost 80 percent of the women active in the pro-life movement at the present time are Catholics. The remainder are Protestants (9 percent), persons who claim no religion (5 percent), and Jews (1 percent). In sharp contrast, 63 percent of pro-choice women say that they have no religion, 22 percent think of themselves as vaguely Protestant, 3 percent are Jewish, and 9 percent have what they call a "personal" religion. We found no one in our sample of pro-choice activists who claimed to be a Catholic at the time of the interviews.

When we asked activists what religion they were raised in as a child, however, a different picture emerged. For example, 20 percent of the pro-choice activists were raised as Catholics, 42 percent were raised as Protestants, and 15 percent were raised in the Jewish faith. In this group that describes itself as predominantly without religious affiliation, therefore, only 14 percent say they were not brought up in any formal religious faith. By the same token, although almost 80 percent of present pro-life activists are Catholic, only 58 percent were raised in that religion (15 percent were raised as Protestants and 3 percent as Jews). Thus, almost 20 percent of the pro-life activists in this study are converts to Catholicism, people who have actively chosen to follow a given religious faith, in striking contrast to pro-choice people, who have actively chosen not to follow any.

Perhaps the single most dramatic difference between the two groups, however, is in the role that religion plays in their lives. Almost three-quarters of the pro-choice people interviewed said that formal religion was either unimportant or completely irrelevant to them, and their attitudes are correlated with behavior: only 25 percent of the pro-choice women said they *ever* attend church, and most of these said they do so only occasionally. Among pro-life people, by contrast, 69 percent said religion was important in their lives, and an additional 22 percent said that it was very important. For pro-life women, too, these attitudes are correlated with behavior: half of those pro-life women interviewed said they attend church regularly once a week, and another 13 percent said they do so even more often. Whereas 80 percent of pro-choice people never attend church, only 2 percent of pro-life advocates never do so.

Keeping in mind that the statistical use of averages has inherent difficulties, we ask, who are the "average" pro-choice and pro-life advocates? When the social background data are looked at carefully, two profiles emerge. The average pro-choice activist is a forty-four-year-old married woman who grew up in a large metropolitan area and whose father was a college graduate. She was married at age twenty-two, has one or two children, and has had some graduate or professional training beyond the B.A. degree. She is married to a professional man, is herself employed in a regular job, and her family income is more than $50,000 a year. She is not religiously active, feels that religion is not important to her, and attends church very rarely if at all.

The average pro-life woman is also a forty-four-year-old married woman who grew up in a large metropolitan area. She married at age seventeen and has three children or more. Her father was a high school graduate, and she has some college education or may have a B.A. degree. She is not employed in the paid labor force and is married to a small businessman or a lower-level white-collar worker; her family income is $30,000 a year. She is Catholic (and may have converted), and her religion is one of the most important aspects of her life: she attends church at least once a week and occasionally more often.

INTERESTS AND PASSIONS

To the social scientist (and perhaps to most of us) these social background characteristics connote lifestyles as well. We intuitively clothe these bare statistics with assumptions about beliefs and values. When we do so, the pro-choice women emerge as educated, affluent, liberal professionals, whose lack of religious affiliation suggests a secular, "modern," or (as pro-life people would have it) "utilitarian" outlook on life. Similarly, the income, education, marital patterns, and religious devotion of pro-life women suggest that they are traditional, hard-working people ("polyester types" to their opponents), who hold conservative views on life. We may be entitled to assume that individuals' social backgrounds act to shape and mold their social attitudes, but it is important to realize that the relationship between social worlds and social values is a very complex one.

Perhaps one example will serve to illustrate the point. A number of pro-life women in this study emphatically rejected an expression that pro-choice women tend to use almost unthinkingly—the expression *unwanted pregnancy*. Pro-life women argued forcefully that a better term would be a *surprise* pregnancy, asserting that although a pregnancy may be momentarily unwanted, the child that results from the pregnancy almost never is. Even such a simple thing—what to call an unanticipated pregnancy—calls into play an individual's values and resources. Keeping in mind our profile of the average pro-life person, it is obvious that a woman who does not work in the paid labor force, who does not have a college degree, whose religion is important to her, and who has already committed herself wholeheartedly to marriage and a large family is well equipped to believe that an unanticipated pregnancy usually becomes a beloved child. Her life is arranged so that for her, this belief is true. This view is consistent not only with her values, which she has held from earliest childhood, but with her social resources as well. It should not be surprising, therefore, that her world view leads her to believe that everyone else can "make room for one more" as easily a she can and that therefore it supports her in her conviction that abortion is cruel, wicked, and self-indulgent.*

It is almost certainly the case that an unplanned pregnancy is never an easy thing for anyone. Keeping in mind the profile of the average pro-choice woman, however, it is evident that a woman who is employed full time, who has an affluent lifestyle that depends in part on her contribution to the family income, and who expects to give a child as good a life as she herself has had with respect to educational, social, and economic advantages will draw on a different reality when she finds herself being skeptical about the ability of the average person to transform unwanted pregnancies into well-loved (and well-cared-for) children.

The relationship between passions and interests is thus more dynamic than it might appear at first. It is true that at one level, pro-choice and pro-life attitudes on abortion are self-serving: activists on each side have different views of the morality of abortion because their chosen lifestyles leave them with different needs for abortion; and both sides have values that provide a moral basis for their abortion needs in particular and their lifestyles in general. But this is only half the story. The values that lead pro-life and pro-choice women into different attitudes toward abortion are the same values that led them at an earlier time to adopt different lifestyles that supported a given view of abortion.

---

*As might be imagined, it is not an easy task to ask people who are anti-abortion activists about their own experiences with a certain kind of unanticipated pregnancy, namely, a premarital pregnancy. Most pro-choice people were quite open about having had such pregnancies; ... their pregnancies—and subsequent abortions—were central to their feelings about abortion. Pro-life women, by contrast, were deeply reluctant to discuss the topic. Several of them, after acknowledging premarital pregnancies, said that they did not want people to think that their attitudes on abortion were merely a product of their personal experiences. Thus we have no comparative figures about the extent to which the values represented here are the product of different experiences or just different opinions. We know only that unanticipated pregnancy was common among pro-choice women, and the interviews suggest that it was not uncommon among pro-life women. The difference in experience is, of course, that those in the first group sought abortions and those in the second group, with only a few exceptions, legitimized their pregnancies with a marriage.

For example, pro-life women have *always* valued family roles very highly and have arranged their lives accordingly. They did not acquire high-level educational and occupational skills, for example, because they married, and they married because their values suggested that this would be the most satisfying life open to them. Similarly, pro-choice women postponed (or avoided) marriage and family roles because they chose to acquire the skills they needed to be successful in the larger world, having concluded that the role of wife and mother was too limited for them. Thus, activists on both sides of the issue are women who have a given set of values about what are the most satisfying and appropriate roles for women, and they have made *life commitments that now limit their ability to change their minds*. Women who have many children and little education, for example, are seriously handicapped in attempting to become doctors or lawyers; women who have reached their late forties with few children or none are limited in their ability to build (or rebuild) a family. For most of these activists, therefore, their position on abortion is the "tip of the iceberg," a shorthand way of supporting and proclaiming not only a complex set of values but a given set of social resources as well.

To put the matter differently, we might say that for pro-life women the traditional division of life into separate male roles and female roles still works, but for pro-choice women it does not. Having made a commitment to the traditional female roles of wife, mother, and homemaker, pro-life women are limited in those kinds of resources—education, class status, recent occupational experiences—they would need to compete in what has traditionally been the male sphere, namely, the paid labor force. The average pro-choice woman, in contrast, is comparatively well endowed with exactly those resources: she is highly educated, she already has a job, and she has recent (and continuous) experience in the job market.

In consequence, anything that supports a traditional division of labor into male and female worlds is, broadly speaking, in the interests of pro-life women because that is where their resources lie. Conversely, such a traditional division of labor, when strictly enforced, is against the interests of pro-choice women because it limits their abilities to use the valuable "male" resources that they have in relative abundance. It is therefore apparent that attitudes toward abortion, even though rooted in childhood experiences, are also intimately related to present-day interests. Women who oppose abortion and seek to make it officially unavailable are declaring, both practically and symbolically, that women's reproductive roles should be given social primacy. Once an embryo is defined as a child and an abortion as the death of a person, almost everything else in a woman's life must "go on hold" during the course of her pregnancy: any attempt to gain "male" resources such as a job, an education, or other skills must be subordinated to her uniquely female responsibility of serving the needs of this newly conceived person. Thus, when personhood is bestowed on the embryo, women's nonreproductive roles are made secondary to their reproductive roles. The act of conception therefore creates a pregnant woman rather than a woman who is pregnant; it creates a woman whose life, in cases where roles or values clash, is defined by the fact that she is —or may become—pregnant.

It is obvious that this view is supportive of women who have already decided that their familial and reproductive roles are the major ones in their lives. By the same token, the costs of defining women's reproductive roles as primary do not seem high to them because they have already chosen to make those roles primary anyway. For example, employers might choose to discriminate against women because they might require maternity leave and thus be unavailable at critical times, but women who have chosen not to work in the paid labor force in the first place can see such discrimination as irrelevant to them.

It is equally obvious that supporting abortion (and believing that the embryo is not a person) is in the vested interested of pro-choice women. Being so well equipped to compete in the male sphere, they perceive any situation that both practically and symbolically affirms the primacy of women's reproductive roles as a real loss to them. Practically, it devalues their social resources. If women are only secondarily in the labor market and must subordinate working to pregnancy, should it occur, then their education, occupation, income, and work become potentially temporary and hence discounted. Working becomes, as it traditionally was perceived to be, a pastime or hobby pursued for "pin money" rather than a central part of their lives. Similarly, if the embryo is defined as a person and the ability to become pregnant is the central one for women, a woman must be prepared to sacrifice some of her own interests to the interests of this newly conceived person.

In short, in a world where men and women have traditionally had different roles to play and where male roles have traditionally been the more socially prestigious and financially rewarded, abortion has become a symbolic marker between those who wish to maintain this division of labor and those who wish to challenge it. Thus, on an intimate level, the pro-life movement is women's version of what was true of peasants in the Vendée, the part of France that remained Royalist during the French Revolution. Charles Tilly has argued that in the Vendée, traditional relationships between nobles and peasants were still mutually satisfying so that the "brave new world" of the French Revolution represented more loss than gain, and the peasants therefore resisted the changes the Revolution heralded. [2] By the same logic, traditional relationships between men and women are still satisfying, rewarding, and meaningful for pro-life women, and they therefore resist the lure of "liberation." For pro-choice women, however, with their access to male resources, a division of labor into the public world of work and the private world of home and hearth seems to promise only restriction to "second-class" citizenship.

Thus, the sides are fundamentally opposed to each other not only on the issue of abortion but also on what abortion *means*. Women who have many "human capital" resources of the traditionally male variety want to see motherhood recognized as a private, discretionary choice. Women who have few of these resources and limited opportunities in the job market want to see motherhood recognized as the most important thing a woman can do. In order for pro-choice women to achieve their goals, therefore, they *must* argue that motherhood is not a primary, inevitable, or "natural" role for all women; for pro-life women to achieve their goals, they *must* argue that it is. In short, the debate rests on the question of whether women's fertility is to be socially recognized as a resource or as a handicap.

To the extent that women who have chosen the larger public world of work have been successful, both legally and in terms of public opinion and, furthermore, are rapidly becoming the numerical majority, pro-life women are put on the defensive. Several pro-life women offered poignant examples of how the world deals with housewives who do not have an official payroll title. Here is what one of them said:

> I was at a party, about two years ago—it still sticks in my mind, you see, because I'm a housewife and I don't work—and I met this girl from England and we got involved in a deep discussion about the English and the Americans and their philosophies and how one has influenced the other, and at the end of the conversation—she was a working gal herself, I forget what she did—and she says, "Where do you work?" I said, "I don't." And she looked at me and said, "You don't work?" I said "No." She said, "You're just a housewife . . . and you can still think like that?" She couldn't believe it, and she sort of gave me a funny look and that was the end of the conversation for the evening. And I've met other people who've had similar experiences. [People seem to think that if] you're at home and you're involved with children all day, your intelligence quotient must be down with them on the floor someplace, and [that] you really don't do much thinking or get yourself involved.

Moreover, there are subtle indications that even the pro-life activists we interviewed had internalized their loss of status as housewives. Only a handful of married pro-life activists also worked at regular jobs outside the home; but fully half of those who were now full-time homemakers, some for as long as thirty years, referred to themselves in terms of the work they had given up when they married or had their first child: "I'm a political scientist," "I'm a social worker," "I'm an accountant." It is noteworthy that no one used the past tense as in "I used to be a social worker": every nonemployed married woman who used her former professional identification used it in the present tense. Since this pattern was not noticed during the interviewing, what the woman themselves had in mind must remain speculative. But it does not seem unreasonable to imagine that this identification is an unconscious bow to the fact that "just plain" individuals, and in particular "just plain housewives," lack the status and credibility of professionals. Ironically, by calling on earlier identifications these women may have been expressing a pervasive cultural value that they oppose as a matter of ideology. They seemed to believe that when it comes to making public statements—or at least public statements to an interviewer who has come to ask you about activities in the abortion debate—*what* you are counts more than *who* you are.

Because of their commitment to their own view of motherhood as a primary social role, pro-life women believe that other women are "casual" about abortions and have them "for convenience." There are no reliable data to confirm whether or not women are "casual" about abortions, but many pro-life people believe this to be the case and relate their activism to their perception of other people's casualness.[3] For example:

> Every time I saw some article [on abortion] I read about it, and I had another friend who had her second abortion in 1977 . . . and both of her abortions were a

matter of convenience, it was inconvenient for her to be pregnant at that time. When I talked to her I said, "O.K., you're married now, your husband has a good job, you want to have children eventually, but if you became pregnant now, you'd have an abortion. Why?" "Because it's inconvenient, this is not when I want to have my child." And that bothered me a lot because she is also very intelligent, graduated magna cum laude, and knew nothing about fetal development.

The assertion that women are "casual" about abortion, one could argue, expresses in a short-hand way a set of beliefs about women and their roles. First, the more people value the personhood of the embryo, the more important must be the reasons for taking its life. Some pro-life people, for example, would accept an abortion when continuation of the pregnancy would cause the death of the mother; they believe that when two lives are in direct conflict, the embryo's life can be considered the more expendable. But not all pro-life people agree, and many say they would not accept abortion even to save the mother's life. (Still others say they accept the idea in principle but would not make that choice in their own lives if faced with it.) For people who accept the personhood of the embryo, any reason besides trading a "life for a life" (and sometimes even that) seems trivial, merely a matter of "convenience."

Second, people who accept the personhood of the embryo see the reasons that pro-abortion people give for ending a pregnancy as simultaneously downgrading the value of the embryo and upgrading everything else but pregnancy. The argument that women need abortion to "control" their fertility means that they intend to subordinate pregnancy, with its inherent unpredictability, to something else. [P]ro-choice activists . . . have told us that something else is participation in the paid labor force. Abortion permits women to engage in paid work on an equal basis with men. With abortion, they may schedule pregnancy in order to take advantage of the kinds of benefits that come with a paid position in the labor force: a paycheck, a title, and a social identity. The pro-life women in this study were often careful to point out that they did not object to "career women." But what they meant by "career women" were women whose *only* responsibilities were in the labor force. Once a woman became a wife and a mother, in their view her primary responsibility was to her home and family.

Third, the pro-life activists we interviewed, the overwhelming majority of whom are full-time homemakers, also felt that women who worked *and* had families could often do so only because women like themselves picked up the slack. Given their place in the social structure, it is not surprising that many of the pro-life women thought that married women who worked outside the home were "selfish"—that they got all the benefits while the homemakers carried the load for them in Boy and Girl Scouts, PTA, and after school, for which their reward was to be treated by the workers as less competent and less interesting persons.*

---

*In fact, pro-life women, especially those recruited after 1972, were *less* likely to be engaged in formal activities such as Scouts, church activities, and PTA than their pro-choice peers. Quite possibly they have in mind more informal kinds of activities, premised on the fact that since they do not work, they are home most of the time.

Abortion therefore strips the veil of sanctity from motherhood. When pregnancy is discretionary—when people are allowed to put anything else they value in front of it—then motherhood has been demoted from a sacred calling to a job.* In effect, the legalization of abortion serves to make men and women more "unisex" by deemphasizing what makes them different—the ability of women to visibly and directly carry the next generation. Thus, pro-choice women are emphatic about their right to compete equally with men without the burden of an unplanned pregnancy, and pro-life women are equally emphatic about their belief that men and women have different roles in life and that pregnancy is a gift instead of a burden.

The pro-life activists we interviewed do not want equality with men in the sense of having exactly the same rights and responsibilities as men do, although they do want equality of status. In fact, to the extent that *all* women have been touched by the women's movement and have become aware of the fact that society often treats women as a class as less capable than men, quite a few said they appreciated the Equal Rights Amendment (ERA), except for its implied stand on abortion. The ERA, in their view, reminded them that women are as valuable *in their own sphere* as men are in theirs. However, to the extent that the ERA was seen as downplaying the differences between men and women, to devalue the female sphere of the home in the face of the male sphere of paid work, others saw it as both demeaning and oppressive to women like themselves. As one of the few married employed pro-life women argued:

> I oppose it [the ERA]. Because I've gotten where I am without it. I don't think I need it. I think a woman should be hired on her merits, not on her sex or race. I don't think we should be hiring on sex or on race. I think we should be taking the competent people that are capable of doing the job. . . . I don't think women should be taking jobs from the breadwinner, you know. I still think that our society should be male . . . the male should be the primary breadwinner. For example, my own husband cannot hope for promotion because he is white and Anglo, you know, I mean white male. He's not going to get a promotion. If he could get the promotion that others of different minorities have gotten over him, I probably wouldn't have to work at all. So from my own point of view, purely selfishly, I think we've got to consider it. On the other hand, if I'm doing the same job [as a man], I expect to get the same pay. But I've always gotten it. So I really don't think that's an issue. I see the ERA as causing us more problems than it's going to [solve]. . . . As I see it, we were on a pedestal, why should we go down to being equal? That's my feeling on the subject.

It is stating the obvious to point out that the more limited the educational credentials a woman has, the more limited the job opportunities are for her, and the more limited the job opportunities, the more attractive motherhood is as a full-time occupation. In motherhood, one can control the content and pace of one's own work, and the job is *intrinsically meaningful*. Compared with a job

---

*The same might be said of all sacred callings—stripped of its layer of the sacred, for example, the job of the clergy is demanding, low status, and underpaid.

clerking in a supermarket (a realistic alternative for women with limited educational credentials) where the work is poorly compensated and often demeaning, motherhood can have compensations that far transcend the monetary ones. As one woman described mothering: "You have this little, rough uncut diamond, and you're the artist shaping and cutting that diamond, and bringing out the lights . . . that's a great challenge."

All the circumstances of her existence will therefore encourage a pro-life woman to highlight the kinds of values and experiences that support childbearing and childrearing and to discount the attraction (such as it is) of paid employment. Her circumstances encourage her to resent the pro-choice view that women's most meaningful and prestigious activities are in the "man's world."

Abortion also has a symbolic dimension that separates the needs and interests of homemakers and workers in the paid labor force. Insofar as abortion allows a woman to get a job. to get training for a job, or to advance in a job, it does more than provide social support for working women over homemakers; it also seems to support the value of economic considerations over moral ones. Many pro-life people interviewed said that although their commitment to traditional family roles meant very real material deprivations to themselves and their families, the moral benefits of such a choice more than made up for it.

> My girls babysit and the boys garden and have paper routes and things like that. I say that if we had a lot of money that would still be my philosophy, though I don't know because we haven't been in that position. But it's a sacrifice to have a larger family. So when I hear these figures that it takes $65,000 from birth to [raise a child], I think that's ridiculous. That's a new bike every year. That's private colleges. That's a complete new outfit when school opens. Well, we've got seven daughters who wear hand-me-downs, and we hope that sometime in their eighteen years at home each one has a new bike somewhere along the line, but otherwise it's hand-me-downs. Those figures are inflated to give those children everything, and I think that's not good for them.

For pro-life people, a world view that puts the economic before the noneconomic hopelessly confuses two different kind of worlds. For them, the private world of family as traditionally experienced is the one place in human society where none of us has a price tag. Home, as Robert Frost pointed out, is where they have to take you in, whatever your social worth. Whether one is a surgeon or a rag picker, the family is, at least ideally, the place where love is unconditional.

Pro-life people and pro-life women in particular have very real reasons to fear such a state of affairs. Not only do they see an achievement-based world as harsh, superficial, and ultimately ruthless; they are relatively less well-equipped to operate in that world. A considerable amount of social science research has suggested, at least in the realm of medical treatment, that there is an increasing tendency to judge people by their official (achieved) worth.[4] Pro-life people have relatively fewer official achievements in part because they have been doing what they see as a moral task, namely, raising children and making a home; and they see themselves as becoming handicapped in a world that discounts not only their social contributions but their personal lives as well.

It is relevant in this context to recall the grounds on which pro-life people argue that the embryo is a baby: that it is genetically human. To insist that the embryo is a baby because it is genetically human is to make a claim that it is both wrong and impossible to make distinctions between humans at all. Protecting the life of the embryo, which is by definition an entity whose social worth is all yet to come, means protecting others who feel that they may be defined as having low social worth; more broadly, it means protecting a legal view of personhood that emphatically rejects social worth criteria.

For the majority of pro-life people we interviewed, the abortions they found most offensive were those of "damaged" embryos. This is because this category so clearly highlights the aforementioned concerns about social worth. To defend a genetically or congenitally damaged embryo from abortion is, in their minds, defending the weakest of the weak, and most pro-life people we interviewed were least prepared to compromise on this category of abortion.

The genetic basis of the embryo's claim to personhood has another, more subtle implication for those on the pro-life side. If genetic humanness equals personhood, then biological facts of life must take precedence over social facts of life. One's destiny is therefore inborn and hence immutable. To give any ground on the embryo's biologically determined babyness, therefore, would by extension call into question the "innate," "natural," and biological basis of women's traditional roles as well.

Pro-choice people, of course, hold a very different view of the matter. For them, social considerations outweigh biological ones: the embryo becomes a baby when it is "viable," that is, capable of achieving a certain degree of social integration with others. This is a world view premised on achievement, but not in the way pro-life people experience the word. Pro-choice people, believing as they do in choice, planning, and human efficacy, believe that biology is simply a minor given to be transcended by human experience. Sex, like race and age, is not an appropriate criterion for sorting people into different rights and responsibilities. Pro-choice people downplay these "natural" ascriptive characteristics, believing that true equality means achievement based on talent, not being restricted to a "women's world," a "black world," or an "old people's world." Such a view, as the profile of pro-choice people has made clear, is entirely consistent with their own lives and achievements.

These differences in social circumstances that separate pro-life from pro-choice women on the core issue of abortion also lead them to have different values on topics that surround abortion, such as sexuality and the use of contraception. With respect to sexuality, for example, the two sides have diametrically opposed values; these values arise from a fundamentally different premise, which is, in turn, tied to the different realities of their social worlds. If pro-choice women have a vested interest in subordinating their reproductive capacities, and pro-life women have a vested interest in highlighting them, we should not be surprised to find that pro-life women believe that the purpose of sex is reproduction whereas pro-choice women believe that its purpose is to promote intimacy and mutual pleasure.

These two views about sex express the same value differences that lead the two sides to have such different views on abortion. If women plan to find their primary role in marriage and the family, then they face a need to create a "moral cartel" when it comes to sex. If sex is freely available outside of marriage, then why should men, as the old saw puts it, buy the cow when the milk is free? If many women are willing to sleep with men outside of marriage, then the regular sexual activity that comes with marriage is much less valuable an incentive to marry. And because pro-life women are traditional women, their primary resource for marriage is the promise of a stable home, with everything it implies: children, regular sex, a "haven in a heartless world."

But pro-life women, like all women, are facing a devaluation of these resources. As American society increasingly becomes a service economy, men can buy the services that a wife traditionally offers. Cooking, cleaning, decorating, and the like can easily be purchased on the open market in a cash transaction. And as sex becomes more open, more casual, and more "amative," it removes one more resource that could previously be obtained only through marriage.

Pro-life women, as we have seen, have both value orientations and social characteristics that make marriage very important. Their alternatives in the public world of work are, on the whole, less attractive. Furthermore, women who stay home full-time and keep house are becoming a financial luxury. Only very wealthy families *or families whose values allow them to place the nontangible benefits of a full-time wife over the tangible benefits of a working wife* can afford to keep one of its earners off the labor market. To pro-life people, the nontangible benefit of having children—and therefore the value of procreative sex—is very important. Thus, a social ethic that promotes more freely available sex undercuts pro-life women two ways: it limits their abilities to get into a marriage in the first place, and it undermines the social value placed on their presence once within a marriage.

For pro-choice women, the situation is reversed. Because they have access to "male" resources such as education and income, they have far less reason to believe that the basic reason for sexuality is to produce children. They plan to have small families anyway, and they and their husbands come from and have married into a social class in which small families are the norm. For a number of overlapping reasons, therefore, pro-choice women believe that the value of sex is not primarily procreative: pro-choice women value the ability of sex to promote human intimacy more (or at least more frequently) than they value the ability of sex to produce babies. But they hold this view because they can afford to. When they bargain for marriage, they use the same resources that they use in the labor market: upper-class status, an education very similar to a man's side-by-side participation in the man's world, and, not least, a salary that substantially increases a family's standard of living.

It is true, therefore, that pro-life people are "anti-sex." They value sex, of course, but they value it for its traditional benefits (babies) rather than for the benefits that pro-choice people associate with it (intimacy). Pro-life people really do want to see "less" sexuality—or at least less open and socially unregulated sexuality—because they think it is morally wrong, they think it distorts the meaning of sex, and they feel that it *threatens the basis on which their own marital bargains are built*.

These differences in social background also explain why the majority of pro-life people we interviewed were opposed to "artificial" contraception, and had chosen to use natural family planning (NFP), the modern-day version of the "rhythm method." To be sure, since NFP is a "morally licit" form of fertility control for Catholics, and many pro-life activists are very orthodox Catholics, NFP is attractive on those grounds alone. But as a group, Catholics are increasingly using contraception in patterns very similar to those of their non-Catholic peers.[5] Furthermore, many non-Catholic pro-life activists told us they used NFP. Opposition to contraception, therefore, and its corollary, the use of NFP, needs to be explained as something other than simple obedience to church dogma.

Given their status as traditional women who do not work outside of the home, the choice of NFP as the preferred method of fertility control is a rational one because NFP enhances their power and status as women. The NFP users we talked with almost uniformly stated that men respect women more when they are using NFP and that the marriage relationship becomes more like a honeymoon. Certain social factors in the lives of pro-life women suggest why his may be so. Because NFP requires abstinence during the fertile period, one effect of using it is that *sex becomes a relatively scarce resource.* Rather than something that is simply there—and taken for granted—sex becomes something that disappears from the relationship for regular periods of time. Therefore, NFP creates incentives for husbands to be close and intimate with their wives. The more insecure a woman and the less support she feels from her husband, the more reasonable it is for her to want to lengthen the period of abstinence to be on the safe side.* The increase in power and status that NFP affords a woman in a traditional marriage was clearly recognized by the activists who use NFP, as these two quotations suggest:

> The rhythm [method] is the most freeing thing a woman can have, if you want me to tell you the honest-to-God truth. Because if she's married to someone that she loves, and she ought to be, then you know [when she abstains] she's got a romance time, she's got a time when she doesn't have to say she has a headache. He's just got to know, hey, either we're going to have another baby and you're going to pay for it or we're going to read our books tonight. And once in a while we're going to get to read our books, that's the way I look at it. I think it's wonderful, I really do, it might not sound too romantic to people, but it is, this is super romantic.

> You know, if you have filet mignon every day, it becomes kind of disinteresting. But if you have to plan around this, you do some things. You study, and you do other things during the fertile part of the cycle. And the husband and wife find out how much they can do in the line of expressing love for one another in other ways, other than genital. And some people can really express a lot of love and do a lot of touching and be very relaxed. Maybe others would find that they can only do a very little touching because they might be stimulated. And so they would have to find out where their level was. But they can have a beautiful relationship.

---

*One NFP counselor described a case to me in which a woman found herself unavailable for sex an average of twenty-five days a month in what seemed a deliberate attempt to use sex to control a spouse's behavior. But the interpretation of oneself as fertile (and hence sexually unavailable unless the spouse wishes to risk the arrival of another child) need not be either calculating or conscious. The more insecure a woman is in her marriage the more insecure she may be about interpreting her fertility signs, both because the insecurity in her marriage translates into a more general insecurity and because she may wish to err "on the safe side" if she is worried about the effects of a pregnancy on a shaky relationship.

NFP also creates an opportunity for both husbands and wives to talk about the wife's fertility so that once again, something that is normally taken for granted can be focused on and valued. Folk wisdom has it that men and women use sexuality in different ways to express their feelings of caring and intimacy: men give love in order to get sex and women give sex in order to get love. If there is some truth to this stereotype (and both popular magazines and that rich source of sociological data, the Dear Abby column, suggest that there is), then it means that men and women often face confusion in their intimate dialogues with one another. Men wonder if their wives really want to have sex with them or are only giving it begrudgingly, out of a sense of "duty." Wives wonder if husbands really love them or merely want them for sexual relief. Natural Family Planning, by making sex periodically unavailable, puts some of these fears to rest. Some women said their husbands actually bring them flowers during the period of abstinence. Though husbands were much less forthcoming on this topic, it would seem reasonable that a woman who has been visibly reassured of her husband's caring for her might approach the renewal of sexual activity with the enthusiasm of someone who knows she is cared for as a whole person, to the husband's benefit and pleasure.

Furthermore, a few mutually discreet conversations during our interviews suggest that during abstinence at least some couples find ways of giving each other sexual pleasure that do not involve actual intercourse and hence the risk of pregnancy. Given traditional patterns of female socialization into sexuality and the fact that pro-life women are both traditional and devout women, these periods of mutual caressing may be as satisfying as intercourse for some women and even more satisfying than intercourse for others.*

The different life circumstances and experiences of pro-life and pro-choice people therefore intimately affect the ways they look at the moral and social dilemmas of contraception. The settings of their lives, for example, suggest that the psychological side benefits of NFP, which do so much to support pro-life values during the practice of contraception, are sought in other ways by pro-choice people. Pro-choice people are slightly older when they marry, and the interviews strongly suggest that they have a considerably more varied sexual experience than pro-life people on average; the use of NFP to discover other facets of sexual expression is therefore largely unnecessary for them. Moreover, what little we know about sexual practices in the United States (from the Kinsey Report) suggests that given the different average levels of education and religious devoutness in the two groups, such sexual activities as "petting" and oral-genital

---

*In short, these interviews were describing both "petting" and oral sex. Feminist literature has called to our attention the fact that traditional notions about sexuality are "male-centered": it is assumed that there will be insertion and that there will be a male ejaculation. Ironically, NFP—the birth control method preferred by the devout, traditional women we interviewed—may come very close to achieving the feminist ideal. Under NFP, the "rules" of "regular" sex are suspended and each couple must discover for themselves what feels good. For a generation of women who were raised when long periods of "necking" and "petting" occurred before—and often instead of—intercourse, NFP may provide a welcome change from genitally centered, male-oriented sexual behavior to more diffuse, body-focused "female" forms of sexual expression.

stimulation may be more frequently encountered among pro-choice people to begin with.*

The life circumstances of the two sides suggest another reason why NFP is popular among pro-life people but not seriously considered by pro-choice people. Pro-choice men and women act on their belief that men and women are equal not only because they have (or should have) equal rights but also because they have substantially similar life experiences. The pro-choice women we met have approximately the same kinds of education as their husbands do, and many of them have the same kinds of jobs—they are lawyers, physicians, college professors, and the like. Even those who do not work in traditionally male occupations have jobs in the paid labor market and thus share common experiences. They and their husbands share many social resources in common: they both have some status outside the home, they both have a paycheck, and they both have a set of peers and friends located in the work world rather than in the family world. In terms of the traditional studies of family power, pro-choice husbands and wives use the same bargaining chips and have roughly equal amounts of them.[6]

Pro-choice women, therefore, value (and can afford) an approach to sexuality that, by sidelining reproduction, diminishes the differences between men and women; they can do this *because they have other resources on which to build a marriage.* Since their value is intimacy and since the daily lives of men and women on the pro-choice side are substantially similar, intimacy in the bedroom is merely an extension of the intimacy of their larger world.

Pro-life women and men, by contrast, tend to live in "separate spheres." Because their lives are based on social and emotional division of labor where each sex has its appropriate work, to accept contraception or abortion would devalue the one secure resource left to these women: the private world of home and hearth. This would be disastrous not only in terms of status but also in terms of meaning: if values about fertility and family are not essential to a marriage, what supports does a traditional marriage have in times of stress? To accept highly effective contraception, which actually and symbolically subordinates the role of children in the family to other needs and goals, would be to cut the ground of meaning out from under at least one (and perhaps both) partners' lives. Therefore, contraception, which sidelines the reproductive capacities of men and women, is both useless and threatening to pro-life people.

THE CORE OF THE DEBATE

In summary, women come to be pro-life and pro-choice activists as the end result of lives that center around different definitions of motherhood. They grow up

---

*Kinsey's data suggest that for males the willingness to engage in oral-genital or manual-genital forms of sexual expression is related to education: the more educated an individual, the more likely he is to have "petted" or engaged in oral sex (Alfred Kinsey, *Sexual Behavior in the Human Male*, pp. 337–81, 535–37). For females, the patterns are more complicated. Educational differences among women disappear when age at marriage is taken into account. But as Kinsey notes: "Among the females in the sample, the chief restraint on petting . . . seems to have been the religious tradition against it." The more devout a woman, the less likely she is to have ever petted (Kinsey, *Sexual Behavior in the Human Female*, pp. 247–48).

with a belief about the nature of the embryo, so events in their lives lead them to believe that the embryo is a unique person, or a fetus; that people are intimately tied to their biological roles, or that these roles are but a minor part of life; that motherhood is the most important and satisfying role open to a woman, or that motherhood is only one of several roles, a burden when defined as the only role. These beliefs and values are rooted in the concrete circumstances of women's lives—their educations, incomes, occupations, and the different marital and family choices they have made along the way—and they work simultaneously to shape those circumstances in turn. Values about the relative place of reason and faith, about the role of actively planning for life versus learning to accept gracefully life's unknowns, of the relative satisfactions inherent in work and family—all of these factors place activists in a specific relationship to the larger world and give them a specific set of resources with which to confront that world.

The simultaneous and on-going modification of both their lives and their values by each other finds these activists located in a specific place in the social world. They are financially successful, or they are not. They become highly educated, or they do not. They become married and have a large family, or they have a small one. And at each step of the way, both their values and their lives have undergone either ratification or revision.

Pro-choice and pro-life activists live in different worlds, and the scope of their lives, as both adults and children, fortifies them in their belief that their own views on abortion are the more correct, more moral, and more reasonable. When added to this is the fact that should "the other side" win, one group of women will see the very real devaluation of their lives and life resources, it is not surprising that the abortion debate has generated so much heat and so little light.

NOTES

1. Granberg, "The Abortion Activists," p. 158.

2. Charles Tilly, *The Vendée*.

3. Many of the pro-life people in this study asserted that women have abortions because they do not wish to have stretch marks or because they want to take a European vacation. While I know of no direct data of how women feel who choose abortions, in the course of research for my previous book (*Taking Chances: Abortion and the Decision Not to Contracept* [1975]), I interviewed over 100 women in deep, unstructured verbatim interviews. In subsequent research, I have talked with or interviewed over 500 women who have had abortions. In my own—and possibly biased—experience, few of these women were "casual" about having an abortion. Some were more conflicted about the abortion decision than others, but for all the women I interviewed, the decision to seek an abortion has been serious, thoughtful, and carefully considered.

4. See, e.g., Fuchs, *Who Shall Live?*; Tristam Engelhardt, *Science, Ethics and Medicine*; Crane, *Sanctity of Social Life*; and Paul Ramsey, *Ethics at the Edges of Life*.

5. Westoff and Bumpass, "Revolution in Birth Control Practices," pp. 41–44.

6. There is a long sociological research tradition on the relative power status of husbands and wives and what contributes to their relative power; see Robert Blood and Donald Wolfe, *Husbands and Wives*; Robert Blood and Robert Hamlin, "The Effects of the Wife's Employment on the Family Power Structure," pp. 347–52; Phyllis Hallenbeck,

"An Analysis of Power Dynamics in Marriage," *Journal of Marriage and the Family* 27 (1966):200–03; and David Heer, "Measurement and Bases of Family Power: An Overview," *Marriage and Family Living* 25 (1963):133–39. For fundamental critiques of this literature, see Constantina Safilios-Rothchild, "Family Sociology or Wives' Family Sociology? A Cross-Cultural Examination of Decision-Making," pp. 290–301; and Dair Gillespie, "Who Has the Power? The Marital Struggle," pp. 445–58.

REFERENCES

Blood, Robert and Robert Hamlin. 1958. "The Effects of the Wife's Employment on the Family Power Structure." *Social Forces* 36:347–52.

Blood, Robert and Donald M. Wolfe. 1960. *Husbands and Wives: The Dynamics of Family Living*. New York: The Free Press.

Crane, Diana. 1975. *The Sanctity of Social Life*. New York: Russell Sage.

Engelhardt, Tristam. 1976. *Science, Ethics, and Medicine*. Hastings-on-Hudson, NY: Institute for Society, Ethics, and Natural Science.

Fuchs, Victor. 1974. *Who Shall Live? Health Economics and Social Choice*. New York: Basic Books.

Gillespie, Dair. 1971. "Who Has the Power? The Marital Struggle." *Journal of Marriage and the Family* 33:445–58.

Granberg, Donald. 1981. "The Abortion Activists." *Family Planning Perspectives* 13:158–61.

Kinsey, Alfred, et al. 1948. *Sexual Behavior in the Human Male*. Philadelphia: W. B. Saunders.

Kinsey, Alfred, et al. 1953. *Sexual Behavior in the Human Female*. Philadelphia: W. B. Saunders.

Luker, Kristin. 1975. *Taking Chances: Abortion and the Decision Not to Contracept*. Berkeley and Los Angeles: University of California Press.

Ramsey, Paul. 1978. *Ethics at the Edges of Life*. New Haven: Yale University Press.

Safilios-Rothchild, Constantina. 1969. "Family Sociology or Wives' Family Sociology? A Cross-Cultural Examination of Decision-Making." *Journal of Marriage and the Family* 29:290–301.

Tilly, Charles. 1964. *The Vendee*. Cambridge, MA: Harvard University Press.

Westoff, Charles and Larry Bumpass. 1969. "The Revolution in Birth Control Practices of U.S. Roman Catholics." *Science* 174:41–44.

31

Teenage Pregnancy in Developed Countries: Determinants and Policy Implications*

Elise Jones et al.

This article summarizes the results of a comparative study of adolescent pregnancy and childbearing in developed countries, undertaken by the Alan Guttmacher Institute (AGI). The study's main purpose was to gain some insight into the determinants of teenage reproductive behavior, especially factors that might be subject to policy changes.

A 1983 article by Charles F. Westoff, Gérard Calot and Andrew D. Foster reported that although adolescent fertility rates have been declining in the United States, as they have in virtually all the countries of Western and northern Europe, teenage fertility is still considerably higher in the United States than in the great majority of other developed countries.[1] There is a large differential within the United States between the rates of white and black teenagers. However, even if only whites are considered, the rates in the United States are still much higher than those in most of the other countries. The gap between the United States and the other countries is greater among younger adolescents (for whom the great majority of births are out of wedlock and, presumably, unintended) than it is among older teenagers. Abortion rates are also higher among U.S. teenagers than among adolescents in the dozen or so countries for which there are data.[2]

Two major questions were suggested by these comparisons: Why are teenage fertility and abortion rates so much higher in the United States than in other developed countries? And, since most teenage pregnancies in the United States are unintended,[3] and their consequences often adverse,[4] what can be learned from the experience of countries with lower adolescent pregnancy rates that might be useful for reducing the number of teenage conceptions in the United States?

The AGI study involved two distinct undertakings: quantitative bivariate and multivariate analyses of the factors associated with adolescent fertility in 37 developed countries, and case studies of teenage pregnancy and its antecedents in five selected countries and the United States.

THE 37-COUNTRY ANALYSIS

The two dependent variables selected for the 37–country† study were cumulative age-specific birthrates for girls under age 18 and those for women 18–19. The

*Jones, Elise, et al. 1985. "Teenage Pregnancy in Developed Countries: Determinants and Policy Implications." *Family Planning Perspectives* 17(2):53–65. © The Alan Guttmacher Institute.

† Australia, Austria, Belgium, Bulgaria, Canada, Chile, Cuba, Czechoslovakia, Denmark, the Federal Republic of Germany, Finland, France, the German Democratic Republic, Greece, Hong Kong, Hungary, Ireland, Israel, Italy, Japan, the Netherlands, New Zealand, Norway, Poland, Portugal, Puerto Rico, Romania, Singapore, Spain, Sweden, Switzerland, Taiwan, the USSR, Great Britain, (England and Wales and, considered separately, Scotland), the United States, and Yugoslavia.

rates are explained in the appendix (page 585). Birthrates rather than pregnancy rates were chosen because abortion data were available for only 13 of the 37 countries. However, it was found that abortion rates and birthrates were highly correlated, so that it seemed reasonable to assume that birthrates are an acceptable proxy for pregnancy rates. Measures for 42 independent variables selected for the quantitative analysis were obtained from published data and from a country-level survey conducted by the AGI designed to supplement inadequately documented areas of information, such as the prevalence of sex education within each country, the availability of contraceptive services for minors and social attitudes that might have a bearing on adolescent sexual activity. The questionnaire was sent to the public affairs officer of the American embassy in each foreign country included in the study, to the embassy of each of these countries in Washington, D.C., and to the family planning organization or other agency responsible for family planning services in each country.

Scatter plots and pairwise relationships between each independent variable and the two dependent variables were examined initially, and on the basis of these results, a multivariate analysis was attempted. Descriptions of the methodology and of the major results of the bivariate analysis are carried in the appendix. The results of the multivariate analysis presented here have to be taken as suggestive rather than conclusive, and they are described only in broad terms.

- The analysis found a positive association between teenage childbearing and the proportion of the labor force employed in agriculture (a variable interpreted as indicating level of socioeconomic development).
- There is a positive relationship between levels of maternity leaves and benefits and the teenage birthrate. (Because the United States does not have a uniform national policy, it was not represented on this variable. In fact, U.S. maternity benefit policies tend to be less liberal than those in most European countries,[5] and, thus, the United Sates would not have fit this pattern.)
- Analysis of the relationship between fertility and openness about sex (defined on the basis of four items: media presentation of female nudity, the extent of nudity on public beaches, sales of sexually explicit literature and media advertising of condoms) in a given society reveals low birthrates in countries found to exemplify the most liberal views.
- More equitable distribution of income (i.e., a greater proportion of a country's total household income received by the poorest 20 percent of the population) is negatively related to the cumulative birthrate for girls under 18. Of the 19 countries for which this information was available, Canada, the United States and New Zealand have the least equitable distribution of income. Of these three countries, the United States has by far the highest teenage birthrate.
- The birthrate for older teenagers is lower where the minimum age for marriage is higher. (Again, the United States was not represented on this variable because the legal age at marriage varies from state to state, although in most states women can marry on their own consent by age 18.)
- Finally, the rate for older teenagers is also somewhat responsive to government policies to increase fertility.

It is notable that the United States differs from most of the countries with comparably high adolescent fertility on four factors. The position of the United States is anomalous with regard to socioeconomic development, one of the most important factors associated with low teenage fertility. Although it is one of the most highly developed countries examined, the United States has a teenage fertility rate much higher than those observed in countries that are comparably modernized; and the U.S. rates are considerably higher than those found in a number of much less developed countries. The inconsonance applies particularly to fertility among younger teenagers, where the U.S. rate falls between those of Romania and Hungary. The relatively high adolescent birthrate in the United States would also suggest, if the experience of the United States were consistent with that of other countries, that the country has a pronatalist fertility policy, high levels of maternity leaves and benefits and a low minimum age at marriage. In fact, the United States has none of these.

The United States fits the general pattern for high teenage fertility in that it is less open about sexual matters than most countries with low teenage birthrates, and a relatively small proportion of its income is distributed to families on the bottom rungs of the economic ladder.

Had better or more complete information been available, it is likely that at least some of the additional variables found to be associated with adolescent fertility in the bivariate analysis would have retained their importance in the multivariate analysis. Certain of them deserve mention because of their policy significance and because they figure prominently in the individual country case studies that follow, for which more detailed information was available. These include restrictions placed on teenagers' access to contraception, the level of religiosity in the country (both associated with high birthrates) and teaching about contraceptives in the schools (associated with low birthrates). It is noteworthy that government subsidy of abortions is *not* associated with teenage fertility.

In the 37 country study, the United States does not appear to be more restrictive than low-fertility countries in the provision of contraceptive services to teenagers; however, comparable data could not be obtained on the provision of contraceptives free of charge or at very low cost—a factor that, as we shall see, appears to be very important in terms of accessibility in the country case studies. Teenagers are much less likely to get free or very low-cost contraceptive services in the United States than in the other five countries studied in detail—all of which have much lower adolescent birthrates and abortion rates than the United States. The very high level of religiosity reported for the United States (the highest of any of the 13 countries for which there are data) is probably one factor underlying the low rating of the United States on openness about sex. It is also notable that the United States scores relatively low among the 37 countries on the measures of availability of contraceptive education in the schools.

COUNTRY CASE STUDIES

The five countries selected for the case studies in addition to the United States— Canada, England and Wales, France, the Netherlands and Sweden—were chosen on the basis of three considerations: Their rates of adolescent pregnancy are considerably lower than that of the United States, and it was believed that sexual activity among young people is not very different; the countries are similar to the United States in general cultural background and stage of economic development; finally, from the investigators' experience with the first phase of the project, it was apparent that for these countries, some crucial data related to adolescent pregnancy were available.

Figures 1, 2 and 3 present, for the United States and each of the five countries, 1981 birthrates, abortion rates and pregnancy rates by single year of age. The exceptional position of the United States is immediately apparent. The U.S. teenage birthrates, as Figure 1 shows, are much higher than those of each of the five countries at every age, by a considerable margin. The contrast is particularly striking for younger teenagers. In fact, the maximum relative difference in the birthrate between the United States and other countries occurs at ages under 15. With more than five births per 1,000 girls aged 14, the U.S. rate is around four times that of Canada, the only other country with as much as one birth per 1,000 girls of comparable age.

Teenagers from the Netherlands clearly have the lowest birthrate at every age. In 1981, Dutch women aged 19 were about as likely to bear a child as were American women aged 15–16. The birthrates are also very low in Sweden, especially among the youngest teenagers. Canada, England and Wales, and France compose an intermediate group. Birthrates are relatively high for Canadian girls aged 14–16, and rise gradually with age. The French rates are low among women up to age 18, but increase very sharply among older teenagers.

In 1981, as Figure 2 shows, the relative positions of the countries with respect to abortion are surprisingly close to the pattern observed for births. The United States has by far the highest rate, and the Netherlands, very much the lowest, at each age. French teenage abortion rates climb steeply with age,* while the Canadian curve is somewhat flatter. The rate for England and Wales rises relatively little after age 17. The chief difference between the patterns for births and abortions involves Sweden, which has age-specific abortion rates as high as, or higher than, those of any of the other countries except the United States.

The teenage pregnancy rates†necessarily follow the same pattern, as Figure 3 reveals. The U. S. rates are distinctly higher than those of the other five countries; the Dutch rates are clearly lower. The French teenage pregnancy rates appear to be low among teenagers 16 and younger, and after that age, to be high. The reverse is true of Canada.

Thus, the six countries represent a rather varied experience. At one extreme is the United States, which has the highest rates of teenage birth, abortion and pregnancy. At the other stands the Netherlands, with very low levels on all three measures. Canada, France, and England and Wales are quite similar to one another, Sweden is notable for its low adolescent birthrates, although its teenage abortion

---

*The relatively low rates among younger teenagers may be due to underreporting at those ages in France.

†Calculated as the sum of births and abortions experienced by women of a given age divided by the midyear estimate of the female population of that age.

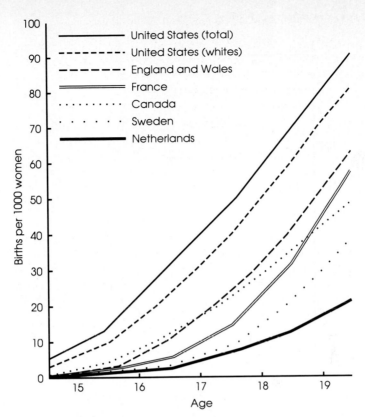

FIGURE 1. Births per 1,000 women under age 20, by woman's age, case-study countries, 1981

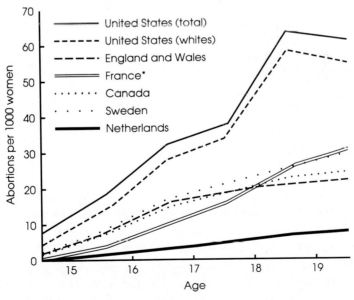

FIGURE 2. Abortions per 1,000 women, by woman's age, 1981

*1980 data

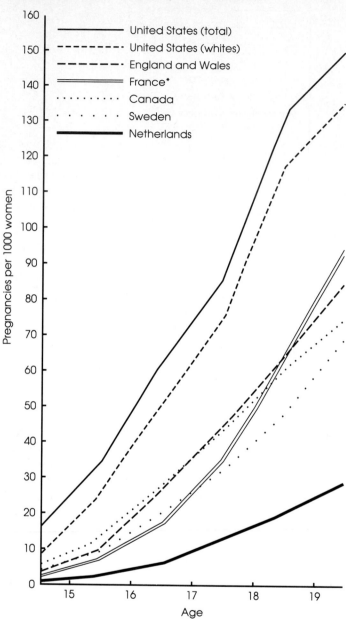

FIGURE 3. Pregnancy rates per 1,000 women by woman's age, 1981

*1980 data

Note: Pregnancies are defined here as birth plus abortions; age is the age at outcome.

rates are generally higher than those reported for any country except the United States. It is noteworthy that the United States is the only country where the incidence of teenage pregnancy has been increasing in recent years. The increase reflects a rise in the abortion rate that has not been completely offset by a decline in the birthrate. For both younger and older teenagers, the disparity between the U.S. pregnancy rates and those for other countries increased somewhat between 1976 and 1981.

In the United States, the pregnancy rates among black teenagers are sufficiently higher than those among whites to influence the rates for the total adolescent population, even though in 1980, black teenagers represented only 14 percent of all 15–19-year-olds. Restriction of the international comparisons to pregnancy rates among white U.S. teenagers reduces the difference between the United States and other countries by about one-fifth. However, the pregnancy rate for white U.S. adolescents remains much higher than the rates for the teenage populations in the other countries, as shown in the table.

Pregnancy rate	15–19	15–17	18–19
U.S. total	96	62	144
U.S. white	83	51	129
England & Wales	45	27	75
France	43	19	79
Canada	44	28	68
Sweden	35	20	59
Netherlands	14	7	25

What is more, some of the other countries studied also have minority populations that appear to have higher-than-average teenage reproductive rates (e.g., Caribbean and Asian women in England), so that it would not be appropriate to compare white U.S. rates with rates for the total adolescent population in those countries.

A common approach was established for the study of the six countries selected for close examination. Detailed information on teenage births and abortions was collected, and a systematic effort was made to assemble quantitative data on the proximate determinants of pregnancy—specifically, the proportion of teenagers cohabiting, rates of sexual activity among those not living together and levels of contraceptive practice. In addition, the investigators sought descriptive material on a number of related topics: policies and practices regarding teenage access to contraceptive and abortion services, the delivery of those services, and the formal and informal provision of sex education. Several aspects of teenage life were explored to try to enhance understanding of certain social and economic considerations that might influence the desire to bear children and contraceptive practice. These include the proportions of young people in school, employment and unemployment patterns, the move away from the family home, and government assistance programs for young people and, particularly, for young unmarried mothers.

Teams of two investigators each visited Canada, England, France, the Netherlands and Sweden for one week and conducted interviews with government officials, statisticians, demographers and other researchers, and family planning, abortion and adolescent health service providers. These interviews provided the opportunity to discuss attitudes and other less tangible factors that might not otherwise have been possible to document, and helped the investigators to identify other sources of data.

The five countries that were visited and the United States have much in common. All are highly developed nations, sharing the benefits and problems of industrialized modern societies. All belong essentially to the cultural tradition of northwestern Europe. All have reached an advanced stage in the process of demographic transition. Life expectancy is over 70 years for men and women of all the countries. Finally, all have fertility levels below that required for replacement. Yet, as Figure 3 demonstrates, teenage pregnancy rates in the six countries are quite diverse. However, the consistency of the six countries' positions in Figures 1 and 2 points to an immediate and important conclusion: The reason that adolescent birthrates are lower in the five other countries than they are in the United States is not more frequent resort to abortion in those countries. Where the birthrate is lower, the abortion rate also tends to be lower. Thus, the explanation of inter-country differences can focus on the determinants of pregnancy as the antecedent of both births and abortions.

The Desire for Pregnancy

Are the differences in adolescent birthrates due to the fact that in some countries, higher proportions of young women choose to become pregnant? The number of marital births per 1,000 teenagers is higher in the United States than in any other of the countries studied, and the proportion of teenagers who are married is at least twice as high in the United States as in the other countries (not shown). Data on teenagers' pregnancy intentions are available only for the United States. In 1980, 76 percent of marital teenage pregnancies and only nine percent of non-marital teenage pregnancies were intended. On the assumption that all pregnancies ending in abortions are unintended, and that a large majority of nonmarital births are the result of unintended pregnancies (except in Sweden, where nonmarital childbearing has traditionally been free of social stigma), the distribution of pregnancy outcomes illustrated in Figure 4 sheds some light on the contribution of unintended pregnancy to the differences among the six countries. The combined fraction of all pregnancies accounted for by abortions and nonmarital births is approximately three-quarters in the United States and Canada, close to two-thirds in England and Wales and France, and only about one-half in the Netherlands. Thus, in England and Wales, France and the Netherlands, unintended pregnancy appears to constitute a smaller pat of adolescent pregnancy than it does in the United States. Even more striking is the fact that the abortion rate alone in the United States is about as high as, or higher than, the overall teenage pregnancy rate in any of the other countries.

Exposure to the Risk of Pregnancy

Figure 5 illustrates some recent findings on levels of sexual activity (defined here as the proportion who have ever had intercourse) among teenagers in the six coun-

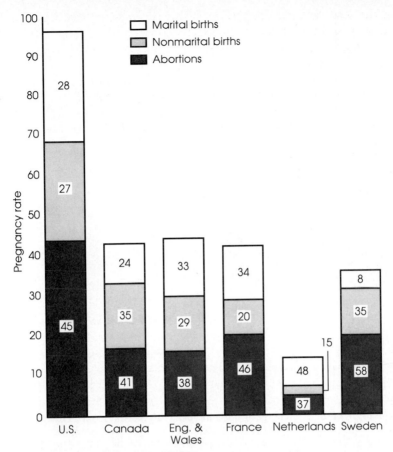

FIGURE 4. Percentage distribution of pregnancies, and pregnancy rates, by outcome,* for woman aged 15–19, 1980/1981

*The rates can be estimated by measuring the height of the bars against the vertical axis. The numbers inside the bars represent the percentage distributions.

tries. The data should be interpreted cautiously, however, as there are numerous problems of comparability and quality. (Two potentially important aspects of sexual activity among adolescents—the number of sexual partners and frequency of intercourse—could not be examined because data on them were not available for most countries.) The most striking observation from the figure is that the differences in sexual activity among teenagers in the six countries do not appear to be nearly as great as the differences in pregnancy rates. Sexual activity is initiated considerably earlier in Sweden than elsewhere. By age 16, around one-third of all Swedish girls have had intercourse, and by age 18, four-fifths have done so. In Canada, by comparison, women may have had their first sexual experience later than the average for all six countries. At ages 16–17, only one out of five girls are sexually active. Smaller proportions of women are reported as having initiated sexual intercourse before the age of 18 in both Great Britain (England, Wales and Scotland) and France than in the United States. However, a rapid catch-up seems to take place, and in France the proportion of young women who have had

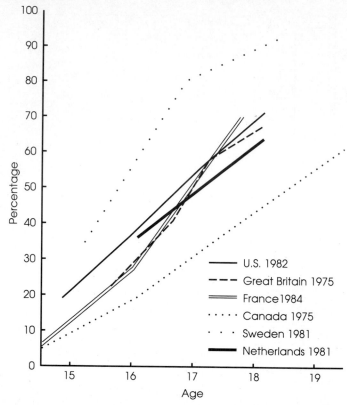

FIGURE 5. Percentage of women ever having had intercourse, by age

intercourse by the time they are 19 appears to be higher than that found in the United States. The median age at first intercourse is very similar for the United States, France, Great Britain and the Netherlands—something under age 18—and is about a year younger in Sweden, and may be about a year higher in Canada.

These data indicate that the variation in adolescent pregnancy rates shown in Figure 3 cannot, by and large, be explained by differences in levels of sexual experience. The examples of the Netherlands and Sweden make it clear that the postponement of first intercourse is not a prerequisite for the avoidance of early pregnancy. It does seem possible that reduced sexual exposure among younger Canadian teenagers is partly responsible for keeping their pregnancy rates relatively low. The difference in pregnancy rates between the Netherlands and Sweden may also be partly attributable to the older age at sexual initiation in the Netherlands.

Contraceptive Use

The data on contraceptive practice, represented schematically in Figure 6, were, likewise, derived from surveys that differed widely in their design and approach to the issue.[6] Nevertheless, it is possible to make some estimates of proportions using any contraceptive method, and proportions using the pill, at various ages. Contraceptive use among French teenagers is probably underestimated because condom use was not included in the published results of the survey. It is likely,

Age	United States		Great Britain	France*		Can-ada	Sweden		Netherlands	
	1976	1979	1976	1979	1980	1976	1978†	1981	1979 1980	1981
	NM‡	NM‡	NM‡	T‡	T‡	T‡	T‡	T‡	T‡	NM‡
	Used at last coitus	Used at last coitus	Use currently	Use regularly	Use regularly	Use currently	Used in last coitus	Used in last 4 wks	Used in last 6 mos	Used at last coitus

Percentage using any method

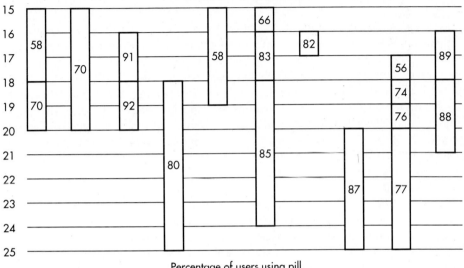

Percentage of users using pill

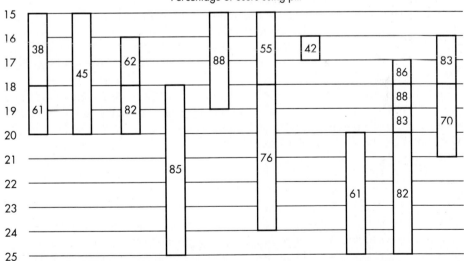

FIGURE 6. Percentage of sexually experienced women using any contraceptive method and among users, percentage using the pill, by age and marital status of woman and occasion of contraceptive use

*Students only, condom use excluded   † Students in one city   ‡ T = all women   NM = never-married woman

Notes: The data should be interpreted cautiously because of problems in their comparability and quality. As an example of how to read this figure, the data for Canada indicate that among all sexually active women, 66 percent of 15-year-olds, 83 percent of 16–17-year-olds and 85 percent of 18–23-year-olds were using some method in 1976.

therefore, that the United States has the lowest level of contraceptive practice among teenagers of all six countries.

In particular, pill use appears to be less widespread among U.S. teenagers than among those in the other countries. This difference suggests that American adolescents use less effective contraceptives to avoid accidental pregnancy, even if they are using a birth control method.

Access to Contraceptive and Abortion Services

Contraceptive services appear to be most accessible to teenagers in England and Wales, the Netherlands and Sweden. In England and Wales and the Netherlands, those seeking care may choose to go either to a general practitioner (limited to their own family doctor in the Netherlands) or to one of a reasonably dense network of clinics. The Dutch clinic system is less extensive than the British one, but it is directed largely toward meeting the special needs of youth, whereas in England and Wales, there are relatively few clinics specially designed for young people. In Sweden, there are two parallel clinic systems, one consisting of the primary health care centers that serve every community, and the other consisting of a less complete network providing contraceptive care and related services to the school-age population.

Canada, France and the United States also have clinic systems, but these appear to be less accessible than those found in the other countries. (In France, however, the clinic system has expanded considerably since 1981.) The Canadian clinic system is uneven, with fairly complete coverage for adolescents in Ontario and Quebec, and scattered services elsewhere. The U.S. clinic network is reasonably accessible in a strictly geographic sense. Moreover, all family planning clinics receiving federal funds are required to serve adolescents. A basic drawback of the U.S. clinic system, however, is that it was developed as a service for the poor, and is often avoided by teenagers who consider clinics places where only welfare clients go.[7]

Condoms are widely available in England and Wales, the Netherlands and Sweden. They not only are available from family planning clinics and pharmacies, but also are sold in supermarkets and other shops and in vending machines. In France and in many parts of Canada and the United States, condoms are less freely available.

Confidentiality was found to be an important issue in every country. Even where attitudes about sex are very open, as in the Netherlands and Sweden, the research teams were told that young people wish to keep their personal sex lives private. The need for confidential services is probably best met in Sweden, where doctors are specifically forbidden to inform parents about an adolescent's request for contraceptive services. Dutch doctors also are required to keep the visit confidential if the teenager requests it; and the services in Dutch clinics are entirely confidential. French official policy stipulates that clinic services for women under age 18 be absolutely confidential. Although the prescription of contraceptives to girls younger than 16 without a requirement that the parents be informed is now being legally contested in Britain, the practice was followed through the period covered by this study, and the British government is seeking to preserve confidentiality for young teenagers. In Canada and the United States, many individual doctors insist on parental consent before they will provide contraceptives to minors. However, most family planning clinics in Canada and the United States provide services to young women without any such restriction.

Like all medical care, contraceptive services, including supplies, are provided free of charge to young people in England and Wales and Sweden. Free services and supplies are available from clinics to French women under age 18; and for older teenagers, most of these expenses are reimbursable under social security. Contraceptive services provided by Dutch family doctors are covered under the national health insurance scheme, but the clinics charge a small fee. Until very recently, no charge was made to have a prescription filled at a pharmacy. In Canada, doctors' services are likewise covered by national medical insurance, and clinic services are free; but all patients except those on welfare have to pay for supplies obtained from pharmacies. The potential expense of obtaining contraceptive services in the United States varies considerably. Indigent teenagers from eligible families are able to get free care through Medicaid, and others do not have to pay anything because of individual clinic policy; otherwise, clinic fees are likely to be modest. On the other hand, consulting a private doctor usually entails appreciable expense, as does purchase of supplies at pharmacies.

An additional observation concerns the central role of the pill everywhere outside the United State. In each country, the research teams were told that the medical profession accepts the pill as a highly appropriate, usually *the most* appropriate, method for adolescents. Moreover, a pelvic examination is not necessarily required before the pill can be prescribed in some of these countries. The emphasis on pill use emerged more clearly from the interviews than from the incomplete statistics on contraceptive use summarized in Figure 6. By contrast, in the United States, there seems to be a good deal of ambivalence about pill use, both on the part of the medical profession and among potential young users. In the United States, medical protocol requires that a pelvic examination be performed before the pill can be prescribed, a procedure some young people find daunting.[8] Whether justified or not, this requirement undoubtedly influences method selection among young women.

Postcoital contraceptive pills have been available at many family planning clinics in the United Kingdom for a number of years. Postcoital IUD insertion and oral contraceptives are available in the clinics run by both the Dutch and the French family planning associations. However, it is unlikely that these methods are sufficiently widely utilized to influence the birthrate appreciably. In Sweden, the morning-after pill is not yet permitted for general use. The federal Food and Drug Administration has not approved postcoital use of pills in the United States, and no plan exists to market them, but they are available in some college health clinics and rape treatment centers.

Geographically, abortion services are most easily accessible in the Netherlands and Sweden. Although services are theoretically in place throughout England and Wales and France, wide differences in the abortion rates by area are believed to be attributable to variation in the availability of abortion facilities. In all three countries, as in Canada and the United States, services are likely to be found in cities. In Canada, England and Wales, and France, abortions typically involve at least an overnight hospital stay.

In Sweden, there is no charge for abortion; Canadian women usually pay only a small portion of the cost; and abortions obtained under the national health service in Britain are also free. However, because of bureaucratic delays in the national health service, almost half of British women choose to pay for an abortion in the private sector. In the Netherlands, the cost of an abortion is borne by the patient but is not high. The same was true in France up until 1982, when the service became free. Most U.S. women must pay for the abortion procedure themselves. For a second-trimester abortion, in particular, the cost may be substantial.

Sex Education

Sweden has the distinction of being the first country in the world to have established an official sex education curriculum in its schools. The curriculum, which is compulsory and extends to all grade levels, give special attention to contraception and the discussion of human and sexual relationships. Perhaps most important, there is a close, carefully established link in Sweden between the schools and contraceptive clinic services for adolescents. None of the other countries comes close to the Swedish model. Sweden established this link in 1975, following liberalization of the abortion law, because of concern that liberalized abortion access might otherwise result in a sharp rise in teenage abortion rates. In fact, adolescent abortion rates have declined dramatically since 1975, whereas the rates for adults have not changed much. (In the other countries studied, teenage abortion rates have *not* fallen during this period.) The Swedish authorities credit the combination of sex education with the adolescent clinic program for the decline.

In Canada, England and Wales, and the United States, school sex education is a community option, and it is essentially up to the local authorities, school principals or individual teachers to determine how much is taught and at what age. In England and Wales, however, there is a national policy favoring the inclusion of topics related to sex and family life in the curriculum, whereas there is no such national policy in Canada and the United States. French policy now mandates broad coverage of sexuality for all adolescents, although in practice, interpretation of this provision similarly devolves on local decision-makers.

The Netherlands is a case apart. Coverage of sex in the school curriculum is limited on the whole to the facts of reproduction in natural science classes. The Dutch government, nevertheless, encourages the teaching of contraception indirectly by subsidizing mobile educational teams that operate under the auspices of the private family planning association. At the same time, in recent years there has been an explosion of materials on contraception and other sex-related topics in the media, much of which is of a responsible and informative nature. Youth surveys show that knowledge of how to avoid pregnancy appears to be virtually universal.

In Sweden, sex education is completely accepted by the vast majority of parents, most of whom themselves had sex education while they were in school. Objections are confined to the immigrant community, for some of whom sex education represents a direct challenge to their own traditions. British law requires schools offering sex education to notify the parents. In the United States, many of the school districts that provide sex education give parents the option of excusing their children from such courses.

THE WIDER CONTEXT

Consideration was given to a number of other social, economic and political factors that appear to be related to the phenomenon of adolescent pregnancy. The investigators who visited the four European countries were struck by the fact that in those countries, the government, as the main provider of preventive and basic health services, perceives its responsibility in the area of adolescent pregnancy to be the provision of contraceptive services to sexually active teenagers. This commitment to action and the enunciation of an unambiguous social policy appear to be associated with a positive public climate surrounding the issue. Teenage childbearing is viewed, in general, to be undesirable, and broad agreement exists that teenagers require help in avoiding pregnancies and births.

Another aspect of government involvement in and commitment to contraceptive services for teenagers has to do with the rationale for such programs. In France, the Netherlands and Sweden, the decision to develop such services was strongly linked to the desire to minimize abortions among young people. In France and the Netherlands, for example, conservative medical groups had shown some reluctance to endorse the provision of contraceptives to young, unmarried women. Apparently, the alternative of rising abortion rates among teenagers helped to persuade them that such services were justified. In Sweden, the connection was made explicit by the government, and the 1975 law that liberalized abortion also laid the groundwork for the development of contraceptive services for young people, with the specific understanding that prevention of the need for abortion could best be achieved by putting safe, effective, confidential services within the reach of all teenagers. In the United States, in contrast, some powerful public figures reflect the view that the availability of contraceptive services acts as an incitement to premarital sexual activity and claim, therefore, that such services actually cause an increase in abortions.

The use of contraceptive services is obviously made simpler in the European countries, as in Canada, by the fact that medical services of all kinds are easily accessible through national health programs, and teenagers, in particular, grow up accustomed to using public health facilities or to visiting their local general practitioner as a matter of course. This combination of ease of accessibility and familiarity with the health care system probably serves to remove many of the social, psychological and financial barriers to contraceptive services experienced by young people in the United States.

There seems to be more tolerance of teenage sexual activity in the European countries visited than there is in most of the United States and in parts of Canada. Such acceptance of adolescent sexuality is unremarkable in a country like Sweden, with its long history of support for sexual freedom, and the absence there of taboos against premarital sex. However, such acceptance represents a considerable break with traditional standards in the Netherlands, France and, in Canada, Quebec. One reason for the more successful experience of the European countries may be that public attention was generally not directly focused on the morality of early sexual activity but, rather, was directed at a search for solutions to prevent increased teenage pregnancy and childbearing.

In the United States, sex tends to be treated as a special topic, and there is much ambivalence: Sex is romantic but also sinful and dirty; it is flaunted but also something to be hidden. This is less true in several European countries, where matter-of-fact attitudes seem to be more prevalent. Again, Sweden is the outstanding example, but the contrast with the United States was evident in most of the countries visited. Survey results tend to bear out this impression, although the questions asked are not directly comparable from country to country. For instance, in 1981, 76 percent of Dutch adults agreed with the statement that "sex is natural—even outside marriage," whereas in 1978, only 39 percent of Americans thought premarital sex was "not wrong at all."[9] These observations tend to confirm the findings of the 37-country study, which found that openness about sex may be an especially important factor in lowering adolescent fertility.

While the association between sexual conservatism and religiosity is not automatic, in the case of the United States the relationship appears to be relatively close. The proportion of the population who attend religious services and feel that God is important in their lives is higher in the United States than in the other case-study countries.[10] Although England and Wales and Sweden have an established church, both countries are more secular in outlook than the United States. Moreover, in the Netherlands, France and Quebec Province, increasing secularization is believed to be an important aspect of recent broad social changes. Fundamentalist groups in America are prominent and highly vocal. Such groups often hold extremely conservative views on sexual behavior, of a sort rarely encountered in most of Western Europe. Both the nature and the intensity of religious feeling in the United States serve to inject an emotional quality into public debate dealing with adolescent sexual behavior that seems to be generally lacking in the other countries. It is notable that religiosity was found to correlate highly with adolescent fertility in the 37-country study, although the number of country observations was small.

Although all six countries included in the survey are parliamentary democracies, the nature of each country's political institutions differs, and there is considerable variation in the way in which public issues are developed and public policies formulated. The U.S. political system appears to foster divisiveness and confrontation at many levels of society, while these elements seem less salient a part of political life in the other countries. In addition, the United States is distinguished by the widespread use of private funds to mount political campaigns and create myriad pressure groups. While the American confrontational style may have its political uses, it makes the resolution of certain emotionally charged issues hard to achieve. Positions tend to become polarized, and the possibilities for creative compromise are narrowed. The most interesting country to contrast with the United States, in terms of political style, is probably the Netherlands. It has strong and diverse religious and political groups, but a complex range of formal and informal conventions exists to defuse and resolve ideological conflicts before these emerge into the open. As a result, through accommodation and negotiation, the Dutch administrations of all political tendencies have, in the past 15 years or so, been able to make birth control services available to teenagers without exacerbating divisions in the society.

Directly related to this issue is the fact that with the exception of Canada, the United States is a much larger country than any of the others, in terms of both its geographic and its population size. In smaller, more compact countries, where lines of communication are more direct, it is easier than in the United States to engage in a national debate that includes all the appropriate parties to the discussion. For example, in the early 1960s, debate within the Dutch medical community over the advisability of prescribing the pill to teenagers quickly resulted in a broad consensus. A similar process would be much harder to implement in the United States. As a result, informing concerned professionals about the terms of a debate may be as hard as keeping the general population up to date on any issue.

Another closely related facet of national life is the extent to which political and administrative power is concentrated in the national government. France is often cited as the epitome of a centralized state, and even the existence of two "nations" within England and Wales is a simple arrangement compared with the federal systems of Canada and the United States. Both countries have two-tiered government structures, with some powers delegated to the central government and some reserved to the provinces or states. This structure has two main consequences: First, major differences can develop within the country in policy-making. Second, the task of giving shape to social change, in terms of public policies and programs, becomes enormously complicated because of the many bureaucracies that must be dealt with and the sometimes indeterminate boundaries of their separate jurisdictions.

Many observers from different backgrounds have suggested that early teenage childbearing in the United States is a response to social anomie and to a sense of hopelessness about the future on the part of large numbers of young people growing up in poverty. In the course of the country visits, the investigators collected information on teenage education and employment patterns, in order to explore further the possible association between career and life opportunities for young people and their attitudes toward reproductive planning. The finding was that educational opportunities in the United States appear to be as great as, or greater than, those in other countries, except, possibly, Sweden. In Sweden, about 85 percent of young people aged 18–19 are pursuing academic or vocational schooling. In Canada and France, most young people leave school at around 18, as they do in the United States, although a higher proportion of U.S. students go on to college. However, in the Netherlands, only about half of girls are still in school at age 18, while in England and Wales, the majority of young people end their full-time schooling at age 16.

The employment situation is difficult to compare or assess, since definitions of labor-force participation and unemployment differ from country to country. The most that can be concluded is that unemployment among the young is considered a very serious problem everywhere, and young people themselves are universally uneasy on this score. The chances of getting and keeping a satisfying or well-paying job do not appear to be worse in the United States than in other countries. To a greater extent than in the United States, however, all the other countries offer assistance to ease the problem, in the form of youth training, unemployment benefits and other kinds of support.

It is often suggested that in the United States, the availability of public assistance for unmarried mothers creates a financial incentive for poor women, especially the young, to bear children outside of marriage. Yet, all the countries studied provide extensive benefits to poor mothers that usually include medical care, food supplements, housing and family allowances. In most cases, the overall level of support appears to be more generous than that provided under the Aid to Families with Dependent Children program in the United States. Benefits in the other countries tend to be available regardless of women's marital or reproductive status, although in England and Wales and in France, at least, special supplementary benefit programs for poor single mothers also exist. In those countries, however, the existence of considerable financial support for out-of-wedlock childbearing does not explain the differences between their teenage birthrates and those of the United States.

The final difference between the United States and the other countries that may be relevant to teenage pregnancy concerns the overall extent and nature of poverty. Poverty to the degree that exists in the United States is essentially unknown in Europe. Regardless of which way the political winds are blowing, Western European governments are committed to the philosophy of the welfare state. The Dutch and the Swedes have been especially successful in achieving reasonably egalitarian societies, but even in England and Wales and France, the contrast between those who are better off and those who are less well off is not so great as it is in the United States. In every country, when respondents were pressed to describe the kind of young woman who would be most likely to bear a child, the answer was the same: adolescents who have been deprived, emotionally as well as economically, and who unrealistically seek gratification and fulfillment in a child of their own. Such explanations are also given in the United States, but they tend to apply to a much larger proportion of people growing up in a culture of poverty. No data are available that would have made it possible to examine adolescent pregnancy in terms of teenagers' family income. However, as noted earlier, the 37-country study found that more equitable distribution of household income is associated with lower teenage fertility—at least among the younger teenagers.

POLICY IMPLICATIONS

The 37-country study and the individual country studies provide convincing evidence that many widely held beliefs about teenage pregnancy cannot explain the large differences in adolescent pregnancy rates found between the United States and other developed countries: Teenagers in these other countries apparently are *not* too immature to use contraceptives consistently and effectively; the level and availability of welfare services does *not* seem correlated with higher adolescent fertility; teenage pregnancy rates are *lower* in countries where there is *greater* availability of contraceptive services and of sex education; levels of adolescent sexual activity in the United States are not very different from those in countries with much *lower* teenage pregnancy rates; although the teenage pregnancy rate of American blacks is much higher than that of whites, this difference does not explain the gap between the pregnancy rates in the United States and the other countries; teenage unemployment appears to be at least as serious a problem in all the countries studied as it is in the United States; and American teenagers have more, or at least as much, schooling as those in most of the countries studied. The other case-study countries have more extensive public health and welfare benefit systems, and they do not have so extensive and economically deprived an underclass as does the United States.

Clearly, then, it *is* possible to achieve lower teenage pregnancy rates even in the presence of high rates of sexual activity, and a number of countries have done so. Although no single factor has been found to be responsible for the differences in adolescent pregnancy rates between the Untied States and the other five countries, is there anything to be learned from these countries' experience that can be applied to improve the situation in the United States?

A number of factors that have been discussed here, of course, are not easily transferable, or are not exportable at all, to the United States: Each of the other five case-study countries is considerably smaller, and all but Canada are more compact than the United States—making rapid dissemination of innovations easier; their populations are less heterogeneous ethnically (though not so homogenous as is commonly assumed—most have substantial minority nonwhite populations, usually with higher–than–average fertility); religion, and the influence of conservative religious bodies, is less pervasive in the other countries than it is in the United States; their governments tend to be more centralized; the provision of wide-ranging social and welfare benefits is firmly established, whether the country is led by parties labeled conservative or liberal; income distribution is less unequal than it is in the United States; and constituencies that oppose contraception, sex education and legal abortion are not so powerful or well funded as they are in the United States.

Some factors associated with low pregnancy rates that *are*, at least theoretically, transferable receive varying levels of emphasis in each country. For example, school sex education appears to be a much more important factor in Sweden than it is in the other countries; a high level of exposure to contraceptive information and sex-related topics through the media is prominent in the Netherlands; condoms are more widely available in England, the Netherlands and Sweden. Access to the pill by teenagers is probably easiest in the Netherlands.

On the other hand, although initiation of sexual activity may begin slightly earlier in the United States than in the other countries (except for Sweden), none of the others have developed official programs designed to discourage teenagers from having sexual relations—a program intervention that is now advocated and subsidized by the U.S. government. The other countries have tended to leave such matters to parents and churches or to teenagers' informed judgments.

By and large, of all the countries studied, Sweden has been the most active in developing programs and policies to reduce teenage pregnancy. These efforts include universal education in sexuality and contraception; development of special clinics—closely associated with the schools—where young people receive contraceptive services and counseling; free, widely available and confidential contraceptive and abortion services; widespread advertising of contraceptives in all media; frank treatment of sex; and availability of condoms from a variety of sources. It is notable that Sweden has *lower* teenage pregnancy rates than have all of the countries examined, except for the Netherlands, although teenagers begin intercourse at earlier ages in Sweden. It is also noteworthy that Sweden is the only one of the countries observed to have shown a rapid decline in teenage abortion rates in recent years, even after its abortion law was liberalized.

The study findings point to several approaches observed in countries other than Sweden that also might help reduce teenage pregnancy rates in the United

States. These include upgrading the family planning clinic system to provide free or low-cost contraceptive services to *all* teenagers who want them, and publicizing the fact that these services are not limited to the poor; establishment of special adolescent clinics, including clinics associated with schools, to provide confidential contraceptive services as part of general health care; encouraging local school districts to provide comprehensive sex education programs, where possible, closely integrated with family planning clinic services; relaxation of restrictions on distribution and advertising of nonprescription contraceptives, especially the condom; dissemination of more realistic information about the health benefits, as well as the health risks, of the pill; and approval of the use of postcoital methods.

In sum, increasing the legitimacy and availability of contraception and sex education (in its broadest sense) is likely to result in declining teenage pregnancy rates. That has been the experience of many countries of Western Europe, and there is no reason to think that such an approach would not also be successful in the United States.

Admittedly, application of any of the program and policy measures that appear to have been effective in other countries is more difficult in the United States nationally, where government authority is far more diffused. But their application may, in fact, be as easy or easier in some states and communities. Efforts need to be directed not just to the federal executive branch of government, but to Congress, the courts, state legislatures, local authorities and school superintendents and principals—as well as to families and such private-sector and charitable enterprises as insurance companies, broadcast and publishing executives, church groups and youth-serving agencies.

Among the most striking of the observations common to the four European countries included in the six-country study is the degree to which the governments of those countries, whatever their political persuasion, have demonstrated the clear-cut will to reduce levels of teenage pregnancy. Pregnancy, rather than adolescent sexual activity itself, is identified as the major problem. Through a number of routes, with varying emphasis on types of effort, the governments of those countries have made a concerted, public effort to help sexually active young people to avoid unintended pregnancy and childbearing. In the United States, in contrast, there has been no well-defined expression of political will. Political and religious leaders, particularly, appear divided over what their primary mission should be: the eradication or discouragement of sexual activity among young unmarried people, or the reduction of teenage pregnancy through promotion of contraceptive use.

American teenagers seem to have inherited the worst of all possible worlds regarding their exposure to messages about sex: Movies, music, radio and TV tell them that sex is romantic, exciting, titillating; premarital sex and cohabitation are visible ways of life among the adults they see and hear about; their own parents or their parents' friends are likely to be divorced or separated but involved in sexual relationships. Yet, at the same time, young people get the message good girls should say no. Almost nothing that they see or hear about sex informs them about contraception or the importance of avoiding pregnancy. For example, they are more likely to hear about abortions than about contraception on the daily TV soap opera. Such messages lead to an ambivalence about sex that stifles communication and exposes young people to increased risk of pregnancy, out-of-wedlock births and abortions.

APPENDIX

Two criteria were applied in defining "developed" countries for the statistical analysis in the 37-country study: a total fertility rate of less than 3.5 children per woman, and a per capita income level of over $2,000 a year. A population size boundary of at least one million was also imposed. Three of the 40 countries that qualified for inclusion—Argentina, Trinidad and Tobago, and Uruguay—were dropped from the analysis because they had no recent data on teenage fertility. Cuba was included despite the fact that no per capita income data were available. Where possible, England and Wales were treated as a separate country from Scotland. It should be stressed that the final group of 37 countries constitute a universe rather than a sample, so that statistical inferences based on sampling theory cannot be made from the findings.

Initially, eight dependent variables* involving teenage birthrates and pregnancy rates were selected for consideration, allowing for the varying coverage and precision of the data. Since the correlation coefficients[†] among these eight variables suggested that the relationship between birthrates and pregnancy rates was quite close—and pregnancy rates were available for fewer than two-fifths of the countries—cumulative birthrates for girls under 18 and for women 18–19 were finally chosen as dependent variables. These were formed by summing the single-year age-specific birthrates across each of the two age spans.

Almost 100 independent variables were initially considered for inclusion in the 37-country study. However, high-quality data for sufficient numbers of countries were not always available, making it necessary to reduce the final number to 42.

A few caveats about the quality of the data used in the bivariate analysis are also in order. It is not possible to tell whether a low correlation indicates the absence of a relationship or is due to shortcomings in the data. In many instances, the measures available are only rough approximations of the concept they were intended to represent, and even though a number of other potential variables were excluded because the data were not comparable from country to country, more subtle forms of noncomparability no doubt remain. In addition, the variables derived from the AGI country survey must be regarded as subject to a considerable margin of error, since they represent informed observation rather than quantitative fact.

It was decided to exclude from the multivariate analysis variables for which 18 or fewer country observations were available and those having a correlation coefficient of less than 0.3 with both dependent variables.

Table 1 shows the correlations between the two dependent and 42 independent variables. The latter are grouped under headings intended to indicate in a general

---

*These were the birthrates for women aged 15–19; cumulative birthrates for women under 20, for women less than 18, and for women 18–19; the pregnancy rate for women aged 15–19; and cumulative pregnancy rates for women 15–19, for women under 20, for women less than 18 and for women 18–19.

[†] The calculation was made only for the countries for which data on adolescent abortion rates were available: Canada, Czechoslovakia, Denmark, England and Wales, Finland, France, Hungary, the Netherlands, New Zealand, Norway, Scotland, Sweden and the United States.

TABLE 1 Zero-order correlations between the independent variables and the cumulative birthrates for women under age 18 and women aged 18–19

Variable	Cumulative birthrate		N
	Women < 18	Women 18–19	
Marriage			
Proportion of females married at ages 15–19	0.83	0.84	37
Minimum age for marriage without parental consent	−0.33	−0.39	24
Childbearing			
Five-year total fertility rate for ages ≥ 20	0.06	0.13	37
Policy to raise fertility	0.25	0.36	35
Liberal policy on maternity leaves and benefits	0.45	0.58	28
Proportion of gov't expenditure on income maintenance and family allowances	−0.19	0.09	17
Paternal financial support (Q)	0.07	0.21	31
Contraception			
Proportion of all currently married using the pill	−0.18	−0.17	20
Proportion of all currently married using condoms	−0.63	−0.58	13
Policy to provide contraceptives for young, unmarried women (Q)	−0.46	−0.44	36
Favorable policy on teaching contraception (Q)	−0.21	−0.06	37
Proportion of female students taught about contraception (Q)	−0.31	−0.17	36
Age at which contraception is taught	0.12	0.17	28
Abortion			
Abortions per woman 15–44*	0.67	0.77	24
Parental consent for abortion not required (Q)	0.01	−0.04	33
Public funding of abortions (Q)	0.05	0.26	29
Sex			
Open about sex (Q)	−0.50	−0.51	37
Minimum age for consensual intercourse†(Q)	0.30	0.24	34
Proportion of female students in coeducational schools (Q)	−0.00	0.04	36
Health			
Population per physician	0.12	0.05	34
Maternal mortality	0.43	0.51	35
Per capita gov't expenditure on health care	−0.13	−0.11	19
Education			
Proportion of secondary-school-age females attending school	−0.13	−0.27	31
Proportion of females 15–19 attending school	−0.20	−0.12	14
Per capita gov't expenditure on education	−0.44	−0.38	18
Social Integration			
Total marital divorce rate	−0.26	−0.27	19
Mortality rate from liver cirrhosis	0.34	0.35	34
Incidence of suicide at ages 15–24	−0.17	−0.15	30
Proportion foreign-born	−0.35	−0.28	19
General social conditions			
Log of population density	−0.18	−0.13	35
Proportion fo cities with populations ≥ 500,000	−0.12	−0.32	34
Proportion of labor force in agriculture	0.60	0.66	34
Religiosity	0.66	0.67	13

TABLE 1 (Continued)

Employment			
Labor-force participation rate for females 15–19	0.28	0.11	15
Labor-force participation rate for males 15–19	0.11	0.02	15
Proportion of labor force female	0.22	0.39	33
Labor-force participation rate for females 35–44	0.35	0.42	18
Overall unemployment rate†	0.15	0.16	27
General economic conditions			
Gross national product per capita	−0.51	−0.61	33
Average annual growth in gross domestic product	−0.16	−0.11	
Proportion of total household income distributed to top 10% of population	0.06	0.00	14
Proportioin of total household income distributed to bottom 20% of population	−0.41	−0.14	19

*Excluding Japan.

†Excluding Puerto Rico.

Note: Q = comes from the AGI country questionnaire.

way the nature of their possible link to adolescent fertility. The variables associated with low adolescent birthrates (ranked according to degree of correlation) are GNP per capita; openness about sex; a government policy to provide contraceptives to young, unmarried women; a high proportion of household income distributed to the bottom 20 percent of the population; a high proportion of the population foreign-born (the last two for younger teenagers only); a high minimum age at marriage without parental consent; a high percentage of women taught about contraception in the schools (for younger teenagers only); and a high percentage of the population living in large cities (for older teenagers only).

Associated with high teenage birthrates are a high percentage of the labor force engaged in agriculture; a generous policy of maternity leaves and benefits; high levels of maternal mortality; a government policy to raise fertility; a high proportion of the labor force composed of women (the last two for older teens only); a high rate of mortality from liver cirrhosis—a proxy for alcoholism; and a high minimum age for consensual intercourse (for younger teenagers only).

Two variables with high correlation coefficients and for which 19 or more country observations were available were not used for the multivariate analysis because of their special status as intermediate variables closely correlated with birthrates. These were the proportion of females married at ages 15–19 and the abortion rate for women aged 15–44.

High correlation coefficients were obtained for the variables proportion of married women whose partner used condoms (negative) and the level of religiosity in the country (positive), but too few countries had this information to meet the requirement for inclusion in the multivariate analysis.

The multivariate analysis was based primarily on ordinary least-squares regression. The approach taken was determined by the need to minimize the problems associated with very small sample size and the substantial amount of missing data. First, step-wise procedures were used to identify the three independent variables having the greatest impact on each dependent variable, and then the remaining independent variables were added one at a time to assess how much variation each of them could explain over and above that accounted for by the initial three. A brief discussion of the results of the multivariate analysis can be found in the text (see pages 565–567).

NOTES

1. C. F. Westoff, G. Calot and A. D. Foster, "Teenage Fertility in Developed Nations," *Family Planning Perspectives*, 15:105, 1983.

2. C. Tietze, *Induced Abortion: A World Review*, 1983, Fifth ed., The Population Council, New York, 1983, Tables 5 and 7.

3. M. Zelnik and J. F. Kantner, "Sexual Activity: Contraceptive Use and Pregnancy Among Metopolitan-Area Teenagers," *Family Planning Perspectives*, 12:230, 1980, Table 6.

4. See, for example: F. F. Furstenberg, Jr., R. Lincoln and J. Menken, eds., *Teenage Sexuality, Pregnancy and Childbearing*, University of Pennsylvania Press, Philadelphia, 1981, pp. 163–300.

5. S. B. Kamerman, A. J. Kahn and P. Kingston, *Maternity Policies and Working Women*, Columbia University Press, New York, 1983.

6. R. F. Badgley, D. F. Caron and M. G. Powell, *Report of the Committee on the Operation of the Abortion Law*, Minister of Supply and Services, Ottawa, 1977; K. Dunnel, *Family Formation*, 1976, Office of Population Censuses and Surveys, Social Survey Division, Her Majesty's Stationery Office, London. 1979: "Amour: La Première fois. . . . " (Sondage SOFRES), *Le Nouvel Observateur*, Mar. 23–29, 1984, pp. 46–53; *Sex in Nederland*, Het Spectrum, Utrecht/Antwerp, 1983; M. Zelnik and J. F. Kantner, "Sexual and Contraceptive Experience of Young Unmarried Women in the United States, 1976 and 1971," *Family Planning Perspectives*, 9:55, 1977, M. Zelnik and J. F. Kantner, 1980, op. cit. (see reference 3); B. Lewin, "The Adolescent Boy and Girl: First and Other Early Experiences with Intercourse from a Representative Sample of Swedish School Adolescents," *Archives of Sexual Behavior*, Vol. 11, No. 5, 1985; and B. Andersch and I. Milsom, "Contraception and Pregnancy Among Young Women in an Urban Swedish Population," *Contraception*, 26:211, 1982.

7. E. E. Kisker, "Teenagers Talk About Sex, Pregnancy and Contraception," *Family Planning Perspectives*, 17:83, 1985.

8. L. S. Zabin and S. D. Clark, Jr., "Why They Delay: A Study of Teenage Family Planning Clinic Patients," *Family Planning Perspectives*, 13:205, 1981, Table 10.

9. *Sex in Nederland*, 1983, op. cit. (see reference 7), Table 4.8, and B. K. Singh, "Trends in Attitudes Towards Premarital Sexual Relations," *Journal of Marriage and the Family*, 42:2, 1980.

10. Center for Applied Research in the Apostolate, "Value Systems Study Group of the Americas," Washington, D.C., July 1982, Table 8.

32

Sneaker Mothers*

Terry M. Williams and William Kornblum

Be ready for responsibility and independence because it's something every woman and girl has to go through alone. And I think that once you have a baby you might as well get ready for a life, your life and someone else's life. You have to try to make a good life for both and to do that, no games and not too much fun, you have to be fully prepared to take care. It slows a young person down a hell of a lot.

—a teenage mother

"Sex is a wonderful experience, a beautiful feeling," writes short, feisty Regina Eugene. "Making love can be extremely beautiful, especially if you have deep feelings for your sex partner. I have never made love to any man that I didn't have deep feelings for."

"Sex, it's a motherfucker," says Regina's friend Yolanda, "especially when you end up with a big stomach."

Both Regina and Yolanda are nineteen, and both have had "big stomachs." They are among the "sneaker mothers"—the 10 percent of 15- to 19-year-olds who become pregnant each year. There are a million others like them. Over 60 percent of these pregnancies result in live births, and in most cases the young woman decides to raise her own child. Usually she does not marry the baby's father.

The sneaker mothers do not consider themselves particularly sexual. For them, sex is part of a recreational pattern that also includes desultory TV watching, frequent marijuana smoking, and the consumption of vast quantities of pizza and pop. The following exchange between Regina and her "man," Vernon, is typical.

Vernon: Are you still going uptown?
Regina: Yes, later on.
Vernon: What time?
Regina: About two.
Vernon: Why so late?
Regina: Because I'm going to wash my hair, I'm hot.
Vernon: Why don't you come over here and wash your hair and do it in the air conditioner?
Regina: You going to come over here and get me?
Vernon: Are you ready?
Regina: No, but by the time you get here I will be.

*Williams, Terry M. and William Kornblum. 1985. "Sneaker Mothers." Pp. 83–96 in *Growing Up Poor*. Lexington, MA: Lexington Books. Reprinted by permission of the publisher. Copyright 1985, D. C. Heath and Company.

This essay is based on extensive research by Lorraine Mayfield among teenage mothers in Louisville, Meridian, and New York City.

(I got dressed and Vernon was here faster than I thought he would be; however, I was ready. We went into the cool house. We smoked a couple of joints and laid in the bed watching TV. TV watching led to love making.)

Vernon: I'm hungry.
Regina: What do you want?
Vernon: Pizza sounds good.
Regina: You going to get one?
Vernon: I guess I will.

(Vernon put his shoes on and left, I sat there and watched TV. When Vernon got back he cooked the pizza. We ate the pizza sitting on the floor acting silly. After eating the pizza, we sat on the couch and smoked a few joints.)

Teenagers like Regina and Yolanda have active sexual lives from an early age—sometimes as early as twelve. Part of the reason for this is lack of adult supervision. As one young mother explained, "I was given a great deal of freedom at an early age. My mother had left my father because he would beat her and my father would stay out of the house for days at a time. Although I had older brothers, I was able to go out and stay out as late as I pleased."

A far more telling reason than lack of supervision is a view of sex that denies its consequences. Teenagers in all of the communities we studied, while they are aware of the consequences of sexual activity, do not take responsibility for them. To them, pregnancy is a sort of occupational hazard. Nowhere is this more evident than in the following exchange between Regina and her aptly nicknamed friend Tiny:

Regina: Do you engage in sex?
Tiny: Yes.
Regina: Do you use protection?
Tiny: No, because I have been on pills for seven and a half years. The doctor told me I need a rest from the pills.
Regina: How often do you have sex?
Tiny: Four times a week.
Regina: Do you engage in oral sex?
Tiny: No, but I will when I get married.

These young women are not promiscuous. Almost without exception, they have sex with only one partner, usually a steady boyfriend. Tiny lived with her parents in a small wood-framed house in Louisville. She often skipped school to have sex with her boyfriend and would on occasion invite him over after her parents went to work. Going steady meant sex on a regular basis with him. For the girls, going out with one boy by age sixteen or seventeen was important socially because unlike the boys, the girls had to have one relationship at a time to avoid the stigma of being "fast." And in most of these communities being "fast" is one step short of being a whore. Sex is a way of pleasing—and in some cases keeping—a man. Often it is looked upon as a gift—a birthday or Christmas present. Our notes about one of the girls, 16-year-old Pestac of Harlem, illustrate this.

Pestac first had sex in December after having dinner with her boyfriend, her close girlfriend, and her girlfriend's boyfriend (they all attend the same school). After dinner they went to a hotel. Pestac wasn't planning to have sex even at this point. She argued while in the room but decided to have sex thinking she was giving her boyfriend a "Christmas present." Before going to her hotel room, her girlfriend offered her one of her birth control pills. Pestac refused the pill. Up until this point, Pestac was a virgin. She didn't think about getting pregnant.

Pestac is a slight, quiet girl who dresses neatly and avoids the life of the streets. Yet like many other teens she neglected to take precautions against becoming pregnant.

Why do so many young women have sex without protection? Surely the sneaker mothers don't intend to get pregnant, at least not consciously. Yet 70 percent of them do not use any form of birth control. By and large, they are either uninformed or misinformed on this subject. They are especially hostile to the pill, claiming that it causes headaches, cancer, blood clots, obesity, ulcers, and a variety of other ailments. The IUD is accused of causing pain, excessive bleeding, and cramping, while the diaphragm is scorned as a "middle-class method" that interferes with sexual spontaneity.

As a result of this very widespread attitude, most of the teenage mothers are pregnant within a year after beginning their sexual lives. Only after giving birth do they seek a birth-control method in order to avoid future pregnancies, usually at the urging of their mothers and fathers, aunts, or sisters to "get something." Since the "something" is unspecified, the choice of a birth control method is often a difficult decision that is greatly influenced by the advice of poorly informed friends.

Of the young mothers we studied, 80 percent were using some form of birth control to prevent future pregnancies. This protection is often used intermittently or incorrectly, however, so that over 40 percent have had second pregnancies that were terminated by abortion.

The extent of misinformation about birth control is surprising given the fact that the majority of the teenage mothers have had a sex education course in school, and half of them received sex education before becoming pregnant. Apparently it didn't sink in, as can be seen in the following comments by teenage mothers:

Barbara, age 17: I had a sex ed course in elementary school. I was confused about some words and I don't remember any talk about contraception, only the pill.

Linda, age 17: I found the course boring and I tried to cut that course as often as possible. I didn't know how it applied to my life. I wish I had listened.

Cynthia, age 15: My teacher taught us about sex and birth control in a hygiene class. We saw some films, but that was it on the topic. We didn't spend much time on it.

Janet, age 14: No one understood, but no one asked any questions.

A visit to a sex education class in a slum high school reveals the source of much of the teenagers' confusion. Often the class takes the form of a study period in which the students construct outlines from their hygiene books. Each student works individually; sometimes they whisper questions to each other if they don't understand a word or concept, but there is little opportunity to discuss human reproduction or birth control methods, and little interaction between the teacher and the students. Under these circumstances not much learning can take place. When teenagers do get accurate information about reproduction and contraception, it is usually from health-care professionals. But the sequence of events is usually pregnancy first, birth control second.

Since most teenage mothers do not intend to become pregnant, their initial reaction to pregnancy is shock and depression, followed fairly soon by acceptance. A typical comment is, "If God wants me to have children, there is nothing I can do about it." In some cases, however, there is a long period of denial—especially among very young mothers who have just begun to menstruate. In these cases acceptance may not occur until the third or fourth month of pregnancy, after a period of immense confusion. There are a few cases. also, in which the initial reaction is largely positive: "I was shocked, but happy."

Pregnant teenagers do not immediately share their feelings with their parents. More often they confide the news of their pregnancy to their girlfriends or sisters. Only after a month or so do they tell their parents. Sometimes the parents find out from other sources. Their daughters are afraid to tell them, and the girls' fear is usually justified by their parents' reactions to the news: "My mother and father argued at each other because I got pregnant. My daddy tried to whip me, my mother tried to work me to death."

In most cases the parents are very despondent about their daughter's pregnancy. By the time they find out about it, it is usually too late to do anything but anticipate having a grandchild. This prospect is generally shocking and disappointing, but eventually, if family resources allow, the grandchild is welcomed. Parental acceptance may be eased by the fact that in many cases the mother herself had her first child in her teens.

Once an adolescent learns that she is pregnant, she frequently has the option of getting an abortion. Overwhelmingly, the young mothers are against abortion, viewing it as criminal, sinful, or both. "I would never kill a baby" is a typical comment, as is "It's like going out in the streets and killing an old person. I think people should be locked up for having an abortion."

Some of the young mothers in rural Mississippi, where legal and safe abortion services are not available, are deterred by economics more than by ethics. As one teenager put it, "I think it's okay [an abortion]. I would have had one myself, if I could have gotten to Jackson. When I realized I was pregnant, it was too late. I was broke anyway."

For some pregnant teenagers, timing is the crucial factor in the decision for or against an abortion. Most abortions, particularly those using the D and C method, are performed during the first trimester of pregnancy. In New York State it is possible to have a legal abortion until the sixth month using the saline method. This method, however, is more expensive, more dangerous, and less available than the D and C. Thus, for most teenagers who consider an abortion, it must occur within the first three months of pregnancy. And as noted earlier, since many teenagers deny the fact of their pregnancy until after the third month, they are left with no choice but to bear the child.

If the pregnancy is not terminated (that is, in the great majority of cases), the young girl becomes a mother. In nine months she makes the transition from childhood to adulthood. Her life is transformed. Gone are the adolescent pleasures of going to movies, partying, spending money on snacks and clothes. Now she is responsible for preparing formulas, feeding her always-hungry infant, and taking care of it almost all the time. Instant maturity.

We do not use the phrase "instant maturity" lightly. For one thing, having a child is a symbol of maturity and (after an initial period of adjustment) is seen as such by the young mother's relatives and friends. Motherhood confers a specific identity where before there may have been only a restless searching; moreover, for better or worse this society regards motherhood as an occupation. This is an important fact in an environment that offers few alternatives to motherhood—a fact that is implicitly recognized by teenagers who postpone sexual activity until after they have graduated from high school.

For some young mothers, the rapid shift from childhood to adulthood is a positive experience. Carol J. of Meridian, a friendly, articulate young woman, is one of the fortunate ones.

> I had been working at a local nursery for over three years, so I had been saving money for [the baby's] arrival. I had moral and financial support from my mother and the child's father. With their support I felt as though I could endure anything. Since we still had a close relationship, his support was vital.
>
> My son Benjamin was born on May 20, 1978, at Anderson Hospital. Until I had gone through labor, I didn't realize my situation. It wasn't until we got home that I suddenly realized that I was a mother. It was a shock to finally see the baby that I had carried for nine months, finally where I could touch him. I had a good delivery, that took only five minutes. All through my pregnancy I read literature on babies, in order to strengthen my background on the subject. I wanted to know all about the do's and don'ts of baby care. After working at a nursery and saving my money, I felt that I could take care of my child or anyone else's child efficiently.
>
> Now my son is 1 1/2 years old. He is steadily growing, learning, and surprising me each and every day. My child is my main motivation for living, because I want to provide for all of his needs. Each day he brings me love, laughter, and joy, and these things make my day brighter and fuller.
>
> Never once have I regretted having my baby. I would never take a moment from my pregnancy. The pregnancy did complicate my life some, but to me it was worth it. Before I became pregnant I planned to join the Army to better my education and skills. These plans haven't changed, they were just delayed.

For most teenagers, becoming pregnant means dropping out of school. Even if they stay in until the baby is born, they drop out afterwards to take care of the child. Yet most mothers express a desire to complete their education—later.

A few pregnant teenagers transfer to special schools for pregnant students. These schools tend to be poorly funded and not very numerous (the five such schools in New York City serve approximately 650 of the 15,000 pregnant teenagers there). Their personnel is limited, and as a result the curriculum is also restricted. Thus the majority simply drop out.

Educators are aware that pregnancy is one of the main reasons that female teenagers drop out of school. In one high school we found that over 75 percent of the girls who became pregnant while attending the school did not graduate. The principal suggested that it is difficult to establish the pregnancy rate for teenagers who have already dropped out. An assistant principal called the surrounding housing projects a "baby factory" where many of his students had become pregnant in the preceding year. The health counselor expressed similar sentiments. Often, like parents, she learns that a teenager is pregnant in the third or fourth month, so that there are few options concerning the outcome of the pregnancy. Although the girls are able to continue their education at their local high schools, the teachers and school authorities do not encourage them to do so.

Many teenage mothers who drop out of school express the opinion that school is boring or that they are tired of it. Quite a number consider their fellow students silly, immature, and not really interested in learning. Adolescent parents who think of school in this fashion are unlikely to return to or remain in school. As one teenage mother put it, "After dropping out, it is difficult to get into the groove of school." An added factor for many young mothers is the fact that returning to school will mean repeating a grade before continuing.

In addition to these psychological barriers to continued education, the young mothers face economic and logistical barriers. Carmen's situation is a good example. Carmen is an attractive 18-year-old Puerto Rican mother with a six-month-old son. When we met her she was interested in returning to school, from which she had dropped out in the seventh month of her pregnancy. During the time she was pregnant she had left her mother's house and found an apartment, which she shared with her boyfriend for three months. Her boyfriend (who eventually left after a quarrel) discouraged her from attending school, saying that it was important for her to stay home and care for the baby. After he left, Carmen found a roommate, Angie, to share her three-and-a-half-room apartment. Angie was an 18-year-old mother with a eighteen-month-old son. Because of her responsibilities as a parent, numerous welfare and hospital appointments, and an active social life, Angie did not provide any help, either emotional or financial, for Carmen. In fact, within two months Carmen asked her to leave because she had not contributed toward the payment of any of the bills, including rent and electricity.

Carmen was left to run the household and take care of her baby. Her dream of returning to school became increasingly remote until she invited two male homosexual friends to live with her. For a while they were helpful. The run-down fourth-floor walkup was painted bright yellow and green. And 16-year-old Jose, who had dropped out of school, volunteered to watch the baby while Carmen returned to the local high school.

During a period of about two months Carmen left her baby with Jose and went to school, struggling to write book reports and do her math. Then she and Jose had a fight and she put him out of her apartment. She dropped out of school again, saying that she felt overwhelmed by trying to do everything herself.

Staying in school is only one of several major problems facing teenage mothers. Even more pressing is the question of how to make a living. Although most of the young mothers have a work history (that is, 75 percent have worked at either a part-time or summer job), eight out of ten are dependent on public assistance for their support. Often the welfare check alone is insufficient to cover expenses. Some of the girls find occasional small jobs to do. Others are low-level drug dealers and hustlers of one kind or another. In addition, a kinship-based support system in low-income black communities provides either complete or partial financial assistance. In most cases the baby's father is unable to provide financial support because he is either not working or does not have enough money to help out.

Many of the young mothers have worked in fast-food chains as cashiers, food processors, or waitresses, or as clerks in local firms and hospitals, or as baby-sitters. But in today's economy even such low-paying jobs are scarce, and as a result most of the sneaker mothers are unemployed. Carol J. describes how it feels to be unemployed after having worked steadily for several years.

I have been working for Smith's Nursery going on four years. I enjoyed my job, working with the small children. Then in the 11th grade I became pregnant. In April, I got laid off. Being laid off is a terrible experience. I would never have made it, if I had not taken my mother's advice. My mother taught us to always save your money, look towards the future. I still have the same ideals.

I was laid off in April of 1978. I was without a paycheck for five months. I went to the unemployment office to see if I could draw my unemployment. The woman I spoke to said that "you must be able to work right now." Here I was, had been working three years at the place and can't even draw my unemployment pennies.

One month and two weeks later, I gave birth to a healthy 6 lb. 3 1/2 ounce baby boy. I still had no income for six weeks. After my six weeks were up, I went back to the unemployment office. This time I was able to sign up, but received my first check after three weeks of going down there for interviews. I was desperate for a job, but none was to be found.

When I finally got my check in June, my income was $112 a month. As hard as things were, every little bit helps. I lived off of unemployment compensation until the first week in September. In September, I went back to my old job at the nursery.

Another teenager expressed the meaning of work for a young mother.

When one doesn't have a job, it can mean being without money a lot of times. There are times when I may want to buy myself something or my baby, but I just can't. It feels pretty bad to walk in a place and want something you can't buy. It is frustrating to go look for work and don't find any. It even hurts worse when I try one particular job and fail, and someone else comes along and gets it.

When I don't have a job I have to depend on others. I hate to depend on welfare, because they only give you $60.00 a month for one child. My parents will help if I ask, but I like to be independent.

I wouldn't want a job as much if I didn't have a child. I like to be able to buy my child some of the things that she wants. I even like to buy little extras for her sometimes, but being jobless, I have to buy just what's needed. When one is jobless that means they can't even save for the future for themselves or family.

I keep hoping that jobs in the area will start hiring. I always go looking for jobs, and when there aren't any available, I feel better knowing that I tried. When I first became jobless it felt bad, but after a while I learned to accept it.

Even when jobs are available, it is difficult to find one at a salary sufficient to cover all of a young mother's expenses. Yolanda's experience is typical:

I had a job as a clerk. I quit because I couldn't make enough to pay my baby-sitter and take care of my baby and me. I didn't think it was fair working all day away from my baby and then not making enough to buy anything, like food and clothes for me and the baby.

For most teenage mothers there is a threshold salary at which it becomes worthwhile to go out to work. Most of the jobs for which they might qualify pay less than that. Only one-fourth of the young mothers in our study had jobs. Usually they worked as typist-receptionists, clerk-typists, or waitresses. Many others expressed interest in obtaining a G.E.D. (equivalent to a high school diploma) and seeking out manpower employment and training programs in which they could learn a specific skill.

The experience of teenage mothers in training programs is generally unfavorable. Few such programs include child-care arrangements that facilitate all-day involvement by the mother. In addition, the programs are reluctant to accept pregnant teenagers and young mothers because they fear that these participants are more likely to have "negative terminations" and that they will be difficult to place. They also believe that parental responsibilities interfere with a teenager's ability to participate fully in such a program. In short, young mothers who attempt to enter job training programs often face discrimination by program officials.

Could all of these problems be avoided if the young mother married the child's father? The answer, in most cases, is no. As noted at the beginning of this essay, it is unusual for poor teenage parents to marry. This is true for many reasons, not the least of which is the young people's own desire for personal freedom—freedom to date others, to continue their education, perhaps to travel or even migrate. The teenagers' parents also generally discourage marriage (forced marriage is unheard of), particularly if the baby's father is not working. In the background is the recognition that teenage marriages are often short-lived.

In reality, marriage has little to offer compared to the relative security to be found in the kinship network, usually combined with welfare benefits. Even if the baby's father has a job, it is usually temporary, poorly paid, and subject to layoffs. As a result, poor teenagers of both sexes tend to view marriage as a goal to be realized at some indefinite future time. As one young father put it—rather sadly—"I'm not ready yet. I still have nothing to offer you or my baby."

The result of this situation is that teenage fathers (if they are aware of their paternity) often enter the kinship network as friends of the family—someone the young mother can call upon for occasional help. While there are some cases in which teenage parents live together, marriage is unlikely unless the couple's economic prospects are relatively secure. This point of view is reflected in our notes on Sue H., an 18-year-old Louisville mother who strongly desires a better standard of living.

> Sue had planned to marry Sidney, the father of her baby. He had been her boyfriend since age 15. Sidney is a 23-year-old high-school dropout. He moved into Sue's apartment as soon as she got it. At the time he wasn't working and couldn't provide anything for the household. Sue decided not to get married right away, thinking that she could do better on her own. She found that Sidney wasn't much help. Sidney has worked for CETA and helped with the bills. At present he is unemployed.
>
> Sue said that Sidney is considering going into the Army. She would like that and would consider marrying him if he did.

Presently, Sue is not happy with Sidney, particularly since he is not working. Sue considers him lazy and would like to have him leave, although she doesn't want to put him out into the cold.

In the end, what it comes down to is the reality of the baby's presence. Sooner or later every teenage mother comes face to face with the fact that her life has changed and that the change is permanent. In conversations with these young women one often hears a note of wistfulness about their lost childhood. They often mention not having free time in which to participate in the activities enjoyed by their friends. At a deeper level, they are out of the mainstream of adolescent life. They spend most of their time caring for the baby—which translates into being virtually alone during most of the day.

When asked how her life has changed, a 16-year-old mother said, "It affected me in every way. I don't have no one to keep [my baby]. I'm young and I like to go out. I can't find a good man for staying home with the baby." Another young mother adds, "I don't never have time for myself, a baby always needs attention." And one of our community research assistants had this to say about her friend LJ: "She's a nice girl and everything. I mean she doesn't smoke, drink, get high or any of those things, but her mother doesn't let her go anywhere. All she do is cook, clean up, and take care of her baby. She's sort of like a modern-day Cinderella."

One result of this situation is an excessive amount of TV watching interspersed with time spent with the child. The following excerpt from the diary of a teenage mother is typical:

> The baby and I got up at 9:00 a.m. I fed her and played with her. By 12:00 she was asleep. So I took a bath, brushed my teeth, ate, combed my hair, and put on some clothes. And watched my stories [soap operas] on TV until 2:00. Then the baby got up so I gave her a bath, combed her hair, put some clothes on her. About 3:00 I fed her again and watched some more TV and talked with my grandmother. Around 4:00 my sister called.

Many young mothers, while they love their babies, describe them as greedy and demanding. They are disappointed when the baby doesn't return their love. This can be quite traumatic for a young woman who already feels isolated from her friends (who are busy with school or work) and her parents (who have not yet accepted the fact that they are grandparents). Often the baby's father has discontinued the relationship and the mother feels abandoned. Carmen expressed these sentiments after her boyfriend left. She was quite depressed and would spend long hours in front of the television set watching game shows, the "stories," and the afternoon movie. She took care of her baby, but during this time she didn't take care of herself. She didn't comb her hair, and she wore the same dark blue sweatshirt and faded jeans every day. Sometimes tears came to her eyes as she spoke of the life she was leading and her feeling that she had no control over it.

For some of the sneaker mothers life is not so difficult. This is especially true if the young woman has the support of other family members—mother, grandmother, sisters—who provide financial support, child care, and other forms of assistance. While there are cases in which the girl's mother or grandmother takes over completely, in other situations the young mother and her relatives are able to maintain a balanced, generally positive relationship. such a relationship can be seen in the following exchange between Judy Stone, a resident of Cotter Homes in Louisville, and her mother:

> (I went out on the porch, looked in the mail box. Both of my checks were there. I went and asked mama to take me to the bank.)
>
> Mother: Girl, don't you know, that is a blessing, you ought to really be thankful. I be right back. You get the baby together while I get myself ready, okay! (So I got the checks cashed, went to the store, put a few outfits in the layaway. Went and ate lunch and rode around for a while, then we went back home.)
>
> Judy: Mama, I sure do thank you. Without your help I don't think we could make it.
>
> Mother: Yes, you could, honey, 'cause God is on your side. You could make it without me. Don't ever say that 'cause you've got more than some others. Be grateful, you hear! I'm going to take a nap. I'll talk to you later.

Despite all the difficulties they face, the sneaker mothers have surprisingly positive attitudes about themselves. In a survey of twenty-five young mothers in New York, we asked several questions aimed at discovering how they felt about themselves. Among other things, they were asked whether they agreed a lot or a little, or disagreed a little or a lot, with the following statements:

1. What happens to me is my own doing.
2. I am able to do things as well as most other people.
3. I have a positive attitude about myself.
4. I feel that I have a number of good qualities.

Overall, the respondents indicated that they felt very good about themselves and did not consider themselves less competent than older mothers. In general, they felt that they are more mature and better able to deal with the world than their contemporaries Renee, a street-wise, self-possessed young woman whose appearance belies her youth, made this very clear:

> Although I am only 17, I feel that I am very mature. I have been on my own for a while and I've done most of the things that my friends are just beginning to do. I feel that I am a woman now. And I want to do the best I can for me and my baby.

Social workers who work with teenage mothers express concern about their emotional condition, their financial difficulties, their interrupted education, and the reactions and supportive capacity of their families. They claim that the teenagers perceive their children as "cute dolls" or possessions. The young mothers are not in touch with the emotional needs and developmental stages of their children. They may overfeed their babies, giving them cereal and whole foods before they can easily digest such foods. One of the major concerns of professionals is that teenage mothers have little understanding of what it means to be a parent, to provide for and love a child. For these and other reasons, greater efforts must be made to locate teenage mothers and assist them in overcoming the barriers they face.

The majority of the young mothers have a work history and know the value and importance of money in raising a family. Almost without exception, they look forward to completing school (usually via the G.E.D.) and going to work. Typical plans for the future are expressed in these comments by teenage mothers:

> I want to go to college and be happy and I hope to be married. But I can't go until I get someone to keep [the baby] because my parents work.

> I want to finish high school and get a job. I'll save some money and get a house in Puerto Rico to raise my family.

Other comments also reflect conventional desires — marriage, family, work:

> I want to have a healthy baby, get married, and go to college.
> I want to have a nursing career and get married with a family.
> I want to get into business school to become a secretary and after getting training, get married.

Most teenage mothers want to work as nurses, secretaries, or accountants. Even when they are unsure of the particular job they want, they envision a life that includes work and family. The majority desire to complete high school, and 75 percent would like to continue their education either in college or in a training program. But returning to school takes on less importance if it will not definitely lead to a job that pays enough to cover both living costs and child care. Judy Stone's comments illustrate this point:

> I learned the lesson my mother was trying to get through my head all of these years. You don't get anything free, rather you can't get something for nothing. I know now you have to get out there and get it on your own. Up to now, I have been lazy, but not any more. I'm going to try my best to find something and go back to school on top of it. I really can't get anywhere without that piece of paper, which I have not got. So then maybe I can go out more than once out of a month, I mean really go out, eat dinner and go out dancing somewhere: have some spending money like I use to. I think I can do it if I really try as long as I keep in my mind who and what I'm doing it for. First my little girl, second myself so maybe we can go some more places that we want to go.
>
> I looked in the paper today, I couldn't find anything. Everything you had to have some kind of training. Like you had to have a high school education or training of some kind or I was too young.
>
> Being unemployed is terrible to me, nothing goes the right way, but I have to get out there and do it. Because nobody else is going to do it for me and I know that now. So I will go back to school and on top of that, when I get out I hope to get a typing job somewhere.

The most serious problem facing young mothers, thus, is not so much how to get into the labor force as how to get sufficient education and/or training to enter the labor force at a salary high enough to support the mother and her child and pay for child care as well. The motivation is there—almost all teenage mothers want to be self-sufficient and some, like Carol J., are very ambitious—but supportive services are lacking. Training programs often discriminate against teenage parents, and day-care facilities are scarce, particularly for children under three, making it difficult for young parents to participate in whatever manpower programs are available. Medical care is available, but teenagers are reluctant to take advantage of it—usually they show up only in an emergency. Hospitals and clinics attempt to reach teenage mothers, but this occurs primarily through the schools—and the young mothers usually have dropped out of school. In sum, although the problems facing teenage parents are numerous and severe, this group is hard to reach and keep track of.

CHAPTER TEN

The Family and the Elderly

33

Older People and Their Families: The New Pioneers*

Ethel Shanas

The theme of this paper is the relationship of older people and their families in the contemporary United States. The title, which really encapsulates the theme, was suggested to me by a thoughtful article by David W. Plath, an anthropologist on the faculty of the University of Illinois at Urbana-Champaign. In discussing the elderly in Japan, Professor Plath (1972) points out that the aged, in Japan, as in many other countries, are treated ambivalently. On the one hand, there are the Confucian precepts that demand honor for the elderly, and for parents in particular. On the other hand, there are the social strains that arise from an increase in both the numbers and the proportion of the elderly in the Japanese population. In his final paragraph, Professor Plath (1972, p. 150) writes:

> Modern society, in Japan as in many nations, has bestowed longevity. It has turned old people loose into new life-span territory. But it has equipped them only with medieval maps, full of freaks and monsters and imaginary harbors. The aged are the true pioneers of our time, and pioneer life is notoriously brutal.

*Shanas, Ethel. 1980. "Older People and Their Families: The New Pioneers." *Journal of Marriage and the Family* 42(1): 9–15. Copyrighted 1980 by National Council on Family Relations,

Burgess Award Address presented at the annual meeting of the National Council on Family Relations in Boston, Massachusetts on August 6, 1979. The 1975 Survey of the Elderly was supported by the U.S. AoA, grant number 90-A-369, and the U.S. Social Security Administration, grant number 10-P-57823. Gloria Heinemann had major responsibility for the preparation of the tabular data.

I have often considered this statement and its implications for the American aged. Ours is a society which, as Irving Rosow states (1976, pp. 457–482), "systematically undermines the position of the elderly and deprives them of major institutional functions." Our society is oriented toward youth. We deprive older people of work, their major source of income, and thus make it impossible for them to compete for goods and services in the marketplace. For older persons who prefer not to work forever, and they are the majority, we downgrade their leisure-time activities and view these as trivial. We accept in the young modes of behavior we condemn or at least frown upon among those in the middle or later years. Barefoot college students on the street do not draw a second glance; barefoot older persons are considered, at best, eccentric and, at worst, mentally incompetent. Discussions about university tenure are confused by the implicit assumption that somehow tenured faculty are all unproductive "old fogies," whereas the ranks of assistant professors abound with unrecognized geniuses. Politicians, as well as performers, undergo hair transplants and hope this will help them look younger. Despite the fact that the men sent to the moon were middle-aged (because, in that strange environment, experience and judgment were deemed to be of utmost importance), we continue to downgrade attributes such as theirs in those we describe as "old."

I agree that the aged in the United States are deprived of major institutional functions. At the same time, I question whether the aged in this country are living in a world with only imaginary harbors as Professor Plath suggests. Are these new pioneers perhaps finding their way to safe havens after all? And, if they are, where are these safe havens for the elderly?

In this paper, I shall try to answer these questions by a consideration of the relations of older persons in the United States and their age distribution. Following this, I shall consider, first, the physical proximity of older persons to their children, siblings, and other relatives; second, family help patterns; third, the four-generation family and some of the role ambiguities it raises for its members; and, finally, what progress the aged as new pioneers are making in their voyage to a safe harbor. Some of the data to be given here comes from the United States Bureau of the Census; the findings on the proximity of older persons and their families, on family help patterns, and on the four-generation family come from three successive nationwide probability surveys of the noninstitutionalized population aged 65 and over, the first of which dates back to 1957, and the most recent of which was completed in 1975. In surveys such as these there are no volunteer subjects. The probability design is such that the chances are 19 out of 20 that the true proportion of any variable will be within the range of estimate reported here, plus and minus one standard deviation. These data then are based on what older people report about themselves, not on what other people say about them.

I should like in this paper to pay tribute to Ernest Watson Burgess, the 1942 president of the National Council on Family Relations, for whom this lecture is named. It was my privilege, first as a student and then as a colleague, to know and work with this extraordinary man. Ernest Burgess died in December, 1966, at the age of 80. From 1916 until his formal retirement in 1951 he taught in the

Department of Sociology at the University of Chicago. After his retirement, until the age of 78, he continued as a consultant at the Industrial Relations Center at that university. Many of the retirement preparation programs now so widely used in government and industry grew out of Dr. Burgess' post-retirement occupation. Ernest Burgess was an innovator in the study of urban sociology, delinquency, gerontology and the family. He himself never married, but many of us were his "intellectual" children and he remained concerned about our work, our welfare, and our families, as long as he lived. At the end, his colleagues and his former students were his family, and they (particularly Donald J. Bogue of the Department of Sociology at the University of Chicago) took the responsibility of providing care and attention to a beloved teacher and sociological pioneer.

THE NUMBERS AND PROPORTIONS
OF OLDER PERSONS

Let us turn to some consideration of the numbers and proportions of older persons in the United States. When is a person old? There is no simple answer to this question. Some 20 years ago the identical question was asked of a cross-section of the American public, aged 21 and over. The findings of that survey are still relevant today. Regardless of his calendar age, the public viewed a man as "young" or "middle-aged" as long as he was vigorous and active. A woman's age, however, was considered to be more closely related to her calendar age. A man, then, is as old as his activities; a woman as old as her birthdays (Shanas 1962). In this country, a calendar age, 65, is used to define the beginning of old age. Other countries use different ages, some less than 65, some more. The use of age 65 rather than another age, for instance, 70, as the mark of old age, then, is a man-made artifact. When the United States enacted its Social Security Legislation in 1935, 65 was selected as the age at which full retirement benefits were available to workers. Sixty-five thus became institutionalized as the threshold of old age.

All the research available, however, shows that people grow old at different rates. One person may be physically old at 60 while another is "young" at 75. The older the age cohort, the less alike are its individual members. There are more differences in functional capacity among persons aged 80 to 90, for example, than among a group of 20-year-olds. Scholars in the field have posited the need for a definition of old age based on function rather than one based on the calendar. However, what the components of such a definition should be are as yet undetermined (Birren and Renner 1977).

Using the calendar definition of old age common in this country, persons aged 65 and over, and, more particularly, persons aged 75 and over, are increasing both in their number and as a proportion of the total population of the United States. We need only look about us in our daily life to see that old people are increasingly visible. For many of us, this visibility of the old is a personal experience, because we have parents and grandparents who may be well over 65. When I began teaching some 30 years ago very few of my senior year students had living grandparents. Now, most of my students have at least one living grandparent, and some even have living great-grandparents.

Census reports document this change in family composition. In 1950, there were about 12.3 million people aged 65 and over. These persons constituted about 8.1 percent of the population, or about one in every 12 or 13 persons. By 1980, there will be about twice as many persons aged 65 and over as there were in 1950, 24.5 million, and they will constitute about 11 percent of the population, or one in every nine Americans. Among every hundred Americans of all ages, then, "11 will be 65 years of age or more."

People aged 80 and over were rare in the United States at the turn of the century. In 1900, most old people were the "young" old, those under 70 or 75. At that time, there were about 21 to 24 persons aged 80 and over for every 100 persons aged 60 to 64. Three-quarters of a century later, the "old-old" had become common. In 1975, there were 49 persons aged 80 and over for every 100 persons aged 60 to 64 (Siegel 1976). The ratio of persons 80 and over to persons 60 to 64 has more than doubled since 1900. Those 80 and over are the great-grandparent generation. There are now more than 2 million Americans 85 years of age and over (Siegel 1976). It is difficult to visualize 2 million people. For comparison purposes it may help to recall that only three of our large cities, New York, Chicago and Los Angeles, have more than 2 million residents.

For those who fear that the United States will become a country of old people in the foreseeable future, that these longevous new pioneers will be the "take-over" generation, demographers forecast that the rapid rise in the proportion of the population aged 65 and over is past. To quote Jacob Siegel of the Bureau of the Census (1976, pp. 1–68), "Statements made in the press and elsewhere that over one-third of the population of the United States will be over 65 years of age in another quarter to half century are unfounded." However unfounded these prophecies about the future, the fact remains that there has been a tremendous growth in the numbers of older people during the past three-quarters of a century, and that these increased numbers have had their effect on contemporary family relationships.

OLDER PARENTS AND THEIR CHILDREN

Among those aged 65 and over today, only about four of every five have living children. Of those who have children, half have only one or two, and half have three or more (Shanas 1978). The old person with children has had different life experiences than the person with no children. These differences continue into old age. The person with children is not *only* a parent; as a parent, he is part of a lineage. Often he or she is the beginning of a lineage of three, four, or even five generations. Ninety-four percent of old people with children are grandparents; 46 percent, great-grandparents. Almost half of all persons aged 65 and over in this country who have living children are thus members of four-generation families. The likelihood of being a great-grandparent increases with age, and among those 80 and over, almost three-fourths are great-grandparents. On the other hand, there are great-grandparents among the "young-old" too. One-fourth of those aged 65 and 66 in 1975 are already great-grandparents (Shanas 1978).

THE LIVING ARRANGEMENTS OF PERSONS OVER 65

Before beginning this discussion of the living arrangements of older people, it is necessary to distinguish between family and household as these terms are used in this essay. For most older people, the family is that group of individuals to whom they are related by blood and marriage. This definition of the family implies that the family includes more than the individual's immediate family, that is, spouse, children, and perhaps siblings. For an older person, his family may include those persons somewhat distantly related by blood or marriage, such as cousins of various degrees, or in-laws, all of whom may be perceived as family members. Nothing in this definition of the family as a network of kin implies that a family must live under the same roof. Those living under the same roof comprise a household. While households of unrelated old people who exchange services and who give one another emotional support as though they were family members are becoming more common, only a small fraction of the elderly live in such arrangements.

Most older people in the United States live in the community, only about 5 to 6 percent live in institutions. About two of every three older men are married and living with their wives. Primarily because women outlive men, only about one of every three older women is married and living with her husband.

In the United States, both older people and their adult children place a value on independent living. Older people stress their desire for such living arrangements. They want to live close enough to children so that they can see them and, especially, see their grandchildren, but they also want to maintain their own households as long as possible. Adult children, for their part, stress their own need for privacy. These desires for independence and privacy are reflected in the living arrangements of older people. Among all older married persons, whether they have children or not, only 12 percent live in a household that includes one or more of their children, while 17 percent of unmarried persons, the single, widowed and divorced, live in such households. Two-thirds of all unmarried persons, whether men or women live alone (Shanas 1978). This two-thirds of all unmarried persons encompasses one of every seven older men, and one of every three older women (Siegel 1976; Glick 1979).

It is not possible to live with children if one has no children. The discussion which follows then focuses on those older people who have children, about four of every five of the noninstitutionalized elderly. While the proportion of old people who live with their children has decreased over the last 20 years, the proportion living close to children has increased substantially. In 1975, the proportion of old people living in the same household with one of their children was 18 percent. Thirty-four percent of all persons over 65 with children, however, live apart from children, but within 10 minutes distance from at least one of them. As a result, in 1975, half of all people with children (52 percent) lived either in the same household with a child, or next door, down the street or a few blocks away. Old people who live alone are commonly considered a particularly vulnerable group among the elderly. Yet, among those old people who have children and who live alone, half are within 10 minutes distance of a child (Shanas 1979b).

Living near adult children is no guarantee that the older parent will see his or her children. In a national interview study in 1975, however, half of all old people with children, including those with children in the same household, saw one of their children the day they were interviewed or the day before that. Three-fourths of older people with children had seen at least one of their children during the week before they were interviewed. Old people (with children) who live alone are equally as likely as those who live in larger households to have seen a child the previous day or within the past week.

Relatives other than children also play an important role in the family life of old people. In 1975, about eight of every 10 old people had living siblings. Those now 75 years of age were themselves part of an average family of five children. With the increase in longevity, many of these brothers and sisters have also survived to old age. Old persons who have never married are especially likely to be close to their siblings. Many live in the same household. Furthermore, while about only one-third of all persons with siblings had seen a brother or sister the week before they were interviewed, among those who had never married, three-fourths saw a brother or sister (Shanas 1979b).

In addition to visiting with children and siblings, old people visit with other relatives who are not among their direct descendants. In 1975, about three of every 10 older persons said that they had seen some relative who was neither a child, a grandchild nor a brother or sister during the previous week.

We know very little about the quality of the interchange either in the households shared by older people and their adult children or in the visits between older people and their children and other relatives. Old people living in the same household with children or relatives may find such an arrangement satisfactory or they may find it unpleasant. In a national survey made some 20 years ago, those older parents who lived in households separate from their children were the most likely to oppose living with a child; those already living in the same household with a child were the least likely to oppose this mode of life. Those older persons who lived with adult children were the most likely of all old persons to say that this is the preferred living arrangement for older people (Shanas 1962). I would guess that we would find much the same attitudes about living arrangements among older people were we to repeat these questions today. People tend to approve of the living arrangement in which they find themselves.

In much the same way, we do not know whether the visits between older people and their children and relatives are brief or lengthy, friendly and warm, or acrimonious and hostile (Shanas 1979b). What we do know is that older parents and their adult children and other relatives do see one another, and that some exchange takes place between them. The nature of such an exchange may just be, as people say, "a visit," or it may involve actual help and services between the generations.

HELP PATTERNS AMONG THE ELDERLY AND THEIR KIN

Help and services across the generations is a continuing feature of family life in the United States (Shanas 1973; Sussman and Burchinal 1962). In 1975, seven of every 10 persons aged 65 and over with children report they gave help to their children, the same proportion reported help to their grandchildren, and five of every 10 reported help to their great-grandchildren. At the same time that old people report giving help to their descendents, a substantial proportion of old persons, again seven of every 10, report receiving help from children. The kinds of help received from children and the help given to children are very similar. These include help with home repairs and housework, care in illness, and various kinds of gifts. In addition, help to children by older people included taking care of grandchildren. Only about two-thirds of those who said they helped their grandchildren or great-grandchildren reported that they actually gave such help during the month before they were interviewed. The nature of such help was personal care described as "baby-sitting," or "having the children stay with me," making things for the grandchildren or great-grandchildren, and giving them money or other gifts.

It should be borne in mind that often the sharing of a home by older parents and an adult child is a form of help although it is usually not reported as such by older people. Such home sharing may mean that the older parent is providing shelter and care for divorced or widowed adult children and their children, in turn, or that adult children are providing shelter and care for indigent or sick parents. As adult children have children of their own they reach a better understanding with their parents. Turning to parents for help seems to become easier. The family, in turn, persists as a major source of help to the elderly in case of illness and in necessary negotiations with bureaucracy despite the fact that, in the United States and in other industrial countries, arrangements are available for outside agencies to fulfill these functions (Shanas 1979a). Parents, as they become unable to satisfy their needs, continue to turn first to their children for care and services.

THE EMERGENCE OF THE
FOUR-GENERATION FAMILY

I want now to discuss the true new pioneers among the elderly and their families. These are the members of the four-generation family. Half of all persons over 65 in the United States with living children are members of such four generation families. Such families are now commonplace, but, as the data on the numbers and proportions of old people have shown, earlier in this century such families were rare. Many persons now in their seventies, eighties and nineties, the great-grandparent generation, will say "I never expected to live so long." In their youth, and even in their young adulthood, very old people were few. Those now among the "old-old" (Neugarten 1974), have no role models that they can use to fashion their own present day roles. In our society, as Irving Rosow (1976 p. 466) has put it, persons "are not socialized to the fate of aging." The lives of the older members of the four-generation families, the presence of great-grandchildren can provide joy and a sense of fulfillment. It can also serve as a source of bewilderment as the life-styles of the young become more and more different from those of the older generation.

The adult children of the oldest generation, those in the grandparent generation, find themselves in the middle. They, too, are new pioneers. Those middle-aged persons who have perhaps looked forward to the time when their children would be grown as a time for freedom from major family responsibilities, now find themselves with new responsibilities, the care and often the financial support of elderly parents. Many persons in the grandparent generation are experiencing some of the stresses associated with their own aging, retirement from work, lessened income, and perhaps health problems. Yet they are expected to be, and often are, the major social support of their own parents. The needs of their own children and grandchildren indeed may conflict with the needs of their elderly parents.

The generation in the middle are parents to their own children; they sometimes must assume the parental roles for their grandchildren and, yet, at the same time, they must be dutiful and loving children to their own parents. The strain attendant to such a role may be considerable. The members of the four-generation family, as it has emerged in contemporary life, are plagued by role ambiguities and by unanticipated demands from its members. Who is the matriarch in such four-generation families? Is it the great-grandmother or is it the grandmother who holds the family together? Which of these two is called "Granny" by great-grandchildren, and which is given another descriptive title? Just as the old tell us that they never expected to live so long, so the generation in the middle tell us that "I've raised my family. I want to spend time with my husband or wife. I want to enjoy my grandchildren. I never expected that when I was a grandparent, I'd have to look after my parents."

SUMMARY AND DISCUSSION

Old people and their families are the new pioneers of our era. They have ventured into uncharted areas of human relationships, and developed systems of exchange and interaction without help or guidance from the so-called helping agencies in our industrial society. Astronauts and space vehicles have guidance systems. Old people and their families have only those traits which distinguish human beings from other animals: love, sympathy, the ability to empathize one with the other.

Between the turn of the century and the present, the number of persons aged 65 and over has increased eightfold; their proportion in the population has increased threefold. The status of old people has increased not at all. It may even have become lessened, as what was once scarce, a very old person, has become commonplace. In most areas, in the marketplace, in the area of work, in social intercourse, the only status of those aged 65 or more is that they are old. Sometimes they are seen as "funny" old people who behave inappropriately in the eyes of younger persons. At other times, they are "cute" old, bright productive and active persons, and, thus, assumed to be like clever children. Society has deprived old people both of responsibility and of function and thus provided the basis for the roleless role of the elderly (Rosow 1976).

There is one area, however, in which old people do have a role and a safe haven. That safe harbor is within the family. the family—spouse, siblings and other kin—serves to integrate old people into society. If people have children, they live close to at least one of their children and see at least one child often. If people have no children, other relatives, siblings, nieces, nephews, or cousins often assume some of the helping functions of children. Friends and neighbors provide social support for people without kin who live alone. Pseudofamilies function to invite people without kin to join them at traditional family gatherings, at Thanksgiving and Christmas parties. The four-generation family, plagued with role ambiguities, supports its members, both young and old, with informal as well as formal help.

The safe harbor for the elderly is constantly under siege.

> Analysis of contemporary and future models of the family structure of the elderly in the United States indicate that, despite the fact that the family is now serving as a major source of help to its elderly members, certainly as the major source of care to those who need nursing and home care, the trend toward further bureaucratization of services to the elderly seems inevitable (Shanas 1977, p. 18).

As more women work, there will be fewer available family caretakers. Yet, as families become less able to fulfill the role of helpers to their aged members, they will seek to modify the bureaucratic structure so that it functions in a way that is more satisfactory to both old people and their kin. The future is uncharted for the old as it is for all of us. Family and kinship ties, however, have been amazingly resilient through the millennia. they may be different for old people in the future from what they are now, but they will continue to provide safe harbor for their members however long they may live.

REFERENCES

Birren, J. E. and V. J. Renner. 1977. "Research on the Psychology of Aging: Principles and Experimentation." Pp. 3–38 in *Handbook of the Psychology of Aging,* edited by J. E. Birren and K. W. Schaie. New York: Van Nostrand-Reinhold.

Glick, P. G. 1979. "The Future Marital Status and Living Arrangements of the Elderly." *The Gerontologist* 19 (3): 301–309.

Neugarten, B. L. 1974. "Age Groups in American Society and the Rise of the Young-Old." *Annals of the American Academy* 415 (September): 187–198.

Plath, D. W. 1972. "Japan: The After Years." Pp. 133–150 in *Aging and Modernization,* edited by D. O. Cowgill and L. D. Holmes. New York: Appleton-Century-Crofts.

Rosow, I. 1976. "Status and Role Change Through the Life Span." Pp. 457–482 in *Handbook of Aging and the Social Sciences,* edited by R. H. Binstock and E. Shanas. New York: Van Nostrand-Reinhold.

Shanas, E. 1962. *The Health of Older People: A Social Survey.* Cambridge: Harvard University Press.

— 1973. "Family-Kin Networks and Aging in Cross-Cultural Perspective," *Journal of Marriage and the Family* 35 (August): 505–511.

— 1977. "The Elderly: Family, Bureaucracy and Family Help Patterns." Paper presented at a meeting of the Institut de la Vie, Vichy, France, April.

— 1978. "A National Survey of the Aged." Final report to the Administration on Aging. Washington, D.C.: U.S. Department of Health, Education and Welfare.

—1979a. "The Family as a Social Support System in Old Age." *The Gerontologist* 19 (2): 169–174.

—1979b. "Social Myth as Hypothesis: The Case of the Family Relations of Old People." *The Gerontologist* 19 (1): 3–9.

Siegel, J. S. 1976. "Demographic Aspects of Aging and the Older Population of the United States." U.S. Bureau of the Census, Current Population Reports, Series P-23, No. 59. Washington, DC: U.S. Government Printing Office.

Sussman, M. B. and L. Burchinal. 1962. "Parental Aid to Married Children: Implications for Family Functioning." *Marriage and Family Living* 24: 320–332.

34

The Future of Grandparenthood*

Andrew Cherlin and Frank Furstenberg, Jr.

Almost three years to the day after our initial visit, we returned to the senior citizen center where we had begun our study of American grandparents. During the interim, we had designed a questionnaire, conducted a nationwide survey by telephone, visited personally with grandparents around the country, analyzed our data, and written most of this book. Still, we wanted to listen to grandparents one last time, to test whether their words would now have a familiar ring, and to clear up a few lingering issues.

So, feeling now like veterans rather than the novices of 1982, we once again parked our car in front of the converted store and went inside to meet a new group of Jewish grandparents. There had been some changes in the neighborhood. In the past few years, several Jewish families had emigrated to this city from the Soviet Union. Our informants were in awe of the relationships between the Russian-Jewish grandparents and their families. One woman, Mrs. Berg, told us:

> We have quite a few Russian friends. Now these friends, invariably the mothers are living with the sons, the daughters, with grandchildren—they're all together. I have noticed such a difference among our Russian friends, who have only been in this country four or five years—these are new immigrants. The grandchildren have great reverence for the grandparents; they live together. When they go on vacation they take the grandparents with them! I'm just shocked! When they go out eating, they take the grandparents with them! When you go to a restaurant, you will see

*Cherlin, Andrew and Frank Furstenberg, Jr. 1986. "The Future of Grandparenthood." Pp. 185–207 in *The New American Grandparent: A Place in the Family, a Life Apart.* New York: Basic Books.

the grandparents with them. And this is such a new experience because we don't go eating with our children. They go their way, we go our way. It's a special occasion when you go out with your children—an anniversary, a birthday.

Her husband added:

The [Russian] grandparents are very much involved with the families of their children. They assume such a responsibility. We know a woman who was a famous surgeon in Russia, she's here in America, and she has that same feeling that she has to take of her grandchild if the mother goes away. She's always obligated to that little girl. Now, you wouldn't find the same thing in America.

The grandparents in the room contrasted this great degree of togetherness, respect, and mutual obligation with the weaker ties they experienced with their own children and grandchildren. Mr. Berg asked:

Does it appear to you that we're disenchanted?

INTERVIEWER: *Do you think you're disenchanted?*

Yes. Disenchanted with the way we expected the family continuity to be—you know, when we were younger, when we had children, and the way it turned out. The lessening of the relationship, the distance between us, the wide abyss between the way my grandchildren think and the way we feel. And the kind of reverence we had toward an old, intelligent, crude grandfather. I had reverence for him because he was my grandfather.

After a number of these contrasts between the fullness of the grandparent-grandchild relationship among the Russian immigrants and the thinness among the Americans, plus some complaining about the material advantages immigrant families had secured through special assistance programs, one of us asked whether anyone in the group would trade places with the immigrants in order to have their type of relationship. The question was met with immediate cries of "No Way!", "No," "I'm satisfied." The questioner pursued the point further: "Why wouldn't you trade places? There are all these strong family ties." A woman replied, "I don't think I could live with my children," and a chorus of "No" and "No way" followed.

Another woman said simply, "It's too late." And in an important sense, she was right. The immigrants' family relationships reminded the Jewish-American grandparents of the idealized picture that they conjure up when asked what family life was like when they were children. Whether or not this picture is accurate as a description of the past, it is clear to most grandparents that it cannot serve as a model for their families today—that, indeed, they would reject this model if it were offered. For the discussion at the senior center illustrated a central contradiction in the lives of American grandparents: like most other Americans, they want intimate, satisfying, stable family ties, but at the same time they want to retain their independence from kin. They want affection and respect from their children and grandchildren, but they do not want to be obligated to them. The price paid for strong family ties by the Russian immigrants—and by family members in developing countries around the world—is a substantial loss of autonomy. It is a price most American grandparents are not willing to pay.

In this regard, they are becoming more and more like their children and grandchildren. Joseph Veroff, Elizabeth Douvan, and Richard A. Kulka analyzed two national surveys about American's feelings of well-being and life satisfaction, conducted in 1957 and 1976. Overall, they found that feelings of well-being among Americans in 1976 were tied to personal growth more than in 1957. Life satisfaction was linked more closely to interpersonal intimacy and less closely to participation in organizations such as the church or social roles such as worker or husband. Moreover, self-reliance and self-expression became more important sources of fulfillment. And as for the greater importance of self-reliance:

> This is no more clearly highlighted than in the case of older people in the society of 1976 who have joined the rest of their population in seeking self-sufficiency as a crucial life value for well-being more than older people in 1957.[1]

We would argue that this change in the basis of older people's sense of well-being is rooted in material changes . . . : the great rise in their standard of living, the increase in longevity, improvements in transportation and communication, and the like. As a result of these trends, many more older Americans have the opportunity to live independent lives. Given this opportunity, they—like their children and grandchildren—are seizing it. Another grandparent at the senior center told us:

> When we were raising children, we figured when the children got married and moved to their own locales, we'd be free to do as we please. All our lives, we've worked for the kids, to make sure they had an education and everything else. Then we find out when we're grandparents they say, "Uh, Mom, Pop, how about baby-sitting? We're going away for a couple of days." Once in a while this is fine, but we wouldn't want to be tied down to that like three or four times a year. And when my wife was baby-sitting for my granddaughter, I was against it because she was coming here to the center on Wednesdays. She was giving up her day; it killed the day even though she was only baby-sitting for five hours or so. . . . And she's depriving herself of her pleasures.

The sense that they deserve to have their pleasures now because they worked hard to raise their children was widespread among the grandparents in our study. Having paid their dues, many—like the grandfather just quoted—felt that they need not be "tied down" too often, need not oblige all their children's demands. Perhaps grandparents in other cultures, if faced with the same opportunities for independence, would make different choices. For example, older people in Taiwan still live with their adult children in substantial, though slowly declining, numbers despite rapid economic development.[2] But personal autonomy has long been a central value in American life, as observers from the time of Tocqueville have noted. And this emphasis on autonomy extends to family relations as well. In a recent study of American individualism, Robert N. Bellah and his colleagues wrote that "free choice in the family, which was already greater in Tocqueville's day than it had been before, is now characteristic of the decisions of all members of the family except the youngest children."[3] Given the central place of personal autonomy in American culture and the improved material circumstances of older people, the shift among grandparents toward greater independence seem inexorable.

We would also argue . . . that the increasing independence of the generations promotes the growth of the companionate style of interaction between grandparents and grandchildren. Informal, affectionate, warm relations are more likely when grandparents and grandchildren are relatively equal in social status, as anthropological studies suggest. Thus, the greater independence of grandparents—their reluctance to assume responsibility except in times of crisis, their exclusion by parents from decision-making, their overall lack of authority—leads to a greater emphasis on personal intimacy and emotional satisfaction with grandchildren. Here again, as the Veroff, Douvan, and Kulka study makes clear, their behavior mirrors that of Americans in general. Grandparents, newly freed from the constraints of economic dependence, blessed with longer lives, and imbued with American values, have joined their juniors in the pursuit of sentiment. The new American grandparent wants to be involved in her grandchildren's lives, but not at the cost of her autonomy.

Some would fault grandparents of this behavior. Arguing on behalf of stronger family ties, conservative critics of the contemporary family have called for a return to "traditional" family values, including the restoration of the authority of old over young and of husbands over wives. Although we respect the moral concern that underlies this position, our research has convinced us that the chances for a large-scale restoration of these traditional values are near zero—particularly insofar as grandparents are concerned. The most outspoken advocate for closer ties between grandparents and grandchildren has been child psychiatrist Arthur Kornhaber. . . . He has warned of a "new social contract" that has, in his opinion, weakened the family:

> A great many grandparents have given up emotional attachments to their grandchildren. They have ceded the power to determine their grandparenting relationship to the grandchildren's parents and, in effect, have turned their backs on an entire generation.[4]

In the book he wrote with journalist Kenneth L. Woodward, he calls for a return to "an ethos which values emotions and emotional attachments," particularly between grandparents and grandchildren.[5]

Kornhaber's critique, though well intentioned and not without basis, is strong on rhetoric but weak on the facts. First, he downplays the positive features of social change. For example, his charge that grandparents have abandoned emotional attachments to their grandchildren is false, as the evidence in this book has amply demonstrated. Again and again, our interviews showed that grandparents have strong attachments to their grandchildren. In a majority of cases, this bond takes the form of a companionate relationship based on regular (though not daily) contact and an informal style of interaction. The grandparents in our survey reported overwhelmingly ... that their relationships with the study children were "closer" and "more friendly" than their own relationships with their grandparents had been when they were children. We learned that grandparents with companionate relationships expressed great contentment with the emotional rewards of grandparenthood, even if they were not completely satisfied with the amount of time they were able to spend with their grandchildren. [We] discovered that the major enemy of grandparents is geographical distance. When grandchildren live nearby, grandparents see them often, even if they do not get along with the children's parents.

Kornhaber ... does not think today's companionate relationships qualify as "real" relationships—thus his charge that grandparents have abandoned their family commitments. But they certainly felt like real relationships to the grandparents we spoke with. One should at least consider the possibility that the greater emphasis on companionship has had the salutary effect of diminishing the stiff, formal style that often dominated intergenerational relations in the past and increasing the salience of love and affection in intergenerational relations today.

Similarly, there is little recognition that the greater independence of the older population usually is experienced by them and most of their children as a positive development. What seems to Kornhaber as detachment is perceived by many grandparents as self-reliance, a quality much valued in American culture. Just a generation or two ago, far fewer grandparents had the economic resources and the good health necessary to live long, independent lives. Now that more do, is it fair to criticize them for enjoying the autonomy that is so highly prized in American society? The older among today's grandparents came of age during the Great Depression and lived through the hardships of World War II. They raised large families during the baby boom and worked to put their children through college. Consequently, it is not surprising that most older Americans are generally content with the trouble-free, independent lives that they now lead. Is there not a great social achievement here, namely, an advance in the quality of life for a previously disadvantaged group of Americans?

Conservative arguments about the family are often stated as if, without any major changes in social structure, moral exhortation alone could alter people's behavior patterns. Kornhaber and Woodward ... are aware that the strong intergenerational ties of the past that they so admire were rooted in economic cooperation among families working hard to subsist. They further acknowledge that as material conditions have improved, intergenerational ties have become less intense. Yet they reject the linkage between material conditions and family relationships, calling merely for the spread of an ethos than would restore the intensive emotional ties of the idealized three-generational unit, as if the power of moral suasion were sufficient to bring about the changes they favor. It is not. To attain the goal they seek, one must consider, in addition, what changes in the social structure would be necessary—and what the social and economic costs would be.

Let us consider, then, what it might take to establish widely the kind of deeper, stronger ties between grandparents and grandchildren that Kornhaber—and, other things being equal, almost everyone else—would like to see. To begin with, our society would have to discourage if not restrict people's geographical movements. Our analyses [have] shown that involved relationships between grand-parents and grandchildren depend most heavily on very frequent contact, which in turn depends very heavily on living nearby. A massive relocation would be required to put enough grandparents and grandchildren near enough to allow for a great increase in contact. Presumably, young adults move to pursue better oppor-tunities, thus improving the general welfare (by more efficiently matching their skills to jobs); and older people relocate for health and recreational reasons. Are we prepared to reduce employment opportunities for improved grandparent-grandchild relations? Would we really consider urging workers to remain in depressed labor markets so that their children would have regular contact with grandparents? How many older people who have worked hard all their lives could be dissuaded from retiring to a condominium in the Sunbelt? We doubt that many Americans would respond to these appeals.

Moreover, even if such appeals were successful, they would not suffice. The involvement of grandparents in families of the past was enhanced when they retained a substantial amount of authority over the lives of their children, often based upon the ownership or control of economic resources. Even today in many developing countries, elders have a great deal of influence over the timing of the major events in their children's lives due to their control over resources.[6] In order to foster intense intergenerational ties, then, our society would have to give the older generation substantial control over resources and allow for older people to have more influence over their children's choice of spouse, timing of marriage, type of work, and place of residence. We suspect that few Americans would accept this degree of influence in their own family decisions.

THE GAINS FROM INTERGENERATIONAL TIES

These, then, are the steps it would take to restore the authority of grandparents as it is sometimes believed to have existed in the past. We stress the "believed" because family historians have cast doubt on the notion that American families ever functioned like families in Japan, India, or China, where reverence and respect for ancestors remains high even today. Still, it is likely that family elders more often wielded influence in day-to-day family dealings a century ago than they do today. Teenaged children were expected to contribute to their parents' support, and elderly parents often continued to receive material support from their adult children and their children's children. Money and services flowed in two directions within the family—to children when they were young and then back to parents as they aged.

Family scholars are not quite certain just when and why this reciprocal flow of resources changed. Some believe that the change occurred gradually as parents lost the ability to employ their children in the family farm or business. Others think that the sustained period of economic growth following World War II reduced the need for intergenerational transfers. Probably, too, the Social Security system, which was devised to insure the economic well-being of the elderly, helped to undermine the traditional pattern of intergenerational exchange. By the middle of this century, relatively few adult children continued to turn over portions of their earnings to their parents. Increasingly, older parents were able to support themselves, and growing numbers of them were able to assist their adult children in establishing careers and launching families.

What do grandparents gain from intergenerational relations today? First, . . . an indirect exchange still is taking place through the Social Security system. The middle generation is paying generously to support the elderly, while preserving the cultural fiction that the elderly are taking care of themselves. This belief reinforces the high value Americans place on the autonomy of family members. Grandparents do not want to rely on their children and grandchildren for economic security.

Second, grandparents are repaid by their children and grandchildren in sentimental currency—love and affection. While we cannot fully document it, we believe that this form of exchange probably has increased over the past several decades. We have argued that emotional ties between the elderly and their grandchildren are more valued than ever before. This does not necessarily mean that they are more gratifying—though we suspect that they often are—but that the standards of what constitutes a "close" relationship have been elevated. As in contemporary marriage, more emotional satisfaction is now expected in intergenerational relations. Yet, as in marriage, the pursuit of sentiment, though personally rewarding, can be elusive and frustrating. As inflation in standards can lead to doubts and disappointments. When our respondents told us about their strong feelings for their grandchildren, we sometimes sensed reservations about whether the feelings were reciprocated. Some grandparents felt less than secure about their place in the family.

Third, grandparents are able to bask in what they perceive as the special achievements of their grandchildren. Though they may see them infrequently, grandparents boast of their grandchildren's success in school, on the athletic field, or in church activities. In the homes we visited, we were shown trophies, merit badges, certificates, and newspaper clippings. We were regaled with stories of school plays, honor rolls, and lucrative summer employment. It was clear that grandchildren's accomplishments had helped to make life worthwhile. To be sure, grandparents understand, as do parents, that children are achieving for themselves. But grandparents are a central part of the audience. Indeed, parents encourage them to share the children's accomplishments. And one of the benefits of this form of exchange is that grandparents who live in Florida or Arizona can receive it nearly as well as those who live next door.

Our conclusion, then, is that there will be no "return" to "traditional" grandparent-grandchild relations on a large scale—and that this is not altogether bad. Substantial benefits have accrued to grandparents and their adult children as a result of the movement toward greater autonomy and companionship. Moreover, the symbolic rewards of grandparenthood are important, even though they are less substantive than the exchange of goods and services. In addition, the costs of widely establishing a strong, influential relationship between grandparents and their progeny are so high that few would support the necessary actions. This is not to deny that real costs are attached to the current state of family relations or that some grandparents have misgivings or discontents about their roles. All family arrangements entail certain costs; we are probably more aware of the costs of ours than ever before. Rather, we wish to emphasize here that even if there are structural weaknesses in the American family (as few would deny), grandparents are not likely to be the agents of change or useful instruments of public policy. Their influence in most families is modest, and the prospects for greatly increasing that influence are slim. Those searching for a means of strengthening the American family will probably have to look elsewhere.

COUNTERCURRENTS

Still, there are some countervailing tendencies that may act to increase modestly the importance of the grandparental role. Those who are inclined to exhortations on behalf of strong bonds between grandparents and grandchildren might take heart from our finding that grandparents with a greater family consciousness saw their grandchildren more often and exchanged more services. These findings showed that there is significant variation in family values among American grandparents, holding economic factors constant. But just how one might foster the spread of a more familistic orientation—assuming that was a shared policy objective—is unclear.

More important, for better or worse, is the trend toward frequent divorce. [D]ivorce in the middle generation creates a need for assistance from the older generation and how grandparents, particularly on the custodial side, respond to that need. The crisis of divorce calls into action the latent support network of the family, in which grandparents play a central part. In essence, divorce recreates a functional role for grandparents similar to the roles they had when higher parental mortality and lower standards of living necessitated more intergenerational assistance. One result . . . is that children in divorced families today tend to develop stronger ties to their custodial grandparents than children in intact families develop with either set of grandparents.

The effect of divorce demonstrate once again that strong, functional intergenerational ties are linked to family crises, low incomes, and instability rather than to health, prosperity, and stability. There is a trade-off here, and we suspect that almost everyone would prefer to see fewer family crises—and less divorce—even at the cost of a weakening of intergenerational ties. Consequently, the latent nature of intergenerational support in most intact families today—the "family watchdog" role of grandparents, in Lillian Troll's phrase—should be seen as an advance in social welfare. It reflects the greater prosperity and (at least until the recent rise in divorce) stability of the nuclear unit and the greater material well-being of the older generation. It would be nice to have one's cake and eat it, too—that is, to have prosperity and family stability and also to retain strong intergenerational ties. But the strong bonds of the past, when they did exist, derived from day-to-day participation in a common family enterprise. Without the need for such participation, intergenerational ties emphasize loving, affectionate, companionate relations with a fund of additional resources held in reserve.

Nevertheless, divorce is creating a more functional role for grandparents in millions of American families. At current rates, about two-fifths of all American children will witness their parents' divorce.... Since most older people have more than one child, the odds are increasingly high that a grandparent will watch at least one child divorce after the birth of grandchildren. The small silver lining in this otherwise dark cloud is that many grandchildren will experience closer ties to some of their grandparents. But . . . this benefit is distributed quite unequally, from the grandparents' point of view. Maternal grandparents, whose daughters usually retain custody following a divorce, stand to benefit most; but paternal grandparents stand to lose. Although some paternal, noncustodial grandparents do establish closer ties, they more commonly become symbolic figures who see their grandchildren infrequently and on ritual occasions. Nor . . . is this situation amenable to legal remedies. High rates of divorce, coupled with current custody patterns, could increase the relative importance of the maternal line in American kinship, an unanticipated, unwanted, though not necessarily harmful effect. All in all, divorce is far from an ideal way to strengthen intergenerational ties.

Another potential crosscurrent is the increasing relative wealth of older Americans. Because of . . . economic trends . . . , the elderly are now a relatively advantaged, though not affluent, group. Should these trends continue, more grandparents will be able to play the role of economic protectors of their grandchildren. They also may be more motivated to do so, as we will discuss, if birth rates remain low and grandchildren are in short supply. The family watchdogs will have more resources with which to act when trouble arises. Even so, we would not expect grandparents in intact families to have more authority over the major decisions in their children's lives. That kind of authority cannot be bought; it requires day-to-day involvement in the grandchildren's lives. Many of today's independent grandparents do not want this type of involvement, nor do their children want them to have it. And some of the grandparents who would like day-to-day involvement live too far away to get it. The typical types of financial aid are likely to be lump-sum transfers for special needs—such as orthodontics, college tuition, or a downpayment on a home—rather than smaller, regular payments. Indeed, only one-fourth of the most affluent grandparents in our survey (those with total family incomes of twenty thousand dollars or more in 1982) reported that they had provided any financial support to the study child's parents in the previous twelve months; and more than half of them did so "occasionally" or "seldom" (as opposed to "regularly").

Thus, grandparents are likely to be increasingly important as a source of financial reserves—an insurance policy against family crises or a source of assistance for major purchases—but not as a source of regular income support. This role is consistent with the independence both grandparents and their adult children value so highly. Occasional large transfers of assets allow grandparents to make an important contribution while retaining most of their regular flow of income for their own use. Occasional transfers also allow adult children to receive valuable assistance without feeling that they are dependent on their parents for support. And by compartmentalizing financial transfers, this system does not interfere with the preferred day-to-day emphasis on companionship.

On a national scale, one might ask whether these intrafamily transfers are likely to redress the growing imbalance between the well-being of children and the well-being of the elderly. Samuel H. Preston has demonstrated that during the 1960s and 1970s, the relative economic position of the elderly improved. In 1970, according to Preston, 16 percent of children under fourteen were living in poverty, compared to 24 percent of persons over sixty-five. But by 1982 the situation had reversed: 23 percent of children were poor, compared to just 15 percent of the elderly. When in-kind payments such as Medicare and food stamps are taken into account, according to Preston, the gap widens further: 17 percent of children were poor in 1982, compared to just 4 percent of the elderly.[7] The gap is a result, in part, of the great increases in Social Security and pension payments. . . . It also results from the growth of single-parent families and from the greater postponement of childbearing among more well-to-do families. Can we rely on private transfers from grandparents to grandchildren to help close the gap?

In our opinion, private, intrafamily transfers can be of only limited help. To be sure, moderately affluent grandparents whose children divorce often will be called upon to help out financially. [G]randparents on the custodial side after a divorce were more likely to be providing support than other grandparents, even several years after the divorce. But the problem is that many disadvantaged children have disadvantaged grandparents. Out-of-wedlock births to teenagers, for example, occur disproportionately in the lower-income segment of the population; in some cases, the paternal grandparents may not even acknowledge (or know about) their son's paternity. In order to reduce substantially the disparity between children and the elderly, grandparents would have to take responsibility for assisting other people's grandchildren whom they do not know and who do not live in their neighborhoods. There is no reason to believe that this will occur on an individual level, not because grandparents are selfish but because, like most other Americans, they confine their personal generosity to their own families and their own communities. Even a sudden plunge in the divorce rate would not eliminate the gap. A fifteen-year study of family economics by the University of Michigan showed that only part of the reduction of children's economic well-being relative to the elderly is a result of changes in family structure.[8] Consequently, the only way to reduce the gap directly is by some type of aggregate transfer from the elderly—or from the even better-off adult population of working age—to children. Policy makers cannot look to private intergenerational transfers to mitigate the poverty that disadvantaged children face.

Grandparents: Supply and Demand

An additional trend that may have a substantial impact on the future of grandparenthood is the sharp decline in the birth rate since the 1950s. At current rates, the average American woman will give birth to fewer than two children, and continued low birth rates will create a growing imbalance between the numbers of grandparents and grandchildren. To illustrate, suppose we had done our survey in 1900, when the birth rate was higher and life expectancy was lower. [W]e would have found that grandparents were in short supply: there were only twenty-seven persons age fifty-five and over for every one hundred children fourteen and under. Moreover, those grandparents who were fortunate enough to have survived were less affluent and had fewer resources to give to their grandchildren. Now let us suppose that we were to redo our survey in the year 2000, and let us assume further that the birth rate has remained low, that gains in adult life expectancy have continued, and the economic situation of the elderly has not deteriorated. We would find that the demand for grandchildren would have increased as more persons lived relatively affluent, long lives but that the supply of grandchildren would have decreased sharply. [T]he Bureau of the Census predicts that by the year 2000 persons fifty-five and over will actually outnumber children fourteen and under.

Thus, the demographic and economic bases of the grandparent-grandchild relationship at the end of this century are likely to be reversed from what existed at the beginning of the century. In the earlier period, grandparents had more claimants on their emotional and material resources and fewer resources to give; in the near future they will have more resources but far fewer claimants. A few generations ago some grandparents must have been overwhelmed by the number of grandchildren they had, but in the 1990s many more will be underwhelmed. On average, given continued low fertility, an older person will have nearly two living adult children, each of whom will have nearly two children. But these averages will conceal important variations. For example, demographer Charles F. Westoff estimates that if current rates continue, about one-fourth of all young women will not bear children.[9] If so, then a substantial minority of older persons will find that only one of their children will give birth to grandchildren—often just one or two.

This short supply of grandchildren may alter the strategies that grandparents pursue. Fewer grandparents will have the option of letting circumstances—such as geographical proximity or how well they get along with their daughters-in-law—determine the nature of their relationships with their grandchildren. The strategy we label selective investment . . . will not be possible as often. Instead, there will be more incentive for grandparents to invest heavily in their first or second grandchild, on the theory that there may not be any others, even if the grandchild does not live nearby. Yet it is very difficult for grandparents to overcome the barriers of distance or a poor relationship with daughters-in-law. There could be an increasing proportion of grandparents who have remote relationships with all their grandchildren. But if older people remain relatively well-off economically and fertility remains low, we would expect to see more grandparents engage in large expenditures such as airplane trips and joint vacations that might maintain ties despite great distances. Grandparents may also become even more accommodating in their relations with their children—even more circumspect, for example, about the norm of noninterference—in order to maintain family ties. Another alternative would be for grandparents to compensate by embracing stepgrandchildren as the best available substitute. [T]he bonds between stepgrandparents and stepgrandchildren appear to vary sharply according to custody arrangements and to the age of the children when their parents remarry. Continued low fertility may promote the assimilation into the family of stepgrandchildren who today might be considered marginal.

All this suggests that the fit between the number of older family members, the resources available to them, and the numbers of children in their families—

between the demand for grandchildren and the supply of same—may have improved and then worsened during this century. At the turn of the century, when grandparents were less numerous and less well-off, the demand for grandparents who could devote time, energy, and resources to their grandchildren may have exceeded the supply. By the end of the century the supply of able, healthy, well-off potential grandparents is likely to exceed the demand. We would speculate that sometime in the very recent past, probably in the 1970s, the balance between the resources and desires of grandparents and the needs of grandchildren may have been at a peak. The grandparents of the 1970s were the first to benefit from the extraordinary increases in Social Security payments that began in the mid-1960s. They also had large numbers of grandchildren because they had given birth to the large baby-boom cohorts in the 1950s. This conjuncture of longevity, relative affluence, and large families may prove to be unique. To a degree, it allowed grandparents to increase their personal autonomy without sacrificing intimacy—to lead independent lives without foregoing intergenerational ties. From the grandchildren's perspective, to be sure, the trends look different: they may benefit in the near future from the increased attention their scarcity seems likely to bring. Thus, a low birth rate, like a high divorce rate, may act to increase somewhat the salience of grandparents to grandchildren's lives. But grandparents as a group, it seems to us, never had it as good as they did in the recent past, and they may never have it as good again.

FORMULATING A NEW DEFINITION OF THE ROLE

Finally, then, what are we to make of the ambiguous situation of the new American grandparent? First, we must reject the notion that grandparenthood is a meaningless, unimportant role. On the contrary, being a grandparent is deeply meaningful. But it must be understood that what makes life experiences "meaningful" in our society has changed in recent decades. Like most other Americans, grandparents increasingly find meaning in their lives through personal fulfillment: they seek self-reliance, and they seek emotionally satisfying interpersonal relationships. Their relationships with grandchildren fit these criteria. Eschewing the role of the authority figure, grandparents concentrate instead on developing relationships based largely on love and affection. Most succeed in establishing rewarding, companionate relationships without compromising the autonomy they also value. Some social commentators argue that we ought to emphasize additional criteria when evaluating our personal well-being—for example, the extent to which we are engaged in efforts to assist others, or the degree to which we have lasting, stable bonds to family and community. But these arguments, valid though they may be, cannot change the fact that grandparents, in their own terms, find companionate relationships meaningful and satisfying. Whether or not it ought to be so, the pursuit of sentiment is central to the meaning of grandparenthood today.

Nevertheless, some grandparents play an active role in helping to rear their grandchildren and in exchanging services with them. Sixteen percent of the grandparents in our survey had this type of "involved" relationship with the study children. Since the grandchildren in the study essentially were selected randomly, an additional fraction of the grandparents must have had involved relationships with other grandchildren not in the study. In order for grandparents to have this functional role, however, a special set of circumstances must exist. Most important, the grandchildren must live quite close by; our findings suggest that, with few exceptions, grandparents cannot take on parentlike authority unless they see their children and grandchildren very frequently. It also helps if the grandparents are younger—hence better able to cope physically with the duties of caring for children—and if they get along well with the grandchild's mother. And it helps if there is a specific need for the grandparents' assistance, as is the case when a divorce occurs in the middle generation. There is not much chance of an involved relationship developing between a sixty-eight-year-old grandmother and a granddaughter who lives with her mother and father an hour's drive away; too many structural constraints prevent it, even if the grandmother wanted it. Thus, it is unrealistic to expect that large numbers of grandparents could play a strong, authoritative, ever-present role in their grandchildren's upbringing.

Is this to be lamented? Readers must answer that question according to their own moral views. But let us make a few observations that, we believe, should temper any feelings of disappointment about the infrequency of strong, functional intergenerational ties. First, . . . the idealized picture of the strong, supportive grandparent of the past is overdrawn. As recently as the turn of the century, far fewer grandchildren had the opportunity to know their grandparents, and most did not live with them. It is misleading to compare the reality of the present to a nostalgic image of the past. Second, it is common for grandparents today to serve as the protectors of their grandchildren—as sources of support in reserve. This latent support may never be activated; but, like a good insurance policy, it is important nevertheless. In fact, given the growing affluence of the elderly, the rise in divorce, and the declining numbers of grandchildren, the protector role is likely to become more salient in the future. Third, the evidence . . . suggests that even if more grandparents played a key functional role, they would have a relatively modest influence over the values of their grandchildren. When even parents have a difficult time combating the influence of the media or the peer group, we cannot expect grandparents to be very effective.

What has happened over the past decades is that grandparents have been swept up in the same social changes that have altered the other major family relationships—wife and husband, parent and child. The increasing economic independence, the greater emphasis on self-reliance, and the search for sentiment that have changed marital relations—making them both more oriented toward intimacy and more brittle—have also changed grandparental relations. In addition, we have seen how the limitations of grandparent-grandchild relations mirror in many ways the difficulties of parent-child relations. Indeed, the final lesson we wish to draw from our study is that the situation of grandparents today demonstrates the pervasiveness of family change. Rooted in our changing social structure and our changing values, the tension between personal autonomy and family bonds now affects all important family relationships. For grandparents, this tension means that they must try to balance their desire for emotionally satisfying relationships with their grandchildren, on the one hand, against their wish to lead, at long last, independent lives. The resolution of this tension is the fundamental problem facing American families today. As our study suggests, there can be no return to the "traditional" family values of the past without alterations in our social structure that few would tolerate. And yet the maintenance of family ties remains important to most of us. This is a problem that requires the attention of all family members and of our society as a whole; we cannot expect grandparents, acting alone, to solve it for us.

NOTES

1. Joseph Veroff, Elizabeth Douvan, and Richard A. Kulka, *The Inner American: A Self Portrait from 1957 to 1976* (New York: Basic Books, 1981), 535. For a similar argument about the changing basis of self-identity in American society see Ralph H. Turner, "The Real Self: From Institution to Impulse," *American Journal of Sociology* 81 (March 1976): 989–1016.

2. Ronald Freedman, Ming-Cheng Chang, and Te-Hsiung Sun, "Household Composition, Extended Kinship, and Reproduction in Taiwan," *Population Studies* 36 (1980): 395–411.

3. Robert N. Bellah et al., *Habits of the Heart: Individualism and Commitment in American Life* (Berkeley: University of California Press, 1985), 90.

4. Arthur Kornhaber, "Grandparenthood and the 'New Social Contract'," in *Grandparenthood,* ed. Vern L. Bengtson and Joan F. Robertson (Beverly Hills, CA: Sage Publications, 1985), 159–71. Quoted at p. 159.

5. Arthur Kornhaber and Kenneth L. Woodward, *Grandparents/Grandchildren: The Vital Connection* (New York: Doubleday, Anchor Press, 1981), 147.

6. For an elaboration of the importance for marriage and fertility of "wealth flows" to and from the older generation, see John C. Caldwell, *Theory of Fertility Decline* (London: Academic Press, 1982).

7. Samuel H. Preston, "Children and the Elderly in the U.S.," *Scientific American* 251 (December 1984): 44–49.

8. Greg J. Duncan, Martha Hill, and Willard Rodgers, "The Changing Economic Status of the Young and Old," paper presented at the Workshop on Demographic Change and the Well-Being of Dependents, National Academy of Sciences, 5–7 September 1985.

9. Charles F. Westoff, "Marriage and Fertility in the Developed Countries," *Scientific American* 239 (December 1978): 51–57.

35

To Be Old and Asian: An Unsettling Life in America*

Florentius Chan

The 1980 census reported that there were 211,736 older Asian and Pacific Islanders aged 65 and over living in the United States. This figure is expected to increase significantly by 1990. The majority of these elderly are foreign-born and many of them are newly arrived immigrants or refugees. Like most of the Asians in this country, they usually live in or near big cities such as San Francisco, Los Angeles and New York.

The Asian elderly who were born in this country have experiences similar to those of other elderly Americans. Typically, they live by themselves and have fairly regular contact with their grown-up children.

The situation of elderly immigrants and refugees, however, is quite different, as is now well known to the mental health professionals who assist them with their problems of adjustment to life in America. Most of the refugees and immigrants who came to this country when already elderly did not intend to come here in the first place. They accompanied children who migrated to this country or followed later when their children sponsored their entry to the United States. They did not know very much about this country and were not well prepared for the changes about to confront them.

As they left their home countries these elderly persons experienced a series of significant losses. Their support networks of relatives and friends were shattered by war or were left behind when they departed. Their status in society and family changed dramatically, along with cultural and financial changes that deeply affected every aspect of their lives.

Elderly refugees from Vietnam, Cambodia and Laos faced additional problems. Unlike most other immigrants, they could not reasonably expect to be able to return to their countries of origin if adjustment to life in the United States proved too difficult.

Severe adjustment problems often induce in the elderly Asians a sense of having lost control over their lives and daily events, increasing their dependency and depression.

Most elderly Asian persons have great difficulty learning English. Except for those who live in Chinatowns or other ethnic communities, English is a necessity if they are to engage in even simple conversations with neighbors, take buses, read newspapers, understand TV programs and carry on the ordinary activities of everyday life. The language problem may keep them at home with little to do, making them dependent on their children or others as interpreters and intermediaries.

*Chan, Florentius. 1988. "To Be Old and Asian: An Unsettling Life in America." *Aging* 358:14–15.

In the balance of this article, the term Asian refers to immigrants and refugees from Asia and the Pacific Islands

Lack of transportation is another major problem. Very few Asian elderly own cars or have drivers' licenses, and if they can't read street signs or subway maps, they probably can't use public transportation. Even keeping appointments with doctors or welfare agencies may be very difficult. The expression "no legs" is commonly used by the Asian elderly who complain of severe handicaps due to lack of transportation.

Problems of cultural adjustment tend to underlie all the other difficulties that Asian elderly immigrants and refugees face. In their home countries they were generally respected and consulted for their wisdom and experience. They usually lived with their adult children and grandchildren and received any care they needed from them. They participated actively in making household decisions and disciplining grandchildren, while enjoying a position of authority in the home.

Their position in this country, however, may be quite different. Although they often live with their children or relatives, the older generation's knowledge may be considered obsolete and their wisdom may be ignored by the younger family members. The elders' religious practices, such as burning paper money and sacrificing live chickens, may seem totally out of place here. They may be allowed to play little role in household decisions. When they get sick they may be regarded as a burden, especially if they do not have health insurance or Medicaid coverage.

Elderly Asian men often come to feel bored and useless because they have few friends and activities and cannot get involved in household events. Elderly Asian women may be challenged on their childrearing practices when they babysit their grandchildren. Their methods and thinking may seem old-fashioned or unsuitable.

Arguments and disagreements tend to erupt more when they are living with their daughters-in-law than when with their sons-in-law. They complain that their daughters-in-law do not live up to traditional virtues and expectations. And the daughters-in-law tend to find the elderly women too bossy and stubborn.

Following are some notes from case histories illustrating some of the difficulties Asian elderly persons face:

A homeless, divorced 80-year-old Filipino man came to the community mental health clinic complaining of sleep disturbance, poor memory and anxiety. He has four children but refuses to live with them, saying they do not respect him and mistreat him. Social Security disability income is his main financial resource. He carries his bags of belongings from place to place and has been mugged several times.

A 63-year-old married Vietnamese woman sought help at the mental health clinic for depression. She and her husband came to the United States in 1985, sponsored by one of their sons. They have five children, two in Vietnam, one in a Thai camp, and two in the United States. They stayed with the son who lived in California until he rejected them because his wife didn't want them in her home any longer. The other married son who lives in Texas also refused to accept them. The couple is now dependent on general relief funds and has very serious financial problems.

A healthy 84-year-old Vietnamese widow has lived in this country since 1978. She was a wealthy business woman in Vietnam. She does not want to live with her children because she does not get along well with them. Currently she lives alone and is able to take care of herself. A devout Buddhist, she maintains an altar with a statue of the Buddha and burns incense there every day. She is extremely concerned that if she should die in this country her soul would never rest. Her children would not visit her burial place often, she believes, and would not burn money there, as is the tradition—they would probably only bring flowers. She speaks of returning to Vietnam in four more years. In Vietnam her soul could rest in peace, she feels. Her greatest fear is that she may die suddenly before returning to Vietnam. Sometimes she goes to the community social services agency to ask for help with a translation or local transportation. At those times she usually tells the community worker she has no friends and feels very lonely.

Such problems and conflicts are not unique, of course, to Asian immigrants and refugees. But they do call for culturally-sensitive assistance of a special kind, tailored to the needs of the older Asians and the process of adjustment they are undergoing.

36
Puerto Rican Elderly Women: Shared Meanings and Informal Supportive Networks*

Melba Sánchez-Ayéndez

Studies of older adults' support systems have seldom taken into account how values within a specific cultural context affect expectations of support and patterns of assistance in social networks. Such networks and supportive relations have cultural dimension reflecting a system of shared meanings. These meanings affect social interaction and the expectations people have of their relationships with others.

Ethnicity and gender affect a person's adjustment to old age. Although sharing a "minority" position produces similar consequences among members of different ethnic minority groups, the groups' diversity lies in their distinctive systems of shared meanings. Studies of older adults in ethnic minority groups have rarely focused on the cultural contents of ethnicity affecting the aging process, particularly

*Sánchez-Ayéndez, Melba. 1986. "Puerto Rican Elderly Women: Shared Meanings and Informal Supportive Networks." Pp. 172–186 in *All American Women: Lives That Divide, Ties That Bind*, edited by Johnetta B. Cole. New York: The Free Press. Reprinted with permission of The Free Press, a division of Macmillan, Inc. Copyright © 1986 by The Free Press.

of women (Barth 1969). Cultural value orientations are central to understanding how minority elders approach growing old and how they meet the physical and emotional changes associated with aging.

This article describes the interplay between values and behavior in family and community of a group of older Puerto Rican women living on low incomes in Boston.[1] It explores how values emphasizing family interdependence and different roles of women and men shape the women's expectations, behavior, and supportive familial and community networks.

BEING A WOMAN IS DIFFERENT FROM BEING A MAN

The women interviewed believe in a dual standard of conduct for men and women. This dual standard is apparent in different attributes assigned to women and men, roles expected of them, and authority exercised by them.

The principal role of men in the family is viewed as that of provider; their main responsibility is economic in nature. Although fathers are expected to be affectionate with their children, child care is not seen to be a man's responsibility. Men are not envisioned within the domestic sphere.

The "ideal" man must be the protector of the family, able to control his emotions and be self-sufficient. Men enjoy more freedom in the public world than do women. From the women's perspective, the ideal of maleness is linked to the concept of *machismo*. This concept assumes men have a stronger sexual drive than women, a need to prove virility by the conquest of women, a dominant position in relation to females, and a belligerent attitude when confronted by male peers.

The women see themselves as subordinate to men and recognize the pre-eminence of male authority. They believe women ought to be patient and largely forbearing in their relations with men, particularly male family members. Patience and forbearance, however, are not confused with passivity or total submissiveness. The elderly Puerto Rican women do not conceive of themselves or other women as "resigned females" but as dynamic beings, continually devising strategies to improve everyday situations within and outside the household.

Rosa Mendoza,[2] now sixty-five, feels no regrets for having decided at thirty years of age and after nine years of marriage not to put up with her husband's heavy drinking any longer. She moved out of her house and went to live with her mother.

> I was patient for many years. I put up with his drunkenness and worked hard to earn money. One day I decided I'd be better off without him. One thing is to be patient, and another to be a complete fool. So I moved out.

Although conscious of their subordinate status to their husbands, wives are also aware of their power and the demands they can make. Ana Fuentes recalls when her husband had a mistress. Ana was thirty-eight.

> I knew he had a mistress in a nearby town. I was patient for a long time, hoping it would end. Most men, sooner or later, have a mistress somewhere. But when

> it didn't end after quite a time and everyone in the neighborhood knew about it, I said "I am fed up!" He came home one evening and the things I told him! I even said I'd go to that woman's house and beat her if I had to.... He knew I was not bluffing; that this was not just another argument. He tried to answer back and I didn't let him. He remained silent.... And you know what? He stopped seeing her! A woman can endure many things for a long time, but the time comes when she has to defend her rights.

These older Puerto Rican women perceive the home as the center around which the female world revolves. Home is the woman's domain; women generally make decisions about household maintenance and men seldom intervene.

Family relations are considered part of the domestic sphere and therefore a female responsibility. The women believe that success in marriage depends on the woman's ability to "make the marriage work."

> A marriage lasts as long as the woman decides it will last. It is us who make a marriage work, who put up with things, who try to make ends meet, who yield.

The norm of female subordination is evident in the view that marriage will last as long as the woman "puts up with things" and deals with marriage from her subordinate status. Good relations with affinal kin are also a woman's responsibility. They are perceived as relations between the wife's domestic unit and other women's domestic units.

Motherhood

Motherhood is seen by these older Puerto Rican women as the central role of women. Their concept of motherhood is based on the female capacity to bear children and on the notion of *marianismo*, which presents the Virgin Mary as a role model (Stevens 1973). *Marianismo* presupposes that it is through motherhood that a woman realizes herself and derives her life's greatest satisfactions.

A woman's reproductive role is viewed as leading her toward more commitment to and a better understanding of her children than is shown by the father. One of the women emphasized this view:

> It is easier for a man to leave his children and form a new home with another woman, or not to be as forgiving of children as a mother is. They will never know what it is like to carry a child inside, feel it growing, and then bring that child into the world. This is why a mother is always willing to forgive and make sacrifices. That creature is a part of you; it nourished from you and came from within you. But it is not so for men. To them, a child is a being they receive once it is born. The attachment can never be the same.

The view that childrearing is their main responsibility in life comes from this conceptualization of the mother-child bond. For the older women, raising children means more than looking after the needs of offspring. It involves being able to offer them every possible opportunity for a better life, during childhood or adulthood, even if this requires personal sacrifices.

As mother and head of the domestic domain, a woman is also responsible for establishing the bases for close and good relations among her children. From childhood through adulthood, the creation and maintenance of family unity among offspring is considered another female responsibility.

FAMILY UNITY AND INTERDEPENDENCE

Family Unity

Ideal family relations are seen as based on two interrelated themes, family unity and family interdependence. Family unity refers to the desirability of close and intimate kin ties, with members getting along well and keeping in frequent contact despite dispersal.

Celebration of holidays and special occasions are seen as opportunities for kin to be together and strengthen family ties. Family members, particularly grandparents, adult children, and grandchildren, are often reunited at Christmas, New Year's, Mother's and Father's days, Easter, and Thanksgiving. Special celebrations like weddings, baptisms, first communions, birthdays, graduations, and funerals occasion reunions with other family members. Whether to celebrate happy or sad events, the older women encourage family gatherings as a way of strengthening kinship ties and fostering family continuity.

The value the women place on family unity is also evident in their desire for frequent interaction with kin members. Visits and telephone calls demonstrate a caring attitude by family members which cements family unity.

Family unity is viewed as contributing to the strengthening of family interdependence. Many of the older women repeat a proverb when referring to family unity: *En la unión está la fuerza.* ("In union there is strength.") They believe that the greater the degree of unity in the family, the greater the emphasis family members will place on interdependence and familial obligation.

Family Interdependence

Despite adaptation to life in a culturally different society, Puerto Rican families in the United States are still defined by strong norms of reciprocity among family members, especially those in the immediate kinship group (Cantor 1979; Carrasquillo 1982; Delgado 1981; Donaldson and Martinez 1980; Sánchez-Ayéndez 1984). Interdependence within the Puerto Rican symbolic framework "fits an orientation to life that stresses that the individual is not capable of doing everything and doing it well. Therefore, he should rely on others for assistance" (Bastida 1979, p. 70). Individualism and self-reliance assume a different meaning from the one prevailing in the dominant U.S. cultural tradition. Individuals in Puerto Rican families will expect and ask for assistance from certain people in their social networks without any derogatory implications for self-esteem.

Family interdependence is a value to which these older Puerto Rican women strongly adhere. It influences patterns of mutual assistance with their children as well as expectations of support. The older women expect to be taken care of during old age by their adult children. The notion of filial duty ensues from the value orientation of interdependence. Adult children are understood to have a responsibility toward their aged parents in exchange for the functions that parents performed for them throughout their upbringing. Expected reciprocity from offspring is intertwined with the concept of filial love and the nature of the parent-child relationship.

Parental duties of childrearing are perceived as inherent in the "parent" role and also lay the basis for long-term reciprocity with children, particularly during old age. The centrality that motherhood has in the lives of the older women contributes to creating great expectations among them of reciprocity from children. More elderly women than men verbalize disappointment when one of their children does not participate in the expected interdependence ties. Disappointment is unlikely to arise when an adult child cannot help due to financial or personal reasons. However, it is bound to arise when a child chooses not to assist the older parent for other reasons.

These older Puerto Rican women stress that good offspring ought to help their parents, contingent upon available resources. Statements such as the following are common:

> Of course I go to my children when I have a problem! To whom would I turn? I raised them and worked very hard to give them the little I could. Now that I am old, they try to help me in whatever they can. . . . Good offspring should help their aged parents as much as they are able to.

Interdependence for Puerto Rican older parents also means helping their children and grandchildren. Many times they provide help when it is not explicitly requested. They are happy when they can perform supportive tasks for their children's families. The child who needs help, no matter how old, is not judged as dependent or a failure.

Reciprocity is not based on strictly equal exchanges. Due to the rapid pace of life, lack of financial resources, or personal problems, adult children are not always able to provide their families with more financial and instrumental assistance than their children are able to provide them. Of utmost importance to the older women is not that their children be able to help all the time, but that they visit or call frequently. They place more emphasis on emotional support from their offspring than on any other form of support.

Gloria Santos, for example, has a son and a daughter. While they do not live in the same state as their mother, they each send her fifty to seventy dollars every month. Yet, she is disappointed with her children and explains why:

> They both have good salaries but call me only once or twice a month. I hardly know my grandchildren. All I ask from them is that they be closer to me, that they

visit and call me more often. They only visit me once a year and only for one or two days. I've told my daughter that instead of sending me money she could call me more often. I was a good mother and worked hard in order for them to get a good education and have everything. All I expected from them was to show me they care, that they love me.

The importance that the older women attach to family interdependence does not imply that they constantly require assistance from children or that they do not value their independence. They prefer to live in their own households rather than with their adult children. They also try to solve as many problems as possible by themselves. But when support is needed, the adult children are expected to assist the aged parent to the degree they are able. This does not engender conflict or lowered self-esteem for the aged adult. Conflict and dissatisfaction are caused when adult children do not offer any support at all.

SEX ROLES AND FAMILIAL SUPPORTIVE NETWORKS

The family is the predominant source of support for most of these older women, providing instrumental and emotional support in daily life as well as assistance during health crises or times of need. Adult children play a central role in providing familial support to old parents. For married women, husbands are also an important component of their support system. At the same time, most of the older women still perform functional roles for their families.

Support from Adult Children

The support and helpfulness expected from offspring is related to perceptions of the difference between men and women. Older women seek different types of assistance from daughters than from sons. Daughters are perceived as being inherently better able to understand their mothers due to their shared status and qualities as women; they are also considered more reliable. Sons are not expected to help as much as daughters or in the same way. When a daughter does not fulfill the obligations expected of her, complaints are more bitter than if the same were true of a son: "Men are different; they do not feel as we feel. But she is a woman; she should know better." Daughters are also expected to visit and/or call more frequently than are sons. As women are linked closely to the domestic domain, they are held responsible for the care of family relations.

Motherhood is perceived as creating an emotional bond among women. When daughters become mothers, the older women anticipate stronger ties and more support from them.

Once a daughter experiences motherhood, she understands the suffering and hardships you underwent for her. Sons will never be able to understand this.

My daughter always helped me. But when she became a mother for the first time, she grew much closer to me. It was then when she was able to understand how much a mother can love.

Most of the older women go to a daughter first when confronted by an emotional problem. Daughters are felt to be more patient and better able to understand them as women. It is not that older women never discuss their emotional problems with their sons, but they prefer to discuss them with their daughters. For example, Juana Rivera has two sons who live in the same city as she and a daughter who resides in Puerto Rico. She and her sons get along well and see each other often. The sons stop by their mother's house every day after work, talk about daily happenings, and assist her with some tasks. However, when a physical exam revealed a breast tumor thought to be malignant, it was to her daughter in Puerto Rico that the old woman expressed her worries. She recalls that time of crisis:

> Eddie was with me when the doctor told me of the possibility of a tumor. I was brave. I didn't want him to see me upset. They [sons] get nervous when I get upset or cry. . . . That evening I called my daughter and talked to her. . . . She was very understanding and comforted me. I can always depend on her to understand me. She is the person who better understands me. My sons are also understanding, but she is a woman and understands more.

Although adult children are sources of assistance during the illnesses of their mothers, it is generally daughters from whom more is expected. Quite often daughters take their sick parent into their homes or stay overnight in the parental household in order to provide better care. Sons, as well as daughters, take the aged parent to the hospital or doctors' offices and buy medicines if necessary. However, it is more often daughters who check on their parents, provide care, and perform household chores when the parent is sick.

When the old women have been hospitalized, adult children living nearby tend to visit the hospital daily. Daughters and daughters-in-law sometimes cook special meals for the sick parent and bring the meals to the hospital. Quite often, adult children living in other states or in Puerto Rico come to help care for the aged parent or be present at the time of an operation. When Juana Rivera had exploratory surgery on her breast, her daughter came from Puerto Rico and stayed with her mother throughout the convalescence. Similarly, when Ana Toledo suffered a stroke and remained unconscious for four days, three of her six children residing in other states came to be with her and their siblings. After her release from the hospital, a daughter from New Jersey stayed at her mother's house for a week. When she left, the children who live near the old woman took turns looking after her.

Most adult children are also helpful in assisting with chores of daily living. At times, the older women give their children money to do the shopping for them. Daughters are more often asked to do these favors and to also buy personal care items and clothes for their mothers. Some adult offspring also assist by depositing Social Security checks, checking post office boxes, and buying money orders.

Support from Elderly Mothers

The Puerto Rican older women play an active role in providing assistance to their adult children. Gender affects the frequency of emotional support offered as well as the dynamics of the support. The older women offer advice more often to daughters than to sons on matters related to childrearing. And the approach used differs according to the children's gender. For example, one older woman stated,

> I never ask my son openly what is wrong with him. I do not want him to think that I believe he needs help to solve his problems; he is a man. . . . Yet, as a mother I worry. It is my duty to listen and offer him advice. With my daughter it is different; I can be more direct. She doesn't have to prove to me that she is self-sufficient.

Another woman expressed similar views:

> Of course I give advice to my sons! When they have had problems with their wives, their children, even among themselves, I listen to them, and tell them what I think. But with my daughters I am more open. You see, if I ask one of my sons what is wrong and he doesn't want to tell me, I don't insist too much; I'll ask later, maybe in a different way; and they will tell me sooner or later. With my daughters, if they don't want to tell me, I insist. They know I am a mother and a woman like them and that I can understand.

Older mothers perceive sons and daughters as in equal need of support. Daughters, however, are understood to face additional problems in areas such as conjugal relations, childrearing, and sexual harassment, due to their status as women.

Emotional support to daughters-in-law is also offered, particularly when they are encountering marriage or childrearing problems. Josefina Montes explains the active role she played in comforting her daughter-in-law, whose husband was having an extramarital affair.

> I told her not to give up, that she had to defend what was hers. I always listened to her and tried to offer some comfort. . . . When my son would come to my home to visit I would ask him "What is wrong with you? Don't you realize what a good mother and wife that woman is?". . . . I made it my business that he did not forget the exceptional woman she is. . . . I told him I didn't want to ever see him with the other one and not to mention her name in front of me. . . . I was on his case for almost two years. . . . All the time I told her to be patient. . . . It took time but he finally broke up with the other one.

When relations between mother and daughters-in-law are not friendly, support is not usually present. Eulalia Valle says that when her son left his wife and children to move in with another woman, there was not much she could do for her daughter-in-law.

> There was not much I could do. What could I tell him? I couldn't say she was nice to me. . . . Once I tried to make him see how much she was hurting and he replied: "Don't defend her. She has never been fond of you and you know it." What could I reply to that? All I said was, "That's true but, still, she must be very hurt." But there was nothing positive to say about her!

Monetary assistance generally flows from the older parent to the adult children, although few old people are able to offer substantial financial help. Direct monetary assistance, rarely exceeding fifty dollars, is less frequent than gift-giving Gift-giving usually takes the form of monetary contributions for specific articles needed by their children or children's families. In this way the older people contribute indirectly to the maintenance of their children's families.

The older women also play an active role in the observance of special family occasions and holidays. On the days preceding the celebration, they are busy cooking traditional Puerto Rican foods. It is expected that those in good health will participate in the preparation of foods. This is especially true on Christmas and Easter when traditional foods are an essential component of the celebrations.

Cooking for offspring is also a part of everyday life. In many of the households, meals prepared in the Puerto Rican tradition are cooked daily "in case children or grandchildren come by." Josefina Montes, for example, cooks a large quantity of food everyday for herself, her husband and their adult children and grandchildren. Her daughters come by after work to visit and pick up their youngest children, who stay with grandparents after school. The youngest daughter eats dinner at her parents' home. The oldest takes enough food home to serve her family. Dõna[3] Josefina's sons frequently drop by after work or during lunch and she always insists that they eat something.

The older women also provide assistance to their children during health crises. When Juana Rivera's son was hospitalized for a hernia operation, she visited the hospital every day, occasionally bringing food she had prepared for him. When her son was released, Dõna Juana stayed in his household throughout his convalescence, caring for him while her daughter-in-law went off to work.

The aged women also assist their children by taking care of grandchildren. Grandchildren go to their grandmother's house after school and stay until their parents stop by after work. If the children are not old enough to walk home by themselves, the grandparent waits for them at school and brings them home. The women also take care of their grandchildren when they are not old enough to attend school or are sick. They see their role as grandmothers as a continuation or reenactment of their role as mothers and childbearers.

The women, despite old age, have a place in the functional structure of their families. The older women's assistance is an important contribution to their children's households and also helps validate the women's sense of their importance and helpfulness.

Mutual Assistance in Elderly Couples

Different conceptions of women and men influence interdependence between husband and wife as well as their daily tasks. Older married women are responsible for domestic tasks and perform household chores. They also take care of grandchildren, grocery shopping, and maintaining family relations. Older married men have among their chores depositing Social Security checks, going to the post office, and buying money orders. Although they stay in the house for long periods, the men go out into the community more often than do their wives. They usually stop at the *bodegas*,[4] which serve as a place for socializing and exchange of information, to buy items needed at home and newspapers from Puerto Rico.

Most married couples have a distinctive newspaper reading pattern. The husband comments on the news to his wife as he reads or after he has finished. Sometimes, after her husband finishes reading and commenting on the news, the older woman reads about it herself. Husbands also inform their wives of ongoing neighborhood events learned on their daily stops at the *bodegas*. Wives, on the other hand, inform husbands of familial events learned through their daily telephone conversations and visits from children and other kin members.

The older couple escort each other to service-providing agencies, even though they are usually accompanied by an adult child, adolescent grandchild, or social worker serving as translator. An older man still perceives himself in the role of "family protector" by escorting the women in his family, particularly his wife.

Older husbands and wives provide each other with emotional assistance. They are daily companions and serve as primary sources of confidence for each other, most often sharing children's and grandchildren's problems, health concerns, or financial worries. The couples do not always agree on solutions or approaches for assisting children when sharing their worries about offspring. Many times the woman serves as a mediator in communicating her husband's problems to adult children. The men tend to keep their problems, particularly financial and emotional ones, to themselves or tell their wives but not their children. This behavior rests upon the notion of men as financially responsible for the family, more self-sufficient, and less emotional than women.

Among the older couples, the husband or wife is generally the principal caregiver during the health crises of their spouse. Carmen Ruiz, for example, suffers from chronic anemia and tires easily. Her husband used to be a cook and has taken responsibility for cooking meals and looking after the household. When Providencia Cruz's husband was hospitalized she spent many hours each day at the hospital, wanting to be certain he was comfortable. She brought meals she had cooked for him, arranged his pillows, rubbed him with bay leaf rubbing alcohol, or watched him as he slept. When he was convalescing at home, she was his principal caregiver. Dõna Providencia suffers from osteoarthritis and gastric acidity. When she is in pain and spends the day in bed, her husband provides most of the assistance she needs. He goes to the drugstore to buy medicine or ingredients used in folk remedies. He knows how to prepare the mint and chamomile teas she drinks when not feeling well. He also rubs her legs and hands with ointments when the arthritic pain is more intense than usual. Furthermore, during the days that Dõna Providencia's ailments last, he performs most of the household chores.

While both spouses live, the couple manages many of their problems on their own. Assistance from other family members with daily chores or help during an illness is less frequent when the woman still lives with her husband than when she lives alone. However, if one or both spouses is ill, help from adult children is more common.

FRIENDS AND NEIGHBORS AS
COMMUNITY SOURCES OF SUPPORT

Friends and neighbors form part of the older women's support network. However, the women differentiate between "neighbors" and "friends." Neighbors, unlike kin and friends, are not an essential component of the network which provides emotional support. They may or may not become friends. Supportive relations with friends involve being instrumental helpers, companions, and confidants. Neighbors are involved only in instrumental help.

Neighbors as Sources of Support

Contact with neighbors takes the form of greetings, occasional visits, and exchanges of food, all of which help to build the basis for reciprocity when and if the need arises. The establishment and maintenance of good relations with neighbors is considered to be important since neighbors are potentially helpful during emergencies or unexpected events. Views such as the following are common: "It is good to get acquainted with your neighbors; you never know when you might need them."

Josefina Rosario, a widow, has lived next door to an older Puerto Rican couple for three years. Exchange of food and occasional visits are part of her interaction with them. Her neighbor's husband, in his mid-sixties, occasionally runs errands for Dõna Josefina, who suffers from rheumatoid arthritis and needs a walker to move around. If she runs out of a specific food item, he goes to the grocery store for her. Other times, he buys stamps, mails letters, or goes to the drugstore to pick up some medicines for her. Although Dõna Josefina cannot reciprocate in the same way, she repays her neighbors by visiting every other week and exchanging food. Her neighbors tell her she is to call them day or night if she ever feels sick. Although glad to have such "good neighbors," as she calls them, she stresses she does not consider them friends and therefore does not confide her personal problems to them.

Supportive Relationships Among Friends

Although friends perform instrumental tasks, the older women believe that a good friend's most important quality is being able to provide emotional support. A friend is someone willing to help during the "good" and "bad" times, and is trustworthy and reserved. Problems may be shared with a friend with the certainty that confidences will not be betrayed. A friend provides emotional support not only during a crises or problem, but in everyday life. Friends are companions, visiting and/or calling on a regular basis.

Friendship for this group of women is determined along gender lines. They tend to be careful about men. Relationships with males outside the immediate familial group are usually kept at a formal level. Mistrust of men is based upon the women's notion of *machismo*. Since men are conceived of as having a stronger sexual drive, the women are wary of the possibility of sexual advances, either physical or verbal. None of the women regards a male as a confidant friend. Many even emphasize the word *amiga* ("female friend") instead of *amigo* ("male friend"). Remarks such as the following are common:

I've never had an *amigo*. Men cannot be trusted too much. They might misunderstand your motives and some even try to make a pass at you.

The few times the women refer to a male as a friend they use the term *amigo de la familia* ("friend of the family"). This expression conveys that the friendly relations are not solely between the woman and the man. The expression is generally used to refer to a close friend of the husband. *Amigos de la familia* may perform instrumental tasks, be present at family gatherings and unhappy events, or drop by to chat with the respondent's husband during the day. However, relations are not based on male-female relationships.

Age similarity is another factor that seems to affect selection of friends. The friendship networks of the older women are mainly composed of people sixty years of age and older. Friends who fill the role of confidant are generally women of a similar age. The women believe that younger generations, generally, have little interest in the elders. They also state that people their own age are better able to understand their problems because they share many of the same difficulties and worries.

Friends often serve as escorts, particularly in the case of women who live alone. Those who know some English serve as translators on some occasions. Close friends also help illiterate friends by reading and writing letters.

Most of the support friends provide one another is of an emotional nature, which involves sharing personal problems. Close friends entrust one another with family and health problems. This exchange occurs when friends either visit or call each other on the telephone. A pattern commonly observed between dyads of friends is daily calls. Many women who live alone usually call the friend during the morning hours, to make sure she is all right and to find out how she is feeling.

Another aspect of the emotional support the older women provide one another is daily companionship, occurring more often among those who live alone. For example, Hilda Montes and Rosa Mendoza sit together from 1:00 to 3:00 in the afternoon to watch soap operas and talk about family events, neighborhood happenings, and household management. At 3:00 P.M., whoever is at the other's apartment leaves because their grandchildren usually arrive from school around 4:00 P.M.

Friends are also supportive during health crises. If they cannot come to visit, they inquire daily about their friend's health by telephone. When their health permits, some friends perform menial household chores and always bring food for the sick person. If the occasion requires it, they prepare and/or administer home remedies. Friends, in this sense, alleviate the stress adult children often feel in assisting their aged mothers, particularly those who live by themselves. Friends take turns among themselves or with kin in taking care of the ill during the daytime. Children generally stay throughout the night.

Exchange ties with female friends include instrumental support, companionship, and problem sharing. Friends, particularly age cohorts, play an important role in the emotional well-being of the elders.

The relevance of culture to experience of old age is seen in the influence of value orientations on the expectations these Puerto Rican women have of themselves and those in their informal supportive networks. The way a group's cultural tradition defines and interprets relationships influences how elders use their networks to secure the support needed in old age. At the same time, the extent to which reality fits culturally-based expectations will contribute, to a large extent, to elders' sense of well-being.

NOTES

1. The article is based on a nineteen-month ethnographic study. The research was supported by the Danforth Foundation; Sigma Xi; the Scientific Research Society; and the Delta Kappa Gamma Society International.

2. All names are fictitious.

3. The deference term *Dõna* followed by the woman's first name is a common way by which to address elderly Puerto Rican women and the one preferred by those who participated in the study.

4. Neighborhood grocery stores, generally owned by Puerto Ricans or other Hispanics, where ethnic foods can be purchased.

REFERENCES

Barth, F. 1969. Introduction to *Ethnic Groups and Boundaries*, edited by F. Barth. Boston: Little, Brown.

Bastida, E. 1979. "Family Integration and Adjustment to Aging Among Hispanic American Elderly." Ph.D. dissertation, University of Kansas.

Cantor, M. H. 1979. "The Informal Support System of New York's Inner City Elderly: Is Ethnicity a Factor?" In *Ethnicity and Aging*, edited by D. L. Gelfand and A. J. Kutzik. New York: Springer.

Carrasquillo, H. 1982. "Perceived Social Reciprocity and Self-Esteem Among Elderly Barrio Antillean Hispanics and Their Familial Informal Networks." Ph.D. dissertation, Syracuse University.

Delgado, M. 1981. "Hispanic Elderly and Natural Support Systems: A Special Focus on Puerto Ricans." Paper presented at the Scientific Meeting of the Boston Society for Gerontological Psychiatry, Boston, MA, November.

Donaldson, E. and E. Martinez 1980. "The Hispanic Elderly of East Harlem" *Aging* 305–306: 6–11.

Sánchez-Ayéndez, M. 1984. "Puerto Rican Elderly Women: Aging in an Ethnic Minority Group in the United States." Ph.D. dissertation, University of Massachusetts at Amherst.

Stevens, E. P. 1973. "Marianismo: The Other Face of Machismo in Latin America." In *Female and Male in Latin America*, edited by A. Pescatello. Pittsburgh: University of Pittsburgh Press.

PART IV

FAMILIES IN CRISIS
AND CHANGE

In this part of the reader, we examine two problematic aspects of marriage and family life. The ensuing articles will illustrate how patriarchy has been a major contributor to marital and familial tensions and problems. Patriarchal ideology supported by economic, social, political, and religious institutions often enables men to exert the upper hand in many aspects of martial and family relationships. Similarly, the domination of older family members over younger ones has often been the consequence of age stratification processes operating in family systems. In Chapter Eleven, Family Violence and Stress, the first four articles deal with the ultimate abuse of marital and familial patterns of stratification and power—family violence.

Intimate violence, whether it takes the form of wife battering or child abuse, can be seen as an irrational outgrowth of the excesses of patriarchal authority. The legitimation of male prerogatives, privilege, authority, and power can be abused, and in the case of wife battering, it is. This results in the severe mistreatment of women. Contemporary American society has just recently discovered the prevalence of marital abuse, which has been hidden from history because the belief that "normal" marriages are happy and well adjusted and that violence is an aberration has led to the underestimation of such abuse. This misunderstanding has further led to the treatment of marital abuse erroneously as a psychologically determined pathology and not as a social phenomenon.

Similarly, child abuse can be seen as a negative consequence of the conceptualization of children and adolescents as essentially inferior and subordinate human beings. Structural characteristics of the private nuclear family also play important contributory roles. Governmental policies and the underlying assumptions of the helping professions, too, often work against the best interests of children.

Murray A. Straus has been one of the most active sociologists in the study of family violence. In an important essay, "Societal Morphogenesis and Intrafamily Violence in Cross-Cultural Perspective," Straus (1977) outlined the major factors that account for family violence. The first three factors relate to internal family dynamics and include the extent of time involvements of family members with each other, the number of activities and interests that the family members share, and the intensity of their involvements and attachments. The fourth factor is sexual inequality, which links male dominance with wife beating. The privacy of the family is listed as the fifth factor. Straus argues that the private family insulates its members from the social control of neighbors and extended kin. He then builds on the relationship between family violence and aggression and various societal patterns. Using cross-cultural data as his source, Straus develops the view that the more pervasive the existence of societal violence, the higher is the level of family violence. Further, there seems to exist a reciprocal relationship between the aggression and violence in the society and the level of violence within the family.

Another point of interest is Straus's assertion that there is a strong link between violence in one family role with violence in other family roles. Thus, in families where violence between husband and wife is prevalent, parents will more likely be violent toward their children. Further, battered or abused children often become parents who batter and abuse their children. Finally, we should note that the growing concern of abuse of elderly parents by their grown children can be seen as a manifestation of the inadequacies of the private family and the declining significance of the elderly in contemporary society.

In Article 33, Murray A. Straus and his colleague Richard J. Gelles provide a sociological profile of the underlying conditions of family violence. We often tend to view incidents of family violence as a consequence of an individual pathology and look first for psychological explanations. Straus and Gelles take the approach that it is of vital importance to understand the underlying sociological patterns accounting for this phenomena. They first examine the social organization of the family to determine what structural features of the modern household are conducive to violence in the home. Then they turn their attention to family and individual characteristics related to intimate violence. Finally, they concern themselves with the spatial and temporal components of family violence—that is, where and when family violence is most likely to occur.

John M. Johnson and Kathleen J. Ferraro, two sociologists who work out of the symbolic interaction perspective of social psychology, are concerned with how individuals continually adapt to situations and how these adaptions affect self concepts. In Article 38, Johnson and Ferraro study the experiences of battered women, who find themselves living through episodic outbursts of violence from their mates. The consequences of that victimization on their sense of identity is the focus of their concern.

In the next article (39), Johnson extends the analysis of the conceptualization of childhood to an understanding of the changing concept of child abuse. He further elaborates by discussing the child maltreatment movement and its impact on family life. What complicates the treatment of child abuse is the prevailing tension between the rights of parents and the intervention of social agencies. Since the privatization of the family, parental rights regarding the rearing of children have been of paramount importance. However, in cases of child maltreatment, society finds itself in a dilemma. Although it may be in the victimized child's best interest, society is reluctant to interfere with parental prerogatives and often leaves the the child in the family and subject to further neglect and abuse. Taking the child from the home, on the other hand, often means subjecting the child to inadequate foster-care programs and institutional facilities. Johnson's paper is concerned with this dilemma.

We return to the subject of the relationship between societal factors and intimate violence in Robert S. Laufer and M.S. Gallops's article (40), "Life-course Effects of Vietnam Combat and Abusive Violence: Marital Patterns." Laufer and Gallops examine the impact of military service in Vietnam and war trauma on marital patterns. They look at the relationship between war and the family and examine the consequences on a number of family variables including abusive violence, marital satisfaction, and rates of marriage and divorce. Here again, we are made aware on how broader societal patterns affect domestic relationships.

The concluding article (41) in this chapter examines the effects of AIDS on parent-child relationships. AIDS—an acronym for "acquired immunity deficiency syndrome"—is a contagious disease that has differential impact in the United States on specific "risk" groups: gays, intravenous drug abusers, and hemophiliacs. For the most part, the societal reaction to this dreadful disease is influenced and distorted by ideological factors relating to homosexuality. Peggy H. Cleveland and her associates address the question of the attitudes of parents who have children in a high-risk category for AIDS (e.g., homosexual men). The article centers around responses of parents of homosexual children to the question, "What would (or did) you do if (when) you discovered your child had AIDS?" The implications for the helping professions are also delineated by the authors.

The final chapter of the book, Chapter Twelve, Divorce, Single Parenthood, and Remarriage, contains four articles. Divorce is a major form of marital dissolution. It represents an ultimate manifestation of marital and familial instability. Divorce has been viewed by some as an indicator of the breakdown of the American family and as a reflection of societal decline. Conversely, others see it as the outcome of a positive individual act, ultimately beneficial to all members and, as such, a sign of societal strength.

Diane Vaughan in her work on "uncoupling" (Article 42) analyzes the social-psychological consequences of divorce. Her research findings have subsequently been incorporated in her best-selling book, *Uncoupling: How Relationships Come Apart*. Vaughan's analysis of "uncoupling" is influenced by Peter L. Berger and Hansfried Kellner's (1964) "Marriage and the Construction of Reality."

Berger and Kellner believe that the contemporary character of marriage originated in the development of a private sphere of existence that is separated from the controls of such public institutions as politics and economics. Marriage is designed to be a haven of security and order. It is a world in which the husband and wife can create their own social reality and social order. This is seen to be of crucial importance to wage earners—it provides them with an environment in which they can gain a sense of control in contrast to their jobs, which are often viewed in terms of powerlessness and unfulfillment, or to politics, which is viewed cynically.

Berger and Kellner argue that the reality of the world is sustained through interaction with significant others. An individual who is deprived of relationships with significant others will feel a sense of anomie and alienation. The marriage relationship is designed to provide a "nomic" versus an "anomic" situation. Here intimacy can occur and a meaningful world can be constructed. In marriage the two participants come together and redefine themselves through the unfolding of the marital relationship and the involvement they have with others.

Vaughan recognizes the extreme importance that marriage has for an individual's emotional and intimate well-being and one's sense of identity. Indeed, marriage American-style demands that psychological intimacy and love become the cornerstones of marriage. As a consequence, the "uncoupling" process that leads to divorce marks a major turning point in the lives of those affected. Vaughan examines this process and sees it in terms of a series of transitions that range from the dissolution of the marital identity to the formation of somewhat problematic new identity.

In a previous reading (Article 14), Lenore Weitzman discussed the feminization of poverty that was an unanticipated consequence of no-fault divorce. No-fault laws give legal recognition to "marital breakdown" as a sufficient justification for divorce. Weitzman's (1985) major finding was that, under no-fault divorce, women and their children are becoming a new underclass. Divorced women are often impoverished by no-fault laws because the courts, in dividing property, interpret "equality" at divorce by disregarding the economic inequalities created during marriage. Further, the equal division of property often forces women to sell their homes to divide what constitutes the couple's only property. Less tangible, and often more valuable, the husband's property and assets such as education, professional licenses, career advancements, pensions, and health insurances are often not taken into account in court decisions. As a result, rather than alleviating the injustice, no-fault exacerbates it.

Terry Arendall's article (42) contains a powerful ethnographic account of the resultant downward mobility of divorced women and their children, which is a consequence of the inadequate level of personal and child support that they have received from absent husbands, social assistance, and other governmental programs. Here again, we see the inextricable links between families and social policy decisions.

The effects of divorce on children and adolescents has long been a concern of sociology. These effects have become an even more urgent matter in light of the continued relatively high divorce rate in the United States and the fact that an increased number of children are affected. In 1971 the number of children involved in divorce exceeded one million, and in recent years divorce has affected over two million children every year. It is estimated that nearly half of all children under the age of 18 will experience divorce in the 1990s.

Judith Wallerstein has been in the forefront of research on children of divorce. Her major work (1989) was written with Sandra Blakeslee and is called *Second Chances: Men, Women & Children A Decade After Divorce*. It was the culmination of her groundbreaking ten-year longitudinal study of divorced parents and their children. The paper reprinted here (Article 44) was the fourth report of her study of 131 children from 60 divorcing families in Northern California and appeared just prior to her book. Here, Wallerstein details her findings on 38 adolescents 16 to 18 years old who experienced separation from families and are now in the transition to young adulthood. The disheartening conclusions that she reaches speak to the often disastrous effects on children as a consequence of their parents' divorce.

There is a myth surrounding remarriage that says the second marriage is more successful than the first—that "love is better the second time around." According to popular opinion, this is so because remarried individuals are now older, wiser, and more mature. Also, it is assumed that divorced persons who remarry will work harder to ensure a more successful second marriage. Yet, as Andrew Cherlin reports (Article 45), the divorce rate for persons who remarry after divorce is higher than for persons who marry for the first time. According to this researcher, insufficient institutional supports and guidelines to ensure optimal success of these marriages account for the high rate of divorce among remarrieds with children. Cherlin observes that family members of such remarriages face unique problems that do not exist in first-marriage families. He believes that the origins of these problems lie in the complex structure of remarried families and the normative inadequacies to define these familial roles and relationships. Cherlin's article points out the necessity for a more systematic investigation of remarriage.

REFERENCES

Berger, Peter L. and Hansfried Kellner. 1964. "Marriage and the Construction of Reality." *Diogenes* 46:1–25.

Straus, Murray A. 1977. "Social Morphogenesis and Intrafamily Violence in Cross-Cultural Perspective." *Annals of the New York Academy of Sciences* 285:719–730.

Vaughan, Diane. 1986. *Uncoupling: How Relationships Come Apart*. New York: Oxford University Press.

Wallerstein, Judith S. and Sandra Blakeslee. 1989. *Second Chances: Men, Women & Children A Decade After Divorce*. New York: Ticknor & Fields.

Weitzman, Lenore. 1985. *The Divorce Revolution: The Unexplored Consequences*. New York: Free Press.

CHAPTER ELEVEN

Family Violence and Stress

37

Profiling Violent Families*

Richard J. Gelles and Murray A. Straus

Each incident of family violence seems to be unique—an uncontrolled explosion of rage, a random expression of anger, an impulse, a volcanic eruption of sadism. Each abuser seems a bit different. The circumstances never seem to be the same. In one home a child may be attacked for talking back to a parent, in another the precipitating incident may be a broken lamp. Wives have been beaten because the food was cold, because the house was cold, because they were cold.

If we reject the notion that violence and abuse are the products of mental illness or intraindividual pathologies, than we implicitly accept the assumption that there is a social pattern that underlies intimate abuse.[1] The public and the media recognize this underlying pattern. Perhaps the most frequently asked question by the press, public, and clinicians who treat cases of domestic abuse is, "What is the profile of a violent parent, husband, wife, family?" . . . [H]umans have an innate desire for social order. They want to live in a predictable world. Even though violence in the home is more socially acceptable than violence in the street and thus, to a degree, more orderly, people still want to know what to look for. What are the signs, indicators, predictors of a battering parent, an abusive husband?

A profile of intimate violence must include at least three dimensions. First, we need to examine the social organization of families in general that contributes to the risk of violence in the home. Second, we review the characteristics of families in particular that make certain families high risk for violence. Third, we discuss the temporal and spatial patterns of intimate violence—where and when violence is most likely to occur.

VIOLENCE AND THE SOCIAL
ORGANIZATION OF THE FAMILY

The myth that violence and love do not coexist in families disguises a great irony about intimacy and violence. There are a number of distinct organizational characteristics of the family that promote intimacy, but at the very same time contribute to the escalation of conflict to violence and injury.[2] Sometimes, the very characteristics that make the family a warm, supportive, and intimate environment also lead to conflict and violence.

The time we spend with our family almost always exceeds the time we spend at work or with nonfamily members. This is particularly true for young children, men and women who are not in the work force, and the very old. From a strictly quantitative point of view, we are at greater risk in the home simply because we spend so much time there. But, time together is not sufficient to lead to violence. What goes on during these times is much more important than simply the minutes, hours, days, weeks, or years spent together.

Not only are we with our parents, partners, and children, but we interact with them over a wide range of activities and interests. Unless you live (and love) with someone, the total range of activities and interests you share are much narrower than intimate, family involvements. While the range of intimate interactions is great, so is the intensity. When the nature of intimate involvement is deep, the stakes of the involvement rise. Failures are more important. Slights, insults, and affronts hurt more. The pain of injury runs deeper. A cutting remark by a family member is likely to hurt more than the same remark in another setting.

We know more about members of our family than we know about any other individuals we ever deal with. We know their fears, wants, desires, frailties. We know what makes them happy, mad, frustrated, content. Likewise, they know the same about us. The depth of knowledge that makes intimacy possible also reveals the vulnerabilities and frailties that make it possible to escalate conflict. If, for instance, our spouse insults us, we know in an instant what to say to get even. We know enough to quickly support a family member, or to damage him. In no other setting is there a greater potential to support and help, or hurt and harm, with a gesture, a phrase, or a cutting remark. Over and over again, the people we talk to point to an attack on their partner's vulnerabilities as precipitating violence:

> If I want to make her feel real bad, I tell her how stupid she is. She can't deal with this, and she hits me.
> We tear each other down all the time. He says things just to hurt me—like how I clean the house. I complain about his work—about how he doesn't make enough money to support us. He gets upset, I get upset, we hit each other.
> If I really want to get her, I call her dirty names or call her trash.

We found, in many of our interviews with members of violent families, that squabbles, arguments, and confrontations escalate rapidly to violence when one partner focused on the other's vulnerabilities. Jane, a thirty-two-year-old mother, found that criticizing her husband's child-care skills often moved an argument to violence:

Well, we would argue about something, anything. If it was about our kids I would say, "But you shouldn't talk, because you don't even know how to take care of them." If I wanted to hurt him I would use that. We use the kids in our fights and it really gets bad. He [her husband] doesn't think the baby loves him. I guess I contribute to that a bit. When the baby start's fussin' my husband will say "Go to your mom." When I throw it up to him that the baby is afraid of him, that's when the fights really get goin'."

It is perhaps the greatest irony of family relations that the quality that allows intimacy—intimate knowledge of social biographies, is also a potential explosive, ready to be set off with the smallest fuse.

The range of family activities includes deciding what television program to watch, who uses the bathroom first, what house to buy, what job to take, how to raise and discipline the children, or what to have for dinner. Whether the activities are sublime or ridiculous, the outcome is often "zero-sum" for the participants. Decisions and decision making across the range of family activities often mean that one person (or group) will win, while another will lose. If a husband takes a new job in another city, his wife may have to give up her job, while the children may have to leave their friends. If her job and the children's friends are more important, then the husband will lose a chance for job advancement or a higher income. While the stakes over which television station to watch or which movie to go to may be smaller, the notion of winning and losing is still there. In fact, some of the most intense family conflicts are over what seem to be the most trivial choices. Joanne, a twenty-five-year-old mother of two toddlers, remembers violent fights over whether she and her husband would talk or watch television:

When I was pregnant the violence was pretty regular. John would come home from work. I would want to talk with him, 'cause I had been cooped up in the house with the baby and being pregnant. He would just want to watch the TV. So he would have the TV on and he didn't want to listen to me. We'd have these big fights. He pushed me out of the way. I would get in front of the TV and he would just throw me on the floor.

We talked to one wife who, after a fight over the television, picked the TV up and threw it at her husband. For a short time at least, they did not have a television to fight over.

Zero-sum activities are not just those that require decisions or choices. Less obvious than choices or decisions, but equally or sometimes more important, are infringements of personal space or personal habits. The messy wife and the neat husband may engage in perpetual zero-sum conflict over the house, the bedroom, and even closet space. How should meals be served? When should the dishes be washed? Who left the hairbrush in the sink? How the toothpaste should be squeezed from the tube and a million other daily conflicts and confrontations end with a winner and a loser.

Imagine you have a co-worker who wears checkered ties with striped shirts, who cannot spell, whose personal hygiene leaves much to be desired. How likely are you to (1) tell him that he should change his habits; (2) order him to change; (3)

spank him, send him to his room, or cut off his paycheck until he does change? Probably never. Yet, were this person your partner, child, or even parent, you would think nothing of getting involved and trying to influence his behavior. While the odd behavior of a friend or co-worker may be cause for some embarrassment, we typically would not think of trying to influence this person unless we had a close relationship with him. Yet, family membership carries with it not only the right, but sometimes the obligation, to influence other members of the family. Consequently, we almost always get involved in interactions in the home that we would certainly ignore or make light of in other settings.

Few people notice that the social structure of the family is unique. First, the family has a balance of both males and females. Other settings have this quality — coeducational schools, for instance. But many of the social institutions we are involved in have an imbalance of males and females. Some settings — automobile assembly lines, for instance — may be predominantly male, while other groups — a typing pool, for instance — may be almost exclusively female. In addition to the fact that intimate settings almost always include males and females, families also typically include a range of ages. Half of all households have children under eighteen years of age in them.[3] Thus the family, more so than almost any other social group or social setting, has the potential for both generational and sex differences and conflicts. The battle between the sexes and the generation gap have long been the source of intimate conflict.

Not only is the family made up of males and females with ages ranging from newborn to elderly, but the family is unique in how it assigns tasks and responsibilities. No other social group expects its members to take on jobs simply on the basis of their age or their sex. In the workplace, at school, and in virtually every other social setting, roles and responsibilities are primarily based on interest, experience, and ability. In the home, duties and responsibilities are primarily tied to age and gender. There are those who argue that there is a biological link between gender and task — that women make better parents than men. Also, the developmental abilities of children certainly preclude their taking on tasks or responsibilities that they are not ready for. But, by and large, the fact that roles and responsibilities are age- and gender-linked is a product of social organization and not biological determinism.

When someone is blocked from doing something that he or she is both interested in and capable of doing, this can be intensely frustrating.[4] When the inequality is socially structured and sanctioned within a society that at the same time espouses equal opportunity and egalitarianism, it can lead to intense conflict and confrontation. Thus, we find that the potential for conflict and violence is especially high in a democratic and egalitarian society that sanctions and supports a male-dominated family system. Even if we did not have values that supported democracy and egalitarianism, the linking of task to gender would produce considerable conflict since not every man is capable of taking on the socially prescribed leadership role in the home; and not every woman is interested in and capable of assuming the primary responsibility for child care.

The greater the inequality, the more one person makes all the decisions and has all the power, the greater the risk of violence. Power, power confrontations, and perceived threats to domination, in fact, are underlying issues in almost all acts of family violence. One incident of nearly deadly family violence captures the meaning of power and power confrontations:

> My husband wanted to think of himself as the head of the household. He thought that the man should wear the pants in the family. Trouble was, he couldn't seem to get his pants on. He had trouble getting a job and almost never could keep one. If I didn't have my job as a waitress, we would have starved. Even though he didn't make no money, he still wanted to control the house and the kids. But it was my money, and I wasn't about to let him spend it on booze or gambling. This really used to tee him off. But he would get the maddest when the kids showed him no respect. He and I argued a lot. One day we argued in the kitchen and my little girl came in. She wanted to watch TV. My husband told her to go to her room. She said, "No, I don't have listen to you!" Well, my husband was red. He picked up a knife and threw it at my little girl. He missed. Then he threw a fork at her and it caught her in the chin. She was bloody and crying, and he was still mad and ran after her. I had to hit him with a chair to get him to stop. He ran out of the house and didn't come back for a week. My little girl still has a scar on her cheek.

You can choose whom to marry, and to a certain extent you may chose to end the marital relationship. Ending a marital relationship, even in the age of no-fault divorce, is not neat and simple. There are social expectations that marriage is a long-term commitment—"until death do us part." There are social pressures that one should "work on a relationship" or "keep the family together for the sake of the children." There are also emotional and financial constraints that keep families together or entrap one partner who would like to leave.

You can be an ex-husband or an ex-wife, but not an ex-parent or an ex-child.[5] Birth relationships are quite obviously involuntary. You cannot choose your parents or your children (with the exception of adoption, and here your choices are still limited).

Faced with conflict, one can fight or flee. Because of the nature of family relations, it is not easy to choose the flight option when conflict erupts. Fighting, then, becomes a main option for resolving intimate conflict.

The organization of the family makes for stress. Some stress is simply developmental—the birth of a child, the maturation of children, the increasing costs of raising children as they grow older, illness, old age, and death. There are also voluntary transitions—taking a new job, a promotion, or moving. Stress occurring outside of the home is often brought into the home—unemployment, trouble with the police, trouble with friends at school, trouble with people at work. We expect a great deal from our families: love, warmth, understanding, nurturing, intimacy, and financial support. These expectations, when they cannot be fulfilled, add to the already high level of stress with which families must cope.

Privacy is the final structural element of modern families that makes them vulnerable to conflict, which can escalate into violence. . . . The nuclear structure of the modern family, and the fact that it is the accepted norm that family relations are private relations, reduces the likelihood that someone will be available to prevent the escalation of family conflict to intimate violence.

We have identified the factors that contribute to the high level of conflict in families. These factors also allow conflicts to become violent and abusive interchanges. By phrasing the discussion differently, we could have presented these factors as also contributing to the closeness and intimacy that people seek in family relations. People who marry and have families seek to spend large amounts of time together, to have deep and long-lasting emotional involvement, to have an intimate and detailed knowledge of another person, and to be able to create some distance between their intimate private lives and the interventions of the outside world.

There are a number of conclusions one can draw from the analysis of the structural factors that raise the risk of conflict and violence in the family. First, there is a link between intimacy and violence. Second is the classic sociological truism—structures affect people. Implicit in the discussion of these factors is that one can explain part of the problem of violence in the home without focusing on the individual psychological status of the perpetrators of violence and abuse. Violence occurs, not just because it is committed by weird, bad, different, or alien people, but because the structure of the modern household is conductive to violent exchanges.

FAMILY AND INDIVIDUAL CHARACTERISTICS RELATED TO INTIMATE VIOLENCE

The structural arrangement of the family makes it possible for violence to occur in all households. However, not all homes are violent. A profile of intimate violence needs to analyze the characteristics of violent individuals and their families.

Volumes could be written inventorying the characteristics that are thought to be related to family violence. The earliest students of child and wife abuse focused on individual personality characteristics.[6] Abusers were described as sadomasochistic, having poor emotional control, self-centered, hypersensitive, dependent, egocentric, narcissistic, and so on. Later, those who studied violence and abuse examined social and social psychological factors such as income, education, age, social stress, and social isolation.[7] Other investigators focused on experience with and exposure to violence. Still others chose to study violence from the point of view of the family level of analysis, examining family size, family power, and family structure.[8]

Sometimes investigators agree on specific characteristics that are believed to be associated with violence; other times the findings are contradictory. There is one thing that researchers agree on—there are a multitude of factors associated with violence in the home.[9] Despite public clamor for a single-factor explanation, no one factor—not mental illness, not experience with violence, not poverty, not stress, and not alcohol or drugs—explains all or most acts of intimate violence.

Abusive Violence Toward Children

Most people who try to explain and understand individual acts of deviant or aberrant behavior such as child abuse immediately turn their focus on the perpetrator. Our culture has a definite "individual level" bias when it comes to trying to explain seemingly unexplainable acts. When someone does something outrageous, weird, or bizarre, our immediate reaction is to look for the answer within that individual. A full understanding of abusive violence, however, requires an examination of not only the violent parent, but the child and family situation.

If one had to come up with a profile of the prototypical abusive parent, it would be a single parent who was young (under thirty), had been married for less than ten years, had his or her first child before the age of eighteen, and was unemployed or employed parttime.[10] If he or she worked, it would be at a manual labor job. Studies show that women are slightly more likely to abuse their children than men. The reason is rather obvious: Women typically spend more time with children. But, even if mothers and fathers spend equal time with children (and this is rare), it is the woman who is typically given the responsibility of caring for and dealing with the children.

Economic adversity and worries about money pervade the typical violent home. Alicia, the thirty-four-year-old wife of an assembly-line worker, has beaten, kicked, and punched both her children. So has her husband Fred. She spoke about the economic problems that hung over their heads:

> He worries about what kind of a job he's going to get, or if he's going to get a job at all. He always worries about supporting the family. I think I worry about it more than he does. . . . It gets him angry and frustrated. He gets angry a lot. I think he gets angry at himself for not providing what he feels we need. He has to take it out on someone, and the kids and me are the most available ones.

We witnessed a more graphic example of the impact of economic stress during one of our in-home interviews with a violent couple. When we entered the living room to begin the interview we could not help but notice the holes in the living room walls. During the course of the interview, Jane, the twenty-four-year-old mother of three children, told us that her husband had been laid off from his job at a local shipyard and had come home, taken out his shotgun, and shot up the living room. Violence had not yet been directed at the children, but as we left and considered the family, we could not help but worry about the future targets of violent outbursts.

Stressful life circumstances are the hallmark of the violent family. The greater the stress individuals are under, the more likely they are to be violent toward their children. Our 1976 survey of violence in the American family included a measure of life stress.[11] Subjects were asked if they had experienced any of a list of eighteen stressful events in the last year, ranging from problems at work, to death of a family member, to problems with children. Experience with stress ranged from households that experienced no stressful event to homes that had experienced thirteen of the eighteen items we discussed. The average experience with stress, however, was modest—about two stressful life events each year. Not surprisingly, the greater the number of stressful events experienced, the greater the rate of abusive violence toward children in the home. More than one out of three families that were unfortunate enough to encounter ten or more stressful events reported using abusive violence toward a child in the previous year. This rate was 100 percent greater than the rate for households experiencing only one stressful incident.

Violent parents are likely to have experienced or been exposed to violence as children. Although this does not predetermine that they will be violent (and likewise, some abusive parents grew up in nonviolent homes), there is the heightened risk that a violent past will lead to a violent future.

One of the more surprising outcomes of our first national survey of family violence was that there was no difference between blacks and whites in the rates of abusive violence toward children. This should not have been the case. First, most official reports of child abuse indicate that blacks are overrepresented in the reports. Also, blacks in the United States have higher rates of unemployment than whites and lower annual incomes—two factors that we know lead to higher risk of abuse. That blacks and whites had the same rate of abusive violence was one of the great mysteries of the survey. A careful examination of the data collected unraveled the apparent mystery. While blacks did indeed encounter economic problems and life stresses at greater rates than whites, they also were more involved in family and community activities than white families. Blacks reported more contact with their relatives and more use of their relatives for financial support and child care. It was apparent that the extensive social networks that black families develop and maintain insulate them from the severe economic stresses they also experience, and thus reduce what otherwise would have been a higher rate of parental violence. [12]

Most of the cases of child abuse we hear about involve very young children. There is nothing that provokes greater sadness and outrage than seeing the battered body of a defenseless infant. The youngest victims evoke the most sympathy and anger, best fit the stereotype of the innocent victim, and are more likely to be publicly identified as victims of abuse. The youngest children are indeed the most likely to be beaten and hurt.

However, the myth that only innocents are victims of abuse hides the teenage victim. Teenagers are equally likely to be abused as children under three years of age. Why are the youngest children and teenagers at the greatest risk of abusive violence? When we explain why the youngest children are likely victims the answer seems to be that they are demanding, produce considerable stress, and cannot be reasoned with verbally. Parents of teenagers offer the same explanation for why they think teenagers as a group are at equally high risk.

Among the younger victims of violence and abuse, there are a number of factors that make them at risk. Low birth weight babies, premature children, handicapped, retarded, and developmentally disabled children run high life-long risk violence and abuse. [13] In fact, the risk is great for any child who is considered different.

If you want to prevent violence and abuse, either have no children or eight or nine. This was the somewhat common sense outcome of our research on family factors related to violence toward children. It is rather obvious that more children create more stress. Why then did we find no violence in the families with eight or nine children? Perhaps people who have the largest families are the kindest, most loving parents. Perhaps they are simply exhausted. A more realistic explanation is that, at a certain point, children become resources that insulate a family from stress. A family with eight or nine children probably did not have them all at once. With a two- or three-year gap between children, a family with eight or more children has older children at home to help care for and raise the infants, babies, and toddlers. If there is a truly extended family form in our society, it is the large family with children ranging from newborn to twenty living in the home.

A final characteristic of violent parents is that they are almost always cut off from the community they live in. Our survey of family violence found that the most violent parents have lived in their community for less than two years. They tend to belong to few, if any, community organizations, and have little contact with friends and relatives. This social isolation cuts them off from any possible source of help to deal with the stresses of intimate living or economic adversity. These parents are not only more vulnerable to stress, their lack of social involvement also means that they are less likely to abandon their violent behavior and conform to community values and standards. Not only are they particularly vulnerable to responding violently to stress, they tend not to see this behavior as inappropriate.

Abusive Violence Between Partners

Dale, wife of a Fortune 500 executive, wrote us so that we would know that wife beating is not confined to only poor households. Her husband beats her regularly. He has hurled dishes at her, thrown her down stairs, and blackened her eyes. When her husband drinks, she often spends the night huddled in the backseat of their Lincoln Continental. Marion lives so far on the other side of the tracks, she might as well be on another planet. She and her husband live five stories up in a run-down tenement. Heat is a luxury that they often cannot afford, and when they can afford it, the heat rarely works. Marion's husband has broken her jaw and ribs, and has shot at her on two occasions. The range of homes where wife beating occurs seems to defy categorization. One can pick up a newspaper and read of wife beating in a lower-class neighborhood and then turn the page and read that the wife of a famous rock musician has filed for divorce claiming she was beaten.

If there is a typical wife beater, he is not a rock musician, actor, football player, or business executive.[14] The typical beater is employed part-time or not at all. His total income is poverty level. He worries about economic security, and he is very dissatisfied with his standard of living. He is young, between the ages of eighteen and twenty-four—the prime age for violent behavior in and out of the home—and has been married for less than ten years. While he tries to dominate the family and hold down what he sees as the husband's position of power, he has few of the economic or social resources that allow for such dominance; not only does his neighbor have a better job and earn more money than he does, but often so does his wife.

Researchers have found that status inconsistency is an important component of the profile of the battering husband.[15] An example of status inconsistency occurs when a man's educational background is much higher than his occupational attainment—a Ph.D. who drives a taxicab for a living. Status inconsistency can also result when a husband does not have as much occupational or educational status as his wife. Researchers Carton Hornung, Claire McCullough, and Taichi Sugimoto report that, contrary to what is generally believed, violence is less common when the wife is at home then when she works. They suggest that status inconsistency explains this finding. Husbands, they note, can be more threatened when their wives work and have an independent source of income and prestige than when they are home and dependent. Conflict and verbal aggression are frequent occurrences in the wife beater's home. Verbal violence and mental abuse are also directed at his spouse. Perhaps the most telling of all attributes of the battering man is that he feels inadequate and sees violence as a culturally acceptable way to be both dominant and powerful.

There is a great tendency to blame the victim in cases of family violence. Battered women have frequently been described as masochistic. The debate over such presumed masochism has raged to the point where a substantial group of psychologists have called for elimination of the diagnostic category "masochist" from the revision of DSM-III, the official description of psychological diagnostic groupings.

There is not much evidence that battered women as a group are more masochistic than other women. There are, however, some distinct psychological attributes found among battered women. Victims of wife beating are often found to be dependent, having low self-esteem, and feeling inadequate or helpless.[16] On the other hand, battered wives have been found to be aggressive, masculine, and frigid. In all likelihood these contradictory findings are the result of the fact that there is precious little research on the consequence of being battered, and the research that has been conducted frequently uses small samples, without comparison groups. This makes generalizing from such research difficult and contradictory findings inevitable.

Another problem with assessing the psychological traits of battered women is the difficulty in determining whether the personalities were present before the battering or were the result of the victimization. . . .

Pregnant women often report being beaten.[17] Pregnancy, however, does not make women vulnerable to violence and battering.[18] When we analyzed the results of the Second National Family Violence Survey we found that age, not pregnancy, is the best predictor of risk of wife beating. Women between the ages of eighteen and twenty-four are more likely to be beaten, whether they are pregnant or not. Women older than twenty-four years of age are less likely to be beaten.

Although pregnant women are not more vulnerable to violence, the nature of the violent attack does appear to change when a woman is pregnant. One of the first interviews we ever conducted still stands out in our minds. The subject was a thirty-year-old woman who had been beaten severely throughout her marriage. The beatings were more severe, and took on a different tone, when she was pregnant: "Oh yeah, he hit me when I was pregnant. It was weird. Usually he just hit me in the face with his fist, but when I was pregnant he used to hit me in the belly."

Perhaps the most controversial finding from our 1975 National Family Violence Survey was the report that a substantial number of women hit and beat their husbands. Since 1975 at least ten additional investigations have confirmed the fact that women hit and beat their husbands.[19] Unfortunately, the data on wife-to-husband violence have been misreported, misinterpreted, and misunderstood. Research uniformly shows that about as many women hit men as men hit women. However, those who report that husband abuse is as common as wife abuse overlook two important facts. First, the greater average size and strength of men and their greater aggressiveness means that a man's punch will probably produce more pain, injury, and harm than a punch by a woman. Second, nearly three-fourths of the violence committed by women is done in self-defense. While violence by women should not be dismissed, neither should it be overlooked or hidden. On occasion, legislators and spokespersons like Phyllis Schlafly have used the data on violence by wives to minimize the need for services for battered women. Such arguments do a great injustice to the victimization of women.

As we said, more often than not a wife who beats her husband has herself been beaten. Her violence is the violence of self-defense. On some occasions she will strike back to protect herself; on others she will strike first, believing that if she does not, she will be badly beaten. Sally, a forty-four-year-old woman married for twenty-five years, recounted how she used violence to protect herself:

> When he hits me, I retaliate. Maybe I don't have the same strength as he does, but I know how to hold my own. I could get hurt, but I am going to go down trying. You know, it's not like there is anyone else here who is going to help me. So . . . I hit him back . . . I pick something up and I hit him.

Marianne does not wait until she is hit. She says she has learned the cues that her husband is about to hit her:

> I know that look he gets when he gets ready to hit me. We've been married for ten years, and I've seen that look of his. So he gets that look, and I get something to hit him with. Once I hit him with a lamp. Another time I stabbed him. Usually I don't get so bad, but I was real fearful that time.

The violence in Marianne's home is not just one way. She has been hospitalized four times as a result of her husband's beatings. Her fears are very real.

The profile of those who engage in violence with their partners is quite similar to the profile of the parents who are abusive toward their children. The greater the stress, the lower the income, the more violence. Also, there is a direct relationship between violence in childhood and the likelihood of becoming a violent adult. Again, we add the caution that although there is a relationship, this does not predetermine that all those who experience violence will grow up to be abusers.

One of the more interesting aspects of the relationship between childhood and adult violence is that *observing* your parents hit one another is a more powerful contributor to the probability of becoming a violent adult than being a victim of violence. The learning experience of seeing your mother and father strike one another is more significant than being hit yourself. Experiencing, and more importantly observing, violence as a child teaches three lessons:

1. Those who love you are also those who hit you, and those you love are people you can hit.
2. Seeing and experiencing violence in your home establishes the moral rightness of hitting those you love.

3. If other means of getting your way, dealing with stress, or expressing yourself do not work, violence is permissible.

The latter lesson ties in well with our finding that stress also leads to an increased risk of violence in the home. One theory holds that people learn to use violence to cope with stress. If this is correct, then stress would be a necessary, but not sufficient, precondition for family violence. In other words, stress alone does not cause violence unless the family members have learned that being violent is both appropriate and also will not meet with negative sanctions. Another theory is that learning to be violent and stress are two independent contributors to intimate violence and abuse.

The sociologists Debra Kalmuss and Judith Seltzer tested these two theories using the data collected for the First National Family Violence Survey.[20] They found that stress and learning are independent contributions to the risk of abusive violence. Moreover, observing and experiencing violence while growing up was a more powerful contributor to the later risk of intimate violence than was life stress.

Lurking beneath the surface of all intimate violence are confrontations and controversies over power. Our statistical evidence shows that the risk of intimate violence is the greatest when all the decision making in a home is concentrated in the hands of one of the partners. Couples who report the most sharing of decisions report the lowest rates of violence. Our evidence goes beyond the statistics. Over and over again, case after case, interview after interview, we hear batterers and victims discuss how power and control were at the core of the events that led up to the use of violence. Violent husbands report that they "need to" hit their wives to show them who is in charge. Some of the victimized wives struggle against domination and precipitate further violence. Other wives tell us that they will actually provoke their husband to violence because they want him to be more dominant. This is not so much a case of the wife being a masochist as it is another example of the conflicts and struggles that occur as couples confront the traditional cultural expectation that the male should be the dominant person in the household. Some couples fight against this prescription, while others fight to preserve it.

NO PLACE TO RUN, NO PLACE TO HIDE

Eleanor began to prepare dinner for her two children and her husband. It was evening on a Saturday night in January. While she grilled hamburgers, her husband Albert walked in. An argument began over whether Eleanor had take Albert's shirts to the cleaners. Eleanor protested she had. Albert said she was lying. Eleanor protested, yelled, and finally said that Albert was drunk so often he never remembered whether his shirts were clean or dirty. Albert lunged at his wife. He pushed her against the stove, grabbed the sizzling burgers, and threw them across the room. He stalked out, slamming the front door behind him. Quiet tension reigned in the house through a dinner of tuna fish sandwiches and some television, and then the children were put to bed. Eleanor went to bed at 11:00 P.M., but could not fall asleep. At around 1:00 A.M. Albert returned home. He was quiet as he removed his clothes and got into bed. Eleanor turned over, her back to Albert. This signaled that she was awake, and another argument began to brew. This time it was over sex. Eleanor resisted. She always resisted when Albert was drunk. Tonight she resisted because she was still angry over the dinnertime argument. Albert lay his heavy arms around Eleanor and she struggled to get free. The quiet, almost silent struggle began to build. Angry whispers, angry gestures, and finally yelling ensued. Eleanor knew that Albert kept a gun in his night table drawer. Once, after a fight, Albert had gone to bed by putting the bullets on Eleanor's nightstand and the gun under his pillow. As the midnight fight escalated, Albert made a gesture toward the night table. For whatever reason, Eleanor thought that this would be the time that Albert would try to shoot her. She dove across the bed, pulled the drawer out of the night table, clawed for the gun as it rattled to the floor, and came to her feet with the gun in her hand. The first shot tore through Albert's right arm, the second slammed into the wall, the third tore away the top of his head. Eleanor stopped firing only after she heard three of four clicks as the hammer struck the now empty cylinders.

This could be a story out of a soap opera or a supermarket newsstand magazine. It is unfortunately, a story repeated two thousand times a year. We have focused on the family structure and the individual and family characteristics that increase the risk of violence in specific households. Eleanor's and Albert's story illustrates the situational structure of intimate violence.

It goes without saying that intimate violence is most likely to occur in intimate settings. Occasionally couples will strike one another in the car. Husbands sometimes grab their wives at a party or on the street. Husbands or wives rarely slap their partners in public. The majority of domestic combat takes place in private, behind closed doors. We have known men and women to stifle their anger and seethe while guests are in the home. As the last guest leaves and the door closes, the fight and the violence erupt.

Eleanor and Albert began their path to their lethal confrontation in the kitchen. When we interviewed couples about the location of violence between partners and toward children, more than half said that the violence occurs in the kitchen. The living room and bedroom were the next most likely scenes. Only the bathroom seemed free from conflict and violence—perhaps because most bathrooms are small, have locks, or most likely because bathrooms are places of individual privacy.

Students of domestic homicide report that the bedroom is the most lethal room in the home. The criminologist Marvin Wolfgang reported that 20 percent of *all* victims of criminal homicide are killed in the bedroom.[21] The kitchen and dining room are the other frequent scenes of lethal violence between family members.

After 8:00 P.M. the risk for family violence increases.[22] This is almost self-evident, since this is also the time when family members are most likely to be together in the home. We found that four out of ten cases of domestic violence occur between 8:00 P.M. and midnight. Eight out of ten domestic fights take place between 5:00 P.M. and 7:00 A.M. Early evening fights occur in the kitchen. The living room becomes the likely setting for evening disputes, and the most violent and most lethal altercations break out in the bedroom, late at night.

The temporal and spatial patterns of intimate violence support our notion that privacy is a key underlying factor that leads to violence. Time and space constrain the options of both the offender and the victim. As the evening wears on, there are fewer places to run to, fewer places to hide. When the first fight broke out between Eleanor and Albert, it was about 5:00 P.M. Albert rushed out of the house in a huff—most likely heading for the neighborhood bar. The bar closed at 1:00 A.M., and that was when Albert went home to his final conflict.

A fight that erupts in the bedroom, in the early morning, constrains both parties. It is too late to stalk out of the home to a bar and too late to run to a friend or family member. The bed and the bedroom offer no protection and previous few places to flee or take cover. It is not surprising that so many of the most violent family fights end there.

Common sense would argue that weekends are the most violent time of the week for families. Common sense would not lead one to assume that the most violent times of the year are Christmas and Easter. When we looked at which day of the week violence was most likely to occur, we found that the empirical evidence was in full support of common sense. Weekends are when families spent the most time together and when the potential for conflicts and conflicts of interest is greatest. Not surprisingly, seven out of ten violent episodes we talked about with family members took place on either Saturday or Sunday. Weekends after a payday can be especially violent. Janice, the mother of an infant daughter, told us about the typical weekend fight:

It starts over money. He gets paid on Friday. So he comes home on Fridays and I ask him for money. I am usually at the stove cooking when he comes home. And, I have no money left. So I asks. This last Friday he said he didn't have no money. I got real mad. I mean, its payday and he has no money? He said he borrowed money and had to pay it back. I said he just must be lyin'. He spends it on booze or gambles it. Other times we fights because he gives me only fifty dollars. I can't feed him and the baby with just fifty dollars. So I got mad and started to yell.

Thus, the days of the week that are the most violent are those that combine the most conflict and violence-producing structural components of family life—time together, privacy, and stress.

Common sense would not suggest that violence is most likely to erupt at times of the year when families celebrate holidays and the spirit of family togetherness. Yet, contrary to common sense, it is the time from Thanksgiving to New Year's Day and again at Easter that violence in the home peaks.

As we conducted our interviews with members of violent homes we heard again and again about violence that occurred around the Christmas tree. Even the Christmas tree became a weapon in some homes:

I remember one particularly violent time. When we were first married. He was out drinking and he came home stinking drunk. I suppose I must have said something. Well, he took a fit. He started putting his fist through the walls. Finally, he just picked up the Christmas tree and threw it at me.

Another woman recalled her most violent experience:

He hit me just before New Year's Day. I don't really recall what went on. We argue a lot. This time it might have been about money, or maybe the kids. Anyway, he got fierce. He punched me again and again. I was bleeding real bad. He had to take me to the hospital. It was the worst time of the year I ever had.

Perhaps people have a clearer memory of a violent event if it happens around a holiday. While this is a plausible explanation for our findings, it is not the complete answer. We have examined weekly reports of hospital admissions for child abuse and neglect, and found that the peak times of year for admissions were the period from Christmas to New Year's Day, and again in the spring around Easter Sunday.

A number of factors may contribute to the likelihood of domestic violence and abuse during the Christmas season. This is a time when families can assume tremendous financial burdens. Purchasing Christmas gifts can either take a toll on a family's resources or plunge a family into debt. Stress can also come from *not* buying gifts and presents. If a family cannot afford gifts expected by children, loved ones, and others, this can be extremely frustrating. The holiday season offers a stark contrast between what is expected and what a family can afford.

Holidays also create nonfinancial stress. Christmas and Easter holidays project images of family harmony, love, and togetherness. Songs, advertisements, and television specials all play up the image of the caring, loving, and even affluent family. A family with deep conflict and trouble may see these images in sad and frustrating contrast with their own lives. We know that prison riots are more likely to occur during holiday seasons, as prisoners apparently become stressed about being separated from family and friends during times of the year when such closeness is expected. Clearly, being with family and friends, but having unmet expectations for love and warmth, can also be extremely frustrating.

Time of day and time of year analysis supports the notion that privacy and stress are important structural contributors to domestic violence. Conflict frequently erupts over a stressful event, during a stressful time of the day, or around a stressful time of year. If the eruption takes place in a private setting, and at a time and place where it is difficult to flee or back down, the conflict can escalate into violence. The more privacy, the greater the power difference, and the few options the victim has in terms of getting help or finding protection, the more the violence can escalate.

The saddest and most frustrating aspect of our analysis of the structural, personal, familial, temporal, and spatial dynamics of intimate violence is that our results seem to say that violence in the home is inevitable. Lessons learned as a child set the stage for using violence as an adult. The structural makeup of the modern family is like a pressure cooker containing and escalating stress and conflict. If violence breaks out late at night, on a weekend, or a holiday, victims often have no place to run, no place to hide.

Our profile of violent families is not quite as bleak as it might seem. First, no one structural factor, personal experience, or situation predetermines that all or any family will be violent. Second, families do not live in a vacuum. Family members and people outside of the home can intervene to turn down the heat under the pressure cooker. We have found that friends, relatives, and neighbors can successfully intervene and reduce the pressure that could lead to violence.

NOTES

1. Two articles that critique the theory that abuse is the product of mental illness or psychopathology are Richard J. Gelles, "Child Abuse as Psychopathology: A Sociological Critique and Reformulation," *American Journal of Orthopsychiatry* 43 (July 1973): 611–21; and J. Spinetta and D. Rigler, "The Child-Abusing Parent: A Psychological Review," *Psychological Bulletin* 77 (April 1972): 296–304.

2. The organizational characteristics of the family that promote both intimacy and conflict were first described in Richard J. Gelles and Murray A. Straus, "Determinants of Violence in the Family: Towards an Integrated Theory," in Wesley Burr, Reuben Hill, F. Ivan Nye, and Ira L. Reiss, eds., *Contemporary Theories About the Family* vol. 1. (New York: Free Press, 1979), 549–81. These ideas were further developed in Murray A. Straus and Gerald T. Hotaling, eds., *The Social Causes of Husband-Wife Violence* (Minneapolis: University of Minnesota Press, 1980); and Richard J. Gelles and Claire Pedrick-Cornell, *Intimate Violence in Families* (Beverly Hills, Calif.: Sage, 1985).

3. U.S. Bureau of the Census, *Statistical Abstract of the United States: 1987*, 107th ed. (Washington, D.C.: Government Printing Office, 1986), chart 45; U.S. Bureau of the Census, *Current Population Report*, ser. P-20, no. 411.

4. This is the classic statement of psychological frustration/aggression theory. The theory has been articulated by J. C. Dollard, L. Doob, N. Miller, O. Mowrer, and R. Sears, *Frustration and Aggression* (New Haven, Conn.: Yale University Press, 1939); and N. E. Miller, "The Frustration-Aggression Hypothesis," *Psychological Review* 48, no. 4 (1941): 337–42. A sociological formulation of the notion that blocked goals can be frustrating can be found in Robert K. Merton, "Social Structure and Anomie," *American Sociological Review* 3 (October 1938): 672–82.

5. This idea was first presented by Alice Rossi in her article, "Transition to Parenthood," *Journal of Marriage and the Family* 30 (February 1968): 26–39.

6. See, for example: Vincent J. Fontana, *The Maltreated Child: The Maltreatment Syndrome in Children* (Springfield, Ill.: Charles C. Thomas, 1971); Richard Galdston, "Observations on Children Who Have Been Physically Abused and Their Parents," *American Journal of Psychiatry* 122, no. 4 (1965): 440–43; Leroy G. Schultz, "The Wife Assaulter," *Journal of Social Therapy* 6, no. 2 (1960): 103–12; Brandt F. Steele and Carl B. Pollock, "A Psychiatric Study of Parents Who Abuse Infants and Small Children," in R. Helfer and C. Henry Kempe, eds., *The Battered Child* (Chicago: University of Chicago Press, 1968), 103–47; and S. R. Zalba, "Battered Children," *Transaction* 8 (July–August 1971): 58–61.

7. See Gelles, "Child Abuse"; and David Gil, "Violence Against Children," *Journal of Marriage and the Family* 33 (November 1971): 637–48.

8. See R. Emerson Dobash and Russell Dobash, *Violence Against Wives: The Case Against Patriarchy* (New York: Free Press, 1979).

9. For a review of the factors related to family violence, see Richard J. Gelles, "Family Violence," in Ralph H. Turner and James F. Short, eds., *Annual Review of Sociology*, vol. 11 (Palo Alto, Calif.: Annual Reviews, Inc. 1985), 347–67; Marc F. Maden and D. F. Wrench, "Significant Findings in Child Abuse Research," *Victimology* 2 (1977): 196–224; and Suzanne K. Steinmetz, "Violence Between Family Members," *Marriage and Family Review* 1 (1978): 1–16.

10. The profile that is presented is a statistical profile. It would be incorrect to assume

that someone who does not fit this profile would not be an abuser. Similarly, someone who fit the profile is likely to abuse, but is not always an abuser. The profile was developed in Murray A. Straus, Richard J. Gelles, and Suzanne K. Steinmetz. *Behind Closed Doors: Violence in the American Family* (Garden City, N.Y.: Anchor Books, 1980).

11. The survey is reported in Straus, Gelles, and Steinmetz, *Behind Closed Doors*. The measure of stress was adapted from T. H. Holmes and R. H. Rahe, "The Social Readjustment Rating Scale," *Journal of Psychosomatic Research* 11 (1967): 213–18.

12. Straus, Gelles, and Steinmetz, *Behind Closed Doors*; and Noel Cazenave and Murray A. Straus, "Race, Class, Network Embeddedness and Family Violence: A Search for Potent Support Systems," *Journal of Comparative Family Studies* 10 (Autumn 1979): 281–300.

13. A review of child factors that are related to physical abuse can be found in W. N. Friedrich and J. A. Boriskin, "The Role of the Child in Abuse: A Review of the Literature," *American Journal of Orthopsychiatry* 46 (October 1976): 580–90.

14. The profile of wife beaters is a statistical profile and was first presented in Straus, Gelles, and Steinmetz, *Behind Closed Doors*.

15. C. A. Hornung, B. C. McCullough, and T. Sugimoto, "Status Relationships in Marriage: Risk Factors in Spouse Abuse," *Journal of Marriage and the Family* 43 (August 1981): 675–92.

16. Lenore Walker, *The Battered Woman* (New York: Harper & Row, 1979).

17. Richard J. Gelles, "Violence and Pregnancy: A Note on the Extent of the Problem and Needed Services," *Family Coordinator* 24 (January 1975): 81–86.

18. When we analyzed the results of the Second National Family Violence Survey, we did find that the rates of violence and abuse were higher among pregnant women than women who were not pregnant. However, when we controlled for age, the differences disappeared. Women under the age of twenty-four years old experienced high rates of violence and abuse, but the rates were the same for pregnant and nonpregnant women. Women over twenty-four years old experienced lower rates of violence, and again, there were no differences between pregnant and nonpregnant women. Thus, the relationship between violence and pregnancy which we first reported in 1975 (Gelles, "Violence and Pregnancy") and which others have reported, turns out to be spurious.

19. Michael David Allan Freeman, *Violence in the Home: A Socio-legal Study* (Farnborough, England: Saxon House, 1979); Richard J. Gelles, *The Violent Home: A Study of Physical Aggression Between Husbands and Wives* (Beverly Hills, Calif.: Sage, 1974); Morgan E. Scott, "The Battered Spouse Syndrome," *Virginia Medical* 107 (January 1980): 41–43; Suzanne Sedge, "Spouse Abuse," in Marilyn R. Block and Jan D. Sinnott, eds., *The Battered Elder Syndrome: An Exploratory Study* (College Park, Md.: Center on Aging, 1979), 33–48; Suzanne K. Steinmetz, "The Battered Husband Syndrome," *Victimology* 2 (1978): 499–509; Straus, Gelles, and Steinmetz, *Behind Closed Doors*; Mary Warren, "Battered Husbands," in Margaret E. Ankeney, ed., *Family Violence: A Cycle of Abuse* (Laramie, Wyo.: College of Education, University of Wyoming, 1979), 76–78.

20. Debra Kalmuss and Judith A. Seltzer, "A Test of Social Learning and Stress Models of Family Violence." (Paper presented at the annual meetings of the American Sociological Association, New York, 1986).

21. Marvin Wolfgang, *Patterns in Criminal Homicide* (Philadelphia: University of Pennsylvania Press, 1958).

22. This analysis was first presented in Gelles, *Violent Home,* chap. 4.

38
The Victimized Self:
The Case of Battered Women*

John M. Johnson and Kathleen J. Ferraro

In existential sociology the self is not fixed but continually changes and adapts to new situations. The self is essentially open to the world of experience, both positive and negative. When the existential self is confronted with challenging or taxing circumstances, it does not usually recoil or shatter. Instead, it struggles to incorporate new experiences into its evolving reality. Battered women provide an excellent example of this. The victimization experienced by battered women illustrates how the existential self moves from one identity to another under varying conditions.[1] Contrary to much of the research and mass-media reporting about battered women, they do not become victims simply by being the recipients of physical violence. In fact, many women live their entire lives experiencing episodic outbursts of violence from their mates without developing the feelings and identity of a victimized self.[2]

The victimized self is a complex mixture of feelings and thoughts based on the individual's overriding feeling of having been violated, exploited, or wronged by another person or persons. It develops when an individual feels a fundamental threat to his or her very being or existence. The actions or situations people interpret as fundamental threats are varied. Some women feel deeply threatened by verbal assaults, while others may come close to death regularly without feeling themselves to be victims (Ferraro 1979).

THE VICTIMIZATION PROCESS

Women who experience repeated violence or abuse without feeling victimized make use of rationalizations and belief systems that allow them to maintain a feeling of being in a good, normal, or at least acceptable marriage. For example, some women play the role of a "caring wife" and view situations of violence

*Johnson, John M. and Kathleen J. Ferraro. 1984. "The Victimized Self: The Case of Battered Women." Pp. 119–130 in *The Existential Self in Society,* edited by Joseph A. Kotarba and Andrea Fontana. Chicago: University of Chicago Press. © 1984 by The University of Chicago. All rights reserved. Reprinted by permission.

as occasions for taking responsibility to "save" their husbands. Others deny the injuries done to them, even relatively serious ones, and act as if the violence had not occurred. Some will acknowledge the existence of the abuse but reject the husband's responsibility, blaming instead external factors, such as unemployment, alcoholism, or mental illness. Others may feel they "had it coming," an attitude commonly based on feelings of submission to the husband's traditionally defined absolute dominance in the home. And some appeal to higher or institutional loyalties, such as religion, the church, or the sanctity of family life. All of these rationalizations are used by individuals to make sense of their feelings, to make rational what might otherwise be seen as irrational. For some women, these rationalizations can sustain a marriage through a lifetime of violence or abuse. Some may go to their graves believing in them, as did over 3,600 victims of family homicides in 1980 (Ferraro 1982).

Some battered women experience a turning point when the violence or abuse done to them comes to be felt as a basic threat, whether to their physical or social self or to both. Such turning points may stem from dramatic events or crises. They may additionally originate from progressive, gradual realizations by women. In all cases, however, the experience of the turning point produces retrospective interpretations of past events, where individuals creatively seek out new understandings of "what went wrong." What had been rationalized as acceptable is recast as dangerous, malicious, perhaps life-threatening. Before this point, many women may have felt guilt concerning their own complicity in their family situations and perhaps hopefulness that things would improve over time. But these feelings commonly change to feelings of fear and despair. The experience of the turning point produces changes in feelings and interpretations. A new sense of self emerges to meet these emergent conditions. While the development of a victimized self is commonly temporary for individuals, at this juncture the self becomes organized around the perceived facts of victimization. Once women develop a victimized self—a new feeling of being exploited and a new interpretation of the causes and consequences of this exploitation–they may become sufficiently motivated to leave violent situations.

An individual's adoption of a victimized self is all-consuming. For the immediate present it tends to override (but not necessarily destroy) other aspects of the self. It becomes an organizing perspective by which all other aspects of life are interpreted or reinterpreted. It has some similarities to what Everett C. Hughes termed "master status," and indeed, for some rare individuals, the victimized self may assume such importance for long periods of time, perhaps even for the remainder of the person's life. But for most, the victimized self is temporary. After leaving a violent relationship a woman soon begins to take practical steps toward recovery and the rebuilding of her life. She must either set up a new, independent household, arrange for marriage counseling, or return to the marriage with renewed optimism that things will be different. These actions militate against continuance of the individual's sense of victimization. Thus, the victimized self tends to be temporary, certainly for those who mobilize their personal and social resources for change.

The victimized self emerges during moments of existential threat, and it dissolves when one takes actions to construct new, safer living conditions. The victimized self emerges when the rationalizations of violence and abuse begin to lose their power; it becomes the all-consuming basis for however long it takes to transcend this period of crisis and threat. It tends to dissolve, over time, for those who change their lives in new, creative ways, although the sense of victimization never disappears altogether. For all who experience it, it becomes incorporated into an individual's biography as lived experience.

CATALYSTS IN THE VICTIMIZATION PROCESS

When the process of victimization begins, events that previously had been defined as acceptable, although unpleasant, aspects of the relationship begin to take on new meanings. Violence, which had been rationalized as either insignificant in its consequences, beyond the abuser's control, or necessary to the relationship or some other value, is now redefined as abuse or battering.

Changing the definition of events is not an isolated process. It is linked to other aspects of the relationship, and, when these aspects change, specific events within the relationship undergo retrospective reinterpretation. As in cases of nonviolent divorce, what was previously accepted as part of the marriage becomes a focus for discontent (see Rasmussen and Ferraro 1979).

There are a number of catalysis that can trigger this redefinition process. Some authors have noted that degree of severity is related to a woman's decision to leave a violent situation (Gelles 1976). However, it is known that women can suffer extremely severe violence for many years without leaving (Pagelow 1981). What does seem significant is a sudden change in the *level of severity*. Women who suddenly realize that their lives are literally in danger may begin the victimization process. At the point where death is imminent, rationalizations to protect the relationship often lose their validity. Life itself is more important to maintain than the relationship. A woman beaten by an alcoholic husband severely over many years explained her decision to leave on the basis of a direct threat to her life:

> It was like a pendulum. He'd swing to the extremes both ways. He'd get drunk and beat me up, then he'd get sober and treat me like a queen. One day he put a gun to my head and pulled the trigger. It wasn't loaded. But that's when I decided I'd had it. I sued for separation of property. I knew what was coming again, so I got out. I didn't want to. I still loved the guy, but I knew I had to for my own sanity.

Of course, many homicides do occur, and in such cases the wife has obviously not correctly interpreted increases in severity as a threat to her life. Increases in severity do not guarantee a reinterpretation of the situation, but they may play a part in the process.

Another catalyst for changing one's definition of violence may be a *change in its visibility*. Creating a web of rationalizations in order to overlook violence is accomplished more easily if no outsiders are present to question their validity. Since most violence between couples occurs in privacy, victims do not have to cope with conflicting interpretations from outsiders. In fact, they may have difficulty in convincing others that they have a problem (Martin 1976; Davidson

1979). However, if the violence does break through the bounds of privacy and occur in the presence of others, it may trigger a reinterpretation process. Having others witness the degradation of violence is humiliating, for it is a public statement of subordination and powerlessness. It may also happen that an objective observer will apply a different definition to the event than what is consistent with the victim's prior rationalizations, and the mere existence of this new definition will call into question the victim's ideas.

The effect of external definitions on a battered woman's beliefs about her situation varies with the source and form of external definitions. The opinions of those who are highly regarded by the victim, either by virtue of a personal relationship or an occupational role, will be the most influential. Disbelief or an unsympathetic response from others tends to suppress a woman's belief that she has been victimized and to encourage her to accept what has happened as normal. However, when outsiders respond with unqualified support and condemnation of the abuser, their definitions can be a potent catalyst toward victimization. Friends and relatives who show genuine concern for the woman's well-being may initiate an awareness of danger that contradicts previous rationalizations. As one woman reported:

> My mother-in-law knew what was going on, but she wouldn't admit it. . . . I said, "Mom, what do you think these bruises are?" and she said, "Well, some people just bruise easy. I do it all the time, bumping into things." . . . and he just denied it, pretended like nothing happened . . . but this time, my neighbor *knew* what happened, she saw it, and when he denied it, she said, "I can't believe it! You know that's not true!" . . . and I was so happy that finally somebody else saw what was goin' on, and I just told him that this time I wasn't gonna come home!

Shelters for battered women are one source of external definitions that contribute to the victimization process. They offer refuge from a violent situation, a place where a woman may contemplate her circumstances and what she wants to do about them. Within a shelter she will come into contact with counselors and other battered women, who are familiar with the rationalization process and with the reluctance to give up the image of a good marriage. In counseling sessions, rap groups, and informal conversations with other residents, women will hear horror stories from others who have already defined themselves as victims. They will be encouraged to express anger over their abuse and to reject responsibility for the violence. A major goal of many shelters is to help women overcome feelings of guilt and inadequacy so that they will make choices in their own best interests. In this atmosphere, violent incidents are reexamined and defined as assaults in which the woman was *victimized* (Ferraro 1981).

The emergence of shelters as a place to escape from violent marriages has also established a catalyst for the victimization process simply by providing a *change in resources*. When there is no practical alternative to remaining married, there is no advantage in defining oneself as a victim. When resources become available, however, it may be beneficial to reassess the value of remaining in the marriage. Roy (1979) found that the most commonly stated reason for remaining in a violent marriage was having no place else to go. Certainly, a change in resources, then, would alter one's response to violence. Not only shelters, but a change in personal circumstances, such as having the last child leave home, getting a grant for school, or finding a job, can be the catalyst for beginning to think differently about violence.

Apart from external influences, there may be *changes in the relationship itself* that initiate the victimization process. Walker (1979), in her discussion of the stages of a battering relationship, has noted that violent incidents are usually followed by periods of remorse and solicitude. Such phases can be very romantic and thus bind the woman to her husband. But as the battering progresses, this phase may shorten or disappear altogether, eliminating the basis for maintaining a positive outlook on the marriage. When the man realizes that he can get away with violence, he may view it as his prerogative and no longer feel and express remorse. Extended periods devoid of any show of kindness or love may alter the woman's feelings toward her attacker so that she eventually begins to define herself as a victim. One shelter resident described her disenchantment with her marriage this way:

> At first, you know, we used to have so much fun together. He has kind've, you know, a magnetic personality, he can be really charming. But it isn't fun anymore. Since the baby came, it's changed completely. He just wants me to stay at home, while he goes out with his friends. He doesn't even talk to me, most of the time. . . . No, I don't think I really love him anymore, not like I did.

Changes in the nature of the relationship may result in a loss of hope that things will get better and lead to feelings of despair. As long as a woman can cling to a hope that the violence will stop, she can delude herself about it. But when these hopes are finally destroyed and she feels only despair, she may begin to interpret violence as victimization. The Al-Anon philosophy, which is designed for spouses of alcoholics, who are often also victims of abuse, emphasizes the importance of "hitting bottom" before a person can make real changes in his or her life. The director of an Al-Anon-organized shelter explained hitting bottom to me:

> Before the Al-Anon program can really be of benefit, a woman has to hit bottom. When you hit bottom, you realize that all of your own efforts to control the situation have failed; you feel helpless and lost and worthless and completely disenchanted with the world. Women can't really be helped unless they're ready for it and want it. Some women come here when things get bad, but they aren't really ready to be committed to Al-Anon yet. Things haven't gotten bad enough for them, and they go right back. We see this all the time.

She stressed that it is not the objective level of violence that determined hitting bottom but, rather, the woman's feelings of despair. Before one can develop a real, effective sense of victimization, it is necessary to feel that the very foundations of the self have been threatened or attacked, that one's very life or social being is endangered. It isn't until that primordial threat has been experienced that it is likely that the individual will be mobilized for effective action, the kind sufficient to break love-bounds or to change external circumstances. Many do not reach this point. In 1980 over 3,600 persons were killed in family homicides. This figure alone indicates that the interpretive processes discussed here are problematic ones for individuals. Violence may never be interpreted as life-threatening even if it eventually has mortal consequences.

THE TURNING POINT

The victimization process involves redefining past events, their meanings, and one's role in them. Violent incidents must be interpreted as violations of one's rights, as unjustified attacks on one's self, and as the responsibility of the attacker in order for a victimized self to emerge. Whatever the original context of the violence, it is now viewed as the most explicit expression of a generalized pattern of abuse. The positive aspects of the relationship fade into the past, the interactional subtleties and nuances become blurred, and the self becomes organized around victimization.

For some, the awareness of the victimized self may begin with a relatively dramatic event, a "turning point," perhaps similar to what anthropologists have termed "culture shock," that heightened existential awareness associated with meeting persons from foreign cultures, when attempts at communication lay bare the artificiality of social conventions. For others, the process may be more gradual. In either case, the result is similar: for the individual, an awareness of the social reality previously taken for granted. For all individuals, almost all of the time, daily life has a certain obdurate, taken-for-granted quality to it. The substance of what is taken for granted varies from culture to culture, even between individuals within a given culture, whether one is an artist or a hod carrier. But for all persons, most of their lives have this taken-for-granted quality, which is occasionally interrupted or broken by crises of one sort or another. The effect of such crises is to reacquaint the individual with the precariousness of this taken-for-granted reality. This is a time of heightened self-consciousness, when things and events, previously assumed to have an "objective" character, seem to be merely human in their nature. Individuals who experience this crisis in their daily life commonly begin elaborate reconstructions and reinterpretations of past events and individuals in their lives. Different features of events are highlighted. Individuals previously idealized are now "demonized," as Jack Douglas has termed it, as facts of their (putative) character are fashioned in such a manner as to make sense of their evil victimizing. For some persons, perhaps only a few major portions of their lives are reinterpreted (such as the meanings of one's courtship and marriage, following a subsequent reinterpretation of battering), while for others the reinterpretation may be "global," encompassing all aspects of one's life and identity, which are now cast in a new light and subject to new understandings. Such a global reconstruction rarely occurs quickly. It commonly takes months, even years. But initiation of the process involves temporarily adopting a victimized self as a "master status" (Hughes 1958), an interpretive frame that overrides all others in importance for the person and provides the foundation for all lesser interpretations. "Being a victim" is a way of relating to the world, a way or organizing one's thoughts and feelings about daily events and persons. Old things are seen in a new way. Old feelings are felt differently now. Old meanings are experienced in a different light. A woman who discussed her marriage while staying at a shelter illustrates this process of reinterpreting the past:

> When I look back on it now, of course, I can see how all along he'd do anything to control me. First it was little things, like wanting me not to wear makeup, then it got so he criticized everything I did. He wouldn't let me drive or handle our money. He wouldn't even let me buy the kids' Christmas presents. I think he wanted me to be his slave, and so he started beating on me to make sure I was scared of him.

Achieving a new sense of a victimized self commonly prepares the way for practical action. While it is true that some individuals seem to find solace and comfort in their interpretations of victimization as such, this is not true for most of those who feel victimized. Feeling victimized threatens one's self, one's sense of competence, and this is usually related to practical actions to see that the victimization stops or does not reoccur. The practical actions taken by individuals vary greatly. One battered woman might leave her husband, establish an independent existence, and perhaps undergo counseling to change relationship patterns that had become habitual over the years. Another might return to the marriage, accepting the husband's claims that he has changed and that he will never hurt her again. Some of those who are victimized join together with others for many purposes, such as setting up self-help groups (e.g., Al-Anon), or for social-movement organization and action. The feeling of victimization underlies social-movement participation in many cases and some political actions as well. Wars, revolutions, and many social movements have started with the feelings of the victimized self.

THE EMOTIONAL CAREER OF THE VICTIMIZED SELF

The cognitive aspects of accepting a victimized self, such as rejecting rationalizations and reinterpreting the past, are tied to the feelings that are created by being battered: The emotional career of the victimized self begins with guilt, shame, and hopefulness, moves to despair and fear, shock and confusion, and finally to relief and sometimes even elation. These feelings are experienced by women who first rationalize violence, then reach a turning point, and finally take action to escape. At any point in her emotional career a woman may decide to cling to rationalizations and a violent marriage. Only about half of the women who enter shelters actually progress along this emotional career to the point of feeling relief that they are no longer in danger. The career path, then, should be viewed as a continuum rather than a fixed sequence through which all battered women pass.

When men beat their wives, they usually have some explanation for their violence even if that explanation seems nonsensical to outsiders. Women are told that their abuse is a natural response to their inadequacies. They are made to feel that they are deficient as women, since they are unable to make their husbands happy. Battered women often feel quite guilty about their marital problems. They feel largely responsible for their husbands' violence and make efforts to control anything that might trigger their displeasure. They feel that the violence is a reflection of their own incompetence or badness. Feelings of guilt and shame are part of the early emotional career of battered victims. At the same time, however, they feel a kind of hopefulness that things will get better. Even the most violent man is nonviolent much of the time, so there is always a basis for believing that violence is exceptional and that the "real" man is not a threat.

> First of all, the first beatings, you can't believe it yourself. I'd go to bed, and I'd cry, and I just couldn't believe this was happening, and I'd wake up the next morning thinking, that couldn't have happened, or maybe it was my fault, it's so unbelievable, that this person that you're married to and you love would do that to you, but yet you can't leave either because ya know, for the other 29 days of the month that person loves you and is with you.

These feelings of guilt and shame mixed with hopefulness give way to despair when the violence continues and the relationship loses all semblance of a loving partnership. At the point of despair, the catalysts described above are most likely to influence a battered woman to make a change.

The turning point in the victimization process, when the self becomes organized around a fundamental threat, is characterized by a penetrating fear. Women who do see their husbands' actions as life-threatening experience a fear that consumes all thoughts and energies. It is felt physiologically in general body achiness, a pain in the pit of the stomach, and tension headaches. There is physical shaking, chills, and inability to eat or sleep. Sometimes the fear is expressed as a numbed shock, in which little is felt or communicated. The belief that her husband is intent on inflicting serious bodily harm explodes the prior self, which is built on rationalizations and the myth of a "good marriage." The self is left without a reality base, in a crisis of ambiguity. The woman is no longer the wife she defined herself to be, but she has not had time to create new meanings for her life. She feels afraid, alone, and confused.

> At that point, I was just panicked, and all I kept thinking was, "Oh God, he's gonna kill me." I could not think straight, I was so tired and achey, I couldn't deal with anything, find a place to move and all that. Thank God my friends took me in and hid me. They took me by the hand and led me through the motions for a few days, just took care of me, because I really felt just sick.

The victimized self is highly vulnerable. Battered women escaping violent situations depend on the nurturance and support of outsiders, sometimes strangers in shelters, to endure the period of fear and shock that follows leaving the marriage. In cases where women do not feel the support of others, an abuser's pleas to come home and try again are especially appealing and often effective. People in great pain and confusion will turn to those who offer warmth. If a violent husband is the only person who appears to offer that warmth, a battered woman will probably return to the relationship. However, if she is able to find and accept a temporary refuge with friends, relatives, or a shelter, she will be in a situation much more conducive to the relief that follows in the wake of a crisis endured.

Once situated in a safe location, with supportive people, fear for her life subsides. Then, perhaps, she will feel relieved to lay down a burden she has carried for months or years. She will be free of the continuous concern to prevent violence by controlling all potentially disturbing events. This sudden relief sometimes turns to feelings of elation and exhilaration when women who have repressed their own desires find themselves free to do as they please. Women in shelters often rejoice at such commonplace events as going shopping, getting their hair done, or taking their children to the park without worrying about their husbands' reactions.

> Boy, tomorrow I'm goin' downtown, and I've got my whole day planned out, and I'm gonna do what *I* wanna do, and if somebody doesn't like it, to Hell with them! You know, I'm having such a good time, I shoulda done this years ago!

The elation that accompanies freedom serves as a wellspring of positive action to begin a new life. The difficult tasks of finding a new home, getting divorced, and, often, finding a job are tackled with energies that had previously been directed toward "keeping the peace." As these activities begin, however, the self moves away from victimization. Active involvement with others to obtain one's own desires is inconsistent with the victimized self. The feelings and perceptions of self required to leave a violent marriage wither away as battered women begin to build a new self in a new situation.

CONCLUSION

Feeling victimized is for most individuals a temporary, transitory stage. There are good reasons for this. While it is of great importance for victimized individuals to achieve and create new understandings of their present and past, and while this itself alleviates some of the sufferings of victimization, there are certain incompatibilities between feeling victimized and being oriented toward practical actions to change one's situation in the world. Feeling victimized implies, for most persons, significant passivity in accepting external definitions and statuses. To change such a situation involves the individual in active, purposive, creative behavior. Since victimization represents a primordial threat to the self, individuals are highly motivated to change these circumstances, and these actions by themselves diminish the sense of victimization. The specific time frame for this transitory period varies. For most wars, revolutions, and social movements, it may be a matter of months or years. For individuals caught in the throes of a violent marriage for decades, the process may take longer, even the remainder of their lives. It makes little difference, however, whether or not the practical actions achieve "success," whether success is defined in terms of revolutionary victory, the success of a social-movement organization, or moving into a new relationship in which violent or abusive acts are absent. The very process of taking practical action inevitably diminishes the individual's sense of victimization and in many cases even brings the emotional career of the victimized self to an end.

There are both similarities and differences between the form of victimization described here and other forms. Battered children, for example, often reinterpret childhood abuse when they reach adulthood; these reinterpretations thus do not occur as the by-product of a turning point in the course of the abuse, as is the case in violent marriages. Those who are assaulted by strangers, such as victims of muggings or rapes, may experience the existential threat to the self in much the same way as battered women do, but there is no prior relationship to reinterpret as a consequence of assuming a victimized self. The feelings and perceptions of these other victimized selves remain largely unexplored. Future studies, detailing the cognitive and emotional experiences of various types of victims, would make possible a more complete, generalized analysis of the victimized self than can be gained by focusing only on battered women.

NOTES

1. We owe a debt of gratitude to David Altheide, Paul Higgins, Mildred Daley Pagelow, and Carol A. B. Warren for comments on an earlier draft of this paper.

2. Data for our respective researches have been gained from direct field observations, depth interviewing, various kinds of official documents, and surveys. More details on the data collection and analyses are to be found in Johnson (1975, 1981) and Ferraro (1979a, 1979b, 1981). An important resource for the research was the personal experience of the authors as cofounders and early leaders (1977–79) of an Arizona shelter for battered women.

REFERENCES

Davidson, Terry. 1978. *Conjugal Crime*. New York: Hawthorn.

Ferraro, Kathleen J. 1979a. "Hard Love: Letting Go of an Abusive Husband." *Frontiers* 4(2):16–18.

———. 1979b. "Physical and Emotional Battering." *California Sociologist* 2(2):134–49.

———. 1981. "Battered Women and the Shelter Movement," Ph.D. dissertation, Department of Sociology, Arizona State University.

———. 1982. "Rationalizing Violence." Unpublished paper.

Gelles, Richard J. 1976. "Abused Wives: Why Do They Stay?" *Journal of Marriage and the Family* 38:659–68.

Hughes, Everett C. 1958. *Men and Their Work*. New York: Free Press.

Johnson, John M. 1975. *Doing Field Research*. New York: Free Press.

———. 1981. "Program Enterprise and Official Cooptation of the Battered Women's Shelter Movement." *American Behavioral Scientist* 24:827–42.

Martin, Del. 1976. *Battered Wives*. San Francisco, CA: Glide.

Pagelow, Mildred Daley. 1981. *Women-Battering*. Beverly Hills, CA: Sage.

Rasmussen, Paul K. and Kathleen J. Ferraro. 1979. "The Divorce Process." *Journal of Alternative Lifestyles* 2:443–60.

Roy, Maria (ed.). 1977. *Battered Women*. New York: Van Nostrand.

Walker, Lenore E. 1979 *The Battered Woman*. New York: Harper and Row.

39
The Changing Concept of Child Abuse and its Impact on the Integrity of Family Life*

John M. Johnson

During the brief span of twenty-five years in the United States, the concept of child abuse has changed dramatically. It has gone from an obscure and hotly contested topic found in arcane medical journals to a position of routine mass-media publicity. Twenty-five years ago most medical doctors, including pediatricians, resisted the legitimacy of the child abuse concept. Today it is widely accepted and discussed by all professionals. It is widely discussed among the citizens as well, and even small schoolchildren talk about child abuse or neglect. Occasionally these children initiate reports to school or police officials, alleging injuries to themselves or others. Clearly these are indices of a massive social change that has occurred over a relatively short period of time.

The social changes concerning child abuse and neglect are intertwined with a "statistical explosion" of officially recognized and officially documented cases. This dramatic increase has led popular and scientific writers to assert a social problem of "epidemic" proportions. The first national study of the incidence of child abuse in the United States was done in 1962 by the American Humane Association. This study documented, for the first eleven months of 1962, a total of 662 cases that were serious enough to warrant some kind of court proceedings. We can thus, by extrapolation, place the 1962 incidence of child abuse at about 720 cases.[1]

The year 1963 marks the beginning of legislative initiative in the field of child abuse. The next decade saw much legislative, governmental, and programmatic action, with the establishment, at the end of the year, of the National Center on Child Abuse and Neglect. Their official statistics for 1973 show an incidence of about 60,000 officially recorded cases of child abuse, a national increase of over 8,300 percent in about ten years. Two years later they produced a national incidence of about 80,000 cases. And the 1976 study by the Department of Health, Education and Welfare put the annual rate at about a million new cases of child abuse and neglect. At the beginning of the 1980s in the United States, estimates of our incidence rate (number of new cases per year) for child abuse and neglect vary between 1 million to 4.5 million cases, and estimates of the prevalence (number of cases at any one time) are commonly two or three times that number. This is the "new math" of family violence in the United States.

*Johnson, John M. 1986. "The Changing Concept of Child Abuse and Its Impact on the Integrity of Family Life." Pp. 257–275 in *The American Family and the State*, edited by Joseph R. Peden and Fred R. Glahe. San Francisco, CA: Pacific Research Institute for Public Policy. Copyright © 1986 by Pacific Research Institute for Public Policy. Reprinted by permission.

Child maltreatment, now the more general term, includes child battering, abuse, neglect, failure to thrive, malnutrition, emotional abuse or neglect, sexual abuses, and a range of other acts or conditions. Child maltreatment is also today a large social movement that includes the activities of many groups: officials, professionals, media personalities, and private citizens. Partisans who promote the causes of the child maltreatment movement want us to think that the officially produced statistics on incidence and prevalence are objective, empirical facts. They wish us to think that a determination of child maltreatment is a scientific assessment made by a trained professional. They wish us to think that assessments of child maltreatment are done without regard to the assessor's values, and that the official statistics are collected without regard for political definitions or realities. But these are the rhetorical promotions of those with partisan interests in this area, those who wish to enlist our support for the political reality they have constructed since the early 1960s. None of these rhetorical claims can be supported by the facts.

Child maltreatment is not an unproblematic, empirical fact. It is a political definition of state legislatures. State officials are the ones mandated by law to respond to and bureaucratically process the child maltreatment claims brought to their attention. They are the ones who take the immediate, practical action in specific cases. They do so on the basis of their professional, bureaucratic, and personal values, as mitigated by situational constraints and resource practicalities. The national incidence and prevalence statistics on child maltreatment do not make any intelligible sense, because they combine incomparable state political definitions and practical decisions by bureaucratic officials at the local level. To understand the proper context of the present situation, it is important to gain a historical perspective on how children have been treated over the centuries. Such a historical perspective not only produces a sense of the relativity of judgments concerning child maltreatment but—and this is more important—provides a grasp of the essentially political and normative nature of a phenomenon so commonly presented as something else. The beating of children is an old phenomenon, but child maltreatment as a social movement that has mapped out new mandates for state authority and intervention is a relatively new phenomenon.

THE ORIGINS OF CHILDHOOD

Today it is taken for granted that "childhood" is a distinct, and even special, state of life. While the centuries have witnessed relatively little change in the manner by which infants and small children have biologically and physically grown, the social and cultural meanings associated with and imputed to "childhood" have changed greatly over time. For about 90 percent of all human history for which there are some records, societies have condoned and practiced infanticide, the intentional killing of infants. Infanticide was practiced for reasons of birth control, religious ceremony, or social policy. The earliest historical records of infanticide date to 7,000 B.C. in Jericho.[2] Infanticide was practiced for well over 8,000 years, and began to disappear only during the Middle Ages. In ancient Sparta, a public official examined newborns to attest to their health and worthiness to draw upon limited societal resources. The unworthy were thrown into the "Valley of Infants." Roman law forbade the raising of deformed infants. Even in later centuries, when the Christian churches redefined and prohibited infanticide, it was practiced clandestinely, and deaths were attributed to "over-laying," or accidental suffocation by the mother.[3]

Recent laws prohibiting infanticide can be found as late as 1843 in Germany, 1870 in Russia, and 1875 in India. Today the practice is largely clandestine and unofficial.

After the Middle Ages, abandonment of infants emerged as a common practice in western cultures. Harris estimates that by 1820 in France about 40,000 infants per year were being legally abandoned by their parents.[4] In the United States the New York Foundling Asylum was established in 1869 to save abandoned infants, who numbered about 1,400 in 1873.[5]

The growth of Christianity is associated with the emergence and development of many forms of child "discipline." The Puritan concept held that newborns, like adults, were born into a state of sin and depravity; hence strict measures were needed to acquaint the young with the ways of God.[6] Physical punishment, restraint, bodily mutilations, whippings, beatings, and the use of many instruments to bring these about were considered "normal" for members of Western cultures between the 1700s and 1900s. Many of these practices and ideologies thrive today. Radbill observes, "It was always taken for granted that parents and guardians had every right to treat their children as they saw fit."[7] This was additionally emphasized by the following thumb rule from American common law:

> If one beats a child until it bleeds, then it will remember the words of its master. But if one beats it to death, then the law applies.[8]

The fundamental ambiguities of legal applications are illustrated by one of the most famous child maltreatment cases in history. In 1875 the American Society for the Prevention of Cruelty to *Animals* (ASPCA) in New York City was asked to intervene for the purpose of protecting Mary Ellen, a nine-year-old girl who had been neglected, beaten, and even slashed with scissors by her foster parents. Earlier efforts to intervene had failed, because the parental rights to child discipline had been heretofore considered absolute by the law. So the ASPCA was asked to intervene to protect Mary Ellen on the argument that she was a member of the animal kingdom, and thus the legitimate recipient of laws already on the books to protect animals. The case received wide media publicity, and paved the way for the founding of the Society for the Prevention of Cruelty to Children (SPCC) in 1876. In the following years, the SPCC emerged as one important element of the growing social movement to prohibit child labor; their efforts were thus directed more to the abuses by employers of children, and only rarely did they concern themselves with the abuses of natural parents. There would have been relatively little public sentiment for the latter at the time. There were 161 local chapters of the SPCC by the turn of the century. These were later consolidated into the Children's Division of the American Humane Association.

THE MODERN DISCOVERY OF CHILD ABUSE

Historical evidence presents a long record of child victimization. The first medical or scientific studies of parental "abuse," however, can be dated from the 1888 article on acute periosteal swelling by Dr. S. West.[9] Later there was the 1946 study by Dr. John Caffey, analyzing the relationship between long bone fractures and subdural hematoma, the hemorrhaging that follows a head injury.[10] These early studies appeared to produce little publicity or concern.

Two medical studies done during the 1950s gained greater recognition.[11] Both asserted, in effect, that certain patterns of traumatic childhood injuries were caused by parental irresponsibility, neglect, indifference, or immaturity. This was an important departure for the medical profession, which, at an earlier time, had interpreted similar injuries as the result of "unspecified" causes.

A watershed point occurred with the 1962 publication of an article, "The Battered Child Syndrome," by C. Henry Kempe and his colleagues at the University of Colorado Medical School.[12] This research, published in a most prestigious and respected medical journal, was accompanied by an official editorial asserting the seriousness of this new medical problem. The characteristic features of the syndrome included traumatic injuries to the head and long bones, commonly done to children under three years of age by parents who had themselves been beaten or abused as children. These parents commonly denied the mistreatment of their own children. The publication of this research article was an important step in legitimizing this problem as an appropriate area of medical intervention.[13] An interesting question is why the medical profession's policy and involvement occurred at this time rather than an earlier one. Pfohl[14] argues that the entrepreneurial efforts of the occupational group of pediatric radiologists were important elements of the social movement at this early stage.

EARLY LEGISLATION

One critical social movement organization is the American Humane Association. The AHA has been active in all phases of the child maltreatment movement from the very beginning. They have conducted research, drawn up early "model legislation" for all governmental levels, published and publicized research and program information, provided "expert witnesses" to state legislatures contemplating legislative initiatives, and served important gatekeeping and liaison functions among and between all the professions through their conferences, workshops, and other communications. Most of these activities occurred under the 24-year leadership of Vincent de Francis, a key figure in the child maltreatment movement. He was one of the participants in an important meeting that occurred in January 1962 in Washington, D.C., at the Department of Health, Education and Welfare (HEW). The purpose of this meeting was to begin exploring the possibility of federal and/or state legislation on child abuse. Included in this meeting were Children's Bureau and HEW officials, members of the pediatric section of the American Medical Association, de Francis of the American Humane Association, and some private parties.[15] The main thrust of this meeting was to encourage legislative initiative to protect medical doctors from potential legal action in cases where they made reports of child maltreatment.

An eventual outcome of the 1962 meeting was a draft of "model legislation," which could be taken back to state legislatures, concerning child abuse reporting, liabilities, mandates, and responsibilities. The year 1963 is an important one for child abuse legislation, as eighteen states proposed and eleven states passed enabling bills on child abuse. During the next two years, thirty-six more states followed, and within the first five years fifty of the U.S. states and territories passed some form of child abuse legislation. This is an impressive social change to occur in such a relatively short period of time. It is interesting to contrast the child abuse legislation with the efforts to pass the Equal Rights Amendment (ERA), which failed to gain the needed two-thirds majority required for a constitutional amendment within a period of *ten years*. The contrast shows that, unlike the hotly contested and disputed ERA, child abuse and neglect are "least common denominator social problems" for large numbers of the American public, involving few conflicts and heated confrontations.[16] They are the kinds of problems everyone can be against. The prevailing definitions and realities of child maltreatment and the appropriate policy response are not contested by the major political parties, ideological positions, major churches, or professional and educational institutions.

As legal phenomena, child abuse and neglect are defined at the *state* level of government and, as with most other state definitions, the statutory concepts and mandates differ greatly from one jurisdiction to another. The early legislation generally mandated the *reporting* by physicians of child abuse or neglect. Many states established penalties for failures to report suspected cases. The new laws at first included few changes to existing statutes concerning delinquency, dependency, neglect, and criminal penalties. Since the early legislative period (1963–65), however, all of the state laws have been changed, modified, or revised on these and many other crucial issues.

THE AMBIGUOUS POLITICAL DEFINITIONS OF ABUSE

By 1965, reporting of child abuse and neglect had been mandated by forty-three of the fifty states.[17] By 1967, forty-nine states had the new laws.[18] As a reasonable assumption, one might think that if something is against the law, and hence the subject of potential legal sanction, the phenomenon in question would be clearly defined. How could officials (or professionals) define, identify, or classify something if the law requiring their identifications did not define it? But this is precisely the case for child abuse and neglect. By 1974, only eighteen of the fifty-three states and U.S. territories specifically defined child abuse and neglect in their statutes.[19] The state laws reflect very little consensus on even the most fundamental terms. The 1975 analysis by Sanford Katz observed the following:

> A large majority of the jurisdictions (45) do not have a statutory definition for the term "neglect" and /or "neglected child." Only eight states define "neglect" . . .

and less then half of the jurisdiction (22) have a "neglected child" definition. . . .
Twenty-three states use some other definition to refer to a "neglected child," such
as "deprived child," "dependent or neglected," or "dependent child."[20]

On common sense grounds, it is easy to understand how a perception of
"child neglect" might be intertwined with an observer's personal values, since a
judgment of "neglect" implies a concept of a "normal home," which is subject
to great ambiguity. A physical child battery, however, is hardly less ambiguous
or problematic. Western legal traditions have long assessed legal culpability on
the basis of determining the *intention* to commit an act. If it can be determined
that an individual was fully and legally capable of intending his or her actions,
and did in fact do so on a given occasion, then we properly hold that individual
accountable for his or her action. If, by contrast, the individual was not capable
of intending the action, whether because of reduced capacity, insanity, or mental
illness, he or she is held blameless, even for the same action. If the individual is
judged capable of forming intentions, but found by a judicial process not to have
done so on a specific occasion, then the individual is held blameless. Examples
of the latter may be "accidents," that is, events that may indeed produce harmful
consequences, even death, but where the judgment is that the act was not a
willful or intentional one. The determination of the caretakers' intention is not
just one of many factors to be considered in making an assessment about child
battering; it is *definitive*. It is only possible to distinguish a "child battery" from
an "accident" by making an assessment of the caretakers' intention to do the
act. As an internal mental state of the individual at the time of engaging in
an act, intent is not directly observable by an outsider, and is thus inherently
problematic (or uncertain). An added complication is that those who are called
in to investigate claims about child abuse are invariably called in after the fact,
when direct evidence of the actor's internal mental state is impossible, and indirect
evidence often ambiguous, contradictory, or uncertain. For these and many other
reasons, then, even the assessments of a physical beating are commonly very
problematic ones.

It is easier to formulate and operationalize an abstract definition when one
is dealing with a more restricted phenomenon, such as a physical battery. New
levels of complexity and ambiguity are introduced when the focus is more broad,
as in "child neglect." For neglect, again, the issues surrounding definition are of
primary importance and logically take precedence over epidemiological or etio-
logical questions. Nevertheless, there is no agreement about the parameters of
child neglect. In some respects the definition of neglect is of greater significance
than that of battering or abuse, since informed "guesstimates" place the ratio of
neglect to abuse cases from three-to-one[21] to ten-to-one.[22] Guesstimates such as
these commonly sidestep the logically and empirically prior question of definition
by taking as an instance of neglect anything so defined by officials at the local
levels, by whatever criteria they may have used.

Those who focus on neglect emphasize either the condition(s) of the parent(s),
such as alcoholism, drug abuse, or psychological problems, or some specific harm
to the children, such as an identifiable physical or psychological harm. To be neglectful means that the parent has failed in some manner to exercise responsibility

over those means within their control. This latter idea about control introduces another level of discretionary judgment into an already complex equation. What about the family that is trying conscientiously and sincerely to provide the basic necessities, but is still unable to do so because of their present condition of poverty, illness, or unemployment? To what extent is their poverty or employment status "within their control"? How does one judge "conscientious" or "sincere" in such a situation? Officials and professionals who routinely make such assessments play an important "gatekeeping" role in the screening of potential child neglect cases.[23] Many studies now show that various kinds of racial, ethnic, social class, and occupational biases creep into such assessments, with the general finding being that official gatekeepers are more likely to "normalize" those persons, behaviors, and situations seen as close to their own lives or circumstances, but are more likely to officially label and bureaucratically process those experienced as more remote from them.[24] This is one of the important factors accounting for the usual overrepresentation of poor and minority persons in official caseloads.[25]

Few states have clear definitions, as we have seen. And there is certainly no agreement between states on definitions. Despite this, however, there have been several important changes to the child abuse and neglect laws since the 1963–65 period of legislative initiative. These changes have occurred in all states. By the 1980s, states have changed, modified, or revised their child abuse and neglect laws two or three times in most cases. One important change concerns the progressive expansion of the mandate to report suspected cases of abuse or neglect. Whereas the early laws commonly required only physicians to report, most laws today require many other professionals as well—any physician (including interns and residents), surgeon, dentist, osteopath, chiropractor, podiatrist, nurse, druggist, pharmacist, laboratory technician, acupuncturist, schoolteacher or school administrator, social worker, and/or "any other person." Another important change involves the increase in the penalties for not reporting. Granting immunity from criminal or civil liability for those who report suspected cases of abuse or neglect is another critical change, now found in all of the state laws. Also, granting doctors and other professionals waivers from the legal or ethical restrictions against revealing confidential communications represents another way by which the law has been changed to encourage reporting to and processing by official, bureaucratic agencies. There have been some other legal changes, too, including revisions of the evidentiary criteria to be used in court cases involving abuse or neglect. These changes have for the most part enhanced and facilitated organizational goals rather than individual or family rights.

Providing incentives as well as sanctions to report abuse and neglect cases, while at the same time ignoring critical matters of defining what it is that is to be reported, has produced many ironic results at local and state levels. After the passage of new laws at the state level, it is common for local and state agencies to experience an initial short-term rate increase of several hundred, even several thousand, percent.[26] This has been observed for crime rates as well, and on many occasions those cities or states with the highest crime rates are those in the process of rationalizing their reporting procedures, or in the process of documenting some "need" for federal or state financial assistance. For child maltreatment, such short-term increases often overwhelm the local bureaucratic resources for responding to or investigating new reports. Such a situation greatly increases the chances of making a "Type II error," that is, failing to diagnose child abuse or neglect when it is in fact present.[27] In given local situations, this may mean that the efforts to stop child maltreatment through enhanced reporting efforts may cause deleterious consequences that may have been otherwise avoided. The bureaucratic welfare state produces many such ironies.

Child maltreatment is not some symptomatic feature of American society, or even of the 1960s and 1970s, but *allegations* of mass maltreatment arose during those two decades. Child maltreatment is thus more usefully seen as a social movement, one that has achieved success at several levels. As such, the current movement is a recent manifestation of the earlier "child saving" movement,[28] a turn-of-the-century moral crusade that asserted the symbolic dominance of middle-class, Christian values. Moral crusades are an indisputable tradition in American history.

The child maltreatment social movement achieved many successes at various state and local levels, as we have seen. The greatest success, however, and the greatest impetus for the movement, came with the 1974 passage of federal legislation: the Child Abuse Prevention and Treatment Act, also informally known as the "Mondale Bill" after its primary sponsor. This federal law (P.L. 93-247) established a National Center on Child Abuse and Neglect, located within the Department of Health, Education and Welfare. The official mandates of the National Center included changes to conduct research on the causes, incidence, and prevalence of child abuse and neglect, and also to compile and publish a summary of pertinent knowledge in this field.[29] It is additionally important to understand that this bill provided $85 million of resources for the child maltreatment movement over a four-year period. This money was spent for research, publication, and program initiative. The latter typically occurred under the auspices of a "demonstration project," whereby the federal government would provide the "seed money" to get a program started and operational for a specified period, usually two to three years, on the theory that once program effectiveness had been established, local funding sources would then step in to continue the program. The $85 million provided a major resource leading to the institutionalization of the child maltreatment social movement. New programs dealing with child maltreatment were started in hospitals,[30] clinics,[31] volunteer programs,[32] day care centers,[33] and entire communities.[34] Programs such as these greatly enhanced local officials' abilities to gain contact with heretofore undefined abuse or neglect cases, through the mechanisms the practitioners term "case finding." And they also greatly enhanced the gatekeeping role of decision makers in local agencies.

AGENCY SCREENING AND CASE FINDING

A somewhat naive view about child abuse and its relationship to community agencies assumes that what is called child abuse or neglect is relatively straightforward and unproblematic. Abuse and neglect are seen to define specific acts, with "abusive" and "neglectful" being considered characteristics of specific individuals who engage in them. Community agencies are assumed to adopt a passive or reactive response to abusive or neglectful acts that precede their interventions in space and time. Community agencies are thought to represent a functional response to the problem, tending to control it.

The available evidence fails to support any of the above assumptions. The formal definitions of abuse and neglect are very ambiguous and problematic. There is very little agreement on the meanings of maltreatment even among the professionals who intervene in such cases. An early study of Viano[35] found dissimilar attitudes and perceptions among the professionals involved. More recently, a very thorough research project found significant differences in the perceptions of child abuse and neglect between the four major occupational groups involved in the investigation, identification, and treatment of maltreatment cases: police, social workers, lawyers, and pediatricians.[36] Some of these differences appeared to be related to the different occupational tasks the professionals commonly performed. This understanding is what led Gelles to propose that "the occupational and organizational mandate of a community agency determines how active it will be in identifying cases of child abuse, how likely the employees of the agency are to label particular cases abuse, and the types of cases which are labeled abuse."[37]

The various occupational groups that find themselves in a situation of receiving, investigating, or otherwise processing child maltreatment cases develop an "occupational ideology" about those cases. This ideology includes a set of perceptions, thoughts, feelings, values, and work experiences that become taken for granted by those in a given work setting. The traditional ideology of social workers tends to be supportive and humanitarian, for example, whereas police and prosecutors tend to be more punitive and legalistic in their orientation.[38] Whatever the abstract or ideological values, however, virtually all child abuse screening occurs in some kind of *organizational context*. This commonly involves sets of formal and informal rules that are routinely used to organize work tasks, recipe knowledge of "the way we do things around here," and limited resources to pursue one course of action over another. Such considerations form a practical work context for all decisions, often determining what gets done in specific instances, even independently of other professional or occupational values. Child protective service professionals may investigate a claim of child neglect and determine that the removal of the child is warranted, for example. But perhaps, at that moment, there are no resources available to effect such a decision (such as emergency or regular foster homes). In such a situation, the placement of the child is highly unlikely, unless the case involves an immediate threat to life, which is rare, or the potential for media publicity.

Child maltreatment investigations in public agencies are always made within a context of limited time and resources. Rare exceptions to this involve those "child abuse horror stories" that receive disproportionate mass media publicity.[39] These involve dramatic injuries or circumstances. One example originated from Cleveland, Tennessee, where a father forced his three-year-old daughter to remain awake and walking for three days. When she asked for water, he forced Tabasco sauce down her throat and stomped on her feet. She died of exhaustion. Another case, out of Long Beach, California, involved the discovery of a seven-year-old girl who had been tied to a chair in her room for her entire life. She had been forced to sleep in her own feces; when found, she weighted only 35 pounds and was unable to talk. A third case, from Los Angeles, involved an infant found to have more than 600 cigarette burns over her body. These are the dramatic, horrible child abuse cases. When they occur, there is usually an instantaneous consensus about what should be done to save the child from immediate danger. But these dramatic cases are statistically very rare, and their unrepresentative publication via the mass media presents a distorted picture of the more routinely encountered cases.

The usual child maltreatment cases routinely encountered in the everyday operations of official agencies tend to involve ambiguities, uncertainties, conflicting accounts about what occurred (or why), nonserious injuries, and living conditions that render judgments cloudy. For these kinds of cases, which clearly constitute the overwhelming statistical majority as well as the dominant work tasks of those confronted with them, there is much room for discretion. Police, emergency room physicians, child protective services' social workers, public health nurses, and others who receive allegation of abuse or neglect essentially serve as "gatekeepers," determining which cases will be screened in or out of the system. At all levels the discretion is great, and decisions are essentially free of review. Officials who make these determinations do so on the bases of their occupational ideology, personal values, and immediate practical situation within the bureaucratic organization. In a situation such as this, an uncanny correspondence exists between the official assessments and the resources available at the moment to "do something."

The gatekeeping functions of local agency decisions are illustrated by the concept of "case finding." This refers to the entrepreneurial initiative exercised by officials to recruit new cases, which would not otherwise be there, into the child protective services' caseloads. Case finding is a concept well known to social work professionals. References to the practice can be found throughout the academic and professional literature. Large numbers of social workers and other health services workers openly advocate the discovery and recruitment of new cases through case finding, on the theory that this is a way to bring needed services to those who either would not know to ask about them or who might be mistaken about whether such interventions would serve their best interests. The very concept and practice of case finding, however, disproves the naive view that officials only passively respond to reports that predate their interventions.

One needs hardly to emphasize that large numbers of citizens do not share the naive view about official interventions in child maltreatment cases. Many individuals and families feel a great sense of injustice concerning the official investigations or interventions in their lives. Such feelings have been common in many minority communities for decades now. In such communities a feeling of discrimination and injustice has persisted for years. The available research tends to support this feeling, showing that official decision-making processes recruit disproportionate numbers of poor and minority families into their caseloads. With respect to decisions on specific cases, perhaps there have always been a few instances of officials who make "Type I errors," that is, who incorrectly label someone a child abuser. But in recent years these numbers have grown to the point where aggrieved parties have organized for counteraction. In Phoenix, Arizona, for example, there is a group known as PAPS, or Parents Against Protective Services. The founders of this group claim a membership of about 2,200 parents who have been angered by the treatment they have received at the hands of child protective services. The very existence of such organizations carries important implications. It shows that the steadily increasing power of the state to intervene in family life has reached such a point that organized opposition to it has developed. It also indicates that the state interventions now extend considerably beyond the traditional target groups for official social control: the poor and certain ethnic communities.

THE IMPACT OF THE CHILD MALTREATMENT MOVEMENT ON THE INTEGRITY OF FAMILY LIFE

All persons familiar with the current facts on child abuse and neglect express agreement on this important point: Existing definitions are imprecise and ambiguous, and there is no consensus about their meanings. What remains hotly disputed, however, is whether this state of affairs represents a desirable or undesirable situation. Those who see advantages to the open-ended nature of the definitions, for example, argue that this permits the flexibility needed to "individualize" decision making in specific cases. A respected scholar in the field of family law, Harry Krause, argues as follows:

> Due to the varied nature of the situations to be covered, the neglect and dependency laws are rarely specific. A legal finding of neglect typically is a composite of many factors and requires a highly individualized judgment on all of the circumstances of each specific case. Statutes *need* to be flexible to provide the necessary broad discretion to the courts.[40]

Advocates of the "open definition" consider it advantageous because decision makers can be sensitive to contextual, local, and emergent features of the situation. There is an implicit assumption here, however, that officials not only act in good faith, but with the "best interests" of the community foremost in mind at all times. At this stage in our history, such claims are more usefully seen as just ignorant—or as self-interested claims by those who wish to extend the powers and authorities of the welfare state, in what they must presume to be their own best interests.

Opponents of "open definitions" are less sanguine about official good faith and judicial wisdom. They tend to emphasize the potential for injustice that resides in statutory ambiguity and official discretion. Michael Wald, who drafted the child protective model legislation promoted by the American Bar Association, is one who advocates such a stance:

> Most state statutes define neglect in broad, vague language, which would seem to allow virtually unlimited intervention. . . . The definitions of neglect offered by legal scholars are equally broad. . . . The absence of precise standards for state intervention is said to be a necessity, even a virtue. . . . It is both possible and desirable to define neglect in more specific terms and with reference to the types of damage that justify intervention. . . . Vague laws increase the likelihood that decisions to intervene will

be made in situations where the child will be harmed by intervention. Because the statutes do not reflect a considered analysis of what types of harm justify the risk of intervention, decision making is left to the ad hoc analysis of social workers and judges.... Their decisions often reflect personal values about children which are not supported by scientific evidence and which result in removing children from environments in which they are doing adequately. Only through carefully drawn statutes, drafted in terms of specific harms to the child, can we limit the possibility of intervention in situations where it would do more harm than good.[41]

These continuing disputes about definitions and the proper authority for state intervention have important consequences. They also provide evidence of the critical impact of the child maltreatment movement on American family life. Never before in history has the power of the state expanded so rapidly into the domain of the family. Never before have so many of the traditional rights and obligations of family life eroded so rapidly. Never before have so many families been caught up in the net of official investigation and case processing; our best estimates today tell us that about 1 million U.S. families receive an official investigation that results in a *substantiated* claim of abuse or neglect *each year*.[42] Several million others are investigated by official agents, which is in and of itself a great source of anxiety, stress, conflict, and stigma. The legal custody and control of children has been taken away from more and more parents through court proceedings, although there is some evidence that these trends are reversing in more recent years. More and more children are now removed from their homes and "placed" in a foster home or other institution; one needs only the most superficial familiarity with this situation to see that such placement decisions tend to follow resource availability; that is, as new facilities or resources are added to the institutional network, more and more of these placement decisions are seen by officials as "needed," or even "necessary."

We are forever interested in the questions about how our society compares to others, or whether the times we live in are better or worse than before. Is there more or less justice for families today? Is the family stronger or weaker? Are our policies more or less humane? These are often the important questions that animate our academic and research interests. Unfortunately perhaps, the evidence about all of these issues is mixed. A historical perspective tends to produce a complex, mixed judgment. Certainly we no longer practice the forms of infanticide, abandonment, enslavement, bodily mutilation, or severe corporal discipline so common throughout history. Most people would see this as representing an improved, more humane condition. On the question of state authority and intervention in family life, the evidence is again mixed. The United States no longer invests forms of virtually unreviewed discretion as we find in the office of the tithingman in Massachusetts in the 1670s, who was given the mandate to personally inspect local families for their moral rectitude and religious obedience.[43] We no longer condone the removal of children from their families, by private parties, without any due process or legal hearing, to be given or sold to other families. Yet this was a sanctioned policy of U.S. Societies for the Prevention of Pauperism at the turn of the century.[44] When seen in this context, perhaps some of the recent legal cases concerning child maltreatment may be judged more humane.

Historical relativism provides a necessary view, but it should not produce in us a paralysis of perspective or action. There is little doubt that basic family relations are once again caught in the throes of social change, and that the integrity of family life is threatened in new and fundamentally different ways. The recent experience with the Child Maltreatment Movement in the United States forces on us one inescapable conclusion: We must stop thinking that governmental actions merely represent functional responses to family problems, tending to control them. Recent empirical evidence leads us to see that governmental efforts may serve to create and sustain some kinds of problems, and specifically in the case of official interventions into family life, they may make problems worse for the individuals involved. This realization produces a new circumspection and caution about the role of governmental action in resolving family problems, and paves the way for more informed political action.

NOTES

1. Vincent de Francis, "Parents Who Abuse Children." *PTA Magazine* 58 (Nov. 1963): 16–18.

2. Lloyd de Mause, ed., *The History of Childhood* (New York: Psychohistory Press. 1974).

3. M. Harris, "Why Men Dominate Women." *New York Times Magazine*, 13 Nov. 1977. pp. 46ff.

4. Ibid., p. 120.

5. Samuel X. Radbill, "A History of Child Abuse and Infanticide," in R. Helfer and C. Kempe, eds., *The Battered Child* (Chicago: University of Chicago Press, 1968), p. 10.

6. Ibid., p. 12.

7. Ibid., p. 4.

8. Ibid.

9. T. Solomon, "History and Demography of Child Abuse." *Pediatrics* 51 (1963): 773–76.

10. John Caffey, "Multiple Fractures in the Long Bones of Infants Suffering from Chronic Subdural Hematoma," *American Journal of Roentgenology* 56 (Aug. 1946): 163–73.

11. Frederick N. Silverman, "Roentgen Manifestations of Unrecognized Skeletal Trauma in Infants," *American Journal of Roentgenology* 69 (March 1953): 413–26: Paul V. Wooley and W. A. Evans Jr., "Significance of Skeletal Lesions in Infants Resembling Those of Traumatic Origin." *Journal of the American Medical Association* 158 (June 1955): 539–43.

12. C. Henry Kempe. et al., "The Battered Child Syndrome." *Journal of the American Medical Association* 181 (July 1962): 17–24.

13. See Stephen J. Pfohl, "The 'Discovery' of Child Abuse." *Social Problems* 24 (Feb. 1977): 310–23: Peter Conrad and Joseph W. Schneider. *Deviance and Medicalization: From Badness to Sickness* (St. Louis: C. V. Mosby Co., 1980). pp. 161–71.

14. Pfohl, *n*. 13.

15. Knowledge of this meeting was gained from personal talks with Vincent de Francis.

16. Jack D. Douglas, *Defining America's Social Problems* (Englewood Cliffs, N.J.: Prentice-Hall, 1974).

17. M. G. Paulsen, "The Legal Framework for Child Protection." *Columbia Law Review* 67 (Jan. 1966): 1–49.

18. Vincent de Francis, *Child Abuse Legislation in the 1970s* (Denver: American Humane Association, 1970).

19. Vincent de Francis and C. I. Lucht, *Child Abuse and Legislation in the 1970s*, rev. ed. (Denver: American Humane Association, 1974).

20. Sanford Katz, "Child Neglect Laws in America," *Family Law Quarterly* 9 (Spring 1975): 295–331.

21. Saad Z. Nagi, *Child Maltreatment in the United States* (New York: Columbia University Press, 1977).

22. V. Cain, "Concern for Children in Placement," *Analysis of Child Abuse and Neglect* (Washington, D.C.: National Center on Child Abuse and Neglect, 1977).

23. Richard J. Gelles, *Family Violence* (Beverly Hills, Calif.: Sage Publications, 1979).

24. See Jeanne M. Giovannoni and Rosina M. Becerra, *Defining Child Abuse* (New York: Free Press, 1979); Gelles, *n.* 22; Alfred Kadushin and John A. Martin, *Child Abuse* (New York: Columbia University Press, 1981).

25. Leroy Pelton, "Child Abuse and Neglect: The Myth of Classlessness," *American Journal of Orthopsychiatry* 48 (Oct. 1978): 608–16.

26. Nagi, *n.* 21.

27. A "Type I Error" would be the labeling and processing of a caretaker as a child abuser who has not in fact abused a child.

28. Anthony M. Platt, *The Child Savers* (Chicago: University of Chicago Press, 1969).

29. Ellen Hoffman, "Policy and Politics: The Child Abuse Prevention and Treatment Act." in Richard Bourne and Eli H. Newberger, eds., *Critical Perspectives on Child Abuse* (Lexington, Mass.: Lexington Books, 1979), pp. 157–70.

30. A. Wolkenstein, "Hospital Acts on Child Abuse," *Journal of the American Hospital Association* 49 (March 1975): 103–6.

31. R. Polakow and D. Peabody, "Behavioral Treatment of Child Abuse," *International Journal of Offender Therapy and Comparative Criminology* 19 (1975): 100–108.

32. C. Hinton and J. Sterling, "Volunteers Serve as an Adjunct to Treatment for Child-Abusing Families," *Hospital and Community Psychiatry* 26 (March 1975): 136–37.

33. Jacobus Ten Broeck, "The Extended Family Center," *Children Today* 3 (April 1974): 2–6.

34. H. Lovens and J. Rako, "A Community Approach to the Prevention of Child Abuse," *Child Welfare* 54 (Feb 1975): 83–87.

35. Emilio Viano, "Attitudes Toward Child Abuse Among American Professionals." (Paper presented at the first meeting of the International Society for Research on Aggression, Toronto, Canada, 1974).

36. Giovannoni and Becerra, *n.* 24.

37. Gelles, *n.* 23, p. 61.

38. The research of Giovannoni and Becerra, *n.* 24, suggests that the traditional differences between the more supportive versus the more punitive professions are dissipating.

39. John M. Johnson, "Mass Media Reports and Deviance." (Paper presented at the annual meeting of the Society for the Study of Social Problems, San Francisco, 1982).

40. Harry D. Krause, *Family Law in a Nutshell* (St. Paul, Minn.: West Publishing Co., 1977), pp. 236–37.

41. Michael Wald, "State Intervention on Behalf of 'Neglected' Children: A Search for Realistic Standards," *Stanford Law Review* 27 (April 1975): 985–1040.

42. Gelles, *n.* 23.

43. Peter Conrad and Joseph W. Schneider, *Deviance and Medicalization: From Badness to Sickness* (St. Louis: C. V. Mosby Co., 1980).

44. Radbill, *n.* 5.

40
Life-Course Effects of Vietnam Combat and Abusive Violence: Marital Patterns*

Robert S. Laufer and M. S. Gallops

Recent research has established the significance of war trauma as a long-term disruptive factor in the lives of Vietnam veterans (Laufer et al. 1981; Laufer, Gallops, and Frey-Wouters 1984; Yager et al. 1984; Laufer, Brett, and Gallops, in press), corroborating the work of several studies (Helzer et al. 1979; Wilson 1978; Kadushin et al. 1981; Nace et al. 1978; Harris 1980). Earlier work focused on posttraumatic stress indicators, psychiatric symptomatology, and behavior problems such as alcohol use, drug use, and post-service arrests and found that a broad pattern of persistent social and psychological disruption is associated with exposure to war trauma. The general literature on the effects of war on Vietnam veterans has been posed, for the most part, in terms of the direct impact of wartime experiences on later conditions. Yet, as we have argued elsewhere (Laufer 1985), the effects of war ought to be conceptualized in terms of how war influences the development of the early adult life structures and how it differentiates a cohort over its life course. The task we undertake in this paper is to specify the effects of military service and war trauma on family patterns in early adult life-course development.

*Laufer, Robert S. and M. S. Gallops. 1985. "Life-Course Effects of Vietnam Combat and Abusive Violence: Marital Patterns." *Journal of Marriage and the Family* (November): 839–851. Copyrighted 1985 by the National Council on Family Relations, 1910 West County Road B, Suite 147, St. Paul, Minnesota 55113. Reprinted by permission.

Do military service in wartime and exposure to war trauma bring about distinct family patterns and problems within the implicated segment of the population? This is the question that is addressed here. The effects of military service are distinguished by exposure to combat, exposure to episodes of abusive violence, and participation in these episodes (abusive violence may be understood generally as the arbitrary use of violence against persons when not necessitated by self-defense).

In this paper we explore five questions: (a) Do military service and war trauma affect the propensity to marry? (b) Do they affect the timing of marriages? (c) Do they affect the propensity to divorce? (d) Do they affect the quality of marital relations? (e) Do marital patterns mediate the effects of war trauma on later psychological well-being?

WAR AND THE FAMILY

Since World War II a number of speculative essays, generally based on demographic trends and case studies, have considered the impact of military service during war upon family patterns and the emergence of family problems (Waller 1940, 1944; Pratt 1944, chap. 8; McDonagh 1946; Hill 1949; Lieberman 1971). The attention given the relationship between war and the family is well justified. As an institution that provides for the material, psychological, and emotional needs of individuals, the family plays an important role in enabling its members to deal with externally produced stress. The impact of war on the family is severe, because it involves a separation of members, a disruption of domestic routine, and a high degree of uncertainty as to the outcome of the process—i.e., will the father, son, or brother who has been taken into the service return; and if he returns, what will be his physical, psychological, and emotional states?

The massive social transformations produced by this century's two world wars created severe social dislocations which directly affected the family. The wave of war marriages, initiated as soldiers were about to leave home, was only one example of how the family was affected (Waller 1944; pp. 131–134, pp. 136–139). While the family is subject to unusual pressures and strains during wartime, it also plays a very important role when the veteran returns, as the veteran must reorient himself to civilian life. When men return from war they usually return to family and friendship networks, so that the individual's readjustment to civilian life is, in the early stages, primarily mediated by the family. It is commonly perceived that the family serves as the first line of civilian therapy for the returning veteran (Pratt 1944; Waller 1944).

The importance of the family in helping men deal with stressful life events, broadly defined, has received considerable confirmation from recent research. Studies of the relationship between family relations and mental health have shown that the rates of mortality from a variety of causes are higher for unmarried than for married males (Gove 1973), the rates of suicide for unmarried and divorced men is higher than among married men (Gove 1972), levels of reported psychiatric symptoms are lower for married males compared with unmarried ones (Lin et al. 1979; Myers et al. 1975), stress events are more likely to lead to psychological symptoms and difficulties among the unmarried rather than the married (Eaton 1978; Gore 1978), and unmarried veterans tend to be more politically alienated than married ones (Fendrich and Axelson 1971).

Examining the role of the family is important in understanding the manner in which the experience of war affects men's lives. To the extent that war is a stressful and traumatic experience, one would expect it to create difficulties in the lives of those exposed to it, through marital strife and divorce or by preventing the creation of marriages. Conversely, marriage offers the veteran an opportunity to harmonize, to some extent, the disjunction he is likely to experience between his social position and that of his nonveteran age peers, in his movement toward adult status. The contradiction between social position and chronological age for veterans is likely to be painfully intense for veterans of war who, in ways often irrelevant to civilian society, have aged dramatically (Wilson 1978; Laufer 1985). Our transcripts indicate that in some cases emotional support, intimacy, and fathering children were fantasized as bringing a release from personal tensions that developed during military service.

The following sections outline the effects we expect military service and exposure to war trauma to exert upon the family lives of veterans and their patterns of seeking and establishing intimacy.

THE EFFECTS OF MILITARY SERVICE

Service in the military during wartime should generate distinctive patterns and/or problems in domestic life for two reasons: among those who have married before their entry, the period of separation may induce tensions and strains in the relationship that have to be resolved upon their return; and, for those who are inducted into the service before they begin their adult careers, the time spent in the military sets back their career clock by a substantial length of time, creating pressures to make up for this delay upon their return to civilian life. These two sources of influence are relevant to all groups who enter the military, whether during wartime or not, since they are due to military service itself; but they are particularly important during periods of conflict because large proportions of men in the armed services do not enter them voluntarily but do so only under compulsion. In this context military service marks an unexpected and generally undesired interruption of their civilian and domestic careers.

Military service during wartime has been identified as having two negative effects on the married lives of veterans. First, it affects the stability of marriages. Separation for those leaving their conjugal families behind requires the wife to make adjustments during the husband's absence. These adjustments may not allow the marriage to return to the status quo. The wife may become more independent and self-reliant and come to assume it her right to shoulder the responsibilities in the family; then, upon the husband's return, the coping skills developed by the wife may create tensions about the husband's appropriate role (Pratt 1944; Hill 1949; McCubbin et al. 1976).

Second, military service affects the timing of veterans' marriages. Those who are inducted into the service before they begin their adult careers have their social lives frozen for a period. Within American society in this century, there commonly has existed a normative pattern in the transition to adulthood which included completing schooling, securing employment, and then getting married and having a family (Hogan 1981). The problem veterans may face upon return is that though they are "chronologically ready for marriage [they are] socially and economically unprepared for it. In trying to compensate for lost time, the separatee may catapult himself into more problems than he can safely handle" (McDonagh 1946, p. 451).

Veterans who return from the service find, when they contact their peer network, that they are two or more years behind in the social process of reaching adulthood although they are still at comparable chronological ages. The veteran's sense of urgency to quickly close that gap may encourage a quick transition to the status of husband and father without considering the social and economic disadvantages such roles produce. Consequently, veterans may attempt to do everything at once instead of moving through the career stages they would have experienced without the advent of military service. In general, serving in the military appears to contribute to a disparity between social and chronological aging in the veteran population (Elder 1978).

THE EFFECTS OF WAR TRAUMA

In the Vietnam War, men were exposed to life-threatening situation, called upon to take the lives of others, exposed to episodes of the abusive treatment of noncombatants, and in some instances themselves participated in the physical abuse of noncombatants. These experiences are sources of trauma and weigh heavily upon the lives of veterans after they return to civilian life. The degree to which men have these experiences and to which such memories and imagery continue to trouble them as civilians may be related to the manner in which they approach and attempt to construct their domestic lives after they return. Consequently exposure to war trauma should have a direct impact on their married lives.

Exposure to war trauma also should affect patterns of intimacy. This should be especially characteristic of those veterans exposed to the more chilling and shocking aspects of war. Particular war experiences such as exposure to combat, death, and acts of physical cruelty are likely to return the veteran to society with problems that directly affect the veteran's capacity to establish and maintain a family. In the long run the trauma of war may be so disruptive that the veteran is unable to maintain a marriage regardless of when he entered it.

Men who have these experiences may find themselves incapable of generating the types of intimacy that they had known before the service. As a study of readjustment of World War II veterans noted:

> The soldier is taught deliberately to kill and to harden himself against softer thoughts . . . Thus, in spite of genuine affection for his wife a returned soldier may find himself . . . strangely undemonstrative and brusque . . . Moreover, he may bring back . . . a streak of hardness and inhumanity to human suffering. (Pratt 1944, pp. 182–183).

This limiting of the emotional scope of the veteran is very likely to limit his inclination to enter marriage or to find an acceptable partner or, once in a marriage, to satisfy the mate's emotional needs and maintain the relationship over time. Veterans with greatest exposure to combat and violence may have immunized themselves to some degree from strong expressive feelings toward others, a characteristic that could contribute to marital difficulties.

It is also possible that those who were traumatized return with an inability to relate emotionally to women and, thus, avoid marriage altogether. The work of psychiatrists with Vietnam veterans and the experience of veteran "rap" groups have shown that many veterans avoid intimate relations because they are seriously concerned with their own vulnerability (Lifton 1973, chap. 9).

The impact of the Vietnam War on men's lives is known to have varied over its course. The character of the war changed as the American involvement escalated from 1965 to 1968, and the character of the enemy changed from local guerilla units to North Vietnamese regulars. In addition, changing attitudes to the conflict in America placed more pressure on servicemen as the moral and political ambiguity of the conflict became publicly evident. Servicemen in the later years of the war, particularly after the Tet Offensive in 1968, were caught between an intensification of the conflict in Vietnam and a decline in popular support in the U.S. Consequently, we hypothesized that the impact of traumatic experiences may have been more pronounced for men who served after 1967 since they were subject to other cross pressures in a changing military and political environment. Previous work found that combat exposure interacted with period of service in affecting levels of posttraumatic stress symptomatology (Laufer et al. 1981), and more recent work also has found period of service to have important effects on postservice adjustment (Stretch 1984).

THE VIETNAM WAR AND MARITAL PROBLEMS

Research on the relationship between war trauma and marital and stress problems among Vietnam veterans has received relatively little attention (the work of Martin 1981, is the exception). However, what little evidence we do have suggests that war trauma does contribute to marital difficulties among Vietnam veterans. The combination of social separation, career disorientation, and personal/psychological traumatization probably make it difficult for veterans to develop their domestic lives as successfully as their civilian counterparts. In terms of the marriage histories of veterans, one would expect to find that the group as a whole has higher rates of marriage failure than nonveterans have and that those exposed to traumatic experiences in Vietnam have higher rates still.

Despite the dearth of empirical work in this area we can formulate a set of expectations as to how wartime service and exposure to war trauma affected patterns of marriage and marital difficulties among veterans. Table 1 outlines these expectations. The effects that social separation due to military service have upon marriage patterns should be constant both for veterans who did and for veterans who did not serve in Vietnam. For those married before they entered the service, there should be a higher rate of marriage disruption and failure in the

TABLE 1. EXPECTED MILITARY SERVICE AND WAR EXPERIENCE EFFECTS ON MARITAL PATTERNS

Variables	Vietnam-era Veterans[a,b]	Vietnam Veterans[b]	
		No War Trauma	War Trauma
Rates of marriage	+	+	−
Rates of divorce	+	+	+
Age at marriage	−	−	−
Satisfaction with marriage	nd	nd	−

Note: + indicates that the rate or characteristic should be higher; − indicates that the rate or characteristic should be lower; "nd" indicates that there should be no difference among groups.

[a] Vietnam-era veterans are those who served in the military during the period of conflict but who never served in the Vietnam theatre of operations.

[b] The reference group against which the patterns in these groups are compared is nonveterans.

form of separation and divorce than among civilians of comparable ages. For those not married before or during service there should be higher rates of marriages beginning immediately after leaving the service. The degree to which veterans marry after leaving the service should lead both to a higher rate of marriage among veterans and to a lower age profile for those veterans who do marry. Those two hypotheses stem from the likelihood that veterans getting married soon after release do so under the impulse to make up for lost time without specifically referring to what their nonveteran peers are doing at the same age. Whereas nonveterans may still be working in the normative sequence of finishing education, finding a job, and then getting married, returning veterans may be concerned with starting their civilian work careers and their families simultaneously. This would lead to both of the characteristics stated above.

Among Vietnam veterans we expect that those who had traumatic experiences in Vietnam either would never enter marriage or would have marriage problems. The personal problems and psychological difficulties that develop as a consequence of exposure to war stress either should prevent veterans from establishing intimate relations with others or should limit their abilities to maintain these relations. To the extent that veterans in this category do marry once they return, the memories, intrusive imagery, and constriction of emotions resulting from their war experiences may create problems in their domestic lives that result either in separation and divorce or in marriages of a less satisfactory character.

If marriage does provide important support functions for the returning veteran, problems associated with military service and with exposure to war trauma should be lower among those men in stable marriages than among those who have been divorced or who have failed to marry. Relatedly, if military service or war trauma strongly contributes to marital disruption and weak familial relations, its long-term effect on psychological and behavioral problems may be transmitted by these factors. Figure 1 outlines these relationships. If the primary effects of military service and war trauma are transmitted through family patterns, the direct effects of military service and war

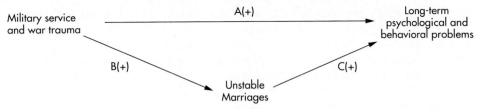

FIGURE 1. THE EXPECTED ROLE OF MARITAL PATTERNS IN TRANSMITTING THE EFFECTS OF WAR STRESS

trauma should become indirect, reflected in a strong relationship between having marital problems and the presence of psychological and behavioral problems.

METHOD

The Sample

Our sample contains 1,259 men who were of draft-eligible age during the Vietnam War. The sample, comprising Vietnam veterans, Vietnam-era veterans, and nonveterans, was drawn from 10 sites[1] chosen to represent four sections of the country on matched economic and demographic characteristics and collected in two waves: the Northeast in 1977 (Wave I, n = 341) and the South, Midwest, and West in 1979 (Wave II, n = 918).[2] Though not a national probability sample, it does represent several regions and city sizes in the continental United States and, at minimum, adequately represents the population in the 10 sites.

The sample was stratified by veteran status, race, age, and education (Wave I only). Random digit dialing techniques were used in each of the 10 locations to screen individuals and collect the sample. If a male who fit an unfilled cell's characteristics lived in the household reached, he was selected for interviewing. The refusal rate to the screening calls was 7.8%; the refusal rate of the interviews was 17.5%. Sample selection by telephone screening continued until the required number in each site cell was obtained (Rothbart 1981).

Due to high costs of collecting a large sample of a relatively rare population (e.g., Vietnam-era veterans) by random probability techniques, multiplicity sampling was used to increase the yield of veterans. If the household contacted did not contain an eligible respondent, the screener asked if a brother, son, or nephew living in the sampling area was a veteran during the Vietnam war. In these cases the kinship unit—not the household unit—was being sampled. If an eligible candidate was obtained by this process and fit the sample requirements, he was interviewed and information was obtained on his kinship network in the area. This allowed the estimation of his probability of being nominated given the random method of selection with respect to those found by contacting households (Rothbart et al. 1982). The Wave II sample contained 290 veterans obtained by contacting households and 213 veterans obtained by kin nomination.

In the following analysis all multiple regression procedures are carried out on unweighted data. Multiple regression allows the statistical control of characteristics on which the sample was stratified. Also, previous work has shown that regression estimates are reliable and only marginally affected by changes in sampling variance produced by weighting (Rothbart 1981, p. 96). When summary characteristics such as means, percentages, and correlations are presented, however, they are based on weighted data, adjusting for both the stratification design and the differential probability of selection in the multiplicity group, to make our sample comparable to the general site populations from which it was drawn.

The Variables

In order to test the effects of military service and war trauma upon the family patterns of our sample, we use five variables:

1. Veteran—coded 1 for those who served in the military but did not serve in Vietnam and 0 otherwise.
2. Vietnam Veteran—coded 1 if the veteran served in Vietnam and 0 otherwise.
3. Combat—a checklist of 10 experiences including such items as "received incoming fire," "encountered mines or boobytraps," and "engaged VC or NVA in a firefight." The full scale ranges from 0 to 14 (four experiences received a weight of 2). The effective range on the scale in our sample was 0 to 13. (A further discussion of the Combat Scale used here is presented in Laufer et al. 1981, app. I.)
4. Exposure—coded 0 if the Vietnam veteran did not witness any episodes of abusive violence and 1 if he did. This variable is limited to witnessing these events only. (The meaning and significance of exposure to abusive violence is elaborated further in Laufer, Gallops, and Frey-Wouters 1984.)
5. Participation—coded 1 if the Vietnam veteran participated in the physical mistreatment of noncombatants, or other uses of abusive violence, and 0 otherwise.

In using these variables in a regression model, two things should be noted. First, both Veteran (Vietnam-era) and Vietnam veteran are coded independently so that they measure the differences between the mean values in these groups and the mean values for nonveterans. If there is a constant effect of military service, the regression effects of both should be parallel, with the same sign and roughly the same magnitude. The significance test of the effect of each is based on comparisons with nonveterans. Second, the two measures of abusive violence— Exposure and Participation—are coded independently; i.e., those who participated were not also coded as exposed. When both arc included in the regression model, they measure the difference between the mean values in these groups and the mean for all Vietnam veterans who had no contact with instances of abusive violence. Our earlier research has shown that the effects of these two experiences are not parallel and cumulative, a relationship we initially expected (Laufer, Gallops, and Frey-Wouters 1984; Laufer, Brett, and Gallops, in press).

The information on marriage deals primarily with the individual's first marriage.

1. Ever Married—coded 1 if the respondent was ever married, 0 otherwise.
2. Age at Marriage—coded as the respondent's age in years when he entered his first marriage.
3. Ever Divorced—coded 1 if the respondent's first marriage ended in divorce or separation, 0 otherwise.
4. Marital Satisfaction—this information was obtained from those men who were married at the time of the interview. This measure is a combination of two items: (a) How often has the thought of a divorce crossed your mind? and (b) All things considered, how satisfied are you with your marriage? Each was coded from (1) Often; Very Unsatisfied to (5) Never; Very Satisfied. Combined as one measure the range was (0) Low to (100) High.

In dealing with the domestic careers of men, it is important to control for background characteristics that may have contributed to their desire and ability to achieve a stable family life. We examined a number of relevant background characteristics, which include race, father's education, whether the respondent came from a single-parent family, whether there were problems in the family of origin, the size of the respondent's family of origin, whether the respondent had problems with authority as a youth, and the age of the respondent. Although several of these variables had effects on the features of marital careers we examined, they did not affect the pattern of relationships found between military service and traumatic experiences and these characteristics.

FINDINGS

The War Experience and Marital Patterns

In its most general form, the question of how military service and the war affected patterns of domestic life can be posed, "How does the probability of entering marriage, and getting divorced or separated, vary by group?" As Table 2 shows, veterans were more likely than nonveterans to have entered marriage, and Vietnam veterans were the most likely: 84% of this group did so, as did 81% of Vietnam-era veterans, while nonveterans were the least likely (only 70% of this group did so). The rates of divorce within the different groups are not as notably different as the rates of marriage. Surprisingly, Vietnam veterans were the lowest (20%), Vietnam-era veterans the highest (27%), with nonveterans falling in between (24%).

These simple comparisons suggest that serving in the military acted to encourage men to enter marriage; however, they do not answer the question of what produced this relationship. Did service in the military encourage quick marriages before induction, or did veterans return to civilian life after service and enter marriage as a result of their prolonged separation from social life? These questions can be answered by examining the ages at which men started their first marriages. Table 3 provides this information. All three groups had equivalent proportions of men entering marriage through the age of 21. By this age one-fifth (21%) to one-fourth (24%) of the men in each group had entered their first marriages. Age

TABLE 2. SELECTED MARITAL CHARACTERISTICS BY VETERAN STATUS

Characteristics	Vietnam Veterans	Vietnam-era Veterans	Nonveterans
Percentage who were ever married	84*[a] (n = 326)[b]	81* (n = 341)	70 (n = 590)
Percentage whose first marriage ended in divorce or separation	20 (n = 277)	27 (n = 270)	24 (n = 423)
Median age in years at first marriage	22.8 (n = 274)	23.6* (n = 268)	22.8 (n = 423)

[a] The percentages are based on weighted data.

[b] The ns are the unweighted number of cases in the category.

*These characteristics of the veteran group is significantly different from those of nonveterans, $p < .05$.

18 to age 21 was the period in which most men entered the service, the median age at induction being 19.5 years and the median length of time served being 34 months. It appears there was not a rush of marriages among men entering the service; it seems safe to conclude, then, that the war-marriage phenomenon was not a pronounced occurrence during the Vietnam war.

The levels of marriage in each group did begin to separate by the time these men were in their early 20s. Beginning at age 22, Vietnam veterans consistently entered marriages more frequently than did their nonveteran counterparts. The ratio of men who had entered marriage among Vietnam veterans vs. among nonveterans was 24:23 at age 21 and 67:56 by age 25. This difference of 11% constituted most of the 14% difference in rates between these two groups (84% vs. 70%) which is shown in Table 2. Thus, most of the difference in rates of marriage between Vietnam veterans and nonveterans can be traced to their actions during the ages of 22 to 25. Among Vietnam veterans this was the period in which most men were returning from military service; for nonveterans this was the period in which they were completing college and finishing their formal education.

The age pattern of entering marriage among Vietnam-era veterans was different from that of Vietnam veterans. With respect to the pattern found among nonveterans, Vietnam-era veterans entered marriages more frequently in the age range of 25 to 28. At age 24 half of both Vietnam-era veterans and nonveterans had been married. Over the next four years Vietnam-era veterans entered marriage more frequently than nonveterans; by age 28, 73% of Vietnam-era veterans had entered marriage, compared with only 65% of nonveterans. This 8% difference in rates represents most of the 11% difference (81% vs. 70%) shown between these two groups in Table 2.

As shown in Table 3, the cumulative rates of marriage by age suggest that Vietnam veterans were more likely to enter marriage during their period of readjustment to civilian life than were Vietnam-era veterans. The hypothesis that men leave military service eager to make up for lost time is corroborated by this pattern. The meaning of the later pattern of increases in marriage among

TABLE 3. CUMULATIVE PROPORTION OF RESPONDENTS MARRIED BY AGE, BY VETERAN STATUS

	Vietnam Veterans	Vietnam-era Veterans	Nonveterans
Age at marriage			
18 or younger	1%[a]	3%	4%
19	7	4	11
20	13	11	17
21	24	21	23
22	37	27	32
23	49	39	41
24	60	50	50
25	67	58	56
26	70	65	60
27	76	70	64
28	78	73	65
29	79	75	67
30 or older	84	81	70
Never married	16%	19%	30%
N	321[b]	337	578

[a] The percentages are based on weighted data.

[b] The *n*s are the unweighted number of cases in the category.

Vietnam-era veterans is less clear. They began to enter marriages more frequently well after they were released from service.

It does not appear that either veteran group was seriously restricted in the marriage market in their early years by military service. The rates of entering marriage in the ages of 18 to 21 were roughly equivalent for all three groups; and rates of marriage for each group were small at age 21, given that men generally enter marriage after the age of 21. Even though most of the veterans in the sample were in the military during the period in which they were 18 to 22, they were just as likely to enter marriages in this period as were their nonveteran counterparts.

The expectation that veterans would tend to marry at earlier ages than non-veterans is not confirmed. Vietnam-era veterans married at a slightly later age than nonveterans (.8 years, or roughly 10 months). On the other hand, the median age at first marriage of Vietnam veterans was exactly that of nonveterans (see Table 2). The interquartile range of the age distribution at first marriage is also very similar for the three groups. For Vietnam veterans and nonveterans, the range is four years (from ages 21 to 25); for Vietnam-era veterans, it is five years (from ages 21 to 26). Veterans do not marry earlier than nonveterans in an absolute sense; however, most veterans spent almost three years in the military between the ages of 19 to 23. The period of military service disrupted their social careers. If we adjust for this period, then we conclude that veterans married relatively earlier in their social careers.

The minimal age-at-marriage difference, in combination with the average duration of service, suggests that those who entered service may have compensated for other career costs by marrying early, relative to the three or so years "lost" in service. Among both Vietnam veterans and Vietnam-era veterans, 10% were married before they entered the service, roughly 30% were married during their enlistment, and another 30% were married within the first 24 months after their release (these percentages are higher than those shown in Table 3 because they are based on the number of men in these groups who ever married). Thus, a large portion of veterans were supporting families within two years of their discharge (about 70% of the men in these groups who would ever marry).

The absence of differences between groups in the rates of divorce, shown in Table 2, runs directly against our expectations. In addition, the appearance of the lowest rate of divorce among Vietnam veterans is surprising. To determine whether there were any important differences among Vietnam veterans due to their war experiences, a regression analysis of the variables Having Been Divorced and Marital Satisfaction on the military service and war experience variables was carried out. The results of this analysis are presented in Table 4. As shown, net of other effects Vietnam veterans were significantly less likely ($b = -.21, p < .001$) to have ever been divorced than nonveterans. Among the war experiences, exposure to combat and participation in abusive violence have significant effects on postservice marital disruption. Combat exposure is related ($b = .03, p < .001$) to higher levels of divorce, while participation is related ($b = -.19, p < .05$) to lower levels of divorce. The effect of serving in Vietnam must be seen in conjunction with the effect of combat exposure. The negative effect of Vietnam-veteran status indicates that veterans with low levels of combat have low rates of divorce. This can be seen when rates of divorce in different combat categories are examined. Of Vietnam veterans with low combat exposure (scores 0 through 3) only 11% had divorced or separated, compared with 18% of those with moderate exposure (scores 4 through 9) and 32% of Vietnam veterans with high combat exposure (scores 10 through 13). While the overall rate of divorce among low-combat Vietnam veterans is lower than among Vietnam-era veterans (27%) or nonveterans (24%), the rate among high-combat Vietnam veterans slightly exceeds the rates in both other groups.

While the effect of combat exposure on divorce is consistent with expectations of the relationship between traumatic experience and subsequent difficulties, the negative effect of participation in abusive violence contradicts this expectation. The reasons for this surprising relationship are not clear. One possibility is that, among veterans with this experience, marriage is used as a buffer against the memories of this trauma.

Table 4 also presents the regression of current marital satisfaction on military service and traumatic experience variables. The findings on this outcome variable are extremely weak, as shown by the low R^2, and at best can be seen as suggestive. It appears that military variables have little impact on the long-term character of relations within the family, at least as measured by feelings of compatibility with the spouse. Vietnam-era veterans are no different from nonveterans in their level of marital satisfaction, while Vietnam veterans report slightly higher levels of satisfaction ($b = 5.90, p < .05$) than their nonveteran counterparts. Once again, the Vietnam veteran effect must be seen in conjunction with the com-

TABLE 4. REGRESSIONS OF BEING DIVORCED OR SEPARATED AND LEVEL OF MARITAL SATISFACTION ON MILITARY SERVICE AND TRAUMATIC EXPERIENCES

	Ever Divorced[a]	Marital Satisfaction[b]
Vietnam-era veteran	$-.01^c$	$-.61$
	$(.01)^d$	$(.01)$
Vietnam veteran	$-.21$***	5.90**
	$(.22)$	$(.12)$
Combat	$.03$***	$-.65$*
	$(.24)$	$(.10)$
Exposure	$.03$	$.57$
	$(.02)$	$(.01)$
Participation	$-.19$**	-5.70
	$(.07)$	$(.04)$
df	961	805
Mean	$.25$	80.8
SD	$-$	21.4
Intercept	$.26$	80.5
R^2	$.03$	$.01$

[a] Ever divorced is a dichotomous variable coded 1 if the respondent's first marraige ended in a divorce or separation. It applies only to respondents who were married at least once. Veterans who were divorced before they entered the service or before they left the military ($n = 18$) were excluded from the analysis.

[b] Marital satisfaction was measured only for those respondents who were married at the time of the interview.

[c] Unstandardized regression coefficient.

[d] Standardized regression coefficient.

*$p < .10$.

**$p < .05$.

***$p < .001$.

bat effect, which is weak and negative ($b = -.65, p < .10$). The mean value of marital satisfaction is 80.3 among nonveterans, 80.9 among Vietnam-era veterans, and 84.7 among Vietnam veterans. For the latter group the mean value of marital satisfaction in the low-combat groups (scores 0 to 3) is 86.7, that in the moderate-combat group (scores 4 through 9) is 87.4, and that in the high-combat groups (scores 10 through 13) is 78.8. The relationship between combat exposure and marital satisfaction is weak and of marginal significance although it is in the expected direction. Again, exposure to abusive violence is nonsignificant, as is participation. While nonsignificant, the latter does have a coefficient in the expected direction unlike its effect on divorce rates.

The negative effect of participation in abusive violence on divorce rates and the absence of an effect arising from exposure to abusive violence is surprising, given the traumatic character of these experiences. Earlier work has shown that such experiences had significant negative effects on the later psychological well-being of Vietnam veterans (Lifton 1973; Shatan 1978; Laufer, Gallops, and Frey-Wouters 1984; Yager et al. 1984). Consequently we expected that marital difficulties would be tied to these experiences in much the same way they were related to combat. Veterans exposed to these traumas return to civilian life with more inner conflicts, questioning, doubts, emotional numbing, and pathological adaptive behaviors. In intimate relations such as marriage, these patterns of feeling and behavior should be revealed most clearly and result in more marital difficulties.

The failure of these experiences to have the predicted effects on this outcome measure—i.e., higher divorce rates net of other factors—led us to pursue a line of analysis suggested by earlier findings (Laufer et al. 1981; Stretch 1984). Previous studies have reported that the period of service sometimes interacts with war trauma. For a measure of period, we divided our sample into two groups: those who served in the military (or nonveterans who had their major period of draft eligibility) before 1968, and those who served in the period after 1967. The year 1968 marked an important transition for American perceptions of the Vietnam war, as well as the character of military experience in Vietnam: this year saw the height of American involvement and intensive warfare, particularly during the Tet offensive; and, at the same time, opposition to the war was escalating in the United States.

Although marital difficulties did not arise from the experience of abusive violence over the entire period of conflict, we expected that this result stemmed from the fact that these experiences had no effect at all before 1968, while having a significant effect after 1967. Doing separate multiple regressions on whether an individual was ever divorced or separated, with the sample divided into two period groups, partially confirmed these expectations (see Table 5). Of those who served before 1968 (this group includes nonveterans who were draft eligible in this period), the effect of exposure to abusive violence was negative but nonsignificant ($b = -.14$); after 1967 the effect was positive and significant ($b = .24, p < .05$). This pattern did not hold for those who participated in abusive violence, however: those who participated before 1968 had slightly lower divorce rates ($b = -.14$), although this effect was not significant; those who participated after 1967 had significantly lower divorce rates ($b = -.25, p < .05$). Combat exposure significantly contributed to higher levels of marital disruption in both periods, but its effect was more pronounced after 1967. Before 1968 the effect of combat was positive and significant ($b = .02, p < .05$), while after 1967 the effect was significant and twice as large ($b = .04, p < .001$).

The utility of these five variables in explaining levels of marital disruption is not great. The model is especially weak with regard to those who served before 1968, the level of explained variance being only .02. The model is slightly more adequate with regard to those who served after 1967, for whom the level of explained variance is a modest .08. The modest ability of the model to explain this aspect of marital careers indicates that, while traumatic experience is not the primary factor shaping the marital careers of these men, it is a significant one.

TABLE 5. REGRESSIONS OF BEING DIVORCED OR SEPARATED BY PERIOD OF SERVICE ON MILITARY SERVICE AND TRAUMATIC EXPERIENCES

	Ever Divorced or Separated	
	Served Before 1968[a]	Served After 1967
Vietnam-era veteran	−.05[b]	.34
	(.05)[c]	(.04)
Vietnam veteran	−.21**	−.25**
	(.21)	(.26)
Combat	.02*	.04***
	(.17)	(.36)
Exposure	−.14	.24*
	(.08)	(.14)
Participation	−.14	−.26*
	(.04)	(.11)
df	517	438
Mean	.26	.23
Intercept	.31	.20
R^2	.02	.08

[a] Nonveterans were assigned their period based on the year in which they turned 19 years old; this was the time of their greatest draft eligibility.

[b] Unstandardized regression coefficient.

[c] Standardized regression coefficient.

*$p < .05$.

**$p < .01$.

***$p < .001$.

Also examined were several controls tapping predispositional factors that could account for variance in marital disruption and levels of exposure to combat. None of those available in the study—including race, age, preservice family history, parents' socioeconomic status, preservice behavioral problems and substance use, and education—weakened the relationship found between combat exposure and marital disruption.

The role of period of service in conditioning the effects of traumatic experience on marital disruption suggested the possibility that the year of military service was merely a proxy for the type of social support the veterans received at homecoming. The effect of traumatic experiences may have been conditioned by the type of civilian environment to which the veteran returned. The decline in popular support for the war after 1967 may have created more pressures on the returning veteran and reinforced the negative aspects of his traumatic military experiences. Conversely, the more supportive civilian environment present before 1968 may have served to mitigate the expression of civilian problems that had their origins in the men's service experiences.

To determine if the effects of traumatic experience on marital disruption were due to the character of the veteran's homecoming experience, two variables measuring the latter were introduced into the model. The first was a scale of three items measuring the veteran's feelings of alienation at homecoming, and the second was a scale of five items measuring the veteran's perception of popular and governmental support of veterans for their service to the country. The inclusion of these variables in the model had no effect on the magnitude of effects attributable to traumatic war experiences. The two homecoming variables did have significant effects on the levels of divorce of men who served before 1968 but did not for those who served after 1967.

Table 6 presents the percentage differences that correspond to the regression findings. Clearly, those who witnessed abusive violence and were exposed to combat after 1967 had much higher rates of marital failure than other groups of Vietnam veterans, Vietnam-era veterans, and nonveterans. Despite the failure of the pattern to include those who participated in abusive violence, the different rates of divorce by level of combat and by exposure to abusive violence after 1967 confirm the importance of the social context in determining, to a degree, how well veterans dealt with their experiences once they returned. As seen in

TABLE 6. LEVELS OF DIVORCE AMONG SELECTED GROUPS, AMONG THOSE EVER MARRIED, BY PERIOD SERVED

	Served Before 1968[a]			Served After 1967		
	Married only Once	Divorced or Separated		Married only Once	Divorced or Separated	
Nonveterans	69%[b]	31%	($n = 247$)[c]	81%	19%	($n = 215$)
Vietnam-era veterans	72	28	($n = 161$)	74	26	($n = 129$)
Vietnam veterans	81	19	($n = 162$)	79	21	($n = 140$)
Vietnam veterans						
Never exposed to abusive violence	80	20	($n = 114$)	87	13	($n = 94$)
Witnessed abusive violence	84	16	($n = 38$)	51	49	($n = 31$)
Participated in abusive violence	83	18	($n = 10$)	81	19	($n = 15$)
Low combat	82	17	($n = 60$)	98	2	($n = 39$)
Moderate combat	81	19	($n = 55$)	83	17	($n = 59$)
Heavy combat	79	21	($n = 47$)	51	49	($n = 42$)

[a] Period of service for nonveterans is defined as those years in which they were most draft eligible, ages 18 to 20.

[b] The percentages are based on weighted data.

[c] The ns are the unweighted number of cases in the category.

Table 6, the group with the highest rate of marital failure was Vietnam veterans exposed to heavy combat in the period after 1967 (49%). The other group with a comparably high rate of divorce was Vietnam veterans who witnessed abusive violence after 1967 (49%).

Social Support and Postservice Problems

This paper has shown that the Vietnam war affected the marital careers of those who served, particularly of those who were exposed to its most severe stresses. In an earlier paper we reported that the features of war experience we have examined here had significant lasting influence upon the likelihood that men would report psychological problems and symptomatology (Laufer, Gallops, and Frey-Wouters 1984). In that analysis we did not consider any factors subsequent to the war experience as possible mediators or contributors to the veterans' ongoing difficulties. It is clear from the literature reviewed above that the family can play a mediating role "in times of crisis that can help prevent mental disorder" (Eaton 1978; p. 230). Veterans who are exposed to high levels of stress during wartime are best served on their return by having a supportive environment to diffuse the tensions and buffer the shocks precipitated by the return to civilian life. The family, before any other social institution, should play this role.

The war's disruptive effect on marriages limits the resources that the veteran has to deal with the past and to reacclimatize himself to civilian life. It is likely that, if the veteran is unable to enter and/or maintain a satisfactory marital relationship, he will be more likely to exhibit continuing evidence of psychological stress.

It is apparent from the findings presented in this paper that combat exposure has an important impact on the domestic lives of Vietnam veterans, specifically in contributing to a higher likelihood of divorce. In other research (Yager et al. 1984; Laufer, Brett, and Gallops, in press), combat exposure was found to contribute to the experience of a number of problems in the year(s) before the interview, including hyperarousal stress symptoms and heavy alcohol consumption. If the long-term effect of combat upon the psychological well-being of veterans is mediated through their family patterns, then including "family" measures in the regression equation should transfer the effect of combat to the "family" measures.[3]

The measures of problems at the time of the interview, used to test the mediating influence of family relations, are (a) the number of hyperarousal stress symptoms reported as having occurred in the year before the interview (range 0 to 7), and (b) the number of months in the two years before the interview that the respondent drank heavily every day (range 0 to 24). We found that combat exposure has a significant direct effect on both of these problems in our earlier work. Figure 2 shows the model of effects when Ever Divorced is tested as an intervening variable in the relationship.[4]

As seen in this figure, men who have had marital difficulties resulting in divorce or separation tend to have more hyperarousal symptoms and to engage in heavy alcohol consumption. In both cases the effect is positive and significant. This finding confirms the argument in the literature that having a stable family

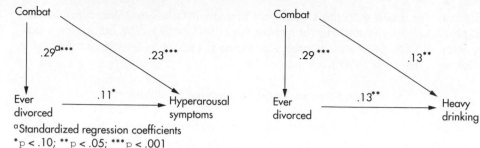

^aStandardized regression coefficients
*p < .10; **p < .05; ***p < .001

FIGURE 2. MODEL OF THE RELATIONSHIP BETWEEN COMBAT EXPOSURE, FAILURE OF FIRST MARRIAGE, AND CURRENT PROBLEMS

environment is an important social resource which helps individuals work through their problems.[5]

At the same time, combat exposure continues to have a significant direct effect on these problem indicators. Its indirect effect through divorce is significant as well, although its primary contribution to current problems is not mediated by its contribution to marital disruption.[6]

The general literature on the importance of family relations in dealing with stress and of their importance for the psychological well-being of the individual is confirmed in our sample. Those who had never married and those who had been divorced or separated report significantly higher levels of psychological and emotional numbing, angry feelings about life, perceived hostility from others, generalized guilt, feelings of demoralization, and the experience of being arrested than those who had one stable marriage. Despite the general differences between these groups, it appears that the effects of traumatic war experiences are not mediated through their effect on the presence or absence of familial support, as hypothesized, but that they maintain direct and enduring effects on the psychological well-being of veterans over and above the effects due to the family situation of the men. This is especially true of combat exposure, which has a direct effect on the likelihood of getting divorced as well as a direct long-term effect on the veteran's psychological state and level of alcohol consumption. In summary, the findings indicate that war trauma and family support have significant and independent effects on the psychological well-being of Vietnam veterans.

DISCUSSION

We began our inquiry into marital patterns of Vietnam veterans to determine if we could gain further insight into the effects of war on career development patterns during the early adult years. These findings enhance our understanding of how the Vietnam War has affected adult development within this generation. At the same time they leave unanswered many questions about the specific mechanisms that tie exposure to war trauma to marital difficulties.

From our analysis we see that Vietnam veterans are more likely to get married than their nonveteran counterparts. This difference in rates of marriage occurred primarily between the ages of 22 and 25, the period when these veterans were leaving the military and returning home. In our view these findings are preliminary evidence that veterans are prone to undertake more early adult life tasks simultaneously than their age peers. The fact that there is little age difference between groups at entry into first marriage further supports this interpretation.

There is some evidence that exposure to war stress significantly contributes to life event crises such as marital disruption. Both combat experience and exposure to abusive violence contribute to the likelihood of divorce, the latter only for those who served after 1967. Participation in abusive violence, by contrast, significantly lowered the likelihood of divorce after 1967. It is possible to speculate on how the psychological responses to these experiences affected the domestic lives of these men, but an examination of psychological difficulties during and after service found that the effect of combat on divorce was not primarily transmitted through these difficulties. We have found a significant relationship between war trauma and marital disruption; but lacking adequate information on the character of marital transitions, we are not able to specify adequately the mechanisms producing this relationship.

Instead of the family environment mediating the effects of war stress, the failure, or absence, of a marriage contributes independently to psychological and behavioral problems. Our test of the role of the family in mediating between traumatic experiences and long-term stress responses showed that the relationships between exposure to trauma and later difficulties was not primarily transmitted through the effect of war trauma on marital disruption. Two interpretations can be made of this finding. One line of reasoning leads to the inference that war trauma as such, regardless of the life experiences of the men once they returned, disrupts the social careers of veterans. From this point of view, war experiences are prime movers in the individual's life; and though subsequent experiences may add to or subtract from the individual's problems, they do not qualitatively change the character of the traumatic experience and its memory.

A second interpretation is that other aspects of veterans' social career—such as their educational or occupational achievement, income level, and employment history—are the primary mediating statuses and conditions regard to their current well-being. In a study of the prevalence of depression, Pearlin and Johnson (1977) found that social and economic strains, in combination with marital status, were major contributors to psychological difficulties. This finding suggests the importance of conditional constraints, in conjunction with the availability of social support, in distinguishing groups with a greater propensity to develop stress reactions. While we found no interaction between war trauma and marital states comparable to their finding that situational stress interacted with marital status, more immediate conditions such as unemployment and income level could work in this fashion.

The analysis here has shown the importance of the Vietnam War for the lives of men who served there. As our research and that of others proceed, we hope to develop a comprehensive, career picture of the impact of war on the life course of veterans. This paper has been concerned with the specification of the role of marriage patterns in this process.

NOTES

1. The sites were Brooklyn, NY; southern Westchester County, NY; Bridgeport, CT; Atlanta, GA; Los Angeles; Chicago; South Bend, IN; the two rural counties adjacent to South Bend; Columbus, GA; and the two rural counties adjacent to Columbus.

2. Our sample also included 83 Chicanos interviewed in the Los Angeles area. This special population is excluded from the present analysis.

3. An alternative formulation of this relationship is that problems attributable to war trauma began during and immediately after the service and lead to later marital instability. In examining a range of stress symptoms that began during or within the first 12 months after service, we found that the direct effect of Combat on Divorce was only slightly diminished by including problem indicators as controls in the regression. The model with which we are concerned here attempts to explain the long-term effects of war trauma on veterans; consequently we want to determine why psychological problems associated with war trauma exist 6 to 14 years after men left the service. We believe that experience and response patterns separated by this amount of time are linked by other experience and life event patterns. For testing this model, measures of the individual's marital career are based on events from the time of leaving the service to the time of the interview; the measures of current problems we use deal with the last 12 or 24 months before the interview.

4. It should be noted that Ever Divorced is a dichotomous variable. Its use as an endogenous variable within a causal model violates the assumption that dependent measures have, at least, an interval character. Despite this we chose this form of presentation for several reasons. First, the conceptual assumptions underlying OLS analysis are flexible, and its regression estimates are particularly robust. Second, a logistic regression performed on Ever Divorced produced a Combat effect with roughly the same standardized coefficient. Third, our concern in this instance is to compare the direct effects of Combat and Divorce on these outcomes. The magnitude of the indirect effect of Combat, through Divorce, is discussed—but only to note its relationship to the direct effect of combat, not its absolute size.

5. We also examined the possibility that, among those married, marital satisfaction and perceived spouse support played an intervening role between war trauma and subsequent psychological and behavioral problems. We found no evidence of such a relationship. Combat exposure was only weakly related to marital satisfaction and not related to perceived spouse support. In addition, neither measure of the quality of the marriage was tied extensively to subsequent problems. Perceived spouse support was only significantly related (negatively) to numbing symptomatology and to perceptions that others were hostile. Marital satisfaction was significantly related to no subsequent problems.

6. Using an interaction term, we also tested whether the slope of Combat differed between the "married only once" and the "first marriage ended in divorce or separation" groups. We found that Combat has a consistent effect in both groups.

REFERENCES

Eaton, W. W. 1978. "Life Events, Social Supports, and Psychiatric Symptoms: A Reanalysis of the New Haven Data." *Journal of Health and Social Behavior* 19:223–234.

Elder, G. 1978. "Historical Change in Life Patterns and Personality." Paper presented at the Eastern Sociological meetings, Philadelphia.

Fendrich, J. M. and L. J. Axelson. 1971. "Marital Status and Political Alienation Among Black Veterans." *American Journal of Sociology* 77:245–261.

Gore, S. 1978. "The Effects of Social Support in Moderating the Health Consequences of Unemployment." *Journal of Health and Social Behavior* 19:157–165.

Gove, W. R. 1972. "The Relationship Between Sex Rules, Marital Status and Mental Health." *Social Forces* 51:33–44.

———. 1973. "Sex, Marital Status, and Mortality." *American Journal of Sociology* 79:45–67.

Harris, L. 1980. *Myths and Realities: A Study of Attitudes Toward Vietnam Era Veterans.* Washington, DC: U.S. Government Printing Office.

Helzer, J., L. Robins, and E. Wish. 1979. "Depression in Viet Nam Veterans and Civilian Controls." *American Journal of Psychiatry* 136:526–529.

Hill, R. 1949. *Families Under Stress: Adjustment to the Crises of War Separation and Reunion.* New York: Harper & Brothers.

Hogan, D. 1981. *Transitions and Social Change: The Early Lives of American Men.* New York: Academic Press.

Kadushin, C., G. Boulanger, and J. Martin. 1981. *Legacies of Vietnam, Vol. IV: Long Term Stress Reactions.* Report submitted to the Veterans Administration. Washington, DC: U.S. Government Printing Office.

Laufer, R. S. 1985. "War, Trauma and Human Development: Vietnam." Cited by S. Sonnenberg, A. Blank, and J. Talbot in *The Trauma of War: Stress and Recovery in Vietnam Veterans,* Washington, DC: American Psychiatric Press.

Laufer, R. S., E. Brett, and M. S. Gallops. "Patterns of Symptomatology Associated with Post-Traumatic Stress Disorder Among Vietnam Veterans Exposed to War Trauma." *American Journal of Psychiatry.*

Laufer, R. S., M. S. Gallops, and E. Frey-Wouters. 1984. "War Stress and Post-War Trauma." *Journal of Health and Social Behavior* 25:65–85.

Laufer, R. S., T. Yager, E. Frey-Wouters, and J. Donnellan. 1981. *Legacies of Vietnam Vol. III: Post-War Trauma: Social and Psychological Problems of Vietnam Veterans and Their Peers.* Washington, DC: U.S. Government Printing Office.

Lieberman, E. J. 1971. "American Families and the Vietnam War." *Journal of Marriage and the Family* 33(November):709–721.

Lifton, R. J. 1973. *Home from the War: Vietnam Veterans. Neither Victims nor Executioners.* New York: Simon and Schuster.

Lin, N., W. M. Ensel, R. S. Simeone, and W. Kuo. 1979. "Social Support, Stressful Life Events, and Illness." *Journal of Health and Social Behavior* 20:108–119.

Martin, J. 1981. "Marital Status, Spouse Support and Mental Health." Chap. 7 in *Legacies of Vietnam, Vol. IV: Long Term Stress Reactions,* edited by C. Kadushin, G. Boulanger, and J. Martin. Washington, DC: U.S. Government Printing Office.

McCubbin, H. I., B. Dahl, G. R. Lester, D. Benson, and M. L. Robertson. 1976. "Coping Repertoires of Families Adapting to Prolonged War-Induced Separations." *Journal of Marriage and the Family* 38 (August):461–471.

McDonagh, E. C. 1946. "The Discharged Serviceman and His Family." *American Journal of Sociology* 51:451–454.

Myers, J. J., J. Lindethon, and M. Pepper. 1975. "Life Events, Social Integration and Psychiatric Symptomatology." *Journal of Health and Social Behavior* 16:421–429.

Nace, E. P., C. P. O'Brien, J. Mintz, N. Ream, and A. L. Meyers. 1978. "Adjustment Among Vietnam Veteran Drug Users Two-Years Post Service." In *Stress Disorders Among Vietnam Veterans*, edited by C. R. Figley. New York: Brunner/Mazel.

Pearlin, L. I. and J. S. Johnson. 1977. "Marital Status, Life-Strains and Depression." *American Sociological Review* 52(October):704–715.

Pratt, G. K. 1944. *Soldier to Civilian: Problems of Readjustment*. New York: Whittlesey House.

Rothbart, G. 1981. "General Methodology." Chap. 2 in *Legacies of Vietnam, Vol. II: Comparative Adjustment of Veterans and Their Peers*, edited by A. Egendorf, C. Kadushin, R. S. Laufer, G. Rothbart, and L. Sloan. Washington, DC: U.S. Government Printing Office.

Rothbart, G. S., M. Fine, and S. Sudman. 1982. "On Finding and Interviewing the Needles in the Haystack: The Use of Multiplicity Sampling." *Public Opinion Quarterly* 46:409–421.

Shatan, C. F. 1978. "Stress Disorders Among Vietnam Veterans: The Emotional Content of Combat Continues." in *Stress Disorders Among Vietnam Veterans*, edited by C. R. Figley. New York: Brunner/Mazel.

Stretch, R. H. 1984. "Post-Traumatic Stress Disorder Among U.S. Army Reserve Vietnam and Vietnam-Era Veterans." Washington, DC: Dept. of Military Psychiatry, Walter Reed Army Medical Center.

Waller, W. 1940. *War and the Family*. New York: The Dryden Press.

————. 1944. *The Veteran Comes Back*. New York: The Dryden Press.

Wilson, J. P. 1978. "Identity, Ideology and Crisis: the Vietnam Veteran in Transition, Part II." Unpublished monograph, Cleveland State University.

Yager, T., R. Laufer, and M. S. Gallops. 1984. "The Effects of War Experience Among Vietnam Veterans." *Archives of General Psychiatry* 41:327–333.

41

If Your Child Had AIDS . . . : Responses of Parents with Homosexual Children*

Peggy H. Cleveland, Lynda Henley Walters, Patsy Skeen, and

Bryan E. Robinson

It has been suggested that the death of an adult child may be the most distressing of all causes of grief (Shanfield, Benjamin, and Swain 1984). With the growing number of persons with AIDS (PWAs), many parents are experiencing this tragedy.

In the first account of AIDS, this disease was referred to as "Gay Related Immuno-Deficiency." Because gay men were initially considered to be the primary risk group for contracting AIDS, attitudes about homosexuality have greatly influenced attitudes toward AIDS as a disease process and toward people with AIDS (Morin, Charles, and Malyon 1984). Furstenberg and Olsen (1984, p. 46) have suggested that attitudes towards AIDS are unrealistic, referring to them as "myth, superstition, and stigma with their attendant attitudes and feelings." It is reasonable to believe that families of PWAs as well as those who have the disease have been affected by such generally held, uninformed attitudes.

Most of the research on AIDS has understandably focused on the victims of the disease (Dilley, Ochitill, Perl, and Volberding 1985; Faulstich 1987; Frierson and Lippmann 1987; Morin, Charles, and Malyon 1984; Nichols 1985; Wilson 1987). With the exception of a few studies (e.g., Robinson, Skeen, and Walters 1987; Robinson, Walters, Skeen, in press), little data exist on the impact of AIDS on the victims' families. As a result, little is known about the families of PWAs. Even less is known about the feelings of families with members who are in a high risk category for AIDS (e.g., homosexual men). This article addresses this issue. Clinicians' reports indicate that the responses of parents and other family members, and even health care professionals, parallel society's responses and range from providing support to antagonism and withdrawal (Furstenberg and Olsen 1984; Sageman 1983).

The focus of this report is the responses of parents of homosexual children to the question, "What would (or did) you do if (when) you discovered your child had AIDS?" This was an open-ended question. Examples of responses are reported; other data from the study are reported as appropriate to gain perspective on the feelings and experiences of these parents.

*Cleveland, Peggy H., Lynda Henley Walters, Patsy Skeen, and Bryan E. Robinson. 1988. "If Your Child Had AIDS...: Responses of Parents with Homosexual Children." *Family Relations* 37(2): 150–153. Copyrighted 1988 by the National Council on Family Relations, 1910 West County Road B, Suite 147, St. Paul, Minnesota 55113. Reprinted by permission.

METHOD

Procedure

Subjects were primarily recruited through the Federation of Parents and Friends of Lesbians and Gays (P-FLAG) and a few from the National Federation of Parents and Friends of Gays (P-FOG). The purpose of these organizations is to help parents and their gay children understand one another and offer mutual support wherever it is needed. In addition, this study used a snowball procedure in which homosexual young adults were asked to supply the names and addresses of their parents (if their parents knew of their homosexuality) and participants were asked to supply names and addresses of other parents they knew who have homosexual child(ren).

Questionnaires, consent forms, and postage-paid envelopes were mailed to individuals and group leaders who distributed them. Participants were assured of anonymity. Questionnaires and consent forms were returned in separate envelopes. Parents were asked not to discuss their responses with each other until all materials had been completed and returned.

It is difficult to calculate a precise return rate since most questionnaires were distributed by second parties, and it could not be determined how many questionnaires were actually distributed. However, the number of questionnaires completed and returned compared to the number of questionnaires mailed to group leaders suggest a return rate of at least 34%.

Sample

Subjects were 763 parents (28% father and 72% mothers) of gay and lesbian children. The ages of parents ranged from 37 to 82 years. Seventy percent of the parents were responding about a male child, 30% were responding about a female child. From parents of female children, responses to the question about AIDS are typified by this one: "I would be devastated—but since lesbian women have the least chance of anyone contracting AIDS, I don't think or worry too much about it." In this article the comments represent only the views of parents of gay men. Thirteen indicated that their son had AIDS; three of the 13 had died.

The majority were Caucasian with Blacks and Hispanics underrepresented. Parents were well-educated with most having more than a high school education. Only 24% had an annual family income of less than $20,000; most reported middle to upper level incomes. More were from the West (41%) than any other region; however, all regions of the United States were represented and the distribution by size of community was fairly even. Most reported that they participate in organized religion with about one-third considering themselves very religious; however, 56% reported that they only rarely or occasionally attend a religious service.

RESULTS

Responses to this question varied from affirmations of love and support to expressions of inability to deal with the issue. The overwhelming majority of these parents said that they would support their children if they contracted AIDS. Because most of these parents belonged to a support group that encouraged love and support, it is especially noteworthy to find that some parents were having some difficulty with their children's homosexuality. However, most who wrote comments regarding what they would do if their children contracted AIDS were, as expected, positive. Statements such as the following express the resolve to "be there" for their children.

> "Help him as much as we could. Bring him home and care for him."
> "Try to help him as best I can. One of my sons lost his mate because of AIDS. The young man was so loving and caring. His folks turned him down. Never did make up with him."

For some, the emotional support extended to the partners as well as to their children. The supportiveness of these parents, evident in the following comments, is reflective of the views of approximately 61% of those who reported that their child was either currently or had been in a committed, spouse-like relationship. Although a minority, some parents said they did not have a good relationship with the partner (12%). Approximately 22% reported that they did not enjoy visiting with the partner, and, of those, 10% said it was because of the homosexuality. Even though these small percentages are important in this particular sample, it is noteworthy that without having been prompted, some parents referred to their desire to be supportive to the partner in the event of AIDS. For example,

> "When and if appropriate, I would get him to the best AIDS clinic immediately, and see that his partner was present, involved, and not blamed."
> "All and everything humanly possible to help, care, and support him and his partner."

Getting the best medical care was often stated as the first response of the parents. The hope of medical success and "cure" was often stated.

> "I would try to get him the best possible medical help and pray as hard as I could."
> "I would advise him to hope (even believe) he might be cured and to go for what appeared to be the most competent treatment available to him."

Many of these parents recognized the enormous impact of an AIDS diagnosis on the patient and family. If they anticipate difficulty with the medical profession and such professionals as morticians (as did 40% of these parents), apparently their concerns are warranted (Coastes, Temoshok, and Mandel 1984; Furstenberg and Olsen 1984). Batchelor (1984a, 1984b) has even suggested that the fears of health care professionals may result in their unrecognized anger toward and withdrawal from families of AIDS patients. Other recent findings have indicated that AIDS-phobia is most prevalent among hospital workers who are older, have low contact with AIDS patients, and have homophobic attitudes (Pleck, O'Donnell, O'Donnell, and Snarey, in press). Potential difficulties not withstanding, these parents recognized that they and other family members would need both medical and psychological assistance.

> "Get help, medical and psychological, for him and for me."
> "Try to find a support group for myself and learn how to cope, how to help. Try to find out about treatment/care options and be sure he was getting reasonable care."
> "Contact Cascade AIDS Project—for up-to-date information."
> "I would probably need counseling so I could, in turn, provide the strongest kind of support for my son."

The parent and child with AIDS are not the only affected family members. Many of the children with AIDS have siblings and grandparents who are likely to experience trauma and need support. Many siblings and grandparents will turn to their parents/children for support and understanding just as they are likely to do in any other crisis. Parents are also likely to feel responsible for the problem and want to respond by helping these family members. Therefore, parents of PWAs must carry a heavy burden as they try to deal with their own needs, with the needs of the AIDS child, and with the needs of other family members. Many parents will require a great deal of support from friends and family as well as counseling and other support-oriented organizations.

A few of the replies indicate some ambivalence in the relationship with their children. This may be an outgrowth of the struggle some families have experienced in dealing with the homosexuality of their children. This struggle may involve some estrangement as parents confront feelings associated with learning that their child is homosexual. Evidence of an ambivalence included such statements as the following:

> "Ask if he wants me to do anything for him . . . Probably keep in a little closer touch—but maybe not. Certainly wouldn't want him to feel pressure to report to me."
> "Be grief stricken. Be afraid—wouldn't accept my love and loyalty and care. Pray for a cure. Fight to carry on."

The stigma and fears associated with AIDS affected decisions about how some parents would react. According to responses to questionnaire items about AIDS, a few parents even indicated that they would not go near their child (3%) and 5% said they would be more cautious of contact with their child. Many more (47%) reported that they would not want anyone outside the family to know about the AIDS diagnosis, and 16% do not want other family members to know. Examples of how parents express these concerns follow.

> "I would support him. I wouldn't tell all people that he had AIDS because I feel it's nobody's business."
> "I don't really know. Probably be sick at heart and pray for a treatment or cure. Would not want everyone to know about it, just family."
> "I would go live with him until cure was found or until his death. I would not have physical contact with my other son for fear I would give it to him."
> "I'd be afraid others would find out and shun me."

"I would not be comfortable sharing the diagnosis with family and friends. Would hopefully be supportive to my child."

However, in spite of the association of AIDS with an alternate lifestyle (Fettner and Check 1985; Pleck et al., in press, Robinson, Walters, and Skeen, in press), many of these parents did not distinguish between AIDS and any other terminal illness. For example,

"The same as I would do if I found out any child had a terminal illness. Be there!"
"I'd care for him the same as for any other serious ailment. I'd help wherever I could physically or monetarily."

Of these parents, thirteen reported that their children have AIDS (all sons)— three had died at the time of data collection. The prevailing emotion is sadness as illustrated in the following quotes:

"I felt my heart was broken and I fell apart. I asked so much for my child but from the onset I took care of him 24 hours a day for 16 months at home and 2 weeks in the hospital."
"Same as always! We've been through six hospitalizations and all is stable at present. He is living at home now."
"A great part of my life is gone and I still *hurt*. I lost a wonderful son and friend."

DISCUSSION

Parental responses to the question addressed in this report indicate the persistence of a bond between parent and child and a grief process about which we know little. Such a bond is considered desirable for family life, but is should be noted that these families may be in the minority. Other reports indicate that over 70% of AIDS patients live alone and over 60% have little or no contact with families of origin (Christ and Wiener 1985; DeVita 1985).

The fact that the majority of those in this sample belong to support groups is very informative. By their membership in such groups, these parents are recognizing their need for contact with others who have similar experiences. As a result of this association, they are not isolated and they are dealing with the issue of their children's homosexuality; moreover, those whose sons have AIDS have a built-in support system that other parents do not.

Even with the support that most have through P-FLAG and P-FOG, the thought of their children contracting AIDS is devastating. Those parents who do not have such support and are unaware of the sexual orientation and lifestyles of their children must certainly experience overwhelming emotion and ambivalence upon hearing that their children have AIDS. Carl (1986) has referred to the "double death" syndrome: Parents learn that a child is homosexual and must deal with the loss of a "normal" child at the same time they must deal with the illness and death of their child as a result of AIDS. This may be particularly true because many parents still consider homosexuality as an indication that something is wrong, in spite of the fact that the American Psychiatric and American

Psychological Associations have shifted homosexuality from their "disorders" list to a "preference" list. Specifically, in this study, some parents always or sometimes thought homosexuality is sick (11%), sinful (14%), or wrong (22%). Their ambivalence is reflected in the fact that 94% always or sometimes thought that homosexuality is normal for some people.

Many of the parents who responded to this question indicate a desire to be supportive but express some ambivalence about how to do so. Adult children often do not live with their parents but are in the new families they have created or in close, family-like communities they have established for themselves. Sometimes these two family systems collide (Carl 1986; Furstenberg and Olson 1984), and there are no established, socially-accepted behavior patterns. Some of the questions raised include: How available can parents be? How much are they needed? How much should they do? What should they do to be most helpful?

The effects of this disease on families, lovers, and friends of the PWA generally are not known; yet there are indications from other illnesses such as cancer that the trauma that affects the patients also affects significant others (Mailick 1979; Northouse 1984; Singer 1983). These parents are experiencing trauma as they react to the illness of their children and as they prepare for their deaths. Parents need support for their own experiences so they can in turn be supportive of their children with AIDS.

Many of these parents recognize a need for resources. They indicate that they would seek out AIDS organizations, information concerning the AIDS process, and adequate medical care. They mention needing names and locations of organizations and agencies providing services.

Some parents need to be helped to come to some resolution of the stigma associated with AIDS and, by association, with the stigma on themselves. Some parents speak of being ashamed and of wishing to keep the diagnosis secret. These parents will be more physically and psychologically isolated than others and may go through an even more difficult bereavement process because of their isolation.

Implications for the Helping Professions

Different types of intervention are needed in order to incorporate all of the needed services for the parents of patients with AIDS. Specialized knowledge is needed by those who treat AIDS patients and their families (Cleveland 1987). Some parents and other family members can benefit from individual counseling sessions when their feelings are very intense and anxiety or depression is the prevailing affect. Conjoint family sessions can be effective in the resolution of "old business" and in helping families to solve problems and support each other as they go through a difficult experience.

Support groups have been cited as a necessary part of the effective treatment of PWAs (DeVita 1985; Lopez and Getzel 1984; Morin 1984). This modality could also be effective for parents; however some parents may choose to cope alone. Support groups can address the parents' strong feelings of pain, anger, grief, and fear, as well as ways in which parents and children can find as much comfort and strength as possible during their remaining days together. During this period, some parents and children have the potential to achieve the most loving relationship they have ever had. Families need help to mobilize their strengths and resources to deal with the situation, to develop new resources, to find and use community services, and to "work on old business" (Furstenberg and Olsen 1984). Sources of accurate information and education are especially important and need to be readily available to parents, other family members, members of the helping professions, and the general public.

Organizations that encourage families of AIDS patients to help each other, especially families who are just learning about the AIDS diagnosis, are useful. As families help others, they in turn draw help and support. The world surrounding AIDS is chiefly a negative one, yet there is a positive aspect that results when a caring, loving relationship marks the termination of the life of a member of the family. After the life of a loved one is over, there is comfort in remembering that everything possible was done to make the life of a child better by the attention, support, and understanding of a loving parent.

REFERENCES

Batchelor, W. F. 1984a. "AIDS." *American Psychologist* 39: 1277–1278.

———. 1984b. "AIDS: A Public Health and Psychological Emergency." *American Psychologist* 39: 1279–1284.

Carl, D. 1986. "Acquired Immune Deficiency Syndrome: A Preliminary Examination of the Effects on Gay Couples and Coupling." *Journal of Marital and Family Therapy* 12: 241–247.

Christ, G. H. and L. S. Wiener. 1985. "Psychological Issues in AIDS." Pp. 275–297 in *AIDS: Etiology, Diagnosis, Treatment, and Prevention*, edited by V. T. DeVita. Philadelphia: Lippincott.

Cleveland, P. H. 1987. Description of the Experiences of AIDS Patients with a Comparison to Terminal Cancer Patients." Unpublished doctoral dissertation, University of Georgia.

Coates, T. J., L. Temoshok, and J. Mandel. 1984. Psychosocial Research Is Essential To Understanding and Treating AIDS." *American Psychologist* 39: 1309–1313.

DeVita, V. T. 1985. *AIDS: Etiology, Diagnosis, Treatment, and Prevention*. Philadelphia: Lippincott.

Dilley, J. W., H. N. Ochitill, M. Perl, and P. A. Volberding. 1985. Findings in Psychiatric Consultations with Patients with Acquired Immune Deficiency Syndrome." *American Journal of Psychiatry* 142: 82–86.

Faulstich, M. E. 1987. "Psychiatric Aspects of AIDS." *American Journal of Psychiatry* 144: 551–556.

Fettner, A. G. and W. A. Check. 1985. The Truth About AIDS: Evolution of an Epidemic. New York: Holt, Rinehart & Winston.

Frierson, R. L. and S. B. Lippmann. 1987. "Psychologic Implications of AIDS." *American Family Physician* 35(3): 109–116.

Furstenberg, A. C. and M. M. Olsen. 1984. "Social Work and AIDS." *Social Work in Health Care* 9(4): 45–62.

Lopez, D. J. and G. S. Getzel. 1984. "Helping Gay AIDS Patients in Crisis." *Social Casework* 65: 387–394.

Mailick, M. 1979. "The Impact of Severe Illness on the Individual and the Family: An Overview." *Social Work in Health Care* 5: 117–127.

Morin, S. F. 1984. AIDS is One City." *American Psychologist* 39: 1294–1297.

Morin, S. F., K. Charles, and A. Malyon. 1984. "The Psychological Impact of AIDS on Gay Men." *American Psychologist* 39: 1288–1293.

Nichols, S. E. 1985. "Psychosocial Reactions of Persons with the Acquired Immunodeficiency Syndrome." *Annals of Internal Medicine* 103: 765–767.

Northouse, L. 1984. "The Impact of Cancer on the Family: An Overview." *International Journal of Psychiatry in Medicine* 14: 215–239.

Pleck, J. H., L. O'Donnell, C. O'Donnell, and J. Snarey. (in press). "AIDS-phobia, Contact with AIDS, and AIDS-Related Job Stress in Hospital Workers." *Journal of Homosexuality.*

Robinson, B. E., P. Skeen, and L. Walters. 1987. "The AIDS Epidemic Hits Home." *Psychology Today* 21: 48–52.

Robinson, B., L. Walters, and P. Skeen. (in press). "Attitudes of Parents Toward Their Homosexual Children and AIDS: A National Study. *Journal of Homosexuality.*

Sagemon, S. 1983. "AIDS: Coping with the Unknown." *Emergency Medicine* (October 30): 165–168, 173–177, 181.

Shanfield, S. B., A. H. Benjamin, and B. J. Swain. 1984. "Parents' Reactions to the Death of an Adult Child from Cancer." *American Journal of Psychiatry* 141: 1092–1094.

Singer, B. A. 1983. "Psychosocial Trauma, Defense Strategies and Treatment Considerations in Cancer Patients and Their Families." *The American Journal of Family Therapy* 11(3): 15–21.

Wilson, T. C. 1987. "Counseling Roles and AIDS." *CAPS Capsule* 2: 2–3.

Divorce, Single Parenthood, and Remarriage

42

Uncoupling:
The Social Construction of Divorce*

Diane Vaughan

Berger and Kellner (1964) describe marriage as a definitional process: two autonomous individuals come together with separate and distinct biographies and begin to construct for themselves a subworld in which they will live as a couple. A redefinition of self occurs as the autonomous identity of the two individuals involved is reconstructed as a mutual identity. This redefinition is externally anticipated and socially legitimated before it actually occurs in the individual's biography.

Previously, significant conversation for each partner came from nonoverlapping circles, and self-realization came from other sources. Together, they begin to construct a private sphere where all significant conversation centers in their relationship with the other. The coupled identity becomes the main source of their self-realization. Their definitions of reality become correlated, for each partner's actions must be projected in conjunction with the other. As their worlds come to be defined around a relationship with a significant other who becomes *the* significant other, all other significant relationships have to be reperceived, regrouped. The result is the construction of a joint biography and a mutually coordinated common memory.

Were this construction of a coupled identity left only to the two participants, the coupling would be precarious indeed. However, the new reality is reinforced through objectivation, that is, "a process by which subjectively experienced meanings become objective to the individual, and, in interaction with others, become common property, and thereby massively objective" (Berger and Kellner

*Vaughan, Diane. 1988."Uncoupling: The Social Construction of Divorce." Pp. 384–403 in *Social Interactions: Readings in Sociology*, 3rd ed., edited by Candace Clark and Howard Robbey. New York: St. Martin's Press. Copyright © 1988 by St. Martin's Press, Inc. Reprinted by permission of St. Martin's Press, Incorporated.

1964, p. 6). Hence, through the use of language in conversation with significant others, the reality of the coupling is constantly validated.

Of perhaps greater significance is that this definition of coupledness becomes taken for granted and is validated again and again, not by explicit articulation, but by conversing around the agreed [upon] definition of reality that has been created. In this way a consistent reality is maintained, ordering the individual's world in such a way that it validates his identity. Marriage, according to Berger and Kellner, is a constructed reality which is "nomosbuilding" (1964, p. 1). That is, it is a social arrangement that contributes order to individual lives, and therefore should be considered as a significant validating relationship for adults in our society.

Social relationships, however, are seldom static. Not only do we move in and out of relationships, but the nature of a particular relationship, though enduring, varies over time. Given that the definitions we create become socially validated and hence constraining, *how do individuals move from a mutual identity, as in marriage, to assume separate, autonomous identities again?* What is the process by which new definitions are created and become validated?

The Berger and Kellner analysis describes a number of interrelated yet distinguishable stages that are involved in the social construction of a mutual identity; for example, the regrouping of all other significant relationships. In much the same way, the *demise* of a relationship should involve distinguishable social processes. Since redefinition of self is basic to both movement into and out of relationships, the social construction of a singular identity also should follow the patterns suggested by Berger and Kellner. This paper is a qualitative examination of this process. Hence, the description that follows bears an implicit test of Berger and Kellner's ideas.

The dimensions of sorrow, anger, personal disorganization, fear, loneliness, and ambiguity that intermingle every separation are well known.[1] Their familiarity does not diminish their importance. Though in real life these cannot be ignored, the researcher has the luxury of selectivity. Here, it is not the pain and disorganization that are to be explored, but the existence of an underlying orderliness.

Though the focus is on divorce, the process examined appears to apply to *any* heterosexual relationship in which the participants have come to define themselves and be defined by others as a couple. The work is exploratory and, as such, not concerned with generalizability. However, the process may apply to homosexual couples as well. Therefore, the term "uncoupling" will be used because it is a more general concept than divorce. Uncoupling applies to the redefinition of self that occurs as mutual identity unravels into singularity, regardless of marital status or sex of the participants.

The formal basis from which this paper developed was in-depth, exploratory interviews. The interviews, ranging from two to six hours, were taped and later analyzed. All of the interviewees were at different stages in the uncoupling process. Most were divorced, though some were still in stages of consideration of divorce. Two of the interviews were based on long-term relationships that never resulted in marriage. All of the relationships were heterosexual. The quality of these interviews has added much depth to the understanding of the separation process. The interviewees were of high intellectual and social level, and their sensitivity and insight have led to much valuable material, otherwise unavailable.

A more informal contribution to the paper comes from personal experiences and the experiences of close friends. Further corroboration has come from autobiographical accounts, newspapers, periodicals, and conversations, which have resulted in a large number of cases illustrating certain points. Additional support has come from individuals who have read or heard the paper with the intent of proving or disproving its contentions by reference to their own cases.

Since the declared purpose here is to abstract the essential features of the process of uncoupling, some simplification is necessary. The separation of a relationship can take several forms. To trace all of them is beyond the scope of this study. Therefore, to narrow the focus, we must first consider the possible variations.

Perhaps the coupled identity was not a major mechanism for self-validation from the outset of the union. Or the relationship may have at one time filled that function, but, as time passed, this coupled identity was insufficient to meet individual needs. Occasionally this fact has implications for both partners simultaneously, and the uncoupling process is initiated by both. More frequently, however, one partner still finds the marriage a major source of stability and identity, while the other finds it inadequate. In this form, one participant takes the role of initiator of the uncoupling process. However, this role may not consistently be held by one partner, but instead may alternate between them, due to the difficulty of uncoupling in the face of external constraints, social pressure not to be the one responsible for the demise of the marriage, and the variability in the self-validating function of the union over time. For the purpose of this study, the form of uncoupling under consideration is that which results when one partner, no longer finding the coupled identity self-validating, takes the role of initiator in the uncoupling process. The other partner, the significant other, still finds the marriage a major source of stability and identity.

UNCOUPLING: THE INITIATION OF THE PROCESS

I was never psychologically married. I always felt strained by attempts that coupled me into a marital unit. I was just never comfortable as "Mrs." I never got used to my last name. I never wanted it. The day after my marriage was probably the most depressed day of my life, because I had lost my singularity. The difference between marriage and a deep relationship, living together, is that you have this ritual, and you achieve a very definite status, and it was *that* that produced my reactions—because I became in the eyes of the world a man's wife. And I was never comfortable and happy with it. It didn't make any difference who the man was.

An early phase in the uncoupling process occurs as one or the other of the partners begins to question the coupled identity. At first internal, the challenging of the created world remains for a time as a doubt within one of the partners in the coupling. Though there is a definition of coupledness, subjectively the coupledness may be experienced differently by each partner. Frequently, these subjective meanings remain internal and unarticulated. Thus, similarly, the initial recognition of the coupling as problematic may be internal and unarticulated, held as a secret. The subworld that has been constructed, for some reason, doesn't "fit."

A process of definition negotiation is begun, initiated by the one who finds the mutual identity an inadequate definition of self. Attempts to negotiate the definition of the coupledness are likely to result in the subjective meaning becoming articulated for the first time, thus moving the redefinition process toward objectivation. The secret, held by the initiator, is shared with the significant other. When this occurs, it allows both participants to engage in the definitional process.

Though the issue is made "public" in that private sphere shared by the two, the initiator frequently finds that a lack of shared definitions of the coupled identity stalemates the negotiations. While the initiator defines the marriage as a problem, the other does not. The renegotiation of the coupled identity cannot proceed unless both agree that the subworld they have constructed needs to be redefined. Perhaps for the significant other, the marriage as it is still provides important self-validation. If so, the initiator must bring the other to the point of sharing a common definition of the marriage as "troubled."

ACCOMPANYING RECONSTRUCTIONS

Though this shared definition is being sought, the fact remains that, for the initiator, the coupled identity fails to provide self-validation. In order to meet this need, the initiator engages in other attempts at redefining the nature of the relationship. Called "accompanying reconstructions," these *may* or *may not* be shared with the significant other. They may begin long before the "secret" of the troubled marriage is shared with the other, in an effort to make an uncomfortable situation more comfortable without disrupting the relationship. Or they may occur subsequent to sharing the secret with the significant other, as a reaction to the failure to redefine the coupledness satisfactorily. Time order for their occurrence is not easily imposed—thus, "accompanying reconstructions."

The initiator's accompanying reconstructions may be directed toward the redefinition of (1) the coupledness itself, (2) the identity of the significant other, or (3) the identity of the initiator. A change in definition of either of the three implies a change in at least one of the others. Though they are presented here separately, they are interactive rather than mutually exclusive and are not easily separable in real life.

The first form of accompanying reconstruction to be considered is the initiator's redefinition of the coupledness itself. One way of redefining the coupledness is by an unarticulated conversion of the agreed-upon norms of the relationship.

> I had reconceptualized what marriage was. I decided sexual fidelity was not essential for marriage. I never told her that. And I didn't even have anyone I was interested in having that intimate a relationship with—I just did a philosophical thing. I just decided it was O.K. for me to have whatever of what quality of other relationship I needed to have. Something like that—of that caliber—was something I could never talk to her about. So I did it all by myself. I read things and decided it. I was at peace with me. I knew that we could stay married, whatever that meant. O.K., I can stay legally tied to you, and I can probably live in this house with you, and I can keep working the way I have been. I decided I can have my life and

still be in this situation with you, but you need some resources, because I realize now I'm not going to be all for you. I don't want to be all for you, and I did tell her that. But I couldn't tell her this total head trip I'd been through because she wouldn't understand.

Or, the coupledness may be redefined by acceptance of the relationship with certain limitations. Boundaries can be imposed on the impact that the relationship will have on the total life space of the initiator.

I finally came to the point where I realized I was never going to have the kind of marriage I had hoped for, the kind of relationship I had hoped for. I didn't want to end it, because of the children, but I wasn't going to let it hurt me any more. I wasn't going to depend on him any more. The children and I were going to be the main unit, and, if he occasionally wanted to participate, fine—and if not, we would go ahead without him. I was no longer willing to let being with him be the determining factor as to whether I was happy or not. I ceased planning our lives around his presence or absence and began looking out for myself.

A second form of accompanying reconstruction occurs when the initiator attempts to redefine the significant other in a way that is more compatible with his own self-validation needs. The initiator may direct efforts toward specific behaviors, such as drinking habits, temper, sexual incompatibilities, or finance management. Or, the redefinition attempt may be of a broader scope.

I was aware of his dependence on the marriage to provide all his happiness, and it wasn't providing it. I wanted him to go to graduate school, but he postponed it, against my wishes. I wanted him to pursue his own life. I didn't want him to sacrifice for me. I wanted him to become more exciting to me in the process. I was aware that I was trying to persuade him to be a different person.

Redefinition of the significant other may either be directed toward maintaining the coupledness, as above, or moving away from it, as is the case following.

The way I defined being a good wife and the way John defined being a good wife were two different quantities. He wanted the house to look like a hotel and I didn't see it that way. He couldn't see why I couldn't meet his needs... When he first asked for a divorce and I refused, he suggested I go back to school. I remembered a man who worked with John who had sent his wife back to school so she could support herself, so he could divorce her. I asked John if he was trying to get rid of me. He didn't answer that. He insisted I go, and I finally went.

A third form of accompanying reconstruction may be directed toward the redefinition of the initiator. Intermingled with attempts at redefinition of the significant other and redefinition of the coupledness itself is the seeking of self-validation outside the marriage by the initiator. A whole set of other behaviors may evolve that have the ultimate effect of moving the relationship away from the coupledness toward a separation of the joint biography.

SELF-VALIDATION OUTSIDE THE MARRIAGE

What was at first internally experienced and recognized as self-minimizing takes a more concrete form and becomes externally expressed in a search for self-maximization. Through investment of self in career, in a cause requiring commitment, in a relationship with a new significant other, in family, in education, or in activities and hobbies, the initiator develops new sources of self-realization. These alternative sources of self-realization confirm not the coupled identity but the singularity of the initiator.

Furthermore, in the move toward a distinct biography, the initiator finds ideological support that reinforces the uncoupling process. Berger and Kellner (1964, p. 3) note the existence of a supporting ideology which lends credence to marriage as a significant validating relationship in our society. That is, the nuclear family is seen as the site of love, sexual fulfillment, and self-realization. In the move toward uncoupling, the initiator finds confirmation for a belief in *self* as a first priority.

> I now see my break with religion as a part of my developing individuality. At the time I was close friends with priests and nuns, most of whom have since left the church. I felt a bitterness toward the church for its definition of marriage. I felt constrained toward a type of marriage that was not best for me.

Whether this ideology first begins within the individual, who then actively *seeks* sources of self-realization that are ideologically congruent, or whether the initiator's own needs come to be met by a serendipitous "elective affinity" of ideas (Weber, 1930), is difficult to say. The interconnections are subtle. The supporting ideology may come from the family of orientation, the women's movement, the peer group, or a new significant other. It may grow directly, as through interaction, or indirectly, as through literature. No matter what the source, the point is that, in turning away from the marriage for self-validation, a separate distinct biography is constructed in interaction with others, and this beginning autonomy is strengthened by a supporting belief system.

The initiator moves toward construction of a separate subworld wherein significant conversation comes from circles which no longer overlap with those of the significant other. And, the significant other is excluded from that separate subworld.

> I shared important things with the children that I didn't share with him. It's almost as if I purposefully punished him by not telling him. Some good thing would happen and I'd come home and tell them and wouldn't tell him.

The initiator's autonomy is further reinforced as the secret of the troubled marriage is shared with others in the separate subworld the initiator is constructing. It may be directly expressed as a confidence exchanged with a close friend, family member, or children, or it may be that the sharing is indirect. Rather than being expressed in significant conversation, the definition of the marriage as troubled is created for others by a variety of mechanisms that relay the message that the initiator is not happily married. The definition of the marriage as problematic becomes further objectivated as the secret, once held only by the initiator, then shared with the significant other, moves to a sphere beyond the couple themselves.

Other moves away occur that deeply threaten the coupled identity for the significant other and at the same time validate the autonomy of the initiator.

> I remember going to a party by myself and feeling comfortable. She never forgot that. I never realized the gravity of that to her.
>
> Graduate school became a symbolic issue. I was going to be a separate entity. That's probably the one thing I wanted to do that got the biggest negative emotional response from him.
>
> All that time I was developing more of a sense of being away from her. I didn't depend on her for any emotional feedback, companionship. I went to plays and movies with friends.

The friendship group, rather than focusing on the coupledness, relies on splintered sources that support separate identities. Though this situation can exist in relationships in which the coupled identity is validating for both participants, the distinction is that, in the process of uncoupling, there may not be shared conversation to link the separate subworld of the initiator with that of the significant other.

These movements away by the initiator heighten a sense of exclusion for the significant other. Deep commitment to other than the coupled identity—to a career, to a cause, to education, to a hobby, to another person—reflects a lessened commitment to the marriage. The initiator's search for self-validation outside the marriage even may be demonstrated symbolically to the significant other by the removal of the wedding ring or by the desire, if the initiator is a woman, to revert to her maiden name. If the initiator's lessened commitment to the coupled identity is reflected in a lessened desire for sexual intimacy, the challenge to the identity of the significant other and the coupledness becomes undeniable. As the significant other recognizes the growing autonomy of the initiator, he, too, comes to accept the definition of the marriage as "troubled."

The roles assumed by each participant have implications for the impact of the uncoupling on each. Whereas the initiator has found other sources of self-realization outside the marriage, usually the significant other has not. The marriage still performs the major self-validating function. The significant other is committed to an ideology that supports the coupled identity. The secret of the "troubled" marriage has not been shared with others as it has by the initiator, meaning for the significant other the relationship in its changed construction remains unobjectivated. The challenge to the identity of the significant other and to the coupledness posed by the initiator may result in increased commitment to the coupled identity for the significant other. With the joint biography already separated in these ways, the couple enters into a period of "trying."

TRYING

Trying is a stage of intense definition negotiation by the partners. Now both share a definition of the marriage as troubled. However, each partner may seek to construct a new reality that is in opposition to that of the other. The significant other tries to negotiate a shared definition of the marriage as savable, whereas the initiator negotiates toward a shared definition that marks the marriage as unsavable. [2]

For the initiator, the uncoupling process is well underway. At some point the partner who originally perceived the coupled identity to be problematic and sought self-validation outside the coupled identity has experienced "psychological divorce." Sociologically, this can be defined as the point at which the individual's newly constructed separate subworld becomes the major nomos-building mechanism in his life space, replacing the nomos-building function of the coupled identity.

The initiator tries subtly to prepare the significant other to live alone. By encouraging the other to make new friends, find a job, get involved in outside activities, or seek additional education, the initiator hopes to decrease the other's commitment to and dependence upon the coupled identity for self-validation and move the other toward autonomy. This stage of preparation is not simply one of cold expediency for the benefit of the initiator, but is based on concern for the significant other and serves to mitigate the pain of the uncoupling process for both the initiator and the other.

For both, there is a hesitancy to sever the ties. In many cases, neither party is fully certain about the termination of the marriage. Mutual uncertainty may be more characteristic of the process. The relationship may weave back and forth between cycles of active trying and passive acceptance of the status quo due to the failure of each to pull the other to a common definition and the inability of either to make the break.

> I didn't want to hurt him. I didn't want to be responsible for the demise of a marriage I no longer wanted. I could have forced him into being the one to achieve the breach, for I realized it was never going to happen by itself.
> I didn't want to be the villain—the one to push her out into the big, bad world. I wanted to make sure she was at the same point I was.
> I kept hoping some alternative would occur so that he would be willing to break. I kept wishing it would happen.

Frequently, in the trying stage, the partners turn to outside help for formal negotiation of the coupled identity. Counseling, though entered into with apparent common purpose, becomes another arena in which the partners attempt to negotiate a shared definition from their separately held definitions of the marriage as savable or unsavable. For the initiator, the counseling may serve as a step in the preparation of the significant other to live alone. Not only does it serve to bring the other to the definition of the marriage as unsavable, but also the counseling provides a resource for the significant other, in the person of the counselor. Often it happens that the other has turned to no one for comfort about the problem marriage. The initiator, sensitive to this need and unable to fill it himself, hopes the counselor will fill this role. The counseling has yet another function. It further objectivates the notion of the coupled identity as problematic.

At some point during this period of trying, the initiator may suggest separation. Yet, separation is not suggested as a formal leave-taking but as a *temporary* separation meant to clarify the relationship for both partners. Again, the concern on the part of the initiator for the significant other appears. Not wanting to hurt, yet recognizing the coupled identity as no longer valid, the temporary separation is encouraged as a further means of bringing the other to accept a definition of the marriage as unsavable, to increase reliance of the other on outside resources of self-realization, and to initiate the physical breach gently.

> Even at that point, at initial separation, I wasn't being honest. I knew fairly certainly that when we separated, it was for good. I let her believe that it was a means for us first finding out what was happening and then eventually possibly getting back together.

Should the initiator be hesitant to suggest a separation, the significant other may finally tire of the ambiguity of the relationship. No longer finding the coupling as it exists self-validating, the significant other may be the one to suggest a separation. The decision to separate may be the result of discussion and planning, or it may occur spontaneously, in a moment of anger. It may be mutually agreed upon, but more often it is not. However it emerges, the decision to separate is a difficult one for both partners.

OBJECTIVATION: RESTRUCTURING
OF THE PRIVATE SPHERE

The separation is a transitional state in which everything needs definition, yet very little is capable of being defined. Economic status, friendship networks, personal habits, and sex life are all patterns of the past which need simultaneous reorganization. However, reorganization is hindered by the ambiguity of the relationship. The off-again, on-again wearing of the wedding rings is symbolic of the indecision in this stage. Each of the partners searches for new roles, without yet being free of the old.

For the initiator who has developed outside resources, the impact of this uncertainty is partially mitigated. For the significant other, who has not spent time in preparation for individual existence, the major self-validating function of the marriage is gone and nothing has emerged as a substitute.

> I had lost my identity somewhere along the way. And I kept losing my identity. I kept letting him make all the decisions. I couldn't work. I wasn't able to be myself. I was letting someone else take over. I didn't have any control over it. I didn't know how to stop it. I was unsure that if anything really happened I could actually make it on my own or not.

The separation precipitates a redefinition of self for the significant other. Without other resources for self-validation, and with the coupled identity now publicly challenged, the significant other begins a restructuring of the private sphere.

This restructuring occurs not only in the social realm but also entails a form of restructuring that is physical, tangible, and symbolic of the break in the coupled identity. For instance, if the initiator has been the one to leave, at some point the significant other begins reordering the residence they shared to suit the needs of one adult rather than two. Furniture is rearranged or thrown out. Closets and drawers are reorganized. A thorough house-cleaning may be undertaken. As the initiator has moved to a new location that reinforces his singularity, the significant other transforms the home that validated the coupling into one that likewise objectivates the new definition. Changes in the physical appearance of either or both partners may be a part of the symbolic restructuring of the private sphere. Weight losses, changes of hair style, or changes in clothing preferences further symbolize the yielding of the mutual identity and the move toward autonomy.

Should the significant other be the one to leave, the move into a new location aids in the redefinition of self as an autonomous individual. For example, the necessity of surviving in a new environment, the eventual emergence of a new set of friends that define and relate to the significant other as a separate being instead of as half of a couple, and the creation of a new residence without the other person are all mechanisms which reinforce autonomy and a definition of singularity.

Though the initiator has long been involved in objectivating a separate reality, frequently for the significant other this stage is just beginning. Seldom does the secret of the troubled marriage become shared with others by this partner until it can no longer be deferred. Although the initiator actively has sought objectivation, the significant other has avoided it. Confronted with actual separation, however, the significant other responds by taking the subjectively experienced meanings and moving them to the objective level—by confiding in others, perhaps in writing, in letters or in diaries—any means that helps the other deal with the new reality.

There are some who must be told of the separation—children, parents, best friends. Not only are the two partners reconstructing their own reality, but they now must reconstruct the reality for others. Conversation provides the mechanism for reconstruction, simultaneously creating common definitions and working as a major objectivating apparatus. The longer the conversation goes on, the more massively real do the objectivations become to the partners. The result is a stabilization of the objectivated reality, as the new definition of uncoupledness continues to move outward.

Uncoupling precipitates a reordering of all other significant relationships. As in coupling, where all other relationships are reperceived and regrouped to account for and support the emergence of *the* significant other, in uncoupling the reordering supports the singularity of each partner. Significant relationships are lost, as former friends of the couple now align with one or the other or refuse to choose between the two. Ties with families of orientation, formerly somewhat attenuated because of the coupling, are frequently renewed. For each of the partners, pressure exists to stabilize characterizations of others and of self so that the world and self are brought toward consistency. Each partner approaches groups that strengthen the new definition each has created, and avoids those that weaken it. The groups with which each partner associates help co-define the new reality.

OBJECTIVATION: THE PUBLIC SPHERE

The uncoupling is further objectivated for the participants as the new definition is legitimized in the public sphere. Two separate households demand public identification as separate identities. New telephone listings, changes of mailing address, separate checking accounts, and charge accounts, for example, are all mechanisms by which the new reality becomes publicly reconstructed.

The decision to initiate legal proceedings confirms the uncoupling by the formal negotiation of a heretofore informally negotiated definition. The adversary process supporting separate identities, custody proceedings, the formal separation of the material base, the final removal of the rings all act as means of moving the new definition from the private to the public sphere. The uncoupling now becomes objectivated not only for the participants and their close intimates, but for casual acquaintances and strangers.

Objectivation acts as a constraint upon whatever social identity has been constructed. It can bind a couple together, or hinder their recoupling, once the uncoupling process has begun. Perhaps this can better be understood by considering the tenuous character of the extramarital affair. The very nature of the relationship is private. The coupling remains a secret shared by the two and seldom becomes objectivated in the public realm. Thus, the responsibility for the maintenance of that coupling usually rests solely with the two participants. When the relationship is no longer self-validating for one of the participants, the uncoupling does not involve a reconstruction of reality for others. The constraints imposed by the objectivation of a marital relationship which function to keep a couple in a marriage do not exist to the same extent in an affair. The fragility of the coupling is enhanced by its limited objectivation.

Berger and Kellner (1964, p. 6) note that the "degree of objectivation will depend on the number and intensity of the social relationships that are its carriers." As the uncoupling process has moved from a nonshared secret held within the initiator to the realm of public knowledge, the degree of objectivation has increased. The result is a continuing decline in the precariousness of the newly constructed reality over time.

DIVORCE: A STAGE IN THE PROCESS

Yet a decrease in precariousness is not synonymous with a completion of the uncoupling process. As marriage, or coupling, is a dramatic act of redefinition of self by two strangers as they move from autonomous identities to the construction of a joint biography, so uncoupling involves yet another redefinition of self as the participants move from mutual identity toward autonomy. It is this redefinition of self, for each participant, that completes the uncoupling. Divorce, then, may not be the final stage. In fact, divorce could be viewed as a nonstatus that is at some point on a continuum ranging from marriage (coupling) as an achieved status, to autonomy (uncoupling), likewise an achieved status. In other words, the uncoupling process might be viewed as a status transformation which is complete when the individual defines his salient status as "single" rather than "divorced." When the individual's newly constructed separate subworld becomes nomos-building— when it creates for the individual a sort of order in which he can experience his life as making sense—the uncoupling process is completed.

The completion of uncoupling does not occur at the same moment for each participant. For either or both of the participants, it may not occur until after the other has created a coupled identity with another person. With that step, the tentativeness is gone.

> When I learned of his intention to remarry, I did not realize how devastated I would be. It was just awful. I remember crying and crying. It was really a very bad thing that I did not know or expect. You really aren't divorced while that other person is still free. You still have a lot of your psychological marriage going—in fact, I'm still in that a little bit because I'm still single.

For some, the uncoupling may never be completed. One or both of the participants may never be able to construct a new and separate subworld that becomes self-validating. Witness, for example, the widow who continues to call herself "Mrs. John Doe," who associates with the same circle of friends, who continues to wear her wedding ring and observes wedding anniversaries. For her, the coupled identity is still a major mechanism for self-validation, even though the partner is gone.

In fact, death as a form of uncoupling may be easier for the significant other to handle than divorce. There exist ritual techniques for dealing with it, and there is no ambiguity. The relationship is gone. There will be no further interaction between the partners. With divorce, or any uncoupling that occurs through the volition of one or both of the partners, the interaction may continue long after the relationship has been formally terminated. For the significant other—the one left behind, without resources for self-validation—the continuing interaction between the partners presents obstacles to autonomy.

> There's a point at which it's over. If your wife dies, you're a lot luckier, I think, because it's over. You either live with it, you kill yourself, or you make your own bed of misery. Unlike losing a wife through death, in divorce, she doesn't die. She keeps resurrecting it. I can't get over it, she won't die. I mean, she won't go away.

CONTINUITIES

Continuities are linkages between the partners that exist despite the formal termination of the coupled identity. Most important of these is the existence of shared loved ones—children, in-laws, and so on. Though in-laws may of necessity be excluded from the separately constructed subworlds, children can rarely be and, in their very existence, present continued substantiation of the coupled identity.

In many cases continuities are actively constructed by one or both of the participants after the formal termination of the relationship. These manufactured linkages speak to the difficulty of totally separating that common biography, by providing a continued mechanism for interaction. They may be constructed as a temporary bridge between the separated subworlds, or they may come to be a permanent interaction pattern. Symbolically, they seem to indicate caring on the part of either or both of the participants.

> The wife moves out. The husband spends his weekend helping her get settled—hanging pictures, moving furniture.

> The husband moves out, leaving his set of tools behind. Several years later, even after his remarriage, the tools are still there, and he comes to borrow them one at a time. The former wife is planning to move within the same city. The tools are boxed up, ready to be taken with her.

> The wife has moved out, but is slow to change her mailing address. Rather than marking her forwarding address on the envelopes and returning them by mail, the husband either delivers them once a week or the wife picks them up.

> The wife moves out. The husband resists dividing property with her that is obviously hers. The conflict necessitates many phone calls and visits.

> The husband moves out. Once a week he comes to the house to visit with the children on an evening when the wife is away. When she gets home, the two of them occasionally go out to dinner.

> A nice part of the marriage was shared shopping trips on Sunday afternoons. After the divorce, they still occasionally go shopping together.

> The holidays during the first year of separation were celebrated as they always had been—with the whole family together.

> During a particularly difficult divorce, the husband noted that he had finally succeeded in finding his wife a decent lawyer.

Continuities present unmeasurable variables in the uncoupling process. In this paper, uncoupling is defined as a reality socially constructed by the participants. The stages that mark the movement from a coupled identity to separate autonomous identities are characterized, using divorce for an ideal-type analysis. Yet, there is no intent to portray uncoupling as a compelling linear process from which there is no turning back. Such conceptualization would deny the human factor inherent in reality construction. Granted, as the original secret is moved from private to public, becoming increasingly objectivated, reconstructing the coupled identity becomes more and more difficult.

Each stage of objectivation acts as the closing of a door. Yet at any stage the process may be interrupted. The initiator may not find mechanisms of self-validation outside the coupling that reinforce his autonomy. Or the self-validation outside the coupling may be the very stuff that allows the initiator to stay *in* the relationship. Or continuities may intervene and reconstruction of the coupled identity may occur, despite the degree of objectivation, as in the following case.

> Ellen met Jack in college. They fell in love and married. Jack had been blind since birth. He had pursued a college career in education and was also a musician. Both admired the independence of the other. In the marriage, she subordinated her career to his and helped him pursue a masters degree, as well as his musical interests. Her time was consumed by his needs—for transportation and the taping and transcribing of music for the musicians in his group. He was teaching at a school for the blind by day and performing as a musician at night. They had a son, and her life, instead of turning outward, as his, revolved around family responsibilities. She gained weight. Jack, after twelve years of marriage, left Ellen for his high school sweetheart. Ellen grieved for a while, then began patching her life. She got a job, established her own credit, went back to college, and lost weight. She saw a lawyer, filed for divorce, joined Parents Without Partners, and began searching out singles groups. She dated. Throughout, Jack and Ellen saw each other occasionally and maintained a sexual relationship. The night before the divorce was final, they reconciled.

The uncoupling never was completed, though all stages of the process occurred, including the public objectivation that results from the initiation of the legal process. Ellen, in constructing an autonomous identity, became again the independent person Jack had first loved.[3] This, together with the continuities that existed between the two, created the basis for a common definition of the coupling as savable.

DISCUSSION

Berger and Kellner describe the process by which two individuals create a coupled identity for themselves. Here, we have started from the point of the coupled identity and examined the process by which people move out of such relationships. Using interview data, we have found that, although the renegotiation of separate realities is a complex web of subtle modifications, clear stages emerge which mark the uncoupling process. The emergent stages are like benchmarks which indicate the increasing objectivation of the changing definitions of reality, as these definitions move from the realm of the private to the public.

Beginning within the intimacy of the dyad, the initial objectivation occurs as the secret of the troubled marriage that the initiator has held is shared with the significant other. With this, the meaning has begun to move from the subjective to the objective. Definition negotiation begins. While attempting to negotiate a common definition, the initiator acts to increase the validation of his identity and place in the world by use of accompanying reconstructions of reality. The autonomy of the initiator increases as he finds self-validation outside the marriage and an ideology that supports the uncoupling. The increased autonomy of the initiator brings the significant other to accept a definition of the marriage as troubled, and they enter into the stage of "trying." The process continues, as counseling and separation further move the new definition into the public sphere.

The telling of others, the symbolic physical signs of the uncoupling, and the initiation of formal legal proceedings validate the increasing separation of the partners as they negotiate a new reality which is different from that constructed private sphere which validated their identity as a couple. Eventually, a redefinition of the mutual identity occurs in such a way that the joint biography is separated into two separate autonomous identities. As Berger and Kellner state that marriage is a dramatic act of redefinition of self by two individuals, so uncoupling is characterized by the same phenomenon. Self-realization, rather than coming from the coupledness, again comes from outside sources. Significant conversation again finds its source in nonoverlapping circles. The new definition of the relationship constructed by the participants has, in interaction with others, become common property.

Language is crucial to this process. Socially constructed worlds need validation. As conversation constantly reconfirms a coupled identity, so also does it act as the major validating mechanism for the move to singularity, not by specific articulation, but by the way in which it comes to revolve around the uncoupled identity as taken for granted.

The notion that the stages uncovered do broadly apply needs to be further confirmed. We need to know whether the process is invariant regardless of the heterosexuality, homosexuality, or social class of couples. Does it also apply for close friends? In what ways does the sex of the interviewer bias the data? Additionally, the stages in the process should be confirmed by interviews with both partners in a coupling. Due to the delicacy of the subject matter, this is difficult. In only one instance were both partners available to be interviewed for this study. Notwithstanding these limitations, the findings which emerge deserve consideration.

Most significant of these is the existence of an underlying order in a phenomenon generally regarded as a chaotic and disorderly process. Undoubtedly the discovery of order was encouraged by the methodology of the study. The information was gained by retrospective analysis on the part of the interviewees. Certainly the passage of time allowed events to be reconstructed in an orderly way that made sense. Nonetheless, as was previously noted, the interviewees were all at various stages in the uncoupling process—some at the "secret" stage and some five years hence. Yet, the stages which are discussed here appeared without fail in every case and have been confirmed repeatedly by the other means described earlier.

In addition to this orderliness, the examination of the process of uncoupling discloses two other little-considered aspects of the process that need to be brought forth and questioned.

One is the caring. Generally, uncoupling is thought of as a conflict-ridden experience that ends as a bitter battle between two adversaries intent on doing each other in. Frequently, this is the case. Yet, the interviews for this study showed that in all cases, even the most emotion generating, again and again the concern of each of the participants for the other revealed itself. Apparently, the patterns of caring and responsibility that emerge between the partners in a coupling are not easily dispelled and in many cases persist throughout the uncoupling process and after, as suggested by the concept of continuities.

A second question that emerges from this examination of uncoupling is related to Berger and Kellner's thesis. They state that, for adults in our society, marriage is a significant validating relationship, one that is nomos-building. Marriage is, in fact, described as "a crucial nomic instrumentality" (1964, p. 4). Though Berger and Kellner at the outset do delimit the focus of their analysis to marriage as an ideal type, the question to be answered is, To what degree is this characterization of marriage appropriate today?

Recall, for example, the quote from one interviewee: "I was never psychologically married. I always felt strained by attempts that coupled me into a marital unit. I was just never comfortable as 'Mrs.' " The interviews for this study suggest that the nomos-building quality assumed to derive from marriage to the individual should be taken as problematic rather than as given. Gouldner (1959) suggests that the parts of a unit vary in the degree to which they are interdependent. His concept of functional autonomy may be extended to illuminate the variable forms that marriage, or coupling, may take and the accompanying degree of nomos. A relationship may exist in which the partners are highly interdependent, and the coupled identity does provide the major mechanism for self-validation, as Berger and Kellner suggest. Yet it is equally as likely that the participants are highly independent, or "loosely coupled" (Weick 1976; Corwin 1977), wherein mechanisms for self-validation originate *outside* the coupling rather than from the coupling itself. The connection between the form of the coupling, the degree to which it is or is not nomos-building, and the subsequent implications for uncoupling should be examined in future research.

NOTES

1. For a sensitive and thought-provoking examination of these as integral components of divorce, see Willard Waller's beautiful qualitative study, *The Old Love and the New*.

2. This statement must be qualified. There are instances when the partners enter a stage of trying with shared definitions of thee marriage as savable. The conditions under which the coupling can be preserved have to be negotiated. If they can arrive at a common definition of the coupling that is agreeable to both, the uncoupling process is terminated. But this analysis is of uncoupling, and there are two alternatives: (1) that they enter with common definitions of the marriage as savable but are not able to negotiate the conditions of the coupling so that the self-validation function is preserved or (2) that they enter the period of trying with opposing definitions, as stated here.

3. Waller interprets this phenomenon by using Jung's conceptualization of the container and the contained, analogous to the roles of initiator and significant other, respectively, in the present discussion. Notes Waller, "Or the contained, complicated by the process of divorcing, may develop those qualities whose lack the container previously deplored" (pp. 163–168).

REFERENCES

Berger, Peter L. and Hansfried Kellner. 1964. "Marriage and the Construction of Reality." *Diogenes* 46:1–23.

Berger, Peter L. and Thomas Luckmann. 1966. *The Social Construction of Reality.* New York: Doubleday.

Bohanon, Paul. 1971. *Divorce and After.* Garden City, NY: Anchor.

Corwin, Ronald G. 1976. "Organizations at Loosely Coupled Systems: Evolution of a Perspective." Paper presented at the Seminar on Educational Organizations as Loosely Coupled Systems, Palo Alto, CA.

Davis, Murray S. 1973. *Intimate Relations.* New York: Free Press.

Epstein, Joseph E. 1975. *Divorce: The American Experience.* London: Jonathan Cape.

Goode, William J. 1956. *Women in Divorce.* New York: Free Press.

Gouldner, Alvin W., 1959. "Organizational Analysis." Pp. 400–428 in *Sociology Today,* edited by R. K. Merton, L. Bloom, and L. S. Cottrell, Jr. New York: Basic Books.

Krantzler, Mel. 1973. *Creative Divorce.* New York: New American Library.

Nichols, Jack. 1975. *Men's Liberation: A New Definition of Masculinity.* New York: Penguin.

Sullivan, Judy. 1974. *Mama Doesn't Live Here Anymore.* New York: Pyramid.

Waller, Willard. 1930. *The Old Love and the New.* Carbondale, IL: Southern Illinois University Press.

Walum, Laurel Richardson. 1977. *The Dynamics of Sex and Gender: A Sociological Perspective.* Chicago: Rand McNally.

Weber, Max. 1930. *The Protestant Ethic and the Spirit of Capitalism.* Translated by Talcott Parsons. New York: Charles Scribner's Sons.

Weick, Karl E. 1976. "Educational Organizations as Loosely Coupled Systems." *Administrative Science Quarterly,* 21:1–19.

Weiss, Robert. 1975. *Marital Separation.* New York: Basic Books.

43

Downward Mobility*

Terry Arendall

These women had assumed that after divorce they would somehow be able to maintain a middle-class life-style for themselves and their children. Those in their twenties and thirties had been confident that they could establish themselves as capable employees and find positions that would provide sufficient incomes. Most of the older women, who had been out of the work force longer, had been less confident about their earning abilities, but they had assumed that the difference between the former family income and their own earnings would be adequately compensated for by court-ordered child support and spousal support payments. In fact, virtually all of the women had assumed that family management and parenting efforts, which had kept most of them from pursuing employment and career development while they were married, would be socially valued and legally recognized in their divorce settlements. What had worried them most was not economic difficulty but the possible psychological effects of divorce on themselves and their children. Still, they had believed that they would probably recover from the emotional trauma of divorcing in a matter of months and would then be able to reorganize their lives successfully.

DRASTICALLY REDUCED INCOMES

But even the women who had worried most about how they would manage financially without their husbands' incomes had not imagined the kind of hardship they would face after divorce. All but two of the sixty women had to cope with a substantial loss of family income. Indeed, 90 percent of them (fifty-six out of sixty) found that divorce immediately pushed them below the poverty line, or close to it. As wives and mothers, they had been largely dependent on their husbands, who had supplied the family's primary income.† Without that source of income, they suffered a drastic reduction in standard of living—an experience not shared by their ex-husbands.[1] Like women generally, they were "declassed" by divorce.

The economic decline experienced by these sixty women, all of whom remained single parents, was not temporary.[2] With caution and careful spending, most could meet their essential monthly expenses. But few had any extra money for dealing with emergencies or unexpected demands, and some continued to fall

---

*Arendall, Terry. 1980. *Mothers and Divorce: Legal, Economic, and Social Dilemmas*. Berkeley, CA: University of California Press. © 1986 The Regents of the University of California.

† According to Lee Rainwater (1984) and the U.S. Bureau of the Census (1985), the earnings of working married wives contribute only 22 percent of the average family's total income. For this reason, poverty, which occurs in only one of nineteen husband-wife families and in only one of nine families maintained by a single father, afflicts almost one of every three families headed by a woman.

further behind, unable even to pay their monthly bills. One of them, divorced for nearly eight years, described her experience this way:

> I've been living hand to mouth all these years, ever since the divorce. I have no savings account. The notion of having one is as foreign to me as insurance — there's no way I can afford insurance. I have an old pickup that I don't drive very often. In the summertime I don't wear nylons to work because I can cut costs there. Together the kids and I have had to struggle and struggle. Supposedly struggle builds character. Well, some things simply aren't character building. There have been times when we've scoured the shag rug to see if we could find a coin to come up with enough to buy milk so we could have cold cereal for dinner. That's not character building.

Although they had been living for a median period of over four years as divorced single parents, only *nine* of these sixty women had managed to halt the economic fall prompted by divorce: four of these nine had even managed to reestablish a standard of living close to what they had had while married. Thus the remaining majority—fifty-one women—had experienced no economic recovery. Few had any savings, and most lived from paycheck to paycheck in a state of constant uncertainty. One of them, a woman in her late forties and divorced more than four years, told me:

> I can't go on like this. There's no way. I can manage for another year, maybe a year and a half, but no more. I don't have the stamina. It's not that I don't have a job. My problem is money, plain and simple. That's all that counts in this situation.

This group of recently divorced mothers was by no means unique. All female-headed households experience high rates of economic hardship, and the gap in median income between female-headed families and other types of families has actually widened between 1960 and 1983.* Part of the reason is obvious: certain fixed costs of maintaining a family—such as utility bills and home mortgages or rent—do not change when the family size declines by one, and many other expenses, such as food and clothing, do not change significantly. Additionally, in most cases when the mother obtained employment, it provided a low income that was substantially reduced by new expenses, such as the costs of transportation and child care.†

---

* Between 1960 and 1983, the median income of female-headed families with no husband present dropped by the following percentages: from 61 to 57 percent of the median income of male-headed families with no wife present, from 43 to 41 percent of the median income of married couples, and from 51 to 38 percent of the median income of married-couple families in which the wife was also employed. In 1983, the median income for female-headed families was $11,484; for male-headed families with no wife present, $20,140; for married-couple families, $26,019; and for married couples in which the wife was employed, $30,340 (U.S. Bureau of the Census, 1985).

†From his Michigan study, David Chambers (1979) concludes that the custodial parent needs 80 percent of the predivorce income to maintain the family's standard of living. The total income of most family units of divorced women and children falls below 50 percent of their former family income. Sweden, in fact, has determined that single-parent families actually need more income than others and provides cash supports that give them incomes comparable to those of two-parent families (Cassetty 1983a).

These women understood how their economic dependency in marriage had contributed to their present economic situation. One of them, who had been married nearly twenty years before divorcing, said:

> Money does wonders in any situation. I'm sure women with more education and better jobs don't have situations quite as desperate as mine. But I quit school when I married and stayed home to raise my children.

Unfortunately, they arrived at such understanding the hard way, through experience. Before divorcing, they had expected to receive "reasonable" child support and had thought they could probably find jobs that paid "reasonable" wages. They had only the vaguest understanding of other women's divorce experiences. Thus two of them said:

> Friends of mine had ended up divorced with children, and they would tell me some of these things. But I had no empathy at all. I might say, "Gee, that doesn't seem fair" or "Gee, that's too bad." But it never *really* hit me how serious it is until it happened to me. So I think there must be a lot of people out there who don't have the foggiest idea what it feels like.
>
> I had no idea how *much* money it takes. You don't have the (husband's) income, but you still have your family. There's the rub.

Their experiences led them to conclude that in America today, divorced women generally must accept a reduced standard of living. And as women with children, they were keenly aware that only remarriage could offer a quick escape from economic hardship.* A mother of three told me:

> I have this really close friend. She was a neighbor and often kept my daughter until I got home from school. She and her husband had two darling little kids. One day he just up and left. Surprised us all—he married his secretary eventually. My friend hadn't worked before, so I helped her get some typing skills. She worked for two weeks and said, "No more." She called me and said, "Well, I'm not going through what you did. I'm getting married." That was like a slap in the face. Gosh, did I look that bad? I started to doubt myself. Was I doing that bad a job? Should I have gone the marriage route? Gone out and gotten a job and then married somebody? I still wonder about that. Things would have been a lot easier financially. The kids would have had a father. And I would have done what society looks at favorably. I don't know. I still don't know what to do.

Economically these women lost their middle-class status, but socially their expectations of themselves and their children remained the same. They still identi-

---

* Research supports the commonsense belief that the surest way to reverse the economic decline resulting from divorce is to remarry (Sawhill 1976; Duncan and Morgan 1974, 1979; Johnson and Minton 1982). Do women remarry because they conclude, pragmatically, that being a single woman is too costly, for themselves and perhaps also for their children? Would fewer women remarry if they could successfully support themselves? The answers to such questions will have interesting political implications.

fied with the middle class, but their low incomes prevented them from participating in middle-clas activities. This contradiction created many dilemmas and conflicts:

> I went to a CETA workshop, and I started crying when all they talked about was how to get a job. A woman came after me in the hallway, and I just bawled. I'd been searching for a job for months. I had a degree and teaching credential, and here I was being told how to fill out a stupid job application. And I had three kids at home that I didn't know how I was going to feed that week and a lovely home I couldn't afford.
>
> I moved here after the divorce because the school had a particularly good program for gifted children. Kids were classed by ability and not just by grade level. So my kid was in a really good spot for what he needed. I didn't realize at the time that I was the only single parent in that group. One reason those kids can achieve at that level is because they have a very stable home life, two parents to work with every child on the enrichment and the projects and the homework. I hate to say this, but it's all socioeconomic. Every kid in there belonged to a high socioeconomic group. Oh, they can rationalize that it's not really like that, but it's completely WASPish, all two parent families where the mothers don't work. Mothers are available to take kids to music lessons, soccer lessons, gymnastic lessons, and all of that whenever it's needed. I had to take my son out of that class. I couldn't keep up the level of activity required of the kids and the parents. The gap was growing greater and greater. If I'd lived like this a long time, I might have known how to cope, but this was all new. And it all came down to money.

The women resented their precarious positions all the more because they knew that their former husbands had experienced no loss in class status or standard of living and could have eased their struggles to support the children:

> Five hundred dollars here or there—or taking over the orthodontist's bills—anything like that would have meant a lot. I don't see why this kid should have to live with jaw and tooth problems because I got a divorce. His jaw had to be totally realigned, so it wasn't just cosmetic. His father could easily have paid that monthly [orthodonist] bill and deducted it. That would have made a tremendous difference. But he wouldn't. By making me suffer, he made his child suffer too.

When the children retained some access to middle-class activities through involvement with their fathers, their mothers had ambivalent feelings. They were grateful that their chldren were not neglected by their fathers and could enjoy some enriching and entertaining activities with them; but they found their former husbands' greater financial resources a painful reminder of how little they themselves could provide. One woman, who had to let her child get free meals through the subsidized school lunch program, despite her many efforts to make more money, told me this:

> His father seldom buys him anything. But his stepmother sometimes does. She can give him all these nice things. She's given him nice books, a stereo headset. I have no idea what her motivation is, but it's a very funny feeling to know that I can't go and buy my son something he would love to have, but this perferct stranger can. And how will that affect my son ultimately? He must know how difficult things are

here, and that I'm not deliberately depriving him. But it's kind of ironic—I helped establish that standard of living, but I end up with none of it, and she has full access to it.

EXPENSES AND ECONOMIZING

Living with a reduced budget was a constant challenge to most of these women because they had no cushion to fall back on if expenses exceeded their incomes. Their savings were depleted soon after they divorced; only twelve of the sixty women I talked to had enough money in savings to cover a full month's expenses. Most said they had radically cut back their spending.[3] The major expenses after divorce were housing, food, and utilities. The women with young children also had substantial child care expenses, and several had unusually high medical bills that were not covered by health insurance.

Within a short time after their divorces, more than one-third of the women— sixteen women living in homes they owned and seven living in rented places—had to move to different housing with their children in order to reduce their expenses. Two of the women had moved more than four times in the first two years after their divorces, always for financial reasons.[4] During marriage, forty-nine of the sixty women had lived in homes owned with their husbands. After divorce, only nine of them retained ownership of the family home. Of these nine, six were able to acquire ownership by buying out their husbands as part of the community property settlement (five of them only because they were able to get financial assistance from their parents); two retained the home by exchanging other community assets for it; and one received the home according to the dictates of the religion she and her husband shared.

Home ownership brought with it many expenses besides mortgage payments. Several women neglected upkeep and repairs for lack of money. A woman who was in her fifties reported this common dilemma:

> I owe $16,000 on this house. I could get about $135,000 for it, so I have a large equity. But it would have taken all of that to get that condominium I looked at, and my payments would still have been about $400 a month. I don't know how I'll be able to keep up the house, financially or physically. The house needs painting, and I can't keep up the yard work. I'd like to move. I'd like a fresh start. But the kids don't want to move, and I can't imagine how I'll handle all of this once they're gone. When the alimony [spousal support] stops, there'll be no way I can manage a move. I'm stuck here now. The mortgage is really low and the interest is only 5 percent.

Two of the mothers reduced expenses by moving their children from private to public schools. Two others were able to keep their children in private schools only after administrators waived the tuition fees. Seven mothers received financial assistance for preschoolers' child care costs, five from private and two from public agencies. One of these women, who worked full-time, had this to say about her expenses:

I'm buying this house. I pay $330 a month for it. Child care for my two kids runs to almost $500 a month. Since I bring home only a little more than $900, there's no way I could make it without the child care assistance. There'd be nothing left.

About half of these women had economic situations so dire that careful budgeting was not enough, and they continued to fall further behind economically. Those living close to the margin managed by paying some bills one month and others the next. Their indebtedness increased, and opportunities for reversing the situation did not appear:

I'm so far in debt. Yes indeed. I keep thinking, why should I worry about the bills? I'll never get out of debt! All I can do is juggle. Without my charge cards, my kids would be bare-assed naked. And school is coming up again. What am I going to do for school clothes? And they've all grown fast this year. . . . I probably owe $3,000 on charge cards, and I still owe rent—I haven't paid this month or last. The landlord I have has been very understanding. He's let us go along as best he can. We've been here four years, and he knows what I'm going through. Over the years, he's given me several eviction notices, but this last time he hired a lawyer and everything. I decided I'd just pitch my tent on the capitol mall in Sacramento and say, "Here I am." I've written my congressman again, because I qualify for subsidized housing. But it'll take forever to get any action on that.

For many, however, even the persistent realities of economic hardship could not extinguish middle-class hopes:

My husband liked really good food and always bought lots and the best. So when he left, it was really hard to cut the kids back. They were used to all that good eating. Now there's often no food in the house, and everybody gets really grouchy when there's no food around. . . . I think I've cut back mostly on activities. I don't go to movies anymore with friends. We've lost $150 a month now because my husband reduced the support. It gets cut from activities—we've stopped doing everything that costs, and there's nowhere else to cut. My phone is shut off. I pay all the bills first and then see what there is for food. . . . I grew up playing the violin, and I'd wanted my kids to have music lessons—piano would be wonderful for them. And my older two kids are very artistic. But lessons are out of the question.

Obtaining credit had been a real problem for many, for the reasons given by this woman, who had worked during the marriage while her husband attended school:

My kids and I were very poor those first years after the divorce. I had taken care of our finances during marriage. But I didn't have accounts in my own name, so I couldn't get credit. I got a job as soon as I could. I was getting $65 a month for child support and paying $175 a month for rent. Between the rent and the child care and the driving to work, I was absolutely broke. I really didn't have enough to live on. I had no benefits either, with my first job. I was living dangerously, and with children. I could barely pay the basic bills. There wasn't enough money for food lots of times. I cried many times because there wasn't enough money. I couldn't get any credit. [When I was married] my husband could get any credit he wanted, but it was on the basis of *my* job, which had the higher income. He couldn't even keep his checkbook balanced, but now I'm the one who can't get credit! It was a hard lesson to learn. Now whenever I get a chance, I tell women to start getting a credit rating.

The woman who told me this, incidentally, had managed to overcome initial impoverishment and gain a middle-class income from her job.

Some women regarded personal possessions such as jewelry, furniture, and cars as things they might sell to meet emergencies or rising indebtedness:

I sold jewelry to have my surgery, to pay for the part that wasn't covered. I still have some silver, and I have some good furniture, which could probably bring something. That's probably what I'd do in an emergency, sell those things. What else do people do?

Teenaged children helped by earning money through odd jobs and babysitting. Older teenagers changed their college plans, and several entered community colleges instead of universities. One woman's daughter was already in the Navy, pursuing her schooling in languages and working as a translator, and the daughter of another was considering military service as a way of saving money for a college education.

Most women compared their own hardship and forced economizing to the economic freedom enjoyed by their ex-husbands. For example:

I know my ex-husband goes somewhere almost every weekend, and he usually takes a friend along. I wonder how he can do that. How can he go somewhere every weekend? The only way I could do that is find a rich man! I couldn't possibly work enough hours to pay for that much stuff. I'd be doing well to finance a [twenty-mile] trip to San Francisco!

There were some exceptions to the general pattern of economic decline. Nine of the sixty women had regained some latitude for discretionary spending, though only three of them had managed this economic reversal without help. These nine were a distinct subgroup; the others did not share their higher standards of living or their feelings and approaches to the future. Still, only two of these nine women had not experienced a major decline in income immediately upon divorcing (or separating). One had been living on welfare because her husband's excessive drinking and erratic behavior had prevented him from holding a job; she found employment immediately after separating from him. The other one had been the primary family wage earner during her marriage.* Four of the women

---

* A recent study by Lee Rainwater (1984, p. 84) shows how economic dependency in a previous marriage makes it difficult for a woman to recover economically from divorce: "By the fourth year that they headed their own families, women who had regular work experience before becoming female heads had family incomes equal to 80 percent of their average family income while a wife. Women who had not worked at all had incomes slightly less than half that of their last married years."

whose incomes had dropped significantly had managed to stop and even reverse the economic decline very soon after divorce because they were granted temporary spousal support awards and acquired some money and assets from their community property settlement; two of them, who had been divorced after more than twenty years of marriage, also received substantial amounts of money from their parents. Although these four did not experience the degree of hardship shared by the others, they did not fully recover their formerly high income levels and therefore also had to alter their life-styles. As one of them said:

> Essentially, I took an $80,000 drop in annual income. And I had to borrow again last year. This year I finally sold the house, and that was really the only way I've made it. My change in life-style has been *tremendous*. Just my heating and electricity bill for our home was $350 a month. We just barely got by on $2,000 a month. I stopped buying household things; I stopped buying clothes for myself. And I rented out a room in the house. It was a huge house, and that helped out. I let the cleaning woman and the gardner go. I didn't paint. I let the property taxes go until I sold the house and paid them then. I quit taking trips. This house I'm in now has much lower operating expenses. My son doesn't have the same things he'd had. His grandparents buy most of his shoes and clothes now. He used to have lots and lots, so it's been a change for him.

Of the other five women who succeeded in improving their economic situations after a few years, three did so entirely through their own work efforts, and the other two managed with help from their former husbands—one took in the child for more than a year while his ex-wife worked at several jobs, and the other accepted a shared parenting arrangement.

EMOTIONAL RESPONSES TO ECONOMIC LOSS

None of the nine women who had experienced substantial economic recovery reported suffering serious emotional changes. Forty-four of the others, however, spoke of frequent struggles with depression and despair. Every one of them attributed these intense feelings, which often seemed overwhelming, directly to the financial hardships that followed divorce. This woman spoke for many others in describing the effects that economic loss had had on her:

> I think about money a great deal. It's amazing. I used to get so bored by people who could only talk about money. Now it's all I think about. It's a perpetual thought, how to get money—not to invest, or to save, but just to live. The interesting thing is that you develop a poverty mentality. That intrigues me. I would never have thought that could happen. But if I had had money, several times in the last year I would have fought what was happening to me in a way I no longer think of fighting. You tend to accept what's coming because there's so much you *have* to accept. You get so you accept everything that comes your way. For example, I accepted at first what I was told about treating this cancer on my face: that the only surgery possible would leave my face disfigured with one side paralyzed. I knew it would ruin any possibility of my teaching if they did that to my face, but I would have just accepted it if a friend hadn't gotten me to go to someone else for consultation. I wouldn't have done that

on my own. That's not how I would have behaved at other times in my life. I think it must happen to a lot of divorced women. It was only this year that I realized how strange this has become. I'm educated. I've come through a wealthy phase of my life, and now here I am, being shuttled around and not even fighting. It continues to fascinate me. After a while, you develop a begging mentality in which you'd like to squeeze money out of anybody. I guess I'm somewhere in the realm of poverty. I know there are poorer people, but I'm pretty well down near the bottom. If I were to lose this job—which is always possible, there's no security to it—I'd be finished. Finished. I'd lose the house. I'd lose everything. There's no way I could survive.

The first year of divorce was traumatic for most, especially because legal uncertainties were mixed with other fears. A vicious circle was common: anxieties brought sleepless nights, and fatigue made the anxieties sharper. Although economic hardship remained, by the end of the first year most of the women had learned to control some of the anxiety surrounding it.*

Depression overtook a majority of these women at some time or other. Their feelings of despair over financial troubles were worsened by concerns for their children. One of them said:

I thought about running away, but who would I have turned my kids over to? I also thought about suicide—especially when the youngest was still a baby and I had so much trouble with child care and it cost me so much. I kept thinking that if I were gone, it would take a major burden off of everybody.

In fact, such despair was a common experience: twenty-six of the sixty women volunteered that they had contemplated suicide at some time after divorce. They mentioned various contributing factors, such as emotional harassment from their husbands and uncertainty about their own abilities and identities, but all said that economic hardship was *the* primary stress that pushed them to the point of desperation.

One mother gave a very detailed account of her experience with suicidal depression, which occurred at a time when she had been barely managing for several months. She would drag herself to work and then collapse in bed when she got home. When she would get out of bed, she told me, the sight of her ten-year-old son sitting in front of the television set, alone in a cold room and eating cold cereal, would send her back to bed, where her exhaustion and despair would be exacerbated by hours of crying. She went on:

I came home to an empty house that night—it was February. I had gotten my son's father to take him that weekend so I could go to my class—the one about learning to

---

*Various studies argue that the first year or so after divorce is the most stressful and traumatic (Hetherington, Cox, and Cox 1976; Wallerstein and Kelly 1979, 1980; Weiss 1979a, 1979b). Additionally, both Pett (1982) and Buehler and Hogan (1980) found that financial concerns were among the factors that limited divorced mothers' emotional recovery from divorce. None of these studies, however, attempts to distinguish the effects of economic uncertainty from more generalized separation emotions.

live as a single person again. I'd hoped that by getting some encouragement, I'd be able to pull myself out of this and find a way to make a better living. About eleven o'clock, I just decided this was no way to live. I couldn't take care of this child. I'd gone to Big Brothers, and they wouldn't take him because he had a father. But his father wasn't seeing him. Family Services weren't any help. The woman there did try to help, I think. She cared. But she'd been married more than twenty-five years and just didn't understand. All I could do in the fifty-minute appointment with her was cry. My attorney wasn't giving me any help or getting me any money. My mother was mad at me—she said it was my fault for leaving my husband.

I just couldn't see it ever being any different, so I decided to kill myself. I'm sure that's not a unique thing. It was the most logical thing in the world. I knew exactly how I was going to do it. I was going to fill the bathtub with warm water and cut my wrists. It would be fine then—that thought was the only thing that made me feel any better. Nothing was as bad as the thought of getting up the next day. So I called my son's father—he was going to bring him back the next day—and I asked him if he thought he could take care of him. I didn't think I gave any evidence [of my feelings] or anything—it wasn't a desperate call for help, or a threatening call, or anything like that, because I'd already made up my mind. I just didn't want him to bring my son in here and find me like that. I wanted him to make some kind of arrangements to take care of him. He didn't say anything on the phone, but in about twenty minutes the doorbell rang. Two young men in blue uniforms were standing there. They wanted to take me to an emergency room. It was a crisis place, they said. They were young and scared themselves and acted like they didn't know what to do.

I guess the shock of realizing how far I'd gone was enough to snap me out of it. I'd spent those twenty minutes [after the phone call] piddling around taking care of some last-minute things, tidying up and so on. It seems that once I made the decision, it gave me such inner peace, such a perfect reconciliation. It seemed the most logical, practical thing in the world. Then their coming stopped me from doing it. I didn't go with them, but they gave me a phone number and told me there were people there who would come and get me anytime.

I've only recently put into perspective what happened. It wasn't so much my inability to cope as it was the convergence of everything in my situation. That person at Family Services did help, actually, when she pointed out that some people who've never had trouble dealing with anything don't know what else to do when they feel like they can't cope. That fit. I'd never had a crisis I couldn't deal with in some way. I'd gotten myself into bad situations before, but I could always see cause-and-effect relationships, and I'd always felt like I could make some changes right away that would change things in my life. In this case, I couldn't figure anything out. I don't even know how to tell you what I thought.

This woman had been divorced before and had not suffered depression; but she had had no child then, no one else for whom she was responsible.

These women who were new to poverty had no ideas about how to cope in their new situations, and they found little help in the society at large. Some of the most desperate were unable to afford professional counseling. One of them said:

At one point during the eviction, I was getting hysterical. I needed help. So I called a program called Women's Stress. Good thing I wasn't really suicidal, because they kept me on hold a long time. They said, "Well, this program is just for women with an alcohol or drug problem. Does that fit you?" I said, "No, but if I don't get help, it will." They said they'd send me a pamphlet, which they did. It cost twenty-five dollars to join. I never did find any help.

The worst personal pain these women suffered came from observing the effects of sudden economic hardship on their children. Here is one woman's poignant account:

I had $950 a month, and the house payment was $760, so there was hardly anything left over. So there we were: my son qualified for free lunches at school. We'd been living on over $4,000 a month, and there we were. That's so humiliating. What that does to the self-esteem of even a child is absolutely unbelievable. And it isn't hidden; everybody knows the situation. They knew at his school that he was the kid with the free lunch coupons....My son is real tall and growing. I really didn't have any money to buy him clothes, and attorneys don't think school clothes are essential. So he was wearing these sweatshirts that were too small for him. Then one day he didn't want to go to school because the kids had been calling him Frankenstein because his arms and legs were hanging out of his clothes—they were too short. That does terrible things to a kid, it really does. We just weren't equipped to cope with it.

But the need to cut costs—on food, clothing, and activities for the children— was not the only source of pain. Most of the mothers reported that their parenting approaches changed and that their emotions became more volatile, and even unstable, in periods of great financial stress. Mothers who went to work full-time resented the inevitable loss of involvement in their children's lives:

I wish I could get over the resentment. [In the first years after the divorce] I spent half the time blaming myself and the other half blaming their father. Because I was so preoccupied, I missed some really good years with them, doing things I'd looked forward to and wanted to do. Those years are gone now.

Some of the mothers also thought the experience of economic hardship after divorce might eventually affect the society at large, as more and more women and children come to share it.[5] For example:

It's not just the mother [who's affected]. It's a whole generation of kids who don't even know how to use a knife and a fork, who don't sit at a table to eat, who don't know how to make conversation with people of different ages. There are so many awful possibilities, and it's a whole society that's affected. I'm not talking about people who have lived for years in poverty. We planned and lived one way with no idea of the other reality. Then this harsh reality hits, and everything becomes a question of survival. I think it must be different if that's all you've experienced. At least then your plans fit your possibilities—that sort of thing. You can't spend your whole day trying to survive and then care anything about what's going on in the world around you. You really can't....Maybe it's going to take 50 percent of the population to be in this shape before we get change. But some of us have to be salvaged, just so we can fight. We can't all be so oppressed by trying to survive that we can't do anything at all.

Although their despair was worsened by concern for their children, it was the children who gave these women their strongest incentive to continue the struggle:

> Sure, I think about suicide. And I'm a smart lady who's been creative and able to do some things to change our situation. But I'm tired—*tired*. And it's real hard. What keeps me alive is my kid. I may be boxed in, but if I give up, what will happen to her? She doesn't deserve that.

Most of these women also admitted to having lost a sense of the future. A fifty-year-old woman, who said she wondered if she would someday become a bag lady, told me:

> That's what I started to say at the beginning—*I don't have a future*. I can sit around and cry about that for a while, but then I have to move on and ask, what am I going to do about it? And there's not much I can do. What career can I start at my age? How do I retrieve all those years spent managing a family?

And another somewhat younger woman said:

> The worst poverty is the poverty of the spirit that sets in when you've been economically poor too long, and it gets to the point where you can't see things turning around.

To avoid this sense of hopelessness, a majority of the sixty women tried not to think about the future and made only short-term plans:

> I learned very quickly that I couldn't think too far into the future or I'd drive myself crazy. The future became,"What will I do next month?" I learned I had to go day to day and just do the best I could. That's been my major technique for coping, and I learned it right away. I've built up some retirement and Social Security through work, thank heavens. But I have to live right now. I just can't think about the future. The worse that can happen is that the state will take care of me, and I'll end up in a crappy old folks' home. But I don't think about that.

Ten of the sixty women—a unique subgroup—said they had not experienced serious depression or despair after divorce. But the reasons they gave simply reemphasize the central importance of economic loss in the lives of divorced women. Four of these ten had various sources of income that protected them from poverty and enabled them to work actively toward improving their situation. Two of them were using income from the divorce property settlement to attend graduate school, and they hoped to regain their former standard of living by pursuing professional careers. Two were receiving financial support from their parents while they sought employment and planned for the possible sale of their homes as part of the property settlement. The remaining six said they were generally optimistic *in spite of* their poor economic positions. Like the others, they found the financial hardships imposed by divorce surprising and difficult to handle; they simply found these hardships easier to cope with than the despair they had known in their marriages.

In summary, these women discovered that the most important change brought about by divorce was an immediate economic decline, which for most of them had not been reversible. Despite their economizing efforts and dramatically altered life-styles, many of them continued to lose ground financially. In addition, economic circumstances had a powerful effect on their emotional lives. Only a very few escaped feelings of despair and hopelessness. Most found that economic uncertainties fostered depression, discouragement, and despair, and nearly all said they had endured periods of intense anxiety over the inadequacy of their income and its effects on the well-being of their children. Most of them felt trapped in their present circumstances and said they had no sense of the future.

NOTES

1. Some other studies that show the adverse economic impacts of divorce on women are Duncan and Morgan (1979); Weitzman (1981, 1985); Spanier and Casto (1979); Eisler (1977); Espenshade (1979); Levitan and Belous (1981); U.S. Commission on Civil Rights (1983); McCarthy (1985). An analysis of the University of Michigan's Panel Study of Income Dynamics, a nationally representative and longitudinal study of five thousand families, concludes: "Former husbands are better off than their wives....even after adjusting for these transfers [child support and alimony], husbands are still better off than their wives" (Hampton 1974, p. 169). Another major study found: "It is only the women and children whose standards of living decline even when the father is making payments.... Four in five fathers can live at or above the Intermediate Standard Budget" (Chambers 1979, p. 48).

2. The University of Michigan Panel Study of Income Dynamics found that the economic decline experienced by women after divorce is not temporary (Duncan and Morgan 1974, 1976, 1978, 1979; Hill 1981). Saul Hoffman and James Holmes (1974, p. 24) state: "Even after adjusting for demographic and environmental variables, female-headed families with children were shown to be two and one-half times as likely to be temporarily poor and twice as likely to be persistently poor as similar families headed by married couples." See also Rainwater (1984); Kamerman (1984); Corcoran, Duncan, and Hill (1984); McCarthy (1985).

3. Various studies have found that reduced consumption of both goods and services is a major response by divorced mothers to economic decline; for example, see Hampton (1976); Espenshade (1979); Masnick and Bane (1980). They spend much less than divorced men do on food, recreation, clothing, and discretionary items (Masnick and Bane 1980). According to McCubbin et al. (1980, p. 866), a 1979 General Mills study reports: "in order to cope with inflation, 75 percent of the single-parent families were cutting back on health-related items (medical care, dental care, etc.)."

4. George Masnick and Mary Jo Bane (1980) note that many single-parent families move several times in two or three years. Buehler and Hogan (1980) note that women and their children frequently move to poorer housing in order to economize following divorce.

5. Michael Smith (1980, p. 80) concludes from his analysis of the Panel Study of Income Dynamics that no emotional recovery period is evident: regardless of the number of years since their divorce, divorced women had lower community participation and efficacy, as well as a greater sense of alienation and loss of control over their lives. He states that powerlessness and limited community participation may be viewed as important indicators of the societal conditions with which single parents must cope.

REFERENCES

Buehler, C. and J. Hogan. 1980. "Managerial Behavior and Stress in Families Headed by Divorced Women: A Proposed Framework." *Family Relations* 29(4):525–532.

Chambers, D. 1979. *Making Fathers Pay: The Enforcement of Child Support*. Chicago: University of Chicago Press.

Corcoran, M., G. Duncan, and M. Hill. 1984. "The Economic Fortunes of Women and Children: Lessons from the Panel Study of Income Dynamics." *Signs* 10(2):232–248.

Duncan, G. and J. Morgan (eds.). 1974. *Five Thousand Families*. Vol. 4. Ann Arbor: University of Michigan Press.

———. 1976. *Five Thousand Families*. Vol. 5. Ann Arbor: University of Michigan Press.

———. 1978. *Five Thousand Families*. Vol. 6. Ann Arbor: University of Michigan Press.

———. 1979. *Five Thousand Families*. Vol. 7. Ann Arbor: University of Michigan Press.

Eisler, R. 1977. *Dissolution: No-Fault Divorce, Marriage, and the Future of Women*. New York: McGraw-Hill.

Espenshade, T. 1979. "The Economic Consequences of Divorce." *Journal of Marriage and the Family* 41(3):615–625.

Hamptom, R. 1974. "Marital Disruption: Some Social and Economic Consequences." In *Five Thousand Families*, Vol. 4. Ann Arbor: University of Michigan Press.

Hetherington, E., M. Cox, and R. Cox. 1976. "Divorced Fathers." *The Family Coordinator* 25:417–428.

———. 1979. "The Development of Children in Mother-Headed Families." *The American Family: Dying or Developing*, edited by D. Reiss and H. Hoffman. New York: Plenum.

Hill, M. 1981. "Some Dynamic Aspects of Poverty." In *Five Thousand Families*, vol. 9, edited by G. Duncan and J. Morgan. Ann Arbor:University of Michigan Press.

Hoffman, S. and J. Holmes. 1974. "Husbands, Wives, and Divorce." In *Five Thousand Families*, vol. 4, edited by G. Duncan and J. Morgan. Ann Arbor: University of Michigan Press.

Johnson, W. and M. Minton. 1982. "The Economic Choice in Divorce: Extended or Blended Family?" *Journal of Divorce* 5(1–2):101–113.

Kamerman, S. 1984. "Women, Children, and Poverty: Public Policies and Female-Headed Families in Industrial Countries." *Signs* 10(2):249–271.

Levitan, S. and R. Belous. 1981. *What's Happening to the American Family?* Baltimore, MD: Johns Hopkins University Press.

McCarthy, L. 1985. *The Feminization of Poverty: Report of the Lieutenant Governor's Task Force on the Feminization of Poverty*. Sacramento: State of California.

McCubbin, H., C. Joy, A. Couble, J. Comeau, J. Patterson, and R. Neidlee. 1980. "Family Stress and Coping: A Decade Review." *Journal of Marriage and the Family* 42:855–871.

Masnick, G. and M. Bane. 1980. *The Nation's Families: 1960–1990*. New York: Auburn House.

Pett, M. 1982. "Predictors of Satisfactory Social Adjustment of Divorced Single Parents." *Journal of Divorce* 5(3): 1–17.

Rainwater, L. 1984. "Mothers' Contributions to the Family Money Economy in Europe and the United States." In *Work and Family*, edited by P. Voydanoff. Palo Alto, CA: Mayfield.

Smith, M. 1980. "The Social Consequences of Single Parenthood: A Longitudinal Perspective." *Family Relations* 29(1):75–81.

Spanier, G. and R. Casto. 1979. "Adjustment to Separation and Divorce: An Analysis of Fifty Case Studies." *Journal of Divorce* 2(3):241–253.

U.S. Bureau of the Census. 1985. *Statistical Abstract of the United States, 1985. National Data Book and Guide to Sources*. Washington, DC: U.S. Government Printing Office.

U.S. Commission on Civil RIghts. 1983. *A Growing Crisis: Disadvantaged Women and Their Children*. Washington, DC: U.S. Government Printing Office.

Wallerstein, J. and J. Kelly. 1979. "Children and Divorce: A Review." *Social Work* (November):468–475.

Weiss, R. 1979a. *Going It Alone: The Family Life and Social Situation of the Single Parent*. New York: Basic Books.

———.1979b. "Growing Up a Little Faster: The Experience of Growing Up in a Single-Parent Household." *Journal of Social Issues* 35(4):97–111.

Weitzman, L. 1981. *The Marriage Contract: Spouses, Lovers, and the Law*. New York: Free Press.

———. 1985. *The Divorce Revolution: The Unexpected Social and Economic Consequences for Women and Children in America*. New York: Free Press.

44

Children of Divorce: Report of a Ten-Year Follow-Up of Early Latency-Age Children*

Judith S. Wallerstein

This is a report from a ten-year longitudinal study of responses of parents and their children to separation and divorce. The study, which began in 1971, was designed to explore the experiences of 60 Northern California families whose 131 children were between $2\frac{1}{2}$ and 18 years of age at the time of the decisive separation. This paper provides the first overview of the early latency age children from that sample, as they appeared a decade later.

Earlier papers have presented findings from the ten-year follow-up of two groups of youngsters: the younger group was of 31 children, preschool at the time of initial separation, who have now reached early adolescence; the older group was of 40 youngsters, later latency, pre-adolescent, and adolescent youngsters at that time, who have now reached young adulthood (Wallerstein 1984, 1985). A third paper described the psychological characteristics and circumstances of the parents at the ten-year mark (Wallerstein 1986).

Focus here is on the psychological and social functioning of 38 young people, 16 girls and 22 boys, most of whom were between 6 and 8 years old at the decisive parental separation. At the ten-year follow-up, these children were between 16 and 18 years old and in the last two years of their high school careers, or just beginning college. During these late adolescent years, they confront the critical developmental tasks of separation from their families and the consolidation of the internal psychological structures and identifications that will enable them to undertake the last stretch on their road to young adulthood. Their attitudes toward themselves and their parents, their views on how their lives have been shaped by the divorce and its many-year aftermath in the postdivorce or remarried family, their aspirations and achievements, the extent to which they look ahead with courage and reasonable self-confidence, and the extent to which their present relationships and their hopes for future intimacy, love, and marriage are dimmed by foreboding—all fall within this present inquiry. The relevance of such broad-based questions has been demonstrated by recent research on the enduring effects of psychic trauma, findings that showed that effects which may not be visible immediately, or even in later specific behavior or symptoms, may, in fact, profoundly influence an individual's subsequent guiding conceptions and personal expectations of the world (Horowitz 1976; Terr 1983).

*Wallerstein, Judith S. 1987. "Children of Divorce: Report of a Ten-Year Follow-Up of Early Latency Age Children." *American Journal of Orthopsychiatry* 37(2):199–211. Copyright © 1987 the American Orthopsychiatric Association, Inc. Reproduced by permission.

I have noted earlier some of the complex problems involved in tracking the enduring influences of early trauma and differentiating these from developmental and situational factors operative at the time of study (Lewis and Wallerstein, "Divorce-Specific"; Wallerstein 1984). Such issues have special relevance to this age group because these young people, standing at the threshold of separation from their families, will inevitably face tasks in the normal course of their own later adolescent development that will recall the critical themes of the marital rupture that they had faced in early latency.

Initial findings from the same study showed that the children who were in early latency at the time of the marital breakdown were preoccupied with issues of loss and separation: loss of the protective family structure and separation from their fathers. Their profound mourning of these losses, which resembled grief reactions among young children to the death of a parent, was accompanied by intense anxiety that jeopardized their recent achievements in the relatively new, challenging world of school and competitive play. The longing for their fathers appeared to reflect intense needs of the children that were unrelated to any particular qualities of the antecedent father-child relationship. Fathers who had been neglectful, or verbally and physically abusive, were as passionately missed as were fathers who had maintained very good relationships with their children. Rising anger toward the mother and fear of the mother also emerged at this initial period. The mother appeared in the play and fantasy of many of these children, especially of the boys, as a powerful and potentially dangerous figure who needed to be appeased or kept at a distance because, from the child's perspective, she had succeeded in vanquishing the powerful father and driving him from the family turf. The children's distress extended to almost every domain of their lives; more than half suffered immediate disruption in their learning and peer relationships at school that lasted the better part of a year. The most distressed responses occurred among the boys and among a significant subgroup of girls whose attachment to the father remained intense and eroticized (Kelly and Wallerstein 1986).

The gravity of these earlier responses, and the fact that these youngsters stand once again at a point in their development where they must confront similar issues of entry into a wider world, but now within the context of the divorced or remarried family, raise certain questions. Will the replaying of earlier themes of separation and loss that inevitably accompany the final phase of adolescence, combined with the need to consolidate identifications (including sexual identifications) in order to move out of the family orbit, revive early anxieties and reopen old conflicts? Will these reverberations from the past, in turn, reinforce the already formidable anxieties of the present? If so, adolescent separation and the demands of the competitive and sexual society of young adulthood that loom ahead may well be especially difficult and painful for these youngsters and for their parents. In a recent paper, I have reported difficulties associated with the issue of separation from the perspective of the unmarried custodial parent who has come to depend on the continuing presence of the adolescent youngsters within the household (Wallerstein 1986). It is possible that certain developmental stages are more difficult for children, as well as for parents, in the divorced and the remarried family. The divorced or remarried family may be less hospitable to certain changes, not because of lesser concern but because, as a family structure, it is more rigid and more vulnerable. It thus has greater difficulty marshalling the strength needed to support the youngsters in their struggle without jeopardizing the delicate balance between the formerly married or newly married couple, or threatening the psychological equilibrium of the individual parent.

METHOD AND SAMPLE

Methods and population of this longitudinal study of 60 families have been reported in earlier publications, along with findings from the assessments at baseline, one year, five years, and ten years (Lewis and Wallerstein, "Issues"; Wallerstein 1984, 1985; Wallerstein and Kelly 1980). At the ten- year mark, 54 (90%) of the original 60 families were located, including 113 children (50 boys and 63 girls). Semistructured interviews of several hours' duration were conducted separately with each family member. These interviews were supplemented with questionnaires for children and parents. Three of the five clinicians who participated in the initial study and in the first and second follow-ups, at the 18-month mark and the five-year mark respectively, interviewed the same youngsters whom they had seen at each of the earlier checkpoints.

One of the earliest papers from this study described the experiences of 26 children who were 7 to 8 years old at the separation and at the one-year mark (Kelly and Wallerstein 1976). Of the 38 children discussed in this paper who were between ages 16 to 18 at the ten-year follow-up, 21 are from that original group of 26. Three of the original group could not be located for interview at the ten-year mark. Because of the variability in the length of time after the divorce when these young people were located and contacted, two others, by the ten-year mark, were older than the 18-year upper age limit of the present group, and are therefore not included in this analysis. Also due to the variable elapsed times between the divorce and the follow-up, the present group includes eleven children who were between 5 and 6 years of age, and six who were between ages 8 and 9, at the time of the separation. The mean length of time since the separation was 10.9 years, with a range of 9.6 to 13.1 years.

FINDINGS

Custody

Following the separation, all of the children were in the legal and physical custody of the mothers. There were only three changes in legal custody during the entire ten-year period. The changes in physical residence were, by contrast, striking. During their adolescence, over 40 percent of these young people, a few more boys than girls, went to live with their fathers. Most stayed a year and then returned to their mothers' homes. But nine of the 38 youngsters (four boys and five girls), approximately one fourth of the entire group, remained in their fathers' homes. These moves to the fathers' homes had many psychological determinants explored later on in this paper.

Visiting

Most of the fathers were geographically accessible to their children. One third of the youngsters lived in the same county as their fathers; another third lived one or two hours away by car. The remainder had fathers who lived at a greater distance, but only 10 percent of the youngsters had fathers who resided out of the state. Access to their fathers was open for almost all of these youngsters, despite continuing bitterness between a substantial minority of the parents (Wallerstein 1986). Only four youngsters had no contact at all with their fathers; for three, this absence reflected the indifference or unavailability of the father; for one, it reflected the mother's continuing prohibition.

Over one third of these young people visited their fathers regularly, one or more times a month. Three boys within this group visited several times a week. A greater number, 57 percent of the girls and 44 percent of the boys, had irregular visits, less than six times a year. The remaining three boys and one girl visited only during school vacations. These findings stand in sharp contrast to those reported in a national study, which indicated that approximately 40 percent of a sample of 13- to 15-year-olds had not been visited at all by their fathers during the preceding five years (Furstenberg and Nord 1982).

The psychological stability of the father was a significant factor in the visiting pattern between father and child. This parallels the finding at the five-year follow-up that the psychological stability of the father was a critical factor in the maintenance of child support payments (Wallerstein and Huntington 1983). Fathers who had been diagnosed in initial and subsequent interviews as severely neurotic, or as character-disordered, were likely to be capricious in their visiting, while the more psychologically intact fathers, whose own lives were stable, tended to visit their children on a regular basis. Nevertheless, it should be noted that some of the more frequently visiting fathers were disturbed men whose psychological dependence on their children, and sometimes on their former wives, had continued over many years. In most instances, visits were arranged mutually by father and adolescent. In a full one–quarter of the cases, however, the entire initiative for contact with the father rested with the youngster.

School Performance

The overwhelming majority of these young people (89 percent) were still in school, almost all of them full-time. Approximately half were in their last two years of high school. One fifth were living at home and attending the local junior college, and another one fifth were enrolled in full-time college programs and living outside the family home. Only four were not in school at all: two of the young men had dropped out during their last two years of high school, and two young women ended their educations with a high school diploma.

Half of these young people were doing well academically. An additional one quarter were doing "C" level work; the school work of the remaining one quarter was poor or failing. Many of the youngsters who were doing mediocre or poor school work were capable of greater achievement. Several of the boys who had been identified earlier as gifted children were poor students during their high school years. We estimated that 40% of the entire sample were underachieving to a significant degree. A similar pattern of shallow aspirations emerged with respect to career choices. Although many of these young people had not yet formulated their plans, several youngsters who surely could have aimed for professional careers were putting aside the idea of college in favor of semi-skilled jobs.

Employment

Three quarters of these young people held part-time jobs. Close to 30 percent of them could be regarded as substantially, if not entirely, self-sufficient economically and another 42 percent had achieved some degree of self-sufficiency. One boy was entirely self-supporting while, at the same time, he attended school full-time. Many expressed the importance to them of financial independence and their awareness of longstanding concerns about money. Ann told us, "I hate being dependent. I will never be dependent on anyone."

Financial Support During College

Despite the high professional status of many of the fathers, economic support and encouragement for these young people during their college years was often absent (Wallerstein and Corbin 1986). Of the youngsters in two-year and four-year college programs, only half received financial help that was appropriate to their fathers' economic means. Among the remainder, many were entirely unsupported by fathers who were well able to provide for them. In these families, only one of the mothers had remarried, and all but one of these mothers were employed at low-paying jobs. The interaction between fathers and children around issues of support after the youngster had reached the age of 18 was always painful for these young people. Typically, they refrained altogether from asking for assistance, hoping that their fathers would be sensitive to their needs. No single youngster took the position that support was his or her right although, given the professional status of the fathers and the socioeconomic standards of the families, economic support would have been taken for granted had the family remained intact.

Feelings of disappointment, bewilderment, and low-keyed resentment toward the fathers were widespread among the college-age youngsters, but overt anger was rare, even when the father was affluent. Charles, the son of a very wealthy architect, told us in sad confusion that he was really worried about money during his forthcoming freshman year at college. He vaguely felt that his father was letting him down by not helping him at all, financially. He did not really understand it, since he knew that his father made a great deal of money.

Psychological and Social Adjustment

Age differences in the psychological and social adjustment of these young people emerged as critical throughout the entire sample at the ten-year mark. Overall, this group and the next older group of youngsters (those who had been in later latency and early adolescence at the breakup and were 19 to 23 years old at the ten-year mark) (Wallerstein 1985), were significantly less well adjusted on a wide range of measures than were the youngest group of children who had been preschoolers at that earlier time and who were presently 11 to 15 years old (Wallerstein 1984).

Sex differences were important. A major scale was developed to assess psychological and social adjustment. It combined the clinician's assessment of the status of the individual's internal functioning (psychological integration, affective stability, strength of the defensive structure, and reality judgement) with overall competence (the way in which the individual child functioned in the various domains of his or her environment, including school and social relationships); on this scale, sex differences were striking (Lewis and Wallerstein, "Divorce Specific"). Of the 16 girls in this group, six were judged to be doing well with respect to psychological intactness and their functioning in their environment; six fell into an uneven category; and four were doing poorly in both regards. Of the 22 boys in this age group, eight were judged to be doing well, three fell into the mixed category, and 11 were doing poorly. Thus, fully one half of the boys, as compared with only one quarter of the girls, were judged to be doing poorly.

What distinguished these young adolescents from the next older and younger age groups in the study was that their profound unhappiness about current relationships and haunted concerns regarding future ones were masked by their overall conformity to social expectations. Among boys, serious delinquency, drug use, alcoholism, and truancy were all relatively low, especially when compared with the much higher incidence of serious trouble with the law among the young men in the next older age group in the study (Wallerstein 1985). Episodic recklessness among the girls, however, was a concern. Forty percent of the girls had three or more boyfriends during their adolescent years; one quarter of the girls had abortions between the ages of 13 and 16, and one girl had a second abortion. In fact, the incidence of abortion during early adolescent years was highest in this age group. At the same time, moderate to clinical levels of depression were highest in this group. There were more suicide attempts between the ages of 13 and 16 than in the other groups. One girl whom we had assessed as acutely depressed and referred for immediate treatment, died shortly thereafter in an "accident" that had all the earmarks of suicide.

There were few differences between boys and girls in their attitudes towards the divorce or their anxieties regarding their present and future relationships. Significant differences emerged, however, in the capacity to seek out and make use of a range of relationships and resources within the environment. Girls were much more likely to reach out to peers, to develop and rely on their friendships, to engage in extracurricular activities, to pursue a range of interests, to become more quickly engaged in dating and sexual relationships. Girls were significantly more likely, as well, to draw psychological support from their mothers. By contrast, a majority of the boys showed considerable caution and holding back from heterosexual relationships and a reserve in their feelings that shaded into emotional constriction, rigidity, and severe loneliness for a significant subgroup.

Memories of the Marital Rupture

Unlike the preschool children, now in early adolescence, who had largely repressed their experiences from that time, only a few youngsters (14 percent) in the original latency group claimed at the ten-year mark to have no memory of the separation (Wallerstein 1984). They did not suffer from the intrusive, sometimes overwhelming images from the past that the older group reported (Wallerstein 1985). However, more than half of the group retained vivid, if somewhat fragmented memories, usually painfully recalled scenes of physical violence between the parents. Often, after recounting a violent scene, the youngster described with sadness the subsequent departure of the father from the home, as if these events formed the tragic, inexorable sequence of divorce: the origin was marital conflict; the outcome was loss of the father, not relief from conflict. Harry told us:

> Fighting is what I remember. I tried to get between them, but Dad would throw me down. I just remember Dad leaving home. It hurt me not to see Dad except a couple of times a week.

Sarah said:

> I remember being sad because they fought. I would wake up and hear glasses being thrown. I was scared at night, but I did not want Dad to go. I wanted him to be around for us.

Youngsters who were doing well in the present were likely to have dimmer, more limited memories. Their statements often reflected conscious efforts at suppression and emotional distancing. Betty told us: "About the divorce. I have blocked it out. I have no idea what caused it and I do not like to think about it." Nora, who was also doing well, said: "All I remember is that my dad moved to a hotel."

Attitudes and Feelings Toward Past and Present

In their unhappiness, their loneliness, their sense of neediness and deprivation, the youngsters now 16 to 18 years old suffered more than the other age groups in the study. The divorce was regarded as the central experience in their lives by over half of these young people, who spoke longingly of their lives in the intact, predivorce family. Some volunteered that their difficulties had escalated through the years, indicating that they had been more protected from parental quarrels when they were younger. An overwhelming majority, boys and girls alike, spoke wistfully of their longing for an ideal intact family. These feelings were unrelated to their judgment of the wisdom of their parents' decision to divorce. The majority, in fact, regarded their parents as incompatible, the divorce as irreversible, and the relationship between the parents as beyond repair. Nevertheless, they often explained a change in one parent's mood as a reflection of a major change in the other parent's life, as if it were self-evident that strong, invisible ties between the divorced parents had lasted over the years or as if their view of their parents, as a couple, had endured. Tom told us, "Mom's been bitchy since Dad's new wife had a baby."

Their sense of powerlessness in the face of the major event in their lives was striking. This was conveyed along with a sad, somewhat stoic acceptance of their experience. Alice said:

> I don't know if divorce is ever a good thing, but if it is going to happen, it is going to happen. If one person wants out, he wants out. It can't be changed. I get depressed when I think about it. I get sad and angry when I think about what happened to me.

The recurring theme was loss of the father, even though there seemed to be almost no link between the father for whom they yearned and the actual father, to whom access was entirely open and who in many instances lived nearby. When asked if she had gained anything from the divorce, Olga said emphatically, "Absolutely no." Asked what she had lost, the girl responded, "My father. Being close to my dad. I wish it were different, but it is not going to change. It is too late." Olga's father lived nearby and she saw him monthly. He paid little attention to her at these meetings, preferring his son.

Larry's father also lived close by. The boy and his mother had asked the father to take Larry into his home, but the father had refused. Larry told us:

> Life has been worse for me than for other kids because I was a divorced kid. Most of my friends had two parents and those kids got the things that they wanted. Not having a dad is tough for me. I wanted to live with him but he would not take me. He never told me why.

Karl, who lived with his mother and stepfather and two older sisters, said, "I needed a father, not because I like him more, but because there was no one in the home like me. That's my true feeling." We were interested that Karl did not include his stepfather in his perspective of someone who would be like him within the home.

Perhaps one clue to the distress expressed by so many youngsters was their sense of the unavailability of the working mother. It was not unusual for the youngster to equate the mother's unavailability with uninterest or rejection. Chuck said that his mother did not care for him. She was busy working all the time. "She does not pay any attention to me. I want her to be a mom with an interest in what I am doing with my life, not just a machine that shells out money." It would appear that the longing for the father may reflect not only feelings about the father, but also the feeling so many of these young people had of being rejected by a busy, working mother who was not available to them, and the overall sense that so many shared of not having been provided with the close support that they wished for and needed from their family during childhood and adolescent years. It is possible that, in the same way that the youngest group of children at the ten-year mark were preoccupied with the idealized family of their fantasies, these youngsters are preoccupied with the lost father as the symbolic equation of the divorce. Their preoccupation with the father, unrelated to the actual quality of their father-child relationships, repeats their responses of ten years earlier.

Finally, although resentment was surely implicit in many of the statements of these young people, overt expressions of anger toward parents, especially toward fathers, was uncommon. One of the distinguishing characteristics of this entire group, particularly the boys, was the muting of anger. This psychological stance parallels the limited acting out among these young people. Speaking of his father, who refused to support his college career unless the boy came to live with him and the new stepmother, even though the tension in the remarriage was very high, Andy said:

> He won't change. He won't allow anything else to come into his mind. I just learn to accept it. Sometimes I feel sorry for him. He really needs a wife. He and his new wife just don't get along.

Sometimes the need to avoid anger pushed youngsters into far-fetched apologies for their parents. Kelly told us how angry her mother had been when Kelly asked to live with her father. She had been ostracized by her mother; she was even asked to eat at a separate table following her request. Kelly confided, "I can't really blame my mom completely. She stayed up all night to take care of me when I was one year old."

Attitudes Toward the Future

Most of these young people believe in romantic love. With few exceptions, they expect to fall in love, marry, and have children of their own. Like most of the other young people in this study, their values are conservative. They do not regard the divorced family as a new social norm. They consider divorce a solution that reflects marital failure, one that should be used only as a last resort when there are children. They agree on divorce when there is physical violence in the family. They believe, on balance, that divorce helps parents, not children. Their values include fidelity and life-long commitment. It is painful for them to acknowledge what many of them know, that one of their parents had been unfaithful during the marriage. Anger at a parent whom they know to have been promiscuous can be very bitter. Describing her father's many affairs, Betty said tartly,

> Some day he won't be able to cultivate all those 21-year-old girls and life will catch up with him. He is going to be an old man and he will be punished.

Close to two thirds of these young people were apprehensive about the possibility of disruption in their own future marriages. Girls were especially fearful that their marriages would not endure. A recurrent theme was a sense of vulnerability and fear of being hurt by romantic relationships. Talking about the future, Brenda said,

> It is hard to make a commitment. All the work and all the trust that is involved. I don't want to get married and do what my mom did. I don't know if marriage will

last or not. How can you be sure that marriage will last? I hate to think of what will happen. I am afraid. I am afraid of being hurt. That's why I am a loner.

One half of the boys and girls were fearful of being betrayed, not only in their future, but in their present relationships as well. Of all the age groups, these youngsters were most worried about repeating their parents' relationships patterns and mistakes. Nancy said, "I always find myself attracted to guys who treat you bad." Maureen said, "A problem I have is not being able to show my feelings. I am afraid that they might get stepped on. Once in a relationship, I feel that I will be afraid of losing it if I get attached." Teresa said, "There is a lonely, shaky part of me. I am afraid of what happened to my parents happening to me."

A repeated fear among the boys, somewhat different from the fear of betrayal that the girls emphasized, was their fear of being unloved. Zachary said, "The divorce made me cautious of my relationships. Whenever I meet a girl, I have the unconscious feeling that when she gets to know me she will not love me."

A substantial minority of these young people, however, felt that they were but little influenced by their parents' failures and were relatively confident about the future. Several sought role models elsewhere in order to build their expectations on a solid ground. Barbara told us that she had selected her grandparents and their long-lasting marriage as the model for her future plans.

I look at my grandparents who have been married 40 years. I don't look at divorce. It does not cross my mind. I don't think, if I got married, I would get a divorce. I don't worry about losing relationships.

Several young people told of their pleasure with the intact families of their boyfriends or girlfriends and their reassurance in finding examples of stable, happy marriages. Susan told us,

My boyfriend has a family and I love his family. His parents have been married a long time. They are Irish. The kids all live at home. It is fun to be around them. I am always over there.

Independence

The forthcoming move toward independence created a great deal of anxiety in these young people. Although many, in accord with Weiss' observations (1984), spoke proudly of their independence as a positive outcome of their parents' divorce, their behavior was often discrepant with their pronouncements. Mary told us "Nobody helped me. Just my own determination and my friends." She had learned from a soccer accident that, "If you want to play, you play in pain." Diana said, "The outcome of the divorce was that to survive I had to be independent." Others told us how they had learned to solve problems on their own. Yet, although most of them were employed at least part-time and taking responsibility for themselves to a high degree, few spoke of *wanting* to establish themselves independently, and only three of these young people had left home to live on their own. Several of the youngsters who spoke bravely of their independence had suffered intensely during their freshman year at college and sought to return home.

A dream of Katherine's, which occurred during her freshman year at an out-of-town college, reveals some of the difficulties faced by these young people who were attempting to establish independence at a time when their own insecurities and need for parenting dominated their thoughts. Katherine told us,

> I had a dream at mid-term. In real life, I told a friend that the first thing I would do when I would get home was that I would hug my dad, and that would be proof that he loved me, and that I loved him. In the dream, I came home and my dad wasn't there. The person who met me said. "Haven't you forgotten that your dad is dead?"

Katherine said that what disturbed her most was not that her dad was dead, but that there was no one to hug her, and she had worried so much about getting home for a hug.

It appears that independent behavior, and the pride young people feel in it, can mask an intense hunger for the further nurturance and powerful feelings of not being sufficiently nurtured to make it on one's own without "playing in pain."

Father-Child Relationships

Whether they visited regularly or sporadically, whether they lived nearby or in a distant state, fathers remained a significant psychological presence in the lives of these young people. This was so despite the fact that well over half of their growing up years had been spent in the divorced family, mostly in the custody of the mother, and despite the fact that almost half had lived for many years with a stepfather. Furthermore, there is evidence in our findings that the need for the father as a benign image, if not a real presence, increased during the adolescent years. Donna, aged 16, said, "I never felt that I needed a dad until this year."

It is important, however, not to confuse the yearning that so many of these young people expressed for a closer relationship with the father with the actual quality of these father-child relationships at the ten-year mark. At that time, visiting patterns were mostly disappointing and had been so for many years. Even among that minority of the youngsters who were visited regularly, some had fathers who showed so little interest or initiative during the visits that these contacts were experienced as rejections. Only a minority, 25 percent of the girls and 30 percent of the boys, enjoyed adequate or good relationships with their fathers. Over half of the group suffered intense feelings of rejection. Yet, with all of this disappointment, most of these youngsters expressed a great deal of affection for their fathers, along with compassion for their failings as parents.

We were interested to find significant links between the relationship with the father and the overall psychological adjustment of boys. Frequency of visiting was unrelated to the level of psychological functioning in boys or girls. But the quality of the father-child relationship was significantly related to good or poor psychological outcome among boys, though not among girls. Poor overall adjustment at the ten-year mark in boys was significantly associated with low self-esteem, poor academic achievement, weak aspirations, and feelings of rejection by the father. At the other end of the spectrum, good psychological functioning was significantly connected with feeling accepted by the father and with an adequate, or better than adequate, father-son relationship. Thus, a boy's perceptions of his father's feeling toward him, and his need for affirmation and encouragement from his father, appeared to be of critical significance at this time.

Several subgroups particularly gravitated toward the father during adolescence. Their overtures were often undertaken with great trepidation and their vulnerability to rejection at these times was striking and often not recognized by either parent.

Disappointment often led to bitterness and great sorrow. One girl became preoccupied with thoughts of suicide following her return from a visit with her indifferent father.

One subgroup among the boys suffered repeated rejections by their fathers, often rejections alternating with invitations. The consequences for this group were tragic. There was only limited evidence of a son's ability to disengage from a capricious relationship with the parent. Paradoxically, the more capricious and rejecting the father, the more intense was the admiration of the child and the more powerful the child's efforts at identification. In fact, identification with the rejecting father, especially one who had been neglectful, abusive and demeaning to the mother, was an all-too-common solution that repeated the phenomenon we had observed at early latency when the same youngsters, as despairing little boys, donned articles of clothing that belonged to the absent father and, in full identification with his role, hurled insults at their distressed mothers.

Unfortunately, the rejection by the father at adolescence had even more devastating effects on the development of these boys, who felt trapped, hurt, and humiliated by their fathers. Dora captured this theme in her family when she confided, "My brothers are just like my father—the anger, the violence, the loss of control." The boys fully identified with the father's demeaning view of women. They were fearful of regressing into the mother's orbit, and they seemed unable to find within themselves sufficient resourcefulness to generate goals and move ahead on their own. Larry was a gifted 17-year-old, who appeared to be drifting aimlessly. Speaking as if the divorce had happened only yesterday, he told us,

> My mom *is* responsible for pushing my dad out of the house and out of my life. I have never forgiven her for this. She is good at getting on my nerves, just the way she got on Dad's nerves.

Larry described his increasingly infrequent contact with his father. On one occasion, he told us, his father telephoned when Larry had been "really drunk" and threatened to "come over and kick [my] rear end off." Larry smiled at this prospect and continued,

> I have a drinking problem. I worry about that. I drink more than my dad did when he was a kid. I drink because it helps me solve my problems. Last week, I broke

up with my girlfriend and I got thoroughly bombed. I think I am probably going to live my life a lot like my dad.

Asked if there were any other parts of his father that he saw in himself, he replied,

Yes, in my relationships with girls. I get angry with them and I want to slap them, or hit them. Once, I hit my girlfriend in the face.

His bitterness about his father's erratic attentions to him often played itself out in aggression toward the women in his family. Once, during Larry's adolescence when his father failed to show up, as promised, at an important school function in which Larry was a participant, the boy became extremely agitated and physically attacked his sister.

For Larry, as well as for other boys who were caught up in an identification with the disturbed parent, the divorce had failed. Though the divorce may indeed have benefited one or both parents by providing the legal and geographical separation that enabled them to restructure their own lives, it failed to separate boys like Larry from their internal need to identify with the abusive father. These identifications have, in fact, been newly infused at adolescence by the boys' developmentally governed needs to consolidate their masculine identity. They have also been strengthened by the unfortunate vicissitudes of the postdivorce father-son relationship and by the intense anxiety felt by these boys at being left with the "demeaned women." The entire psychological constellation at the close of adolescence appears to repeat the boys' experiences at the marital rupture, ten years earlier, but with more grave and lasting consequences.

A range of complex motivations led these young people to turn to their fathers at this developmental stage. Another subgroup consisted of boys whose ties to their mothers had been close and protective over many years. They now sought a closer relationship and identification with their fathers to facilitate the psychological separation from the mother and the transition to manhood. The relationship with the father has an enormous potential value for the boy at this time: it can provide an identification figure and a relationship that can encourage the boy to undertake the first slippery steps towards independence. Where the father failed, in reality, to meet the boy's needs for a benign and virtuous figure for identification, it was not uncommon for the boy to invent the father image that he needed.

Jim's father had sought divorce after many years of infidelity and frequent absences from the family. The mother had opposed the divorce out of her intense love for her husband and her anxiety at being left with three children to care for. Jim had been very close to his mother for many years and treated her with unfailing love and kindness. He told us when he was twelve years old, "I stuck with Mom and tried to help her because Dad left her all alone." At age 17, the boy startled us with an entirely new version of his history. He said,

I never could understand how Dad could marry Mom, after she forced him to leave the East Coast and move out here. I still have not figured it out. Maybe Mom does not like men. I worried about whether Mom is gay, because she did not like my Dad, or me. My Dad and I have become very good friends. He is like me, and he is honest with me and tells me both sides of the story.

A third subgroup of youngsters who gravitated towards the father included those who were living with a psychologically deteriorating mother, or who were experiencing serious conflicts in their relationships. Some went in search of a more permissive household. Those who left the mother's home often ran the gauntlet of her anger and humiliation; the move was rarely easy, for parent or child. At the opposite end, the father who received them was often unprepared for the responsibility of an adolescent, especially one "in flight." The new situation often represented a great challenge and, when successful, improved circumstances for both parent and child, and reflected the resourcefulness and capacity for psychological growth of both. We were interested to find that although it has been argued that the child in the divorced family lacks the buffering presence of the other parent, in a significant number of instances (one fourth of the group) these youngsters had been successful in their turn to the father for the help that they needed. Both parent and youngster profited from the second chance in their renewed relationship.

Edward, who had lived for years with a disturbed mother, told us,

There was yelling and screaming every day. I had to leave because there was no harmony in the house. [Since he has left, he has had] some sad realizations, having to do with the whole concept of what a mother is and should be. I started to realize that I was not an extension of my mom. That I was my own person. My mom is dominant and has a hard time accepting that a person has other things in their lives besides their mother. My dad is loving and caring, but he has been disconnected in the past. He has not grown up, and he had some growing up to do since the divorce, but he came to see that he wanted to be with the kids, not just every weekend, not just a "sugar daddy." My dad is very valuable to me. He is a good and generous man. He is a loving and caring friend. He is proud of me, and I love him very much.

Edward was doing very well.

CONCLUSIONS

This is the fourth report from a ten-year longitudinal study of 131 children from 60 divorcing families in Northern California. Findings have been presented regarding 38 young people, 16 boys and 22 girls, who were 16–18 years old at the ten-year follow-up and who had experienced marital rupture during their early latency years. Most of these young people are in school full-time, live at home, hold part-time jobs, and are law-abiding. Most have remained in the legal and physical custody of their mothers. The one quarter who now reside with their fathers made the changeover during their adolescent years.

Feelings of sadness, of neediness, of a sense of their own vulnerability, were expressed by the majority of these young people. Although two thirds of their lives have been spent in the divorced or remarried family, they spoke sorrowfully of their loss of the intact family and the consequent lack of opportunity for a close relationship with the father. They spoke wistfully of the more nurturing, protective environment that they envision in intact families. Anxieties about relationships with the opposite sex, marriage, and personal commitments ran very high. A central concern was fear of betrayal in relationships, both present and future, and of being hurt and abandoned. Although few differences were noted between boys and girls in attitudes toward the divorce and anxieties about the future, the girls seemed more able at this developmental stage to draw sustenance from their social relationships and from their relationships with their custodial mothers. Girls were more likely to become involved in dating and sexual relationships. Boys were far more likely to be lonely and to hold back in their relationships with girls. They showed more reserve, even constriction, in their capacity to feel or to express affection and anger. Half of the boys and one fourth of the girls were considered poorly adjusted and at high risk at the time of the ten-year follow-up.

Although, for the majority, relationships with the father were poor, the psychological significance of the father had persisted and appeared to have gained importance during the adolescent years for both sexes, but especially for the boys. Frequency of visiting with the father was not related to psychological outcome in boys or girls, but the quality of the relationship between father and son was significantly linked to both good and poor adjustment in boys. During adolescent years, a significant subgroup of boys and girls left troubled or unrewarding relationships with mothers to live with fathers under circumstances that were more suitable to their needs. A second subgroup of boys who had close ties with the mother also sought closer contact with the father at adolescence, in or outside his home, in order to facilitate the psychological separation from the mother and the move towards greater independence. Another subgroup of boys was unable to disengage from an intense, negative identification with an abusive, rejecting parent. These identifications appeared to have been strengthened and consolidated during adolescence by the impact of the adolescent boy's intense need for his father and the psychopathological interaction of the father-son relationship over the years. In instances where the mother had been the victim of the father's abuse, she may have benefited greatly from the divorce; but for the son, trapped by the complex dynamics of the identification process with a disturbed father, the divorce had failed.

Separation from the divorced family and transition into young adulthood is especially painful for these young people. They are burdened by intense worries about failure in their present and future relationships, by their sense of having been insufficiently nurtured and encouraged during their years of growing up, and by an overall sense of their own powerlessness. They have realistic concerns about their college years. In the process of negotiating their important steps away from the custodial mother and the regressive pull of early relationships, the boys are haunted by their earlier separation from the father at a critical time; they experience a renewed, intense need for his reassuring presence, encouragement and protection. Although it is likely that many of these young men will make the transition to psychological independence successfully, the evidence in these findings is that a significant number will enter adulthood with lowered expectations of themselves and others and that they will suffer psychological conflicts that will impair their capacities for the love and intimacy for which they long. Many will need psychological treatment.

One interesting finding that emerged was that the ebb and flow of the parent-child relationship that exists in the intact family may persist to some extent within the divorced family, despite geographical distances or remarriage, and that young people during their various developmental stages still turn to the appropriate parent for support, regardless of the legal status that divides the family. Thus, the divorced family has retained some capacity to buffer and protect the child if the parent whose help is sought is stable, available, and responsive to the child's need. Failure of that parent to respond appropriately can represent a bitter, even tragic, disappointment.

REFERENCES

Furstenberg, F. and C. Nord. 1982. "The Life Course of Children of Divorce: Marital Disruption and Parental Contact." Presented to the Population Association of America, San Diego, CA.

Horowitz, M. 1976. *Stress Response Syndromes*. New York: Jason Aronson.

Kelly, J. and J. Wallerstein. 1976. "The Effects of Parental Divorce: Experiences of the Child in Early Latency." *American Journal of Orthopsychiatry* 46:20–32.

Lewis, J. and J. Wallerstein. In Press. "Divorce-Specific Assessment of Families." In *The Bio-Psycho-Social Assessment of Children*, edited by C. Kestenbaum. New York: New York University Press.

Lewis, J. and J. Wallerstein. In Press. "Methodological Issues in Longitudinal Research on Divorced Families." In *Advances in Family Intervention, Assessment and Theory*, vol. 4, edited by J. P. Vincent. Greenwich, CT: JAI Press.

Terr, L. 1983. "Chowchilla Revisited: The Effects of Psychic Trauma 4 Years After a School Bus Kidnapping." *American Journal of Psychiatry* 140:1543–1550.

Wallerstein, J. 1954. "Children of Divorce: Preliminary Report of a 10-Year Follow-Up of Young Children." *American Journal of Orthopsychiatry* 54:444–458.

———. 1985. "Children of Divorce: Preliminary Report of a 10-Year Follow-Up of Older Children and Adolescents." *Journal of the American Academy of Child Psychiatry* 24:545–553.

———. 1986. "Women After Divorce: Preliminary Report from a 10-Year Follow-Up." *American Journal of Orthopsychiatry* 56:65–77.

Wallerstein, J. and S. Corbin. 1986. "Father-Child Relationships After Divorce: Child Support and Educational Opportunities." *Family Law Quarterly* 20:109–128.

Wallerstein, J. and D. Huntington. 1983. "Bread and Roses: Nonfinancial Issues Related to Fathers' Economic Support of Their Children Following Divorce." In *The Parental Child Support Obligation: Research, Practice, and Social Policy*, edited by J. Cassetty. Lexington, MA: D. C. Heath.

Wallerstein, J. and J. Kelly. 1980. *Surviving the Breakup*. New York: Basic Books.

Weiss, R. 1979. *Going It Alone*. New York: Basic Books.

45

Remarriage as an Incomplete Institution*

Andrew Cherlin

Sociologists believe that social institutions shape people's behavior in important ways. Gerth and Mills (1953, p. 173) wrote that institutions are organizations of social roles which "imprint their stamps upon the individual, modifying his external conduct as well as his inner life." More recently, Berger and Luckmann (1966) argued that institutions define not only acceptable behavior, as Gerth and Mills believed, but also objective reality itself. Social institutions range from political and economic systems to religion and language. And displayed prominently in any sociologist's catalogue of institutions is a fundamental form of social organization, the family.

The institution of the family provides social control of reproduction and child rearing. It also provides family members with guidelines for proper behavior in everyday family life, and, presumably, these guidelines contribute to the unity and stability of families. But in recent years, sociologists have de-emphasized the institutional basis of family unity in the United States. According to many scholars, contemporary families are held together more by consensus and mutual affection than by formal, institutional controls.

The main source of this viewpoint is an influential text by Ernest Burgess and Harvey Locke which appeared in 1945. They wrote:

> The central thesis of this volume is that the family in historical times has been, and at present is, in transition from an institution to a companionship. In the past, the important factors unifying the family have been external, formal, and authoritarian, as the law, the mores, public opinion, tradition, the authority of the family head, rigid discipline, and elaborate ritual. At present, in the new emerging form of the companionship family, its unity inheres less and less in community pressures and more and more in such interpersonal relationships as the mutual affection, the sympathetic understanding, and the comradeship of its members. (p. vii)

In the institutional family, Burgess and Locke stated, unity derived from the unchallenged authority of the patriarch, which was supported by strong social pressure. But, they argued, with urbanization and the decline of patriarchal authority, a democratic family has emerged which creates its own unity from interpersonal relations.

Many subsequent studies have retained the idea of the companionship family in some form, such as the equalitarian family of Blood and Wolfe (1960) or the symmetrical family of Young and Wilmott (1973). Common to all is the notion that patriarchal authority has declined and sex roles have become less segregated. Historical studies of family life demonstrate that the authority of the husband was

*Cherlin, Andrew. 1978. "Remarriage as an Incomplete Institution." *American Journal of Sociology* 84 (3):634–650. Published by The University of Chicago Press. © 1978 by The University of Chicago.

indeed stronger in the preindustrial West than it is now (see, e.g., Ariès 1962; Shorter 1975). As for today, numerous studies of "family power" have attempted to show that authority and power are shared more equally between spouses (see Blood and Wolfe 1960). Although these studies have been criticized (Safilios-Rothschild 1970), no one has claimed that patriarchal authority is as strong now as the historical record indicates it once was. Even if we believe that husbands still have more authority than wives, we can nevertheless agree that patriarchal authority seems to have declined in the United States in this century.

But it does not follow that institutional sources of family unity have declined also. Burgess and Locke reached this conclusion in part because of their assumption that the patriarch was the transmitter of social norms and values to his family. With the decline of the patriarch, so they believed, a vital institutional link between family and society was broken. This argument is similar to the perspective of Gerth and Mills, who wrote that a set of social roles becomes an institution when it is stabilized by a "head" who wields authority over the members. It follows from this premise that if the head loses his authority, the institutional nature of family life will become problematic.

Yet institutionalized patterns of behavior clearly persist in family life, despite the trend away from patriarchy and segregated sex roles. As others have noted (Dyer and Urban 1958; Nye and Berardo 1973), the equalitarian pattern may be as firmly institutionalized now as the traditional pattern was in the past. In the terms of Berger and Luckmann, most family behavior today is habitualized action which is accepted as typical by all members—that is, it is institutionalized behavior. In most everyday situations, parents and children base their behavior on social norms: parents know how harshly to discipline their children, and children learn from parents and friends which parental rules are fair and which to protest. These sources of institutionalization in the contemporary American family have received little attention from students of family unity, just as family members themselves pay little attention to them.

The presence of these habitualized patterns directly affects family unity. "Habitualization," Berger and Luckmann wrote, "carries with it the important psychological gain that choices are narrowed" (1966, p. 53). With choices narrowed, family members face fewer decisions which will cause disagreements and, correspondingly, have less difficulty maintaining family unity. Thus, institutional support for family unity exists through the routinization of everyday behavior even though the husband is no longer the unchallenged agent of social control.

Nowhere in contemporary family life is the psychological gain from habitualization more evident than in the families of remarried spouses and their children, where, paradoxically, habitualized behavior is often absent. We know that the unity of families of remarriages which follow a divorce is often precarious—as evidenced by the higher divorce rate for these families than for families of first marriages (U.S. Bureau of the Census 1976). And in the last few decades, remarriage after divorce—as opposed to remarriage after widowhood—has become the predominant form of remarriage. In this paper, I will argue that the higher divorce rate or remarriages after divorce is a consequence of the incomplete institutionalization of remarriage after divorce in our society. The institution of the family in the United States has developed in response to the needs of families of first marriages and families of remarriages after widowhood. But because of the complex structure, families of remarriages after divorce that include children from previous marriages must solve problems unknown to other types of families. For many of these problems, such as proper kinship terms, authority to discipline stepchildren, and legal relationships, no institutionalized solutions have emerged. As a result, there is more opportunity for disagreements and divisions among family members and more strain in many remarriages after divorce.

The incomplete institutionalization of remarriage after divorce reveals, by way of contrast, the high degree of institutionalization still present in first marriages. Family members, especially those in first marriages, rely on a wide range of habitualized behaviors to assist them in solving the common problems of family life. We take these behavioral patterns for granted until their absence forces us to create solutions on our own. Only then do we see the continuing importance of institutionalized patterns of family behavior for maintaining family unity.

I cannot provide definitive proof of the hypothesis linking the higher divorce rate for remarriages after divorce to incomplete institutionalization. There is very little quantitative information concerning remarriages. In fact, we do not even know how many stepparents and stepchildren there are in the United States. Nor has there ever been a large, random-sample survey designed with families of remarriages in mind. (Bernard's 1956 book on remarriage, for example, was based on information supplied nonrandomly by third parties.) There are, nevertheless, several studies which do provide valuable information, and there is much indirect evidence bearing on the plausibility of this hypothesis and of alternative explanations. I will review this evidence, and I will also refer occasionally to information I collected through personal interviews with a small, nonrandom sample of remarried couples and family counselors in the northeast. Despite the lack of data, I believe that the problems of families of remarriages are worth examining, especially given the recent increases in divorce and remarriage rates. In the hope that this article will stimulate further investigations, I will also present suggestions for future resesarch.

THE PROBLEM OF FAMILY UNITY

Remarriages have been common in the United States since its beginnings, but until this century almost all remarriages followed widowhood. In the Plymouth Colony, for instance, about one-third of all men and one-quarter of all women who lived full lifetimes remarried after the death of a spouse, but there was little divorce (Demos 1970). Even as late as the 1920s, more brides and grooms were remarrying after widowhood than after divorce, according to estimates by Jacobson (1959). Since then, however, a continued increase in divorce (Norton and Glick 1976) has altered this pattern. By 1975, 84 percent of all brides who were remarrying were previously divorced, and 16 percent were widowed. For grooms who were remarrying in 1975, 86 percent were previously divorced (U.S. National Center for Health Statistics 1977). Thus, it is only recently that remarriage after divorce has become the predominant form of remarriage.

And since the turn of the century, remarriages after divorce have increased as a proportion of all marriages. In 1900 only 3 percent of all brides—including both the single and previously married—were divorced (Jacobson 1959). In 1930, 9 percent of all brides were divorced (Jacobson 1959), and in 1975, 25 percent of all brides were divorced (U.S. National Center for Health Statistics 1977). As a result, in seven million families in 1970 one or both spouses had remarried after a divorce (U.S. Bureau of the Census 1973). Most of this increase is due to the rise in the divorce rate, but some part is due to the greater tendency of divorced and widowed adults to remarry. The remarriage rate for divorced and widowed women was about 50 percent higher in the mid-1970s than in 1940 (Norton and Glick 1976).

At the same time, the percentage of divorces which involved at least one child increased from 46 percent in 1950 to 60 percent in 1974 (U.S. National Center for Health Statistics 1953, 1977). The increase in the percentage of divorces which involve children means that more families of remarriages after divorce now have stepchildren. Although it is not possible with available data to calculate the exact number of families with stepchildren, we do know that in 1970 8.9 million children lived in two-parent families where one or both parents had been previously divorced (U.S. Bureau of the Census 1973). Some of these children— who constituted 15 percent of all children living in two-parent families—were from previous marriages, and others were from the remarriages.

Can these families of remarriages after divorce, many of which include children from previous marriages, maintain unity as well as do families of first marriages? Not according to the divorce rate. A number of studies have shown a greater risk of separation and divorce for remarriages after divorce (Becker, Landes, and Michael 1976; Bumpass and Sweet 1972; Cherlin 1977; Monahan 1958). Remarriages after widowhood appear, in contrast, to have a lower divorce rate than first marriages (Monahan 1958). A recent Bureau of the Census report (U.S. Bureau of the Census 1976) estimated that about 33 percent of all first marriages among people 25–35 may end in divorce, while about 40 percent of remarriages after divorce among people this age may end in divorce. The estimates are based on current rates of divorce, which could, of course, change greatly in the future.[1]

Conventional wisdom, however, seems to be that remarriages are more successful than first marriages. In a small, nonrandom sample of family counselors and remarried couples, I found most to be surprised at the news that divorce was more prevalent in remarriages. There are some plausible reasons for this popular misconception. Those who remarry are older, on the average, than those marrying for the first time and are presumably more mature. They have had more time to search the marriage market and to determine their own needs and preferences. In addition, divorced men may be in a better financial position and command greater work skills than younger, never-married men. (Divorced women who are supporting children, however, are often in a worse financial position—see Hoffman [1977].)

But despite these advantages, the divorce rate is higher in remarriages after divorce. The reported differences are often modest, but they appear consistently throughout 20 years of research. And the meaning of marital dissolution for family unity is clear: when a marriages dissolves, unity ends. The converse, though, is not necessarily true: a family may have a low degree of unity but remain nominally intact. Even with this limitation, I submit that the divorce rate is the best objective indicator of differences in family unity between remarriages and first marriages.

There are indicators of family unity other than divorce, but their meaning is less clear and their measurement is more difficult. There is the survey research tradition, for example, of asking people how happy or satisfied they are with their marriages. The invariable result is that almost everyone reports that they are very happy (see, e.g., Bradburn and Caplovitz 1965; Glenn 1975; Campbell, Converse, and Rodgers 1976). It may be that our high rate of divorce increases the general level of marital satisfaction by dissolving unsatisfactory marriages. But it is also possible that the satisfaction ratings are inflated by the reluctance of some respondents to admit that their marriages are less than fully satisfying. Marriage is an important part of life for most adults—the respondents in the Campbell et al. (1976) national sample rated it second only to health as the most important aspect of their lives—and people may be reluctant to admit publicly that their marriage is troubled.

Several recent studies, nevertheless, have shown that levels of satisfaction and happiness are lower among the remarried, although the differences typically are small. Besides the Campbell et al. study, these include Glenn and Weaver (1977), who found modest differences in marital happiness in the 1973, 1974, and 1975 General Social Surveys conducted by the National Opinion Research Center. They reported that for women, the difference between those who were remarried and those who were in a first marriage was statistically significant, while for men the difference was smaller and not significant. In addition, Renne (1971) reported that remarried, previously divorced persons were less happy with their marriages than those in first marriages in a probability sample of 4,452 Alameda County, California, households. Again, the differences were modest, but they were consistent within categories of age, sex, and race. No tests of significance were reported.

The higher divorce rate suggests that maintaining family unity is more difficult for families of remarriages after divorce. And the lower levels of marital satisfaction, which must be interpreted cautiously, also support this hypothesis. It is true, nevertheless, that many remarriages work well, and that the majority of remarriages will not end in divorce. And we must remember that the divorce rate is also at an all-time high for first marriages. But there is a difference of degree between remarriages and first marriages which appears consistently in research. We must ask why families of remarriages after divorce seem to have more difficulty maintaining family unity than do families of first marriages. Several explanations have been proposed, and we will now assess the available evidence for each.

PREVIOUS EXPLANATIONS

One explanation, favored until recently by many psychiatrists, is that the problems of remarried people arise from personality disorders which preceded their marriages (see Bergler 1948). People in troubled marriages, according to this view, have unresolved personal conflicts which must be treated before a successful marriage can be achieved. Their problems lead them to marry second spouses who may be superficially quite different from their first spouse but are characterologically quite similar. As a result, this theory states, remarried people repeat the problems of their first marriages.

If this explanation were correct, one would expect that people in remarriages would show higher levels of psychiatric symptomatology than people in first marriages. But there is little evidence of this. On the contrary, Overall (1971) reported that in a sample of 2,000 clients seeking help for psychiatric problems, currently remarried people showed lower levels of psychopathology on a general rating scale than persons in first marriages and currently divorced persons. These findings, of course, apply only to people who sought psychiatric help. And it may be, as Overall noted, that the differences emerged because remarried people are more likely to seek help for less serious problems. The findings, nevertheless, weaken the psychoanalytic interpretation of the problems of remarried life.

On the other hand, Monahan (1958) and Cherlin (1977) reported that the divorce rate was considerably higher for people in their third marriages who had divorced twice than for people in their second marriages. Perhaps personality disorders among some of those who marry several times prevent them from achieving a successful marriage. But even with the currently high rates of divorce and remarriage, only a small proportion of all adults marry more than twice. About 10% of all adults in 1975 had married twice, but less than 2% had married three or more times (U.S. Bureau of the Census 1976).

Most remarried people, then, are in a second marriage. And the large number of people now divorcing and entering a second marriage also undercuts the psychoanalytic interpretation. If current rates hold, about one-third of all young married people will become divorced, and about four-fifths of these will remarry. It is hard to believe that the recent increases in divorce and remarriage are due to the sudden spread of marriage-threatening personality disorders to a large part of the young adult population. I conclude, instead, that the psychoanalytic explanation for the rise in divorce and the difficulties of remarried spouses and their children is at best incomplete.[2]

A second possible explanation is that once a person had divorced he or she is less hesitant to do so again. Having divorced once, a person knows how to get divorced and what to expect from family members, friends, and the courts. This explanation is plausible and probably accounts for some of the difference in divorce rates. But it does not account for all of the research findings on remarriage, such as the finding of Becker et al. (1976) that the presence of children from a previous marriage increased the probability of divorce for women in remarriages, while the presence of children from the new marriage reduced the probability of divorce. I will discuss the implications of this study below, but let me note here that a general decrease in the reluctance of remarried persons to divorce would not explain this finding. Moreover, the previously divorced may be more hesitant to divorce again because of the stigma attached to divorcing twice. Several remarried people I interviewed expressed great reluctance to divorce a second time. They reasoned that friends and relatives excused one divorce but would judge them incompetent at marriage after two divorces.

Yet another explanation for the higher divorce rate is the belief that many remarried men are deficient at fulfilling their economic responsibilities. We know that divorce is more likely in families where the husband has low earnings (Goode 1956). Some remarried men, therefore, may be unable to earn a sufficient amount of money to support a family. It is conceivable that this inability to be a successful breadwinner could account for all of the divorce rate differential, but statistical studies of divorce suggest otherwise. Three recent multivariate analyses of survey data on divorce have shown that remarried persons still had a higher probability of divorce or separation, independent of controls for such socioeconomic variables as husband's earnings (Becker et al. 1976), husband's educational attainment (Bumpass and Sweet 1972), and husband's and wife's earnings, employment status, and savings (Cherlin 1977). These analyses show that controlling for low earnings can reduce the difference in divorce probabilities, but they also show that low earnings cannot fully explain the difference. It is possible, nevertheless, that a given amount of income must be spread thinner in many remarriages, because of child-support or alimony payments (although the remarried couple also may be receiving these payments). But this type of financial strain must be distinguished from the questionable notion that many remarried husbands are inherently unable to provide for a wife and children.

INSTITUTIONAL SUPPORT

The unsatisfactory nature of all these explanations leads us to consider one more interpretation. I hypothesize that the difficulties of couples in remarriage after divorce stem from a lack of institutionalized guidelines for solving many common problems of their remarried life. The lack of institutional support is less serious when neither spouse has a child from from a previous marriage. In this case, the family of remarriage closely resembles families of first marriages, and most of the norms for first marriages apply. But when at least one spouse has children from a previous marriage, family life often differs sharply from first marriages. Frequently, as I will show, family members face problems quite unlike those in first marriages—problems for which institutionalized solutions do not exist. And without accepted solutions to their problems, families of remarriages must resolve difficult issues by themselves. As a result, solving everyday problems is sometimes impossible without engendering conflict and confusion among family members.

The complex structure of families of remarriages after divorce which include children from a previous marriage has been noted by others (Bernard 1956; Bohannan 1970; Duberman 1975). These families are expanded in the number of social roles and relationships they possess and also are expanded in space over more than one household. The additional social roles include stepparents, stepchildren, stepsiblings, and the new spouses of noncustodial parents, among others. And the links between the households are the children of previous marriages. These children are commonly in the custody of one parent—usually the mother—but they normally visit the noncustodial parent regularly. Thus they promote communication among the divorced parents, the new stepparent, and the noncustodial parent's new spouse.

Family relationships can be quite complex, because the new kin in a remarriage after divorce do not, in general, replace the kin from the first marriage as they do in a remarriage after widowhood. Rather, they add to the existing kin (Fast and Cain 1966). But this complexity alone does not necessarily imply that problems of family unity will develop. While families of remarriages may appear complicated to Americans, there are many societies in which complicated kinship rules and family patterns coexist with a functioning, stable family system (Bohannan 1963; Fox 1967).

In most of these societies, however, familial roles and relationships are well defined. Family life may seem complex to Westerners, but activity is regulated by established patterns of behavior. The central difference, then, between families of remarriages in the United States and complicated family situations in other societies is the lack of institutionalized social regulation of remarried life in this country. Our society, oriented toward first marriages, provides little guidance on problems peculiar to remarriages, especially remarriages after divorce.

In order to illustrate the incomplete institutionalization of remarriage and its consequences for family life, let us examine two of the major institutions in society: language and the law. "Language," Gerth and Mills (1953, p. 305) wrote, "is necessary to the operations of institutions. For the symbols used in institutions coordinate the roles that compose them, and justify the enactment of these roles by the members of the institution." Where no adequate terms exist for an important social role, the institutional support for this role is deficient, and general acceptance of the role as a legitimate pattern of activity is questionable.

Consider English terms for the roles peculiar to remarriage after divorce. The term "stepparent," as Bohannan (1970) has observed, originally meant a person who replaced a dead parent, not a person who was an additional parent. And the negative connotations of the "stepparent," especially the "stepmother," are well known (Bernard 1956; Smith 1953). Yet there are no other terms in use. In some situations, no term exists for a child to use in addressing a stepparent. If the child calls her mother "mom," for example, what should she call her stepmother? This lack of appropriate terms for parents in remarriages after divorce can have negative consequences for family functioning. In one family I interviewed, the wife's children wanted to call their stepfather "dad," but the stepfather's own children, who also lived in the household, refused to allow this usage. To them, sharing the term "dad" represented a threat to their claim on their father's attention and affection. The dispute caused bad feelings, and it impaired the father's ability to act as a parent to all the children in the household.

For more extended relationships, the lack of appropriate terms is even more acute. At least the word "stepparent," however inadequate, has a widely accepted meaning. But there is no term a child living with his mother can use to describe his relationship to the woman his father remarried after he divorced the child's mother. And, not surprisingly, the rights and duties of the child and this woman toward each other are unclear. Nor is the problem limited to kinship terms. Suppose a child's parents both remarry and he alternates between their households under a joint custody arrangement. Where, then, is his "home"? And who are the members of his "family"? These linguistic inadequacies correspond to the absence of widely accepted definitions for many of the roles and relationships in families of remarriage. The absence of proper terms is both a symptom and a cause of some of the problems of remarried life.

As for the law, it is both a means of social control and an indicator of accepted patterns of behavior. It was to the law, for instance, that Durkheim turned for evidence on the forms of social solidarity. When we examine family law, we find a set of traditional guidelines, based on precedent, which define the rights and duties of family members. But as Weitzman (1974) has shown, implicit in the precedents is the assumption that the marriage in question is a first marriage. For example, Weitzman found no provisions for several problems of remarriage, such as balancing the financial obligations of husbands to their spouses and children from current and previous marriages, defining the wife's obligations to husbands and children from the new and the old marriages, and reconciling the competing claims of current and ex-spouses for shares of the estate of a deceased spouse.

Legal regulations concerning incest and consanguineal marriage are also inadequate for families of remarriages. In all states marriage and sexual relations are prohibited between persons closely related by blood, but in many states these restrictions do not cover sexual relations or marriage between other family members in a remarriage—between a stepmother and a stepson, for example, or between two stepchildren (Goldstein and Katz 1965). Mead (1970), among others, has argued that incest taboos serve the important function of allowing children to develop affection for and identification with other family members without the risk of sexual exploitation. She suggested that current beliefs about incest—as embodied in law and social norms—fail to provide adequate security and protection for children in households of remarriage.[3]

The law, then, ignores the special problems of families of remarriages after divorce. It assumes, for the most part, that remarriages are similar to first marriages. Families of remarriages after divorce, consequently, often must deal with problems such as financial obligations or sexual relations without legal regulations or clear legal precedent. The law, like the language, offers incomplete institutional support to families of remarriages.

In addition, other customs and conventions of family life are deficient when applied to remarriages after divorce. Stepparents, for example, have difficulty determining their proper disciplinary relationship to stepchildren. One woman I interviewed, determined not to show favoritism toward her own children, disciplined them more harshly than her stepchildren. Other couples who had children from the wife's previous marriage reported that the stepfather had difficulty establishing himself as a disciplinarian in the household. Fast and Cain (1966), in a study of about 50 case records from child-guidance settings, noted many uncertainties among stepparents about appropriate role behavior. They theorized that the uncertainties derived from the sharing of the role of parent between the stepparent and the noncustodial, biological parent. Years ago, when most remarriages took place after widowhood, this sharing did not exist. Now, even though most remarriages follow divorce, generally accepted guidelines for sharing parenthood still have not emerged.

There is other evidence consistent with the idea that the incomplete institutionalization of remarriage after divorce may underlie the difficulties of families of remarriages. Becker et al. (1976) analyzed the Survey of Economic Opportunity, a nationwide study of approximately 30,000 households. As I mentioned above, they found that the presence of children from a previous marriage increased the probability of divorce for women in remarriages, while the presence of children from the new marriage reduced the probability of divorce. This is as we would expect, since children from a previous marriage expand the family across households and complicate the structure of family roles and relationships. But children born into the new marriage bring none of these complications. Consequently, only children from a previous marriage should add to the special problems of families of remarriages.[4]

In addition, Goetting (1978a, 1978b) studies the attitudes of remarried people toward relationships among adults who are associated by broken marital ties, such as ex-spouses and the people ex-spouses remarry. Bohannan (1970) has called these people "quasi-kin." Goetting presented hypothetical situations involving the behavior of quasi-kin to 90 remarried men and 90 remarried women who were white, previously divorced, and who had children from previous marriages. The subjects were asked to approve, disapprove, or express indifference about the behavior in each situation. Goetting then arbitrarily decided that the respondents reached "consensus" on a given situation if any of the three possible response categories received more than half of all responses. But even by this lenient definition, consensus was not reached on the proper behavior in most of the hypothetical situations. For example, in situations involving conversations between a person's present spouse and his or her ex-spouse, the only consensus of the respondents was that the pair should say "hello." Beyond that, there was no consensus on whether they should engage in polite conversation in public places or on the telephone or whether the ex-spouse should be invited into the new spouse's home while waiting to pick up his or her children. Since meetings of various quasi-kin must occur regularly in the lives of most respondents, their disagreement is indicative of their own confusion about how to act in common family situations.

Still, there are many aspects of remarried life which are similar to life in first marriages, and these are subject to established rules of behavior. Even some of the unique aspects of remarriage may be regulated by social norms—such as the norms concerning the size and nature of wedding ceremonies in remarriages (Hollingshead 1952). Furthermore, as Goode (1956) noted, remarriage is itself an institutional solution to the ambiguous status of the divorced (and not remarried) parent. But the day-to-day life of remarried adults and their children also includes many problems for which there are no institutionalized solutions. And since members of a household of remarriage often have competing or conflicting interests (Bernard 1956), the lack of consensual solutions can make these problems more serious than they otherwise would be. One anthropologist, noting the lack of relevant social norms, wrote, "the present situation approaches chaos, with each individual set of families having to work out its own destiny without any realistic guidelines" (Bohannan 1970, p. 137).

DISCUSSION AND SUGGESTIONS FOR RESEARCH

The lack of institutionalized support for remarriage after divorce from language, the law, and custom is apparent. But when institutional support for family life exists, we take it for granted. People in first marriages rarely stop to notice that a full set of kinship terms exists, that the law regulates their relationships, or that custom dictates much of their behavior toward spouses and children. Because they pay little attention to it, the institutional nature of everyday life in first marriages can be easily underestimated. But such support contributes to the unity of first marriages despite the decline of the patriarch, who was the agent of social control in past time. Institutional guidelines become manifest not only through the transmission of social pressure by a family head but also through the general acceptance of certain habitual behavior patterns as typical of family life. Since this latter process is an ongoing characteristic of social life, the pure "companionship" family—which, in fairness, Burgess and Locke defined only as an ideal type—will never emerge. We have seen this by examining the contrasting case of remarriage after divorce. In this type of marriage, institutional support is noticeably lacking in several respects, and this deficiency has direct consequences for proper family functioning. I have tried to show how the incomplete institutionalization of remarriage after divorce makes the maintenance of family unity more difficult.

One of the first tasks for future research on remarriage is to establish some basic social demographic facts: what proportion of remarried couples have children present from a previous marriage, what proportion have children present from the remarriage, how many children visit noncustodial parents, how frequent these visits are, and so on. As I mentioned, there is no reliable information on these questions now. The U. S. Bureau of the Census, for example, has not discriminated in most of its surveys between parents and stepparents or between children and stepchildren. Yet until figures are available, we can only guess at the number of families which face potential difficulties because of complex living arrangements.

And if we reinterviewed families of remarriage some time after obtaining this information from them, we could begin to test the importance of institutional support for family unity. It follows from the argument advanced here that the more complex the family's situation—the more quasi-kin who live nearby, the more frequently adults and children interact with quasi-kin, the more likely each remarried spouse is to have children from a previous marriage—the more serious becomes the lack of institutional guidelines. Thus, adults in remarriages with a more complex structure should be more likely to divorce or separate in the future, other things being equal. Also, a more complex structure might increase the financial strain on family members, so their earnings and financial obligations should be carefully assessed.

But beyond collecting this fundamental information, we need to discover, by a variety of means, what norms are emerging concerning remarriage and how they emerge. Content analyses of literature, for example, or close study of changes in the language and the law may be illuminating. Just in the past few years, discussion groups, adult education courses, newsletters, and self-help books for remarried parents have proliferated. Whether these developments are central to the institutionalization of remarriage remains to be seen, but they represent possible sources of information about institutionalization which should be monitored. In addition, detailed ethnographic studies could allow us to uncover emerging patterns of institutionalization among families of remarriages.

And in all these investigations of the institutionalization of remarried life, we must develop a perspective different from that of traditional family research. In much past research—starting with the work of Burgess and others—family sociologists have been concerned primarily with the interpersonal relations of family members, especially of husbands and wives (Lasch 1977). But sociologists' theories—and their research strategies— having assumed, for the most part, that interpersonal relations in families can be accounted for without many references to social institutions. Thus, Burgess and Locke (1945) popularized the notion of the companionship family, whose stability depended largely on what went on within the household. And Locke (1951) measured marital adjustment through a questionnaire which focused largely on such personal characteristics as adaptability and sociability. Yet in order to understand family life—whether in first marriages or remarriages—we must explicitly consider the influences of social institutions on husbands and wives and on parents and children.

We need to know what the institutional links are between family and society which transmit social norms about everyday behavior. That is, we need to know exactly how patterns of family behavior come to be accepted and how proper solutions for family problems come to be taken for granted. And the recent rise in the number of remarriages after divorce may provide us with a natural laboratory for observing this process of institutionalization. As remarriage after divorce becomes more common, remarried parents and their children probably will generate standards of conduct in conjunction with the larger society. By observing these developments, we can improve our understanding of the sources of unity in married—and remarried—life.

NOTES

1. A study by McCarthy (1977), however, suggests that remarriages may be more stable than first marriages for blacks. Using life-table techniques on data from 10,000 women under age 45 collected in the 1973 Survey of Family Growth, McCarthy reported that the probability of separation and divorce during the first 15 years of marriage is lower for blacks in remarriages than in first marriages, but is about 50 percent higher for whites in remarriages than for whites in first marriages.

2. Despite the lack of convincing evidence, I am reluctant to discount this explanation completely. Clinical psychologists and psychiatrists with whom I have talked insist that many troubled married persons they have treated had made the same mistakes twice and were in need of therapy to resolve long-standing problems. Their clinical experience should not be ignored, but this "divorce-proness" syndrome seems inadequate as a complete explanation for the greater problems of remarried people.

3. Bernard (1956) noted this problem in the preface to the reprinted edition of her book on remarriage. "Institutional patterns," she wrote, "are needed to help remarried parents establish relationships with one another conducive to the protection of their children."

4. In an earlier paper (Cherlin 1977), I found that children affected the probability that a woman in a first marriage or remarriage would divorce only when the children were of preschool age. But the National Longitudinal Surveys of Mature Women, from which this analysis was drawn, contained no information about whether the children of remarried wives were from the woman's previous or current marriage. Since the Becker et al. (1976) results showed that his distinction is crucial, we cannot draw any relevant inferences about children and remarriage from my earlier study.

REFERENCES

Ariès, Philippe. 1962. *Centuries of Childhood*. New York: Knopf.

Becker, G., E. Landes, and R. Michael. 1976. "Economics of Marital Instability." Working Paper No. 153. Stanford, CA: National Bureau of Economic Research.

Berger, Peter L. and Thomas Luckmann. 1966. *The Social Construction of Reality*. New York: Doubleday.

Bergler, Edmund. 1948. *Divorce Won't Help*. New York: Harper & Bros.

Bernard, Jessie. 1956. *Remarriage*. New York: Dryden.

Blood, Robert O. and Donald M. Wolfe. 1960. *Husbands and Wives*. New York: Free Press.

Bohannan, Paul. 1963. *Social Antropology*. New York: Holt, Rinehart & Winston.

————. 1970. "Divorce Chains, Households of Remarriage, and Multiple Divorces." Pp. 127–39 in *Divorce and After*, edited by Paul Bohannan. New York: Doubleday.

Bradburn, Norman, and David Caplovitz. 1965. *Reports on Happiness*. Chicago: Aldine.

Bumpass, L. L. and A. Sweet. 1972. "Differentials in Marital Instability: 1970." *American Sociological Review* 37 (December): 754–66.

Burgess, Ernest W. and Harvey J. Locke. 1945. *The Family: From Institution to Companionship*. New York: American.

Campbell, Angus, Philip E. Converse, and Willard L. Rodgers. 1976. *The Quality of American Life*. New York: Russell Sage.

Cherlin, A. 1977. "The Effects of Children on Marital Dissolution." *Demography* 14 (August): 265–72.

Demos, John. 1970. *A Little Commonwealth: Family Life in Plymouth Colony*. New York: Oxford University Press.

Duberman, Lucile. 1975. *The Reconstructed Family*. Chicago: Nelson-Hall.

Dyer, W. G. and D. Urban. 1958. "The Institutionalization of Equalitarian Family Norms." *Journal of Marriage and Family Living* 20 (February): 53–58.

Fast, I. and A. C. Cain. 1966. "The Stepparent Role: Potential for Disturbances in Family Functioning." *American Journal of Orthopsychiatry* 36 (April): 485–91.

Fox, Robin. 1967. *Kinship and Marriage*. Baltimore: Penguin.

Gerth, Hans and C. Wright Mills. 1953. *Character and Social Structure*. New York: Harcourt, Brace & Co.

Glenn, N. 1975. "The Contribution of Marriage to the Psychological Well-Being of Males and Females." *Journal of Marriage and the Family* 37 (August): 594–601.

Glenn, N. and C. Weaver. 1977. "The Marital Happiness of Remarried Divorced Persons." *Journal of Marriage and the Family* 39 (May): 331–37.

Goetting, Ann. 1978a. "The Normative Integration of the Former Spouse Relationship." Paper presented at the annual meeting of the American Sociological Association. San Francisco, September 4–8.

————. 1978b. "The Normative Integration of Two Divorce Chain Relationships." Paper presented at the annual meeting of the Southwestern Sociological Association, Houston, April 12–15.

Goldstein, Joseph, and Jay Katz. 1965. *The Family and the Law*. New York: Free Press.

Goode, William J. 1956. *Women in Divorce*. New York: Free Press.

Hoffman, S. 1977. "Marital Instability and the Economic Status of Women." *Demography* 14 (February): 67–76.

Hollingshead, A. B. 1952. "Marital Status and Wedding Behavior." *Marriage and Family Living* (November): 308–11.

Jacobson, Paul H. 1959. *American Marriage and Divorce*. New York: Rinehart.

Lasch, Christopher. 1977. *Haven in a Heartless World: The Family Beseiged*. New York: Basic.

Locke, Harvey, J. 1951. *Predicting Adjustment in Marriage: A Comparison of a Divorced and a Happily Married Group*. New York: Holt.

McCarthy, J. F. 1977. "A Comparison of Dissolution of First and Second Marriages." Paper presented at the 1977 annual meeting of the Population Association of America, St. Louis, April 21–23.

Mead, M. 1970. "Anomalies in American Postdivorce Relationships." Pp. 107–25 in *Divorce and After*, edited by Paul Bohannan. New York: Doubleday.

Monahan, T. P. 1958. "The Changing Nature and Instability of Remarriages." *Eugenics Quarterly* 5:73–85.

Norton, A. J and P. C. Glick. 1976. "Marital Instability: Past, Present, and Future." *Journal of Social Issues* 32 (Winter): 5–20.

Nye, F. Ivan and Felix M. Berardo. 1973. *The Family: Its Structure and Interaction*. New York: Macmillan.

Overall, J. E. 1971. "Associations between Marital History and the Nature of Manifest Psychopathology. *Journal of Abnormal Psychology* 78 (2): 213–21.

Renne, K. S. 1971. "Health and Marital Experience in an Urban Population." *Journal of Marriage and the Family* 33 (May): 338–50.

Safilios-Rothschild, Constantina. 1970. "The Study of Family Power Structure: A Review 1960–1969." *Journal of Marriage and the Family* 32 (November): 539–52.

Shorter, Edward. 1975. *The Making of the Modern Family*. New York: Basic.

Smith, William C. 1953. *The Stepchild*. Chicago: University of Chicago Press.

U.S. Bureau of the Census. 1973. *U.S. Census of the Population: 1970. Persons by Family Characteristics*. Final Report PC(2)-4B. Washington, DC: Government Printing Office.

———. 1976. *Number, Timing, and Duration of Marriages and Divorces in the United States: June 1975*. Current Population Reports, Series P-20. No. 297. Washington DC: Government Printing Office.

U.S. National Center for Health Statistics. 1953. *Vital Statistics of the United States, 1950*. Vol. 2. *Marriage, Divorce, Natality, Fetal Mortality, and Infant Mortality Data*. Washington DC: Government Printing Office.

———. 1977. *Visual Statistic Report. Advance Report. Final Marriage Statistics, 1975*. Washington, DC: Government Printing Office.

Weitzman, L. J. 1974. "Legal Regulation of Marriage: Tradition and Change." *California Law Review* 62: 1169–1288.

Young, Michael and Peter Wilmott. 1973. *The Symmetrical Family*. New York: Pantheon.